JAZZ

The Essential Companion

JAZZ

The Essential Companion

Ian Carr
Digby Fairweather
Brian Priestley

GRAFTON BOOKS
A Division of the Collins Publishing Group

LONDON GLASGOW
TORONTO SYDNEY AUCKLAND

Grafton Books
A Division of the Collins Publishing Group
8 Grafton Street, London W1X 3LA

Published by Grafton Books 1987

British Library Cataloguing in Publication Data

Carr, Ian, *1933–*
Jazz: the essential companion.
1. Jazz music—Dictionaries
I. Title II. Fairweather, Digby
III. Priestley, Brian, *1946–*
785.42′03′21 ML102.J3

ISBN 0-246-12741-4

Typeset by CG Graphic Services, Tring, Bucks
Printed in Great Britain by
William Collins Sons Ltd,
Westerhill, Glasgow

Contents

Introduction

Interest in jazz has grown hugely in recent years and many people – both musicians and non-musicians – have come to the music for the first time. There was clearly a great need for a guide to its turbulent history and the idea of a single-volume comprehensive dictionary of jazz written by musicians was originated by John Latimer Smith who recruited myself, Brian Priestley and Digby Fairweather for the purpose. He nursed the project into fruition and also wrote the entries on the three authors.

Although only as old as the century, jazz has grown and even overgrown so rapidly, that a newcomer to it might well feel bewildered by its proliferation of styles, stars and differing approaches to music-making. Indeed, even apparently knowledgeable people often sound confused and unsure about the essence of the music. All kinds of questions are constantly raised without ever being satisfactorily answered: is there such a thing as 'real' or 'true' jazz, and does any one style have a monopoly of that 'truth' and 'reality'? Are acoustic instruments somehow superior to electric ones? Was jazz-rock-fusion a gigantic aberration or a movement as valid and influential as bebop?

The problem is that in a mere 80 years or so, the music has moved from the simple structures and harmonies of its beginnings to the sophistication and subtleties of the 1920s and 1930s, the complexities of bebop and post-bop music in the 1940s and 1950s, outright abstraction in the 1960s, jazz-rock-fusion in the 1970s and the pluralism of the post-fusion period. With each successive decade, the scope of the music has expanded causing the very word 'jazz' to require regular reappraisal. And further confusion is caused by the fact that even when a phase or movement has passed its creative peak, it is still not over and done with: virtually all styles and approaches, however ancient or recent, continue to exist simultaneously. Furthermore, any radical innovation is often accompanied by a retreat into the safety of nostalgia: with the advent of bebop in the 1940s there was also a traditional jazz revival (a re-creation of New Orleans, Chicago and Dixieland styles), and with the fusion and pluralism of the 1970s and 1980s came also a revival of bebop. The newcomer trying to pick his or her way through this labyrinth requires a handbook which gives the facts, which clarifies, demystifies and defines, and which gives answers to fundamental questions about artistic value. That is what we have set out to provide in this companion.

This is the first time that a jazz dictionary has been written entirely by musicians and the advantage of this, we believe, is that the authors have crucial insights into the process of music-making: the problems of creativity and the conditions (physical, financial and cultural) which affect and shape the lives of musicians. In so far as the major figures and key movements are concerned, we three writers are in general agreement; it is only in minor matters that we might disagree. We have striven for factual accuracy at all times, but at the same time, when value judgements were necessary, we felt free to express any strongly held opinions. We decided against attempting a 'house-style' of writing, believing that one of the strengths of the book would be the differences in individual style of the three authors; that is why each entry is signed with the writer's initials. Digby's style, for example, is expansive, vivid and discursive, whereas Brian's mode of expression is more compressed, so that though his entries may seem shorter, their pith is often highly concentrated.

Although the three of us are interested in all aspects of jazz and its history, for the purposes of this mammoth task it was essential to divide up the field into broad areas of responsibility. Thus, stylistic developments of jazz from its beginnings to the 1940s were largely Digby's responsibility; Brian covered the 1940s and 1950s, but overlapped both with Digby and with my own province which was from 1960 to 1985–6. The heart of the book is, of course, the biographies of individual musicians; all major innovators and virtually all leading players on the international scene are included. Entries on American musicians naturally predominate, but as jazz has become a world phenomenon and is now an integral part of the culture of many other countries which bring to it their own flavour and identity, there are probably more non-Americans in this dictionary than in any other. We used two broad criteria for inclusion: musicians who have made an impact internationally, and also those who, though unknown or little known internationally, have made some particularly distinctive contribution to the music. We have included very few people from the realm of blues and gospel music, covering only those with a clear jazz connection.

We have also tried to make the book as relevant to the present as possible by including a number of gifted musicians from the rising generation of players. When biographical details were not available in current reference works or periodicals, we sent out questionnaires to musicians of all styles and persuasions and received replies from six continents: North and South America, Europe, Asia, Africa and the Antipodes. The questionnaires did not merely seek facts; they also gave the recipients the opportunity of informing us what they considered to be their most important recordings and career landmarks. Only a handful of questionnaires failed to come back to us and in these cases, if we could not find the relevant information it was, of course, impossible to write an entry. We are aware that there may therefore be regrettable omissions, and hope in future editions to make them good.

At the end of each biographical entry, we have listed the subject's most representative recordings. With dead or long-established artists, their key recordings have usually been obvious and only one or two LPs have been listed. With certain major figures it was necessary to list a number of their LPs, and with other artists nearer to the present time we sometimes listed several albums because it is not yet clear which are the most typical. We have also tried to give the labels of the most recent reissues of old material.

While the biographies are the backbone of the book, a vitally important part is the definition of words and phrases, the explanation of various terms and the essays on key subjects. Words such as 'riff' and 'chorus', highly abstract terms such as 'swing' and 'funky', are all succinctly and clearly defined and explained; there are essays on phenomena such as 'dance bands', and on movements and styles like 'bebop', 'free jazz', 'jazz-rock-fusion', putting each in clear historical and musical perspective. In a sense, these analytical and explanatory entries are essential for a fuller understanding of the biographies.

Where appropriate, we have recommended biographical and autobiographical books, and also various useful historical and analytical works. We decided not to include lists of the many publications of transcribed solos and sketch-scores which have proliferated in recent years. They are easily available and interested people can find them without much effort.

Now that jazz has a substantial history, it is important that enthusiasts and musicians have a clear understanding of it and a perception of the past as part of the present. Indeed, without a knowledge of the past we cannot properly understand the present. And a musician should function not only with his own generation in his bones, but also with a sense of the music's entire history existing simultaneously behind (or even within) the work of its living practitioners. Each new generation of players subtly shifts the balance of the whole existing order, creating a need for perennial reappraisals of the key historical figures. And each new step, style or movement magnifies rather than diminishes the prime creators of jazz so that as time goes by we slowly appreciate more and more the truly extraordinary achievements of Louis Armstrong, Bix Beiderbecke, John Coltrane, Miles Davis, Duke Ellington, Dizzy Gillespie, Coleman Hawkins, Charlie Parker, and Lester Young, among others who, in a basically unsympathetic environment, created a new music and set its indelible imprint on the twentieth century. Brian, Digby and I believe that this book is an act of homage to them and also to all other jazz musicians, because they too are part of this remarkable family.

Ian Carr
December 1986

Note on using this book

bar	baritone sax
clt	clarinet
dms	drums
gtr	guitar
MOR	middle-of-the-road
nda	no date(s) available
perc	percussion
r & b	rhythm-and-blues
tmb	trombone
tnr	tenor sax
TOBA	Theater Owners' Booking Association
tpt	trumpet
vln	violin

Entries are in letter-by-letter alphabetical order, with spaces and hyphens ignored. Names beginning with 'Mc-' are arranged as though they were prefixed 'Mac-', and 'St' as though they were spelt 'Saint'. People are listed and ordered under their familiar working names: **Smith, Stuff (Hezekiah)** follows **Smith, Ruthie**; **Turner, Big Joe** precedes **Turner, Bruce**; well-known nicknames are given in brackets with quotation marks – ('Satchmo'). Where there are two or more people with the same names, order is by date of birth.

Comprehensive cross-referencing is not offered, but where reference to another name will give useful additional information, that name is preceded by an asterisk.

In the discographies, when no leader is listed it means that the biographee was the leader for the recording session(s).

A

AACM, see Abrams, Muhal Richard.

A & R (Artists & Repertoire) An A & R man is the talent scout for a recording company. He discovers and signs up artists, and also monitors the kind of musical material they record. [IC]

Abercrombie, John L., acoustic and electric guitars, electric 12-string guitar, mandolin guitar. b. Portchester, New York, 16 December 1944. Started on guitar at 14 with lessons from a local teacher. Played in rock bands while at school. 1962–6, at the Berklee School of Music, studied guitar with Jack Petersen. 1967–8, he stayed in Boston working with organist Johnny 'Hammond' Smith; 1969, in New York, played briefly with Mike and Randy Brecker in the band Dreams. 1970–1, spent a year and a half with Chico Hamilton, making his first trip to Europe with him and playing the Montreux festival. 1971–3, worked with Jeremy Steig, Gil Evans and Gato Barbieri; 1973–5, recorded with Dave Liebman twice, spent a year with Billy Cobham's band, toured Europe with Jack DeJohnette, and led his own trio and quartet. 1974, began his long and fruitful association with ECM, recording his first album as leader for the label. In the later 1970s and the 1980s, Abercrombie toured and recorded with fellow guitarist Ralph Towner, always with very fine artistic results. Abercrombie's early influences were Jim Hall, Barney Kessel, Tal Farlow; later ones were Pat Martino, George Benson, Larry Coryell and John McLaughlin, among others. He is at home with any area from bebop to rock to free improvisation, and he is also a composer of quality. [IC]

With Cobham, DeJohnette, Liebman, Barbieri, Dreams, Michal Urbaniak and others; as leader, *Timeless* (1974); *Gateway* (1975); Abercrombie/Towner, *Sargasso Sea* (1976); *Gateway 2* (1977); solo, *Characters* (1977); *Arcade* (1978); Abercrombie/Towner, *Five Years Later* (1982); feat. Mike Brecker, *Night* (1984), all ECM

Abrahams, Brian Stanley, drums, percussion, voice. b. Cape Town, 26 June 1947. Father a guitarist. Began at 13 with local Cape bands, and was more noted for his singing. He developed as a drummer by backing singers and dancers in the early 1970s. Then played with a trio in Swaziland where he accompanied Sarah Vaughan and Nancy Wilson. Came to the UK in 1975. Since then has worked with the John Taylor quartet, Ronnie Scott quintet, Chris Hunter band, Jazz Afrika, Dudu Pukwana's Zila, Johnny Dyani's Witchdoctor's Son, the Brotherhood of Breath, and in the 1980s began leading his own group, District 6. He admires Max Roach, Art Blakey, Jack DeJohnette, and has also been inspired by Ellington, Monk and Chris McGregor. Abrahams listens to 'most contemporary music, including classics'. He enjoys teaching and doing workshops, and continues 'to spread the rich culture of South African folk music'. Compositions, 'A Calling to Rise' ('Woza Wena'), 'Ilanga' ('The Sun'), 'Bayete Ezululand'. [IC]

With Brotherhood of Breath, *Yes Please* (1982), In & Out, Paris; with District 6, *Akuzwakale (Let It Be Heard)* (1984), D6, London

Abrams, Muhal Richard, piano, composer, clarinet, cello. b. Chicago, 19 September 1930. Studied piano from age 17 and spent four years at Chicago Music College. Began playing professionally in 1948, and was soon composing and arranging for bands as well. 1961, formed the Experimental Band, which included Eddie Harris, Donald Garrett, Victor Sproles and Roscoe Mitchell, and was a rehearsal group for the city's improvisers. This grew into a more comprehensive organization called the Association for the Advancement of Creative Music (AACM). It began as a co-operative to help Chicago musicians to promote and present their own music which could not be heard through established commercial channels, but rapidly developed into a social force serving the black community through music. As well as organizing festivals and concerts, Abrams and the AACM set up a school for young musicians, thus giving direction and structure to a hitherto haphazard and amorphous scene. In this, Abrams was the moral as well as the musical influence; he encouraged trombonist George Lewis to take up extra-musical studies – in this case, German philosophy; and saxophonist Joseph Jarman has described, in an often-quoted statement, how he was helped: 'Until I had the first meeting with Richard Abrams, I was like all the rest of the "hip" ghetto niggers; I was cool, I took dope, I smoked pot, etc . . . In having the chance to work in the Experimental Band with Richard and the other musicians there, I found something with meaning/reason for doing.'

Several important groups and many leading

Muhal Richard Abrams

musicians have emerged from the AACM, including the *Art Ensemble of Chicago, Air (see THREADGILL, HENRY), and Leroy Jenkins, Anthony Braxton, Chico Freeman, Ray Anderson.

Richard Abrams remained an *éminence grise* in Chicago throughout the 1960s and early 1970s, teaching, working as a pianist and often accompanying visiting soloists. 1973, toured with his group in Europe. 1976, left Chicago, moving to New York. 1978, appeared at the Montreux festival and at last began to get some international recognition as a pianist.

His piano style incorporates the entire black tradition from ragtime, boogie-woogie and the stride school to bebop and free, totally abstract, improvisation. His influences range from James P. Johnson, Willie 'The Lion' Smith and Art Tatum to Nat Cole and Bud Powell. His conception is totally contemporary, but contains the roots of the past. [IC]

With AEC, Braxton, Jarman, Marion Brown, Eddie Harris and others; *Levels and Degrees of Light* (1967); *Young at Heart Wise in Time* (1969); *Things to Come from Those Now Gone* (1970), all Delmark; *Creative Construction Company* (1970), Muse; *Sightsong* (1975), Black Saint; *Muhal Richard Abrams* (1977), Black Saint

Abstraction, see FREE JAZZ.

A cappella A term borrowed from European church music, and used to describe both unaccompanied gospel singing and unaccompanied r & b vocal groups. Sometimes applied by extension to instrumental work which is completely solo, and sometimes misspelled in a variety of ways, including as one word. [BP]

Adams, George Rufus, tenor sax, flute, bass clarinet. b. Covington, Georgia, 29 April 1940. Started on piano at 11, and was soon playing it for the church choir; took up sax at school, playing with the high-school band and r & b funk in a night club where he heard blues singers such as Howlin' Wolf, Lightnin' Hopkins and others. He won a scholarship to Clark College where he graduated in music. 1961, spent the summer vacation touring with blues singer Sam Cooke. 1963, moved to Ohio, working with organ groups; 1966, toured Europe with organist Hank Marr; guitarist James 'Blood' Ulmer was in the band. 1968, moved to New York City, working with Roy Haynes, Gil Evans, Art Blakey. He continued to work and record with Evans in the later 1970s. 1973–6, he was with Charles Mingus, and later said: 'My association with Mingus as a musician and as a person – I consider that as one of the mainsprings of my musical life.' After Mingus he freelanced for a while in New York, then played with McCoy Tyner. In the late 1970s and the 1980s he was leading his own groups. 1979, played at NY Jazz Festival and in the 1980s toured internationally with a quartet which included pianist Don Pullen. With Mingus, Evans and his own groups he has played major festivals in the USA and Europe. In the early 1980s on many occasions he even treated the audience to a vocal blues: Adams's playing has the vocal inflexions and power of his blues and gospel roots, as well as the harmonic and linear freedom of the leading post-Coltrane saxophonists. Other influences are Charlie Parker, Ben Webster and Coleman Hawkins. [IC]

With Mingus, Evans, Tyner, Haynes; *Jazz Confronto 22* (1975), Horo; *Suite for Swingers* (1975), Horo; *Paradise Space Shuttle* (1979), Timeless/Muse; *Sound Suggestions* (1979), ECM

Adams, Pepper (Park), baritone sax. b. Highland Park, Illinois, 8 October 1930; d. 10 September 1986, of lung cancer. Played in early adolescence in Rochester, New York, then in Detroit with Lucky Thompson at age 16 (1947). Also six weeks touring with Lionel Hampton (1947). Before and after army service (1951–3), much gigging with fellow Detroit youngsters Donald Byrd, Kenny Burrell, Tommy Flanagan, Elvin Jones etc. Played with Stan Kenton (1956), Maynard Ferguson, Chet Baker, first albums under own name on West Coast (1957). Based in New York from 1958, worked with Benny Goodman (1958, 1959), occasional member of Charles Mingus groups (1959, 1962, 1963). Co-led quintet with Donald Byrd (1958–62), then some studio work. Founder member of Thad Jones–Mel Lewis band (1965–78, including

Cannonball Adderley (*right*) and Nat Adderley

European tours), also recorded while in Europe under own name (1973, 1976). Undertook solo tours in USA, Europe and Japan in 1980s. A typical product of the post-bop era, Adams was one of very few players to attempt this style on the baritone. His hard, dry-sounding tone enhanced the razor-edged precision of his timing and his unstoppable steam-roller lines. [BP]

Reflectory (1978), Muse

Adderley, Cannonball (Julian Edwin), alto and soprano sax. b. Tampa, Florida, 15 September 1928; d. 8 August 1975. Was school music instructor in Fort Lauderdale both before and after army service, leading own groups part-time. Encouraged by Eddie Vinson and others to move to New York, Adderley did so in 1955 (shortly after the death of Charlie Parker) and made an immediate impact. Formed nationally touring quintet including brother Nat Adderley

(1956–7), then joined Miles Davis (1957–9). In late 1959, Cannonball re-formed quintet with Nat, a partnership which with changing rhythm-sections retained considerable popularity until his death from a stroke.

Adderley's solo playing was initially much influenced by Charlie Parker, although his less emphatic accents and rounded tone revealed an appreciation of Benny Carter; rhythmically, the strutting phraseology of Vinson and Louis Jordan left its mark, as on many others of Cannonball's generation. He made all this into a homogeneous style, capable in the late 1950s of absorbing further influences such as aspects of John Coltrane's and even Ornette Coleman's work. In different ways, both of these approaches accorded with Adderley's penchant for melody and a highly diffused sense of decoration, which sometimes left his lines devoid of breathing spaces for the listener.

Leading his own group, however, he showed that he had learned much from associating with Davis (one of Adderley's most famous albums, *Somethin' Else*, was Miles's last small-group record under someone else's leadership). His use of the rhythm-section, in particular, gave musical substance to the 1960s style of 'soul jazz', with which Cannonball was especially identified. Many observers were inclined to write off such developments as motivated purely by commercial zeal, but much of Adderley's work stands up better than other contemporary offerings. Although most of the popular tunes played by the quintet were written by band members, his own 'Sermonette' and 'Sack o' Woe' were widely used by other groups. [BP]

Somethin' Else (1958), Blue Note; *Cannonball and Coltrane* (1959), Mercury; *Mercy, Mercy, Mercy* (1967), Capitol

Adderley, Nat(haniel), cornet. b. Tampa, Florida, 25 November 1931. Work with Lionel Hampton (1954–8) and Woody Herman (1959) seems overshadowed by the time spent in his elder brother's group (1955–7 and 1959–75). Since Cannonball's death, Nat has continued the spirit of their collaboration, either leading his own group or as a guest soloist, visiting Europe in 1982 and 1985. Except when working in big bands, Nat has preferred the mellower sound of the cornet to that of trumpet, and has produced an interesting amalgam of Dizzy Gillespie, Clark Terry and Miles Davis, sounding at his best when not following any one of these too closely. He is also the composer of 'Work Song' and 'Jive Samba', frequently attributed to Cannonball, and his son Nat Adderley Jnr. (b. 22 May 1955) is a promising keyboard player. [BP]

Don't Look Back (1976), Steeplechase

Africa In one sense, Africa is the source of all jazz, since the early creators and most of the subsequent innovators were descended from people forcibly removed from Africa, mainly by British slave traders. (Is this what we mean by the UK contribution to jazz?) Such research as there has been, and that is not much, does appear to corroborate the fact that the rhythmic complexity implicit in all jazz (and explicit in Afro-Caribbean and Afro-Latin musics) is the same complexity that is found in various African traditional styles.

More vaguely, the idea of their African heritage has inspired jazz performers differently at different periods. In the 1920s Duke Ellington was taking the tourist-attraction exotica of the Cotton Club shows and using it as inspiration for genuine musical advances. The 1940s saw Dizzy Gillespie (consciously) and Charlie Parker (intuitively) effecting a musical rapprochement with actual Afro-Caribbean styles, while in the 1960s at the height of the US civil rights movement there was conscious musical and spiritual identification with Africa on the part of North American musicians, and even playing visits to Africa by Duke Ellington, Randy Weston, Archie Shepp and others.

But jazz is not an African music. Indeed, it has never been popular there and, since independence, most African countries have evolved their own contemporary styles, borrowing freely from Western music and now feeding back into it. The main exception is in Southern Africa where urbanized workers were encouraged to listen to and imitate American popular music and, as the racialist régime became increasingly repressive, a local version of jazz came to have a life of its own and to express the feelings of the majority group and some white sympathisers. Ironically, none of this music is officially exported, so that the work of performers such as Dollar Brand (Abdullah Ibrahim), Hugh Masekela, Dudu Pukwana, Chris McGregor has only become known as they themselves have emigrated to Europe and the US. [BP]

Afro-Latin The term covers a huge variety of music, resulting from the combination of elements of African styles with the Spanish, Portuguese and even French cultures transplanted to South and Central America. The blend was achieved earlier and more thoroughly than anything in North American music before the 1970s. For this reason, watered-down South American music was being successfully exported to the US (and Europe) from the time of the tango in the 1910s.

However, since it was a question of 'time' in the metrical sense, there were of course hints of Afro polyrhythms in ragtime and early New Orleans jazz, not to mention occasional borrowings from South American rhythms such as the habañera. So it was only to be expected that, by the 1930s, jazzmen including Duke Ellington were interested in new imports from the Latin countries like the rumba and, what is more, bands from those countries who settled in the US began incorporating jazz-influenced improvisation. In this way, the stage was set for the first real collaborations, joining the innovators of bebop such as Dizzy Gillespie and Charlie Parker with the innovators of the mambo such as Machito.

For a while, progress in this direction was sporadic but, since the early 1960s with the introduction of the bugalu (and its soft-core contemporary, the bossa nova), there has been a continuous interchange in the US between jazz and Afro-Latin musicians. As with any fusion, the lowest common denominator often seems to predominate but, more than ever before, even the creative performers who emerge on each side have knowledge of both fields. What may be even more significant in the long run is that in the last two decades, especially in Paris and London, musicians from Africa itself have been collaborating with players of a jazz/Afro-Latin background, and the latest fusions from various African countries have achieved some success in the US.

Both Africa and Latin America are vast areas, and both still produce distinct regional styles in the way that North America used to before it became so homogenized. Possibilities for interaction are therefore endless, and it would be a rash commentator who predicted the effect all this will have on jazz; but the book below gives some idea of the ground covered so far. [BP]

Roberts, John Storm, *The Latin Tinge* (OUP, 1979)

Ahola, Sylvester, cornet, trumpet. b. Gloucester, Massachusetts, 24 May 1902. 'One hell of a trumpet player', in Pee Wee Erwin's words, he was easily combining the virtues of lead trumpeter and outstanding jazz soloist by 1925 in New York. He worked with Frank E. Ward's orchestra, Peter van Steeden, the California Ramblers, among many others, and also replaced the great Frank Guarente with Paul Specht's orchestra, which featured the ground-breaking small group the Georgians. After a period in 1927 with the legendary and short-lived Adrian Rollini New Yorkers (featuring Bix Beiderbecke, Frankie Trumbauer, Joe Venuti *et al.*), he came to England to join first the Savoy Orpheans and later Ambrose. British records of the time are (in the words of Warren Vaché Snr.) 'saturated with his work': – he recorded over 3000 (mostly unlisted) sides in the UK between 1927 and 1931. Finally a petition circulated by British trumpeters barred him, as an American, from recording other than with his bandleader Ambrose. 'Hooley' returned home, and picked up the threads with Ray Noble, Peter van Steeden (for NBC's brand new Bing Crosby radio show) and a full book of session work. Happy and wealthy, he retired to his Massachusetts home where, in the mid-1980s, he was living amid his collection of brass instruments and keeping his lip in trim with the Cape Anne Symphony Orchestra. Ahola recorded over 4000 sides in his career, which is the subject of a comprehensive discography by Brian Rust. [DF]

Jazz in Britain: the 1920s, Parlophone

Airshot or **Aircheck** The name given to a recording taken from a live music broadcast. Extremely significant in the radio industry of the 1930s and 1940s, and of great importance to the bands who benefited from the exposure, these broadcasts were initially taken down by individual listeners (as compared to transcription recordings, performed by the musicians specifically for radio use). Later they came to be exchanged between collectors and, from the 1960s onwards, provided a valuable source of vintage material for albums, though usually without remuneration to those who took part. Without them, most of us would never have heard Ellington playing for dancers or Parker at Birdland. [BP]

Akiyoshi, Toshiko, piano, composer. b. Dairen, Manchuria, 12 December 1929. Moved to Japan (1946) and became involved in jazz with various groups, then own group from 1951. Encouraged by Oscar Peterson to move to US, studied at Berklee School (1956–9) and with mother of Serge Chaloff. Formed Toshiko–Mariano quartet co-led by Charlie Mariano, whom she married (1959), and spent a year together in Japan (1961). Worked several months with Charles Mingus (1962, including Town Hall concert), then returned to Japan for three years. In New York again, did radio series and wrote material for specially assembled big band (1967). Formed new quartet with second husband Lew Tabackin (1970). Moving to Los Angeles (1972), ran big band of top studio musicians, making occasional live appearances and several albums. Returned to New York (1981), forming new big band still co-led by Tabackin but with material composed exclusively by Akiyoshi.

Although her piano work is extremely competent and clearly inspired by Bud Powell and later stylists, her writing is far more individual. Here the influence of Gil Evans can be detected, but the atmosphere engendered is by no means the same, in part because of specifically oriental-sounding textures especially in the use of woodwind and percussion. More profoundly, the spaciousness and melodic grace of her best material seems to reflect her background in a manner which is less selfconscious. [BP]

Kogun (1975); *Sumi-e* (1977), both RCA

Film: *Jazz is My Native Language* (dir. Renee Cho, 1984)

Albany, Joe (Joseph Albani), piano. b. Atlantic City, 24 January 1924. A post-war associate of Charlie Parker and Lester Young, with whom he can be heard on one airshot and one studio session respectively. Also worked with Benny

Toshiko Akiyoshi

Carter (1944), Georgie Auld (1945). Stan Getz (1947). Following an almost unbroken absence of 25 years from the jazz scene, Albany emerged again in the 1970s to forge a solo career. Still in many respects an unreconstructed bopper, he has the clarity of thought typical of keyboard players influenced by saxophonists such as Parker and Young. The brilliant touch and rhythmic vitality of his right-hand work have been highlighted by a number of albums and a documentary film, and have attained a peak only hinted at in his mid-1940s work. [BP]

Bird Lives! (1979), Interplay

Film: *Joe Albany . . . A Jazz Life* (dir. Carole Langer, 1980)

Alcorn, Alvin Elmore, trumpet. b. New Orleans, 7 September 1912. After a grounding with brass bands (including George Williams's) he worked with, among others, Armand J. Piron's orchestra, then spent six years with trumpeter Don Albert's successful Ellington-style New Orleans-based swing band – a sensational Southern success which recorded for Vocalion in 1936. Before, and after, World War II, Alcorn worked for Papa Celestin, Alphonse Picou and others. 1954, joined Kid Ory in California, replacing Teddy Buckner, for a spell of favourable reviews, club and concert appearances and fine recordings which established his name world-wide. Alcorn appeared in *The Benny Goodman Story* (1955), with Ory again in 1956, and continued to work regularly (including a spell with George Lewis in 1958) until the 1960s; 1966, toured Europe with the New Orleans All Stars and in 1969 was making guest appearances in New York. From 1974 onwards he was resident, and playing marvellously, in New Orleans, at the Marriott Hotel on Canal Street: 'the best session in New Orleans', said Owen Bryce in 1982. Alcorn's brother plays alto saxophone, his son trumpet. [DF]

Any with Kid Ory, including *Kid Ory's Creole Jazz Band 1956*, Vogue/Good Time Jazz

Alexander, Monty, piano. b. Kingston, Jamaica, 6 June 1944. A dynamic performer who made an early mark in the USA in the 1960s. Frequently associated as a sideman with Ray Brown and Milt Jackson, he has also recorded a considerable quantity of albums under his own name. The strong influence of Oscar Peterson and an appropriately fluent technique seem, on the basis of records, to be the sum total of Alexander's style but, as often with unpretentious players steeped in swing, the results can be highly compelling in person. [BP]

Triple Treat (1982), Concord

Ali, Rashied (Robert Patterson), drums, congas. b. Philadelphia, 1 July 1935. Mother sang with Jimmie Lunceford. He worked with local groups and r & b bands; 1953, first jazz gigs with his own group. 1963, moved to New York, working with Pharoah Sanders, Don Cherry, Paul Bley, Bill Dixon, Archie Shepp, Earl Hines, Marion Brown and Sun Ra. 1965–7, second percussionist in John Coltrane's group, then with Alice Coltrane trio. 1968, toured in Europe with his own quartet, also worked with Sonny Rollins. 1969, with Jackie McLean; continued leading his own groups; 1972, formed Survival Records and organized New York Jazz Musicians' Festival. 1973, opened his own loft, Ali's Alley/Studio 77; continued workshops, concerts and occasional lectures in mid-1970s. [IC]

With Coltrane, Shepp, Bud Powell, A. Coltrane; Rashied Ali quintet, *Rashied Ali – Moon Flight* (1975); *Rashied Ali – NY Ain't So Bad* (1975); with Leroy Jenkins, *Swift are the Winds of Life* (1975), all Survival

Allen, Henry James 'Red', trumpet, vocals, composer. b. New Orleans, 7 January 1908; d. New York City, 17 April 1967. One of the best and brightest young trumpeters in New Orleans by the early 1920s (his father ran a famous brass band in the city from 1907 to 1940), he first moved North to join King Oliver's Dixie Syncopators in 1927. Moved back to New Orleans to work with pianist Walter 'Fats' Pichon and Fate Marable, but Loren Watson, a Victor talent scout, signed him as Victor's much-needed 'answer' to Louis Armstrong. Allen travelled to New York and recorded with Luis Russell's orchestra, which he then joined full time. The orchestra, with old friends like Paul Barbarin, Greely Walton and Russell himself, felt like home. 'It was the happiest band I ever worked in', Allen remembered later. '. . . It was also the most swinging band in New York – it put the musicians in an uproar!' So did their young trumpet star whose then unique 'modern style', all slurs, atonal twists and growls, was a real Armstrong alternative: it showed up dramatically in Russell classics like 'Jersey Lightning' and on Allen's own solo sides with his New Yorkers. In 1933, tempted by money and prestige, Allen joined Fletcher Henderson. The stay (which involved great exchanges with Coleman Hawkins) lasted a year, then came another 3 with Lucky Millinder (during which Allen recorded his hit 'Ride Red Ride', originally a poorly reviewed B-side), and in 1937 he moved back to Russell as featured artist and warm-up man for Louis Armstrong, who by now was fronting Russell's aggregation. Allen was allowed a set a night to feature himself before Armstrong took the stand, but he kept busy as a freelance too, recording solo for Perfect and Vocalion, working with Joe Marsala in a mixed group, and all up and down 52nd Street. In 1940 Russell's band was sacked en bloc by Armstrong's manager Joe Glaser, and for the last 27 years of his life Allen led his own bands and worked solo. His sextet, formed that year (including, among others, Ed Hall, J. C. Higginbotham and Ken Kersey) quickly became successful – it had a modern approach for its day – and worked regularly for 14 years commuting between Boston, Chicago, San Francisco and New York. By 1954, Allen found himself working regularly at the Metropole, New York, a noisy musicians' bar which featured two or more jazz bands at once time in a more or less continuous policy, and in all styles. Allen's group – featuring Coleman Hawkins, Buster Bailey and J. C. Higginbotham – entertained most nights, and perceptive listeners noted that Allen's approach, amid the noise, was refining itself into something wonderful: a collage of blues phrases, rocket-flares, subterranean rumbles, growls and flutters, often delivered in a determined whisper: records from the period, for example 'I Cover the Waterfront' of March 1957, show clearly what seemed to be new. The 1960s signalled a great Red Allen revival. With a quartet (the most popular format for swing trumpeters since Jonah Jones's) he recorded for Prestige, was featured in *Downbeat* in a complimentary session-commentary by Martin Williams ('Condition Red-Allen, that is') and reviewed with five stars soon after. A second (now classic) album, *Feelin' Good*, quickly turned into a legend and was given the seal of approval by modern trumpeter Don Ellis, 'Red Allen is the most avant-garde trumpet player in New York!' In the 1960s he continued his New York clubwork fairly regularly: visits to England in 1963, 1964 and 1966 (his first had been with Kid Ory in 1959) produced as much love for his gentle personality and humour as respect for his music. His last visit to England, in tandem with Sammy Price, came in 1967 when it was plain that Allen was playing at reduced power: he died later that year of cancer. [DF]

Henry Red Allen, vol. 5 (1957), RCA; *Feelin' Good* (1965), CBS

See Williams, Martin, *Jazz Masters of New Orleans* (Macmillan, 1967, repr. Da Capo, 1979); Balliett, Whitney, *Improvising* (OUP, 1977)

Allen, Pete (Peter), clarinet, alto and soprano sax, leader, vocals. b. nr. Newbury, Berks, 23 November 1954. Son of banjoist Bernie Allen, he set up his Dixieland band after formative years in the West Country, some with trumpeter Rod Mason. Equipped with a sound business sense and ambition, as well as a hard-driving clarinet style sometimes reminiscent of Ed Hall, Allen presents a high-powered popular-based

Henry 'Red' Allen

jazz show which, by virtue of gifted marketing as well as ability, has steadily attained the status and pulling-power of men 20 years his senior such as Kenny Ball and Terry Lightfoot. Allen's band reworks the standard repertoire of classic jazz with skill and flair. Regular professional colleagues on the road with Allen's show include entertainers such as Beryl Bryden and Tommy Burton: fine players who have worked with him include Ian Hunter-Randall, Chris Hodgkins (tpts), Mick Cooke (tmb), John Armatage (dms). Since his line-up stabilized, around 1983, Allen's band has achieved a new cohesion. [DF]

Down in Honky-Tonk Town! (1979), Black Lion

Allison, Mose John, Jnr., piano, voice, composer; also trumpet. b. Tippo, Mississippi, 11 November 1927. Piano lessons from age five; played trumpet with Dixieland band at high school. Steeped in the blues and black music of the Mississippi area, also listening to Nat Cole's trio and the beboppers. After college (Louisiana State University) he played all over the South until 1956 when he moved to New York. 1956–9, worked with Stan Getz, Gerry Mulligan, Al Cohn, Zoot Sims, led his own trios around New York, worked with local rhythm-sections in Paris, Stockholm and Copenhagen. Through the 1960s, 1970s and into the 1980s he continued to work with his trio in clubs in the USA and occasionally in Europe.

His favourites include blues singers such as Sonny Boy Williamson and Tampa Red, as well as Ellington and Monk, and his singing and playing blend all these influences. Everything he does is understated, with a superbly swinging time-feel. His soft voice has the rhythms, the throwaway (half-spoken) words and the inflexions of the country blues, but he projects a sophisticated, wry form of self-communing in the setting of his inherently 'modern' trio. Compositions: 'Parchman Farm'; 'If You Live'; 'Everybody Cryin' Mercy'; 'Look What You Made Me Do'; 'I Don't Worry About a Thing'; 'Powerhouse'; 'Hello There, Universe'. [IC]

Mose Allison Sings the Seventh Son (1963), Prestige; *The Best of Mose Allison* (1960s), Atlantic; *Retrospective* (1960), Columbia; *Middle Class White Boy* (1982), Elektra Musician

Altschul, Barry, drums, b. Bronx, New York, 6 January 1943. Began on drums at 11; studied with Charli Persip. 1964–70, worked with Paul

Bley, going deeply into the free (abstract) improvisation of the day, and was also involved with the Jazz Composers' Guild, 1964–8 (see MANTLER, MICHAEL). 1968, went to Europe, playing bebop and working with Carmell Jones, Leo Wright and Johnny Griffin. Back in the US he studied with Sam Ulano for nine months. 1969, worked with Sonny Criss and Hampton Hawes in California and Tony Scott in New York. 1970–2, with Circle, a group led by Chick Corea and including Dave Holland and Anthony Braxton, which toured the USA and Europe, recording a live double album in Paris. 1972, Corea left the group, and the remaining three members with Sam Rivers recorded *Conference of the Birds*, an album of Dave Holland's compositions.

1974–6, Altschul and Holland worked with the Braxton quartet (with Kenny Wheeler) and also with the Sam Rivers trio, continuing with Rivers after the quartet broke up. 1975, Altschul did much teaching and wrote a conceptual study book for drums. 1978, he split from the Rivers group, and that was Altschul's last job as a sideman. While with Rivers, he had been leading a quartet with Ray Anderson (tmb), Brian Smith (bass), Anthony Davis (piano); 1979, Smith was replaced by Rick Rozie and the group recorded an LP, *For Stu*. After Davis and Rozie left, Altschul led a trio with Anderson and bassist Mark Helias which in 1980 toured Europe. 1981, he toured with Art Pepper, and continued leading the trio.

Altschul has studied African, Indian, Brazilian and Caribbean music, incorporating elements from them into his work. Although he began in the 1960s avant-garde, he eventually (like so many others from that period) re-examined the entire spectrum of jazz history, going back into bebop, hard bop and swing. He told Lee Jeske: 'The avant-garde was a period that was necessary to extend the vocabulary of the musicians themselves . . . After a while the avant-gardists become the contemporary, then they become the mainstream.' [IC]

With Corea, Buddy Guy, Rivers, Bley; with Circle, *Paris Concert* (1971), ECM; with Braxton, *The Complete Braxton* (1971), Arista/Freedom; *Five Pieces* (1974), Arista; with Holland, *Conference of the Birds* (1972), ECM; as leader, *You Can't Name Your Own Tune* (1977), Muse; *Another Time, Another Place* (1978), Muse; *For Stu* (1979), Soul Note

Ambrosetti, Franco, trumpet, fluegelhorn, composer. b. Lugano, Switzerland, 10 December 1941. Father, Flavio Ambrosetti, a saxophonist who played opposite Charlie Parker at the 1949 Paris Jazz Festival. Classical piano lessons for eight years until 16; self-taught on trumpet from 17. 1962, began playing at Zurich's African Club, and also commenced a long association with his father, G. Gruntz and Daniel Humair, which developed in 1972 into the George Gruntz Concert Jazz Band. Since the 1960s he has continued to play in his father's quintet and to lead his own groups.

Ambrosetti is a brilliantly assured player in the neo-bop mould. His main influence in terms of sound, articulation and phrasing seems to be Freddie Hubbard, but with a harmon mute the spirit of Miles Davis (*circa* the mid-1960s) imbues his work. He often has leading Americans as well as Europeans in his groups and on his records, and his 1983 album *Wings*, with Mike Brecker, Kenny Kirkland, Humair, John Clark and Buster Williams, shows him at his best, as both player and small-group composer. 1985, led an all-star band at the Berlin Festival which included Humair, Dave Holland, Gordon Beck, Dave Liebman.

Ambrosetti has a degree in economics from the University of Basle, and also works an eight-hour day as an executive of his family's firm, Ettore Ambrosetti & Sons, which produces steel wheels for cars and industrial and agricultural vehicles. He has said, 'I am not able to play only music or to be only an industrialist. I need both.' [IC]

With G. Gruntz, G. Azzolini, Flavio Ambrosetti; *Heartbop* (with P. Woods, H. Galper, 1981); *Wings* (1983), both Enja

Ammons, Albert C., piano. b. Chicago, 23 September 1907; d. Chicago, 2 December 1949. One of the fathers of boogie-woogie, he was a brilliant versatile pianist who worked in Chicago clubs as a soloist in the 1920s and later on, around the turn of the decade, with territory bands and orchestras including Louis Banks's, 1930–4. 1934–8 he led his own band in Chicago (including a residency at the Club DeLisa) and made his first records for Decca in 1936 featuring Guy Kelly (tpt), Israel Crosby (bass) and others. Ammons's powerful 'shouting' style and natural gift for boogie was ideal for the eight-to-the-bar commercial era about to dawn, and from 1938 he moved to New York to appear at Carnegie Hall and regularly at Café Society, often with a frequent colleague, Pete Johnson, and sometimes in trio with Meade Lux Lewis. He remained successful all through the 1940s (despite, says John Chilton, temporary hand paralysis in mid-decade) and continued touring, with residencies in Hollywood and Chicago, and recording (his last sides, with Crosby again, were made for Mercury in 1949), until he became seriously ill. [DF]

King of Boogie and Blues (1939–49), Oldie Blues

Ammons, Gene (Eugene) ('Jug'), tenor sax. b. Chicago, 14 April 1925; d. 23 July 1974. Played with Billy Eckstine band (1944–7), then worked in Chicago recording under his own name and with his father, Albert Ammons. Featured in Woody Herman band (1949), then co-led two-tenor septet with Sonny Stitt (1950–2). Continued appearing with own group, or as visiting soloist, and recording with all-star line-ups until imprisonment for drug offences (1964–9). Visited Montreux festival (1973) and was working steadily until shortly before his death, from cancer terminated by pneumonia.

Ammons's approach can be said to derive from both Lester Young and Ben Webster, with something of the latter's tone applied to the lines of the former. The underlying simplicity and directness common to these models fed a style which soon took on a life of its own, and became very popular with black record-buyers and jukebox patrons. Although he was ideally suited for it, Ammons leaned less towards straight rhythm-and-blues than some of his contemporaries. His ballad playing was especially emotive but, although his melodic gifts were in some senses obvious, they were never short of subtleties appealing to the more jazz-minded audience. While Ammons's career ended before he had gained favour outside the US, he founded a 'Chicago school' of tenor which influenced numerous players of the next generation such as Johnny Griffin and Clifford Jordan, before becoming an unrecognized part of the international language of jazz (as, indeed, did his 1950 tune 'Gravy' which was the basis for the standard 'Walkin'', copyrighted by his manager Richard Carpenter). [BP]

Juganthology (1955–7); *The Big Sound* (1958), both Prestige

Andersen, Arild, double bass. b. Oslo, Norway, 27 October 1945. At college he specialized in electronic engineering, but studied music privately with George Russell. 1967–73, played with Jan Garbarek's quartet and trio, and at the same time worked with singer Karin Krog. 1973–4, worked in the USA with Sam Rivers and Paul Bley. 1974, formed his own group with Scandinavian musicians: Pàl Thowsen, Jon Balke, Juhani Aaltonen (Finland), Knut Riisnes. 1979, member of a quartet with Kenny Wheeler, Paul Motian and pianist Steve Dobrogosz. 1981, member of another all-star quartet with Bill Frisell, John Taylor and Alphonse Mouzon. With his fellow-countryman drummer Jon Christensen, Andersen co-led a quintet in 1983. 1969, voted Musician of the Year in Norway; 1975, the European magazine *Jazz Forum* voted him No. 1 European bass player. His main influences are Miles Davis, Don Cherry and Paul Bley. [IC]

Five LPs with Jan Garbarek; with Karin Krog, Terje Rypdal, Don Cherry, Sam Rivers, Sheila Jordan, Bill Frisell, David Darling; *Clouds in My Head* (1975); *Shimri* (1976); *Green Shading into Blue* (1978); *Lifelines* (1980); *A Molde Concert* (1981), all ECM

Anderson, Cat (William Alonzo), trumpet. b. Greenville, South Carolina, 12 September 1916; d. 29 April 1981. Taught to play in Jenkins' Orphanage, South Carolina, he soon after toured with a small Orphanage-based group, the Carolina Cotton Pickers. Other early professional engagements came from guitarist Hartley Toots, Claude Hopkins, Lucky Millinder, Erskine Hawkins (who was jealous of Anderson's stratospheric range and fired him) and Lionel Hampton. 1944, Anderson succumbed to Ellington's persuasion and joined him at the Earle Theater in Philadelphia. From then on his trumpet, capable of playing more than five octaves, became a vital tone colour in Ellington's musical palette, ready to double a lead line two octaves up or simply supply altissimo colour to Ellington's tone poems. Like Maynard Ferguson some years later, Anderson saw playing in the trumpet's super-register as a mental exercise which any good player could acquire, but, like Ferguson again, he was much more than just a high-note man; he possessed a huge, beautiful sound all the way through the trumpet's register and – more than Ferguson ever did – had mastered the arts of half-valve and plungermute playing to perfect Ellingtonian level. It was a noise that Ellington delighted in and used to fantastical effect on trumpet showpieces such as 'El Gato', 'Trumpet No End' and 'Jam with Sam': since Anderson died his approach to highnote playing has seldom been copied by others. For most of his life with Ellington, Anderson, a highly-strung man of unbendable standards, played the lead book, to the apparent disapproval of Cootie Williams at the other end of the trumpet section. After Ellington's death he continued to work in studios and often made welcome solo appearances where his solo talents were heard in a wider variety of roles and, as always, to magnificent effect. [DF]

Old Folks (1979), All Life

See Dance, Stanley, *The World of Duke Ellington* (Scribner's, 1970, repr. Da Capo, 1980)

Anderson, Ivie Marie, vocals. b. Gilroy, California, 10 July 1905; d. Los Angeles, 28 December 1949. From the early 1920s she appeared as a soubrette at the Cotton Club, in reviews such as Sissle and Blake's *Shuffle Along* and as a band singer with leaders such as Anson Weeks and Curtis Mosby and with Paul Howard's Quality Serenaders. The night she joined Duke Ellington, a lucky 13 February 1931 at the Paramount Theater, New York, the band broke every attendance record and from then on, in Ellington's words, 'Ivie was our good-luck charm.' Slim, beautiful and dignified, always dressed in white on stage, she sang with surprising strength and, said Helen Dance, 'her voice became as much a part of the Ellington band as did the saxes of Carney and Hodges.' Her part in a 1930s Ellington show included a crosstalk act with drummer Sonny Greer (which he refused to carry on with anyone else after she left), Ellington hits such as 'A Lonely Co-ed' and 'I'm Checkin' Out, Goombye!' and often a moving version of 'Stormy Weather' (borrowed from Ethel Waters at the Cotton Club), which according to Ellington, 'stopped the show cold' in

London and France (1933). There are numerous records of Anderson with Duke: she was the first to record 'It Don't Mean a Thing' with him in 1932. Harry Carney said, 'She looked very angelic and above it all, yet backstage and on the bus, in hotels, restaurants everywhere, she was always regular 100 per cent! There was no side to her!' She left Ellington in 1942 to open a Los Angeles restaurant and continued singing for a while, despite chronic asthma, but died much too young. [DF]

Duke Ellington Presents Ivie Anderson (1932–40), CBS (double)

Anderson, Ray, trombone, alto trombone, slide trumpet, cornet, tuba. b. Chicago, 1952. Took up trombone at age eight, playing in school bands with fellow pupil and trombonist George Lewis. He had classical lessons, but listened to mainstreamers such as Vic Dickenson and Trummy Young on record. Eventually began attending concerts of the AACM (see ABRAMS, MUHAL RICHARD), and also immersed himself in Chicago blues. During a year at Macalester College, Minneapolis, played in funk bands after hours, then went to California, also playing in funk bands and working with drummer Charles Moffett and others. 1972, arrived in New York, sat in with Mingus, studied and freelanced. 1977, began working with both Barry Altschul's and Anthony Braxton's groups, but still freelanced mostly on the NY Latin scene. 1979, led his own group at the Moers festival in West Germany; 1980, toured and played festivals in Europe with Barry Altschul. Anderson won the *Downbeat* critics' poll on trombone in 1981, as a 'Talent Deserving Wider Recognition'. He is an example of the new pluralism: a player with tremendous stamina and great technical ability who is equally at home with music ranging from Braxton's totally scored pieces, to free (abstract) improvisation, Latin music for dancers, neo-bop and funk bands. [IC]

With Altschul, *Another Time, Another Place* (1978), Muse; with Braxton, *Seven Compositions, 1978*, Moers Music; as leader, *Harrisburg Half Life* (1979), Moers; with Slickaphonics, *Modern Life* (1983), Enja

Archey, Jimmy (James), trombone, b. Norfolk, Virginia, 12 October 1902; d. Amityville, New York, 16 November 1967. Made his début in New York in 1927, with Edgar Hayes's orchestra, and worked with Fletcher Henderson's second band, Henderson's Rainbow Orchestra, as featured soloist. His first notable records with James P. Johnson's Orchestra (featuring King Oliver and Fats Waller), and Oliver's studio bands, revealed a strong, consistently shouting player, with technique to spare and progressive ideas. For the next seven years from 1930 Archey worked with Luis Russell's orchestra, and moved on to a star-studded selection of aristocratic big bands, including those of Benny Carter, Claude Hopkins, Coleman Hawkins, Duke Ellington (depping for Tricky Sam Nanton) and Cab Calloway; by the late 1940s, after marvellous recordings with Mutt Carey's New Yorkers, a residency on Rudy Blesh's This Is Jazz radio show, and an appearance with Mezz Mezzrow's band in Nice, he was more and more often thought of as a New Orleans revivalist, rather than the sophisticated big-band player he could be. 1948, joined young Bob Wilber's revivalist band; 1950, took over the group for work in the USA and abroad; for seven years from 1955, worked with Earl Hines's Dixieland-based band in San Francisco (including a long spell at Club Hangover, one of the city's two big jazz centres). Early 1960s, suffered a long illness, but re-emerged to tour the USA and Canada with Dixieland bands again, including a European tour for the New Orleans All Stars, during which he was still a dominant feature. 'Although his notes are produced in a manner worthy of the bop machine-gunners,' wrote J. C. Hillman in *Jazz Journal* in 1966, 'his style is surprisingly close to Jim Robinson, though neater and more accurate. His solos were powerful and inventive, and the ensembles really brought out the best in him!' [DF]

Giants of Traditional Jazz (1947), Savoy (double)

Ardley, Neil Richard, composer. b. Carshalton, Surrey, 26 May 1937. 1959, B.Sc., Bristol University. 1960–1, studied arranging and composition with Ray Premru. 1964–70, director of the New Jazz Orchestra (NJO). From 1969, composed music for his own groups formed for recordings, broadcasts and tours. During the 1970s he also built up an electronic studio, composing music mainly for television. Ardley has almost always earned his living apart from music, as a writer of information books (about 60 to date) on science, computers, natural history and music. His main influences are Stravinsky, Gil Evans, Duke Ellington, and he also admires Mike Gibbs. His *Greek Variations* (1969) is a composition in six parts for a 9-piece jazz group and string quartet, based on a motif from a Greek folk song. *A Symphony of Amaranths* (1971), deploying a 25-piece band with strings, received the first Arts Council of Great Britain award for a jazz recording. Then came two compositions which are a fascinating mélange of acoustic instruments and electronics: *Kaleidoscope of Rainbows* (1975, Gull), which was based on Balinese scales and written for a 13-piece ensemble, and *The Harmony of the Spheres* (1978, Decca), for a 9-piece ensemble plus the voices of Pepi Lemer and Norma Winstone. [IC]

With NJO, *Western Reunion* (1965), Decca, and *Le Déjeuner sur l'herbe* (1968), MGM Verve; *The Greek Variations* (1969), Columbia; *A Symphony of Amaranths* (1971), Regal Zonophone

Neil Ardley

Armatage, John, drums. b. Newcastle upon Tyne, 5 August 1929. Turned professional in 1957 with John Chilton and soon after joined Bruce Turner's Jump Band, with whom he recorded, made a film, *Living Jazz* (1962), and toured until the band's break-up. From then on Armatage worked with Alan Elsdon's band, freelanced busily, and continued – quite unobtrusively – to make a living from jazz, touring abroad, playing regularly in the 1970s and 1980s with Pete Allen's band, with Terry Lightfoot (an old colleague) and, all too occasionally, parading his second skill, as a band arranger. One of Britain's best swing drummers, he plays in the loose, lithe idiom of Sid Catlett and Dave Tough. [DF]

Armstrong, Lil (*née* Lillian Hardin), piano, vocals. b. Memphis, Tennessee, 3 February 1898; d. Chicago, 27 August 1971. She worked in Chicago as a classically trained piano demonstrator for Jones's Store on 35th and State. An ultra-modern jazz pianist for her time (and 'an excellent musician', says Crawford Wethington) who had left ragtime behind, she worked early on with Sugar Johnny's Creole Orchestra, the toast of Chicago for $55 a week (her wage at Jones's had been $3) and then with Freddie Keppard's sensational Original Creole Orchestra, in her element at last: 'Lil always had a grin a mile wide as she bent over the keyboard', remembers Mezz Mezzrow. Lil Hardin met Louis Armstrong, young and diffident, playing second trumpet in King Oliver's Creole Jazz Band for which she played piano, and after Oliver let fall that 'as long as Louis's in my band I'm still King!' she encouraged the reluctant Armstrong to make the break ('I don't want to be married to no *second* trumpet player'). They married on 5 February 1924; a year later Louis was back from a spell with Fletcher Henderson in New York and a banner appeared in front of the Dreamland in Chicago advertising 'Louis Armstrong – the world's greatest jazz cornettist' – with Lil Hardin's band. Armstrong had swapped one leader for another. Lil kept a loving and watchful eye on her husband's career: when a rival trumpeter featured top Es at a nearby cabaret, Hardin had Armstrong 'make top Fs at home'. But he was ribbed by his fellow bandsmen because he worked for his wife and this led to uncomfortable on-stage confrontations: by 1931 relations were strained and by 1938 they were divorced. Lil sued Armstrong for royalties on tunes co-composed while they were married (and won), billed his 1934 musical successor, Jonah Jones, as 'Louis Armstrong the Second' at the Lafayette Theater, New York, and relentlessly advertised herself as 'Mrs Louis Armstrong' for future projects.

Armstrong took it well. Lil's career – following a post-graduate degree in music – included an all-male band, an all-female band and a post as house pianist for Decca from 1936. In Chicago in 1940 she opened a restaurant, the Swing Shack, and for the last 30 years of her life was a celebrated club pianist around Chicago and a likeable raconteuse. She died of a heart attack while taking part in a Chicago memorial concert to her late husband. [DF]

The Louis Armstrong Legend, 1925–9, World Records (4 records, boxed set)

Armstrong, Louis Daniel ('Satchmo'), trumpet, vocals, composer. b. New Orleans, *c.* 4 July 1900; d. Corona, New York, 6 July 1971. Born on Independence Day 1900 (he may have decided the exact day for himself), he sang on the New Orleans streets in a boyhood quartet and in 1913 was admitted to the Colored Waifs' home for firing a gun into the air. In the home he learned the trumpet, and by four years later was challenging every trumpet king in his home town, from Freddie Keppard to Joe Oliver, his first father-figure, whom he replaced in Kid Ory's band in 1919. Oliver, by now 'King' Oliver, invited Louis in 1922 to join him in Chicago to play second trumpet. Tempting as it is to echo Nat Gonella's incredulous comment, 'I can't imagine Louis playing second trumpet to anyone!', Oliver was able to teach Armstrong a little; the regular harmonic experience of playing second (his ear, even then, was faultless) and, above all, the importance of playing straight lead, as Oliver did, in 'whole notes', were lessons that Armstrong was to remember for life. Experience was by now, however imperceptibly, toughening the young man up: his second wife Lil Hardin (above) helped to focus an inbuilt streak of ambition and he learned, once at least from Oliver, who, it transpired, was 'creaming' his sidemen's wages, that people could be devious – necessary knowledge for a survivor. Although he loved Oliver until the end, by 1924 Armstrong had made the jump to New York and Fletcher Henderson's orchestra. It was hot city company for a country boy, although he had the humour and talent to counter mockery ('I thought that meant "pound plenty"!', he quipped, when the stern Henderson ticked him off for a missed 'pp' dynamic) and somewhere along the way he decided he was the best, and got ready to defend his title if necessary. 'Louis played the Regal Theater in Chicago,' remembers Danny Barker, 'and they had this fantastic trumpeter Reuben Reeves in the pit. So in the overture they put Reuben Reeves on stage doing some of Louis's tunes. Louis listened – then when he came on he said, "Tiger Rag". Played about thirty choruses! The next show? No overture!'

In 1925, Armstrong, already a recording star, began dates with Okeh with his Hot Five and Seven (featuring Johnny Dodds, Kid Ory and his wife Lil until Earl Hines replaced her). The music on masterpieces such as 'Cornet Chop Suey', 'Potato Head Blues', 'SOL Blues' and 'West End Blues' turned jazz into a soloist's art form and set new standards for trumpeters world-wide: Armstrong, at the peak of his young form, peeled off top Cs as easy as breathing (previously they were rare) and pulled out technical *tours de force* which never turned into notes for their own sake. His singing introduced individuality to popular vocals and, just for good measure (when he dropped the music one day at a recording session), he invented scat singing. Best of all was his melodic inspiration: his creations were still being analysed, harmonized and itemized as perfection 50 years on. Rather than playing ever higher and harder, Armstrong simplified his creations, polishing each phrase to perfection while keeping his strength for the knockout punch and by 1930 he was a New York star, with imitators all around him. But his business life was at a temporary impasse. Then, in 1935, he found his Godfather-figure, a powerful, often ruthless Mafia operator, Joe Glaser, who was to steer his client's fortunes for 35 more years. In 1935, with Glaser's approval, Louis teamed with Luis Russell's orchestra, an aggregation of old New Orleans friends, and for five years he was to tour and record with them: the records are classics, and helped to get Armstrong into films such as *Pennies from Heaven* (1936), *Artists and Models* (1937) and others.

In 1940, Glaser's office brusquely sacked the band and Louis put together another. It contained younger 'modernists' such as John Brown (alto), Dexter Gordon (tnr) and Arvell Shaw, a long Louis associate, on bass, with Velma Middleton sharing the singing, and it lasted until summer 1947. But big bands were on a downward slide, Armstrong found leading his a headache, and in 1947 promoter Ernie Anderson presented him with a small band (directed by Bobby Hackett) at New York's Town Hall. The acclaim that greeted the decision signalled the end of his big-band career, and for the last 24 years of his life, Louis led his All Stars, a 6-piece band which featured, to begin with, a heady mixture of real stars ('too many make bad friends', said Armstrong ruefully later) including Jack Teagarden and Earl Hines. It developed into a more controllable and supportive team featuring, among others at various times, Barney Bigard and Ed Hall (clt) and, a strong right arm, Trummy Young (tmb). With his All Stars, Armstrong presented a tightly arranged show which, right down to repertoire and solos, seldom varied in later years, a policy which was sometimes criticized. But great records (perhaps his best) made with the All Stars, such as *Plays W. C. Handy*, *Plays Fats*, and a club set, *At the Crescendo*, turned into jazz anthems, and solos such as *Louis and the Good Book* and its superior follow-up *Louis and the Angels* revealed Armstrong at a wonderful late peak. The All Stars (at his own wish) maintained a crippling touring schedule and in 1959 he had his

Louis Armstrong

first heart attack. For his last ten years, amid hit parade successes, unabated touring and recurring illness, Armstrong gradually slowed down: by 1969, when he visited Britain for the last time, it was noticeable that his trumpet playing, still painfully beautiful, was rationed and that he was looking older. He died in bed (smiling) on 6 July 1971.

Impossible to remember Satch without remembering the man: 'He was a very joyous host,' says Ruby Braff, 'even in his dressing room with 50 people standing round.' It is time to kill off the legend that Armstrong's big heart was a pose: says Barney Bigard, 'There never was any hidden side to him. He came "as is".' Another legend deserves demolition; that Louis was simply the lucky one of countless talents in and around New Orleans (Jabbo Smith and Punch Miller are two cited contenders). The records prove otherwise. A recent suggestion

Art Ensemble of Chicago

has been that recurrent lip trouble (which Armstrong certainly suffered from) caused a musical decline from the 1930s on: performances from the 1930s to the end demonstrate his continuing achievement. Finally, the old accusation that Louis Armstrong was an 'Uncle Tom' (a black who pandered to the white man's image of his race): as Joe Muryani, his later clarinettist, says, 'Louis Armstrong was *nobody's* nigger!'

'He left an undying testimony to the human condition in the America of his time': Wynton Marsalis's way of saying, in 1985, that Louis was simply the greatest jazz trumpeter ever and, with Charlie Parker and Duke Ellington, the most influential jazzman of the classic era. [DF]

The Louis Armstrong Legend, 1925–9, World Records (4 records, boxed set); and any, from before or after, on which he sings, plays or speaks.

See Armstrong, Louis, *Satchmo: My Life in New Orleans* (Peter Davies, 1955); Jones, Max, and Chilton, John, *Louis: The Louis Armstrong Story 1900–71* (Studio Vista, 1971)

Arrangement covers a multitude of musical operations. In fact, the same ambiguity exists in non-jazz music, probably because a strong melody is seen by most people as more identifiable than its presentation, and the presentation (unless the tune is old enough to be in the public domain) cannot be copyrighted, whereas a melody can. Therefore, a new arrangement may refer to a slight redistribution of instruments (as on one of Ellington's many re-orchestrations of 'Mood Indigo') or it may mean taking a simple popular melody as the basis of an elaborate composition (such as Duke's 'arrangement' of 'Sidewalks of New York').

Aspects which would be less significant in other musics can have substantial impact on the content of a jazz performance, for instance in the several versions of Gillespie's 'Night in Tunisia' done with rhythmic patterns different from the original conception. Naturally, there is a considerable overlap between arrangement and composition in jazz, the question of quality in both areas often being determined by whether the result stimulates high-grade improvisation or not. [BP]

Art Ensemble of Chicago Saxist Roscoe Mitchell had been involved with the AACM (see ABRAMS, MUHAL RICHARD) since its inception, and in 1966, Lester Bowie (tpt) moved to Chicago, gravitated to the AACM and joined Mitchell's band. 1969, with bassist Malachi Favors and saxist Joseph Jarman, Mitchell and Bowie formed the Art Ensemble of Chicago. They moved to Paris, which in 1969 had a flourishing jazz scene and was a haven for black US musicians, and there they found their drummer, Don Moye. They stayed in Paris for 18 months, recorded twelve albums, appeared individually on LPs with several other expatriates, and when they returned to the USA at the end of 1971 the AEC and its members had laid the foundations of a solid international reputation.

The Ensemble showed a way out of the cul-de-sac of abstraction, and became one of the key groups of the 1970s and 1980s. Its inclusive, pluralistic music fused elements from free jazz and from the whole jazz tradition going right back to New Orleans, and there were also strong ethnic – particularly African – ingredients. Their performances also presented the music with brilliant theatricality; the stage crammed with both conventional instruments and all kinds of percussion and ethnic instruments, including gongs, whistles, log drums, and the musicians, their faces painted in African ceremonial designs, wearing outlandish hats and colourful African robes. David Spitzer wrote: 'The members of the group produce musical sounds which run the gamut from the traditional to the absurd and the surreal. They also include valid, humorous, vocal discourses and cries, as well as atypical sounds produced on traditional instruments.'

Since 1971 the group has toured and played major festivals all over the world, making a great impact and gaining a large international following. They have recorded for major labels including Atlantic and, since 1978, ECM on which they have three superb albums; during the mid-1970s they ran their own AECO record label for a while. Their LPs have received many awards including Record of the Year, 1970, from the Académie de Jazz Française for *People in Sorrow*; Album of the Year, *Melody Maker*, 1973–4, for *Bap Tizum*; *Full Force* was awarded Record of the Year (1980) by *Stereo Review*, *Melody Maker* and the *Downbeat* critics' poll, and also gained the Grand Prix Diamant du Disque de Montreux, 1981. [IC]

A Jackson in your House (1969), Affinity; *People in Sorrow* (1969), Nessa; *Reese and the Smooth Ones* (1969), Affinity; *Les Stances à Sophie* (1970), Nessa; *Live, Parts 1 & 2* (1970), Affinity; *Bap Tizum* (1972), Atlantic; *Kabalaba* (1974), AECO; *Nice Guys* (1978); *Full Force* (1980); *Urban Bushmen* (1980), all ECM

Arvanitas, Georges, piano. b. Marseilles, France, 13 June 1931. 1954, moved to Paris and began backing US visitors and residents. Recorded own first two albums with Art Taylor (1958) and Louis Hayes (1959), then led own quintet (1959–62). Married to American singer Barbara Belgrave, made two working visits to USA (1964–5, 1966), touring with Ted Curson and Yusef Lateef groups and singer Lloyd Price. Returning to Paris, involved in studio work and formed own trio which specialized in backing visiting musicians such as Dexter Gordon and Johnny Griffin, both live and occasionally on record. Though known chiefly for his driving accompaniments, Arvanitas is an excellent post-bop soloist with an attack reminiscent of Kenny Drew. [BP]

Dexter Gordon/Sonny Grey, *Live* (1973), Spotlite

Ashby, Harold Kenneth, tenor sax, b. Kansas City, 27 March 1925. He is often associated with the style of Ben Webster: his two brothers (Herbert and Alec) both worked with Webster, early on he listened to Webster in Chicago clubs, and Webster later sat in regularly with Ashby's quartet in Kansas City. By that time Ashby had worked with Walter Johnson's band and was doing the rounds with r & b groups. 1957, moved to New York, into a room adjacent to Webster and began a regular working association. 1958, Webster introduced him to Duke Ellington and two years later Ashby began depping in the orchestra, recording with Ellington alumni such as Webster, Johnny Hodges and Lawrence Brown, working in specific Ellingtonian projects (including the *My People* show) and joining permanently on 5 July 1968. He stayed until Ellington's death in 1974. Freelance work followed, with Benny Goodman, Sy Oliver and others, and as a soloist in New York jazz rooms. 1985, Ashby was making the rounds of jazz festivals, including Nice where he scored a monumental hit in 1986 playing driving, Ben Webster-inspired tenor. 'Harold must surely rank among the great unsung masters of jazz," says Eddie Cook. [DF]

Lawrence Brown, *Inspired Abandon* (1965), Jasmine

See Dance, Stanley, *The World of Duke Ellington* (Scribner's, 1970, repr. Da Capo, 1980)

Association for the Advancement of Creative Music, see ABRAMS, MUHAL RICHARD.

Assunto, Frank, Jack and John, see DUKES OF DIXIELAND.

Atonality The absence of a key signature or tonal centre, which has been attempted in some composed jazz but rarely with success. The only unforced development of atonality in jazz has taken place in some instances of 'free jazz', especially the collective improvisations of large groups of musicians; even then, such structural signposts as occur spontaneously often consist of hints at a common tonality. Certainly, in smaller 'free' groups, greater rhythmic freedom and freedom from predetermined structures have been sought, but atonality is not high on the agenda. Composers who have striven to achieve atonal jazz even complain that Ornette Coleman is not 'advanced' enough in this respect but, of course, he has been far more influential than the atonalists. [BP]

Auld, Georgie (John Altwerger), saxes, clarinet. b. Toronto, 19 May 1919. He came to prominence with Bunny Berigan's orchestra in 1937 playing swing saxophone that recalled two major influences, Coleman Hawkins and Ben Pollack's underrated Larry Binyon. 1939, joined Artie Shaw, taking over leadership for three months after Shaw's abdication, before moving to Benny Goodman in 1940 (he recorded classic sides with Goodman's sextet that year). After another short spell with Shaw he joined the army briefly in 1943 but came out to form his own band (1943–6) which significantly included young modern jazzmen, including Erroll Garner, Dizzy Gillespie and Al Porcino. Auld aligned himself firmly with the bebop movement, playing modern jazz at the Three Deuces and running his own Troubadour Club on 52nd Street before joining Billy Eckstine's magnificent big band. After a role on Broadway in *The Rat Race* (1949), Auld worked busily with his own quintet (1950–1), featuring Frank Rosolino and Tiny Kahn, then, because of lung trouble, moved to the sunnier climate of California to open his own club, the Melody Room. For the rest of the 1950s studio work, big-band and solo appearances kept him busy, and by 1967 he was musical director for Tony Martin. In the 1970s he became a star in Japan, undertaking over a dozen tours and recording 16 albums by 1975; two years later he took a leading soundtrack and onscreen role in the movie *New York, New York* (1977). A regular string of solo albums such as *Music for Winners* and a follow-up, *One for the Losers*, charts his musical course in the 1970s and 1980s. [DF]

Austin, Lovie (*née* Cora Calhoun), piano, arranger. b. Chattanooga, Tennessee, 19 September 1887; d. Chicago, 10 July 1972. A pioneer jazzwoman, she received a thorough music education at Roger Williams College, Nashville, and then at Knoxville College, before touring vaudeville circuits backing her husband's act and directing her own shows including *Lovie Austin's Revue* which had a long run at New York's Club Alabam. She then settled in Chicago, working as house pianist for Paramount Records, playing piano for Ma Rainey, Ida Cox and Ethel Waters, and composing hits such as 'Graveyard Blues' for Bessie Smith. 'Lovie wrote – and played – a mess of blues,' Alberta Hunter confirms. For over 20 years she was leader of the pit orchestra at Chicago's Monogram Theater and Mary Lou Williams remembers, 'seeing this great woman in the pit conducting a group of five or six men, a cigarette in her mouth and her legs crossed, playing the show with her left hand and writing music for the next act with her right'. Austin's many rampaging New Orleans-style records (featuring men such as Tommy Ladnier, Johnny Dodds and Jimmy O'Bryant) are classics, but she found herself out of fashion by the early 1930s with very little copyright protection to ensure royalties on her compositions. During World War II she had to work in a war factory, and after that became a dance school pianist. Her last records were made in Chicago in 1961. [DF]

Lovie Austin's Blues Serenaders (1924–6), Classic Jazz Masters

See Dahl, Linda, *Stormy Weather* (Quartet, 1984)

Australian Jazz The few times that Australian jazz has come to Europe it has usually made an impression. British revivalists post-war remember with special pleasure the collaborations of British trumpeter Humphrey Lyttelton with Australian pianist Graeme Bell and the almost disturbingly original contributions of such Bell sidemen as Ade Monsbourgh. Later Australians to make an impact in Europe (in their different ways) included singer Judith Durham and saxophonist Bob Bertles (from Ian Carr's Nucleus), but such musicians, top-class though they are, represent only the tip of an iceberg: in Australia itself a jazz scene flourishes which (it could be argued) produces the most stimulating music of any outside America. In 1985 the most universally rated performers included Bob Barnard (a post-war trumpeter of world-class talent who plays naturally in the Hackett–Braff area but regularly works studios as an in-demand lead player too), his brother Len Barnard (a drummer of comparable ability), Don Burrows (reeds and flute, who leads his own quartet), Errol Buddle (a saxophonic equivalent to Britain's Tubby Hayes), as well as, of course, bandleaders such as Graeme Bell, and leader-arrangers John Sangster, Dave Dallwitz and others. Highly rated Australian originals include Alan Nash, Eric Holroyd, Roger Bell (tpts), Ken Herron, Bob McIvor, John Costelloe (tmbs), John McCarthy, Graeme Lyall, Tony Buchanan, Paul Furniss (reeds), Col Nolan, Tony Gould, Chris Taperell (piano), among many others. Perhaps the most famous centre of activity for Australian jazz is the Sydney Jazz Club (opened in 1953 on the premises of the Real Estate Institute) which published its own magazine, *The Quarterly Rag*, from 1955 to 1970 and still flourishes. A host of other clubs ran in its shadow and equivalent jazz centres may be found in Perth, Melbourne, Brisbane and elsewhere. While senior performers such as Ade Monsbourgh, Roger Bell and others are now heard less often, their work is continued by other, younger men, including Tom Baker, an ex-trumpeter who, within a matter of months, turned into a saxophonist of scary ability, and a healthy host of other young hopefuls. One of the most enjoyable Australian jazz institutions is their annual Convention, a huge meeting of Australian (and sometimes international) Dixielanders which chooses a new location every year and confines itself primarily to the classic end of jazz music. But modern jazz flourishes in Australia too, notably in a hugely successful rock-based jazz band, Galapagos Duck, which achieved pop-star status in the early 1980s. [DF]

Any including John Sangster, *Lord of the Rings*, vols. 1–3 (1976–8) EMI

See Linehan, Norm, *Australian Jazz Picture Book* (Child and Henry, 1980)

Autrey, Herman, trumpet, vocals. b. Evergreen, Alabama, 4 December 1904; d. New York, 14 June 1980. He had had a very successful career for ten years from 1923 (with shows, dance bands, and his own group in Florida) and was working at Smalls' Paradise with Charlie Johnson's orchestra in 1934 when Fats Waller came talent-spotting with his new Victor recording contract. He hired Autrey on the spot. From then on came five glorious years of 'House Full' signs, record crowds, films, touring and recording sessions (often of unfamiliar material taken care of in a take or two). 'Fats was awful good to me', remembers Autrey. 'He treated me like a son!' Waller treated all his men well; on one occasion he bought Autrey an expensive trumpet which he kept for over 30 years. Autrey regularly doubled with other bands while Fats appeared solo and after Waller died he worked with Stuff Smith, played up and down 52nd Street, and became well known as a bandleader himself in Canada. In 1954 he was badly hurt in a car crash, but came back triumphantly and in the 1960s played with the immensely successful Saints and Sinners, a neat swing band featuring Rudy Powell and the great Vic Dickenson: their records are a delight. In the 1970s Autrey was busy as ever in New York; but most listeners will remember him for the commanding, rough-edged and occasionally wild trumpet that enlivened so many Waller creations. [DF]

Fats Waller, vol. 6 (1930–5), RCA

Avant-garde, see FREE JAZZ.

Axe A now outdated term for a musical instrument, used especially but not exclusively for brass or horns which performers can carry in one hand. Presumably dating from the era of 'cutting contests', when you used your axe to mow down the opposition. [BP]

Ayler, Albert, tenor, soprano and alto sax, voice, bagpipes, composer. b. Cleveland, Ohio, 13 July 1936; d. New York, 25 November 1970. His father Edward Ayler played sax and violin and sang; his brother Donald Ayler is a trumpet player. Albert began on alto sax at age seven; at ten he began a seven-year study period at the Academy of Music with Benny Miller, who had once played with Charlie Parker and Dizzy Gillespie. As a teenager he began playing with r & b bands including Lloyd Pearson's Counts of Rhythm and Little Walter (Jacobs). His early influences were Lester Young, Sidney Bechet, Wardell Gray and Charlie Parker, and in Cleveland he was nicknamed 'Little Bird'. 1958–61, did army service, playing in a Special Services band, and during this period he switched to tenor sax. After demobilization he found little sympathy for his unconventional musical ideas in the USA, and in 1962 left for Sweden where he worked with a commercial band and played his own music after hours. He made his first recordings there in October, and in January 1963 recorded in Copenhagen the album *My Name is Albert Ayler*, which has been called 'one of the classics of the new music'. He met Cecil Taylor in Scandinavia and began playing with him in New York.

Ayler's reputation, which had been made in Europe, followed him back to the USA, and he began to record regularly. He was a member of the Jazz Composers' Guild (see MANTLER, MICHAEL). 1964, with Don Cherry, Gary Peacock (bass) and Sunny Murray (dms), toured in Holland, Sweden and Denmark. 1965, formed a new group in the USA, with his brother Donald, saxophonist Charles Tyler, bassist Lewis Worrell and Murray again on drums, which recorded one of his most influential albums, *Bells*, live at a Town Hall concert. By this time controversy was raging about Ayler, ranging from assertions that he couldn't play and was a charlatan, to claims that he was the new Messiah of jazz.

Until about 1967, Ayler's music was a mixture of uncompromising abstraction and elements from traditional forms such as folk dances, marches, folk songs, and the dirges of old New Orleans funeral processions. As a saxophonist his true innovations were timbral, textural, and in the climate of feeling that he engendered. He had a huge, emotive sound with a strong vibrato, and he could move with rippling ease from gruff, honking low notes to hoarse screams in the extreme upper register – all the characteristics of r & b tenor sax playing abstracted and taken to their ultimate expression. In his work there is always a sense of violence barely under control, and he himself said in the early 1960s: 'It's not about notes any more. It's about feelings.' His tonal distortions and wild expressiveness spawned many imitators and disciples on the free jazz scene, particularly in Europe. It has been said that he was in many ways closer to Bubber Miley and Tricky Sam Nanton (both of whom used tonal distortion expressively) than he was to Charlie Parker, Miles Davis or Sonny Rollins. Ayler's music, however, always seems unfinished and incomplete, as if it is perhaps the raw material out of which an art might be made. It lacks the necessary self-editing process, and much of it is too long and monotonous.

Like several other leading players on the free jazz scene, Ayler began to turn away from abstraction in the later 1960s, and re-examined his musical roots. His work began to show strong elements from gospel music and r & b, and on his 1968 album *New Grass* he both talks – preaching religion – and sings with a nice little blues/gospel backing band which includes electric bass, Joe Newman on trumpet and Pretty Purdie on drums. He was accused by his old colleagues of 'selling out', but it is highly unlikely that he was capable of such shallowness. Ayler was a driven man, deeply religious, with a powerful premonition of his own imminent death and the sincerity of one who can do only what he does. He died in mysterious circumstances: in November 1970 he had not been seen for 20 days when his body was found floating in the East River, New York. He had died by drowning.

Ayler has had a considerable influence, parti-

Albert Ayler

cularly on saxophonists. He certainly influenced John Coltrane, who admired him, and who, after he had recorded his album *Ascension* (1965), told Ayler, 'I found I was playing just like you.' Through Coltrane, Ayler's spirit and sound have touched countless subsequent musicians. [IC]

My Name is Albert Ayler (1963), Fantasy; Ayler/Don Cherry, *Vibrations* (1964), Arista Freedom; *Witches and Devils* (1964), Arista Freedom; *Spiritual Unity* (1964); *Bells* (1965); *Spirits Rejoice* (1965), all ESP; *New Grass* (1968), Impulse

B

Bailey, Benny (Ernest Harold), trumpet. b. Cleveland, Ohio, 13 August 1925. Early work as a teenager in r & b context led to joining Jay McShann (1947), Dizzy Gillespie big band (1947–8) and Lionel Hampton (1949–53). Remained in Europe after Hampton tour of 1953 and worked in radio studio bands, then joined Quincy Jones's band which débuted in Paris and toured in USA (1959–61). Returned to Europe and completed many years of studio work in Sweden, Germany and Switzerland; during this period, played on all the engagements of the Kenny Clarke–Francy Boland band. More recently, has made occasional small-group records and has worked in USA again. In big-band circles Bailey is revered for his section-leading ability, but his solo improvising has been vastly underrated. From a bebop-inspired approach he has fashioned a very individual style full of long lines and angular melodies, and his mannerism of dropping two octaves in the space of one note is instantly recognizable, even in the most uninspiring studio bands. [BP]

Serenade to a Planet (1977), Ego

Bailey, Buster (William C.), clarinet, saxes. b. Memphis, Tennessee, 19 July 1902; d. Brooklyn, New York, 12 April 1967. He acquired his legendary lightning technique from a classical teacher, Franz Schoepp, who taught at Chicago Music College (two or three years later another Schoepp pupil was Benny Goodman), and by 1917 was touring with W. C. Handy's famous showband. Work with Erskine Tate and King Oliver followed and then in October 1924, one week after Louis Armstrong, Bailey joined Fletcher Henderson. In Henderson's technically demanding orchestra his speed and near-classical accuracy of execution became a byword, and he moved into the select and invincible A-team of Henderson soloists headed by Coleman Hawkins. With short breaks he remained until 1937, when he found another showcase in the perfectly polished and phenomenally successful John Kirby band. With Kirby came a starry round of cabaret work, hit records and weekly radio exposure. Once again, amid the intricate Charlie Shavers creations for Kirby, Bailey's woody, occasionally reedy and always precise playing found the perfect setting. After the war he led his own band again on 52nd Street, spent two years with Wilbur de Paris and struck up a regular relationship with trumpeter Henry 'Red' Allen, as well as lending his technique to concerts with the Sauter-Finegan orchestra, pitwork with the Ziegfeld Theater orchestra, and symphony concerts. From 1954 he was a regular member of Red Allen's band at New York's fast and furious Metropole sessions, and took part in definitive mainstream recordings with Taft Jordan, Pee Wee Erwin, Hawkins, Allen and others. After more freelancing with Wild Bill Davison, the Saints and Sinners and others, Bailey, prosperous, elegant, of stately mien, ended his career with Louis Armstrong, with whom he had joined Fletcher Henderson 40 years before, playing his supporting role as perfectly as ever. [DF]

All About Memphis (1958), Affinity

Bailey, Derek, guitar. b. Sheffield, Yorkshire, 29 January 1930. Grandfather a professional pianist/banjoist; uncle a professional guitarist. 1941–52, studied music with C. H. C. Biltcliffe and guitar with John Duarte, among others. 1952–65, worked as a guitar soloist, accompanist or with orchestras in every kind of musical context: clubs, concert halls, dance halls, theatres, radio, TV and recording studios. From 1963 he became increasingly interested in the possibilities of freely improvised music: he has said, 'I have had the good fortune to work with most of the leading German blasters, American groovers, Dutch acrobats and English kaleidoscopists in this field.'

Since 1965 he has performed solo concerts in all major cities of Europe, Japan and the USA. 1970, formed, jointly with Evan Parker and Tony Oxley, Incus Records, the first independent, musician-owned record company in Britain. 1976, formed Company, a changing ensemble of improvising musicians featuring players from Europe, North and South America, Africa and Japan. In the 1960s he worked with the Spontaneous Music Ensemble, but since then has gradually withdrawn from group music, preferring to play solo electric guitar and only occasionally performing in duos with people to whom he feels a strong affinity: Evan Parker, Steve Lacy and Tony Coe are among the few.

He has pursued the austere path of total improvisation and abstraction with monolithic integrity, becoming one of the masters in that field. Yet, despite the severity of his approach, his music is often alive with drama, intelligence and anarchic humour; ironically, his album *View from 6 Windows* (1982, Metalanguage), was nominated for a Grammy award. Bailey has also

Derek Bailey

written an important and controversial book on improvisation, examining it in all its manifestations, from the European classical tradition to vernacular music of all kinds – ethnic, rock, jazz and free improvisation. It has been translated into Italian, French, Japanese and Dutch. [IC]

Since 1968, over 60 albums on various labels: with Tony Coe (clarinet in C), *Time* (1979), Incus; solo acoustic guitar, *Aida* (1980), Incus; with *Music Improvisation Company* (1970), ECM; with Evan Parker and Han Bennink, *The Topography of the Lungs* (1970), Incus; with Lacy, *Company 4* (1977), Incus

See Bailey, Derek, *Improvisation – its Nature and Practice in Music* (Moorland Publishing, 1980; Prentice-Hall, USA, 1983)

Bailey, Mildred (*née* Mildred Rinker), vocals. b. Tekoa, nr. Seattle, Washington, 27 February 1907; d. Poughkeepsie, New York, 12 December 1951. Mildred Rinker and her brother Al went to school in Spokane (where Bing Crosby attended a Jesuit college). Later she sang in local cabarets such as Charlie Dale's and on local radio before sending a demonstration record to Paul Whiteman who was persuaded to hire her by what he heard and by his newly hired 'Rhythm Boys', Rinker, Crosby and Harry Barris. Beautifully featured (she signed early photographs 'Face Bailey') but very fat, she had, said Crosby and most of her contemporaries, a 'heart as big as Yankee Stadium'. From 1929 for the next four years she sang with Whiteman; a 1932 hit, 'Rockin' Chair', dubbed her 'The Rockin' Chair Lady', scarcely the most attractive image for a young woman. In 1933, almost comically fat, she married the diminutive Red Norvo (contemporary publicity shots of the couple are determinedly comedic) and with him was to achieve more fame with hits like 'Weekend of a Private Secretary'. She was Norvo's featured band singer, 1936–9. But for Bailey it was an insecure marriage. 'As salty as a fishwife', according to her perceptive biographer Bucklin Moon, she blamed any lack of success on her appearance, and treated all around her to shows of deep affection alternating with towering outbursts of blackmouthed rage. The retiring, eager-to-please Norvo once confided to cornettist Rex Stewart that 'Mildred was really two people – one, a warm solicitous wife, the other a moody and excitable artist.'

Bailey, the first prominent female band singer (as Hoagy Carmichael says), was a big star for most of the 1930s. Her records outsold most other female singers of the period apart from Billie Holiday, a singer for whom she had the highest musical (if not personal) respect. She had radio series of her own, a distinguished list of recorded accompanists and more money than she could spend. By 1939, though, her partnership with Norvo showed signs of cracking. She had cut short a 1938 tour to return to New York amid nervous strain and bad feeling among her accompanists, and by late 1939 was a solo singer and featured star on Benny Goodman's Camel Caravan programme. Her divorce was finalized in 1943. Despite continuing clubwork around New York (at Café Society, the Blue Angel and elsewhere) her career was on a downhill swing, complicated by a liver complaint and a hint of heart trouble. By 1948, according to Irving Townsend, she was living with her beloved dogs in a ground-floor apartment on East 31st Street, NY, lonely, but still as unpredictably kind or angry, and beginning to be ill. In 1949 she was taken to hospital near death (Bing Crosby and Frank Sinatra made arrangements for her care and paid the bills), and despite returns to work with Joe Marsala and Ralph Burns she never really got better and died penniless, in 1951, of liver and heart failure. Women's liberation and the 1980s might have understood her career better than the 1930s and 1940s could. [DF]

Mildred Bailey: Her Greatest Performances, 1929–46, CBS

See Dance, Stanley, *The World of Swing* (Scribner's, 1974, repr. Da Capo, 1979)

Baker, Chet (Chesney H.), trumpet, fluegelhorn, vocals. b. Yale, Oklahoma, 23 December 1929. After musical study and army service, played briefly with Charlie Parker (1952) then spent a year with the first Gerry Mulligan quartet. With Mulligan out of commission in 1953, Baker formed his own quartet (1953–6). His career was intermittent in the late 1950s and 1960s owing to involvement with

Mildred Bailey

narcotics, and most of his time in the last three decades has been spent in Europe, although he continues to visit the USA.

Baker was acclaimed as a 'great white hope' at the tender age of 23, a burden from which his image has never really recovered. Not one of nature's bandleaders, he seldom asserts his authority and has taken part in some highly unsatisfying performances and albums. In the same way that his solo style is still in thrall to early Miles Davis, much of his favourite repertoire is selected from tunes recorded by Miles. Fragile to the point of transparency, like his singing, the trumpet work treads a tightrope between affirmation and apathy but, when the surroundings are right, Baker's lyrical playing can easily make the listener forget all reservations. [BP]

Baker/Art Pepper, *Playboys* (1956), Boplicity; *Daybreak* (1979), Steeplechase

Baker, David Nathaniel, Jnr., trombone, cello, composer. b. Indianapolis, Indiana, 21 December 1931. Played with Indianapolis natives Wes Montgomery and Slide Hampton, toured on trombone with Buddy Johnson, Stan Kenton (1956), Maynard Ferguson (1957), Lionel Hampton and Quincy Jones (1961). 1960–2, was member of George Russell sextet until muscular problem forced him to concentrate on cello. Became enormously energetic teacher/theoretician as author of numerous textbooks and solo transcriptions, and as chairman of jazz department of Indiana University from 1966. Probably the first musician with an established performing reputation to move full-time into jazz education, Baker had compositions such as 'LeRoi' and 'Honesty' recorded by other musicians. Especially while with Russell, he displayed a brilliant technique and was one of the first trombonists to incorporate avant-garde effects such as slides, smears, rips and fall-offs. [BP]

George Russell, *Ezz-thetics* (1961), Riverside/OJC

Baker, Ginger (Peter), drums. b. Lewisham, London, 19 August 1940. Interested in blues and jazz while at school and took up drums. Early 1960s, played with Alexis Korner and then Graham Bond. 1966, formed Cream with Eric Clapton and Jack Bruce: the group became immensely popular in the USA and won gold awards for all its albums. It disbanded in 1968 at the height of its success. 1969, with Clapton, Stevie Winwood and Rick Grech, Baker formed Blind Faith, touring in UK and USA. After that group broke up, Baker formed Air Force, which played Afro-jazz-flavoured music and featured some leading jazz musicians including saxist Harold McNair. By the 1980s, Baker was living in semi-retirement on a farm in Italy. [IC]

With Cream, *Heavy Cream*, *Off the Top* (1967), *Wheels of Fire* (1968), all Polydor

Baker, Kenny, trumpet, cornet, fluegelhorn, composer, leader. b. Withernsea, East Yorkshire, 1 March 1921. He was first heard (on record) in a British public jam session of 1941, and quickly established an unbeatable reputation in London clubs. Brass band trained, with faultless technical command, the young Baker was lead trumpeter with Ted Heath's post-war orchestra (such *tours de force* as 'Bakerloo Non-stop' are still well remembered), and in the 1950s led his own Baker's Dozen for which he played lead and solos and wrote the library. By the 1950s Baker was regularly in studios, but his numerous jazz recordings (with a quartet for Parlophone, with groups of all kinds for Nixa and others) are world-class, a confident replay of Bunny Berigan without the errors and range to spare. So good was Baker that when the Musicians' Union were trying to justify their ban on American players working in Britain, they were able to ask, 'While we have Kenny Baker who needs Louis?' In the 1960s and 1970s he was still on call for film and studio work (a famous appearance on soundtrack for Baker was a long hot-trumpet solo mimed by Kay Kendall in the film *Genevieve*, 1954), but he regularly emerged to play jazz clubs, often with co-trumpeter John McLevey. He formed *The Best of British Jazz*, a show (with Don Lusher and Betty Smith) which toured regularly from 1976, and after the death of Harry James in 1983 was asked by the James Foundation to take over their orchestra. A small fighting-cock of a man (he once elbowed Benny Goodman out of the way for persistently misjudging the tempo of a Baker feature on British concerts), Baker is a world-class lead trumpeter, solo performer and improviser. [DF]

The Phase 4 World of Kenny Baker (1962–77), Decca

Baker, Shorty (Harold), trumpet. b. St Louis, Missouri, 26 May 1913; d. New York, 8 November 1966. One of the great line of St Louis trumpeters which begins with Charlie Creath in the 1920s and goes on to Miles Davis in the 1980s, Baker's main influences were Louis Armstrong and Joe Smith, both men of beautiful sound, and Baker, working in their image, began his career on riverboats, with Fate Marable, and on the road, with Erskine Tate, Don Redman, Teddy Wilson and Andy Kirk (he later married Mary Lou Williams, Kirk's pianist). 'He was an excellent section man,' says Clark Terry, 'and they all loved having him around; he was such a happy humorous man!' The first of countless stays with Duke Ellington began in 1942 and Baker was one of the most popular figures in the orchestra. His glassy-clear tone (which he achieved with a rare Hein mouthpiece, deep, thin, hard to handle and produced in St Louis) was often featured in Ellington niceties like 'Mr Gentle and Mr Cool' (with Ray Nance, his close friend), 'All Heart' and Hoagy Carmichael's 'Stardust'. Perhaps it was Baker's long and happy association with Ellington that regularly gave him the heart to leave, however. 'When you leave Duke's organization,' he told Stanley Dance, 'you feel very confident playing in any other band.' Some of his freelance years were spent with Ben Webster, Teddy Wilson, and Johnny Hodges' small band. In 1964, while Baker was at the Embers with a quartet, throat trouble put him in hospital. He was cheerful to visitors and still busy planning a future, but cancer had taken hold. [DF]

Billy Strayhorn, *Cue for Saxophone* (1959), Felsted

See Dance, Stanley, *The World of Duke Ellington* (Scribner's, 1970, rep. Da Capo, 1980)

Baldock, Ken (Kenneth Ernest), piano, double bass, bass guitar, educator. b. London, 5 April 1932. Mother played piano. Piano lessons at age six; studied piano and bass at the Guildhall School of Music and Drama. During the

1960s, he was associated with John Dankworth for nine years, playing TV, festival and recording dates; 1975–6, with the Ronnie Scott quartet; since 1981, has been with the Bobby Wellins quartet; has also led his own occasional groups, and has, since 1975, been double bass tutor at the Barry (Wales) summer school; also teaches piano. Baldock has worked with many other leading musicians, including Coleman Hawkins, Ben Webster, Benny Carter, Lockjaw Davis, Milt Jackson, Joe Pass, Barney Kessel, Cleo Laine, Anita O'Day and Joe Williams. He represented the UK at the 1972 and 1973 Montreux Jazz Festivals playing and recording with Teddy Wilson, Stephane Grappelli, Bill Coleman and others. In 1976 and 1977, appeared with Oscar Peterson in two TV series. [IC]

With Gordon Beck, Al Haig, Buddy DeFranco, Phil Seamen and many others; with Teddy Wilson, *Runnin' Wild* (1973) Black Lion; with Barney Kessel, *Summertime in Montreux* (1973) Black Lion; with *Jay McShann and Al Casey* (1984), JSP

Ball, Kenny (Kenneth), trumpet, vocals, bandleader. b. Ilford, Essex, 22 May 1930. Started his career in bands led by Charlie Galbraith, Sid Phillips and Eric Delaney before forming his own in 1958. It quickly set a new standard for British Dixieland of the period: sidemen such as Dave Jones (clt), John Bennett (tmb) and Ron Weatherburn (piano) seemed to come from nowhere and easily equalled the red-hot trumpet of their leader, who sounded as technically assured as the players he loved, Louis Armstrong, Kenny Baker and Clifford Brown (a highly eclectic set of influences for the period). Signed to Jack Fallon's Cana agency, the band quickly produced a hit single for Pye ('I love you, Samantha' from *High Society*). More followed (including 'Midnight in Moscow', 'March of the Siamese Children' and 'So do I'), and Ball's band rapidly became the most successful jazz act of the Trad boom. After the rock set in, Ball worked in cabaret, conquered a worrying spell of lip trouble and by 1968 was back to full form supporting Louis Armstrong at London concerts. Changes in his band personnel brought in clarinettist Andy Cooper (replacing Jones) and Johnny Parker (replacing Weatherburn). In the 1970s he continued to tour jazz clubs and theatres in Britain and Europe: peak spots on TV shows such as Morecambe and Wise and Saturday Night at the Mill and regular appearances on Royal Variety Shows kept him in the public eye, and by the 1980s the trumpeter had become what every jazzman would like to be, a much-loved household name. Like Acker Bilk, Ball recorded commercial material almost on a separate basis from his jazz output, but much of everything he issued is worth hearing. One album with strings, for example, (*A Friend to You*) features good songs such as 'Nina Never Knew', appealing slightly vulnerable singing and weathered trumpet. In 1985 Kenny Ball's was the first British band to tour in the Soviet Union, where he was received with rapture. [DF]

Ballad, a slowish popular song, or an original jazz composition in that style or at least that tempo. As instrumental virtuosity has increased and with it the range of tempos used, 'ballad tempo' has become slower and slower. When Louis Armstrong recorded the first jazz version of 'Body and Soul' in 1930, it moved along at 120 beats per minute, but when Freddie Hubbard did the millionth version of the same tune in 1981 the acceptable tempo had dropped to 48 bpm.

A slow ballad and a slow blues played at exactly the same tempo will probably not feel the same, the blues having more pent-up power and the ballad more relaxed lyricism. [BP]

Ballamy, Iain Mark, soprano, alto and tenor sax, flute, piano. b. Guildford, Surrey, 20 February 1964. Father a pianist. Self-taught; began on piano at age six, switching to alto sax at 14. 1983, started his own quartet, the Iains, which includes Django Bates on keyboards; also a founder member of the big band Loose Tubes. Has also played with Gordon Beck, John Taylor, Stan Sulzmann, Gil Evans, Jim Mullen, Bill Bruford and John Stevens, among others. The Iains toured the UK in October 1985, and in November played at the Baden-Baden New Jazz Meeting; 1986, the group toured Morocco, and Ballamy also toured Japan with Bruford. Since 1985, he has been a member of Billy Jenkins's Voice of God Collective. In 1985 Ballamy was awarded the John Dankworth cup for the most promising Young Musician soloist. His favourites include Roland Kirk, Charlie Parker, John Coltrane and John Surman, and other inspirations include his own musical associates, Miles Davis, Gil Evans, Charles Ives and others. [IC]

With Bruford; with *Loose Tubes* (1984), Loose Tubes; with Billy Jenkins's Voice of God Collective, *Greenwich* (1985), Wood Wharf; *Uncommerciality* (1986), All Music

Banks, Billy (William), vocals. b. Alton, Illinois, *c*.1908; d. Tokyo, 19 October 1967. A protégé of Irving Mills, who heard him in Cleveland and brought him to New York to open at Connie's Inn in 1932, Banks is remembered best as titular head of the Rhythmakers, a legendary studio group starring Henry 'Red' Allen and Fats Waller which recorded for Mills that year. To the sessions, often cited since by record companies as 'the hottest jazz ever recorded', Banks contributed high-pitched intense vocals (he was a part-time female impersonator). 1934–8, after a brief return to Cleveland to run his parents' shoe shop, he toured with bandleader Noble Sissle. From 1938 for twelve years he was featured cabaret star at Billy Rose's legendary Diamond Horseshoe bar and by 1952 was touring Europe, including Holland, France and

Britain (where he appeared and recorded, including two sides with Freddy Randall's band). After more touring, including Asia and Australia, he settled in Japan where he died. [DF]

Billy Banks and his Rhythmakers (1932), VJM

Barbarin, (Adolphe) Paul, drums, leader, composer. b. New Orleans, 5 May 1899; d. 10 February 1969. By his teens New Orleans' most famous drummer was already a familiar figure in the Young Olympia Brass Band, and in 1917 he struck out for Chicago to work its clubs and cabarets with, among others, Freddie Keppard and Jimmie Noone. Then it was back to New Orleans, to Chicago again to work with King Oliver's Dixie Syncopators, home again and finally his most prestigious trip so far, to join Luis Russell's newly-formed band with Henry 'Red' Allen in New York. Records with Russell such as 'Panama' and 'Jersey Lightning' illustrate his driving New Orleans-based approach. So do classics like 'Knockin' a Jug' and 'Mahogany Hall Stomp' in which Louis Armstrong sounds particularly happy. 1929–32, and again 1935 (with Louis again), Barbarin provided Russell with the 'good old New Orleans up-and-down' beloved of Jimmie Lunceford, but then returned home again to lead his own band. From then on, with regular trips north to play with Bechet and Allen, guest celebrity spots with Art Hodes in Chicago (1953), and bandleading enterprises for clubs such as Child's in New York, Barbarin was happy to base himself, when he could, in hometown New Orleans. There he led parades, formed his own successful band, played clubs, and regularly toured the US state capitals as a billtopper.

In 1955 he formed his own Onward Brass Band: it became his mission to see his band march in the whites-only Proteus carnival procession that precedes Mardi Gras. The year they finally did, 1969, Barbarin collapsed on parade and died. [DF]

Paul Barbarin: recorded in New Orleans, vol. 1 (1956), Good Time Jazz

Barber, Chris, trombone, bass trumpet, bass, vocals, composer, arranger. b. Welwyn Garden City, Herts, 17 April 1930. He formed his first band in 1948; by 1951 it featured two fine trumpeters, Ben Cohen and Dick Hawdon, later a senior tutor at Leeds Music College, and the records they made are worth looking for. After a brief attempt to team up with Ken Colyer in 1953 however ('the whole band was sacked or sacked Ken, depending on who was telling the story,' says George Melly), Barber brought in trumpeter Pat Halcox, a strong and latterly versatile player. From that day his band, featuring blues singer Ottilie Patterson, clarinettist Monty Sunshine, Barber's own bucolic trombone and banjoist-singer Lonnie Donegan (replaced by Eddie Smith after 'Rock Island Line' recorded for a Barber album turned Donegan into a pop star), was set fair for success. It featured a broadly-based adventurous repertoire (reminiscent of the kind of policy Wilbur de Paris operated in the USA), and quickly produced 'turntable hits' like 'Whistling Rufus', a jaunty cakewalk, 'Bobbie Shafto' and two for Monty Sunshine, 'Hushabye' and 'Petite Fleur', which did much to launch the Trad boom of the late 1950s and ensured Sunshine a successful bandleading career of his own. All through the boom years, Barber's band, now with Ian Wheeler on clarinet, remained at the top of the popularity polls (despite a lack of hit-parade singles) and after the Beatles invasion of 1962, it was Barber who most cleverly and courageously coped with the switch in fashion.

While other bands resigned themselves to cabaret-style re-runs of old glories, Barber, whose knowledge of, involvement in, and affection for the blues predated the whole 1960s rediscovery by 20 years, quickly re-formed as Chris Barber's Jazz and Blues Band, brought in an electric rhythm-section (featuring a fine blues guitarist, John Slaughter) and played on regardless, combining his previous repertoire with contemporary blues-based material. The band's performances of the period are remarkable for their eclecticism: *Battersea Rain Dance*, which contained tunes by John Handy, a contemporary alto-saxophonist, and *Drat that Fratle Rat* which corralled modern rock players such as Tony Ashton alongside his regular band members. By now these included an outstanding young Nottingham-based reedman, John Crocker, and Pete York, a versatile young rock drummer who had worked with Spencer Davis. In the 1970s and 1980s Barber continued to work on new jazz projects: a six-volume autobiographical set for Black Lion which traced the history of the Barber band from year one, regular new tours including *Echoes of Ellington* (a collaboration with Ellingtonians Russell Procope and Wild Bill Davis) and a stimulating teaming of Trummy Young with pianist John Lewis (who wrote a suite for the Barber band which back in the 1950s would have been cheerfully dismissed as impossible). In the 1980s came the highly successful *Take Me Back to New Orleans* package with singer/pianist Dr John, which received, as do most of Barber's projects, comprehensive radio, TV and record coverage.

Barber's career over 40 years has been unflaggingly successful, thanks to his canny business sense, American-style bandleading policy, which keeps an eye on fashion without bowing to it too extravagantly, and all-round 'entertainment without compromise' standards. While created in the image of the great American masters, his music is an important oeuvre of its own in international jazz terms. [DF]

Can't We Get Together? (1954–84), Timeless Traditional (double)

Barbieri, Gato (Leandro J.), tenor sax, composer. b. Rosario, Argentina, 28 November

Chris Barber

1934. Uncle played tenor sax. Family moved to Buenos Aires. Took up clarinet at 12 after hearing a recording of Charlie Parker's 'Now's the Time'. Private lessons for five years, also studying alto sax and composition, then at 20 he took up tenor sax. He rejected the music of his homeland, and soon became Argentina's leading jazz musician, playing in Lalo Schifrin's orchestra, then leading bands of his own and working with visiting American stars. After seven months in Brazil, he and his Italian-born wife went in 1962 to Europe, living in Rome. His reputation grew; 1963, met Don Cherry, working with him for the next few years. With Cherry, Barbieri went deeply into the avant-garde music of the time – free (abstract) improvisation heavily influenced by Ornette Coleman – and the recordings he made then with Cherry have been described as 'among the seminal works of the "new music"'. 1967, after recording the album *In Search of Mystery* under his own name, Barbieri began to move away from abstraction and to explore his own neglected cultural roots. He has said, 'After this record I felt something was wrong and I had to make a choice. I always liked to play melody and improvisation and rhythm . . . in Argentina I [had] played everything: tango, mambo, Brazilian music, guaracha, etc . . . So slowly, slowly, I changed.' He began incorporating the rhythms, harmonies and melodic flavour of South American music into his own work, forging a new and more powerful identity in the process. His tenor sound became even warmer and more resonant, giving his driving, impassioned style a lyrical, more human dimension, and his music was enriched by a greater range of textures, colours and rhythms. 1969, recorded his first important album, calling it *The Third World*, then returned to Argentina to go more deeply into his roots. 1972, composed and played the music for Bernardo Bertolucci's film *Last Tango in Paris*, and the album won him a Grammy award. The film music changed him overnight from a cult figure into an international star, and he returned to South America to make a series of albums with local musicians and native instruments in Buenos Aires and Rio de Janeiro. Since then he has recorded and toured largely with musicians from South America, playing festivals there and in the USA and Europe. Barbieri's music must be seen as part of the post-abstraction phase of jazz, and as one of the first examples of the new and beneficial influence of Latin-American musicians on the music – an influence which grew rapidly during the later 1970s and shows no sign of diminishing in the 1980s. [IC]

With Carla Bley and Gary Burton, three with Cherry, one with Charlie Haden's Liberation Music Orchestra; *In Search of Mystery* (1967), ESP; *The Third World* (1969), Flying Dutchman; *El Pampero* (1971), Flying Dutchman; *Last Tango in Paris* (1972), United Artists; *Chapter One: Latin America* (1973); *Chapter Two: Hasta Siempre* (1974); *Chapter Three: Viva Emiliano* (1975); *Chapter Four: Alive in New York* (1976), all ABC Impulse

Barefield, Eddie (Edward Emmanuel), saxes, clarinet, arranger. b. Scandia, Iowa, 12 December 1909. He worked first in territory bands in the late 1920s and by 1930 was with Bernie Young's band when he first heard Lester Young and Art Tatum, two primary influences. 1932, travelled to New York with Bennie Moten then with the Cotton Pickers (at the time they included Roy Eldridge and young brother Joe) and the following year joined Cab Calloway for three years. For the rest of the 1930s Barefield was constantly to be found in the best company and bands, including Fletcher Henderson, Don Redman (he also became musical director for Ella Fitzgerald in 1942), and Coleman Hawkins. For much of the rest of the 1940s he worked in studios and for Broadway shows as musical director. Throughout the 1950s he was MD for Cab Calloway, toured, played in studios and freelanced with a variety of top bands (including the Dukes of Dixieland) and remained very busy with Sammy Price, the *Jazz Train* production, in films and leading bands of his own. By the late 1970s Barefield was appearing in the New York production of *One mo' time*, and producing fine new albums, one appropriately and happily titled *The Indestructible Eddie Barefield* for Harry Lim's Famous Door label. A lifelong friend of Ben Webster, Barefield now concentrates on tenor exclusively and like another Webster associate, Budd Johnson, deserves to be much better known than he is. [DF]

The Indestructible Eddie Barefield (1977), Famous Door

See Dance, Stanley, *The World of Count Basie* (Scribner's, New York, Sidgwick & Jackson, London, 1980)

Barker, Danny (Daniel), guitar, banjo, composer. b. New Orleans, 13 January 1909. By 1930 in New York after a New Orleans apprenticeship and some time in Chicago with – among others – 'Li'l' Brother' Montgomery, he was busy with clubwork, but apart from a contract with Mae West's show ('the first chance I had to make a little loot in the depression!' he remembered later) was often working for a few cents a night in the hard years. From this slow financial start, Barker moved into the big bands: Benny Carter, Lucky Millinder and in 1939 Cab Calloway, who called him 'a fabulous player': Barker stayed for seven years. Then came a further spell accompanying Blue Lu, his singer wife, and regular work with companion New Orleans men such as his uncle Paul Barbarin, Albert Nicholas and Wilbur de Paris, actor Conrad Janis, and as a single, a duo and full-time bandleader at Jimmy Ryan's in the early 1960s. In 1965 Barker moved back to New Orleans to play and lead parades (he was Grand Marshal for the Congo Square Brass Band in 1969), coached the Fairview Baptist Youth Band, and by 1977 was still leading his French Market Jazz Band in Tradition Hall, soloing like a virtuoso and leading the ensemble.

Just as important as his performing career, he is a devoted researcher and author who cherishes the jazz life, sees its music as a discipline to be valued and studied and its people as of colossal and often neglected importance. In this second role, Barker was for many years assistant curator of the New Orleans jazz museum, a seasoned commentator for TV, radio and educational outlets, and co-wrote (with Jack Buerkle) the best study of New Orleans music, *Bourbon Street Black* (OUP, 1973). 'A fine teacher of the unwritten history of colour and of music,' said Studs Terkel. [DF]

Danny Barker's Band (1986), Period

See Barker, Danny, *A Life in Jazz* (Macmillan, 1986)

Barker, Stan (Stanley), piano. b. Clitheroe, Lancashire, 24 May 1926. A fine eclectic jazz pianist who works with his trio in the Midlands and regularly backs American visitors such as Billy Butterfield, Al Grey and Buddy Tate, he is also co-director of a successful educational organization, Jazz College, which operates in schools, colleges and universities throughout the Midlands and North of England (as well as the southern regions more regularly in 1986). His activities include regular teaching for the Royal Northern College of Music, Merseyside Arts, South Wales Arts Association, Belfast School of Music and Southport Arts Centre, where since 1979 he has been Artist in Residence, as well as regular appearances on the club circuit with his trio, and solo for radio and TV. [DF]

With Digby Fairweather, *Let's Duet* (1984), Essex Records

Barlow, Dale, tenor and soprano sax, composer, b. Sydney, Australia, 25 December 1959. Father a saxophonist/clarinettist. Started on piano at an early age; studied classical flute and clarinet; played alto sax until 16, then switched to tenor. Private tuition, and also took the Jazz

Diploma Studies course at New South Wales Conservatorium. Played Monterey Jazz Festival, USA, in 1979, as featured soloist with a young Australian band. Recorded and played with many leading Australian jazz groups. 1982–3, studied and played in New York. Has toured Europe and the USA extensively with various groups. Played a concert with Sonny Stitt and Richie Cole, which was recorded. Also played and recorded with Cedar Walton and Billy Higgins. Currently leading own groups in the UK and Europe. Barlow's favourites are John Coltrane, Sonny Rollins, Wayne Shorter, Joe Henderson and 'anyone who's any good'. Other inspirations: Miles Davis, Stravinsky, Bartók, Hancock, Bach, African and South American music. [IC]

Dale Barlow with the Cedar Walton Trio (1985), Criss Cross; with the Benders (recorded in Sydney), *E* (1982), Hot

Barnes, George, guitar. b. Chicago Heights, Illinois, 17 July 1921; d. 1977. He won a Tommy Dorsey Amateur Swing Contest when he was 16, but by that time had been on the road for three years with his own quartet. 1938, recorded with blues singers Washboard Sam, Big Bill Broonzy and Jazz Gillum while working as a staffman for NBC in Chicago and carried on with staffwork (plus a stint with Bud Freeman) until 1942 when he was called up. After demobilization he went back to the studios, broadcast with his nifty progressive octet and played each week on the Plantation Party Show. By 1951 he had graduated to New York, working for TV and radio and recording with Louis Armstrong (whose *Musical Autobiography* set features him), Yank Lawson, Ernie Royal, Kai Winding and Bobby Hackett. Barnes's clipped electric guitar with its blues-based phrasing would have fitted rock and roll perfectly but, in public at least, he stayed faithful to his jazz roots and in the early 1960s formed a guitar duo for concerts and clubs with veteran master Carl Kress. After Kress's death in 1965 he carried on the idea with a younger partner, Bucky Pizzarelli. The lovely music they made, and their spectacular breakup after a quarrel, are both bemusedly reported by Whitney Balliett in *New York Notes* (1972). 'The guitarists' swan set at the tiny St Regis room', he wrote, 'was played not on their instruments but on each other!' 1973, Barnes teamed with Ruby Braff in a dazzling quartet, one of the great small groups in all jazz. By 1975, though, the finely honed sensitivities of the co-leaders had drawn sparks and the group ended. Barnes died soon after of a heart attack. [DF]

The Best I've Heard: the Braff–Barnes Quartet (1973–4), Vogue Jazz (double)

Barnes, John, saxes, clarinet. b. Manchester, 15 May 1932. A 'strict' New Orleans-style clarinettist in his early years, he began his career with the Manchester-based Zenith Six in 1952 and played with them for three years before joining Mike Daniels's Delta Jazzmen, 1955–61, and Alan Elsdon (with whom he turned professional), 1961–4. By this time it was plain that Barnes's talents were developing and expanding, and they found their full showcase after he joined Alex Welsh's band, replacing Archie Semple in 1964. Welsh's first album with his new lineup (*Strike One*, 1966) dramatically revealed Barnes not just as a vibrant clarinettist but a fiery alto saxophonist with strong overtones of Willie Smith and (perhaps best of all) a world-class baritone saxophonist whose dark-toned fluency seemed to combine all the best of Mulligan and Carney without aping either of them. In 1967, Rex Stewart (who had recently toured with Welsh's band) labelled Barnes in *Downbeat* as 'outstanding'. The same year he figured largely in *Downbeat*'s critics' poll. For the next 11 years he was a focal point of Welsh's finest-ever band, played with it at the Newport Jazz Festival, toured Britain and Europe and produced a string of fine recordings. He also formed a strong musical partnership with Roy Williams, just as capable of speeding through the Gerry Mulligan repertoire as playing 'Muskrat Ramble'. 1977, he left Welsh to rejoin Alan Elsdon and Keith Nichols's newly formed Midnite Follies Orchestra and in 1979 joined Humphrey Lyttelton's band. [DF]

Alex Welsh, *In Concert in Dresden* (1977), Black Lion (double)

Barnet, Charlie (Charles Daly), saxes, vocals. b. New York City, 26 October 1913. He walks into jazz history around 1930 as the prototype Goodtime Charlie, making the rounds of Harlem, touring with a wild and kindred spirit, trumpeter Jack Purvis, and assembling bands for projects in and out of New York. 'A happy-go-lucky millionaire', says Billie Holiday appreciatively, 'living it up, and making money talk.' It was typical of Barnet that at his first meeting with Holiday he insisted on breaking colour-bar restrictions by drinking with her and Teddy Wilson in the whites-only area of their club, and for the rest of his career he was to remain a committed supporter of good music, black or white. For much of the 1930s Barnet, a saxophonist who loved Hawkins, Armstrong and Ellington, found his career moving slowly: his most notable venture was to play the Apollo, previously reserved for black bands, in 1934. 'That engagement opened up a whole new area – one no other white band had', he recalled later. '[And] after our record of "Cherokee" came out in 1939 we began playing the whole of the black theatre circuit.' His band also played on tour, and for collegiate strongholds such as Glen Island Casino where in 1935, with a mixed personnel (featuring John Kirby and Frankie Newton), he played to a cool reception. For four more years that was the pattern. 'I was with Charlie in the spring of 1939,' recalls Billy May, 'and business was terrible. Glenn Miller was getting all of it down at Glen Island Casino. Charlie used to say half-kiddingly, "Let's run Miller out of business." And so we did crazy musical things like playing "Sunrise Serenade", one of Glenn's big numbers, and Charlie would blow the melody and the rest of the band would be playing Duke Ellington's "Azure".' Later in 1939 Barnet's band had the chance to replace Count Basie at New York's Famous Door, caused a sensation (Bluebird records issued a new Barnet single every week at the period, including his big hit 'Cherokee' arranged by May), and later that year the band moved triumphantly back into the Apollo. He was soon established as a hitmaker with other bestsellers like 'Redskin Rhumba', 'Wings over Manhattan', 'It's a Wonderful World' and his famous 'Skyliner', featuring a soprano-led saxophone section, an unusual voicing in its day. In what he called the 'chaotic forties' Barnet was still discovering and signing new talent (from singer/dancer Bunny Briggs and Lena Horne to young bebop men like Dodo Marmarosa and Buddy DeFranco), and playing more or less as he pleased. But the US draft had a debilitating effect on his band: musicians were constantly called up and the new generation that replaced them were often happier to play in a style that Barnet found rather too contrived. 'I held out against the bebop influence until 1949,' he wrote later, 'but had to go along with it then because none of the newer musicians knew how to approach big band playing except in that idiom. But I had a horror of ending up in Stan Kenton's bag.' That was what Capitol Records thought he should do (they had lost Kenton's services in 1948), but Barnet's reaction was exactly what could be expected from a Johnny Hodges lover who didn't need the money. He broke up his band at the end of a two-week engagement at the Apollo in 1949, to genuine regret on all sides, and moved into management, bought a chain of hotels and played what he wanted to. Charlie Barnet's occasional returns to bandleading in the 1960s and 1970s were few but worth watching for. His autobiography (along with George Melly's *Owning Up*) is the most irresistibly naughty book ever written by a jazzman. [DF]

Charlie Barnet, vol. 1. (1939–42), RCA

See Dance, Stanley (ed.), *Those Swinging Years: the Autobiography of Charlie Barnet* (Louisiana State University Press, 1984)

Barron, Kenny (Kenneth), piano, composer, educator. b. Philadelphia, 9 June 1943. Started on piano at 12; studied with a sister of pianist Ray Bryant. 1957, his first job was with Mel Melvin's orchestra, a jazz-oriented r & b outfit, of which Barron's saxophonist older brother Bill was a member. 1959, worked briefly with Philly Joe Jones; 1960, worked one week with Yusef Lateef in Detroit. 1961, moved to New York, working with Bill Barron and Ted Curson; also that year with James Moody, Lee Morgan, Roy Haynes and Lou Donaldson. Moody recommended him to Dizzy Gillespie, and Barron replaced Lalo Schifrin in the trumpeter's quintet staying for four years (1962–6). Tours and LPs with Gillespie brought him to international notice. 1966–70, worked with Freddie Hubbard; 1970–5, with Yusef Lateef; 1976, joined the Ron Carter quartet, staying until it broke up in 1980. From 1973, a full-time instructor at Rutgers University, teaching theory, keyboard harmony and piano. Has also worked with many others, including Milt Jackson, Jimmy Heath, Stan Getz, Buddy Rich, Esther Marrow. [IC]

Over fifty LPs as a sideman with Gillespie, Moody, Carter, Hubbard, Lateef, Joe Henderson, Sonny Fortune, Bill Barron and many others; *Sunset to Dawn* (1973); *Peruvian Blue* (1974); *Lucifer* (1975), all Muse

Bartz, Gary Lee, saxes, composer, voice. b. Baltimore, Maryland, 26 September 1940. Father ran local jazz club. He got an alto sax at 11. At 17 began 18 months at the Juilliard School, NYC. Back in Baltimore, studied at Peabody Conservatory. First professional work with Max Roach–Abbey Lincoln, followed by a stint with Art Blakey, 1965–6. Worked with Roach again, also McCoy Tyner and Blue Mitchell, 1968–9. August 1970, joined Miles Davis, remaining with him until late 1971. 1972, won US and UK polls on alto sax. Formed and led his own group, Ntu Troop, which achieved international popularity and appeared at major festivals, including Kongsberg and Montreux, 1973, Berkeley, 1974. Has also composed music for TV. He was strongly featured with Davis and made a big impact with his excellent solo work. With Ntu Troop he stated that he was not playing jazz, but American music. In the later 1970s, he had a recording contract with Capitol and made records which were definitely not jazz: they were essays in the currently fashionable disco-funk spiced with the occasional improvised solo. [IC]

With Miles Davis, *Live-Evil* (1970), CBS; as leader, *Libra* (1967); *Another Earth* (1968); *Harlem Bush Music – Taifa* (1970); *Harlem Bush Music – Uhuru* (1970/71), all Milestone; *Ju-Ju Street Songs* (1972); *Singerella – A Ghetto Fairytale* (1973/74), both Prestige; *Love Affair* (1978), Capitol

Basie, Count (William), piano, organ. b. Red Bank, New Jersey, 21 August 1904; d. 26 April 1984. Became professional musician in early 1920s, playing in Asbury Park, New Jersey, and in New York clubs. Then touring as accompanist for vaudeville, including two years with Gonzelle White (1925–7). Settled in Kansas City, working in local theatres, then joined Walter Page's Blue Devils on tour in Dallas (1928–9). Moved to Elmer Payne band, along with Eddie Durham, both of them going on to Bennie Moten (1929–34) during which period other Blue Devils

Count Basie

such as bassist Page, trumpeter Hot Lips Page, Jimmy Rushing, Buster Smith and Lester Young also joined Moten. These musicians formed nucleus of Basie's own Kansas City groups (first in 1934 and again, after Moten's death, 1935–6), when they were augmented by baritonist Jack Washington, Jo Jones, Buck Clayton and Herschel Evans. Signed to national band agency and record contract, Basie moved to New York (late 1936), quickly enlarging to 12-piece by addition of other key figures, rhythm guitarist Freddie Green and lead saxophonist Earl Warren. Work at Roseland Ballroom (1937) and Famous Door nightclub (1938) gradually established Basie's reputation, and the band's character was maintained by the arrival of Harry Edison and Dicky Wells (1938) and replacement of Evans and Young by Buddy Tate (1939) and Don Byas (1940).

Conditions of World War II caused more rapid personnel turnover, though many of Basie's new recruits in the 1940s were unique soloists, especially Vic Dickenson and saxists Lucky Thompson, Illinois Jacquet and Paul Gonsalves. For economic reasons, the big band was folded and Basie led an octet (1950–1) before starting a new 16-piece line-up (1952); significant members who joined this outfit during 1950s included Ernie Wilkins, Frank Foster, Thad Jones (these three also arranging), Joe Newman, Eddie Davis and Joe Williams. First of many European tours (1954) and a couple of extremely successful records gave the necessary impetus for the band to remain in business for a further three decades, although economic considerations in mid- and late 1960s dictated the recording of several albums backing middle-of-the-road singers. 1970s, Basie played in many all-star sessions without the band, but his only absences from its public appearances were occasioned by illness, which caused him in his last years to perform from a motorized wheelchair.

Always underrated as a pianist, Basie received informal guidance as a teenager from Fats Waller (exactly three months older), and early records with Moten and a few of his own show him playing excellent 'stride piano'. But the style forever associated with him is slimmed down by comparison; and, simultaneously influencing later developments in jazz pianism, it was impossible to achieve except with a cohesive and balanced rhythm-section. The amazing mobility and drive of the Green/Page/Jones combination, who were together for most of the period 1937–49, enabled Basie also to prod the band pianistically in a way which – though heard in the work of other Kansas City players such as Mary Lou Williams and Pete Johnson, and even Earl Hines – was brought to perfection by the Count.

The crucial role of the rhythm-section in his first famous big band was magnified because the ensemble functioned with the freedom of a traditional sextet. Soloists were continually being supported by spontaneous 'riffs', a feature particularly prevalent in Kansas City jazz, and some of these were then memorized as 'head arrangements' which later became famous. ('One O'Clock Jump', the band's theme-tune, was partly created in this way by Buster Smith and first organized on paper by Buck Clayton, though copyrighted by Basie.) By the late 1930s, however, as it became desirable for the popular instrumental numbers (and, even more so, the arrangements for vocalists other than the veteran Rushing) to assume a fixed form, scores were commissioned first from Eddie Durham and Buster Smith, then from outside writers such as Andy Gibson and Buster Harding who were also working for many others including white bands. Basie was saved from anonymity by his unique rhythm-section, and gradually the new 1950s unit pared down the prolix arrangements of the late swing era so that its best performances made predictability a virtue, just like the predictability of the 12-bar blues which still inspired much of its repertoire.

If imitation is the sincerest form of flattery, Basie's achievement has been the most fawned-over, whether by rehearsal bands, youth bands, semi-professional bands or studio-produced bands all round the world. It will be interesting to see how Frank Foster, the current leader, maintains the most authentic of the imitations while perpetuating the vitality of the original. [BP]

Swinging The Blues (1937–9), Affinity; *Basie Boogie* (1941–67), CBS; *Sixteen Men Swinging* (1952–54), Verve; *Basie At Birdland* (1961), Vogue; *Standing Ovation* (1969), Jasmine; *For The First Time* (1974), Pablo

See Dance, Stanley, *The World of Count Basie* (New York and London, 1980); Morgan, Alun, *Count Basie* (Tunbridge Wells, New York, 1984); Murray, Albert, *Good Morning Blues: the Autobiography of Count Basie* (London, 1986); Sheridan, Chris, *Count Basie: A Bio-Discography* (London, 1986)

Film: *To the Count of Basie* (dir. John Jeremy, 1980)

Basso, Gianni, tenor sax. b. Asti, Italy, 24 May 1931. Educ. Conservatorio di Asti. Co-led a quintet with trumpeter Oscar Valdambrini (Basso–Valdambrini quintet) which, 1955–60, played at the Taverna Mexico in Milan featuring occasional US soloists. The quintet, one of the best groups in Italy, remained active into the 1960s. Basso worked as sideman with many visiting leaders, including Maynard Ferguson, Chet Baker, Gerry Mulligan and Kenny Clarke. He appeared with Ferguson in a film, *La prima notte di quiete*. He performed at jazz festivals throughout Europe. In the 1980s he was active as a studio musician in Rome, but still playing club dates. [IC]

With Slide Hampton, Chet Baker, Frank Rosolino; 13 albums with Valdambrini for Italian labels, two of which were issued on US Verve: *Buddy Collette in Italy with Basso–Valdambrini* (1961), Ricordi; *The Best Modern Jazz in Italy* (1959), Italian RCA

Bates, Django (Leon), piano, synthesizers, trumpet. b. Beckenham, Kent, 2 October 1960. Heard jazz records at home when very young and played piano by ear. 1971–7, studied trumpet, piano and violin at Centre for Young Musicians, London. 1977–8, young musicians course at Morley College. Went to Royal College of Music to spend four years studying composition, but left, disenchanted, after two weeks. 1981, with Tim Whitehead's Borderline staying for three and a half years. 1983, joined Dudu Pukwana's Zila, something he had dreamed of since the age of eight. 1983, founder member of Loose Tubes, a 21-piece ensemble for which he does much of the composing. 1984, joined First House, a young quartet which won the third European Jazz Competition at Leverkusen, West Germany. His tastes run from

Keith Jarrett and Bill Evans to Geri Allen and Glenn Gould, and from Dudu Pukwana and other African musicians to Charles Ives and many soul and Motown artists. This catholicity is reflected in Bates's brilliantly promising work both as instrumentalist and composer. [IC]

With Tim Whitehead, *English People* (1982), Spotlite; with Dudu Pukwana, *Life in Bracknell and Willisau* (1983), Jika; with Ken Stubbs, *First House* (1985), ECM; *Loose Tubes* (1984), Loose Tubes

Batiste, Alvin, clarinet, sax, piano, composer. (nda). A working musician in New Orleans from around 1950, and a hugely-gifted clarinettist, his appearances in the media are rare and his music under-recorded. His work, rather like Tony Coe's in Britain, is brilliant and eclectic, based on a cross-culture of classic and modern jazz and including synthetic music and contemporary classical devices. Batiste lives and teaches in Baton Rouge and the album listed below gives an intriguing glimpse of his composition and (occasional) improvisation. His extended works include three 'New Orleans Suites' written for the New Orleans Philharmonic; other regular musical colleagues include Billy Cobham (with whom he has recorded) and Ornette Coleman, a frequent collaborator. [DF]

Alvin Batiste: Musique d'Afrique Nouvelle Orléans (1985), India-Navigation

Bauduc, Ray, drums, composer. b. New Orleans, 18 June 1906. He worked around his hometown with leaders such as Johnny Bayersdorffer (as well as guitarist Nappy Lamare, a lifelong friend) before coming to New York in 1926 with the Scranton Sirens. By 1928 (after time with bandleader Fred Rich as drummer and featured dancer) he had taken over the drum chair from his new leader Ben Pollack (while Pollack conducted) and stayed until 1934 when he left, with most of the rest of the band, to join Bob Crosby. With Crosby, Bauduc's sensational New Orleans style found its perfect frame: a collage of clicking woodblocks, press rolls, rimshots, splash and Chinese cymbals. He became a central figure in Crosby's band, often directing the musical traffic, offering ideas and laying down guidelines. After Crosby's band broke up in 1942, Bauduc served in the army, then worked with a big band, with his own swing quartet (he was tired of the Dixieland tag), with Crosby again, Jimmy Dorsey, 1948, and Jack Teagarden, 1952–5. Then came a spell co-leading with Lamare: a highly successful band which lasted until 1960 when Bauduc moved out to California, a regular base, and played clubs. By 1970 he was living in Texas and semi-retired. [DF]

Bob Crosby, *South Rampart Street Parade* (1935–42), EMI

See Chilton, John, *Stomp Off, Let's Go* (Jazz Book Services, 1983)

Bauer, Billy (William Henry), guitar. b. New York City, 14 November 1915. Played with a number of big bands from 1939, including Woody Herman (1944–6), with Chubby Jackson group (1947) and occasionally with Benny Goodman, but main jazz association with Lennie Tristano trio/sextet (1946–9). One of the few original guitarists to emerge in the 1940s, Bauer avoided the elastic phrasing of the Charlie Christian school. Obtaining a rather ugly metallic sound which was the equivalent of Tristano's glassy piano tone, he aspired to a mirror-image of the pianist, but without achieving a similar idiosyncratic strength. Apart from recording with J. J. Johnson–Kai Winding (1954) and Cootie Williams–Rex Stewart (1957), and reunions with Tristano and Lee Konitz, has been occupied with session work. Many of the original compositions of Konitz, Tristano etc. are registered with William H. Bauer Publishing Co. [BP]

Lennie Tristano, *The Rarest Trio/Quartet Sessions* (1946–7), Raretone

Beat (1) In European terminology, beats are individual pulses within a bar; the time signature 4/4 indicates 4 beats each a ¼-note in value. These beats can be either a 'down-beat' or an 'up-beat' (see DOWN and UP). The up-beat is also sometimes described as the 'off-beat' (down-beat being replaced by 'on-beat') or as the 'after-beat' or, more picturesquely, as the 'back-beat': the last name conveys an image of bouncing back either spatially or psychologically, as indeed does the term 'up-beat'.

(2) 'The beat', however, describes the quality of the overall flow of a performance. The phrase 'So long as it's got the beat' (or 'a beat') gives the over-simplified impression that the main pulse is the chief thing to listen for. But, in all Afro-American music influenced by jazz, the time-signature is only the basis for a continuous interplay of counter-rhythms. It is in this sense that 'the beat' is usually understood. [BP]

Beau, Heinie (Henry John), composer, clarinet, saxophones, arranger. b. Calvary, Wisconsin, 8 March 1911. One of the best (and most neglected) Dixieland-to-swing clarinettists, he came from a big-band background (with Tommy Dorsey, 1940–3) and later settled in Hollywood where he worked as a freelance arranger and musician in radio, TV and recording. He rapidly gravitated to the jazz-based areas regularly occupied by arranger Paul Weston, recorded with great singers such as Peggy Lee and Frank Sinatra, with a variety of jazz bands and, most notably for jazz fans, regularly with Red Nichols. 'Red and his music were my first introduction to jazz and my biggest influence', Beau wrote later (his first arrangement ever was a note-for-note copy of Nichols's 'Washboard Blues' for a family band) and after a first stint with the cornettist in 1940, in Richmond,

Virginia, he was to form a long professional and personal friendship with him. This was to result in some now classic recordings from the late 1950s in which Beau not only re-arranged many of Nichols's greatest hits but also wrote new compositions which lovingly retained Nichols's favourite devices: tympani, mellophone, bass saxophone lead and so on: all the records are indispensable. After Nichols's death, Beau continued his studio commitments and in the 1970s visited Europe (including England where he sat in at top London jazz clubs). [DF]

Red Nichols, *Meet the Five Pennies* (1959), Capitol

Bebop (or Bop: both versions are equally current).

(1) The classic style which came to fruition in New York in the early 1940s, masterminded by Dizzy Gillespie and Kenny Clarke and brought to life by Charlie Parker. Its emergence was the result of much open-ended jamming (at after-hours clubs such as Minton's and Monroe's) and some theoretical discussion with likeminded souls including Thelonious Monk, Tadd Dameron and Mary Lou Williams. Its arrival was somewhat masked by the wartime popularity of increasingly formularized big-band swing; on the other hand, the 1942–3 musicians' union strike against recordings (often cited as a delaying factor) actually encouraged the formation of small specialist labels which, from 1944, put bebop on record at an earlier stage of development than most previous jazz styles.

Although the new style created consternation and hostility among many established musicians (plus interest and encouragement from others), it was a direct outgrowth of later 1930s jazz. Contributory factors included the harmonic elaboration of Coleman Hawkins, Art Tatum and Duke Ellington; the melodic freedom of such contrasting players as Lester Young and Roy Eldridge; and the airtight looseness of the Basie band rhythm-section with Jo Jones. The work of more truly transitional figures including Charlie Christian, Jimmy Blanton and the John Kirby Sextet (especially Charlie Shavers and Billy Kyle) needs to be set beside the then increasing importance of US-based Afro-Latin bands, for a full appreciation of bebop's expansion of jazz vocabulary. And, although the chordal extensions and the angular lines which went with them caused the strongest reaction at the time, it has become clear in retrospect that their greater feel for polyrhythms was these players' most lasting contribution.

Historically, bebop was the first kind of jazz whose performers were, to some extent, artistic elitists – but this has to be seen in context with the short-lived social gains of black Americans during World War II, as a musical attempt to build a bridgehead for greater respect of black contributions to US society. Initially the attempt seemed doomed to total failure, and yet not only has every subsequent jazz style been indelibly marked by bebop, but the combined influence of these jazz styles on more popular music of the last ten years has been enormous.

(2) Inevitably, but somewhat confusingly, 'bebop' has also been associated with various styles of dancing. There is no particular connection with any one kind of jazz, or indeed of rock, for 'bopping' used in this sense tends to drift in and out of fashion, and indiscriminately describes dancing to Miles Davis and Art Blakey or to Little Richard records. [BP]

Bechet, Sidney, soprano sax, clarinet. b. New Orleans, 14 May 1897; d. Paris, 14 May 1959. Very early on he heard powerful trumpeters such as Freddie Keppard in New Orleans. Lessons followed with Lorenzo Tio, Louis Nelson and George Baquet, and soon he was playing with every leading light in his home town and himself teaching (Larry Shields and Jimmie Noone were two pupils). By 1917 he was in Chicago and there joined Will Marion Cook's orchestra, with whom he travelled in 1919 to New York and then to Europe. In London, with Cook, that year the young clarinettist found a straight soprano saxophone in a junkshop, liked it, and began to feature it onstage in a stately version of 'Song of Songs'. He made headlines. The young Ernst Ansermet was enthralled with Bechet's sound, so was the Prince of Wales, and the object of all this attention (so he said) played for the king at Buckingham Palace. 'It was funny to look at your money and see someone you knew', he mused later, but after deportation for minor assault the love affair was over: 'On the boat', he wrote, 'I took all the English money I had and dropped it overboard.' Back in New York, Bechet worked with revues, with James P. Johnson, with Duke Ellington (who would have liked to have him in the band) and taught Johnny Hodges. In 1925 came his first trip to Paris to play for the famous *Revue Nègre*; then four years of globetrotting in Russia, Germany and France as musical director for the *Revue* and as a bandsman, before 1929 when, in Paris, he was gaoled for 11 months for a shooting offence. He emerged a bitter man.

He worked with Noble Sissle regularly over the next ten years and during the period struck up a firm friendship with trumpeter Tommy Ladnier, a fellow-traveller, wit and survivor. With Ladnier in New York he co-led bands in clubs, put together the Bechet–Ladnier Feetwarmers for a spell at Savoy Ballroom and opened a tailor's shop, as well as getting back together with his old teacher Lorenzo Tio who had come to New York to work at the Nest. By the end of the decade, Bechet was working along 52nd Street with friends including Joe Marsala, Ladnier, Bobby Hackett and Eddie Condon and in 1940 he made some historic sides with Louis Armstrong: two powerful giants established as stars who saw no need to bend the knee to one another. 'A man like Louis,' said Bechet later, with just a trace of guile, 'he's not just a

Sidney Bechet

musicianer any more. He's got himself a name, and he's got to live up to that name. I don't even blame him!' Most of the other players on titles such as 'Coal Cart Blues' and 'Down in Honky-Tonk Town' knew what was happening and seldom talked about the results: jazz temperament was showing its claws. In the early 1940s Bechet did well enough, playing clubs, dances, parties and in a band with Vic Dickenson as well as, during the war, appearing regularly for Eddie Condon's Town Hall concerts, and briefly in 1945 at the Savoy Club, Boston, with Bunk Johnson. Johnson turned up drunk and brought in his manager Gene Williams when the pace got hot; trumpeter Johnny Windhurst completed the residency.

By that time Bechet had settled in Brooklyn and began teaching to help his pocket. He taught aspiring saxophonists like Richard Hadlock and Bob Wilber, his most famous pupil who actually moved into a spare room in Bechet's house and took a daily lesson. But the old master was far from busy. In 1946 he had taken part in a jazz-based Broadway play, *Hear That Trumpet*, worked Jimmy Ryan's and clubs up and down 52nd Street as well as back in Chicago. 1949 was his turning point. That year he was welcomed like a son at the Salle Pleyel Jazz Festival in Paris, and after one more trip back to New York his mind was set. In November 1949 Sidney Bechet went back to Paris (stopping off in London to play with a determined Humphrey Lyttelton on an illegal London stage) and once settled in began working with André Rewelliotty. The approval was hysterical. In 1951 Bechet remarried, a German woman, at Antibes (there was never any shortage of girls), quickly acquired a manager, Claude Wolff (who later married Petula Clark), and turned into a French hero of Chevalieresque proportions. In 1955 his music for a ballet, *La Nuit est une sorcière* ('an extended piece,' says Bob Wilber, 'which he worked on, so far as I can see, all his life'), was performed. He travelled back to America to star with Bob Scobey *et al.* at festivals, and by the late 1950s, in Paris, police had to be called in whenever he played in public. When he died in 1959, of cancer, a square in Antibes was named for him, and a statue erected in the park.

Around Bechet's life there hangs an aura of other-worldliness, chiefly the result of his rambling, poetic autobiography *Treat it Gentle*, in which he portrayed himself as a kind of jazz nature boy, wandering a strange land of his own creation. The truth was harder. Bechet was a thinker, and capable of being however he felt like being at will: 'Some people say Sidney was the most temperamental son-of-a-bitch in music,' says Barney Bigard, 'others say he was the nicest man you ever met.' Whatever aspect of his personality Bechet chose to display, he was above all a man of personal and musical authority, and very few trumpeters, apart from Louis Armstrong who brooked no opposition, were ever able to blow him down. His jazz contribution is gigantic. His compositions were melodically stronger than those of any other classic jazz musician, his creation of a vocabulary for his instrument was as great an achievement as Coleman Hawkins's for tenor, his records are majestic. Bob Wilber, his one-time pupil, has done much to recall Bechet's greatest repertoire (an often neglected area): without Wilber's work, and, of course, Bechet himself, jazz would be poorer. [DF]

Bechet of New Orleans (1932–41), RCA

See Bechet, Sidney, *Treat it Gentle* (Corgi, 1960); Williams, Martin, *Jazz Masters of New Orleans* (Macmillan, 1967, repr. Da Capo, 1979)

Beck, Gordon James, piano, electric piano, synthesizers, composer. b. London, 16 September 1938. Father played violin. Self-taught. After nine years as a design draughtsman in aero-engineering, became a professional musician. At first worked with groups in London. 1962, joined the Tubby Hayes quintet and with it made his first tours abroad including the San Remo festival. 1965, formed his own trio which worked regularly as the house rhythm-section in the Ronnie Scott Club, accompanying singers and soloists. 1967, made his own first albums and began working extensively as a studio musician. 1969–72, with Phil Woods's European Rhythm Machine, doing festivals, concerts, radio and TV and clubs throughout Europe, and touring the USA, 1971. 1972, formed his own group, Gyroscope, and re-formed his trio.

Since 1974, Beck has worked, recorded and composed for many people including Lena Horne, Phil Woods, Gary Burton, Cleo Laine, Mel Tormé, Mike Gibbs, Clark Terry, Charles Tolliver, Alan Holdsworth, Don Sebesky, Helen Merrill and Didier Lockwood. In the early 1970s he was a member of Piano Conclave, the 6-keyboard group led by George Gruntz. 1985, with Holdsworth he toured California and Japan, and with Didier Lockwood he recorded an album in New York with Cecil McBee and Billy Hart, after which the group toured Europe extensively.

Beck has been active in jazz education for some years and became co-organizer of the Treforest Summer School. Since 1978 he has recorded for the French label JMS, because during the 1970s he toured a great deal in France, building up a big reputation and audience there. Beck is one of a tiny handful of British musicians with a really solid international reputation, which in the 1980s seems to be burgeoning rapidly. His many influences include Herbie Hancock, Bill Evans, Keith Jarrett, Chick Corea, Tommy Flanagan, Art Tatum, Bud Powell, McCoy Tyner, Horace Silver, and he is in the same league – technically brilliant, with an apparently inexhaustible flow of ideas, great lyricism, and tremendous rhythmic drive. Other inspirational figures for him are Gary Burton, Ravel and Debussy. He has over 40 compositions on LPs, several of them on other people's albums, including 'Here Comes the Mallet Man' (Gary Burton), 'Executive Suite' (Phil Woods), 'The Day When the World Comes Alive' (Cleo Laine). [IC]

With Tubby Hayes, Annie Ross, Ronnie Scott, Nucleus, Piano Conclave; *Experiments with Pops* (1967), Major/Minor; *Gyroscope* (1968), Morgan; *The French Connection* (1978), Owl; *Sunbird* (1979); *The Things You See* (1980); *Celebration* (1984), all JMS; *Seven Steps to Evans* (1979), MPS; with Phil Woods, *Live at Frankfurt* (1971), Embryo; with Don Sebesky, *Three Works for Jazz Soloists and Orchestra* (1979), Gryphon; Helen Merrill/Gordon Beck, *No Tears, No Goodbyes* (1984), Owl

Beckett, Harry (Harold Winston), trumpet, fluegelhorn, piano. b. Barbados, West Indies, 30 May 1935. Private music lessons. Came to UK in 1954 and played in night clubs. 1961, worked with Mingus in London, making the film *All Night Long*. Early 1960s, joined Graham Collier, playing in his various groups for several years. Since then he has played with most leading UK musicians including John Surman, the New Jazz Orchestra, Mike Westbrook, Nucleus, Stan Tracey, Chris MacGregor's Brotherhood of Breath, Mike Gibbs, Elton Dean, Dudu Pukwana's Zila, Ronnie Scott and John Dankworth. Beckett also leads groups of his own, varying in size from trio to sextet or more. He has played at festivals and toured all over Western and Eastern Europe as well as Scandinavia, the Middle East and India. He has received Arts Council bursaries to compose, perform and record his own works. He has also been active in jazz education, taking workshops and giving lectures and recitals in schools and colleges. Beckett's playing is all quicksilver and lyricism; he can run the gamut from wild aggression to great delicacy, and his concept encompasses most areas from bebop and chord changes to modal and free playing. [IC]

With Surman, Collier, Brotherhood of Breath, Ray Russell and others; seven under his own name, including *Themes for Fega* (1972), RCA; *Joy Unlimited* (1974), Cadillac; *Memories of Bacares* (1976), Ogun; *Got It Made* (1977), Ogun

Beiderbecke, Bix (Leon Bix), cornet, piano, composer, b. Davenport, Iowa, 10 March 1903; d. 7 August 1931. High School in Davenport, then to Lake Forest Academy near Chicago for a year. He came from a prosperous middle-class family and his mother was an accomplished pianist. He was a 'natural' musician, largely self-taught on piano from early childhood and on cornet which he began playing at 15. He was inspired by recordings of the Original Dixieland Jazz Band and their trumpet player Nick La Rocca, and heard music on the riverboats that came up the Mississippi from Memphis, St Louis and New Orleans. He certainly heard Louis Armstrong on one of these riverboats and also a white trumpet-player called Emmett Hardy whom Bix later acknowledged as an influence, but who never recorded. In 1923 Beiderbecke was star soloist with the Wolverines, with whom he made his first records, and came to New York to play at Roseland. 1925, he was with Charlie Straight's commercial orchestra in Chicago and spent much time listening to, and sitting in with, the pioneer black musicians there – King Oliver, Louis Armstrong, Jimmie Noone and others. 1926, with Frankie Trumbauer's orchestra at the Arcadia Ballroom, St Louis. After working with Jean Goldkette in Detroit, he joined Paul Whiteman's band as featured soloist, 1928–30; but with many absences due to ill-health caused by the alcoholism which ultimately killed him. The last year of his life was spent in Davenport and New York, gigging with Glen Gray's Casa Loma Orchestra and others. He died of pneumonia and was buried in Davenport.

Bix was appreciated by only a handful of musicians and fans during his brief lifetime. Some years after his death, Dorothy Baker's novel *Young Man with a Horn*, which was inspired by but not based on his life story, began the whole process which was to make him into a legendary figure. Musically he was already an immortal – a seminal influence and an inspiration to many other musicians. He was jazz's first great lyricist; the hallmarks of his style and music are delicacy of phrase and nuance, wonderfully poised rhythmic sophistication and rich sonority. For the first time in the history of that noble and martial instrument, the trumpet (cornet) projected an almost feminine sensitivity and a new, inward-looking thoughtfulness. Bix's emotional and technical palette was smaller than that of Louis Armstrong, whose epic imagination was pushing his trumpet technique to the extreme limits. But Bix had a burnished, bell-like sound, a sure attack, a natural sense of swing, and although he always played well within his technical abilities, his sound and the sweet logic of his thought made him one of the major jazz soloists. This line of playing, begun by Bix and his saxophonist friend Frankie Trumbauer, has been carried on by Bobby Hackett, Lester Young, Charlie Parker, Miles Davis and others right down to the present day. Bix was probably the first white musician ever to be admired and imitated by black jazzmen: Rex Stewart and others learned to play his most famous solo (the Trumbauer record of 'Singing the Blues') note for note. As a pianist and composer, Bix was one of the first jazzmen to be influenced by Debussy's harmonic ideas; the irony was that because his ear was so good, because he was such a 'natural', he never learned to read music very well, and even his own compositions for piano had to be written down for him. Bill Challis, Jean Goldkette's arranger, transcribed the only Beiderbecke compositions we have, a mere five – and Bix nearly drove him to distraction because he never played one of them the same way twice. His most famous composition is 'In a Mist'. Although the piano pieces have great charm, it is by his cornet solos that Bix Beiderbecke must be judged: his major contribution on cornet keeps the piano pieces alive.

Possibly because of the influence of his family, Bix seemed to aspire to the state of classical music while always feeling inferior to it. Had he been more disciplined, he might have continued to develop as a player and composer. He was a man of enormous talent, but meagre character or self-discipline, and his creative despair, induced by technical inadequacy and lack of vision, made him take refuge in alcohol. All of his work is still available on record on various labels, but the most comprehensive edition is on the Italian Joker label, which presents Bix Beiderbecke's complete recorded work in chronological order. The definitive biography is Richard M. Sudhalter and Philip R. Evans with William Dean-Myatt, *Bix, Man and Legend* (Quartet Books, 1974). [IC]

Film: *Bix – Ain't None Of Them Play Like That* (dir. Brigitte Berman, 1981)

Beirach, Richie (Richard), piano, electric keyboards, composer. b. Brooklyn, New York, 1947. Classical piano lessons from age six; he heard Red Garland, Miles Davis and John Coltrane and became interested in jazz; studied at Berklee, Boston, then took a degree in theory and composition at the Manhattan School of Music, New York, followed by a one-year postgraduate fellowship which enabled him to study with Stan Getz, Dave Holland and Jack DeJohnette. April 1974, became a member of Dave Liebman's Lookout Farm, and began playing electric piano. Lookout Farm toured widely in Europe and played major festivals. Beirach's influences include Art Tatum, Bud Powell, Paul Bley, Bill Evans, Chick Corea, Herbie Hancock and McCoy Tyner; other inspirations are Schoenberg, Berg, Scriabin, Debussy, Ravel, Bartók, early Miles Davis and Coltrane, Charlie Parker, James Brown and Sly Stone. [IC]

With Getz, Jeremy Steig, Freddie Hubbard, Lee Konitz; *Lookout Farm* (1974); with Lookout Farm, *Drum Ode*, (1975); Richard Beirach trio, *Eon* (1975), all ECM; Liebman/Beirach, *Forgotten Fantasies* (1975), Horizon

Bellson, Louie Paul (Louis Balassoni), drums, composer. b. Rock Falls, Illinois, 26 July 1924. Copious big-band experience with Benny Goodman (1943, 1946), Tommy Dorsey (1947–9) and Harry James (1950–1). Also co-led sextet with former Dorsey colleague Charlie Shavers (1950). Joined Ellington band following final departure of Sonny Greer (1951–3). Having married singer Pearl Bailey in London in 1952, spent much of the next years acting as her musical director with his own band. Also made tours with Jazz at the Philharmonic (1955, 1967, and in Europe 1972), rejoined Dorsey (1955–6 and posthumous Dorsey band 1964), Ellington (1965–6) and James (1966). Since 1960s, has been involved in much educational and demonstration work, and has led own big band in US and abroad (European tours 1979 and 1980), for which he arranges most of the material himself.

Bellson first became noted as a composer through his features with the early 1950s Ellington band, 'The Hawk Talks' (title actually inspired by Harry James) and 'Skin Deep'; the dovetailing of the writing with his dynamic drumming of the period was particularly impressive. His participation in casual small-group recordings results far too often in merely ticking off the up-beats, instead of providing real propulsive power. As well as having an unfortunate influence on some other players, this is a far cry from Bellson's more creative drumming in a big-band context. [BP]

Big Band Jazz from the Summit (1962), Vogue; *Thunderbird* (1963), Jasmine

Beneke, Tex (Gordon), tenor sax, vocals. b. Fort Worth, Texas, 12 February 1914. He came to fame after he joined Glenn Miller's newly re-formed orchestra of 1938 as featured vocalist doubling tenor, at $52.50 a week. Beneke's charming Southern-sunny voice became the voice of Miller's orchestra on immortal hits like 'Chattanooga Choo Choo', 'I gotta gal in Kalamazoo' and 'Don't sit under the apple tree' (despite his self-confessed inability to remember words), and his booting blues-flavoured tenor was always heavily featured by Miller, sometimes to the chagrin of section mate Al Klink. Beneke, a humorous and relaxed youngster in his twenties, was popular with all the band (including the leader) and despite featured roles in films such as *Sun Valley Serenade* (1941) and *Orchestra Wives* (1942), after which he topped polls in *Downbeat* and *Metronome*, steadfastly refused to become big-headed: 'Tex's big ambition', says drummer Maurice Purtill, 'was to get back to Texas, eat some chili, and play some blues.' Beneke served in the US Navy during World War II (he never played in Miller's AAF orchestra). In 1946 he was requested by the Miller estate to take the Glenn Miller orchestra back on the road including an only slightly reduced string section of twelve and a French horn (all 13 had been dropped by 1949). With this sometimes bop-flavoured band, and later on with his own, broadcasting and recording, Beneke's career carried on successfully until the 1970s. [DF]

Tex Beneke and his Orchestra, *Shooting Star* (1948), Magic Records

Bennett, Cuban (Theodore), trumpet. b. 1902; d. Pittsburgh, 28 November 1965. 'You could call him the first of the moderns': Roy Eldridge talking about Benny Carter's cousin, Cuban Bennett, a trumpeter of phenomenal harmonic knowledge, lip and endurance, who predated Dizzy Gillespie by ten years. 'He played changes like I've never heard', said Dickie Wells, and Benny Carter agreed: 'Cuban was the greatest', he told Stanley Dance. 'You wouldn't believe that anyone could play that way in the twenties, yet it's hard to talk about him if you've nothing to substantiate it with. He was so advanced. They're doing today what he did then!' Bennett never recorded, never seems to have worked steadily with a band (apart, possibly, from an obscure spell with Bingie Madison in a New York taxi dance hall), and he drank a lot. He was a jazz nomad who enjoyed the free and easy life in clubs, experimenting and working underground. 'He just liked to hang around and blow in the joints,' says Dickie Wells, 'and the joints finally gave out. Later I understand he was on a farm his people left him.' [DF]

Bennink, Han, percussion. b. Zaandam, Netherlands, 17 April 1942. Has played with Ben Webster, Don Byas, Johnny Griffin, Lee Konitz, Sonny Rollins, John Tchicai, Cecil Taylor, Don Cherry, Dexter Gordon, Gary Peacock, Paul Bley, Steve Lacy, Eric Dolphy, Evan Parker, Peter Brötzmann and many others. Bennink has been mostly identified with the free (abstract) improvisation scene in Europe. [IC]

With Derek Bailey, E. Parker, D. Gordon, Manfred Schoof, Alex von Schlippenbach and others; with Dolphy, *Last Date* (1964), Fontana; Brötzmann/Bennink, *Ein halber Hund kann nicht pinkeln* (1977) FMP; *Han Bennink Solo* (1978), FMP

Benson, George, guitar, vocals. b. Pittsburgh, Pennsylvania, 22 March 1943. Singing and playing ukulele as a child, cut first vocal records at 11 for r & b label. Studying guitar from then on, Benson at 19 was already touring with Jack McDuff group (1962–5). Formed own quartet including Lonnie Smith on organ (1965), recording under own name and taking part in Spirituals to Swing Anniversary Concert (1967). Began series of increasingly successful middle-of-the-road albums (from 1968), *Breezin'* breaking sales records for instrumental discs (1976). Capped this by concentrating increasingly on singing in a style closely modelled on Stevie Wonder.

It is untrue, however, to say that Benson has never looked back for, as well as playing at the Kool Festival (1985), he has made in the 1980s some instrumental-only recordings so far unreleased by his producers. And (like Nat Cole, an illustrious predecessor with a similar career pattern) many of his more commercial efforts include fine jazz solos, usually in unison with his scatting. But, especially when heard in extended improvisation, the influence of Wes Montgomery and Tal Farlow still fires some remarkably fluent and inspired playing. [BP]

The Electrifying George Benson (1973), Affinity

Berg, Bob, tenor and soprano sax. b. Brooklyn, New York, 1951. Played in junior high school band and began listening to jazz at age 13; dropped out of High School of Performing Arts; at 18, went to Juilliard School for a year on a special non-academic totally music programme. Influenced by the later Coltrane, he became deeply involved in free jazz from 1966 to the end of the decade when, he told Mark Gilbert, 'I got totally sick of free jazz and went back and really studied the classics like 1950s Miles and Coltrane, and the Bird things.' Throughout the 1970s he wanted to play only acoustic bebop, and was deeply opposed to the jazz-rock-fusion music of the time. 1974–6, worked with Horace Silver; 1976–81, with Cedar Walton's quartet, touring and playing festivals internationally; 1983–5, with Miles Davis he toured world-wide playing most major festivals. Talking of joining Davis's electric fusion group, Berg said, 'I needed a change, and I always felt I had the ability to do it and not just play straightahead jazz. Playing with Miles is different from being in a fusion band because you don't have to play funk licks.'

Bob Berg is one of the most gifted of the post-Coltrane generation of saxophonists, with flawless technique, great harmonic awareness, a beautifully poised sense of time and a massive, emotive sound. [IC]

With Sam Jones, Kenny Drew, John McNeil; three with Horace Silver; six with Cedar Walton, including *Eastern Rebellion 2* (1977), Timeless; as leader, *Steppin'* (1982), Red; with Billy Higgins, *Soweto* (1983), Red; with Miles Davis, *You're Under Arrest* (1985), CBS

Berger, Karl Hans, piano, vibes, composer, percussion, educator. b. Heidelberg, Germany, 30 March 1935. Started on piano, taking up vibes in 1960; 1948–54, Heidelberg Conservatory; 1955–63, musicology and sociology, University of Heidelberg; PhD, 1963. Inspired to take up vibes by French vibist Michel Hausser, with whom he played in Germany and Paris. Berger was steeped in the work of Ornette Coleman, and he moved to Paris in March 1965, met Don Cherry and played with him for 18 months. Autumn 1966, played with Steve Lacy for a month, then followed Cherry to New York, working with him, Roswell Rudd, Marion Brown, David Izenzon, Sam Rivers and others. With drummer Horacee Arnold, played school and college concerts with a group funded by Young Audiences Inc., 1967–71; also taught for two years at the New School for Social Research, conducting improvisation classes.

1971, with Coleman, Berger formed the Creative Music Foundation, moving in 1973 to Woodstock, where he set up Creative Music Studio to give full-time classes in all aspects of music including its relation to the dance. Over 30 leading musicians have instructed there on a temporary basis, among them Sam Rivers, George Russell, Roscoe Mitchell, John Cage, Richard Teitelbaum, Lee Konitz and Steve Lacy, and they have usually created large orchestral works with the students.

Berger is a virtuoso player who has always been associated with the more abstract side of improvisation. He has led his own groups from time to time since 1966, has won several US jazz polls, and has toured extensively in Europe and Canada, playing many festivals including Prague, Molde, Pori, Antibes, Frankfurt, Berlin. [IC]

With Lee Konitz, John McLaughlin, John Surman and others; with Don Cherry, *Symphony for Improvisers* (1966), Blue Note; as leader, *With Silence* (1972), Enja; *Changing the Time* (1977), Horo; solo, *Interludes* (1977), FMP; Karl Berger/Dave Holland, *All Kinds of Time* (1976), Sackville; with Musica Elettronica Viva, *United Patchwork* (1977), Horo

Berigan, Bunny (Rowland Bernart), trumpet, vocals. b. Hilbert, Calumet, Wisconsin, 2 November 1908; d. New York City, 2 June 1942. At the start of his short career he worked with college bands and in 1928 was heard by bandleader Hal Kemp. Kemp's pianist John Scott Trotter (later Bing Crosby's MD) remembers: 'Kemp didn't hire Bunny, because he had the tinniest, most ear-splitting tone you ever heard', but two years later Berigan had acquired one of the hugest, most generous sounds any jazz trumpeter ever had and Kemp hired him for a trip to Europe (including Britain) and hotel work in New York. Berigan's records from this period show a full-formed talent at play. In 1931 he joined Fred Rich's CBS studio band and continued working busily in studios before joining Paul Whiteman's highly successful, and by now very commercial, orchestra as a late replacement for Bix Beiderbecke. The arrangement was not a success: Berigan felt fettered by the limited solo space he was offered, disliked Whiteman's musical policy, and in any case was seldom happy when he worked for others. So he left again and returned to studio work. By June 1935 he was playing for Benny Goodman (and drinking heavily) and he was in on that great night when Goodman, after ten months of touring, first sent the crowds wild at the Palomar Ballroom in Los Angeles. 'When Bunny stood up and blew "Sometimes I'm happy" and "King Porter Stomp",' recalled Goodman, 'the place exploded!' But Berigan had leader ideas of his own (trumpeter Pee Wee Erwin joined Goodman in his place), and in 1936, after a spell back in the studios and work in the evening for Red McKenzie, he floated a big band: it sank at the rehearsal stage. That year he topped the *Metronome* poll with five times as many votes as his nearest competitor (at a period when Louis Armstrong was at his peak): a first recording of 'I can't get started', with a small group, had caught the public's attention, and in June he began a set of appearances on the networked Saturday Night Swing Club for CBS. From 1937 Berigan's big band, on the road at last, toured, albeit to mixed reviews. With it he was to record on 7 August 1937 a second, definitive 'I can't get started': it was to remain his classic. But his live appearances too were often of unbeatable brilliance. 'Bunny's band stole the show from us at the Savoy', recalls Haywood Henry who was with Erskine Hawkins at the period. 'There were only three bands that could do that: Duke, Lionel – and Bunny. We didn't prepare for Bunny 'cos we thought we had him! But Buddy Rich and Georgie Auld were with him, and the house came down. As for Bunny I've no doubt he was the best white trumpeter.' At the end of 1940, however, Berigan was bankrupt; he rejoined Tommy Dorsey's band for six months, but on 20 August left abruptly after an NBC broadcast: 'I couldn't bring him round,' said hard-man Dorsey with an unfamiliar note of real regret, 'so I had to let him go. I hated to do it.' Berigan was Dorsey's most vital cornerman (his solos three years before on Dorsey sides like 'Marie' had helped to seal his leader's future), but his reasons for leaving sounded rebelliously familiar and no doubt inflamed by alcohol. 'There wasn't enough chance to play', he said irritably. 'Most of the time I was just sitting there waiting for choruses.' By 1941, George T. Simon was able to report on Berigan's newest band, and observe that Berigan had shrunk away ('he must have lost at least thirty pounds'), that he put in a deputy for the first half of the show, and (said Henry 'Red' Allen) was soon after playing sitting down. (Trumpet authority, Charles Colin, has suggested that later in his career Berigan may have suffered spells of temporary mental imbalance.) On 1 June 1942 he was scheduled to play at New York's Manhattan Center: the band turned up but Bunny never did. Seriously ill with cirrhosis and heavy haemorrhaging (he had been drinking cheap 'rotgut' liquor in his last, poorer days) he was rushed to Polyclinic Hospital and died there: Tommy Dorsey paid the funeral expenses.

Louis Armstrong and Bunny Berigan may have been trumpet talents of a similar mettle, but there the resemblance stopped. Armstrong was black: Berigan was white. Armstrong, underneath his easy-going bonhomie, had a streak of steel: Berigan had none. Armstrong saw his career as a 'hustle', a means of survival to be jealously guarded: Berigan, for whom most things from trumpet playing to girls came easily, looked at life more casually. Armstrong's solos were polished setpieces: Berigan's were audacious creations which either equalled Armstrong's for technique and inspiration or developed so fast that they aborted. Berigan remains, with Bix Beiderbecke, the trumpet tragedy of the 1930s: a super-talent which, like Beiderbecke's, blew itself away too soon leaving Armstrong at the top of the heap to offer a rare criticism of his potential rival: 'Bunny was great, but he had no business dying *that* young.' [DF]

Bunny Berigan and his Orchestra (1937–9), RCA

The best summary of Berigan's career is John Chilton's Grammy-winning notes for a Time-Life collection of Berigan's sides, currently unavailable in Britain. Another good survey is Danca, Vince, *Bunny: A Bio-discography of Bunny Berigan* (Danca, 1978)

Berman, Sonny (Saul), trumpet. b. New Haven, Connecticut, 21 April 1924; d. 16 January 1947. Played as a teenager with big bands such as Tommy Dorsey and Benny Goodman. Was working with the Woody Herman band (1945–7) at the time of his death following a drug overdose. One of the promising young soloists of the 'Second Herd', Sonny's presence can be felt on a small number of Herman band and small-group tracks, and on one informal session (see below). His fiery, Gillespie-inspired playing held out unfulfilled promise, and still stands up to scrutiny. [BP]

Beautiful Jewish Music (1946), Onyx

Bernhardt, Clyde Edric Barron, trombone, vocals. b. Goldhill, North Carolina, 11 July 1905. A veteran of touring shows in the early 1920s and a fine swing trombonist, he moved to New York in 1928, joined King Oliver in 1931, worked with Marion Hardy's Alabamians, then spent three years with Vernon Andrade, 1934–7. Thereafter he worked regularly for Edgar Hayes, Cecil Scott, Luis Russell, Claude Hopkins and Dud Bascomb, among others, and by the 1950s was leading his own r & b-slanted groups around clubs. In the late 1960s he attracted more attention with his Harlem Blues and Jazz Band featuring Viola Wells (professionally known as 'Miss Rhapsody'), who until then had turned up only on a few obscure recordings for Savoy in the 1940s. The outfit, containing seasoned veterans like Franc Williams (tpt, ex-Duke Ellington), Charlie Holmes (alto) and Tommy Benford (dms), recorded, toured and achieved huge publicity due in part to a British champion, critic Derrick Stewart-Baxter. In the 1980s Bernhardt was touring with the Legends of Jazz, but his ex-band was successful still, touring with Al Casey and pianist Gene Rodgers added to the ranks and sometimes with honorary British members like Roy Williams, Danny Moss, Stan Greig and Jim Shepherd. [DF]

Sittin' on top of the world! (1975), Barron

Berry, Bill (William R.), trumpet, fluegelhorn, vibes, composer, leader. b. Benton Harbor, Michigan, 14 September 1930. A young veteran of Duke Ellington's orchestra, which he joined in 1962, trumpeter Berry (who also often plays cornet for preference) worked in studios for much of the 1960s (including Merv Griffin's TV show for which Bobby Rosengarden was MD) and in 1971 formed the LA Big Band, a highly successful aggregation. In the 1970s and 1980s he developed a solo career, involving small group recordings and European tours as a single where his schooled approach, creative flair (which takes in most of the best mainstream influences from Armstrong to Joe Newman) and reliability won him a big reputation. In 1985 he was in Britain to work London venues. [DF]

Berry, Chu (Leon), tenor sax. b. Wheeling, West Virginia, 13 September 1910; d. Conneaut, Ohio, 30 October 1941. He arrived in New York in 1930, carrying his tenor in a red velvet bootbag strung at the top and wearing a goatee beard which gave him a Chinese look: the nickname 'Chu' came from Billy Stewart's impression that Berry looked like Chu Chin Chow. After spells with several bands (including immortal recordings with Spike Hughes's pickup bands for Decca) he majored with Benny Carter and Teddy Hill at the Savoy, and in November 1935, against offers from Duke Ellington, joined Fletcher Henderson. By then he had become close friends with the young Roy Eldridge – 'When Fletcher wanted Chu he had to take Roy too', recalls Walter C. Allen – and the two would terrorize New York jam sessions after hours, cutting down opposition with deadly skill. Berry's style ('based on riff patterns and speed', according to Milt Hinton) was spotted by Hinton's new boss Cab Calloway, who hired him in 1937 and drew a word portrait of him in later years: 'Chu was a big guy and he sometimes wore glasses. His suits never quite fit right and he had a way of half-smiling and looking down his nose at you thru' the glasses.' Apart from his tenor skills, Berry became a vital straw-boss in Calloway's entourage. 'Chu was very frank and Cab liked him', says Hinton. 'He was a swapper, a real saving-man, and he used to swap arrangements with Chick Webb which he thought would fit Cab's band. He was very much responsible for us having good music in the band. Chu had the kind of confidence that made Cab listen!' And Berry's saxophone was well-nigh unbeatable by then. Fortunately, Berry recorded prolifically: with Eldridge, with Lionel Hampton and with Calloway on at least one classic outing, 'I don't stand a ghost of a chance with you'. When he suffered severe head injuries in a car crash with Andy Brown, another Calloway saxophonist, on 27 October 1941 and died four days later, it was for Calloway, 'like losing a brother, someone I had joked with and hollered at. There was a quiet around the band for weeks and we left his chair empty.'

Chu Berry is still underrated. He was the only jazz tenor saxophonist who presented a real challenge to the omnipotent Coleman Hawkins on his own full-blown, fast-fingered master terms, although Berry's sound was in some ways different from his rival's: blowzier, fuller, with a more emotive vibrato and a strange crying sound in his frequently-used upper register. But he missed the late 1940s onset of jazz intellectualism by a few years and died very young without being dramatically different enough from Hawkins to be thought of as an intellectual alternative. And he worked, by and large, in second-rank bands. But he was – the ultimate accolade – a musician's musician. 'Chu was about the best,' said Coleman Hawkins. [DF]

The Calloway Years 1937–41, Meritt (double)

Berry, Emmett, trumpet. b. Macon, Georgia, 23 July 1915. His fiery, full-toned and flawless creations were enough to guarantee him the soloist's chair with Fletcher Henderson, 1936–9, replacing the unstoppable Roy Eldridge: a formidable challenge. From short stints with Horace Henderson and Earl Hines he moved to Teddy Wilson's Café Society sextet for two years of radio, records and live dates, and then to Raymond Scott's much publicized CBS band; the first integrated band of its kind. 1945–50, Berry worked with Count Basie, then with Buck Clayton in the legendary small band that Jimmy Rushing led at the Savoy (Britain was to see this band practically person for person on its 1959 tour). 1951–4, he toured with Johnny Hodges' fine small band, then the following year with Sammy Price's Bluesicians in Europe (a rare album by Price, *A Real Jam Session* is a copybook sample of Berry at his best), and all through the decade he took part in countless jazz and session recordings in New York and Los Angeles with everyone from Count Basie to Gil Evans (admirers may have spotted him backing Miles Davis in Evans's orchestra on a much-transmitted New York TV show). In the 1960s Berry was busily freelancing still, but since 1970, when he retired to Cleveland, jazz has apparently been the poorer for his absence. Like Bobby Hackett, Dick Ruedebusch and Joe Wilder, he deserves to be more than a trumpet-specialist's delight. [DF]

Sam Price and his Bluesicians (1955), Vogue

Berton, Vic (Victor Cohen), drums, percussion, vibes. b. Chicago, 6 May 1896; d. California, 26 December 1951. He had played percussion in the Alhambra Theater, Milwaukee, by the time he was eight, and during World War I for Sousa's Navy band; by the time he (briefly) took over management of the Wolverines, as well as the drum stool from Vic Moore in 1924, he was a senior figure in the jazz firmament. He also acquired, temporarily, an (even) larger-than-life reputation when in 1931 he was arrested for smoking marijuana with Louis Armstrong. Frank Driggs tells us that he regularly dabbled in occultism and 'often greeted his students in flowing black robes'. A highly gifted drummer-percussionist, Berton's recorded work with Red Nichols (featuring pedal-tympani on sides such as 'That's No Bargain' and 'Boneyard Shuffle') and others made him the best-remembered white jazz drummer of the 1920s and helped to pave the way for later 'personality drummers' such as Gene Krupa. From 1930, after work with Roger Wolfe Kahn, Paul Whiteman and others, he moved into studio work at Paramount and later Twentieth Century-Fox. Berton was a powerful personality in his own right: a cocksure businessman with a fast-talking line in hard sell. [DF]

Red Nichols and his Five Pennies (1926–30), Coral

Best, Denzil DeCosta, drums, composer. b. New York City, 27 April 1917; d. 24 May 1965. Took up drums only in 1943, after playing piano, trumpet, bass; worked with Ben Webster (1943–4), Coleman Hawkins (1944–5), Illinois Jacquet (1946) and Chubby Jackson (1947). Also freelance recording with such as Lee Konitz. After record date with George Shearing (1948), founder member of Shearing quintet (1949–52, terminated by car accident). Then played with Artie Shaw group (1954) and Erroll Garner trio (1956–7). Despite further gigging with singer Nina Simone and Tyree Glenn, Best was gradually crippled by calcium deposits in his wrists, and met his death falling down steps in the New York subway. In his heyday a driving but discreet drummer, he specialized in playing with brushes rather than sticks. He was also the composer of such bebop anthems as 'Move', 'Wee' (aka 'Allen's Alley') and 'Dee Dee's Dance'; his tune '45° Angle' was recorded by Herbie Nichols and Mary Lou Williams, and he co-wrote 'Bemsha Swing' with Thelonious Monk, his colleague in the 1944 Hawkins group. [BP]

Coleman Hawkins, *Hollywood Stampede* (1945), Capitol

Best, Johnny (John McClanian), trumpet. b. Shelby, North Carolina, 20 October 1913. From the mid-1930s (he started his 'name career' with a young Les Brown in 1934) Best worked with a string of top-ranking swing bands including Artie Shaw, Charlie Barnet, Glenn Miller, the US Navy band during the war and then, after demobilization, with Benny Goodman. Like Billy Butterfield, for whom he subbed later in the World's Greatest Jazz Band, Best combined the strength of a lead trumpeter with high-powered solo ability (a valuable and by no means commonplace double ability), and with all the above bands his intense, rather Butterfield-like solo work was featured heavily. After the war, Best joined NBC for studio work, played regularly for leaders such as Jerry Gray, Billy May (an old friend) and Bob Crosby (with whom he toured Japan in 1964) and worked in night clubs including the Honeybucket in San Diego. A regular associate of the World's Greatest Jazz Band in the 1970s, Best was still playing regularly in the 1980s despite a serious fall in 1982 which (says John Chilton) confined him to a wheelchair. 'A sort of cross between Bunny Berigan and Bobby Hackett!' Thus George Chisholm on one of the best and most underrated swing trumpeters. [DF]

The Sound of Jazz All-Stars (1977), Jazz Connoisseur Cassettes

B flat On the main brass instruments, trumpet and trombone, B flat is the home key: in other words, the key in which the most important notes of the major scale can be produced without use of the valves or slide, and where a minimum use of these produces the remainder of the scale. Thus, brass players usually learn to play in this key first, and then in F which is almost as easy, and many of them go through life feeling that even a complex music such as jazz is somehow less demanding in these two keys.

Although the mechanics are different, B flat is also the home key on tenor and soprano saxophone and on clarinet, while on alto and baritone saxophone B flat is in the same relationship to their home key as F is for trumpet and trombone.

The crucial role of these instruments in early

jazz, and their general dominance in later periods, explains the huge number of blues in B flat – some of them even called that, for want of any more inspired title – and the equally huge number of 'I Got Rhythm' variants in the same key (see RHYTHM). Hence also the expression, 'Not your standard B-flat gig/situation/person etc.' [BP]

Bickert, Ed (Edward Isaac), guitar. b. Manitoba, Canada, 29 November 1932. One of the brightest guitar talents to emerge in the 1980s, he worked regularly in Toronto from the 1950s on, in studios and regularly with clarinettist Phil Nimmons and reedman Moe Koffman as well as, later in the 1970s, trombonist Rob McConnell and Paul Desmond. By the mid-1970s, however, Leonard Feather was still able to sum up his reputation as 'mainly local, but he is highly regarded by the Americans who have played with him'. An album with Rosemary Clooney (*Sings Harold Arlen*, 1983, Concord) unobtrusively introduced Bickert's talents to a wider audience: his quiet assurance, flowing lines (recalling Kenny Burrell and Jim Hall, as much as Charlie Christian) and innate musicality showed up on equal terms with better recognized players such as Dave McKenna and Jake Hanna and quickly turned him into an international 'new star' at over 50. From then on Bickert appeared regularly on Concord, not only with Scott Hamilton, Warren Vaché *et al.*, but frequently as a leader and soloist in his own right. [DF]

The Ed Bickert 5 at Toronto's Bourbon Street (1983), Concord

Bigard, Barney (Albany Leon), clarinet, tenor sax, b. Villere Street, New Orleans, 3 March 1906; d. Culver City, California, 27 June 1980. He was taught clarinet by Lorenzo Tio Jnr., the finest teacher in New Orleans, but early in his career bought a new 'novelty instrument', a tenor saxophone, and featured himself in a slaptonguing duo with bandleader-clarinettist Albert Nicholas at Tom Anderson's Café in New Orleans. Soon after, the two of them were invited to join King Oliver in Chicago's Plantation Club and Oliver bought Bigard a brand new Albert-system clarinet and hired him as a clarinettist. When Oliver found himself short of work in 1927, Bigard freelanced then joined Duke Ellington in New York for his first Cotton Club season. 'Barney had that woody tone that Pop always adored', said Mercer Ellington, and something else besides: a creative imagination for inventions which later became a part of Ellington compositions. Theme two of 'Mood Indigo', the athletic opening of 'East St Louis Toodle-oo' (a routine for comedian 'Pigmeat' Markham) and 'C-Jam Blues' were all from ideas contributed by Bigard to the creative free-for-all that was the early Ellington band. 'Ellington's got Barney Bigard, a good New Orleans boy sitting right by him telling him what to do',

Barney Bigard

said Jelly Roll Morton, a naughty overstatement which had a germ of truth in it. Bigard left Ellington in 1942, having helped create immortalities like 'Barney goin' easy!', 'Across the track blues' and 'Clarinet Lament' (his favourites) and after relaunching Kid Ory, recording with him and a part in the film *New Orleans* (1947), joined Louis Armstrong and his All Stars for five happy years. During that time his translucent tone, snaky mobility and celebrated 'waterfalls' were integral to Armstrong's show, but by the time he left Bigard was exhausted by travel and drinking heavily. After a rest and spells with Ben Pollack and Cozy Cole he was back with Louis again in 1960 (and, for Trummy Young, 'sounding a whole lot better than before'), but left again in autumn 1961 and after more freelancing gave up full-time music in 1965. He came back again regularly for tours, guest appearances, full-scale features in the music press, radio and TV work, until he died in 1980 when perhaps the greatest Tio pupil of all was lost to jazz. It may be that one more vital aspect of Bigard was afterwards run to earth by Jo Jones: 'Barney made the clarinet famous. This was *before* Benny Goodman.' [DF]

Barney Going Easy (1937–40), Tax

See Bigard, Barney (ed. Barry Martyn), *With Louis and the Duke* (Macmillan, 1985)

Big Band One of the most popular formats for the propagation of jazz, the big band now stands somewhat apart from the majority of small-group performances. But it was not always so: the earliest big bands, such as those of Fletcher Henderson and Duke Ellington, were only slightly larger than King Oliver's 8-piece Creole Jazz Band.

The discovery that reed instruments in particular sounded more impressive playing in pre-arranged harmony led the 3 saxes/3 brass (plus 4 rhythm) line-up of mid-1920s Henderson and Ellington to become 4 saxes/6 brass by the late 1930s. In the bands of the swing era improvised solos tended to be seen as enhancing the ensemble, rather than the reverse (which was also true, at least at the time). As the size of big bands increased still further (to 5 saxes/8–10 brass by the mid-1940s) they lagged behind the stylistic developments in small-group jazz which they often helped to popularize subsequently.

The appearance of occasional bands, such as Count Basie in the mid-1930s or Lionel Hampton in the 1940s, which function like 'large small-groups' and whose comparative simplicity and excitement seem to arise from the sheer joy of playing together, only emphasizes the norm of big bands as vehicles principally for either one leading soloist or for an arranger or composer. Either way the possible delights are so inviting that, despite the daunting economics of getting 19 or more musicians to work together, the big-band idea seems destined never to die. [BP]

Bilk, Acker (Bernard Stanley), clarinet, vocals, bandleader. b. Pensford, Somerset, 28 January 1929. He began his career in the mid-1950s working with Ken Colyer, and soon after formed his own band. A hit record, 'Summer Set' co-written by Bilk and pianist Dave Collett, climbed to number eight in the British hit parade, and Bilk's band shot to success, aided by a gifted publicist, Peter Leslie (he later worked for the Beatles), who clothed them in Edwardian outfits and bowler hats. Bilk was the biggest star of Britain's Trad boom, with a string of shuffle-beat hit records (recalling one of his biggest favourites, Louis Prima) and, most important of all in the long term, a Denis Preston engineered title 'Stranger on the Shore', which Bilk wrote (and originally titled) for his daughter Jenny. Later it was used in a children's TV serial and became his biggest success (he now fondly calls it 'my old-age pension'). His band played in films and on TV and radio until the advent of the Beatles, when Bilk moved into cabaret, played jazz clubs on spare nights, and built up a similarly fanatical following in Europe. His band of the late 1960s (featuring Bruce Turner and trumpeter-musical director Colin Smith, as well as pianist-arranger, Barney Bates) was one of the best British mainstream bands ever. By the late 1970s Bilk was still leading his jazz band wherever possible (trumpeter Rod Mason replaced Smith in 1970), and recording with them as well as regularly with large string orchestras: he easily surpasses Bobby Hackett as the jazzman to have recorded most with strings and produced another huge hit, 'Aria', in 1976. After Rod Mason left his band, Bilk hired a much underrated British trumpeter, Mike Cotton, and trombonist/singer Campbell Burnap replaced longtime sideman Johnny Mortimer. Together they formed another great Bilk band, still as busy in 1986. [DF]

Acker Bilk in Holland (1983), Timeless Traditional

Biscoe, Chris (Christopher Dennis), alto, soprano and baritone sax, alto clarinet, piccolo, flute, tenor sax. b. East Barnet, Herts, 5 February 1947. Started on alto in 1963 and was entirely self-taught. Studied English and education at Sussex University, 1965–8, then moved to London. 1970–3, played with National Youth Jazz Orchestra then began working professionally with various London groups. 1979–85, worked with Mike Westbrook's various bands. Formed his own quartet in 1980. 1983–5, also worked with Chris McGregor's Brotherhood of Breath. Began composing in 1969, and writes most of the material for his own group. Toured Poland with NYJO, France and Britain with the Brotherhood, and with Westbrook has played in Western Europe, Scandinavia, New York and Australia. [IC]

With Mike Westbrook, *The Westbrook Blake* (1980), Original; with Westbrook Orchestra, *The Cortege* (1982), Original; *A Little Westbrook Music* (1983), Westbrook; Westbrook Orchestra, *On Duke's Birthday* (1984), Hat Art; *Chris Biscoe Quintet and Duo* (1985), (CDBCI cassette only); Westbrook Trio, *Love for Sale* (1986), Hat Art (double)

Bishop, Walter, Jnr., piano. b. New York City, 10 April 1927. Son of Jamaican-born songwriter of the same name (composer of 'Swing, Brother, Swing'). An early disciple of Bud Powell, Bishop was the pianist most frequently employed by Charlie Parker during the first half of the 1950s, when he also recorded with Miles Davis. Still active in the 1980s as a group sideman and at his most effective as such. Stylistically important for his incorporation of Erroll Garner's right-hand chording into the bop piano style, he influenced Red Garland and those who followed him, but his own work has been unjustly neglected. [BP]

Hot House (1977–8), Muse

Black Benny, drums. (nda). A legendary bass drummer around 1915 with the New Orleans Brass Band, who supposedly played louder and stronger than any other in the city. Benny was a lowlife who spent regular time in gaol and sometimes was released by the police for important parades. But he carried a gun and on one occasion at least shot a bystander during a Canal

Street marchpast. A pen-portrait of Benny, one of Louis Armstrong's early minders, appears in Armstrong's autobiography, *Satchmo: My Life in New Orleans*. 'Benny got killed', recalls Pops Foster. 'He hit this woman and then turned his back on her and she cut him down.' [DF]

Blackwell, Ed(ward Joseph), drums. b. New Orleans, 1927 (or 1929). Late 1940s gigging with Plas Johnson, Roy Brown and Ellis Marsalis in New Orleans, where he first met Ornette Coleman. 1951, moved to Los Angeles, rehearsing regularly with Coleman but had returned home at time of Coleman's first records and first New York appearances. On tour with Ray Charles (1957), freelance gigging and r & b session work in New Orleans with such as Earl King, Huey 'Piano' Smith (late 1950s). Joined Coleman quartet in New York (1960–2), also recording with John Coltrane–Don Cherry and Eric Dolphy–Booker Little. Worked with Cherry quartet (1965–6) and Randy Weston (1965–7, including tours in Africa), lived in Morocco with Weston during 1968. Rejoined Coleman (1967–8, 1970–3), briefly with Thelonious Monk, Alice Coltrane. Teaching (from 1972) at Wesleyan University, playing activity restricted through use of kidney machine. From 1976, regular participant in group Old and New Dreams with Cherry, Dewey Redman and Charlie Haden, playing material associated with Coleman.

Blackwell's most important work, historically speaking, may have been with Coleman, whose early music thrived on the drummer's responsive alertness. However, the same control and clarity that made him so suitable in that context appears in all Blackwell's contributions. Tonally, he gets a very alive sound from the drums, which may derive from his interest in early New Orleans players such as Paul Barbarin, Baby Dodds and Zutty Singleton. Certainly the variety of situations in which Blackwell has featured speaks not only for his versatility but for his virtues. [BP]

Ornette Coleman, *This Is Our Music* (1960), Atlantic; Cherry/Blackwell, *Mu Pts.1/2* (1969), Affinity

Blake, Eubie (James Hubert), piano, composer. b. Baltimore, Maryland, 7 February 1883; d. Brooklyn, New York, 12 February 1983. Ragtime's centenarian began on a home harmonium in Baltimore playing hymns, but the rhythms of a revolutionary new music were all around him. On the local streets he heard brass bands 'raggin' the hell out of the music': in saloons and dance halls later he heard the virtuoso ragtime piano professors who ceremoniously spread their coats out, velvet lining upwards, dusted off the keys with a new silk handkerchief and sat down to produce magic. Early masters like 'One Leg Willie' (Joseph) pointed the way for Blake: a trained classical pianist, Joseph had stopped trying to follow up his degree in music in a white man's world, and after a phenomenal three years at Boston Conservatory had taken to ragtime and drink. His showstopper was 'Stars and Stripes Forever' (an ironic choice) played in march time, ragtime and boogie, and for Blake he was only equalled once 60 years on into jazz history – by Johnny Guarnieri. Blake learned his craft, as he had to, away from home in sporting houses (including three years at Aggie Shelton's) and wrote his first rag, 'The Charleston Rag', around 1899. By the 1900s, young, ambitious and talented, he was touring with medicine shows, accompanying singers such as Madison Reed, and playing for Baltimore hotels. His piano show by then encompassed classical themes in ragtime, popular tunes of the day, flash ragtime specialities, a classical waltz and perhaps a Bert Williams recitation. Early songs he wrote included 'Poor Jimmy Green' (1908) and two very successful rags, 'Chevy Chase' and 'Fizz Water Rag'. In 1915, Eubie teamed with an ambitious young entrepreneur, Noble Sissle, for vaudeville appearances. Earl Hines remembers Blake well at the time: 'He used to wear a racoon coat and a derby and he always carried a cane. He was the first one I ever saw playing piano with one hand and conducting with the other. He used to lift his hands high off the keyboard, which was my first lesson in the value of showmanship. He and Sissle were all the rage when they came to town.' By 1921, Blake and Sissle were on Broadway with a colossal success, *Shuffle Along*, the first all-black musical, starring Florence Mills and featuring comedy duo Miller and Lyles. Auditions for *Shuffle*

Eubie Blake

Along stretched three times round the theatre, and its success was to pave the way for more black extravaganzas, among them *Revue Nègre* (in which Sidney Bechet appeared), *Plantation Review*, *Rhapsody in Black* and *Bamville Review*. While Sissle continued his solo treks around Europe, Blake stayed in New York to write prolifically for such hit shows as the *Blackbirds Review*, producing hits like 'Memories of you' (with Andy Razaf, 1930) and 'You're lucky to me'. He was to work with Sissle again, though, up to World War II, assembling more shows, but then retired to study the Schillinger system beloved of Glenn Miller at New York University, where he won his degree.

In 1969 John Hammond recorded a vital double album *86 years of Eubie Blake* for Columbia. The LP, featuring his songs, solo piano, reminiscences and a reunion with Sissle, paved the way for a Blake revival in the ragtime-conscious early 1970s, and so did a successful appearance at the New Orleans Jazz Festival, 1970: that year Blake was awarded the annual James P. Johnson award. Two years later he won the Duke Ellington medal, and was writing new rags and travelling internationally to appear at jazz festivals and on TV and radio: in 1976 with Terry Waldo he collaborated on an authoritative book, *This is Ragtime*, started his own record label and replaced Rudolf Friml as ASCAP's oldest living member. Perhaps his greatest triumph was reserved for 1978 when a full-scale Broadway review *Eubie* (which came to London and was televised worldwide) strung his songs together in a vivid 'song by song' presentation which brought back all the unbridled glories of *Shuffle Along*. In 1981, Blake received the Presidential Medal of Honour. He died just five clear days after his one-hundredth birthday. [DF]

Eubie Blake, Blues and Rags: his earliest piano rolls, 1917–21, vol. 1, Biograph

See Waldo, Terry, *This is Ragtime* (Hawthorn Books, 1976)

Blake, Ran, piano, keyboards, composer, educator. b. Springfield, Massachusetts, 20 April 1935. Began on piano at age four; studied with many teachers, but mainly self-taught. Early influences were classical music (particularly 20th-century) and the black gospel music of the Church of God in Christ at Hartford, Connecticut. He graduated from Bard College, where he was the first student to major in jazz; also spent several of his college summers at the Lenox School of Jazz, which had been opened by John Lewis and Gunther Schuller. 1957, began a long association with singer Jeanne Lee, and they were among the first to attempt total voice and piano improvisation. They toured Europe in 1963 and achieved some recognition there, but success eluded them in the USA. Since the late 1960s, he has been a member of the staff of the New England Conservatory of Music of which Schuller is president. At first he taught improvisation and acted as co-director of the conservatory's community service projects, then in 1973 he was made chairperson of the Third Stream Department. He has defined Third Stream as 'an improvised synthesis of ethnic cabaret or Afro-American music with what has been called for the last few years European avant-garde.'

Blake collaborated with tenor saxophonist Ricky Ford off and on in the 1970s, and has worked with singer Eleni Odoni, but he generally prefers to perform solo. His favourites include George Russell, Thelonious Monk, Ray Charles and Max Roach. [IC]

Ran Blake Plays Solo Piano (1965), ESP; *Crystal Trip* (1977), Horo; *Open City* (1977), Horo; *Rapport* (1979), Arista/Novus

Blakey, Art(hur) (aka Abdullah Ibn Buhaina, 'Bu'), drums. b. Pittsburgh, Pennsylvania, 11 October 1919. Starting out a self-taught pianist, Blakey was already leading a big band at 15; suddenly displaced in his own group by Erroll Garner, he migrated to drums. After working with several local bands, member of Mary Lou Williams's first New York group (1942). Big-band experience followed, with Fletcher Henderson (1943–4) and the adventurous young outfit of Billy Eckstine (a founder member in 1944, Blakey stayed until the band's demise in 1947). Briefly led own big band, the 17 Messengers, and recorded under own name for Blue Note (1947). Also freelance gigging and records with such as Tadd Dameron–Fats Navarro, Thelonious Monk, Charlie Parker, Miles Davis, Horace Silver, and longer stints with Lucky Millinder (1949) and Buddy DeFranco (1952–3). Occasionally leading own groups in New York and on out-of-town gigs, including live recording with Clifford Brown, Silver *et al.* (1954).

A Horace Silver studio date (1954) caused the formation of the Jazz Messengers as a co-operative with Blakey, Silver, Kenny Dorham (later Donald Byrd), Hank Mobley and Doug Watkins, until the other four left (mid-1956) and the Messengers became the trade name for all Blakey's subsequent groups. Although there has been a fairly steady turnover of personnel, the proportion of major soloists is high: even a selective list must include Jackie McLean, Johnny Griffin, Wayne Shorter, John Gilmore, Billy Harper, Bobby Watson, Lee Morgan, Freddie Hubbard, Woody Shaw, Wynton Marsalis, Curtis Fuller, Slide Hampton, Cedar Walton, Keith Jarrett, Chick Corea, Joanne Brackeen. Blakey has occasionally appeared with special reunions of former Messengers (at Kool Festival, 1981, in Japan, 1983, and at the Blue Note re-launch, 1985) and for one tour the group became a 10-piece band (1980). But the basic quintet (or, more often since 1961, sextet) sound of the Messengers became the virtual definition of the style known as 'hard bop'.

Although he continued to freelance on re-

Art Blakey

cords, notably with Sonny Rollins (1957), Milt Jackson (1957), Cannonball Adderley (1958) and Hank Mobley (1960), Blakey has rarely been heard in public away from the Jazz Messengers since 1955; the major exception was with the Giants of Jazz (1971–2). His own brilliant playing has remained largely unchanged for three decades and his solo work, in its concentration on the snare drum, is a reminder that his style was formed during the swing era. Yet his accompaniment relies on the rhythmic complexity of bebop. For, in addition to the driving beat of his right hand and left foot (and even the left hand on the snare, at medium tempos such as 'Moanin' '), Blakey introduces all manner of cross-rhythms behind a soloist. If the soloist's inspiration begins to flag, Blakey lifts him on to another plane – as Johnny Griffin put it, 'He'd make one of those rolls and say, "No, you can't stop yourself *now*!" '

These effects used to be considered an unwelcome distraction by some listeners (and by critics not attuned to polyrhythms). Indeed, certain youthful band members who were not quite ready for their task may have been swamped by such a tidal wave of percussion. But those who were adequately prepared clearly relished the challenge, and emerged even stronger after the ordeal. Most important of all, perhaps, is that in his long career Blakey has always exuded excitement, but always channelled it to enhance the ensemble, just as the swing-era drummers did. As a result the ensemble that he leads – no matter what the personnel at any particular moment – has become one of the cornerstones of the jazz tradition. [BP]

A Night at Birdland, vols. 1/2 (1954); *Moanin'* (1958); *Free For All* (1964), all Blue Note; *Straight Ahead* (1981), Concord

Blanchard, Terence, trumpet, composer. b. New Orleans, March 1962. Studied piano from age five, composition from 15. Took up trumpet in 1976 at New Orleans Center for Creative Arts run by Ellis Marsalis, then in 1980 won Pee Wee Russell Scholarship to Rutgers University in New Jersey. Recommended by Paul Jeffrey, played with Lionel Hampton (1980–2) while still a student. Joined Art Blakey as trumpeter and musical director, replacing Wynton Marsalis (1982–6). Left after four years to form own quintet with Blakey sideman Donald Harrison, with whom he had made three albums.

Initially, Blanchard's arrival on the national scene was inevitably overshadowed by his precocious predecessor from New Orleans; but, all comparisons with Marsalis left aside, it was soon evident that Blanchard was uncommonly talented for one so young (20 when he joined Blakey). He showed an early absorption of Clifford Brown and the 1950s Miles Davis along with more fashionable neo-bop archetypes such as Freddie Hubbard and Woody Shaw; although the latter predominate in his more mature work, he combines their excitement with an intriguing edge of reserve in his tone-quality. He was also an extremely capable front-man for the Jazz Messengers and, shortly before he left, Blanchard had expanded Blakey's band to a septet for the first time in its long history. His writing for this line-up and for his quintet albums again reveals a strong neo-bop influence with some individual touches. [BP]

Art Blakey, *New York Scene* (1984); Blanchard/ Donald Harrison, *Discernment* (1984), both Concord

Blanton, Jimmy (James), bass. b. Chattanooga, Tennessee, October 1918; d. 30 July 1942. Studied violin as a child, switched to bass while in college and played with Tennessee State Collegians (1936–7). Also worked during summer vacations with Fate Marable (1936–9), left college to play full-time with Jeter–Pillars band in St Louis (1937–9). Joined Duke Ellington (October 1939), but after only two years, was admitted to hospital with ultimately fatal tuberculosis.

The crucial figure in giving the bass greater prominence, Blanton was not only in the right place at the right time, but he was clearly the right candidate. Previously John Kirby and the two bassists from Chicago, Milt Hinton and Israel Crosby, had been moving towards more melodic 'walking lines', while the great Basie band of the late 1930s had shown the advantage of allowing Walter Page to be heard as the foundation of the rhythm-section. Blanton, however, combined the melodic tendencies of the first group with the marvellously alive pulse of Page, and a beautiful rounded tone which enhanced his brief solo passages. His facility in all these fields could not have had such a speedy impact if Ellington had not known immediately how to exploit it (and taken the trouble to have him exceptionally well captured by the recording engineers of the period – and by the public address systems on live performances). As a result Blanton set new standards of technique and fluency, but he also set the ball in motion for the development of contemporary bass playing. [BP]

Duke Ellington, *The Indispensable, vols. 5/6* (1940), RCA

Bley, Carla (*née* Carla Borg), composer, piano, organ, synthesizers. b. Oakland, California, 11 May 1938. Father a piano teacher and church organist; he gave her piano lessons as soon as she could walk. After age five she had no formal lessons, but played hymns in churches and sang in church choirs. She became interested in jazz at 17: 'I liked Miles Davis and Thelonious Monk, people who had only a few notes and chose them well.' She went to New York, working as a waitress, and in 1957 married pianist Paul Bley who encouraged her to start composing, which she did in 1959. She began to devote all her time and energy to music in 1964, after being inspired by Ornette Coleman and Don Cherry, and she worked with Charles Moffett and Pharoah Sanders at a New York club in January of that year. Other musicians began to play and record her compositions, among them George Russell, Jimmy Giuffre and Art Farmer.

With trumpeter-composer Michael Mantler (who was to become her second husband), she was co-leader of the Jazz Composers' Orchestra from December 1964, and wrote her first orchestral piece, 'Roast', for it. The JCO (see MANTLER), was an attempt to give the free (abstract) music of the day an orchestral setting, and at this point in her career Carla Bley was deeply involved with the free jazz scene. January 1965, she went to Holland to record and do radio and TV work. Back in the USA the JCO played a series of concerts in New York and appeared at the Newport Jazz Festival. Late 1965, she returned to Europe, playing in Germany and Italy, and forming a quintet with Mantler and Steve Lacy. 1966, while touring Europe with Peter Brötzmann and Peter Kovald, playing high-energy free jazz, she suddenly became disenchanted with total abstraction. She went back to the USA and began working on her composition *A Genuine Tong Funeral*. Later she said: 'That's when my life started. I stopped being part of the stream I was in and struck out as a protest to that stream.' *A Genuine Tong Funeral* (subtitled *Dark Opera Without Words*), was recorded for RCA in November 1967 by the Gary Burton quartet augmented by Gato Barbieri, Jimmy Knepper, Steve Lacy, Howard Johnson, Mantler and Bley.

From this point on, she was more of a composer than an instrumentalist. Also in 1967 she began working on her massive composition *Escalator Over the Hill*. 1969, she arranged all the music on Charlie Haden's *Liberation Music Orchestra* album, and also composed some of it. She spent three years composing and recording *Escalator Over the Hill*, completing it in June 1971, and it was released as a triple album set on

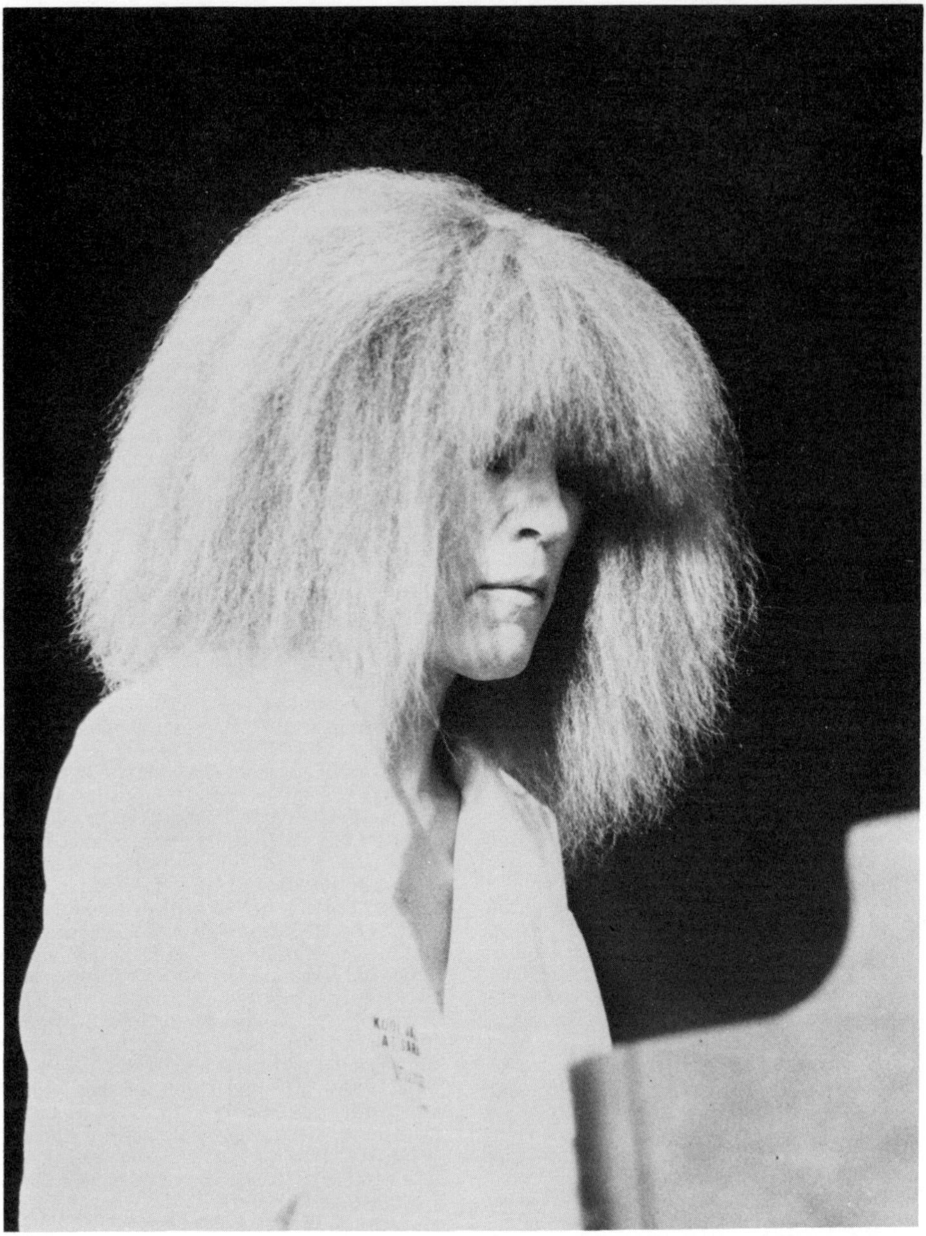

Carla Bley

the record label that she and Mantler created: JCOA Records. *Escalator* was inspired by lyrics by Paul Haines, and is a kind of jazz opera, which J. E. Berendt has called 'the largest complete work that has so far emerged from within jazz'. It was also a kind of summary of her musical ideas to date, using jazz and rock musicians, and covering the gamut from abstraction to set structures and harmonies, rock rhythms and elements from ethnic (Indian) music. In 1973 it was awarded the French Oscar du Disque de Jazz.

Also in 1973, with Don Cherry, she played on the film score of Jodorowski's *Holy Mountain*, and with Mantler set up Watt Records to handle their own compositions separately from their JCOA label, which was used to release the music of other people. She was commissioned to write a piece for classical musicians, and produced '3/4' which was performed at the Alice Tully Hall in 1974, with Keith Jarrett playing the solo part. Later that year she had a short stint playing with the Jack Bruce band.

From 1976 she led her own bands which usually included French horn and tuba as well as trumpet and reeds, touring and playing major festivals internationally. 1985, she completed an opera based on Malcolm Lowry's novel *Under the Volcano*, which was given its première in Los Angeles.

Carla Bley, from the moment she began composing in the early 1960s, was an original with an extraordinary melodic flair. Two classics of that decade, 'Sing me Softly of the Blues' and 'Ad Infinitum', show her genius for creating evocative and memorable tunes and 'Ida Lupino' and 'Wrong Key Donkey' have the same qualities. She developed slowly into one of the most important band leaders and composing-arranging talents on the entire jazz scene. Her early influences were hymns and church music, and later Erik Satie's *Parade* (1917), of which she has said, 'For a long time it was almost the only music I listened to.' But she has stated that her greatest influences were the Beatles' *Sergeant Pepper's Lonely Hearts Club Band* and *Magical Mystery Tour*, and it was these, with the Satie, which gave her earlier orchestral music more of a European than an Afro-American flavour. The theatricality and parody in her work are European in origin as are the discontinuous rhythms of some of her earlier work. During the 1970s there was a gradual strengthening of the Afro-American rhythms and her music gained enormously in pith and impact, becoming brilliantly concentrated after the diffuseness of *Tropic Appetites* (1973–4). Beginning with *Dinner Music* in 1976, she released a series of magnificent albums which still goes on in the 1980s. Although her medium-sized bands have an instrumentation similar to the Gil Evans bands, and although her writing for lower instruments such as trombone and tuba is, like Evans's, superb and crucial to her music, her orchestral sound is all her own and instantly recognizable. [IC]

Escalator Over the Hill (1969–71), JCOA; *Tropic Appetites* (1973–4); *Dinner Music* (1976); *The Carla Bley Band European Tour 1977*; *Musique Mécanique* (1978); *Social Studies* (1981); *Carla Bley Live!* (1981); *Heavy Heart* (1984), all Watt

Bley, Paul, piano, synthesizer, composer. b. Montreal, 10 November 1932. Began on violin at age five, piano at eight, junior diploma at McGill Conservatory at eleven; 1950, studied composition and conducting at Juilliard School, New York. In the later 1950s he was associated with the burgeoning avant-garde movement, playing with Charles Mingus, Ornette Coleman, Don Cherry, Jimmy Giuffre, Don Ellis, Sonny Rollins and Gary Peacock. He also encouraged his wife, Carla Bley, to begin composing. 1964–5, member of the Jazz Composers' Guild, and also led his own groups which included Steve Swallow, Pete La Roca and Giuseppe Logan. He toured Japan with Rollins, 1963, and Europe with his own quintet, 1965.

In the 1970s he pioneered electronics, playing solo concerts using acoustic piano and three electric keyboards, and for a time was closely associated with Annette Peacock, who sang with him. The duo appeared at festivals in the USA and Europe. 1973–5, toured Europe twice playing solo acoustic piano at festivals and on TV. 1979, again toured Europe playing solo acoustic piano and appearing at festivals including Ljubljana, Yugoslavia.

Although he first came to prominence with the 1960s avant-garde, Bley is steeped in jazz history and is thoroughly at home with all approaches from the abstract and non-tonal to the diatonic and harmonic. He has always been something of a loner, restlessly exploring different avenues of improvisation. 1975, formed his own production company, Improvising Artists Inc. (IAI), to release records of his own and of other artists. [IC]

With Mingus, Giuffre, Rollins, George Russell, Don Ellis; *Paul Bley with Gary Peacock* (1970); solo piano, *Open to Love* (1973), both ECM; as leader, *Quiet Song* (1974); *Alone Again* (1975), both IAI; *Synthesizer Show* (nda); Bley/Annette Peacock, *I'm the One* (1971), both RCA

Blowers, Johnny (John), drums, percussion. b. Spartanburg, South Carolina, 21 April 1911. He came to New York to join Lou McGarity in 1937, and the following year worked for Bobby Hackett at Nick's, for Bunny Berigan's orchestra and others. One of the very best Dixieland drummers (in the school of Leeman, Fatool *et al.*), from 1940 he was a busy studio man working for CBS and others but turned up regularly on fine Dixieland recording dates for Eddie Condon, Louis Armstrong, Billie Holiday and others. From the mid-1960s he could be heard regularly in clubs such as Condon's and in 1981 came to Europe, and made the rounds of the London jazz scene to universal delight. [DF]

Warren Vaché Snr., *Jazz: it's a wonderful sound* (1977), Starfire

Blue Note Records Given the huge number of specialist jazz record labels during the last 50 years, it is perhaps surprising how few have been sufficiently long-lived or single-minded to have become a definition of the music they purvey. Blue Note, founded in 1939, is one of the exceptions and, although there are alternative descriptions of the style concerned, the phrase 'Blue Note jazz' immediately conjures up a specific sound.

The company recorded boogie, small-group swing and bebop for several years before becoming, in the early 1950s, the contractual home of many of the most important post-boppers such as Horace Silver and Art Blakey. As these musicians and the company's owners (Alfred Lion and the late Francis Wolff) actively sought out younger performers in the same mould, they played a large part in helping to develop what was then becoming known as 'hard bop'. But the combination of hard-boppers with the 'soul jazz' of organist Jimmy Smith and his followers was also a part of the Blue Note sound from around 1956 to 1966.

In the mid-1960s also, a somewhat different style associated with Miles Davis alumni such as Jackie McLean, Herbie Hancock and Wayne Shorter was described as the Blue Note 'school' to distinguish their kind of modal-based 'free jazz' from the more thorough-going changes wrought by the simultaneous work of Albert Ayler *et al*. But though this music is still very influential (and still being beneficially reissued), its identification with Blue Note Records was short-lived compared to the earlier style. What remains to be seen is whether their renewed recording activity from 1985 onwards (after a hiatus of several years) will add to or modify the definition of Blue Note jazz. [BP]

Blue notes are usually defined as the flattened third and flattened seventh of the scale in any particular key. (The flattened fifth is also heard as a blue note when used as a melodic replacement or variation of the normal fifth, but not when it is a harmonic colouring in dense chordal textures.)

It is the melodic context which highlights the impact of these notes, and historically they are not so much an exact note as audibly bent or slurred; if played on an instrument rather than sung, they are usually underlined by a squeezed, growled or otherwise vocalized tone. Their use not only predated the appearance of 'blues' music as such, but also occurs in gospel, soul and rock, as well as in jazz of all periods, whether in the 12-bar blues format or not. While they stand out clearly against the major chords typical of most vocal blues and jazz-blues, they are not dependent on the major; the later development of minor-key blues sequences in no way lessens their use or their effectiveness.

For this reason, it is misleading to talk of *the* 'blues scale'. In a major-key blues, the blue notes exist alongside and in addition to the notes of the major scale, whereas in a minor blues they duplicate some of the notes already included in the minor scale. The mathematically minded will observe that the former situation gives a 10-note scale (9 or 8, if not all the blue notes are used) while the latter could be a 7-note scale. Or less, since a scale with 6 notes or only 5 (such as the pentatonic minor) can equally sound like a blues scale.

At the other end of the spectrum, in more contemporary chromatic jazz any one of the 12 divisions of a scale can be made to appear in context as a blue note, given the necessary prominence and vocalized articulation. [BP]

Blues (1) Blues is a traditional Afro-American music which first coalesced in the early 1900s and continues to undergo healthy development and change today. Originally a predominantly vocal expression accompanied, if at all, by the singer's own guitar or piano (indeed, its immediate predecessors were totally unaccompanied vocals), it has gradually admitted more and more instrumental work over the decades. Nevertheless, a blues band's instrumental-only numbers are merely a prelude or an interlude to the vocals, a situation that is reversed in most jazz performances.

Although the development of blues has been parallel to, rather than closely interlinked with, that of jazz, they have frequently interacted during their history. For instance, when the blues groups of the 1930s added the occasional trumpet and saxophone solos, the influence of Kansas City jazz led to the formation of 'rhythm-and-blues'. Conversely, most significant changes in jazz have been accompanied by a new influx of blues influence: Louis Armstrong's innovations and those of Charlie Parker and Ornette Coleman would have meant less if they had not also instinctively incorporated elements of blues style in their playing.

In this sense, blues is a feeling, but not merely one narrow emotional area. Blues phraseology, either vocal or instrumental, being more honest and realistic than more popular music, expresses ambiguous emotions, as implied by titles such as 'Laughing to Keep from Crying' (Lester Young). It is the combination of openness and ambiguity which is the unique quality of the blues and the reason for its world-wide influence.

(2) A blues, on the other hand, is not a particular tune but a specific chorus structure of 12 bars continually repeated, which was borrowed initially from folk blues. It was, in fact, the input of early jazz instrumentalists that was responsible for its length becoming fixed at 12 bars, rather than 11½ or 13 bars.

Because of its short repetitive form (and also because of the emotional climate associated with vocal blues), it has always been regarded as a test of the jazz improviser's creativity and/or authenticity. The form has been so pervasive, however, that already by the 1930s it had moved beyond any necessary connection with the traditional style and become a form adaptable to abstract improvisations just like any other. A comparison of two pieces such as 'Chasin' the Trane' and 'Tunji', both by John Coltrane, shows the range of response available to one player within the blues form. For this reason, any one example of an instrumental blues is often referred to by jazz musicians as 'a 12-bar' rather than 'a blues'.

A couple of standard sequences have sometimes been referred to, mainly by traditional jazz players, as a 16-bar blues (the sequence of 'How Come You Do Me?' or 'Doxy') or a 32-bar blues, simply because they were used so frequently at one period; but otherwise they have nothing in common with a blues. There is, however, such a thing as a 24-bar blues which occurs when the tempo is doubled but the rate of the chord changes is not: Coltrane's 'Tunji' is in fact an example of this.

The blues can be either (1) blues or (2) a blues, according to the context. Jazz musicians saying, 'Let's play the blues' do not mean, 'Let us play some traditional folk music', but rather, 'Let us do a 12-bar'. (Although, of course, if they actually say 'the blues', it may come out more bluesy than if they had said 'a 12-bar'.) Incidentally, tune titles can be misleading. Especially in the 1920s, when blues were first acknowledged by the music industry, but also later, numerous items have used the word which were neither (1) nor (2). [BP]

Blythe, Arthur Murray, alto sax, composer; also soprano sax. b. Los Angeles, 5 July 1940. Studied with local saxophonists. He worked with Horace Tapscott in LA, 1963–73; also with Stanley Crouch and the Black Music Infinity, 1967–73; began leading his own groups in 1970. 1974, moved to New York working with Leon Thomas, Julius Hemphill and Chico Hamilton, with whom he visited California in the summer of 1975. He was with the Gil Evans orchestra, 1976–80, recording several albums with him and touring and playing festivals in the USA and Europe; 1978–80, worked occasionally with groups led by Lester Bowie and Jack DeJohnette. He was also working and recording with his own groups. 1979, began recording for Columbia and was still with the company in 1985.

Blythe is one of the most gifted alto saxists to have emerged in the 1970s. His playing has all the emotional power of the blues and gospel music, and great harmonic awareness allied to the linear freedom of abstract improvisation, a combination of qualities which has made him much in demand. He is also a fine composer. Three of his Columbia albums, *Lenox Avenue Breakdown*, *Illusions* and *Elaborations*, use unusual instrumentations, including tuba and cello, and must rank with the most creative small-group music of their time. His influences include Coltrane, Charlie Parker, Miles Davis, Monk, Ellington and Eric Dolphy. [IC]

The Grip and *Metamorphosis* (both 1977), India-Navigation; *Lenox Avenue Breakdown* (1979); *Illusions* (1980); *Elaborations* (1982); *Put Sunshine In It* (1985), all Columbia; with Bowie, *The Fifth Power* (1978), Black Saint; with Gil Evans, *Live at the Public Theater (New York 1980), vols. 1 & 2*, Trio; with Jack DeJohnette, *Special Edition* (1980), ECM

Blythe, Jimmy (James Louis), piano, composer. b. Louisville, Kentucky. *c.* 1901; d. Chicago, 21 June 1931. He was a house pianist in the 1920s for companies such as Paramount and Champion and recorded an enormous number of sides as a soloist, accompanist (to singers such as Trixie Smith) and as a bandleader: his studio groups include the State Street Ramblers, Washboard Band and Washboard Ragamuffins. The groups corralled, besides his regular percussionist Jimmy Bertrand, star names including Natty Dominique, the legendary Stump Evans and the Dodds Brothers. Those names give a clue to his subsequent obscurity; like Lovie Austin and Clarence Williams, Jimmy Blythe seems to have been a victim of musical fashion. [DF]

Cutting the Boogie: Piano Blues and Boogie Woogie (1924–41), New World

Boland, Francy (François), piano, arranger. b. Namur, Belgium, 6 November 1929. Played at Paris Jazz Fair, 1949, and contributed arrangements to record dates by Bobby Jaspar and others, 1950s. 1955–6, worked with Chet Baker in Europe following death of Richard Twardzik and began writing charts for radio studio bands such as Kurt Edelhagen. This led to series of albums and transcription recordings featuring Kenny Clarke (from 1961) gradually leading to live appearances with all-star Clarke–Boland big band, which revealed Boland as a retiring but effective ensemble pianist. However, his reputation rests exclusively on his arranging ability and, as well as maintaining an excellent balance between the band sound and the need to feature his renowned soloists, he was especially noted for his improvisatory and involved writing for the saxophone section. Although there was a comparative lack of invention in his original compositions, Boland's qualities show through strongly in his arrangements of standards that in other people's hands were already hackneyed; in his hands they come up fresh as new. [BP]

Clarke/Boland, *Live at Ronnie Scott's* (1969), MPS

Bolden, Buddy (Charles Joseph), cornet. b. New Orleans, 6 September 1877; d. Jackson, Louisiana, 4 November 1931. According to his legends, the supposed first-ever jazz trumpeter, young, handsome, with his shirt 'busted open to the waist so all the girls to see that red flannel undervest' (Jelly Roll Morton), paraded the streets of New Orleans, four or five women on his arm, callin' his chillun home with a trumpet sound that could be heard 14 miles away on a clear night. In spare time he ran a barbershop and a scandal sheet, and he went spectacularly insane on a 1905 street parade.

All the above is standard Bolden legend, and fine copy, and it seems a pity that most of it is untrue. A piece of clear-eyed research by Don

Marquis (see below) finally revealed the truth: Bolden never ran a barber's shop, although his first bandleader Charlie Galloway did, and Bolden was often in there. Rather than being a scandal sheet editor, Bolden was a part time plasterer and labourer, and no trumpet, even on a clear night, could possibly penetrate for more than a quarter of a mile.

The facts unearthed by Marquis reveal that Bolden was raised at 2309 First Street in New Orleans and left school in 1890. All around him were brass bands, street hawkers' cries, church revival meetings and the ragtime of leaders such as John Robichaux. He was taught cornet by Manuel Hall, a friend of his mother's, and played jobs early in his career with Charlie Galloway's band, a small dance group that included Albert Glennie, later a Bolden sideman on string bass. Bolden by degrees took over leadership of the band, retaining Galloway (gtr), Frank Lewis (vln) and in 1897 Willie Cornish (valve tmb). A cylinder recording, which Cornish swore was made before 1898, has never been traced.

At this time Bolden was young, big and striking-looking (he had a child by Harriet Oliver in 1897) and was developing his powerful cornet playing. What he sounded like is conjecture, but his improvisation, if any, would have been primitive, harmonically elementary (probably confined to melody embellishment) and with a rhythmic approach reflecting the current ragtime vogue. But Bolden was a riveting performer of personal charisma and crowd-pleasing musical power. Marquis proves that by 1900 he was playing all over New Orleans in saloons and dance halls, parks and cabarets, for every stratum of black New Orleans. A friendly, gregarious man, he was known as 'King' Bolden by 1904 and for two years after was taking more and more work in the uncomfortable knowledge that younger men like Freddie Keppard and King Oliver were coming up fast and doing new things. Bolden began to drink more, to behave eccentrically, and in 1906 during a Labor Day parade which he never completed was put under arrest for dementiae. He was soon released and lived at home for another year, but there was no more playing. Bolden moved himself and his family into a rougher area of New Orleans on 1st Street and began drinking heavily: a report in the local paper of an attack on his mother and mother-in-law by the cornettist preceded a phone call to the police by Mrs Bolden on 13 March 1907, and that day Buddy Bolden was taken first to gaol, then to Jackson Mental Institute in New Orleans. He remained there for 24 years and died of cerebral arterial sclerosis. [DF]

See Marquis, Don, *In Search of Buddy Bolden* (Da Capo, 1978)

Bonano, Sharkey (Joseph), trumpet, vocals, bandleader. b. Milneburg, Louisiana, 9 April 1904; d. New Orleans, 27 March 1972. He was active in his home town by 1920 (as well as in New York briefly that year with Eddie Edwards) and all through the 1920s played with fine local bands like the New Orleans Harmony Kings and the Prima–Sharkey Orchestra (with Louis Prima's brother Leon); he also auditioned unsuccessfully as a replacement for Bix Beiderbecke in the Wolverines in 1924. Bonano made regular forays into the 'big time' early on, including a spell with Jean Goldkette in 1927, and by 1936 was leading his own band in New York. Isolated references of the period seem to indicate that he may have talked a greater game than he played. Nevertheless, Bonano was a fine hot trumpeter and after the dawn of the New Orleans revival he turned into a highly successful solo act and bandleader, travelling back to New York and Chicago for prestige engagements but still basing himself at home. All through the 1950s he produced a string of albums and singles which became near best-sellers, and often featured blues singer Lizzie Miles and 'Bugle' Sam deKemel, a well-known local attraction. He played the New Orleans Jazz Festival in 1969, three years before he died. [DF]

Midnight on Bourbon Street (1952), Capitol

Bond, Graham John Clifton, alto sax, piano, Hammond organ, voice. b. Romford, Essex, 28 October 1937; d. 8 May 1974. Parents unknown; adopted by Edwin and Edith Bond, from Dr Barnardo's Home. Foster-mother played piano. Lessons on piano, cello, oboe. Played in school orchestra, largely self-taught on sax. Active in London area, 1961–2, with Don Rendell quintet. 1962, with Alexis Korner's Blues Incorporated, which included Jack Bruce (bass) and Ginger Baker (dms). 1963, left Korner taking Bruce and Baker with him, to start his own group, Graham Bond Organization. At first guitarist John McLaughlin was with the group, but after a few months he was replaced by saxophonist Dick Heckstall-Smith. GBO II was formed in 1966, with Jon Hiseman on drums. 1967–9, Bond led various pick-up groups, and visited USA, jamming with Jimi Hendrix, Jefferson Airplane, Dr John, Buddy Miles, among others. 1970–1, with Ginger Baker's Air Force. 1971–3, formed various short-lived groups. Bond's two greatest influences were Charlie Parker and Ray Charles, and his music was shot through with elements from the blues and hot gospel, as well as with passionate improvisatory aspects coming out of Parker but veering towards the contemporary avant-garde. He was something of a charismatic figure and one of the pioneers of improvisation on the popular music scene. His later years were clouded by a growing obsession with the occult, mystical learning and magic, which was most probably a direct or indirect cause of his death: in mysterious circumstances, he fell under a London underground train. [IC]

The Sound of '65 (1965), Columbia; *There's a Bond Between Us* (1966), Columbia; *Love is the*

Law (1968), Pulsar; *Mighty Graham Bond* (1968), Pulsar; *Solid Bond* (1970), Warner Bros

Boogie-woogie, or 'boogie', was originally a jazz-related solo piano form, featuring round and round bass (often eight-to-the-bar) in the left hand, punctuated by rhythmic, often repetitive, right-hand figures. Repeated bass was a frequent device of early ragtime professors, who sometimes called it 'the sixteens'; early ragtime compositions like Joplin's 'Solace Rag' feature a repeated bass, and (says Clarence Williams) music like boogie-woogie was played around the turn of the century in the lumber and railroad camps of the American Midwest. By the 1920s boogie-woogie had become formalized, due in part to the efforts of Albert Ammons and Meade 'Lux' Lewis, and in 1928 the first important boogie records were issued (Lewis's 'Honky-Tonk Train Blues', Pinetop Smith's 'Pinetop's Boogie-woogie').

But it was not until ten years later, after a 1938 Carnegie Hall concert which teamed Ammons, Lewis and Pete Johnson, that the international craze for eight-to-the-bar began. Over the next 15 years boogie became a commercial hit: artists from the Andrews Sisters ('Boogie-woogie Bugle Boy') to Will Bradley ('Down the road apiece') re-created the music with everything from a solo piano to a big band. Most important though, boogie was to supply several fundamental elements to rock and roll. The use of a straight-quaver rhythm feel (as, for example, Albert Ammons used it) replaced the concept of 'jazz-swing' with a kind of shuffling rock rhythm later 'introduced' by rock artists like Huey Smith (one of his first hits was 'Rockin' pneumonia and boogie-woogie flu') and Frankie Ford. By then artists such as Louis Jordan and Lips Page had naturally identified with boogie, and they had been using its devices for ten years before 'Rock around the Clock' was even thought of. Boogie remained popular for 20 years more: Humphrey Lyttelton's 'Bad Penny Blues', a hit in 1956, and 'Lady Madonna', a hit for the Beatles in 1967, showed how the form survived unaltered; and the rock and roll revival of the 1970s preserved it securely once again.

'Boogie-woogie' was simultaneously (or perhaps first) applied to various forms of dancing. As with the word 'bebop' in this connection, it covers virtually any style that moves the whole body and not just the feet. [DF]

Boogie Woogie Masters 1928–41, Affinity

Bop, see BEBOP.

Bose, Sterling 'Bozo' (Belmont), trumpet. b. Florence, Alabama, 23 February 1906; d. St Petersburg, Florida, June 1958. Certainly his credentials are top notch: he worked early on for Jean Goldkette, for Ben Pollack in 1930 and with Joe Haymes's highly disciplined band until Tommy Dorsey took it over in 1935. For the rest of the decade he seems to have moved quickly in and out of most of the best bands: a few months with Benny Goodman, Glenn Miller, Bobby Hackett, Bob Zurke and Bud Freeman until the early 1940s, by which time he was back in New York with small groups led by Miff Mole, Art Hodes and others at Nick's Club. For the last 13 years of his life, Bose freelanced between Chicago, New York and Mobile, led his own band in Florida and worked clubs, but his reputation seemed to have vanished with the war years and his post-war activities, largely unrecorded and undocumented, are a sad echo of a potentially good career. The only anecdotes we have of the pre-war Bose seem to be drunken ones – he was once dragged out of the sea near death from trying to play his trumpet to the fishes, and as a 1930s Decca house musician he was part of an alcoholic quintet known as the 'Falling-Down Five' – but appearances on other people's record dates provide a tantalizing glimpse of what he had to offer. [DF]

Miff Mole and his Dixieland Orchestra (1944), Brunswick

Bossa nova A style of Brazilian popular song most successful in the early 1960s. Strangely cool by comparison with other exportable Afro-Latin rhythms, and distantly influenced by the harmonic language of US West Coast jazz, it soon acquired a permanent place in international middle-of-the-road music. It has also repaid its debt to West Coast by entering the repertoire of all easy-listening jazz players everywhere, as in the phrase: 'Let's do an up-tempo piece first, then something medium followed by a ballad, and then we can brighten things up with a bossa.' [BP]

Bostic, Earl, alto sax, arranger. b. Tulsa, Oklahoma, 25 April 1913; d. 28 October 1965. Played alto while in high school, and while at Xavier University, New Orleans, added trumpet, guitar etc. Worked in several territory bands including Bennie Moten (briefly, 1933) and Fate Marable (1935–6). 1938, in New York, joined bands of Don Redman and Edgar Hayes; 1939, made record début with Lionel Hampton group including Charlie Christian. Led own groups, played and arranged for Hot Lips Page (1941). After a year with Hampton band (1943–4), busy with freelance recording and arranging (including work for Artie Shaw, Paul Whiteman, Louis Prima etc.) 1945, formed regular band, making first records under own name with enlarged all-star band; next year began cutting discs with his septet, so successfully that he stayed with the same label for the remainder of his career. Band members usually had to take a back seat to Bostic himself on records, but among those who gained worthwhile experience with him were Jaki Byard, Jimmy Cobb, Johnny Coles, John Coltrane, Benny Golson, Blue Mitchell, Stanley Turrentine.

Admired by fellow saxophonists for his mastery of the instrument, Bostic also had a considerable influence on r & b styles. His early 1940s hit composition 'Let me off Uptown' was typical of the Louis Jordan era, but his own playing took the vibrant tone and the special effects of Southwestern tenor players and turned them into a way of life. His 1945 solo on 'The Man I Love' shows him beginning to apply this method to well-known standard songs, a policy which, with the addition of a heavy up-beat, paid off handsomely in 'Temptation' (1948) and 'Flamingo' (1951). In an era when 99 per cent of hit records were vocal, Bostic kept a distinct jazz influence alive in popular music. [BP]

That's Earl, Brother (1943–5), Spotlite; *Earl Blows a Fuse* (1946–57), Charly

Boswell Sisters: Connee (originally Connie), vocals, various instruments, b. New Orleans, 3 December 1907; d. New York, 11 October 1976; **Martha**, b. 1908, piano, vocals; **Helvetia**, violin, vocals. They grew up comfortably in white New Orleans, learning black music from their black staff. Connee, because of polio, was to stay in a wheelchair for life. All three sisters played instruments: Martha piano, Helvetia (Vet) banjo, guitar and violin, and Connee saxophone, cello, trombone and piano. Connee's finest instrument, though, was her voice (very early on she had recorded 'Crying Blues' with Martha) and not long after all three sisters were in Los Angeles for a five-nights-a-week radio series. With other broadcasting commitments for CBS the girls were constantly on air, and they discovered their close-blended timbre one night when Connee lost her high notes during a cold: singing at half-volume close to a microphone produced their unique sound. In 1931 at the Paramount Theater, New York, the trio created a sensation: they were signed by Brunswick Records and CBS radio, and appeared on the first-ever American TV transmission. Their work over the next five years was to be the model for dozens of 'sister acts', from Andrews to Beverley, which flourished for the next 20 years. Most of the Boswell Sisters' 75 or so Brunswick records are now classics, recorded between midnight and dawn after live radio or theatre shows with stars such as Bunny Berigan, the Dorseys, Mannie Klein and the underrated Larry Binyon. Connee wrote their arrangements, neat and complex but with plenty of room for hot solos, and at one point imposed a liquor ban on sessions (it was broken by Artie Bernstein, who kept a bottle of scotch in a trap door at the back of his bass). Now at the peak of their popularity, the sisters made films, including *The Big Broadcast of 1932*, *Moulin Rouge* (1934) and *Transatlantic Merry Go Round* (1934); they appeared twice in Britain and in Holland (where they recorded, respectively with Ambrose and the Ramblers). By the mid-1930s all three were married, Connee to Harold Leedy, their manager (to whom she was devoted for 40 years); thereafter she embarked on a highly successful solo career, including radio, TV, films (*Artists and Models*, 1937; *Syncopation*, 1942), cabaret and records (with Bing Crosby, Bob Crosby, Victor Young and Ben Pollack). Her jazz treatment of light classical items such as 'Martha' ('Ah! so pure') 'My Little Gypsy Sweetheart' and 'Ah! Sweet Mystery of Life' were early examples of their kind and caused controversy as well as consternation to Decca's prim A & R man Jack Kapp. In the 1950s Connee took a leading role in a successful TV series, *Pete Kelly's Blues* (as Savannah Brown, opposite Jack Webb), and worked tirelessly for charity, but retired after her husband's death, which rapidly aged her, and died 18 months later. Perhaps her greatest disciple was Ella Fitzgerald who said 'Who influenced me? There was only one – Connee Boswell! She was doing things that no one else was doing at the time!' Those vital things included singing correctly, rather than belting, as the older acoustic-bound blues singers had to do. Connee Boswell was the first of the microphone-based singers and, as Chris Ellis and Michael Brooks have noted, she exerted a vital influence over the new 1930s generation of popular song-stylists. [DF]

The Boswell Sisters, 1932–4, Biograph

Bowie, Lester, trumpet, fluegelhorn, kelphorn, vocals, percussion, composer. b. Frederick, Maryland, 11 October 1941. Brought up in Little Rock, Arkansas, and St Louis, Missouri. Began playing at age five; at 16 led a youth group; in St Louis he used to practise his trumpet by an open window in the hope that Louis Armstrong might pass by and discover him. After military service he worked with r & b bands and also with his wife, singer Fontella Bass. He played on r & b sessions for Chess Records; also helped to form BAG (Black Artist Group) and the Great Black Music Orchestra in St Louis. 1966, moved to Chicago, got involved with AACM (see ABRAMS, MUHAL RICHARD), and joined the band of saxist Roscoe Mitchell. In the later 1960s he and Mitchell were founder-members of the *Art Ensemble of Chicago, one of the key groups of the 1970s and 1980s. 1969, Bowie recorded with Archie Shepp, Sunny Murray, Jimmy Lyons, Cecil Taylor, among others. He has also done intermittent solo projects and recordings over the years. He composed, conducted and recorded 'Gettin' to know y'all' with the 50-piece Baden-Baden Free Jazz Orchestra in 1969, performing it again at the 1970 Frankfurt Jazz Festival. 1974, toured Senegal, performing with African drummers; 1979, played a New York concert with his 59-piece Sho Nuff Orchestra; he has also recorded with Jack DeJohnette and Fela Kuti, among others.

Bowie is a flamboyant performer with a flair for comedy and musical parody, and became a major contributor to the theatrical side of the

Art Ensemble's concerts. He is also a fine trumpet player with a beautifully rounded tone and a technique and imagination which encompass the whole trumpet tradition from Bubber Miley's growls to Miles Davis's musings, and the whole improvising field from blues and popular songs to the most severe abstraction. [IC]

With AEC; *Numbers 1 & 2* (1967), Nessa; *Fast Last* (1974), Muse; *The 5th Power* (1978), Black Saint; *The Great Pretender* (1981); *All the Magic* (1982); with Jack DeJohnette, *New Directions* (1978), all ECM

Bowman, Dave (David W.), piano. b. Buffalo, New York, 8 September 1914; d. 28 December 1964. A great jazz pianist who worked in the musical area of Bushkin, Schroeder *et al.*, he studied at Hamilton Conservatory, Ontario, and the Pittsburgh Music Institute, then toured Britain with Jack Hylton's band before moving into Nick's Club, New York, in 1936. There he worked with Bobby Hackett, and the Summa Cum Laude Orchestra until 1940 when he joined Jack Teagarden's band. Months with Joe Marsala and Muggsy Spanier followed in 1941, after which Bowman became a staffman for ABC and NBC, often working as accompanist to singer Perry Como. From 1954 he worked with Bud Freeman's trio then moved to Florida to freelance and was working for Phil Napoleon in 1964 as well as in a Miami hotel band when, three days after Christmas, his car plunged into a drainage canal near Miami and he drowned. [DF]

Bud Freeman, *Chicagoans in New York* (1935–40), Dawn Club

Boyle, Gary, guitar, composer. b. Patna, India, 24 November 1941. Family moved to London when he was eight. Started on guitar at 15 with private lessons; 1967–9, studied at Leeds College of Music after working for twelve months with Brian Auger and Julie Driscoll, 1966. 1970–1, returned to work with Auger. 1970–3, with Mike Westbrook, Mike Gibbs, recorded with Stomu Yamashta. 1973–5, formed his own jazz-rock group Isotope, which toured in Europe. 1975, moved to Manchester and freelanced. Often works in duo and other formations with John Etheridge. 1978, Boyle's solo album *The Dancer* received the Montreux Jazz/Pop Award. His favourite guitarists are John McLaughlin, Robben Ford, Mike Stern, and other inspirations are Miles Davis and Joe Zawinul. [IC]

With Yamashta and others; with Isotope, *Illusion* (1974); solo, *The Dancer* (1978); *Electric Glide* (1979), all Gull

Brackeen, Joanne (*née* Joanne Grogan), piano, composer. b. Ventura, California, 26 July 1938. As an adolescent, learned piano by copying Frankie Carle records and making her own 'inner music'. A few private lessons, but left Los Angeles Conservatory of Music after only three days. By 1958 she was doing West Coast club dates with Dexter Gordon, Harold Land and others. 1959, with Teddy Edwards and Charles Lloyd, then gave up performing to be wife of saxist Charles Brackeen and mother to four children. 1965, moved to New York and began to play in public again. 1969, with Woody Shaw and Dave Liebman. 1969–71, with Art Blakey's Jazz Messengers. 1972–5, with Joe Henderson. 1975, joined Stan Getz, who brought her to the attention of a wider public, particularly in Europe where she was much appreciated. By 1977 she had established herself as a major solo voice, receiving much critical recognition. Leonard Feather has commented that she is as important to the 1980s as Bill Evans and Herbie Hancock were to the 1960s, and McCoy Tyner and Keith Jarrett to the 1970s. Joanne Brackeen has said: 'I prefer using my own material to standards. Different songs are like babies, and I feel better playing one that I created and nurtured than one I adopted, no matter how good it is.' [IC]

With Art Blakey, *Jazz Messengers 70* (1970), Catalyst; with Stan Getz, *Gold* (1977), Inner City; as leader, *Snooze* (1975), Choice; *Mythical Magic* (1977), PA/USA; *Tring-a-Ling* (1977), Choice; *Aft* (1978), Timeless/Muse; *Prism* (1979), Choice; *Keyed In* (1979), Tappan Zee

Bradford, Bobby Lee, trumpet. b. Cleveland, Mississippi, 19 July 1934. Brought up in Dallas from age 12, played in high school and college with Cedar Walton, David Newman etc.; gigging with Buster Smith and others. 1953, moved to Los Angeles, began collaborating with Ornette Coleman and appeared with Wardell Gray, Gerald Wilson, Eric Dolphy. After military service and further studies, replaced Don Cherry with Coleman quartet in New York (1961–3). Back on West Coast, co-led group with clarinettist John Carter (1965–71), then visits to Europe (1971, 1972–4, 1986, recording each time with John Stevens). Later teaching in Los Angeles and leading own groups. None of Bradford's early 1960s work with Coleman was recorded, although he was on Ornette's 1971 *Science Fiction* and *Broken Shadows* sessions; but his dates under his own name reveal a thoughtful and melodic player who benefited from the 'free jazz' experience to define his own individual style. [BP]

Lost in L.A. (1983), Soul Note

Film: *The New Music* (dir. Peter Bull, 1980)

Bradford, Perry 'Mule' (John Henry), piano, composer. b. Montgomery, Alabama, 14 February 1893; d. Queens, New York, 20 April 1970. 'One of those old honky-tonk pianists that played with one finger', says Pops Foster, he travelled between the South and New York in the 1910s playing for shows, rent parties, saloons and singers. He came to New York to stay around 1920, while managing vaudeville singer Mamie Smith, and it was her recording of 'Crazy Blues' (written by Bradford as part of the score for his show *The Maid of Harlem*) which single-handed launched the 1920s blues craze, race recordings, Smith's career and Bradford's. From then on he toured with Mamie Smith and worked busily as a black talent scout, song-plugger, publisher (in 1923 he was gaoled for infringement of copyright laws) and composer. Some of his famous compositions include 'That Thing Called Love', 'Evil Blues' and 'You can't keep a good man down'. Bradford recorded as a bandleader in the 1920s, under the collective title Perry Bradford's Jazz Phools: the 'phools' included Louis Armstrong, Don Redman, Charlie Green and James P. Johnson. [DF]

Louis Armstrong, *Young Louis: the Sideman* (1924–7), MCA

See Bradford, Perry, *Born with the Blues* (Oak, 1965)

Bradley, Will (Wilbur Schwichtenberg), trombone, composer. b. Newton, New Jersey, 12 July 1912. After work from 1931 with CBS as a staffman he joined Ray Noble's new American orchestra in 1935; his section mate was Glenn Miller. 'He can do more things better than any trombone player I've ever heard', said Miller then, and Bradley stayed in demand in studios until 1939 when he formed a band with drummer Ray McKinley which quickly created a successful style of its own playing big band boogie. But Bradley enjoyed playing ballads as well as up-tempo tunes and had a questing musical ear which was later to take him into the world of contemporary classical composition. 'He is as fluent as the early Teagarden, as graceful as Dorsey even in the fastest of passages and as imaginative as McGarity at his Goodman best' (from a fan letter to *Metronome* magazine in 1946). From 1942 on he returned to studio work, playing the Tonight show, studying composition and pursuing a spare-time hobby of gemstone culture. [DF]

With John Guarnieri, *Big Band Boogie* (1959), RCA

Braff, Ruby (Reuben), trumpet. b. Boston, Massachusetts, 16 March 1927. He was working around Boston in the late 1940s, but it was some now classic records by Vic Dickenson's septet in 1953–4 that brought him dramatically into the spotlight and invented the term 'mainstream' single-handed. However, the 1950s were less than kind to Braff in working terms: the critical acclaim that surrounded his prolific recordings was seldom reflected in his datesheet. He arrived at a time when all players of his age were expected to sound like Dizzy Gillespie or Clifford Brown: his viable swing-based alternative was ignored by jazz fashion. For the next few years he worked on and off at jazz festivals, in clubs and on radio and TV (as well as playing an acting role in *Pipe Dreams* on Broadway in 1955–6), but by 1960 was able to report to Leonard Feather that he had been 'almost continuously out of work for five years'. If so, it showed no effect on his recorded output, which was the most revolutionary of any trumpeter/cornettist operating in his jazz area at the time: albums such as *Holiday in Braff* (a re-creation of Billie Holiday splendours with Bob Wilber's saxophone section), *Easy Now!* (on which he teamed with Roy Eldridge without being either bested or cowed) and *Ruby Braff – featuring Dave McKenna* (which shows him at his hard-blowing 1950s best) prove it. By the 1960s Braff was working more regularly: with George Wein's Newport All Stars (very early on he formed a love-hate relationship with Wein's determined piano playing) and often in Europe as a soloist, where one of his happiest partnerships was with Alex Welsh's fine British band. In the 1970s, now established as a star solo cornettist who appeared often with pianist Dick Hyman and the New York Jazz Repertory Company, he formed one of his few regular groups, with guitarist George Barnes. The Braff–Barnes quartet, in its short, sometimes stormy career (both leaders were quick-tempered artists) created small-group jazz to set alongside Louis Armstrong's Hot Five and the small groups of Benny Goodman and Teddy Wilson: music that was delicate but never precious, strong but never strident, tasteful but never effete. After quarrels parted the leaders, Braff returned to solo performance, working in the USA with chosen equals such as Hyman, and in Europe with gifted accompanists such as Canadian guitarist Ed Bickert and British pianist Brian Lemon.

An accomplished pianist himself, Braff is choosy about the people he plays with and sometimes quick to voice his views, but those who criticize him for that should remember that they are the views of 'the best trumpeter walking now', in Warren Vaché's words. In the 1980s Braff made a conscious decision to work only with those whose musical viewpoint matched his own. Collaborations with pianist/pipe organist Hyman produced classics such as *America the Beautiful* (a masterpiece), a Crosby set with strings, *Swingin' on a Star*, for Peter Boizot's Pizza label, which Armstrong could scarcely have bettered in his different way, and late duets with pianist Gene de Novi.

Braff is probably the most artistic trumpeter (more correctly, cornettist) to emerge since Louis Armstrong, who in fact represented everything that Braff respects in music: honesty, lyricism, strength, sound, and the kind of polished-jewel melodic creations that Braff later called 'the adoration of the melody'. But Braff, unlike most late impressionists, not only absorbed Armstrong's philosophies but constructively added to them. First, he developed a

Ruby Braff

mobile facility which revolutionized the technique of many trumpeters in the 1950s but never toppled over into the 'fast fingering' that Armstrong justly dismissed. Second, he introduced a sound for one specification in the low cornet register that is as arresting as Armstrong's but different: a cello-round tone-cavern that no trumpeter had achieved before. Third, he evolved, like Bobby Hackett, an individual harmonic route through chords which avoided the stock devices of bebop and were challenging and inimitable. [DF]

With Dick Hyman, *America the Beautiful* (1984), Concord

See Balliett, Whitney, *Alec Wilder and his Friends* (Houghton Mifflin, 1974)

Brand, Dollar, see IBRAHIM, ABDULLAH.

Brass Most generations of jazz musicians have followed the European terminology in using the word 'brass' to describe only trumpets, trombones, tubas etc., excluding the saxophone family (despite their construction).

To most rock or post-rock musicians, however, 'brass' covers virtually everything that is not a stringed or rhythm instrument. Therefore, the phrase 'brass section' has different connotations, according to who uses it. [BP]

Braud, Wellman (originally Breaux), string bass. b. St James Parish, Louisiana, 25 January 1891; d. Los Angeles, 29 October 1966. First on violin, then on bass, he played early on in Tom Anderson's New Orleans saloon, moved to Chicago in 1917 to work with Sugar Johnnie and Charlie Elgar's band, and by 1923 was on tour with James P. Johnson's *Plantation Days* review. After three more years with Will Vodery, vaudevillian Wilbur Sweatman, Jelly Roll Morton and others, he joined Duke Ellington in 1927 and became a stylish focus of attention as well as a musical pacesetter. 'The way he was slapping the bass!' recalls Mercer Ellington. 'When they recorded he always made sure he was close to the mike and it's amazing how his sound still comes through on those old records.' Braud's impact had (with Pops Foster a little later) a colossal effect on younger contemporaries like Milt Hinton and in Britain Tiny Winters, and he set a style for most pre-Blanton bassists. A dignified and kindly man when he was old, Braud had once been a voluble and enthusiastic salesman for himself and others: after leaving Ellington in 1935 he managed the Spirits of Rhythm, ran his own restaurant, got involved in other Harlem business ventures and led his own trio. Although officially retired from 1944 he remained active in jazz, touring with Kid Ory in 1956 and returning to regular gigs after a 1961 heart attack. 'I just worshipped him – he was my mentor', said Hinton later. 'He had such dignity and power – a real New Orleans gentleman.' [DF]

Duke Ellington at the Cotton Club (1929–31), RCA

Braxton, Anthony, alto, soprano and sopranino sax, clarinet, contrabass clarinet, flute, composer, and vocals, percussion, accordion, harmonica musette. b. Chicago, 4 June 1945. 1959–64, lessons with Jack Gell of the Chicago School of Music and studied harmony and composition at Chicago Musical College and philosophy at Roosevelt University. He met Roscoe Mitchell and Jack DeJohnette while at Wilson Junior College; early influences were Paul Desmond, Coltrane, Schoenberg, then Miles Davis, Eric Dolphy, Lee Konitz and Jackie McLean. 1964–6, in the army he played in bands and began leading small groups.

1966, back in Chicago, he joined the AACM (see ABRAMS, MUHAL RICHARD) and has said of that experience: 'There was a degree of unification among musicians in Chicago that wasn't attainable in New York . . . There was so much communication and interchange, and careful study and research . . . It wasn't as competitive.' 1968, he created a milestone in jazz history when he recorded a double LP of solo alto saxophone, *For Alto*; it was not released until 1971, after which the fashion grew for solo instrumental performances. 1969, went to Paris with the Creative Construction Company, which included Leroy Jenkins (vln), Leo Smith (tpt) and Steve McCall (dms), but the group had little success there. Braxton has said, 'Our music was perceived as being cold, and that has stuck with me.'

Back in the USA he went to New York at Ornette Coleman's invitation, staying at the latter's house for a while. Then for a year, Braxton gave up music and worked as a chess hustler in Washington Square Park, New York. 1970, began an informal association with Chick Corea, studying scores by Stockhausen, Boulez, Xenakis and Schoenberg, as well as playing together. Then he joined Corea's newly formed group Circle, which included Dave Holland and Barry Altschul. Circle lasted two years (1970–2) and played in the USA and France, where the group recorded a live double album. In the early 1970s he also worked with the Italian group Musica Elettronica Viva, playing contemporary classical and improvised music.

For Alto was highly praised on its release, won several accolades, including the Gold Disc award from Japanese music critics, and by 1972 was one of the best-selling albums of the small independent label Delmark Records. That year, Braxton made his concert début as leader playing at the Town Hall, New York, in duo, trio and quintet formations; he also played solo at Carnegie Hall. Since then he has continued to lead his own groups, touring and playing festivals in the USA, Canada and Europe. In the mid-1970s he led a quartet with Kenny Wheeler (tpt), Holland and Altschul, until in 1976, Wheeler left and his place was taken by trombonist George Lewis. Braxton has also worked in duo with British guitarist Derek Bailey.

1974, Braxton signed a recording contract with Arista Records and moved to Woodstock. 1975, with the quartet, toured Europe and played festivals including Graz and Hamburg; in September his trio played at the concert of Arista jazz artists in New York, and were the only acoustic group in a programme otherwise entirely made up of heavily electronic jazz-rock-fusion bands. The trio, with Holland and Altschul, seemed like an oasis of sanity in a desert of decibels, and their severely abstract music was warmly received.

Braxton is as much a composer as an improviser, and has used mathematical relationships,

Anthony Braxton

The Brecker Brothers (Randy on trumpet, Mike on tenor sax)

diagrams and formulae as a basis for both composing and playing. He is one of the first black musicians working in abstraction to acknowledge a debt to contemporary European art music, and his music often seems to have a kind of wilful intellectualism. He has been accused of an inability to swing, and Gary Giddins has written: 'His heavy involvement with the fashions of the European avant-garde seemed to stifle the exuberant vitality of his best work.' Whether he swings or not, his restless creativity is constantly seeking new outlets, there is much humour in his work and he is continually doing the unexpected. The range of his talent is vast: at one end of the spectrum there are the solo saxophone performances, at the other, totally composed works for huge ensembles such as his *For Four Orchestras,* which has been described as 'a colossal work, longer than any of Gustav Mahler's symphonies and larger in instrumentation than most of Richard Wagner's operas'. [IC]

With Dave Holland, Max Roach, Circle, Derek Bailey, Muhal Richard Abrams, Roscoe Mitchell, Joseph Jarman, Gunter Hampel, Creative Construction Company and others; *For Alto* (1968), Delmark; *The Complete Braxton* (1971), Arista; *New York Fall 1974*, Arista; playing standards, *In the Tradition, vols. 1 & 2* (1974), Steeplechase; *Five Pieces* (1974); *Creative Music Orchestra* (1976); *For Four Orchestras* (1978); *Alto Saxophone Improvisations* (1979), all Arista; *Performance 9/1/79*, hat HUT

Breaks An essential ingredient of good jazz, according to Jelly Roll Morton, and although he exaggerated, it is perhaps a pity they are not used more. A break consists of the rhythm-section marking the first beat of a bar and then remaining silent for the rest of the bar (or longer), while the soloist fills the space alone. Equally, the 'break' describes what the soloist plays during the gap, which acquires an inevitable charge of tension that is then resolved as the rhythm-section piles in again. Instances abound in early jazz; the 4-bar break following the interlude of 'Night in Tunisia' is the most famous later example.

The idea more or less died out with the democratization of 'free jazz', but surfaced again more recently in the 1974–5 Miles Davis bands; on albums such as *Agartha*, Davis would stop the rhythm-section briefly during someone else's solo. This was done on a totally random basis, unlike the obviously programmed breaks in earlier jazz where the anticipation of the break by both soloist and audience is part of the fun. [BP]

Brecker, Mike, tenor sax, flute, soprano sax, piano. b. Philadelphia, Pennsylvania, 29 March 1949. Father a pianist and both parents jazz buffs. Studied with Vince Trombetta, 1965–9, and Joe Allard. At first interested in rock – Cream and Jimi Hendrix, then King Curtis,

Junior Walker and Coltrane. Spent one year at University of Indiana; 1970, went to New York where his brother, trumpeter Randy Brecker, had been based for four years. First professional job was with r & b band led by Edwin Birdsong. 1970, with Billy Cobham. Worked in a jazz-rock group called Dreams, which functioned for two years or so and also recorded, but had no success. 1973, with James Taylor. 1973–4, with Horace Silver. 1974–5, with Billy Cobham; worked with Yoko Ono in Japan, 1974. With Randy, formed the Brecker Brothers, which became one of the most successful jazz-rock-fusion groups of the mid-1970s. At the end of the decade, he was a member of the all-star group Steps, which eventually changed its name to Steps Ahead. This was formed to do a Japanese tour, and the original personnel included Steve Gadd (dms), Eddie Gomez (bass), Mike Mainieri (vibes). When Gadd left, Peter Erskine joined on drums, and there have been various keyboard players. Steps Ahead became one of the most successful bands of the early 1980s, touring and playing festivals all over the world. Their first albums were recorded in Japan and imported into the USA, but they eventually signed with a US company.

Brecker developed into perhaps the most comprehensive saxophone talent of the 1970s and 1980s, with a burnished, incisive sound and a fluency and drive which are unsurpassed. He can set his stamp on virtually any kind of context – big band, small group, electronic jazz-rock – which is why he has been one of the busiest studio musicians and certainly the most recorded saxophonist since 1975. [IC]

With Mike Gibbs, Hal Galper, Kenny Wheeler, Horace Silver and many others; *The Brecker Brothers* (1974); *Back to Back* (1975), both Arista; with Steps Ahead, *Steps Ahead* (1983); *Modern Times* (1984), both Elektra Musician

Brecker, Randy, trumpet, piano, drums. b. Philadelphia, Pennsylvania, 27 November 1945. Took up trumpet in third grade at high school; played gigs with r & b bands while still at school. 1963–5, at University of Indiana, playing in the big band and small groups; private lessons with David Baker. The Indiana big band won a competition at Notre Dame Festival and did a US State Department tour of Europe and the Middle East, after which Brecker stayed on in Europe for three months working as a single. Back in the USA, he moved to New York City working with Blood Sweat and Tears, 1966; Horace Silver, 1967, 1969, 1973; Janis Joplin, Duke Pearson, Clark Terry big bands, 1968; Stevie Wonder and Art Blakey, 1970; with his brother, saxophonist Mike Brecker, in a jazz-rock group Dreams until 1972. In the early 1970s he was also with Larry Coryell's Eleventh House and Billy Cobham's group, and he worked with Deodato, Johnny and Edgar Winter; also very active as a studio musician playing in brass sections on albums of many artists including James Brown and Gladys Knight and the Pips. 1974, with Mike Brecker, formed the hugely successful jazz-rock group the Brecker Brothers.

In the later 1970s the Brecker brothers opened a successful club in New York. As well as continuing to do studio work, they have also worked together as sidemen in acoustic bands playing neo-bop; 1978, in this capacity, they recorded a magnificent live album (*Speak with a Single Voice*) with a group led by Hal Galper.

Randy Brecker's style comes out of the Clifford Brown/Freddie Hubbard school, and he is a virtuoso performer who has many fine acoustic and electric (amplified trumpet) solos on record. [IC]

With Silver, Pearson, and others; *The Brecker Brothers* (1974); *Back to Back* (1975), both Arista; with Larry Coryell, *Introducing the Eleventh House* (1974), Vanguard; with Billy Cobham, *Crosswinds* (1974), Columbia; with Hal Galper, *Speak with a Single Voice* (1978), Enja

Brookmeyer, Bob (Robert), valve-trombone, arranger (and piano). b. Kansas City, 19 December 1929. After working as pianist with several big bands (1951–2), joined Stan Getz quintet (1953, also late 1954). Work with Gerry Mulligan quartet/sextet (1954, 1955–7), followed by Jimmy Giuffre trio (1957–8). Began freelancing in New York as player and arranger, toured with Gerry Mulligan big band (1960–1) for which he also wrote. Co-leader with Clark Terry of occasional quintet (1961–6), also further tours with Mulligan. Founder member of Thad Jones–Mel Lewis band (1965–7, contributing arrangements), while becoming more active as freelance writer and studio musician, first in New York then (from 1968) in Los Angeles. Increased jazz profile once more after returning to New York (late 1970s), formed own quartet and wrote new arrangements for Mel Lewis band from 1979.

Brookmeyer's valve-trombone sound initially seems rather cold and unemotional, but is capable of considerable variation – from the deliberately deadpan tone which he uses for unaccented and apparently aimless Tristanoesque doodling to the warm yet fuzzy quality shown when injecting some swing-era phrasing. It is no accident that his best solos result from a mixture of these approaches, combined with the occasional full-throated shout. Nor is it an accident that one of his best albums is called *Traditionalism Revisited*, for he has always displayed a liking for the uncomplicated humour which pervades some early jazz, particularly the work of its trombonists. This tendency blended especially well with Clark Terry during their partnership, and it shows also in his arranging, which marries the influences of early Gil Evans and Gerry Mulligan in a way that makes them appear almost over-serious by comparison. Of Brookmeyer's own tunes, 'Open Country' (recorded with both Mulligan and Getz) and 'Jive

Hoot' have enjoyed popularity with other players. [BP]

Traditionalism Revisited (1957), Affinity; *Gloomy Sunday and Other Bright Moments* (1961), Verve; *Bob Brookmeyer and Friends* (1964), CBS

Brooks, Tina (Harold Floyd), tenor sax. b. Fayetteville, North Carolina, 7 June 1932; d. 13 August 1974. Younger brother of tenorman David (Bubba) Brooks, Jnr., who played with Sonny Thompson (1950s) and Bill Doggett (1970s–1980s). Tina, as he was known since childhood, moved with family to New York (1944) and, after playing with schoolmates, toured with Sonny Thompson (1950–1), Charles Brown, Joe Morris, Amos Milburn and Lionel Hampton (1955). Then, associating with Benny Harris and Elmo Hope, worked in various Bronx and Harlem clubs (1956–7) and recorded with Jimmy Smith ('The Sermon' etc, 1958) and Kenny Burrell. After a brief recording career lasting until 1961, slid into obscurity progressively reinforced by drug problems. The conviction and fluency of his playing, somewhat reminiscent of Hank Mobley, were until recently undervalued (only one album under his own name was released during his lifetime). But re-issues, followed by first-time issues of sessions previously withheld, have led to a renewed interest in his work. [BP]

Complete Blue Note Recordings of Tina Brooks Quintets (1958–61), Mosaic

Brötzmann, Peter, saxes, clarinet. b. Remscheid, Germany, 6 March 1941. Studied painting at art school in Wuppertal; self-taught as a musician. He began playing traditional jazz and swing at 18, but graduated rapidly to the free jazz of the 1960s, and since then has stayed with abstraction. 1966, worked with Carla Bley, Michael Mantler and Steve Lacy, touring Europe with the group Jazz Realities; subsequently with Don Cherry and most leading European free improvisers. From 1968, led his own trio with Fred van Hove (piano) and Han Bennink (dms). Brötzmann has also worked and recorded with Globe Unity Orchestra and Albert Mangelsdorff. Since the late 1960s he has been a member of Free Music Production (FMP), a musicians' collective concerned with promoting abstract music nationally and internationally, and which produces records and organizes concerts and festivals. [IC]

Brötzmann trio, *Balls* (1970); trio, with A. Mangelsdorff, *Outspan Number 1* (1974); *Brötzmann Solo* (1976); Brötzmann/Bennink, *Ein halber Hund kann nicht pinkeln* (1977), all FMP

Brown, Boyce, alto sax. b. Chicago, 16 April 1910; d. Hillside, Illinois, 30 January 1959. A jazz eccentric with an angular playing style who for most of his life stayed in Chicago. He worked through the 1930s and 40s in good company including Wingy Manone, Paul Mares and Danny Alvin, as well as leading his own bands, but recorded only a few sides (with Wild Bill Davison amongst others) before entering a Servite monastery in 1953. In 1956, as 'Brother Matthew', he emerged to make his only album and appear on TV with Eddie Condon who remembered him later: 'a slow reader, blind in one eye with about one tenth vision in the other! But he was an intellectual who listened to Delius and wrote poetry.' Some of that poetry, reprinted in Condon's scrapbook, suggests that Brown was no stranger to earthly pleasures. He died of a heart attack. [DF]

Eddie Condon, *With Brother Matthew* (1956), ABC Paramount

Brown, Cleo(patra), piano, vocals. b. Meridian, Mississippi, 8 December 1909 (or 1907). When her Baptist minister father moved to Chicago (1919), she played piano in church and learned boogie from her pianist brother. She also worked for touring show, and from late 1920s had residencies in Chicago clubs and on radio. 1935, replacement for Fats Waller on his New York radio series: as a result began recording. Worked in New York, Chicago, Los Angeles, San Francisco, Las Vegas regularly (apart from early 1940s illness) until 1953, gaining international popularity. Took up full-time nursing, then, after retirement in 1973, played and sang religious 'inspirational music' under name C. Patra Brown. Her version of 'Pinetop's Boogie-woogie' influenced many subsequent players, male and female; it is all the more surprising that she only ever made 24 tracks under her own name (18 in one year, 1935–6). The singing is cute rather than profound (providing an unmistakable cue for Rose Murphy and Nellie Lutcher), but the driving piano work is what really counts. [BP]

(4 tracks by Brown) *Kings and Queens of Ivory* (1935–40), MCA

(2 tracks by Brown), *Piano Portraits, vol. 2* (1935), Affinity

Brown, Clifford, trumpet, composer. b. Wilmington, Delaware, 30 October 1930; d. 26 June 1956. Father an amateur musician, gave him a trumpet when he was 15. He studied trumpet privately in Wilmington, also taking lessons in jazz harmony, theory, piano, vibes and bass. By 1948 he was playing gigs in Philadelphia with people such as Miles Davis, Kenny Dorham, Max Roach, J. J. Johnson and Fats Navarro. The latter encouraged and influenced him. 1949, entered Maryland State University to study music, and did some arranging for the college band. June 1950–May 1951, he was in hospital after a car crash which almost killed him. Dizzy Gillespie and others encouraged him to recover and resume playing. 1952–3, played trumpet and piano with r & b group, Chris Powell and his Blue Flames; briefly worked and recorded with Tadd Dameron; August–December 1953, joined Lionel Hampton's band, touring Europe with it, and recording as leader with a French rhythm section. Early 1954, he was briefly with the Art Blakey quintet, recording two magnificent live albums with them (*A Night at Birdland*, vols. I & II); mid-1954, joined Max Roach in a group that became known as the Clifford Brown–Max Roach quintet, spending the rest of his life with it. He won the New Star award in the *Downbeat* critics' poll in the same year.

Clifford Brown had genius as both a trumpet soloist and a composer/bandleader. He absorbed his main influences (Gillespie and Navarro) very rapidly, and by the age of 22 was already very much himself – an original stylist with his own sound. His was one of the fullest and most beautiful trumpet sounds in jazz, and it was this which brought him nearer to Navarro than Gillespie. The latter had always sacrificed fullness of sound in order to achieve almost supernatural speed, flexibility and range; Navarro and Brown sought for tonal beauty, with Brown having just the edge in terms of breadth and resonance: a crackling, brassy sound with plenty of vibrato. He had an excellent range, great stamina, superb execution and an apparently inexhaustible capacity for melodic invention which expressed itself fluently at any tempo – breakneck, medium or slow. But above all, his music exuded warmth and joy, and it is these qualities which gave his brilliance such human eloquence.

The quintet he co-led with Max Roach, one of the finest groups of the 1950s, included pianist Richie Powell (Bud Powell's brother), bassist George Morrow and, at various times, saxists Sonny Stitt, Harold Land and Sonny Rollins. During its two-year existence, Brown became more and more himself, the sound gaining in fullness and beauty, the technique in sureness, and his ideas becoming more daring. Some of the live recordings of the group rank with the very greatest. Brown was also an excellent composer for small groups, and several of his pieces have become part of the standard jazz repertoire: 'Joy Spring', 'Daahoud', 'Sandu', among others. As a trumpet stylist, his influence lives on in the work of Lee Morgan, Freddie Hubbard and Wynton Marsalis, and every subsequent jazz trumpeter has been influenced by him either directly or indirectly. His music reflected his personality and character: he was clean-living, disciplined, and had a warm gentle disposition which made him much loved by his associates. He was killed in a road accident at the age of 25. [IC]

Clifford Brown in Paris (1953), Prestige; with Art Blakey, *A Night at Birdland* (vols. I & II, 1954), Blue Note; *Clifford Brown & Max Roach Inc* (1954); with Maynard Ferguson and Clark Terry, *Clifford Brown Jam Session* (1954); Brown/Roach quintet, *Jordu* (1954–5), all Trip; *Study in Brown* (1955), Emarcy; *Clifford Brown with Strings* (1955), Trip; *Clifford Brown and Max Roach at Basin Street* (1956), Trip

Brown, Lawrence, trombone. b. Lawrence, Kansas, 3 August 1907. He began his career in bands led by Charlie Echols and Paul Howard. The serious-minded son of a minister (he never smoked, gambled or drank), Brown had studied to be a doctor and loved the cello, a sound and approach which he applied to the trombone. When he became a kingpin of Duke Ellington's mighty trombone section in 1932 he was christened 'Deacon' for his mournful demeanour and given a new feature by his leader every year until he left. They included 'Ducky wucky', 'Slippery horn', 'Sheikh of Araby', 'Yearning for love', his own composition 'Golden Cress' and many others. Brown's style was revolutionary in its speed (a 1929 record by Paul Howard, 'Charley's Idea', based on 'Tiger Rag', was already Brown at his fastest), creamy tone, neurotic vibrato and range: he later reluctantly took over Tricky Sam Nanton's role as plunger specialist. 'I don't like using the plunger,' he said, 'but I imitate the tops: Tricky Sam. That buzzing breaks your lip down and you have to wait a little while to get back to normal.' Brown left Ellington in 1951 ('I was tired of the sameness of the big band', he said), and joined Johnny Hodges' breakaway small group until 1955 when he took 'the best job in the business', a staff position replacing Warren Covington at CBS. But in 1960 he was back with Ellington for another ten years until he left again with a Deaconesque pronouncement: 'We have to realize that being popular is nowadays more important than producing anything of value.' After 1970 he was active in business consultancy, took part in the Nixon campaign and later took up the post of recording agent for Hollywood's branch of AFM. Brown's solo recordings, with Hodges, Joe Turner or Jackie Gleason for just three samples, are high trombone art; his smooth yet highly personal creations an incalculable influence on trombonists of character from Tommy Dorsey to Bill Harris. [DF]

Inspired Abandon (1965), Jasmine

See Dance, Stanley, *The World of Duke Ellington* (Scribner's, 1970, repr. Da Capo, 1980)

Brown, Marion, alto sax, composer, ethnomusicologist. b. Atlanta, Georgia, 8 September 1935. Mother sang in church, gospel groups. Studied sax, clarinet and oboe at school and college. Also studied music education, political science, economics and history at Clark College and Howard University. Played in an army band and, 1957, with Johnny Hodges in Atlanta. Went to New York City, becoming involved with the free (abstract) improvisation of the day and recording with Archie Shepp (*Fire Music*) and John Coltrane (*Ascension*). Led his own group in the mid-1960s. Then spent some years in Europe, playing and recording. While there, became deeply interested in African music. 1970, returned to USA where he has taught and studied oral tradition, linguistics and compositional disciplines in African music. Also explored the possibilities of African instruments, and invented his own instruments. [IC]

Marion Brown quartet, *Why Not* (1966), ESP; *Afternoon of a Georgia Faun* (1970), ECM; *Three for Shepp* (1966), Impulse; *Geechee Recollections* (1973), Impulse; *Duets* (1976), Arista Freedom

Brown, Marshall Richard, leader, composer, arranger, educator, valve-trombone. b. Framingham, Massachusetts, 21 December 1920; d. New York City, 13 December 1983. In the earlier 1950s he was a musical educationalist. As bandmaster for high school bands, one of which, Farmingdale, played the Newport Jazz Festival in 1957, he was an innovator in the youth jazz movement. 1959, led the Newport Jazz Festival Youth Band. 1960s, worked in eclectic adult company, including Ruby Braff, Eddie Condon, Roy Eldridge and, in particular, with a Gerry Mulligan-style pianoless quartet showcasing a new-style Pee Wee Russell and featuring Brown's own compositions. 1970s, worked just as easily with Lee Konitz's quintet for whom again he wrote the book. His compositional talents produced several quite successful pop songs (in America); in a jazz context Brown was a shining-toned, technically able soloist who, like Bob Wilber, Dick Cary and Rusty Dedrick, was often to be found at the inspirational centre of intelligent jazz projects. [DF]

With Pee Wee Russell, *New Groove* (1962), Columbia

Brown, Pete (James Ostend), alto and tenor sax, trumpet, violin. b. Baltimore, Maryland, 9 November 1906; d. New York City, 20 September 1963. Some swing musicians survived the onslaught of bebop more comfortably than others. Because Charlie Parker, its central figure, was an alto-saxophonist, he presented a challenge to his predecessors which it was necessary either to ignore (as Johnny Hodges calmly did) or to come to terms with. Of the swingmen who plumped for the second option Pete Brown is perhaps the most uncomfortable example.

He played piano first, and came to New York in 1927 with Bernie Robinson's band, by which time he was doubling trumpet and saxophone: for the next ten years he worked for lesser-known leaders such as Charlie Skeets and Fred Moore and struck up a strong friendship with trumpeter Frankie Newton which found its way on to record from the mid-1930s onward. Together they joined John Kirby's first band, but it was a brief stay and a year later (1938) Brown was once again leading his own groups up and down 52nd Street and by 1940 co-leading with Newton at Kelly's Stables. Over the next ten years he stayed busy enough: he commuted between Boston, Chicago and New York with and without Newton, briefly fronted Louis Jordan's band in 1943, and into the 1950s continued clubwork. Up to about this time his style was a grit-toned, happy statement of all the best qualities of swing; and he single-handedly invented the 'jump style' of alto. But then his style seemed to take on a change for the worse: his sound coarsened and elements of Parker's innovations appeared, then disappeared, from his solo work, uncomfortably like an unwelcome spectre at a feast. On a 1954 recording date for Bethlehem, Brown's selection of repertoire, as much as his style, hovers uncertainly between contemporary vehicles ('There will never be another you') and more welcomingly familiar old standbys ('The world is waiting for the sunrise') and his solo contributions are dwarfed by trumpeter Joe Wilder. Brown was to make only one more record, for Verve in 1959, before he died. In later years he was ill, too, from diabetes and weight problems, and he spent a lot of time teaching as well as playing club residencies. But on Joe Turner's *Boss of the Blues* album from the very period when, according to copybook critical theory, Brown was no longer a force to be reckoned with, surrounded by such compatible friends as Walter Page, Lawrence Brown and Pete Johnson, he sounds just as good as he ever did: more confirmation of Jo Jones's unarguable truism that like-minded musicians together make a mockery of fashion. [DF]

Joe Turner, *Boss of the Blues* (1956), Atlantic Jazzlore

Brown, Ray(mond Matthews), bass, cello. b. Pittsburgh, Pennsylvania, 13 October 1926. After gigging with local bands, was just 19 when he began working with Dizzy Gillespie (1945–7). 1947–51, formed own trio to tour with Ella Fitzgerald, to whom he was married 1948–52. 1951–66, worked with Oscar Peterson trio, also recording prolifically with others. 1966, settled in Los Angeles and, as well as continuing to record and perform in public, became involved in personal management of such as Quincy Jones, Milt Jackson and the then re-formed Modern Jazz Quartet. Founder member of the L.A.4 (1974), also led own trio for special engagements, often with Monty Alexander, later with pianist Gene Harris. Also occasionally producer of albums by Jackson and others.

One of the immediate successors of Jimmy Blanton, Brown stepped on to the New York small-group scene as Oscar Pettiford left it in order to join Ellington. Ray's conception did not add significantly to the Blanton style except for a more bluesy inflection in his solos, although this became rather overblown in some of his later recordings. But what he did triumphantly was to take the full-toned rhythm playing and build it to a peak of perfection that few have equalled. [BP]

All Star Big Band (1962), Verve; Duke Ellington/Brown, *This One's for Blanton* (1972), Pablo

Brown, Sandy, clarinet, bass clarinet, vocals, composer, leader. b. Izatnagar, India, 25 February 1929; d. London, 15 March 1975. He grew up in Edinburgh and came south to London in 1954 with pianist Stan Greig and trumpeter Al Fairweather to form the Fairweather–Brown All Stars. A musician of questing harmonic sense and total authority, and a world-class blues player, he was quick to move musically from an early revivalist paraphrase of Louis Armstrong's Hot Five to a more sophisticated 'mainstream' area: his compositions of the late 1950s (and albums such as *McJazz* and *Dr McJazz*) were and still are highly original, essential jazz listening. By the 1960s Brown's band, featuring front-rank British players such as Tony Milliner (tmb), Brian Lemon (piano), Tony Coe (tnr) and Fairweather, had reached a peak: one more album, *The Incredible McJazz*, represents this creative zenith. By then Brown was busily pursuing his second career as an acoustic architect (his firm, Sandy Brown Associates, designed hundreds of recording studios for Britain's BBC and world-wide) and playing less often. But his regular return to play clubs and jazz festivals and to record, including such late masterpieces as 'Hair at its hairiest!', with George Chisholm and Kenny Wheeler, and his last, a seminal quartet recording with Brian Lemon's trio, showed that his genius never dimmed. His health, however, did. By the mid-1970s Brown had become seriously ill; in March 1975 he began winding up his affairs and he died in bed one Saturday afternoon watching Scotland lose to England in the Calcutta Cup. His collection of writings (below) helps to illuminate the mind of this brilliant and complex jazzman. [DF]

With the Brian Lemon Trio (1971), Hep

See Brown, Sandy, ed. David Binns, *The McJazz Manuscripts* (Faber, 1979)

Brown, Tom, trombone, bass. b. New Orleans, 3 June 1888; d. 25 March 1958. He was very active in New Orleans in the first years of the century, playing for parades, brass bands and later in Chicago (among others) at Lamb's Café, a stronghold for bands. He is remembered particularly for being the first New Orleans bandleader to present his band in Chicago: 'A fine group,' Ed Garland remembers, 'and Brown played good trombone; he tried to copy Ory.' Brown's Chicago band featured Larry Shields who later swapped jobs with Alcide Yellow Nunez to join the Original Dixieland Jazz Band. When an offer came to Brown to visit Reisenweber's cabaret in New York his band had broken up, and he recommended the ODJB who went on to fame and fortune; Brown continued an active career in New Orleans, with Ray Miller, Harry A. Yerkes, and later regularly with Johnny Wiggs. His newer records for GHB, Southland and Oriole are worth hearing. [DF]

Brown, Vernon, trombone. b. Venice, Illinois, 6 January 1907; d. Los Angeles, 18 May 1979. The most stylish trombonist of Benny Goodman's late 1930s band had already been playing in good company for ten years before he joined Goodman: with Frank Trumbauer and Bix Beiderbecke at the Arcadia Ballroom, St Louis, in 1926, then with Jean Goldkette in 1928. He never made the logical career move of his friends – into Paul Whiteman's orchestra – but instead freelanced for ten years before signing with Goodman in 1937 for a two-year stay in which his warm-toned, sophisticated style (midway between Cutty Cutshall and Jack Teagarden) was well featured on record. After Goodman he worked with Artie Shaw (1940), Muggsy Spanier (1941–2) and soon after began a career in radio and TV staffwork with regular returns for Goodman reunions. He was still active in the early 1970s. [DF]

Benny Goodman, *Carnegie Hall Jazz Concert, 1938*, CBS (double)

Brubeck, Dave (David Warren), piano, composer. b. Concord, California, 6 December 1920. A group leader of unparalleled popularity in the 1950s and 1960s, Brubeck did much to promote the success (and respectability) of jazz with the white middle-class audience. Beginning as a composition student with Darius Milhaud, he led experimental and strongly European-influenced jazz groups in San Francisco in the late 1940s, before his quartet featuring Paul Desmond established him as an international attraction. After Desmond left in 1967, first Gerry Mulligan became a member of the group and later Dave's own sons, Darius (keyboards, b. 14 June 1947), Chris (trombone, bass, b. 19 March 1952) and Danny (drums, b. 4 May 1955). In the 1980s reedman Jerry Bergonzi and former San Francisco colleague Bill Smith have toured with Brubeck.

Although a prolific writer, and forever associated with his hit record of Desmond's 'Take Five', Brubeck's only compositions to have become standards were the two covered by Miles Davis, 'In Your Own Sweet Way' and 'The Duke'. Similarly the popularization of 'odd' time-signatures (5, 7 or 9 beats per bar) and of two instruments improvising simultaneously (in his case, saxophone and piano) were not achieved by Brubeck alone. As for his piano work, Dave in his early days often lacked the technique to carry out his ideas, except when indulging in heavy chording; in later years, a greater sense of relaxation imparted more ease, and swing, to his execution. [BP]

Brubeck/Demond (1952–3), Fantasy; *Time Out* (1959), CBS

Bruce, Jack (John Symon Asher), bass, vocals, composer, keyboards, synthesizer, harmonica. b. Glasgow, 14 May 1943. Royal Scottish Academy of Music at 17, studying cello and composition. 1962, with Alexis Korner's Blues Incorporated; 1963–5, with the Graham Bond Organization. Worked briefly with John Mayall and Manfred Mann, before forming Cream with Ginger Baker and Eric Clapton. After Cream broke up he was an original member of Tony Williams's Lifetime, which included John McLaughlin and Larry Young. When that first Lifetime disbanded, Bruce pursued a solo career using various combinations of friends including John Marshall, Chris Spedding, Larry Coryell and Jon Hiseman. He also performed on Carla Bley's album *Escalator Over the Hill*. From mid-1970s, started a series of shortlived bands. Bruce is an immensely talented musician who only occasionally realizes his full potential. He is an excellent singer, a masterful songwriter, a very good composer/arranger for small groups and big bands, and with Cream he brought bass guitar playing to a new level of brilliance. [IC]

With Cream, Lifetime, Bley; *Songs for a Tailor* (1970); *Things we Like* (1971); *Harmony Row* (1971), all Polydor; with Kip Hanrahan, *Desire Develops an Edge* (1983), American Clave

Brüninghaus, Rainer, piano, synthesizers. b. Bad Pyrmont, West Germany, 21 November 1949. He studied classical piano at Cologne Conservatory. 1973–6, with Volker Kriegel's Spectrum; 1975–80, Eberhard Weber's Colours; 1978–81, Manfred Schoof's quintet. Since 1981, Brüninghaus has been leading his own trio which includes Markus Stockhausen (tpt) and Fredy Studer (dms). 1983, awarded the jazz prize of the South West German Radio Station. 1984, his album *Continuum* received the German Record Critics' prize. He also composes and arranges for radio big bands and for symphony orchestras, and does some teaching at a music college in Cologne. He has worked with many other leading jazz musicians including Archie Shepp, George Adams, Kenny Wheeler, Charlie Mariano, Carla Bley, Toots Thielemans, Albert Mangelsdorff, Bobby McFerrin. [IC]

With Mariano, Schoof, Kriegel, five with Weber, to whose music Brüninghaus has made a vital contribution; with Eberhard Weber, *Yellow Fields* (1977); *Silent Feet* (1979); *Little Movements* (1980); under his own name, *Freigeweht* (1980); *Continuum* (1983), all ECM

Brunis, Georg (George Clarence Brunies), trombone, vocals. b. New Orleans, 6 February 1902; d. Chicago, 19 November 1974. Best known of the five Brunies brothers (all from New Orleans, all musicians) he played at eight with Papa Jack Laine's 'Junior band'. 11 years on, with Paul Mares, he was part of the Friars Society Orchestra with Mel Stitzel and drummer Ben Pollack that turned into the New Orleans Rhythm Kings. Then came the first long stint with clarinettist Ted Lewis, 1924–34, whose much-maligned act was none the less a headliner, and for Brunis one lesson in presentation. In 1934 he was with another master showman, Louis Prima at the Famous Door, and from 1936 began a long residency at Nick's. By now his playing, 'on the nose, never mixed up with a lot of phony tricks', as Amy Lee said, was complemented by cut-up routines: playing trombone with his foot, bullfrog-voiced songs, unscheduled parades into the Ladies room and invitations to (lighter) customers to stand on his stomach. But he always played 'like it was his last night on earth', said Matty Walsh, and he forged two classic partnerships at the period: with Muggsy Spanier's Ragtimers for five and a half months (and 16 great records) and with Wild Bill Davison in 1944 for definitive recordings on Commodore. By 1943, Brunis was with Lewis again, then at Eddie Condon's, 1947–9, and for nine years after that he played at Club Eleven Eleven (1951–9) in Chicago. For the next 15 years (despite illness in the late 1960s), he stayed busy, continuing to define the role of a trombone in Dixieland ensemble ('George's taste in jazz ranges from New Orleans to New Orleans' said Bud Freeman) and perfectly embodying the sophisticated end of tailgate trombone. [DF]

Muggsy Spanier, *The Great Sixteen* (1939), RCA

Brunskill, Bill (William), trumpet, leader. b. East London, 2 February 1920. He personifies the proud amateur traditions of British revivalism. A local government officer by day (until 1985 when he retired), he has played New Orleans jazz to generations of London jazz fans since the 1940s, working most of the major venues. In 1984 he was the central figure in a TV documentary, written by George Melly and researched by John Chilton, *Whatever happened to Bill Brunskill?*, tracing the story of British revivalist jazz. His band in 1985 contained Mike Pointon (tmb), Les Allen (clt), Bill Stagg (banjo) and Hugh Crozier (piano). [DF]

Bryant, Ray (Raphael), piano. b. Philadelphia, 24 December 1931. Coming from a musical family, with a sister who sang gospel music, he became known to colleagues as house pianist at Philadelphia's Blue Note club, where he worked with elder brother Tom (bass, b. 21 May 1930; d. 3 January 1982). This led to recordings with Miles Davis, Sonny Rollins, Carmen McRae, Coleman Hawkins, Jo Jones etc., and to a prolific career as trio leader and soloist. One of the few pianists of his generation to show an affinity for unaccompanied playing, Bryant has a wide-ranging left hand and a straightforward harmonic vocabulary which suggests predecessors such as Teddy Wilson. More rhythmically outgoing than the latter, he was able to incorporate aspects of gospel keyboard work into a mainstream jazz style, rather than the other way around and without sounding merely derivative. His 1959 hit record 'Little Susie' is just one example among many of Bryant's genuinely happy-sounding approach. [BP]

Hot Turkey (1975), Black & Blue

Bryant, Willie (William Steven), vocals, leader, compere. b. New Orleans, 30 August 1908; d. Los Angeles, 9 February 1964. He began his career as a dancer and first fronted his own big band at the famous Howard Theater, Washington. From 1933 he was in New York, first as a dancer and revue artist, and from 1934 as leader of a big band which worked clubs including the Ubangi and more notably the Savoy Ballroom. The band had arrangements by Teddy Wilson (including a Benny Carter-ish 'Liza' featuring the saxophone section) and starred musicians such as Wilson, Cozy Cole, Benny Carter, Ben Webster, Edgar Battle and Taft Jordan; Bryant himself was no musician, but his likeable personality and good looks won him jobs after the band broke up in late 1938 as MC at the Apollo, disc jockey and actor. His band, including Panama Francis on drums, re-formed 1946–8, after which Bryant resumed his freelance career. [DF]

Bryce, Owen, trumpet, bandleader. b. Woolwich, London, 8 August 1920. He partnered Reg Rigden and briefly Humphrey Lyttelton in the first George Webb Dixielanders, re-formed in 1949 as the Original Dixielanders, and in 1956 formed his own band from the High Society Jazz Band. In later decades he also published his own instructional tutors, wrote widely for the jazz press and – from his floating barge-home and elsewhere – set up residential jazz courses; in 1986 he played regularly again, including for George Webb reunions. [DF]

Any with George Webb

Bryden, Beryl, washboard, vocals. b. Norwich, Norfolk, 11 May 1926. Britain's 'Queen of the Blues' is one of the most colourful figures in European jazz. Her big, friendly voice, wide-ranging repertoire (which runs from Bessie Smith to pleasing 1930s standard tunes such as 'Miss Brown to you') and professional presentation have taken her a long way from the days in post-war London when she first sang with George Webb's Dixielanders, Humphrey Lyttelton and most of the rest. Her career has been based as much in Europe as Britain: in Paris, 1953–4, she sang for Lionel Hampton and around the clubs and later, in Holland and Germany, worked with such famous bands as Fatty George's and the Tremble Kids. During the 1960s she played the Antibes festival, toured the Far East and Africa in 1965 and paid her first visit to New York in 1970. Then came a busy decade when Bryden – a tirelessly cheerful career woman – weathered the changes in jazz and popular music tastes as successfully as ever: she continued her European travels, recorded prolifically for Ted Easton's Riff label in Holland (where she was crowned 'Queen of Jazz' in 1978) and others, appeared regularly at South Bank concerts in London, often with her close friends Alex Welsh and his band, and won the BBC Jazz Society's Musician of the Year award. In the 1980s, appearing at festivals, jazz clubs and regularly with Pete Allen's band in a new production, *Jazzin' Around*, on Britain's theatre circuit, Beryl Bryden happily showed no sign of slowing up. [DF]

Way Down Yonder in New Orleans (1975), (with the Piccadilly Six) Elite Special.

Buckner, Milt(on), piano, organ, arranger. b. St Louis, Missouri, 10 July 1915; d. 27 July 1977. Raised in Detroit from age nine, he was the younger brother of altoist Ted Buckner, who played with the Jimmie Lunceford band (not to be confused with the unrelated Teddy Buckner, below). Played and arranged for many Detroit-based bands from 1930, including McKinney's Cotton Pickers. Came to fame with Lionel Hampton band (1941–8, 1950–2). In between, led own 17-piece band, later reducing to tentet (1949–50). From 1952, led organ trio (his 1955 edition included Sam Woodyard, who promptly joined Ellington, and saxist Danny Turner, who was later in the Basie band). Continued with this format for the rest of his life, teaming up with Illinois Jacquet from 1971. Extremely popular in Europe from late 1960s, Buckner was one of the pioneers of the electric organ in jazz and its use in replacing a big-band brass section, and his early arranging experience clearly influenced this conception. [BP]

Green Onions (1975), Black & Blue

Buckner, Teddy (John Edward), trumpet, fluegelhorn, vocals. b. Sherman, Texas, 16 July 1909. Like most of his generation, Buckner grew up in the shadow of Louis Armstrong, but unlike some of his contemporaries (Henry 'Red' Allen or Rex Stewart, for example) never felt the need to develop an alternative route through jazz to his idol's. On the contrary, Buckner, a trumpeter of enormous strength, technique and natural fire, declared his allegiance to Armstrong very early on (by 1936 he was working as Louis' stand-in on the film *Pennies from Heaven*) and all the way through his career was regularly to be heard singing and playing the praises of his inspiration: in Lionel Hampton's bebop band of 1948 (where he determinedly played an Armstrong-style feature), with Kid Ory's band, 1949–54 (where his stunning trumpet is genuinely difficult to distinguish from Armstrong's), in Armstrong-style tributes at Gene Norman's Dixieland festivals, and, as late as 1975, in a tribute film for ABC, *Louis Armstrong – Chicago Style!*.

After work with territory-bandleader Speed

Webb he had played around the West Coast, went to Shanghai with Buck Clayton's band in 1934, and a year later took over Lionel Hampton's at Paradise Club, Los Angeles. In the 1940s he was regularly to be found with r & b shows as well as with big bands led by Benny Carter, Gerald Wilson and others. He led his own bands all through the 1950s and 1960s (after 1965 he was regularly at Disneyland) and in the 1970s was still busy in California. From the 1930s to the 1970s he appeared in numerous films. Clearly Buckner's espousal of traditional jazz during the revival was never in the interests of limited technique: a huge-toned, sometimes flashy performer with a fondness (unlike Armstrong) for muted effects, he was capable of playing more or less anything. [DF]

A Salute to Louis Armstrong (1958), Vogue

Bunn, Teddy (Theodore Leroy), guitar, vocals. b. Freeport, Long Island, 1909; d. Lancaster, California, 20 July 1978. The most important black guitarist of the 1930s before Charlie Christian, his work is still often neglected, perhaps because Eddie Lang had created such a gigantic impression just before him and the new revolutions of Christian were soon to make the older man appear just a little out of fashion. But Bunn's music is fondly remembered by musicians and critics everywhere. 'He was a true guitar master', says Max Jones. 'The urge he gave to a band, his rhythmic support, whether heard in a washboard band, swing combo, blues or big-band context, was nearly as impressive as his beautiful soloing.' Bunn's solo talents in the 1930s were featured with the Spirits of Rhythm (his cutting-toned single-string creations were their strongest solo voice) and he made definitive contributions to record sessions by the Mezzrow–Ladnier quintet of the same period. By August 1940, when he recorded with Lionel Hampton, Bunn had changed permanently to electric guitar. For the next ten years he played in various re-formations of the Spirits and with his own small groups, and by the mid-1950s was following the new road for guitar into rhythm-and-blues and rock and roll, working with Jack McVea, Edgar Hayes and others, and with touring rock and roll shows. By the late 1960s Bunn worked less often: he suffered a mild stroke in 1970, and it was followed by three heart attacks which rendered him partially blind and paralysed. He died after ten years' illness, almost forgotten, except, says Max Jones, a faithful fan, 'among musicians and collectors who remember his top-flight solos and accompaniments'. [DF]

Spirits of Rhythm, 1932–4, JSP

Burbank, Albert, clarinet. b. New Orleans, 25 March 1902; d. 15 August 1976. He was a pupil of Lorenzo Tio in 1916, then played in the city and resorts around New Orleans all through the 1920s. During the depression he worked with drummer Kid Milton's band and after the war (during which he served in the US Navy) was regularly with trumpeter Herb Morand. During the 1950s he worked with internationally famous names including Paul Barbarin and Kid Ory (in 1954), but thereafter moved back home to play for local leaders such as Octave Crosby and Bill Matthews and brass bands like the Eureka and Young Tuxedo, as well as a long stint with Papa French's jazz band. Regularly with the Preservation Hall band in the early 1970s (when he toured Australia with them), Burbank played right up until 1975 when he suffered a stroke; but he kept on singing until he died. [DF]

Burnap, Campbell Crichton MacKinnon, trombone, vocals. b. Derby, 10 September 1939. He played around New Zealand and Australia before coming to Britain, via New Orleans, in the 1960s to work for a variety of leaders including Terry Lightfoot, Monty Sunshine and Alan Elsdon, as well as leading his own quintet with saxophonist Geoff Simkins and freelancing with leaders such as Alex Welsh. He played whenever possible with the trombone quintet Five-a-Slide and from 1980 joined Acker Bilk. Blessed with considerable personal charm, good looks and a natural ability to front a band, Burnap became a valuable asset to Bilk, and in 1985 was still busily touring recording and appearing on TV with his leader. One of Britain's most stylish trombonists, he plays in a burry combination of Jack Teagarden and Bill Harris and sings with a lazy-charming delivery akin to Teagarden's own. [DF]

Acker Bilk in Holland (1983), Timeless Traditional (double)

Burrage, Ronnie (James Renaldo), drums, piano, percussion: vibes, marimba, timpani, congas, berimbau, tavil. b. St Louis, Missouri, 19 October 1959. Mother a classical pianist and several uncles musicians. Studied advanced theory at U. City High, Washington University. Scholarship to North Texas State, Howard University, where he spent one semester before moving to New York City. At age nine, he performed with Duke Ellington, and until he died, Ellington wrote encouraging Burrage's interest in music. Sang in St Louis Cathedral boys' choir; worked with funk and r & b groups. 1980–3, worked with St Louis Metropolitan Jazz Quintet, accompanying many visiting soloists including Arthur Blythe, Jackie McLean, Andrew Hill, Jaco Pastorius, McCoy Tyner. 1983, worked for a month with Chico Freeman. 1983–5, with Woody Shaw's quintet. By the early 1980s, Burrage already had a tremendous reputation among US musicians and by 1985 had worked with most contemporary stars from Pat Metheny to Lester Bowie and members of the World Saxophone Quartet. He has already led several groups of his own. 1982, played with the Young Lions at the Kool Jazz Festival, New

York. 1984, opened the Kool Jazz Festival, Philadelphia, with his own group Burrage Ensemble. 1986, toured Europe with his own Third Kind of Blue including John Purcell (reeds) and Anthony Cox (bass), in which Burrage also sang his own compositions. His composition 'Endless Flight' was written for McCoy Tyner, and was recorded on the Young Lions' double album. Burrage's influences range from Jack DeJohnette, Art Blakey, Max Roach, Elvin Jones to Bobby Hutcherson, Herbie Hancock, Egberto Gismonti, Milton Nascimento, Toots Thielemans and Mozart. [IC]

With Chico Freeman, *Destiny Dance* (1981), Contemporary; three tracks on *Kevin Eubanks Guitarist* (1982), Elektra Musician; with *Young Lions at Carnegie Hall* (1982), Elektra Musician; with *Jackie McLean* (1985), Doll House

Burrell, Kenny (Kenneth Earl), guitar (and vocal). b. Detroit, Michigan, 31 July 1931. Part of the 1950s exodus from Detroit, he made his first recording there with visiting Dizzy Gillespie (1951). Worked locally, then (1955) briefly with Oscar Peterson trio during illness of Herb Ellis and moved to New York, freelancing and recording prolifically. 1957, with Benny Goodman; since then has worked under own name with trio/quartet but formed particular associations on record, especially with Jimmy Smith. Own records have occasionally included either big-band backing (by such as Gil Evans or Don Sebesky) or all-star small groups. Toured Europe with own group (1969), Japan (1970, 1975), and both with Newport All Stars (1972). Since 1973, teaching and doing studio work in California. Reunions with Smith at Blue Note re-launch, Kool Festival (1985) and European tour (1985).

Burrell never achieved the wide popular appeal of a Wes Montgomery or a George Benson (despite his vocal work in early 1960s). Utterly reliable in an accompanying role, he gives the same impression of complete infallibility when soloing. Managing to be both boppy and bluesy without being boring, he has furthered the Charlie Christian style better than almost anyone else. [BP]

Kenny Burrell with John Coltrane (1958), Prestige; *Ellington is Forever, vol. 1* (1975), Fantasy

Burton, Gary, vibraphone, composer, educator. b. Anderson, Indiana, 23 January 1943. Began on piano (self-taught) at age six; studied composition and piano at high school; self-taught on vibes. Attended the Berklee School, Boston, at the beginning of the 1960s, where he met composer/arranger Mike Gibbs, beginning a long and fruitful association. 1963, toured the USA and Japan with George Shearing. 1964, Shearing recorded an LP (*Out of the Woods*) of Burton's compositions. 1964–6, with Stan Getz quartet, including an appearance at the White House and in two films, *The Hanged Man* and *Get Yourself a College Girl*. 1967, formed his own quartet with Larry Coryell (gtr), Steve Swallow (bass) and Bob Moses (dms), and the fully mature Burton sound and style were clearly evident for the first time. The quartet's music had all the jazz virtues – harmonic sophistication, swing, good dynamics – but it also fused elements from rock and country music, creating a fresh, attractive, totally contemporary sound, and anticipating the jazz-rock movement of the 1970s.

Gary Burton

Burton himself was generally recognized as being the new voice on vibes. He asserted that he was not influenced by other vibists, and that his main inspiration had been pianist Bill Evans. In fact, his whole approach to the vibes was pianistic, with brilliantly fleet linear runs and rich four-mallet chording that was without precedent in jazz. Later he explained the genesis of this: 'I played a lot at home by myself when I was first learning. I naturally started filling things in and accompanying myself because it sounded too empty as a single line instrument.'

Also in 1967, he asked Carla Bley to arrange her *A Genuine Tong Funeral* for his quartet augmented by Gato Barbieri, Jimmy Knepper, Steve Lacy, Howard Johnson, Michael Mantler and Carla Bley herself. It was recorded in November and this was Carla Bley's first major exposure on an LP; it was also the beginning of a long association with Burton who would go on playing and recording her compositions over the years. Since 1970, Burton has also played solo concerts, and has worked in duo with Keith Jarrett and frequently with Chick Corea.

Between 1971 and 1975 he toured in Japan, Australia, the UK and Western and Eastern Europe. 1974–6, recorded and toured with his quartet featuring bassist Eberhard Weber as soloist and melodist and fifth member of the group. 1974, with long-time friend and associate Steve Swallow, he recorded a superb duo album of which he said: 'I think frankly that *Hotel Hello* is going to turn out to be the masterpiece album of any that I've done . . . It strikes me as the best representation of my playing that I've ever gotten on record.' In fact the early 1970s were something of a rebirth for him; he began recording for Manfred Eicher and ECM, and for the first time the actual sound of his vibes was captured on record.

During the 1960s and early 1970s he was active as an educator, conducting workshops and presenting lecture/concert programmes with his quartet at universities all over the USA. 1971, he became a permanent staff member at Berklee, and in 1985 he was made Dean of Curriculum there. In the late 1970s and the 1980s, he toured in duo with Chick Corea, visiting Europe and Japan, as well as playing many cities in the USA. 1982, he was featured soloist on Corea's 'Lyric Suite' for piano, vibes and string quartet. He has also visited Russia, playing solo concerts at the US embassy for invited Russian musicians and critics. In the mid-1980s his quartet included Steve Swallow, Adam Nussbaum (dms) and the young Japanese pianist Makoto Ozone.

Burton is not only a great player and fine bandleader, but an inspirational figure, a discoverer of new talent and a catalyst through whom people can focus and find themselves. Many leading musicians have emerged from his groups and his projects, including Bob Moses, Larry Coryell, Pat Metheny, Mike Gibbs, Carla Bley, Tiger Okoshi, Danny Gottlieb. He is a major stylist on vibes, and he was one of the initiators of the trend of playing without a rhythm section. [IC]

Country Roads and Other Places (1967), RCA; *A Genuine Tong Funeral* (1967), RCA; *The New Quartet* (1973); quartet plus Weber, *Ring* (1974); Burton/Swallow, *Hotel Hello* (1974); Burton/Ralph Towner, *Matchbook* (1975); quartet, *Times Square* (1977); Chick Corea/Burton, *In Concert, Zurich, October 28 1979*; quartet, *Picture This* (1982), all ECM; with Mike Gibbs orchestra, *In the Public Interest* (1973), Polydor

Bushkin, Joe (Joseph), piano, composer, trumpet. b. New York City, 7 November 1916. He was first spotted by Artie Shaw around 1935 as 'a very young, bright-eyed, intense kid who hung out with the Chicago crowd'. Bushkin, whose childhood loves included softball and trumpet as well as piano, was on 52nd Street with Bunny Berigan, Eddie Condon, Muggsy Spanier and Joe Marsala. In 1940 Tommy Dorsey, whose raids on Marsala's bands were frequent and a standing joke, hired him. In Dorsey's band Bushkin recorded over 100 sides, wrote 'Oh look at me now' (a gem) for Frank Sinatra and, according to Sinatra, 'introduced the band to pernod! Suddenly all the Coca Cola turned green!' During the war he directed a successful GI show, *Winged Victory*, which toured the Pacific and Japan, and wrote 'Hot time in the town of Berlin' with John de Vries (a small hit for Crosby and Sinatra). In 1946 he joined Benny Goodman, taught a young Burt Bacharach to play jazz in spare moments, and acted in a jazzman's Broadway play, *Rat Race*, with Georgie Auld and others. From 1950 he was regularly at the Embers (with Jo Jones, Charles Mingus *et al.*), a small club into which, Jonah Jones recalls, 'nobody else but Joe would take a trumpet'. The 'muted jazz' which resulted set a lucrative trend for Jones soon after, and a pattern for trumpet-led quartets for ten years after that. Bushkin's solo albums of the period, often with strings (such as *Midnite Rhapsody* and *Listen to the Quiet*), were commercial hits and ensured his continuing solo career through the 1960s and 1970s at the Embers, in New York and Las Vegas. By 1970, partly retired, he was in Hawaii breeding horses, but returned triumphantly to back Bing Crosby at London's Palladium, in New York and Norway and for radio and TV spectaculars. A small classic album (below) on which Bushkin's piano, songs, trumpet and reminiscing are irrestible recalls this period. In the 1980s Bushkin was as busy as ever and in 1985 his new quartet featured Warren Vaché Jnr. [DF]

Celebrates 100 Years of Recorded Sound (1977), United Artists

Butterfield, Billy (Charles William), trumpet, fluegelhorn, leader. b. Middleton, Ohio, 14 January 1917. He took up music at 13 and played in campus bands while he studied medicine. During a stint with Austin Wylie, an eccentric bandleader who also featured Claude Thornhill and Artie Shaw early in their careers, he was spotted by Bob Crosby's band and joined them in autumn 1937 in Cleveland. Crosby featured Butterfield's wide-range, huge-toned trumpet (notably on a Bob Haggart tune 'I'm Free', later retitled 'What's New?') until 1940 when Artie Shaw made an offer. Butterfield, who had already recorded the soundtrack for a Shaw film, *Second Chorus*, with Bobby Hackett, moved over, stayed for six months and recorded more classics including 'Stardust'. By 1941 he was with Benny Goodman until petrol rationing and the draft meant less work and Joe Glaser, Louis Armstrong's powerful manager, helped him back into studio work, but Butterfield had his eye on a band of his own and after the war formed one with clarinettist Bill Stegmeyer. 'But the whole thing came to a shuddering stop', he told his old friend Alan Littlejohn later. 'It was very much a one-man concern and I had to do everything: set the band up, take it down, drive the bus – even take vocals!' With relief, but in debt, he moved back to studio work (often with Hackett at ABC, a much-loved team), doubling up with small bands at Nick's and Condon's, and with a 6-piece band featuring saxophonist Nick Caiazza for dates in colleges around Norfolk. The 1950s were perhaps Butterfield's greatest recorded decade: with Condon, Jackie Gleason and Ray Conniff he produced work of matchless taste, fire and invention which echoed Louis Armstrong but had ideas of its own. In 1968 he was invited to join the World's Greatest Jazz Band, 'at its best one of the finest groups I ever worked with', he said, and here his playing, especially early on, took on new fire: flaring, daring, high-register bursts which complemented Yank Lawson's hectoring co-lead to perfection. In the 1970s came regular partnerships with Flip Phillips (a favourite), solo tours and prolific recording in Europe, and a weathered maturity which, once in a while, fluffed up the edges of his tone attractively. Butterfield's gifts are still a natural extension of Armstrong's: strength (he is a fine lead trumpeter, too), warm, buttered tone, and a magician's ability to pull melodic creations of arresting originality like a conjuror from battered jazz hats. With Bobby Hackett, he is the most artistic swing trumpeter of post-war America. [DF]

In a Mellow Tone (1975), DSC

See Chilton, John, *Stomp Off, Let's Go* (Jazz Book Services, 1983)

Byard, Jaki (John), piano, saxes, arranger, etc. b. Worcester, Massachusetts, 15 June 1922. An enormously versatile musician who was working professionally from age 15, before army service in World War II. Toured on piano with Earl Bostic in the late 1940s and played tenor saxophone throughout the 1950s in Boston's Herb Pomeroy band (for which he wrote 'Aluminium Baby', a second cousin to 'Satin Doll'). After replacing Joe Zawinul with the Maynard Ferguson band, 1959, Byard began recording albums under his own name and, although finding a sympathetic forum for pianistic virtuosity during two stints with Charles Mingus (1962–5 and 1970), is heard to best advantage as a soloist. Has also led his own big band, the Apollo Stompers, and taught at New England Conservatory. Byard's familiarity with the whole gamut of jazz pianists from contemporary players to Tatum and Waller (see his 'A.T.F.W.Y.O.U.' on various Mingus concert albums) is matched by his knowledge of European music; any or all of this is called upon in Byard's kaleidoscopic performances. [BP]

To Them – To Us (1981), Soul Note

Film: *Anything for Jazz* (dir. Dan Algrant, 1980)

Byas, Don (Carlos Wesley), tenor sax, b. Muskogee, Oklahoma, 21 October 1912; d. Amsterdam, 24 August 1972. Early experience with Bennie Moten, Walter Page and his own band before switching from alto to tenor, 1933. Settled in California and worked in succession with Lionel Hampton (1935), Eddie Barefield and Buck Clayton (1936). 1937, moved to New York, playing with numerous name bands such as Don Redman, Lucky Millinder, Andy Kirk and Benny Carter. Made considerable impact by replacing Lester Young in Count Basie band (1941–3), and during these three years became heavily involved in New York's 'underground' scene at Minton's and elsewhere. 1944, played in Dizzy Gillespie's first small group on 52nd Street; 1945, replaced Gillespie in quintet with Charlie Parker and led own quartet/quintet, recording prolifically under own name and others'. Widely regarded as 'the' tenor player of the period, superior to current work of either Coleman Hawkins or Lester Young. 1946, while visiting Europe with Redman small group decided to settle in Paris (later Amsterdam) and became the first American jazz superstar there since Hawkins. Frequent solo appearances, also played Paris Jazz Fair, 1949, with Hot Lips Page, toured Europe with Ellington band (1950) and with Jazz at the Philharmonic (1960). Returned only once to US (1970), featured at Newport Festival and with Art Blakey (including Japanese tour in 1971), before his death from lung cancer.

Although derived ultimately from Hawkins, Byas's style was more involved harmonically, a fact attributable to the direct influence of Art Tatum; Johnny Griffin has commented: 'I used to say Don was the Tatum of the saxophone . . . He was using his harmonic solutions.' In this respect he could justifiably claim to have had a decisive effect on Parker; and while his on-the-beat accentuation was shunned by Parker, it came back with a vengeance in the work of the Coltrane school. His huge tone could sometimes sound unwieldy at fast tempos, but it was particularly sumptuous on the ballads which were the source of his post-war popularity, first in the US and then in Europe. [BP]

Midnight at Minton's (1941), Onyx; *Savoy Jam Party* (1944–6), Savoy; Don Byas/Bud Powell, *A Tribute to Cannonball* (1961), CBS

Byrd, Charlie (Charles L.), guitar. b. Suffolk, Virginia, 16 September 1925. Played guitar from age 10, toured with name groups including Joe Marsala (1947–9). Then studied European guitar music (including with Andrés Segovia) and settled in Washington, DC, working there in clubs and recording for locally-based label. With Woody Herman sextet (1958–9), including UK tour with Anglo-American Herd and Monterey Festival (both 1959). Returned to Washington, and did South American tour for State Department; contact with Brazilian popular music enabled him to appear on first Stan Getz album of bossa nova (1962), whose enormous success caused lawsuit over royalties. Continued leading own trio and recording for major labels, often with augmented backing. Compared with either his jazz contemporaries or expert bossa-nova guitarists such as João

Gilberto or Luiz Bonfa, Byrd sounds unbearably stiff but his chief attraction lies in the use of the unamplified finger-style sound in a semi-jazz context. [BP]

Bossa Nova Pelos Passoros (1962), Riverside/OJC

Byrd, Donald, trumpet, fluegelhorn, educator, composer. b. Detroit, Michigan, 9 December 1932. Educated at Wayne University and Manhattan School of Music, came to national and international prominence with Art Blakey's Jazz Messengers in the mid-1950s. Also worked with many leading modernists including Max Roach, John Coltrane, Red Garland, Pepper Adams, Sonny Rollins and Thelonious Monk. By 1958 he was also leading his own quintet, played festivals in Belgium and France, toured Sweden and took part in one German and two French films. Continued to lead his own groups and tour internationally during the 1960s; also did a great deal of teaching at jazz clinics and at the Music and Art High School, NYC. 1963, studied with Nadia Boulanger in Paris and in the US acquired two educational degrees. 1971, received his PhD in college teaching and administration from Columbia University School of Education, then took up the post of chairman of the Black Music Department at Howard University, Washington, DC.

1973, recorded a jazz-rock-soul album entitled *Black Byrd* for Blue Note, which became the best-selling LP in the company's entire history, rocketing him to super-stardom. He made a few more albums in the same vein and toured in the US and internationally, but success did not unsettle him and he continued steadily with his educational and self-educational work, studying law, and lecturing at various campuses on education, black music, and law as it applies to music and musicians, and conducting workshops. He left Howard in the autumn of 1975, but has continued to teach at university level.

Byrd's main influences are Dizzy Gillespie, Miles Davis and Clifford Brown, and his work in the 1950s and 1960s revealed immense assurance and lyricism. [IC]

With many people, including Art Blakey, Horace Silver, Coltrane, Monk, Pepper Adams, Michel Legrand; with Rollins, *Sonny Rollins* (1957); as leader, *Chant* (1961); *A New Perspective* (1963); *Black Byrd* (1973), all Blue Note

C

Cables, George Andrew, piano. b. New York City, 14 November 1944. After studying at High School of Performing Arts and Mannes College, worked with both Art Blakey and Max Roach (mid-1960s, recording with both early 1970s). Played regularly with Sonny Rollins (1969), Joe Henderson (1969–71), Freddie Hubbard (1971–6, 1980). Backed Dexter Gordon for two years after his return to US (1977–9), and Art Pepper in New York (1977) and for last three years of his career (1979–82, recording two duo albums with Pepper). As well as being a prolific composer for others, Cables occasionally appears under his own name and is an invaluable sideman. His backing is always intensely rhythmic and supportive, and his solo work is sure-footed and stimulating. [BP]

Art Pepper/George Cables, *Goin' Home* (1982), Galaxy

Caceres, Ernie (Ernesto), clarinet, baritone and alto sax. b. Rockport, Texas, 22 November 1911; d. Texas, 10 January 1971. He worked with his family (one brother, Emilio, played violin, the other, Pinero, played trumpet and piano) in the early 1930s around Detroit and later New York. There, in 1938 he joined Bobby Hackett's band for the start of a musical relationship which lasted, on and off, for 30 years. A booming-toned agile player, and a skilled, versatile musician who read music fluently, Caceres was with Harry Carney the first baritone stylist to achieve a solo reputation; but his sound, less lush and more edgy than Carney's, was heard in a wider variety of contexts than his black contemporary's: with, among others, Jack Teagarden (1939), Bob Zurke, Glenn Miller (1940–2) and later with Benny Goodman, Tommy Dorsey and Woody Herman. By 1948, Caceres was winner of a *Metronome* poll and the following year won again against strong opposition from the burgeoning bebop movement. Although he was capable of standing his ground in such company, as he shows on a 1949 Metronome All Stars recording date, 'Overtime' and 'Victory Ball', his style gravitated more naturally to swing and Dixieland and from 1946, when he moved into Nick's Club in New York, he was more and more associated with Eddie Condon's circle of 'timeless' jazzmen. With them he recorded regularly, he led his own quartet at the Hickory Log in 1949 and from 1950 for six years was a staffman and featured artist on Garry Moore's TV show. In 1956–7 he played for Bobby Hackett's Henry Hudson band (his brother Pinero also appeared with them) and kept working all through the 1960s with Billy Butterfield and later with Jim Cullum's Happy Jazz Band. [DF]

Hackett/Condon, *Jam Session* (1948), Aircheck

Caiazza, Nick, tenor sax, clarinet. b. New Castle, Pennsylvania, 20 March 1914. He was featured with Joe Haymes's well-drilled orchestra in his early twenties, but is best remembered for his flowing contributions to Muggsy Spanier's Ragtimers (November–December 1939) which – along with Bernie Billings's and Ray McKinstry's (two other neglected players) – helped to characterize Spanier's classic 'Great Sixteen' recordings. Caiazza, a disciplined big-band player and one of the best white saxophonists, remained highly successful through the 1940s, recording for V-Discs with Armstrong, Teagarden and others, working as a staffman for NBC and CBS and from 1950 to 1959 for Paul Whiteman at ABC, as well as recording and appearing in small groups led by Billy Butterfield, Benny Goodman and others. By the late 1960s he was teaching at Berklee School of Music [DF]

Muggsy Spanier, *The Great Sixteen* (1939), RCA

Caldwell, Happy (Albert), tenor sax, clarinet. b. Chicago, 25 July 1903; d. 29 December 1978. 'A great and unheralded influence on tenor saxophone' (said Rex Stewart) and certainly one of the most gifted players in the formative years of his instrument. 'He was playing like mad', affirms Coleman Hawkins, and all through the 1920s and 1930s Caldwell stayed busy, touring with Bernie Young's band, then with Mamie Smith and later with a succession of fine American big bands including Fletcher Henderson's, Vernon Andrade's, Charlie Johnson's and Tiny Bradshaw's: he also appeared on such classic records as Louis Armstrong's 'Knockin' a jug', sides with Jack Bland's Rhythmakers (from 1932, featuring Henry 'Red' Allen) and even Jelly Roll Morton's 1939 remake of 'Winin' Boy Blues'. In the 1920s Caldwell (a former clarinet pupil of Buster Bailey) was all over New York playing clubs, dance schools and recording, and cornettist Stewart draws a word picture of the two of them commuting from band to band and surviving: 'It was Happy and Rex against the world! [But] Happy knew his way around. We spent part of each day finding a sheltered place to sleep and the rest of the time hustling hot dog money!' Recorded examples of Caldwell early on sound much like Hawkins, but there is little evidence that he kept up his former admirer's relentless musical progression: by 1939 he was leading 'a little band in the back room of Minton's': according to Kenny Clarke, 'a rather drab place frequented by old men, [until] when Teddy Hill took over in 1941 he asked me to bring in a band.' Caldwell at 37 was hardly old, but his style (rather like Prince Robinson's) had never quite kept up with Hawkins, and no records exist to chart his reactions to bebop. But around New York his name stayed well known for years longer: he regularly led a band at Smalls' Paradise, 1950–3, and was a familiar face playing for New York functions until he died. [DF]

Billy Banks, *The Rhythmakers* (1932), VJM

California Ramblers They were managed by Ed Kirkeby, who later became manager to Fats Waller. At its height the band contained a rich selection of white stars, including Red Nichols, the Dorseys, Adrian Rollini (who took up bass saxophone at Kirkeby's request and featured it with the band) and drummer Stan King; from 1921 they played at the Pelham Bay Park, Westchester County, which Kirkeby renamed the California Ramblers Inn. Throughout the ensuing decade the California Ramblers – with a huge variety of players – recorded literally hundreds of sides for a plethora of different labels (sometimes under the pseudonym 'The Golden Gate Orchestra') and much of it stands the test of jazz time. In the 1970s and 1980s in the USA, cornettist Dick Sudhalter re-formed the Ramblers for concerts and club dates using some of their most attractive material. [DF]

Miss Annabelle Lee: The California Ramblers 1925–7, Biograph

Callender, Red (George Sylvester), bass, tuba. b. Haynesville, Virginia, 6 March 1916. Went to school in New Jersey, then touring band job at 17. Settled on West Coast, working with, among others, Buck Clayton (1936), Louis Armstrong (1937–8), Lester Young (1941–3), his own trio (1944–6), Erroll Garner (1946–7), Johnny Otis (1947) and Cee Pee Johnson (1947). Led own band in Hawaii (1947–8, 1949–50) and in San Francisco (1948), also did production work for small record companies. Much recording, including with Charlie Parker (1947) and last albums of Art Tatum (1955–6). Everything mentioned so far on string bass but, becoming heavily involved in session work from 1950s onwards, he also used tuba with everyone from Frank Sinatra to Stan Kenton to Stevie Wonder; live appearances on tuba, such as with Mingus and Monk (Monterey festival, 1964) and James Newton (from 1980, including 1981 European tour), maintained his strong jazz connection.

Following the premature death of the slightly younger Jimmy Blanton, Callender first drew favourable attention through his 1942 trio recording with Lester Young and Nat Cole. His style combines a Blantonesque approach to melody and timing with a penetrating pizzicato tone which strongly influenced his friend and pupil Charles Mingus. [BP]

Charlie Parker, *On Dial, vol.2* (1947), Spotlite; *Red Callender Speaks Low* (1957), Red

See Callender, Red, and Cohen, Elaine, *Unfinished Dream: The Musical World of Red Callender* (Quartet, 1985)

Calloway, Cab (Cabell), vocals, leader. b. Rochester, New York, 25 December 1907. He began his long and distinguished jazz career as a hustler and part-time singer in Baltimore's clubland. 1927, he joined an all-male quartet in the famous black revue *Plantation Days* and when they arrived in Chicago stayed on to work solo as singer, drummer and MC in the Dreamland and Sunset Cafés. 1929, while introducing the Sunset shows, he took over leadership of the Alabamians, an 11-piece band from Chicago: it was a happy period. Once in New York, though, the Alabamians fared badly against tough musical opposition. They parted company with Calloway, who at Louis Armstrong's recommendation joined the company of Connie's Hot Chocolates at Connie's Inn, then, spring 1930, went into the Savoy as contracted frontman for the Missourians, another touring band that was to form the base for Calloway's great orchestra. In the Savoy he developed a spectacular new line in showmanship, got noticed by the Mafia who ran it and found himself forcibly transferred to the Cotton Club as relief band to Duke Ellington's. As work at the Cotton Club regularized, Calloway took over leadership of the Missourians (previously they had worked as a co-operative) and filled them out with spectacular cornermen: Reuben Reeves (a showman trumpeter who, says Rex Stewart, played like Al Hirt), Ed Swayzee (a trombonist from Sam Wooding's globetrotting orchestra), trumpeter Doc Cheatham and pianist Benny Payne, a longtime partner. From 1931 the band began recording and broadcasting for network radio and turned into a smash hit: their theme song 'Minnie the Moocher', a creation by Calloway and Irving Mills based on a previously successful routine for 'St James Infirmary', was to become Calloway's lifelong *pièce de résistance*. For the next decade and a half his band – noisy, extrovert, fronted by its wild-haired, white-suited conductor – made headlines at the Cotton Club, in theatres countrywide, in films and on radio, and Calloway's singalong specialities and high, histrionic tenor voice worked to hysterical onstage approval – even if, from time to time, his highly-paid sidemen had reservations about it. Conditions on the road were often appalling (especially for black bands) but morale stayed high. And Calloway – personally if not always

Cab Calloway

musically – was loved and respected by his musicians: 'This is the kind of guy he was', says Benny Payne. 'You could get drunk with him and bring him home on your back – but next day when he raised his hand for the downbeat he didn't want to know what had happened the night before!' The band spent 40–50 weeks a year on the road and produced a string of hit records, 'The Lady with the Fan', 'Za-zuh-Zaz' and others, many of them containing explicit references to drugs when that was still highly unacceptable. Perhaps the best Calloway bands of all played after 1940 producing classic sides, often with solo contributions from Milt Hinton, Hilton Jefferson, Chu Berry, Jonah Jones and others.

By 1947 Calloway's regular bandleading days were coming to an end. 1948, he reduced to a septet, then a trio, and one brief big-band revival was a flop. His solo career, though, hardly faltered. From 1952–4 he played Sportin' Life in a *Porgy and Bess* revival opposite Leontyne Price, toured with the show regularly thereafter and in 1965 was warm-up man for the Harlem Globetrotters before spending three years playing Horace Vandergelder opposite Pearl Bailey in an all-black production of *Hello, Dolly!* In the 1970s he appeared on Broadway in *Bubbling Brown Sugar*, cameoed in the marvellous Belushi/Aykroyd rock and roll fantasy *The Blues Brothers* and in 1985 was a consultant for Francis Ford Coppola's film *The Cotton Club*; that year he visited Britain for a television spectacular, singing his famous hits. Calloway is a survivor – in 1986 he featured in TV commercials – whose contribution to jazz history deserves a second look. Not only was he (like Earl Hines, Wilbur de Paris and others) a vocational bandleader, but he treated his men to wages higher than did any other bandleader of the swing years: his name remains universally popular among the musicians who knew him. [DF]

Sixteen Cab Calloway Classics (1939–41), Epic

See Calloway, Cab, and Rollins, Bryant, *Of Minnie the Moocher and Me* (Crowell, 1976)

Candido (Candido Camero), bongo, conga drums. b. Regal, Havana, 22 April 1921. Went to USA in the 1950s, playing with Dizzy Gillespie, Stan Kenton, Billy Taylor. Continued with his own groups, then with other leaders including Sonny Rollins and Elvin Jones. One of the most accomplished Latin percussionists, he has played and recorded with many of the big names in jazz and pop including Duke Ellington, Tony Bennett, Machito and Tito Puente. He played the Newport Jazz Festival–New York with Kenton in 1975. [IC]

Drum Fever (nda), Poly; *Beautiful* (nda), United Artists; with David Amram, *No More Walls* (nda), RCA

Cárdenas, Steve (Steven Abelardo), guitar. b. Kansas City, Missouri, 5 February 1959. Mainly self-taught, but some music theory at high school, and two years of private theory lessons. Played in high school and junior college jazz bands, winning the 'Most Outstanding Musician' award in 1978 and 1979 at Central States Jazz Festival. In summer 1982, taught guitar at two Jamey Aebersold jazz camps; in the autumn did a 43-city tour with guitarist Phil Keaggy. 1984, formed his own trio with Forest Stewart on electric bass and Scott Robinson on drums. In summer 1984, he led the S. Cárdenas quartet at the Montreux Jazz Festival. He has also worked with Carmell Jones, Carl Fontana, Eddie Harris, Jimmy Hamilton, Clifford Jordan, Dave Liebman, Slide Hampton and others. His favourites include Jim Hall, John Scofield, Mick Goodrick and Wes Montgomery, and particular inspirations are Keith Jarrett, Wayne Shorter and Bill Evans. [IC]

With Gary Foster, *Kansas City Connections* (1985), Revelation

Carey, Mutt (Thomas), trumpet. b. Hahnville, Louisiana, 1891; d. Elsinore, California, 3 September 1948. His brother Jack ran the Crescent Brass Band in New Orleans, but he took up trumpet late, at 22. He worked first with Frankie Dusen, Joe Oliver, Jimmy Brown and Bebe Ridgeley in clubs and on parades. In 1914 he joined Kid Ory to begin a (sometimes fiery) partnership of more than 30 years. Carey, with his mellow-toned mid-range playing spiced up with muted effects, was one of the most popular New Orleans trumpetmen, with an often-mentioned gift for playing softly but he could play loudly too and emulated his friend King Oliver's muted techniques until he became the self-named 'Blues King of New Orleans'. Carey moved to California in 1919 to join Kid Ory, and when Oliver himself came to California in 1921 to cover jobs for Ory, audiences dismissed him as just a Carey imitator: Oliver quickly left for Chicago and greater things. From 1925 Carey took over Ory's small group, renamed it the Jeffersonians and expanded to big-band size for work in the silent film studios; during a quiet spell in the 1930s he combined music at weekends with work as a Pullman porter and mailman. He returned to Ory's band for the Standard Oil broadcasts (narrated by Orson Welles) which accelerated the revivalism of the mid-1940s and remained a much-loved star until he died. Recordings of Mutt Carey's New Yorkers (with Ed Hall), made just after he left Ory in 1947 to form his own band are marvellous illustrations of a great jazz trumpeter. [DF]

8 tracks with Carey's New Yorkers, *Giants of Traditional Jazz* (1947) Savoy (double)

Carisi, Johnny (John E.), arranger, composer (and trumpet). b. Hasbrouck Heights, New Jersey, 23 February 1922. Played in several big bands including Glenn Miller service band (1943–6) and Claude Thornhill's. 1948, began formal study of composition while writing for record dates by Miles Davis and Brew Moore. Later jazz associations include playing and writing for Urbie Green big-band album (1956, one tune from which was used on *Miles Ahead*) and three pieces for Gil Evans date (1960); also wrote more conventional album for trumpeter Marvin Stamm (1968). Carisi has been involved in all aspects of music from pop to ballet, and his compositions include a saxophone quartet and a tuba concerto. His jazz output has been minuscule but, thanks to his association with Davis and Evans, his thought-provoking work with medium-sized ensembles has received due attention. [BP]

Evans/Carisi/Cecil Taylor, *Into the Hot* (1961), Impulse

Carmichael, Hoagy (Hoagland Howard), songwriter, vocalist, piano. b. Bloomington, Indiana, 11 November 1899; d. Palm Springs, California, 28 December 1981. In his early years as an aspiring lawyer, he worshipped the young Bix Beiderbecke (who, with the Wolverines, recorded Carmichael's first composition 'Free Wheeling', later titled 'Riverboat Shuffle'). Soon after, the young composer – abandoning law and moving into the young 1920s jazz circles – had written at least one classic duet, 'Rockin' Chair', which he recorded with Louis Armstrong. From the very start his compositions were marked by musical references to the jazz he loved: 'Stardust', the 1929 masterpiece that sealed his songwriting future, quotes directly from a Louis Armstrong solo (bar 4 is bar 26 of Armstrong's 'Potato Head Blues' solo); 'Skylark', played in strict straight quavers, turns into a Bix Beiderbecke pastiche. The lyrics, too, sometimes included jazz references: 'Riverboat Shuffle' celebrates Coleman Hawkins and Louis Jordan, 'The Monkey Song' cites Beiderbecke and Charlie Parker ('Bird') in quick succession. (Carmichael's muse is often quirky: as well as monkeys, the listener runs up against mice, spiders, whales and the whole menagerie of his 1951 award-winning fantasy, co-composed with Johnny Mercer, 'In the cool cool cool of the evening'.) Some of his songs tackled unusually challenging subjects ('Rockin' Chair' for example – like 'Shh! the old man's sleepin'' and 'Little old lady' later – reflected his preoccupation with old age), and this seemed to give more impact to his excursions into the standard territory of love-songs, such as 'One Morning in May'.

A huge list of compositions after 'Stardust', all through the 1930s, established Carmichael in Hollywood as well as Tin Pan Alley and by the 1940s he was playing effective cameo roles in enduring films such as Howard Hawks's *To Have and Have Not* (1945) as well as in more forgettable ones like Michael Curtiz's *Young Man with a Horn* (1950, ostensibly based on the life of Bix Beiderbecke). In the 1940s his Decca sides were regularly staffed by stars such as Dick Cathcart and Eddie Miller, and at least one 1950s album teamed him with modern jazzmen including Art Pepper, Jimmy Rowles and Don Fagerquist. Regular radio shows and television and solo appearances in the USA and Europe kept him busy all through the 1950s and it was only with the coming of the Beatles in 1962 that Carmichael at last sat back on his royalties. Since his retirement, and his death 20 years later, his songs have continued to be steady favourites with jazz instrumentalists and singers. [DF]

Sixteen Classic Tracks (1942–50), MCA

See Carmichael, Hoagy, *The Stardust Road* (repr. Midland Books, 1983)

Carney, Harry Howell, baritone sax, clarinet, bass clarinet, alto. b. Boston, 1 April 1910; d. New York City, 8 October 1974. He began playing the clarinet in youth bands in Boston; a few doors away lived Johnny Hodges and Charlie Holmes and all three made exploratory New York trips in 1927 to visit the Rhythm Club. Carney played other venues too – the Savoy, in a relief band and at the Bamboo Inn, where Duke Ellington heard him and invited the young saxophonist to join the band for a trip back to Boston. Once there Ellington persuaded Carney's parents to let their son join him on the road: a first contract involved Ellington in pro-parentia guardian duties. He used his protégé to play alto first, alongside Rudy Jackson, then third alto (after Otto Hardwicke had joined the band yet again) but Carney had his eye on the big baritone saxophone. 'I wanted to impress everyone with the idea that the baritone was *necessary*,' he said. Ellington quickly fell for Carney's huge sound, modelled in the top register on Coleman Hawkins, in the bottom on Adrian Rollini: apart from a clarinet solo on 'Rockin' in Rhythm' he played little else but baritone for his leader for the next 45 years. A cultured, knowledgeable and good-natured man who grew older gracefully, Carney, said Rex Stewart in the 1960s, 'has the look of a man who has lived in nothing but comfort'. Jimmy Staples added: 'He has a characteristic not always evident in some famous musicians – humility!' In later years Carney became Ellington's closest associate, because he drove Ellington everywhere. Long drives of up to 600 miles cemented the friendship: Ellington would sit alongside to compose, think or sleep, and the only time his driver got agitated was when his employer was late for the pickup. 'He's a great fellow,' said Carney, 'and it's not only been an education being with him but also a great pleasure. At times I've been ashamed to take the money!' After Ellington died in 1974, Carney told Don George: 'This is the worst day of my life. Without Duke I have nothing to live for.' His own death four months after was predictable. 'Carney died of bereavement,' said Whitney Balliett. Of course, Carney's contribution to Ellington's *oeuvre* was and remains immeasurable: his huge sound, which shouldered and sometimes led Ellington's saxophones, was with that of Johnny Hodges the most irreplaceable of his leader's woodwind voices. [DF]

Any with Ellington

See Stewart, Rex, *Jazz Masters of the 1930s* (Macmillan, 1972, repr. Da Capo, 1982); Dance, Stanley, *The World of Duke Ellington* (Scribner's, 1970, repr. Da Capo, 1980)

Carr, Ian, trumpet, fluegelhorn, keyboards, composer, writer, educator. b. Dumfries, Scotland, 21 April 1933. Younger brother, Mike Carr, a pianist and composer. Self-taught on trumpet from age 17. 1952–6, studied at King's College, Newcastle-upon-Tyne, taking degree in English Literature and diploma in education. 1960–62 played with the EmCee Five, based in Newcastle, then moved to London, joining Don Rendell. He became co-leader of the Rendell–Carr quintet in 1963, staying with it until July 1969; the group made five albums and played international festivals including Antibes, 1968. 1962–70, he also played and recorded with the New Jazz Orchestra, Michael Garrick, Neil Ardley, Guy Warren of Ghana (Ghanaba), John Stevens and Trevor Watts among others, and worked with Joe Harriott, John McLaughlin, Mike Westbrook and Don Byas.

September 1969, Carr formed his group Nucleus which pioneered jazz-rock-fusion and the use of electronics. In January 1970, the group recorded their first album, *Elastic Rock*, which made a big impact in Europe; June 1970, Nucleus won first prize at the Montreux International Jazz Festival; in July they performed at the Newport Festival and at the Village Gate in New York. Leonard Feather later wrote: 'Nucleus has been a seminal influence in Europe and elsewhere.'

During the 1970s, Nucleus toured throughout Europe, playing major festivals and appearing on radio and TV. 1974, an augmented Nucleus toured the UK for the ACGB Contemporary Music Network, performing Carr's long composition, *Labyrinth*. 1978, Nucleus spent three weeks in India playing two nights at the first Jazz Yatra in Bombay, followed by concerts in Calcutta and Delhi. 1984, Nucleus did a seven-week British Council tour of Latin America playing concerts and conducting workshops; their concert in Mexico City was filmed for TV. 1985, Nucleus played for one week at the Rome spring festival, and recorded a live album at the Stuttgart festival.

Since 1975, Carr has been a member of the *United Jazz and Rock Ensemble; since 1981, he has directed weekly workshops for gifted teenagers at Interchange in North London; since 1982, he has been an associate professor at the Guildhall School of Music and Drama, giving individual tuition and workshops in improvisation, composition and performance. He has had many composing commissions and written for all sizes of ensemble ranging from small groups to full orchestra with strings; in 1986 he composed *Spirit of Place* for string ensemble and soloists Tony Coe and Eberhard Weber, and the work was performed at Bracknell classical and jazz festivals.

Carr's book on Miles Davis is generally regarded as a classic of jazz biography. August 1982, he was given the Calabria award for 'outstanding contribution in the field of jazz'. [JLS]

Over 45, including six with UJRE; with Nucleus, *Elastic Rock* (1970); *Solar Plexus* (1970); *Belladonna* (1972); *Labyrinth* (1973); *Roots* (1973); *Snakehips Etcetera* (1975), all Phonogram Vertigo; *In Flagrante Delicto* (1977); *Out of the Long Dark* (1978), both Capitol; *Awakening* (1980); *Live at the Theaterhaus* (1985), both Mood

See *Music Outside: Contemporary Jazz in Britain* (Latimer New Dimensions, London, 1973); *Miles Davis, a critical biography* (Quartet Books, London, 1982; Paladin, London, paperback, 1984; Morrow, New York, 1982)

Carr, Mike (Michael Anthony), organ, piano, vibes, etc. b. South Shields, Durham, 7 December 1937. Self-taught on piano, Carr organized Newcastle-based group Emcee Five (1960–2) which included Malcolm Cecil (who later worked with Jim Hall and Stevie Wonder) and elder brother Ian Carr. Played in London (on organ) with Herbie Goins (1966) and own trio including John McLaughlin (1967). Accompanied Coleman Hawkins (on piano, 1967) and Don Byas (1968, during long stay in Portugal). Duo with Tony Crombie (1969–70), becoming Ronnie Scott trio (1971–5, including Carnegie Hall concert 1974). Toured UK with Kenny Clarke trio (1978), also gigged and/or recorded with Buddy Tate, Illinois Jacquet, Eddie Davis, Johnny Griffin, Arnett Cobb, Sonny Payne, Art Taylor, Jimmy Witherspoon etc. His own trios have included Jim Mullen, Dick Morrissey, Peter King, Tony Coe. 1980, formed jazz-funk recording group Cargo, making successful singles and album (1985) featuring Peter King and Ronnie Scott.

A dynamic performer whose pedal work emulates Jimmy Smith, although his right-hand lines are more bebop-oriented than most organists. Recently he has also incorporated electric piano, causing no less a personage than Oscar Peterson to comment, 'I have never heard an organist in the States who has all that swinging, the organ, the electric piano, and the bass pedals.' [BP]

Live at Ronnie Scott's (1979), Spotlite

Carter, Benny (Bennett Lester), alto sax, trumpet, arranger, composer; also recorded on tenor sax, clarinet, trombone, piano. b. New York City, 8 August 1907. He took lessons from Harold Procter and a couple of other teachers, it seems on a semi-casual basis. Carter's inspirations for trumpet (which he played first) included Bubber Miley and his own cousin Cuban Bennett, who very early on showed him what could be done with harmony while they played together in jam sessions: for saxophone the young Benny adored Frank Trumbauer – like Carter himself, an elegant, technically flawless and tasteful player. After tentative beginnings (Rex Stewart remembers him being dismissed from the stand to pass out handbills at John O'Connor's club), Carter developed fast as both musician and arranger and by 1928 was easily playing in demanding situations (from Fletcher Henderson's band to Duke Ellington's) and making an impression with his arrangements. ('I started off by writing saxophone choruses along the chords', he said later; the device was to remain a favourite all his life.) By 1928 he had his own band, too, working at New York's Arcadia Ballroom, and re-formed it regularly over the next eight years for specific projects, as well as working with and arranging for most of the great bands of the era: his own groups became a guarantee of musical excellence. 'If you made Benny Carter's band in those days the stamp was on you,' says Danny Barker. 'Then you could go with Chick Webb or Fletcher or any of the other bands. It was like major and minor league baseball.' Carter – quiet-mannered, easy-going, soft-spoken and affable, but confidently aware of his own abilities – moved in and out of great bands, including Charlie Johnson's, Chick Webb's, Fletcher Henderson's, until 1935, when he sailed for Paris to join Willie

Lewis's Orchestra at Chez Florence. A year later he took up the job of staff arranger for Henry Hall's BBC Dance Orchestra to which, from March 1936, he contributed as many as six new arrangements a week: recordings of the period, such as the revolutionary 'Waltzing the Blues', are still much re-issued. Then came two years in Holland, Belgium, Scandinavia and France before a return to the USA in 1938 – with violinist Eddie South on board the *Ile de France* – after which he formed a big band. Carter's project (just like South's big band earlier in the decade) was an elegant musical success but not a commercial one; perhaps it was just too refined for the 'killer-diller' years. 'And he probably came home too late', says Dave Dexter. 'There were so many swing bands being booked by 1939 that his great organization never seemed to get the right bookings nor the network radio time to make it a favourite.' And it was led by a black. In 1941 he cut down to a sextet and by 1943 was leading a band at Billy Berg's club on the West Coast. 'I found myself concentrating more on the big-band concept, writing and arranging,' said Carter. When he was offered work writing for films (including *Stormy Weather* in 1943) by Twentieth Century-Fox he eagerly accepted, and in 1945 moved to Hollywood permanently to write in the day and play club residencies at night. Over the next forty years he was to write scores for films including *The Snows of Kilimanjaro* (1952), *The Five Pennies* (1959), *Flower Drum Song* (1961), *Buck and the Preacher* (1971), and television music for series such as *Bob Hope Presents*, *M-Squad*, *Ironside*, *Banyon* and numerous 'specials'. But he was far from lost to the jazz world after the 1940s; he continued to lead his own bands, toured and recorded for Norman Granz, worked solo, and went on contributing such essential recordings to the jazz shelves as *Further Definitions* (which re-created Carter classics from 1937 including 'Honeysuckle Rose', teamed him with Coleman Hawkins and again revealed his saxophone-writing skills), *Additions to Further Definitions* and *Kansas City Suite*, which he wrote in 1961 for Count Basie to five-star reviews. In the 1970s he toured Europe and Japan, signed recording contracts with Norman Granz (for Pablo) and in 1985 was back in England to play and record.

A classic alto-saxophonist, Benny Carter – along with Willie Smith and Johnny Hodges – made the most artistic contribution ever to swing saxophone. All through his career he presented an elegant alternative to his two contemporaries: where Smith devoured solos with a greedy surging urgency and Hodges catwalked a sequence with sinewy sensual grace, Carter negotiated lines with agile panache, his improvisation a graceful exercise in perfection; and he is a superb trumpeter, as well as a great saxophonist. 'He's still an affable and courtly gentleman', says Stewart. 'His gentility seems to be out of a forgotten age. He moves with the grace and poise of those accustomed to walking with kings. Perhaps that's why those who know him best call him "King".' [DF]

Swinging at Maida Vale (1936–7), Jasmine; *Benny Carter: Jazz Giant* (1957), Contemporary

See Berger, Morroe, *et al.*, *Benny Carter* (2 vols., Scarecrow Press, 1982); Dance, Stanley, *The World of Swing* (Scribner's, 1974, repr. Da Capo, 1979); Stewart, Rex, *Jazz Masters of the 1930s* (Macmillan, 1972, repr. Da Capo, 1982)

Carter, Betty (*née* Lillie Mae Jones), singer. b. Flint, Michigan, 16 May 1930. Studied piano, began working as singer in Detroit clubs (1946), sat in with Dizzy Gillespie big band and Charlie Parker quintet. 1948–51, toured with Lionel Hampton, making record début and writing occasional arrangements for band. Working in various nightclubs and theatres, then touring and recording with Ray Charles (1961) and appearances in Japan (1963) and Europe (1964). After retiring from performance for marriage and raising children (late 1960s), returned to greater success from 1970. As well as forming own Bet-Car Records (1969), started to work exclusively with hand-picked trio, including such pianists as John Hicks, Danny Mixon, Mulgrew Miller and (1985) Benny Green.

Considered until the 1970s to be too far-out for even the jazz public, Carter has seen the taste-makers catch up with her. In a style initially inspired by Billie Holiday and especially Sarah Vaughan, she sings in a way which is more instrumentally conceived than any other vocalist using largely standard material; this is not merely true of her scatting (which prompted Hampton to rename her 'Betty Bebop') but, even more so, of her fragmentation of a given tune and lyrics. Miraculously, the lyrics survive and are sometimes enhanced by the process, although this depends (like melodic decoration) on the original being familiar to listeners, many of whom find the result too mannered. But Carter's melodic improvisations, combined with her husky, saxophone-like voice quality, often create marvellous effects which would be denied to anyone less audacious. [BP]

Modern Sound of Betty Carter (1960), ABC; *Whatever Happened to Love?* (*c.* 1982), Bet-Car

Film: . . . *But then, she's Betty Carter* (dir. Michelle Parkerson, 1980)

Carter, John Wallace, clarinet, alto. b. Fort Worth, Texas, 24 September 1929. Played with Ornette Coleman and Charles Moffett (late 1940s). Holds BA in music from Lincoln University, Missouri, and MA in music education from University of Colorado; also studied at North Texas State and California State University. Based on West Coast since early 1960s, formed quartet with Bobby Bradford (1965), then own groups from 1973. Member of James

Newton woodwind quintet (since 1980, touring Europe, 1981). 1982, after teaching music in public school system, founded the Wind College in Los Angeles, whose tutors include Newton, Charles Owens, John Nunez and Red Callender. Callender, who once described working alongside Carter and Newton as his most enjoyable experience since playing with Art Tatum, has said of Carter; 'I had never heard anybody with such control on the clarinet . . . His complete mastery of the instrument is astounding.' [BP]

Dauhwe (1982), Black Saint

Film: *The New Music* (dir. Peter Bull, 1980)

Carter, Ron (Ronald Levin), bass, cello, bass guitar, composer (and violin, clarinet, trombone, tuba). b. Ferndale, Michigan, 4 May 1937. Began on cello at age ten, and was soon playing chamber concerts; at Cass Technical High School in Detroit he changed to double-bass. 1956–9, studied at Eastman School of Music, Rochester, NY, graduating B.Mus. Played and recorded with Eastman Philharmonia Orchestra before first professional jazz engagement with Chico Hamilton, 1959. 1960–2, freelanced with many people including Eric Dolphy, with whom he recorded several times on cello, Cannonball Adderley, Jaki Byard, Randy Weston, Bobby Timmons, Mal Waldron. He earned an M.Mus. at the Manhattan School of Music, 1961. Musicians quickly recognized Carter's outstanding qualities – his perfectly poised sense of time, brilliant technique, and a sound so resonant that in ballads it seemed as if the notes were being artificially sustained – but it was not until he joined Miles Davis in 1963 that he came to prominence in the USA and internationally.

He stayed with Davis's quintet until 1968 and, with Tony Williams on drums and Herbie Hancock on piano, made up what has been called perhaps the greatest jazz-time-playing rhythm-section ever. By the mid-1960s each of the three men was the dominant influence on his instrument, and they had, as a unit, transformed rhythm-section playing; they swung as never before, and they took outrageous liberties with the pulse without ever losing the beat, playing with a freedom bordering on, but never disintegrating into, total abstraction. It was a way of playing which required immense virtuosity and it spawned disciples and would-be imitators through successive decades.

Carter, like everyone else who has played with Davis, was magnified by the association, and played on a series of classic albums, making an important contribution to them. He also had time to freelance, and in 1965, played in Europe with Friedrich Gulda. He continued to be active in education and was on the faculty of several summer clinics.

Early 1970s, Carter worked with the New York Bass Choir, Lena Horne for her New York appearances, Michel Legrand, the New York Jazz Quartet, and freelanced with Stanley Turrentine, Hubert Laws, George Benson and others; he recorded for CTI Records, and toured with some of their artists in Europe and Japan. Throughout the jazz-rock-fusion boom, the acoustic bass always remained his first love and first choice, but he did double occasionally on electric bass, practising it only one hour a week 'just to stay in tune'.

1976, he formed his first quartet with Kenny Barron (piano), Buster Williams (bass), Ben Riley (dms). Carter was the main soloist and melodist, playing piccolo bass, which he tuned higher than a standard acoustic bass, and which therefore projects more clearly over a rhythm-section. 1977, he was reunited with Herbie Hancock and Tony Williams in the all-star group VSOP, which also included Wayne Shorter and Freddie Hubbard. This toured world-wide and recorded a studio and a live album. 1978, he also toured with an all-star quartet led by Sonny Rollins and including McCoy Tyner and Al Foster. Since the later 1970s he has usually done an all-star tour every summer.

1981, he was again reunited with Hancock and Williams, when the Hancock quartet, featuring Wynton Marsalis (tpt) toured the USA, Europe and Japan, where they recorded a double album. Carter also played on Marsalis's 1984 album *Hot House Flowers*, and assisted Robert Freedman with the arrangements for a large string ensemble plus French horn, tuba and woodwind. He remained active in education, with private students and academic engagements. 1983, he deputized for John Lewis at City College, teaching Jazz History after World War II and three other more practical classes: small group; advanced improvisation; rhythm-section. [IC]

Over 500 albums with very many people including Dolphy, M. Tyner, Legrand, H. Silver, F. Gulda, Laws, F. Hubbard, M. Jackson, Roberta Flack, Aretha Franklin; with Miles Davis 15 albums including *My Funny Valentine* (1964); *ESP* (1965); *Miles Smiles* (1966); *Nefertiti* (1967); *Miles in the Sky* (1968), all CBS; with Hancock/Williams, *VSOP Live under the Sky* (1977); *Herbie Hancock Quartet* (1981), both CBS; as leader, *A Song for You* (1978), Milestone; *All Blues* (1973), CTI; *Etudes* (1983), Elektra Musician

Cartwright, Deirdre Josephine, guitar. b. London, 27 July 1956. Family musical. Piano lessons as a child; self-taught on guitar. 1973–81, played with various London small groups and big bands. 1981, joined the Guest Stars, an all-women fusion band. 1983, she was the guitar presenter for the BBC TV workshop series Rockschool, writing and recording the book and cassette. 1984, the Guest Stars toured US East Coast. The band and its first album received acclaim in the UK. Influences: Jimi Hendrix, Pat Metheny, Charlie Christian, Alan Holdsworth, among others; also Mingus, Pastorius, and her associates in the Guest Stars. [IC]

The Guest Stars (1984); *Out at Night* (1985), both Guest Stars

Carver, Wayman Alexander, flute, saxes, clarinet. b. Portsmouth, Virginia, 25 December 1905; d. 6 May 1967. Although a flute and piccolo specialist called Flutes Morton was playing regularly at the Sunset Café, Chicago, in the mid-1920s, Carver was among the first jazz flautists of note and the first to be featured on record. He took up the instrument at 14 and after a stay with Elmer Snowden (1931–2) joined Benny Carter for two years, featuring his innovatory instrument (in jazz terms) on Spike Hughes's 1933 session in New York that produced 'Sweet Sue Just You'. 1934–40, Carver worked for Chick Webb and Ella Fitzgerald, contributing arrangements such as 'My Heart Belongs to Daddy' and 'Down Home Rag'. After quitting full-time bandwork he turned to teaching, then later became professor of music at Clark College, Georgia, and taught there until he died: two prominent Carver pupils are George Adams and Marion Brown. [DF]

Spike Hughes and his All-American Orchestra (1933), Jasmine

Cary, Dick (Richard Durant), piano, alto horn, trumpet, arranger. b. Hartford, Connecticut, 10 July 1916. He began his professional jazz life with Wild Bill Davison in 1941 at Nick's Club, New York. After work with Benny Goodman, Joe Marsala, Brad Gowans and the Casa Loma Orchestra he joined the army at Fort Dix and in the army band acquired his famous second instrument, an alto horn. His main instrument, though, was still the piano and in 1947 he joined Louis Armstrong for Ernie Anderson's first All Stars concert at New York's Town Hall. He 'worked with Louis for several months – until the job got into a routine'. With typical integrity he swapped the highly-paid piano chair with Earl Hines, and then spent time studying twelve-tone theory with Stefan Wolpe. Regular work with Jimmy Dorsey, Tony Parenti, Muggsy Spanier and Eddie Condon followed and then a partnership which gave Cary the eclectic headroom he needed – with Bobby Hackett, resident at the Henry Hudson Hotel, New York. After this peak, Cary moved out to Los Angeles to pursue freelance arranging, work with Eddie Condon again, and rehearsals with groups of interested people: his accumulated book contained nearly 1000 arrangements. The 1970s brought a Cary resurgence: he worked jazz festivals, toured Europe as a soloist and recorded beautifully for the Dutch Riff label (on, among other instruments, the intriguing F trumpet he found in a pawnshop). Cary's enquiring musical mind and high standards have fashioned a career of faultless excellence. His 1980s activities have included more festivals, rehearsal bands (with Dick Cathcart and others) and more thinking. [DF]

The Amazing Dick Cary (1975), Riff; *The Music Man goes Dixieland* (1957/8), Fortune; any with Hackett

Casa Loma Orchestra A co-operative, masterminded by popular six-foot saxophonist Glen 'Spike' Gray, which laid the groundwork for such later successful swing kings as Benny Goodman. Named for a never-to-be-opened hotel, the Casa Lomans were formed by Gray from an orchestra contracted to Jean Goldkette, the Orange Blossoms, and in 1929 were booked into New York's Roseland Ballroom by the Tommy Rockwell–Cork O'Keefe office. There they were heard by Bob Stevens, an Okeh talent scout who offered them a contract: between then and 1931 (with a book written by talented guitarist Gene Gifford) the Casa Lomans built their sound up, adding cornermen such as clarinettist Clarence Hutchenrider, trombonist-singer Pee Wee Hunt, Sonny Dunham (a spectacular high-note trumpeter) and singer Kenny Sargent. The great years for Casa Loma were 1931–5: they produced strings of records for Victor, Brunswick and Decca, broadcast on the Camel Cigarette programme and played summers at a collegiate heaven, Glen Island Casino. Here the Casa Lomans' impeccably drilled music – murmuring sentimental items mixed in with swing specialities such as 'White Jazz' (later covered by Lew Stone) – became the anthems of a generation, and easily survived Benny Goodman's high-powered onslaught of a year or two later. By 1935 the Casa Loma Orchestra was resident at the Rainbow Room on top of New York's Radio City; soon after, Glen Gray took over fronting the band from violinist Mel Jenssen (a 1939 hit for the band, two months ahead of Glenn Miller, was 'Sun Valley Serenade'). In the 1940s key men like Dunham went out on their own, the draft took more, but Gray replaced them with fine young talent such as pianist Lou Carter, guitarist Herb Ellis and singer Eugenie Baird, as well as tried and trusted players like cornettists Red Nichols and Bobby Hackett, both of whom featured with the orchestra in 1944. Gray retired from touring in 1950 but continued to record regularly with his orchestra until he died of cancer in 1963; later Capitol albums featuring Jonah Jones, Conrad Gozzo, Si Zentner, Nick Fatool and other stars are worth finding. [DF]

The Casa Loma Band (1930–6), Bandstand

Casey, Al (Albert Aloysius), guitar. b. Louisville, Kentucky, 15 September 1915. Two uncles and two aunts sang in a gospel quartet for a nightly show on Radio WLW, Cincinatti; on the show they befriended Fats Waller who was in search of a guitarist and they recommended their nephew. 'Fats said, "If you finish high school and get your diploma with decent grades, you've got the job!" ' recalls Casey, who still reveres Waller's memory; until graduation in 1933 he played with his new boss on records and in school holidays. From 1934 until 1942 (with a year away in 1939), Casey's playful chorded acoustic guitar solos were the most graceful feature of Fats Waller's Rhythm. His nine years with Waller included countless records ('Buck Jumpin' ', a clever feature based on guitar harmonics was a small hit), films and sellout concert tours. When Waller died in 1943, Casey laid off work, but came back with Clarence Profit's trio, which he later took over, replacing Profit with Sammy Clanton, and found himself often playing alongside young bebop stars such as Fats Navarro. The same year he won the *Esquire* magazine guitarist's poll and featured in a famous All-American Award Winners' concert, sponsored by Leonard Feather at the New York Metropolitan Opera House. After the war and the fall of 52nd Street it was 'back to all kinds of jobs, weekend gigs and so on' followed by four years with King Curtis (1957–61) playing r & b, and more of the same with drummer Curley Hamner's sextet, including a long New York residency. In the early 1970s Casey worked part-time, then gave up completely for two years, but in 1980 – despite a leg injury sustained by falling upstairs – he resumed a busy round of solo work in England (masterminded by promoters Dave Bennett and Peter Carr); by 1986 he was playing annually to packed British clubs and back home with the highly successful Harlem Blues and Jazz Band. [DF]

Six Swinging Strings (1981), JSP

See Dance, Stanley, *The World of Swing* (Scribner's, 1974, repr. Da Capo, 1979)

Castle, Geoff (Geoffrey Charles), piano, electric piano, synthesizers. b. London, 8 June 1949. Parents both musical. B.Sc. (Eng.), Queen Mary College, London University. Eight years' private classical tuition; two years' jazz tuition with Tubby Hayes, Don Rendell, Graham Collier. 1967–70, with NYJO; 1970–4, with Graham Collier's band which won the Press Prize and came second in the main jury prize at Montreux, 1971. 1974–82, worked with Nucleus, also gigged with other UK musicians and formed his own group, Strange Fruit, 1977. With Nucleus he toured and played festivals all over Western and Eastern Europe, and spent three weeks in India, 1978. 1983–4, worked with Brian Smith's quartet in New Zealand, and wrote and produced the music for a NZ film, *Checkmate.* His most important composition is his 1981 suite *Impressions of New York.* He has also been involved as a teacher on occasional jazz courses, and has taken classes at the Guildhall School of Music, London. [IC]

With Graham Collier and six with Nucleus; *Paz are Back* (1980), Spotlite; *Brian Smith Quartet* (1984), Ode, NZ; with Strange Fruit, *Debut* (1982), President

Cathcart, Dick (Charles Richard), trumpet. b. Michigan City, Indiana, 6 November 1924. He began his career with the USAAF band, Alvino Rey and Ray McKinley and was lead trumpeter with Bob Crosby's post-war big band, a Basie-style ensemble arranged by Tommy Todd which owed nothing to Crosby's pre-war Dixieland approach. 1946–9, Cathcart worked for the MGM film studios, then with Ben Pollack, Ray Noble and Frank de Vol. The kind of versatility, technique, taste and creativity implied in such different jobs came to the fore in 1952 when Cathcart was invited to direct the music and ghost the trumpet for a radio series, *Pete Kelly's Blues*, which brought his perfectly smooth and graceful concept and glass-clear tone dramatically to the public ear. Thereafter, apart from a spell on the road with the Modernaires (he is a fine singer with a life-long interest in the art), Cathcart was the offstage trumpet for a Pete Kelly decade that included a still-watchable feature film (1955) and in 1959 a long TV series, starring William Reynolds as cornettist Kelly and Connee Boswell as blues singer Savannah Brown. A string of faultless albums for RCA Victor and Warner Bros, including music from these productions, and later just good music by Pete Kelly's Big Seven (as Cathcart's band became known) featured stars such as Eddie Miller, Matty Matlock, Moe Schneider, Ray Sherman, Nick Fatool and George Van Eps; they worked together regularly in a variety of contexts including sessions for Paul Weston (often for Capitol) and Harry James. The music that resulted was sublimely good: so was another uncannily brilliant album by Cathcart with arranger Warren Barker's orchestra, *Bix MCMLIX.* Later in the 1960s Cathcart was regrettably absent from recording (although he kept on singing) but in 1985 was back to full playing form with Dick Cary's rehearsal band, at Sacramento's 1985/6 Jazz Festival with a re-formed Big Seven and blowing around the festival circuit. [DF]

Pete Kelly at Home (1956), RCA.

Catherine, Philip, acoustic and electric guitars, guitar synthesizer. b. London, 27 October 1942, to English mother and Belgian father: resident in Brussels after World War II. Inspired at first by Django Reinhardt and René Thomas. During the 1960s he played with various Belgian musicians including Jack Sels and Fats Sadi, after turning professional at 17 and touring with organist Lou Bennett. Inspired by John McLaughlin and Larry Coryell, he began playing jazz-rock, working with Jean-Luc Ponty, 1970–2. Then studied for a year at the Berklee School in Boston, USA. 1973, back in Europe, founded with Charlie Mariano and Jasper van't Hof, the group Pork Pie, which had great success in Europe, touring and playing festivals, including the Berlin Festival, 1974. Also played with the Mike Gibbs band and Klaus Doldinger's Jubilee. 1975, made his first album as leader, with van't Hof, Mariano, John Lee (bass) and Gerry Brown (dms), and his second

Philip Catherine (*right*), with Jasper van't Hof (*left*) and Charlie Mariano (*centre*)

album with the same personnel in 1976. That year he played a spontaneous duo with Larry Coryell at the Berlin Festival, making a big impression. They then recorded together and toured Europe twice, also playing major festivals including Montreux, 1977, Newport, USA, and Bilzen, Belgium, 1978. Since then, Catherine has worked and recorded in a trio with Mariano and van't Hof, and also freelances. [IC]

With Toots Thielemans, Joachim Kuhn, Chris Hinze; *September Man* (1975), Atlantic; *Guitars* (1976), Atlantic; with Pork Pie, *The Door is Open* (1975), MPS; with Coryell, *Twin House* (1977), Atlantic; *Splendid* (1978), Elektra; with Mariano/van't Hof, *Sleep my Love* (1979), CMP; *Philip Catherine, Chet Baker, Jean Louis Rassinfosse* (1983), LDH; Niels-Henning Ørsted Pedersen/Catherine, *The Viking* (1983), Pablo

Catlett, Big Sid (Sidney), drums, b. Evansville, Indiana, 17 January 1910; d. Chicago, 25 March 1951. He came to New York from Chicago in 1930 to join Elmer Snowden. An easy-going soft-hearted giant, often dressed in green chalk-striped suits and bright flowered ties selected from his huge wardrobe, Catlett's contribution to Snowden's band was, even by then, musically aware. 'He was a musician's drummer', says Rex Stewart. 'He would ask you, "What kind of rhythm shall I play for you?" That was as soon as you came in the band and after you'd told him you'd get the same thing every night.' Catlett combined music with a strong line in showmanship: beautiful controlled movement punctuated with verbal asides, cavernous rimshots to accompany 'business' and a giant powder puff for his armpits; the combination ensured him work with the élite 1930s bands from Fletcher Henderson to Benny Goodman, and in all of them Catlett became a centre of musical and personal attention. 'Though he was such a powerful fellow he could play very lightly and delicately without sounding weak,' says Max Kaminsky, 'and his generosity matched his size. He'd give you the shirt off his back if you needed it!' Billie Holiday added the slyest tribute: 'He wasn't called Big Sid because he was 6′ 2″ you know!' (In fact he was 6′ 4″.) It was the 1940s bebop revolution that most clearly pinpointed Catlett's versatility. Where the traditional–modern conflicts of jazz fashion helped to kill Dave Tough, the easy-going Catlett simply crossed 52nd Street and sat in, as a matter of course, with brothers Charlie Parker and Dizzy Gillespie. 'Sid was the first guy I was aware of who was the complete drummer', says Billy Taylor. 'He could play any style. I remember when Buddy Rich was with Tommy Dorsey he used to cut all the drummers but not Sid! It used to annoy Buddy so much. He'd play all over his head and then Sid would gently play his simple melodic lines on drums – and make his point!'

Catlett played literally nonstop all through the 1940s (he seldom bothered to go to bed) including two years, 1947–9, with Louis Armstrong's All Stars, where he got on well with his leader despite a chronic inability to be onstage for curtain up. By the late 1940s Catlett was visibly ill, took time away from the All Stars after a heart attack and was replaced by Glaser's office with Cozy Cole: shortly after his ritual Christmas trip back to visit his mother in 1950 he collapsed in the wings of the Chicago Opera House at a Hot Lips Page benefit and died: he was 41. Catlett loved sport, and his son (a giant of 6′ 8″) became an outstanding baseball player for Notre Dame University in the later 1960s. [DF]

Satchmo at Symphony Hall (1947), MCA Coral

See Stewart, Rex, *Jazz Masters of the 1930s* (Macmillan, 1972, repr. Da Capo 1982); Balliett, Whitney, *Improvising* (OUP, 1977)

Celestin, Papa (Oscar), trumpet, vocals. b. La Fourche, Louisiana, 1 January 1884; d. New Orleans, 15 December 1954. A legend of New Orleans jazz and a strong lead trumpeter, who early on was famous for his off-centre embouchure, he was with the Algiers Brass Band by the early 1900s, with Henry Allen Senior's Olympia band soon after and led the band at Tuxedo Hall, 1910–13. Not long after, his Tuxedo Brass Band became one of the city's most popular bands, and in 1917 the Original Tuxedo Orchestra – which he co-led with trombonist William 'Bebe' Ridgely – began playing dances for white society, featuring star names like Zutty Singleton, Kid Shots Madison, Manuel Manetta and Paul Barnes. Celestin recorded a lot in the 1920s for Okeh and Columbia, toured widely and remained a big New Orleans attraction, but in the Depression years he retired from full-time music. He worked in shipyards during the war, and after, with the onset of revivalism, reorganized his band for a late burst of success. He recorded again for De Luxe in 1947, and by 1949 was starring on Bourbon Street at the Paddock Lounge, recording regularly and doing TV and radio work. 'Oscar "Papa" Celestin, now well on the way to his 70s has the jazz world on its toes', wrote John A. Provenzano then. Celestin played for President Eisenhower in 1953: a bust of him bought by the New Orleans Jazz Foundation stands today in the Delgado Museum, New Orleans. [DF]

The Sound of New Orleans, vol. 3 (1925–45), CBS

Challis, Bill (William H.), arranger, piano, saxophone, clarinet. b. Wilkes Barre, Pennsylvania, 8 July 1904. A self-taught pianist, Challis – along with Tom Satterfield, Lennie Hayton and Matty Malneck – played a central role in creating a style for Paul Whiteman's great orchestra of 1927–30. Challis's highly (if occasionally determinedly) modernistic arrangements were always charming at least, as well as ingenious, and often much more than that. Scores such as 'Changes', 'Oh Miss Hannah' and 'San' (with its celebrated trumpet trio for the Dorseys and Bix Beiderbecke) were notable for their brilliant exploitation of tone colours, unconventional voicing and revolutionary harmonies (in jazz terms) and proved that, in Dick Sudhalter's words, 'Challis was easily on a par with Don Redman and other outstanding black orchestrators'; indeed, it could be argued that most of Challis's work is much more complex and daring than the contemporary output of Redman or even Duke Ellington, neither of whom was faced with writing for orchestras as huge as Whiteman's. Even the more contrived moments in Challis's 1920s work are hard to dislike, and his settings for Beiderbecke, Trumbauer and their brilliant contemporaries are often ravishing. He had already worked alongside them for a year in Jean Goldkette's band from 1926 before joining Whiteman, and after leaving in 1930 began working as a full-time arranger, writing for a variety of top-line bands including Fletcher Henderson, the Dorseys and Glen Gray's Casa Loma Orchestra. Challis's later work for such artists as Bobby Hackett (in 1946), stripped of its obligation to break new ground, is a mature delight. In 1986 he was no longer arranging because of failing sight, but still fit and active. [DF]

The Bix Beiderbecke Legend (1924–30), RCA Victor

See Sudhalter, Richard M., *Bix: Man and Legend* (Quartet, 1974)

Chaloff, Serge, baritone sax. b. Boston, 24 November 1923; d. 16 July 1957. Father was symphonic musician, mother a noted piano teacher. Played with several big bands as a teenager, then Boyd Raeburn (1944–5), Georgie Auld (1945–6), Jimmy Dorsey (1946–7). Some small-group recording both before and during stay with Woody Herman (1947–9), then with Count Basie (1950). In early 1950s returned to Boston and, after a few years' inactivity, did some teaching and made further albums under own name; his final date, a reunion of the Herman band Four Brothers (February 1957), found him crippled by spinal paralysis. Herman's popularity had helped Chaloff become the first baritonist to make a reputation during the bebop era. Unlike some who followed, he avoided the mistake of forcing endless streams of notes through the horn at a pace which neutralized its characteristic sound. Instead, he built on the baritone's tonal richness and, especially in his later work, attained a profundity associated with few players of any instrument during this period. [BP]

Blue Serge (1956), Affinity

Chambers, Henderson Charles, trombone. b. Alexandria, Louisiana, 1 May 1908; d. New

York City, 19 October 1967. His career began in territory bands in the 1930s (such as Speed Webb's and Zack Whyte's) and Al Sears's group in Kentucky (1935–6) and in 1941 he joined Louis Armstrong's big band for two years. From then on he worked in a starry selection of orchestras and small bands including those of Don Redman (1943), Ed Hall (1944–8), Lucky Millinder, Count Basie and Cab Calloway, as well as Duke Ellington in 1957, Mercer Ellington (1959), Ray Charles (1961–3) and Count Basie (1964–6). Perhaps because his soloing was never as highly individual as, say, Dickie Wells's or Vic Dickenson's, Chambers never quite achieved their high reputation; he is a neglected name, and a rare valuable chance to study his solo powers turns up on the first of Buck Clayton's immortal *Jam Sessions* where he partners Urbie Green in 'Hucklebuck' and 'Robbins' Nest'. [DF]

Buck Clayton Jam Session (1953), CBS

Chambers, Joe (Joseph Arthur), drums (and piano). b. Stoneacre, Virginia, 25 June 1942. Studied in Philadelphia and Washington, where he did regular gigging (1960–3). Moved to New York, playing with Eric Dolphy, Freddie Hubbard, Lou Donaldson, Jimmy Giuffre, Andrew Hill etc. Working with Bobby Hutcherson (1965–70, including European tour, 1970, and eight albums); also recording with many others such as Archie Shepp, Wayne Shorter, Joe Henderson. Since 1970, member of Max Roach's percussion group M'Boom, to which he contributes compositions. 1974, appeared at Carnegie Hall (playing own suite *The Almoravid*); at Moers Festival, 1982. Has made one multi-instrumental album playing keyboards and percussion, and one of solo piano. Chambers's qualities as a sensitive but dynamic drummer were compared by Archie Shepp to the work of Roy Haynes, which was high praise indeed; while McCoy Tyner observed, 'Probably because he's also a pianist and composer himself . . . he knows how to listen to what a writer wants in a performance.' [BP]

The Almoravid (1973), Muse

Chambers, Paul Laurence Dunbar, Jnr., bass. b. Pittsburgh, Pennsylvania, 22 April 1935; d. 4 January 1969. Grew up in Detroit, where he studied tuba. Toured with Paul Quinichette (1954), Bennie Green (1955), J. J. Johnson–Kai Winding (1955) and George Wallington (1955). Joined the Miles Davis quintet and remained seven and a half years (1955–63). Enormously prolific recording career, especially in late 1950s, despite problems of being heroin user. Then working regularly with Wynton Kelly trio (1963–6), continued freelance gigging in New York, with Tony Scott, Barry Harris etc., until shortly before his premature death.

'Mr P.C.', as he was called in Coltrane's tune-title, was one of the most influential rhythm-section players ever. In addition to his springy articulation and propulsive time-feeling, his oblique walking lines made interesting detours around the more obvious notes that other bassists used. At slow tempos, the fill-in phrases which Jimmy Blanton had introduced on bass were converted by Chambers into upper-register countermelodies, and indeed even his up-tempo lines were often strong enough to be described in the same way. In featured solos (and he was one of the first bassists to be accorded these on a regular basis, often several times per album) he added new and exceptionally horn-like bebop phrasing to the bass repertoire. Although his bowed tone and phrasing left something to be desired, he certainly helped to popularize the greater use of the bow, and his pizzicato playing set new standards for rhythm-sections all over the world. [BP]

Whims of Chambers (1956), Blue Note; *Ease It* (1959), Affinity

Changes The only changes described by that word alone are harmonic ones (tempo changes would have to be spelled out with both words). But 'the changes' means specifically the exact series of chords which makes up the required sequence for a particular piece. Whereas rhythm-section instrumentalists have to 'play the changes', the front-line soloists may feel free to ignore them to a certain extent, although they at least need to 'know the changes' in order to ignore them. [BP]

Charles, Dennis, drums, percussion. b. St Croix, Virgin Islands, 4 December 1933. 1945, moved to New York, already playing congas; self-taught on drumkit from 1954. 1955–60, worked with Cecil Taylor group, also gigging with Afro-Latin and Afro-Caribbean groups in Harlem. Recorded albums with Gil Evans (1959) and Sonny Rollins (1962, playing calypsos); live work with Steve Lacy quartet (1963–4), Archie Shepp, Don Cherry etc. Then out of music for long period before returning (1980s) with, among others, the Jazz Doctors (including saxophonist Frank Lowe and violinist Billy Bang). Charles's straightahead but admirably loose style was a useful foil for the early Cecil Taylor and proved highly suitable to a number of different contexts. [BP]

Jazz Doctors, *Intensive Care* (1983), Cadillac

Charles, Ray (Ray Charles Robinson), vocals, piano, arranger (and alto sax). b. Albany, Georgia, 23 September 1932. Blind from childhood, began playing piano self-taught. Brought up in Florida and attended blind school, becoming freelance entertainer at 15. Travelled to West Coast, formed his McSon trio in Seattle (1949) and made first recordings. Also recorded using front-line band of Lowell Fulson, with whom he toured (1950–1), and backed Guitar Slim on record (1953). Otherwise working as a single (1951–4), followed by formation of 7-piece band, backing Ruth Brown (1954). Played for dances, r & b package shows, appeared at Newport festival, 1958, with own band after recording with top jazz soloists. Increasing popular success with white audiences led to creation of own big band (1961) which, with backing vocalists and featured singers such as Betty Carter (1961) and Billy Preston (1966–8), toured internationally. Still maintaining links with jazz in occasional recordings, appeared at Kool Festival, 1985.

Most of Charles's records from around 1960 have extremely middle-of-the-road accompaniment with massed strings and heavenly choirs, but his ability to sing in his own way anything from 'You are my Sunshine' to 'Georgia on my Mind' proves the universality of jazz singing in the tradition of Louis Armstrong and Billie Holiday. But Ray Charles also merits a place for his instrumental work. The same kind of far-reaching fusion created by his vocal style (gospel + blues + jazz = soul) occurred equally effortlessly in his keyboard playing, even though this never made the same impact as his singing. Charles's 1950s instrumental albums provided a considerable boost to the recognition of gospel's influence on hard bop, and indeed on the swing and r & b bands that inspired the hard boppers in the first place. [BP]

Charles/Milt Jackson, *Soul Meeting* (1957), Atlantic; *Live in Concert* (1964), ABC

Charles, Teddy (Theodore Charles Cohen), vibraharp, composer. b. Chicopee Falls, Massachusetts, 13 April 1928. Worked on vibes (also piano or drums) with various big bands including Benny Goodman, Chubby Jackson, Artie Shaw and Buddy DeFranco (1948–51, all as 'Teddy Cohen'). From 1951, small-group activity with Oscar Pettiford, Roy Eldridge, Slim Gaillard etc., while studying composition. Led own quartet from 1953, and associated with Jazz Composers' Workshop (1953–5) with Teo Macero, Charles Mingus; appeared with this group at Newport festival (1955, 1956) and wrote arrangements for Miles Davis album produced by Mingus (1955). Having produced his own albums in 1953 (with Wardell Gray, Shorty Rogers etc.), specialized in production from 1956; as well as conventional line-ups such as Pepper Adams/Donald Byrd (since reissued as by Herbie Hancock) and Booker Little/Booker Ervin, he often created unusual groups, for instance three trumpets and rhythm, or John Coltrane and two baritones, or *The Soul of Jazz Percussion*. These sessions often featured Charles's own writing and were rather less arid than his experimental work of the early 1950s, but his vibes playing was frequently more interesting than his arranging. [BP]

Charles/Shorty Rogers, *Collaboration: West* (1953), Prestige/OJC

Charlesworth, Dick (Richard), clarinet, tenor sax. b. Sheffield, Yorkshire, 8 January 1932. He moved to London in 1952 and played in dance and jazz bands including Jim Weller's in 1956 before forming his own, Dick Charlesworth's Jazzmen, that year. Twelve months later they won the South London Jazz Band Championship, turned professional in 1959 and soon after signed a recording contract with EMI. Featuring a bowler-hatted, pinstriped band uniform and a re-marketed image as Dick Charlesworth's City Gents, the band became comfortably successful (although it never reached the Trad boom heights of Barber, Bilk and Ball) and featured excellent sidemen such as Dave Keir (tmb) and Robert Masters (later a highly successful agent) playing mellifluous trumpet. Charlesworth's musical policy featured interesting, often out-of-the-way repertoire and remained well known until the Beatles invasion of 1962 laid the jazz world temporarily to waste. Charlesworth worked on P & O liners, 1964–9, then ran a music bar in Spain which became a regular stopping-off point for jazzmen in transit. From 1976 when he came home he played all over London's club and pub scene. [DF]

Chase, Tommy (Thomas), drums. b. Manchester, 22 March 1947. Initially inspired by Clifford Brown track 'Clifford's Axe', Chase is a largely self-taught drummer. Professional at 17, playing in summer shows, cabaret and on cruise liners. Based in London from early 1970s, gigging regularly with guitarist Dave Cliff, saxist Ray Warleigh, Art Themen and Harry Beckett; formed own sextet including these four (1975). Worked with visiting Americans Joe Albany, Al Haig and Jon Eardley, also recording with latter and playing with him in Germany. Own quartet featuring saxist Alan Barnes (1983–6) gained considerable success with younger listeners. Won Musical Trades Association award (1984) and *Wire* awards for Best Group/Best Album (1986). Chase's drumming has been influenced by Max Roach, Art Blakey, Elvin Jones (also Kenny Clarke, Philly Joe Jones, Roy Haynes); other personal favourites include Sonny Rollins, Roland Kirk, Duke Ellington, Art Tatum. A tireless and unwavering campaigner for acoustic bebop, he says, 'I'm tired of playing complicated figures, now I just want to swing like mad.' [BP]

Drive! (1985), Paladin

Chase chorus, see FOURS

Cheatham, Doc (Adolphus Anthony), trumpet. b. Nashville, Tennessee, 13 June 1905. He worked first in vaudeville theatres backing visiting blues singers (including both Clara and Bessie Smith) and playing for burlesque shows. By 1926, in Chicago, he was still occasionally trying saxophone, until the influence of Louis Armstrong and Freddie Keppard took over;

soon after, on trumpet now, he was recording with Ma Rainey and soaking up music. After short stays with Bobby Lee and Wilbur de Paris he travelled to Europe with Sam Wooding (good friend Tommy Ladnier shared the trumpet solos), then came back to New York to work with Marion Hardy: recalls Dickie Wells, 'He was such a *nice* trumpet player, beautiful tone!' Cheatham – a slim, trim almost frail man – played lead for the next ten years of his life (with McKinney's Cotton Pickers and, 1933–9, with Cab Calloway), but then had a breakdown. So he took a rest before joining Teddy Wilson and then Eddie Heywood, both of whom used Cheatham's delicate style to great advantage. By 1945, out of sympathy with bebop, he took a job with the Post Office, worked out some dental problems, opened a New York teaching studio and took stock in general. He was soon back and, perhaps surprisingly, playing the jazz solos with a variety of Latin-American bands including Ricardo Rey's, Marcelino Guerra's, Machito's and Perez Prado's. By the 1950s he was swinging again, working for Wilbur de Paris (playing second to Sidney), Sammy Price and Herbie Mann, then led his own band for five years at Broadway's International Hotel. 1966–7 with Benny Goodman, then Cheatham came back to work with Red Balaban at Your Father's Moustache and in the 1970s began to build an international soloist's reputation as a result of records, touring and a general public feeling that his career was worth celebrating. The perfect father-figure for classic jazz, charming, urbane, musically faultless, Cheatham is a spiritual brother to Louis Armstrong as his late records attest. [DF]

The Fabulous Doc Cheatham (1983), Parkwood

See Dance, Stanley, *The World of Swing* (Scribner's, 1974, repr. Da Capo, 1979)

Cherry, Don (Donald E.), trumpet, piano, organ, wooden flutes, doussn'gouni, melodica, voice. b. Oklahoma City, 18 November 1936. Started on trumpet at junior high school. As a teenager, played piano in r & b band with drummer Billy Higgins. 1956, they began playing with Ornette Coleman. 1959, Cherry and Coleman spent the summer at the Lenox School of Music, and in the autumn made their New York début in a quartet with Charlie Haden and Higgins. Cherry worked with Coleman, also recording a series of seminal albums with him, until the end of 1961. He played briefly with John Coltrane, Steve Lacy and Sonny Rollins. 1963, founder member of the New York Contemporary Five, which included Archie Shepp and John Tchicai and which toured and recorded in Europe before disbanding in early 1964. Cherry returned to Europe with Albert Ayler, then formed a group with Gato Barbieri which lasted until autumn 1966, recording in Europe and New York. He recorded with George Russell at a concert in Stuttgart, 1965; worked with Giorgio Gaslini in Milan the following year. The rest of the 1960s he spent gypsy fashion, wandering the world playing and soaking up its music; as well as commuting between Europe and the USA, he travelled to Africa and Asia. He and his wife Moki eventually settled in Sweden in the early 1970s, living in a schoolhouse, working an organic farm, doing music programmes for children on radio and TV and taking music workshops on the road to schools.

From the mid-1960s Cherry became more and more deeply involved in ethnic music, studying techniques and learning to play instruments from different cultures such as Tibet, China, Africa and India. In Sweden he acquired a doussn'gouni, a hunter's guitar from Mali, with a calabash soundbox, six strings and a rattle, and began to feature it regularly. 1973, he and his wife (voice and percussion) gave a concert of Organic Music Theatre in Central Park, New York, as part of the Newport Jazz Festival. They covered the stage with multi-coloured banners and involved several children in the performance. Percussion, voices and Cherry's trumpet were utilized in an unclassifiable mélange.

From the early 1970s he and his wife and their associates rarely played clubs, but divided their time between working with children, teaching and playing festivals. Cherry explained: 'When we travel in Europe, Moki does the environments for the show, trying to work on all the senses, with incense for smells, and tapestries you can touch and see. Moki has made tapestries with the songs on them so that people can learn to sing them.' When working with children, Cherry tried to introduce them to the music of different lands, from Africa to India to Tibet to Brazil.

He still kept in touch with the USA, and in 1975 played a two-week engagement at the Five Spot in New York with a quartet which included Billy Higgins, Hakim Jami (bass), Frank Lowe (reeds), with Cherry also playing some electric piano as well as trumpet. 1976, he began working and recording with a group of his (and Ornette Coleman's) old associates: Dewey Redman (reeds), Charlie Haden (bass) and Ed Blackwell (dms). Their first album for ECM was entitled *Old and New Dreams*, and this became the name of the band which toured, played some festivals and recorded a live album, *Playing* (ECM), in 1980. The music of this group featured many of the old Ornette Coleman compositions, but also pieces written by Cherry, Coleman and Haden.

In the later 1970s he began a fruitful association with Collin Walcott, who was also steeped in the ethnic musics of the world, and who played sitar, tabla and percussion. 1977, Cherry played on Walcott's album *Grazing Dreams* (ECM), which is one of the most perfect fusions of elements from ethnic music with the harmonies and structural sense of jazz. On this small masterpiece, Cherry's playing on trumpet, wood flute and doussn'gouni, is given superb

Don Cherry

coherence and pith by the clearly defined contexts. 1978, he and Walcott formed a trio with Brazilian percussionist Nana Vasconcelos, calling it Codona. They played concerts and eventually recorded three albums on ECM.

1982, he received a (US) National Endowment grant to work in Watts, where he was brought up, visiting many schools and introducing black children to the music of Thelonious Monk, Charlie Parker and Ornette Coleman.

Don Cherry is a natural and an original in both his music and his life. Everything he does seems to come directly from the heart, with the same immediate response as birdsong, and in this sense he is a man at one with himself; and his art seems to be an attempt to become at one with the world outside himself. Like all the main innovators in jazz, he is also a fairly prolific composer. From the moment he appeared on the scene with Coleman at the end of the 1950s he showed a virtually fully-formed original trumpet style, and his playing has always been full of lyricism and freshly honed phrases. He always swings, and if he is sometimes rather diffuse, it is a benign fault coming out of his 'street music' philosophy of the social and disarming function of music. He says, 'I'm a world musician', and he calls his music 'Primal Music'. He is a major force in two areas: as a trumpet stylist he has had a huge influence; and he is one of the pioneers of the growing movement in jazz to know and absorb vital elements of ethnic music. [IC]

Musicisangam Europa; Cherry/Ed Blackwell, *El Corazon* (1982), ECM; *Don Cherry* (1975), Horizon; *Hear and Now* (1976), Atlantic; *Symphony for Improvisers* (1966), Blue Note; *Relativity Suite* (1973), JCOA; 11 albums with Coleman, including *Change of the Century* (1960), Atlantic; with Coltrane, *The Avant-Garde* (1960), Atlantic; with Jazz Composers' Orchestra, *Escalator Over The Hill* (1971), JCOA

Chescoe, Laurie, drums, bandleader. b. London, 18 April 1933. He worked professionally from the late 1950s in a wide variety of classic-style jazz bands from Monty Sunshine's (1960–4) and Bruce Turner's (1965) to Bob Wallis's (1966–70) and George Webb's Dixielanders in their 1970s re-formation. By the middle of that decade he was a regular colleague of pianist Keith Nichols and, as well as working with longstanding groups such as the Black Bottom Stompers, had joined Nichols's Midnite Follies Orchestra as well as playing on the pianist's touring shows, regularly for Alan Elsdon's band and more and more often organizing his own groups featuring Alan Elsdon (tpt) and Dave Jones (clt). By the mid-1980s, Chescoe – who works by day – was featured with Nichols's newest presentation (a re-creation of King Oliver's Dixie Syncopators), with the Midnite Follies Orchestra on their occasional appearances and with the Alex Welsh Memorial Band: he had worked with Welsh for the last two years of the trumpeter's career (1981–3). A Cliff Leeman-style player who delights in the drum philosophies of such seminal figures as Baby Dodds and plays with all their attention to shades of sound and dynamic, Chescoe upholds fine traditions of Dixieland jazz drumming that could easily disappear. [DF]

Midnite Follies Orchestra, *Hotter than Hades* (1978), EMI.

Chicago has at least three distinct musical connotations, even leaving aside the fact that most of what we regard as classic New Orleans jazz was actually recorded in Chicago, by musicians who moved there in the 1910s and 1920s. This, however, is not what is meant by 'Chicago jazz', but rather the closely related style played by the first generation of white musicians to pick up on the New Orleans innovations. Often considered to be more solo-oriented and less relaxed rhythmically, the music of Jimmy McPartland and others (and of the later Eddie Condon groups) became sufficiently influential, even on the 1950s Armstrong All Stars, to have more adherents world-wide than the 'authentic' New Orleans style.

Though seldom acknowledged, Chicago was also in the 1930s the home of a particular jump-band music (typified by the Harlem Hamfats) which combined jazz horns and drums with blues singer-guitarists. This style, influencing the output of even Big Bill Broonzy, led to the post-war outcropping of 'Chicago blues' which, through the work of its guitarists and bassists, had a considerable impact on later rock and jazz-rock; likewise, horn players who have worked in blues bands, and the freedom and power of vocalists like Muddy Waters, also had an effect on 'free jazz'.

For while it is true that Chicago had a thriving bebop scene, particularly strong in tenor players such as Gene Ammons, it is not known for a regional accent in bebop. In the free jazz area, however, Chicago has made another celebrated contribution and, during the second half of the 1960s, Anthony Braxton, Muhal Richard Abrams and the members of the Art Ensemble were putting things together in a way that was not being done elsewhere. Now, however, the Chicago style is so widely imitated that it has become virtually the main thread of American free jazz in the last 20 years. [BP]

Chilton, John, trumpet, fluegelhorn, author, leader, arranger, composer. b. London, 16 July 1932. He came to prominence with Bruce Turner's Jump Band (1958–63); with Turner he recorded classics such as *Jumping at the NFT*, made a film, *Living Jazz*, and toured consistently. Later in the 1960s he worked with big bands led by Alex Welsh and Mike Daniels, led his own band, the Swing Kings (1966–8), which toured with Americans such as Charlie Shavers, and opened his own Bloomsbury Book Shop in

Holborn, London, selling to jazz collectors. In 1971, with Max Jones, he produced his first big book, *Louis*, a detailed biography/critique of Louis Armstrong: a year later came his *Who's Who of Jazz: Storyville to Swing Street* (4th edn 1985), a painstaking factual encyclopedia of jazzmen born before 1920 which quickly became a standard source. Then, in quick succession, came a wealth of accurate and definitive studies, including *Billie's Blues* (1975), *McKinney's Music* (1978), *Teach Yourself Jazz* (1979), *A Jazz Nursery: the Story of the Jenkins Orphanage Bands* (1980) and *Stomp Off Let's Go!: the Story of Bob Crosby's Bobcats* (1983). Such an output would grace a full-time author, but all through this prolific period Chilton played busily as musical director for George Melly, a partnership which began informally at a London pub, New Merlins Cave, and in 1974 (after a best-selling LP, *Nuts!*, Warner Bros) turned into the most successful jazz act of the decade. Throughout the period Chilton's organizational powers and regular songwriting have been a potent force behind Melly's throne; his trumpet playing (a crackling-to-fractured mix of Cootie Williams, Rex Stewart and Armstrong) has been constantly featured on TV, radio, records, and very successfully in America, Australia and the Far East at all the major jazz venues and festivals. He is a jazz historian to set alongside Leonard Feather and Stanley Dance. [DF]

George Melly, *Makin' Whoopee* (1982), PRT

Chisholm, George, trombone. b. Glasgow, 29 March 1915. He joined Teddy Joyce in 1936, Ambrose in 1938 and was soon leading his own groups for recording sessions, by then it was clear that, in Leonard Feather's words, Chisholm was 'a superlative musician with an ageless style'. It showed up to advantage on sides that the young trombonist made with Fats Waller in London in 1938, and by 1941 he was leading the trombone section and arranging for the Squadronaires, Britain's RAF-based dance orchestra (his duets with Eric Breeze became a central feature of the show). After the war Chisholm freelanced, then in 1952 joined the BBC Show Band where – on the BBC's revolutionary Goon Show – he was able to indulge his natural gift for comedy, often taking speaking roles (he remained a close friend and occasional partner to comedian Spike Milligan); in 1956 he played alongside Louis Armstrong at London's Royal Festival Hall (for the Hungarian Relief Fund concert) and soon after began a long TV residency with his Jazzers on the hugely popular Black and White Minstrel Show doing comedy routines. The decision then caused a certain amount of pompous controversy among jazz critics: in retrospect it was an enjoyable natural extension of Chisholm's flair for comedy. Throughout the 1960s and 1970s Chisholm recorded for himself, played clubs, concerts and in studios, and by the later decade was touring in tribute concerts to Louis Armstrong on London's South Bank and countrywide, leading his own Gentlemen of Jazz, guesting at US jazz festivals such as Colorado; after heart bypass surgery in 1982 he was back to full strength, touring with Keith Smith in mid-decade and in 1985 was awarded the OBE. Chisholm's majestic tone, athletic, biting style and use of what became known as Chisholm intervals (based on the emphasis of lower neighbour tones in his lines) are an irreplaceable feature of British jazz; he is one of the few truly international-standard jazz figures (along with Sandy Brown, Kenny Baker and Peter King) to emerge from Great Britain. [DF]

In a Mellow Mood (1974), Peerless-Velvet.

Chittison, Herman, piano. b. Flemingsburg, Kentucky, 1909; d. Cleveland, Ohio, 8 March 1967. Early on in his career he worked with Zack Whyte's famous territory band (it also contained, at various times, stars such as Sy Oliver and Quentin Jackson) and stayed for three years until 1931. Working as accompanist to singers Ethel Waters and Adelaide Hall, as well as comedian Stepin Fetchit, he attracted great attention and by 1934 was starring with bandleader Willie Lewis in Paris as well as touring with Louis Armstrong. (His contribution to Armstrong's show was a crowd-pleaser and, said agent N. J. Canetti, may have been the cause of the trumpeter's premature return to New York, an uncharitable thought which nevertheless gives some idea of Chittison's solo powers.) After he left Lewis in 1938, Chittison took ex-members of Lewis's band, including Bill Coleman, to Egypt for a two-year stay, returning home in 1941; for the last 25 years of his life he led his own trio around New York, helped by a weekly appearance on a popular series, *Casey – Crime Photographer*, which ran for seven years on CBS radio. He recorded regularly too, often in a likeable 'pop' format recalling Eddie Heywood: his last album was in 1964, three years before his death. [DF]

Willie Lewis and his Entertainers (1935–7), Swing Disques (double).

Chorus In jazz parlance, 'a chorus' means once through the entire tune, whether this is 12 bars, 32 bars or longer. This use of the term dates from the days when every popular song was published with a verse (usually of a throw-away nature and usually omitted) followed by 'the chorus'.

The word also became an abbreviation for solo chorus, as in 'X's brilliant chorus on Y's otherwise boring version of "Z".' As soon as this usage was established, it was applied to any length of solo, so that X's chorus might in fact last for several choruses. [BP]

Christensen, Jon, drums. b. Oslo, 20 March 1943. Self-taught. 1960, won the Norwegian

Jazz Amateur Competition. 1961–5, played at clubs and festivals in Norway with local and international musicians, including Bud Powell, Dexter Gordon, Sonny Stitt, Don Ellis, Don Byas, Jan Garbarek, Karin Krog and Kenny Dorham. 1964, appeared at Antibes festival with Karin Krog. 1966–8, played in Sweden with Monica Zetterlund, the Steve Kuhn trio and George Russell's sextet and big band. 1970–3, with Jan Garbarek quartet. 1970–85, made some 30 LPs on ECM and toured with Garbarek, Terje Rypdal, Eberhard Weber, Ralph Towner, Enrico Rava, Keith Jarrett, Miroslav Vitous, John Surman. 1967, won the Norwegian Jazz Federation's 'Buddy' prize. 1973–84, the Polish magazine *Jazz Forum* voted him No. 1 on drums every year. Christensen has every virtue as a drummer; great rhythmic power and extreme sensitivity. He can handle any area, rock, jazz, free, with immense musicality, and always projects without ever obtruding. During the 1970s he was a member of three of the most important and influential groups in jazz at that time: Keith Jarrett's European quartet, Eberhard Weber's Colours and Jan Garbarek's quartet; and he played a key role on some classic albums. Favourite drummers are Buddy Rich, Art Blakey, Elvin Jones, Philly Joe Jones, Tony Williams and Jack DeJohnette, and other influences are George Russell, Gil Evans, Wayne Shorter, Garbarek and Jarrett. [IC]

With George Russell big band and sextet, Steve Kuhn, Miroslav Vitous; with Garbarek, *Dansere* (1975); *Afric Pepperbird* (1970); *Sart* (1972); *Witchi Tai To* (1973); *Paths – Prints* (1982); with Jarrett, *Belonging* (1975); *My Song* (1978); *Nude Ants* (1980); with Towner, *Solstice* (1975); with Weber, *Yellow Fields* (1975), all ECM

Christian, Charlie (Charles), guitar. b. Dallas, Texas, 29 July 1916; d. New York, 2 March 1942. Christian, the seminal influence on modern jazz guitarists until the 1960s, was professional by 1934 in the Oklahoma City area, toured with Anna Mae Winburn's band, Alphonso Trent (on bass), Lloyd Hunter and Nat Towles, and by 1937 was specializing on electric guitar, often with Lesley Sheffield's band, meanwhile jamming in Benny Hooper's basement on Walton Street with another legend, tenorist Dick Wilson. John Hammond introduced him to Benny Goodman on a recording date to little avail, but the same night Hammond and bassist Artie Bernstein smuggled Christian's amplifier – and later Christian himself, in his purple suit – on stage at the Victor Hugo Hotel, Beverley Hills, for a 90-minute version of 'Rose Room': Goodman hired Christian there and then at $150 a week as the newest star with his sextet. The guitarist's appetite for music was as inexhaustible as it was for girls, goodtime and late nights. Soon after, Minton's Playhouse, the shrine of bebop, managed by Teddy Hill, was flourishing; Christian was brought to the club by pianist Mel Powell and became a fixture. Every Monday, when the Goodman band took a night off from their residency at Pennsylvania Hotel in Meadowbrook, NY, the young guitarist would create immortal music there (some of it recorded and regularly issued since). Most other nights he was there after work and frequently played all day too, just for good measure. 'Later when I was in New York,' says Mary Lou Williams, 'I'd look Charlie up and we'd go to a basement room in the Dewey Square hotel usually around ten in the morning and sometimes we'd jam, just the two of us, until eleven at night. It smelled down there and the rats ran over our feet and only ten keys on the piano played – but we just didn't pay any attention!'

In October 1940 Christian was coughing persistently and Goodman's doctors had spotted TB on one lung but touring continued until he was taken ill on a tour of the Midwest and admitted first to New York's Bellevue Hospital, then to the Seaview Sanatorium on Staten Island. Visiting 'wellwishers' smuggled in marijuana, drink and even girls, and in early 1942 smuggled Christian out to a party: he contracted pneumonia and died. 'He was a sweet loving man with few defences against the world', remembers Hammond. 'His only resource was music and when he was unable to play he was unable to live.' Christian's funeral was in Harlem: he was buried in the cheapest coffin available. But his influence – typically enough – on a generation of then-modern guitarists was huge. He was the first to establish a mature vocabulary for electric guitar which younger players such as Jim Hall and Barney Kessel had cause to be grateful for, and it was only with the emergence of a rock-based guitar vocabulary in the 1960s that Christian's approach fell into historic perspective. Dizzy Gillespie, who loved him, makes a less fashionable yet perceptive point: 'Charlie was *bad*! He knew the blues and he knew how to do the swing. He had a great sense of harmony and he lifted up the guitar to a solo voice in jazz . . . but he never showed me a total knowledge of the harmonic possibilities of the instrument.' However, Christian's flowing lines, pawky sound and rhythmic grace (very like his friend and influence Lester Young) carried him to jazz immortality. [DF]

Live 1939–41, Festival

See Shapiro, Nat, and Hentoff, Nat, *The Jazz Makers* (Rinehart, 1957, repr. Da Capo, 1979)

Christie, Ian, see CHRISTIE, KEITH.

Christie, Keith, trombone. b. Blackpool, 6 January 1931; d. London, 16 December 1980. He began his high-pressure career as an explosive revivalist with Humphrey Lyttelton's band (his features of the period such as 'The Dormouse', written by Lyttelton, are fondly remembered), then moved on to form the Christie Brothers Stompers (with brother Ian on clarinet), but by the mid-1950s was rapidly broadening his approach. In 1953 he was ready to join John Dankworth's highly modern-for-the-period big band, then Tommy Whittle, then freelanced around London's club scene and by 1957 was partnering Don Lusher in Ted Heath's unfaultable trombone section. After he left Heath, Christie moved into studio work and played regularly with Tubby Hayes's big band; 1970–2, he toured Europe with Benny Goodman, when not continuing a wide-based variety of activities which veered from work with Kenny Wheeler's big band to recreating Jelly Roll Morton's Red Hot Peppers (under pianist Max Harris) for American choreographer Twyla Tharp. By the late 1970s he was working in the London production of the jazz-based show *Bubbling Brown Sugar*: there he suffered an accident one night when he fell off the raised theatre set. He returned to work after he recovered, including concerts with the *Best of British Jazz* package and others, but alcoholism had claimed him and he died in 1980. His brother Ian (b. 24 June 1927) became a respected Fleet Street television critic after early years with Humphrey Lyttelton, Mick Mulligan and the Christie Brothers Stompers, among others, and in the 1980s returned to regular performing with Graham Tayar's Crouch End All Stars and recording with Wally Fawkes. [DF]

Humphrey Lyttelton, *A Tribute to Humph* (1949–50), Dormouse

Chromatic The opposite of diatonic, in which only the notes of a specific major or minor scale are used. In diatonic music, therefore, the appearance of notes outside the starting scale entails modulation to another key, as in a song like 'All the Things you Are', whereas chromatic chords allow the use of non-scale notes without changing key.

Chromatic chords (especially the diminished chord) were part of jazz as early as the 1920s. In fundamentally diatonic chord-sequences, most of the passing chords in the original version and the substitute chords inserted by jazz musicians are liable to be chromatic. Their use, however, has been less than essential in jazz, although more fashionable at some periods than others, and late 1940s examples such as Bud Powell's 'Dance of the Infidels' (or even John Coltrane's late 1950s pieces of the 'Giant Steps' vintage) are far more chromatically complex than the average jazz material of the period.

What is important to note is the frequent independence of melodic improvisation from the underlying chords. As early as the 1920s Louis Armstrong implied passing chords which were not used by the rhythm-section at hand, whereas King Oliver would diatonically ignore a passing chord if he felt like it. Broadly speaking, Armstrong led to Hawkins, Parker and Coltrane, while Oliver inspired Lester Young, Ornette Coleman etc., and neither school plays 'on the chords' in the way we have been brought up to believe. In fact, both of these different tendencies are present in the free chromatic playing (and chromatic free playing) of more recent times, which is a forcible reminder that the root meaning of the word 'chromatic' is not to do with rules but with colouring. [BP]

Circular breathing A technique used by some players of wind instruments, usually reed players, but also occasionally brass players. It consists of breathing in through the nose while the cheeks push air out through the instrument, thus enabling the player to produce an unbroken column of air. This means that a note can be held indefinitely, because a player need not pause in order to breathe. The technique has only a limited artistic use, because most music needs 'breathing' pauses in order to come fully alive. [IC]

Clare, Kenny, drums. b. UK, 8 June 1929; d. 21 December 1984. A consummate big-band drummer. 1949–54, worked with Oscar Rabin band; 1954–5, with Jack Parnell; 1955–60, with the Johnny Dankworth orchestra; 1962–5, the Ted Heath band; 1967–72, with the Clarke–Boland band; 1973–4, with a big band led by the German trombonist/composer Peter Herbolzheimer. Clare also worked with the Bobby Lamb–Ray Premru orchestra. He played on a superb LP with Ella Fitzgerald, *Can't Buy me Love*, and he became the permanent UK drummer for Henry Mancini, involved in all the 'Pink Panther' film scores. He also played on film soundtracks scored by Michel Legrand. In the 1980s he was still working with John Dankworth and Cleo Laine. Earlier he had spent three years in the USA working with Basie, Herman and Ellington while backing singer Tom Jones. [IC]

With Lamb–Premru, Dankworth, Stephane Grappelli; with Clarke–Boland, *Off Limits* (1970), Polydor; with Herbolzheimer, *Live at Ronnie Scott's* (1974), MPS

Clark, Garnet, piano. b. Washington, DC, *c.* 1914; d. France, 1938. He was a child prodigy who at the age of 16 was playing piano and arranging for Tommy Myles's band in Washington. He came to New York in 1933, worked at Pod's and Jerry's Club that year and caused a sensation, but in 1935 emigrated to Europe where – with Benny Carter in Paris – he briefly joined Willie Lewis's Entertainers and with Bill Coleman and Django Reinhardt made his one and only record session (apart, says Dan Morgenstern, from an 'obscure Alex Hill big band session' the year previously). After solo work and time as accompanist for Adelaide Hall touring Switzerland, Clark went mad, was committed to an insane asylum and died at 24. [DF]

Django Reinhardt and the American Jazz Giants (1935–8), Prestige

Kenny Clarke

Clark, Sonny (Conrad Yeatis), piano. b. Herminie, Pennsylvania, 21 July 1931; d. 13 January 1963. 1953, made record début on West Coast with Wardell Gray, then regular pianist with Buddy DeFranco, replacing Kenny Drew. 1957, settled in New York and participated in numerous album sessions, notably for Blue Note Records. Much admired by other pianists – Bill Evans's 'NYC's No Lark' was titled in memory of Clark, whose premature death was hastened by alcohol abuse, an attempt to counteract dependency on heroin. Both his right-hand lines and driving accompaniments contain hints of Horace Silver and Hampton Hawes, although arrived at independently, and his rhythmic ebullience and melodic sense are more than a match for either of them. [BP]

Leapin' and Lopin' (1961), Blue Note

Clarke, Kenny (Kenneth Spearman, 'Klook') (aka Liaqat Ali Salaam), drums, composer (and vibraphone etc.). b. Pittsburgh, Pennsylvania, 9 January 1914; d. 26 January 1985. After gigging locally, worked briefly with Roy Eldridge (1935) and then with Jeter–Pillars band. In New York joined Edgar Hayes (1937–8), touring Europe with him and making records under own name in Stockholm (1938). 1939, with Claude Hopkins; 1940–1, Teddy Hill band; 1941, led house group at Minton's, using Thelonious Monk and encouraging advanced sitters-in such as Dizzy Gillespie, Charlie Christian, Charlie Parker etc. Briefly with Louis Armstrong, Ella Fitzgerald band (both 1941), then Benny Carter sextet (1941–2); in both the latter, worked alongside Gillespie. 1943, with Henry 'Red' Allen's group in Chicago, with Coleman Hawkins and under own name in New York. After army service in Europe, played with Gillespie big band (1946, European tour 1948). Remained in Paris several months before working with Tadd Dameron (New York 1948–9, Paris Jazz Fair, 1949). Spent more time in France, where he married, and played in US from 1951 with Billy Eckstine and with Milt Jackson, in trio with John Lewis which also backed Parker (1951–2). Recordings by Jackson led to formation of Modern Jazz Quartet, Clarke leaving in 1955 because of freelance gigging and recording; in the jazz record boom of the mid-1950s he cut well over 100 albums in the space of a year.

1956, settled in France, doing much studio work and live appearances with visiting Americans including Miles Davis (1957) and Jazz from Carnegie Hall group (1958). Played regularly with Bud Powell and Oscar Pettiford (later Pierre Michelot), known unofficially as the Three Bosses (1959–60). Then worked opposite Powell with own organ/guitar/drums trio, an instrumentation he maintained for several years (appearing in England with organist Eddie Louiss, 1967; with Mike Carr, 1978). Also ran intermittent big band co-led by Francy Boland (1961–72) whose surprisingly stable all-star line-up included, over the years, Johnny Griffin, Tony Coe, Ronnie Scott, Benny Bailey, Art Farmer, Ake Persson, Jimmy Woode and second drummer Kenny Clare; known initially through records and radio transcriptions, the band also undertook (from 1966) many live appearances and cut one live album. Clarke continued to freelance, recording, for instance, with Dexter Gordon (1963, 1973) and Gillespie (1974), and operated own teaching studio in Paris. Made brief return visits to US in 1972, for dedication of commemorative plaques on 52nd Street (1979) and for Kool Festival (1984). Living in semi-retirement near Paris at the time of his death.

Although originally prized as the founder of bebop drumming in the early 1940s, Kenny rapidly became the embodiment of straight-ahead playing. Even his sometimes insistent snare-drum commentary was essentially supportive, just as his bass-drum helped to underline rather than dictate: his full nickname 'Klookmop' describes a rim-shot on the snare followed by the bass-drum, and the sounds were used literally as punctuation of others' phrases rather than a statement in themselves. The fact that Clarke was initially inspired by Jo Jones (even down to the very idea of punctuating improvisations) doubtless explains why he was such a superb big-band drummer, never flashy or even noisy but always appropriate. But perhaps the greatest joy of his playing, most clearly audible on small-group recordings, was the pulse of his cymbal work, so marvellously alive yet effortless that fellow musicians called it his 'heartbeat'.

Clarke wrote a number of tunes that were recorded by others, but is especially noted as co-composer of two key early bop items, 'Epistrophy' (aka 'Fly Right') with Thelonious Monk and 'Salt Peanuts' with Dizzy Gillespie. Both pieces are built around the cross-rhythm of 3 against 4, which was the source of so much of the freedom of bebop. [BP]

Paris Be-bop Sessions (1948–50), Prestige; Milt Jackson, *Opus de Jazz* (1955), Savoy; *Kenny Clarke Meets the Detroit Jazzmen* (1956), Savoy; Clarke/Boland, *Live at Ronnie Scott's* (1969), MPS

Clarke, Stanley M., bass, bass guitar, keyboards. b. Philadelphia, 30 June 1951. Studied bass while at school, also at local music academy. Played with rock groups in late 1960s. 1970, spent six months with Horace Silver, then a year with Joe Henderson, followed by periods with Pharoah Sanders and Stan Getz. Clarke came to real national and international prominence with Chick Corea's Return to Forever, of which he was an original member. A master of both acoustic and electric basses, he was the new star in the early 1970s, winning polls in both categories. He soon had his own contract with CBS, and began to record a series of highly produced albums using some of the leading jazz, rock and Latin instrumentalists of the time. In the later 1970s and after, he made a series of joint albums with George Duke. He has done many international tours, appearing at festivals in the USA and Europe. Influences, Jimmy Blanton, Oscar Pettiford, Paul Chambers, Scott La Faro, John Coltrane, Miles Davis. [IC]

With Corea, Getz, Sanders, Dexter Gordon, Joe Farrell; *Stanley Clarke* (1974); *Journey to Love* (1975); *School Days* (1976); *Modern Man* (1978); *I Wanna Play for You* (1979), all CBS

Classic/Classical simply means generally acknowledged as great, but, since the ability to discern greatness requires historical distance, the term is applied retrospectively to specific styles (in drama, the visual arts and so on). In European music, 'classical' strictly refers to the heyday of the sonata form and the early symphonic style, but it is used loosely for all European composed music up to and including the time when the tradition began to fall apart after World War I; as a term covering this whole area, the expression 'straight music' actually has much to commend it.

'Classic jazz' is a description which recognizes that this same quality can be perceived in jazz – not only in the recorded masterpieces by the key figures of jazz history, but indeed in their whole approach; in some people's usage, 'classic jazz' refers only to music of the 1920s, while to many others it covers all music not influenced by bebop and its aftermath. However, the broader term 'black classical music' was coined in the 1960s to include everything from ragtime to the avant-garde, in order to distinguish this 'serious' music from more popular forms of black music. The distinction may perhaps be tainted with the élitism attached to the classical music of other continents, but it may also be a necessary antidote to the stereotypes of the US music industry. [BP]

Clayton, Buck (Wilbur Dorsey), trumpet, arranger, composer. b. Parsons, Kansas, 12 November 1911. One of the greatest classic trumpeters, he came from a musical family and was taught the trumpet by Bob Russell (from George E. Lee's band). In early years he worked for bands led by Duke Ellighew, Lavern Floyd in California, Charlie Echols (a famous territory band) and promoter Earl Dancer, and then at 21, went to China for two years leading his own band. Back in California he did the same at Frank Sebastian's Cotton Club, before joining

Buck Clayton

Count Basie at the Reno Club, Kansas City, in 1936 as a replacement for Hot Lips Page. By 1937 Basie's band was successful in New York, and Clayton stayed with them until he was called up, 1943–6; he spent his army years in bands led by pianist Dave Martin and Sy Oliver. On discharge he joined Norman Granz's newly formed Jazz at the Philharmonic show, playing the testing trumpet spectaculars Granz expected, and as he once joked, 'keeping Lester Young and Coleman Hawkins apart!' From 1947 he was back in New York and in 1948 played at the Savoy Ballroom with Jimmy Rushing's 'good-sounding band', which a decade later was to form the basis of a band with which he toured Europe. Then in the 1950s Clayton partnered Joe Bushkin in the first of the pianist's influential Embers quartets and worked at Lou Terrassi's with Tony Parenti ('he taught me Dixieland') and with two highly contrasted clarinettists, Benny Goodman and Mezz Mezzrow. He is best remembered at this period for a set of irreplaceable recordings in which he and kindred spirits from the swing era played chorus after chorus on standard tunes: the resulting *Buck Clayton Jam Sessions* (often one tune per side of an album) cemented the mainstream jazz boom and illustrated the value of extended performances in jazz recording.

In 1959 Clayton toured with a memorable team (including Emmett Berry, Dickie Wells and Buddy Tate) which visited England and recorded classic albums such as *Songs for Swingers*. In the 1960s he worked and recorded with Eddie Condon, toured Europe as a soloist (including tours of Britain with old friend Humphrey Lyttelton) and played jazz festivals, before the first signs of lip trouble surfaced in 1969. By the 1970s this became a disturbing recurring condition (during one operation Clayton had 39 stitches in his top lip) and the problem reached its height in 1979 when, after a month in Denmark, Clayton applied himself more to teaching, arranging (Lyttelton commissions included), guest lectures and directing recording sessions. [DF]

Buck Clayton Jam Session (1953), CBS

See Buck Clayton with Nancy Miller Elliott, *Buck Clayton's Jazz World* (Macmillan, 1986)

Cless, Rod (George Roderick), clarinet, saxes. b. Lennox, Iowa, 20 May 1907; d. New York City, 8 December 1944. He began his short, often brilliant, musical life learning violin, then cornet, then saxophone and clarinet, which he played in the high school orchestra. At school and university in Iowa he was a star pupil: good at maths, captain of the baseball team, a promising swimmer and diver, and after university he moved to Des Moines, where in 1925 the Wolverines played a six-week residency at Riverview Park Ballroom. Cless went there every night, befriended Frank Teschemacher, and two years later took the plunge in Chicago, rooming with Tesch and working with him in Charles Pierce's orchestra and others. There were a few records ('Jazz me blues' with Teschemacher, Krupa and Mezzrow is one), but Cless survived the Depression none too happily with teaching and playing for dance band bounces. By the début of Muggsy Spanier's brilliant band at the Sherman (Cless's work on their 16 Bluebird recordings is legendary and near unsurpassable) he had suffered a broken marriage (to Bud Freeman's sister) and was cultivating a drinking problem. For the next four years, however, Cless continued to work where he belonged, on the jazz circuit, with Art Hodes, Bobby Hackett, Wild Bill Davison and Max Kaminsky, among others. One night in early December 1944, Kaminsky noticed the clarinettist very drunk and offered to walk him home. Cless, always shy and retiring, refused and Kaminsky reluctantly let him go. Cless fell backwards over a balustrade on the way to his flat and died four days later at the age of 37. [DF]

Muggsy Spanier, *The Great Sixteen* (1939), RCA

Cleveland, Jimmy (James), trombone. b. Wartrace, Tennessee, 3 May 1926. A member of the Lionel Hampton band (1949–53), Cleveland afterwards became an in-demand freelance soloist on the New York recording scene. This provided entry into the general session world and, apart from a few months with the Quincy Jones band in Europe (1959–60), this has continued to be his mode of employment. He moved to Los Angeles at the end of the 1960s, and occasionally emerges in all-star West Coast big bands. In terms of technical prowess, Cleveland is probably the most dazzling disciple of J. J.

Johnson and, especially at slower tempos, shows a real flair for jazz solo work. [BP]

Introducing Jimmy Cleveland (1955), Emarcy

Clouds of Joy, see KIRK, ANDY

Clyne, Jeff, double bass, bass guitar. b. London, 29 January 1937. Mainly self-taught, but some short periods studying with orchestral players. 1955, bandsman in the 3rd Hussars. Played in London with Tony Crombie's Rockets and with Stan Tracey. 1958, joined the Jazz Couriers, a group co-led by Tubby Hayes and Ronnie Scott. Continued to work with Hayes's various groups for about ten years. In the early 1960s Clyne also worked with such avant-garde groups as SME and Amalgam, led by John Stevens and Trevor Watts. Mid-1960s, with the Stan Tracey quartet, playing on the classic *Under Milk Wood* album. In the later 1960s he worked with Gordon Beck, Tony Kinsey, John McLaughlin and Tony Oxley. Towards the end of the decade, took up bass guitar, joining Nucleus at its beginning in 1969, and staying until 1971. The group won first prize at the Montreux festival, 1970, playing at the Newport (USA) festival the same year, and at the Village Gate in New York. Also played with Keith Tippett, Gary Boyle's Isotope, and other UK musicians. 1976, with Pepi Lemer, formed Turning Point, a fusion band for which he composed much of the music. He has accompanied singers Blossom Dearie, Marion Montgomery, Annie Ross and Norma Winstone, and worked with many US musicians, including Lucky Thompson, Zoot Sims, Phil Woods, Jim Hall, Lockjaw Davis, Tal Farlow, and with the Belgian, Toots Thielemans. His favourite string bassists are Scott La Faro, Eddie Gomez and Marc Johnson, and on bass guitar, Jaco Pastorius. [IC]

With Hayes, *Tubby's Groove* (1959), Tempo; *100% Proof* (1966), Fontana; with Stan Tracey, *Under Milk Wood* (1965), Steam; with Watts/Stevens, *Springboard* (1966), Polydor; with Beck/McLaughlin, *Experiments with Pops* (1967), Major-Minor; with Beck/Tony Oxley, *Gyroscope* (1968), Morgan; with Nucleus, *Elastic Rock* (1970); *We'll Talk about it Later* (1970), both Vertigo; with Turning Point, *Creatures of the Night* (1977); *Silent Promise* (1978), both Gull

Cobb(s), Arnett(e) Cleophus, tenor sax. b. Houston, Texas, 10 August 1918. After working with the Texas-based bands of Chester Boone (1934–6) and Milt Larkin (1936–42, including West Coast period fronted by Floyd Ray), Cobb succeeded his former Larkin colleague Illinois Jacquet with Lionel Hampton (1942–7). Then formed his own 7-piece band until interrupted by serious illness (1948–50). Re-formed successfully, only to be disabled (1956) by car crash. Despite frequent hospitalization and permanent reliance on crutches, Cobb has continued to work in the 1970s and 1980s as soloist, making tours of Europe and taking part (1978 onwards) in all-star reunions with Hampton.

One of the many tenor saxists from Texas who share certain characteristics, such as emphatic phrasing and a vocalized tone capable of everything from seductive whispers to joyous shouts. Cobb, along with the somewhat younger Jacquet, virtually defined which aspects of the style were to be incorporated in the standard r & b approach, and the efforts of his own group, including the hit 'Smooth Sailing', were largely aimed at this audience. His more recent work has demonstrated convincingly that, without abandoning the virtues of r & b, he is more than capable of creating extended jazz solos. [BP]

The Fabulous Apollo Sessions (1947), Vogue; *The Wild Man from Texas* (1976), Black & Blue

Cobb, Jimmy (Wilbur James), drums. b. Washington, DC, 20 January 1929. After working with leading local musicians, toured with Earl Bostic (1951). Then with Dinah Washington, to whom he was married and acted as musical director (1951–5). Freelancing in New York before joining Cannonball Adderley (1957–8). Briefly with Stan Getz and Dizzy Gillespie until following Cannonball into Miles Davis group (1958–63). 1963–71, played regularly with Wynton Kelly until the latter's death. Accompanied Sarah Vaughan in 1970s, plus copious freelance work including 1981 tour of Japan with Kenny Drew and Kool Festival, 1985. Cobb's strength lies in his time playing, which is very much out of the Kenny Clarke school. Less of a living metronome than Clarke, he even sounds compelling while slowing down (especially when partnered by Paul Chambers in the Davis and Kelly groups). Although perfectly capable of well-constructed improvisations based largely on the snare drum, Cobb is rarely in the solo spotlight. But the way in which he uses accents to steady or to spur other soloists is a delight, not only to them but to the attentive listener. [BP]

Miles Davis, *Friday Night and Saturday Night at the Blackhawk* (1961), CBS

Cobham, Billy (William), drums, composer. b. Panama, 16 May 1944. Father a pianist; the family moved to New York City when Cobham was three. He began on percussion when still a toddler and at eight was adept enough to play publicly with his father. 1959, got his first complete drum set when he went to the High School of Music and Art. School friends included future jazz stars George Cables (piano), Jimmy Owens (tpt), Eddie Gomez (bass). After high school he went into the army, playing with a military band until his demobilization, 1968, when he joined the Horace Silver quintet.

Billy Cobham

Stayed with Silver for eight months, working in the USA and touring Europe, and Cobham's brilliant playing began to attract much attention. After leaving Silver, he became active as a session musician playing on film and TV soundtracks and advertising jingles. 1969–70, with Randy and Mike Brecker, formed and worked with a jazz-rock group called Dreams, and in the same period also played on some key Miles Davis albums including *Bitches Brew, Live-Evil, Jack Johnson.* 1971, founder-member of John McLaughlin's Mahavishnu Orchestra, which many consider to have been the greatest jazz-rock-fusion group of all. Cobham made a vital contribution to the group's music which was innovative and enormously influential.

When the first Mahavishnu Orchestra disbanded in 1973, Cobham began leading his own bands and recording under his own name, and his first album, *Spectrum,* is one of the classics of the jazz-rock genre. 1974–5, toured the USA and Europe with his own groups, playing concerts and major festivals. September 1975, formed a new group, Spectrum, which included George Duke (keyboards) and John Scofield (gtr), but in the later 1970s he stopped leading groups and freelanced. He also conducted drum clinics and did some teaching. Early 1980s, living in Switzerland and freelancing in Europe. 1984–5, played with German trumpeter Johannes Faber's group Consortium, recording one album with them. Left Consortium to lead his own group again, and recorded a highly successful album called *Warning.*

Cobham was the dominant drummer of the first half of the 1970s, spawning disciples and imitators all over the world. His playing combines great power and rhythmic clarity with a most musical sensitivity and subtlety. With the Mahavishnu Orchestra, the integration of his drums with the ensemble, and his magnificent handling of asymmetry (in both rhythms and structures), set new standards of excellence for everyone.

His early influences were Stan Levey, Sonny Payne, Gus Johnson, Jo Jones, and other inspirations include Miles Davis and Tito Puente. [IC]

With Silver, George Benson, Ron Carter, Deodato, Freddie Hubbard, Randy Weston, Milt Jackson and many others; with John McLaughlin, *My Goal's Beyond* (1970), Elektra Musician; with Mahavishnu Orchestra, *The Inner Mounting Flame* (1971); *Birds of Fire* (1972); *Between Nothingness and Eternity* (1972), all CBS; as leader, *Spectrum* (1973); *Total Eclipse* (1974); *Crosswinds* (1974); *Shabazz* (1975), all Atlantic; *Warning* (1985), GRP

Coe, Tony (Anthony George), saxes (mainly tenor), clarinet, bass clarinet, composer, b. Canterbury, Kent, 29 November 1934. Father played clarinet and sax. Private lessons on clarinet; played in school orchestra. Self-taught on sax. Studied composition with Donald Leggatt, Alfred Nieman, Richard Rodney Bennett, Vinco Globokar. 1953–6, National Service, playing in an army band. 1957–62, with Humphrey Lyttelton's band, touring the USA, UK and Europe. 1962–4, led his own group, and was featured soloist in 1964 with Birmingham Symphony Orchestra in *Rhapsody in Blue*. 1965, Count Basie offered him a place in the Basie band sax section and only red tape stopped him from taking up the offer. 1966–9, with the John Dankworth orchestra. 1967, joined the Kenny Clarke–Francy Boland band, staying until its break-up in 1973. During the 1970s he began working with Derek Bailey's Company, a free (abstract) improvisation group, and with Stan Tracey, as well as leading a series of groups of his own including (with Kenny Wheeler) Coe, Wheeler & Co, Three (with Bob Cornford), Coe, Oxley & Co and Axel. 1978, toured in Europe with the United Jazz and Rock Ensemble. 1983, toured the UK with the Mike Gibbs band. 1984, went to the USA to be one of the featured soloists on Bob Moses' album, *Visit with the Great Spirit*. He has also worked intermittently with Matrix, a small ensemble formed in 1971 by clarinettist Alan Hacker, which is not a jazz group but has a wide-ranging repertoire of early, classical and contemporary music. With Matrix, Coe has performed at the Edinburgh Festival, done broadcasts for the BBC and ORTF (Paris), and has played the music for films such as *The Devils* (1970) and *The Boy Friend* (1971). He is also the featured tenor sax soloist in Henry Mancini's music for the 'Pink Panther' films.

Coe is a player of astonishing versatility and brilliance. He began as a mainstreamer with Lyttelton and others, and was influenced by Barney Bigard and Johnny Hodges, but he very rapidly assimilated the innovations and stylistic developments of Charlie Parker and Paul Gonsalves, among others. Other inspirations are Alan Hacker, Debussy, Berg, Boulez, Louis Armstrong. Associating with Derek Bailey and others, he also became one of the finest exponents of free (abstract) improvisation. And he has remained catholic in his tastes and protean in his abilities: he can function with perfect ease in any of these categories – with a mainstream group playing a standard tune, with a post-Coltrane small group or a jazz-rock band, with a freely improvising ensemble, or with a European art music chamber group such as Matrix.

He is also an immensely gifted composer and has written many pieces over the years for his own groups, and also compositions for Matrix, the Danish Radio Big Band and the Metropole Orchestra and Skymasters in Holland. In 1975 he was given a composition grant by the Arts Council of Great Britain, and wrote *Zeitgeist*, an extended work deftly fusing jazz and rock elements with techniques from European art music, and deploying a very large orchestra including woodwind and cellos. The piece was first performed and recorded in 1976. The composer Richard Rodney Bennett has written: 'The dedication of the work to Alban Berg seems highly significant. Berg's music grew from a brilliantly fertile imagination controlled by a beautifully planned and articulated structure. *Zeitgeist* possesses precisely these admirable qualities.' Other compositions are 'Invention on an Ostinato Rhythm', 'The Jolly Corner', 'The Buds of Time'.

Coe is a sophisticate who, behind a smokescreen of vagueness, hides an incisive, chess-player's mind. By the mid-1980s he was generally considered to be the finest and most original living clarinettist in jazz, and one of the most individual stylists on tenor sax. He always improvises compositionally, with an overall view of the music and of his place in it. [IC]

An excellent example of his clarinet playing is on 'Rainbow 5' from Neil Ardley's *Kaleidoscope of Rainbows* (1975), Gull, and his tenor playing can be heard at its best on 'Lay-by', from Stan Tracey's big-band tribute to Ellington, *We Love You Madly* (1969), EMI, and on 'A Rose Without A Thorn' from *Stan Tracey Now* (1983),

Tony Coe

Steam; as leader, *Zeitgeist* (1976), EMI; *Tournée du Chat* (1982), Nato; Coe/Oxley/Laurence & Co, *Nutty on Willisau* (1983), Hat Art; *Le Chat se retourne* (1984), Nato; with Peter Herbolzheimer, *Jazz Gala Concert '79*, BID; with Deny Levaillant, *Barium Circus* (1984), Nato; with Tracey, *The Crompton Suite* (1982), Steam

Cohen, Alan, composer, arranger, soprano and tenor saxophone. b. London, 25 November 1934. A graduate of the Royal Academy of Music, he formed a band to appear at Ronnie Scott's Club in 1967 and quickly became known as an important British arranger supplying scores for Humphrey Lyttelton, the New Jazz Orchestra and American visitors such as Bing Crosby. In 1972 Cohen's recorded re-creation of Ellington's 'Black, Brown and Beige' suite (featuring British-based jazzmen like Olaf Vas, Harry Beckett and others) won high praise and he continued writing on a semi-freelance basis until 1978, when he formed the Midnite Follies Orchestra with Keith Nichols. The MFO, featuring Alan Elsdon, John Barnes, Pete Strange and others, recorded, toured and played major repertory concerts for six years after which Cohen arranged for Charlie Watts's Big Band (1985), wrote an extended composition for 'Music at Leasowe's Bank' (1986) and, that year, formed his own quintet, playing soprano saxophone. A technically able theorist with a strong ear to historic values in jazz, Cohen is one of the most important British arrangers. [DF]

Midnite Follies Orchestra, *Hotter than Hades* (1978), EMI

Cohn, Al(vin Gilbert), tenor sax, arranger. b. Brooklyn, New York City, 24 November 1925. A sideman with several big bands including Georgie Auld (1944–6), Buddy Rich (1947), Woody Herman (1948–9) and Artie Shaw (1949–50). Thereafter mainly busy as an arranger, making many jazz recordings in the 1950s and doing mostly non-jazz work since then. Has also appeared frequently as tenor soloist, and co-featured (from the late 1950s) with fellow Herman and Shaw colleague Zoot Sims or (in the 1980s) with his son, guitarist Joe Cohn.

As a jazz writer Al has created such notable big-band pieces as 'The Goof and I', used by both Rich and Herman, and the small-group numbers written for his own recordings include the standard 'The Underdog' (aka 'Ah Moore', dedicated to his then wife, singer Marilyn Moore). His work on tenor was sometimes compared unfavourably with that of Sims, but any apparent lack of fluency was amply compensated by the melodic intelligence of his Young-derived style. Since his recent return to more regular playing, the same quality has been emphasized by a more meaty tone reminiscent of such players as Buddy Tate. [BP]

The Progressive Al Cohn (1950–3), Savoy; *Nonpareil* (1981), Concord

Cole, Cozy (William Randolph), drums. b. East Orange, New Jersey, 17 October 1909; d. Columbus, Ohio, 29 January 1981. He was first inspired by Sonny Greer with Duke Ellington's band and moved to New York in 1926 where he worked as a barber and shipping clerk while building his musical career and taking lessons with Charlie Brooks, the pit drummer at Lincoln Theater. Always a swift-thinking and absorbed drummer, Cole never missed an opportunity to study (later he went to Juilliard and in 1954 opened a New York drum tuition school with Gene Krupa) and by the early 1930s he was building a big reputation with bands led by Blanche Calloway, Benny Carter at Connie's Inn, Willie Bryant (1935–6) and, from 1936, with Stuff Smith and Jonah Jones at the Onyx (their re-recorded version of 'I'se a muggin' ' with Cole hit big). From 1938, Cole worked with Cab Calloway, from 1942 with Raymond Scott's 'integrated' band at CBS, and by 1944 he was busy with film and pitwork, playing for the *Carmen Jones* show, in Billy Rose's Ziegfeld Theater (with Don Byas) and briefly in 1946 with Benny Goodman doing the eight-a-day at New York's Paramount Theater. By 1949 he had replaced Sid Catlett with Louis Armstrong's All Stars for a three-year stay and all through the 1950s played in studios and taught drums. 1957, he toured Europe with Earl Hines and Jack Teagarden and in 1958 had a surprise hit record of his own, 'Topsy', arranged by Dick Hyman and financed by Alan Hartwell, a fan from the Metropole where Cole regularly appeared. Thereafter he toured with his own band (featuring tenorist George Kelly), went to Africa in 1962 and by 1969 had rejoined Jonah Jones at the Embers. In the 1970s Cole stayed active: he played for a 1973 Calloway reunion at Newport Jazz Festival, New York, and in 1976 for a *Night in New Orleans* package starring Benny Carter which toured the UK. One of the greatest classic drummers, he belongs in the class of Catlett, Singleton *et al.* [DF]

Louis Armstrong, *Satchmo at Pasadena* (1951), Ace of Hearts

See Dance, Stanley, *The World of Swing* (Scribner's, 1974, repr. Da Capo, 1979)

Cole(s), Nat 'King' (Nathaniel Adams), piano, singer. b. Montgomery, Alabama, 17 March 1917; d. 15 February 1965. Like both Jimmy and Tommy Dorsey, whose solo work moved beyond the realm of jazz, Cole's brilliant piano style set new standards for players of his instrument. They admired his playing unreservedly, while other listeners were distracted by the popularity of his vocals (also widely influential but fairly insignificant in the development of jazz singing).

The inspiration of Earl Hines can be clearly heard in Cole's one early recording as a sideman (for his elder brother Eddie). But by the time he began leading his trio in 1939, Nat – in common with Billy Kyle at the same period – was taking a key role in turning the idea of 'trumpet-style' right-hand lines into a conception more akin to the saxophone or clarinet. Simultaneously, the left-hand punctuations became more streamlined and predictable than those of Hines, but the smoothness of the whole approach consolidated the piano's vocabulary in a way that was crucial for its adaptation to bebop.

Cole's popularity is evidenced by the fact that his line-up of piano, guitar (initially Oscar Moore) and bass dictated the trio format for countless performers from Art Tatum to Oscar Peterson. But far more significant is Cole's direct influence on the pianists of a whole generation, including those later influential in their own right – namely Peterson, Powell, Horace Silver and Bill Evans. [BP]

Trio Days (1940–1), Affinity; *Nat King Cole meets the Master Saxes* (1942–4), Phoenix/Spotlite; *Trio Days* (1944–9), Capitol

Cole, Richie (Richard), alto sax (and tenor, baritone). b. Trenton, New Jersey, 29 February 1948. Studied alto as teenager with Phil Woods (mid-1960s), later did some gigging with him (mid-1970s). 1976, began recording under own name. 1976–9, led regular backing group for Eddie Jefferson; has since collaborated with Manhattan Transfer. 1979, formed own group, Alto Madness, based in San Francisco since 1981 but touring internationally. An impressive technician, Cole's heated playing is an unfortunate vulgarization of the work of Woods and others closer to the bebop source, so that prolonged exposure to his style may be rather wearing. [BP]

Return to Alto Acres (1982), Palo Alto

Coleman, Bill (William Johnson), trumpet, fluegelhorn, vocals. b. Centerville, Paris, Kentucky, 4 August 1904; d. Toulouse, France, 24 August 1981. He played the clarinet early on (perhaps his later mobile approach to trumpet reflected the fact), but like Doc Cheatham became a permanent brass convert after he heard Louis Armstrong. 'My first inspiration,' he remembered later, 'and "Money Blues" with Fletcher Henderson was my first impression of him!' 1927, Coleman came to New York with brothers Cecil and Lloyd Scott in a great band including another fine trumpeter, Frankie Newton: together they often made short work of better-known opposition. And for the next five years his darting, quicksilver creations graced such fine New York bands as Lucky Millinder's, Benny Carter's and Charlie Johnson's; his sides with Fats Waller at this period dwarf the efforts of Waller's lesser trumpeters. 1935, he moved to Paris, his base for the next five years, to work with Freddie Taylor and the great Willie Lewis orchestra. There he found none of the travails of black musicians in New York; 'it was a mellow, cultural city where you were accepted for what you were!' He recorded solos with Garnet Clark, Dickie Wells and Lewis's orchestra, guested and recorded with the Hot Club of France quintet and became a celebrity. After a year in Egypt from 1939 he came back to New York in 1940 to work with such stellar names as Teddy Wilson, Ellis Larkins, Andy Kirk, Benny Carter, Teddy Wilson, Coleman Hawkins, Lester Young, Mary Lou Williams and Sy Oliver. Perhaps the rise of bebop, with its emergent trumpet Turks such as Dizzy Gillespie (who surpassed him in technique if not elegance), made life less comfortable for Coleman than it had been in Paris, and in 1948, in response to a telegram from Charles Delaunay, he returned to play for the opening of a Paris night club and stayed on to live in France. From there he commuted regularly to other European countries, among them Belgium, Switzerland and Holland, and his 1950s recordings show a new, rounded confidence and maturity (his sextet sides with Guy Lafitte and others from 1955 are simply perfect). Coleman went on recording and performing all over Europe, including well-remembered trips to Britain in the 1960s with Bruce Turner's Jump Band. In the year he died his adopted home town Limeray pronounced him an honorary free citizen. [DF]

Bill Coleman à Paris 1936–8, vols. 1/2, EMI

See Coleman, Bill, *Trumpet Story* (1981)

Coleman, George, tenor sax (and alto). b. Memphis, Tennessee, 8 March 1935. After early experience in blues bands, including touring with B. B. King (1952, 1955–6), he moved to Chicago with Booker Little (1957). Joined Max Roach quintet (1958–9), Slide Hampton octet (1959–61), Wild Bill Davis (1962). 1963–4, member of Miles Davis quintet, sideman with Lionel Hampton (1964), Lee Morgan, Elvin Jones, Shirley Scott, Cedar Walton. Has led own quintet, quartet and octet, and worked as visiting soloist with local rhythm-sections.

An extremely fluent post-bop stylist with a beautifully even tone, whose ability to run the changes at lightning speed has been the envy of many other players. He is also capable of considerable sensitivity at slower tempos, and of occasional recourse to his blues roots. [BP]

Live at Ronnie Scott's (1978), Pye

Coleman, Ornette, alto sax, composer, tenor sax, trumpet, violin. b. Fort Worth, Texas, 19 March 1930. Began on alto at 14, largely self-taught; played in his school marching band with fellow students and future jazz musicians Dewey Redman, Charles Moffett and Prince Lasha. 1946, took up tenor sax, inspired by the best local tenor player, Thomas 'Red' Connors, who taught him the elements of bebop and introduced him to the work of Charlie Parker. Worked in Connors' band for a while, playing mostly blues; also worked with r & b groups, eventually forming his own and backing singers

Ornette Coleman

such as Big Joe Turner. 1949, toured on tenor with a minstrel show and was left stranded in New Orleans. He eventually got a job with Pee Wee Crayton's r & b band, leaving it in Los Angeles where, apart from one brief period back in Fort Worth, he made his home until 1959. There he did a variety of non-musical jobs while studying theory and harmony textbooks, and working on his own music. Coleman's concept was so unorthodox that most musicians dismissed and derided him, and it was not until the mid-1950s that he found his regular playing associates. 1953–4, he began playing with trumpeter Bobby Bradford and drummer Ed Blackwell; then, after working briefly with Paul Bley, he began regular private sessions with Don Cherry (tpt), Billy Higgins (dms) and Charlie Haden (bass), who ultimately became the Ornette Coleman quartet.

1958, bassist Red Mitchell helped Coleman to get his first recording contract with the Los Angeles company Contemporary Records, and the two albums on that label, *Something Else!* and *Tomorrow is the Question*, served notice on the jazz world that a radical new talent had arrived. Coleman was championed by Nat Hentoff, one of the most eminent jazz critics of the 1950s, and he was befriended and helped by John Lewis and Gunther Schuller. He signed with Atlantic Records, who sponsored his attendance (with Don Cherry) at the Lenox (Massachusetts) School of Jazz in August 1959. In the autumn of that year, Coleman took his quartet into the Five Spot in New York and, in an explosion of publicity and controversy, 'free jazz' became an established fact. 1959–62, Coleman recorded seven albums for Atlantic and played with his quartet in the New York area and at the Newport and Monterey jazz festivals. Then he retired from performing for two years.

Coleman arrived on the New York scene at 29 years old with his musical concept fully formed.

No one except his immediate associates had witnessed his gradual development, and most critics and musicians were unprepared for such a radical new sound. His quartet had no chordal instrument – no piano or guitar – and his music was non-harmonic; there were no chords, no harmonic sequences, no chordal structures at all. His highly original compositions embodied other new factors: rhythmic accents were displaced in unexpected ways, melodic phrases often had unusual, asymmetrical lengths, and bass and drums sometimes took a much more melodic role than previously, either phrasing with the horns or in counterpoint to them. To cap it all, Coleman and Cherry played with fluency, maturity, and a kind of freedom which showed that this was their natural mode of expression: compositions, solos, whole performances were all of a piece.

The traditional features and familiar roots in Coleman's music were at first overlooked. It was not entirely abstract: although there were no harmonies, it was often tonal, the improvisation taking place in a basic key and often in common time with the superbly swinging rhythm-section of Haden and either Higgins or Blackwell. Coleman and Cherry, too, always swung mightily, and their phrases were shot through with the human cry of the blues. The influence of Charlie Parker and Thelonious Monk was evident in the music, and nearly all Coleman's compositions were either based on the blues or were variations on the AABA format of popular songs. Furthermore, the Coleman quartet's performances always 'breathed' beautifully, creating and releasing tension with great artistry.

Coleman's early music was enormously influential, affecting and inspiring musicians on all instruments, and stimulating the whole free jazz movement in the USA and Europe. John Coltrane visited the Five Spot regularly to hear Coleman, became friendly with him, and the two of them played together a great deal. His approach did not negate more conventionally structured music, but could simply create another dimension to it, which is why his influence was also potent among non-free players of all persuasions.

1963–4, he took up trumpet and violin, and after studying them for two years, emerged from retirement in 1965, appearing at the Village Vanguard, New York, with a trio featuring David Izenzon (bass) and Charles Moffett (dms). He took the trio to Europe, visiting several countries and recording a live double album at the Golden Circle in Stockholm, Sweden. At the Fairfield Halls in Croydon, Surrey, a chamber group played a totally scored Coleman composition, which consisted (in accordance with his 'harmolodic theory') of a series of interweaving melodic lines with no underlying harmonic structure.

In the later 1960s he led a quartet with Dewey Redman (tnr), Charlie Haden and either Ed Blackwell or Coleman's son Denardo on drums. 1967, he played at the Village Theater with his quartet and the Philadelphia Woodwind Quintet; 1969, there was a brief reunion with Don Cherry for a New York University concert. 1971, he opened his own Artist House in the SoHo section of Manhattan as a centre for exhibitions and concerts. He seemed to find more fulfilment in composing than in performing at this time, and spent much time at home writing and doing most of his playing there. 1972, his quartet performed with a symphony orchestra at the Newport Jazz Festival, New York, playing his *Skies of America*, composed in accordance with his harmolodic theory. From 1975, using electric bass and guitars, he began to work with the rock rhythms of the day, in what became known as his Prime Time band. But the results of Coleman's rock experiments are extremely patchy; the old compositional skill is little in evidence, and interacting lines which might sound attractive in an acoustic band often seem cluttered and monotonous in an electric rock group.

1985, the Prime Time band opened a week-long festival in Coleman's honour at Hartford, Connecticut. He was presented with the key to the city, and a documentary film, *Ornette: Made in America*, directed by Shirley Clarke, was shown. The core of the Hartford festival was a performance of three of Coleman's chamber pieces: a 1962 string quartet, *Dedication to Poets and Writers: The Sacred Mind of Johnny Dolphin*, a 1983 work, *Time Design*, for string quartet and percussion, written in memory of Buckminster Fuller, and a 1984 work for strings, two trumpets and percussion. 1984, he was also given the key to his home town, Fort Worth.

Ornette Coleman's debut was so stunning that the rest of his career, going in fits and starts as it has, with long reclusive periods, seems something of an anticlimax. His most intensely creative work was done in the 1950s, culminating in his New York appearances (1959–62), and the nine seminal albums recorded 1958–61. His profoundly original music seemed to flow out of him effortlessly and naturally. It split the music world into those who thought he was the new Messiah (John Lewis, Leonard Bernstein and others), and those who thought he was, if not the Devil incarnate, then at least a charlatan who could not really play. The resulting publicity rocketed Coleman to international stardom before he had left American shores. Nothing else he would ever do would place him so firmly in the centre of the stage again. There has been little development in his subsequent acoustic music, and his use of trumpet and violin, as well as alto, seems like a desperate search for new colours and textures. His supporters make all kinds of claims for the idiosyncratically 'creative' way he uses the new instruments, but his alto playing is vastly superior.

He admires European classical music, and has aspired to compose in that tradition since the early 1960s. In fact, Coleman is first and foremost a composer, but his compositions are born from his playing and improvising. *Harmolody offers an inevitably limited approach to music-making, and his compositions in this vein have not received recognition from the classical music establishment. There is no doubt, however, about the quality of his best compositions for small group; they rank among the finest pieces in jazz and several of them have entered the general repertoire – 'Tears Inside', 'Ramblin'' and 'Una Muy Bonita', for example. But most of them were written before he invented a theory of music-making.

Ornette Coleman's influence continues to show itself all over the jazz spectrum. Musicians not only listen to his music and learn from it, they also seek him out to study with him and discuss their musical ideas. As with his friends John Coltrane and Albert Ayler, his commitment is total, and he has made his music, to adapt Val Wilmer's expression, 'as serious as his life'. [IC]

Something Else (1958), Contemporary; *The Shape of Jazz to Come* (1959); *Change of the Century* (1959); *Free Jazz* (1960), all Atlantic; *Chappaqua Suite* (1965), CBS; *At the Golden Circle, vol. 1* (1965), Blue Note; *The Empty Foxhole* (1966), Blue Note; *Saints and Soldiers* (1967), RCA Red Seal; *Skies of America* (1972), Columbia; *Dancing in your Head* (1975), A & M/ Horizon

Coles, Johnny (John), trumpet, fluegelhorn. b. Trenton, New Jersey, 3 July 1926. Resident in Philadelphia in the 1940s, then worked with leading r & b bands such as Eddie Vinson (1948–51), Bull Moose Jackson (1952) and Earl Bostic (1955–6). Time with James Moody (1956–8) led to important solo contribution in Gil Evans albums and working band (1958–60). With Charles Mingus briefly (1964), George Coleman (1966), Herbie Hancock sextet (1968–9). Other famous affiliations include Ray Charles (1969–70 and mid-1970s), Duke Ellington (1970–4), Art Blakey (1976), and the Count Basie band from 1985. Early 1980s, appeared with both Dameronia and Mingus Dynasty. An underrated and extremely effective improviser, influenced by Miles Davis and probably Kenny Dorham; his tonal variety is capable of expressing a lot in a few notes, but he does not lack in fluent technique when required. [BP]

Frank Wess/Coles, *Two at the Top* (1983), Uptown

Collette, Buddy (William Marcel), tenor, clarinet, flute (and other saxes). b. Los Angeles, 6 August 1921. Worked with several LA groups before becoming leader of navy band (1942–5). 1946, member of short-lived co-operative group with Britt Woodman, Charles Mingus etc., then extensive freelancing and session work. Became first black musician to hold permanent position in a West Coast studio band (1951–5). Founder member of popular Chico Hamilton quintet (1955–6), then returned to freelance playing, teaching and composing. Assembled big bands for Monterey festivals, led by Mingus and by Monk (1964), Dizzy Gillespie (1965), Gil Evans (1966). A discreet, swinging saxophonist of the Lester Young school, Collette is also a brilliant clarinettist and flautist who has made a better case than many post-swing players for the use of these instruments in jazz. [BP]

Blockbuster (1973), RGB

Collie, Max, trombone, vocals, leader. b. Melbourne, Australia, 21 February 1931. His most remarkable achievement (like Pete Allen's a decade later) was to build a national reputation for his New Orleans-style band at a time when demand for new names working in that jazz area was really nil. Collie, a hardswinging, rudimentary trombonist with a degree in marketing, set out to persuade the jazz public that they needed him, and he did it well. By dint of a long residency at Chelsea's Trafalgar pub, a string of LPs (first for Black Lion, then others), then a self-financed tour of the USA which received blanket coverage in *Melody Maker* (it culminated in a 'World Championship of Jazz' contest which he won), and a hard-swinging, chummily-presented show, Collie had soon amassed a huge and devoted following for his hardworking band. By the 1980s the World Champion – now a highly successful and well-paid act – was looking for fresh achievements and in 1983 he opened the Dixie Strand Café with American tycoon Sam Johnson: it was one of his few unsuccessful ventures. Soon he was back on the road in full swing playing the kind of rough-edged revivalist music which all too often in the British 1950s polished itself out of its convictions. In 1985 Collie completed more than 100 performances of his new presentation, *New Orleans Mardi Gras*, in collaboration with two other committed New Orleans figureheads, Ken Colyer and Cy Laurie. [DF]

World Champions of Jazz (1976), Black Lion (double)

Collier, Graham (James), composer, director, keyboards, (ex-bassist). b. Tynemouth, Durham, 21 February 1937. Father, a drummer for silent movies, then a semi-pro for the rest of his life, encouraged him to play trumpet in local orchestras. Joined the army as a band boy at 16 and spent six years (three in Hong Kong) with army bands which included dance music and jazz. 1961, won a *Downbeat* scholarship to the Berklee School of Music, USA, where he studied with Herb Pomeroy, becoming the school's first British graduate in 1963. Returned to the UK and since 1964 has led his own bands known as Graham Collier Music and varying in size from six or seven to twelve and sometimes very big ensembles. His personnel has included most leading British musicians such as John Surman, John Marshall, Mike Gibbs, Kenny Wheeler, and sometimes players from Europe and the USA including Ted Curson, Palle Mikkelborg and Manfred Schoof. Collier's ensembles have appeared at major festivals and played concerts in very many countries. 1967, he was the first jazz composer to win an Arts Council bursary, and wrote *Workpoints* for a 12-piece band. 1976, formed his own record company, Mosaic Records, which produced not only Collier's music but also the work of some of his contemporaries and associates: Howard Riley, Stan Sulzmann, Roger Dean and Alan Wakeman. 1971, his band won two prizes at the Montreux Jazz Festival, the Press prize and the second main jury prize. As a composer he has had commissions from many major festivals as well as from most European radio stations. He has also composed for TV commercials, documentary films and stage plays. Collier is very active as an educator, running workshops and conducting seminars or giving talks in the UK, Europe and the USA. He has written four books, including *Inside Jazz*, a guide for the lay person (Quartet Books, 1973), and *Jazz – a Student's and Teacher's Guide* (Cambridge University Press, 1975, rev. 1978; also Norwegian and German translations).

Collier's favourite composers are Ellington and Mingus, and other inspirations are Lutoslawski, Penderecki, Shostakovich and Miles Davis. [IC]

Songs for my Father (1970), Fontana; *Mosaics* (1971), Fontana; *Darius* (1974); *Midnight Blue* (1975); *New Conditions* (1976); *Symphony of Scorpions* (1976); *Day of the Dead* (1978), all Mosaic

Collins, Cal, guitar. b. Tennessee, *c.* 1930. He grew up in Tennessee, listening to country and western music, but became aware of jazz early on and was playing the electric guitar for fun by 13. In the 1950s he worked commercially with a quartet, playing jazz wherever possible, and after two years in the army settled in Cincinnati for club work, studio dates and session work for local radio and TV. His first international claim to fame was a three-year spell with Benny Goodman (on Jack Sheldon's recommendation) where he found himself in the company of Scott Hamilton, Warren Vaché, John Bunch, Keter Betts and Spike Moore. Here Carl Jefferson heard him for the first time and signed him to Concord for a set of lovely jazz-filled dates with his new colleagues. As a star with the Concord All Stars, with Rosemary Clooney and regularly featured as a soloist in his own right, Collins is an asset to jazz. [DF]

Any on Concord label

Collins, Lee, trumpet, vocals. b. New Orleans, 17 October 1901; d. Chicago, 3 July 1960. Although he never achieved the commercial recognition of Armstrong or Red Allen (and, of course, was never quite as good), he was a highly rated player in New Orleans from the early 1920s and in 1924 went to Chicago, where he replaced Louis Armstrong with King Oliver's band and recorded with Jelly Roll Morton. Back in New Orleans, he had built a big reputation by the late 1920s, working with an A-team of local heroes: Dave Jones, Earl Humphrey and Theodore Purnell. 1930, in New York, he briefly replaced Henry 'Red' Allen in Luis Russell's orchestra. All through the 1930s he was in Chicago, working with the Dodds brothers, Zutty Singleton, Dave Peyton, and leading his own bands, and shortly after the war he was resident at Chicago's Victory Club. In later years he had a variety of prestigious jobs with top names, including Kid Ory (1948) and Mezz Mezzrow (all round Europe 1951). Despite failing health – he was suffering from the emphysema which was to finish first his career and then his life – he played on through the 1950s relentlessly, at Club Hangover, San Francisco, then finally back in Chicago. A fine trumpeter, much influenced by Bunk Johnson, Collins wrote an autobiography (see below) which throws much light on a dedicated professional jazzman. [DF]

A. J. Piron/Louis Dumaine/Jones/Collins, *New Orleans* (1923–9), Collectors Classics

See Collins, Lee, with Gillis and Minor, *Oh Didn't He Ramble?* (University of Illinois Press, 1974)

Collins, Shad (Lester Rallington), trumpet. b. Elizabeth, New Jersey, 27 June 1910; d. New York City, June 1978. The son of a minister, he played early on in Charlie Dixon's band and all through the 1930s with a front-rank collection of big bands including those of Chick Webb, Benny Carter, Teddy Hill, Don Redman, Count Basie (1938–40) and regularly in the 1940s with Cab Calloway, as well as, later in the 1950s, with r & b leaders such as Sam 'The Man' Taylor, until in the 1960s he left full-time music to work as a cab-driver. Collins was one of the most respected trumpeters of the swing era, although he never wished to move with the times (Dizzy Gillespie makes some cutting remarks about Collins's reaction to his youthful experiments when they worked together with Teddy Hill). Unfortunately his recorded dates often seemed coincidentally to be with more famous trumpeters, who in one way or another overshadowed him: a 1937 Paris session with Dickie Wells ('Devil and the Deep Blue Sea' *et al.*) shows Bill Coleman in a form so devastating that it leaves little room for anyone else, and a later date with Vic Dickenson (in 1953 for John Hammond) fanfared the emergence of Ruby Braff, beside whose legato runs and fat, full tone Collins's legitimate swing-style phrasing and punchy delivery featured on a few tracks sound unfairly pedestrian. It would be wise, however, to avoid accepting the accidental picture of jazz history that presents itself through the occasional data of recording sessions and keep an ear out for whatever Shad Collins music is left unassessed. A fine sample of his fat-toned, strong performance is to be found on *Basie Reunions*. [DF]

Basie Reunions (with Paul Quinichette) (1982), Prestige

Coltrane, Alice (*née* McLeod), piano, organ, harp. b. Detroit, Michigan, 27 August 1937. Worked in Detroit with trio, and with female vibist Terry Pollard. Was touring with Terry Gibbs quartet (1962–3) at the start of her association with John Coltrane (they were married after his divorce in 1966). After playing piano in his group from late 1965 until his death, she formed her own groups and recorded regularly (1968–late 1970s). Far less active of late, she initially exploited one aspect of the music her husband had produced in his final years, and gradually turned it into something more suitable as a background for prayer or meditation. By the early 1970s she was sufficiently confident of this direction to issue an album of John Coltrane overdubbed with her own arrangements for strings, and in the album below she re-orchestrated a piece by Stravinsky (under 'divine instruction' following a visitation from the late composer). [BP]

Lord of Lords (1972), Impulse

Coltrane, John William ('Trane'), tenor and soprano sax, composer (and alto). b. Hamlet, North Carolina, 23 September 1926; d. 17 July 1967. Moved to Philadelphia after graduating from high school, began formal saxophone study and gigging on alto. Spent part of military service in navy band (1945–6), then toured with King Kolax (1946–7) and Eddie Vinson (1947–8). Back in Philadelphia, rehearsed with Jimmy Heath big band (1948), then (alongside Heath and other Philadelphians) joined Dizzy Gillespie big band (1949–50). Remained when Gillespie cut down to sextet (1950–1) and switched permanently to tenor, which he had previously used while with Vinson. Further touring with Gay Crosse (1952), Earl Bostic (1952) and Johnny Hodges (1953–4), alternating with stays in Philadelphia and work with local musicians, including briefly Jimmy Smith (1955). Became member of new Miles Davis quintet (autumn 1955–early 1957) and began to record prolifically with Davis, Paul Chambers etc.

Early 1957, during final stay at home, Coltrane abandoned his long-standing addiction to alcohol and hard drugs, and experienced a spiritual awakening which had immediate musical consequences. He laid the foundations for most of his later work (in collaboration with Philadelphia pianist McCoy Tyner) and recorded the first of many albums under his own name. He also performed with Thelonious Monk on records and then live (1957), subsequently rejoining Miles Davis (early 1958–spring 1960). At this stage the John Coltrane quartet was formed, the classic line-up consisting of Tyner (who joined in summer 1960), drummer Elvin Jones (autumn 1960) and bassist Jimmy Garrison (end of 1961). Despite the financial and artistic success of this group, which made four tours of Europe, Trane was continually seeking to expand his musical horizons; Eric Dolphy had been an added member for a while (1961–2) and, after regularly inviting younger, more free-thinking players to join in his live performances and (with the album *Ascension*) also on record, Coltrane radically changed his personnel. Autumn–winter 1965, he introduced first Pharoah Sanders on tenor, then Rashied Ali on drums and his second wife, Alice Coltrane, on piano. Only a year later, however, he began to decline engagements on the grounds of fatigue and, shortly afterwards, died of cancer of the liver.

Though the stylistic detail of Coltrane's playing varied considerably over the years, the one common thread was its intensity. On the evidence of eyewitnesses and his lamentably few pre-Miles recordings, this was as true of his first struggles as it was during the experimentation of his last years. Some of the earliest documentation of Trane, even while with Davis, sounds comparatively unformed, as if adapting the honking approach derived via Dexter Gordon from Lester Young in order to incorporate flowing Charlie-Parker-out-of-Don-Byas lines. This conflict between a relatively rigid rhythmic feel and an advanced harmonic conception was only resolved when, around 1957, Coltrane developed sufficient fluency to overcome the apparent obstacles. In fact the speed and accuracy of his execution became the envy of saxophonists of many musical persuasions, and it was only achieved through becoming obsessively devoted to technical mastery; Lee Konitz said, '[He must have been] an eight- or ten-hour-a-day practiser to play the way he did.'

It is sometimes forgotten that Trane could also display an admirable restraint in his interpretation of standard popular ballads, and yet do so without losing intensity. Some of his original ballads, notably 'Naima' (1959), exemplify this ability, but it was probably only as a relief from the relentless harmonic exploration of 'Giant Steps' (composed 1957) that he was able to attain such classical restraint. The sound which most typifies his mature work, however, is of restless, sometimes anguished floods of notes (usually with an explicit or implied fast-tempo feel) which, although harmonically correct, are not melodically appealing or even rhythmically interesting in any obvious way. Rather, there is a full frontal assault on all these technical categories, just as much as on the listener's senses; the well-known description 'sheets of sound' is significant for, although the individual notes are precise, the approach heralds the desire to go beyond fixed pitch to pure emotion. How far Coltrane was ever a member of the mid-1960s avant-garde is likely to remain a controversial question owing to his untimely death, but he certainly facilitated its arrival.

John Coltrane

What he did do, indisputably, was to become the leading exponent of the 'modal' school of improvisation. Although his approach was at first dismissed as merely 'playing scales', Coltrane's sense of architectural balance used the style organically and totally convincingly. A third original tune to have been widely used by others, 'Impressions' (1961), is really just an excuse for extensive examination of one scale (or mode) and, as with its companion piece, the themeless blues 'Chasin' the Trane', the recorded version broke all conventions about the length of continuous improvisation which an audience could be expected to take. Undoubtedly this prolixity was aided by Trane's interest in Eastern music; although he modestly disclaimed precedence in this area, it was he who popularized the use of the soprano saxophone played with a distinctly oriental tone and also legitimized the idea of jazzmen gaining inspiration from such musicians as the sitarist Ravi Shankar. And, just as Indian improvisers need their

Ken Colyer

rapport with a good tabla player, Coltrane found his ideal percussionist in Elvin Jones, without whom his most emotionally exhaustive (and self-exhausting) work would have been inconceivable.

Both in length of performance and in expanding the horizons of jazz in the direction of 'world music', Coltrane has had an enormous influence, for good and bad, on younger players of all instruments. While he also begat a huge number of outright imitators (as did Armstrong and Parker before him), his encouragement of lesser-known musicians more 'modern' than himself set a new and exemplary standard of selflessness. Perhaps this is why no single performer has come along to dominate the succeeding decades as he dominated the 1960s. [BP]

First Recordings (1951–6), Durium; *Blue Train* (1957), Blue Note; *Giant Steps* (1959), Atlantic; *My Favorite Things* (1960), Atlantic; *Africa/Brass* (1961); *Impressions* (1961); *Duke Ellington and John Coltrane* (1962), all Impulse/Jasmine; *A Love Supreme* (1964), Impulse; *Ascension* (1965), Impulse/Jasmine

See Priestley, Brian, *John Coltrane* (Apollo, 1987); Simpkins, Cuthbert, *Coltrane: a Biography* (Herndon House, 1975)

Colville, Randolph, clarinet, alto, tenor, soprano sax, arranger. b. Glasgow, 23 May 1942. He graduated from the Northern School of Music in Manchester and later taught clarinet at his old alma mater, now reformed as the Royal Northern College of Music. Around Manchester he played in anything from solo recitals to circus bands, and was a later member of two famous Manchester-based units, the Jazz Aces and the Saints Jazz Band; he also toured Britain in 1967 with Teddy Wilson. After his move south in the late 1970s Colville's warm tone, elegant improvisation and Matty Matlock-inspired approach produced a string of offers and by the 1980s he was working regularly with Keith Nichols's Ragtime Orchestra, the Midnite Follies Orchestra (co-led by Nichols and Alan Cohen), Alan Elsdon's band and from 1984 as an occasional substitute for Bruce Turner in Humphrey Lyttelton's band. Apart from his clarinet skills, Colville is a trained and painstaking arranger whose work has been featured by the Midnite Follies Orchestra, Elsdon, the all-trombone band Five-a-Slide and his own sextet. [DF]

Humphrey Lyttelton, *Echoes of the Duke* (1984), Calligraph

Colyer, Ken (Kenneth), trumpet, guitar, vocals, leader. b. Great Yarmouth, Norfolk, 18 April 1928. The spiritual and musical leader of British New Orleans jazz, he very early on made it clear where his deep musical allegiances lay. 'Ken played traditional, not revivalist jazz', says George Melly. 'His wavery vibrato and basic melodic approach was based on Bunk Johnson.' Colyer's love was for the pure music of New

Orleans and after an initial, at the time controversial, period of bandleading ('to ears attuned to Morton's Red Hot Peppers,' says Melly, 'Ken's band was a horrible noise!') he rejoined the Merchant Navy, deserted in Mobile, Alabama, and took a Greyhound bus to New Orleans, where he sat in with such old masters as George Lewis and recorded with Emile Barnes and others. 'The logical thing was to get there while the old men were still playing,' said Colyer later, 'and that's what I did!' He was deported from the USA, came back to London, and after a brief collaboration with Chris Barber (whose ideals were different from his), formed his own band and began touring, playing clubs and concerts and recording. For the next three decades this was, broadly speaking, to be Colyer's career pattern. In 1957 he toured Britain with George Lewis (a close friend), continued recording busily all through the decade, and produced a number of British classics with his band and skiffle group, as well as leading London's best jazz brass band. The collapse of the Trad boom in 1962 made very little difference to Colyer's progress: as his aims, to begin with, had nothing to do with commercial appeal, commercial interests affected him not a whit. All through the 1960s he continued touring Europe, playing clubs and concerts, worked the British circuit, too, and recorded for a variety of independent labels, as well as regularly going back to his spiritual home, New Orleans. After a bout of stomach cancer he was forced to retire temporarily, but by the end of the 1970s he was back to full power, and in the 1980s was assuming legendary status in Britain. [DF]

In New Orleans (1953), Dawn Club

Commercial is a state of mind, not a style of music. In the mouths of musicians, the word is usually negative (and in the mouths of jazz fans, always), for it seldom refers to the useful aptitude for commerce demonstrated by being able to understand a royalty statement or count the heads of a paying audience.

On the contrary, it describes the person or the music deliberately geared to maximizing royalties and audiences, and therefore usually requiring conscious exaggeration of characteristics thought to be successful. Popular fashion being what it is, many performers are more commercial at some periods than at others. But it is also worth pointing out that jazz (like most other Afro-American music) is capable of operating on several levels at once, so that some music which is obviously commercial in intent can still be worth listening to for its own sake many decades later. [BP]

Commodore A record label occupying a pioneering position in jazz history, founded by Milton 'Milt' Gabler in 1935 and named after the Commodore Music Shop, a New York radio-cum-novelty store that Gabler's father had opened in 1926 and subsequently handed on to his son. The label set out to fill a gap in commercial recorded production by recording only hot small-band jazz rather than the commercial swing fare with which larger record companies were becoming exclusively preoccupied. Gabler's first recording session on 18 January 1938, featuring Eddie Condon's band, was in part a result of his knowledge that a small specialist public existed for such music: he had been the first to reissue, from 1935 on, a series of hot jazz classics under the logo 'United Hot Clubs of America' from a huge purchase of 20,000 Okeh deletions which he had bought as a job lot from Columbia. By 1940, Gabler's dual operation (reissues and new recordings) had won him a huge reputation and in 1941 he was signed by Decca Records as a stock co-ordinator and A & R man. This enabled him to help major artists like Billie Holiday to record for Decca, but he kept his interest in the Commodore Music Shop, working there every evening and Saturdays as well as enlarging his activities as a jazz promoter (from 1940 for five years he was the organizer for Jimmy Ryan's weekly jam sessions). Early classics on Commodore included sessions by Condon, Bud Freeman and numerous others as well as artistic masterpieces by Billie Holiday, including 'Strange Fruit' from 1939 with Frankie Newton's band. By the 1950s Gabler's Commodore label had broadened its artistic sights to include more contemporary performers (Frank Wess was one) and valuable earlier material recorded on the label was, from the 1960s on, regularly the subject of reissue programmes: in the 1970s on the Atlantic label in a brief abortive series and in the 1980s, more successfully, on American Columbia and Germany's TelDec. [DF]

Composition The term is used indiscriminately in jazz circles to cover anything from a complex original tune to a simple but memorable riff. There are also works which show more obvious compositional effort, some of symphonic length, but hardly any of them worth the paper they are written on.

Very often the most effective jazz writers may appear to be merely rearranging familiar materials, and there is a sense in which the really successful jazz composition is one where the written matter and the improvised content blend into a unified and seamless whole. Few composers have come within touching distance of this holy grail, except for Duke Ellington, Charles Mingus, George Russell and one or two younger writer/performers. For this concept to work it seems to require the active presence of the writer directing the performers, and to have been created with specific collaborators in mind: the European definition of a composition as something put down on paper in order that anyone will be able to play it is neatly turned on its head in jazz practice.

Eddie Condon

Historically, the few important figures in this category often appear (in retrospect) to have both summarized what is best about the jazz of a certain period, and to have predicted certain subsequent developments. How far they actually inspire the next round of improvised innovation is debatable, and certainly it seems that new developments in jazz have to be improvisational, not compositional, to achieve any widespread application.

However, it can be argued that the thought processes of, say, Count Basie or Miles Davis make them significant composers, just as much as Ellington or Russell, even though the former organized their bands through their own playing and not on paper. They are at least more important than those would-be composers of various periods who have taken snapshots of what they like about jazz and pasted them together with European compositional techniques. [BP]

Condon, Eddie (Albert Edwin), guitar, banjo, composer, leader, entrepreneur. b. Goodland, Indiana, 16 November 1905; d. New York City, 4 August 1973. The figurehead of Chicago jazz, he was a professional jazz banjoist at 17 (with Hollis Peavey's Jazz Bandits) and by the 1920s had built a circle of gifted young friends around Chicago, including Frank Teschemacher, Jimmy McPartland and Bud Freeman. On 10 December 1927 he co-led (with Red McKenzie) the first Chicago-style jazz records of all, 'although,' he qualified later on, 'we were just a bunch of musicians who happened to be in Chicago at the time!' By 1928 he was in New York working briefly and unhappily with Red Nichols, then more contentedly with Red McKenzie's Mound City Blue Blowers. With McKenzie, a kindred fighting spirit, Condon helped to set up great multiracial recording dates with black musicians such as Louis Armstrong, Leonard Davis and Happy Cauldwell alongside white ones including Jack Teagarden, Joe Sullivan and Gene Krupa: classics like 'Knockin' a Jug' and 'Mahogany Hall Stomp' were the result. In the early to mid-1930s he was busy sorting out his musical life and convictions up and down 52nd Street and by 1938 had formed two significant relationships: one with record producer Milt Gabler, who amended his Commodore reissue policy to record Condon for the first time, and the other with club owner Nick Rongetti, at whose influential club he opened that year with Bobby Hackett. Nick's – or 'Sizzlin's' as Condon called it – was a noisy cheerful club and the guitarist made it his base of operations for the next eight years, combining work there with exploratory hotel concerts at the Park Lane and Belmont, co-promoted by Paul Smith and Ernie Anderson. In 1939 came the most polished of Condon's bands to date, the Summa Cum Laude (the name means 'graduated with honour'), formed after a Princeton fraternity dance and made up of some of Condon's most compatible partners: Max Kaminsky, Bud Freeman, Pee Wee Russell *et al.* The band recorded, toured and played onstage for a now attractive but then unsuccessful musical, *Swingin' the Dream*, starring Maxine Sullivan and Louis Armstrong, which, said Condon, 'was open on Broadway for about three minutes!' By 1942 he had cemented a third professional relationship, with manager-publicist Ernie Anderson, and together they presented a Fats Waller concert at Carnegie Hall (a modest success) and soon after a set of Town Hall concerts, the last of which was televised for CBS: 'A few weeks later,' Condon recalled, 'jazz was the hit of television.' The concerts developed and extended all through the war years, were broadcast and transcribed on disc, making a valuable contribution to America's morale and presenting Condon's determined policy of desegregated, free-spirit jazz.

In 1945 he opened his own club on West 3rd Street, round the corner from his Washington Square home, and it became the late spot for an in crowd of stars: Robert Mitchum, John Steinbeck, Yul Brynner, Bing Crosby and Johnny Mercer were steady habitués. Once there – looking sharp in his formal suit and invariable bow tie – Condon would circulate, chatting in his bewildering fast staccato, laying groundwork for new plans (he called it 'parish business'), filling his pockets with tiny indecipherable memos and on occasion playing guitar. The band, on a stand at one end of the room, played long, loudly, beautifully. House cornettist Wild Bill Davison recalls: 'I've gone in there and felt like death but three minutes in and I forgot my illness! It went on till 4.00 every morning, never stopped swinging, people screaming and whiskey flying. It was New Year's Eve every day!' From the late 1940s Condon's name became international. Thanks to Anderson and personal manager John O'Connor, by 1948 he had his own TV programme, the Eddie Condon Floorshow, a best-selling autobiography (see below) and soon a column in the *New York Journal-American*, 'Pro and Condon'. In the 1950s he began a long, fruitful recording relationship with George Avakian of Columbia: it produced albums which ever since have defined Condon's music, and were in their time revolutionary with their inclusion of Condon's spoken comments at the ends of tracks (*Bixieland* and *Jam Session, Coast to Coast* are two examples). From that time he devoted himself to his club, to touring and to occasional writing: in 1957, *Eddie Condon's Treasury of Jazz*, a classic compilation, was published. The author, with his group, toured Britain, presenting faultless music which critics seemed to prefer to underplay while they sensationalized Condon's legendary drinking abilities (readers who want a fair commentary on the tour should read Condon's own account, or Humphrey Lyttelton's). Back home, Condon had grown tired of New York and began commuting to work three days and nights a week from a big rambling house on the Jersey shore where he lived lazily and enjoyed a steady stream of callers from Muggsy Spanier to Bing Crosby (the period, with others, is enchantingly captured in Condon's last *Scrapbook of Jazz*: a must). But he continued to pursue a busy schedule – touring Australia, New Zealand and Japan in 1964 (on stage once in Japan he was introduced as 'The king of bop and the mayor of Greenwich Village'), and that year was taken into hospital, severely ill. A lightning recovery allowed him to appear at his own Carnegie Hall benefit concert, but the following year he was ill again, and gently slowed down until his final trip to hospital in 1973.

It would be hard to overestimate Condon's jazz contribution. He created an image for Chicago jazz and, more important, a collection of faultless recorded jazz music. He was fiercely loyal to the musicians he loved, created a professional frame for them to shine in, and was a fine judge of humanity who liked the good things about people: genuineness, creativity, humility. 'And', says Sidney Bechet, whose cause Condon championed, 'he was a real fine musicianer.' The matter of Condon's guitar playing (he called the instrument his 'pork chop') is sometimes overlooked, but, says Bobby Hackett, 'Eddie was the greatest rhythm guitarist you ever heard.' No one who knows the records will forget that sweet and plangent chime, nor the man who played it. [DF]

At the Jazz Band Ball (1944–50), Decca/Telefunken

See Condon, Eddie, with Thomas Sugrue, *We Called it Music* (Davies, 1948)

Conniff, Ray, trombone, arranger. b. Attleboro, Massachusetts, 6 November 1916. He began his celebrated career with Bunny Berigan's band in 1937 – he later called the band 'a gang of naughty little boys' – then joined Bob Crosby, 1939–40. A period with Artie Shaw followed (a notable Conniff solo is the striking, tight-muted outburst on Shaw's 'Beyond the Blue Horizon' from 1941), then another leading his own octet, then prolific work as a studio man. In the mid-1950s Conniff invented an orchestral device which became widely imitated: a choir of men's voices set against a women's choir, singing currently popular songs in a wordless swing-style paraphrase, block harmony or unison, along with a trumpet, trombone or sax section. This highly successful formula had little to offer jazz followers but on at least two recorded occasions Conniff teamed up again with his old Bob Crosby colleague Billy Butterfield. Two successful albums, *Just Kiddin' Around* and *Mr Conniff meets Mr Butterfield*, resulted: both made the best-seller lists and both are well worth hearing. [DF]

Mr Conniff meets Mr Butterfield (1958–9), Philips

Contrapuntal, see COUNTERPOINT.

Cook, Junior (Herman), tenor sax. b. Pensacola, Florida, 22 July 1934. After a brief stay with Dizzy Gillespie (1958), worked for ten years with basically one group, first as Horace Silver quintet (1958–64), then as Blue Mitchell quintet (1964–9). Then taught at Berklee School, plus gigging with Freddie Hubbard (1971–5), Elvin Jones, George Coleman. Has co-led quintets with Louis Hayes (1975–6) and Bill Hardman (1979–81), was featured with Michael Weiss quartet (1985). An extremely competent and exciting player who runs the risk of sounding somewhat anonymous, but only through his complete mastery of post-bop tenor styles. [BP]

Good Cookin' (1979), Muse

Cook, Willie (John), trumpet. b. Tangipahoa, Louisiana, 11 November 1923. His first band after leaving school was King Perry's Fletcher Henderson-style orchestra, after which he moved to Jay McShann in early 1943 and then to Earl Hines, 1943–7. 'My first real influence on trumpet was Harry James,' he told Stanley Dance later, 'then Louis Armstrong and a little later on Charlie Spivak. I always did like melodic playing and I guess I intended to be a first horn man from the beginning.' After Hines he worked with Jimmie Lunceford's orchestra for six months, then with Dizzy Gillespie (1948–50), Gerald Wilson and Billie Holiday, as her MD for a year, before joining Duke Ellington in 1951. From then until Ellington's death he was regularly coming and going: 'I was out of the band several times up to 1958, then I left for a year and a half. I came back in 1960 for a little while and then again in 1961. In 1962 I went back for about three weeks and then it was a long time to 1 September 1968!' 'Willie Cook has always been potentially the best first trumpeter in the business', said Ellington. '. . . his taste as a soloist is quickly proved to anyone who listens to his records.' Cook's ability was won over a long period, although in his formative years his regular duties as lead trumpeter, and the presence in Ellington's orchestra of outstanding soloists such as Clark Terry, helped to hide his own solo strength. In the decade after Ellington died he toured Europe as a soloist, recorded prolifically in Sweden and elsewhere, and became far better known as a soloist, working in Britain at top clubs such as Pizza Express in 1985 and, that year, attending the annual Duke Ellington Convention at Oldham, Lancashire, with fellow guests Bob Wilber and Jimmy Hamilton. [DF]

Cooke, Micky (Michael), trombone. b. Hyde, Cheshire, 6 August 1945. He worked with Terry Lightfoot's band in the 1960s, where his shouting Abe Lincoln-influenced style attracted much attention: later, after freelance work for leaders including Dave Shepherd, Lennie Hastings, Pete Allen and Alan Elsdon, he joined Keith Smith's Hefty Jazz with whom he has worked regularly since, taking part in all of Smith's highly successful ventures and touring the USA with him in 1985. He is one of the hottest and most technically able British trombonists. [DF]

Any with Keith Smith

Cool describes the ability of certain jazz improvisers to sound more detached and less 'hot' than their colleagues. This is partly a question of tone-colour, and the veiled enthusiasm of Bix Beiderbecke or Lester Young is a far cry from Armstrong's and Hawkins's extrovert declamations (even in their most reflective moments). With or without a particularly cool tone, however, the same impression can be created by drifting behind the beat, which not only sounds 'laid-back' but is probably also the source of that expression. Because of its appropriateness to much 1950s jazz, 'cool' then became a general term of approval unrelated to music.

It is possible, though less easily achieved, for an entire ensemble to have this quality, as in the Gil Evans arrangements for the Miles Davis 1948 band described (nearly 25 years after the arrival of Bix Beiderbecke) as 'The Birth of the Cool'; but much of what followed in the West Coast movement almost caused the death of the cool. Nevertheless, the approach constantly resurfaces, for instance in the work of Wayne Shorter, and as in his case many of the most successful jazz performances present a subtle and continually shifting blend of both hot and cool elements. [BP]

Coon–Sanders Nighthawks A highly successful jazz-based dance orchestra, co-led by drummer Carlton Coon and pianist Joe Sanders, originally formed in Kansas City after World War I. Resident at the Muehlebach Hotel, the band also broadcast for station WDAF from 1921, and their polished, sometimes hot music was quickly in such demand that they secured a long residency at Chicago's Blackhawk Restaurant from 1926. From here they broadcast regularly and gained a following among jazz lovers everywhere: many of their arrangements, 'Brainstorm' for one, were published as 'stocks' (i.e. standard arrangements for purchase by amateur, and sometimes professional, orchestras in search of repertoire). Coon died on 5 May 1932, after an operation on a septic tooth, but Sanders took over leadership, billed the orchestra as the Original Nighthawks and remained active in the Midwest until 1950 (with regular trips back to the Blackhawk). He died in

Kansas of a stroke in May 1965 but ex-members of the orchestra (e.g. Leonard Schwartz) are still active. [DF]

Cooper, Alan, B♭, E♭ and bass-clarinet. b. Leeds, 15 February 1931. A veteran of the Yorkshire Jazz Band, Anglo-American Alliance and Temperance Seven (which suited his naturally zany sense of humour). His intriguing gaspipe lower register and stifled bronchial sound in the upper were the perfect expression for his piquant, very melodic and defiantly original ideas. A naturally eccentric but highly talented player, Cooper is – after Sandy Brown – the most original clarinettist (and bass-clarinettist) on Britain's classic jazz scene. [DF]

Digby Fairweather, *Songs for Sandy* (1982), Hep

Cooper, Lindsay, bassoon, piano, sopranino and alto sax, oboe, composer. b. London, 3 March 1951. Played with National Youth Orchestra; studied at Dartington College and Royal Academy of Music. Brief career as freelance classical bassoonist followed by various pop, theatre and improvised music groups, 1970–3; 1974–8, with Henry Cow; 1977–82, the Feminist Improvising Group; 1979–83, Mike Westbrook orchestra; from 1984, Westbrook Rossini; 1981–4, Maarten Altena octet; 1982–5, David Thomas and the Pedestrians. Since 1984 she has led her own group, the Lindsay Cooper Film Music Orchestra. She has also worked with Derek Bailey's group Company, and with Maggie Nicols, Irene Schweizer, Joelle Leandre, George Lewis, John Zorn, Lol Coxhill, Georgie Born, Lauren Newton, among others. She has written many scores for films and TV, including *The Gold Diggers* (1983), directed by Sally Potter; also several compositions for dance and theatre including *Face On* (1983), a dance show by Maedee Dupres. Her favourites are Irene Schweizer on piano, and saxists Coxhill, Evan Parker, Steve Lacy; other inspirations include Westbrook, Carla Bley, Nicols and Robert Wyatt. [IC]

With Cow, Westbrook, Altena octet and others; *Rags* (1980), re/arc; *The Gold Diggers* (1983), Sync Pulse; *Music for Other Occasions* (1986), Sync Pulse; Cooper/Nicols/Leandre, *Live at the Bastille* (1984), Sync Pulse; with David Thomas and the Pedestrians, *More Places Forever* (1984), Rough Trade

Corea, Chick (Armando Anthony), piano, composer, electric keyboards, drums. b. Chelsea, Massachusetts, 12 June 1941. Father a musician. Began on piano at age six, drums at eight. 1962–6, worked with Mongo Santamaria, Willie Bobo, Blue Mitchell, Herbie Mann. 1967, recorded with Stan Getz and also started leading his own groups. 1968–70, worked with Miles Davis, touring internationally, appearing at most major festivals, and playing on some of the trumpeter's most important and influential albums, including *Filles de Kilimanjaro, In a Silent Way, Bitches Brew, Live-Evil.*

Until he joined Davis, Corea had been known on the New York scene as a brilliant acoustic pianist notable for his composing, his familiarity with Latin idioms, and for an eclectic style compounded of his main influences: Tatum, Hancock, Tyner, Monk, Bud Powell, Bill Evans. His 1968 trio album, *Now He Sings, Now He Sobs* (Solid State), shows his consummate ability at that time and also hints at his growing interest in the freer and more European aspects of the contemporary avant-garde.

The exposure with Davis made him an international jazz star, establishing him as one of the leading performers on electric keyboards, and the group's non-harmonic, often polytonal jazz-rock music gave Corea the freedom to explore abstraction as much as he wished. In 1970 he and bassist Dave Holland left the Davis band to form Circle, with Anthony Braxton (reeds) and Barry Altschul (dms), which, for the most part, went even more deeply into the European vein of abstraction. It created an acoustic music which often had no relation to Afro-American forms such as the blues or gospels, no coherent physical rhythmic grooves, but which featured much scurrying and chittering non-tonal improvisation. Circle toured in the USA and Europe, recording a live double-album in Paris, and two studio LPs for Blue Note, but towards the end of 1971, Corea left the group suddenly. Years later, recalling this period, he said to John Toner, 'When I see an artist using his energies and technique to create a music way beyond the ability of people to connect with it, I see his abilities being wasted.'

He played briefly with the Stan Getz quartet, then at the beginning of 1972, with Stanley Clarke (bass) and Airto Moreira from the Getz group, Airto's wife Flora Purim, and Joe Farrell, he formed Return to Forever, an electric, jazz-rock group with a strong Latin flavour, and one of the most delightful and original fusion groups of the 1970s. Its music combined elements from rock, jazz, Latin and classical music, and although the group started out playing to tiny audiences at the Village Vanguard, Manhattan, they toured Japan later in 1972, playing to 3000 people in Tokyo, and became one of the most successful groups of the decade. RTF went through several changes of personnel and included Bill Connors, Steve Gadd, Al DiMeola, Lenny White and Gayle Moran among its members. The final version broke up in 1980, but there was a reunion tour in 1983.

In the later 1970s and early 1980s Corea began concentrating again on acoustic piano and toured world-wide in duo with Herbie Hancock and with Gary Burton. 1980–5, he also collaborated with Mike Brecker, Steve Gadd, Eddie Gomez, Roy Haynes, Miroslav Vitous, Keith Jarrett, Friedrich Gulda and various classical

Chick Corea

musicians. 1984, he recorded Mozart's concerto for two pianos and orchestra, and in 1985 he composed his own 3-movement piano concerto, which had its premiere in the USA in February 1986 and was performed later that year at the Music Joy Festival, Japan. Also in 1986 he returned to electric keyboards, launching his new Elektric Band with bassist John Patitucci and drummer Dave Weckl.

Chick Corea ranks with Herbie Hancock and Keith Jarrett as one of the leading keyboard virtuosi and composer-bandleaders since the late 1960s. He is one of the most original and gifted composers in jazz, and many of his pieces have entered the general jazz repertoire, including 'Spain', 'La Fiesta', 'What Games shall we Play Today', 'Spanish Song', 'Tones for Joan's Bones', 'Return to Forever'. He told John Toner in 1974, 'What I am striving for is incorporating the discipline and beauty of the symphony orchestra and classical composers – the subtlety and beauty of harmony, melody and form – with the looseness and rhythmic dancing quality of jazz and more folky musics.' He has been involved in the study of Scientology since 1971. [IC]

With Mann, Hubert Laws, Sonny Stitt, Getz, Hancock, Davis and others; with Circle, *Paris Concert* (1971), ECM; with Return to Forever, *Return to Forever* (1972), ECM; *Hymn of the Seventh Galaxy* (1973), Polydor; with Gary Burton, *Lyric Suite for Sextet* (1982); *In Concert, Zurich* (1979); as leader, *Piano Improvisations, vols. 1 & 2* (1971), all ECM; *The Leprechaun* (1976), Polydor; *My Spanish Heart* (1976), Polydor; *Children's Songs* (1983), ECM

Cornford, Bob (Robert Leslie), piano, keyboards, composer/arranger. b. Brazil, 15 May 1940; d. London, 18 July 1983. Parents lived in Brazil until retirement; mother played piano. Studied at Royal College of Music, London. Became interested in jazz after hearing Bill Evans. Worked as pianist-arranger for John Dankworth in early 1960s. Wrote many arrangements for BBC featuring singers including Mark Murphy, Sandra King, Norma Winstone, Elaine Delmar, and soloists including Tony Coe, Bobby Wellins, Kenny Wheeler. 1969, with Danish State Radio Orchestra he performed three broadcasts of his own music and a public concert. Mid-1970s, the North German Radio Orchestra (NDR) performed Cornford's 30-minute composition *Coalescence* in a broadcast and concert in memory of Ben Webster; 1982, they performed a broadcast and concert of his *In Memoriam*, in memory of Bill Evans. From 1977 he was a member of Tony Coe's small group Axel, and also played in groups with Wellins, Wheeler, Alan Skidmore, Phil Lee and others. June 1983, played with Lee Konitz at the Canteen in London. A month later, Cornford died of a heart attack at the age of only 43. His favourite pianists were Bill Evans and Herbie Hancock, and other particular inspirations were Gil Evans, Miles Davis, Ben Webster, Tony Coe, Webern, Debussy, Ravel, Pat Smythe, Ken Wheeler and Peter Warlock. Cornford had a consuming interest in all types of music, and he was also fond of reading, good food, wine and cats. He was a superb composer-arranger and a sensitive pianist. If he had a fault, it is probably that he lacked essential ego, which is why so little of his work is available on record. [IC]

Coalescence NDR. Die Jazz Werkstätten (Jazz workshops, 1969–70); with Tony Coe, *Tournée du Chat* (1981), Nato French: Cornford plays piano on one track, 'The Jolly Corner'; with Ken Wheeler, *Windmill Tilter* (1968), Fontana; with *Michael Gibbs* (1969), Deram

Corny A pretty corny word by now, though not totally lost from everyday conversation, its normal usage was created by white jazzmen of the 1920s. Just as corn-fed chickens are supposed to be healthier and therefore better for those who consume them, so corn-fed music (later shortened to corny) was totally innocuous and devoid of the 'unhealthy' associations of jazz. Of course, it was its supposed depravity that attracted most of the young white audience to the music in the first place, and the generation gap which was evident after World War I assured jazz of its status as something to shock the bourgeois. So, in the eyes of bright young things who danced to jazz and drank illegal Prohibition booze, the older generation (or youngsters pure enough to remain above temptation) were corn-fed; but, to the few dedicated musicians who entered the emotional depths of jazz, it was the fans who were themselves corny. [BP]

Coryell, Larry, guitar, composer. b. Galveston, Texas, 2 April 1943. Family moved to state of Washington in 1950. Some guitar lessons, but mostly self-taught. At 15 he joined a rock and roll group run by 17-year-old Mike Mandel. Studied journalism at University of Washington in Seattle, playing in rock and jazz groups. Left university before his final year, and moved to New York in 1965, joining Chico Hamilton. 1966, with Bob Moses and Jim Pepper, he formed Free Spirits, possibly the first electric jazz-rock group. Then he and Moses joined Gary Burton's quartet, touring internationally with it 1967–8. He played briefly with Herbie Mann, recording with him *Memphis Underground*, one of the seminal albums of the period, then formed his own group Foreplay, with saxist Steve Marcus and Mike Mandel (keyboards).

1970, he recorded the album *Spaces*, with John McLaughlin, Chick Corea, Miroslav Vitous and Billy Cobham. 1973, formed his jazz-rock group the Eleventh House, which included Mandel, Randy Brecker and Alphonse Mouzon. The group had much success, touring extensively, with four visits to Europe and one to Japan.

When it broke up, Coryell concentrated on acoustic guitar only for some years. He toured in Europe in 1975 playing solo acoustic guitar, and began playing duos with Philip Catherine in 1976, touring Europe twice with him and playing major festivals including Montreux, 1977, Bilzen (Belgium) and Newport (USA), 1978. Coryell also toured in trio with McLaughlin and Paco De Lucia. Late 1970s, played on two of Mingus's albums; 1979, recorded with guitarist John Scofield. In the 1980s he even recorded (for Nippon Phonogram) some classical pieces – his versions of Rimsky-Korsakov's *Scheherazade*, Stravinsky's *Firebird*, *Petrushka* and *The Rite of Spring*. By the mid-1980s Coryell was touring, once more on electric guitar, with a trio consisting of Mouzon and French bass guitarist Bunny Brunel.

Coryell's career has been dogged by crises of both confidence and identity, because he has rarely been able to unify the opposing facets of his enormous talent. He has been, at one time and another, the brash, loud, electrified rock-and-roller, the urbane jazz soloist, the sensitive acoustic guitarist, the classical performer: in a sense, his dilemma is the dilemma of jazz today. But with all his anguish and soul-searching since he appeared on the scene in the mid-1960s, he has been one of the most consistently interesting performers – a brilliant and compelling soloist with a superb technique, and the ability to surprise delightfully. [IC]

With Gary Burton, *A Genuine Tong Funeral* (1967), RCA; with Herbie Mann, *Memphis Underground* (1968), Atlantic; with *The Jazz Composers' Orchestra* (1968), JCOA; as leader, *Spaces* (1969), Vanguard; *Introducing the Eleventh House* (1974), Vanguard; with P. Catherine, *Twin House* (1977), Atlantic; solo, *Standing Ovation* (1978), Mood; with J. Scofield, *Tributaries* (1979), Arista

Costa, Eddie (Edwin James), piano, vibraharp. b. Atlas, Pennsylvania, 14 August 1930; d. 28 July 1962. Played with Joe Venuti in New York (1949), then after army service freelance work with Kai Winding etc. Worked and recorded with Tal Farlow trio (1956–8), Woody Herman sextet (1958–9) and own trio. Was becoming more in demand for studio work by the time of his death in a car accident. Costa's piano style, long underrated, was characterized by a combination of percussiveness and mobility; the sound particularly identified with him was the use of the lower half of the keyboard for fast-running bebop lines (sometimes in octave unison), but his attacking accompaniments were also noteworthy. [BP]

The Swinging Guitar of Tal Farlow (1956), Verve

Cotton, Mike (Michael), trumpet, fluegelhorn, harmonica, vocalist, leader. b. Hackney, London, 12 August 1939. From early years as a Dixieland bandleader in 1961 he cannily moved with the times, changed to a music format embracing rock and roll, rhythm and blues and soul music and in 1964 re-formed his band as the Mike Cotton Sound. 1964–71, his group was highly successful; although they never became hit paraders they backed a succession of American soul visitors including Doris Troy, Solomon Burke and Sugar Pie DeSanto. After Cotton broke up his band he freelanced briefly, then joined the Kinks, a British rock legend whose leader Ray Davies (composer of 'You Really Got Me', 'Waterloo Sunset' and other classics) had a weakness for jazz. After two more successful years Cotton came back to jazz, took over Bill Nile's band briefly and then joined Acker Bilk in 1973. A strong, powerful soloist with an enviable range and occasional interest in electronic experiments (at one point he used a set-up similar to trumpeter Don Ellis's), he works naturally in the mainstream area occupied in America by players such as Bill Berry, and although sometimes underrated never fails to impress. [DF]

Any with Acker Bilk

Counterpoint Sometimes referred to in connection with jazz, counterpoint means the interweaving of different melodic lines. Another European musical term, 'polyphonic', describes this kind of overall texture, while 'contrapuntal' draws attention to the detail of the interweaving.

Although present in many styles including New Orleans and free jazz, melodic counterpoint is not essential to jazz. Rhythmic counterpoint is, on the other hand, and can be savoured in all jazz. [BP]

Cox, Ida, vocals. b. Cedartown, Georgia, 1889; d. Knoxville, Tennessee, 10 November 1967. She began her career with minstrel shows, then made the transition to vaudeville and by the early 1920s was a star of the TOBA circuit. Bill-topping in the 1920s, her show was built on a formula, 'three letters each name, three jokes between songs, three songs!', and many of those songs were hits like 'Monkey Man Blues', popular in the Midwest in 1924: others were 'Death Letter Blues', 'Black Crepe Blues', 'Coffin Blues' and 'Graveyard Bound Blues' – a macabre commercial formula and an intriguing link between the Victorian way of death and hit-making 'death discs', such as 'Gloomy Sunday' or 'Ebony Eyes', a decade or three later. Ida Cox recorded regularly for Paramount 1923–9 – accompanists included Lovie Austin, and Fletcher Henderson's group in 1925 – and toured successfully with her own tent show through the 1930s. John Hammond brought her to New York in 1939 to play Café Society, broadcast, make records with Hot Lips Page and others (including the marvellous 'Four Day Creep') and appear in the epoch-making Spirituals to Swing concert on Christmas Eve 1939 at Carnegie Hall. Two years on she was still touring successfully with her *Raising Cain!* and *Darktown Scandals* shows until she suffered a stroke in Buffalo in 1944. She came out of retirement for a last recording for Riverside with Coleman Hawkins, Roy Eldridge and Sammy Price (substituting for her long-time accompanist, husband Jesse Crump). [DF]

With the Coleman Hawkins Quintet (1961), Riverside

Coxhill, Lol (Lowen), soprano and other saxes, vocals. b. Portsmouth, Hants, 19 September 1932. Studied sax and theory with Aubrey Frank. 1962–9, played solo saxophone, also worked with several r & b groups including Otis Spann and Alexis Korner. 1970–3, played duos with David Bedford and others, continued solo sax, spent one year as musical director for Welfare State Theatre, did some acting with various companies. 1974–6, worked with Chris MacGregor's Brotherhood of Breath, also did occasional gigs with rock groups including Henry Cow and Hatfield and the North. 1977–85, continued solo sax, also with Trevor Watts's Moire Music, gigs with Tony Coe, Evan Parker, Derek Bailey and others. Member of the Melody Four with Coe and Steve Beresford. Has also made music for films and TV. He was the subject of an Arts Council of Great Britain documentary film, *Frog Dance*. 1983, toured Japan solo and with Totsuzen Danball. Favourite sopranos, Sidney Bechet, Lucky Thompson, Evan Parker, Steve Lacy. Other inspirations, Pee Wee Russell, Edgard Varese, Ornette Coleman. [IC]

With Tony Coe, Mischa Mengelberg and others, *Instant Replay* (1982) (double); under his own name, *The Dunois Solos* (1982); *Coucou* (1983); *10 : 02* (1984), all Nato France

Crane, Ray(mond), trumpet, piano. b. Skegness, Lincolnshire, 31 October 1930. A fine Nottinghamshire-based trumpeter who moved south in 1963 to join Bruce Turner's Jump Band. After Turner broke up the band, Crane stayed in London, working regularly with pick-up groups including Brian Lemon's, and in the 1970s was a mainstay of Stan Greig's London Jazz Big Band, by which time his naturally hot, Roy Eldridge-influenced style had broadened to encompass Rex Stewart (a favourite) as easily as Harry James. One of the best British swing trumpeters with a broad eclectic interest in most areas of jazz. [DF]

Bruce Turner Jump Band, *Going Places* (1963), Philips

Cranshaw, Bob (Melbourne Robert), bass. b. Evanston, Illinois, 10 December 1932. Worked around Chicago with players such as Eddie Harris. 1957–60, co-led the Modern Jazz Two plus Three (MJT+3) with drummer Walter Perkins. Moved to New York, played regularly with Carmen McRae (1961), Sonny Rollins (1961–2, recordings up to 1965). 1962–3, with Junior Mance trio (including backing Joe Williams). Prolific freelance recording in this period led to full-time involvement in studio scene from mid-1960s. Further spell with Rollins (1972–4, including 1973 Japanese and 1974 European tours), and continued studio, club and Broadway stage work.

An intensely rhythmic performer whose lines, though never deliberately attention-seeking, were admirably straightahead. A couple of key albums which include established figures coming to terms with 'free jazz' have Cranshaw as their most conservative element, namely Rollins's *Our Man in Jazz* (1962) and Grachan Moncur's *Evolution* (1963). But the solid virtues of his playing are perhaps best appreciated in slightly more conventional albums such as those below. [BP]

Lee Morgan, *The Sidewinder* (1963), Blue Note; Sonny Rollins, *Now's the Time* (1964), RCA

Crawford, Jimmy (James Strickland), drums. b. Memphis, Tennessee, 14 January 1910; d. 28 January 1980. He began his career in Jimmie Lunceford's band of promising pupils at Manassas County High School and worked the hard road upwards with Lunceford until their first great successes at the Lafayette Theater, New York, in 1933 and the Cotton Club in 1934. He stayed with Lunceford until the great breakup in 1943 then, with Shelly Manne's help, made the difficult transition back to small-group work – 'my greatest achievement,' he told Stanley Dance later. After demobilization in 1945 he worked with Edmond Hall, Harry James and for Fletcher Henderson's sextet and from then on in a succession of Broadway shows, including *Pal Joey*, *Gypsy*, *Jamaica*, *Delilah*, combining this with regular recording and small-group work wherever possible. Crawford's jazz contribution is comparable to Milt Hinton's: a master whose presence was always a guarantee of professionalism and inspiration. [DF]

The Complete Jimmie Lunceford 1939–40, CBS (4 records, boxed set)

See Dance, Stanley *The World of Swing* (Scribner's, 1974, repr. Da Capo, 1979)

Crawford, Ray (Holland R.), guitar (and tenor). b. Pittsburgh, Pennsylvania, 7 February 1924. 1941–3, played tenor with Fletcher Henderson band. Forced by ill-health to give up saxophone, switched to guitar and worked with Ahmad Jamal in the Four Strings (1949–50) and the Jamal trio (1951–5). Settled in New York, playing with Jimmy Smith, Tony Scott and Gil Evans, with whom he recorded two key sessions (*Old Wine, New Bottles* and *Out of the Cool*, 1959–60). Early 1960s, moved to Los Angeles, teaching and playing but remaining in obscurity.

After the late 1970s Japanese release of his previously unissued album from 1961, Crawford cut two new records on the West Coast. A still undiscovered talent, his playing is unhurried and unhackneyed; on leaving Jamal, he was replaced not by another guitar but a drummer, and he remains the only guitarist to have added a distinctive voice to Gil Evans's music. [BP]

I Know Pres (1961), Candid

Crawley, Wilton, clarinet. b. Smithfield, Virginia, *c.* 1900; d. (nda). One of the more bizarre figures in jazz history, Crawley (who recorded with Jelly Roll Morton) was really a variety artist who toured with great success through the 1920s and 1930s; he also recorded solo sides with, among others, Eddie Lang. Crawley's clarinet playing (rather like Ted Lewis's or Wilbur Sweatman's) was determinedly comedic, making great use of slap-tonguing, exaggerated glissandi and other popular 1920s effects, and his music-hall act was based on these and his abilities as a contortionist. Legend has it (and it may be true) that Crawley was unable to separate his contortionist's tricks from his clarinet playing and so proved extremely difficult to record in studio conditions: however he managed it and a collection of his solo sides (with Lang and others) is planned. [DF]

Crawley Clarinetmoan (1927–8), Harlequin

Crimmins, Roy, trombone. b. London, 2 August 1929. Early in the 1950s he worked with Mick Mulligan and Freddy Randall before joining Alex Welsh to play a concert at the Royal Festival Hall. In the early years of Welsh's band, Crimmins was a strong guiding light and musical influence and he partnered Welsh for 11 years until April 1965 when he took his own band to Germany for a season in Lübeck: the season turned into a 13-year stay. Later in the period Crimmins gave up music for three years but was tempted back to playing by trumpeter Oscar Klein, re-formed his own band (the Roy King Dixielanders) and then moved into studio work until 1978 when he came back to England to freelance. Almost immediately he was invited by Alex Welsh to rejoin the band and stayed with his old friend until their last job together at Nottingham, shortly before Welsh's death in 1982. Crimmins then freelanced, working regularly with Harry Gold, with the trombone quintet Five-a-Slide and with his own five-piece. [DF]

Alex Welsh, *Echoes of Chicago* (1962), EMI

Criss, Sonny (William), alto and soprano sax. b. Memphis, Tennessee, 23 October 1927; d. 19 November 1977, from self-inflicted gunshot. Late 1940s, worked on West Coast with Johnny Otis, Howard McGhee, Billy Eckstine etc. Led own groups intermittently; 1955, toured with Buddy Rich quintet. 1962–5, lived in Europe, then resumed playing and recording in USA. Also did rehabilitation work with young offenders, made further tour of Europe (1974) and appeared with Dizzy Gillespie at Monterey festival (1977). One of the first generation of altoists to be deeply marked by Parker, Criss came up initially with an awkward compromise between the rhythmic approaches of Parker and Willie Smith (the direct comparison between Criss and his idol on Parker's *Inglewood Jam* is revealing). His later work achieved a more homogeneous style while retaining great intensity of delivery. [BP]

Out of Nowhere (1975), Muse

Critchinson, John, acoustic and electric piano. b. London, 24 December 1934. He had early piano lessons, but was more at home playing by ear and so was ultimately self-taught. For years he had various non-musical jobs, playing piano as a semi-pro; 1979, joined Ronnie Scott's quartet; 1980–3, worked with Morrissey–Mullen. Continued working with the Scott quintet and joined Martin Drew's band. His favourite pianists include Herbie Hancock, John Taylor and Gordon Beck, and he has derived inspiration from Miles Davis, Gil Evans, Joni Mitchell and Cannonball Adderley, among others. [IC]

With Scott and Morrissey–Mullen; *Summer Afternoon* (1982); *New Night* (1984), both Coda

Crombie, Tony (Anthony John), drums, composer. b. London, 27 August 1925. Mother was silent movie pianist. Self-taught. Toured with Lena Horne, Carmen McRae, Annie Ross and others. Led his own bands in the mid-1950s and in 1959 his Jazz Inc which included Bobby Wellins and Stan Tracey. Also wrote original scores for TV films and feature films. 1963, led his own band in Israel with Jeff Clyne and Pete Lemer. Has done many European tours with jazz and pop artists including Tony Bennett and Jack Jones. Also worked with Coleman Hawkins, Ben Webster, Jimmy Witherspoon and others at the Ronnie Scott Club. Since 1970s, has worked with Georgie Fame's Blue Flames. Compositions include 'So Near So Far', recorded by Miles Davis; 'Debs Delight', rec. Paul Gonsalves; 'Child's Fancy', rec. Ray Nance; 'That Tune', 'Restless Girl', rec. Stephane Grappelli. Leonard Feather has described Crombie as 'Outstandingly imaginative drummer; talented leader, writer and pianist'. [IC]

Crosby, Bing (Harry Lillis), vocals, actor. b. Tacoma, Washington, 2 May 1903; d. Madrid, Spain, 14 October 1977. He played drums in his local high school band, then explored singing. At Gonzaga University (run by strict Jesuit priests) while studying law he met Al Rinker, with whom he teamed in a double act; in Los Angeles Paul Whiteman heard them, teamed the duo with Harry Barris, and the Rhythm Boys were on their way. They had a highly successful period performing and recording with Whiteman, but after a dispute with Abe Frank, the boss of the Coconut Grove where the trio was appearing, Crosby found himself suspended. Coincidentally, Everett Crosby interested William Paley (director of CBS) in his brother's voice; Paley heard Bing and signed him for a series of 15-minute CBS radio programmes. Jack Kapp heard him on the shows and signed Crosby to Brunswick Records. Crosby's pre-Brunswick work is full of heights – the soaring, unlimitable vocal resources of his Hollywood recordings ('Black Moonlight' is a melodramatic masterpiece) and, best of all, the jazz sides with Bix, the Rhythm Boys ('Changes', 'Ain't no sweet man', 'From Monday on') and Whiteman-based small groups: 'Listening to Bing on the 1932 recording of "Some of These Days" with Trumbauer and Lang behind him,' says Sid Colin, 'you can hear him express all his jazz aspirations!' The Kapp signing – and possibly the death of Eddie Lang, whose jazz guitar he loved and regularly employed – was coincidental with Crosby's honing of his early pyrotechnic approach: from the approach (or onslaught) of a young musical Turk with all the ardour of Jolson but much more taste and technique, his singing gradually adjusted itself to the casual, pipe-smoking image of later life. Perhaps this was a reaction to Kapp's regular contractual demands for startling and sometimes poor material: 'He had me doing things that I thought insane,' said Bing later, 'Herbert, Friml, and Viennese waltzes.' No doubt it was also a bid to conserve creative energy. Crosby was becoming (rather like Elvis Presley, 25 years on) the property of America: his defences against the commercial machine were to 'sing down' as well as, on occasion, to parade a steely gaze and justifiably determined cutoff.

He made his first film, *The Big Broadcast*, in 1932; there were more than 60 to follow. A great deal of Bing Crosby's commercial output thereafter is what America wanted: perfect but unadorned readings of sometimes great, sometimes poor songs which people could hum. No coincidence that his most reactive performances from then on came in duos with other competitive stars and that his most relaxed and humorous work (on radio, records and TV) often seemed to re-appear with the jazz musicians he loved: in films, *Rhythm on the River* (1940, with Wingy Manone), *The Birth of the Blues* (1941, based, just, on the Original Dixieland Jazz Band), *Holiday Inn* (1942, with Bob Crosby's orchestra, but not Bob) and *High Society* (1956, with Louis Armstrong, among others). On records, and often in radio shows with the likes of Red Nichols and Connee Boswell, there were countless confirmations of his claim: 'When all's done, my favourite music is Dixieland!' Even jazz fans who find later Crosby (at least sometimes) too bland for comfort notice the warmth back in his voice on albums with Bob Scobey, sides with Condon, Matty Matlock, Louis Jordan and Wingy Manone. Best of all are his duets with Louis Armstrong, which reveal in four bars the 1928 Bing that never went away. By the 1970s Crosby ran a baseball club and golf tournaments, and he slowed down before a dramatic return to performance just before his death. Ruby Braff heard him at the London Palladium and pronounced him 'the greatest popular singer ever'. [DF]

The Chronological Bing Crosby (1920s–1930s), Jonzo

See Crosby, Bing, *Call Me Lucky* (Simon and Schuster, 1953)

Crosby, Bob (George Robert), vocals, leader. b. Spokane, Washington, 25 August 1913. He had had early experience as a singer with Anson Weeks and the Dorsey brothers (including the intractable Tommy) when in 1935 he was invited to act as frontman for a group of musicians led by Gil Rodin who had left Ben Pollack after a 1934 dispute: they were to form Bob Crosby's Band and breakaway small group, the Bobcats, and included Yank Lawson, Matty Matlock and Dean Kincaide. The chance to front a group of go-ahead groundbreaking jazzmen, to sing regularly and create his own identity was an attractive option. For the next seven years, Bob Crosby – despite initial inexperience which gave him trouble even counting off the band – learned his profession. A likeable, plum-toned singer with a natural jazz feeling (although he lacked his brother Bing's technique), Crosby was a charming presenter, recorded prolifically and very soon knew that his career was a success on its own terms (no doubt Bing envied his brother all that jazz). The band broke up in 1942, and after the war Bob went out as a solo: he worked radio and TV, led his own big bands (including an up-to-the-minute post-war aggregation owing little to Dixieland) and regularly got the Bobcats together for happy reunions. By 1985 he was touring festivals (with Parke Frankenfield's band playing the book) and starring at the White House for President Reagan. Crosby's name is synonymous with the best of Dixieland. [DF]

South Rampart Street Parade (1935–42), EMI

See Chilton, John, *Stomp Off, Let's Go* (Jazz Book Services, 1983)

Crosby, Israel, bass. b. Chicago, 19 January 1919; d. 11 August 1962. He took up the bass at 15 and a year later was noticed by John Hammond as 'the phenomenal 16-year-old bass player' who worked with Albert Ammons at Club de Lisa, Chicago. That year (1935) Hammond booked him on a record date with Gene Krupa which was to produce a small jazz classic, 'Blues for Israel', and Crosby attracted widespread attention as a result: 'He plays with a rare speed and accuracy and unusual precision,' noted

Hugues Panassié, 'and he improvises very rich countermelodies behind the soloists.' From Fletcher Henderson (1936–8) Crosby moved to the Three Sharps and a Flat, Horace Henderson's orchestra (1940), Teddy Wilson's group (1940–2) and Raymond Scott's multi-racial studio group at CBS: for most of the 1940s he was to work regularly in studios. In 1951 he began a long partnership with high-speed modern pianist Ahmad Jamal which lasted on and off until 1962. That year he joined George Shearing and recorded with him (as well as with progressive arranger Bill Russo) but died of a heart attack two months later. A neglected bass virtuoso, who pre-dated Jimmy Blanton. [DF]

Any with Jamal

Cross-rhythm, see POLYRHYTHM.

Crouch, Stanley, drums. b. Los Angeles, 14 December 1945. Began playing drums at 20, while working as actor with Jayne Cortez (former wife of Ornette Coleman). Gigging with various musicians led to formation of co-operative, the Quartet (1967), with Arthur Blythe and Coleman sideman Bobby Bradford. When teaching drama at Claremont College, led Black Music Infinity (1969–75), including James Newton and David Murray. 1975, moved to New York with Murray trio; almost immediately began writing about jazz for *Village Voice*, to which he has been a regular contributor ever since. Now much less active as a player, Crouch's reputation rests on his criticism, including some absorbing record sleeve-notes. His wide knowledge and interests within black music (contemporary gospel singer Andrae Crouch is his cousin) make it appropriate that he is the first musician, established initially as a performer, to have become more influential as a critic. [BP]

Various (1 track each with Crouch): *Wildflowers, vols. 2 & 4* (1976), Douglas

Cullum, Jim (James), cornet, leader. b. San Antonio, Texas, 20 September 1941. He is the second-generation leader of a famous San Antonio-based jazzband, Jim Cullum's Happy Jazz, originally formed by his father, clarinettist Jim Cullum Snr, who began playing in his college band (immortalized by Johnny Mercer in his song 'Jamboree Jones' after he heard them at a 1934 New York football game) and afterwards played for Jack Teagarden, but gave up professional music to run his successful family grocery business. He later formed a family band with his son, Jim Jnr., playing cornet and in 1969 he founded a record company to record his band and other important musical events worth preserving (they included a musical meeting for brothers Emilio and Ernie Caceres). Jim Cullum Jnr. has carried on the traditions of his father's band and owns – with other members including clarinettist Allan Vaché – a hugely successful jazz room open seven nights a week in the Landing Hotel on San Antonio's plush River Walk. Recent albums for Jim Cullum's Jazz Band (they dropped the 'Happy') include a delightful Christmas selection featuring Cullum, Vaché and trombonist Randy Reinhardt (see below). [DF]

'Tis the season to be jamming (1985), World Jazz

Cupido, Josefina, drums, voice. b. London, 21 July 1951. Spanish parents; stepmother a dancer. Self-taught. Started as a dancer at 16 in a flamenco group. Played guitar. Took up drums at 19; also began singing. Played with various London-based groups, including Red Brass and Elephant; in the 1980s joined the Guest Stars, an all-women fusion group. 1984, the Guest Stars toured the US East Coast. 1985, they were support group to Jan Garbarek for his London concert. Favourites are Dannie Richmond, Grady Tate, Billie Holiday, Aretha Franklin, Betty Smith, Art Blakey among others; also Roland Kirk, Mingus, Weather Report, Joan Armatrading, Quincy Jones, all her associates and many others. [IC]

The Guest Stars (1984); *Out at Night* (1985), both Guest Stars

Curson, Ted (Theodore), trumpet, piccolo trumpet, fluegelhorn. b. Philadelphia, 3 June 1935. Went to Granoff Musical Conservatory, studied privately with Jimmy Heath. 1950s, to New York, working with Mal Waldron, Red Garland, Philly Joe Jones and Cecil Taylor. 1959–60, with Charles Mingus's group, which included Eric Dolphy. Curson made his first recordings with Mingus in 1960, playing on some classic tracks such as 'Folk Forms No.1'. 1960–5, co-led a band with Bill Barron, also played with Max Roach and led his own groups. In the late 1960s and during the 1970s he spent much time in Europe, playing concerts, clubs and festivals all over the continent. 1973, he was a member of the Schauspielhaus theatre orchestra in Zurich. Also played clubs in Paris and New York City with Chris Woods, Andrew Hill, Lee Konitz, Kenny Barron. He has always been concerned to promote interest in jazz and to encourage young musicians, playing and lecturing at campuses of the University of California, Vallekilde Music School, Denmark, and the University of Vermont. 1974, sponsored the first US appearance of Arne Domnerus group from Sweden. In the 1980s, presenting new stars on his radio show (WKCR-FM 89.9) in NYC. He won a US jazz poll New Star award, 1966; 1973, the first foreign musician to be awarded a grant from the Finnish government, at the Pori festival. With Gato Barbieri and Aldo Romano, appeared in a film, *Notes for a Film on Jazz*. His compositions include 'Tears for Dolphy', 'Marjo', 'Reava's Waltz', 'Song of the Lonely'. Curson is at home with all kinds of playing approaches because he has always lived adventurously, experimenting and pushing musical frontiers to their limits without losing touch with the roots of jazz. His favourites are Rex Stewart on cornet and Clifford Brown, trumpet, and he cites as other influences Mingus, Monk, Andrew Hill and Teo Macero. [IC]

With Archie Shepp, Sal Nistico, Nick Brignola, Pepper Adams, Andrew Hill and many others; *Tears for Dolphy* (1964), Fontana; *Quicksand* (nda), Atlantic; *Blue Piccolo and Fireball* (1976), Why Not; *Jubilant Power* (1976), Inner City; *Ted Curson Trio* (1979), Interplay; *I Heard Mingus* (1980), Interplay

Curtis, King (Curtis Ousley), tenor and soprano sax. b. Fort Worth, Texas, 7 February 1934; d. 14 August 1971, stabbed by trespasser outside his New York house. Not to be confused with tenor saxist Harold Ousley (b. 23 January 1929), Curtis was a childhood friend of Ornette Coleman. Led own group (*c.* 1950), toured with Lionel Hampton for three months (*c.* 1953), settled in New York and led trio containing Horace Silver (1954). Became involved in session work (predominantly as featured soloist) with the Coasters vocal group and many more; replaced Red Prysock in Alan Freed show band. Live appearances regularly at Smalls' Paradise club (late 1950s) and at Apollo Theater, Harlem (early 1960s); musical director for Aretha Franklin (late 1960s) and studio producer for her and others. Curtis earned his reputation for the superb appropriateness of brief solos on r & b and pop records (though, as many of these were overdubbed, appropriate did not necessarily mean spontaneous); his background knowledge of the 'Texas tenor' tradition, however, emerges strongly on his occasional jazz albums such as the following. [BP]

The New Scene of King Curtis (1960), New Jazz/OJC

Cut (1) To make a recording, as in the pre-tape days a disc was actually engraved at the same time as the musicians played. Apart from the brief renaissance of direct-cut recordings in the late 1970s, the terminology has been outdated for 40 years; yet it survives in the language, often in conjunction with another archaic term in the phrase 'We're cutting some sides tomorrow' (which implies that each tune occupies one whole side of a disc, as when jazz was recorded for 78 rpm or 45 rpm singles). The verb can also be used without an object: 'We're cutting tomorrow.'

(2) To demonstrate superiority over other players of the same instrument. So-called 'cutting contests' developed spontaneously out of the more friendly jamming situation. Two of the most legendary instances were those involving Coleman Hawkins in December 1933 at the Cherry Blossom, Kansas City (which he lost), and in July 1939 at Puss Johnson's in Harlem (which he won).

Sometimes, however, they were not so spontaneous. Both Roy Eldridge and Chu Berry in the mid-1930s, and Dizzy Gillespie and friends in the early 1940s, were known to go out after their paid gigs looking for bands to ambush with their superior musicianship. And, because the genuinely competitive nature of these encounters refined players' skills to a remarkable degree, the virtuosity of the very best soloists of this period was cultivated to such an extent that it went over the heads of most of their potential audience. Producer Norman Granz, however, in his Jazz at the Philharmonic packages from the mid-1940s to the mid-1950s managed to emphasize the excitement rather than the musicianship, and replaced the spontaneity with twice-nightly exhibition matches. [BP]

Cutshall, Cutty (Robert Dewees), trombone. b. Huntington County, Pennsylvania, 29 December 1911; d. Toronto, 16 August 1968. A busy professional by his mid-20s, he came to fame when he joined Benny Goodman in 1940. Replacing Red Gingler, he joined Lou McGarity to form Goodman's finest trombone team of all and stayed for two years until call-up: after discharge he rejoined Goodman briefly, then freelanced with Billy Butterfield and Jimmy Dorsey's Dixielanders, among others (a later replacement was Frank Rehak). In 1949, he joined Eddie Condon, and the almost continuous 20-year spell with Condon that followed is the one for which he is best loved and remembered: there are records to spare, and in England the memories of a mighty 1957 tour with his guitarist-leader. In the 1960s he was again freelance; he died while he was working with Condon once more at the Colonial Tavern, Toronto. Cutshall is one of three swing trombonists – Lou McGarity and Abe Lincoln were the others – whose best work was aesthetically, technically and harmonically comparable to Jack Teagarden's without quite possessing that smooth and elusive genius-stroke. A courteous, humorous professional, his explosive creativity remains an influence on fine players such as George Chisholm. [DF]

Hackett/Condon, *Jam Session* (1948), Aircheck

Cyrille, Andrew, drums, composer. b. Brooklyn, New York, 10 November 1939. Studied privately, 1952–7, and with Philly Joe Jones, 1958. Worked with Nellie Lutcher, Roland Hanna, Illinois Jacquet, Walt Dickerson, Bill Barron, Rahsaan Roland Kirk, 1959–63. Came to prominence with Cecil Taylor, working with him for ten years, 1965–75. During the 1960s, also worked with Stanley Turrentine, Gary Bartz, Junior Mance and many others. 1971, formed Dialogue of the Drums, a percussion trio with Milford Graves and Rashied Ali. Also led his own groups and was active in education in the 1970s: artist in residence at Antioch College, Ohio. Toured and played major festivals in Europe and Japan with Cecil Taylor. 1975, formed his own group, Maono (= feelings), which had a broader musical base. Since 1975, has worked with many people including Leroy Jenkins and Muhal Richard Abrams. 1977, toured Europe and recorded with the Carla Bley band. Cyrille is a consummate percussionist who, after going deeply into free music, returned to basic jazz disciplines. [IC]

With Coleman Hawkins, Walt Dickerson, Bill Barron, Jazz Composers' Orchestra, Marion Brown, Cecil Taylor, Grachan Moncur and others; with Carla Bley, *European Tour 1977*, Watt; as leader, *The Navigator* (1984), Soul Note

D

Daily, Pete (Thaman Pierce), cornet. b. Portland, Indiana, 5 May 1911; d. 23 August 1986. He started on baritone horn, later played tuba and bass saxophone and borrowed his first cornet from a girl in his high school band. By 1930 he was a talent to watch, formed a close musical relationship with pianist Frank Melrose in Chicago and Calumet City, and by the end of the decade had spent time with Bud Freeman, Boyce Bown and Art Van Damme as well as leading his own bands. After the war he organized his own West Coast based group, which quickly achieved commercial success and recorded regularly through the first half of the 1950s, featuring such fine Chicago-style players as Warren Smith, Nappy Lamare, Joe Darensbourg and Jerry Fuller. Early 1960s, Daily switched over to valve trombone and moved to Indiana, continuing regular work with Smoky Stover's band and appearing in the mid-1970s at Sacramento's Jazz Festival. After a stroke early in the 1980s (John Chilton tells us) he was playing less, but his records – like those of Phil Napoleon, another underrated white trumpeter – are worth searching for. [DF]

Dallwitz, Dave (David), piano, composer, leader. b. Adelaide, Australia, 25 October 1914. Australia's ragtime conservative to set beside John Sangster, the heady progressive. Dallwitz runs a scholarly ragtime orchestra which plays the classic rags and his own compositions in the style. He also writes original material in the contemporary mainstream area, and always uses the very best of his Australian colleagues to play it on record: Sangster, Bob and Len Barnard and their peers. There are several excellent recordings by Dallwitz on Swaggie. [DF]

Da Mango, Linda, see MALONE, LINDA.

Dameron, Tadd (Tadley Ewing Peake), composer, arranger, piano. b. Cleveland, Ohio, 21 February 1917; d. 8 March 1965. Gigging locally as pianist with legendary trumpeter Freddie Webster (mid-1930s), then touring with Zack Whyte, Blanche Calloway bands and writing arrangements. 1939, worked in New York with Vido Musso band; 1939–41, arranger for Harlan Leonard band. Began contributing to other famous bands such as those of Jimmie Lunceford, Georgie Auld, Billy Eckstine, Count Basie (including one of Dameron's best-known originals, 'Good Bait'). Occasional sitting-in on piano with Dizzy Gillespie and Charlie Parker led to recording of his 'Hot House' (1945), and arrangements for Gillespie's big band (1945–7). 1947, regular gigging with Babs Gonzales's Three Bips and a Bop (Dameron on piano and backing vocals) and recordings with own quintet/sextet under own name and Fats Navarro's (1947). Nightclub residency with sextet (summer–autumn 1948), augmented to 10-piece (early 1949, with Miles Davis replacing Navarro). Co-led quintet with Davis at Paris Jazz Fair, 1949; encouraged by Kenny Clarke, stayed in Europe several months and wrote briefly for Ted Heath band. Back in New York (late 1949), writing for Artie Shaw, singer Pearl Bailey and others, then doubled on piano and arranging for Bull Moose Jackson group (1951–2). 1953, led own 9-piece band featuring Clifford Brown, Philly Joe Jones etc. in Atlantic City, then less active because of drug problems; wrote for Max Roach–Clifford Brown and for Carmen McRae (1956) and recorded two albums, then imprisoned for three years. Released 1960, arranged albums by Sonny Stitt, Blue Mitchell, Milt Jackson etc., and his own last recording (1962), but worked infrequently in last couple of years preceding his death from cancer.

Sadly undervalued during his lifetime, except by fellow musicians, Dameron was a unique contributor at the crossroads between swing and bebop. The lasting qualities of 'Good Bait' and 'Hot House', though claimed as being written before the crystallization of bop, did reflect its harmonic language (like a number of his lesser-known lines), but rhythmically they are close to the swing era. Many of Dameron's most representative items such as 'Tadd's Delight' (aka 'Sid's Delight') and 'Lady Bird', though beautifully melodic, are built almost entirely of notes derived from his typically lush chords; similarly, his piano style gained its interest from the use of harmony rather than independent lines. In this respect, Dameron was a strong if unacknowledged influence on the compositions of Horace Silver and many of the 'hard bop' writers, as well as on Benny Golson, Gigi Gryce, Paul Jeffrey and others who emulated him more directly. Many of his 9-piece orchestrations were re-created note for note by arrangers Don Sickler and John Oddo for the 1980s group Dameronia led by Philly Joe Jones. [BP]

The Fabulous Fats Navarro, vol.1 (1947–8), Blue Note; *Fontainebleau* (1956), Prestige/OJC; *The Magic Touch* (1962), Riverside/OJC

D'Amico, Hank (Henry), b. Rochester, New York, 21 March 1915. A highly able clarinettist who works broadly in Benny Goodman's style, he worked with Red Norvo on and off until 1939, then joined Bob Crosby in 1940 before time with Tommy Dorsey, his own band, Leo Brown, Benny Goodman, Raymond Scott's multi-racial studio group and others in 1943. From that year until 1955 he worked as a staffman for ABC, then played clubs, worked on TV and radio sessions and freelanced. [DF]

Dance Bands Although jazz and dancing were regularly linked until the flowering of rock and roll, dance bands occupy their own private echelon in jazz history. From the 1920s such bands, organized to provide copybook replays of popular material at the correct tempo for dancers (not necessarily jazz fans) to enjoy perfecting their steps, were a necessary part of America's and Europe's social scene. What they played was functional music with strong emphasis on a singable re-creation of the melody, and jazz – particularly early on – was often heard as an anti-social irrelevance. However, American bandleaders such as Paul Specht, Roger Wolfe Kahn and dozens of others (as well as such studio bands as Fred Rich's, the California Ramblers and the multifarious Denza Dance Bands) often staffed their orchestras with top-rank jazzmen – Mannie Klein, Sylvester Ahola, Red Nichols, Jack Teagarden, the Dorseys, Frank Signorelli *et al.* – and hunting down their short solo contributions to otherwise mediocre records, as well as records of dance bands that reveal overall jazz feeling and arranging flair has become a study in itself: in Europe the VJM label has regularly issued examples of the genre, known collectively as 'hot dance'. Many of the most important contributors to American 'hot dance' – Benny Goodman, the Dorseys and so on – went on later to create their own star reputations and survived post-war, working either in studios or as jazz soloists in their own right.

Up to the war, the story in Europe – and particularly in Britain – was much the same. Jazz remained a specialist music played by fine musicians who made their living working for West End dance bands and, by and large, let their hair down in the small hours playing clubs such as the Nest, the Bag o' Nails and Shim Sham: records of British bands of the period (Ambrose, Lew Stone, Ray Noble, Roy Fox and others) like their American parallels are often spiced with jazz solos at least and sometimes are magnificent jazz in their own right. The most dramatic and regrettable development in Britain post-war was the wholesale fashionable discarding of the pre-war musicians, who in the wake of crusading revivalism, which condemned commercially-based music of any kind, and bebop, which set store by modernism for its own sake, found themselves prematurely consigned to retirement. A highly selective list of British talents who found their careers faltering as a result of jazz trends could include the following: (tpt) Nat Gonella, Bruts Gonella, Max Goldberg, Norman Payne, Arthur Mouncey, Jack Jackson; (sax/clt) Harry Hayes, Buddy Featherstonehaugh, Derek Neville, Freddy Gardner, Benny Winestone, Don Barrigo, Pat Smuts, Philip Buchel, Andy McDevitt, Joe Crossman; (tmb) Lew Davis, Don Macaffer, Joe Ferrie; (piano) Eddie Carroll, Harold Hood, Stanley Black, Jack Penn; (bass) Dick Ball, Tommy Bromley, Dick Escott; (dms) Sid Heager, Max Bacon, Jock Jacobson. Many such pre-war stars changed their career direction from choice (Buchel became a choreographer, Jackson a broadcaster, Black a respected orchestral conductor of light music), but many others were consigned to pit-work, or to alternative career choices to music, and in the climate of the 1950s were given no chance by a brittle post-war jazz world to show what they could do. The 1970s were to bring about a late re-appraisal: American cornettist Richard Sudhalter corralled veterans such as Harry Gold, Pat Dodd, Tommy McQuater, George Elliot and Jock Cummings into his New Paul Whiteman Orchestra and wrote revealingly about the injustice of the two previous decades. In the 1980s late renewed interest was focused on such gifted veterans as Harry Gold, Nat Gonella and Tiny Winters, but British jazz fans certainly missed some good music in the interim. [DF]

See McCarthy, Albert, *The Dance Band Era* (November Books, 1971)

D'Andrea, Franco (Francesco), piano. b. Merano, Italy, 8 March 1941. Mother fond of classical music, and piano player. Self-taught. Began playing piano at 17 after having tried trumpet, clarinet, bass and sax. 1963, first professional job with Nunzio Rotundo at Rome radio station. 1964–5, played with Gato Barbieri in his avant-garde phase. 1968–72, co-led the Modern Art Trio, an avant-garde group. 1972–7, with Perigeo, a jazz-rock group. 1978, formed own trio while beginning to perform solo concerts and teaching intensively. 1981, formed his own quartet with Tino Tracanna (saxes), Attilio Zanchi (bass), Gianni Cazzola (dms), touring with it extensively in Italy and Europe, and playing several international festivals including North Sea, Holland; Edmonton, Canada; Umbria, Italy; Zagreb, Yugoslavia. Also played with Lee Konitz, Johnny Griffin, Steve Lacy, Enrico Rava, Pepper Adams, Conte Candoli, Frank Rosolino, Max Roach, Jean-Luc Ponty, Toots Thielemans, among others. 1982 and 1984, voted Best Italian Jazz Musician in the magazine *Musica Jazz*; 1982, received the Radio Uno jazz prize. His albums *Es* and *No Idea of Time* won the Italian critics' award. D'Andrea has composed many pieces, and in 1984 was commissioned by the Teatro Lirico di Cagliari to collaborate with contemporary composer Luca Francesconi and African percussionist Fode Youla, to create a piece based on the interaction of different musical languages. His favourite pianists range from James P. Johnson, Monk and Lennie Tristano to Hancock, Tyner, Jarrett and Martial Solal, and other inspirations are Mingus, Miles Davis and Coltrane. [IC]

With Barbieri, Konitz, Candoli, Rosolino, Griffin, Rava, Roach and others; five albums with Perigeo; *Modern Art Trio* (1971), Vedette; solo, *Nuvolao* (1978), Carosello; trio, *From East to West* (1979), Atlantic; solo, *Es* (1981); with Barry Altschul/Mark Helias, *My One and Only Love* (1983); with Tino Tracanna/Altschul/Helias, *No Idea of Time* (1984), all Red

Dandridge, Putney (Louis), piano, vocals. b. Richmond, Virginia, 13 January 1902; d. New Jersey, 15 February 1946. A vaudeville artist in the 1920s, he also worked as accompanist to tapdancer Bill Robinson in the early 1930s, led his own band and from 1935 had solo residencies up and down 52nd Street, at the Hickory House and elsewhere. His records, modelled on Fats Waller and his Rhythm, are less well known than they should be and well worth searching for: recorded in 1935–6, they feature superior repertoire, Dandridge's engaging singing and a string of star accompanists including Roy Eldridge, Dick Clark, Bobby Stark, Henry 'Red' Allen, Chu Berry, Ben Webster, Joe Marsala, Dave Barbour and Cozy Cole, as well as specially recruited pianists including Teddy Wilson, Ram Ramirez and Clyde Hart. A neglected corner of the swing era. [DF]

Putney Dandridge, vol. 3 (1936), Rarities

Daniels, Joe (Joseph), drums, bandleader. b. Zeerust, Transvaal, South Africa, 1908. He took up drums at 11 and the same year played Frascati's Restaurant, London, before teenage work with bands led by Al Kaplan and others in London clubs including Moody's, Tottenham Court Road. In 1926 he teamed with trumpeter Max Goldberg in a small group and soon after played with Fred Elizalde (at Oxford), Al Tabor and Billy Mason before joining Harry Roy (1931–7). His famous Hotshots, featuring Daniels's spectacular 'Drumnastics', were initially formed during this period for EMI studio recordings and continued throughout the war when he served in the RAF and ran a quintet. After the war Daniels formed his Dixieland Group (featuring at various times Dave Shepherd, Alan Wickham and others) and recorded for the Parlophone 'Rhythm Style' series. In later years he ran a band at Butlin's Holiday Camp and in 1983 appeared with Denny Wright, Tiny Winters in an American film success *Top Secret.* [DF]

Stepping Out to Swing, 1940–5, Saville

Daniels, Mike, trumpet, leader. b. 13 April 1929. He led a superior British revivalist jazz band of the 1950s and early 1960s which (like Bruce Turner's Jump Band) achieved near-legendary status after 1955 for its clean and convincing re-creation of the Morton/Oliver/Armstrong repertoire. Featuring fine players such as John Barnes (clt/reeds) and Gordon Blundy (tmb) as well as Daniels's own uncluttered Oliver-style lead, the Delta Jazzmen recorded to great effect and played clubs and concerts, winning an erudite and sensitive collection of aficionados; so did Daniels's big band which featured later stars such as John Chilton and Keith Nichols, and played regularly in the London area. (Long after Daniels's abdication it continued under the direction of saxophonist Trevor Swayle.) After Daniels gave up and went abroad his band remained a hallowed memory: a bio-discography by Mike Bowen easily sold out its first printing 20 years after the last note was thought to have been played. 1985, Daniels paid a trip back to Britain, worked a string of provincial dates and, with his band reassembled to a man, found queues stretching round the building for his appearances at London's Pizza Express. [DF]

Delta Jazzmen 1957–9 (1986)

See Bowen, Mike, *The Mike Daniels Delta Jazz Band* (Bowen, 1982)

Dankworth, John Philip William, alto sax, clarinet, arranger. b. 20 September 1927. Played clarinet in trad bands (mid-1940s), studied at Royal Academy of Music. Interested in bebop, worked on transatlantic liners to hear music in New York. In Tito Burns sextet alongside Ronnie Scott, also some arranging for Ted Heath. Founder member of Club 11 (1948–50); formed Johnny Dankworth Seven (1950–3). Own big band (1953–64), featuring singer Cleo Laine (they married in 1958); big band reformed for annual engagements till 1971. Began writing film scores from 1959, increasingly busy mid-1960s to mid-1970s. From 1971, also acting as musical director for Laine's tours of USA, Australia etc. Occasionally working with Dankworth recently, his and Laine's son Alec Dankworth (b. 15 May 1960) has developed into a fine bassist.

John's own alto work, reflecting the influence of Charlie Parker and perhaps Lee Konitz, retains a light, nonchalant tone and a considerable inventive edge. Though sometimes too fussy, his early writing for septet and big band at its best encouraged relaxed and idiomatic performances from such notable contributors as Don Rendell, Kenny Clare, Kenny Wheeler. In its heyday, the big band also developed inventive head arrangements of classic Ellington and Basie warhorses, which were performed during its brief US visit for the Newport festival, 1959. [BP]

Johnny Dankworth Seven and Orchestra (1953–7), EMI; *Zodiac Variations* (1964), Sepia

John Dankworth and Cleo Laine

Darensbourg, Joe (Joseph), clarinet, saxes. b. Baton Rouge, Louisiana, 9 July 1906; d. Van Nuys, California, 24 May 1985. He was active in New Orleans by the 1920s, working with such as Buddy Petit, Fate Marable, Charlie Creath and Jelly Roll Morton, as well as for medicine shows and, from around 1925, Mutt Carey's Jeffersonians in Los Angeles. In the 1930s, like many of his gifted contemporaries, he played all the saxophones instead of clarinet (saxophones were much more fashionable), led bands around Seattle, Vancouver and the West Coast, worked on cruise liners and taught a star pupil, saxophonist Dick Wilson, who was later to work with Andy Kirk. Darensbourg's move back to traditional jazz came in the wake of America's jazz revival: he worked with pianist Johnny Wittwer around Seattle and then joined Kid Ory in 1944 for the first of several stints spread over ten years, doubled up with pianist Joe Liggins, comedian Redd Foxx and Wingy Manone, and after more freelancing started his own band, the Dixie Flyers, in 1956. Thereafter he became a familiar figure at Disneyland, on a mock-up riverboat, playing with the Young Men of New Orleans, worked for three years with Louis Armstrong (he was on the record of 'Hello, Dolly!') and from the 1970s worked at Disneyland again and with Barry Martyn's Jazz Legends, as well as at festivals before heart trouble slowed him down. On clarinet, Darensbourg is remembered well for his featuring of the 'slap-tongue' technique: a reed-players' showstopper in the 1920s which very few of its users (they included Albert Nicholas and Barney Bigard) bothered to carry over to later decades. Darensbourg continued to feature it however, and a highly successful single release – 'Yellow Dog Blues' by Darensbourg's Dixie Flyers – repopularized the sound in 1958. [DF]

Joe Darensbourg and his Dixie Flyers (1958), Vogue

Darling, David, cello, composer. b. Elkhart, Indiana, 4 March 1941. Piano lessons at age four and began on cello when ten. Led his own dance bands in high school, playing bass and alto sax;

studied classical cello at Indiana University; 1965, graduated from Indiana State College with advanced degree in music education; 1966–9, taught in US public schools; 1969–70, faculty cellist and community orchestra conductor at Western Kentucky University; 1970–8, worked with the Paul Winter Consort, touring extensively throughout the USA and recording four albums. After leaving Winter, began to compose more and several of his pieces for large orchestra were played by the Indianapolis and Cincinnati symphony orchestras. 1979, played on Ralph Towner's album *Old Friends, New Friends*, with Kenny Wheeler, Eddie Gomez and Michael Di Pasqua. 1980, with Di Pasqua (dms), Dave Samuels (vibraharp) and Paul McCandless (reeds), Darling co-founded the group Gallery, which recorded for ECM, 1981, and toured the USA and Europe, 1982.

Darling plays both the traditional cello and an 8-string solid-bodied cello of his own design which is amplified and filtered through various electronic attachments such as echoplex, ring modulator and fuzz box, so that he is able to combine elements from the classical tradition with jazz, rock and other elements. [IC]

Solo, *Journal October* (1979); *Cycles* (1981), both ECM; with Paul Winter, *Road* (nda), A & M

Wolfgang Dauner

Dash, St Julian Bennett, tenor sax. b. Charleston, South Carolina, 9 April 1916; d. New York City, 25 February 1974. The greater part of his career was spent in Erskine Hawkins's orchestra, which he joined in 1938, emerging occasionally to record as a soloist: later – after Hawkins reduced to a small group – he led his own band and recorded with his own quintet in 1970, but afterwards retired from music. His principal influence, Chu Berry, is clearly audible in his own style which shows up to advantage on Buck Clayton's 1953 'Hucklebuck' jam session. [DF]

Buck Clayton Jam Session (1953), CBS

Dauner, Wolfgang, piano, synthesizers, composer. b. Stuttgart, Germany, 30 December 1935. Brought up by his aunt, who was a piano teacher and gave him lessons from his fifth year. First worked as a mechanic, but took up music professionally in 1957 when he was offered a tour with a commercial band. 1958, studied trumpet and piano briefly at Stuttgart College of Music, but as a jazz musician largely self-taught. Initially, Bill Evans was his main influence, but Dauner's restless energy and interest in experimentation and the theatrical side of performance soon led him to evolve his own musical climate and method of procedure. 1963, formed his own trio, with Eberhard Weber and Fred Braceful, and its unconventional performances caused a sensation at German festivals. He also worked with visiting American and European jazz stars, and had begun composing, not only music, but also some bizarre, even outrageous events. In the second half of the 1960s, he destroyed a violin and burned a piano on stage, on one occasion, and on another he covered the heads of one of Germany's most renowned choirs in nylon stockings so that they could only emit noises. During this period he devised and recorded *Free Action*, for a septet featuring Jean-Luc Ponty, *Psalmus Spei*, for choir and jazz group for the 1968 Berlin festival, and *Dauner-eschingen*, for jazz soloists and choir, for the 1970 Donaueschingen Music Festival. Since 1969, Dauner has led the Stuttgart Radio jazz group, doing at least one broadcast a month with guest soloists such as Chick Corea, Ponty, Michal Urbaniak, Zbigniew Seifert. 1970, formed his group Et Cetera, which combined electronics with rock rhythms. He has conducted many workshops for children, bringing out their creativity and helping them to improvise; 1974, had his own TV show, Glotzmusik, for children.

1975, he founded the United Jazz and Rock Ensemble (UJRE) to play on a Stuttgart Sunday TV show for young people directed by his friend Werner Schretzmeier. The band became so popular that it began to tour regularly, and to record it Dauner got together with three other members (Volker Kriegel, Albert Mangelsdorff, Ack van Rooyen) and Schretzmeier, to form their own record company, Mood Records. Dauner also composes music for films, television and plays. In the later 1970s he wrote *The Primal Scream* for symphony orchestra, choir, prepared tapes, solo voice and solo violin (Seifert), and this was premiered at the Berlin Festival. 1985, he wrote *Trans Tanz* for symphony orchestra plus solo trombone (Mangelsdorff) and solo piano (himself). He plays many solo piano concerts and he also often works with Mangelsdorff in duo, trio and quartet formations. With the German All Stars he has toured South America and Asia, and with his own groups and the UJRE he has played festivals all over Western and Eastern Europe. He has also won several prizes including Star of the Year 1971, from the *Münchner Abendzeitung*; 1972 and 1973, Musician of the Year, German *Sounds* poll; 1981 he was awarded the stipendium of Hamburg.

His favourite pianist is Glenn Gould, and other inspirations are Coltrane, Webern, Debussy, Ravel. Dauner's is a massive talent embracing (as both player and composer) every facet of contemporary music-making. In 1978 he collaborated with the composer Rolfe Unkel in creating new background music for F. W. Murnau's classic silent movie *Faust* (1926), Unkel composing the acoustic score and Dauner the integrated electronic music. His hobby is painting, he is deeply interested in the theatre, and both pursuits inspire and inform his music. [IC]

Six with UJRE; *Dream Talk* (1964), CBS; with J. L. Ponty, *Sunday Walk* (1968), MPS; *Für* (1969), Calig; *Output* (1970), ECM; with Mangelsdorff/Elvin Jones/Eddie Gomez, *A Jazz Tune I Hope* (1978), MPS; *Wolfgang Dauner Solo* (1978); *Dauner–Mangelsdorff* (1982); *Dauner Solo Piano* (1983) (also CD), all Mood

Davenport, Cow-Cow (Charles), piano, vocals, composer. b. Anniston, Alabama, 26 April 1895; d. Cleveland, Ohio, 2 December 1956. His career, which began in vaudeville, was dogged by bad health, bad luck and a spell in gaol, but by the 1940s, at the height of the boogie boom, he was a regular broadcaster and club attraction. He composed 'Cow-cow Boogie', a big hit for Ella Mae Morse and Ella Fitzgerald in the 1940s, and part-composed 'I'll be glad when you're dead, you rascal you' and 'Mama don't allow'. [DF]

Davern, Kenny (John Kenneth), clarinet, saxes. b. Huntingdon, Long Island, New York, 7 January 1935. He fell under the spell of Benny Goodman when young, then of Pee Wee Russell, whom he heard on a Ted Husing programme. His first professional job was with Jack Teagarden (who always encouraged good young players), thereafter he played on the New York club circuit, including Nick's and Eddie Condon's, and Central Plaza with stars including Billy Butterfield, Wild Bill Davison, Pee Wee Erwin, Condon and Dick Wellstood. Davern first achieved world-wide recognition in the highly successful supergroup Soprano Summit, which he co-led with Bob Wilber. The end of the group (after nine albums and three years' universal success) signalled his disenchantment with saxophone and the beginning of a solo career playing clarinet only. In recent years he toured Europe with the Blue Three (Dick Wellstood and Bobby Rosengarden) and as a soloist; his 1984 album *The Very Thought of You* won a Phonographic Industries award. Tempting as it is to bracket Davern and Wilber together, there are worlds of difference between them. Whereas Wilber ploughs the rich soils of Armstrong and Bechet, Davern walks the wilder byways of such eccentrics as Pee Wee Russell and Rex Stewart. His playing and stage demeanour (slim fingers lifted high off the keys, mobile shoulders) recall Russell, too, but Davern is his own man. Witty, sometimes acerbic, always eclectic, he has explored avant-garde jazz to great recorded effect, yet runs a deadly campaign against less justifiable contemporary jazz trends (such as amplification in every form). A classicist of deep conviction, he is a purist in the true sense. [DF]

The Very Thought of You (1984), Milton Keynes Music Series

Davies, John R. T. ('Ristic'), trumpet, trombone, saxes, piano, banjo. b. Wivelsfield, Sussex, 20 March 1927. He worked very early on with Mick Mulligan's band before in 1949 joining the revolutionary (for its time) Crane River Jazz Band, which set out to replay real New Orleans jazz properly and was still doing so, with line-up unaltered, in 1985. Around the same period he formed the first of his two record companies (Ristic), which produced a number of fine issues (some of them now rare), spent time in bands led by Steve Lane and Cy Laurie and from 1956 joined Sandy Brown's band for what he later said were 'the sixteen most valuable months in my career: Sandy was a super-giant.' From Brown's band Davies joined the Temperance Seven for eight more years as arranger/multi-instrumentalist and from the mid-1960s worked regularly with cornettist Dick Sudhalter, in the Anglo-American Alliance (his favourite), the New Paul Whiteman Orchestra (playing the role of Frank Trumbauer) and elsewhere. Then in 1972 he began work on his second company, Retrieval Records, which now regularly issues specialized material such as hot dance music – often from old masters cleaned and restored to mint playing quality by Davies's own expert processes. And although his appearances became a little rarer, Ristic's activities are worth searching out: his work is always hallmarked with conviction, intelligence and aesthetic judgement. He continued to appear with the Crane River Jazz Band, recorded (among others) with Jimmie Noone Jnr. in 1985, and runs his own band, John R. T.'s Gentle Jazz, which (he says) 'just once, by mistake, played with a drummer!' (other regular members include trombonist Jim Shepherd and another senior master of British jazz who knows what good jazz is, guitarist Nevil Skrimshire). [DF]

New Paul Whiteman Orchestra (featuring Dick Sudhalter), *Running Wild* (1975), Argo

Davis, Anthony, piano, composer. b. Paterson, New Jersey, 1951. Father a university professor, so he was brought up in campus towns of Princeton (NJ) and State College, Pennsylvania. His father knew Art Tatum; pianist Billy Taylor was a neighbour. Davis studied classical piano as a child; graduated in music at Yale in early 1970s, meeting and playing with trombonist George Lewis and others while he was there. 1974–7, played with trumpeter Leo Smith's band New Delta Ahkri, recording two albums; 1975, led his own quartet with Ed Blackwell (dms), Mark Helias (bass), Jay Hoggard (vibes). 1977, moved to New York City, performing with Oliver Lake, Anthony Braxton, Barry Altschul, Chico Freeman and Lewis; he also joined Leroy Jenkins's trio, staying with it until 1979. 1978, recorded his first album as leader, *Song for the Old World*. From the late 1970s into the 1980s Davis ran a duo, led a quartet with flute player James Newton, and played solo piano concerts. 1981, formed his octet Episteme to play his compositions and also pieces by other composers such as Earle Howard and Alvin Singleton. Davis has said: 'Although Ornette Coleman's melodic and linear innovations are important because they freed music from the regularly occurring bebop changes and bar lengths, we're now getting to a period in music where the harmonic dimensions are coming back. I hear almost everything I play as being tonal . . . Most of my own music is composed – written. I think that improvisation is one compositional tool within the framework of a given piece.' 1982, he was teaching two days a week at Yale: composition and history of creative music from 1900. 1985, his opera *X*, based on the life of Malcolm X, had its first performance in the USA.

His influences are Tatum, Monk, Mingus, Cecil Taylor and Ellington, among others; other inspirations are Messiaen, Chopin and Stravinsky. [IC]

With James Newton, Jay Hoggard, Leroy Jenkins, George Lewis and Leo Smith; *Song for the Old World* (1978), India-Navigation; *Past Lives* (1978), Red; *Of Blues and Dreams*, (1978), Sackville; solo, *Lady of the Mirrors* (1980), India-Navigation; *Episteme* (1981), Gramavision

Davis, Art(hur), bass. b. Harrisburg, Pennsylvania, 12 May 1934. After studying at the Juilliard and Manhattan schools of music, toured with Max Roach (1958–9) and Dizzy Gillespie (1959–61). In succeeding years worked with several folk singers and with Lena Horne, becoming a radio studio musician and playing in symphony orchestras. 1969–79, inactive in music 'for reasons connected with racial politics' (he had been the first black string-player to be a full staff member of the New York studio scene). A splendidly rhythmic performer, Davis amply justified John Coltrane's choice of him as occasional second bassist (1961, 1964–5), and he deserves to be far better known for his jazz work. [BP]

Resurgence (1979), Muse

Davis, Lem (Lemuel Arthur), alto sax. b. Tampa, Florida, 22 June 1914; d. New York City, 16 January 1970. His career began in the 1940s (with pianist Nat Jaffe) at a time when bebop was making some latter-day swing-based musicians sound listless and dull. Players such as Roy Eldridge, Bill Coleman and particularly Pete Brown suffered crises of identity at the period and some of Davis's later work (very like Brown's) sounds as if he was trying, rather uncomfortably, to come to terms with modernity without quite believing in it. A star of Coleman Hawkins's septet in 1943, and later with Eddie Heywood's small group (which became hugely successful) he was constantly working in the best company all through the 1940s and made a late extended appearance on Buck Clayton's 1953 'Hucklebuck' recording, by which time, sadly, his lines sound incomplete and his tone suggests that even his breathing had its emotional reservations about what he played. 'Davis is one of the great swing altos gone modern,' wrote annotator/producer George Avakian, 'and his occasional bop phrases kept us all on our toes.' It was a kind way of putting things. Davis – as he deserved to – stayed busy around New York through the 1950s, but little more was heard from him thereafter: listeners who want the best of him should search out titles from the earlier 1940s before jazz fashion seems, on recorded evidence at least, to have taken its toll of his exuberant creativity. [DF]

Davis, 'Lockjaw' (Eddie), tenor sax. b. New York City, 2 March 1921; d. 1986. After stays with Cootie Williams (1942–4) and Andy Kirk (1945–6), began leading own group and recording under own name in 1946. Joined Count Basie band (1952–3) and returned on several occasions, later doubling as saxist and road manager (1957, 1964–5, 1966, 1967–73). While his own leader again, had one of the first permanent tenor-and-organ trios (1955–60, though he had already recorded in this format in 1949). Co-led two-tenor quintet with Johnny Griffin (1960–2), then gave up playing to work as a booking agent (1963–4). Resumed appearances as guest soloist between stints with Basie, sometimes teaming up with Roy Eldridge (1974) and Harry Edison (1975–82).

A tough and trenchant stylist who seemed to have learned early on to emulate the Texas tenors such as Illinois Jacquet and Arnett Cobb, resembling them in his mid-1940s work especially. But he rapidly developed an individual and inimitable tone quality, by turns mellow and exasperated, which enhanced his jerky and somewhat repetitive phrasing. At ballad tempo Lockjaw showed familiarity with the achievements of Hawkins and especially Webster, as the tone becomes the chief vehicle for interpretation. [BP]

Eddie Davis/Johnny Griffin, *Tough Tenors* (1960–2), Milestone; *Light and Lovely* (1975), Black & Blue

Davis, Miles Dewey, trumpet, keyboards, composer, leader; also fluegelhorn. b. Alton, Illinois, 25 May 1926. Family moved to East St Louis in 1927. Wealthy middle-class background: grandfather was a landowner; father a successful dentist who also owned a ranch; mother played violin and his sister played piano. His father gave him a trumpet for his 13th birthday, and he had private lessons from Elwood Buchanan. He played in his high school band; also with r & b band, Eddie Randall's Blue Devils, in St Louis, 1941–3, while still at school. He was befriended by Clark Terry who influenced his sound and style; also met Dizzy Gillespie and Charlie Parker when the Billy Eckstine band played in St Louis.

September 1944, his father sent him to New York to study at the Juilliard School of Music, but he soon left there in order to play in the small clubs on 52nd Street with Coleman Hawkins and others, but mainly with Parker. November 1945, at 19, he was in the Parker quintet which recorded the first true bebop tracks, including the classic blues performance 'Now's the Time', which established Davis immediately as a master of understatement and an alternative trumpet stylist to Gillespie. 1946–8, he worked mostly with Parker, playing on all of the saxophonist's finest sextet and quintet recordings. He left Parker's group in late 1948, and began leading his own groups in New York, including a 9-piece band which created a revolutionary new sound.

The nonet grew out of extensive discussions between Davis and a small coterie of the most vital young talents of the day, who met informally at Gil Evans's apartment. Some, including Evans, Gerry Mulligan and Lee Konitz, were from the Claude Thornhill band which used French horns and tuba, and the aim was to achieve a full orchestral palette from a minimum number of instruments. The result was an instrumentation new to jazz: French horn, trumpet, trombone, tuba, alto and baritone saxes, piano, bass and drums. The nonet's urbane sound, the subtle, innovatory scoring, and the calm, unhurried solos, seemed to be a reaction against the frenetic excesses of bebop, and ushered in what came to be called the 'cool school' of jazz. This was perhaps the first example of key musicians of the time focusing and finding themselves through Miles Davis. The band was a total failure as a working unit, its only public appearances being a two-week engagement at the Royal Roost, September 1948, and one week a year later at the Clique Club. However, several tracks were recorded for Capitol and released on 78 rpms, spawning a host of imitators and admirers. Years later they were issued on an LP under the title *Birth of the Cool*, which has since become recognized as a classic album, and which has sold steadily throughout successive decades. The nonet established Davis as a leader and a talent quite separate from Charlie Parker.

He continued to work with various small groups on a casual basis in New York, and in 1949 played at the Paris Jazz Festival, his first international exposure. But then his brilliantly promising career suddenly lost all impetus and direction, and for four years (1949–53) he hardly worked at all. 1954 saw the beginning of his fully mature style: from that year until the end of the decade there was a succession of recorded masterpieces which astonished and delighted musicians and laymen alike, opened up several new avenues of musical development, influencing subsequent generations of jazzmen all over the world, and brought Davis a huge audience, many of whom knew little about jazz in general.

1955–6 saw the first great Miles Davis quintet, with John Coltrane, Red Garland, Paul Chambers and Philly Joe Jones, a group so brimful of new ideas that they recorded six influential albums in a twelve-month period. 1957, he played and recorded the soundtrack for Louis Malle's film *Lift to the Scaffold*, and in collaboration with Gil Evans recorded their first orchestral masterpiece, *Miles Ahead*, which was followed by two others – *Porgy and Bess* (1958) and *Sketches of Spain* (1959–60). In the last two years of the decade there were also two albums by the great Miles Davis sextet (with Coltrane and Cannonball Adderley), *Milestones* and *Kind of Blue*, both seminal, but the latter probably the most influential LP in jazz history. During the latter half of the 1950s Davis became the dominating figure in jazz: his rhythm-sections were regarded as the key units of the time, and his quintet and sextet were generally recognized as the leading groups of the period. The orchestral works with Gil Evans were not only innovative – creating new sounds, textures and techniques – but they also brought the integration of soloist and ensemble to a new and sustained peak. With *Kind of Blue*, Davis had fully established the relevance and beauty of modal improvisation (see MODAL JAZZ), and it soon became part of the current jazz language. He had also introduced (for the first time in 1954) a totally new instrumental sound – that of the metal harmon mute (without its stem) played close to the microphone, and had established the fluegelhorn, which he played on *Miles Ahead*, as an important expressive instrument: by the early 1960s harmon mutes and fluegelhorns were employed ubiquitously in jazz.

1963–4, Davis gradually formed a new quintet, yet again drawing together some of the most gifted young musicians of the time: Herbie Hancock (piano), Ron Carter (bass), Tony Wil-

Miles Davis

liams (dms) and Wayne Shorter (saxes). This particular rhythm-section is generally considered to be perhaps the greatest time-playing unit in jazz, and its brilliant fluidity can be heard on a series of live albums (1963–4) on which Davis and the group explore conventional structures – standard tunes, ballads, modal pieces and blues – so radically that they are sometimes taken to the verge of disintegration. The greatest of these LPs, and one of the finest live recordings in jazz history, is *My Funny Valentine* (1964). From 1965, Davis and his group began perfecting a new way of playing which came to be called 'time-no changes'. This was a form of abstraction in that the improvisation occurred in regular time, but without prearranged harmonies; in other words, there were composed themes, the group played in 4/4 or 3/4 at various tempos, but after the theme statement, the soloist and the pianist and bassist were free to choose what notes or chords they wanted. This approach added yet another dimension to the current jazz language and soon had practitioners everywhere. Its genesis and development are documented on four studio albums Davis recorded 1965–7. Leonard Feather commented in the later 1960s that Davis had taken small group improvisation to such a pitch of brilliance that he had 'nowhere to look except down'.

Up to this point virtually all Davis's small-group music had been based on themes which related clearly to popular song structures, but in 1968 he began to think more in terms of longer pieces, often without written themes. He also began to change the instrumentation of his group, using electric keyboards, electric guitars, multiple percussion and sometimes Indian musicians and instruments (sitar, tabla etc.). The harmonic and linear abstraction remained, but he employed rock rhythms which created a coherent pulse, giving his music a human face. Yet again, some of the most gifted of the current generation of players were drawn to his band: John McLaughlin, Chick Corea, Keith Jarrett, Dave Holland, Jack DeJohnette, Billy Cobham, Dave Liebman, Joe Zawinul, and others. In two years of furious creative activity, 1969–70, Davis recorded more than 20 LP sides, focusing and launching the jazz-rock-fusion movement. The key albums which had a global influence were *In a Silent Way*, *Bitches Brew* and, to a lesser extent, *Live-Evil* and *Jack Johnson*. Davis continued exploring this vein until 1975, when illness and physical and creative exhaustion incapacitated him. He was inactive until 1980 when he began to perform again.

In the 1980s he felt his way slowly into a new phase which was like a summary of his whole career. He steadily regained all his trumpet magnificence – the huge singing sound, the stamina, the use of the entire range from the lowest notes to the extreme upper register, and his characteristic gift for epigrammatic melodic phrases. Once more he drew to his band some key people from the current generation: Bill Evans and Bob Berg (saxes), Mike Stern and John Scofield (gtrs), Marcus Miller and Daryl 'The Munch' Jones (bass gtrs). He returned to using structures related to popular songs, and on his recordings he functioned more as a producer-composer-arranger than ever before. His studio albums, such as *Decoy* and *You're Under Arrest*, are highly organized, with an immense attention to detail and considerable complexity, yet they seem like blueprints for the looser live performances where the magic and the music really happen. Since his return, Miles Davis has toured once or twice a year in the USA, Europe and Japan, playing to huge and ecstatic crowds everywhere. Although he still employs electronics and rock rhythms, the whole of his past glows in the music, and yet he is neither coasting nor purveying nostalgia. Some of his most eloquent and moving playing has been done on these 1980s tours, and he is still pushing himself to the limit. For his London appearance in 1985, he was on stage for over five hours either playing or actively directing his band.

Miles Davis is a unique figure in jazz because his creativity and his influence as both player and conceptualist have been sustained over four decades (1945–85), and he has introduced the idea of permanent conceptual development. That is why he has been an inspirational figure for successive generations of musicians since the 1940s. With Louis Armstrong and Dizzy Gillespie, he is one of the three most influential trumpet players, but whereas the first two each introduced basically one stylistic approach, Davis has evolved at least three interrelated trumpet styles: the lyrical minimalist approach of 'Bag's Groove' (1954) or of his work on *Kind of Blue* (1959); the voluble brilliance and dramatic use of space of the live albums (1961–4); the abstraction, chromaticism and the electric trumpet of the late 1960s and early 1970s. Few, if any, players can match his emotional scope, which ranges from the extreme violence of 'What I Say' (*Live-Evil*) to the melancholy introspection of ballad performances such as 'Blue in Green' (*Kind of Blue*), the ominous disquiet of 'The Buzzard Song' (*Porgy and Bess*), or the sheer joy of 'Straight no Chaser' (*Milestones*).

His development is minutely documented by his huge body of recorded work, and every phase has its masterpieces which have defined areas and set standards for other musicians. Marcuse has said, 'The truth of art lies in its power to break the monopoly of established reality to define what is real', and Davis's work has broken this monopoly in decade after decade, forcing people to ask 'Is it Jazz?', and causing them to revise and expand their ideas of the music's identity and possibilities. [IC]

With Charlie Parker, Charles Mingus, Michel Legrand and others; *Birth of the Cool* (1949/50), Capitol; quintet, *Cookin'* and *Relaxin'* (1956), Prestige/OJC; with Gil Evans and orchestra, *Miles Ahead* (1957), *Porgy and Bess* (1958). *Sketches of Spain*, (1959/60); sextet, *Milestones* (1958), *Kind of Blue* (1959); quintet, *My Funny Valentine* (1964), *Miles Smiles* (1965), *Nefertiti* (1967), *Filles de Kilimanjaro*, (1968); group, *In a Silent Way* (1969), *Bitches Brew* (1969), *We Want Miles* (1981), *Decoy* (1984), all CBS

See Carr, Ian, *Miles Davis, A Critical Biography* (Quartet Books, London, 1982, Paladin, London, paperback, 1984, Morrow, New York, 1982)

Davis, Richard, bass. b. Chicago, Illinois, 15 April 1930. Part of the generation of Chicago musicians that included Johnny Griffin, John Gilmore and Clifford Jordan, Davis played in local symphony orchestras as well as with local pianists Ahmad Jamal (1953–4) and Don Shirley (1954–6). Then toured and recorded with Charlie Ventura (1956), Sarah Vaughan (1957–60, including tour of Europe) and Kenny Burrell (1959). Freelancing in New York from 1960; brief engagement with Eric Dolphy (1961) led to important 1963–4 albums together. Also formed recording association with Jaki Byard and Alan Dawson, backing Booker Ervin, Roland Kirk etc. (1963–6). Became heavily involved in session work for artists as varied as Igor Stravinsky and Van Morrison, while gigging with Thad Jones–Mel Lewis band (1966–72). Teaching in university from mid-1970s, Davis returned to Chicago; apart from appearances in film *Jazz In Exile* (1982) and at Chicago Jazz Festival, 1984, has been very selective about his jazz work.

Possessed of an enormous sound and a springy beat, he was the most dominant bassist to appear since Charles Mingus, and required a flexible yet driving drummer such as Dawson or Elvin Jones in order to be heard at his best. In these favourable circumstances, Davis was fond of breaking up the beat in a manner probably inspired by fellow Chicagoan Wilbur Ware, and his accompaniments as well as solos usually mixed high-register notes (including double-stops) with the low sounds of the open strings. At times, when surrounded by less suitable collaborators, Davis's work could sound too mannered, but his great contribution and influence should not be overlooked. [BP]

Elvin Jones/Davis, *Heavy Sounds* (1967), Impulse; *As One* (1975), Muse

Davis, Wild Bill (William Strethan), piano, organ, arranger. b. Glasgow, Missouri, 24 November 1918. Studied music at Tuskegee Institute and Wiley College, Texas (late 1930s), playing guitar and arranging for Milt Larkin band before their departure to West Coast. Davis moved to Chicago, doing some arrangements for Earl Hines band (early 1940s). Joined Louis Jordan group as pianist/arranger (1945–8), then returned to Chicago and began playing electric organ; recorded on organ guesting with

Wild Bill Davison

Jordan (1950) and had piano backing from Duke Ellington on one of his own first records (1951). Formed successful organ/guitar/drums trio (1951), working at Birdland and in Atlantic City etc. Occasional arrangements for Ellington, Count Basie and others; from 1961, series of albums with Johnny Hodges. Joined Ellington band for several months, playing featured organ solos (1969–70), then resumed own trio. Worked with Lionel Hampton 10-piece band (1979), also teamed in tenor/organ/drums trios with Illinois Jacquet, Eddie Davis, Guy Lafitte etc. Davis's dynamic arranging is best known via his organ version of 'April in Paris' as transcribed for the Basie band, but the same forthright qualities permeate all his playing. In addition, he deserves to be honoured as a pioneer, for of the pianists of the late swing/early r & b era he switched on to the organ earlier than either Milt Buckner or Bill Doggett. [BP]

Impulsions (1972), Black & Blue

Davison, Wild Bill (William Edward), cornet. b. Defiance, Ohio, 5 January 1906. From the early 1920s he was building lip and career with, among others, the Ohio Lucky Seven, the Chubb–Steinberg Orchestra (for which Davison recorded at 18 for Okeh), the Seattle Harmony Kings and Benny Meroff's Chicago-based orchestra (where he first met Eddie Condon). For most of the 1930s he was in Milwaukee, billed as 'Trumpet-King' Davison, and despite a lip injury in 1939 (he was hit in the mouth, appropriately for Milwaukee, by a flying beer mug) had arrived in New York by 1941. Work at Nick's saloon and with an Original Dixieland Jazz Band re-creation for the Katherine Dunham show culminated in 12 sides for Commodore recorded a week before his 38th birthday in 1944: brilliant recordings with Georg Brunis showing that Davison had found a new style of his own. A two-year spell in the army followed, and after discharge he joined Eddie Condon's house band in 1945. For the long nights and hard musical pace of Condon's club Davison was perfect: a commanding front man and personality; a tough and reliable lead cornettist that Condon could count on; above all an original. His physico-musical style – growls, rips, flares, long tones brusquely cut with a peremptory shake, all giving way to a heart-on-sleeve Irish sentimentality on ballads – personified Condon's Chicago jazz image and was quickly singled out for star treatment. TV presenter Garry Moore first recorded Davison with strings (for a compendium album *My Kind of Music* with, among others, Percy Faith) and this session lit the way for two more incandescent dates, *With Strings Attached* and the enchanting *Pretty Wild*, an irreplaceable jazz classic. Along with gold-standard Condon recordings and quartet dates of his own, by 1960 Davison – with his wife Anne as manager – was a soloist. Despite regular reunions with Condon he began a new lifetime pattern of bandleading and touring, appearing between 1965 and 1975 with over 100 bands and recording over 20 new albums: in the UK these were often with Alex Welsh's great band, including two lifelong colleagues Fred Hunt and Lennie Hastings. Living in Denmark in the 1970s Davison – a thorough professional despite his hard-drinking image – was working as busily as ever. Honoured by 1980 with Carnegie Hall concerts, Davison was still globetrotting in 1983 and after a short illness played the 1985 festivals and a 1986 British tour in fine form.

Because Wild Bill Davison made his name in a jazz age still dominated by the omnipotent Armstrong, his work was occasionally downgraded as a less effective paraphrase of the Armstrong prototype. In fact Davison's style is a brilliant alternative to Armstrong's which, though it was once based on admiration – 'just to make one note sound like Louis is enough to accomplish in one lifetime' he once said with typically rash generosity – long since outgrew its creative inspiration to become a perfect self-sufficient entity. [DF]

Chicago Jazz (1978), Philips

Dawson, Alan, drums and vibes. b. Marietta, Pennsylvania, 14 July 1929. Studied at Charles Alden Drum Studio in Boston, 1947; also studied vibes there, 1949. 1949–52, played with local and army dance bands; 1953, played with Lionel Hampton for three months, making his first trips to Africa and Europe and his first recording – with Clifford Brown and Gigi Gryce. Late 1953–1956, worked with Sabby Lewis. 1957–75, taught at the Berklee School of Music in Boston. During the 1960s he worked with Earl Hines, Booker Ervin, Teddy Wilson, Jaki Byard, Phil Woods, Sonny Stitt, Frank Foster and others. At the 1965 Berlin Jazz Festival, he worked with Sonny Rollins and Bill Evans. 1968–74, he was a member of the Dave Brubeck quartet, touring world-wide and playing major festivals. Dawson has all the virtues as a player – beautiful time, taste and great stamina – but his genius is for teaching. His first student was Tony Williams, and he has also taught Harvey Mason, Joe La Barbera, and many other leading drummers. His favourites are Jo Jones, Sid Catlett, Max Roach, Roy Haynes. [IC]

With Quincy Jones, Brubeck/Gerry Mulligan, Byard, Ervin, Dexter Gordon, Hank Jones and others; with Gigi Gryce Orchestra/Clifford Brown, *The Paris Collection* (1953), Inner City Jazz; with Phil Woods, *Musique du Bois* (1974), Muse

Dean, Elton, saxello, alto sax. b. Nottingham, 28 October 1945. Self-taught. 1967, worked with Long John Baldry's Bluesology. His long association with Keith Tippett began in 1968. Dean was with Soft Machine, 1969–72, after which he began leading his own group Just Us. 1972, joined the London Jazz Composers' Orchestra. 1974, led his own quartet with Louis Moholo, Harry Miller and Tippett, and the following year formed his 9-piece band Ninesense, which included Mongezi Feza, Alan Skidmore and Marc Charig. 1976, co-led a group (El Skid) with Alan Skidmore; 1977, worked with the Carla Bley band. Dean has toured extensively in Europe with various groups. 1985, toured Italy with his quintet, which included Harry Beckett. His favourite saxists are Coltrane and Joe Henderson, and other inspirations have been Miles Davis, Bill Evans and Keith Tippett. [IC]

With Tippett, Carla Bley, three with Soft Machine; with Ninesense, *Oh for the Edge* (1976); *Happy Daze* (1977); quartet, *They All be on this Old Road* (1976), all Ogun; quintet, *Boundaries* (1981), Japo

Dean, Roger Thornton, piano, synthesizer, double-bass, vibraphone. b. Manchester, 6 September 1948. Studied biology at Cambridge University. Private music lessons. Began performing at Cambridge in late 1960s. From 1973, with Graham Collier Music. 1975, formed his own group Lysis. Also worked with London Jazz Composers' Orchestra, Barry Guy, Tony Oxley, Derek Bailey, Harry Beckett, Terje Rypdal, Arild Andersen, Ted Curson, Tony Scott, Tony Coe and others. Has toured playing solo piano concerts in Scandinavia, Australia, Israel and the UK. Also a critic and writer, a performer in contemporary composed music, and a composer with works played in many countries. Among his favourite players are Cecil Taylor, Bill Evans, Barre Phillips and Walt Dickerson. Other influences are Webern, Cage, Coltrane, Miles Davis. Dean is professor of cell biology at Brunel University. [IC]

With Collier, *Midnight Blue* (1975), Mosaic; with Lysis, *Cycles* (1977), Mosaic; *Lysis play Dualyses* (1978), Soma; *Lysis Plus* (1979), Mosaic

Dedrick, Rusty (Lyle F.), trumpet, composer. b. Delevan, New York, 7 December 1918. He trained with big bands led by Dick Stabile, Red Norvo, Claude Thornhill and Ray McKinley among others, then after the war worked for NBC TV. From 1950 he produced a small number of fine records (including duets with Don Elliott and a solo review of *The Trumpet Greats*), but it was after 1970 – when he began appearing at jazz festivals again – that the jazz public saw more of him. By then Dedrick had formed a partnership with Bill Borden of Monmouth Evergreen; some later albums for Borden (including *Back Home Again*, a last date for Lee Wiley, an Isham Jones collection, and three volumes of an Irving Berlin chronology with Bob Wilber) show off his broad-based generous trumpet style to perfection. Dedrick, like Bob Wilber and Dick Cary, is often found at the centre of constructive jazz enterprises: since 1971 he has directed jazz studies at Manhattan College of Music. [DF]

Twelve Isham Jones Evergreens (nda), Monmouth Evergreen

Deems, Barrett, drums. b. Springfield, Illinois, 1 March 1914. Often billed as 'the world's fastest drummer', Deems tends to be thought of as a post-war 'new star' who came to fame with Louis Armstrong's All Stars (he appeared with them in the 1956 film *High Society*). In fact he was working professionally by the late 1920s (with Paul Ash) and led his own bands around Chicago in the 1930s before joining Joe Venuti for seven years from 1937. Then came work with a variety of top leaders including Jimmy Dorsey (1945), Red Norvo (1948) and Muggsy Spanier (1951–4). After his four-year spell with Armstrong – during which he contributed to such great records as *Satch plays Fats* and *Louis Armstrong plays W.C. Handy* – Deems led his own band again, at Chicago's Brass Rail club, worked with Jack Teagarden, 1960–4, and from 1964 formed a working partnership with the Dukes of Dixieland. In the 1970s and 1980s he was still a drum force to reckon with, working around Chicago, his home base, with a variety of groups including Joe Kelly's Gaslight Band (1970), playing and recording with Art Hodes and touring in tribute packages such as Keith Smith's 'Wonderful World of Louis Armstrong'. [DF]

Louis Armstrong, *Satch plays Fats* (1955), CBS

DeFranco, Buddy (Boniface Ferdinand Leonardo), clarinet (and alto sax, bass-clarinet). b. Camden, New Jersey, 17 February 1923. Played with several name bands on alto including Gene Krupa (*c*. 1942–3), Charlie Barnet (1943–4) and Tommy Dorsey (three stints in 1944–8, featured regularly on clarinet). In between, prolific small-group work in California, New York, Chicago. Member of Count Basie octet (1950–1), playing in film short but not allowed on screen with otherwise all-black group (replaced by Marshall Royal). Formed own big band (1951), then quartet with Art Blakey on drums and pianist Kenny Drew, later Sonny Clark (1952–5). Settled on West Coast, led new quartet (1961–4), then became leader of Glenn Miller 'ghost band' (1966–74). Involved in educational work in late 1970s and occasional work as soloist; several tours of Europe in 1980s. A consummate technician who invariably provokes the envy of struggling performers, DeFranco incurs the same criticism of technique without taste which can be levelled against Oscar Peterson and Buddy Rich. In addition, wind instruments in jazz have benefited from non-standard tone quality employed to enhance the player's structures and to express his emotional depths, whereas the mechanical perfection of DeFranco appeals mainly to listeners with different priorities. [BP]

Groovin' (1984), Hep

Defries, David Colin Walter, trumpet, fluegelhorn, tenor horn, percussion. b. London, 24 May 1952. Father and mother both musical. Defries sang in his school choir and played with Surrey County Youth Orchestra; he attended various jazz courses and spent two terms as a student at Leeds College of Music. 1970s, worked with various groups in London, including Julian Bahula's Jabula, Don Weller's Major Surgery and Dudu Pukwana's Zila. 1981, with guitarist Mark Wood, founded the group Sunwind, which the following year won first prize in the Greater London Arts Association jazz competition. Early 1980s, joined Chris MacGregor's Brotherhood of Breath, and has also played with Rip Rig & Panic, the Breakfast Band and Loose Tubes. His favourites range from Louis Armstrong to Miles Davis, Clark Terry to Mongezi Feza, and he names Chris MacGregor, Hermeto Pascoal and Collin Walcott as inspirational figures. [IC]

With Brotherhood of Breath, Rip Rig & Panic; with Sunwind, *The Sun Below* (1983), MMC; *The Secret City* (1985), MMC

DeJohnette, Jack, drums, piano, composer, melodica, voice. b. Chicago, 9 August 1942. Classical piano lessons for ten years; graduate of the American Conservatory of Music, Chicago. Began playing drums with high school concert band, after being inspired by Max Roach. During his early years in Chicago, he covered the whole spectrum, playing everything from r & b to free jazz, and he was practising four hours on piano and four hours on drums every day. 1966, moved to New York, playing drums with organist John Patton; later he gigged with Jackie McLean and singers Betty Carter and Abbey Lincoln. Late 1966–1969, with the Charles Lloyd quartet, which included Keith Jarrett and Ron McClure, and it was his exposure with this group that established his national and international reputation. The Lloyd quartet was the first jazz group to play in US rock concert halls, and the group also toured Europe six times, the Far East once, and was the first band of modern jazz musicians to play in Russia. DeJohnette also gigged around New York with Coltrane, Monk, Freddie Hubbard, Bill Evans, Jarrett, Chick Corea and Stan Getz.

August 1969, played on Miles Davis's seminal album *Bitches Brew*, and in April 1970 joined the Davis band, staying with it until the summer of 1971. During this period he began leading his own groups and as well as playing drums, performed on melodica, piano, clavinet and organ. After leaving Davis, he led his own band, Compost, touring in the USA and internationally. During the 1970s he became virtually one of the house drummers for ECM records, appearing as sideman with many people, including Kenny Wheeler, John Abercrombie, Jan Garbarek, George Adams. He also began recording for ECM as leader, and the first album by his quartet New Directions, with Abercrombie, Lester Bowie and Eddie Gomez, received the Prix du Jazz Contemporain de l'Académie Charles Cros, 1979. From 1980 he formed a group with varying personnel, calling it Jack DeJohnette's Special Edition, which recorded a series of magnificent albums.

DeJohnette is one of the most gifted and complete musicians in jazz. As a drummer, he has everything – a perfectly poised sense of time, an unerring instinct for knowing when to sustain a rhythm and when to disturb the pulse, and he always plays orchestrally with immense attention to detail. As well as Roach, his early favourites were Philly Joe Jones and Elvin Jones, and he embodies all their virtues and has added his own dimension, becoming a master of every style and genre from r & b to rock, ethnic, reggae, bebop and free improvisation. An example of his sheer power is the track 'What I Say' from the Miles Davis album *Live-Evil*, on which DeJohnette sustains a ferocious rock pulse for 15 minutes and then plays a long drum solo. Not surprisingly most contemporary drummers cite him as one of their favourite drummers. He is also an excellent pianist and a considerably talented composer, who with his Special Edition recordings has created some of the most interesting jazz of the 1980s. His composing is as consummate as his playing and just as diverse. [IC]

With Bill Evans, Charles Lloyd, Joe Henderson, Freddie Hubbard, Miroslav Vitous, Miles Davis and many others; *Pictures* (1976); *New Directions* (1978); Special Edition, *Tin Can Alley* (1980), *Inflation Blues* (1982), *Album Album* (1984), all ECM; *The DeJohnette Complex* (1968), Milestone; with Compost, *Take Off Your Body* (1972), Columbia

de Paris, Sidney, trumpet, tuba, vocals. b. Crawfordsville, Indiana, 30 May 1905; d. New York City, 13 September 1967. He was in New York from 1925; 1926–31, worked with Charlie Johnson (the longtime bandleader at Smalls' Paradise), with Fletcher Henderson (replacing Louis Armstrong's replacement Rex Stewart in late 1931), then with Don Redman's band (with whom he recorded classics such as 'Cherry', 'Four or five times' and 'Shimme sha wabble'). For the ten years after 1936 his career diversified, with work for bandleaders as different as Mezz Mezzrow and Charlie Barnet, leading his own groups and playing in theatre orchestras. All this thoroughly equipped him for the demands of his brother Wilbur de Paris's New New Orleans Jazz Band, which formed in 1947 and for the next 16 years was a success playing everything from blues to light classics (for a long time the band carried a second trumpet player, Doc Cheatham). De Paris's fluent creativity, unique rhythmic sense, range and attractive New Orleans vibrato are all over his brother's successful albums. He remains a neglected talent. [DF]

De Paris Dixie (1944–51), Blue Note

de Paris, Wilbur, trombone, leader, occasionally drums. b. Crawfordsville, Indiana, 11 January 1900; d. New York City, 3 January 1973. He began his career around 1912 in carnival bands and tent shows and heard a feast of music on his travels: canny, observant and with a strong sense of what was commercial, he soon had 'eyes to be a bandleader' (in Dickie Wells's words) and by 1925 had his very own band, Wilbur de Paris' Cotton Pickers, at the Cinderella Ballroom, NY. For the next 18 years he was planning, and working as a sideman for other leaders, including three years in Luis Russell's orchestra (alongside a future sideman, banjoist Lee Blair) backing master-showman Louis Armstrong. 1943, he formed a band briefly with brother Sidney, left it for two years to join Duke Ellington, playing Tricky Sam Nanton's role (by all accounts with moderate success) and finally in 1947 put together his New New Orleans Band to make new discoveries within old traditions: 'We try to play as the early New Orleans masters would if they were alive today,' he explained later. The de Paris band, completed when Omer Simeon, an underrated soloist, replaced saxophonist Franz Jackson, sounded like no one but themselves: often using unorthodox instruments (Wilber Kirk's harmonica, the leader's valve trombone, his brother's tuba) and unusual repertoire (originals, classical pastiches, pop tunes), they produced, in Brian Rust's words, 'forthright mellow music – an object lesson to most of our revivalists'. Many UK revivalists – Chris Barber for one – learned much from the de Paris formula and it laid the foundations for the style and approach of Britain's Trad boom bands from 1960 on. In New York the band broke records with a famous 11-year residency at Jimmy Ryan's (after the death of Simeon, Garvin Bushell joined the band) and de Paris signed a lucrative contract with Atlantic Records which gave free and successful rein to his formulas: every record he made at the period is a small classic. When Jimmy Ryan's finally made a change, de Paris continued bandleading in other New York clubs until shortly before his death. [DF]

The Wild Jazz Age (1960), Atlantic/London

Desmond, Paul (Paul Breitenfeld), alto sax. b. San Francisco, 25 November 1924; d. 30 May 1977. Studied clarinet at high school and college, rehearsed and recorded with Dave Brubeck octet (1948–50). Worked with bands locally, then added to Brubeck's regular trio from 1951. Left after 16 years in order to freelance, rejoining Brubeck for specific tours (1972, 1973, 1975). Also appeared in concert with Modern Jazz Quartet (1971) and worked occasionally under own name in New York and Toronto before his death from cancer.

It was only too easy to think of Desmond as merely the best thing in a not very interesting group, and certainly his effortless superiority when matched against Brubeck was the most easily noticeable aspect of his work; the extreme popularity of his tune 'Take Five' (now an anthem of street musicians) did nothing to lessen his identification with the pianist's group. But, despite a certain over-cleverness in his musical humour, he was a much more intuitive soloist, capable of great invention and swing, much akin to Zoot Sims. One of a whole generation of saxophonists initially inspired by Lester Young, he was also marked by Lee Konitz but used a purer, more forthright tone. He was also the only altoist in the early 1950s (apart from Earl Bostic) employing the upper harmonics of the instrument, and it was probably the questing nature of his improvisation that attracted Anthony Braxton, an early admirer. Away from Brubeck, for instance in his quartet partnerships with Gerry Mulligan and Jim Hall, there was an added relaxation and gentleness to his playing which was well exploited in a series of middle-of-the-road albums made during his last decade. [BP]

Take Ten (1963–4), RCA; *Paul Desmond Quartet Live* (1975), Horizon

Paul Desmond

Deuchar, Jimmy (James), trumpet, fluegelhorn, mellophonium, composer, arranger. b. Dundee, Scotland, 26 June 1930. Family musical; he had trumpet lessons and played around the Dundee area. Moved to London in 1950, playing with the Johnny Dankworth Seven. 1952–5, worked with Jack Parnell, Ronnie Scott and Tony Crombie; 1956, toured with Lionel Hampton; 1957, toured the USA with Scott, then joined Kurt Edelhagen's radio orchestra at Cologne. 1960–2, again worked with Scott; 1962–6, with Tubby Hayes. From 1966, worked as soloist and staff arranger with the Edelhagen orchestra; 1965–71, he also worked with the occasional big band led by Kenny Clarke and Francy Boland. He returned to the UK in 1971, and moved back to Scotland during the 1970s. In the 1980s he was active in London. During the mid-1960s Deuchar played with the Benny Golson orchestra on TV in the UK. [IC]

With Tubby Hayes, Zoot Sims, Edelhagen, Clarke–Boland

Dickenson, Vic (Victor), trombone, vocals. b. Xenia, Ohio, 6 August 1906; d. New York City, 16 November 1984. One of the first jazz trombonists (like Dickie Wells) to use the inbuilt humour of the slide trombone to full artistic effect, he heard Mamie Smith's Jazz Hounds while still at school but felt, he said, 'the trombone part was too limited. So I learned what everybody played on the records – the sax and clarinets too!' A natural 'ear' player with little formal training, he worked early on in territory bands (including Speed Webb's and Zack Whyte's); 1930s, with fine big bands like those of Bennie Moten, Blanche Calloway (Cab's most successful sister) and Claude Hopkins; 1940s with Eddie Heywood and others. After a spell of illness in 1947 he was 'house-trombonist' at the Savoy, Boston from 1949, then worked in and around the area with such as Buster Bailey, Bobby Hackett and the McPartlands before coming back to New York for work at the Metropole (replacing J. C. Higginbotham) and

Vic Dickenson

eight years with the very successful Saints and Sinners. Then came stints with Bobby Hackett again, Eddie Condon, the World's Greatest Jazz Band, and, from 1975, Red Balaban and Cats at Condon's. Dickenson, like his frequent colleague Bobby Hackett, was one of the best loved and respected jazzmen in the music's history. Famous for an encyclopedic knowledge of songs, he delivered everything with fluent assurance, burry tone and a droll repertoire of humorous inventions of which he never sounded tired. Benny Morton, who described him as 'The Will Rogers of the trombone', said: 'Vic has more to say on the trombone than anybody I know. He gets musicians laughing when he plays, yet he can say the most serious things with a touch of humour.' Dickenson's humour – as well as his kindness and humility – was as well loved offstage as on. 'One night Vic was late back on the stand,' recalls Warren Vaché, a lifelong fan and regular colleague, 'and the club owner bawled him out, quite rudely. Vic just smiled and tiptoed back onto the stand. And you know what he played? "I apologize"!' Dickenson's favourite phrase was 'Music am a bitch!'; so in the nicest way was he. [DF]

Vic Dickenson Showcase (1954), Vanguard

See Balliett, Whitney, *Jelly Roll, Jabbo and Fats* (OUP, 1983); Dance, Stanley, *The World of Swing* (Scribner's, 1974, repr. Da Capo, 1979)

Dickerson, Carroll, violin, leader. b. 1895; d. October 1957. Primarily remembered as the leader of a Chicago orchestra in the 1920s which featured Louis Armstrong and subsequently travelled with him to New York, he was a strict disciplinarian who demanded the best. He made an impressive onstage figure, dressed in a velvet smock with circular rhinestones studding the back and a tam-o-shanter completing his outfit, but his violin playing was less impressive than his wardrobe, and when Dickerson got drunk (which he frequently did) Earl Hines remembers that, 'He sometimes didn't know if he was using the front of the bow or the back!' Resident bandleader at the Sunset Café, 1922–4, Dickerson then took his orchestra on the road for a 48-week tour of the Pantages Theater circuit and when he arrived back in Chicago was the centre of attention: at the Sunset Café once again, and featuring Louis Armstrong, he was in charge of a high-powered show until Joe Glaser impatiently sacked him and made Armstrong leader instead. Dickerson took over at the Savoy Dance Hall, Armstrong rejoined him, and soon after, in early 1929, Armstrong, Dickerson and the band travelled to New York to join the *Great Day* company. After a season at Connie's Inn they disbanded, but Dickerson stayed in New York to try his luck, briefly led the Mills Blue Rhythm Band, then toured with King Oliver. By 1935 he was back in Chicago and stayed there until he died, leading bands in clubs and dance halls. [DF]

The Louis Armstrong Legend, vol.4, 1925–9, World Records

Dillard, Bill (William), trumpet, vocals. b. Pennsylvania, 20 July 1911. A New York performer by 1929, he worked early on with Jelly Roll Morton and all through the 1930s with a selection of fine big bands including Luis Russell's (1931–2), Benny Carter's (1933) and Teddy Hill's (1934–8). While he was with Hill, Dillard became friends with Dizzy Gillespie, who remembers him: 'Bill was beautiful – played first trumpet and he'd show me how to hold notes out, how to sing on the trumpet. He helped me change the little things I did that weren't professional.' After three more years working with more star names, including Coleman Hawkins and Louis Armstrong, Dillard embarked on an acting career which took him into Broadway shows such as *Carmen Jones* (1943) and Kurt Weill's *Lost in the Stars* (1950) and radio series (*Love of Life* and others), besides regular commitments with his own big band and freelancing. During the 1980s he continued his stage work in the show *One mo' time* (replacing Jabbo Smith who had appeared in the New York production) touring Europe and Australia, and recording in London for producer Dave Bennett with British guitarist Denny Wright and others. [DF]

DiMeola, Al, guitar. b. Bergenfield, New Jersey, July 1954. Started on drums; inspired by the Beatles, took up guitar at age nine. Private lessons, but no formal classical training. At 15, playing country music on pedal steel guitar, but heard the current Miles Davis band with Chick Corea and knew immediately that 'that was the new sound I wanted to get into.' Went to the Berklee School of Music and, while there in 1973, worked with Barry Miles and Joe Kaye's Neophonic Orchestra. 1974, joined Corea's Return to Forever. In the later 1970s he led his own groups and toured in trio with John McLaughlin and Paco DeLucia, playing acoustic guitar in international concert halls. In the mid-1980s, he led his own group, Al DiMeola Project, with Airto Moreira (perc), Danny Gottlieb (dms), Phil Markowitz (keyboards) and Ron McClure (bass), touring internationally with it. DiMeola was influenced by classical guitarists, Julian Bream in particular, and also by Larry Coryell, who helped and encouraged him. Like McLaughlin and Coryell, he is equally at home with acoustic and electric guitars, and is a virtuoso on both. [IC]

With RTF, McLaughlin/DeLucia; *Mediterranean Sundance* (1976); *Elegant Gypsy* (1976); *Friday Night in San Francisco* (1981); *Electric Rendezvous* (1982); *Tour de Force* (1982), all CBS

Di Pasqua, Michael, drums, percussion. b. Orlando, Florida, 4 May 1953. Father played tenor sax; brother, drums. 1969–75, played with Zoot Sims–Al Cohn quintet, Don Elliott, Gerry Mulligan and Chet Baker, Jackie Cain and Roy Kral, among others. 1976–80, co-led group Double Image with Dave Friedman, Dave Samuels and Harvie Swartz. 1981, co-led group Gallery with Dave Samuels and Paul McCandless. 1982, joined Eberhard Weber's Later That Evening band. From 1982 with Jan Garbarek's group. Favourites, Jack DeJohnette, Nana Vasconcelos, Trilok Gurtu, Tony Williams, Philly Joe Jones; other inspirations, Miles Davis, Keith Jarrett, Bill Evans. Composition, 'A Last Game' recorded with Gallery. [IC]

With Don Elliott, *Rejuvenation* (1975), CBS; *Double Image* (1977), Enja; Double Image, *Dawn* (1979); with Ralph Towner, *Old Friends, New Friends* (1979); *Gallery* 1981; with Weber, *Later That Evening* (1982); with Garbarek, *Wayfarer* (1983); *It's OK to Listen to the Grey Voice* (1984), all ECM

Dirty describes, in early jazz, a style of playing incorporating particular tonal effects which are the opposite of a so-called pure tone. A 'hot' tone is not pure either, but especially bright and vibrant; a dirty tone, on the other hand, includes growls and squeezed notes (and combinations of the two) liable to evoke a gut reaction from the listener, and is often used as a brief contrast to the player's normal style.

The implication of earthiness, and the rural roots that go with it, compares interestingly with the later, more citified term 'funky' in its musical connotations. [BP]

Disley, Diz (William Charles), guitar, bandleader. b. Winnipeg, Manitoba, 27 May 1931. He spent his young days in Wales and Yorkshire. A gifted cartoonist (he graduated from Leeds College of Art and later featured his work in the *Radio Times*, *Spectator*, *Melody Maker* and *Jazz Journal*) he played early on with the Yorkshire Jazz Band, then as freelance soloist and occasional sideman with all the best British bands of the 1950s (Welsh, Brown, Ball, as well as Bob Cort and Nancy Whiskey) and often led his own Hot Club-style string quintets. In the 1960s he became a popular figure in folk clubs, an occasional radio presenter (he also introduced the Beatles on their first London concert) and was the first to reintroduce Stephane Grappelli to the British music scene – and international stardom again – in June 1973, when he organized a tour of folk clubs for the violinist backed by his own trio (Denny Wright, John Hawkesworth, briefly, and Disley himself). Thereafter he worked regularly as guitarist-partner to Grappelli, led occasional bands of his own in between and in 1985 was consultant for a projected full-length film (for First Film Company) about Reinhardt. There could be no better consultant: one of the great eccentrics of British acoustic music, Disley is one of Django's spiritual sons. [DF]

Stephane Grappelli, *I Got Rhythm* (1973), Black Lion (double)

Dixieland (1) 'Dixie's Land' – a song written by Dan Emmett in 1859 – immortalized the estates (on Manhattan Island) of slavetrader Jonathan Dixie, who often sold his slaves to go South; later the song was taken up by the Confederates in the Civil War. Coincidentally, 'Dixie's line', drawn by two British astronomers Mason and Dixon, came to represent the dividing line between free American states and those Southern ones that still practised slavery. Between them the two nicknames supplied another for America's South which in turn passed into jazz lore. [DF]

(2) More than most, a word which has different shades of meaning according to who is using it. Basically, it denotes the standardized and internationalized version of Chicago-style jazz of the 1920s, with extrovert, even brash ensemble improvisations framing solo statements that are far more prevalent than in the New Orleans style (typified by the King Oliver Creole Band or even by the contrarily-named Original Dixieland Band).

In American terminology, Dixieland is also a blanket description for anything descended from early New Orleans jazz and, in the mouths of Americans who earn their living playing it, it is not a disparaging term. It only becomes that when spoken by adherents of the revival of 'genuine' New Orleans and by fans of the later generations of New Orleans-born players who benefited from the revival.

The same ambiguities surround the use of the word 'Trad', which is the European term for European Dixieland. [BP]

Dixon, Bill (William Robert), trumpet, composer, scholar, educator. b. Nantucket, Massachusetts, 5 October 1925. Mother a writer and blues singer; family moved to New York in 1933. Dixon began on trumpet at 18; studied painting at Boston University. After army service, which took him to Europe for a year, he studied at the Hartnett School of Music, 1946–51. Freelanced around New York as trumpeter and arranger; also led his own groups; befriended Cecil Taylor in 1958, working with him subsequently. Early 1960s, collaborated with Archie Shepp; 1964, organized the Jazz Composers' Guild (see MANTLER, MICHAEL), which aimed to promote the new free jazz and to improve the working conditions of the avant-garde musicians who created it. 1966, Dixon premiered his composition 'Pomegranate' at the Newport Jazz Festival with dancer Judith Dunn, and this performance led to a contract with RCA, and his orchestral recording *Intents and Purposes*, which was highly acclaimed.

1968, he took up a teaching post at Bennington College, Vermont, and there during the 1970s he established a Black Music department with its own building. He also created the occasional post of musician in residence, which has been filled by Jimmy Lyons, Jimmy Garrison, Alan Shorter, Alan Silva and others. 1976, Dixon, with Stephen Horenstein (tenor sax) and Alan Silva (bass), performed his *Autumn Sequence, from a Paris Diary*, at the Paris annual autumn festival. The piece attempted to show musical development as contemporary history and the music was presented in sections on five successive nights. 1980, he led a septet at the Verona Jazz Ottanta festival. [IC]

With Archie Shepp, *Peace* (1962), Savoy; Bill Dixon orchestra, *Intents and Purposes* (1966–7), RCA; *Bill Dixon 7-tette* (1964), Savoy; *For Friends* (1976), Pipe Records; with Cecil Taylor, *Conquistador* (1966), Blue Note

Dodds, Baby (Warren), drums. b. Robson Street, New Orleans, 24 December 1898; d. Chicago, 14 February 1959. The younger brother of clarinettist Johnny Dodds, and always a bad young brother, Baby Dodds began

Baby Dodds

drinking early on, bought his first drums at the age of 16 and played in Willie Hightower's band that year for ice-creams. He was soon playing all over New Orleans in a showy instrumental style that used every one of his drums, then in Fate Marable's highly able Streckfus orchestra and by 1922 with King Oliver's great Creole Jazz Band (Oliver's records clearly show up Dodds's ground-breaking talent). After the financial quarrel that broke up Oliver's band, Baby Dodds was around Chicago for 20 years (often with his disciplinarian elder brother: 'very hard for me', he said ruefully), and supplementing income where necessary working with a taxi firm. In 1945, in New York to work with Bunk Johnson, his style was still controversial: 'the way he played drums behind the band was a solo in itself', says George Wettling. The approach was disturbing to Johnson (and to other musicians, including Lester Young, who also preferred a discreet tick) but it rang a bell for the liberated role of African drums in modern and avant-garde jazz. In 1947 on a Rudi Blesh show, Dodds listened with interest to Max Roach; his 1953 ambition, 'to work out a drum symphony for five or six drummers', finds an echo in Roach's own M'Boom percussion ensemble. From 1949 Dodds suffered a series of strokes; 'actually physically he's about 95,' said Jo Jones. 'He did more living than three men!' [DF]

Baby Dodds Trio (1946), Riverside

See Gara, Larry, *The Baby Dodds Story* (1959)

Dodds, Johnny (John M), clarinet, occasionally alto sax. b. Waverly, Louisiana, 12 April 1892; d. Chicago, 8 August 1940. He sang 'real high tenor' in the family quartet, then graduated to penny whistle and clarinet, which despite early lessons from Lorenzo Tio he always played by ear. After ten years in and around New Orleans (from 1910 with, among others, Frank Dusen, Kid Ory and Billy Mael's vaudeville troupe) he joined King Oliver's Creole Jazz Band in Chicago and stayed for three years: his throbbing, fervent clarinet recorded more than 40 sides for Oliver for Gennett, Columbia, Okeh and Paramount. When he left in 1924, after a pay disagreement, it was to begin – for several years at least – a prosperous and successful solo career at Burt Kelly's Stables, a wealthy, Mafia-controlled club on Chicago's Rush Street. Dodds combined his residency at Kelly's, and occasionally other small South Side clubs, with regular studio work, recording with his own band, with Jelly Roll Morton, Lovie Austin, and with Louis Armstrong (for whom he recorded all the Hot Five and Seven classics). He took music very seriously, insisted on regular rehearsals for his own band and refused to tolerate drunkenness or slack behaviour from his younger brother Baby, whom he kept on a tight rein. 'I'd say they did regard themselves as artists in the sense we use the term today', says Garvin Bushell. 'They knew they were doing something new that nobody else could do!' This was less true by 1930, although by that time the canny Dodds had invested his money wisely in property, including a block of flats. Nevertheless, work and income were getting harder to come by and Dodds began a round of tireless hustling, and playing – for saloons, clubs, rent parties and jam sessions: one regular fan in Chicago was Benny Goodman. By 1935, with Goodman's own rise to fame, the craze for sophisticated big-band swing, and a new brilliant clarinet star, Jimmie Noone, making headlines in Chicago, Dodds's once-fashionable currency was under question. In 1938 (perhaps a glimmer of the forthcoming revival) he recorded in New York with Charlie Shavers, there were more records in Chicago the year after and a late residency with old friends Lonnie Johnson and Natty Dominique at the Hayes Hotel, but soon after Dodds suffered a stroke. He died the following year, missing the jazz revival by a whisker; his style of playing lives on in the work of aficionados such as Kenny Davern and (in particular) Cy Laurie. [DF]

Johnny Dodds, vols. 1/2 (1926–40), MCA

Doggett, Bill (William Ballard), piano, organ, arranger. b. Philadelphia, 16 February 1916. After playing with local groups, led own locally-based big band (1938) which then toured for a year under Lucky Millinder before breaking up. With Jimmy Mundy big band (1939), then with new Millinder band (1940–2). Arranged for Ink Spots vocal group (1942–4), and freelance for Louis Armstrong, Lionel Hampton, Count

Basie. Recorded on Johnny Otis's first big-band session (1945) during West Coast stay, and four times with early Illinois Jacquet groups (1945–7); replaced Wild Bill Davis in Louis Jordan band (1948–51). Inspired by Davis, took up organ and recorded with Eddie Davis and Ella Fitzgerald (1951). Led own quintet (octet from 1958) with great success in r&b field, his 1956 record 'Honky Tonk' being of classic simplicity. Not much of Doggett's early big-band writing (even for Millinder) has been positively identified as his, but there can be no doubt that this talent carried over directly into his own small group. [BP]

Gon' Doggett (1955–60), Charly

Doldinger, Klaus, tenor and soprano sax, composer, also clarinet, keyboards, synthesizer, mellotron. b. Berlin, 12 May 1936. Studied piano from 1947, clarinet from 1952, at the Robert Schumann Conservatory, Dusseldorf. 1960s, did jazz workshops with visiting Americans such as Kenny Clarke, Max Roach, Donald Byrd and others. Toured in Europe, North Africa, Middle East and South America with his own quintet. 1970, formed a jazz-rock group, which from 1971 was known as Passport, and played festivals and TV in Europe and the Far East. A prolific composer, since the mid-1970s he has spent most of his time writing music for major feature films and TV series such as *Das Boot.* Influenced by Sidney Bechet, Charlie Parker, John Coltrane, Ornette Coleman, Gil Evans and Miles Davis. Doldinger has won many German jazz and rock polls. [IC]

Doldinger Jubilee Concert (1973–4), Atco; *Cross Collateral* (1974), Atco; *Passport et al/ Doldinger Jubilee '75*, Atlantic

Dolphy, Eric Allan, alto sax, bass-clarinet, flute, clarinet, etc. b. Los Angeles, 20 June 1928; d. Berlin, 29 June 1964, as a result of uraemia and/or undiagnosed diabetes. Began playing clarinet in junior school, and studied with noted ex-Les Hite bandsman Lloyd Reese. Playing experience with various West Coast groups, including bebop-influenced Roy Porter big band (1948–9), and with army bands (1950–2). Gigging with Gerald Wilson, Buddy Collette and own groups led to joining the popular Chico Hamilton quintet in early 1958. Late 1959, settled in New York, then worked with Charles Mingus small groups (and big band on record); also busy recording under his own name and for others. Freelance work from late 1960, including albums with Max Roach and George Russell; led own quintet and did solo tour of Germany and Scandinavia. After contributing to Coltrane's 1961 recordings, became full member of his group, autumn 1961–spring 1962. Further period of freelance gigging (though little recording), including European straight music and work with John Lewis's Orchestra USA. Rejoined Mingus early 1964 in time for his tour of

Eric Dolphy

Europe, after which Dolphy undertook his own engagements in the remaining weeks of his life.

Despite a mere six years on the US national scene, Dolphy has had as much long-term influence as other prematurely deceased artists, Beiderbecke, Blanton, Christian, Navarro. This is partly because of the manner in which he defined a role for such hitherto peripheral instruments as the flute and bass-clarinet, that is, the role they would fill in the new jazz of the last two decades. It is also not unconnected with the mere fact of being a convincing multi-instrumentalist. Virtually all previous such musicians were identified with one main instrument to which their others were clearly secondary: Dolphy was a force to be reckoned with on each of his three main horns, and the tendency of players since his time (reedmen especially) to make a virtue of versatility stems mostly from him.

His work on alto is the most easily distinguishable from his predecessors. He had great admiration for Charlie Parker but only occasionally referred directly to his style; instead of Parker's precise and taut rhythmic mechanism, Dolphy came on like a conveyor belt running too fast (like Ornette Coleman or John Coltrane, his timing was more often in 'even 8ths' than 'dotted 8ths'). Unlike Ornette or Trane, however, he relished playing on strict chord sequences while appearing not to follow them strictly. In a famous interview, he once said, 'I play notes that would not ordinarily be said to be in a given key, but I hear them as proper. I don't think I "leave the changes" as the expression goes; every note I play has some reference to the chords of the piece.'

The huge, guffawing tone he used also carried over to his bass-clarinet playing, and in the middle register of both instruments it was evident that the combination of tone and phrasing closely resembled human speech patterns, whether of weighty philosophizing or garrulous chatter. The second is more typical of the flute work because of its pitch range, which has perhaps made this aspect of Dolphy harder to hear for those listeners unconvinced of the importance of the instrument itself. But the significance of his contribution in the eyes of fellow flautists can hardly be overestimated.

Like most jazz players since about 1960, he wrote a large number of original compositions which were only ever performed by his own groups. But the younger generation of 'free' players, many of whom have reverted to the use of chord changes but in a loosely defined manner, has reflected the influence of Eric Dolphy more and more. [BP]

Outward Bound (1960), New Jazz/OJC; *Out There* (1960), New Jazz/OJC; *Great Concert of Eric Dolphy* (1961), Prestige (triple); *Music Matador* (1963), Affinity; *Out to Lunch* (1964), Blue Note

See Simosko, Vladimir, and Tepperman, Barry, *Eric Dolphy: A Musical Biography and Discography* (Smithsonian Institution, New York, 1971)

Dominique, Natty (Anatie), trumpet. b. New Orleans, 2 August 1896; d. Chicago, 30 August 1982. An able, versatile trumpeter who studied with New Orleans' best teacher Manuel Perez, he moved to Chicago in 1913 and all through the 1920s was an in-demand talent. He was good enough to tour with Carroll Dickerson's orchestra, playing their complicated written book ('Poet and Peasant', *Rhapsody in Blue* etc) and later, for Dickerson again, played second trumpet to Louis Armstrong at Sunset Café. He also worked with the two leading Chicago-based clarinettists, Jimmie Noone and Johnny Dodds, forming a partnership with Dodds that lasted until the clarinettist's death. (There are lots of his records at this time with Noone, Dodds, Jelly Roll Morton, Jimmy Bertrand, Jimmy Blythe, Jasper Taylor, Sippie Wallace and others.) In the 1940s Dominique retired to work as a porter at Chicago airport, but by 1950 he was playing again – notably in his self-led Creole Dance Band with Baby Dodds, Volly de Faut, Preston Jackson and Jasper Taylor, which in 1953 was still playing weekends around the city. Dominique was apparently last active at jazz concerts in the mid-1960s. [DF]

Johnny Dodds (1926–8), VJM

Donahue, Sam (Samuel Koontz), tenor sax, trumpet, arranger. b. Detroit, Michigan, 18 March 1918; d. Reno, Nevada, 22 March 1974. He began with Gene Krupa (1938–40) and worked with Harry James and Benny Goodman before he joined the navy in 1942. He led the US Navy Dance Band, which toured Europe throughout the war years and achieved a legendary reputation: most listeners put it ahead of Glenn Miller's AAF band for jazz feeling, swing and adventurousness. Donahue led the band until 1946, when he re-formed his own, and all through the 1950s he worked for top leaders like Tommy Dorsey and Billy May. 1961–5, after a spell with Stan Kenton, he fronted the Tommy Dorsey Memorial Band (featuring Frank Sinatra Jnr. and Charlie Shavers) and thereafter carried on bandleading, as well as working for the Playboy chain of clubs, until he died. Donahue's long career was a success, but his saxophone playing was seldom quoted as a major jazz influence: like Tony Pastor and Tex Beneke he worked most happily in a swing style which by the end of the war had been superseded by the new giants of bebop. But Donahue was canny enough, and a good enough leader, to weather the fickleness of jazz fashion: a considerable achievement on its own. [DF]

Hollywood Hop (1944–8), Hep

Donaldson, Lou, alto sax. b. Badin, North Carolina, 1 November 1926. Moved to New York in early 1950s, recording sessions for Milt Jackson, Thelonious Monk and, continuously from 1952, under own name. Also worked briefly with Art Blakey (1954) and Charles Mingus (1956), and led own group with little interruption from mid-1950s onwards. Made first tours of Europe in 1980s. Initially strongly influenced by Charlie Parker, Donaldson had a more strident tone which suited ideally his simplification of Parker's lines. Concentrating on blues phrasing hitherto associated more with r & b tenor saxists, he helped to create an alto approach to 'soul jazz'; throughout the 1960s his backing group usually contained an organist (and more often than not an extra percussionist), but since the late 1970s he has used a pianist once more. Historically, Donaldson can be seen to have paved the way for such altoists as Cannonball Adderley, Gary Bartz and even David Sanborn. [BP]

Blues Walk (1958), Blue Note

Dorham, Kenny (McKinley Howard), trumpet, composer. b. Fairfield, Texas, 30 August 1924; d. 5 December 1972. Parents musical; started on piano at age seven, trumpet at high school. 1945–8, with Dizzy Gillespie, Billy Eckstine, Lionel Hampton, Mercer Ellington. 1948–50, replaced Miles Davis in the Charlie Parker quintet, playing with Parker at the Paris Jazz Festival, 1949. Freelanced in New York during early 1950s. 1954, founder-member of Art Blakey's Jazz Messengers; 1956–8, replaced Clifford Brown in the Max Roach quintet. During the late 1950s and the 1960s, led various groups of his own, composed and played music for some films, worked with Joe Henderson and Hank Mobley, toured internationally and played major festivals. He died of kidney failure.

Dorham was one of the first bebop trumpeters, and had something of the fleetness of Gillespie and the sonority of Miles Davis. By the beginning of the 1950s he had absorbed his influences and found his own individual voice on trumpet. He was a brilliant player who was never glib, and could project great lyricism even at fast tempos, producing astonishingly long lines of fluid triplets. He was also a magnificent blues player, because his fluidity of execution was accompanied by all the tonal inflexions of the vocal blues tradition. Dorham influenced and inspired countless trumpeters all over the world, but never broke through to a wider audience or even got all the recognition he was due, because he was always overshadowed by Davis and Fats Navarro in the 1940s and Clifford Brown and others in the 1950s and 1960s. He was a fine composer, and at least one of his pieces, 'Blue Bossa', has become part of the general jazz repertoire. [IC]

He played on some of the key albums of the 1950s, in particular, *Horace Silver and the Jazz Messengers* (1954), Blue Note, and *Max Roach 4 Plays Charlie Parker* (1957–8), Mercury: both include wonderful examples of Dorham's mature playing; also with Parker, Monk, Oliver Nelson, Tadd Dameron, J. J. Johnson, Sonny Rollins, Sonny Stitt, Cedar Walton, Cecil Taylor, Joe Henderson; *Max Roach + 4* (1956), Trip; *Kenny Dorham Memorial Album* (1960), Xanadu; *Ease It* (1961), Muse

Dorsey, Jimmy (James), clarinet, alto sax, occasionally trumpet. b. Shenandoah, Pennsylvania, 29 February 1904; d. New York City, 12 June 1957. He worked for most of his early years with his brother Tommy in Dorsey's Novelty Six, the Scranton Sirens (a jazz-based group which often featured sitters-in such as Joe Venuti and Eddie Lang), the California Ramblers (a prototype big band, managed by Ed Kirkeby) and from 1925 in studios and big bands led by Jean Goldkette, Paul Whiteman and others. From 1934 he co-led the Dorsey Brothers orchestra with Tommy, but after a quarrel over the tempo for a then popular song, 'I'll never say "never again" again', took over leadership, replaced his brother with trombonist Bobby Byrne and in 1935 became resident band on the Kraft Music Hall programme starring Bing Crosby. From then on Jimmy Dorsey – a milder man than his brother, often quiet and shy, with a well-formed sense of humour but still deep – led a succession of highly successful bands, had a number of hits (e.g. 'Amapola', 'So rare', and 'Green Eyes' over ten years) and in 1937 supplied the soundtrack music (with an augmented orchestra) for the Fred Astaire–Ginger Rogers box-office success *Shall We Dance?* A good part of Dorsey's success was attributable to his singers Bob Eberly and Helen O'Connell: as a clarinettist he never seriously competed with masters like Goodman and Shaw, and later recordings (with his marvellous Dorseyland band) reveal an occasionally stilted turn of phrase; from the mid-1930s he concentrated heavily on alto. But his band featured a succession of fine if lesser-known jazzmen, including tenor saxophonist Herbie Haymer, trumpeter Shorty Sherock, drummer Ray McKinley and lead trumpeter Ralph Muzillo; after Eberly and O'Connell had left, other fine singers such as Kitty Kallen, Bob Hughes and Bob Carroll replaced them. By 1943, Dorsey's band had reached its peak, and it remained highly successful until after the war when bright young stars such as Herb Ellis and Lou Carter joined the ranks. As late as 1948, Dorsey was still organizing new bands (at the period his brass section featured Maynard Ferguson and Charlie Teagarden together), but also featuring more regularly a small Dixieland unit, Jimmy Dorsey's Dixielanders, which that year played a season at Tommy Dorsey's own Casino Garden ballroom near Los Angeles in Santa Monica (their records featuring Teagarden are tremendous). From 1953, Jimmy Dorsey, no longer a bandleader, was once again featured in a soloist's set with his brother's orchestra (in the wake of a 1947 biographical Hollywood movie they billed themselves as 'The Fabulous Dorseys') and after his brother's death once more took over leadership briefly. [DF]

Jimmy Dorsey and his Orchestra (1949), Big Band Archives

See Sanford, Herb, *Tommy and Jimmy: the Dorsey Years* (Ian Allan, 1972, repr. Da Capo, 1980)

Dorsey, Tommy (Thomas), trombone, trumpet. b. Shenandoah, Pennsylvania, 19 November 1905; d. Greenwich, Connecticut, 26 November 1956. With his younger brother Jimmy he spent his early years around Scranton, later worked with famous bands led by Paul Whiteman and Jean Goldkette and from 1934 formed, with his brother again, the Dorsey Brothers orchestra: the project was dissolved after a quarrel during a Glenn Island Casino residency. From there Dorsey took over Joe Haymes's orchestra – 'a very disciplined band', says Charlie Barnet – and began his ambitious climb. First he brought in arranger Axel Stordahl, trumpeter Joe Bauer, arranger/guitarist Carmen Mastren and singer Jack Leonard, and continued building all through the 1930s. By offering blank cheques to talent he wanted from other orchestras he brought in such stars as Bud Freeman, Max Kaminsky, Yank Lawson, Ziggy Elman and Pee Wee Erwin, a succession of great singers, including Frank Sinatra, Dick Haymes, Jo Stafford and the Pied Pipers, and arranger Sy Oliver. The result was a highly versatile, sternly drilled jazz orchestra; 'of all the hundreds of bands Tommy's could do more things better than anyone else,' says George T. Simon. Dorsey was himself a mine of professional promotion tactics which at various times in-

Tommy Dorsey

cluded an 'Amateur Swing Contest' held nationwide, programmes dedicated to specific songwriters and subjects (on his long Raleigh–Kool radio series) and in 1939 a dual bandshow with Jimmy (they had been reconciled in 1937). The result was a string of hits, notably his theme song, 'I'm getting sentimental over you', 'Song of India', 'Marie' and 'Sunny Side of the Street' featuring The Sentimentalists (later the Clark Sisters). By 1941, Dorsey had taken over his own bookings and opened his own Santa Monica ballroom, by 1942 he had added a string section to his orchestra, and by 1945 he had added Charlie Shavers – a much valued cornerman – to his show. He stayed successful enough for the rest of the decade: in 1947 a Hollywood fantasy, *The Fabulous Dorseys*, starred both brothers and in the same year they introduced 'classical' works like 'Dorsey Concerto' (Leo Shuken) and 'The Quest' (Roy Harris) in concerts. From May 1953 the Dorsey Brothers worked together again – under Tommy's banner, 'featuring' Jimmy – until 1956, when Tommy Dorsey choked to death in his sleep at 51.

Dorsey himself was billed as 'The Sentimental Gentleman of Swing' after his famous theme song, but he was neither sentimental, nor a gentleman: 'a totally cold person', says Bob Crosby, who sang with the Dorsey Brothers orchestra. Few accounts of Dorsey fail to mention his (necessary but) ruthless drive for perfection, his enjoyment of others' discomfiture (he once sent a mock birthday cake to songwriter Johnny Mercer's table filled with old leadsheets of Mercer's less successful songs) and his unshakeable ambition. As a trombonist Dorsey was technically unfaultable: he invented a smooth-as-silk upper register ability which (*pace* Lawrence Brown) was revolutionary for its time and was framed in such classics as his signature tune and 'Song of India'. But his jazz ideas were limited, based on an affection for fine 1920s players such as Miff Mole, whose talents had been in part at least eclipsed by Jack Teagarden, a musician with whom Dorsey never (for once) tried to compete.

The Tommy Dorsey Memorial Band, under leaders Warren Covington and Sam Donahue, remained successful until the mid-1960s featuring Charlie Shavers and singer Frank Sinatra Jnr. [DF]

Tommy Dorsey and his Orchestra, vols. 1/2 (1935–47) RCA (2 doubles)

See Sanford, Herb, *Tommy and Jimmy: the Dorsey Years* (Ian Allen, 1972, repr. Da Capo, 1980)

Double Tempo/Double Time, see TEMPO.

Douglas, Jim (James), guitar, banjo. b. Gifford, East Lothian, 13 May 1942. He worked early on with the Clyde Valley Stompers and in 1964 joined Alex Welsh with whom he remained until the trumpeter's death in 1982. One of Britain's most elegant and experienced jazz guitarists, he worked in Welsh's band with a string of American visitors from Earl Hines to Ruby Braff, all of whom highly praised Douglas's innate musicality, softly supportive rhythm guitar and solo abilities which ran the gamut from swift single-string lines to lightly-floating chorded creations recalling Kress and Van Eps. Douglas works with the Alex Welsh Memorial Band, Alan Elsdon's Jazzmen, and freelances. [DF]

Any with Alex Welsh; *Freddy Randall and his Famous Jazz Band* (1971), Rediffusion

Douglas, Tommy (Thomas), clarinet, reeds, leader. b. Eskridge, Kansas, 9 November 1911. Of all the territory bandleaders, Douglas, who formed his first band in Kansas City in 1930, achieved the highest reputation as a soloist. A spectacular technician – he was a graduate of Boston Conservatory where star names Johnny Hodges, Harry Carney and others had been contemporaries – Douglas played early on as a sideman for Jelly Roll Morton and later Bennie Moten (as well as Duke Ellington for weeks in 1951), but for much of his life he has worked as a leader: young sidemen who gained experience in his bands included Jo Jones and Charlie Parker. Parker, according to biographer Ross Russell, learned much from Douglas. 'Tommy was the kind of man who could play anything. He could play all of the saxophones. He knew his harmony inside out. Charlie took his place . . . watching the leader's fingers . . . asking questions . . . calling him "Mr Douglas".' Douglas disbanded his orchestra in 1937, but soon re-formed and, apart from a late 1930s stint as MD for George E. Lee, led bands regularly into the 1970s. Why this magnificent musician never progressed to the starry end of jazz history has regularly been conjectured: perhaps his preference for Kansas rather than the fast pace of New York was one reason. [DF]

Down (1) A slow tempo. Possibly the choice of expression is linked to the use of 'down' or 'lowdown' to indicate depression or degradation.

(2) The down-beat is the first beat of a performance, or else the first beat of each bar (sometimes referred to as 'one'). There is a non-musical usage of this connotation too, as in the rather dated expression 'a down cat', meaning a person sufficiently aware and reliable to know where 'one' is. [BP]

Downes, Bob (Robert George), concert, alto and bass flute, Chinese, Japanese and South American bamboo flute; tenor, alto and soprano sax. b. Plymouth, Devon, 22 July 1937. His first inspiration was his mother's 'lovely singing voice', but he was basically self-taught. At 19 he took up saxophone and in 1968 began to devote most of his energy to the flute. 1969–70, played with the Mike Westbrook band; 1969, also formed his own Open Music Trio. Since 1974 he has performed mainly as a solo artist (unaccompanied flutes) in Germany where he took up residence in the late 1970s. He formed his Alternative Medicine Quintet in 1978, and in 1984 his Flute Orchestra in Germany. Downes is something of a maverick, and although he admits to being inspired by sax players such as Sonny Rollins, Fathead Newman and Roland Kirk, he admires no flautists. His other influences are Horace Silver, Stan Kenton, and Miles Davis's late 1950s music, but Downes's music also owes much to rock, vocal blues and ethnic music of various kinds, and his emotional range can veer from lyricism to the more abrasive aspects of 'free' jazz. He has composed many scores for contemporary dance companies including the Ballet Rambert (UK), and lists his most representative recent compositions as *Pulse Suite* and *New York Suite*. [IC]

With Ray Russell and the London Jazz Composers' Orchestra; *Dream Journey* (1969), Philips; *Diversions* (1972); *Solo* (1982), both Openian

Drew, Kenny (Kenneth Sidney), piano. b. New York City, 28 August 1928. Accompanist of Lester Young and Buddy DeFranco in the early 1950s, then worked on the West Coast for a couple of years before returning to New York. During this period appeared on important albums by John Coltrane (*Blue Train*) and Dexter Gordon, among others, and continued to record prolifically after making his home in Copenhagen from 1964. Co-owner of Copenhagen-based Matrix record label. A dynamic and sought-after accompanist, Drew is also an exciting soloist somewhat influenced by Bud Powell and Hampton Hawes, with a special fondness for long right-hand lines full of rhythmic verve. [BP]

And Far Away (1983), Soul Note

Drew, Martin, drums, b. Northampton, 11 February 1944. He first became interested in drums when he was five or six years old, took lessons at 11, studying for three years with George Fierstone, and played his first professional engagement at 12. Over the years he has played countless engagements at the Ronnie Scott Club in London, accompanying many major artists. By the mid-1980s, Drew was the regular drummer with several groups: Ronnie Scott's quintet, with which he had been playing for several years, the Oscar Peterson trio, the guitarist Joe Pass and his own band, which included John Critchinson, Ron Mathewson, Dick Morrissey and Jim Mullen. He has worked with innumerable musicians of all styles and persuasions, from singers such as Ella Fitzgerald and Nina Simone to mainstreamers such as Harry Edison and Buddy Tate, and more contemporary stylists such as the Brecker brothers, Freddie Hubbard and Gil Evans. He lists among his main influences Art Blakey, Elvin Jones, Steve Gadd, Buddy Rich and Jack DeJohnette. He has also derived particular inspiration from Cedar Walton, John Coltrane and Sonny Rollins. [IC]

With Red Rodney, Joe Pass, Bill Watrous, Ronnie Scott and several with Oscar Peterson; *Martin Drew Band* (1977), Lee Lambert; with Oscar Peterson, *Big Four in Japan* (1982), Pablo; with John Critchinson, *Summer Afternoon* (1983), Coda

Drootin, Buzzy (Benjamin), drums. b. 22 April 1920. He came along ten years after the first generation of great Dixieland drummers – which included Dave Tough and Cliff Leeman – but he belongs in their class. He was first noticed nationally during a four-year term at Eddie Condon's, 1947–51, and all through the 1950s his swing-to-Dixieland style backed the classiest of his contemporaries: Billy Butterfield, old friend Ruby Braff and Bobby Hackett among others. They all liked Drootin's loose, athletic time-sense, sensitive attention to dynamics and history-conscious style, at a time when younger players were dropping bebop bombs, and he appeared on such classic records as Hackett's *Jazz Ultimate* with Jack Teagarden, held down a residency at George Wein's Boston Jazz Club, 1953–5, and worked all over New York between times with kindred spirits Ralph Sutton, Pee Wee Erwin, Wild Bill Davison *et al.* In the 1960s Drootin joined the Newport All Stars (under Wein with Braff), formed his own Jazz Family with Herman Autrey and Benny Morton, 1967–9, and in the 1970s was back in Boston running his Drootin Brothers Orchestra with relations Al and Sonny. [DF]

Ruby Braff, *Featuring Dave McKenna* (1956), Jasmine

Dudek, Gerd (Gerhard Rochus), tenor and soprano sax, and clarinet, flute, shehnai. b. Gr. Dobern, Germany, 28 September 1938. Brother, Ossi Dudek, plays trumpet. Private clarinet lessons at 15; 1954, went to music school in Siegen. 1960–4, worked with Berlin Jazz quintet. During later 1960s worked with Kurt Edelhagen, touring Russia with him; Manfred Schoof quintet; Globe Unity Orchestra; Wolfgang Dauner; Albert Mangelsdorff; Don Cherry; George Russell; also led his own groups. 1977–81, with Alan Skidmore in the European Jazz Consensus and the European Jazz Quintet. 1985, toured with the Tony Oxley quintet including Enrico Rava, Joachim Kuhn and Ali Haurand. Dudek is one of the most accomplished European saxophonists. Influences include Coltrane, Miles Davis, Charlie Parker, Ornette Coleman, Cherry and Albert Ayler. [IC]

With EJC and EJQ, Schoof, Kuhn, Baden-Baden Free Jazz Orchestra; Globe Unity Special, vol. 1, *Evidence* (1975); *Gerd Dudek-Open* (1977); both FMP

Dudziak, Urszula, voice, percussion, synthesizer, composer. b. Straconka, Poland, 22 October 1943. Studied piano at music school in Zielona-Gora. Private singing lessons for two years. Inspired by Ella Fitzgerald whom she heard on Willis Conover's Voice of America Jazz Hour. Later, Miles Davis was a big influence. Married to Michal Urbaniak and worked with his group travelling throughout Europe from 1965. They played jazz festivals in Warsaw, 1969–72; Molde, 1971; various others in France and Italy. She and Urbaniak went to live in the USA in the autumn of 1973. Her wordless singing made an immediate impact in America, and was described by Herb Nolan in *Downbeat* as 'four-octave vocal soundscape with its lyricless myriad of scats, squawks, groans, screeches, mellow harmonies, subtle counterpoint and wild improvisations'. [IC]

Urszula (1974), Arista; with Adam Makowicz (piano), *Newborn Light* (nda); with Michal Urbaniak, *Fusion III* (nda); *Atma* (nda); *Fusion* (nda); all Columbia; *Heritage* (1977), MPS

Duke, George, keyboards, synthesizer, composer, voice. b. San Rafael, California, 12 January 1946. B.Mus. in composition from San Francisco Conservatory, 1967. Worked with his trio in SF, accompanying stars such as Dizzy Gillespie, Bobby Hutcherson and Kenny Dorham. 1969, played with Jean-Luc Ponty, after which the trio broke up. After spending eight months with the Don Ellis band, Duke began recording with Frank Zappa and joined the Mothers of Invention, 1970–5, with one year away (1971–2) to tour with Cannonball Adderley. During this period he began working with his own groups. 1975, co-led a group with Billy Cobham, and also began a long association with bassist Stanley Clarke which led to a series of joint albums in the 1980s. By the late 1970s he was an international star with his own electronic jazz/rock/funk/soul group touring and playing festivals in Europe and elsewhere. Duke is a highly accomplished player and composer, and cites as influences Ravel, Stravinsky, Stockhausen, Herbie Hancock, Miles Davis and Zappa among others. However, his later albums, particularly the collaborations with Clarke, have moved more towards easy-listening disco music; it is pop music sometimes flavoured with jazz improvisation; no questions asked, no doubts or darker thoughts disturbing the glossy surface. [IC]

With Zappa, Flora Purim, Airto Moreira, Eddie Henderson; with *Jean-Luc Ponty Experience* (1970), Liberty; *Faces in Reflection* (1974); *The Aura will Prevail* (1976); *She Heard My Cry* (1975–6), all BASF; *A Brazilian Love Affair* (1979); *Guardian of the Light* (1983); *The Clarke/Duke Project* (1981); *The Clarke/Duke Project II* (1983), all CBS

Dukes of Dixieland A commercially and musically successful group formed in New Orleans in 1948 by teenage brothers Frank and Fred Assunto; they won a Horace Heidt talent contest and toured with Heidt before settling in New Orleans (under the management of their father and second trombonist 'Papa Jac' Assunto) to turn professional. Their biggest break came with a signing to the Audio Fidelity label, which provided them with huge and deserved publicity. The Dukes' Audio Fidelity-inspired logo 'you have to hear it to believe it' naturally got short shrift from the jazz press, but their music was never less than enjoyable and – in its early days – reminiscent of the Yerba Buena Jazz Band. Later on record and/or live the band featured (besides the considerable talent of trumpeter/singer Frank Assunto) proven names such as Jerry Fuller (clt), Herb Ellis and Jim Hall (gtrs) and Gene Schroeder (piano). Their well-played, timeless jazz is well preserved on fine records such as *Breakin' it up on Broadway* (featuring Assunto's assured trumpet and rather Torméish singing) and *Now Hear This!*: early, more rumbustious sessions including those with Louis Armstrong are also well worth hearing. Sadly, Fred Assunto died young in 1966, his brother Frank in 1974. Papa Jac gave up his connection with the group and retired to teach; he died in 1985. A team of reconstituted Dukes, led by trumpeter Mike Vax and featuring New Orleans clarinettist Otis Bazoon, still played successfully at their New Orleans club Dukes' Place in the late 1970s. In 1985 they were re-formed as an inter-racial group for Hollywood appearances. They included Frank Trapani (tpt), Frank Hooks (tmb), Phamons Lambert (piano/vocals) and others. [DF]

Now Hear This (1962), Columbia

Dunbar, Ted (Earl Theodore), guitar, composer. b. Port Arthur, Texas, 17 January 1937. Self-taught. Degree in pharmacy from Texas Southern University, where he played trumpet and guitar in jazz groups. 1963, studied the Lydian concept with David Baker in Indianapolis. Worked with Baker, Red Garland, Billy Harper and others; 1966, moved to New York. Worked in theatre orchestras, in music education and in small groups and big bands with leading players, including Jimmy Heath and McCoy Tyner. 1970–3, with Gil Evans orchestra; 1971–2, with Tony Williams's Lifetime. Dunbar is on the academic staff of the Music Department at Livingston College, Rutgers University in New Brunswick, New Jersey. His influences range from Wes Montgomery, T-Bone Walker and B. B. King, to Miles Davis, Ellington, Baker and Tony Williams. [IC]

With Tyner, Williams, Curtis Fuller, Lou Donaldson and others; with Don Patterson, *The Return of Don Patterson* (1972), Muse; with Albert Heath, *Kwanza* (1973), Muse; with Gil Evans, *Svengali* (1973), Atlantic; with Kenny Barron, *Peruvian Blue* (1974), Muse

Duncan, Hank (Henry James), piano. b. Bowling Green, Kentucky, 26 October 1894; d. New York, 7 June 1968. One of the creators of stride piano, he ran his own band in Louisville and after coming to New York in the mid-1920s worked for bandleader 'Fess' Williams for five years, then with King Oliver, Charles 'Fat Man' Turner and the Bechet–Ladnier Feetwarmers at the Savoy, and he was second pianist on tour with Fats Waller's big band. For much of the rest of his long life he turned up in small groups (for example, Zutty Singleton's trio in 1939) or as a soloist in New York clubs including Nick's (1947–55 and again 1956–63) and the Metropole (in between). After leaving Nick's he continued to work solo until a long terminal illness. [DF]

Sidney Bechet, *The Blue Bechet* (1932–41), RCA

Dunn, Blind Willie, see LANG, EDDIE.

Durham, Eddie, guitar, trombone, arranger. b. San Marcos, Texas, 19 August 1908. As a teenager played guitar and then trombone with six siblings in the Durham Brothers band. Toured from mid-1920s with circus bands and top territory groups including Walter Page's Blue Devils, moving (along with Count Basie) to Elmer Payne band and then Bennie Moten (1929–33). Briefly with Cab Calloway, Andy Kirk, Willie Bryant, two years with Jimmie Lunceford (1935–7) and a year with Basie (1937–8); in all these bands, contributed arrangements and trombone section-work plus occasional guitar solos. Then freelance writer for Artie Shaw, Glenn Miller etc. and in 1940s leader of various bands including the International Sweethearts of Rhythm and later his own all-women group. After further freelancing, led own groups from 1957, joined Buddy Tate band (1970s) and Harlem Jazz and Blues Band (1980s), including touring and recording in Europe.

An important but neglected figure in the development of jazz guitar, he devised a non-electric method of amplification so that his contributions to the 1929 Moten records leap out with a verve worthy of Charlie Christian – and in a bluesy style which must surely have influenced him. But Durham was better known to his colleagues as an arranger, responsible for the classic 'Moten Swing' and such Basie numbers as 'Sent for you Yesterday' and 'Topsy'. Although not his own composition, he also scored possibly the most famous swing-era arrangement, the Glenn Miller version of 'In the Mood'. [BP]

Bennie Moten, *The Complete, vols. 3/4* (1928–30), RCA; Count Basie, *Swinging the Blues* (1937–9), Affinity

Dutch Swing College Band Europe's longest playing jazz band was formed on 5 May 1945 under the leadership of Peter Schilperoort (clt/saxes). Early members of the band included guitarist Wout Steenhuis (now a successful session musician and soloist), trumpeter Kees van Dorser, clarinettist Dim Kesber and the brilliant Jan Morks who combined outstanding solo clarinet talent with a career in the law (he died in 1984). From 1952, Schilperoort formed a long partnership with guitarist/banjoist Arie Ligthart, and by the late 1950s the DSC was well established as a commercially successful and highly rated unit. By 1959 more key men were in and out of the ranks including a fiery Armstrong-inspired trumpeter, Oscar Klein, and fluent trombonist Dick Kaart (who died in 1985) whose brother Ray (a brilliant lyric trumpeter whose life was complicated by a severe road accident and alcohol problems) was to join, replacing Klein, in 1963. In the 1960s the repertoire of the DSC, always eclectic, broadened further to include popular and rock repertoire; 1968, Ray Kaart was replaced by Bert de Koort, later a successful touring soloist, whose understanding of Bobby Hackett's vocabulary is close to uncanny. In the 1970s the DSC career reached a status peak. Schilperoort formed his own record company, DSC Productions, to produce a string of impressive albums (some with Americans including Billy Butterfield, Joe Venuti and Teddy Wilson; others, self-inspired ideas, explored unusual areas such as country and western and one with full military band). The European touring continued, and Peter Schilperoort was knighted by Queen Juliana of the Netherlands for his contributions to jazz. In the 1980s the DSC wagon continued to roll smoothly along: featuring British cornettist Rod Mason until 1985 when cornettist Sytze von Duin and trombonist Bert Boeren joined, they were still presenting polished highly arranged repertoire with all the skill of their American inspirers. [DF]

The Dutch Swing College Story, 1945–68, Philips

Dutrey, Honoré, trombone. b. New Orleans, 1894; d. Chicago, 21 July 1935. Early work in New Orleans in brass bands and small groups was followed by a spell in the US Navy during 1917, involving him in a powder-room accident which severely damaged his lungs. From then on Dutrey used an inhaler, but was fit enough to join King Oliver's great band in Chicago in 1920, made all the classic records with Oliver's Creole Jazz Band and after the split with Oliver in 1924 led his own band at Lincoln Gardens before spending time with other Chicago-based stars, including Johnny Dodds, Louis Armstrong and Carroll Dickerson's big band. He gave up music in 1930 and died before he was 40 from a recurrence of his disability. [DF]

King Oliver and his Creole Jazz Band: the Okeh Sessions, 1923, EMI World Records

Duvivier, George B., bass, arranger. b. New York City, 17 August 1920; d. 11 July 1985. Studied violin and composition as teenager, also playing bass with Royal Baron Orchestra (*c.* 1937). Turned professional, worked with Coleman Hawkins band (1941), Lucky Millinder (1941–2). Wrote arrangements for Jimmie Lunceford (and played on one recording) while in army (1943–5), then full-time writer for Lunceford (1945–7). Full-time on bass from 1950 with singers Nellie Lutcher, Pearl Bailey, Billy Eckstine and Lena Horne. Also jazz appearances and recordings with Terry Gibbs (1952), Bud Powell (1953–6, including assisting with arrangements), albums with Eric Dolphy and Ron Carter (1960). Primarily involved from 1950s in non-jazz studio work, but also appeared at several jazz festivals in USA and Europe. Duvivier's excellence was proven by the breadth of his associations over a long career. As well as having the ability to be simultaneously interesting and unflamboyant, he made the creation of a driving pulse appear effortless. [BP]

Arnett Cobb, *Keep on Pushin'* (1984), BeeHive

Dyani, Johnny, bass, vocals, composer. b. East London, South Africa, 30 November 1945; d. 1986. (See PUKWANA, D., and MOHOLO, L.) He joined Chris McGregor's Blue Notes in 1962, and left SA with them in 1965, going to Europe and playing in France and Switzerland before settling in Britain. He spent five years based in London working mostly with the avant-garde of the time, freely improvised abstract music in small-group settings. He continued with the Blue Notes, but also played with the Spontaneous Music Ensemble, 1969, and the Musicians' Co-op, 1971. He toured South America with Steve Lacy, Enrico Rava and Louis Moholo (dms), and the quartet recorded an album in 1968. But he was beginning to feel that the Blue Notes were coming too much under the influence of the American free players, and losing touch with their African roots. So in the early 1970s he moved to Denmark, working with John Tchicai and Don Cherry, and also with others, including Abdullah Ibrahim (Dollar Brand), of whom Dyani said, 'Only Abdullah Ibrahim and Makhaya Ntshoko are being true to themselves. They are the ones working for Africa. With them there is a real exchange – as with Don [Cherry] – we don't seem to need to talk, we just communicate.' He also worked with David Murray and Joseph Jarman, and led various groups of his own. Dyani was something of a visionary, and his music has a flavour and feeling all its own. It fuses elements from contemporary jazz with a spaciousness and rhythmic coherence which were rarely evident in the 'free' jazz of the 1960s. It is music of the heart, never of the glands, the expression of an exile's joy, anger and sorrow. [IC]

With Steve Lacy, *Forest and the Zoo* (1966), ESP; with Blue Notes, *Very Urgent* (1967), Polydor; *Blue Notes for Mongezi* (1975), Ogun; Mongezi Feza/Dyani/Okay Temiz, *Music for Xaba* (1972), Sonet; Ibrahim/Dyani duo, *Good News from Africa* (1973), Enja; *Witchdoctor's Son* (1978); with Cherry/Pukwana/Ntshoko, *Song for Biko* (1978); with Ed Epstein/Churchill Jolebe, *Mbizo* (1981), all Steeplechase

E

Eager, Allen, tenor sax (and alto). b. New York City, 27 January 1927. Experience with name bands such as Tommy Dorsey while still a teenager, then played on 52nd Street (1945) and began to make records under own name (1946). Worked with Buddy Rich (1947, 1952) and Tadd Dameron group (1948). Intermittent playing in New York (1953–5, 1957), Paris (mid-1950s), Los Angeles (mid-1960s, where he appeared on Frank Zappa's first album) and Miami (1970s). Activities in the meantime included skiing, riding and car-racing, but made brief jazz comeback in early 1980s including European tour (1982). A disciple of Lester Young who, in the late 1940s, made a distinctive and memorable contribution. [BP]

Renaissance (1982), Uptown

Eckstine, Billy (William Clarence), vocals, trumpet, valve-trombone (and guitar). b. Pittsburgh, Pennsylvania, 8 July 1914. Not to be confused with the 1920s ragtime pianist Willie Eckstein (which is how Billy's family name was originally spelled), the singer worked in Washington (early 1930s), Buffalo, Detroit (1937) and then Chicago (1938). Found fame with Earl Hines band (1939–43), singing ballads but scoring particularly with a smooth and sexy blues 'Jelly, Jelly'. Leaving Hines, he soon formed his own big band (1944–7) with first Dizzy Gillespie and then Budd Johnson as musical director; a short list of the most important musicians who played with him includes Charlie Parker, Dexter Gordon, Gene Ammons, Sonny Stitt, Fats Navarro, Miles Davis and Art Blakey. The septet he fronted next had Wardell Gray on tenor (1947), and thereafter he toured internationally as soloist with jazz-based accompanists such as pianist Bobby Tucker (1950s–1960s) and drummer Charli Persip (late 1960s–early 1970s). Very successful with black audiences throughout the 1940s, when he was easily the most imitated of singers, Eckstine's more middle-of-the-road backing on later records made him an enormous superstar. It is to his credit, therefore, that his performances still include regular reference to his instrumental work. [BP]

Mr B and the Band (1945–7), Savoy

ECM, see EUROPE.

Edison, Harry 'Sweets', trumpet. b. Columbus, Ohio, 10 October 1915. He was born half Red Indian (like Lee Wiley and Jack Teagarden) and fell under the spell of Louis Armstrong after hearing him on Bessie Smith records and live, with Bennie Moten, at Valley Dale dance hall, Ohio. Early on he worked in the best territory bands (among them Jeter–Pillars, Earl Hood and Morrison's Grenadiers), then moved to New York and after six months with Lucky Millinder joined Count Basie in June 1938. He remained until 1950 when Basie disbanded to form a small group and Edison found himself, to his shock, without a band or a father-figure, but with a wife and family to support. He took work with Norman Granz's Jazz at the Philharmonic and Josephine Baker, as her MD, and from 1952, helped and encouraged by Manny Klein, he began regular studio work, a permanent association with Frank Sinatra and played for a clutch of other singers. (Edison, along with Bobby Hackett, is one of the few master trumpet-accompanists and his witty obbligati, on records of the period, would be impossible to count.) By late 1958 he was recording regularly as a soloist, led a quintet again at Birdland, in the 1960s continued his heavy studio commitments as well as regularly appearances at jazz festivals (solo and with his own quartet), with JATP, with Count Basie as guest soloist, and regularly for American TV's Hollywood Palace show. In the 1970s he also made numerous tours with Lockjaw Davis and Benny Carter and taught regularly at Yale for the Duke Ellington Fellowship. A natural player, rather like Louis Armstrong, Edison is one of the most distinctive voices in jazz: single-handed he developed a vocabulary for the harmon mute. One of the fascinating studies of classic jazz is to chart his stylistic development: his young trumpet playing is blustery-wild: in maturity (like Armstrong again) it achieved controlled perfection with a rare gift for 'stretching out' in extended solos without losing creative steam. [DF]

The Inventive Mr Edison (1953), Pacific Jazz

See Dance, Stanley, *The World of Count Basie* (Sidgwick and Jackson, 1980)

Edwards, Teddy (Theodore Marcus), tenor sax, arranger. b. Jackson, Mississippi, 26 April 1924. Worked with many territory bands before moving to Los Angeles (1944). Switched from alto to join Howard McGhee (1945–7), recording with him and on two-tenor session with Dexter Gordon (1947). Played in groups led by Red Callender (1948), Benny Carter, Gerald Wilson, Max Roach–Clifford Brown (1954). Own quartet active in Los Angeles (1958–61), occasional appearances under own name thereafter. Has continued to be in demand for recording and live work with a wide variety of artists including Carter, Wilson, Benny Goodman (1964), Milt Jackson (1969–76), Jimmy Smith (1972), Sarah Vaughan (1974) and Tom Waits (1982). Made solo tour of Europe in 1984.

As well as being a dependable back-up artist, Edwards is a forthright soloist who has been consistently undervalued. His typical Southwestern sound reveals an affinity for the blues and the tone quality that goes with it, but this is only the background to an extremely fluent use of post-bop vocabulary. [BP]

Teddy's Ready (1959), Boplicity/Contemporary

Egan, Mark, bass, trumpet. b. Brockton, Massachusetts, 14 January 1951. His mother and father, sister and brothers all played musical instruments. He started on trumpet at ten and took up bass at 16, playing in local r & b bands. He had private music lessons from 12 to 18, then studied with Jerry Coker at the University of Miami, taking a bachelor's degree in applied music. Bass became his main instrument and for two years he played with Ira Sullivan's group. 1976, moved to New York, touring and recording with the Pointer Sisters and Dave Sanborn. 1977, joined Pat Metheny's group and toured with it extensively for three and a half years. He left the group in 1980 to pursue a solo and freelance career. Since then he has worked with many leading musicians, including Stan Getz, Flora and Airto Moreira, Jim Hall, the Gil Evans orchestra (1983–5), Randy Brecker, Bill Evans (the saxophonist) and John McLaughlin. 1982, with drummer Danny Gottlieb, Egan formed and co-led a group called Elements. With the Gil Evans band he toured Japan, 1983 and 1984, on the same bill with Miles Davis and Herbie Hancock. Egan has spent much time studying ethnic music (from Bali, South India, Africa, Brazil) and with Gottlieb has spent long periods in Kauai, Hawaii, 'playing music in nature in valleys, during very extreme weather conditions (wind, rain etc.)'. Among his favourite bassists are Dave Holland, Steve Swallow, Paul McCartney and Anthony Jackson, and he has derived inspiration from Miles Davis, Duke Ellington, John Coltrane, Stravinsky and Debussy. Two of his best compositions are 'Colorwheel' and 'Valley Hymn'. [IC]

With Steve Grossman, Gil Evans, Bill Evans, Sonny Fortune, Jim Hall, Pat Metheny and others; with Elements, *Elements* (1982), Antilles; *Forward Motion* (1983), Antilles; solo bass, *Mosaic* (1984), Hip Pocket

Eldridge, Joe (Joseph), alto sax, violin. b. Pittsburgh, Pennsylvania, 1908; d. 5 March 1952. He worked in a variety of territory bands around Pittsburgh (he also paid a visit to New York in 1927 with Henry Saparo's group) and in 1933 formed the Eldridge Brothers Rhythm Team with his younger brother Roy in Pittsburgh. Soon after, they together joined McKinney's Cotton Pickers and later in 1936 Joe joined Roy's band in Chicago and moved to New York with it, 1938–40. From then on he worked with Zutty Singleton in New York, with Roy again and with Hot Lips Page and lived for a while in Canada in the late 1940s before moving back to New York shortly before he died. 'I never did know the real cause,' said Roy later. 'He had got real overweight, drinking wine and stuff – it could have been his heart. I'd go to play something and I'd remember the things he had taught me like running the changes. [He was] *down* you know!' [DF]

Roy Eldridge, *Heckler's Hop* (1935–40), Tax

Eldridge, 'Roy' (David), trumpet, fluegelhorn, vocals, drums, piano. b. Pittsburgh, Pennsylvania, 30 January 1911. He forms – in jazz lore at least – the link between Louis Armstrong and Dizzy Gillespie, but in fact the young Roy Eldridge, who (said Doc Cheatham) 'began tearing up Chicago in the 1920s', liked Red Nichols, Rex Stewart, Coleman Hawkins and Benny Carter more than Armstrong. He worked to start with (on trumpet and drums) in carnival, circus and dance bands, one of which, the Nighthawk Syncopators, played a lightning trumpet transcription of Coleman Hawkins's 'Stampede'. From the first, Eldridge was impressed by speed and range; he liked Jabbo Smith and later remembered being worn out by the older man in a cutting contest. 'Little Jazz', as he was soon to be dubbed by bandleader Elmer Snowden, worked his way up through the territory bands of Zack Whyte, Lawrence 'Speed' Webb *et al.* and by 1931 had arrived in New York to work with Snowden, McKinney's Cotton Pickers and Teddy Hill. In Hill's band he became close friends with Chu Berry, and the two would go out on the town to cut down opposition; it was a vocation that Eldridge would continue to pursue all his playing life. With Berry he joined Fletcher Henderson's band in 1935 and one year later opened with his own band at the Three Deuces in Chicago, with broadcasts seven nights a week. By this time his formidable stamina, range and waspish attack were the talk of New York and in 1939 he reopened at the Arcadia Ballroom with an augmented band, broadcasting most days and dominating jam sessions in spare moments. By 1941, back in Chicago, he had joined Gene Krupa's orchestra for a successful but traumatic spell: Krupa hired him after an ignominious trouncing in battle with Jimmie Lunceford's band, and from then on used Eldridge as a cornerman, featuring his stratospheric trumpet

Roy Eldridge

and show drumming and teaming him in a centre-stage double-act with young hip singer Anita O'Day. This on occasion produced temperament problems, but it was more than these that drove Eldridge from the band. The appalling conditions to which black musicians were subjected on tour caused the volatile trumpeter to suffer a nervous breakdown and after one more brief stint with Artie Shaw's band in 1944 he promised: 'As long as I'm in America I'll never in my life work with a white band again.'

The period overall was an unhappy one for him. Soon after his own big band folded ('they couldn't hold their whiskey', he said later): worse still he was starting (like Dave Tough) to question his musical validity in the fast-moving bebop revolution. One night at Minton's Dizzy Gillespie cut him in public: soon after, on a 1949 Jazz at the Philharmonic tour, bebop trumpeter Howard McGhee began taunting Eldridge and didn't let up. For a sensitive and vulnerable competitor like 'Little Jazz' it was a crisis point. 'I felt I was out of step. I was torn whether I should do that sort of thing, or go for myself. It stopped being fun anymore.' So, as Bill Coleman was to do, he took a long sabbatical in France. It worked, and from 1951 Eldridge was regularly with JATP again, his phenomenal range and endurance making him the greatest ever trumpeter of Norman Granz's show. He worked regularly with old colleague Coleman Hawkins and in 1956 at Café Bohemia was keenly disappointed that Miles Davis wasn't appearing opposite him. 'If it were possible,' recalled Nat Hentoff, 'he'd have tried for a cutting contest with Buddy Bolden!' 1960–5, he had his own quintet, backed Ella Fitzgerald, joined Count Basie briefly, and from 1966 led a quintet again with Richie Kamuca. From this period it was occasionally possible to hear that for 'Little Jazz' the trumpet sometimes felt heavier (on a 1967 visit to the UK his first-house notes sounded hard to get); but in 1970 came the start of a long residency at Jimmy Ryan's, and six years on (according to Lee Jeske) he was still taking on all comers until a stroke in 1980 curtailed his playing. [DF]

The Early Years (1935–49), CBS

See Shapiro, Nat, and Hentoff, Nat, *The Jazz*

Makers (Rinehart, 1957, repr. Da Capo, 1979); Lyttelton, Humphrey, *The Best of Jazz 2: Enter the Giants* (Robson, 1981); Dance, Stanley, *The World of Swing* (Scribner's, 1974, repr. Da Capo, 1979).

Electronics Electricity was first used in jazz to amplify the sound of acoustic instruments through public address systems and, by means of electrical recording in the later 1920s, to reproduce acoustic music on 78 rpm discs. But the very acts of amplifying and of recording also involve the electrical treatment of acoustic sound. This initial relationship of acoustic instruments with electronic treatment at live concerts and in the recording studio has grown steadily in sophistication since the 1920s. For example, the metal harmon mute made famous by Miles Davis is played acoustically, but it only gains its full tonal expressiveness when it is placed very close to a sensitive microphone and amplified. Without that electronic 'treatment' the harmon has virtually no tonal interest or expressivity.

From the 1930s on, instruments began to be amplified by the direct use of electrical power: the electric guitar was invented, and later the electric bass and electric piano. The very first all-electric instrument was the electric organ, which was a kind of primitive synthesizer: its sound was created electronically and then amplified. With electric instruments, players began to have more and more control over their own sound, and since the 1950s an enormous number of devices have been invented for the direct treatment of instrumental sound: fuzz boxes, wah-wah pedals, phasers, echoplexes, octave-dividers etc. Since the 1960s synthesizers have developed from their first primitive manifestations into enormously sophisticated instruments. With synthesizers a small group can have all the resources of a full orchestra at its disposal, as well as a vast array of other sounds which the players can discover for themselves. Joe Zawinul has discovered many original ways of creating synthesized sounds, which he thinks of as 'native instruments not yet discovered'.

The inherent conservatism of many jazz musicians made them attack and reject the use of electronics in music – just as, earlier in the century, the introduction of the saxophone into jazz groups had caused an outcry. But synthesizers are a resource to be used, just like any other, and the quality of the music they produce depends entirely on the quality of the musician who uses them. In the hands of a master like Zawinul, they enhance the haunting quality of some of his music, taking on human overtones and communicating human feelings.

With the jazz-rock-fusion movement of the 1970s, electronics were established as a major ingredient and a massive tonal resource, and the often magnificent results can be heard in the music of Miles Davis, Weather Report, Herbie Hancock, Return to Forever and the Mahavishnu Orchestra, to name a few. [IC]

Elizalde, Fred (Federico), piano, composer, leader. b. Manila, Philippines, 1907. He formed his all-British 'Quinquaginta Ramblers', an undergraduate jazz band, for a Cambridge Footlights Club ball in 1927. The novelty of a fully-fledged British jazz band (featuring, incidentally, star cricket blue Maurice Allom on saxophone) created a sensation, and Elizalde became a headliner: in 1927 he recorded, wrote regularly for *Melody Maker*, composed a suite, *The Heart of a Nigger*, for Ambrose's orchestra (which had a good press, and was recorded but then withdrawn after one public performance), and in October that year made more records with an Ambrose contingent (including Nichols-style trumpeter and future DJ Jack Jackson). Then Elizalde took a band into the Savoy with a nucleus of US musicians including Chelsea Quealey, Bobby Davis and – direct from a failed bandleading stint back home – Adrian Rollini. Elizalde's impressive band, led by the youthful pianist in the reflection from a glass-fronted piano, influenced young British musicians such as Harry Gold, who sneaked backstage to listen to Rollini and to learn. But it was too hot for the Savoy's dignified music policy (a ten-year strait-jacket for young would-be jazzmen), and in 1929 Elizalde was politely asked to leave. After one final concert at Shepherd's Bush Empire he moved to Spain, studied under Manuel de Falla and, as Federico Elizalde, became a reputable classical conductor. [DF]

Jazz at the Savoy: the 20s (1927–8), Decca

Ellington, Duke (Edward Kennedy), composer, arranger, piano. b. Washington, DC, 29 April 1899; d. 24 May 1974. After studying piano as a child, he became interested in local ragtimers such as Lester Dishman, for whom he deputized at 15. Working as a freelance sign-painter from 1917, began assembling groups to play for dances; met drummer Sonny Greer from New Jersey (1919) who encouraged Duke's ambition to become a professional musician. Played together (with early hometown associates Otto Hardwicke and Arthur Whetsol) in Wisconsin and Atlantic City before settling in New York (1923), working first as sextet under Elmer Snowden (also from Washington) then as embryonic Duke Ellington and his Washingtonians (1924). Successful nightclub residencies culminated in a long stay at the Cotton Club with an enlarged, 10-piece, band (from end 1927), with regular broadcasts establishing his reputation nationally. Lengthy absences from New York in order to tour West Coast and make first film appearance (1930, replaced at Cotton Club by Cab Calloway) and for tours of Europe and Southern US (both 1933, replaced by Jimmie Lunceford). US tours playing at theatres, hotels and dances virtually constant from 1934, broken

Duke Ellington

by further work at the Cotton Club (1937, 1938 – the latter season the first time Duke contributed songs as well as backing music for dancers) and by second tour of Europe (1939). During second half of 1930s, band numbers had increased to 15 with two basses. Played for and wrote score of revue *Jump For Joy* (1941) and musical comedy *Beggars' Holiday* (1947).

Series of annual concerts at Carnegie Hall (early 1943–end 1948) and one at Metropolitan Opera House (1951), each occasion the premiere of an extended composition. Temporary inactivity of big band (1948) while Ellington toured UK with Ray Nance, Kay Davis and local trio; the reconvened band was his largest ever (18 pieces, dropping to 16 by European tour 1950, usually 15 thereafter). Retirement from band of Sonny Greer (1951) and simultaneous temporary departure of long-term members Johnny Hodges and Lawrence Brown, all playing in Hodges' own group. Declining popularity of Duke's band in US was arrested by a newsworthy Newport festival appearance (1956). He became the first black composer commissioned to write major film soundtracks (notably *Anatomy of a Murder*, 1959) and TV series theme-music. (Benny Carter had preceded him but as an uncredited 'ghost-writer'.) Further foreign tours multiplied: Europe (1958, 1962–71 annually and 1973); Middle East and India (1963); Japan (1964, 1970); West Africa (1966); South America (1968); Australia (1970); Soviet Union (1971). Ellington continued to produce quantities of new pieces and suites, including 'sacred concerts' in various cathedrals, and to appear in public until a couple of months before his death from cancer.

First recorded soon after the start of his bandleading career, Duke seems to have been initially inspired by the successful white dance bands of the 1920s and their rather maudlin (and middle-class) view of what jazz was all about. However, the arrival of Sidney Bechet (1925), Joe Nanton (1926–46) and especially the continued presence of Bubber Miley from the Elmer Snowden days (1924–9) introduced him, virtually for the first time in his life, to the passion and poetry of black jazz. Early masterpieces such as 'Black and Tan Fantasy' (co-written with Miley) are compounds of both approaches, and ever afterwards Ellington performed not one but several stylistic balancing acts. Additional soloists in the next few years – Harry Carney (1927–74), Barney Bigard (1927–42), Johnny Hodges (1928–51, 1955–70), Cootie Williams (1929–40, 1962–74), Lawrence Brown (1932–51, 1960–70) and Rex Stewart (1934–45) – were all sophisticated technically but, all being influenced by Louis Armstrong, were also in touch with the earthy roots of his music. Ellington responded with (or, rather, used their talents to help him come up with) such widely differing successes as 'Mood Indigo', 'It Don't Mean a Thing', 'Sophisticated Lady' and countless instrumental-only conceptions.

A significant new wave of contributors who signed up within a few months of one another included Ben Webster (1940–3, 1948–9), Jimmy Blanton (1939–41) and Duke's writing collaborator Billy Strayhorn (1939–67); they brought him up to date with the jazz of the late 1930s and, particularly in the case of Blanton and Strayhorn, foreshadowed many of the rhythmic and harmonic developments of the 1940s. Ellington's compositional penchant for cannibalizing what they had to offer and in turn stretching their abilities – in virtuoso vehicles such as 'Cotton Tail', 'In a Mellotone' and 'Perdido' (tune by Juan Tizol arranged by Duke) – surfaced again a decade later with the induction of established 'modernists' such as Clark Terry (1951–9) and Paul Gonsalves (1950–74). Fewer Ellington standards may have emerged thereafter (and those that did were less innovative, e.g. 'Satin Doll') but items from *Such Sweet Thunder* and *Suite Thursday* were dramatic demonstrations of his facility for keeping up with the times and yet sounding always like himself. As late as 1966–7, the *Far East Suite* and 'La Plus Belle Africaine' showed him convincingly coming to terms with modal jazz, and also with the increasing popularity of the Latin-jazz crossover which he and Tizol had started off with 'Caravan' back in 1936.

Combining all these innovations within the ongoing history of one band is only half the story, despite the fact that no other figure managed to be creatively involved in so many different stages of jazz development. If it was merely a matter of anthologizing typical phrases of various jazz styles, then numerous other arrangers have achieved this – indeed, that is what arrangers are for. But Ellington set his sights much higher, absorbing the utterances of his hired soloists into his own compositional expression so that the two frequently became indistinguishable. And this was possible because his sensitivity to notes (therefore, to harmony and rhythm) was matched by his sensitivity to textures. In this way, saying that Duke 'always sounded like himself' is tantamount to saying that he sounded like Harry Carney and Johnny Hodges and Cootie Williams . . . But it is at least arguable that they would have sounded less like themselves, had it not been for Duke continually showing them in the best light and thus encouraging them to play at their best.

This is an area in which very few writers have ever tried to emulate Ellington; other aspects of his work have proved more influential, if not always beneficially so. The concept of a specially written series (or suite) of shortish pieces, interlinked either musically or merely by circumstance, has inspired many of those looking for a way of lending spurious dignity to their normal output. Similarly, the idea of featuring just one soloist per piece, which Duke inaugurated with four 'concertos' in 1936 (and came to rely on increasingly thereafter), found immediate favour with several other big bands in the swing era. Less farreaching was the effect of his longer compositions, starting as far back as the two quite different versions of 'Creole Rhapsody' in 1931; Ellington's own successful follow-ups included 'Reminiscing in Tempo' (1935), 'Diminuendo and Crescendo in Blue' (1937), 'Black, Brown and Beige' (1943) and 'Tone Parallel to Harlem' (1951). The retention of a jazz feel despite a minimum of improvisation in these larger structures seems to have eluded other writers.

The crucial factor in Ellington's evolution was his enormous receptivity to everything he ever heard (and saw and felt, hence his choice of evocative titles); as a result, while there was a consistent, and no doubt fairly egotistical, emotional core, his sources of inspiration were constantly expanding. Just as an improviser has to learn to think while on his feet, so Duke learned how to write his kind of jazz while doing it. Indeed, perhaps the writing process is more easily understood by comparing it with his own solo work on piano, and by contrasting the brief and rather bland pseudo-ragtime contributions on his earliest recordings with the dynamic and totally original playing on two albums thrown together in a few hours with Charles Mingus/Max Roach and with John Coltrane/Elvin Jones. It may well be that the small school of pianists who have learned from Duke's use of the instrument – Thelonious Monk, Randy Weston, Abdullah Ibrahim, Stan Tracey, Cecil Taylor and a few others – have perpetuated the spirit of Ellington more meaningfully than those who try to copy his composition and orchestration.

One of the problems in considering Ellington's achievement is that it exists on an astonishing variety of levels. Not only do the writing and playing offer a convenient contrast: for each extended work there are several straight-ahead ballads, simple in conception but immensely sophisticated in their execution. And the number of different uses Duke found for the 12-bar blues is bewildering to behold. Then there is his success as a songwriter (which subsidized the continued existence of the Ellington band in its last 25 years or so): some of the few titles mentioned above had lyrics added and became twice as popular, as did numerous other standards; the quality and quantity of his song output places Duke in the Gershwin and Porter category. However, his uniqueness lies not only in the breadth and universality of the music which reached the greatest number of listeners, but in those irreplaceable and inimitable icons such as 'Harlem Air Shaft', 'Concerto for Cootie' and 'Ko-Ko', all recorded within a few months in 1940, which have been an inspiration to several generations of jazz musicians. [BP]

The Indispensable, vols.1/2 (1927–9), RCA; *The Indispensable, vols.3/4* (1930–4), RCA; *The Complete, vol.3* (1930–2), CBS; *The Complete, vol.7* (1936–7), CBS; *The Indispensable, vols.5/6* (1940), RCA; *Carnegie Hall Concert* (1943), Prestige; *Such Sweet Thunder* (1957), CBS; Ellington/Mingus/Roach, *Money Jungle* (1962), Blue Note; *Duke Ellington and John Coltrane* (1962), Impulse; *The Far East Suite* (1966), RCA

See Ellington, Duke, *Music is my Mistress* (Doubleday, 1973); Ellington, Mercer, with Stanley Dance, *Duke Ellington in Person* (Houghton Mifflin, 1978); Dance, Stanley, *The World of Duke Ellington* (Scribner's, 1970, repr. Da Capo, 1980); Jewell, Derek, *Duke* (Elm Tree Books, 1977)

Film: *On the Road with Duke Ellington* (dir. Robert Drew, 1974)

Ellington, Mercer Kennedy, trumpet, composer, arranger. b. Washington, DC, 11 March 1919. Studied informally with his father Duke Ellington, 'Pigeons and Peppers' at age 18 becoming his first piece to be recorded by Duke (with Cootie Williams group, 1937). Spent several periods leading his own bands (1939, 1946–9, 1959), often hiring musicians later employed by Duke such as Clark Terry, Harold Ashby, Wendell Marshall, Joe Benjamin and singer Al Hibbler, also non-Ducal notables Dizzy Gillespie, Kenny Dorham, Idrees Sulieman, Chico Hamilton, Charles Mingus and Carmen McRae. Also worked as road manager for Cootie Williams band (1941–3, 1954), musical director for singer Della Reese (1960–2) and DJ with a daily show in New York (1962–5). Periods working for his father in 1940–1, contributing original compositions; 1950, playing E-flat horn; 1955–9, general assistant and copyist; 1965–74, trumpeter and road manager.

On Duke's death, Mercer took over his band on a regular basis, making European tours (1975, 1977). He also published a memoir of his father (see above). Early 1980s, original conductor of house band for Broadway musical of Duke tunes, *Sophisticated Ladies*. Although conditions may not now be so favourable for full-time continuance of a band under Mercer's leadership, it is important to remember the masterly pieces written by him in his early twenties, such as 'Things Ain't What They Used To Be', 'Jumpin' Punkins', 'Moon Mist' and especially 'Blue Serge'. [BP]

Duke Ellington, *The Indispensable, vols.7/8* (1941), RCA; *Continuum* (1974–5), Fantasy

Ellis, Chris (Christopher), vocals. b. Shrewsbury, Shropshire, 25 December 1928. His rather too infrequent singing appearances have included spells with Alan Elsdon, the Anglo-American Alliance (leader Dick Sudhalter), the New Paul Whiteman Orchestra (ditto), extended periods in pubs and clubs singing with like-minded musicians such as Keith Nichols and Alan Leat, the Midnite Follies Orchestra (at the Northsea Jazz Festival) and more recently with Tiny Winters' Kettners Five and Orchestra. For many years Ellis has worked on and off as a record producer for EMI and during the 1960s and 1970s often fought hard for worthwhile talent to be recorded: musicians to benefit from his kindly, unobtrusive but dedicated championship included Keith Ingham, Susannah McCorkle and Keith Nichols. Ellis's compilations of classic recordings (including most of Louis Armstrong's 1920s output, most of Bix Beiderbecke's and hundreds of others) set new standards for reissues at their period: so did his later – highly skilful – production of records for visiting Americans such as Ginger Rogers, Elaine Stritch and Sammy Cahn. Ellis's name on a production is a guarantee of worth: his scholarly knowledge – of everything from songs to the backwaters of jazz discography – is encyclopaedic. [DF]

New Paul Whiteman Orchestra, *Running Wild* (1975), Argo

Ellis, Don (Donald Johnson), trumpet, drums, composer. b. Los Angeles, 25 July 1934; d. 17 December 1978. Played trumpet in high school dance bands; 1956, graduated B.Mus. in composition at Boston University. 1956–60, worked in various big bands including Maynard Ferguson's. 1961–2, in New York he worked with George Russell, establishing himself as an interesting new voice on trumpet, and recording one of the seminal albums of the 1960s with Russell's sextet, *Ezz-thetic* (1961), which included Eric Dolphy, Dave Baker, Steve Swallow and drummer Joe Hunt. His early influences were Gillespie, Navarro and Clark Terry, among others, and Ellis displayed a brilliant conventional technique plus an interest in tonal and structural experimentation. He also began leading his own small groups in the early 1960s. 1964, he went back to Los Angeles, beginning postgraduate studies at UCLA, and studying Indian music with Hari Har Rao. He formed the Hindustani Jazz Sextet, one of the first groups to fuse elements from Indian music and jazz. He also became active in music education, teaching both privately and at UCLA and other academic institutions.

From 1965, began leading a series of big bands which made a strong impression internationally, playing major festivals in Europe. He also introduced a series of new devices and new approaches into big-band music. With rocky rhythms, multiple percussion, electronic instruments such as Fender-Rhodes piano, clavinet, ring modulator, phaser and other devices, and the use of odd, asymmetrical time signatures, he anticipated most of the elements of the jazz-rock movement of the 1970s. He also used an electric (amplified) string quartet on occasion, and deployed a vocal quartet as an instrumental section. From 1966, Ellis used a four-valve trumpet which could produce quarter-tones; he used these in solos and also, from time to time, had the entire trumpet section on four-valve horns playing in quarter-tones. He also used sitar and elements from Indian music in his big-band music, sometimes taking asymmetry to extraordinary lengths. He told J. E. Berendt, 'I reasoned that since it was possible to play in a meter such as a 9, divided 2–2–2–3, it would then be possible to play in meters of even greater length, and this led to the development of such meters as 3–3–2–2–2–1–2–2–2 (19). To arrive at this particular division of 19, I tried many different patterns, but this was the one that swung the most. The longest meter I have attempted to date is a piece in 85.' On one of his best albums, *Electric Bath* (1968), not one piece is in common time, yet the music seems effortless and natural, and its range is broad – from a very funky eastern-sounding blues in 7/4 ('Turkish Bath') and a fast funky piece in 5/4 ('Indian Lady'), to spacey, out-of-time sections and the more floating asymmetry of 'New Horizons' and 'Open Beauty'.

Ellis was immensely articulate: he wrote and spoke about music in magazines such as *Downbeat* and on campuses, and from the early 1960s appeared many times on TV, with and without his bands, not only in the USA, but also in Berlin, Hamburg, Paris, Montreal, Antibes and other places. He also remained active in education, teaching theory, composition, arranging and trumpet in New York and Los Angeles. He was a prolific composer, writing for his own bands and groups, and also for other ensembles and institutions: *Contrasts for Two Orchestras and Trumpet*, for Zubin Mehta and the Los Angeles Philharmonic; *Reach*, a cantata for chorus and orchestra for the Berlin Jazz Festival; and many others. He scored the soundtracks for several films including *The French Connection* (1972).

Early in 1975, Ellis suffered a serious heart attack which incapacitated him for many months. He began to do more composing, but by the end of the year had begun playing again. In February 1978 he appeared with a small group at the first Jazz Yatra in Bombay, once more using his four-valve trumpet and featuring asymmetrical rhythms. He played with all his old brilliance and fire, giving a sparkling performance. He died later that year.

Don Ellis was a man of great energy and intelligence, and an inspiring band leader. He helped to re-invigorate jazz by introducing elements from ethnic (particularly Indian) music, by widening its rhythmic possibilities and by deploying the tonal palette of electronics. He was, without doubt, a virtuoso trumpet player, but in some ways his sound lacked warmth, and his big-band music, for all its tremendous brilliance and spirit, seems more the product of mind and will than of the mysteriously sensuous feeling which, for example, imbues the work of Duke Ellington, Miles Davis and Gil Evans. [IC]

With Russell, Charles Mingus and others; *How Time Passes* (1960), Candid; Don Ellis Orchestra at Monterey, *Live in 3 2/3/4* (1966), Pacific Jazz; *Electric Bath* (1968); *Shock Treatment* (1968); *Don Ellis at Fillmore* (1970); *Tears of Joy* (1971), all CBS; *Haiku* (1973), BASF

Ellis, Herb (Mitchell Herbert), guitar. b. McKinley, Texas, 4 August 1921. Studied at North Texas State College alongside Jimmy Giuffre and arranger Gene Roland. Played with Casa Loma Orchestra and Jimmy Dorsey band (mid-1940s) and then with the Soft Winds trio, co-composers of 'Detour Ahead' recorded by Billie Holiday. Joined Oscar Peterson on departure of Barney Kessel (1953–8), then backed singers Ella Fitzgerald and Julie London. Involved in studio work on West Coast from 1960s, with occasional small-group appearances often with Ray Brown from early 1970s onwards. During his period of maximum jazz activity, Ellis was highly regarded as a gutsy guitarist, whose unforced blues inflections made him a natural Charlie Christian disciple. [BP]

Nothing but the Blues (1957), Verve

Elman, 'Ziggy' (Harry Finkelman), trumpet, multi-instrumentalist. b. Philadelphia, 26 May 1914; d. Van Nuys, California, 26 June 1968. He began his career (on trombone) with Alex Bartha's house band at Atlantic City's Steel Pier ballroom; 1936, moved to Benny Goodman, replacing lead trumpeter Pee Wee Erwin. He stayed with Goodman for four years, completing (with Harry James who joined one month later) the royal trumpet triumvirate of Elman/James/Chris Griffin that topped Goodman's greatest band. 1938, as featured soloist, Elman recorded 16 highly successful sides for Bluebird (an RCA subsidiary): two of these, at least, 'Fraulich in Swing' and 'Bublitchki', were to be incorporated into Goodman's repertoire as the thrilling 'And the angels sing' (words by Johnny Mercer) and 'Who'll buy my Bublitchki?' (Elman also played clarinet for Goodman on occasion: reputedly for a live performance of 'Bach Goes to Town' he learned the instrument in one day.) 1940–7, regularly with Tommy Dorsey, usually leading the trumpet section. From 1947, Elman – big, bluff, likeable, always smoking a big cigar – based himself in Los Angeles. He had two unsuccessful tries at running his own big band, at a time when big bands were winding down anyway and badly affected by the second American Federation of Musicians recording ban (1948), so he worked instead in MGM's studios, directed the band for Dinah Shore and Bing Crosby radio shows, and recorded: one late album, *Tribute to Benny Goodman* by Jess Stacy and the famous Sidemen, shows his creative flame burning bright as ever. He appeared in *The Benny Goodman Story* (1955), although his playing was dubbed by Manny Klein, and in later years kept active until a nervous breakdown and drinking problems finally put out the flame. Elman personifies the Jewish 'fraulich' trumpet style. [DF]

And the Angels Sing (1938–9), Sunbeam

Elsdon, Alan, trumpet, fluegelhorn, leader, vocals. b. Chiswick, London, 15 October 1934. He worked in the 1950s with Cy Laurie, Graham Stewart and Terry Lightfoot before forming his own band in 1961, shortly before the British Trad boom ended. For that reason his band never quite achieved the popular status of earlier arrivals such as Barber, Bilk and Ball, but established a high musical reputation which – after the Beatles – gave Elsdon the option to work in cabaret with a variety of popular singers including Cilla Black, the Isley Brothers and Dionne Warwicke. Later in the 1960s, as well as busily working the jazz circuits, Elsdon's band became a temporary backing group for George Melly: he continued to play for clubs and concerts with and without his band and in 1978 joined the Midnite Follies Orchestra, a move which focused attention on his strength, technique and versatility. Elsdon's recreation of jazz roles from Louis Armstrong to Cootie Williams were filled with flair and inspiration and in the 1980s he became a regular working partner to leader Keith Nichols. At Christmas 1985 he led his band for a short season at the London Palladium. [DF]

Jazz Journeymen (1977), Black Lion

Energy/High-energy Music During the 1960s, with the rise of free (abstract) improvisation, which made the hitherto accepted criteria for judging musical performances seem irrelevant, the word 'energy' began to be used as a term of approbation: a performance with energy was 'good', and a high-energy performance was 'very good'. This use of the words among certain groups of musicians and fans has carried on into the post-abstract period of jazz, yet no one seems to have considered the simple fact that inferior performances and inferior music may yet have a high energy level, while exquisite music has often been produced with little apparent expenditure of energy. [IC]

Eric(s)son, Rolf(e), trumpet, b. Stockholm, 29 August 1922. Took up trumpet at age nine and heard Louis Armstrong in Stockholm (1933), turned professional in 1943. Moved to USA (1947–50, 1953–66), also touring Sweden with Charlie Parker (1950) and with Duke Jordan, Cecil Payne etc. (1956). In USA, sideman with many big bands including Benny Carter, Charlie Barnet (1949), Charlie Ventura (1950), Woody Herman (1950), Harry James, Stan Kenton (1959), Maynard Ferguson (1960–1). Small-group work with Lighthouse All Stars (1953, replacing Shorty Rogers), Dexter Gordon, Curtis Counce–Harold Land (1958), and the 10-piece Charles Mingus band (1962–3). Regular member of Duke Ellington band (1963–4), rehearsed and recorded with Rod Levitt octet (1963–5). Then led own Swedish big band (late 1960s), followed by radio studio work in Berlin into 1980s and further playing visits to USA. Already a bright, boppish soloist in his twenties, Ericson's contact with the very best American musicians has helped to form a markedly individual style. [BP]

Stockholm Sweetnin' (1984), Dragon

Erskine, Peter, drums. b. Somers Point, New Jersey, 5 June 1954. At age six attended Stan Kenton National Stage Band Camps, and continued doing so each summer for several years; studied with Alan Dawson and others; also attended Interlochen Arts Academy at Indiana University. 1972, joined Stan Kenton orchestra, touring the USA, Europe and Japan, and teaching at Kenton clinics. Erskine was with Weather Report, 1978–82, in one of the its most vital and creative phases. 1979, began playing with Steps (including Mike Brecker, Mike Mainieri and Eddie Gomez), later renamed Steps Ahead. With Jaco Pastorius in Weather Report, Erskine formed one of the finest rhythm-sections of the 1970s and early 1980s, and exposure with the group brought him to world-wide attention. In the 1980s he has continued with Steps Ahead, touring in Japan, the USA and Europe. His favourites are Elvin Jones, Mel Lewis, Billy Cobham and Grady Tate among others. [IC]

With Kenton and many others; with Weather Report, *8.30* (1979); *Night Passage* (1980); *Weather Report* (1982), all CBS; with Steps Ahead, *Steps Ahead* (1983), Elektra Musician

Ervin, Booker Telleferro, Jnr., tenor sax, composer. b. Denison, Texas, 31 October 1930; d. 31 July 1970. After playing trombone and then taking up tenor during service in air force (1949–53), studied at Berklee (1954) and toured with Ernie Fields (1955). Then worked in Dallas, Denver and Pittsburgh until moving to New York (1958). Immediately recommended to Charles Mingus who employed him for several periods (1958–9, 1960, 1962, 1963, 1964 twice). Also played with pianists Roland Hanna (1959) and Randy Weston (1960, 1964). Work under own name from 1960 including live gigs and recording in Europe (1964–6, 1968). Was performing again in USA at time of death from kidney disease.

Although his father Booker Ervin Snr. played alongside the great Buddy Tate, Booker Jnr.'s style is far removed from the bluesy mainstream playing identified with other 'Texas tenors'. Though his tone is subject to similar inflexions, it is not merely hot but scalding, and his line and time feeling owe something to both Dexter Gordon and John Coltrane. His original compositions and solos on others' material reflect a sophisticated sense of harmony and polytonality as well as the explicit emotionalism he projects. [BP]

The Freedom and Space Sessions (1963–4), Prestige

Erwin, Pee Wee (George), trumpet. b. Falls City, Nebraska, 30 May 1913; d. Teaneck, New Jersey, 20 June 1981. A superb technician for his period, Erwin was learning the trumpet from his father by age four and at eight was featured on Kansas City radio with the Coon–Sanders Nighthawks. At 18 he made the New York trip to join Joe Haymes's band, worked with Isham Jones and Freddy Martin, and by 1935 was with Benny Goodman, happily playing lead and solos for the famous 'Let's Dance' programmes. 1936, a second stint with Ray Noble's orchestra for which Glenn Miller was fixer and staff arranger. (Miller, at Erwin's request, wrote his trumpet high and voiced with the saxophones; when Erwin's successor couldn't play the parts they were given to the clarinettist, and Miller's sound – which he credited to Erwin – came to be.) For the remainder of the 1930s Erwin was first trumpeter for Goodman, Ray Noble and Tommy Dorsey (replacing Bunny Berigan, an indicator of his ability) then took over Berigan's band for two years from 1940. 1942–9, he was in the studios (as an almost permanent deputy for Manny Klein) and then led the band at Nick's Saloon for ten years from 1949: at this period there were many fine Erwin recordings including his definitive Jelly Roll Morton tribute with Kenny Davern. In the 1960s he continued busy studio work (including replacing Bobby Hackett on Jackie Gleason's later recordings), ran a trumpet school with Chris Griffin in New Jersey (his most famous and well-loved pupil is Warren Vaché Jnr.) and played festivals. From the early 1970s he worked with the NYJRC, on fourth trumpet ('There was a time', he told British promoter Vic Smith, 'when I couldn't wait to run up on the stand and play first! Now I walk up and play fourth!'), and in his last years was with Warren Vaché Snr.'s band around New Jersey.

A warm-hearted and funny man whom everybody loved, Erwin died of cancer: his work lives on in Warren Vaché Jnr. [DF]

Classic Jazz by Pee Wee in New York (1980), Qualtro Music

Etheridge, John Michael Glyn, guitars. b. London, 12 January 1948. Father played piano. History of art degree at Essex University. He began playing guitar at school and was self-taught. 1971–4, with progressive jazz-rock groups in London. 1975–8, with Soft Machine. 1977–81, touring with Stephane Grappelli. 1980–1, his own group, Second Vision. 1982, solo concerts in Australia and duo dates with bassist Brian Torff in USA. 1983, formed his own trio which toured England, 1984. Also 1984, concerts with re-formed Soft Machine. 1985, duo work with Gary Boyle and with a quartet. He is a regular teacher on many jazz courses. Etheridge is a fine, all-round player, equally at home on electric and acoustic guitar; his influences range from Django Reinhardt to John McLaughlin. [IC]

With Soft Machine, Grappelli and Didier Lockwood; electric guitar, with Second Vision, *First Steps* (1980), Chrysalis; acoustic guitar, with Grappelli, *Live at Carnegie Hall* (1983), Dr Jazz

Eubanks, Kevin Tyrone, guitar. b. Philadelphia, 15 November 1957. Mother, Vera Eubanks, a D.Mus., his uncles are Ray and Tommy Bryant. Studied at Berklee and with Ted Dunbar. From 14 to 22 his biggest influence was John McLaughlin and the Mahavishnu Orchestra, then he began to listen to Wes Montgomery. 1980–1 with Art Blakey's Jazz Messengers; played briefly with Roy Haynes and Slide Hampton. 1982, toured with Sam Rivers whose free-improvising concept radically altered Eubanks's ideas about music. 1983, toured UK with the Mike Gibbs band. He has played with numerous other musicians, and has been leading his own group since 1983. Other influences are George Benson, Segovia, Oscar Peterson, Mahler and Bartók. Eubanks has already shown himself to be an interesting composer. [IC]

With Art Blakey Big Band, *Live at Montreux* (1980), Timeless; *Kevin Eubanks – Guitarist* (1982), Elektra Musician; *Opening Night* (1985), GRP

Europe has always been vitally important to jazz, and since the 1960s, its influence has increased dramatically and its role become more dynamic. The first serious critical appraisals of jazz were made by Europeans. In 1919 the Swiss conductor Ernst Ansermet heard Sidney Bechet in London, recognized his genius immediately and wrote an ecstatic review in the Swiss *Revue Romande*. The first book on jazz was written by a Belgian, Robert Goffin, in 1932, and the first jazz magazine was started in France during the late 1920s, edited by Hugues Panassié. The first jazz discography was compiled by another Frenchman, Charles Delaunay, in 1936. This general tendency, of Europeans pointing out the quality of American music to Americans, has continued to varying degrees in subsequent decades. In a 1954 review, for example, the French critic André Hodeir was the first to proclaim in print the quality of Gil Evans who, at that time, was living and working in total obscurity in the USA. The Art Ensemble of Chicago first came to prominence in France in 1970 before they had made any impact in America.

Since about 1960, however, Europe has also produced musicians of its own who, in terms of ability, originality and influence, have become key figures in jazz. The first European with this kind of stature was, of course, Django Reinhardt; by the 1980s the list was long and distinguished: Albert Mangelsdorff and Eberhard Weber from Germany, John McLaughlin and John Surman from the UK, Joe Zawinul from Austria, Jan Garbarek from Norway, Jean-Luc Ponty from France and Zbigniew Seifert from Poland are a few of the most important names. Although influenced and inspired by US musicians, these Europeans have produced music which is very different in identity from the usual American jazz, and one of the reasons is that Europe offers a very different aesthetic climate. The gladiatorial competitiveness of the American scene, where musicians must, in the current jargon, 'fight for their space', does not exist in Europe. Instead, the atmosphere is more expansive and reflective, the struggle is not with other musicians but with old, received ideas, and the whole continent from east to west and north to south is steeped in the emotional resonance of folk music and classical music. These 'European' qualities have also leavened the work of some of the finest US jazz musicians: Bix Beiderbecke and Duke Ellington were familiar with the impressionism of Debussy and Ravel, while the work of Miles Davis and Gil Evans shows the influence of classical music and of folk music not only from Europe but also from other continents.

Since the beginning of the 1970s the German ECM record label, and its visionary producer Manfred Eicher, have also helped to shift the centre of gravity from the USA to Europe. At a time when the major record companies in America were recording and releasing only jazz-rock-fusion, Eicher had a programme of releases which ranged from abstraction and the avant-garde to acoustic groups and fusion. When Keith Jarrett's contract was terminated by Columbia in 1972 he went straight to ECM, and it was only then that his full musical persona could express itself, revealing not only his joyous rhythms and his blues and gospel roots, but also his other influence – the romantic melancholy of the classical tradition. Sales of his solo piano albums were soon running to six figures, and his European quartet, with Garbarek, Palle Danielsson and Jon Christensen, was recording some of the finest small-group music of the decade. Many other US musicians also recorded for ECM, including Ralph Towner, John Abercrombie, the Art Ensemble of Chicago, Pat Metheny, Sam Rivers, Chick Corea and Gary Burton, and the major US companies were made to see that there was a very substantial audience for a wide variety of jazz. In a sense, ECM was carrying on from where the crucially important US label Blue Note had stopped at the beginning of the 1970s: Blue Note, of course, was started and run by two Europeans, Alfred Lion and Francis Wolff, refugees from Nazi Germany.

When John McLaughlin was asked in 1975 why he had moved back from the USA to live in Europe again, he said that in America jazz was often regarded as a commodity by the big companies, whereas in Europe it was regarded as an art. With the exception perhaps of the UK, where jazz seems to be regarded as the Cinderella of the arts, the European media in general are generous with their coverage. And even in the UK, the ACGB Contemporary Music Network tours have made much brilliant contemporary jazz available to the British public. As a direct result of this expansive and sympathetic climate, some of the finest and most influential groups of the 1970s and 1980s have been based in Europe, and they have often had mixed European and American personnel; as well as Keith Jarrett's Belonging band, there have been Eberhard Weber's Colours, the Jan Garbarek quartet, and various line-ups led by Albert Mangelsdorff and by John Surman. [IC]

Evans, Bill (William John), piano, composer. b. Plainfield, New Jersey, 16 August 1929; d. 15 September 1980. An enormously influential figure who seemingly sprang upon the jazz scene fully formed. Made his first solo album in 1956 shortly after joining Tony Scott, whom he rejoined briefly in 1959 following a crucial eight months with Miles Davis. Also made important contributions to projects by such as Charles Mingus (*East Coasting*) and George Russell ('All About Rosie', *Jazz in the Space Age* etc.). Led own trio from 1959, apart from brief drug-related absences; after several years of stomach ulcer and liver problems, re-addiction preceded death at the peak of his career.

Evans's recordings with Davis had a decisive effect on the trumpeter, as well as vice versa, despite comprising less than two whole albums (the *Jazz Track* session and *Kind of Blue*). His harmonic approach, especially, was significant in softening the edges of conventional sequences and pointing the way for pianists to cope with modal jazz; it also dictated the emotional content of his innovations, which became almost too rarefied at times and can be seen as foreshadowing the restrained gestures of much European jazz of the 1970s and 1980s. Archie Shepp articulated a widely held view when saying, 'I think Bill's best work was done with the Miles Davis Quintet. A good deal of that energy seems to me to have gone by the way . . . I like him on ballad material . . . but Debussy and Satie have already done those things.'

An extraordinarily prophetic example of Evans's affinity with these composers is 'Peace Piece' (from *Everybody Digs Bill Evans*), whose improvised melody unfolds over a completely open-ended aharmonic background. His up-tempo playing betrays the early inspiration of Bud Powell, Horace Silver, even of Nat Cole, but the shape and length of his lines shows his admiration for Lennie Tristano. Far more expressive than Tristano, Evans displays a wide range of touch and accentuation; the singing tone of his right-hand work and his left-hand voicings were utterly distinctive although universally imitated. Similarly, the interplay within his trio (initially with bassist Scott La Faro, later Eddie Gomez) added a new sound to the vocabulary of rhythm-section work.

Although he was a prolific composer, Evans's creations are closely bound to his style of improvisation and not many have become standard material. 'Blue in Green', written for *Kind of Blue*, is an exception, as is 'Waltz for Debby' (to which lyrics were added by Gene Lees), and others are worthy of wider usage such as 'Turn Out the Stars'. But the combination of strength and sensitivity in his playing is ultimately what will be remembered about Evans and, since a whole generation of keyboard artists absorbed aspects of his style (from Herbie Hancock to Keith Jarrett), it is necessary to listen repeatedly to his early recordings in order to appreciate his unique contribution. [BP]

Everybody Digs Bill Evans (1958); *Portrait in Jazz* (1959); *Waltz for Debby* (1961), all Riverside/OJC; *Conversations with Myself* (1963), Verve

Bill Evans (piano)

Evans, Bill, tenor and soprano sax, flute, keyboards, composer. b. Clarendon Hills, Illinois, 1957. Began on piano at age five, later taking up clarinet and tenor sax. He played classical piano concerts at 16; after one year studying music at North Texas State University he transferred to William Paterson College in New Jersey; also studied sax with Dave Liebman, who recommended Evans to Miles Davis. After graduating, Evans joined Davis in 1980, staying with him until 1984. From 1984, worked with John McLaughlin's re-formed Mahavishnu Orchestra, and also led his own groups and recorded albums under his own name. With Davis he did several major tours taking in the USA, Europe and Japan, appearing at all leading festivals and on television in almost every country in which the band played. Davis has said of Evans, 'He's one of the greatest musicians I've ever come upon'; he is certainly one of the most gifted players to have emerged in the 1980s. He also shows signs of developing into an interesting composer. [IC]

With Miles Davis, *The Man with the Horn* (1980); *We Want Miles* (1981) (double); *Star People* (1983), all CBS; as leader, *Living on the Crest of a Wave* (1983), Elektra Musician; *The Alternative Man* (1985), Blue Note

Evans, Gil (Ian Ernest Gilmore Green), composer, piano. b. Toronto, 13 May 1912, of Australian parentage. Family moved to Stockton, California. After hearing some Louis Armstrong records he became interested in jazz at 14; self-taught as a composer/arranger. 1933–8, led his own band in Stockton, and when it was taken over by Skinnay Ennis, stayed on as arranger until 1941. Then worked as arranger with the Claude Thornhill orchestra until 1948, except for three years' army service (1943–6). As well as the usual big-band line-up of brass, reeds and rhythm, the Thornhill orchestra employed French horns and tuba, and Evans soon became noticed by musicians for the variety and originality of the tonal textures of his arrangements.

1947, Evans was the central figure in a series of discussions with some of the leading young players of the day, including Gerry Mulligan, John Lewis and Miles Davis. They wanted to use the smallest number of instruments possible to get a fully orchestral sound, and this resulted in a 9-piece band under Davis's leadership which made a series of classic recordings and launched the 'cool' school of jazz at the beginning of the 1950s. It comprised trumpet, trombone, French horn, tuba, alto sax, baritone sax, piano, bass and drums, and Evans arranged two of the pieces in its repertoire, 'Moondreams' and 'Boplicity'. French critic André Hodeir wrote in 1954: ' "Boplicity" is enough to qualify Gil Evans as one of jazz's greatest composer/arrangers.'

In the USA, however, Evans still worked in obscurity as a freelance arranger. No critics noticed him or wrote about him. He also spent the first half of the 1950s filling in the gaps in his musical education – listening to much recorded music, reading musical history, biographies and criticism. Then, again in collaboration with Miles Davis and using a 19-piece orchestra which included French horns, tuba and woodwind, he recorded three albums which rank with the finest orchestral music of the 20th century: *Miles Ahead* (1957), *Porgy and Bess* (1958), and *Sketches of Spain* (1959–60). All three were like concertos for trumpet (or fluegelhorn); Davis was the only soloist, and his contribution and the orchestral setting were brilliantly integrated. British critic Max Harrison pointed out that Evans could handle the orchestra with 'a freedom and plasticity that have been surpassed only in a very few works such as Stockhausen's "Gruppen für drei Orchester" ', and that Evans's 'endless mixtures of sound . . . are new not only to jazz writing but to all orchestral music'. In the USA, too, critics were lavish with their praise, and Evans, then in his late forties, at last became well enough known to lead his own bands on recording sessions and for concerts.

1961, his orchestra performed with Miles Davis, at the latter's Carnegie Hall concert which was recorded for a live album. He collaborated with Davis on another studio album, *Quiet Nights*, which neither of them felt happy about, and also on the music for a play, *The Time of the Barracudas*, which had a brief run in Los Angeles but never reached New York. Evans recorded some albums of his own, and wrote arrangements for other artists including Kenny Burrell and Astrud Gilberto. 1966, he played festivals and concerts with his orchestra in California; 1968, played a concert in New York and was reunited with Davis for a concert at UCLA. But these were rare performances; during the late 1960s he spent most of his time writing.

1970, he began weekly performances at the Village Vanguard, usually with larger ensembles composed of some of New York's leading contemporary players. These sessions went on throughout the 1970s and into the 1980s, whenever Evans was at home. At this stage in his career his music often featured rock rhythms extensively, with multiple percussion and electric bass and piano; from 1971 he went even more deeply into electronics, using synthesizers and blending them with acoustic instruments. 1971, he toured Europe with his orchestra, appearing in Sweden, Denmark, Holland and West Germany, and playing at the Berlin festival.

1972, his orchestra played concerts in New York and Long Island; he was named a founding artist of the John F. Kennedy Center for the Performing Arts; he visited Japan, taking only Billy Harper and Hannibal Peterson with him, and toured and recorded with Japanese musicians. 1973–5, the New York Jazz Repertory

Gil Evans

Company put on three Evans concerts featuring different themes: 'Jazz In The Rock Age'; 'Gil Evans Retrospective'; 'The Music of Jimi Hendrix'. Just before Hendrix died in 1970, negotiations had been in progress for the Evans orchestra to record with the guitarist. An album of Hendrix tunes was ultimately made in 1974, featuring two arrangements by Evans and six by other members of his orchestra. 1973, Evans conducted TV and radio broadcasts of his arrangements by the Swedish Radio Orchestra. 1976, he toured Europe with his orchestra, recording a live album in Warsaw; 1978, he made his first appearance in the UK, touring for the Arts Council of Great Britain's Contemporary Music Network in February and recording a live double album at the Royal Festival Hall. Five months later he played a series of major European festivals including the North Sea, at The Hague, and Antibes. Spring 1983, he led an orchestra made up of British musicians, playing at the Camden Festival, London, touring the UK and recording a live album. Four months later he brought his US band over to play at the Bracknell festival, UK, and tour in Europe. 1985, he spent several months in London arranging and recording music for the British film of Colin MacInnes's book *Absolute Beginners*.

Almost every aspect of Gil Evans's extraordinary career reverses the normal pattern. He was virtually unknown and unseen until, at the age of 45, he recorded his first full-blooded masterpiece (*Miles Ahead*) with Miles Davis; although a competent pianist, he is not a virtuoso, and he only began playing professionally in 1952, when he was 40; he did not lead bands of his own until he was almost 50; his most intense period of public performance began ten years later and showed no sign of diminishing in his seventies.

He once said, 'Every form, even though it becomes traditional and finally becomes academic, originally came from someone's spirit who created the form. Then it was picked up and taught in schools after that. But all form originated from spirit.' Everything Evans does comes from this 'spirit', which is why his music always sounds so freshly alive. Although primarily a writer, he loves fluidity and improvisation because, like Duke Ellington, he wants music to be in a state of becoming. This is why he was the perfect collaborator for Miles Davis – who is primarily a player who loves composition – and Evans also made a significant contribution to some of Davis's small-group music including the album *Filles de Kilimanjaro*.

His orchestral writing is notable for the highly mobile lines for bass instruments, the subtle inner-voicings of chords, unusual blending of instruments, and a sense of time and dynamics so fine that the music seems to 'breathe' naturally, as if improvised rather than written. All these qualities are evident on what are unquestionably his supreme compositional achievements – the three orchestral albums with Miles Davis, which have had huge and incalculable influence on all kinds of music and musicians.

Since then, Evans's own ensembles have become generally looser as he became more and more interested in improvisation, and this is evident in his own studio album *The Individualism of Gil Evans* (1963–4), which maintains orchestral coherence while allowing considerable freedom for soloists. A similar balance is maintained ten years later on a studio album which brilliantly combines electronic and acoustic instruments, *Svengali* (an anagram of 'Gil Evans' invented by Gerry Mulligan). In the live albums of the 1970s and 1980s the format grows freer, the improvisation longer and the orchestral sections more skeletal, but even then the music is still identifiably that of Gil Evans. His various groups have created some of the most vital performances in jazz since the early 1970s, and his improvising, adventurous spirit has delighted audiences and inspired musicians all over the globe. [IC]

With Miles Davis, *Miles Ahead* (1957); *Porgy and Bess* (1958); *Sketches of Spain* (1960), all CBS; as leader, *Pacific Standard Time* (1958–9), Blue Note (double); *Out of the Cool* (1960), Impulse; *The Individualism of Gil Evans* (1963–4), Verve (double); *Masabumi Kikuchi and Gil Evans* (1972), Japanese Philips; *Svengali* (1973), Atlantic; Gil Evans orchestra with Steve Lacy, *Parabola* (1978), Horo; *Live at New York Public Theater* (1980), Japanese Trio (double)

Evans, Herschel, tenor sax, alto sax, clarinet. b. Denton, Texas, 1909; d. New York, 9 February 1939. Early on he played with territory bands in Texas, sometimes on tenor, sometimes on an alto that, according to Buddy Tate, had 'about a hundred rubber bands around it. But Herschel was always sharp as a tack!' By the mid-1930s he was working with name bands such as Bennie Moten, Dave Peyton, Charlie Echols, Buck Clayton and Lionel Hampton. 1936, he joined Count Basie to form a well-remembered team with Lester Young which, for its supposed rivalries, still makes a musicians' talking point. Musically and personally they were very different. Evans, direct, blustery, a man's man, inclined to call a spade a shovel, would tear up a band part if he couldn't read it: Young, a superior reader, looked at the world through humorous half-closed eyes, seldom pushed his views and acted out his philosophy, 'to each his own'. Their music, which echoed their personal contrasts to the note, instituted Basie's lifelong tradition of battling tenor saxophones which was to pass into general jazz lore: but, says Jo Jones, 'There was no real friction: Lester and Herschel were brothers in rivalry!' Evans's fulsome hit record 'Blue and Sentimental' reflects his heart-on-sleeve tenor to perfection ('a kind of first-tenor sound,' said Dickie Wells); but he was not with Basie long. Late in 1938 he became ill with dropsy and, said Dickie Wells, 'swelled up so he couldn't get his hat on! It could have been cured if he'd gone to the doctor earlier.' Buddy Tate, his replacement, dreamed that Evans had died and that a telegram came from Basie offering him the tenor chair. It arrived in 1939. [DF]

Count Basie, *Swingin' the Blues* (1937–9), Affinity

Evans, 'Stomp', 'Stump' or **'Stumpy' (Paul Anderson)**, saxes. b. Lawrence, Kansas, 18 October 1904; d. Douglas, Kansas, 29 August 1928. Stump Evans, so called because of his tiny build, played first in Kansas City's Lawrence High School band, then moved to Chicago. A potentially brilliant soloist and a good reader, he was soon a featured player with Erskine Tate's Vendome Orchestra (featuring Louis Armstrong and show trumpeter Reuben Reeves), King Oliver, Jimmy Wade, and Carroll Dickerson's orchestra at Sunset Café, featuring Louis Armstrong again, and Earl Hines. 'Stumpy Evans played beautiful tenor,' remembered Hines. 'Everyone was trying to get him then.' Evans recorded too, with Oliver, Dickerson, Jelly Roll Morton, Jimmy Blythe, and for a time was MD at the Moulin Rouge Club. But he contracted TB while working with Tate and moved back to Kansas where he died at only 24. His highest accolade may have come from Coleman Hawkins who acknowledged Evans as an influence. [DF]

The Complete Jelly Roll Morton, vols. 1/2, 3/4 (1926–7), RCA (2 doubles)

Evans, Sue, drums, percussion. b. New York City, 7 July 1951. Father a music teacher. Piano lessons as a child and began on drums at 11. Studied with Warren Smith at the Third Street Drum School, also with Morris Lang and others. 1969–73, played drums in Judy Collins's backing group in US and Europe. 1972–4, percussion with the Steve Kuhn quartet. She also worked with the Jazz Composers' Orchestra, and recorded with James Brown, Roswell Rudd, Billy Cobham, Blood Sweat and Tears and others. From the late 1960s until 1978, she played percussion and sometimes drums with Gil Evans. Favourites are Elvin Jones, Tony Williams, Max Roach, Airto Moreira, Billy Higgins, Gil Evans and Ornette Coleman. She once said, 'I use percussion for melody and colours. I'm not a timekeeper, per se', but she played drums with the Evans orchestra in Warsaw (1976) and during their European tour in the summer of 1978, and kept time very happily. [IC]

With Steve Kuhn, Bobby Jones and others; with Gil Evans, *Svengali* (1973), Atlantic; *The Gil Evans Orchestra plays the music of Jimi Hendrix* (1974), RCA; *There Comes a Time* (1975), RCA

Ewell, Don (Donald Tyson), piano. b. Baltimore, Maryland, 14 November 1916; d. Deerfield, Florida, 9 August 1983. Tempting as it is to bracket Ewell with Ralph Sutton as the two premier latter-day piano jazz revivalists, Ewell was active around Baltimore by the mid-1930s – ten years or so before Sutton's career got under way – and his inspirations were different. Sutton reworks the disciplines of Waller and Beiderbecke; Ewell delighted in the New Orleans-based music of Jelly Roll Morton and his peers. He also chose very often to work in ethnic surroundings, began his post-war career alongside Bunk Johnson and George Lewis and worked regularly thereafter with New Orleans-based musicians such as Bechet and Kid Ory, as well as such hard-blowing leaders as Doc Evans, George Brunis and Muggsy Spanier. Ewell's piano style – surprisingly delicate and academically perfect – was showcased in Jack Teagarden's marvellous band from 1956 and, despite occasional ideological brushes with trumpeter Don Goldie, he stayed with Teagarden until 1962. There are fine LPs from the 1950s (*Music to Listen to Don Ewell By* and a fine session with Jimmy Yancey's widow Mama Yancey) which illustrate his barrelhouse arts to perfection. After Teagarden's death, Ewell moved back to New Orleans and played there in hotels and for bands, also making regular European tours: one of his last was undertaken to pay for costly cancer treatments for his daughter. She died, and Ewell, sadly disillusioned, carried on working in a daze. Soon after, he suffered several strokes and died too. [DF]

Music to Listen to Don Ewell By (1956), Good Time Jazz; *Quintet* (1971), Jazzology

F

Faber, Johannes Jakob, trumpet, fluegelhorn, piano, violin, composer. b. Munich, West Germany, 7 November 1952. Father a composer. Began on trumpet at age ten; studied at Richard Strauss Conservatory, Munich, at the University for the Performing Arts and Music in Graz, Austria, and at the Berklee College of Music, Boston. First fully professional job at 18, playing in the orchestra for various musicals; also working with Wolfgang Dauner, Sal Nistico, Dusko Goykovich, Mal Waldron, among others; from 1980, member of the Stuttgart Radio Orchestra; 1985, formed his own group, Johannes Faber's Consortium, featuring Billy Cobham on drums. Faber toured with the United Jazz and Rock Ensemble, 1983 and 1984. Received the Baden-Württemburg Jazz Prize, 1985. His favourites range from Louis Armstrong and Maurice André to Miles Davis, Don Cherry, Clifford Brown and Freddie Hubbard. Other inspirations are John Coltrane, Charlie Parker and Joe Pass. [IC]

With Sinto, *Sonho Negro* (1978), Anayana; with Gunter Lenz's Springtime, *Znel* (1979), Mood; *Roaring Plenties* (1980), L & R; with UJRE, *Opus Sechs* (1984), Mood; as leader, *Consortium* (1985), Mood

Faddis, Jon(athan), trumpet, fluegelhorn. b. Oakland, California, 24 July 1953. Studied trumpet from age eight, played with r & b groups and rehearsal big bands from 13. Toured with Lionel Hampton (1971–2), then settled in New York. Worked with Gil Evans (1972), Charles Mingus (including European tour, 1972) and Thad Jones–Mel Lewis, for whom he played lead trumpet (1972–5). 1974, began guesting with Dizzy Gillespie, recording with him and Oscar Peterson. Already involved in studio work, specialized in this field until early 1980s, before emerging on jazz scene again. Appeared at Chicago festival, 1985, and toured Europe with Jimmy Smith quintet (autumn 1985). Initially influenced markedly by Gillespie, even before he played with him, Faddis possesses all the ensemble qualities of big-band players as well as a dazzling upper-register technique. His resurgent jazz work exhibits his brilliant combination of exuberance and discipline, and is now individual stylistically. [BP]

Legacy (1985), Concord

Fairweather, Al (Alastair), trumpet, arranger, composer, leader. b. Edinburgh, 12 June 1927. He is most famous for his long partnership with Scots clarinettist Sandy Brown, which began in Edinburgh then moved to London to produce the most creative mainstream jazz in Britain in the years 1956–64. Fairweather – a forthright, powerful trumpeter who played in the Armstrong mode – took over leadership of the band as Brown's preoccupation with acoustic architecture grew: he also produced many of the neat arrangements which encapsulated Brown's often startling ideas: LPs such as *Doctor McJazz* (1960) featuring 17 classy miniatures, show the partnership at its working peak. After he left Brown, Fairweather worked for Acker Bilk in the mid-1960s, then reverted to full-time teaching, playing in his spare time. In the 1970s he was featured soloist and a highly effective arranger for Stan Greig's London Jazz Big Band, took part in Sandy Brown reunions, freelanced around London's clubs and pubs and, following a severe heart attack in 1983, was back to full playing strength in 1985. He is not related to Digby Fairweather (below). [DF]

Digby Fairweather, *Songs for Sandy*, (1982), Hep

Fairweather, Digby, cornet. b. Rochford, Essex, 25 April 1946. He worked for seven years in all kinds of Essex-based bands from New Orleans-style to avant-garde jazz, with his own band, Dig's Half Dozen (1971), and latterly with Eggy Ley, Hugh Rainey, Eric Silk, Gene Allen, Ron Russell, Lennie Hastings, Dave Shepherd and Alex Welsh, with whom he formed a fondly-remembered friendship (he recorded his first album as deputy trumpeter with Welsh's band in 1975 for Rediffusion). After turning professional on 1 January 1977, he was a founder member of Keith Nichols's Midnite Follies Orchestra, joined the co-operative quartet Velvet, with Len Skeat, Denny Wright and Ike Isaacs, and recorded solo albums: in 1979 he was awarded the BBC Jazz Society's Musician of the Year trophy and for two years after was placed in polls in *Jazz Journal International*. From that year he became involved in jazz education (as co-director, with pianist Stan Barker, of a non-profit-making educational trust, Jazz College) and at the same period joined the Pizza All Stars for three years. After leaving he led his own quartet, re-formed the Kettners Five with veteran bassist Tiny Winters, toured and appeared on TV with a Nat Gonella tribute (starring Nat), taught more busily, and worked for Brian Priestley's septet (featuring Don Rendell). By 1985 – as well as trumpeting – he was the author of a successful new trumpet tutor, *How to Play Trumpet* (Elm Tree Books), broadcast busily (including deps for Humphrey Lyttelton on BBC Radio 2's Best of Jazz and a lengthy World Service series) and had produced three new albums, one of which (*Let's Duet* with Stan Barker) was voted into a shortlist of 'Editor's Records of the Year' for the American *Cadence* magazine. He has contributed short pieces to a variety of recent books. [JLS]

Fallon, Jack, bass. b. London, Ontario, 13 October 1917. He arrived in Britain with the Canadian air force in 1944 and soon after joined Ted Heath's orchestra for two years. His highly modern-for-its-period bass playing attracted huge attention and after leaving Heath in 1946 he worked all over with the cream of British jazz talent, toured and played concerts with visiting talent such as Duke Ellington, Django Reinhardt, Lena Horne, Sarah Vaughan, Maxine Sullivan and Mary Lou Williams, and as staff bassist for the Lansdowne label in the 1950s recorded with Josh White, Jack Elliott and Britishers Kenny Baker, Bruce Turner, Humphrey Lyttelton *et al*. From 1952, Fallon ran his highly successful Cana Agency, which later represented stars like Kenny Ball (as well as the Beatles and the Rolling Stones for occasional work in their early days) and also pursued a busy third career, as a country and western violinist working with Johnny Duncan and others on concerts, radio and TV series. Freelance jazz work, including Bix Curtis's Jazz at the Prom, Jack Parnell's Big Band, and light orchestral work with Frank Chacksfield, Ron Goodwin and others kept Fallon busy and, despite concentrating on his agency in the 1960s, he was often persuaded out of retirement by Lennie Felix (as well as the Beatles with whom he recorded in 1968) and later in the 1980s by pianist Stan Greig, Digby Fairweather and others. [DF]

Farley and Riley: Eddie (Edward J.) Farley, trumpet, vocals, composer. b. Newark, New Jersey, 16 July 1904; and Mike (Michael) Riley, trombone, trumpet, vocals. b. Fall River, Massachusetts, 5 January 1904; d. Torrance, California, 2 September 1984. When the Onyx Club on 52nd Street reopened after a fire in 1935 the resident group assembled by Red McKenzie contained Eddie Condon (gtr), Eddie Farley (tpt/vocals) and Mike Riley (tmb). While rehearsing for the reopening, singer Ruth Lee introduced the band to a novelty song, 'The music goes round and round', written (it later transpired) by Chicago trumpeter Red Hodgson. After trying out the tune and adding their own chords (from 'Dinah') the group appropriated the song for themselves. Condon, appalled by Riley and Farley's cutup antics on stage, left the band soon after ('they poured water over each other, scuffled, mugged and did everything but play music', he said in horror), but the duo recorded their novelty. It became the biggest commercial hit in 1930s jazz history, sold over 100,000 copies, and focused society's attention on 'The Street': during 1935–6 'House Full' signs were constantly up at the Onyx, clubs opened in droves, and the upper set turned right for 52nd Street instead of left into Harlem. Paramount made a film of the song in 1936 and two years later the Casa Lomans were still featuring it, sung by Pee Wee Hunt, with special material by Sammy Cahn. (By that time correct authorship of the song had been amicably reestablished.) Both Riley and Farley formed bands of their own: Mike Farley was active in Chicago until the 1950s. [DF]

Farlow, Tal(mage Holt), guitar. b. Greensboro, North Carolina, 7 June 1921. Only took up guitar at age 21, worked with pianist/singer Dardanelle Breckenbridge (1947), then with Margie Hyams trio (1948) and Buddy DeFranco sextet (1949). With innovative Red Norvo trio (1950–3) and Norvo's quintet (1954–5), in between with Artie Shaw's last Gramercy Five; during latter period, made first records under own name. Then formed trio including pianist Eddie Costa, which worked in 1956 and 1958 with a break for Farlow's retirement; this became virtually complete for a decade, as he became a freelance signpainter (possibly the only jazzman with this alternative career since Duke Ellington). Occasional local gigs and recording (1967) led to Newport festival appearances and touring with George Wein group (1969). Still performing only part-time and teaching, has recorded more regularly since 1976 and undertaken European tours, both with Norvo (1982) and alone (1985, 1986).

An extremely fluent improviser who grasped the essential rhythmic variety of bebop, Tal fell into the trap (especially with his own 1950s group) of using too many notes with a minimum of inflection, for all the world like those transitional mid-1940s guitarists who recorded with Dizzy Gillespie and/or Charlie Parker. Nowadays, while retaining all his facility, Farlow allows far more lyricism into his playing, and the result is correspondingly more captivating. [BP]

The Swinging Guitar of Tal Farlow (1956), Verve; *A Sign of the Times* (1976), Concord

Film: *Talmage Farlow* (dir. Lorenzo DeStefano, 1981)

Farmer, Addison Gerald, bass. b. Council Bluffs, Iowa, 21 August 1928; d. suddenly New York City, 20 February 1963. Twin brother of Art Farmer (below). 1950s, freelanced in New York, playing with Charlie Parker, Miles Davis, Benny Carter, Howard McGhee and many others. 1959–60, with the Art Farmer–Benny Golson Jazztet. 1960–2, worked with Mose Allison and others. Farmer played bass on one of the finest albums of the 1950s under his brother's leadership – *Modern Art* (1958, United Artists), with Benny Golson, Bill Evans and Dave Bailey (dms). [IC]

With Allison, Gene Ammons, Teo Macero, Mal Waldron, Stan Getz; Art Farmer quartet, *Portrait of Art Farmer* (1958), Contemporary

Farmer, Art(hur Stewart), fluegelhorn, trumpet. b. Council Bluffs, Iowa, 21 August 1928. Brought up in Phoenix, Arizona, moved to Los Angeles (1945) with twin brother Addison (above). Art's late-1940s playing experience included the bands of Johnny Otis, Jay McShann, Roy Porter, Gerald Wilson and Benny Carter. 1951–2, gigging and recording with Wardell Gray. 1952–3, toured with Lionel Hampton, cutting discs with Clifford Brown and under own name with other Hampton sidemen including Gigi Gryce. Settled in New York; worked in succession with Gryce (1954–6), Horace Silver (1956–8) and Gerry Mulligan (1958–9); appeared on albums with writers as different as George Russell and Quincy Jones. Became co-leader of the Jazztet with Benny Golson (1959–62), then quartet with Jim Hall (later Steve Kuhn) (1962–5). First solo tours of Europe (1965, 1966) plus work in US with quintet including Jimmy Heath. Member of Austrian Radio Orchestra from 1968, also appearing solo and with Kenny Clarke–Francy Boland and Peter Herbolzheimer bands, and making brief returns to US. 1980s, spent more time in US, reuniting with Benny Golson and appearing under own name, usually with quartet.

The gentle surface of Farmer's playing has been mistaken for blandness by some, and his 1953 recording with Clifford Brown (*Memorial Album*, Prestige/OJC) finds him seemingly at a disadvantage. But even at this stage he was markedly individual and, though inspired by the 'modal' implications of early Miles Davis, he also foreshadowed the wistfulness of later Kenny Dorham, with phrasing behind the beat and achingly wide melodic leaps. As his work matured in the late 1950s, there was an apparent lack of attack in his articulation which, perversely, enhanced the unusual shapes of Farmer's lines. The final touch was added when in the early 1960s he began to solo on fluegel exclusively (trumpet was still used for big-band section-work) so that what had sounded merely forlorn was given a further profundity. Since then, Farmer has managed to broaden his emotional range with growing strength and even glimpses of something approaching gaiety, without jettisoning his unique style. [BP]

Portrait of Art Farmer (1958), Contemporary; *Sing Me Softly of the Blues* (1965), Atlantic; *Moose the Mooche* (1982), Concord

Art Farmer

Farrell, Joe (Joseph Carl Firrantello), tenor and soprano sax, flute. b. Chicago Heights, Illinois, 16 December 1937; d. 10 January 1986 of bone cancer. Played with Ira Sullivan and others in Chicago before moving to New York (1960); joined Maynard Ferguson band (1960–1). Then with Slide Hampton octet (1962), Charles Mingus sextet (1964), George Russell sextet (1964), Jaki Byard quartet (1965). A founder member of Thad Jones–Mel Lewis band (1966–7), he also toured with Elvin Jones trio (1967–71). Work with Chick Corea (on whose first album he played in 1966) including the first Return to Forever (1972–3) and enlarged edition (1977–8). Making own albums regularly from 1970, moved to California (late 1970s) and became heavily involved in studio work. After a period of reassessment, reverted to more frequent jazz playing and co-led European tours with Louis Hayes (1983) and Woody Shaw (1985). Farrell was a driving force on his main instrument, the tenor, and his improvisations reflected an intelligent appreciation of both Coltrane and Rollins. [BP]

Farrell/Hayes, *Vim 'n Vigor* (1983), Timeless

Fatool, Nick (Nicholas), drums. b. Milbury, Massachusetts, 2 January 1915. He learnt his craft with big bands led by Benny Goodman (1939–40), Artie Shaw (1940–1), Les Brown, Alvino Rey, Eddie Miller *et al.*, and later worked in studios (as a staffman on Bing Crosby shows for one example) and for Dick Cathcart in the *Pete Kelly's Blues* radio/TV/film hit of the 1950s. From the 1960s he was a regular associate of Bob Crosby as well as working with Pete Fountain and other kindred Dixieland spirits, and in 1985 toured Europe with a re-formed Crosby-ish band led by Yank Lawson and Bob Haggart. Fatool has time, taste, controlled use of percussion colours which (in concept if not volume) recalls Baby Dodds, and above all the ability to propel a band unrelentingly at the kind of level over which an acoustic guitar can still be comfortably heard. [DF]

Favors, Malachi, bass; also banjo, zither, bells, gongs, log drum, whistles, bicycle horns, voice. b. Chicago, 22 August 1937. Began playing after high school. 1958–60, worked with pianist Andrew Hill; met Roscoe Mitchell and Muhal Richard Abrams in 1961 and worked with Abrams's big Experimental Band which evolved into the AACM (see ABRAMS, MUHAL RICHARD). He joined the Roscoe Mitchell Art Ensemble, which evolved into the *Art Ensemble of Chicago, one of the most important groups of the 1970s and 1980s. [IC]

With AEC, Mitchell, Joseph Jarman and Lester Bowie

Favre, Pierre, drums. b. Le Locle, Switzerland, 2 June 1937. Began on drums at 15, turning professional at 17. Worked with various European bands and at 19 was percussionist in the Basle Radio orchestra. 1960, freelanced in Paris; 1961, in Rome with the American Jazz Ensemble; 1962, joined the Max Greger band. Also played and recorded with George Gruntz, Chet Baker, Bud Powell, Lou Bennett and many others. 1966–70, worked with Irene Schweizer; Peter Kowald; Evan Parker; played at international festivals; did lecture tours in Europe, USA and Japan; headed the Paiste Drummer Service. 1970–5, performed with Michel Portal, John Tchicai; member of the Zurich Radio Orchestra; composed music for theatrical productions; played solo concerts; worked with Interchange (Joachim Kuhn, Peter Warren); collaborated with contemporary composers U. Lehmann, R. Boesch, U. Schneider. 1976, worked with dancers, and performed more frequently with Albert Mangelsdorff. Since then he has also worked in duo with various partners including L. Francioli, J. Hager, Stu Martin, T. V. Gopalkrishna, E. Henz, R. Zosso, and played solo concerts in North and South America, Asia and Europe. He also conducts rhythm workshops and has worked with the groups Drum Orchestra, Music By and Madrugada. [IC]

With Portal, John Surman, Benny Bailey, Mal Waldron and others; trio, *Santana* (1968), FMP; solo *Drum Conversation* (1970), Calig; with Manfred Schoof, *European Echoes* (1969), FMP; with Terumaso Hino, *Vibrations* (1971), Enja

Fawkes, Wally (Walter), clarinet, soprano sax. b. Vancouver, 21 June 1924. He was first heard in the George Webb band (with Ed Harvey, Humphrey Lyttelton and Owen Bryce) and subsequently joined Humphrey Lyttelton, with whom his throbbing broad-toned clarinet found a perfect showcase: records with Lyttelton – from 1947 to 1955 – are British jazz classics. That year Fawkes decided to give up full-time music to pursue his other love, cartoon drawing; for nearly forty years he has drawn 'Flook' for the *Daily Mail* and wins numerous awards for his gentle creations (like Lyttelton, Fawkes usually wields a kindly pen). But he still found time for the clarinet: in the late 1950s Wally Fawkes' Troglodytes (featuring Spike MacIntosh, tpt) and collaborations with Bruce Turner produced British jazz of special quality, and fortunately records too. In the 1960s Fawkes played regularly at New Merlins Cave, a Clerkenwell jazz centre, and for Humphrey Lyttelton reunions, and in the early 1970s was a founder member of John Chilton's Feetwarmers, often in tandem with an old professional partner, George Melly. By the 1980s he was still regularly to be heard playing magnificently in old pubs around London, sometimes with Graham Tayar's Crouch End All Stars: in 1984 more reunions with Lyttelton produced a great album, *It Seems Like Yesterday*, and another with clarinettist-journalist Ian Christie, *That's the Blues Old Man*. Fawkes's fondness for people over professionalism and natural gravitation to small clubs can never quite hide his formidable talent; in 1985 he was duetting at New Merlins Cave with Kenny Davern on equal terms. [DF]

Humphrey Lyttelton, *A Tribute to Humph, vol. 1* (1949–50), Dormouse

Fazola, Irving (Irving Henry Prestopnik), clarinet, saxes. b. New Orleans, 10 December 1912; d. 20 March 1949. The *nom de plume* was a Louis Prima massacre of 'fah-so-lah', a reference to Prestopnik's classical training. He began in New Orleans in the 1920s (playing with Prima, Armand Hug, Julian Lane and Sharkey Bonano, among others), went to Ben Pollack's training band in 1935, to Glenn Miller (a frequent sparring partner) in 1937 and, after several returns to New Orleans, to Bob Crosby's band in 1938, where he stayed all of two years until a spectacular fight with Ray Conniff. 1941, he spent a year with another New Orleans man, Claude Thornhill, then returned to his Dixieland roots with (among others) Muggsy Spanier and George Brunis. He went back to New Orleans in 1943 and for the last five years of his life played all the best jobs in the city. With a sound like honey and a virtuoso's technique, Irving Fazola was arguably the finest clarinettist to emerge in the swing era; but he was unmarketable and unapproachable – 'We used to call him Gloomy Gus,' says Charlie Cordilla. Fat, taciturn, quick-tempered, violent when it suited him, he had few ambitions beyond food, drink, girls and Dixieland jazz, and in all of them (in John Chilton's marvellous phrase) 'he thought in double portions'. High blood pressure and cirrhosis of the liver ended his music at the age of 36. [DF]

Bob Crosby, *South Rampart Street Parade* (1938–9), MCA

See Chilton, John, *Stomp Off, Let's Go!* (Jazz Book Services, 1983)

Feld, Morey, drums. b. Cleveland, Ohio, 15 August 1915; d. Colorado, 28 March 1971. He belongs with such as Cliff Leeman, Nick Fatool and Buzzy Drootin in the echelons of great Dixieland drummers. From a grounding in 1936 with Ben Pollack – the university of so many later great names – he worked on and up with Joe Haymes, the Summa Cum Laude band in 1940, then Benny Goodman (1943–5), Eddie Condon (1946 and after), Billy Butterfield, Peanuts Hucko, Bobby Hackett and as a staffman for ABC, 1955–60. In the 1960s he returned to Goodman, to Condon's, led his own bands and opened a drum school before moving to Denver, Colorado, in 1968 where he joined Peanuts Hucko's quintet and was founder drummer with the World's Greatest Jazz Band. He died in a fire at his home. [DF]

Feldman, Vic(tor Stanley), piano, vibraharp, drums, percussion. b. London, 7 April 1934. One of quite a long list of British keyboard players who made their home in the USA, Feldman emigrated in order to join Woody Herman in 1955. Previously the child prodigy of a highly musical family (playing professionally from the age of seven), he had been a significant contributor to the UK scene, working with Ted Heath and Ronnie Scott (1954–5). Feldman settled in Los Angeles in 1957 and, with few breaks such as six months with Cannonball Adderley (1960–1), has specialized in session work as a miscellaneous percussionist. His tune 'Seven Steps to Heaven' (recorded by Miles Davis) has become a standard. [BP]

Your Smile (1973), Choice

Felix, Lennie, piano, b. London, 1920; d. 1981. He made his début playing in nightclubs pre-war and after 1945 quickly established a reputation as a weathered piano-entertainer. A devotee of Fats Waller among others – he looked like Waller and in later years visibly cultivated his mannerisms if not his girth – Felix liked working in trios and his albums of the 1950s (for example *That Cat Felix!* and *Cat on a Hot Tin Piano*, also featuring Tony Coe) showed that his influences included not only Waller but great soloists such as Art Tatum, Earl Hines and Teddy Wilson. He was less commonly to be found in bands: one likeable exception on record and briefly in person was Nat Gonella's 1960 Armstrong-style group, in which Felix played the Hines role with great gusto, using his fine technique to its best. In the 1960s and 1970s he continued to work solo, playing London nightclubs (the Las Vegas for one) and jazz clubs as well as travelling abroad for long periods to work in Denmark, Germany and elsewhere: he also toured England with Ruby Braff – one occasion on which Felix's accompanying style was swiftly at odds with his guest. Just before Christmas 1980 Felix was leaving the 606 Club in Fulham, London, when he was knocked down by a speeding car. He died in hospital three months later. [DF]

That Cat Felix! (1958), Nixa

Ferguson, Maynard, trumpet, big-band leader, baritone horn, valve trombone. b. Montreal, 4 May 1928. Studied at French Conservatory of Music, Montreal. He came to international notice with the Stan Kenton band which featured him prominently 1950–3. Ferguson had brilliant technical abilities and specialized in screaming high notes which he seemed to be able to produce and sustain at will: his prowess in the upper register was, in fact, unequalled, at that time. 1953–6, he freelanced in Los Angeles; 1957, began leading big bands and continued until 1965, when economics forced him to work with a sextet. In the later 1960s, he moved to the UK, working with an Anglo-American big band which toured the USA in 1971, and also played in Western and Eastern Europe. He moved back to the USA in the early 1970s, again leading big bands and featuring a programme of current jazz-rock and pop hits as well as some updated material from his past. Ferguson's music often has more to do with athletics than aesthetics, and his bands play brash, brassy, high-energy music. He has been intermittently active in education, conducting instrumental clinics and group workshops. In sympathetic company, he is capable of fine and sensitive solo work. [IC]

With Kenton and others; *Dimensions* (1954), Trip; *Around the Horn* (1955–6), Trip; *M. F. Horn* (1971), Columbia; *Chameleon* (1974), Columbia

Feza, Mongezi, trumpet, flute. b. Queenstown, South Africa, 1945; d. London, 14 December 1975. Got his first trumpet at age eight. At 16, was already playing with groups. 1962, joined Chris McGregor's Blue Notes (see PUKWANA, D., and MOHOLO, L.). 1963, the Blue Notes won the Best Group Award at SA's National Jazz Festival; 1965, they left for Europe and played in France and Switzerland before settling in Britain. Feza continued working with McGregor's sextet, and his larger group the Brotherhood of Breath, also with Pukwana's groups Spear and Assagai and Keith Tippett's Centipede. 1972, he worked in Denmark with bassist Johnny Dyani and Turkish percussionist Okay Temiz. With McGregor and others he toured and played festivals throughout the UK and Europe. Mongezi was a dynamic soloist, and his style fused elements from kwela, bebop and free (abstract) jazz, into a highly individual synthesis. His premature death deprived the European scene of one of its most adventurous and benign musicians. [IC]

With Pukwana, Robert Wyatt and Bahula; with Blue Notes, *Very Urgent* (1968), Polydor; with Brotherhood of Breath, *Brotherhood of Breath* (1971), RCA Neon; *Brotherhood* (1972), RCA

Ella Fitzgerald

Victor; *Live at Willisau* (1974), Ogun; Feza/Dyani/Temiz, *Music for Xaba* (1972), Sonet

Film is an invaluable source of reference for watching performers not easily (or no longer) accessible in the flesh. Its apparent superiority as compared to records, however, has to be balanced against the terrible scarcity of jazz on film. The entire history of jazz exists on disc, apart from one or two holes, and even when the records are not available in the market-place they are preserved in archives and frequently reappear for the benefit of new generations of listeners. But even if the whole repertoire of jazz on film finds its way eventually on to videos for the private consumer, it will be a mere drop in the ocean.

Whether the performers are on good or bad form, therefore, becomes a secondary consideration to the question of whether they are on film at all. Pending any further discoveries, Charlie Parker playing on screen consists of just one number; for Art Tatum, 12 bars; while Bix Beiderbecke exists on film only in a silent home movie. Another small disadvantage is that, for most Hollywood feature films, musicians' work had to be recorded first and then mimed for the cameras, sometimes even by different players. The most reliable and exhaustive documentation of this medium is to be found in the book below, which lists everything of the slightest relevance, whether available or not. [BP]

See Meeker, David, *Jazz in the Movies*, 3rd edn.

Fischer, Clare, piano, organ, arranger. b. Durand, Michigan, 22 October 1928. Studied music at Michigan State University. Moved to Los Angeles (1957), wrote arrangements and was accompanist for Hi-Los vocal group (late 1950s). Also arranger/conductor for albums by Donald Byrd (1957, first released 1980) and Dizzy Gillespie (1960). Led own occasional big band (1960s) but, as well as freelance arranging, chiefly known as keyboard player specializing in trio and solo work. Fischer has taken a particularly close interest in Brazilian music, living there and studying Portuguese, and one of his bossa-nova originals, 'Pensativa', has become something of a standard. His playing is a thoughtful but unstilted extension of methods associated with Lennie Tristano and Bill Evans. [BP]

The State of his Art (1973), Revelation

Fitzgerald, Ella, vocals. b. Newport News, Virginia, 25 April 1918. In 1934 she won $25 singing 'Judy' on an amateur night at Harlem's Apollo Theater, as the result of a dare, and her ingenuous charm, crystal-clear diction and translucent voice (which she had noticed first and liked in Connee Boswell, her primary influence) also won her a job with Tiny Bradshaw's band, after an audition at Harlem's Opera House. Soon after, Benny Carter and comedian Bardu Ali, who fronted Chick Webb's band, brought her to the attention of Webb, who let her sing on a one-nighter at Yale University, then for a week at the Savoy Ballroom and finally hired her permanently to sing with his orchestra (he also became her guardian after her mother died). During a hospital stay for Webb in 1938, Ella dressed up a nursery-rhyme routine, 'A-tisket, a-tasket', with arranger Van Alexander, and after it became Webb's biggest hit he was happy to build his show around her: when he died in 1939 she took over his band for two years before going solo.

For the next 45 years she was to establish a queenly reputation as America's finest female interpreter of popular song. From 1948, as a part of Norman Granz's organization, she became almost as well known for her improvisatory powers (on high-speed scat extravaganzas such as 'Lady Be Good' and 'Flying Home') as for her *lieder*-esque interpretations of great songs which were always guaranteed to win the approval of their composers. Fitzgerald continued to tour with Granz through the 1950s, record for a variety of labels and team regularly with Louis Armstrong and others for great duets, but her greatest triumphs were reserved for Granz: from the late 1950s he financed the famous and seminal 'songbook' albums dedicated to the works of George Gershwin, Harold Arlen, Johnny Mercer, Jerome Kern, Cole Porter, Irving Berlin and Duke Ellington. The records stand as perfect monuments to their composers and, as Benny Green said later, her 'perfect intonation, natural ear for harmony, vast vocal range and purity of tone helped to make Ella's versions of these beautifully witty, gay, sad, lovingly-wrought songs the definitive versions'. (Several tracks from the 'Songbooks' including 'Manhattan' and 'Ev'ry time we say goodbye', became long-term 'turntable hits'.) In the 1960s Ella continued to tour festivals, jazz rooms and concert halls internationally, her voice broadening with the years, her act extending into a finely-honed cabaret formula featuring long-term accompanists such as Tommy Flanagan, Keeter Betts and for a while Joe Pass. Into the 1980s it was possible to hear a new rough edge to her voice which, though it indicated the sad and inevitable passage of time, seemed to lend a new profundity to much of what she did: took away the very occasional feeling, with earlier Fitzgerald insouciances, that all was just a little too right with the world. In autumn 1986 she was admitted to intensive care for heart trouble. [DF]

Any of the classic 'Songbook' collections

Flanagan, Tommy Lee, piano. b. Detroit, Michigan, 16 March 1930. Work as a teenager in Detroit quickly established his reputation as a sensitive and stimulating accompanist. This led to recordings and live appearances with J. J. Johnson, Miles Davis (*Collectors' Items*), Sonny Rollins (*Saxophone Colossus*) and Coleman Hawkins. For a long time Flanagan's skill in backing soloists involved total immersion in servicing singers, notably Tony Bennett and Ella Fitzgerald (1963–5 and 1968–75). From the mid-1970s, however, life as an independent trio leader and soloist has produced many fine albums, in which Flanagan's surprisingly delicate touch combines with rhythmic resilience to create a uniquely refined approach to bebop piano. [BP]

Eclypso (1977), Enja

Folk Once upon a time all music was folk music, in the sense of being made by the community for the community without a thought for monetary or artistic considerations. This is how jazz started; and it started to stop being solely that as soon as it was born, or at least as soon as it was employed in bordellos to put customers in the mood.

The folk revival, which began in the US in the 1930s, not only had a significant impact on the subsequent appreciation of blues but played a small part in encouraging the 1940s New Orleans jazz revival (although, in both cases, the emphasis was on the meaningful sociology of these art-forms rather than on the unique Afro-American music itself). Since that period, contact has been fairly minimal although one or two musicians originally from the folk field have shown some affinity for jazz, such as mandolinist David Grisman and the singer (and former violinist) Maria Muldaur.

Beginning in the 1960s, however, jazz musicians have taken a new interest in folk music, either of European countries or more exotic cultures usually classified as 'world music'. [BP]

Ford, Ricky (Richard Allen), tenor sax. b. Boston, Massachusetts, 4 March 1954. Studied locally at New England Conservatory, making record début with Gunther Schuller (1974) and subsequently recording for tutors Jaki Byard and Ran Blake. First touring job with Mercer Ellington (1974–6). Member of Charles Mingus quintet until leader's illness (1976–7), then Dannie Richmond quintet (1978–81). Also played with and wrote arrangements for Lionel Hampton big band (from 1981) and with Mingus Dynasty (from 1982, including two European tours). Several albums and live gigs with own groups, European appearances under own name (1982, 1985) and Abdullah Ibrahim's group Ekaya (1986). Ford's playing, already highly competent by the time of his Ellington stint, was considerably stretched while with Mingus. Now he has an all-embracing style which mixes modal jazz and bebop but also enabled him to stand alongside Illinois Jacquet and Arnett Cobb in the 1981 Hampton band. Described by Ran Blake as 'a marvellous player', Ford's increasing maturity gives the impression that the best is yet to come. [BP]

Interpretations (1982), Muse

Foresythe, Reginald, composer, arranger, piano. b. London, 28 May 1907; d. 28 December 1958. Son of a British father and West Indian mother, Foresythe, who carried a cane and an Eton accent with equal aplomb, played piano in American nightclubs in the 1920s until he met Earl Hines in Chicago, 1930. Hines took Foresythe under his wing and into his home, wrote 'Deep Forest' with him and introduced him to Paul Whiteman, who signed him to play extended classical pieces ('Rhapsody in Blue' included) as well as his own quirky, aristocratically titled creations – 'Dodging a Divorcee', 'Serenade to a Wealthy Widow' etc. – on stage with the orchestra. Charlie Carpenter (Hines's manager) remembers him refusing to accept second-class treatment when ordered to dine in the kitchens of Chicago's College Inn: 'How dare you have the audacity to call me a negro! Must I show you my passport? I'm an Englishman, and I'll go straight to the Embassy and cause this place more trouble than you can stand!' By 1933, Foresythe was regularly in London as well as New York (he returned to Whiteman for a second spell in 1934) and a year later was a British fixture, bandleading at the 400 Club in London's West End and making appearances in British films until the war when he joined the RAF as an intelligence officer. After the war he worked in British nightclubs, his life complicated by alcoholism and homosexuality. [DF]

Formanek, Michael, double bass. b. San Francisco, 7 May 1958. Studied bass privately in San Francisco and New York. First professional engagement in 1974 in SF with saxist Norman Williams, then worked with Eddie Henderson, Joe Henderson, Tony Williams and Dave Liebman; 1978, moved to New York, working with Tom Harrell, Herbie Mann, Chet Baker, Bob Moses and Bill Connors. February 1980 to January 1981, recorded and performed as soloist and accompanist with the Media Band at West German Radio in Cologne. 1982, joined Gallery, which included Paul McCandless, David Darling, David Samuels and Michael DiPasqua. [IC]

Forrest, Jimmy (James Robert, Jnr.), tenor sax. b. St Louis, Missouri, 24 January 1920; d. 26 August 1980. Worked with several St Louis bands such as Fate Marable as a teenager, then with Jay McShann (1941–2, including visit to New York in 1942). Played in Andy Kirk (1943–7) and Duke Ellington bands (1949–50). 1950s, led own group in St Louis, then with Harry Edison quintet. After returning to St Louis for several years, joined Count Basie (1973–8) then appeared as soloist (sometimes with Al Grey) until his death.

Forrest was the first person to record the r & b standard 'Night Train', which combines two Ellington tunes 'That's the Blues Old Man' and 'Happy-Go-Lucky Local'. The style that made the number a hit used his typical 'Southwestern tenor' tone to project lines full of blues and bop, which proved very adaptable to a number of different settings. [BP]

Out of the Forrest (1961), Prestige/OJC

Fortune, Sonny, soprano and alto sax, flute. b. Philadelphia, 19 May 1939. Studied at Wurlitzer's and Granoff School of Music, and privately. Began working locally in r & b groups; 1967, moved to New York. Spent ten weeks with Elvin Jones, after which he joined Mongo Santamaria in 1968, staying for two years. 1970, worked with singer Leon Thomas; 1971–3, with McCoy Tyner, after which he played for a few months with Roy Brooks, led his own group briefly, then played with Buddy Rich for five months in 1974; August, joined Miles Davis. He stayed with Davis until midsummer 1975, when illness incapacitated the trumpeter and he disbanded. Fortune has also played with George Benson, Roy Ayers, Oliver Nelson, Pharoah Sanders among others. With Davis he toured and played festivals in the US, Europe and Japan. [IC]

With Santamaria, *Stone Soul* (nda), CBS; with Benson, *Other Side of Abbey Road* (nda), A & M; with Tyner, *Sahara* (1972), Milestone; with Davis, *Agharta* (1975), CBS; as leader, *Awakening* (1975), A & M

Fosdick, Dudley, mellophone. b. Liberty, Indiana, 1902; d. 27 June 1957. Although the mellophone has paid isolated visits into jazz history over the years – Don Elliott featured one, bands as far apart as Lew Stone's and Stan Kenton's used sections of them, and later Dixieland players such as Jack Coon determinedly doubled on one – Fosdick was the true 'father of mellophone'. He was a fine trained musician who worked in the 1920s with Red Nichols, Don Voorhees and Roger Wolfe Kahn and recorded prolifically as a soloist with Nichols and others. From the early 1930s for another 20 years he combined studio work with a 10-year stay with Guy Lombardo's Royal Canadians and by the mid-1950s was teaching full-time at Roerich Academy of Arts. [DF]

Foster, Al (Aloysius), drums; also tenor sax, piano, bass. b. Richmond, Virginia, 18 January 1944. Family moved to New York when he was five. Father played bass; uncle, Ron Jefferson, played drums. No formal lessons, but learned from watching Jefferson practise. First professional work with Hugh Masekela in 1960; then with Ted Curson. 1962–4, with Illinois Jacquet; 1964–5, with Blue Mitchell, and briefly Erskine Hawkins. 1966, with Lou Donaldson, then with Kai Winding at the Playboy Club in New York, after which he spent five years with the Earl May quartet in a club called the Cellar. During that time he turned down offers to join Cannonball Adderley and Horace Silver because he did not wish to leave his family in order to tour. 1972, Miles Davis heard the band in the Cellar, and that was the beginning of Foster's long association with Davis. After playing on *On the Corner*, he stayed with the band, touring in the USA, Europe and Japan, until it broke up because of Davis's ill-health in 1975. From then until 1980, Foster led his own groups at the Cellar, and worked with other people. When Davis resurfaced in 1980, Foster was soon back in the band, staying with it until early 1985. His influences on drums are Max Roach and Art Taylor, and other inspirations are Davis, Sonny Rollins, Sly Stone, Coleman Hawkins, Art Tatum, Bud Powell, Lester Young. Foster is a magnificent all-round drummer, capable of handling anything from bebop, to free form and jazz-rock. He understood the later music of Miles Davis perfectly, and made an immense contribution to it. His rapport with Davis was such that the transitions from one piece to another in live performance always seemed to happen like magic. [IC]

With Davis, *Get Up With It* (1974); *We Want Miles* (1982); *Star People* (1983); *Decoy* (1984), all CBS; with Freddie Hubbard, *Outpost* (1980), Enja

Foster, Frank Benjamin, tenor and soprano sax, arranger. b. Cincinnati, Ohio, 23 September 1928. After studying at Wilberforce University, played with Wardell Gray, Elvin Jones etc. in Detroit (1949). Army service (1951–3) was followed by joining Count Basie, with whom he played and arranged for 11 years (1953–64). Since then, has been successful freelance writer, contributing to albums by Sarah Vaughan and Frank Sinatra, and has been involved in educational work in New York and elsewhere. As well as playing with Elvin Jones (1970–2 and later albums) and Thad Jones–Mel Lewis (1972, 1975), has led own small groups and Living Color and The Loud Minority big bands, visiting Europe and Japan several times; one of own albums recorded in Japan fronting Jones–Lewis band. Also co-led quintet with Frank Wess from 1983 and appeared in Europe as member of Jimmy Smith quintet (1985). Mid-1986, he took over from Thad Jones as leader of the Basie band.

As a writer, Foster has created a large body of work, and it is perhaps a pity (except financially) that he is always identified with one enormously popular standard, 'Shiny Stockings'. His solo work has been consistently excellent since his early days with Basie and an important 1954 session with Thelonious Monk ('Locomotive' etc.). At that period his tone and phrasing suggested a slightly harder-edged Wardell Gray, but from the early 1960s he has managed to incorporate the phraseology (and the facility) of John Coltrane without being dominated by it, which cannot be said of many players. [BP]

Twelve Shades of Black (1977), Leo; *Roots, Branches and Dances* (1978), BeeHive

Foster, Pops (George Murphy), bass, tuba. b. McCall, Louisiana, 18 May *c.* 1892; d. San Francisco, 30 October 1969. He was born on a sugar plantation 68 miles north of New Orleans and played cello in a family trio completed by brother Willy on guitar and sister Elizabeth on mandolin. By 1905 he was specializing on double bass and from 1908 worked regularly with the Magnolia Band, King Oliver, Kid Ory, Jack Carey and Armand J. Piron, as well as on riverboats from 1910. By 1918 he was regularly with Fate Marable's Streckfus showband and soon after upriver in St Louis with Charlie Creath and Ed Allen's Whispering Gold Band: with Allen he played tuba to combat the fashionable three-saxophone frontline. (The later sad saga of Allen's band, incidentally, is told in Dickie Wells's *Night People*.) Foster was busy all through the 1920s (with Kid Ory and others), moved to New York to join King Oliver in 1928 and one year on joined Luis Russell's New Orleans-based orchestra for 11 years (backing Louis Armstrong from 1935). In the 1940s he was reduced to subway portering, but with the jazz revival moved back into the spotlight to work with Sidney Bechet, Art Hodes, for Rudi Blesh's influential This is Jazz programmes and then – after a visit to Nice with Mezz Mezzrow – for Bob Wilber (Jimmy Archey later took over the band). Thereafter Foster played in New York and in San Francisco, with Earl Hines at the Hangover Club, 1956–61, where Hines showed him some new approaches to bass. For his last few years, however, Foster, with Well-

Pops Foster

man Braud, was the emblem of the good old New Orleans slap bass that held sway until the 1930s, travelling from his California home to tour America and Europe. [DF]

Luis Russell and his Orchestra 1926–30/1930–4 (2 LPs), both VJM

See Foster, Pops, as told to Tom Stoddard, *The Autobiography of a New Orleans Jazzman* (University of California Press, 1971)

Fountain, Pete (Peter Dewey, Jnr.), clarinet, saxes. b. New Orleans, 3 July 1930. He began in his hometown New Orleans in the mid-1940s (with Monk Hazel's Band, the Junior Dixieland Band, Phil Zito and others) and worked with the Basin Street Six, 1950–4. His international success began in 1957 when he teamed up with Lawrence Welk for live appearances, records and a long, nationally networked TV series for ABC which featured him in a Dixieland group drawn from Welk's band: the series lasted until 1959. The contract with Welk landed him a prestigious recording deal with Coral which lasted through the 1960s: his club, Pete's Place, at 231 Bourbon Street opened at the same period. Throughout the 1960s Fountain was a familiar figure on American TV and radio: a clarinet counterpart to New Orleans' newest trumpet king Al Hirt (with whom he worked frequently), and in the 1970s he was headlining at his own club (alternating with two months a year at Las Vegas), appearing on TV specials with such superstars as Bing Crosby, Bob Hope and Johnny Carson, and living comfortably in New Orleans' plush Garden district.

Because some jazz critics regard commercial success as unforgivable, Fountain – a peach-toned clarinettist and musical son of such artists as Irving Fazola and Matty Matlock – is often ignored. But 'Never mind what people say about him,' says Wild Bill Davison, 'he's a fine clarinettist, fine tone, lovely ideas – and he can really play the blues when the mood takes him!' [DF]

South Rampart Street Parade (1963), Coral

See Fountain, Pete and Neely, Bill, *Closer Walk: The Pete Fountain Story* (H. Regnery, 1972)

Fours The practice of breaking up an improvised chorus into a mere four bars of solo by one instrument followed by four bars from another and so on. This takes place usually, if at all, at medium to up-tempo and usually after each player has had a full-length solo earlier in the same piece.

Until 1950 or so this was always called a 'chase chorus', which gave a pleasing picture of hornmen chasing each other's tails melodically (and was a useful expression because it covered the less usual 'eights' and 'twos' as well as fours). However, Lester Young and Charlie Parker led the way in the late 1940s to the now standard practice of 'taking fours' with first a horn player, then the drummer, then horn player, then drummer, etc. As a result, the chase image is less apt and has been replaced by a call-and-response pattern in which the drums are the constant factor. [BP]

Fowlkes, Charlie (Charles Baker), baritone sax. b. New York City, 16 February 1916; d. Dallas, Texas, 9 February 1980. Never noted for his solo abilities, Fowlkes was best known as the long-time baritone saxophonist with Count Basie's orchestra: he joined in 1953 and, except for the years 1969–75, stayed until he died. Before then he had worked long stints with Tiny Bradshaw (1938–44), Lionel Hampton (1944–8) and Arnett Cobb (1948–51) and a rare chance to hear his pleasant if unremarkable soloing turns up on Buck Clayton's 'Hucklebuck'/'Robbins' Nest' (see below). [DF]

Buck Clayton Jam Session (1953), CBS

France, Nic (Nicholas Michael), drums, percussion, piano, steel pan. b. Standon, Herts, 30 March 1956. He was a cathedral chorister 1964–9 and took a degree in music at Cambridge College of Arts and Technology. 1978–80, he worked with various groups in the Cambridge area, including the Trevor Kaye quartet which won first prize at the San Sebastian jazz competition. 1980–2, worked with Nucleus, touring in the UK and Europe. He took part in a television drum workshop with Billy Cobham.

During the 1980s he also worked with Chucho Merchan's Macondo, which won the Greater London Arts Association Young Jazz Musicians' Award, 1981, and with Sunwind, which won the same award in 1983. 1984, Macondo won the European Young Jazz Group competition, and played Detroit Kool Jazz Festival. He also works with several other London-based groups, including Loose Tubes and Working Week. He is an excellent teacher and enjoys doing workshops. [IC]

With L. Shankar and Tim Whitehead; with Nucleus, *Awakening* (1980), Mood; with Sunwind, *The Sun Below* (1983), MMC; *Loose Tubes* (1984), LTLP

Francis, Panama (David Albert), drums. b. Miami, Florida, 21 December 1918. He played early on for revival meetings in his church before joining saxophonist George Kelly's band the Cavaliers (their principal influence was Chick Webb) in Florida. Francis moved to New York in 1938 and a year later joined Roy Eldridge's band at the Arcadia Ballroom, recorded with them and, because he often wore a favourite Panama hat, acquired his lifelong nickname from his leader. Late 1939–46, he worked with Lucky Millinder's riff-proud band at the Savoy: 'It was mostly the Savoy Sultans opposite us: only eight pieces but from the time they hit to the time they finished they were swinging!' Francis loved the Sultans (including their famous riveted Chinese cymbal) and after he left formed his own version of the group (with Jesse Drakes, tpt, and Elwyn Frazier, alto) but with little success, and five years with Cab Calloway followed. From 1953, with the help of percussionist Fred Albright, he began a studio career, often gravitating to r & b ('until people forgot I ever played jazz', he once said ruefully), doubled as house drummer at Central Plaza and widened his studio connections gradually to work with Sy Oliver, Perez Prado, Ray Charles *et al.* 1967–70, he worked for Dinah Shore, from 1973 with Sy Oliver, the NYJRC and in 1976 re-formed his own Savoy Sultans (including George Kelly), this time with huge success: they headlined at festivals, topped polls, and made best-selling records. [DF]

With his Savoy Sultans, *Gettin' in the Groove!* (1979), Black & Blue

See Dance, Stanley, *The World of Swing* (Scribner's, 1974, repr. Da Capo, 1979)

Frankenfield, Parke, piano, vibes, trumpet, trombone, saxophones, clarinet, drums, vocals arranger, bandleader. b. Allentown, Pennsylvania, 6 July 1929. He led bands around Pennsylvania from 1950, including the Dixieland All Stars featuring Ben Ventura (tpt) and Bob Levine (reeds) and a 13-piece big band which recreates swing music of the 1930s and 1940s. Regularly appearing at major US jazz festivals (including Kool and Sacramento), his small group works the rounds of clubs, concerts and riverboat cruises; Frankenfield himself promotes concerts and festivals, runs his own record and cassette label and writes all his own arrangements. In 1985 his band affiliated with Bob Crosby to form the New Bob Cats, who appeared that year at Ronald Reagan's Presidential inauguration at the White House; at the same period Frankenfield moved his operations base to Florida and plays there with Billy Butterfield, John Mince, Chubby Jackson *et al.* [DF]

Jazz at Green Pond (featuring Maxine Sullivan), (1985), Ekrop

Franklin, Aretha, vocals, piano. b. Memphis, Tennessee, 1942. Father C. L. Franklin, pastor of the New Bethel Baptist church and a revered figure in gospel music. From early childhood she sang in choirs, and from 14 was a featured soloist with her father's touring gospel troupe. At 18 she changed to secular music, recording her first album for Columbia in 1960. She received immediate acclaim in jazz circles and was frequently compared to Ray Charles and Dinah Washington. Early 1960s, played mostly in clubs, but after signing with Atlantic records (1966) she had a hit single and album (*I Never Loved a Man the Way I Love You*) in 1967, which made her a superstar overnight. She toured major concert halls all over the USA and Europe, with tumultuous receptions everywhere. By the mid-1970s she had six gold LPs (each having sold a million) and had had 14 hit singles. 1968, the Revd Martin Luther King presented her with a special Southern Christian Leadership Council Award. She has also done TV shows in the US with Duke Ellington, Dinah Shore, Bob Hope and others, and appeared at benefit concerts.

Her singing is a unique combination of the raw, direct and intensely personal style of the country blues, and the more polished, professional, outgoing style of the urban blues, and it is shot through with the exultation of her gospel roots. Her voice is a marvellously expressive instrument which can move instantly from a sweet murmur to jubilant shouts which dominate an ensemble. She projects extreme emotion, but it is always finely controlled, and she is a brilliant exponent of the gospel 'call and response' technique, playing 'preacher' to her vocal backing group's 'congregation'. Her backing bands are always perfect for her purposes, and many of her performances have such a unity and completeness, such a sense of form, that they are among the finest examples of the genre she helped to create. [IC]

I Never Loved a Man the Way I Love You (1967); *Aretha Arrives* (1967); *Lady Soul* (1968); *Aretha in Paris* (1968), all Atlantic

Free Jazz (Improvised Music/Abstraction/ Avant-garde) The term 'free jazz' means improvisation not based on a predetermined, underlying harmonic structure, and without a fixed number of bar-lines – i.e. with no predetermined structural length. There are other variable factors: 1) It may be tonal (occurring in a particular key); or non-tonal (in no particular key and sometimes simply noise i.e. non-musical sound); or polytonal (in several keys simultaneously). 2) It may be in a regular time with recurring rhythmic patterns and/or a fixed pulse; or it may be out-of-time, with a 'free' and irregular temporal momentum. 3) There may or may not be composed themes and/or predetermined textural and spatial considerations for the improvisation.

After the tight structures and the strongly harmonic basis of bebop, a feeling grew during the 1950s that the current jazz language had exhausted itself, and musicians began seeking new approaches to improvisation and music-making. As early as 1949, pianist Lennie Tristano's sextet had recorded a wholly improvised piece, 'Intuition', which began in total abstraction, then slowly evolved into a key centre and tempo. During the 1950s Charles Mingus, pianist Cecil Taylor and others had begun experimenting in this direction. The free jazz movement in the USA was eventually launched in 1959 by Ornette Coleman, who arrived in New York with a conception that was fully realized and a quartet which thoroughly understood the new idiom.

The father of European free jazz was the West Indian alto saxophonist Joe Harriott, who worked out his ideas in 1959, recorded his album *Free Form* in 1960, and played his new music at European festivals in the early 1960s. Harriott's music was different from Coleman's in several important respects. Coleman's grew out of the Afro-American tradition: though harmonically abstract, it was imbued with the feeling of the blues and gospel music, and it usually took place in regular time, swinging beautifully. Harriott's was often totally abstract and had no regular rhythm, it sometimes featured silence as an integral part of the music, fused Afro-Caribbean elements with the angularity and dissonance of 20th-century avant-garde classical music and occasionally included unaccompanied solo improvisation by any one of the members of his quintet.

European free jazz in the 1960s tended to follow this road of total abstraction, and some practitioners disassociated themselves from jazz, calling their activity 'free improvisation' and its results 'improvised music'. There were two main branches of European improvised music: on the one hand, the aggressive anarchism of, for example, Peter Brötzmann and his associates, which expressed itself in violent, non-tonal collective improvisation; on the other, the gentler iconoclastic humour and wit of Derek Bailey and Evan Parker, or the irreverent, good-natured clowning of theatrical performers such as Wolfgang Dauner. Europe also had its followers of Ornette Coleman.

In the USA the more abstract variants of free jazz, even though some white musicians were involved, became known as 'black music' and was identified with the radical protest of the black community against white oppression. This, too, resulted in violent collective improvisations. Val Wilmer has written, 'The dominant factor in most Black music is that the performer be aggressive.' The spokesman of this movement was the black writer, LeRoi Jones (Amiri Baraka), and some of the leading exponents were Cecil Taylor, Archie Shepp, Albert Ayler, and drummers Milford Graves and Sunny Murray. J. E. Berendt has pointed out that 'Besides the protest, there are the hymnlike religious fervour of John Coltrane, the joyous air of the folk musician in Albert Ayler, the intellectual, and yet humorous "coolness" of Paul Bley or Ran Blake, the cosmic amplitude of Sun Ra, the sensibility of Carla Bley.'

By the late 1960s free jazz had established its own mannerisms and clichés, becoming a known quantity; and because of the absence of clear rules and the lack of criteria for judging performances, it attracted a number of charlatans and inferior players. By the end of the decade, Coltrane and Ayler were dead, and many of its other exponents, including Harriott, C. Bley, P. Bley, Abdullah Ibrahim (Dollar Brand), Gato Barbieri and Dauner, had turned away from abstraction to seek other modes of expression. However, many of the key figures in free music continued to develop their conception and to perform their music internationally.

Abstraction threw all the old rules out, attempting to wipe the slate clean and start afresh, and this necessary purge helped to shake the jazz world out of its complacency and inertia. Musicians of all ages and all styles were forced to re-examine themselves and their music. Free jazz enriched the existing jazz language with a new dimension – that of abstraction, which has, since the 1960s, become a part of the vocabulary of most musicians. [IC]

See Wilmer, Valerie, *As Serious as your Life: The Story of the New Jazz* (Allison & Busby, 1977)

Freeman, Bud (Lawrence), tenor sax, clarinet, composer. b. Chicago, 13 April 1906. He took up C melody saxophone in 1923 and by 1925 had changed to tenor. Somewhere in between Eddie Condon heard him playing 'a saxophone green with corrosion [which] sounded the way it looked', but a year later Freeman's sound and technique had improved dramatically. For the next nine years he was working with a formidable list of leaders (including Red Nichols, Meyer Davis, Roger Wolfe Kahn, Ben Pollack, Zez Confrey, Joe Venuti and Gene Kardos) and regularly recording: focal points charting his progress are 'Sugar/Nobody's Sweetheart' by the McKenzie–Condon Chicagoans, their first recording in 1927, and a hit recording from 1933 'The Eel' based on a deceptive *'trompe l'oreille'*

Bud Freeman

which he has used ever since. From Joe Haymes's influential band, also featuring young trumpet turk Pee Wee Erwin, Freeman joined Ray Noble, in July 1935 at New York's Rainbow Room, then moved on to Tommy Dorsey's great band in 1936, then to Benny Goodman for nine months in 1938. But he quickly tired of nine shows a night and left to front the immortal Summa Cum Laude orchestra for hotel work and, surprisingly, a spot in a Broadway musical based on Shakespeare's *A Midsummer Night's Dream*. *Swingin' the Dream*, which also starred Louis Armstrong and Maxine Sullivan, ran for only a few performances, but for Freeman (a closet actor who sported a near-British accent) the chance of an appearance on Broadway in an English-based production must have been seductive.

From 1940 came more freelancing, then two years in the army (he led service bands) and from 1945 regular appearances at Eddie Condon's. Despite his frequent association with Condon on record, Freeman carefully forged a solo career of his own: he also led his own bands around New York and Chicago, recorded prolifically under his own name, took solo work in Peru and Chile and even found time to study under Lennie Tristano. By the early 1960s he was a globetrotter, travelling light as a respected soloist and creating best-selling albums (just one of hundreds of Freeman beauties is *Something Tender*, with guitarists Carl Kress and George Barnes, which achieved a five-star *Downbeat* rating). In 1968 he was a founder member of the World's Greatest Jazz Band and stayed for three years before solo work prevailed. In the 1970s he lived in London for a while before going back to Chicago to settle. At 80, Freeman was still full of suave Anglicized charm and precise humour and playing as strongly and beautifully as ever. He remains, along with Coleman Hawkins, the most recognizable creator of a tenor-saxophone style back in the 1920s. The style was to affect a generation of white saxophonists, including Eddie Miller, Boomie Richman, Nick Caiazza and Tony Pastor, and created the white vocabulary for prebop tenor. Most remarkably it presented – as Bix Beiderbecke did to Louis Armstrong – an alternative to the monolith created by Hawkins and has gone on doing so ever since. [DF]

The Commodore Years (1938–9), London (double)

See Freeman, Bud, *If you know of a better life, please tell me!* (Bashall Eaves, 1976)

Freeman, Chico (Earl, Jnr.), tenor and soprano sax. b. Chicago, 17 July 1949. Son of saxophonist Von Freeman. Began on trumpet, switching to tenor while at Northwestern University; studied with Muhal Richard Abrams and Joe Daley (early 1970s); holds master's degree in composition from Governors State University. 1976, appeared successfully with university group at Notre Dame festival and in Brazil. Settled in New York, working with bassist Cecil McBee (regularly from 1976), Elvin Jones, Sam Rivers, Don Pullen and Sun Ra. Toured Europe with Jones, with AACM big band (1979) and with own quartet (1979, 1980). One of the featured musicians in the Young Lions concert (1982) which, as with the second album listed below, included Wynton Marsalis.

Like almost every other young tenor player, Freeman initially mirrored the work of John Coltrane but is both more individual and more versatile than most of his contemporaries. With a tone that, though not reminiscent of his father's, is recognizably of the Chicago school, Chico is able to incorporate mainstream virtues without imitating specific earlier players. As well as being probably the first jazzman of his generation to record an album of standards (see first album below), he seems engaged on a long-term consolidation which may be only now reaching fruition. [BP]

Spirit Sensitive (1978), India Navigation; *Destiny's Dance* (1981), Contemporary

Freeman, Von (Earl Lavon), tenor sax. b. Chicago, 3 October 1922. Worked with Horace Henderson group (late 1940s) and Sun Ra band (early 1950s). During same period, played with his brothers, drummer Bruz (Eldridge) Freeman and guitarist George Freeman; group's successive pianists were Ahmad Jamal, Andrew Hill and Muhal Richard Abrams. Early 1960s, toured with vocalist Milt Trenier of the Trenier

Brothers. From 1970s has appeared briefly in New York and Europe, but remains based in Chicago. An unsung progenitor of the 'Chicago tenor' style along with Gene Ammons (a couple of years his junior), he has a very personal, rather querulous tone which is sometimes echoed by Johnny Griffin, and tremendous fluency which must have impressed his son Chico (above). [BP]

Young and Foolish (1977), Daybreak

Frisell, Bill (William Richard), guitar. b. Baltimore, Maryland, 18 March 1951. Grew up in Denver, Colorado. Father played tuba and string bass. Frisell began on clarinet, later saxophone, before taking up guitar. Music major at University of North Colorado (1969–71). Diploma in arranging and composition from Berklee College, 1977, and received the Harris Stanton guitar award the same year. Private guitar lessons with Jim Hall, Johnny Smith and Dale Bruning. Frisell is one of the most accomplished and sought-after young American guitarists. Since the late 1970s he has performed in the USA and throughout Europe with leading contemporary players such as Paul Motian, Jan Garbarek, Eberhard Weber, Bob Moses, Charlie Haden's Liberation Music Orchestra, Michael Mantler, Carla Bley, Mike Gibbs' orchestra, Julius Hemphill's Jah band, Gunter Hampel's Galaxie Dream Band, Lyle Mays, John Scofield, Peter Erskine and others. His favourite guitarists are Wes Montgomery, Hall and Jimi Hendrix. [IC]

With Garbarek, Weber, Moses and others; *Amarcord Nino Rota* (1981), Hannibal; *In Line* (1983); *Rambler* (1985); with Paul Motian, *Psalm* (1982), all ECM; *The Story of Maryam* (1983), Soul Note; *It Should've Happened a Long Time Ago* (1984), ECM

Frishberg, Dave, piano, composer, lyricist, vocals. b. St Paul, Minnesota, 23 March 1933. After giving up his job in journalism for full-time music he worked as intermission pianist at Eddie Condon's for a year, was with Bud Freeman's quartet and with Gene Krupa, and worked regularly at the Metropole, besides taking his first steps in witty song-writing: an early success, the drily delightful 'Peel me a grape', cemented his professional credibility and personal good relations with likeminded song people such as Blossom Dearie (for whom it was a hit) and Bob Dorough. In the 1960s he worked for Ben Webster, and with Al Cohn and Zoot Sims for a long famous stay at New York's Half-Note. 1971, left New York to write for a weekly TV show. Then (a testimony to Frishberg's broad mind, humour and open ears) 'I joined Herb Alpert. When I heard the personnel I jumped at the chance. I loved it – it was the most fun I'd had. I got a solo spot and played some of my Jelly Roll Morton stuff.' A solo career was becoming more important to him: two 1970s albums, *Getting Some Fun out of Life* and *You're a Lucky Guy* focused attention on his witty jazz ear, connoisseur's taste in songs and sandy avuncular singing (as well as on his own irresistible jazz *tendresse* 'Dear Bix'). They were followed, no less remarkably, by three valuable (but never precious) albums of original songs, sung by himself: *Oklahoma Toad* (now a collector's item) and the *Dave Frishberg Song Book* vols. 1 and 2. Frishberg's re-emergence as a pianist-singer of Carmichael-esque proportions on the American and European club circuits has been one of the jollier and more comforting aspects of 1980s jazz. [DF]

Dave Frishberg Song Book, vol. 1 (1981), Omnisound

Front-line The front-line of a group consists of all those players not in the rhythm-section. In a jam-session situation, the front-line could run to ten or more musicians; but even eight horns, if working from organized arrangements, would no longer be a front-line but the horn section of a small big-band. [BP]

Fuller, Curtis DuBois, trombone. b. Detroit, Michigan, 14 December 1934. Played with Kenny Burrell and with Yusef Lateef's Detroit quintet (1955–6). Moved to New York in 1957 and within a year had worked for Miles Davis, Dizzy Gillespie, Sonny Rollins and (1958) Lester Young. Immediately began recording prolifically, including sessions with Bud Powell and John Coltrane. Became founder member of the Jazztet with Art Farmer–Benny Golson (1959–60), then with Art Blakey's Jazz Messengers (1961–5). Less active on jazz scene thereafter, but more recording under own name followed in 1970s. Touring with Count Basie (late 1970s and early 1980s), Lionel Hampton (1979), Kai Winding (1980) and with Jazztet (1982), plus freelancing in New York.

Fuller has a style which exploits the technical discoveries of J. J. Johnson but in a more subdued manner. His phrasing is sometimes clipped and repetitive at up-tempo, but with slower vehicles his melodic approach is very distinctive. [BP]

Fire and Filigree (1978), Beehive

Funk/Funky This may derive from the obsolete English word funk = smoke, steam, stench. In jazz and rock the term 'funky' signifies music which is extremely physical and 'dirty' – the rhythms are strong, clear and hypnotic and the phrasing of the melodic and chordal instruments is bluesy and very vocalized. The whole musical idea of funk derives from the blues; blue notes are not sung or played straight, but are bent and slurred expressively – so that the notes and the feeling they express become almost tangible with the sweat and smell and sheer physicality of human experience.

'Funk' and 'funky' first came into real prominence during the 1950s when, as a reaction against the 'straight' and European sound of much 'cool' jazz, musicians turned once more to the vernacular roots of the music, incorporating elements from the blues, the hot gospels and the worksongs. Horace Silver, in his work with Art Blakey and Miles Davis in the early 1950s as both player and composer, was one of the prime movers of this reinvigoration of jazz, and one of his compositions was actually called 'Opus de Funk'. By the end of that decade, however, everyone was trying to be funky, and the result was much stale and sterile music which had all the mannerisms of funk without any of the substance.

Since then, funk has reappeared in various forms, and its quality and validity have always depended entirely on the quality of the musicians who express themselves in that way. With great artists – Miles Davis, Joe Zawinul, Herbie Hancock, among others – it has often been an integral part of their great music; with mediocrities it can, and has, produced mediocre results. [IC]

G

Gadd, Steve, drums. b. Rochester, New York, 1945. Uncle, a drummer in the army, encouraged him. Drum lessons from age seven; sat in with Dizzy Gillespie at 11. Studied music at Eastman College, Rochester, playing in wind ensemble and concert band, and at nights in a club with Chick Corea, Chuck Mangione, Joe Romano and Frank Polero. After college, drafted into army and spent three years in a military band. After the army, gigged and worked with a big band in Rochester. 1972, formed a trio with Tony Levin and Mike Holmes, going to New York with it. The trio fizzled out, but Gadd began to work extensively as a studio musician. He also played with Corea's first Return to Forever. 1970s and 1980s, toured internationally, recorded with Paul Simon and with Al DiMeola's Electric Rendezvous Band. By the end of the 1970s Gadd was the most in-demand and probably the most imitated drummer in the world. In Japan transcriptions of his solos were on sale, and all the leading Japanese drummers were sounding like him. Chick Corea commented: 'Every drummer wants to play like Gadd because he plays perfect . . . He has brought orchestral and compositional thinking to the drum kit while at the same time having a great imagination and a great ability to swing.' Gadd's favourites are Elvin Jones, Tony Williams, Jack DeJohnette, Buddy Rich, Louie Bellson, among others. [IC]

With many singers, including Aretha Franklin, Stevie Wonder, Barbra Streisand, Paul McCartney and Paul Simon; with Corea, *Three Quartets* (1981), Warner Bros; *My Spanish Heart* (1976); *Friends* (1978); *The Mad Hatter* (1978), all Polydor; with George Benson, *In Concert* (1975), CTI; with Stuff, *Stuff* (nda), Warner Bros; with DiMeola, *Electric Rendezvous* (1982), Columbia; with Carla Bley, *Dinner Music* (1976), Watt

Gaillard, Slim (Bulee), vocals, piano, guitar, vibes, tenor sax, composer. b. Detroit, Michigan, 4 January 1916. In the mid-1930s he worked as a solo variety act, playing guitar and tap-dancing simultaneously: a bizarre combination which, early on, reflected Gaillard's comedic view of life. 'Slim and Slam', his double-act with bassist Slam Stewart, 1938–43, caused a sensation and landed a long series on Radio WNEW. Gaillard presented his routines in 'vout', an invented jive talk which finished off every other word with 'oreenee', mugged through incomprehensible songs, notably his own huge hit 'Flat Fleet Floogie', and – right in the middle – would veer off into manic machine-gun Spanish patter and high-speed jive talk. Gaillard's songs – often about food ('Avocado Seed Soup Symphony', 'Matzoh Balls' and 'Yip Roc Heresy' which he composed from an Armenian menu), machinery ('Cement mixer', 'Poppity-pop! Moto-Cikkle') or just marvellous nonsense ('Ya Ha Ha' or 'Laughing in Rhythm') – were completely original. His later successes including 'Down by the Station', a charming children's chant, made him a star from 1944 in Los Angeles clubs where Hollywood stars dropped in nightly and where he worked with bassist Bam Brown and sometimes singer Leo Watson. He had already appeared in films himself – *Star Spangled Rhythm* (1942), *Hellzapoppin* (1942) and others – but by 1947, with a divorce pending and other personal problems, he appeared less often in public, worked from time to time as an MC, comedian and singer and by the early 1960s was running a motel in San Diego: later he bought an orange farm near Seattle. The isolated records he made during the period (one with a fine big band) have now started to reappear as a result of Alastair Robertson's reissuing his earlier sides on the Hep label in the early 1980s. A familiar face from the TV series *Roots – the Next Generations*, he made a lengthy UK tour (to sellout audiences) in 1982, playing guitar, piano (with the backs of his hands) and singing his old hits. He re-recorded for Robertson, made a number of TV appearances presenting and performing and with his striking looks (he uncannily resembles Walt Disney's Uncle Remus), dark-brown voice and gently surreal comedy caused as big a hit as he had 40 years ago. By 1985 he was commuting from country to country, playing jazz festivals, concerts and clubs and spreading joy. [DF]

Slim and Slam, vol.1 (1938–9), Tax; *McVouty: Slim and Bam* (1945–6), Hep

Galloway, Jim, saxes, clarinet. He took up the clarinet in his teens in Glasgow (Forrie Cairns was an occasional clarinet colleague) and later doubled on alto sax playing with local bands such as the Jazzmakers. 1965, moved to Canada, where he added soprano and baritone sax to his collection and set about broadening his experience. 1976, he was asked to take a band to the

Slim Gaillard

Montreux festival (including Buddy Tate and Jay McShann), followed by a trip to Nice for George Wein and a long European tour with Tate again. From then on he was a regular at jazz festivals everywhere, touring Europe as a soloist and at home in Canada leading his own quartet, sextet and big band (Jim Galloway's Wee Big Band) often featuring his wife on bass. A committed jazzman who eschews studio work, Galloway includes among his principal influences on record Armstrong, Teagarden, Ed Hall, Coleman Hawkins, Don Byas, Ben Webster, Lester Young, Ellington, Basie and Lunceford. In 1985 a Galloway commission, *Hot and Suite*, featuring himself, two jazz bands, and a symphony orchestra, was *pièce de résistance* at Edinburgh's annual jazz festival. [DF]

Featuring Jay McShann (1981), Sackville

Galper, Hal (Harold), piano, keyboards, composer. b. Salem, Massachusetts, 18 April 1938. Classical studies, 1945–8; Berklee School of Music, 1955–8; private tuition with Jaki Byard, Herb Pomeroy and others. With Pomeroy big band and small group in Boston, also with Sam Rivers quartet, Tony Williams, Chet Baker; played European festivals with Bobby Hutcherson, Joe Henderson, Stan Getz, Randy Brecker, Attila Zoller. Accompanied many singers including Joe Williams, Anita O'Day, Chris Connor. 1972–5, with the Cannonball Adderley quintet, in which he replaced George Duke. Also played with Lee Konitz, John Scofield and Billy Hart. Since 1982, member of Phil Woods Quintet. Galper is a highly accomplished player, at home with any idiom from jazz and rock to abstraction. His album *Reach Out*, featuring the Brecker brothers, presents his playing and writing at their best. [IC]

With Adderley; with Sam Rivers, *A New Conception* (1966), Blue Note; with Randy Brecker, *Score* (1968), United Artists; with Chet Baker, *Baby Breeze* (1964), Limelight; as leader, *Reach Out* (1976), Steeplechase; *Now Hear This* (1977); *Ivory Forest* (1979); *Speak with a Single Voice* (1981), all Enja

Ganelin Trio: formed in 1971 in the USSR by: Vyacheslav Ganelin, piano, basset, electric guitar, percussion, composer. b. Kraskov, USSR, 1944. Began on piano at age four. Has played jazz since 1961. Graduated from the Vilnius Conservatory. Member of USSR Composers' Union. Has written a number of operas and film scores. Vladimir Chekasin, reeds, trombone, violin, whistle, percussion, voice, composer. b. Sverdlovsk, USSR, 1947. Began on violin at age six; clarinet at 11; alto sax at 18. Graduated from Sverdlovsk Conservatory. Has played jazz since 1967. 1970, he won first prize at the international competition organized by the Czechoslovak Society of Composers. He teaches at a conservatory and directs an orchestra. Vladimir Tarasov, drums, percussion. b. Archangelsk, USSR, 1947. Self-taught. Plays drums with the Lithuanian Radio Symphony Orchestra and the Lithuanian State Symphony Orchestra.

These three virtuosi create a kind of abstract music which grows out of the European free jazz movement of the 1960s but has its own very different identity. Composition seems to play a more important role in the Ganelin's music, and every piece, every album, is different, offering a tremendous variety of textures, timbres, instrumental combinations and approaches. They are capable of good time-playing and occasionally set up some nice sustained rhythms, and their performances can range from grotesque parody and burlesque to the wide-eyed simplicity of children's nursery songs or the romantic melancholy of European – and particularly Slavonic – folk music and classical music. They are steeped in jazz history, which also echoes through their performances. In particular, although their music is sometimes totally abstract and often semi-abstract, there is always a sense of form and an intelligent use of space, so that tension is created and released satisfactorily.

1976, they performed at the Warsaw Jazz Jamboree and their first album, *Con Anima*, was released in the USSR. By the 1980s they were playing concerts both in the Soviet Union and abroad. 1980, they performed at the West Berlin Jazz Festival, to an ecstatic audience; J. E. Berendt wrote: 'With three musicians playing approximately 15 instruments with a breathtaking intensity, building their set to a euphoric climax, it was the wildest and yet the best organized and most professional free jazz I've heard in years.' 1981, they played in Italy; 1983, toured Romania, broadcasting there on Radio Cluj; 1984, they toured the UK for the ACGB Contemporary Music Network. The trio is very popular in Russian intellectual circles.

Because the official Soviet record label Melodiya is reluctant to release their albums in the USSR a London company, Leo Records, has undertaken to release and distribute not only their LPs, but those of other Russian jazz musicians, in Britain and the West. [IC]

Strictly for our Friends (1978); *Con Fuoco – Live in Moscow and Berlin* (1978–80); *Live in Leningrad, Pts. 1/2* (1980) (double); *Vide* (1981); *Baltic Triangle* (1981); *Live in East Germany* (1981); *New Wine* (1982), all Leo

Ganley, Allan, drums, composer, arranger. b. Tolworth, Surrey, 11 March 1931. Mainly self-taught, but in 1970 he did one semester at the Berklee School, Boston, USA. He worked with Jack Parnell's band and the Ambrose orchestra in the early 1950s and then joined the first John Dankworth orchestra, staying with it for two years. Then he formed a quintet called the Jazzmakers which lasted two years and did a major US tour. In the early 1960s he was with the new Tubby Hayes quintet, was busy as a studio musician and had begun composing and arranging. He has worked with many leading musicians, including Stan Getz, Freddie Hubbard, Roland Kirk, Al Cohn, Clark Terry, Dizzy Gillespie, Jim Hall. Ganley is still very active as a player, but his main interest is arranging/composing and he writes regularly for the BBC Radio Big Band. [IC]

With John Dankworth, Kenny Davern, Stephane Grappelli, Albert Mangelsdorff, Bill Watrous and others; with Tubby Hayes quintet, *Down in the Village* and *Late Spot at Scott's* (1962), Fontana; with Jim Hall/Ron Carter/Art Farmer, *Commitment* (1976), Horizon; with Al Haig, *Stablemates* (1977), Spotlite

Garbarek, Jan, soprano, tenor and bass sax, flutes. b. Norway, 4 March 1947. Self-taught. After hearing John Coltrane on the radio in 1961, he wanted to play saxophone. 1962, he won a competition for amateur jazz players, which led to his first professional work. He enrolled at Oslo University, but soon dropped out because he was getting too much work as a musician. Since the early 1960s he has always led groups of his own, mostly with Jon Christensen (dms), Terje Rypdal (gtr) and Arild Andersen (bass). He also worked with George Russell, who was resident in Scandinavia for four years in the later 1960s, and studied Russell's book *The Lydian Chromatic Concept of Tonal Organisation*. He also played with singer Karin Krog. 1970, Garbarek was given a government grant to go to the USA and listen to jazz, and began recording for ECM: he has been with the label ever since. He has also worked with Chick Corea and Don Cherry. In the mid-1970s, with Keith Jarrett, Palle Danielsson (bass) and Jon Christensen, he played on two classic albums, *Belonging* and *My Song*, and Garbarek's work on these established him as one of the major saxophone voices of the post-Coltrane period. This quartet became known as the Belonging band, and it toured in Europe and the USA towards the end of the decade, recording a live double album of new material at the Village Vanguard, New York City. In the 1980s Garbarek led a very distinguished quartet with Eberhard Weber on bass, first Christensen, then Michael Di Pasqua, on drums and percussion, and a series of guitarists including Bill Frisell, Moss Trout and David Torn. His favourites are Johnny Hodges, John Coltrane, Albert Ayler, Pharoah Sanders, Archie Shepp, Gene Ammons, and other inspirations are Miles Davis, Ornette Coleman and Jarrett.

Garbarek's mature work is a perfect blend of the old (the roots of the music) and the new – fresh ways of expressing those roots. Manfred Eicher, his ECM producer, has described him as 'a very ascetic person, with an ascetic appearance, and an ascetic sound'. The asceticism is in the spareness of his phrasing, but not in the feeling that underlies it. Garbarek does not play 'licks' (preconceived or habitual patterns), but his improvisations sound like distilled thought – ideas conceived, edited and expressed on the spur of each moment. Underneath this icy clarity he burns with a feeling which is the more potent for being so tightly controlled. Every note, every phrase is meant; there is no rhetoric, only poetry. And the intense feeling is conveyed in the extraordinary tonal quality of his work; he employs a great variety of subtle inflexions, timbres and ways of articulating notes which are emotionally eloquent. He is a fine small-group composer, and his writing bears the same characteristics as his playing. His music is an affirmation, and it is full of resonances from the past – echoes of Nordic folksong, old church music, half-forgotten things from long ago. [IC]

With Keith Jarrett, *Belonging* (1974); *My Song* (1977); with Ralph Towner, *Solstice* (1976); Garbarek/Towner, *Dis* (1978); with Egberto Gismonti/Charlie Haden, *Magico* (1979); quartet, *Paths, Prints* (1981); *Wayfarer* (1983); with Shankar, *Song for Everyone* (1984), all ECM

Garland, Ed(ward Bertram) 'Montudi', bass. b. New Orleans, 9 January 1885; d. Los Angeles, 22 January 1980. The father of jazz double-bass, his first instrument was 'a stick attached to a hole in a milk can with a string run to the top'. At 15 he was playing bass drum in Frank Duson's Eagle Band (bass drummer Black Benny was in it too), but soon specialized on double-bass and worked with Buddy Bolden at Hank's Saloon, Funky Butt Hall and all over Storyville for $2.50 a night. He played with Buddy Petit, Manuel

Perez, King Oliver and Kid Ory's Brownskin Babes before pioneering around the South with Mabel Lee Lane's vaudeville troupe and by 1917 was raising a riot in Chicago with Sugar Johnny's Creole Band: 'Montudi, Tubby Hall and I beat out a rhythm that put the Bechuana tribes of Africa to shame', Lil Hardin Armstrong recalled later. Garland went to California with King Oliver in 1921 to help Kid Ory out with a double booking, liked the climate as well as the music, and stayed. From 1922, when (with Ory) he recorded the first ever black New Orleans jazz for the Spikes Brothers' Sunshine label ('Ory's Creole Trombone' and 'Society Blues'), Montudi lived on America's West Coast for 50 years, working with Ory and others, leading his own One-Eleven Club band, and playing mood music on silent film sets in Hollywood. In the 1930s came a spell of Hollywood parties and a quieter period until he reteamed with Kid Ory for the Standard Oil Broadcasts, compered by Orson Welles, which helped to establish the American jazz revival. From then on, with stars including Ory, Earl Hines, Turk Murphy, Joe Darensbourg and Andrew Blakeney, Garland worked constantly. In 1974 he was still touring Europe and America (with Barry Martyn), still weighing just 130lbs, nearly blind but still immaculate (he was nicknamed after a legendary New Orleans dandy). In September that year he was honoured by President Gerald Ford as 'the oldest living sideman' during a concert. [DF]

Kid Ory's Creole Jazz Band Live at Club Hangover (1953), Dawn Club

Garland, Joe (Joseph Copeland), tenor, baritone and bass sax, arranger. b. Norfolk, Virginia, 15 August 1903; d. 21 April 1977. 'One of the greatest musicians I ever worked with', says Louis Armstrong. Garland's career resembles Eddie Barefield's in more ways than one: both men were outstanding soloists for their period, experienced musical directors, and more than competent arrangers, as well as versatile multireedmen. Garland's New York career began in 1925 with Elmer Snowden's band at the Bamville Club and from then on he was a mainstay of the competitive music scene with a variety of leaders and (1932–6) with Mills' Blue Rhythm Band, under Lucky Millinder. Then came yearlong stays with Edgar Hayes (1937) and Don Redman (1938) before in 1939 he joined Louis Armstrong's big band for an association which – more or less regularly – was to last until 1947. After Luis Russell's connection with Armstrong was severed in late 1940, Garland took over musical direction of Armstrong's orchestra too and, says Louis, 'he couldn't stand hearing wrong notes! He'd make a funny noise in his throat – and that cat didn't need telling again!' After Armstrong gave up his big band in 1947, Garland – by now well known as the composer of Glenn Miller's hit 'In the Mood' and later Les Brown's theme 'Leapfrog' – worked for Claude Hopkins and as musical director again, this time for Earl Hines, in 1948. But from the early 1950s he left full-time music and put together bands for fun (one, in 1959, featured Clyde Bernhardt and Charlie Holmes and played around New Jersey) as well as cultivating an interest in photography, a study in which he gained three degrees. An achiever and a highly competent professional throughout his career, Joe Garland and his music deserve re-assessment. [DF]

Any with Armstrong's big band, 1939–47

Garland, Red (William M.), piano. b. Dallas, Texas, 13 May 1923; d. 23 April 1984 following heart attack. A rather idiosyncratic stylist, whose wide influence stemmed from his work in the Miles Davis group (1955–8). Previously had accompanied several name soloists in Philadelphia and Boston, and toured with Eddie Vinson in the late 1940s, alongside John Coltrane. By the time of his first recordings with Davis, Garland was strongly indebted to Ahmad Jamal (perhaps also to Parker's pianist Walter Bishop) and his use of boppish but tinkly solo lines was actively encouraged by Miles; so too was his right-hand chording which, however, had a distinctive sound due to the frequent inclusion of 'wrong' notes. After a period of success as a trio leader in the early 1960s Garland returned first to Philadelphia and then to Dallas, and despite being 'rediscovered' he seldom recaptured the jaunty confidence of his 1950s recordings. [BP]

Red Garland's Piano (1957), Prestige/OJC

Garner, Erroll Louis, piano. b. Pittsburgh, Pennsylvania, 15 June 1921; d. 2 January 1977. Recognized in early childhood as a gifted musician, Garner had an elder brother (Linton, b. 25 March 1915) who also became a professional pianist. Erroll appeared from the age of 10 with the Kan-D-Kids entertainers on KQV Radio, and at 16 joined local saxist Leroy Brown. After work with singers and piano duettists, moved to New York in 1944 and achieved immediate nightclub success. Apart from a year with Slam Stewart (1944–5) and the occasional all-star jam session, worked only as soloist or leader of his own trio and, thanks to strong management, graduated in the 1950s from nightclubs to top-class hotels and international concert tours.

Garner may have been inspired by the example of Earl Hines, a fellow Pittsburgh resident but 18 years his senior, and there were resemblances in their elastic approach to timing and the use of right-hand octaves. Erroll's style, however, was unique and had neither obvious forerunners nor competent imitators (although at an amateur level more players attempted to imitate him than any other pianist in jazz history). A key factor in his sound was the independence of his springy but rock-steady left hand from the seemingly wayward melodies of the right. Whether in ultra-slow ballads or

Erroll Garner

rampant up-tempo improvisation, this never failed to convey a humorous and titillating attitude to both the material at hand and the audience.

Although his tune 'Misty' rapidly became a standard with singers, it was never a favourite with fellow instrumentalists. But Erroll was a jazz musician through and through, his popular appeal arising directly from his playing. It was achieved without the aid of jocular vocals or ingratiating announcements, in the manner of Armstrong or Waller (the only comparable figures in terms of earning universal affection), and it seems equally unlikely that he tailored his music to the demands of success. He merely found the way to people's hearts and never lost it. [BP]

Misty (1951–7), CBS; *Concert by the Sea* (1955), CBS; *A Night at the Movies* (1965), Bulldog

See Doran, James M., *Erroll Garner: The Most Happy Piano* (Scarecrow Press, 1985)

Garrick, Michael, piano, pipe organ, keyboards, composer. b. Enfield, Middlesex, 30 May 1933. Parents both musical. Garrick took a BA in English literature at London University, but as a musician he was self-taught, except for some classes at the Ivor Mairants School of Dance Music. In the 1970s he attended the Berklee School, Boston, as a mature student. He began leading small groups in the late 1950s and was one of the pioneers of Poetry and Jazz concerts, working with various British poets and leading a quintet which included Joe Harriott and Shake Keane. 1965–9, pianist with the Rendell–Carr quintet; from 1966, regularly leading his own sextet. He is a prolific composer, and several of his compositions were an important part of the Rendell–Carr repertoire. 1967, he composed *Jazz Praises*, a cycle of religious pieces for his sextet and a large choir, which was performed and recorded in St Paul's Cathedral, London, the following year. As well as being deeply versed in jazz and church music, Garrick has studied Indian music and several of his compositions are inspired by Indian scales and techniques. He is very active in jazz education, teaching at schools and on short courses. Among his favourite pianists are Bill Evans, John Taylor, Duke Ellington and Herbie Hancock, and he also cites John Lewis and Kenny Wheeler as inspirational figures. Poetry is an abiding interest for him and he has for years been studying Rudolf Steiner's Anthroposophy. Some of Garrick's best and best known compositions are *Dusk Fire*, *Black Marigolds*, *Cold Mountain*, all small-group pieces, and bigger works such as 'Jazz Praises', 'Mr Smith's Apocalypse', 'Zodiac of Angels'. [IC]

Four with Rendell–Carr; as leader, 14 albums including *Black Marigolds* (1966), Argo; *Jazz Praises* (1968), Airborne; *Mr Smith's Apocalypse* (1971), Argo; *You've Changed* (1978), Hep

Garrison, Jimmy (James Emory), bass, b. Miami, Florida, 3 March 1934; d. 7 April 1976, of lung cancer. He was raised in Philadelphia where he played with local groups until 1958, when Philly Joe Jones brought him to New York. There he gigged with various people, including Lennie Tristano, Benny Golson, Bill Evans, Kenny Dorham, but only began to be noticed when he joined Ornette Coleman's group at the Five Spot. Coltrane sat in with Coleman's group and liked Garrison so much that he offered him the job with his own quartet. 1961–6, he was a fundamental force in Coltrane's group, and Elvin Jones commented, 'He was the turning point . . . his aggressiveness, his attitude toward the instrument gave us all a lift.' Garrison left in the summer of 1966, and co-led a group with Hampton Hawes for six months. Then, with Archie Shepp's group, he toured and played festivals in the US and Europe, 1967–8; with Elvin Jones trio, 1968–9; taught for a year (1970–1) at both Bennington College and Wesleyan University, performing as soloist at Bennington graduation ceremony; 1972, with Alice Coltrane; rejoined Jones, 1973–4. Then ill-health beset him; he had trouble with a hand in late 1974 and a lung operation in 1975.

Garrison played the bass as a bass – as the rock-solid fundament of a band. He was not interested in the Scott La Faro style which 'liberated' the instrument from the 'tyranny' of roots, giving it a front-line role. Talking of Garrison's role in the Coltrane quartet, McCoy Tyner has said, 'He was like the pivot in the group. He had excellent time, good supportive work, knew the function of the bass.' Yet Garrison was also a powerful soloist both pizzicato and with a bow, and he was a master of double and multiple stopping, strumming the instrument with his thumb like a guitar. [IC]

With Coltrane on Impulse; with Shepp, *There's a Trumpet in my Soul* (1975), Arista; Jones/Garrison sextet, *Illumination* (1963), Impulse; with Jones, *Puttin' it Together* (1968); *The Ultimate* (1968), both Blue Note

Gaskin, Leonard, bass. b. Brooklyn, New York, 25 August 1920. A bassist remarkable for his versatility – and latterly a teacher of note – he took up bass in high school and worked first among the emergent bebop generation of the early 1940s including Duke Jordan, Dizzy Gillespie and Charlie Parker. He remained busy for another ten years, recording with Miles Davis and others, and in 1956 joined Eddie Condon with whom he toured in 1957 as well as staying busy with studio work. In the 1960s and after he remained a central figure in New York's bass fraternity and by the late 1970s was touring Europe, among others with the Oliver Jackson trio. [DF]

Gaslini, Giorgio, piano, composer, synthesizer. b. Milan, 22 October 1929. Piano lessons as a child; studied composition at Milan Conservatory of Music. Appeared at Florence Jazz Festival, 1947, with his own trio. 1957–60, active as a player and composer and a conductor of symphony orchestras. He composed and played the music for Antonioni's film *La Notte* (1960). From 1963, led his own quartet. 1965, wrote and performed the music for another film, Vermuccio's *Un Amore*. During the 1960s Gaslini took his music to the people, playing with his quartet in factories, hospitals, universities, cinemas and concert halls, in an attempt to make jazz part of the fabric of Italian life. He has played many festivals in Italy and elsewhere in Europe. He has also worked with Gato Barbieri, Max Roach, Don Cherry and others, and has been active in music education. He wrote the first Italian jazz opera, *Colloquio con Malcolm X*, which was performed in Genoa and recorded in 1970. He was friendly with Eric Dolphy, and after the saxophonist's death, composed 'I Remember Dolphy'. His favourites include Hines, Monk, Tristano and Coltrane, and other influences are Schoenberg, Varese, Webern and Ives.

Gaslini is a consummate pianist and composer, and his concept in both capacities is pluralistic; he is at home with any area or context – classical, neo-bop, total or partial abstraction. He remains active and at the height of his powers in the 1980s and has produced what Sam Syers has called 'three of the most outstanding albums of the decade' (see below). [IC]

Gaslini Plays Monk (1981), Soul Note; duo with Anthony Braxton, *Four Pieces* (1981), Dische della Quercia; *Schumann Reflections* (1984), Soul Note

Gay, Al (Albert), clarinet, tenor, alto and soprano sax. b. London, 25 February 1928. An original member of the Jive Bombers which won the *Melody Maker* All British championship of 1946, Gay later worked with Freddy Randall (1953–6), then Bobby Mickleburgh, Laurie Gold, Joe Daniels, Harry Gold, and caused a stir when in 1961 he joined Bob Wallis's younger Storyville Jazzmen, for whom he provided an elegant dash of sophistication. By 1965 Gay had joined more kindred spirits in Alex Welsh's new band: with Welsh he recorded prolifically, broadcast on radio and TV, toured alongside great American visitors including Earl Hines and Ruby Braff and produced a lot of definitive work. 1970s–1980s, he was freelance again, working with Stan Greig's large and small groups, Randall again and Ron Russell's band before rejoining Welsh in 1977, replacing John Barnes. He also led his own quartet for BBC work and clubs and in 1978 toured with the World's Greatest Jazz Band. Along with Danny Moss, Al Gay is Britain's most distinguished mainstream tenorman, but where Moss paints in the deep oils of Ben Webster or Arnett Cobb, Gay's lines come in more overt watercolour, somewhere between Zoot Sims and Eddie Miller. [DF]

At Home with Alex Welsh (1968), EMI

Geller, Herb(ert), alto and soprano sax, flute. b. Los Angeles, 2 November 1928. After working with Joe Venuti (1946) and others, moved to New York and played with Claude Thornhill, Billy May etc. 1951, returned to Los Angeles and was prominent with several small groups; led occasional quartet with his pianist wife Lorraine (*née* Walsh, b. 11 September 1928; d. 10 October 1958). Then on tour with Benny Goodman, Herb also played for Louie Bellson (1959, 1961), followed by move to Europe (1962); after studio work in Berlin, has worked since 1965 in studio bands of NDR (Hamburg) under various leaders including Peter Herbolzheimer. In the 1950s Geller was more Parker-influenced than many altoists based on the West Coast and, though not over-exposed as a soloist recently, has updated his style considerably. [BP]

Rhyme and Reason (1975), Discovery

Getz, Stan(ley), tenor sax. b. Philadelphia, 2 February 1927. Big-band experience began at age 15 and included work with Jack Teagarden (1943), Stan Kenton (1944–5), Jimmy Dorsey (1945), Benny Goodman (1945–6). Made first recordings under own name at 19. Joined Woody Herman band (1947–9), then began leading own quartet/quintet. Also worked as soloist in Scandinavia (1951), with Kenton (winter 1953–4) and with Jazz at the Philharmonic (1957–8, including

Stan Getz (Buddy Rich on drums)

trip to Europe). Out of circulation during 1954 owing to drug offences, Getz remained in Europe for three years (1958–61) and settled in Copenhagen. Returned to US to lead own quartet and make popular albums with Charlie Byrd, Luiz Bonfa, João and Astrud Gilberto (1962–4). Members of his regular group included Gary Burton (1964–6); Chick Corea (1966–7, 1971–72), Stanley Cowell (1969), Joanne Brackeen (1975–7) and Lou Levy (1981–3); Steve Swallow (1965–6), Miroslav Vitous (1968–9), Stanley Clarke (1972); Roy Haynes (1966–7), Jack DeJohnette (1969, 1975), Tony Williams (1972) and Billy Hart (1975–8). 1972, Getz started producing and leasing his own albums, and since then his successes of the 1960s have enabled him to live in semi-retirement and re-form his group for specific engagements. Artist in residence at Stanford University (1986).

Getz is one of the most renowned of jazzmen, and one of comparatively few who have achieved widespread acclaim while retaining the admiration of their fellow musicians. The reasons lie, on both sides, in his appealing sense of melody and his often exquisite tone. Neither was attained overnight, and many of his early records are closely based on the vocabulary of Lester Young but with a less expressive sound. But as early as the 1948 'Early Autumn' with Herman and his 1951 recordings in Sweden, the distinctive featherweight tone matches the floating quality of the lines. In the second half of the 1950s a more metallic ring underlines the acquisition of some overt blues influence, and both aspects are blended into a new melodic refinement in his mature 1960s style.

Despite the enormous popularity of his bossa nova albums of this period, such material always formed a small proportion of his repertoire. The paramount importance of melody in the pop outings and the much greater rhythmic development in his other work, especially live, created an artistic tension which gives his playing its present all-encompassing strength. Certainly his sound quality displays an extraordinary combination of emotive colour and cutting edge. [BP]

Getz/James Moody, *Tenor Contrasts* (1951), Esquire; *Focus* (1961), Verve: *Captain Marvel* (1972), Columbia/Verve; *The Dolphin* (1981), Concord

Ghanaba (aka **Guy Warren of Ghana**), drums, African percussion, composer, b. Accra, Ghana, 4 May 1923. At the Government Elementary Boys' School, Accra, 1928–39, and was leader of the school band in his last two years; 1940, drummer with the Accra Rhythmic Orchestra; 1941, won a teacher-training scholarship to Achimota College, Accra, but dropped out in 1943; visited the USA that year while working for the US army; 1943–52, back in Africa, he worked as a reporter, newspaper editor, radio disc-jockey, and musician – playing with one of the most famous African jazz groups, the Tempos. 1950, he spent some time in London, playing with Kenny Graham's Afro-Cubists. 1953, he took his own band, the Afro-Cubists, to play at the inauguration of President W. Tubman of Liberia, and stayed on there in the capital, Monrovia, working as a disc-jockey. 1955, he went to Chicago, joining the Gene Esposito band as co-leader, percussionist and arranger; 1956, with this band he recorded his album *Africa Speaks, America Answers*, which sold over a million copies and includes his composition 'That Happy Feeling'; 1957, he moved to New York, leading his own trio at the African Room and recording his classic album *Themes for African Drums* (1958). In the USA he was associated with many of the leading musicians of the time including Max Roach, Dizzy Gillespie, Lester Young and Billie Holiday. Since the early 1960s Ghanaba has lived on the outskirts of Accra, returning to the UK and USA only occasionally to record or play concerts.

Ghanaba has created a music all his own; it is profoundly African, but it is leavened with the linear improvisation of jazz and with some European harmonic elements. His music also has a surprisingly wide emotional and tonal scope, ranging from the violent energy and passion of 'Burning Bush' (percussion, brass, sax) to gentle tone poems such as 'I Love the Silence' (voice, African xylophone and guitar) and the joyous lilt of 'That Happy Feeling'. Historically, he is one of the fathers of black pride and was the main African influence on jazz in the USA and Europe in the 1950s. Max Roach wrote in 1974: 'I met Ghanaba in Chicago in

Ghanaba

1956 . . . Ghanaba was so far ahead of what we were all doing, that none of us understood what he was saying – that in order for Afro-American music to be stronger, it must cross-fertilize with its African origins . . . We ignored him. Seventeen years later, Black Music in America has turned to Africa for inspiration and rejuvenation, and the African sound of Ghanaba is now being imitated all over the United States wherever Afro-American music is played.' In 1981, Ghanaba was anointed as an Odomankoma Kyrema (a Divine Drummer) by Aklowa, the African Heritage Village based at Takely, near London. [IC]

Africa Speaks, America Answers (1956), Decca; *Themes for African Drums* (1958), RCA-Victor; *Afro-Jazz* (1968), Columbia; *The African Zoundz of Guy Warren of Ghana* (1972), EMI; *That Happy Feeling* (1978), Safari Records; *Ghanaba! Live at the Arts Centre, Accra!!* (1980), Safari

See Guy Warren of Ghana, *I Have a Story to Tell* (Guinea Press, Accra, 1966)

Gibbs, Mike (Michael Clement Irving), trombone, piano, composer/arranger. b. Salisbury, S. Rhodesia (now Zimbabwe), 25 September 1937. Piano lessons from age seven for ten years; trombone from 17. 1959–62, at Berklee School of Music, Boston; 1961, full scholarship to Lenox School of Jazz, where he studied with Gunther Schuller, George Russell, J. J. Johnson; also private studies in composition with Schuller. 1962, graduated from Berklee with Prof. Dip. in arranging and composition, and recorded his first album as arranger – for Gary Burton, with Phil Woods, Tommy Flanagan, Joe Morello. 1963, B.Mus. from Boston Conservatory; scholarship to Tanglewood Summer School studying with Aaron Copland, Iannis Xenakis, Schuller and Lukas Foss. Briefly back to Rhodesia, then he moved to UK in 1965, playing trombone with Graham Collier, John Dankworth, Cleo Laine, Tubby Hayes and working as a studio musician for radio, TV, films and albums – also getting arranging work in all those contexts. 1968–74, with his own bands he played concerts and clubs and did radio broadcasts in the UK and Europe; also performed his music with the radio big bands of Denmark, Sweden and Hamburg, and with the Hanover Radio Symphony Orchestra. Early 1970s, he won several *Melody Maker* awards, including best Big Band, Musician of the Year, First Arranger, First Composer; his LP *In the Public Interest* was voted best album of 1974.

By the late 1960s Gibbs was generally recognized as being one of the leading younger composer/arrangers in jazz. He had already absorbed his main influences (Gil Evans and Olivier Messaien – particularly the 'Turangalila') and found his own sound and style. His buoyant rock rhythms and his use of asymmetry anticipated the jazz-rock movement of the 1970s, and compositions such as 'Family Joy', 'Oh Boy!' and 'Tanglewood '63', showed an extraordinary melodic gift as well as great orchestral sonority. In particular, his writing for the lower instruments was often powerfully dramatic, and his work already showed considerable emotional resonance, ranging from the ominous brooding of 'On the Third Day' to the irrepressible high spirits of 'Family Joy', one of the most joyous compositions in jazz or any other music.

1974, he moved to the USA to take up the post of composer in residence at Berklee, but continued to do occasional tours and concerts with his own bands. 1975–8, he played the Berlin festival and twice toured the UK; 1978–81, he performed his music with the radio orchestras of Sweden, Finland and Cologne; 1982, he produced guitarist Kevin Eubanks's first solo album, and acted as musical director for the Young Lions at the Kool Jazz Festival concert, Carnegie Hall, producing a live double album for them.

1983, he resigned from his Berklee post to freelance in New York as composer/arranger/producer, and co-produced saxist Bill Evans's first album; his composition 'Interviews', commissioned by the Foundation of New American Music, was performed by the Orchestra (Los Angeles). By 1984, Gibbs had become a globe-trotting orchestrator and producer, commuting between the USA and Europe. He orchestrated a ballet for John Dankworth, and also Michael Mantler's composition for orchestra and soloists 'Twenty Five'; Gibbs conducted the first performance of this with the Cologne Radio Symphony Orchestra featuring Carla Bley, Steve Swallow, Nick Mason, Bill Frisell and Mantler.

Mike Gibbs

1985, he orchestrated Pat Metheny's film score for *Twice in a Lifetime*, and also John McLaughlin's Concerto for Guitar for the Los Angeles Philharmonic. He also moved back to London that year.

Mike Gibbs has composed and arranged music for four feature films, and for two ballets for the Ballet Rambert, London. His compositions have also been recorded by Gary Burton, Stan Getz, Cleo Laine, John Dankworth, Stanley Clarke and others. He has worked as an arranger on albums for many people including Joni Mitchell, Lenny White, Michael Walden, Peter Gabriel, Jaco Pastorius, Sister Sledge, Mantler and McLaughlin. Favourite trombonists are J. J. Johnson, Roswell Rudd, Chris Pyne, and other influences are Charles Ives, Miles Davis and Weather Report. [IC]

Michael Gibbs (1968), Deram; *Tanglewood '63* (1970), Deram; *Just Ahead* (1972), Polydor; Gibbs/Burton, *In The Public Interest* (1973), Polydor; *Will Power* (1974), Argo; with Burton, *Seven Songs for Quartet and Chamber Orchestra* (1974), ECM; Gibbs, *The Only Chrome Waterfall Orchestra* (1976), Bronze

Gibbs, Terry (Julius Gubenko), vibraharp (and drums). b. Brooklyn, New Jersey, 13 October 1924. From a musical family, won radio amateur contest at 12 and played drums professionally before army service in World War II. Small-group work on 52nd Street (1945–6) followed by touring jobs with Tommy Dorsey, Chubby Jackson, Buddy Rich (1948) and Woody Herman band (1948–9). Led own groups, also with Charlie Shavers–Louie Bellson and Benny Goodman (1951–2). Then own quintet/quartet and, after settling in Los Angeles (1957), part-time big band composed of jazz-inclined studio musicians. From 1964, became musical director on various television shows. An early enthusiast of bebop, Gibbs was nevertheless closer rhythmically to Lionel Hampton than Milt Jackson, but frequently an inventive soloist. His big band, which often included Mel Lewis on drums, was a precursor of the similar organization run by Lewis and Thad Jones, and was excellent of its kind. [BP]

Take It from Me (1964), Jasmine

Gig An engagement or a job. It may be 'a one-off gig' or 'a regular gig' or even a residency (the same band being employed at least one night every week at the same venue). It may be 'a money gig' or 'a jazz gig', and rarely do the twain ever meet.

Worst of all, from many musicians' point of view, would be having to take 'a day gig' (which does not mean playing jazz in the daytime but, on the contrary, living the 9-to-5 life) in order to support their musical activities. However, as more and more established performers undertake music teaching to a greater or lesser extent, the great divide has become a little blurred. [BP]

Gilberto, Astrud, vocals. b. Bahia, Brazil, 1940. Family moved to Rio when she was two. Her professional début as a singer occurred in 1963, at the beginning of the bossa nova impact on jazz, when she was asked to sing the English lyrics to 'The Girl from Ipanema' on an album Stan Getz was making with her then husband João Gilberto. Her deadpan delivery and girlish voice were an instant hit, and she subsequently toured several times with Getz, and played international festivals. [IC]

New Stan Getz quartet, featuring Astrud Gilberto, *Getz Au Go Go* (1964), Verve

Gilberto, João, vocals, guitar. b. Juaseiro, Bahia, Brazil, June 1931. First played drums in a local band, then taught himself guitar, developing into a solo performer. He evolved the style of singing and guitar rhythms that came to be associated in the late 1950s in Brazil, and the early 1960s in the US, with the bossa nova (new wave) movement. Gilberto came to the US in 1963 and recorded an influential album with Stan Getz which remained a best-seller for several years. [IC]

Getz/Gilberto (1963), Verve

Gillespie, Dizzy (John Birks), trumpet, composer, vocals, conga, piano. b. Cheraw, South Carolina, 21 October 1917. Father an amateur

Dizzy Gillespie

musician who played bass, mandolin, drums, piano, and through him Gillespie gained a working knowledge of several instruments; but he died when Dizzy was ten, and the boy was mostly self-taught as a musician. He started on trombone at 12½ and on trumpet about a year later. At 16 he won a scholarship (for sports and music) to Laurinburg Institute in North Carolina, and spent two years there playing music but not studying it. From 1935 he lived in Philadelphia, playing in small groups and a big band led by Frank Fairfax. He developed precociously and was soon a virtuoso soloist in the style of his idol Roy Eldridge, whose role in the Teddy Hill band he inherited early in 1937; he stayed with Hill for two years, visiting Europe and recording his first solos with the band. 1939–41, he was one of the three instrumental stars in Cab Calloway's band and his style was beginning to develop some of the elements of bebop; during this period he also began writing big-band arrangements, became friends with Charlie Parker, and was already sitting in at Minton's Playhouse, where he, Thelonious Monk, Kenny Clarke and others were working out their revolutionary new ideas. 1941–3, he was with various big bands including Benny Carter, Charlie Barnet, Lucky Millinder and Earl Hines; 1944, he worked with small groups on 52nd Street; June 1944, he joined Billy Eckstine's band, and by the end of that year Gillespie's fame had spread among musicians and fans, and bebop had gained cult status.

He left Eckstine in early 1945 and led a small group at the Three Deuces, then formed and toured with his first big band; in May, with his All Star Quintet which included Charlie Parker, Al Haig (piano), Curley Russell (bass), Sid Catlett (dms), he recorded the first full-blooded bebop tracks including 'Shaw 'Nuff', 'Salt Peanuts' and 'Hot House', which shook up the jazz world with their brilliant and alien virtuosity. December 1945, Gillespie took his sextet to California for eight weeks, with Parker, Milt Jackson (vibes), Ray Brown (bass), Haig and Stan Levey (dms), but the new music was so foreign to audiences that it had a very mixed reception. 1946, he re-formed a big band, touring and recording with it, and playing two months in Scandinavia at the beginning of 1948; it disbanded early in 1950.

The 1940s were for Gillespie a period of sustained and almost superhuman creative energy during which he changed the face of jazz in three ways: first, he created a totally original trumpet style which took virtuosity to undreamed-of limits, redefining the technical possibilities of the instrument; second, with Parker and others he established bebop as the valid contemporary style for both small groups and big bands; third, he changed the way jazz musicians behaved towards one another: whereas previous generations of musicians had been reluctant to share their knowledge with up-and-coming players, Gillespie proselytized, taught, encouraged musicians on all instruments, drawing them into the music and recommending them for various jobs. His generosity and his confidence in his own abilities were such that he assisted and nurtured the talents of potential rivals including Fats Navarro, Kenny Dorham, Miles Davis, Clifford Brown, and later Lee Morgan and Jon Faddis. If Bird was the intuitive genius of bebop, Dizzy was the organizing genius, the passionate rational force.

Virtually all his important compositions were written in that creative heyday – 'Night in Tunisia', 'Groovin' High', 'Woody 'n You', 'Salt Peanuts', 'Blue 'n Boogie', and others, most of which have become standard themes in the subsequent jazz repertoire. His solo style had reached its fully mature glory by the mid-1940s: the trumpet had never before been played with such speed, such flexibility, dynamism and drama. The whole essence of a Gillespie solo was cliff-hanging suspense: the phrases and the angle of approach were perpetually varied, breakneck runs were followed by pauses, by huge interval leaps, by long, immensely high notes, by slurs and smears and bluesy phrases; he was always taking listeners by surprise, always shocking them with a new thought. His lightning reflexes and superb ear meant that his instrumental execution matched his thought in its power and speed. And he was concerned at all times with swing – even when he was taking the most daring liberties with the pulse or beat, his phrases never failed to swing. Gillespie's magnificent sense of time and the emotional intensity of his playing came from childhood roots. His parents were Methodists, but as a boy he used to sneak off every Sunday to the uninhibited services in the Sanctified Church. He said later: 'The Sanctified Church had a deep significance for me musically. I first learned the meaning of rhythm there and all about how music could transport people spiritually.'

Since 1950 he has mostly led small groups, worked as a soloist with Norman Granz's Jazz at the Philharmonic, led occasional big bands and played one-off special projects at festivals and concerts. 1956, he formed a big band and did two long tours for the US State Department, the first from March to May in Pakistan, Lebanon, Syria, Iran, Turkey, Yugoslavia and Greece, the second in Latin America that autumn. This was the first time that the US government had used a jazz ensemble as its cultural representative, and as the tours were immensely successful they continued to use jazz in this capacity; a significant change in the music's status in America. Gillespie kept the big band going until January 1958, when he resumed leading a quintet.

During the early 1960s his pianist was the Argentinian Lalo Schifrin, a composer who wrote several pieces for Gillespie including 'Gillespiana' which was performed at the Monterey Jazz Festival, 1961, 'Tunisian Fantasy', an orchestral version of Dizzy's early composition 'Night in Tunisia', and in 1962 'The New Continent' which featured Gillespie as soloist with a large orchestra conducted by Benny Carter. The same year, Dizzy improvised a solo trumpet soundtrack for a short film showing the Dutch painter Karel Appel at work, which won first prize at the Berlin Film Festival. During the 1960s he also did projects with Gil Fuller, who had been the chief arranger of Gillespie's 1940s band, and took part in educational television shows.

During the 1970s he continued to tour worldwide and to appear at major festivals everywhere, both as a soloist and with his own groups. 1975, Gillespie was given the equivalent of a painter's retrospective exhibition: this was a 'Tribute to Dizzy Gillespie' concert in September at the Avery Fisher Hall, New York, and consisted of big-band and small-group performances featuring him with friends and associates from different stages in his career including Percy and Jimmy Heath, James Moody, John Lewis, Max Roach, Stan Getz and Lalo Schifrin. The same year, the award Musician of the Year from the Institute of High Fidelity was presented to him by Miles Davis in San Francisco. He had also received an honorary doctorate from Rutgers University in 1970, and the Handel Medallion from New York City in 1972.

Dizzy Gillespie is one of the most important figures in the entire history of jazz and, like Louis Armstrong and Miles Davis, he has influenced players on all instruments. There are other parallels with Louis; in fact, Gillespie's whole career is like a magnification and extension of Armstrong's. Louis created a whole trumpet style and a complete musical language in his small group recordings of 1925–8, and then spent the next decade refining and polishing it, after which there were no significant changes or developments. During the 1940s Dizzy created a new trumpet style and, with Parker and others, a new language for small groups and big bands; during the 1950s he continued refining his art, after which there were few significant changes. Dizzy has always been much more the conscious artist than Louis, and so there have been interesting new compositions since the 1940s ('Con Alma', 'Kush', 'Brother King') and some ambitious musical projects, but his playing and his conception have remained, in essence, the same. Both he and Louis have been accused by solemn jazz purists of demeaning themselves by clowning and humour in an attempt to 'commercialize' their music. Such accusations betray a dismal lack of understanding. To both men humour and clowning were the natural outcome of their high spirits and the way they viewed the world; and humour is a way of distancing and dealing with an often unsympathetic and sometimes openly hostile environment. The dizziness of Dizzy has helped him to survive, and he has done so without ever really breaking through to a wider audience: his has always been the cult following of the jazz world. Great artists are always of their time, never ahead of it; the general public always lags behind. In the 1980s, now that bebop is history, a known quantity, fixed and safe, it is becoming more popular, and its surviving creator, Dizzy Gillespie, is at last beginning to get his due recognition from a wider public. [IC]

Dizzy Gillespie, vols 1–2 (small groups, big bands and Metronome All Stars) (1946–9), RCA; *Dizzy Gillespie, vol. 3* (big band Paris concert) (1948), Jazz Reactivation; *Dizzy Gillespie and his Orchestra, Body and Soul* (with Sarah Vaughan) (1949), Bulldog; *Dee Gee Days, the Savoy Sessions* (1951–2), Savoy; with Parker/Powell/Mingus/Roach, *Quintet of the Year – Jazz at Massey Hall* (1953), Debut/OJC; Eldridge/Gillespie, *Trumpet Kings* (1954), Verve (double); *Dizzy Gillespie: World Statesman* (1956), Columbia; *The Greatest Trumpet of them All* (1957), Verve; Gillespie and his orchestra, *Portrait of Duke Ellington* (1960), Verve; *Dizzy on the French Riviera* (1962), Philips; quintet/James Moody, *Swing Low Sweet Cadillac* (1967), Impulse; *Giants of Jazz* (1972), Concord

See Gillespie, Dizzy, with Al Fraser, *DIZZY, To Be or Not To Bop, the autobiography of Dizzy Gillespie* (Doubleday, New York, 1979, W. H. Allen, London, 1980, Quartet, London, paperback, 1982)

Gilmore, John, tenor sax, drums. b. Summit, Mississippi, 28 September 1931. Raised from age two in Chicago, played saxophone in school and clarinet in army (1948–52). Worked with Earl Hines group (1952), then began in 1953 playing in quartet with Sun Ra, with whom he has been associated almost continuously ever since. Regular member of Art Blakey group (1964–5, including European tour). Has also recorded with Freddie Hubbard, Andrew Hill, Pete La Roca (album reissued as by Chick Corea) and under own name.

Apart from his role as auxiliary drummer with Sun Ra, Gilmore is known for two rather different styles of tenor playing. On performances of a straight-ahead post-bop character (which includes many of those with Sun Ra), he runs the changes with a fluency and tone halfway between Johnny Griffin and Wardell Gray. On more abstract material, he is capable of long passages based exclusively on high-register squeals, the aspect of his work which he claims influenced Coltrane. Especially when heard live, Gilmore is one of the few musicians who carries sufficient conviction to encompass both approaches. [BP]

Blowing in from Chicago (1957), Blue Note; Sun Ra, *Pictures of Infinity* (1968), Black Lion

Gismonti, Egberto, guitar, piano, Indian organ, vocals, percussion, composer. b. Carmo, Rio de Janeiro, Brazil, 5 December 1947. All his family were musical, playing popular Brazilian songs and some classical music. He had piano lessons from age six, studying classical music for 15 years; then spent two years in Paris, studying orchestration and analysis with Nadia Boulanger; also studied one year with composer Jean Barlaque. Back in Brazil he worked as an arranger and a concert artist. Gismonti was attracted by Ravel's ideas of orchestration and chord voicings, but at the same time was drawn to his Brazilian musical heritage – in particular to 'choro', a Brazilian form of funk music. 1967, he took up 6-string classical guitar in order to play choro, and in 1973 switched to 8-string guitar which has a range of five octaves, enabling him to play all kinds of moving bass lines, drones and inversions of chords. 1973–5, he experimented with different tunings and searched for new sounds, using flutes, kalimbas (thumb pianos), voice, bells etc. He also listened to Django Reinhardt, Jimi Hendrix, Wes Montgomery and John McLaughlin.

Gismonti has recorded and performed extensively in Brazil, and worked with Airto Moreira, Flora Purim and Paul Horn. 1976, he spent four weeks with the Xingu Indians in the Amazon jungle before recording his first album for ECM, *Danca Das Cabecas*, and has said, 'They influenced me a lot in ways of approaching my instruments, and in approaching myself. You can hear all of those tribal sounds . . . That particular album is like a walk through the jungle.' *DDC* was nominated Album of the Year by *Stereo Review* and also received the Grosser Deutscher Schallplattenpreis. 1979, with Charlie Haden (bass) and Jan Garbarek (reeds), he recorded two albums and toured Europe, also appearing at the Berlin Jazz Festival. 1981, he again toured throughout Europe with that trio. He has also composed and played background music for 11 films.

Gismonti is a virtuoso performer with a very pianistic guitar style, and his music is a delicate fusion of all the influences he has absorbed – folk music, classical, jazz, blues, African, Brazilian and various other ethnic musics. [IC]

Danca Das Cabecas (1976); *Sol Do Meio Dia* (featuring Nana Vasconcelos/Jan Garbarek/Collin Walcott/Ralph Towner) (1977); *Solo* (1978); with Garbarek/Haden, *Magico* (1979); *Folk Songs* (1979); *Sanfona* (1980/1); *Duas Vozes* (with Vasconcelos) (1984), all ECM

Giuffre, Jimmy (James Peter), clarinet, tenor sax, composer (and baritone sax, flute). b. Dallas, Texas, 26 April 1921. Studied music at North Texas College, played with name bands such as Jimmy Dorsey (1947), Buddy Rich (1948) and Woody Herman (1949). Settled on West Coast and worked with Lighthouse All Stars (1951–2), Shorty Rogers (1953–5) and recorded under own name. Led regular trio with Jim Hall and either Bob Brookmeyer or various bassists (1956–9); later trios with Paul Bley and Steve Swallow (1960–2), Don Friedman and Barre Phillips (1964–5), Kiyoshi Tokunaga and Randy Kaye (1970s). Active since 1960s as composer and academic, teaching at New England Conservatory in late 1970s–early 1980s.

Giuffre's career has covered many different phases, and it is perhaps understandable that not all have been equally noteworthy. His excellence as a straightforward big-band writer is exemplified by his classic original for Herman, 'Four Brothers', and its less well-known follow-up 'Four Others'. In the early 1950s and the 1960s Giuffre was an avowed experimentalist and, whether with the West Coast thinkers or the New York avant-garde, he sounded less than convincing; similarly, his composed works for large ensemble ('Pharaoh', 'Suspensions' and 'Hex') seem somewhat barren. But the subdued clarinettist and saxist, who discovered a folksy element in the work of Lester Young, mined one narrow vein that was not without its charm, as the continuing popularity of 'The Train and the River' demonstrates. [BP]

The Jimmy Giuffre 3 (1956), Atlantic; *Dragonfly* (1983), Soul Note

Gleason, Jackie, musical director. b. Brooklyn, New York, 26 February 1916. A survivor of burlesque shows who became a highly-rated TV and film actor (some of his best-known films include *The Hustler*, 1961, *Smokey and the Bandit*, 1977, *The Toy*, 1984), Gleason's recorded jazz connections stretch back to the 1950s when, to tie in with a long-running American TV series, Music for the Love Hours (for which he conducted a big string orchestra), Capitol Records produced a series of Gleason albums. Featuring a similarly lush string orchestra, and in the early days cornettist Bobby Hackett, the albums became best-sellers, but have been persistently downgraded since: 'the results belong more to the category of mood music than jazz music', says critic Jorgen Jepsen, a widely accepted view. But early Gleason albums such as *Rendezvous*, *Music to Make you Misty* and of course *Music for the Love Hours* contain irreplaceable examples of an irresistible combination, Bobby Hackett and the great American ballad. After financial disagreements ended the partnership, Gleason – a long-time jazz buff, 52nd Street habitué and smart operator – used other soloists including Pee Wee Erwin (who took over from Hackett), Don Goldie, Lawrence Brown, Toots Mondello, Charlie Ventura, Hank Jones and Jimmy Cleveland. The albums remain – right down to their kitschy covers – essential collectors' items. [DF]

Jackie Gleason Presents Music to Make you Misty (*c.* 1954), Capitol

Glenn, Tyree (Evans Tyree), trombone, vibes, vocals. b. Corsicana, Texas, 23 November 1912; d. Englewood, New Jersey, 18 May 1974. In his early years he worked with Tommy Myles, Charlie Echols, pianist Booker Coleman's Bellhops, Eddie Barefield's big band, Eddie Mallory, and two top names: Benny Carter, at the Harlem Savoy in 1939, and Lionel Hampton at the Paradise Nightclub, Los Angeles, with trumpeter Teddy Buckner. 1939–46, he worked with Cab Calloway's best big band, leading a trombone section of Quentin Jackson, Keg Johnson and Claude Jones, and playing the trombone features in Calloway's small group the Cab Jivers: after the war he was in Don Redman's band around Europe (along with Don Byas) and then, in 1947 joined Duke Ellington. He played the Tricky Sam Nanton role with academic perfection for four years, then left Ellington in Chicago in 1951 and from the year after was active in studio work (including Jack Sperling's CBS radio show, playing vibes), led his own quartet at the Embers and a quintet with Shorty Baker around New York, and, like Joe Bushkin and Georgie Auld, took up acting part-time. In 1965 he joined Louis Armstrong, playing vibes and trombone and unselfishly subjugating his solo career (there were regular solo albums by now) to do for Louis what Trummy Young had done before him. After Armstrong's death,

Glenn led his own small group until February 1974. He died six days before Duke Ellington and was laid to rest, amid much grieving, in the same funeral home as Ellington and Paul Gonsalves. His sons, Roger Glenn (flute/vibes) and Tyree Glenn Jnr., a tenor saxophonist, keep their underrated but popular father's memory alive, the latter with new issues such as *Great Jazz Classics – Great Automobiles* on the US Ty-Glo label: other fine memories are Glenn's own compositions, including 'Sultry Serenade' and 'Tyree's Blues', among many. [DF]

Tyree Glenn and his Orchestra (1957), World Record Club

Globe Unity Orchestra A large ensemble concerned with the freer end of the jazz spectrum, founded by German pianist Alexander von Schlippenbach in 1966 to perform his composition *Globe Unity* at the Berlin festival. It developed into an international ensemble with leading musicians from Germany, UK, USA, and Italy, including Albert Mangelsdorff, Kenny Wheeler, Evan Parker, Manfred Schoof, Paul Rutherford. It performed at the World Exhibition in Osaka, Japan, 1970. Until 1974 it worked mostly in Germany. 1975, Rheims festival with guest artists Enrico Rava and Anthony Braxton. 1977, a ten-day tour of the UK. Since then the orchestra has played several concerts in Paris, and festivals in Grenoble, Rome, Bologna, Berlin, Moers and Lisbon, and has toured the Far East for the Goethe Institute, and performed at Jazz Yatra in Bombay, India. [IC]

Globe Unity (1966), MPS; *Live in Wuppertal* (1973); *Hamburg '74*; *Evidence* (1975); *Into the Valley* (1975); *Pearl* (1977), all FMP; *Local Fair* (1975), PO Torch; *Improvisations* (1977), Japo; *Compositions* (1979), Japo

Godding, Brian, electric and acoustic guitars, guitar synthesizer. b. Wales, 19 August 1945. Self-taught, he started in a rock band in the 1960s. At the beginning of the 1970s he played in Keith Tippett's Centipede, and joined Mike Westbrook's Solid Gold Cadillac. He has continued working with Westbrook's various bands since then. Godding has also worked with many other UK musicians. He has co-written numerous songs with Kevin Coyne. His taste in guitarists runs from McLaughlin and Allan Holdsworth to Jeff Beck and Jimi Hendrix. [IC]

Mike Westbrook Orchestra, *Citadel/Room 315* (1975), RCA; *The Cortege* (1982), Original; *On Duke's Birthday* (1985), Hat Art

Gold, Harry, bass, tenor saxophones, clarinet, reeds, leader, arranger, composer. b. London, 26 February 1907. He played early on with a British dance band, the Metronomes, at the Astoria, Charing Cross Road, and later with Roy Fox and Geraldo. His Pieces of Eight (in which he played tenor as well as bass sax) was formed first in 1940 as band-within-a-band for Oscar Rabin, and featured early on such well-known names as Geoff Love (tmb), Norrie Paramor (piano) and Bert Weedon (gtr). They achieved solid commercial success but in jazz terms sometimes fell between the two stools of post-war jazz revivalism, for which they were too polished, and modern jazz. Gold, a busy worker in the music industry and in-demand arranger, rather slipped from view in the 1960s until Dick Sudhalter (a champion of pre-war British musicians) featured him in the New Paul Whiteman Orchestra, 1975. Soon after Gold re-formed his Pieces of Eight, with trumpeter Al Wynette and other old colleagues Bob Lazell and Don Lowes, for a trial run at the Yorkshire Grey pub in the Gray's Inn Road, and a successful round of albums, festival appearances and broadcasts into the 1980s re-established the Pieces of Eight under Gold's firm leadership as Britain's most polished Dixieland band. [DF]

Octagonal Gold (1980), Black Lion

Goldberg, Stu, keyboards, composer. b. Massachusetts, 1954, raised in Seattle, Washington. Began on piano and trombone at age ten; at 12 took up organ, influenced by Jimmy Smith and Jimmy McGriff, but continued to study classical music. At 16 he was featured at the Monterey Jazz Festival in a quartet with Ray Brown, Louie Bellson and Mundell Lowe. He studied jazz for two and a half years at the University of Utah, graduating *magnum cum laude*. 1974, moved to Los Angeles and joined John McLaughlin's Mahavishnu Orchestra, touring the USA and Europe with it in 1975, then leaving to freelance. Since then has toured the US with Miroslav Vitous, Europe with Alphonse Mouzon, and worked with Al DiMeola. 1978, he joined Freddie Hubbard; also played a successful series of solo concerts in Europe and recorded his first album as leader. Influences include Herbie Hancock and Joe Zawinul. [IC]

With Mouzon, Charlie Mariano and others; with Mahavishnu, *Inner Worlds* (1975), Columbia; with McLaughlin, *Johnny McLaughlin; Electric Guitarist* (1978), Columbia; *Stu Goldberg: Solos, Duos and Trio* (with L. Coryell/L. Subramaniam) (1978), MPS

Goldie, Don (Donald Elliott Goldfield), trumpet. b. Newark, New Jersey, 5 February 1930. He was the son of Harry 'Goldie' Goldfield, Paul Whiteman's assistant conductor, entertainer-comedian and trumpet player, who at one stage was short-listed to lead Bob Crosby's future band. After playing in a wide variety of groups, from country blues to Lester Lanin and Buddy Rich (a regular colleague), Don joined Jack Teagarden in 1959, fulfilling the leader's need for a sure-lipped trumpet player with showman experience and ideas to spare. With Teagarden, Goldie recorded brilliantly (his solos on set pieces such as 'Blue Dawn', 'High Society' and 'Riverboat Shuffle' are startlingly brilliant), often playing his solos into a muffler mute of his own invention which gave him a distinctive shaded sound. His work with Teagarden (right up to their last album together, *Think Well of Me*, a Willard Robison collection) focused attention on Goldie's brilliance (his technique in all but range was close to Al Hirt's or Charlie Shavers') and after Teagarden's death more fine recordings followed for Argo, and for Jackie Gleason. In the 1970s Goldie was trumpet king of Miami; in the 1980s he continued to lead his own Jazz Express 6-piece and played festivals (including Sacramento, 1985). A Goldie solo is a joyful model of melodic ingenuity spiced with perky-tongued triplets, audacious vibrato and rhythmic awareness: sometimes in the early days with Teagarden his approach was simply too exuberant for tight-lipped jazz critics. [DF]

The Legendary Jack Teagarden (1960–1), Roulette (double)

Goldkette, Jean, leader, piano. b. Valenciennes, France, 18 March 1899; d. Santa Barbara, California, 24 March 1962. A classically-trained French pianist, he spent his childhood years in Greece and Russia, arrived in America in 1911 at the age of 12 and a few years later, leading a dance band in Chicago, caught the eye and ear of entrepreneur Edgar Benson who led the mightily successful Benson Orchestra of Chicago. Goldkette – bespectacled, full of charm and quick with business acumen – became Benson's MD, moved to Detroit to run a second Benson orchestra there, and after a successful run at the Book-Cadillac Hotel acquired the lease of an unfinished Chinese restaurant. This he converted into the Graystone Ballroom (which quickly became the premier Detroit venue for visiting bands) and Goldkette staffed it with his Victor Recording Orchestra, which achieved a legendary reputation (on one famous occasion they 'cut' Fletcher Henderson's band on Henderson's home ground at New York's Roseland). The orchestra – a fantastic collection of stars including at various times Bix Beiderbecke, Frank Trumbauer, Danny Polo, Joe Venuti, Eddie Lang, Tommy and Jimmy Dorsey, Don Murray, Bill Rank and arranger Bill Challis – did record for Victor but the records (at the behest of Victor's A & R man Eddie King) were often confined to commercial titles. Goldkette widened his operations quickly and dramatically: according to Rex Stewart, 'he created several orchestras, built many ballrooms and operated through the Midwest on such a large scale that he became the most important impresario in the area bounded by Buffalo, Chicago, Toronto and New York.' By the 1930s Goldkette had stopped creating bands (most of the Victor Orchestra was with Whiteman by 1928) and confined himself to agency work and classical piano performance. [DF]

The Bix Beiderbecke Legend (1924–7), RCA Victor

See Stewart, Rex, *Jazz Masters of the 30s* (Macmillan, 1972, repr. Da Capo, 1982)

Golson, Benny, tenor sax, composer, arranger. b. Philadelphia, 25 January 1929. First toured with r & b band of singer Bull Moose Jackson. Did summer season with Tadd Dameron (1953), then with Lionel Hampton band (1953–4). Briefly replaced his friend John Coltrane with Johnny Hodges (1954) and replaced Stanley Turrentine with Earl Bostic (1954–6). Played and arranged for Dizzy Gillespie big band (1956–early 1958), also during this period writing for record sessions by Donald Byrd, Oscar Pettiford, Art Farmer etc. Following 18 months with Art Blakey (1958–9), his own quintet with Curtis Fuller became the Jazztet through addition of Farmer (1959–62). Gradually gave up playing to concentrate on writing, first for jazz-related big-band and vocal albums, then for television commercials and serials. Then returned to playing in late 1970s, making records and touring including visits to Europe (1982 with reunited Jazztet, 1985 solo).

Golson's tenor work originally followed the lines of Lucky Thompson, and then adopted some of the Byas-derived developments of Coltrane. But it took second place to his writing even in the 1950s, when he created many well-received originals reminiscent of the harmonic approach of Dameron (though his actual arrangements more often recalled John Lewis). His tunes were frequently recorded by others at this period and then fell into disuse, as with those of his colleague Gigi Gryce. 'I Remember Clifford', inspired by Clifford Brown, is the most long-lived, although the modal 'Killer Joe' has been more successful with non-jazz listeners. [BP]

Benny Golson's New York Scene (1958), Contemporary/OJC; Jazztet, *Moment to Moment* (1983), Soul Note

Gomez, Eddie (Edgar), bass. b. Santurce, Puerto Rico, 4 October 1944. Brought up in New York, joined Newport Festival Youth Band at age 14 (1959–61), studied at Juilliard School (1963). Gigged with Rufus Jones sextet (1963), Marian McPartland trio (1964), Gary McFarland sextet (1965). Also active on 'free jazz' scene with Paul Bley (1964–5), recording with him and with Giuseppe Logan (both featuring drummer Milford Graves). Then joined Bill Evans trio and remained for over a decade (1966–77). Continued to make albums with other performers such as Jazz Composers' Orchestra, Jeremy Steig, Bennie Wallace etc. Chosen by Charles Mingus to deputize for him shortly before his death (1978). Increasingly busy with studio work from late 1970s onwards, Gomez was a founder member of group Steps (later Steps Ahead) and made several tours of Japan and Europe with them (1979–84).

His early work followed the example of Scott La Faro in exploiting the upper range of the bass and playing it with the melodic fluency expected of any other instrument. It was fitting, therefore, that he inherited La Faro's position with Bill Evans, for he seemed (perhaps because of superior amplification) to further this approach with even greater aptitude and authority. Moving gradually into the fusion area, he demonstrated that in the right hands the amplified acoustic bass loses nothing in comparison with the electric axes of Jaco Pastorius or Eberhard Weber. He now seems less flamboyant than either of these players, though his technique remains as staggering as ever. [BP]

Bill Evans, *California Here I Come* (1967), Verve; Steps Ahead, *Modern Times* (1984), Musician

Gonella, Nat (Nathaniel Charles), trumpet, mellophone, leader, vocals. b. London, 7 March 1908. He was born in a rough area of Bow, London, brought up in a Board of Guardians school and played first in a junior review band (Archie Pitt's Busby Boys). He became intrigued by jazz and Louis Armstrong after hearing 'Wild Man Blues' in a Nottingham record shop while on tour. (At 15, Gonella even resembled Louis physically.) After Pitt broke up the band in 1928, Gonella joined Bob Dryden's band at the Dreamland, Margate (Dryden was later to play drums in the Georgians), left to join Archie Alexander's band at Brighton, and was signed by Billy Cotton (with whom he first recorded) for a season at the Streatham Locarno. After two more career jumps (with Roy Fox and headlining success with Lew Stone's band), Gonella formed his Georgians: first as a band-within-a-band for Lew Stone, later as an independent unit featuring Pat Smuts (tenor) and Harold 'Babe' Hood (piano). The Georgians – hugely successful – packed theatres, broadcast and appeared in films up to the war: Gonella's trumpet – a highly original variant of the Armstrong prototype – would later inspire Humphrey Lyttelton, Kenny Ball and others. After the war, Gonella's big band, the New Georgians, operated successfully enough until – in line with jazz fashion – he formed a bebop band – a brief and unhappy flirtation with what he was later to call 'gas oven music'. Then came a spell on the halls with comedians Max Miller and Leon Cortes until in 1959 his jazz career was relaunched by agent Lyn Dutton with a 6-piece Armstrong-style New Georgians, an appearance on TV in This is Your Life and a record contract with EMI (including an Armstrong-style 'Autobiography' album produced by Denis Preston). Gonella's newly-found success was curtailed by the eruption of the Beatles and the collapse of the Trad boom. For the next 15 years he lived in Lancashire, recorded infrequently and played northern clubs: in 1977 a trip to Holland (for Ted Easton) put his newly-recorded 'Oh Monah' at number 5 in the Dutch hit parade. In 1984 a tour by Digby Fairweather's New Georgians celebrated his music: in 1985 a biography by Ron Brown, television and a set of reissues (lovingly assembled by EMI's Hugh Palmer and others) continued the celebration. [DF]

Nat Gonella

Mister Rhythm Man (1934–5), EMI

See Brown, Ron, with Cyril Brown, *Georgia on my Mind: the Nat Gonella Story* (Milestone, 1985)

Gonsalves, Paul, tenor sax (and guitar). b. Boston, Massachusetts, 12 July 1920; d. London, 14 May 1974. Played in Boston's Sabby Lewis band both before and after World War II service. Then joined Count Basie (1946–9), followed by several months with Dizzy Gillespie (1949–50) and 24 years with Duke Ellington. Most of his few brief absences during this long period were associated with drug and alcohol addiction but, thanks to Ellington's tolerance and encouragement, he was musically more in control than many others in his situation.

Although Gonsalves initially guaranteed himself a place in Duke's band through his knowledge of Ben Webster's work, it was the harmonically involved experimentation of Don Byas which most strongly influenced him. His development of this approach, however, was more extreme than anyone else of a similar persuasion. Every note could be justified logically, but the angularity of Paul's style was such that he was flirting with atonality long before either Coltrane or Dolphy. As a result, he has received belated recognition from much younger players such as David Murray.

One of the roles taken by Gonsalves in the Ellington band was that of the combative and inexhaustible rabble-rouser featured, from the early 1950s onwards, in extended versions of 'Take the A Train' and 'Diminuendo and Crescendo in Blue', the latter becoming especially popular. While these medium up tempos were very suitable for highlighting his serpentine phrasing, it was on ballads especially that his vocalized but fragile tone was most affecting. In addition, they allowed free rein to his polyrhythmic skill, so that the slow 'Happy Reunion' or 'Chelsea Bridge' became saxophone showpieces in the grand tradition, but sounding like no one else before or since. [BP]

Gettin' Together (1960), Jazzland/OJC; Gonsalves/Ray Nance, *Just a-Sittin' and a-Rockin'* (1970), Black Lion

Gonzales, Babs (Lee Brown), vocals. b. Newark, New Jersey, 27 October 1919; d. 23 January 1980. After singing in various clubs on both East and West Coasts, organized own group, Three Bips and a Bop, including Tadd Dameron and Rudy Williams (1946–8), who first recorded 'Oop-Pop-A-Da' later covered by Dizzy Gillespie. Vocalist and road manager with James Moody band (from 1951); also participated in record sessions by Jimmy Smith, Bennie Green, Johnny Griffin. Working as soloist thereafter, including frequent visits to Europe; one of first US performers at Ronnie Scott's (1962). Usually published his own albums on a variety of labels, as well as two books which he also distributed. A tireless promoter and pusher of jazz into unlikely outlets, his efforts in that direction were probably more important than his actual performing. Several other activities on the fringe of showbusiness included work as chauffeur to actor Errol Flynn; for fuller details, see his autobiographies (below). [BP]

Bennie Green, *Soul Stirrin'* (1958), Blue Note

See Gonzales, Babs, *I, Paid My Dues . . . Good Times, No Bread* (Expubidence, 1967); Gonzales, Babs, *Movin' On Down de Line* (Expubidence, 1975)

Goode, Coleridge (George Emmerson), violin, bass. b. Jamaica, 29 November 1914. Father organist and choral conductor, mother a soprano. Started on violin. 1934–40, electrical engineering at Glasgow University, Scotland. 1940, studied bass privately. 1945–6, played and broadcast with the Stephane Grappelli quartet and recorded with Django Reinhardt and the Quintet of the Hot Club of France. 1958, began his long association with Joe Harriott's quintet which pioneered abstract, free-form jazz, then in the mid-1960s blazed another new trail with Indo-Jazz Fusions, playing festivals all over Europe. In the 1960s Goode also worked and recorded with Michael Garrick. He pioneered double-bass amplification, first using it on a broadcast in 1946. Favourite bassists are Jimmy Blanton, Slam Stewart and Ray Brown, and like Stewart, Goode usually plays bowed solos singing in octave unison with his bass. [IC]

Four 78 rpm tracks with the Hot Club of France, six LPs with Michael Garrick, nine with Joe Harriott, including *Free Form* (1960), Jazzland; *Indo-Jazz Suite* (1965), Columbia

Benny Goodman

Goodman, Benny (Benjamin David), clarinet, alto sax. b. Chicago, 30 May 1909; d. 20 June 1986. He took up the clarinet at 11, studied under a great teacher, Franz Schoepp (who also taught Buster Bailey and Jimmie Noone), and by 13 was working professionally. Apart from Frank Teschemacher – who in any case lacked Goodman's steel nerves – there was no clarinettist in Chicago to challenge his potential, and by 1925 he was working for Ben Pollack, a man six years his senior (and less talented) who quickly latched on to Goodman as a central feature of his show. Goodman – still a jazz missionary, ambitious, and with a healthy disregard for authority as well as an ego – treated his leader with ill-concealed disregard, took recording dates using Pollack's men but never Pollack, and in 1929 resigned (along with Jimmy McPartland) after his aggrieved leader had complained that his protégés had appeared on stage in grubby shoes. From then on Goodman worked with Red

Nichols, then in the studios for five years, using the money he earned to support his mother and 11 brothers and sisters after his father had been killed in a taxi accident. In 1934 – at twenty-five – he was leading his own band for Billy Rose's Music Hall which broadcast weekly for NBC and attracted attention with a closing hour of hot arrangements. The night that Goodman, despairing after a nondescript tour, threw in one of his hottest at a dance at the Palomar Ballroom, Los Angeles, he caused a riot in the student audience. For the next five years, first in Chicago, then in New York, he dramatically achieved a national, then an international reputation, playing (to riots again) at the Paramount Theater, New York, and in 1938 at a legendary (recorded) Carnegie Hall concert at a time when jazz was still largely foreign to concert-hall settings. By now Goodman, with the aid of John Hammond, a rich young talent scout, had strengthened his team to include trumpeter Harry James, showman-drummer Gene Krupa (one of his nearest friends in the period) and, in a much-publicized but important step, black musicians such as Teddy Wilson and Lionel Hampton; the Benny Goodman small groups – featuring Wilson, Hampton and Krupa and a dramatic later addition, electric guitarist Charlie Christian among others – created a second revolutionary new sound of the period.

By now Goodman was also beginning to acquire a near-legendary reputation (among musicians) for being 'difficult'. Singer Helen Forrest left, so she said, 'to avoid a nervous breakdown', Harry James had left in 1938 claiming that he'd 'never really understood Benny' and pianist Jess Stacy was later to remember of the period: 'Benny was a terrific leader – but if I'd had any spunk I'd probably have thrown the piano at him!' Goodman, a reticent, often aloof man, was a skilled perfectionist who expected the best, and may have seen his own early struggles as a justification for not being soft with others: he also insisted (not unreasonably) on being the centre of attention in any orchestra he formed. By 1940 (after a bout of back trouble) he had rebuilt his orchestra, and although the replacement names never created the definitive impact of first-generation stars such as James and Krupa, newer additions including Cootie Williams, Billy Butterfield, Lou McGarity, Jimmy Maxwell, Charlie Queener, Aaron Sachs, Red Norvo, John Best, Peanuts Hucko and Frank Beach continued to set unfaultable standards: a later 1942 hit for his new singer Peggy Lee was a blues-based 'Why don't you do right?' By the end of the decade Goodman was determinedly (and effectively) incorporating bebop into his programmes, featuring titles such as 'Undercurrent Blues', 'Shishkabop' and 'Oo-bla-dee' and musicians such as Doug Mettome, Milt Bernhardt and Wardell Gray. As well as accommodating the vagaries of jazz fashion he was moving into the world of classical music. In 1942 he had been scheduled to play concerts with José Iturbi and in 1947 commissioned Béla Bartók to write 'Contrasts for clarinet, violin and piano'. As a classical performer, Goodman could fully explore his first love – clarinet playing – away from the pressures of bandleading and was safe from the swiftly changing jazz times. From then on, during three hugely successful decades of international touring, there was regular evidence of Goodman as a sometimes absent-minded and shortfused professor. He also appeared in films (including *A Song is Born*, 1947) and in 1955 Hollywood filmed *The Benny Goodman Story*; after more than a decade of overseas touring in 1962 the King of Swing toured Russia for the US State Department – huge triumphs to set alongside the occasional press which questioned Goodman's pattern of leadership.

By 1964 Benny Goodman was appearing in classical concerts with his daughter Rachel (to whom he had once dedicated his little swing tune 'Rachel's Dream') and continued to tour Europe through the 1960s and 1970s: a 1978 Carnegie Hall concert, 40 years on from the great original, was amiably chaotic. In the 1980s he was still mounting occasional concerts and shining brightly in another new small group featuring Scott Hamilton and Warren Vaché, still playing as brilliantly as ever, and still, as he was in Harry James's 1938 observation, 'practising more than 15 times more than the entire Goodman orchestra combined'. Although late Benny Goodman conveys little of the hot urgency that informs his early work – his later playing sometimes levels into a mildly interested urbanity – he remained the old master of the jazz clarinet: a virtuoso who, according to Warren Vaché, could still play rings around the opposition right up to his death. [DF]

Carnegie Hall Concert, 1938, CBS (double)

See Connor, D. Russell, and Hicks, Warren W., *Benny Goodman On the Record* (Arlington, 1969); *Benny: King of Swing*, introd. Stanley Baron, (Thames & Hudson, 1979)

Gordon, Dexter Keith, tenor and soprano sax. b. Los Angeles, 27 February 1923. Joined new Lionel Hampton band at age 17 (1940–3). Then briefly with Lee Young sextet (1943) and toured with bands of Fletcher Henderson (1943–4), Louis Armstrong (1944) and Billy Eckstine (1944–5). Moved to New York as freelance soloist, working with Charlie Parker and others (1945) and making regular recordings under own name. Returned to Los Angeles (1946), freelancing with drummer/singer Cee Pee Johnson (1947) and others. Started informal partnership with Wardell Gray lasting on and off until 1952, when Gordon began first of two sentences for drug offences (1952–4, 1956–60). Both comebacks led to recordings, those of 1960–2 being particularly well received. First trip to Europe (autumn 1962) found Gordon settling in Copenhagen for a total of 14 years with only brief returns to USA in 1965, 1969 and 1970. Huge acclaim for his visit of 1976–7 encouraged him to move back and, after several years of successful playing, he was virtually in retirement from 1983 until taking the lead role of US musician in Franco-American film *Round Midnight* (1986).

Dexter's style in the mid-1940s was probably the most popular approach to the tenor, influencing many players whose primary allegiance was to Lester Young (such as Sonny Stitt, early Stan Getz and especially John Coltrane). His combination of bop-inspired lines with an essentially pre-bop time feeling produced an inherent tension which was excruciatingly enjoyable. His tone quality, always vibrantly hot even when playing ballads, remained virtually unchanged for 40 years, despite adopting a few mannerisms from Coltrane in the 1960s and occasionally taking up the soprano. His authoritative delivery, however, only increased with the passing years. [BP]

Long Tall Dexter (1945–7), Savoy; *Our Man in Paris* (1963), Blue Note; *Homecoming* (1976), CBS

Gospel One of the absolutely central expressions of Afro-American music, gospel has a longer continuous history than either jazz or blues. Though not under the same name, it can trace its roots back to the pre-ragtime spirituals such as 'Walk all over God's Heaven', and to 18th-century English Protestant hymns including 'Amazing Grace'.

What is more remarkable is that both these forms of material continued to evolve well into the second half of the 20th century, unlike the minstrel-show music which was their secular equivalent. Obviously, the consciousness underlying black secular music has had to reflect greater changes than the eternal message of religious music, yet the latter has never been unaffected by the society it serves and there has been a constant musical cross-fertilization between what became gospel and what became jazz and blues.

This is a vast subject which has yet to be studied in any depth. But it is worth remarking, for instance, the place of spirituals in the repertoire of early New Orleans marching bands; the jazz-blues background of gospel 'founder' Thomas A. Dorsey (b. 1 July 1899) and the jazz-blues awareness of great soloists such as Mahalia Jackson; and the call-and-response patterns which ensemble jazz borrowed from choral gospel music. Indeed, the whole tension between ensemble and soloist (and the question of whether the latter becomes a superstar at the expense of the former) is another way in which gospel runs parallel to jazz; it also provides a way past the lyrics and into the musical beauties of gospel. [BP]

Gottlieb, Danny, drums, b. New York City, 18 April 1953, raised in Union, New Jersey. Began on drums at 14, playing in high school band; during his last years at school, studied with Joe Morello and Mel Lewis. 1971, went to University of Miami, Florida, graduating B.Mus. in 1975; while there, he played with Paul Bley, Jaco Pastorius, Ira Sullivan, Pat Metheny, and also gained much experience playing shows on Miami Beach. 1975, moved to New York working with Joe Farrell, Clark Terry, Pat Martino and others. 1976, joined the Gary Burton quartet; 1978, toured Europe with Eberhard Weber's Colours. With Pat Metheny, he broke away from Burton's group in order to form the Pat Metheny Group, with Lyle Mays and Mark Egan. The group toured extensively in the USA, Europe and Japan and played most major festivals, becoming one of the most successful jazz groups of the 1970s and early 1980s. He left Metheny and from 1984 was a member of John McLaughlin's reconstituted Mahavishnu Orchestra. [IC]

With Gary Burton, *Passengers* (1976); with Metheny, *Watercolors* (1977); *Pat Metheny Group* (1978); *American Garage* (1980), all ECM; with McLaughlin, *Mahavishnu* (1984), Warner Bros

Goudie, Big Boy (Frank), tenor sax, clarinet, trumpet. b. Royville, Louisiana, 13 September 1899; d. San Francisco, 9 January 1964. He was taught trumpet by Bunk Johnson, was working in Papa Celestin's Tuxedo Band by 1910, played in New Orleans for ten years and by 1921 was touring with minstrel shows. 1925, he moved to Paris and from there played in Europe with a variety of famous leaders including Noble Sissle, Sam Wooding and Willie Lewis until the outbreak of war, when he took refuge in Brazil and Argentina. 1946, he was back in France working for Arthur Briggs, Glyn Paque (in Switzerland) and Bill Coleman, among others; 1951–6, led his own band in Berlin. That year he came back to America and San Francisco to play with more than 20 different bands and run a furniture upholstery business from home. [DF]

Willie Lewis and His Entertainers (1935–7), Swing-Disques

Gowans, Brad (Arthur Bradford), valve trombone, clarinet, cornet, saxes. b. Billerica, Massachusetts, 3 December 1903; d. Los Angeles, 8 September 1954. A dandy who sported a small gaucho moustache and was mad on sports cars, in the 1920s he played all his instruments in bands led by Tommy de Rosa, Jimmy Durante, Mal Hallett, Joe Venuti and others. He retired for a time before coming back to join Bobby Hackett in Boston's first great jazz band at the Theatrical Club in 1936: from then on, valve-trombone was his first choice. In New York by 1938 he was working for Hackett again,

Wingy Manone and Eddie Condon, and the year after was founder member of one of the best bands that ever played anywhere, the Summa Cum Laude led by Bud Freeman. From then on he was regularly at the heart of 52nd Street life, played on Jimmy Ryan's first ever jam session (with Shavers, Higginbotham, Hackett and others), worked as staff arranger – very successfully – for Ray McKinley and played for Condon (on his first jazz concerts, at the opening of his new club and everywhere else too) for much of the rest of the 1940s. Spells with Jimmy Dorsey (in 1948) and Nappy Lamare (from 1949) followed, by which time Gowans was living in Los Angeles. His last date was with Ed Skrivanek's band in 1954: he died of cancer after a long illness. [DF]

Condon/Jimmy McPartland/George Wettling, *Chicago Jazz* (1939–40), Coral

Goykovich, Dusko (Dusan Gojkovic), trumpet, composer. b. Jajce, Yugoslavia, 14 October 1931. Active in Europe during the 1950s. 1961–3, studied at Berklee School of Music; played with Maynard Ferguson, 1963–4; with Woody Herman, 1964–6. Played in Europe for eight months with Sal Nistico in International Jazz Quintet, 1966; then with Clarke–Boland band until it disbanded in 1973. Also worked with Mal Waldron, Jimmy Woode, Philly Joe Jones and others. From 1967, lived in Europe, leading his own groups, composing, arranging and teaching. Co-led a Euro-American 12-piece band with Slide Hampton, 1974–5. Influences are Roy Eldridge, Dizzy Gillespie, Kenny Dorham, Clifford Brown and Miles Davis. Goykovich is a fine all-round player, at home with big bands and small groups. With his own groups he has combined elements from Slavonic folk music, both rhythmic and melodic, to produce a highly individual synthesis. His album *Swinging Macedonia* has all the jazz virtues, but is strongly flavoured with Eastern European rhythms and scales. [IC]

With Clarke–Boland, Herman and others; as leader, *Swinging Macedonia* (1966), Enja; Alvin Queen/Goykovich, *A Day in Holland* (1983), Nilva

Grappelli, Stephane, violin. b. Paris, 26 January 1908. He played harmonium at ten, acquired his first ¾-size violin at 12 and soon after was studying at the Paris Conservatoire where he majored in *solfège*. At 16 he was working summer seasons, playing in silent cinemas and in Paris courtyards for centimes until Stephane Mougin, a young fellow musician, introduced him into the Gregorians, a big band modelled on Jack Hylton's and led by a flamboyant French dancer-entrepreneur Gregor, in which Grappelli first played piano, then violin. Soon after, at the Croix du Sud club, he met Django Reinhardt and one night at the Hotel Claridge their acquaintance turned into a musical partnership. 'We were all in the dressing room waiting to go on,' Grappelli remembered later, 'and Django was as usual plucking at his guitar. I just started improvising on the chords, and Louis Vola thought it would be fun to add his bass fiddle to our duo: he joined in and so did Django's brother. Thus was born a new jazz!' The little group (with the addition of a third guitarist, first Roger Chaput, then a variety of others) was adopted by the newly-formed Hot Club of France which presented it at a Salle Pleyel concert (with Coleman Hawkins); from then on the Quintette du Hot Club de France, as it became known, was a sensational success at chic clubs such as Bricktop's and Chez Florence playing its quiet but spectacularly creative music. The partnership between Grappelli and Reinhardt often threatened to founder: Grappelli – conscientious, hard-working, reliable and never really one of the boys – played to lengths that suggested rivalry with Reinhardt and worried constantly about his partner's gypsy tendencies. But they worked together, recording prolifically and achieving international fame until 1939 when, caught on the hop by the war, Grappelli stayed in London. 'I don't think he did very much to begin with,' says Denny Wright, his guitarist-partner of the 1940s and 1970s, 'but later he played the club at 96 Piccadilly and then moved into Hatchett's with George Shearing and a quartet (including me for a year) and worked all through the Blitz. After that he took the show on tour of the Moss Empires.' By 1946, Grappelli and Reinhardt were reunited for concerts in Britain and at home, but the guitarist seemed to have lost the urgent motivation of pre-war, enjoyed fishing and painting as much as working and, despite regular recording and clubwork, their partnership operated on a more casual basis until, just before a projected American trip, Reinhardt died. Since then, said Grappelli in 1964, 'I've passed my time between Paris, Italy and England, working steadily: nightclubs, concerts, radio and TV.' It seemed as if his career had reached a comfortable plateau, but in 1972 British-based guitarist Diz Disley, a lifelong Reinhardt follower, brought Grappelli to Britain to play the rounds of local folk clubs (jazz clubs expressed little interest in the idea) with a Reinhardt-style quartet featuring, apart from himself, Denny Wright (gtr) and John Hawkesworth (bass). After the unexpected success of that tour – 'it was the first time he'd gone back to the Hot Club format,' explains Wright – Grappelli rapidly turned back into a superstar, played Carnegie Hall in 1974 and with his quartet – Disley, Wright (later Ike Isaacs) and Len Skeat (bass) – toured America and Europe playing the best halls and theatres. Grappelli albums soon to follow included collaborations with talents as different as Bill Coleman, Gary Burton and Teresa Brewer: prestige sets with Yehudi Menuhin also sold hotly (Menuhin's solos were pre-written). As the 1980s progress Grappelli's soaring improvisational talent – backed by Martin Taylor as well as Disley – seems to have matured like vintage French wine: his colossal technique, sculptured lines and elegant repertoire are one of jazz's most gracefully creative sounds. [DF]

Feeling + Finesse = Jazz (1962), Atlantic Jazzlore; or any from the 1970s/80s

Graves, Milford Robert, drums, percussion. b. Jamaica, New York, 20 August 1941. Self-taught, initially playing congas and subsequently studying Indian tabla as well as drum-kit. Worked on dance gigs, also with Hugh Masekela and Miriam Makeba (early 1960s). Then involved in avant-garde scene with New York Art Quartet, Paul Bley, making albums with them and with reedman Giuseppe Logan (the last-mentioned being first jazz recording of Graves, Eddie Gomez and Don Pullen). Also with original 1964 edition of Jazz Composers' Orchestra Association. Performed in duo with Don Pullen (1966), duo with Andrew Cyrille, trio with Cyrille and Rashied Ali. With Albert Ayler (1967–8), regular duo work with reed-player Hugh Glover. Taught at Black Arts Repertory Theatre (late 1960s) and at Bennington College, Vermont, alongside Bill Dixon (1970s). Tours of Europe (1973, 1974) and Japan (1977). From 1983, played with all-percussion quartet Pieces of Time featuring Andrew Cyrille, Don Moye and Kenny Clarke (later Philly Joe Jones).

Probably the most influential of the early 'free jazz' drummers, Graves has a highly mobile style which is not perceived in any schematic manner. Technically complex and demanding, his playing nevertheless interacts constantly with the musical activity around him and thus stimulates further activity, without being overbearing. As a soloist he has been a pioneer of extended percussion-only performances from the time of his first album. [BP]

Percussion Duo (1964), ESP

Gray, Glen, see CASA LOMA ORCHESTRA.

Gray, Wardell, tenor sax. b. Oklahoma City, 13 February 1921; d. 25 May 1955. Raised in Detroit and, after working locally, toured with Earl Hines band (1943–5). Settled on West Coast and made first records under own name (1946, only released in Europe). Freelancing with Benny Carter (mid-1940s, 1955), Billy Eckstine septet (1947) and others, regular jam-sessions and recording from 1947 with Dexter Gordon. Briefly with Benny Goodman, Count Basie, Tadd Dameron (all 1948), then longer stays with Goodman (1949) and Basie octet (1950–1). Further gigs on West Coast during last years. Cause of death rumoured to be drug overdose while working in Las Vegas in company with heroin addict, dancer Teddy Hale (not to be confused with bandleader Teddy Hill).

Though not as immediately influential as his partner Gordon, Wardell converted their common interest in Lester Young into a more mobile style than most of his contemporaries. His great fluency, combined with a mellow yet compact tone, enabled him to fit easily in a bebop context, and to bring its flavour into the swing-oriented groups with which he usually worked. His tune 'Twisted', now a standard thanks to singers Annie Ross and Joni Mitchell, is an excellent example of Gray at his best. [BP]

Memorial, vols. 1/2 (1949–53), Prestige/OJC

Green, Bennie, trombone. b. Chicago, 16 April 1923; d. 23 March 1977. Joined Chicago-based Earl Hines band at 19 (1942–3, when sidemen included Gillespie and Parker), rejoined several times (1946–8, 1951–3). Worked with Charlie Ventura (replacing Kai Winding, 1948–9), Gene Ammons–Sonny Stitt (1950) and own quintets from mid-1950s to early 1960s. After a period of inactivity, reappeared with own group (1968) and played with Duke Ellington (1969), before working in Las Vegas hotel bands. Green was probably the first trombonist to consort with beboppers, and the first whose ear enabled him to adopt aspects of their harmonic approach. Nevertheless he retained a swing-era phraseology and a warm singing tone, which adapted well to the r & b-influenced repertoire of his later groups. [BP]

J. J. Johnson/Winding/Green/Willie Dennis, *Four Trombones* (1953), Prestige

Green, Charlie 'Big' (or **'Long'**), trombone. b. Omaha, Nebraska. *c.* 1900; d. New York, February 1936. He had a thorough training in tent and carnival shows around Omaha and by the time he joined Fletcher Henderson in 1924 was one of the finest blues players ever. One of the 'A'-team of Henderson's soloists (along with Coleman Hawkins, Buster Bailey, Joe Smith and Louis Armstrong), he was humorously unflappable, with a vast appetite for life, food and drink, and the ability to make a joke of practically anything, including, says Dickie Wells, his own mortality. Green's blues can be heard to perfection on a number of sides made with Bessie Smith (his most famous recorded feature with her was 'Trombone Cholly') and with all the other blues singers for whom Henderson was staff pianist at Black Swan. But more than that he was a fine all-round trained player who could play almost anything in any key, read a score at sight and play a straight waltz just as well as he could play jazz. Green, who relished solo playing and tended to make short work of opposition, saved most of his energetic rivalries for music; he kept a feud going with tubaist Ralph Escudero (who, says Louis Armstrong, sometimes doubled Green's trombone parts on his tuba) and later sparred with Jimmy Harrison. After he left Henderson for the last time in 1930, 'Big' Green worked with heavyweight bands led by Don Redman, Chick Webb, Benny Carter and others and was working with Kaiser Marshall's band when in 1936 he passed out on his doorstep one snowy night and froze to death. [DF]

Fletcher Henderson, *A Study in Frustration* (1923–38), CBS (4 records, boxed set)

Green, Dave (David John), double bass. b. London, 5 March 1942. He had no formal lessons, started playing at 16 and turned professional four years later. 1963–9, he was with the Rendell–Carr quintet; 1965–83, with Humphrey Lyttelton's band; 1967–78, with Stan Tracey's quintet, octet and big band; from 1964 on, with Michael Garrick. He formed his own band, Fingers, in 1979, and did a British Council tour of Yugoslavia with it in 1984. Green has also worked with many Americans from mainstreamers such as Benny Goodman, Coleman Hawkins, Ben Webster, Pee Wee Russell, to modernists such as Roland Kirk, Sonny Rollins, George Coleman and Milt Jackson. He played at the Nice Jazz Festival, 1984, and the following year he played with the Jim Galloway–Carl Fontana group at the Berne Jazz Festival. In the summer of 1985 he toured Europe with Didier Lockwood and Gordon Beck. His favourite bassists are Jimmy Blanton, Ron Carter, Charlie Haden, and Wilbur Ware is also an influence. [IC]

With Ben Webster, *Webster's Dictionary* (1970), Pye; with Stan Tracey, *Under Milk Wood* (1976), Steam; as leader, *Fingers Remember Mingus* (1979), Spotlite; with Marvin Hannibal Peterson, *Poem Song* (1981), Mole

Green, Freddie (Frederick William), acoustic guitar. b. Charleston, South Carolina, 31 March 1911. He came to New York in his teens, working by day as an upholsterer and by night in jazz clubs including the Yeah Man, Exclusive Club and Black Cat in Greenwich Village. There he was heard by impresario John Hammond, who recommended him to Basie as a replacement for Claude 'Fiddler' Williams. Basie reluctantly auditioned him in a Roseland dressing room – and the next day Green was on the band bus bound for Pittsburgh. He stayed for 13 years, cementing the smooth pulse of Basie's all-American rhythm-section: 'They had a kind of throb going,' says Nat Pierce, 'no one instrument louder than the other, so it was a real section!' 'Freddie, Walter and Jo would follow Basie until he hit the right tempo, and when he started they *kept* it', emphasizes Harry Edison. In future years when less reliable timekeepers joined Basie, Green's metronomic guitar was his leader's familiar rock. Comfortable in the Basie band – he played softball in the band team, went swimming with friend Harry Edison and crabbing with Preston Love (as well as having a love-affair with Billie Holiday early on) – it was a shock to Green when Basie's small group of 1950 excluded him: he climbed back on the stand one night, uninvited, and never allowed himself to be left out again. For the next 35 years the sight of 'Old Freddie Green sitting there like a sheep dog looking round to see that nothing is going wrong' (Don Byas) was as familiar as the confident ring of chords produced by his agile left hand on the guitar strings. He stayed until Basie died, and in 1985 was still recording, in Manhattan Transfer's tribute to Basie, 'Rambo'. [DF]

Any with Count Basie

Green, Grant, guitar. b. St Louis, Missouri, 6 June 1931; d. 31 January 1979. Worked with Jimmy Forrest in home-town (1950s), making record début when Forrest cut Chicago session with Elvin Jones etc (1959). Played in organ groups of Sam Lazar (1960) and Jack McDuff (1961), recording with them and with Lou Donaldson, Stanley Turrentine and drummer Dave Bailey. Began making albums under own name, including such musicians as Yusef Lateef, Joe Henderson, Hank Mobley, Herbie Hancock, McCoy Tyner, Elvin Jones, and organists John Patton and Larry Young. Career interrupted by drug problems (late 1960s) but enjoyed most popularity in 1970s until hospitalization (1978). Some later recordings have really tedious pseudo-funk backings, Green graces them with the performances they deserve; but he was capable of moving in very fast company musically, and some albums, unreleased at the time, which have appeared recently (mostly in Japan) make this even more evident. [BP]

Born to be Blue (1962), Blue Note

Green, Urbie (Urban Clifford), trombone, bandleader. b. Mobile, Alabama, 8 August 1926. A trombone student by the age of 12, he progressed with amazing speed: after four years with Gene Krupa (1946–50), he joined Woody Herman, taking over Bill Harris's featured chair. At not much over 24 he had developed the perfected approach of Jack Teagarden without sounding like either an imitator or an exhibitionist. As with Teagarden, everything Green played sounded like the only musical way to play it, and he added some new gifts of his own to Teagarden's master-method: an ability to play high up in the trombone super-register without effort (and never for effect), an ear-boggling speed of execution, and a joyfully developed use of the slide – more pronounced than Teagarden's – which was specially welcome in an era when most of Green's contemporaries were trying to sound like valve-trombonists. All this was quickly spotted by musicians and critics; Green won the *Downbeat* New Star poll for 1954 and soon after was a regular colleague of Benny Goodman, appeared in *The Benny Goodman*

Story (1955) and led Goodman's orchestra for a three-month tour in 1957. By then – working in studios as well as with his own orchestra – Green was a star in his own right, appeared on record with musicians 20 years his senior (including Buck Clayton and Jimmy Rushing) and produced a string of albums of his own which have since turned into trombonists' textbooks. By the 1960s he was often bandleading still, fronting Tommy Dorsey's orchestra, and in 1969 was with a rock-based small group at New York's Riverboat experimenting with electronic octave-dividers. From the 1970s Green – who by now had taken up farming too – was most often to be seen and heard teaching at clinics, leading his own small groups, appearing at prestigious one-offs, including Duke Ellington's 70th birthday celebrations at the White House, and playing the best jazz festivals: his regular reappearances on record are always brilliant. [DF]

Urbie Green and Twenty-one Trombones! (1968), Project 3

Greer, Sonny (William Alexander), drums. b. Long Branch, New Jersey, 13 December *c.* 1895; d. New York, 23 March 1982. Duke Ellington's first drummer, and for many his greatest ever, Greer was four years older than Ellington and arrived in New York with Elmer Snowden's band well before the young pianist. So he was well qualified to become a senior member of Ellington's 'family': a fast-talking hipster who knew the latest jive talk, hustled in pool halls to get his drums out of hock and drank with the best. Greer worked with Ellington's 5-piece Washingtonians, a band he loved for their quiet and subtle arrangements, and then moved, with a few reservations, into the Cotton Club with the augmented orchestra, for which he built up a $3000 edifice of drums supplied by Indiana's Leedy Drum Company (for whom Greer was a designer), chimes, vibes, tympani and gong. To see him at the centre of Ellington's highly dramatic presentation recalled an African giant beating sacrificial drums, and was an inspiration to later drummer-showmen like Gene Krupa. Greer, a powerful drummer, was fundamental to all Ellington's greatest work until 1950: that year, conscious of Greer's heavy drinking and occasional fallibility in performance, as well as changing fashion, Ellington took a second drummer, Butch Ballard, on a Scandinavian tour. The bad quarrel that followed – much worse than their regular 'cussings-out' according to Mercer Ellington – ended the partnership. For the next 20 years Greer freelanced with Johnny Hodges' small band, Red Allen, Tyree Glenn and others, and appeared in films (including *The Night They Raided Minsky's* and an 11-minute feature, *Sonny*, for Midget productions, both in 1968). From 1974 he joined Ellington scholar Brooks Kerr for a hugely successful tribute to his old boss which conquered the USA. 'I never heard a better drummer for the Ellington band than Sonny Greer', says Don Byas. 'It was funny, for alone or with another band he was nothing exceptional. But he fitted with the Duke as has no one else!' [DF]

Any with Duke Ellington

See Dance, Stanley, *The World of Duke Ellington* (Scribner's, 1970, repr. Da Capo, 1980)

Greig, Stan (Stanley Mackay), piano, drums bandleader. b. 12 August 1930. He grew up in Edinburgh, joined Sandy Brown's school band at Royal High School in 1945 and came south to London to join Ken Colyer (on drums) in 1954. From then on he worked with Humphrey Lyttelton (1955–6), the Fairweather–Brown All Stars (1956–60), Acker Bilk (1960–8) and from 1969 had his own trio and quintet (featuring Colin Smith and Al Gay), playing mainstream jazz and specializing in boogie-woogie. 1975, Greig formed the London Jazz Big Band, a top-rate 15-piece orchestra (with arrangements by him, John Picard, Al Fairweather, Tony Milliner and others) which played clubs, concerts and a BBC Jazz Club; but despite such musicians as Picard, Milliner, Fairweather, Gay and Smith in the ranks it never achieved the recognition it deserved and was never recorded. In 1985, Greig – a highly respected member of Britain's senior jazz community – had completed a spell with George Melly and was once again with Humphrey Lyttelton [DF]

Blues Every Time (1985), Calligraph

Grey, Al (Albert Thornton), trombone. b. Aldie, Virginia, 6 June 1925. His early years, during World War II, were spent in a Navy band and after demobilization he joined Benny Carter: subsequently he worked with Lucky Millinder, Jimmie Lunceford, Arnett Cobb and Lionel Hampton, then, after a spell with Dizzy Gillespie, 1956–7, he joined Count Basie, a vital career move. His pungent plungermute contributions to Basie masterpieces such as 'Blues in Hoss' Flat' made Grey the most striking band soloist of the period along with Lockjaw Davis. He stayed until 1961, by which time he had established an international reputation and recorded – as leader – albums such as *Thinking Man's Trombone*. After 1961 he worked in studios, toured for Jazz at the Philharmonic, played occasionally with George Wein's Newport All Stars and built his soloist's reputation on TV and as winner of a *Downbeat* poll: by the mid-1970s he was touring regularly with Jimmy Forrest in duo and in the 1980s, after Forrest's death, teamed with Buddy Tate for more tandem appearances. A regular star of the festival and club circuit from then on, Grey still commutes tirelessly from country to country, always producing the same high-octane performances, and enjoying his fame. A booting, high energy soloist – often billed in the 1980s as 'The last of the great plungers' – Grey is a post-war jazzman who works often (as his

Al Grey

byline suggests) in the trombonistic area previously occupied by such great names as 'Tricky Sam' Nanton. In 1985 – as for many years past – he was resident for several weeks at Peter Boizot's Pizza Express, London, again with Buddy Tate and in 1986 appeared at the Edinburgh Jazz Festival and all over the festival circuit. [DF]

With Tony Coe, *Live at Pizza Express* (1979), Pizza Express

See Dance, Stanley, *The World of Count Basie* (Sidgwick & Jackson, 1980)

Griffin, Chris (Gordon), trumpet. b. Binghampton, New York, 31 October 1915. A new trumpet talent on the 1930s New York scene – he was playing with Charlie Barnet's big band in his late teens – from 1936, Griffin formed one-third of Benny Goodman's legendary trumpet section with Harry James and Ziggy Elman. With Goodman he was featured sparingly – although programme items such as 'Blue Skies' and 'Blue Room' included solos for him – but it would have been difficult for any trumpeter not to be at times overshadowed by the bravura presence of James ('Sing Sing Sing' and others) and Elman ('And the Angels Sing') and reviewers of the time, including George T. Simon, occasionally – and rather unnecessarily – drew attention to the fact. Griffin was 'a thorough musician' (in Dave Barbour's phrase) and after he left Goodman in 1939 concentrated on studio work, following up an earlier connection with CBS; he stayed with the company for 30 years and co-ran a trumpet school with Pee Wee Erwin in the 1960s and 1970s. After Erwin's death in 1981, Griffin replaced his partner in Warren Vaché Senior's small group based in New Jersey – a valuable late opportunity to hear his solo talents in the kind of setting they deserved. [DF]

Benny Goodman, *Carnegie Hall Concert, 1938*, CBS (double)

Griffin, Johnny (John Arnold III), tenor sax. b. Chicago, 24 April, 1928. On the road at age 17 with Lionel Hampton (1945–7), then with breakaway Hampton group of trumpeter Joe Morris (1947–50) which enjoyed great success in r & b field. After stays with Jo Jones (1950) and Arnett Cobb (1951), was stationed in Hawaii (1952–4) and returned to Chicago, leading his own group and also working there with Thelonious Monk (1955). Toured with Art Blakey (1957), then Monk quartet (1958). Worked as soloist in Chicago and elsewhere, until formation of Eddie Davis–Johnny Griffin quintet (1960–2). Autumn 1963, followed in footsteps of Dexter Gordon by touring Europe and staying on, based in Holland and then France. Regular member of Kenny Clarke–Francy Boland band (1967–72) and other occasional all-star groups. Also guest soloist with various European rhythm-sections, sometimes reunited with Eddie Davis (1977, 1984) and Arnett Cobb (1984). From 1978 onwards, began to spend part of each year touring in USA with own quartet.

Although he is fully conversant with the tenor tradition of Hawkins, Byas, Webster and Young, it has often been remarked how close in spirit Griffin's playing is to that of Charlie Parker. The headlong rush of ideas, and the rhythmic variety and freedom that goes with them, all point in this direction. In addition his tone combines a vocalized sound with a slightly hysterical edge that, at his best, can evoke almost uncontrollable exhilaration – except perhaps for other tenor players, since Griffin is one of the fastest and most accurate ever on his instrument. [BP]

You Leave Me Breathless (1967), Black Lion; *Return of the Griffin* (1978), Galaxy

Grimes, Henry Alonzo, bass. b. Philadelphia, 3 November 1935. Studied at Juilliard School (1953) and gigged with Arnett Cobb, Willis Jackson. Played with Gerry Mulligan quartet (1957), Charles Mingus (with Mingus on piano, 1957), Tony Scott (1958), Sonny Rollins trio (1958–9, including 1958 Newport festival where he also backed Thelonious Monk). Worked with Cecil Taylor (1961–2), then rejoined Rollins, whose group then included Don Cherry (1962–3, including European tour). Gigging with Steve Lacy quartet (1963) and further work with Taylor. During 1965 recorded with, among others, Albert Ayler, Archie Shepp, Frank Wright, Mose Allison, Perry Robinson and first of three albums with Cherry. Appears to have been inactive in jazz since the late 1960s, which is a cause for great regret since the strength gained from his wide experience was evident in whatever context he performed. [BP]

Sonny Rollins, *Live in Stockholm* (1959), Dragon; Cecil Taylor, *Unit Structures* (1966), Blue Note

Grimes, Tiny (Lloyd), guitar, vocals. b. Newport News, Virginia, 7 July 1916. He started playing four-string guitar ('I always tell people I can't afford the other two strings', was his standard explanation) in 1937, after several years as a drummer, and taught himself everything he knew. Eight months later he joined a string group, The Cats and a Fiddle, but soon after teamed with Slam Stewart (after Stewart's former partner Slim Gaillard had gone into the army) and the two of them then joined Art Tatum to form a legendary trio: their fantastic interplay and Tatum's occasional stylish singing were, in Frank Driggs's words, 'the talk of the jazz world'. After Tatum, Grimes's bluesy guitar was all over 52nd Street until clubs began closing: when work slowed he went to Cleveland and in Atlantic City formed an embryo rock and roll show, The Rocking Highlanders, who played in kilts and anticipated acts such as Jackie Dennis and Lord Rockingham's Eleven by ten good years. In the 1950s Grimes continued touring and playing small-group residencies until a serious illness in 1964, but he recovered in two years to return to New York clubland, and to one-nighters with Jay McShann and Milt Buckner. From 1970 he was back in the swing of jazz festivals and club dates with Earl Hines and others. [DF]

One is Never too Old to Swing (1977), Sonet

See Dance, Stanley, *The World of Swing* (Scribner's, 1974, repr. Da Capo, 1979)

Grossman, Steve(n), saxes, b. Brooklyn, New York, 18 January 1951. Started on alto in 1959, studying with brother Hal, who later taught at Berklee. Took up soprano sax at 15 and tenor a year later. November 1969, made his first recording with Miles Davis. March to September 1970, member of Davis's group, playing on some key albums. 1971, with Lonnie Liston Smith; 1971–3, with Elvin Jones; 1975, formed Stone Alliance with Gene Perla and Don Alias. Influences, Coltrane, Rollins, Wayne Shorter. Grossman was much maligned by critics during his stint with Miles Davis, yet, although only 19, he made a very positive contribution to the music, playing with great emotional intensity and creating some excellent melodic lines. [IC]

As leader, *Some Shapes to Come* (1973); *Terra Firma* (1975–6), both PM; with Davis, *Jack Johnson, Live-Evil, Miles Davis at Fillmore* (all 1970), all CBS; with Jones, *Merry-Go-Round* (1971); *Live at the Lighthouse* (1972), both Blue Note

Grosz, Marty, guitar, banjo, vocals, composer. b. Berlin, 28 February 1930. A fine rhythm guitarist (one of the few left) and constantly surprising soloist, he worked for years in Chicago in comparative obscurity. Although early albums such as *Hooray for Bix* on Riverside clearly showed where he was bound, it was after Grosz joined Soprano Summit at the invitation of Bob Wilber that his name started turning up in jazz households. He took an active part in Wilber's project, writing a number of fine arrangements, but after three years and eight more albums went back to freelancing around New York, often with Dick Sudhalter (including Sudhalter's New California Ramblers), Kenny Davern, and his own groups. His later solo albums (notably *I hope Gabriel likes my music!* by Marty Grosz's Blue Angels) featured numerous Grosz trademarks: enquiring repertoire, intriguing originals written by him, friendly, very jazzy singing, and fine arranging as well as a likeable sleeve cover of his own devising. Grosz is also (like Wellstood and Sudhalter) a jazz journalist whose writings mark him out as something extraordinary: in recent years just one musical project with Sudhalter, a kindred spirit, is the Classic Jazz Quartet or Bourgeois Scum featuring clarinettist Joe Muryani and pianist Dick Wellstood: quality music with a sense of humour. [DF]

I hope Gabriel likes my music! (1981), Aviva

Gruntz, George Paul, piano, church organ, harpsichord, Rhodes piano, synthesizer, composer. b. Basle, Switzerland, 24 June 1932. Studied music at Basle and Zurich Conservatories. Won several prizes at Zurich jazz festivals during the 1950s, but did not become a fully professional musician until 1963. He was a member of the European all-star group called Newport International Band, performing at the Newport Festival and in New York. Since then he has appeared at most major jazz festivals throughout the world. 1968–9, he was a member of Phil Woods's original European Rhythm Machine. Since 1970 he has also been Musical Director of the Zurich Schauspielhaus; and since January 1972 he has been artistic director/producer of the Berlin Jazz Festival. Also in 1972, Gruntz, together with Swiss musicians Flavio and Franco Ambrosetti and Daniel Humair, formed an all-star big band called the Band which toured Europe that year and in 1976. 1978, he took the band over, calling it the George Gruntz Concert Jazz Band. 1973, he created the Piano Conclave: from a pool of ten leading European pianists, he drew six for the Conclave performances, and they used 20 keyboard instruments from harpsichord to synthesizer, working with a rhythm-section. The Conclave played major festivals all over Europe. He has also played with Don Cherry, Roland Kirk, Mel Lewis and others.

Gruntz is a prolific composer/arranger, writing for all kinds of ensembles from small groups and big bands to symphony orchestras. 1974, he was given an Arts Council of Great Britain composition award and wrote *The Rape of Lucrece* which was performed in London in 1975 at the Shakespeare birthday celebrations concert at Southwark Cathedral. 1977, he was commissioned to write a long piece for a percussion orchestra, and the premiere of *Percussion Profiles* was given at the Monterey festival. He has also written a jazz opera and a ballet work, collaborated with various composers including Hans Werner Henze, and composed for art-film soundtracks and for contemporary theatrical productions. He has won polls in the USA and Europe for composing, arranging, his keyboard work and his big band. [IC]

Noon in Tunisia (1967), MPS; *Jazz Goes Baroque* (1964), Philips; Piano Conclave, *Palais Anthology* (1976), MPS; Concert Jazz Band, *Live at the Quartier Latin, Berlin* (1980), MPS; *Theatre* (1983), ECM; with Phil Woods, *At the Montreux Jazz Festival* (1969), MGM

Gryce, Gigi, alto sax, flute, composer. b. Pensacola, Florida, 28 November 1927; d. 17 March 1983. After extensive studies including in Paris, his reputation was secured by his stays with Tadd Dameron and Lionel Hampton (both 1953), the latter also giving rise to many small-group recordings by band members arranged by Gryce and Quincy Jones. Wrote and played for Oscar Pettiford band (1955–7), and during same period co-led Jazz Lab quintet with Donald Byrd, expanding to 9-piece line-up for records. Led own quintet (1959–61), but then became less active on music scene. Gryce's alto work, although passionate and articulate in a Parkerian vein, was largely overshadowed by his writing, which appeared on albums by Clifford Brown, Art Farmer, J. J. Johnson etc. In particular a couple of tunes, 'Speculation' and 'Nica's Tempo', enjoyed a considerable vogue in the mid-1950s and were recorded by several groups. [BP]

The Rat Race Blues (1960), New Jazz/OJC

Guarente, Frank (Francesco Saverio), trumpet. b. Montemilleto, Southern Italy, 5 October 1893; d. USA, 21 July 1942. According to John Chilton, he came to the USA in 1910 and while living in New Orleans in 1914 took advice from King Oliver. After a lot of freelance work he joined violinist Paul Specht's highly successful orchestra in 1921 and became the centrepiece of Specht's hot band-within-a-band, the Georgians. Including trombonist Russ Morgan and pianist Arthur Schutt the Georgians recorded for Columbia, played a long residency at the Alamec Hotel on Broadway and visited London for a 1923 summer season. 1924–7, Guarente led the New Georgians in their own right in America and Europe, including a 1926 summer in Scheveningen (a Dutch jazz stronghold that later played host to jazzmen such as Ray Noble and Nat Gonella); 1927, he came to London to join the original Savoy Orpheans (alongside trumpeter Max Goldberg). After a trip to Prague the group broke up on return to London and Guarente took his Oliver-flavoured trumpet into the Savoy and other major London venues before returning to the USA in 1928. For the next 12 years he was active in studio work with (among others) Victor Young and the Dorseys: a period of ill health caused his retirement early in the 1940s. [DF]

George Gruntz

And the Georgians, 1922–7, VJLP (3 volumes, cassette only)

Guarnieri, Johnny (John Albert), piano, composer. b. New York City, 23 March 1917; d. 7 January 1985. He heard Fats Waller when he was 15 and turned professional two years later to work with George Hall, Farley and Riley ('a comedy band and not really for me'), Benny Goodman in 1939 and Artie Shaw in 1940. Shaw had got himself a remarkable pianist (and harpsichordist on the immortal 'Gramercy 5' titles) who at the drop of a downbeat could play in any style to order. Versatility and a vivid imagination assured him work and after a non-stop period seeing in 'the dark hours to dawn' along 52nd Street, doubling with Raymond Scott's CBS orchestra (he slept in a CBS lounge to make the calls) and recording all over, Guarnieri moved into studio work as a staffman for NBC. His jazz interests never flagged, however, and through the 1950s occasional albums illustrated his bravura abilities: 'in performance he might offer a lighter-than-air "My Funny Valentine" with the left hand only, a 5/4 treatment of "Maple Leaf Rag" and then perhaps "I'm just wild about Harry" with a dozen key changes', observed critic Floyd Levin. In later years, Guarnieri, a warm-hearted and enthusiastic communicator of his love for music and people, taught selflessly: his pupils responded by financing a label, TazJazz, to record him. By 1970 the pianist had recorded an album of 5/4 originals, composed a 5/4 piano concerto premiered in Los Angeles in 1970, and by the early 1970s was enchanting visitors at the Tail of the Cock club in Studio City, California, where he worked regularly until 1982. He collapsed and died suddenly on a date with Dick Sudhalter in New York: there was great grief. [DF]

Gullin, Lars Gunnar Victor, baritone sax, composer (and piano). b. Visby, Sweden, 4 May 1928; d. 17 May 1976. Began on clarinet and played alto regularly until taking up the baritone at age 21. Played with Arne Domnerus sextet including Rolf Ericson (1951–3), then formed own quintet (1953). Thereafter worked principally as guest soloist with local rhythm-sections, also frequent recording including with visiting Americans such as Clifford Brown. Toured in Italy with Chet Baker (1959), and subsequently made considerable impression as composer. Much of Gullin's career was shadowed by narcotics (the fictional saxist of the Swedish film *Sven Klang's Combo* is based on Gullin) and some periods in which he was inactive as a player were only survived with the aid of artists' grants from the Swedish government.

The first European musician after Django Reinhardt to have an impact in the USA without relocating there, Gullin has never been duplicated or surpassed. His facility and relaxation, especially in the 1950s, were able to make the baritone feel like a delicately handled tenor. But his tone (thanks to the Tristano influence detectable in many Swedish and German musicians of this period) was so light and pure that it recalled not so much a tenor as altoist Lee Konitz. Konitz in turn was an admirer of Gullin, and participated in a posthumous album of Gullin tunes, under the title of one of them, *Dedicated to Lee* (1984, Dragon). Local commentators detect the inspiration not only of folk-music but of 19th-century Swedish composers in Gullin's distinctive writing. [BP]

The Great Lars Gullin, vol.1 (1955–6), Dragon; *Jazz Amour Affair* (1968), Odeon

Gurtu, Trilok, percussion, tabla, drums, conga. b. Bombay, India, 30 October 1951. Grandparents, mother and brother all musical. Studied tabla with Ahmed Jan Thirakwa; in jazz, percussion and conga, he was self-taught. Tabla from age six, regularly accompanying his mother and other musicians at his home; 1965, with his brother led a percussion group in Bombay; influenced by Miles Davis and John Coltrane (*Coltrane Plays the Blues*), he began playing jazz; 1973, went to Europe with an Indian jazz-rock-ethnic group, staying in Italy until 1975. He went to the USA in 1976, playing with various jazz groups in New York, and beginning his long association with Charlie Mariano; worked with Don Cherry, Barre Phillips; was active as a teacher in NY; played Woodstock every year until 1982; in the 1980s he has played the New York Kool Jazz Festival with Lee Konitz, worked with Karl Berger, with Mariano and Philip Catherine, and with Archie Shepp. He has also toured Europe with Nana Vasconcelos in duo with break dancers, with a quartet including L. Shankar, J. Garbarek and Vasconcelos, and with Mariano and Jasper van't Hof. In the mid-1980s, Gurtu was working with Rainer Brüninghaus (keyboards) and John Abercrombie (gtr), and was also a member of the group Oregon, in which he replaced the late Collin Walcott. Gurtu's favourites are A. J. Thirakwa, Roy Haynes and Elvin Jones; other inspirations are Chopin, Ellington, Shobha Gurtu (his mother), Miles Davis, Booker Little, Ahmad Jamal and the music of Africa.

Compositions: 'Paschlove' dedicated to Collin Walcott; and a commission for the West German Radio with Airto Moreira and Flora Purim. [IC]

With Barre Phillips, *Three Day Moon* (1978), ECM; with Family of Percussion, *Here Comes the Family* (1979), Nagara; with Catherine/Mariano/Toots Thielemans, *End of August* (1981), WEA; Shankar/Garbarek/Zakir Hussain/Gurtu, *Song for Everyone* (1984), ECM

Guy, Barry John, double-bass, violone, composer. b. London, 22 April 1947. Became interested in jazz at school. Studied double-bass and composition at the Guildhall School of Music and Drama. Mid-1960s, began playing with John Stevens and Trevor Watts in the Spontaneous Music Ensemble, which was totally dedicated to 'free' (i.e. abstract) improvisation. Since then, he has pursued a dual career on the European art music circuit and on the free improvisation circuit. He has also worked with the Howard Riley trio, Bob Downes's Open Music, Trevor Watts's Amalgam, Iskra 1903, and various groups with Tony Oxley, Evan Parker and Peter Kowald.

By the end of the 1960s it was becoming apparent that there was not much of an audience for improvised abstract music and, faced with an unsympathetic world, the players drew together for mutual support in an organization called the Musicians' Co-operative. Guy was a founder member and, to celebrate the event, he composed *Ode* for a 21-piece ensemble of free improvisers which he called the London Jazz Composers' Orchestra. In fact he was following a precedent created in the USA by Michael Mantler in 1964, when he formed an ensemble, calling it the Jazz Composers' Orchestra. The aim of both orchestras was to try to explore the relationship of individual improvisers to organized ensemble sound and to translate abstraction from a small-group setting to an orchestral one. The situation was complicated in the British ensemble by the fact that several of its members were ideologically opposed to any kind

Barry Guy

of formal composition at all. The LJCO has undergone various transformations over the years, and has appeared at festivals in the UK and Europe.

Guy has composed many pieces for 'classical' ensembles of all sizes, and he has composed several works for the LJCO, including *Polyhymnia* and *Four Pieces for Orchestra*. He received the Radcliffe Music Award, 1973, first prize for *String Quartet III*. He is a virtuoso player, often giving solo concerts. Among his influences he names Charles Mingus, Scott La Faro, Gary Peacock, Albert Ayler, Eric Dolphy, Ornette Coleman, John Coltrane, Bill Evans, and all his UK improvising associates. [IC]

With Parker, Downes, Oxley, Amalgam, Iskra 1903 and others; LJCO, *Ode* (1972), Incus; *Stringer* (1984), FMP/SA; solo bass/violone, *Statements V–VI* (1976), Incus; Guy/Riley/Wachsmann, *Improvisations are Forever Now* (1977), Vinyl; with Riley, *Facets* (1979–81), Impetus; Kowald/Guy, *Paintings* (1981), FMP

Guy, Fred, guitar, banjo. b. Burkesville, Georgia, 23 May 1897; d. Chicago, 22 November 1971. At the start of his career he worked with Joseph Smith's band in New York, then led his own before joining Duke Ellington in 1925. A close friend of Ellington's, Guy provided a stabilizing influence in the early days of the Famous Orchestra. 'He was one of the more mature, level-headed people in the band', says Mercer Ellington. 'He had a very dry sense of humour, but it was never exercised at anyone else's expense. [And] although he was serious-minded he was a great one for anecdotes and memories of humorous happenings!' Guy switched to guitar in the mid-1930s after Eddie Lang's influence had been widely acknowledged and played it regularly thereafter until he left Ellington in 1949 to work for 20 years as a dance hall manager. When he committed suicide it was a severe shock to his leader in his declining years. [DF]

Any with Ellington

Gwaltney, Tommy (Thomas), alto and tenor sax, clarinet, vibes, xylophone. b. Norfolk, Virginia, *c.* 1925. From 1945 he was an active performer in and out of Washington, DC, with bands led by Benny Goodman, Billy Butterfield and Bobby Hackett (including Hackett's legendary Henry Hudson band in which he regularly replaced Bob Wilber) before basing himself in Norfolk, Virginia, around 1960 to lead jazz and dance bands. At this period he produced at least one album, *Goin' to Kansas City*, which turned into a collectors' classic: its carefully researched repertoire, fine arrangements (some by Tom Newsom, another neglected reedman who worked for Vincent Lopez and, later, regularly with the World's Greatest Jazz Band) and line-up – mixing established KC men such as Buck Clayton and Dickie Wells along with younger men including John Bunch and Charlie Byrd – showed Gwaltney as a potential performer/researcher to rival Wilber. In ensuing years, however, less was heard from him out of America than should have been: in 1965 he began a long residency at Washington's Blues Alley and used the club as a platform to help re-launch singer Maxine Sullivan – an intelligent move, reflecting his strong sense of history and musical judgement. Luckily Gwaltney has appeared on record frequently enough to be researchable. [DF]

Goin' to Kansas City (1960), Riverside

H

Hackett, Bobby (Robert Leo), cornet, trumpet, guitar, ukulele, banjo. b. Providence, Rhode Island, 31 January 1915; d. Chatham, Massachusetts, 7 June 1976. In the early years of his career he was almost as well-known for his guitar playing (no doubt the groundbase for his love of correct chords and infallible harmonic sense): he first specialized on cornet while working in a trio with Pee Wee Russell in Boston, 1933. By the mid-1930s his translucent sound, subtle harmonic twists and elegant lines seemed to make him the natural successor to Bix Beiderbecke (in fact his primary influence was always Louis Armstrong) and for the rest of the decade he worked with bandleaders such as Horace Heidt, briefly led his own orchestra and made the rounds of New York's club circuit. 1941–2, he played acoustic guitar, then cornet, for Glenn Miller, a close friend. By 1944, when he joined Glen Gray's Casa Lomans, Hackett had a severe drink problem which helped to induce the diabetes that would eventually kill him. But he controlled his habit and by 1946 was a staffman for ABC (with Billy Butterfield), worked regularly at Eddie Condon's and other clubs and in 1947 was MD for Louis Armstrong's revolutionary Town Hall concert as well as second cornettist. During the 1940s Hackett's gift for playing second made him a regular companion and recording colleague to Armstrong, who supplied the best one-line reason for having him there: 'Bobby's got more ingredients!' he said. From 1951 some of Hackett's greatest recordings were made for Jackie Gleason's 'mood music' albums such as *Music for Lovers Only*. The sessions, for which Hackett was paid only just above union scale, became best-sellers, and Gleason's failure to cut him in on the deal caused a deep rift between them, but every one of their collaborations is a must for Hackett students. He later perpetuated the sound on records with pipe-organ played by Glenn Osser, and recorded with strings until the end of his career – but not for Gleason. While he combined studio and clubwork, Hackett produced more 1950s masterpieces with Jack Teagarden (*Coast to Coast* with its roaming 'I guess I'll have to change my plan' might just be the greatest Dixieland record ever) and by 1956 was leading a band at the Henry Hudson Hotel, featuring clarinettist Tommy Gwaltney (later replaced by Bob Wilber) and staff arranger Dick Cary. Formed at a natural peak in his career, Hackett's Henry Hudson band is remembered nearly as well as Muggsy Spanier's Ragtimers (albeit their repertoire and style differed greatly) but it broke up a year later and he returned to studio work, a spell with Benny Goodman (1962–3), another for Ray McKinley and in 1965 became 'official accompanist' for Tony Bennett. In the late 1960s Hackett ran a quintet with Vic Dickenson, guested with the World's Greatest Jazz Band, and played on the Cape with Dave McKenna: 1974, a European tour teamed him with fellow cornettist Dick Sudhalter, and 18 months later he was dead from alcoholic complications triggering diabetes.

Hackett was universally loved by the jazz community for his graceful, unobtrusive music – and for his inability to say anything bad about anyone (once, in a musician's test case, Hackett was asked about Hitler: 'Well', he said after a pause, 'he was the best in his *field*.'). He was the perfect accompanist – singers from Teresa Brewer to Lee Wiley adored him – and defined jazz taste with every note he played; seldom did the fire disappear from the perfection. [DF]

Coast to Coast (1955), EMI

See Balliett, Whitney, *Alec Wilder and his Friends* (Houghton Mifflin, 1968)

Haden, Charlie (Charles Edward), bass. b. Shenandoah, Iowa, 6 August 1937. Born into a musical family, he played on daily radio show as a child. Moved to Los Angeles, worked with Art Pepper (1957), Elmo Hope, Hampton Hawes (1958–9). Regular gigs with Paul Bley group (1957–9) including briefly Ornette Coleman and Don Cherry. With the classic Coleman quartet (1958–60) and rejoined him on several occasions from 1966 (European tour with two basses, Haden and David Izenzon, 1968). After curing his drug addiction at Synanon Foundation (early 1960s) Charlie undertook counselling of addicts while resuming regular playing with Denny Zeitlin (1964–6). Worked with Jazz Composers' Orchestra Association (late 1960s) and in 1969 assembled group of members to record *Liberation Music Orchestra* album; a similar line-up toured Europe in 1982 and 1985. Frequent appearances and recording with Alice Coltrane (1968–72) and Keith Jarrett quartet (1967–75). Recorded series of duo sessions with Coleman, Jarrett, Hawes etc. (1975–6), and first album (1976) of Old and New Dreams quartet (Cherry, Haden, Dewey Redman, Ed Blackwell) led to touring from 1979 onwards. Also recording and

Bobby Hackett

tour (1982–3) with trio including Jan Garbarek and guitarist Egberto Gismonti.

A powerful yet extremely adaptable player, Haden was probably the first to apply the freedoms of the 'avant-garde' to the role of bassist. Accepting the traditional task of being supportive but stimulating, he went one step further and, by his intuitive choice of phrases, suggested new directions for the other participants in collective improvisation. Although he expressed admiration for Wilbur Ware, there was little of Ware's work to model himself upon when Haden began to make an impact, and all of it was in a bebop context. Haden's group playing was at first paramount, though Coleman quartet pieces such as 'Lonely Woman' and 'Ramblin'' hinted at the bassist's virtuoso capabilities. While his ability in group playing is undiminished, he has since developed into a riveting soloist and, despite concentrating more than most of his contemporaries on the lower and middle range of the instrument, displays a ravishingly beautiful tone. [BP]

The Golden Number (1976), Horizon; *Old and New Dreams* (1979), ECM

Hadi, Shafi (aka **Curtis Porter**), tenor and alto sax. b. Philadelphia, 21 September 1929. After touring with leading r & b bands such as Paul Williams (*c.* 1951) and the Griffin Brothers, settled in New York and joined Charles Mingus (late 1956–8 and 1959). Thought to have been inactive in music since early 1960s. Apart from recordings with Mingus and Hank Mobley, and his solo saxophone work for the film *Shadows* (1959), little is known of Hadi. But his distinctive mixture of bop and blues, combined with a very individual tone, is likely to remain in the memory of anyone who has ever heard him. [BP]

Charles Mingus, *Tijuana Moods* (1957), RCA

Haggart, Bob (Robert Sherwood), bass, composer, arranger. b. New York City, 13 March 1914. He began as a guitar player – his teacher was George Van Eps – and then taught himself bass in high school. At school and after, he heard the finest jazz on record (including Louis Armstrong's Hot Five which made a lifelong impression) and soon after was making his way in professional music, working all kinds of gigs, becoming well known as a bright new bass talent and turning down offers from Benny Goodman and Tommy Dorsey: 'I felt I wasn't ready', he later told John Chilton. In 1935 he became a founder member of Bob Crosby's band, which introduced Dixieland to the swing-happy 1930s (and thus presaged the 1940s jazz revival). He recorded the classic hit 'Big Noise from Winnetka' (which with its whistling/drumsticks on bass strings routine was to become a standard showpiece for Dixieland bands ever after) and composed/arranged much of Crosby's most distinguished repertoire: 'South Rampart Street Parade' (a creation with Ray Bauduc, scribbled on a hotel tablecloth which he then took home), 'Dogtown Blues' and 'Diga diga doo' are three examples. From 1942 (when Crosby's band broke up), Haggart became a busy studio musician working with popular and jazz giants such as Bing Crosby, Duke Ellington and Louis Armstrong, and from 1950 with Yank Lawson for records with the Lawson–Haggart Jazz Band which Dixieland aficionados often call the best ever of their kind. In between he was a familiar bass at Crosby reunions (including a famous one at New York's Rainbow Grill in 1966), and at every Dick Gibson jazz party in Colorado from their 1963 inception: in 1968 the house band from these parties turned, at Gibson's instigation, into the World's Greatest Jazz Band, which Haggart co-led with enormous musical success and occasional personal reservations for ten years. In the 1980s he was happy to be back in a re-formed Lawson–Haggart Jazz Band producing a touching, reminiscent LP for George Buck, *Sentimental Journey*, and bandleading still, as well as touring Europe alone and with friends. [DF]

The Legendary Lawson–Haggart Jazz Band (1952–3), MCA Coral (double); *Sentimental Journey* (1980), Jazzology

See Chilton, John, *Stomp Off Let's Go!* (Jazz Book Services, 1983)

Haig, Al (Allan W.), piano. b. Newark, New Jersey, 22 July 1924; d. 16 November 1982. One of the first pianists to develop an idiomatic bop style, he was active with Dizzy Gillespie and Charlie Parker by late 1944. After service under the leadership of Gillespie (1944–6), Parker (1948–50, including his first trip to Europe) and Stan Getz (1949–51), much of his time was spent playing solo background music or in non-jazz organizations. Only in the last decade of his life, he experienced a personal renaissance which led to many foreign tours and frequent recording. The contradictions of his career were evident quite early on, for some of his work as a featured performer in his own right seems to err on the side of caution, especially when using standard songs. However, when backing superior soloists (Parker *At the Royal Roost* or Getz *At Storyville*) or dealing with specifically jazz-based material, he displays a special combination of commanding calm and dynamic drive. [BP]

Expressly Ellington (1978), Spotlite

Haim, John, cornet, leader. b. London, 1929; d. London, January 1949. He formed his first band in 1945 and was one of the brightest talents of post-war revivalist London; in the 1947 *Melody Maker* dance band contest he won an individual award for solo performance. Haim's band, including his brother Gerry (tuba) and banjoist Eric Silk, was creating a stir around London's clubs when a morbid and inexplicable error occurred: the *Melody Maker* reported his death in a headline. Haim had never told his sidemen he was in fact suffering from a lung disorder: days later he did die as the result of a heart attack brought on by his condition. He was 19. 'A memorial record was issued on Delta 6,' recalled Rex Harris, 'entitled "Blues for Johnny" – but it gives no indication of the lusty sound which the band made in the flesh.' That Haim's replacement for the tribute was Freddy Randall, however, gives a hint of the high level of Haim's performance. [DF]

Hakim, Sadik (aka **Argonne Thornton**), piano. b. Duluth, Minnesota, 15 July 1922; d. 20 June 1983. Active on New York's 52nd Street scene in the mid-1940s, under his then name of Thornton. Participated in significant record sessions by Charlie Parker and Lester Young, also regular work and recording with Ben Webster and Lockjaw Davis. Later with the James Moody band (1951–4) and Buddy Tate band (1955–60). Resident in Canada from the late 1960s, except for visit to Europe in 1972, until returning to New York during late 1970s. A prolific writer in his later years, Hakim also wrote the tune 'Eronel' recorded by and credited to Thelonious Monk. His 1940s style, though indicative of the problems of adapting to bebop, was strongly individual and possibly more interesting than his later work. [BP]

Lester Young and his Tenor Sax, vol. 2 (1947–8), Aladdin

Halcox, Pat, trumpet, fluegelhorn, cornet, arranger, leader. b. Chelsea, London, 17 March 1930. He joined Chris Barber in 1954 from the Albemarle Jazz Band and has stayed with him ever since: he also tours annually with the Chris Barber Summer Band (minus Barber). A New Orleans-based player to begin with, Halcox rapidly broadened his approach with Barber's, until by the 1960s he was as skilled at playing in a neo-rock setting as he was at leading a collective ensemble. His solo work with Barber – fiery, creative, and latterly with an impressive range – is one of the delights of British traditional jazz. Because of Barber's catholic musical tastes, Halcox has had every opportunity to parade his broad-based abilities, and he remains – musically as well as personally – one of Britain's best loved and respected trumpeters. [DF]

Any with Chris Barber

Hall, Ed(mond), clarinet, baritone sax. b. Cadiz Street, New Orleans, 15 May 1901; d. Boston, 11 February 1967. He came from a family of four clarinet-playing sons (two surviving brothers are clarinettist Herbie and saxophonist Clarence, who later worked with Fats Domino). His father, Edward Hall, was a member of the great Onward Brass Band which played in New York (in 1891) as well as New Orleans. From 1919, Ed Hall – playing an Albert system like many of his New Orleans colleagues – worked in a variety of bands (including Jack Carey, Lee Collins, Buddy Petit, Chris Kelly and Kid Thomas) over a wide area and finally came to New York with Alonzo Ross in 1928. From here he jobbed around, and by 1930 was working with Claude Hopkins. Despite the often appalling touring conditions suffered by black musicians in the 1930s Hall stayed with Hopkins until 1935, when Chauncey Haughton replaced him. Much of his work for the next ten years or so was New York-based, with Lucky Millinder, Zutty Singleton and Joe Sullivan; in 1940 he joined Henry 'Red' Allen's brand new band and in 1941 Teddy Wilson's classy sextet, which broadcast and recorded regularly. 1944–6, Hall led his own group (including Jimmy Crawford) for a famous New York residency at Café Society (uptown and downtown), and after four more years in Boston joined Eddie Condon, 1950–5, and Louis Armstrong's All Stars (replacing Barney Bigard) for three years after that. The Armstrong schedule encouraged Hall to think about retirement in 1958, but in the 1960s he was still busy working with Condon, with his own quartet around New York and touring abroad until his sudden death. A calm and placid man, much loved by all who met him, whose grittily fierce clarinet playing always came as a surprise, Hall practised yoga and inner cleanliness (one practice observed by Steve Voce involved swallowing a roll of clean bandage inch by inch then pulling it back up again). He suffered a heart attack after shovelling snow from his driveway and was dead on arrival at hospital. [DF]

At Club Hangover (1954), Storyville

Hall, Jim (James Stanley), guitar. b. Buffalo, New York, 12 December 1930. After playing local bands, moved to Los Angeles (1955). First prominent with Chico Hamilton quintet (1955–6), then member of Jimmy Giuffre trio (1956–9). Part of Ella Fitzgerald rhythm-section (1960–1), also working in New York in duo with Lee Konitz. Half a year with new Sonny Rollins group (1961–2), then co-led quartet with Art Farmer (1962–4). Recordings with all aforementioned and with Gerry Mulligan, Bill Evans etc. Settled into New York studio work, also own trio gigs frequently since 1965 including numerous tours abroad (Ronnie Scott's, 1966; Berlin, 1967, 1969; Japan, 1976 etc). Duo appearances and records since 1972 with Ron Carter, and much unaccompanied playing.

Hall is definitely not one of those after-Christian, after-bebop, afternoon-nap guitarists. In fact, far from blinding the listener with science and technique, he is often so subtle in the use of both as to bypass some listeners altogether. His extremely mellow sound often disguises his rhythmic and harmonic finesse and, like the very best players of conventional frameworks, he manages to sound totally free within them. Backing other soloists, too, his choice of textures is usually unexpected but sounds absolutely right; both this ability and his fine contrapuntal sense are best revealed alongside musicians who share the same qualities, such as Sonny Rollins or Bill Evans or indeed Ron Carter. [BP]

Evans/Hall, *Undercurrent* (1959), United Artists; Hall/Carter, *Telephone* (1982), Concord

Hallberg, Bengt, piano, organ. b. Gothenburg, Sweden, 13 September 1932. Already active on the Swedish jazz scene as a teenager, he gained attention abroad through his recordings with Stan Getz (*Tenor Contrasts*, 1951, Esquire) and Clifford Brown (*Memorial*, 1953, Prestige/OJC). 1950s, worked and recorded regularly with Lars Gullin and Arne Domnerus while, since then, he has made his living largely as a composer and session musician. Despite this, his enthusiasm for jazz remains undiminished, and the freshness of his early work has matured into a style of considerable originality. Whereas the harmonically updated Teddy Wilson approach of the 1950s was already very distinctive, Hallberg's later playing (especially unaccompanied) is a totally individual amalgam of many elements from stride to post-modal jazz. [BP]

On His Own (1976), Phontastic

Hamilton, Chico (Foreststorn), drums. b. Los Angeles, 21 September 1921. While still in high school, played regularly with band including fellow students Dexter Gordon, Ernie Royal, Buddy Collette and Charles Mingus, later Illinois Jacquet. Then freelancing with Floyd Ray, Lionel Hampton, Slim Gaillard (1941) and others until army service (1942–6). Worked with Jimmy Mundy band, briefly with Count Basie, and with Lester Young (all 1946). Toured with singer Lena Horne (1948–55) and, based in Los Angeles between tours, did studio work and played with Charlie Barnet and original Gerry Mulligan quartet (1952–3). Formed own quintet (1955), which became popular internationally through use of flute/clarinet and cello; replacing cello with trombone (1962) to achieve harder sound, Hamilton toured regularly until mid-1960s and then, usually with two reeds, again in early 1970s. Since then active in writing advertising jingles and film music, Hamilton's original reputation as an excellent Jo Jones-tutored drummer has been largely forgotten. His quintet veered constantly between being the unacceptable face of capitulation to European influence and an acceptable forum for aspiring improvisers. In the latter field, Chico deserves credit for offering their first touring opportunities to such interesting musicians as Buddy Collette, Jim Hall, Paul Horn, Eric Dolphy, Ron Carter, Charles Lloyd, Gabor Szabo, John Abercrombie and Arthur Blythe. [BP]

Gongs East (1958), Discovery

Hamilton, Jimmy (James), clarinet, tenor sax, arranger. b. Dillon, South Carolina, 25 May 1917. Brought up in Philadelphia, studied piano and brass instruments, playing latter with local bands (mid-1930s). Switched to saxophone and clarinet, worked for Lucky Millinder and Jimmy Mundy (both 1939, concurrently with Bill Doggett). Member of Teddy Wilson sextet (1940–2), then with Eddie Heywood, Yank Porter groups. Joined Duke Ellington (1943), filling post vacated eight months earlier by Barney Bigard and remaining till 1968. Freelance arranging and playing, then teaching music in public schools in Virgin Islands (1970s–80s). Special guest at Ellington Conference in Manchester, UK (1985).

In performance, Hamilton often exhibited something of a split personality. His comparatively rare tenor solos sounded like the better r & b players; on clarinet, however, he had an academically correct tone and admirable fluency, and the possible jazz deficiencies of this approach were cleverly minimized by Duke Ellington during his long tenure. Some of his features within the band were initially composed by Hamilton himself, such as 'Air Conditioned Jungle' and 'Ad Lib On Nippon'. [BP]

Duke Ellington, *The Cosmic Scene* (1959), CBS; *It's About Time* (1961), Swingville

Hamilton, John 'Bugs', trumpet, b. St Louis, Missouri, 8 March 1911; d. St Louis, 15 August 1947. His short career, spanning only 15 years, included New York spells with Billy Kato, Chick Webb and Kaiser Marshall in the early 1930s before the period for which he is best remembered: four years with Fats Waller, 1938–42, replacing Herman Autrey. Hamilton's style – on record anyway – was close to Autrey's, although a few degrees more elegant and musical on occasion. Very little more was heard from him after Waller's death, apart from a brief spell with Eddie South's fine small group: he died of tuberculosis at only 36. [DF]

Any with Waller

Hamilton, Scott, tenor sax. b. New England, 12 September 1954. He played first around New England, then moved to New York to follow up connections with Roy Eldridge, Tiny Grimes, Carol Sloane and John Bunch. Bunch recommended him to Benny Goodman and Hamilton joined him. By then he had already met his frequent partner, cornettist Warren Vaché, for the first time in a New York jazz club. While with Goodman, Hamilton signed a contract with Concord Records, and the huge publicity that followed (promoting him and Vaché as mainstream Messiahs) guaranteed them both a heady round of appearances at clubs, festivals and recordings in America and Europe. It was difficult to understand how – from a post-Beatles generation – a tenor-saxophonist of such stunning maturity could have emerged whose natural vocabulary was evidently that of Ben Webster, Lester Young, Don Byas and Zoot Sims. The demands placed on young Hamilton – not much more than 20 years old – were heavy: that he resisted falling permanently into a whisky bottle to allay the pressure is a tribute to his inner strength. By the early 1980s he was working at full force with the Concord Super Band, with his own quintet of young mainstreamers and recording superbly with Bob Wilber, Buddy Tate, Rosemary Clooney, Warren Vaché and alone. By 1985 he was with the Newport Jazz Festival All Stars (George Wein at the piano), busily recording, touring and making the festival rounds. [DF]

Hamilton/Vaché, *With Scott's Band in NYC* (1978), Concord

Hammer, Jan, piano, electric keyboards, synthesizer, drums, composer. b. Prague, Czechoslovakia, 17 April 1948. Mother a jazz singer; father a doctor who played vibes. Began on piano at age four; also took up drums. As a teenager he was influenced by the Beatles, Jimi Hendrix and James Brown, then by Coltrane and Elvin Jones. He played in a trio with Miroslav and Alan Vitous during high school. Studied classical composition and piano at Prague Conservatory; won an international music competition in Vienna in 1966, and won scholarship to the Berklee College of Music. 1967, played at Warsaw Jazz Jamboree with Stuff Smith. When the Russians invaded Czechoslovakia in 1968, he left for the USA, working around Boston and attending some classes at Berklee. 1970–1, with Sarah Vaughan, touring USA, Canada and Japan. Then based himself in New York, working with Jeremy Steig, Elvin Jones, and others. May 1971–December 1973, he was with the Mahavishnu Orchestra (see McLaughlin, John); then with Billy Cobham's Spectrum until the autumn of 1975. Since then he has led his own groups, touring in the USA and internationally.

Hammer is a virtuoso performer: equally at home with acoustic and electric music, he can handle all areas of improvisation from abstraction to conventional forms, and he is a master of the complex asymmetry of jazz-rock-fusion. He made an important contribution to some of the classic albums of the 1970s with the Mahavishnu Orchestra and with Cobham. [IC]

With Jerry Goodman, Stanley Clarke, John Abercrombie, Steig, Jones; with Mahavishnu, *The Inner Mounting Flame* (1971), CBS; *Birds of Fire* (1972), CBS; as leader, *Black Sheep* (1979), Asylum; *Hammer* (1980), Asylum; Hammer/Neal Schon, *Untold Passion* (1981), CBS; Hammer/Schon, *Here to Stay* (1982), CBS; Hammer/James Young, *City Slicker* (1986), Gem

Hampel, Gunter, vibraphone, clarinet and bass-clarinet, saxes, flutes, piano, composer. b. Göttingen, Germany, 31 August 1937. Grandfather a multi-instrumental street musician. Studied music from 1948, also architecture. Led his own band from 1958, touring Germany and Europe. In the 1960s he became deeply committed to free jazz, his group improvising collective, abstract music. Guitarist John McLaughlin worked with him for six months during the mid-1960s. Hampel toured extensively for the Goethe Institute in Africa, Asia and South America. At the 1972 Munich Olympic Games and Berlin Jazz Festival he played solo (unaccompanied) concerts. His wife, singer Jeanne Lee, has also worked in his group. Early 1970s, started his Galaxie Dream Band. At the end of the 1960s he formed Birth Records to put out his own music. He has composed music for films, and appeared at most major international festivals. Hampel lives in New York for half each year and in Germany for the other half. [IC]

As leader (with Anthony Braxton/Willem Breuker/J. Lee etc.), *The 8th of July* (1969); *Ballet Symphony No. 5* (1971); with Galaxie Dream Band (including Enrico Rava), *Angel* (1972); *Out from Under* (1974); *Cosmic Dancer* (1975); *Transformation* (1976); *All is Real* (1978), all Birth

Hampton, Lionel, vibes, drums, piano, vocals. b. Louisville, Kentucky, 12 April 1909. He was raised in the Catholic Church and was sent to school at the Holy Rosary Academy in Kenosha, Wisconsin, where he was taught snare-drum rudiments by a strict Dominican nun. Back in Chicago he joined the Chicago Defender Newsboys' Band and learned tympani (and, significantly, marimba) under Major N. Clark-Smith. Spare evenings were spent watching his idol and occasional teacher, percussionist Jimmy Ber-

Lionel Hampton

trand, at the nearby Vendome Theater. Then, he said, 'My uncle Richard Morgan' (who later shared Bessie Smith's turbulent life) 'bought me everything: silk shirts, the finest clothes, my first marimba and my first set of drums – it had a light in it!' (like Bertrand's). Soon after, Hampton was working with bands led by Detroit Shannon, Curtis Mosby, Vernon Elkins, Paul Howard and Reb Spikes before joining Les Hite to back Louis Armstrong at the Los Angeles Cotton Club. There he met dancer Gladys Riddle, who was to become his wife and gifted business manager: she bought a 'little set of vibes', encouraged him to practise them and then sent him to the University of Southern California to study theory. Thereafter Hampton formed his own band (finding that that was the only way to feature himself as he wished on vibes); in 1936 he was offered a residency at the Paradise Café in Los Angeles and one night Benny Goodman came in: 'The next thing I knew Benny was on stage playing clarinet, Gene Krupa was at the drums and Teddy Wilson was at the piano.' They recorded together and six weeks later Hampton was featured artist with Benny Goodman's quartet on the Camel Cigarette programme. A year later RCA offered their new star *carte blanche* to record whenever he was in New York with whoever he pleased: the 90 resulting sides (along with Teddy Wilson's, Billie Holiday's and Mildred Bailey's) are the best records of the Swing era at its zenith, and feature practically every star of the period as well as Hampton's likeable singing. He was with Benny Goodman until 1940 (creating the kind of excitement that jazz had seldom experienced until then) and then – with Goodman's blessing – left to start his own highly successful big band, which in 1986 was the longest established orchestra in jazz history.

Over the years, Hampton's band became a legendary university for young talent, including Charles Mingus, Art Farmer, Joe Newman, Illinois Jacquet, Dexter Gordon, Lee Young, Ernie Royal, Clark Terry, Joe Williams and Dinah Washington: 'They all got a living and a chance,' said Hampton later, 'and I didn't hold 'em back, but I was strict and I disciplined 'em!' – vital in the wild jazz years of the 1940s when, for the first time, hard drugs and a whole new hipster image for young musicians were taking hold (and toll) of the post-war jazz generation. There are only occasional rumours of Hampton being too hard on his sidemen: a famous story exists of Clifford Brown escaping down a fire-escape after his leader had imposed a ban on members of his band recording in Paris in 1953, and had posted a lookout in the hotel lobby to prevent his sidemen from sneaking out of the hotel. By and large, though, Hampton led a happy band, as well as a tight ship, which very early on cornered a market later to be occupied by rock and roll. A Hampton hit record, 'Flying Home' from 1942, clearly established his formula: high energy, screaming brass, rhythmic trademarks which could drive an audience to fever pitch and the kind of near-hysterical excitement that Hampton had first created with Goodman's quartet. Hampton's big band was, in a sense, a rock and roll band still conforming to jazz conventions – just as Dinah Washington (had she lived in the 1970s) would certainly have been a soul singer.

All through the 1960s Hampton's band remained hugely successful, appearing at all the best festivals (including Newport, 1967 and 1972): he also led a successful small group, Lionel Hampton's Inner Circle, at clubs and festivals, played regularly at Benny Goodman reunions (Newport, 1973, for example), recorded regularly with all-star small groups (*You better know it*, starring Hank Jones, Clark Terry and Ben Webster, is a late classic) and was often to be seen in Europe. By the mid-1970s his lifelong services to music were reaping tangible rewards: he ran his own highly successful publishing companies, his own record label, Who's Who in Jazz, and had founded the Lionel Hampton Development Corporation which erected two multi-million apartment complexes in Harlem and by 1980 was planning a full-scale university. By the mid-1980s, Dr Lionel Hampton (the doctorate came from Pepperdine College, California) was moving in the senior circles of New York politics as well as leading his big band around the jazz circuits of the world. [DF]

Historic Recording Sessions 1937–9, vol. 1, RCA (3 records, boxed set); any big band album led by Hampton

See Dance, Stanley, *The World of Swing* (Scribner's, 1974, repr. Da Capo, 1979)

Hampton, Slide (Locksley Wellington), trombone, tuba, arranger. b. Jeannette, Pennsylvania, 21 April 1932. With Buddy Johnson (1955–6) and Lionel Hampton bands (1956–7). Played and arranged for Maynard Ferguson (1957–9), then formed own octet (1959–62). After working as musical director for singer Lloyd Price and freelance arranging, joined Woody Herman (1968) and toured Europe with him; settled there, doing much arranging for radio studio bands and playing in all-star contexts. Returned to New York (1977) and began leading his own World of Trombones 12-piece group, also involved in jazz education. One of the few prominent left-handed trombonists, Hampton has an amazingly fluent technique but, unlike some of the busier players on his instrument, is blessed with a fine melodic sense too. [BP]

The Fabulous (1969), Pathe

Hancock, Herbie (Herbert Jeffrey), keyboards, electronics, composer. b. Chicago, 12 April 1940. His parents, sister and brother were musical. He had piano lessons from age seven, making rapid progress; at 11 he played Mozart's D major piano concerto with the Chicago Symphony Orchestra, and in his teens performed in Bach's Brandenburg Concerto no. 2 in F major. He attended Grinnell College, gradu-

Herbie Hancock

ating first in electrical engineering, then in music composition. January 1961, he went to New York with trumpeter Donald Byrd and made an immediate impact. He worked with Phil Woods and Oliver Nelson, and recorded his first album as leader, *Takin' Off* (Blue Note), which has been described as 'one of the most accomplished and stunning débuts in the annals of jazz'. One of the tracks, 'Watermelon Man', became a hit single and versions have since been recorded by more than 200 artists. He worked briefly, 1962–3, with Eric Dolphy; May 1963, joined the Miles Davis quintet, which included Ron Carter, Tony Williams and, later, Wayne Shorter. He stayed with Davis for five and a half years, leaving in 1968, but continuing to play on some later record sessions. His time with Davis established him internationally as one of the most important pianists of the time, and also as a fine composer of small-group material. Throughout the 1960s he also continued to record under his own name, and several of his compositions became part of the jazz repertoire: 'The Sorcerer', 'Riot', 'Canteloupe Island', 'Dolphin Dance', 'Maiden Voyage' and 'Speak Like a Child'.

When he left the Miles Davis group, Hancock led a sextet which included Eddie Henderson (tpt, fluegelhorn), Benny Maupin (reeds and flutes), Julian Priester (tmb), Billy Hart (dms) and Buster Williams (bass), touring and playing festivals in the USA and Europe. With this group he began to feature electronics more and more as a source of colour and atmosphere, but although the music was excellent, alternating spacey free sections with some marvellously rhythmic passages, there were not enough bookings to make the sextet viable economically. The jazz scene was in such a parlous state at the time that even though his albums sold reasonably well, though he was recognized internationally as one of the leading forces in the music and continued to win polls and receive honours (among others an honorary doctorate from his old university, Grinnell in Des Moines, Iowa), he lacked the status, financial or otherwise, to keep the sextet together. He disbanded it in June 1973, forming a quartet with Maupin on reeds, and featuring funky rhythms and electronic sounds. It was not just money that made Hancock change tack; he had done much soul-searching and analysed his own situation ruthlessly. He was upset that friends had his albums on their shelves, but never played them. He said: 'I realized that I could never be a genius in the class of Miles, Charlie Parker or Coltrane, so I might just as well forget about becoming a legend and just be satisfied to create some music to make people happy. I no longer wanted to write the Great American Masterpiece.'

Ironically, he immediately created a small American masterpiece with his new group's first recording, *Headhunters*, which became the best-selling jazz album in history. The first track, 'Chameleon', also became a hit single, and it became part of the jazz repertoire of the 1970s and after – and both album and hit single were instrumental records as opposed to vocal ones. The music was heavily electronic, with electric bass, keyboards and synthesizers, and it featured the kind of hypnotically repeating interlocking rhythms which Hancock admired so much in the music of Sly Stone. The whole sound was composed and orchestrated with immense care, and improvised solos were beautifully integrated into performances which embodied all Hancock's virtues: superb time and flawlessly executed rhythms, graceful melodies, brilliantly creative and catchy riffs, and an atmosphere of urbane contemplation laced with joy. *Headhunters* was a radical new sound and it radically transformed Hancock's fortunes, turning him into a superstar with a huge international following. He and his group toured as the main attraction in major concert halls throughout the USA, Europe and Japan, and made some more best-selling instrumental albums.

In the later 1970s Hancock began to make albums with vocals, his music became much more pop-orientated and, indeed, his popularity was huge at this point. But at the same time he began to play and record acoustically again and work with old associates. In 1977, he initiated and toured world-wide with VSOP – the old Miles Davis band with Freddie Hubbard standing in for Davis. Later he toured with Chick Corea, performing acoustic piano duets; 1982, he toured Europe and Japan with a quartet made up of himself, Tony Williams, Ron Carter and Wynton Marsalis.

In the mid-1980s he continued to make heavily electronic funky hit records and to break new ground. Collaborating with a rock group called Material, he co-wrote a tune, 'Rockit', which inspired an award-winning video and helped to make the album *Future Shock* a best-seller. This is where Hancock's restless creativity seems to find its main satisfaction – pioneering new electronic music. [IC]

With many people including Wayne Shorter, G. Benson, T. Williams, Wes Montgomery; 17 with Miles Davis, including *My Funny Valentine* (1964), CBS; *Filles de Kilimanjaro* (1968), CBS; as leader, *Maiden Voyage* (1965), Blue Note; sextet, *Crossings* (1972), Warner Bros; *Headhunters* (1973); *Thrust* (1974); *The Quintet/VSOP Live* (1977), all CBS; *Corea/Hancock* (1978), Polydor; *Herbie Hancock Quartet* (1982), CBS (double); *Sound System* (1984), CBS

Handy, 'Captain' John, alto sax, clarinet. b. Pass Christian, Missouri, 24 June 1900; d. New York City, 12 January 1971. He first specialized on alto saxophone in the late 1920s (having played clarinet as well in a variety of bands including Kid Rena's, Kid Howard's and his own at the Entertainer's Club in 1925) and during the 1930s played his new speciality with his own group, the Louisiana Shakers, on tour and resident at La Vida Dance Hall, New Orleans. By the 1960s he was regularly to be heard with trumpeter Kid Sheik Cola's band, as well as at Preservation Hall. He achieved international popularity after touring Europe as a successful soloist in the mid-1960s, playing with a variety of New Orleans-style bands: his gutty, hard-swinging approach (which sometimes recalled Pete Brown, as well as Johnny Hodges and Sidney Bechet by turn) was an eloquent reminder that saxophones – the bane of hard-line jazz revivalists in the 1950s – had never really been out of place in a New Orleans ensemble. He played the Newport Jazz Festival, 1970, with the Preservation Hall Jazz Band, where his stomping, timeless style created a sensation. Regular LPs during the 1960s provided a permanent record of his talent, just in time. [DF]

Kid Thomas Valentine/Captain John Handy: *The December Band, vol. 2* (1965), Jazz Crusade

Handy, John, reeds, composer, educator; and flute, piano, voice, percussion. b. Dallas, Texas, 3 February 1933. (No relation to 'Captain' John Handy, above.) Self-taught on clarinet from 13; began on alto sax in 1949; studied theory at college. Moved to New York 1958, working with Mingus, 1958–9. Formed his own group in 1959, playing around New York and, 1961, doing a US Government tour of Europe. He worked in Sweden and Denmark as a soloist. 1963, soloist with Santa Clara Symphony Orchestra and San Francisco State College Symphonic Band. 1964, soloist with Mingus at Monterey Jazz Festival. In San Francisco, 1965, he formed his own quintet with Michael White on violin, making a tremendous impact at Monterey. 1966–7, he toured with the Monterey All Stars in the US, and played in Gunther Schuller's opera *The Visitation.* 1968, he formed a new band with Mike Nock, White, Ron McClure, who broke away two years later to form one of the first jazz-rock groups, Fourth Way. In 1970, Handy finished writing his Concerto for Jazz Soloist and Orchestra, playing with the San Francisco Symphony Orchestra for its premiere; 1971, he performed it with the Stockton Symphony Orchestra and in 1972 with the New Orleans Symphony Orchestra. Since 1971 he has collaborated with Indian musician Ali Akbar Khan (sarod – a guitar-like Indian instrument), forming a group called Rainbow. 1980–1, Rainbow also included violinist L. Subramaniam.

Since 1968, Handy has been active as an educator in California, teaching courses in jazz history, black music and improvisation at various universities and conservatories. He was a judge at the Monterey High School Jazz Festival, 1973–4; he also devotes his summer months to festivals, acting as judge at various secondary school jazz gatherings. He has also played major festivals with his various groups and collaborators all over the US and Europe.

Handy was initially thoroughly schooled in bebop, but with Mingus he rapidly developed a more flexible and adventurous approach. With an alto sound somewhere between that of Parker and Eric Dolphy, he is an impassioned soloist with a highly individual style and a concept which can embrace anything from bebop to abstraction, Indian music or contemporary classical. [IC]

With Mingus, *Mingus Ah Um* (1959); *Mingus Dynasty* (1959); as leader, *Live at the Monterey Jazz Festival* (1965); *New View* (1967), all CBS; *Karuna Supreme* (1975), MPS; *Hard Work* (1976), Impulse

Handy, W. C. (William Christopher), composer, bandleader, cornet. b. Muscle Shoals, Alabama, 16 November 1873; d. 28 March 1958. Known as 'The Father of the Blues', W. C. Handy was the composer – or at least the copyrighter – of a huge number of classic blues themes, beginning with 'St Louis Blues', 'Memphis Blues' (originally known as 'Mr Crump', his first success and an electioneering song), 'Beale Street Blues', 'Old Miss Rag', 'Chantez les bas' and many others. At a century's distance it may never be established what passages among these compositions actually were Handy's own inventions: 'Handy is not the inventor of the genre,' says Isaac Goldberg, '[but] he was the first to set down jazz on paper – to fix the quality of the various breaks, as these wildly filled in pauses were named. With a succession of blues he fixed the genre.' The inspiration for many of Handy's songs came from folk tunes, rural blues and others that he heard from street performers and any number of other wandering sources, but he brought discipline and structure to what he heard. After the success of 'Memphis Blues' in 1912 – and soon after, in 1914, his masterpiece, 'St Louis Blues' – Handy, a highly trained bandmaster and cornettist, opened a publishing firm in Memphis with Harry Pace: in 1918 the operation moved up to New York, where it flourished on Broadway as Handy Brothers Music Company Inc. From the 1920s Handy suffered periods of blindness, but carried on busily with his publishing concerns and played for concerts and tours all the way through the 1930s: he also recorded in 1939 with J. C. Higginbotham and others. After a subway accident in 1943, when he fell on the track, he became a more elusive figure, turning up at special concerts to hear his great inventions played by musicians such as Eddie Condon. Handy's autobiography *Father of the Blues* was first published in 1941: an engrossing portrait of old America, it carries the reader into an irresistibly fascinating world as vivid as a Currier and Ives print. In 1958 Paramount filmed *St Louis Blues*, an approximation of Handy's story starring Nat 'King' Cole and Eartha Kitt: in 1960 a statue of Handy was unveiled in Memphis. The best document of Handy's compositions is Louis Armstrong's *Plays W. C. Handy* collection from 1954, but the album below contains fascinating personal reminiscences by this gentle Father of the Blues. [DF]

Father of the Blues: a musical autobiography (1952–3), DRG

See Handy, W. C., *Father of the Blues* (Sidgwick & Jackson, Jazz Book Club Edition, 1961)

Hanna, Jake (John), drums, b. Roxbury, Massachusetts, 4 April 1931. A Boston-based musician until the late 1950s, he worked with Marian McPartland and Woody Herman before (in 1964) starting a ten-year stint on American TV's Merv Griffin Show. During that period he worked in an impressively eclectic variety of settings from the Clark Terry–Bob Brookmeyer quintet and Maynard Ferguson to the Oscar Peterson trio in 1974, and by later in the decade was working regularly with the stable of young stars that included Warren Vaché and Scott Hamilton for Carl Jefferson's Concord label and live with the Concord Super Band. Hanna's understanding of every area of jazz drums – from Baby Dodds to Ed Thigpen and beyond – makes him a riveting performer to hear and see. Like Louie Bellson, he functions equally happily in a big band or small group, and although he emerged too late into the jazz scene to achieve quite the reputation of Buddy Rich, Bellson and their peers, his talents are comparable. [DF]

Concord Super Band Live in Tokyo (1979), Concord

Hanna, Sir Roland P., piano, composer. b. Detroit, Michigan, 10 February 1932. Played regularly in Detroit and elsewhere before studying at music college in mid-1950s. Worked with Benny Goodman (1958), Charles Mingus (1959, and for recording 1971). Led own trios and duos regularly from 1959, also with Thad Jones–Mel Lewis (1967–74). Toured as soloist in Europe and Africa (1968–9); 1974, founded New York Jazz Quartet with Frank Wess, Ron Carter, drummer Ben Riley. In addition to several albums under his own name, Hanna is notable for backing work in ensemble contexts which is always exciting and to the point. As a soloist, he displays an improvisatory flair in various European 'classical' styles besides his brilliant jazz work. His knighthood was bestowed by the President of Liberia. [BP]

Perugia (1974), Black Lion/Freedom

Hard Bop A term coined in the late 1950s for the then current consolidation of bop, after its more effete tendencies had been effectively hived off by the 'cool' West Coast musicians and by East Coasters such as the Modern Jazz Quartet.

The positive aspects of hard bop involved its exaggeration of early bop's polyrhythmic vitality, especially in the accompaniments of bandleaders Art Blakey, Max Roach and Horace Silver, and the resilience of soloists such as Sonny Rollins or Lee Morgan. This was more palatable than the 1940s style partly because of the apparent simplicity of much of the original material written for these groups. Heard alongside the occasional Parker tune which they retained in their repertoire, a typical hard-bop composition sounded closer to r & b (but with post-bop improvisation) while some even harked back directly to the 'jump bands' of the 1930s. This, incidentally, is why it became fashionable in the 1980s for a new generation of listeners to dance to hard-bop records made as much as 25 years earlier, a fashion which began in London and threatens to spread to the rest of the jazz world. [BP]

Harding, Buster (Lavere), arranger, piano. b. Ontario, Canada, 19 March 1917; d. 14 November 1965. Brought up in Cleveland, where he started his own band as a teenager. After work in Buffalo and Boston, arranged for Teddy Wilson big band (1939–40). Also wrote for Coleman Hawkins band and for Cab Calloway (1941–2); turning freelance, contributed arrangements to Roy Eldridge, Artie Shaw, Count Basie, Calloway, Dizzy Gillespie etc. Musical director for record sessions by Billie Holiday (1949, also playing piano for her in 1951) and Gillespie (1954). Apart from playing briefly with Jonah Jones (early 1960s), was restricted by illness although continuing to write. Harding's block-chord voicing for brass focused the Calloway band during one of its best periods, and helped to set the style of the post-war Basie band; his 1947 'Mr Roberts' Roost' for Basie was adapted in the later jukebox hit 'Paradise Squat'. [BP]

The Indispensable Count Basie (1927–50), RCA

Hardman, Bill (William Franklin, Jnr.), trumpet. b. Cleveland, Ohio, 6 April 1933. Frequent affiliations with Charles Mingus (1956, 1969–70 and big band in 1972) and with Art Blakey (1956–8, 1966–9, 1970, 1975–6). Also briefly with Horace Silver, Lloyd Price big band, several years with Lou Donaldson (1959–66). Has run his own group, the Brass Company, and played in USA and Europe with Junior Cook (1979–81). An admirer of Clifford Brown, Hardman in his early work had a limited phraseology and a peculiarly acrid tone which were very identifiable. He has built on this foundation to become a wide-ranging stylist who deserves to be more widely known. [BP]

Home (1978), Muse

Hardwicke, Otto 'Toby', alto, bass and baritone sax. b. Washington, DC, 31 May 1904; d. 5 August 1970. A childhood friend of Duke Ellington, he began as a bass player in Carroll's Columbia Orchestra and was persuaded to take up C-melody saxophone by Ellington around 1920. 'Toby was a great saxophone player so far as tone and execution were concerned,' says Mercer Ellington, 'and he was also valuable from the standpoint of thought and ideas.' But Hardwicke, for a variety of reasons (wanderlust, a variety of girlfriends or drinking) would disappear at inconvenient moments in Ellington's early career-building campaign. After 1928 he went to Europe, worked with Noble Sissle and Nekka Shaw and by 1930 was leading his own band, featuring a five-man saxophone section – an innovation – in Harlem. (His band once bested Ellington's in a famous battle, and may have helped Ellington towards his idea for an enlarged saxophone section later on.) When he rejoined Ellington in 1932, Hardwicke found Johnny Hodges leading the section and the band more of an autocracy than the freewheeling club it had been ten years before. But he stayed with Ellington, on the whole very happily, until 1946 when the demands of travel, increased drinking and increasing arguments with Ellington caused a crack in his friendship with his leader. Eventually he left the band for good and retired. [DF]

Duke Ellington, *Hot from Harlem* (1927–30), World Records (double)

See Dance, Stanley, *The World of Duke Ellington* (Scribner's, 1970, repr. Da Capo, 1980)

Hardy, Emmett Louis, cornet. b. Gretna, New Orleans, 12 June 1903; d. New Orleans, 16 June 1925. The best-remembered 'fact' about the legendary Emmett Hardy is that he influenced the young Bix Beiderbecke, but as no records of his work exist the sharply divided opinions that research has stimulated are hard to quantify one way or the other. As Hardy was a graduate of Papa Jack Laine's 'Children', a New Orleans university for young jazzmen (so was Nick La Rocca who unquestionably influenced Beiderbecke) and later on regularly worked on the steamship SS *Capitol*, which he first joined in Beiderbecke's home town, Davenport, Iowa, it seems certain enough that Bix heard him at least and may well have been inspired by him, if only temporarily. Hardy – after a brief visit to Chicago, where an attempt to join the New Orleans Rhythm Kings was foiled by the American Federation of Musicians – returned to New Orleans and died soon after of tuberculosis at just 22. [DF]

Harlem Hamfats, see MORAND, HERB.

Harmolodics A theory formulated by Ornette Coleman and derived from his practice as an improvising musician: each instrument in an ensemble is both a melody and a rhythm instrument; players abandon their traditional roles and instruments which normally accompany share as lead voices in creating the music. No instruments play a supportive/accompanying role and the resulting music comprises contrapuntal lines. Harmonic consonance and resolution become irrelevant, the emphasis being on creating interacting lines. [IC]

Harmonics Apart from being founded on the same laws of physics, harmonics have nothing to do with considerations of harmony (see below). The principles are most easily understood in connection with stringed instruments, where the act of lightly touching a string at its midpoint sets both halves vibrating at twice the frequency, i.e. exactly one octave higher than its normal pitch. Used only for special effects, these harmonics created on guitar, violin or bass (even on piano, by playing the strings themselves 'under the lid') have a veiled but ringing tone when compared to the normal method of note production on such instruments.

Harmonics are an everyday fact of life for brass players who blow down tubes with valves or slides attached, e.g. trumpets, trombones etc. For the valves and slides only change the instruments' pitch by half an octave at most, and all other variations of pitch are made by manipulation of the mouthpiece. The lowest available notes (used occasionally by cornettists Rex Stewart and Nat Adderley, and more frequently by trombonists but mostly in big-band arrangements) are rather rude, flatulent sounds called fundamentals; everything else from the low register to the extreme high register is achieved by using the lips to double and redouble the frequency of vibrations, thereby producing a series of harmonics of the fundamental note.

The term is most often employed in connection with the reeds, such as clarinet or saxophones. Here, producing harmonics by accidentally overblowing is heard simply as a squeak, but the controlled use of overblowing (absolutely forbidden in European technique) has become one of the joys of jazz saxophone. Again it involves a different tone quality, thinner and more urgent, as can be heard in the occasional extra-high notes of Charlie Parker, Paul Desmond or Eric Dolphy. Particularly on tenor saxophone, where their production is easier, extending the upper range with harmonics has become almost mandatory. Illinois Jacquet first made them a speciality in the 1940s, since when they have gone into the vocabulary of funk saxists everywhere, but quite different expressive use has been made of them by both John Coltrane and Stan Getz.

Beginning in the 1930s, Lester Young also introduced the harmonics derived from his very lowest notes, which came out not extremely high but in the middle range of his instrument. He, and others who picked up the idea from him, including Sonny Rollins, exploited the difference of tone from the normal middle-range sound of the instrument. (See also MULTIPHONICS.) [BP]

Harmony The idea of selected notes sounding together to form chords is the great European additive to Afro-American music. It may have been less than totally essential to blues although, by the time they were first recorded, a succession of accompanying chords was fairly standard. The style that came to be known as gospel, on the other hand, had since its earliest beginnings a harmonic content, but treated it with increasing freedom as time went on.

Jazz has always had something of an ambivalent relationship to harmony. For the first 50-odd years of the century, rhythm-section instruments scrupulously observed the chord-changes of a particular piece, while the horns often played with an independence inspired by the blues singers. During the same period, most of the major innovators from Armstrong onwards showed an increasing sophistication in their handling of harmony but, in various ways, avoided being dominated by this concern; Lester Young, in fact, used his harmonic sophistication to work against the chords at times, just as blues-based riffs had often done. However, in the wake of bebop, many lesser players of the 1950s (it is hard now to remember their names, and they have not earned a place elsewhere in this book) seemed over-worried by chordal correctness, which is no doubt one reason why the new styles of the late 1950s (free and modal jazz) attempted to abandon harmony altogether.

It is interesting to note, however, that harmony has made several comebacks since then, and to set that fact alongside George Russell's suggestion that jazz improvisation has always been more scale-based than chord-based. Perhaps the truth is that the use of harmony in jazz is less of a guiding light than in most

European music, and more a matter of texture. [BP]

Harper, Billy, tenor sax, flute, vocals, composer. b. Houston, Texas, 17 January 1943. Family and relations all sing; he was soloist in the church choir. Began on saxophone at 12; lessons at high school, and he played in the school marching and jazz band, 1959–61. At North Texas State University, 1961–5, graduating B.Mus. in saxophone and theory; he also did special jazz studies there. He played with r & b bands; 1966, moved to New York. 1967–mid-1970s, worked with Gil Evans, touring Japan with him in 1972, and playing on several Evans albums including that classic mélange of acoustic and electric instruments, *Svengali* (1973). 1968–70, he also worked with Art Blakey and toured Japan with him. 1971, he joined the Thad Jones–Mel Lewis big band, touring Europe with them in 1973. He led groups of his own in the early 1970s and worked with Max Roach, Lee Morgan, Elvin Jones and others. 1975, he took his quintet to Europe, performing throughout Scandinavia, and also in the Netherlands, France and Italy.

He has been active in music education since the mid-1960s teaching improvisation, sax and flute, privately and in schools and colleges. With his own and various other groups he has played major festivals in the USA, Europe and North Africa. Harper is a fine composer, and Gil Evans has arranged and recorded some of his pieces including the blues/gospel masterpiece 'Thoroughbred' (on the *Svengali* album), one of the definitive performances of 1970s fusion music. Harper's influences include Rollins, Coltrane and Gil Evans. [IC]

With Jones/Lewis, Max Roach, Lee Morgan, Randy Weston, Art Blakey and others; with Gil Evans, *Masabumi Kikuchi and Gil Evans* (1972), Japanese Philips; *Svengali* (1973), Atlantic; as leader, *Capra Black* (1973), Strata-East; *Black Saint* (1975), Black Saint

Harrell, Tom (Thomas), trumpet, fluegelhorn. b. Urbana, Illinois, 16 June 1946. Moved to San Francisco area with family at age five. Joined Woody Herman (1970–1) and Horace Silver (1973–7). Also with Azteca, Arnie Lawrence's Treasure Island, National Jazz Ensemble, studio work. Phil Woods quartet was expanded to quintet by addition of Harrell (1983–). His style was described by Horace Silver: 'He's got his own thing, but you can hear Dizzy, Miles, Hubbard, Kenny Dorham, Blue [Mitchell] and Clifford [Brown].' Very fluent technically, Harrell's playing neverthless gives the impression of understatement and restrained lyricism. [BP]

Moon Alley (1985), Criss Cross

Harriott, Joe (Arthurlin), alto and baritone sax, piano, composer. b. Jamaica, West Indies, 15 July 1928; d. Southampton, Hants, 2 January 1973. Studied clarinet at school, then played saxophone in dance bands. Emigrated to UK in 1951, freelancing in London. 1954, played at the Paris festival with Tony Kinsey; 1955, worked with Ronnie Scott and others; 1959, toured UK with Modern Jazz Quartet. He began leading his own groups in 1958; performed with his quintet at the 1959 San Remo Jazz Festival, after which he contracted tuberculosis and spent six months in hospital. He had begun as a Parker-inspired altoist, and by the end of the 1950s was a very fine player in the conventional post-bebop mould: everything in common time (4/4 or 3/4), themes played at the beginning and end of pieces, improvisation based closely on harmonic sequences. In hospital he conceived the idea of a music (written and improvised) without set rhythmic and harmonic patterns – abstract music – and immediately began composing 'free-form' pieces. Once out of hospital in late 1959 he began rehearsing the pieces with his quintet which comprised Shake Keane (tpt/fluegelhorn), Pat Smythe (piano), Coleridge Goode (bass) and Phil Seamen (dms), all of whom grasped the new concept immediately. They recorded the album *Free Form* in 1960; *Abstract* (1962) received great critical acclaim in the USA.

Joe Harriott

Harriott's abstract music was nothing like the free form jazz created by Ornette Coleman around the same time. Coleman's was shot through with the blues and the Afro-American tradition and, although harmonically abstract, it usually featured a swinging rhythm-section, thus occurring in clearly defined time. Harriott's abstraction often had no regular rhythm, sometimes featured total silences as an integral part of the music, fused Afro-Caribbean elements with the jagged lines and dissonances of Western European avant-garde music, and occasionally included solo (i.e. totally unaccompanied) improvisation by any one of the five players. Abstraction simply added a new dimension to the Harriott quintet's music, and the group often juxtaposed conventionally structured pieces with free-form ones. In the early 1960s they performed the new music at several festivals in Europe.

During the mid-1960s Harriott pioneered yet another trend-setting innovation, collaborating with the Indian violinist and composer John Mayer to create Indo-Jazz Fusions. Using a sextet of jazz musicians and a quartet of Indian musicians, they compounded elements from jazz and Indian music into a rich new synthesis. Three albums were recorded and, again, the 10-piece fusion group performed at many European festivals.

Joe Harriott was a compelling and original soloist with a searing, passionate sound, an inexhaustible fund of rhythmic and melodic ideas and great technical mastery. He was perfectly at home in any context – big band, small group or fusion orchestra – and the master of any idiom, whether conventional, abstract or mixed genre. He was also an important innovator, the father of European free jazz as opposed to the American kind, and one of the first jazz musicians to revitalize his music by integrating it with elements from ethnic music. Unfortunately, his achievements went virtually unrecognized in the UK, and he neither worked enough nor made enough money to survive comfortably. It became impossible for him to lead a regular group, and he was forced to travel around as a soloist playing with local rhythm-sections in provincial towns, sleeping on people's couches or their floors, or wherever he could. In this sense, his last years were horribly similar to those of Charlie Parker, and perhaps even more tragically lonely. He died of cancer at the age of 44. [IC]

Free Form (1960), Jazzland; *Abstract* (1962); *Movement* (1963); *High Spirits* (1964); *Indo-Jazz Suite* (1965); *Indo-Jazz Fusions* (1966); *Indo-Jazz Fusions II* (1967), all Columbia; *Swings High* (1967), Melodisc

Harris, Barry Doyle, piano. b. Detroit, Michigan, 15 December 1929. Like his contemporary and fellow Detroiter Tommy Flanagan, an important second-generation bop stylist. After brief tours with Max Roach in 1956 and Cannonball Adderley in 1960, moved to New York and has remained there teaching and playing mostly under his own name. Became the favourite accompanist of Coleman Hawkins in the mid-1960s; deputized for Thelonious Monk in rehearsals of New York Jazz Repertory Company tribute in 1974. Over the years, Harris has shown an increasing affinity for the music of Monk, in addition to his close involvement in the styles of Powell and Parker. While less intense than either of these players, Harris has a beautifully crisp and lithe approach which readily explains his influence on a number of young players. Since 1982, he has run the Jazz Cultural Centre, a combined nightclub and school in New York. [BP]

For the Moment (1984), Uptown

Harris, Beaver (William Godvin), drums. b. Pittsburgh, Pennsylvania, 20 April 1936. Mother a dancer who played piano. He played clarinet and alto sax as a teenager; became involved in baseball, playing in all major black leagues – his nickname derives from his baseball days. Played baseball and drums while in the US army. After discharge, moved to New York in 1963, working with Sonny Rollins, Thelonious Monk, Joe Henderson, Freddie Hubbard and others. Joined Archie Shepp in 1966, touring Europe with him, and also working with Albert Ayler there. Also worked with Sonny Stitt, Dexter Gordon, Clark Terry. At the end of the 1960s, he formed a co-operative group with Grachan Moncur III, the 360 Degree Experience. 1970, he played with Shepp for LeRoi Jones's play *Slave Ship*; 1973 for Aishah Rahman's *Lady Day: A Musical Tragedy*. 1973, he also did the Newport Jazz Festival tour of Japan with Shepp, Konitz, Gato Barbieri and others. Influences include Kenny Clarke, Max Roach, Roy Haynes, Sonny Rollins. Harris has composed lyrics and music for some Shepp albums. [IC]

With Ayler, Steve Lacy, Pharoah Sanders, Barbieri, Marion Brown, Roswell Rudd and others; with Shepp, *Montreux One* (1975), Arista; as leader, *In Sanity* (1976), Black Saint (double)

Harris, Benny (Benjamin), trumpet, composer. b. New York City, 23 April 1919; d. 11 February 1975. With Tiny Bradshaw (1939), Earl Hines (1941 and 1942–3), small-group work on 52nd Street with Coleman Hawkins, Don Byas etc. Took part in important early bebop record session by Clyde Hart All Stars (December 1944), later intermittent activity as player, e.g. with Charlie Parker (1951–2). Harris contributed to bop repertoire by combining the chords of 'How High the Moon' with Parker's solo on 'Jumpin' Blues' to create 'Ornithology'. Other compositions include 'Little Benny' (aka 'Bud's Bubble' aka 'Crazeology'), 'Reets and I' and 'Wahoo'. [BP]

Don Byas (4 tracks with Harris), *Savoy Jam Party* (1944–6), Savoy

Harris, Bill (Willard Palmer), trombone. b. Philadelphia, 28 October 1916; d. 19 September

1973. Came to prominence as one of the leading soloists of the Woody Herman band, rejoining several times during his career (1944–6, 1948–50, 1956–8, 1959). Co-led groups with Charlie Ventura (1947) and bassist Chubby Jackson (1953), and made annual tours with Jazz at the Philharmonic (1950–4). 1960s, was occupied playing in backing bands at various Las Vegas nightspots, then retired to Florida.

Harris's style was especially distinctive during the period of his greatest popularity, the late 1940s and early 1950s. Though not unaware of bebop, he based himself firmly on swing-era greats such as J. C. Higginbotham. His forthright delivery, complete with a variety of articulation and slurring, conveyed his frequently outrageous sense of humour, reminiscent of a vulgarized Vic Dickenson. Nowadays overlooked except by Herman fans, Harris's always enjoyable solo work deserves wider recognition. [BP]

Bill Harris and Friends (1957), Fantasy/OJC

Harris, Eddie, tenor sax, electric piano, organ, reed trumpet, voice, composer. b. Chicago, 20 October 1936. Studied piano with a cousin and sang with choirs and gospel groups in Baptist churches. At high school, played vibes, clarinet and tenor sax. Professional début as pianist with Gene Ammons. In the 1950s he toured all over France and Germany with the 7th Army Symphony Orchestra. Back in Chicago as a civilian, in 1960 he recorded a single of the movie theme 'Exodus' and it became a national hit, selling a million copies. This commercial success badly damaged his reputation in the jazz community, and since then Harris has always been something of a loner – following his own path and starting trends rather than following them. During the 1960s he earned more contumely by using rock rhythms and experimenting with electronics – which were anathema to the reactionary purism of the jazz scene. At the Newport Jazz Festival, 1970, he also astonished the crowd with another of his technical innovations – a trumpet and fluegelhorn each played with a reed instead of the usual mouthpiece. Although he patented this idea, and one or two people did use the hybrid instruments, the reed trumpet never really caught on, perhaps largely because its sound and attack lacked the true characteristics of the trumpet. As a result of the prejudice against Harris he has rarely, if ever, received any serious critical attention, only the dismissive variety. He is an excellent player, a master of electronics and a prolific composer with a large body of work on record. His magnificent composition 'Freedom Jazz Dance' was recorded by Miles Davis in the mid-1960s, and has since become part of the repertoire and consciousness of subsequent generations of musicians. [IC]

The Best of Eddie Harris (nda); *The Electrifying Eddie Harris* (1967); *Excursions* (nda); *Free Speech* (1970); *Live At Newport* (1970); *Silver Cycles* (nda); *E.H. in the UK* (1972), all Atlantic

Harrison, Donald, alto and soprano sax, composer. b. New Orleans, Louisiana, 23 June 1960. Studied under Ellis Marsalis and Alvin Batiste in New Orleans while still at school, and at Berklee College (1979–80). Worked with Roy Haynes (1980–1), Jack McDuff (1981), then joined Art Blakey (1982–6). As well as recording with Jazz Messengers, co-led albums with fellow Messenger Terence Blanchard, with whom he also played in quintet. Like many of the younger black American jazzmen, Harrison has a strong sense of the tradition, for example arranging 'When the Saints' for the Blanchard/Harrison album *Discernment* and featuring himself on weighty standards such as 'Body and Soul' (on Blakey's *Blue Night*) and 'I Can't Get Started'. But, stylistically, he is firmly of the post-Dolphy generation, with a heated tone to his improvisations and an impressive command of high harmonics. [BP]

Art Blakey, *Blue Night* (1985), Timeless; Harrison/Terence Blanchard, *Nascence* (1986), Epic

Harrison, Jimmy (James Henry), trombone, vocals. b. Louisville, Kentucky, 17 October 1900; d. New York City, 23 July 1931. He had varied early experience, including carnival bands (for which he developed a stand-up Bert Williams routine) and on occasion trio and duo work which helped to develop his trombone technique, revolutionary for its time, often played high up near the trumpet register, fast and melodic and very much in the style of Louis Armstrong. After arriving in New York in 1923 (with Fess Williams's band) he played Ed Small's Sugarcane Club with his best friend June Clark (young 'Bill' Basie played the piano), with Duke Ellington briefly, and with a variety of other bands including Elmer Snowden's. In 1927, Harrison joined Fletcher Henderson, was fired for his slow reading, then later re-hired: he became Henderson's star trombone soloist, a funny and likeable cornerman, and close buddy of Coleman Hawkins, who arranged 'Singin' in the Rain' and several other songs to spotlight Harrison's Bert Williams-style routines. Jack Teagarden and Harrison became inseparable friends: they must have been an attractive pair, immaculately suited, easy-going, always laughing and partying: the trombone titans of their generation. And, evidently, they had things to show one another. They played together in clubs and rent parties (where Teagarden loved the soul food), often with Coleman Hawkins pumping a piano accompaniment. In 1930, however, Harrison became ill and a year later he died of stomach cancer. He remained a primary influence on black trombonists for ten more years. [DF]

Fletcher Henderson, *A Study in Frustration* (1923–38), CBS (4 records, boxed set)

See Stewart, Rex, *Jazz Masters of the 30s* (Macmillan, 1972, repr. Da Capo, 1982)

Hart, Billy (William W.), drums. b. Washington, DC, 29 November 1940. Early professional work with local saxophonist Buck Hill (to whom he returned the favour 20 years later by setting up Hill's album début), and with singer Shirley Horn. Worked briefly with the Montgomery Brothers (1961), then with Jimmy Smith (1964–6, including European tour), Wes Montgomery (1966–8). Gigging with Eddie Harris, Pharoah Sanders and Marian McPartland, joined Herbie Hancock sextet (1969–73), then with McCoy Tyner (1973–4), Stan Getz (1974–7). Also freelance appearances and recording with a wide variety of musicians, including in Europe. Hart is equally capable of straight-ahead time playing with a creative flair, and of the more impressionistic approach. His wide sensibilities are well illustrated by the first album issued under his own name (below). [BP]

Enchance (1977), Horizon

Hart, Clyde, piano, arranger. b. Baltimore, Maryland, 1910; d. 19 March 1945. Played with big bands including Blanche Calloway's (1931–5). Based in New York from 1936, recorded with such important soloists as Henry 'Red' Allen, Billie Holiday, Stuff Smith, Lionel Hampton, Chu Berry, Roy Eldridge and Lester Young. Replaced Billy Kyle with the John Kirby Sextet (1942) and was working with Tiny Grimes's group when Charlie Parker was added for his small-band recording in 1944. During the last couple of months before his death from tuberculosis, Hart cut the only discs under his own name, including the first studio appearance of Parker and Gillespie together. An unhackneyed player who demonstrated the continuity between 1930s jazz and bebop. [BP]

Charlie Parker, *Complete Savoy Studio Sessions, vol. 1* (1944–5), Savoy

Harvey, Eddie (Edward Thomas), trombone, piano, composer/arranger, educator. b. Blackpool, Lancashire, 15 November 1925. Mother played piano and sang. He began in traditional jazz and was a founder member of George Webb's Dixielanders, 1943–6. After National Service with the RAF played with Freddy Randall, 1949–50, then graduated to modern jazz, playing with Vic Lewis. He was a founder member of the Johnny Dankworth Seven in 1950, and worked with Dankworth's big band until the mid-1950s. During the later 1950s and the 1960s, he worked with many leading jazz musicians including Don Rendell and Tubby Hayes, and toured with Woody Herman's Anglo-American Herd and the Maynard Ferguson big band. He has written arrangements for many people including Humphrey Lyttelton (in whose band he played piano for a time) and the Jack Parnell Orchestra at Associated Television. Harvey is very active in education, running regular courses and annual summer schools; he has given regular lectures on jazz at the City Literary Institute, London, and from the early 1970s until 1985 he was assistant Music Master at Haileybury College, Hertfordshire. He has written one book: *Teach Yourself Jazz Piano*, London, 1974. [IC]

LPs with Dankworth and Lyttelton

Hastings, Lennie (Leonard), drums, piano, leader. b. London, 5 January 1927; d. 14 July 1978. He worked around the British post-war modern jazz scene, before joining Freddy Randall's band during their Cooks Ferry Inn tenure. A natural devotee of the style of Cliff Leeman, he moved to Alex Welsh's band in 1954 and (apart from isolated bandleading spells, a stint with Nat Gonella in the early 1960s and time with Johnny Duncan's Blue Grass Boys at the same period) stayed with Welsh, with whom he became a much-loved cornerman, until 1973 when a patch of ill health caused him to leave temporarily: he was replaced by Roger Nobes. From then on Hastings led his own band, toured with American visitors including Wild Bill Davison, Ruby Braff and Soprano Summit, broadcast regularly, worked with Fred Hunt's trio, and was often to be found at Pizza Express. Hastings's lunatic sense of humour – one speciality, originating with Welsh's band, was to sing Tauberesque songs in cod-German, wearing a battered German helmet and half a crown for a monocle – was almost as well known as the Dixieland drumming which made him a favourite with American visitors. He collapsed from a stroke in 1978 and died six weeks later in hospital. [DF]

Any with Alex Welsh; *Always the Best* (1978), Dawn Club

Haurand, Ali (Alfred Antonius Josef), bass, composer. b. Viersen, Germany, 15 November 1943. His mother an amateur pianist. 1965–71, Haurand studied music at Volkswangschule at Essen. 1969, started his own trio playing concerts in Germany, San Sebastian, Belgium and France. He started his own group, Third Eye, in 1970 and, with different personnel, the group has continued into the mid-1980s. It has included Kenny Wheeler, Alan Skidmore, Tony Levin, Gerd Dudek, among others, over the years. Since 1977, Haurand has been a member of the European Jazz Quintet; since 1978, with SOH, a trio consisting of Skidmore, Tony Oxley and himself, from time to time augmented to a quartet with either Wheeler or John Surman. 1985, Haurand founded the Quintet with Joachim Kühn and Enrico Rava. He has also worked with many other leading European and American musicians. With his trio he won prizes at the 1969 festivals in San Sebastian and Bilzen (Belgium). He cites bassists Charles Mingus and Jimmy Garrison as his main initial inspiration, but is also influenced by John Coltrane and his quartet, Bill Evans and Gil Evans. [IC]

25 albums, many under his own name and by his own groups, including, *Ali Haurand Solo* (1974), Naked Metram; *Third Eye Live* (with Wheeler/Skidmore) (1982), View; *SOH Live at Neuss* (1981), View; *The Quartet* (1985), Konnex

Havens, Bob, trombone, vibes. b. Quincy, Illinois, 3 May 1930. Early work around Chicago in the mid-1950s was followed by a spell with Ralph Flanagan's orchestra, and while working with Flanagan, Havens found himself in New Orleans for a month's residency. He fell in love with the city, moved there to live in 1956 and joined George Girard's band: when Girard became ill the following year, Havens moved over to join Al Hirt's spectacular group, which had also featured young clarinettist Pete Fountain, by then a featured star with Lawrence Welk. 1959, after enormous success with Hirt's much-recorded group, Havens joined Welk too (one of his specialities was a high-speed 'Tiger Rag') and stayed for over 20 years, appearing on TV regularly and doubling up with studio work in spare moments. In the 1980s he became first call for the kind of classic Dixieland that Bob Crosby patented (in 1985 he worked with Crosby, Dick Cathcart and Don Goldie) and leads his own band, besides teaching, conducting clinics and work as a soloist with high school and college bands. A highly gifted all-round trombonist, Havens names his early influences as 'Dorsey I guess, and then came Bill Harris. But Jack Teagarden – along with Lou McGarity – was the biggest influence of all.' [DF]

Pete Fountain, *Standing Room Only!* (1965), Coral

Hawdon, Dick (Richard), trumpet, fluegelhorn, bass, mellophone. b. Leeds, Yorkshire, 27 August 1927. His brilliant career began post-war in the Yorkshire Jazz Band (leader Bob Barclay) and Chris Barber's two-trumpet group (his partner was Ben Cohen), as well as bands led by himself and with the well remembered Christie Brothers' Stompers. By 1951 he was living in London and developing his style to encompass the modern jazz players he loved: Clifford Brown, Fats Navarro and a Scottish mentor, Jimmy Deuchar: only three years after playing highly convincing, classic-style music with the Stompers, Hawdon was working and recording with Don Rendell's band, for Tubby Hayes's octet (in 1955) and recording with Hayes playing advanced contemporary material. By a year later, after work with Ivor and Basil Kirchin, he was featured soloist for Johnny Dankworth, then, 1960–2, lead trumpet. Curiously, this astonishing stylistic development caused less controversy than Hawdon's decision in 1962 to join Terry Lightfoot's (traditional) Jazzmen, which made headlines in the jazz press of the time: he was sensible enough to ignore them and carried on – like Humphrey Lyttelton in a less well-publicized reverse order – 'playing as he pleased'. In the late 1960s, after another stint with Dankworth, then years playing lead at the Prince of Wales Theatre in London and a spell as MD at Batley Variety Club, Hawdon became a senior lecturer back home at Leeds College of Music. He also took up bass, and now makes regular appearances at Midlands jazz clubs backing Americans such as Art Farmer. In the mid-1980s he remains one of the best trumpeters in the country, with a weathered style taking in the best of his long, eclectic career. [DF]

Tubby Hayes, *After Lights Out* (1956), Jasmine

Hawes, Hampton, piano. b. Los Angeles, 13 November 1928; d. 22 May 1977. One of the few influential black musicians to have remained resident on the West Coast of the USA. Began gigging as a teenager with r & b saxist Big Jay McNeely, and worked briefly with Charlie Parker (1947). In the early 1950s Hawes was successfully employed by the figureheads of the budding 'West Coast movement', Shorty Rogers and Howard Rumsey's Lighthouse All Stars. After army service in Japan, formed his own trio with Red Mitchell on bass, which made a series of impressive albums. Incarcerated in the late 1950s for drug offences and released in 1963 through executive clemency of President Kennedy, Hawes began recording again for Contemporary but found the jazz scene changed and less welcoming. A privately arranged round-the-world tour (1967–8) led to Hawes cutting half a dozen albums in Europe and Japan but on return to the USA he remained in unwarranted obscurity. Recording again in the early 1970s, Hawes took up electric piano; visited Europe again in 1971, and for the Montreux festival, 1973, with other Prestige artists (Dexter Gordon, Gene Ammons). The ups and downs of his career were detailed in his short but moving autobiography.

In his début recording (Dexter Gordon/Wardell Gray, *The Hunt*, 1947, Savoy) the germ of Hawes's mature style is quite discernible. His most renowned work in the 1950s found him combining the glittering precision of Bud Powell and Charlie Parker with some of the blues tinge later associated with 'funky' pianists. This development ran parallel to the work of Horace Silver at the same period, and indeed Hawes's sense of timing was then very similar to that of Silver, but the Hawes right hand was usually more florid and boppish, influencing Oscar Peterson. On his comeback during the 1960s Hawes adopted some of the then popular mannerisms derived from Bill Evans which, as with his espousal of the electric keyboard in the 1970s, did not mix well with his earlier, eminently percussive approach. He can hardly be overestimated, however, as an important figure in jazz piano history. [BP]

This is Hampton Hawes, vol. 2 (1955–6), Contemporary; *Four!* (1958), Contemporary/OJC

See Hawes, Hampton, and Asher, Don, *Raise Up Off Me* (Coward, McCann, 1973, repr. Da Capo, 1979)

Hawkins, Coleman Randolph, tenor sax. b. St Joseph, Missouri, 21 November *c.* 1901; d. New York City, 19 May 1969. 'He's the person who played the tenor saxophone, who woke you up and let you know there was a tenor saxophone', says Lester Young, Hawkins's principal rival for the first 30 years of jazz history. Hawkins himself created what was, to begin with, an omnipotent vocabulary for the tenor, and for 45 years he maintained and consolidated his lead.

He was playing to audiences by the age of 12, for school dances and developing his master's technique. Still in his early teens, he was regularly in Kansas and travelling at weekends over to Chicago where he heard young pacesetters such as Stomp Evans, Buster Bailey (renowned for his speed), Happy Caldwell, and headlining acts including Sophie Tucker and Ted Lewis, a Hawkins favourite. 1921, he joined Mamie Smith's Jazz Hounds, a hit-making touring group, and went on the road soaking up experience from the music all around him. (In later years Hawkins claimed that with Mamie Smith he was young enough to need a guardian: in fact he was 20 and, by his own admission, 'as big as I am now', an example of Hawkins's sly habit of lopping years off his age.) 1924, he joined Fletcher Henderson for ten years and instantly, with his developing style and roller-coaster speed, became a star of the orchestra: one of the team of omnipotent Henderson 'killers' that included his old idol Buster Bailey and trombonist Jimmy Harrison, who became a close friend. In Henderson's orchestra, Hawkins exercised his cool ear for the abilities of those around him like a dignified, omnipotent pedagogue; he always dressed in the most expensive clothes, drove the fastest car on Henderson's tours and quickly established himself as the Attila of jazz saxophone, ruthlessly cutting down opposition rash enough to challenge him. His contribution to the unbridled stomping power of Henderson's orchestra was mighty, as demonstrated by an early classic, 'Stampede'. In spare moments the killer also arranged for Henderson's band, including a Bert Williams pastiche of 'Singin' in the Rain' for Jimmy Harrison which, he owned, 'sounded a little different!'

By 1934 he was becoming disillusioned with Henderson, sent a telegram to 'Jack Hylton, London, England' (on the advice of June Clark, Henderson's bass player) and on 29 March stepped off the *Ile de France* to begin a five-year tour of Europe in the UK. He played the London Palladium with Hylton's band and for the next five years was to work not only in England but in Holland, France, Denmark (his favourite), Switzerland, Sweden and elsewhere. Away from the American downgrading of his race, Hawkins could cut the dash he felt he deserved but in 1939 he made his leisurely way back to Chicago: 'Fletcher was playin'! He knew I was out in the audience and sent a waiter with a note saying, "Don't you think it's about time the leave of absence is over?" And signed his name at the bottom!' While he was re-establishing his saxophone supremacy at Kelly's Stables on 52nd Street in 1939, Hawkins recorded the side forever to be most associated with his name. 'Body and Soul', which he used as a ten-chorus feature at Kelly's, was recorded in a two-chorus abbreviation for RCA Victor and the record – a prototype of 1939 jazz saxophone, with subtly amended changes, graceful swooping Hawk-like improvisations and perfectly faultless execution – became a jazz classic to place alongside Armstrong's 'West End Blues'.

Hawkins's involvement with bebop in the years that followed was confident, swift, all-embracing. Where other musicians (Dave Tough or Roy Eldridge) felt inadequate and bruised by the revolution, modern jazz supplied Hawkins with the new harmonic challenges he needed to bite on. By 1943 he led a sextet with Don Byas, Thelonious Monk and trumpeter Benny Harris, and he took an active interest in the careers of young musicians such as Fats Navarro, Oscar Pettiford, Max Roach and Dizzy Gillespie. He was also regularly with Norman Granz's Jazz at the Philharmonic from 1946 (with Lester Young), led a quintet with frequent colleague Roy Eldridge and continued to forge a solo career which never suffered serious decline. Even when Hawkins's heavy-toned, gruff saxophone in the fashion-conscious 1950s occasionally seemed to take second place to young jazz Turks such as Stan Getz or Zoot Sims, there was never any serious doubt that he was still the finest exponent of his instrument anywhere in the world of jazz. In the 1960s, as undeposed King of New York, he was playing hotels and still recording prolifically with much younger men including Thad Jones and even Sonny Rollins, and beating them at their own game. Even the kinder revolution of rock and roll did nothing to shake his aplomb: 'rock doesn't sound too bad,' he said at the time, 'but I don't think the right people are playing it yet'. Later in his career, bearded like the prophet he was, Hawkins continued handing down his huge-toned jazz commandments until in 1969, ominously taciturn and worn thin from a permanent diet of lentil soup and brandy, he died. [DF]

Coleman Hawkins, 1930–41, CBS (double)

See Shapiro, Nat, and Hentoff, Nat, *The Jazz*

Makers (Rinehart, 1957, repr. Da Capo, 1979); Stewart, Rex, *Jazz Masters of the 30s* (Macmillan 1972, repr. Da Capo, 1982); Lyttelton, Humphrey, *The Best of Jazz: Enter the Giants* (Robson, 1981); Dance, Stanley, *The World of Swing* (Scribner's, 1974, repr. Da Capo, 1979); Villetard, Jean François, *Coleman Hawkins*: vol. 1 *1922–44*, vol. 2 *1945–57* (Micrography, 1985)

Hawkins, Erskine Ramsay, trumpet, bandleader. b. Birmingham, Alabama, 26 July 1914. In the 1930s a new generation of young trumpeters grew up in America whose speciality was impersonating Louis Armstrong. One of the best was Hawkins, a fine trained player, who had taken up trumpet at 13 and was soon able to deliver a high-powered parody of Armstrong's showier *tours-de-force* such as 'Shine' with its 100 top Cs rounded off with a super-F. 'That's what Erskine was doing all through the South', remembers Dud Bascomb, who was later himself to become featured soloist with Hawkins's big band, formed from a college group based at Alabama State Teachers' College, which first came to New York in 1934. The 'Bama State Collegians, as they were first known, opened at Harlem's Opera House, a vaudeville theatre, on 11 August that year, worked a variety of clubs thereafter (including the Ubangi in 1935) and began recording for Vocalion; after the death of Chick Webb their manager Moe Gale booked them into the Savoy Ballroom where they were to take over Webb's old position as unofficial house band. More success followed, including a record contract for the prestigious Bluebird label, and throughout the 1940s (with regular trips from New York around the South) Hawkins's rocking band, dispensing the same kind of gutbucket swing that Fletcher Henderson had featured at Roseland ten years before, regularly drew record crowds and easily dwarfed more famous names like Count Basie. A string of successful records – including 'Tuxedo Junction' (1939, co-composed by Hawkins, William Johnson, Dud Bascomb and Julian Dash), 'Someone's Rockin' My Dreamboat' (1941) and 'Tippin' In' (1945) – ensured Hawkins's popularity for another decade, and his band, featuring Dud Bascomb (tpt), 'Haywood' Henry (bar) and Avery Parrish (piano), easily survived the big-band decline until 1955, when reduction to a small-group format at last became essential. From 1960, Hawkins – a spectacular technician who, said trumpeter Sammy Lowe, 'had the potential to become a legend' – led a quartet at the Embers and continued recording, re-forming his orchestra and working hotels with his small group: in the 1970s he was still playing strong and guested at the 1979 Nice Jazz Festival. [DF]

Complete Erskine Hawkins (1938–9), RCA Black & White

Hayes, Clancy (Clarence Leonard), banjo, vocals, composer. b. Caney, nr. Parsons, Kansas, 14 November 1908; d. San Francisco, 13 March 1972. The banjo playing seventh son of a seventh son, he began his career in vaudeville in the early 1920s and from 1928 (as 'Bob Sheridan') was presenter for shows such as Mother's Cakes and Cookies and Tune Termites for NBC Radio, San Francisco. Ten years on he was frontman for Lu Watters's big band and remained with Watters for 12 more years all the way through the era of the Yerba Buena Jazz Band, singing and playing banjo and drums; then, after Bob Scobey broke away from Watters to form his hugely successful Frisco Jazz Band, Hayes's lazy vocalizing and humorous 'point material' became central to Scobey's show. With Scobey he recorded over 200 titles including, on occasion, his own marvellous compositions: two fine examples are 'Ten to one it's Tennessee', recorded by no less than Hoagy Carmichael, and the surreal 'Huggin' and a-Chalkin'', recorded by both Carmichael and Johnny Mercer. Sadly, Hayes never had a hit record himself (although *Downbeat* voted him 'New Star' singer of 1954), but continued working for Scobey until 1959 when he finally took up a solo career based in San Francisco but with regular trips away, to Chicago, around the Playboy Club circuit and to jazz festivals. After ten well-recorded solo years Hayes died of mouth cancer: his last record, 'Washboard Blues' with the Ten Greats of Jazz is as good as anything he ever did. [DF]

Swingin' Minstrel (1963), Good Time Jazz/Vogue

Hayes, Louis Sedell, drums. b. Detroit, Michigan, 31 May 1937. With Detroit-based Yusef Lateef quintet at age 18 (1955–6), then touring with Horace Silver (1956–9). Also freelance recording during this period, including with John Coltrane and Cecil Taylor. Member of Cannonball Adderley quintet (1959–65) until joining Oscar Peterson trio (1965–7, 1971–2). Co-led Jazz Communicators group with Freddie Hubbard–Joe Henderson (1967–8), later with Hubbard quintet (1970–1). Co-led quintet with Junior Cook (1975–6), who was succeeded by Woody Shaw (1976–7), later co-led quartet with Joe Farrell (1983–4). As well as continued freelance work, toured with McCoy Tyner trio (1985–). An alert and driving accompanist since his earliest professional days, Hayes rapidly matured into a versatile and dependable group player whose work is consistently exciting. [BP]

The Real Thing (1977), Muse

Hayes, Tubby (Edward Brian), tenor sax, flute, vibraphone, composer. b. London, 30 January 1935; d. 8 June 1973. Father a musician. Started on violin at age eight; changed to tenor at 12 and turned professional at 15. 1951, joined Kenny Baker; later with the big bands of Ambrose, Vic Lewis, Jack Parnell. Led his own

Tubby Hayes

octet, April 1955–October 1956, touring the UK with it. Encouraged by Victor Feldman, began playing vibes in December 1956. With Ronnie Scott he co-led the Jazz Couriers, 1957–9; he toured Germany with Kurt Edelhagen in 1959. His international reputation grew rapidly, and he was the first British contemporary soloist to appear at regular intervals in the USA: he played at the Half Note, New York, 1961, 1962 and 1964; also at Boston Jazz Workshop, 1964, and Shelly's Manne-Hole, Los Angeles, 1965.

In London he led his own big band, for which he did most of the writing; had his own TV series, 1961–2 and 1963. He deputized for Paul Gonsalves with the Ellington orchestra at the Royal Festival Hall in February 1964. With Mingus, Brubeck and others, he appeared in the film *All Night Long* (1961) and with his own quintet in *The Beauty Jungle* (1964) and *Dr Terror's House of Horrors* (1965). He played at many major festivals in Europe including Antibes, 1962, Lugano, 1963, Vienna with Friedrich Gulda, 1964, 1965, Berlin, 1964. At the end of the 1960s he underwent open-heart surgery and was out of action 1969–71, when he began working again. He died while undergoing a second heart operation.

Tubby was a virtuoso performer on tenor and flute, an excellent vibist, and a composer/arranger of rare talent. He could play with great sensitivity, and his technique and knowledge were such that he could compete on equal terms with most US musicians: he twice recorded as leader of all-American groups which included Clark Terry, Roland Kirk and James Moody. He also had the energy and courage to assert himself and his music in a basically unsympathetic environment – which the UK certainly was in so far as 'modern' jazz was concerned. He was a charismatic big-band leader, and he also led some distinguished small groups including two particularly fine quartets: one in the late 1950s which included Terry Shannon (piano), Jeff Clyne (bass), and Phil Seamen or Bill Eyden (dms); one in the later 1960s with Mike Pyne (piano), Ron Mathewson (bass) and Tony Levin (dms). His early influences were Charlie Parker, Sonny Rollins, Stan Getz. [IC]

Many as leader, including *Tubby Hayes and the Jazz Couriers* (1958), London; quartet, *Tubby's Groove* (1959), Tempo; with Clark Terry *et al.*, *Tubbs in NY* (1961); quintet, *Late Spot at Scott's* (1962); with Kirk/Moody *et al.*, *Tubby Hayes and the Allstars: Return Visit* (1962); orchestra, *100% Proof* (1966); quartet, *Mexican Green* (1967); *The Tubby Hayes Orchestra* (1969), all Fontana

Haynes, Roy Owen, drums. b. Roxbury, Massachusetts, 13 March 1926. Worked in Boston with Sabby Lewis band, also Frankie Newton and Pete Brown (early 1940s). Toured with Luis Russell (1945–7) and Lester Young sextet (1947–9). Gigged in New York with Kai Winding (1949), recording with him, Bud Powell and others. Joined Charlie Parker quintet (1949–50), rhythm-section also working with Wardell Gray and Stan Getz. After a hiatus, became regular drummer for Sarah Vaughan (1953–8), then freelancing with Miles Davis, Lee Konitz, Thelonious Monk (1958). Led own trio and quartet, and in next few years also appeared with George Shearing, Lennie Tristano, Kenny Burrell, Getz (1961) and Coltrane (1961, 1963). Regular touring with Getz (1965–7) and with Gary Burton quartet (1967, 1968). Since then, has continued to lead his own Hip Ensemble, including such players as George Adams and Hannibal Peterson (1972).

Still much in demand for freelance work with other musicians, his distinctive sound and style have been extremely influential on the generation of drummers whose main allegiance may seem to be to Max Roach. Frequently lighter and crisper than Roach, due to choosing instruments suitable to his small physical stature, Roy manages to be intelligently insistent and provocative in accompaniment without overpowering the soloist. His own solo work is brilliantly conceived to combine a feeling of continual suspense with absolute relaxation. [BP]

Thelonious Monk: In Action (1958), Riverside/OJC; *Out of the Afternoon* (1962), Jasmine

Head (1) 'A head' is short for 'head arrangement', that is, an arrangement worked out collectively (or dictated by one band member to the others) and then memorized. There are also spontaneous head arrangements but, unless at least some parts are retained in later performance, only one audience will ever hear them. And, of course, there may be head-arranged riffs or interludes incorporated into a previously written arrangement.

(2) Where a performance consists of theme/solos/theme, in that order, the opening section (perhaps including an arranged introduction as well as the theme) is referred to as 'the head', and for the final section the performers 'go back to the head' (in European classical music, *da capo*: Italian, 'from the head'). Only if the head is also a head arrangement do (1) and (2) correspond. [BP]

Heard, J. C. (James Charles), drums. b. Dayton, Ohio, 8 October 1917. His topline career began in 1939 with Teddy Wilson's band, after which he moved through an aristocratic selection of successors including Benny Carter's (1942), Cab Calloway's (1942–5) and his own sextet (1946–7). 1946–53, he was regularly with Norman Granz's Jazz at the Philharmonic and then moved to Japan to lead his own band, which included for a while the Japanese pianist Toshiko. 1957, he returned to New York to work as a single, played with Coleman Hawkins's quintet (co-led by Roy Eldridge) and renewed acquaintance with JATP, as well as gigging with society leader Lester Lanin: from 1961 he worked with Teddy Wilson again for a year, then with pianist Dorothy Donegan and led bands in Las Vegas and Detroit. In the 1970s Heard continued to lead, toured Europe in 1975 with an all-star band and continued this highly successful pattern into the 1980s. While never achieving the international name of a Jo Jones or Gene Krupa, Heard is – rather like Gus Johnson – a drummer who knows every inch of his art, plays with the graceful movement of a ballet dancer in rhythm and since the death of Jo Jones is the keeper of a musical flame that threatens to be extinguished with the passage of jazz time. [DF]

Heath, Al 'Tootie' (Albert), drums. b. Philadelphia, 31 May 1935. Younger brother of Jimmy and Percy Heath, Albert moved to New York (1957) making record début with fellow Philadelphian John Coltrane. Toured with J. J. Johnson (1958–60), then trio gigs with Cedar Walton and Bobby Timmons (1961). Emigrated to Europe (1965), working with George Russell and pianist Friedrich Gulda, also residency with Kenny Drew in Copenhagen (1967–8). Returned to US, became original drummer of Herbie Hancock sextet (1968–9), then joined Yusef Lateef quartet (1970–4). Recorded in Copenhagen with Kenny Drew and Anthony Braxton (1974), remaining in Europe for a year before joining Heath Brothers group (1975). Left the group (1978) for further freelance work, rejoining them from time to time. Also a composer in his own right, Heath is a dynamic and driving drummer who has developed the Kenny Clarke style of discreet directness. Never unduly attracting attention to himself, he is extremely versatile and supportive in whatever musical situation he encompasses. [BP]

Kwanza (1973), Muse

Heath, Jimmy (James Edward), tenor and soprano sax, flute, composer, arranger. b. Philadelphia, 25 October 1926. Played on alto with Nat Towles (mid-1940s) and Howard McGhee sextet (1947–8). Wrote for and led own big band in Philadelphia (1948–9, also fronted briefly by Howard McGhee in New York), then joined Dizzy Gillespie (1949–50). Freelance writing and recording, now on tenor, including for Miles Davis (1953). Further writing, e.g. for Chet Baker (1956) and Art Blakey (1957), during absence from playing. On return, worked for Davis, Kenny Dorham, Gil Evans (all 1959), began making albums under own name as well as writing for others'. Recording and gigging partnerships with Milt Jackson and Art Farmer from mid-1960s, also much educational work in college and for Jazzmobile project. Member of Heath Brothers group from 1975, plus continued composition and arranging, including for George Benson at Kool festival (1985).

Jimmy's excellence as a player was first noticed on alto in the late 1940s, when he was known in Philadelphia as 'Little Bird'. While extremely competent on soprano and flute, he is most effective on tenor and his tough post-bop style is a match for many better-known players. His playing, however, has frequently been overshadowed by arranging which, whether for big band or quintet, is always able to draw the best from the resources available. Among the many Heath tunes recorded by other musicians, 'C.T.A.' and 'Gingerbread Boy' were both used by Miles Davis and have since become standards. Jimmy's son, percussionist Mtume, also worked with Davis in the 1970s and is now a successful producer of soul and funk records. [BP]

Really Big (1960), Riverside; Heath Brothers, *Brotherly Love* (1982), Antilles

Heath, Percy, bass. b. Wilmington, N. Carolina, 30 April 1923. Only began serious study of music (1946) after air force service. Worked alongside younger brother Jimmy in Howard McGhee sextet and big band (1947–8), then freelancing in New York with Miles Davis, Fats Navarro, J. J. Johnson. Joined Dizzy Gillespie sextet (1950–2), followed by freelance gigging and records with Milt Jackson, Davis, Clifford Brown, Thelonious Monk, Charlie Parker and many others. Founder member of Modern Jazz Quartet (1952, touring group from 1954–74); during this period also recording and occasional gigs with Jimmy Heath. Then with Sarah Vaughan (1975), the Heath Brothers band (1975–82), then with re-formed MJQ.

Although the pattern of his career has caused him to be unfairly pigeonholed, 'Big P' (the name of Jimmy Heath's tune dedicated to him) was and is a superb bass player. All the basic jazz virtues of relaxation and buoyancy come across in his straightahead playing which, whether with the MJQ or others, reveals considerable admiration for Ray Brown. In addition, the demands made by the more ambitious aspects of the MJQ's repertoire not only brought the bass into greater prominence, without straining its traditional vocabulary, but drew particularly fine performances from Percy. [BP]

Miles Davis, *Bags' Groove* (1954), Prestige/OJC; Modern Jazz Quartet, *Echoes* (1984), Pablo

Hefti, Neal, composer, arranger, trumpet. b. Hastings, Nebraska, 29 October 1922. Teenage arrangements bought by black bandleader Nat Towles (late 1930s). Later wrote for Earl Hines (early 1940s), both playing and writing for several bands including Charlie Barnet (1942, briefly) and Woody Herman (1944–6). Then writing for short-lived Charlie Ventura big band (1946), Harry James (1948–9) and Count Basie (1950–62). Recorded under own name from 1951 and led band on live appearances, featuring vocalist wife Frances Wayne. By late 1950s had become involved full-time in writing for television and films. Before this, however, his work for the Basie band (especially pieces such as 'Whirlybird' and 'Li'l Darlin' ') made him one of the best-known non-playing arrangers, and the model for many lesser writers such as Sammy Nestico. He also wrote the rather banal 'Repetition' (1947) which went into the repertoire of Charlie Parker's with-strings group. [BP]

Coral Reef (1951–2), Jasmine

Hemphill, Julius, alto sax, composer, b. Fort Worth, Texas, 1940. Studied clarinet in early 1950s. Worked with various Texas bands and also with Ike Turner. 1968, he moved to St Louis, becoming a member of BAG (Black Artists Group) with Lester Bowie and Oliver Lake. Early 1970s, played with Anthony Braxton in Chicago, and also worked in Paris and Sweden. Hemphill is also something of a lyricist and poet, and in 1972 he presented his *Kawaida*, a collage of instrumental music, voices, dance and drama, at Washington University, St Louis. 1977, he was a co-founder of the World Saxophone Quartet, with Hamiett Bluiett, Oliver Lake and David Murray. This group built up a substantial international following, appearing at major festivals all over the world, and continuing into the mid-1980s. [IC]

With Braxton, Bowie, Kool and the Gang; as leader, *'Coon Bid'Ness* (1972), Arista; with World Saxophone Quartet, *Point of No Return* (1977), Moers Music; *Steppin' with the World Saxophone Quartet* (1978), Black Saint

Henderson, Eddie (Edward Jackson), trumpet, fluegelhorn, composer. b. New York City, 26 October 1940. Studied trumpet at school, 1950–4; then theory and trumpet at San Francisco Conservatory, 1954–7. 1958–61, served in the air force; encouraged by Miles Davis to take an interest in jazz. 1961–4, studied at University of California, Berkeley, graduating B.Sc. in zoology; 1964–8, at Howard University, Washington, graduating MD in medicine. During the summer vacations, played with John Handy. 1968, played with Handy and Philly Joe Jones. 1970–3, with Herbie Hancock's sextet, recording, touring internationally, and playing major festivals. He also worked with Pharoah Sanders, Joe Henderson and others. 1973, played for six months with Art Blakey's Jazz Messengers. From 1974, led his own groups, and recorded a series of albums as leader for Capitol Records. He continued to work in his medical capacity both as a general practitioner and as a psychiatrist. Influences, Miles Davis, Freddie Hubbard, Lee Morgan, Coltrane. [IC]

With Hancock, *Crossings* (1972), Warner Bros; as leader, *Comin' Through* (1977), Capitol; *Mahal* (1978), Capitol

Henderson, Fletcher Hamilton ('Smack'), piano, arranger, composer. b. Cuthbert, Georgia, 18 December 1897; d. New York City, 28 December 1952. He came to New York in 1920 with hopes of a career in chemistry, but in 1921 took a job as recording manager for Black Swan Records, a black record label owned by Harry Pace: by 1923 he was well known as the freelance pianist and MD who, in an organized, no-nonsense fashion, made sense of the material handed to him by a succession of blues singers (from Bessie Smith on) who recorded for his label. He was more than just an administrator: a highly trained and skilled musician with a shrewd eye for talent, a gift for leadership and his eye on a big band. By 1924 he had auditioned for the Club Alabam, assumed leadership of the band there and later that year took up residency at New York's Roseland with a band which, by the year's end, contained an unbeatable 'A'-team of soloists including Coleman Hawkins, Buster Bailey, Charlie 'Big' Green and Louis Armstrong, just up from Chicago. Armstrong survived with the super-confident city-slicker Hendersonians on talent and a sense of humour (later victims such as John Kirby were often pilloried even more unmercifully than Louis); but you had to be good to play with Fletcher Henderson, as Pee Wee Russell found out one night when he sat in for Coleman Hawkins. 'My God, those scores. They were written in six flats, eight flats – I never saw anything like it! Buster Bailey was next to me and after a couple of numbers I told him, "Man, I came up here to have a good time, not to work. Where's Hawkins?" ' But the Fletcher Henderson band never sounded academic. It was a powerhouse rhythm machine which could be sloppy, but which delivered a beat that could drive dancers to exhaustion. As time went on, and more talent emerged, the band broadened its approach with more sophisticated arrangements by Henderson himself, Benny Carter and others and new material 'swapped' with other bands such as Jean Goldkette's and the Casa Lomans; by 1934 they were playing (and recording) in a more disciplined fashion (although, for Hawkins at least, the band had lost much of its stompability). But Henderson had had more problems to contend with: personnel changes (after temperamental/financial traumas) and, more seriously, a car accident in 1928 in which he was badly injured. The accident seems to have deeply affected his hard-driving ambitious streak: until then he and wife Leora had run his band as a private operation, independent of agents, sending letters, phoning busily and hustling the night away; afterwards he seemed to slow up. By the mid-1930s Henderson, now working in a variety of provincial venues including Grand Terrace Ballroom in 1936, was better known as a staff arranger for Benny Goodman (he contributed classics to Goodman's first library) and he joined his young champion briefly on piano in 1939. Through the 1940s he ran bands still around New York and Chicago, arranged for lots of newer bands, and by 1950 had a sextet at New York's Café Society. That year he suffered a stroke and although Benny Goodman, with benefits and appeals, kept his name before the public, Henderson died at 55. [DF]

A Study in Frustration (1923–38), CBS (4 records, boxed set)

See Stewart, Rex, *Jazz Masters of the 30s* (Macmillan, 1972, repr. Da Capo, 1982); Allen, Walter C., *Hendersonia* (Walter C. Allen, 1973)

Henderson, Horace, piano, arranger, composer. b. Cuthbert, Georgia, 22 November 1904. He formed his first band on campus at Wilberforce University in the 1920s and was established in New York bandleading by the turn of the decade (later Don Redman took over leadership): then, until the war, he worked for Redman and for his brother Fletcher Henderson, as well as regularly organizing bands of his own. After military service he was accompanist for Lena Horne, then re-formed his orchestras until the failing scene for big bands reduced him to a small group. While he recorded seldom and rarely appeared in New York, Henderson toured throughout the 1950s and 1960s with groups of various sizes and in the late 1960s was active in and around Denver, Colorado. He earned a fine reputation as an arranger whose work was often used by great bandleaders such as Benny Goodman, Charlie Barnet, Tommy Dorsey, Earl Hines, Jimmie Lunceford and his brother. [DF]

Henderson, Joe (Joseph A.), tenor sax, composer, and soprano sax, flute. b. Lima, Ohio, 24 April 1937. Brother also a saxophonist. He first came to prominence co-leading a group with Kenny Dorham, 1962–3; with Horace Silver, 1964–6; co-led Jazz Communicators with Freddie Hubbard, 1967–8; with Herbie Hancock sextet, 1969–70. 1971, he spent four months with Blood Sweat and Tears. Since 1970 he has led his own groups. In the mid-1970s he moved to California and became active in music education. 1979, he toured Europe with his quartet, playing major festivals including Lubljana, Yugoslavia. 1985, he played with Herbie Hancock, Ron Carter and Tony Williams at the televised concert *One Night with Blue Note*, to celebrate the relaunching of the Blue Note label.

Henderson is one of the most gifted of the post-Coltrane saxophonists. He rapidly absorbed his main influences – Sonny Rollins, John Coltrane and Ornette Coleman – finding his own voice and approach on tenor sax. He was exposed to a great variety of music as a child and adolescent, and told Ray Townley: 'I heard a lot of country and western music on the radio . . . A lot of rhythm and blues, a lot of Chuck Berry, Bo Diddley, and all those real *deep* blues players . . . when I went to College [Wayne State University in Detroit], I got just a bit more esoteric – Indian music, Balinese music.' His playing transcends categories, incorporating elements from bebop, r & b, abstraction, rock and ethnic music. He has an extraordinary melodic gift, and his work never sounds like exercises or 'licks' because he is a master of thematic development, and all his solos combine fine logic with surprise. [IC]

With Dorham, Lee Morgan, Silver, Flora Purim and others; as leader, *Joe Henderson in Japan* (1971); *Black is the Colour* (1972); Henderson/Alice Coltrane, *The Elements* (1973), all Milestone; Henderson/Carter/Chick Corea/Billy Higgins, *Mirror Mirror* (1980), MPS

Hendricks, Jon (John Carl), vocals, lyricist. b. Newark, Ohio, 16 September 1921. Brought up in Toledo from age 11, singing on local radio at that period. After high school and frequent performing, army service (1942–6) was followed by law studies; dissuaded from latter by praise from Charlie Parker. Self-taught as a drummer, led own groups in Rochester and Toledo. Based in New York from 1952 as part-time songwriter, his 'I Want You To Be My Baby' (lyrics added to earlier jazz tune 'Rag Mop') was recorded by Louis Jordan. Gave up day job (1957) after recording his own lyricized versions of 'Four Brothers' and Sam 'The Man' Taylor's tenor solo on r & b disc 'Cloudburst' (by Claude Cloud and his Thunderclaps); his backing group for the occasion, Dave Lambert Singers, then narrowed down to Lambert, Hendricks and Ross, first on records and then (1958) as working unit, with Hendricks adding words to classics by Count Basie, Horace Silver, Miles Davis, Art Blakey etc. After Dave Lambert's departure (1964), Hendricks active as soloist including residence in Europe (1967–73); briefly teamed up with Annie Ross and Georgie Fame (1968). Before return to US, had involved his wife and daughter in a new singing group, which in late 1970s included non-family members such as Bobby McFerrin; since 1979, has also written for and guested with Manhattan Transfer. Of his hundreds of lyrics added to jazz solos (sometimes termed vocalese), many brilliantly mirror the rhythmic contours of the original instrumentals, and their success on this level excuses the lack of verbal profundity. [BP]

Lambert/Hendricks/Ross, *The Swingers!* (1959), Affinity; Manhattan Transfer, *Vocalese* (1985), Atlantic

Henry, Ernie (Ernest Albert), alto sax. b. Brooklyn, New York, 3 September 1926; d. 29 December 1957. A worthy associate of important composer/bandleaders such as Tadd Dameron (1947), Dizzy Gillespie (1948–9 and 1956–7), Charles Mingus and Thelonious Monk (both 1956). Despite the brevity of his career, and a gap in the middle of it following work with Illinois Jacquet in the early 1950s, Henry stands out as an intelligent adapter of the style of Charlie Parker. As such, he pointed to some of the developments effected in the 1950s by Sonny Rollins (their one recording together, Monk's *Brilliant Corners*, is thought-provoking in this respect) and to the emotional intensity of Jackie McLean. [BP]

Last Chorus (1956–7), Riverside/OJC

Herman, Woody (Woodrow Charles), clarinet, alto and soprano sax, vocals. b. Milwaukee, Wisconsin, 16 May 1913. A child singer in vaudeville, learning saxophone from age 11. Played in numerous touring bands from 15, ending with Isham Jones until Jones retired from leading (1934–6); members of the band who wished to continue elected Herman as leader. Despite changes in personnel, worked steadily until 1946, when economic difficulties forced him to follow up his success as singer. Formed new band (1947–9), followed by small group; further records as singer accompanied by studio groups. New regular band, now called the Third Herd (1950–8, recording for own Mars label, 1952–4), followed by sextet which was augmented for records and for European tour (1959). Fourth Herd, formed 1961, continued in existence until 1980s although, during 1970s, it became customary to take annual breaks and then re-convene; hence non-numerical designation of Swinging Herd and finally Thundering Herd. The latter was featured with many former sidemen in a 40th anniversary concert at Carnegie Hall (1976) and a 50th anniversary celebration at Hollywood Bowl (1986).

Herman managed the difficult feat of maintaining a feeling of continuity between his different bands, while allowing a gradual stylistic evolution to take place over the decades. This reflects in part his openness to the desires of his soloists, but also his talent-spotting ability in

Woody Herman

terms of section players, which paid off early on in performances such as 'At the Woodchoppers' Ball'; although his publicity catchphrase 'The Band that Plays the Blues' might have justifiably been claimed by Basie, Herman's first band and his down-to-earth clarinet work (as opposed to Goodman and Shaw) did much to live up to it. It was not until the mid-1940s that the band acquired other strong soloists such as Bill Harris and Flip Phillips, along with a bunch of slightly younger men (and two women, Margie Hyams and trumpeter Billie Rogers) who leavened the late swing era with a new excitement on pieces such as 'The Good Earth' and 'Caldonia' – the latter a slightly boppish approach to a Louis Jordan hit which was also still the blues.

The band of the late 1940s, identified in retrospect as the Four Brothers era, was the first large unit anywhere to reflect the then increasing influence of Lester Young by featuring such promising players as Stan Getz, Zoot Sims and Serge Chaloff. And, in the mid-1950s, Herman and musical director Nat Pierce acknowledged the ascendancy of East Coast 'hard bop' with the first of several Horace Silver tunes, 'Opus De Funk' (i.e. the blues yet again). The traditional aspect of the big-band sound was always adhered to and, still more so, the drive and dynamism of a rhythm-section style which was modernized almost imperceptibly, like the repertoire. The early 1960s found Herman adopting pieces by Monk ('Blue Monk'), Mingus ('Better Get it in Your Soul') and Herbie Hancock ('Watermelon Man'), and by the 1970s the young generation working for him introduced Coltrane pieces including 'Giant Steps', while

Woody himself took up the soprano sax, playing it with the same hint of Johnny Hodges which always informed his alto work. And, throughout this entire development, he answered nightly requests for 'Woodchoppers' Ball', and continually made it and his current musicians sound just as lively as in the 1930s. A considerable achievement, unequalled by any other white bandleader. [BP]

The Band that Plays the Blues (1937–42), Affinity; *Best of Woody Herman* (1945–7), CBS; *Road Band* (1955), Capitol; *Woody's Winners* (1965), CBS

See Voce, Steve, *Woody Herman* (Apollo, 1986)

Heywood, Eddie (Edward, Jnr.), piano, composer, arranger. b. Atlanta, Georgia, 4 December 1915. His father, Eddie Heywood Snr., played piano, trumpet and saxophone, recorded prolifically in the 1920s with his own Atlanta-based band and was MD for vaudeville team Butterbeans and Susie. Eddie Jnr. played piano in his father's 81 Theater orchestra when his father was away on tour and five years later joined Clarence Love's orchestra with whom he came to New York in 1937. Thereafter he worked with Benny Carter's short-lived big band and for Zutty Singleton and Georgie Auld at the Three Deuces and by 1941 had his own group at New York's Village Vanguard. This sextet – including Doc Cheatham, Lem Davis and Vic Dickenson – achieved great success at New York's Café Society Downtown and from 1943 they recorded classic sides with Billie Holiday, Ella Fitzgerald, Bing Crosby and the Andrews Sisters, as well as a hit version of 'Begin the Beguine' which turned them into bill-toppers in their own right. From 1947, Heywood was afflicted with arthritic paralysis of the hands: when the trouble cleared he found a 1950s comeback difficult and (with the encouragement of Cole Porter) began to develop a gift for composition. Several big hits, including 'Canadian Sunset', 'Land of Dreams' and 'Soft Summer Breeze' (a huge American success), all featuring the Heywood trademark of repeated bass and a simple right-hand theme, re-established him, and a string of expensively-produced US albums for Mercury, Sunset and RCA Victor followed: they were an inspiration for later arrangers such as Britisher Johnny Pearson. By the 1960s Heywood found himself out of step with popular trends (although one more big hit at least, 'My Guy' by Mary Wells, drew largely from Heywood's 'Canadian Sunset') and once more fighting health problems and arthritis. But he re-emerged triumphantly in the 1970s for New York clubwork and an appearance at the Newport Jazz Festival, New York, 1974. [DF]

Canadian Sunset (1958), RCA Victor

See Dance, Stanley, *The World of Swing* (Scribner's, 1974, repr. Da Capo, 1979)

Higginbotham, J. C. (Jack), trombone. b. Social Circle, nr. Atlanta, Georgia, 11 May 1906; d. New York, 26 May 1973. His career began in 1921 with Neal Montgomery's orchestra in Georgia, and he had worked all over, with vaudeville troupes, tent shows and jazz bands, by the time he got to New York in 1928. There he joined Henry 'Red' Allen (a lifelong friend) in Luis Russell's orchestra at Club Saratoga and stayed until 1931 (classic sides including 'I can't give you anything but love', 'Bessie couldn't help it' and 'St Louis Blues', all with Louis Armstrong, are rich dividends from the period). For the next six years Higgy's huge sound, confident range and pawky tone were to be heard in Fletcher Henderson's orchestra, with Benny Carter (he was sacked for sending a love-note by mistake to the clubowner's wife) and Lucky Millinder; in 1937 came a request from Louis Armstrong for more collaboration. Higginbotham re-joined Luis Russell's orchestra (by this time it was backing Armstrong full-time) and stayed until the whole band was dismissed without ceremony by Armstrong's manager Joe Glaser in 1940. Then came seven years working with Red Allen in a high-octane small band, at Café Society, Kelly's Stables, the Garrick Lounge, Chicago, and Jimmy Ryan's. George Hoefer points up the fascinating duality of Higginbotham at this period: 'While he could arrive in New York in 1947 for an Esquire concert with two cases – one holding his trombone, the other containing nine bottles of whiskey – and wind up playing seated on the floor, he could write at the same time in a national magazine an article entitled "Some of my best friends are enemies!" illustrating a sensitive and keen judgment of the racial situation as applying to Negro musicians.' By the mid-1950s Higginbotham, working with Red Allen again at the noisy Metropole jazz bar in New York, was suffering from an unfashionable period of obscurity: a contemporary album, *Callin' the Blues* with Tiny Grimes, sounds unhappy and forced. During the 1960s, however, he was active at clubs and festivals: illness in 1971 stopped his 50-year career. [DF]

Fletcher Henderson, *A Study in Frustration* (1923–38), CBS (4 records, boxed set)

Higgins, Billy, drums. b. Los Angeles, California, 11 October 1936. After playing with r & b bands, joined Red Mitchell quartet (1957). Replaced departing Ed Blackwell with Ornette Coleman, performed on Ornette's early West Coast-recorded studio albums (1958–9) and appeared with him during New York nightclub residency (1959–60). Left Coleman to work with Thelonious Monk quartet (1960) and John Coltrane quartet (1960). Also with Sonny Rollins & Co (1962–3, including European tour). Many freelance gigs and albums (1960s) with such as Dexter Gordon, Hank Mobley, Donald Byrd, Herbie Hancock and Lee Morgan (including original recordings of both 'Watermelon Man' and 'The Sidewinder'). Regular association with Cedar Walton, beginning 1966, continued usually with bassist Sam Jones (later Dave Williams) through 1970s and early 1980s. Copious freelance recording with and without these favourite associates.

As long ago as 1957, Red Mitchell said, 'Billy Higgins, I think, is really destined to be recognized as one of the great drummers in the country . . . He has great imagination and is a wonderful group player as well as being able to solo.' The apparent flexibility required to work for the many leading stylists who have employed Higgins is very real; but, more than that, it is a reflection of the responsiveness present in his playing at any given moment. The dancing pulse of his cymbals is sufficiently mesmeric to make soloists of whatever persuasion totally relaxed in his company, and any group of which he is a member functions at its optimum level. [BP]

Dexter Gordon, *Go!* (1962), Blue Note; *Mr Billy Higgins* (1985), Riza

High Energy Music, see ENERGY.

Hill(e), Andrew, piano, composer. b. Port au Prince, Haiti, 30 June 1937. Raised in Chicago from age four. Worked with Paul Williams r & b blues band (1953), and played alongside such Chicago musicians as Gene Ammons, Von Freeman, Johnny Griffin, Malachi Favors etc. during 1950s. On tour with Dinah Washington (1961), also accompanied singers Al Hibbler and Johnny Hartman in New York. In Los Angeles (1962–3), working with Roland Kirk, saxist Jimmy Woods and others. Returning to New York, played with Joe Henderson (1963) and began recording under own name. Was active in California again in late 1960s, then composer in residence at Colgate University (1970–1) and lecturing at other colleges. Involved with New York State Council for the Arts (1972–3) and Smithsonian Institution (1973–4). Visits to Montreux festival, 1975, Japan (1976) and Italy (1980). Living again on West Coast in 1980s.

Hill is one of a strong line of pianist/composers who, like Thelonious Monk or Cecil Taylor, are impossible to categorize except as individualists. Although he produces recognizable, even catchy 'tunes', these are very much part of his improvisational playing style, and vice versa. Whether he is implying Caribbean rhythms or using a more abstract approach, he always seems totally controlled and totally spontaneous. He commented in an interview: 'I can't see limiting myself to one harmonic or rhythmic conception . . . As far as I'm concerned, my thing is to create a situation to play in, as interesting a situation as possible.' His success is demonstrated by the manner in which he stimulates different players in his various groups, and equally the manner in which he uses different aspects of the piano. [BP]

Point of Departure (1964), Blue Note; *Strange Serenade* (1980), Soul Note

Hill, Chippie (Bertha), vocals. b. Charleston, South Carolina, *c.* 1900; d. New York City, 7 May 1950. One of 16 children, by 1916 she was working in New York at Leroy's club in Harlem. Later she was on the road with Ma Rainey's show, moved to Chicago around 1925 and recorded important titles with Louis Armstrong and Richard M. Jones, including 'Lonesome All Alone', 'Trouble in Mind', 'Georgia Man' and a collector's favourite, 'Pratt City Blues': regular work in Chicago at the period included spells with King Oliver, one-night stands opposite Ma Rainey and club and theatre work. She retired to marry in the late 1920s, and worked spasmodically thereafter until in 1946 she was rediscovered by Rudi Blesh, sang on his This is Jazz series, recorded for his Circle label (including 'Blues Around the Clock', a thematic predecessor to 'Rock Around the Clock') and scored a huge success at the Village Vanguard, 1947, then the 1948 Paris Jazz Festival. Back in New York she was the victim of a hit-and-run driver and as a result died in the Harlem Hospital. [DF]

Jazz Sounds of the Twenties, vol. 4: The Blues Singers (1923–31), Parlophone

Hill, Teddy (Theodore), saxes, bandleader. b. Birmingham, Alabama, 7 December 1909; d. Cleveland, Ohio, 19 May 1978. He was a competent saxophonist in New York by 1927, worked with Luis Russell, 1928–9, and formed his own band in 1932 which played the Savoy regularly as well as nearby clubs such as the Ubangi. In 1936 they visited Florida with great success, recorded for Bluebird in 1937, and that year toured Europe as well as acquiring a young Eldridge-inspired trumpeter, Dizzy Gillespie. By now Hill was fronting the band rather than playing, exercising his business acumen in a competitive world, and attracting attention with his charm and good looks. The band was full of stars such as Chu Berry, Bill Coleman, Roy Eldridge, Frank Newton and Cecil Scott throughout most of the 1930s, but it lacked the combination of luck and individuality necessary for long-term survival: his manager Moe Gale, when faced with the option of promoting either Hill or the second band in his stable, Erskine Hawkins's, opted for the latter and despite fairly regular returns to the Savoy (Webb's old haunt) some of the steam went out of Teddy Hill's orchestra. They broke up in 1940 after the World's Fair, and a year later Hill took over management of Minton's Playhouse, dispensed with Happy Caldwell's band which had been resident, and turned the room over to the young musicians with whose aims he sympathized. Youthful giants such as Dizzy Gillespie, Kenny Clarke, Thelonious Monk and Charlie Christian worked out their ideas under Hill's tolerant eye and, though little more was heard from him, it was an honourable epitaph: Minton's occupies a central position in jazz development. [DF]

Hines, Earl Kenneth 'Fatha', piano, vocals, composer. b. Duquesne, Pennsylvania, 28 December 1903; d. Oakland, California, 22 April 1983. He grew up in Pittsburgh, where he was inspired by Sissle and Blake revues, and by the age of 21 was leading a band at the Entertainer's Club in Chicago: his precocious talent was to make him, with Louis Armstrong, the most spectacular star to brighten Chicago in the 1920s. For several years, on and off, Hines was Armstrong's close associate (he even invented a style of jazz piano known as 'trumpet style'), but it was significant that, from the very start, their relationship was often compounded by professional rivalry: their early duets, such as 'Weatherbird Rag' (1928) with its squally multi-directional rhythmic challenges, are plainly two masters fighting their way to an on-record draw, and even 'My Monday Date', a Hines composition from the same year, was ribbingly composed to commemorate Armstrong's inability to remember appointments. Hines was MD for Louis Armstrong's Stompers at Sunset Café, Chicago, and worked with Jimmie Noone's hit-making band in 1927. Right at the end of 1928 he took his own band into Chicago's Grand Terrace Ballroom, fulfilling his ambition to be a band-leader.

For the next 12 years the Mafia-controlled Grand Terrace was Hines's home: 'So far as I know', says Jo Jones, 'Earl had to play with a knife at his throat and a gun at his back the whole time he was in Chicago.' If this was the case, Hines made the best of it. He formed a regular association with Reginald Foresythe (who co-wrote Hines's ingenious theme song 'Deep Forest'), expanded to big band size, MC'd, broadcast regularly all through his tenure, ran shows with Valaida Snow (key soloists for Hines at the period included Trummy Young, Budd Johnson, Walter Fuller and Quinn Wilson) and earned a lot of money. Later, after he left the Grand Terrace, Hines contemplated a double act with Billy Eckstine but instead (like Eckstine) went on to lead another big band full of young modern jazzmen including Dizzy Gillespie, Charlie Parker, Wardell Gray and singer Johnny Hartman, until he disbanded in 1947 to run a club in Chicago. That year Joe Glaser approached Hines to ask him to rejoin Armstrong, and he agreed, but both leaders had come too far and formed too many views to give as much as was necessary. 'More than once', says Humphrey Lyttleton, recalling the All Stars at Nice, 'Earl Hines's exuberance was curbed by Louis with a sharp "Cut it, boy!" ' Hines in turn was 'a little upset' that Armstrong had no desire to resume their previous carefree existence 'running together', resented the discipline of Armstrong and the Glaser organization, and left in 1951. 'I didn't think the new contract they offered me was like it should have been', he explained later. '. . . They wanted to list me merely as a sideman!' He formed a group in Los Angeles before moving into the Hangover Club to front a back-to-the-roots Dixieland band for the next five years: his group included Darnell Howard (clt), Jimmy Archey (tmb), Pops Foster (bass) and a variety of trumpeters including Muggsy Spanier and Eddie Smith.

Earl Hines

For the rest of the 1950s Hines toured, (including Europe, 1957) but it was a grey period: his Oakland nightclub, the Music Crossroads, folded ('when they began to realize I was a Negro owner'), and he thought of taking a store. Then in 1964 Stanley Dance engineered the engagement that saved Hines's career: three concerts solo and with a quartet featuring Budd Johnson at New York's Little Theater. The concerts, which caught Hines at his peak, and refocused attention on his genius as a soloist, sold out; and a long piece in the *New Yorker* by Whitney Balliett, a season at Birdland and a set of recordings for Dance turned the pianist back into the publicly acknowledged jazzmaster he deserved to be. Albums he had recorded attained five-star ratings in *Downbeat*, and by the end of the decade he was a jetsetter (including British visits in 1965, 1967 and 1968). Other honours for Hines included election to the '*Downbeat* Hall of Fame' in 1966, a tour of Russia, a meeting with the Pope, and in the 1970s tours of Italy, Japan and Australia. A 1976 appearance at the White House for President Ford featured his new discovery, singer Marva Josie. By the 1980s Hines was owning up to feeling tired, but entertained determinedly until the weekend he died at 79. By that time his reputation as the greatest pianist after Art Tatum in the annals of classic jazz was far too secure to die with him. [DF]

Tour De Force (1972), Black Lion

See Dance, Stanley, *The World of Earl Hines* (Scribner's, 1977); Balliett, Whitney, *Improvising* (OUP, 1977)

Hino, Motohiko, drums. b. Tokyo, Japan, 3 January 1946. Brother of trumpeter Terumasa Hino. Began on drums at age ten; turned professional at 17. Worked with various bands including K. Saijo's quartet, then played in his brother's group until it disbanded in 1975. He led his own trio, playing extensively in jazz clubs. From 1972, voted top Japanese drummer in *Swing Journal* polls. 1978, moved to the USA, working with Joe Henderson, Chuck Rainey, Hal Galper, Ronnie Mathews and others. 1979, joined Hugh Masekela's band; since 1980, a regular member of Joanne Brackeen's trio. Influences, Terumasa Hino, Tony Williams, Elvin Jones. [IC]

With Joe Henderson, Lew Tabackin, Mal Waldron and others; several with Terumasa Hino; as leader, *Flush* (nda), Trio

Hino, Terumasa, trumpet, fluegelhorn, composer. b. Tokyo, Japan, 25 October 1942. Father, Bin Hino, a tap-dancer and trumpet player; brother Motohiko Hino, drummer. Father taught him to tap-dance at age four; he began on trumpet at nine. His greatest loves became Miles Davis and Louis Armstrong, but he also studied the work of Clifford Brown, Lee Morgan, John Coltrane and Freddie Hubbard, transcribing their solos for himself. He told Sally Placksin in 1985; 'it took a long time to transcribe the solos. But that was a great help . . . little by little, one note by one note, you're copying. His [Coltrane's] information came through my heart, then I never forget that.' He played with various bands and groups during the later 1950s and early 1960s, then joined the Hideo Shiraki quintet, the top Japanese jazz group. 1965, with Shiraki, he played the Berlin Jazz Festival and recorded for the German label MPS. 1964–5, he also led his own group and recorded *Hinology*, which won two awards including a Golden Disc. In the later 1960s, he left Shiraki in order to concentrate on his own group, which started with a residency in a small jazz coffee shop in Tokyo. He established himself rapidly as Japan's top trumpeter, working with his own group and with American musicians, doing TV shows and playing on film soundtracks.

1975, he moved to the USA, working with Gil Evans, Jackie McLean, and others. Late 1970s, he was a member of Dave Liebman's group, touring internationally with it and playing major festivals. 1979, they did a two-month tour in Europe, culminating in a performance at the Lubljana festival, Yugoslavia. 1980s, Hino was spending half his time in the USA and half in Japan, where he was still extremely popular.

Hino's other influences include bassist Reggie Workman, and his style is a synthesis of elements from Miles Davis, Coltrane and Freddie Hubbard. He has a magnificent technique, a full, singing sound, and a concept that can embrace any kind of improvisation from neo-bop to abstraction, ballads and fusion. He said to S. Placksin: 'I want to be as simple as possible. Still now, there are so many notes I'm playing, so many notes I don't need. But it's very hard to throw away . . . and always for me very important is space, quiet . . . Miles does the same thing, Stravinsky, whoever, great people. Painters know how to make space. That's the whole idea of art, I think. Space and simplicity. That's why I love Duke Ellington and Satchmo, because of the space.' [IC]

With Liebman and others; as leader, *Vibrations* (1971), Enja; *Taro's Mood* (1973), Enja; *Speak to Loneliness* (1975); *Live in Concert* (1975); *Hogiuta* (1976), all East Wind

Hinton, Milt(on John), bass. b. Vicksburg, Mississippi, 23 June 1910. He took up the bass in high school, studied music at Northwest University and worked early on with bands led by Boyd Atkins and Tiny Parham. From 1931 he was bassist for the 'Dark Angel of the violin', Eddie South, then for three great trumpeters, Jabbo Smith, Guy Kelly and an ailing Freddie Keppard. After a spell with Zutty Singleton's trio at Chicago's Three Deuces, Hinton joined Cab Calloway in 1936 and stayed – albeit with mixed feelings – for 15 years. The band, the highest-paid in swingdom, played its nightly show competently and Hinton was featured in the Cab Jivers, Calloway's small band (another member, briefly, was Dizzy Gillespie with whom Hinton worked out new sequences in the pre-Minton years). He stayed with Calloway until 1951, when the whole band was fired, and afterwards moved into the New York club scene (with Joe Bushkin at the Embers), worked briefly with Count Basie and for two short tours with Louis Armstrong's All Stars. In 1954, tired of touring, he took a staff job at CBS, recording thousands of sides including both Billie Holiday's last sessions (with Ray Ellis) and Bobby Darin's most famous hits from 'Mack the Knife' on. He also worked with Sam Jones, Ron Carter and Richard Davis in the now defunct New York Bass Violin Choir. Throughout the 1970s and into the 1980s Hinton was as busy as ever: in 1985 he stopped the show at London's Pizza Express, singing, reminiscing and playing the bass as perfectly as ever; in 1986 he appeared at the Edinburgh Jazz Festival. [DF]

The Golden Era of Dixieland Jazz (1958), Gala

See Dance, Stanley, *The World of Swing* (Scribner's 1974, repr. Da Capo, 1979)

Chris Hinze

Hinze, Chris (Christiaan Herbert), flute, composer. b. Hilversum, Netherlands, 30 June 1938. Father a child-prodigy violinist who later became a conductor. Hinze studied flute at the Royal Conservatory in The Hague; afterwards he studied arranging at Berklee, Boston. At the Montreux Jazz Festival, 1970, he won the Press Prize as Best Soloist; 1971, he launched his jazz-rock-fusion group Chris Hinze Combination at the Lake Geneva Casino; 1972, for the Holland Festival he was commissioned to compose a suite, *Live Music Now*, for 42 musicians and string orchestra, and for this composition he received the Beethoven Award of the City of Bonn.

During the 1970s Hinze also composed and recorded other symphonic works, including *Parcival*, *New York* and *Silhouettes*, which was recorded with the London Philharmonic Orchestra and arranged by Michael Gibbs; he also made three LPs in Japan, three in India and several in the USA, after which he went to live in New York in 1976. In the later 1970s he made several tours of the Benelux countries with a group called Chris Hinze and Friends and a programme entitled 'Music from the Past till Now'. 1980, he collaborated with Peter Tosh in recording a reggae album, and also formed a duo with German guitarist Sigi Schwab. 1983, the Chris Hinze Combination with Schwab made a 40-concert tour of Holland and Germany. 1985, Hinze included Indian and African musicians in his Combination, touring widely in Europe with a programme called 'African-Indian and World Fusion' and recording a double album, *Saliah*. Hinze also works as record producer for other musicians.

His favourite jazz flautist is James Moody, with whom he has recorded, and other inspirations are Miles Davis, Duke Ellington, Gil Evans, Gunther Schuller and J. S. Bach. [IC]

Combination, *Stoned Flute* (1971); *Virgin Sacrifice* (1972); *Mange* (1974); with the LSO, *Silhouettes* (1977); live recording in the Ellora Caves in India, *Flute and Mantras* (1979); with Peter Tosh, *World Sound and Power* (1980); *Chris Hinze/Sigi Schwab Duo* (1980); with the London String Orchestra, *Mirror of Dreams* (1982); *Saliah* (1985), all Keystone

Hip The opposite of square; an earlier form of the same word, 'hep', was the opposite of what was then corny. Claimed by some to derive from the Oriental habit of balancing opium on that part of the anatomy, 'hip' is actually more likely to be a rhythmic exclamation related to scat-singing – compare 'hip, hip' with 'hey, hey'. Since it came into use in the jazz world of the 1940s, it has designated all the musicality and/or attitudes most desirable in the inner circle of currently fashionable players. Equally, it can be applied, especially when talking among themselves, to suitably aware fans.

However, like all complimentary adjectives, it has a double edge. The only difference between hip as a sincere description, and hip meaning 'would-be hip', lies in the intonation and authority of the person speaking. The noun 'hipster' acquired early on a fairly negative connotation (its abbreviation 'hippie' even more so), and was only ever applied to non-musicians. The lyric of Dave Frishberg's song says it all: 'When it was hip to be hep, I was hep.' [BP]

Hirt, Al (Alois Maxwell), trumpet. b. New Orleans, Louisiana, 7 November 1922. He took up the trumpet at eight and, after sitting enthralled through Benny Goodman's 1938 Carnegie Hall concert, trained at Cincinnati Conservatory of Music: for the next 20 years came work with the New Orleans Symphony Orchestra, with the Dawnbusters Radio Orchestra, touring with Horace Heidt, whose talent contests he won for weeks in succession, and club residencies all over New Orleans. In between there were stints with Tommy Dorsey, Jimmy Dorsey and Ray McKinley (with whom he toured Europe for a year) and in 1958 a vital contract with Audio Fidelity (they also signed the Dukes of Dixieland). This contract ensured Hirt (and the Dukes) a period of blanket publicity in hi-fi magazines and turned him into a new star. By 1960 he was settled in New Orleans with his family, running his own club, and signed to RCA Victor for a set of albums and singles which made him the most talked-about trumpet man of the 1960s. Singles such as 'Java' became hits, LPs with popular figures such as Anne-Margret and Chet Atkins followed, but Hirt's roots in jazz were always audible; and splendid albums, including *Horn-a-plenty* (arranged by Billy May, which pitted Hirt against a trumpet team of Manny Klein, Conrad Gozzo, Frank Beach and Uan Rasey), were issued. In the late 1960s Hirt's progress was temporarily slowed by a lip injury sustained in a street parade, but a few years later he was back in stratospheric form at his club on Bourbon Street. Hirt is often dismissed by jazz critics, because he was commercially successful and because his chosen way of performing is wrongly dubbed as 'vulgar' by tight-lipped critics. In fact his jazz recordings are usually fun at least, often much more, and always worth hearing. [DF]

Twenty Hits (1983), Audio Fidelity

Hiseman, Jon (Philip John), drums. b. Woolwich, London, 21 June 1944. Family on father's side included music hall artists, 1900–30, and dance-band musicians, in the 1930s and 1940s. Studied violin and piano until 13; self-taught on drums. Amateur jazz, blues and dance bands, 1958–65. Founder member of New Jazz Orchestra (NJO) 1964–9. 1966–7, with Graham Bond Organisation, then with Georgie Fame and the Blue Flames, 1967–8. Six months playing with John Mayall's Bluesbreakers in 1968, then started his own group, Colosseum, which continued until 1971. Then spent a year doing studio session work. Started another group of his own, Tempest, at the beginning of 1973, disbanding at the end of 1974. 1975, he joined the United Jazz and Rock Ensemble (UJRE) at its inception. 1975–8, again led his own group, Colosseum II. He first met Barbara Thompson in the NJO in 1964, and they later married. 1979, he joined her group Paraphernalia, and has continued with it and with the UJRE. Since 1977 both he and Barbara Thompson have worked intermittently for Andrew Lloyd Webber on various projects including *Variations* and the musical *Cats* (1981). From the early 1960s Hiseman was associated with Mike Taylor (pianist and composer), playing in his quartet and recording with him. During the 1960s there were also trio projects with Hiseman, Jack Bruce and John Surman.

Hiseman is a drummer of tremendous power and stamina, and has what musicians call 'great chops'. He is equally at home in jazz or rock contexts, though his early influences were mostly jazz drummers such as Joe Morello, Roy Haynes and Elvin Jones, and he was steeped in Coltrane's music. Later influences were Joni Mitchell, Stevie Wonder, Lenny White and Ellington. Hiseman's great energy is mental as well as physical, and extends to the business and organizational side of the music. He has his own record company (TM Records), his own 24TK analog/digital recording studio, a music publishing company, a PA hire company, and he provides management and agency for Barbara Thompson. Since 1983 he has been deeply involved in engineering and producing in the studio. [IC]

Two with NJO, five with UJRE; with Mike Taylor, *Pendulum* (1965), EMI; with Jack Bruce, *Songs for a Tailor* (1967); *Things We Like* (1968), both Polydor; *Colosseum Live* (1971), Bronze; with Colosseum II, *Electric Savage* (1976), MCA; with Paraphernalia, *Live in Concert* (1980), MCA; with Brazilian musicians, *A Night in the Sun* (1981), Kuckuck; with Thompson/Argent, *Shadow Show* (1984), TM

Hodes, Art (Arthur W.), piano. b. Nikoliev, Russia, 14 November 1904. 'The South Side of Chicago became my alma mater', he once declared with typical romanticism, remembering his early career when work with Wingy Manone and Dick Voynow's Wolverines and any number of lesser bands combined for Hodes with soaking in the music of bar-room piano professors in Chicago's gangster-controlled South Side clubs. By 1938 he had arrived in New York to work up and down 52nd Street, but was soon widening his activities to work as a jazz DJ (from the early 1940s) and to edit (with Dale Curran and Harold Hersey) a vital jazz magazine, *The Jazz Record*, which presented realistic but loving portraits of classic jazz musicians at work. In spare moments Hodes found time to become a pioneering lecturer, talking about jazz in schools and colleges, and stayed in New York until 1950 when he decided to move back to the Chicago area.

Johnny Hodges

From 1959 he was resident at Bob Scobey's Chicago nightclub, playing solo, bandleading all over, writing for *Downbeat* magazine, hosting an educational TV series (one programme, *Plain ol' Blues*, won an Emmy) and teaching piano. Since 1970 he has been busily leading again, touring Europe as a soloist and by 1981 playing in New York once more, at Hanratty's. [DF]

Someone to Watch Over Me (1981), Muse

See Hodes, Art (ed.), and Hansen, Chadwick, *Selections from the Gutter* (University of California Press, 1977)

Hodges, Johnny 'Rabbit' (Cornelius Hodge), alto and soprano sax, composer. b. Cambridge, Massachusetts, 25 July 1907; d. New York City, 11 May 1970. He lived on Hammond Street, Boston, in what later turned out to be a saxophonists' ghetto: Howard Johnson, Toots Mondello, Charlie Holmes and Harry Carney were all near neighbours. Very early in his career Hodges met Sidney Bechet (who was working in Boston for burlesque entrepreneur Jimmy Cooper), asked for lessons, and later worked at his Club Bechet, New York, filling in for the older man's late arrivals, and playing duets such as 'I found a new baby' or 'Everybody loves my baby' after he arrived. Hodges was still living in Boston, where Duke Ellington first heard the precocious young saxophonist and signed him on 18 May 1928 to replace Otto Hardwicke. Self-confident and gloriously talented, he was already playing with the poise that would last him a lifetime. Seated impassively at the centre of Ellington's saxophone section, Hodges (nicknamed 'Rabbit' because of his taste for lettuce and tomato sandwiches) directed his section through all of Ellington's creations for the next 22 years, his rich tone, flawless technique and soaring creativity providing Ellington's saxophonic trump-card. A set of small-group recordings (part of a fashionable trend for bands-within-bands) issued in 1938 and 1939 portray his divinely sensual art perfectly: 'soul music with no ifs or buts', was Helen Dance's description of classic Hodges titles such as 'Jeep's Blues', 'Empty Ballroom Blues', 'Hodge Podge' and 'Krum Elbow Blues', recorded with an Ellington contingent, which offer a last chance to hear him playing his first instrument, soprano saxophone (he gave it up in 1940 when Ellington began featuring his alto so heavily that another instrument turned into a burden).

In 1948, while Ellington was touring Britain with a variety show following a serious operation, Hodges was offered a residency at the Apollo Bar on 125th Street, New York, with a small band into which he invited Lawrence Brown, Sonny Greer and other old friends. The 'House Full' signs were up most nights, and soon after – in the wake of rows with Ellington's band and in a lean period for big bands generally – Hodges decided to take a band out on his own. It lasted from 1951 for four successful years but, said Hodges, 'It was a whole lot of work! – and a whole lot of headaches too!' In August 1955 he rejoined Ellington, his stately, blues-inflected creations scoring a huge hit at the 1956 Newport Jazz Festival, and apparently bringing a new creative thrust to his leader's writing: recordings such as *Such Sweet Thunder* (1957), *Jazz Party* (1959) and *Nutcracker Suite* (1960) might have been possible without Hodges but would never have been so great. In the mid-1960s, however, his health began to deteriorate: three hospital spells and doctors' warnings went unheeded as Hodges continued to follow Ellington's punishing schedule. He died while visiting the dentist. 'Because of this great loss', Ellington mourned, 'our band will never sound the same. May God bless this beautiful giant in his own identity.' [DF]

The Big Sound (1957), Polydor

See Dance, Stanley, *The World of Duke Ellington* (Scribner's, 1970, repr. Da Capo, 1980)

Hodgkinson, Colin, bass guitar, voice, composer. b. Peterborough, Cambridgeshire, 14 October 1945. Self-taught. First professional job in 1966 with a jazz trio. 1969, he began working with Alexis Korner in various formations ranging from their brilliant and popular duo to quartets and larger groups. This relationship continued until Korner's terminal illness in 1983. Hodgkinson was a founder member of the group Back Door, 1972–7, with Ron Aspery (reeds) and Tony Hicks (dms). They played the Montreux Festival and did numerous tours of the USA and Europe. 1978, Hodgkinson began working with Jan Hammer, and continued with him in the 1980s. From 1985 he also worked with Brian Auger's Blues Reunion. He composed several pieces for Back Door; with Hammer, he says, he 'writes more lyrics than tunes'.

Hodgkinson is a magnetic performer; an extraordinary virtuoso of the bass guitar, with an engaging vocal style, everything he does is shot through with blues feeling and the sheer joy of music-making. His favourites are Mingus and Eddie Gomez, and particular inspirations are Hammer and Miles Davis. [IC]

With Back Door, *Back Door* (1972), Warner Bros; with Hammer, *Black Sheep* (1979), Asylum; *Hammer* (1980), Asylum; Hammer/Neal Schon, *Here to Stay* (1982), CBS; Hammer/James Young, *City Slicker* (1986), Gem

Holdsworth, Allan, guitar, SyntheAxe, violin, composer. b. Leeds, Yorkshire, 6 August 1946. Father, the late Sam Holdsworth, played piano and taught him chords and scales. He started on saxophone and clarinet; took up guitar at age 17. He wanted the guitar to sound like a sax, more as if he were blowing it than plucking it, and so from the beginning he experimented with electronics. He played around the Leeds area, then came to London at the end of the 1960s. He was one of the pioneers of jazz-rock-fusion in the early 1970s. 1972, he worked briefly with Nucleus, playing on the album *Belladonna*, then left to join Jon Hiseman's Colosseum until November 1973, when he joined Soft Machine, leaving in March 1975 to join Tony Williams's Lifetime in the USA. From 1976 he was with British groups, UK and Bill Bruford's various bands. He also worked and recorded with Jean-Luc Ponty. At the end of the 1970s he was again with Tony Williams, then settled in the USA and led his own bands. 1985, his group, with Gordon Beck on keyboards, toured California and then Japan. Holdsworth acquired a considerable cult reputation during the 1970s, playing most major festivals, and touring internationally as a sideman. In the 1980s, as leader of his own groups, his brilliance became more universally recognized. He is a highly individual stylist, with a gloriously fluid technique and an endless flow of linear ideas. He has said: 'I tend to hear flurries of notes as a whole, from beginning to end, rather than hearing one note after the other.' [IC]

With UK, Soft Machine, Gong, Bill Bruford, Colosseum; with Tony Williams, *Believe It* (1975), Columbia; with Ponty, *Enigmatic Ocean* (1977), Atlantic; as leader, *Velvet Darkness* (1979), CTI; *Road Games* (1980), Warner Bros; *IOU* (1982), AH; *Metal Fatigue* (1984), Enigma; *Atavachron* (1985), Enigma

Holiday, Billie ('Lady Day'), vocals, composer. b. Baltimore, Maryland, 7 April 1915; d. New York City, 17 July 1959. Her early life is obscure, but was apparently a hard one: she was confined to an institution as a victim of childhood rape and became a prostitute in her early teens. By November 1933, when she made her first sides with Benny Goodman ('Your mother's son-in-law'/'Riffin' the Scotch'), she had discovered that although she was 'scared to death' of recording, singing could save her from servility, cleaning steps or whoring. By July 1935, when she made her first great records with friends like Buck Clayton, Lester Young (a platonic soul-brother) and canny Teddy Wilson, the thought still rang joyously in her performances. She signed with Joe Glaser, Louis Armstrong's manager, in 1935 and toured with Count Basie in 1937 and with Artie Shaw (briefly her lover) in 1938. The road was insupportable for her: she bitterly resented the second-class treatment that Shaw, as an ambitious leader, was prepared to negotiate with, and from 1939 turned herself into a solo act at Barney Josephson's multi-racial Café Society club. Despite a hit record, 'Strange Fruit' (1939), a striking anti-lynching song understandably close to her heart, which struck like a hammer on ears attuned to Ella Fitzgerald's satchel-swinging 'A-tisket, a-tasket', Billie was ill-equipped for a solo career: her progress through a series of 1940s night clubs – Famous Door, Kelly's Stables, Billy Berg's, Downbeat, Spotlite and a clutch of others – helped to cement a heroin habit, heavy drinking and her desperate search for a husband/father-figure. With plenty of spending money to spare, a sexual athlete, and in many ways still a child (she avidly read comics), Billie was an easy target for a

Billie Holiday

succession of men – Jimmy Monroe, trumpeter Joe Guy, practised lowlife John Levy, finally Louis McKay, a mafioso heavy – who came, used her and went: she was helplessly dependent on each in turn. As early as the 1940s it was easy to hear that her talent was being remorselessly eaten away, that spontaneous fountain that not even she was sure how to control ('When you open your mouth, you never know what's going to happen', she wrote later). 'Billie is not singing her best, nor does she sing often enough', scolded *Downbeat* magazine in 1944. By this time she was visibly addicted to heroin: in 1947, after being arrested for drug use, she took a cure in Alderson Reformatory, West Virginia. The resulting notoriety terrified her: by the time she played a packed Carnegie Hall Concert in 1948 (to a thunderous ovation) she was beginning to believe that audiences came to see the scars on her arms (which she hid under long gloves) rather than to hear her voice.

Billie desperately wanted to work in films and the previous year had played a maid in *New Orleans*: she had been prepared to settle for any reasonable part ('But she's a cute maid!' she told Leonard Feather). Servant roles were of course standard for black performers (until Sidney Poitier's time), but Billie must have felt the indignity and resented the interference of white people who made her feel guilty for accepting it. She responded with the film's only dignified and worthwhile performance, taking out her resentment on-set but off-camera. By 1952 (after taking a second cure at Belmont Sanatorium) she was working clubs again and had signed with Norman Granz, who was to record her regularly for five years. She was out of sympathy with the intellectualism of modern jazz and hated the rhythm-sections who professed ignorance of her tunes, but as a natural talent lacked the musical knowledge to discuss the problems: no wonder that her voice sometimes sounded like a sad caricature. Granz summed up the stance that her admirers gladly adopted: 'It was obvious to me that she was less of a singer physically – but you have to use a different set of values. A singer's range might become more narrow – but their understanding might become more profound!' In 1953 Billie's *Comeback Story* was networked on TV; in 1954 she toured Europe, including Britain; by 1956, when her bitter-flavoured autobiography *Lady Sings the Blues* was published, she was working harder than ever. In 1957 a TV jazz show re-united her with Lester Young, and the momentary vision is still terribly moving: Billie looks disarmingly lovely (she was still only 42) as she nods approval at Young's languid lines. By 1958 she was living alone near Central Park, New York, with her chihuahua (she had recently been refused permission to adopt a child and sometimes fed her dog from a baby's bottle). On 31 May 1959 she collapsed and was taken to hospital where, on her deathbed, she was arrested for possession of narcotics.

At her peak, in the swing-happy 1930s, Billie Holiday was unquestionably the greatest jazz singer of them all, an avant-garde artist of her time who polished unremarkable popular songs into iridescent gems. She ecstatically recreated her songs' melodies in a small, worldly voice that, in Barney Josephson's words, 'rang like a bell and went a mile'; she conveyed a vulnerability which, as kind Johnny Mercer once said, 'made you feel she needed help'; and she projected an intoxicating sensuality when she sang lines like 'If you wanna make love, OK' in 'Too Hot for Words'. Outwardly she was strong, proud and independent (only Lena Horne in early pictures shares that defiant tilt of the head), but unlike Horne – and other contemporaries who, like Ethel Waters, fought the system on its own doubtful terms – Billie's insecurities led her to drink, drugs and a succession of men, making her an easy target for a witch-hunting white society. Naïve as it normally is to equate singers with their songs, Billie's numbers bear out her own assertion that 'anything I do sing – it's part of my life!' Songs like 'Loverman, oh where can you be?' (a long-time stayer in her act), her own hymn to forgiveness for male infidelity 'Don't Explain', and 'T'ain't nobody's business if I do' all seem central to the devastating problems that quickly killed her.

Hollywood (needlessly and inexplicably) rewrote her story for the film *Lady Sings the Blues* (1972), starring Diana Ross. [DF]

The Golden Years, vols. 1/2 (1933–42). CBS (6 records, 2 boxed sets)

See Chilton, John, *Billie's Blues* (Quartet, 1975); Holiday, Billie, with William Dufty, *Lady Sings the Blues* (Penguin, 1984)

Holland, Dave, bass, cello, composer, and piano, guitar, bass guitar. b. Wolverhampton, Staffordshire, 1 October 1946. Studied at Guildhall School of Music and Drama, London, 1965–8, also performing in orchestral and chamber music concerts; principal bassist in college orchestra. Became active on London jazz scene, working with John Surman, Kenny Wheeler, Evan Parker, Ronnie Scott, Tubby Hayes and others. He already had all the virtues – beautiful tone, perfect time, harmonic knowledge and a brilliant technique – when Miles Davis heard him in London in the summer of 1968, and invited him to New York to join his quintet. He worked with Davis from September 1968 to the autumn of 1970, playing on some of the trumpeter's key albums including *In a Silent Way* and *Bitches Brew* (both CBS), then left with Chick Corea to form Circle with Barry Altschul and Anthony Braxton. Circle toured in the USA and Europe, then broke up when Corea left in 1972. Holland and the other members, with the addition of Sam Rivers, recorded Holland's album *Conference of the Birds*, a classic of acoustic, semi-abstract music.

During the 1970s Holland worked with the Sam Rivers trio, touring world-wide and play-

Dave Holland

ing major festivals, and began to feature cello as well as bass. During the 1980s he began leading his own group which included Kenny Wheeler, Julian Priester and saxophonist Steve Coleman. This toured extensively in the USA and Europe. 1985, Holland worked with a mixed European/American group led by Franco Ambrosetti, which performed at the Berlin Festival. Since the early 1980s Holland has been organizing tutor at the Banff summer school, Canada, and his groups have formed the core of the tutorial staff there. He also teaches privately.

His favourites range from Mingus and Scott La Faro to Ray Brown and Paul Chambers; other influences are Davis, Coltrane, Monk, Ellington, Dolphy and various classical composers. [IC]

With Barre Phillips, Derek Bailey, Braxton, Davis and others; with Circle, *Paris Concert* (1971) (double); quartet, *Conference of the Birds* (1972); with Collin Walcott, *Cloud Dance* (1975); solo bass, *Emerald Tears* (1977); with Kenny Wheeler, *Deer Wan* (1977); with Sam Rivers, *Contrasts* (1980); solo cello, *Life Cycle* (1982); quintet, *Jumpin' In* (1984), all ECM

Holland, Peanuts (Herbert Lee), trumpet, vocals, composer. b. Norfolk, Virginia, 9 February 1910; d. Sweden, 7 February 1979. A veteran of Alphonso Trent's territory band (he joined in 1928 and stayed with breaks for five years), Holland led his own very successful showband, 1938, and, over ten years, lent his powerful talent to a variety of top bandleaders including Jimmie Lunceford, Willie Bryant, Coleman Hawkins and Fletcher Henderson (1941) as well as Charlie Barnet – a close friend and regular employer – 1941–6. That year he travelled to Europe as lead trumpeter for Don Redman and settled there, commuting between Paris and Scandinavia with his own small group and regularly recording with names as diverse as Mezz Mezzrow, Don Byas, Billy Taylor and Claude Bolling. [DF]

With Michel Attenoux (1952), Swing

Holmes, Charlie (Charles William), alto and soprano sax, clarinet, oboe, flute. b. Boston, 27 January 1910; d. Boston, September 1985. He lived on Tremont Street around the corner from Johnny Hodges in 1920s Boston and first played the oboe in local orchestras. He then took up an easier option, the fashionable alto saxophone, and began visiting New York with another near neighbour, Harry Carney. There he worked with bands led by Billy Fowler, George Howe, Luis Russell, Lew Henry (at the Savoy) and guitarist Henri Saparo, before joining Russell's band again at Casper Holstein's Saratoga Club. The Russell band – a romping, stomping New Orleans family – felt like home to Holmes and he stayed, with one short break in 1932, until 1940 (backing Louis Armstrong for the last five years) until Joe Glaser, Armstrong's manager, dismissed the band *en bloc*. After a quiet period back in Boston, Holmes worked with Cootie Williams and others and, briefly, John Kirby in 1947, playing an old tattered book, the remnant of former glories. His last record for a long time was made in 1952 with Al Sears ('a lot of people thought it was Johnny Hodges', he said wistfully later) and Holmes retired soon after to work on Wall Street. 'I never cared about making records', he told Stanley Dance later. '. . . I liked to play where people were dancing and not paying attention to you.' In the 1970s he was persuaded to perform and record with Clyde Bernhardt's Harlem Jazz and Blues Band. The records show no lack of musical talent: perhaps lack of confidence or of driving ambition had more to do with the decline of his career. [DF]

Luis Russell and his Orchestra, 1926–30/1930–4 (2 LPs), VJM

See Dance, Stanley, *The World of Swing* (Scribner's, 1974, repr. Da Capo, 1979)

Hope, Elmo (St Elmo Sylvester), piano, composer. b. New York City, 27 June 1923; d. 19 May 1967. Boyhood friend of Bud Powell, Hope also studied European music. First toured with Joe Morris r & b band that included Johnny Griffin, Philly Joe Jones (1948–9). Freelance gigging and recording with Sonny Rollins, Clifford Brown and under own name during 1950s; moved to Los Angeles (1957–60), working with Harold Land, Lionel Hampton etc. Returning to New York, recorded with all-star group and in duo with his wife, pianist Bertha Hope, but was also imprisoned for drug offences. Remaining intermittently active until his death, Hope was strongly marked by the influence of Powell and especially Thelonious Monk; but he had a personal sound at the piano and was an interesting, and greatly underrated, composer. [BP]

Last Sessions, vols.1/2 (1966), Inner City

Hopkins, Claude Driskett, piano, leader, arranger, composer. b. Alexandria, Virginia, 24 August 1903; d. New York, 19 February 1984. A childhood friend of Rex Stewart in Washington, he was bandleading by 1924 and in 1925 travelled round Europe with Sidney Bechet in the *Revue Nègre*, returned to the USA to work in dancing schools and clubs in New York and Washington and toured for the Theater Owners' Booking Association (TOBA) with the *Ginger Snaps* review. By 1927, in Atlantic City, he had set his band's style – 'I always stressed cup mutes and soft rhythm' – and the formula spelled outstanding success for the band, at New York's Savoy Ballroom, then at Roseland for three years from 1931. Here the band reached a popularity peak, appearing in films and employing Bill Challis, Paul Whiteman's premier arranger, to swell their book: from Roseland they took over from Cab Calloway at the Cotton Club, bringing in Russell 'Pops' Smith (the old reliable lead trumpeter from Fletcher Henderson's orchestra) and popular falsetto singer Orlando Smith. From 1937 the Hopkins band took to the road, playing to packed houses: Hopkins himself – a tough streetwise bandleader who once achieved the near-impossible double of punching both Cab Calloway and Joe Glaser – doubled as a staff arranger for CBS. He continued bandleading until the boom was over, then in 1947 reverted to small-band work, touring with reviews, and backing familiar faces such as Sol Yaged, Herman Autrey and Henry 'Red' Allen at the Metropole. (One familiar but delightful record from the period, issued by Gala as *The Golden Era of Dixieland Jazz*, with Pee Wee Erwin and Buster Bailey, allows an extended view of Hopkins's fleet piano, moving from Waller to Basie and back with easy grace.) In the 1960s and 1970s this work pattern prevailed: but a tour of Europe in 1982 with Earle Warren and Dicky Wells revealed a sad and disillusioned Hopkins, his wife dead, his motivation gone. [DF]

Let's Jam (1961), Fontana

See Dance, Stanley, *The World of Swing* (Scribner's, 1974, repr. Da Capo, 1979)

Horn Centuries ago, this was a generic term for simple brass instruments without valves or slide, such as the posthorn or the alphorn. It is applied by jazz people, however, to any instrument that can be blown (including, but not very often, the so-called French horn and English horn). The actual players of wind instruments in a jazz group are referred to as 'the hornmen' or 'the horns'. [BP]

Horn, Paul, flute (and alto sax, clarinet), b. New York City, 17 March 1930. After studies at music college and work with Sauter–Finegan orchestra, replaced Buddy Collette in Chico Hamilton quintet (1956–8). Studio work in Los Angeles, and appearances and recordings with own groups from 1957. Became one of first musicians after Mary Lou Williams to be featured in church performances of jazz (1964); also one of first jazzmen after Tony Scott to play in Far East countries (1968). Has also performed in China and Russia, and runs his own Golden Flute record label. Horn has a notably pretty sound, which is his chief means of communication with his large and broadly-based following. [BP]

Traveller (1985), Golden Flute

Hot The ability to 'play hot' was a vital, but not indispensable, part of the early jazzmen's equipment. An important factor consists of emphatic rhythmic phrasing with the use of relatively obvious syncopation. In addition, but only available to horn-players, certain instrumental tone-colours (usually with a brilliant edge, but also including the ability to play 'dirty') sounded automatically hot when combined with the necessary phrasing. Of course, since this produced an enthusiastic response from listeners, musicians who did not instinctively play hot, often learned how to 'get hot' for their featured solos; on the other hand, the tone and timing of some players sounds hot from their very first notes, even when they try to be 'cool'.

Although the expression is usually confined to traditional styles, the description applies equally to much rhythm-and-blues and 'modern–mainstream' playing. But the term has fallen into disuse, largely because in the last 25 years the tonal and dynamic range has become so wide; the more frenetic avant-garde players have been hotter-than-hot, while ECM cool has almost reached absolute zero. [BP]

Hot lick, see Licks.

Howard, Darnell, clarinet, violin, saxes. b. Chicago, 25 July *c.* 1895; d. San Francisco, 2 September 1966. As well-known to musicians for his violin playing as his huge-toned clarinet (which in approach and vibrato sometimes seems to echo the sound of his unusual double), he was studying violin by 1902 and after a lot of varied work was good enough to play for W. C. Handy's famous orchestra on Handy's first New York recordings in 1917. For the next six years he was playing and touring with, among others, his former teacher Charlie Elgar, who led a band at Chicago's Dreamland Ballroom in 1921, with James P. Johnson's touring review *Plantation Days* in 1923, and by the middle 1920s with top leaders including King Oliver, Carroll Dickerson and Erskine Tate. In 1931 he joined Earl Hines's brilliant big band, and there he stayed until 1937, playing alto saxophone, featuring his violin, and taking a small group from Hines's orchestra on tour each summer when the Grand Terrace was closed. From the early 1940s Howard opened a shop and awaited the dawn of the revival when, concentrating on clarinet alone, he worked with Kid Ory, Muggsy Spanier and Bob Scobey. 1955–62, he was back with Hines at the Hangover Club, San Francisco, and worked regularly after then (including a tour of Europe with the New Orleans All Stars) until his death from a brain tumour. [DF]

Earl Hines, *Swing Masters* (1961), Riverside

Howard, Kid (Avery), trumpet. b. 22 April 1908; d. New Orleans, 28 March 1966. He began as a drummer and worked early on in bands led by Andrew Morgan and trumpeter Chris Kelly. He was so impressed by Kelly that he switched instruments and later became a regular with the Young Tuxedo Brass Band, Allen's Brass Band and others, as well as in small groups and a brass band of his own. 1930s, he played in clubs and theatres, recorded with George Lewis in 1943 and worked with him regularly from 1952. A familiar figure at Preservation Hall in the early 1960s, Howard's hot, driving style was – and is – held in high regard. His funeral, attended by three brass bands, the Eureka, Olympia and Onward, was one of the biggest ever processions in his home town. [DF]

Any with Lewis

Freddie Hubbard

Hubbard, Freddie (Frederick Dewayne), trumpet, fluegelhorn, composer and piano. b. Indianapolis, Indiana, 7 April 1938. His first professional engagements were with Wes and Monk Montgomery in Indianapolis; he also used to go to Chicago every Sunday to blow at a club where Bunky Green, Frank Strozier and trumpeter Booker Little worked. He moved to New York at the end of the 1950s, sharing rooms with Eric Dolphy for 18 months. He was with Sonny Rollins for four months in 1959; then played with Slide Hampton, J. J. Johnson, Quincy Jones, and in 1961 joined Art Blakey's Jazz Messengers, staying with them for a few years and rapidly establishing a national and international reputation. 1961, he won the *Downbeat* New Star Award for trumpet. Although Hubbard's prime influences were Clifford Brown and Little, he also learned much from Dolphy, and has said: 'He opened me up with the register playing, intervallic playing. I was making two-octave jumps, because he was doing that on the clarinet and bass clarinet. He had me practising from books . . . and he had me interested in Ravi Shankar, which helped me play modally.'

Hubbard's début in jazz was even more remarkable than the bald facts indicate. He not only worked with some of the leading and most influential players (Wes Montgomery, Rollins and Blakey), but at only 22 he walked straight into the history books as well: in December 1960, with Dolphy, he participated in the Ornette Coleman double quartet album *Free Jazz*, one of the great seminal albums of the early 1960s avant-garde; and only two months later, again with Dolphy, Hubbard played an equally important part in another classic and influential recording – Oliver Nelson's *Blues and the Abstract Truth*. Even at that early stage Hubbard's style was fully formed: he had absorbed his influences and created his own sound; a crisp, full-blooded, brassy tone, a highly personal way of rhythmic inflexion, a brilliantly fleet technique, and a vocabulary of tonal resources and effects which were new to the trumpet. He was also perfectly at home with chords and set structures and with semi or total abstraction.

After leaving Blakey he led his own groups for a while, then joined Max Roach; he rejoined Blakey to tour Europe and Japan, and in 1965 worked in Austria with Friedrich Gulda. With Jones he also played on the soundtrack of the film *The Pawnbroker* (1965). In the mid-1960s Hubbard played on yet more classic and seminal albums: with Dolphy, *Out to Lunch*; with Coltrane, *Ascension*; and with Herbie Hancock, *Maiden Voyage* and *Empyrean Isles*. 1966–70, he recorded a series of his own albums for Atlantic, and his music began to show rock influences. During the 1970s he toured internationally with his own groups, playing major festivals, and also made more recordings for CTI and later Columbia. 1972, he moved to California, and the same year his album *First Light* won a Grammy award as the best jazz performance of the year by a small group. In the later 1970s he was leading a group of young unknown musicians who functioned more as a backing band for a 'star' than as collaborators in the act of making music, and his music was heavily electronic and rock-based. Several of his associates from the 1960s had become huge international stars – Herbie Hancock, Wayne Shorter (with Weather Report) and others – with the jazz-rock-fusion movement of the 1970s which they had helped to create, and Hubbard was looking for that kind of stardom and a hit record. He was doomed to disappointment, and in the 1980s was performing once more with an acoustic group playing the contemporary neo-bop at which he excels.

1977, he was reunited with old friends Herbie Hancock, Wayne Shorter, Ron Carter and Tony Williams, in an acoustic band called VSOP which toured world-wide and recorded; 1985, there was a similar reunion for a concert to celebrate the relaunching of the old Blue Note record catalogue. The concert was filmed for television and shown internationally. Autumn 1985, Hubbard was one of the main attractions at the Berlin Festival, leading his own acoustic group and playing with great mastery.

As a trumpet player, Freddie Hubbard is an important stylist, and several subsequent players, including Charles Tolliver, Randy Brecker, Woody Shaw and Wynton Marsalis are indebted to him. Virtuosity and versatility are the hallmarks of his highly individual style and, because of this, he has seemed at times to be all circumference and no centre, which is one of his weaknesses as a bandleader: no central, driving vision or profound commitment to a particular musical direction. He told Howard Mandel: 'My problem has been switching my music, but that's also what keeps me going, *being able to play a little bit of everything*. I want to play a little bit of rock, I want to play a *lot* of jazz, I want to play a little bit of soul. That way I get to meet so many different types of people.' As a result, much of his jazz-rock-fusion output sounds like easy-listening mood music; it is impeccably performed, but has no demons (or daimon), and therefore lacks the necessary emotional tension. All his most important recordings – which include several of the crucially influential albums of the 1960s – are with other leaders. [IC]

With Rollins, Shorter, Sam Rivers, Bobby Hutcherson, Andrew Hill, Roach, Dexter Gordon, Randy Weston and others; with Coleman double quartet, *Free Jazz* (1960), Atlantic; with Nelson, *Blues and the Abstract Truth* (1961), Impulse; with Dolphy, *Out to Lunch* (1964), Blue Note; with Coltrane, *Ascension* (1965), Impulse; with Hancock, *Maiden Voyage* (1965), Blue Note; *VSOP the Quintet – Live* (1977), Columbia; as leader, *Ready for Freddie* (1961), Blue Note; *Backlash* (1966), Atlantic; *First Light* (1972), CTI; *Ride Like The Wind* (1981), Elektra Musician

Hubble, Eddie (John Edgar), trombone. b. Santa Barbara, California, 6 April 1928. He was an early associate of Bob Wilber: they met at Scarsdale High School and worked together briefly in the school jazz band (Dick Wellstood was the pianist). The start of Hubble's career proper came in 1947 when he worked for nine months with singer Red McKenzie at Jimmy Ryan's: the band included a brilliant young trumpeter, Johnny Windhurst, who became Hubble's close friend. For the next few years the trombonist worked around, with Alvino Rey and Buddy Rich among others, but more often alongside Windhurst at the Storyville Club, Boston, or in Windhurst's Riverboat Five, commuting between Ohio and New York. He also worked with Billy Maxted's band, with Phil Napoleon's fine band in the late 1950s at Napoleon's Retreat in Miami, and led his own small group round Fort Lauderdale. By 1966, Hubble was playing with the Dukes of Dixieland, after the death of trombonist Fred Assunto. He stayed a year, then settled in New Jersey with George Morrow's band, and in 1968 was a founder member of the World's Greatest Jazz Band. Since 1970 Hubble has been a freelance: in 1974 he toured Europe with the Kings of Jazz, but his fine Teagarden-style playing is heard too seldom. [DF]

World's Greatest Jazz Band (1971), Atlantic

Hucko, Peanuts (Michael Andrew), clarinet, tenor sax. b. Syracuse, New York, 7 April 1918. He began his career playing smooth tenor saxophone (his early influences were Bud Freeman and Eddie Miller) with trombonist Jack Jenney and later with Will Bradley, Joe Marsala (at the Hickory House), Charlie Spivak ('a most beautiful trumpeter who led a fine band') and Bob Chester before in 1941 he joined the air force. Here he concentrated more on clarinet ('because we did a lot of marching in sand which was awkward with the tenor') and soon after, in Glenn Miller's AAF band was featuring his new speciality in a breakneck 'Stealin' Apples' with Miller's Uptown Hall Gang. He reverted to tenor for spells with Benny Goodman (his section mate was Stan Getz) and Ray McKinley before joining Eddie Condon (on clarinet), 1947–50, filling in for Pee Wee Russell. After Condon, came five years as a studio man for CBS and ABC, where Hucko met Louis Armstrong: in 1958 he joined Armstrong's All Stars for two years. From 1960, Peanuts (the nickname came from his schoolboy love of them) divided his time between Condon and studio work, played Condon's club with his own group, and from 1966 was regularly at Dick Gibson's Colorado jazz parties playing with the Ten Greats of Jazz, later the World's Greatest Jazz Band. In the 1970s he led the Glenn Miller Orchestra at home and abroad, played clarinet solos for Lawrence Welk, worked the studios, and opened his own nightclub, Peanuts Hucko's Navarre, featuring

Ralph Sutton and his singer-wife Louise Tobin. The 1980s brought renewed success: European tours, solo and with his award-winning Pied Piper quintet, work with Syd Lawrence's highly capable Miller-style British orchestra, and best-selling recordings. A clarinet master who never lets the fire disappear from his perfect technique, Hucko forms a distinguished link between Benny Goodman and post-war virtuosi such as Bob Wilber. [DF]

Stealin' Apples (*c*. 1982), Zodiac

Hughes, Spike (Patrick C.), composer, bass. b. London, 1908. A self-taught double-bassist (he played a German string bass made of tin), he arranged for British dance bands before auditioning for Philip Lewis at Decca in 1928. The records that followed by Spike Hughes's Decca-Dents, featuring trumpeter Max Goldberg and an outstanding talent, Philip Buchel (who played alto, tap-danced and later with wife Betty choreographed British musical films including Herbert Wilcox's *Spring in Park Lane*, 1948), are fine examples of British 'chamber jazz'. For the next few years Hughes was busy: touring Holland with his band, writing and orchestrating music for C. B. Cochran and Noël Coward and (in a more specifically jazz vein) interesting items such as *A Harlem Symphony* (composed, as Hughes was quick to point out, on William Walton's piano); in 1932 came a jazz ballet, *High Yellow*, which innovatively juxtaposed jazz and classically-trained players in the same piece and became a society hit. From that year Hughes played bass regularly for Jack Hylton's band, until in 1933 he went to New York. He stayed with John Hammond, wrote songs with Ned Washington (including 'Let's Drink to Love') and, most importantly, recorded 14 masterpieces of Ellingtonian stature with Benny Carter's band, which included such stars as Dickie Wells, Coleman Hawkins, Chu Berry and Henry 'Red' Allen: every title is a classic. 'I left jazz behind at the moment I was enjoying it most: the moment when all love affairs should end', wrote Hughes 15 years later. He seems to have been too bright, too much a trained musician, to take the early excesses of jazz (and the limitations of his own bass-playing) easily in his stride. His entertaining autobiography, larded with classical references, eyebrow-raising chauvinism and determinedly 'modern' attitudes, is a wonderfully entertaining book that ends with a detailed critique of Toscanini: a penance, presumably, for his Bohemian dealings with jazz. He became a pillar of straight music's establishment. [DF]

All American Orchestra (1933), Decca

See Hughes, Spike, *Second Movement* (Museum Press, 1951)

Humair, Daniel, drums, composer. b. Geneva, Switzerland, 23 May 1938. From age seven, played clarinet and drums, and committed him-

Daniel Humair (*right*) with Bobby Jaspar (*left*) and René Thomas (*centre*)

self to jazz after winning a competition for young amateurs. By 1958 he was regularly accompanying Americans in Paris clubs, including a long spell at the Chat Qui Pêche with Lucky Thompson. 1962, he became France's number one drummer in both talent and popularity. He played with the Swingle Singers in the early 1960s, appearing at numerous European festivals. In the late 1960s and early 1970s he was a regular member of Phil Woods's European Rhythm Machine. Also worked with Herbie Mann, Lee Konitz, Anthony Braxton, Roy Eldridge, Stephane Grappelli, Joachim Kuhn and his own group. He has played on the soundtracks of several films, including Bertolucci's *Last Tango in Paris* (1972). Since the mid-1960s he has also had a second career as a successful professional painter. He has won various US and European jazz polls. His main influences are Elvin Jones, Roy Haynes and Philly Joe Jones. [IC]

With Martial Solal, Chet Baker, Jean-Luc Ponty, Lucky Thompson, Swingle Singers, Attila Zoller, George Gruntz, Jim Hall and others; *Phil Woods in Frankfurt* (1970), Atlantic; Beck/Humair/Mathewson trio, *All in the Morning* (1971), Dire-Italian

Humble, Derek, alto sax, clarinet. b. Livingston, Durham, 1931; d. 22 February 1971. Professional at age 16, toured with bands of Teddy Foster, Vic Lewis (1951), Kathy Stobart (1951). Member of Ronnie Scott band (1953–6), also recording with Vic Feldman and others. Joined Kurt Edelhagen radio band (1957–67), also recording regularly with Kenny Clark–Francy Boland from 1961; began touring with them and freelancing from 1967. Died from after-effects of street violence, despite temporary recovery and work in UK with Phil Seamen quartet (1970–1). Ronnie Scott described Humble after his death as 'the complete lead alto saxophonist and a great soloist'. [BP]

Kenny Clarke/Francy Boland, *Live at Ronnie Scott's* (1969), MPS

Humes, Helen, vocals, piano. b. Louisville, Kentucky, 23 June 1913; d. Santa Monica, California, 9 September 1981. She fell under the spell of Ethel Waters early in her career, and recorded four sides for Okeh in Chicago when she was just 14. In the early 1930s she worked with Stuff Smith and Jonah Jones, Vernon Andrade, and with tenorist Al Sears's band in Cincinnati, where Count Basie hired her in 1938 to replace Billie Holiday. With Basie, Humes worked New York theatres, clubs and the Famous Door until 1941, left to work with Teddy Wilson, Art Tatum and others, and by 1944 was touring with package shows, featuring the high-powered blues singing that was her trademark. By 1947 she was in California with Norman Granz's Jazz at the Philharmonic and that year recorded pioneer r & b sides for John Hammond: from then on she was often to be associated with the style, and often toured with blues packages (including a 1962 show with T-Bone Walker, John Lee Hooker and Brownie McGhee). But her jazz approach – clear-toned, rhythmic, note-perfect – also won her regular work with Red Norvo in the 1950s and 1960s, touring Australia with him in 1956 before moving there to live in 1964. She returned to the USA after her mother became ill in 1967 and was soon singing again: in 1973 she scored a huge success at New York's Newport Jazz Festival in a 'Tribute to Count Basie'. The dividends that followed included new recordings, headline appearances at New York's Cookery, the Nice Jazz Festival and European tours, including a visit to Ronnie Scott's in 1978. [DF]

Songs I Like to Sing (1960), Contemporary

See Dance, Stanley, *The World of Count Basie* (Sidgwick & Jackson, 1980)

Hunt, Fred, piano, bandleader. b. London, 21 September 1923; d. Weybridge, Surrey, 25 April 1986. He worked first with clarinettist Cy Laurie's quartet in the early 1950s before joining Alex Welsh's gold-standard Dixieland band in 1954. For the next 20 years or more his fine jazz piano – a mix of Hines, Hodes, Bushkin and his own recipes – was a central feature of Welsh's band. Several earlier recordings, including the classic *Music for Night People*, featuring Welsh and Archie Semple, and a highly collectable solo outing, *Pearls on Velvet* for Doug Dobell, show off Hunt's high-toned talent: Hines-ish flourishes, grumbling blues interludes and chiming declamations. From the mid-1960s, and the formation of Welsh's second great band (featuring John Barnes and Roy Williams), American visitors toured constantly in their company and all – from Peanuts Hucko to Ruby Braff – were unanimous in their praise of Hunt's musicianly understanding and highly creative performance. His filigree-to-muscular piano solos were for long a cherished centrepoint of Welsh's concerts (as were their legendary trumpet–piano duets such as 'Sleepy Time Gal'), but in the later 1970s he left to build a solo career and began a busy round of club and concert performances at home and abroad, recording a second trio album *Yesterdays* and more with Wild Bill Davison and returning occasionally for Welsh reunions. From 1983 terminal cancer made Hunt's appearances rarer; by 1985 he could no longer perform. [DF]

Pearls on Velvet (1968), 77; *Yesterdays* (1979), Erus

Hunter, Chris (Christopher Lionel Robert), alto, tenor and soprano sax, flute. b. London, 21 February 1957. First saxophone at age 12. At 16, began two years of private lessons with Les Evans. Began taking part in jazz workshops and studying improvisation with Don Rendell. At 19, joined NYJO, touring Europe and the USSR. 1978–9, with Mike Westbrook Brass Band touring East Berlin, Scandinavia, Europe in general. Early 1980s, he began doing studio work, mostly as a soloist. 1983, with the Gil Evans British Orchestra, and then in New York for one week with the Westbrook Brass Band. Same year, toured Japan with Gil Evans; October 1983, he moved to New York. 1984, again toured Japan with Gil Evans orchestra featuring Jaco Pastorius, then he joined the Michel Camilo sextet which featured Lew Soloff. 1982, he worked as soloist with Metropole Orchestra, Holland; 1984, he was soloist with Cologne Radio Orchestra for a Mike Gibbs project. Hunter's progress has been meteoric: in six years (1976–83) he moved from being a closet saxophonist to a world platform. But he has the talent, intensity of commitment and vision necessary to make it to the top and stay there. His favourite saxophonists are Cannonball Adderley, Mike Brecker, Jan Garbarek, Charlie Parker, Dave Sanborn and Tom Scott. [IC]

With Westbrook, *Mama Chicago* (1979), RCA; under own name, *Early Days* (1980), Original; *The Warriors* (1981), Ensign; with Gil Evans, *The British Orchestra* (1983), Mole Jazz; *Gil Evans and the Monday Night Orchestra Live at Sweet Basil* (1984), King; *The Michel Camilo Sextet* (1985), King

Hunter-Randall, Ian, trumpet. b. Clapham, London, 3 January 1938. A long-term playing partner to clarinettist Terry Lightfoot (he also worked for clarinettist Pete Allen in the early 1980s), he is one of the finest trumpet talents of British classic jazz. The crackling tone, formidable range and fresh creativity of his

Armstrong-based performance mark him out as a British best and his talents after 20 years deserve wider recognition. In the 1970s his partnership with Mick Cooke (for Lightfoot) produced a near-unbeatable brass team. [DF]

With Terry Lighfoot, Pete Allen

Hurley, Clyde L. trumpet. b. Fort Worth, Texas, 3 September 1916; d. September 1963. Inspired by Louis Armstrong, he played in local bands around his hometown before joining Ben Pollack in 1937 to replace Harry James. Glenn Miller signed him in 1939 for what was to be a none-too-happy stay and Hurley moved to Tommy Dorsey's band for a year from 1940, then to Artie Shaw's in 1941, and a year after that back to Hollywood to take studio work. For the next 13 years he was a Hollywood staffman, and freelance for NBC-TV, but still found time to work the jazz circuit, notably with Ralph Sutton at Club Hangover in 1954, with Matty Matlock's marvellous studio band, the Rampart Street Paraders, and as a guest with Bob Scobey's Frisco band for other special recording assignments at the same period. Hurley may also be heard on Hollywood soundtracks such as *Drum Crazy: the Gene Krupa Story* (1959) and *The Five Pennies* (1959) starring Danny Kaye and Louis Armstrong. [DF]

Live at Club Hangover (1954), Jazz Archives

Husband, Gary Peter, drums, piano. b. Leeds, Yorkshire, 14 June 1960. Father, Peter Husband, was flute player and composer; mother was a dancer. Started on piano at age seven, with private (classical) teacher; studied theory with his father. Took up drums at age ten. Since the late 1970s, he has worked with many leading UK musicians in London, including Gordon Beck, Jim Mullen, Barbara Thompson and Allan Holdsworth. He has toured Europe with Barbara Thompson, and with Holdsworth's group has done tours of the USA and also recorded albums. Husband's influences and inspirations range widely, including Bill Evans (piano), Paul McCartney, John McLaughlin, Jan Hammer, John Coltrane, Holdsworth, Stan Kenton, much Eastern and Western classical music, Frank Sinatra and much pop music. He considers piano and drums to be equally his main instruments, and he has great technical facility on both. [IC]

With Holdsworth, *Allan Holdsworth IOU* (1982), AH; *Metal Fatigue* (1984), Enigma; *Atavachron* (1985), Enigma; with John Themis, *Ulysses and the Cyclops* (1984), Coda

Hutcherson, Bobby (Robert), vibes, marimba, b. Los Angeles, 27 January 1941. Brought up in Pasadena. Piano lessons from age nine, but only became interested in jazz after hearing a Milt Jackson record. Started on vibes while at school, getting some tips from Dave Pike and some help with harmony from a local pianist. He worked locally with saxists Curtis Amy and Charles Lloyd, then played in San Francisco with the Al Grey–Billy Mitchell group, going with it to New York in 1961 and playing at Birdland. 1964, he played on Eric Dolphy's seminal album *Out to Lunch.* He freelanced in New York for another year, playing with Archie Shepp, Hank Mobley, Charles Tolliver and Jackie McLean, among others. Back on the West Coast, he worked with small groups and played in Gil Fuller's big band at the Monterey Jazz Festival, 1965. He won some US polls as new star and best vibist in the mid-1960s. In the later 1960s he began to record regularly under his own name for Blue Note. 1968–71, he co-led a quintet with Harold Land. When the group split up, Hutcherson stayed in San Francisco leading small groups.

He is a fleet, technically excellent player, who has always performed to a consistently high standard, but since the end of the 1960s he has faded into the backwaters of the jazz scene. [IC]

With Eric Dolphy, *Out to Lunch* (1964); as leader, *Spiral* (1968); *Happenings* (1966); *Total Eclipse* (1967); *Linger Lane* (1974), all Blue Note

Hyams, Margie (Marjorie), vibes. b. New York City, 1923. Early career not well documented, playing with group in Atlantic City when 'discovered' by Woody Herman. Played one year with Herman band (1944–5), replaced by Red Norvo when she formed own trio (1945–8, including for a while Tal Farlow). Took part in all-women groups led by Mary Lou Williams, on record and at Carnegie Hall (1947); member of George Shearing quintet, staying 18 months (1949–50). Since women-only big bands were so prevalent in the late 1930s and during World War II, it is hardly surprising that many of their members were capable of joining previously all-male bands – in practice, however, this happened even more rarely than black musicians joining white bands, though there was clearly less resistance from the public. Hyams's vibes solos were a distinct aural asset to both Herman and Shearing (her trio apparently made no records), but she married trumpeter Rolf Ericson and promptly retired from active playing. [BP]

George Shearing, *Lullaby of Birdland* (1949–50), Verve

Hyman, Dick (Richard Roven), piano, composer, organ, clarinet. b. New York City, 8 March 1927. His name first came to the notice of jazz people in the 1950s when, as a staffman for WMCA, MGM and NBC, his output (sometimes linked to jazz and sometimes not) gave little indication either of his worldclass ability or his eclectic jazz interests: an early pointer was 'History of Jazz' concerts for which he collaborated with critic/commentator Leonard Feather. Throughout the 1960s Hyman (in tune with the times) was again involved in a bewilderingly wide vista of highly stimulating musical areas, including free jazz (an album, *Children of All Ages*, was issued on Embryo), jazz-rock, symphonic composition (he wrote a piano concerto, recorded for Command Records) and early experimentation with synthesizers: some results of those highly successful experiments may be heard on another album, *The Electric Eclectics of Dick Hyman*. His colossal all-round abilities however were thrown into clearer relief when after 1970 he began to re-examine the classic areas of jazz with the New York Jazz Repertory Company and a series of concerts and albums which recreated the music of Louis Armstrong, James P. Johnson, Jelly Roll Morton and Scott Joplin. By the late 1970s Hyman's work had placed him alongside Bob Wilber as the most dedicated and scholarly of jazz researchers, whose serious study of his subject never robbed him of the joy in its performance. In the late 1970s Hyman's Perfect Jazz Quintet was a delightful addition to America's classic small groups: in the 1980s he has shone as a virtuoso performer (whose technical command closely resembles Art Tatum's), often in the company of Ruby Braff with whom he has created duet music (on piano and sometimes pipe organ) as profound as that created by Hines and Armstrong. In 1985 he recorded programmes for British TV, solo (*The Ragtime Professor*) and with Braff. [DF]

The Perfect Jazz Repertory Quintet Plays Irving Berlin (1979), World Jazz

I

Ibrahim, Abdullah (aka **Dollar Brand**), piano, composer; also Indian–African flute, soprano sax, cello, voice. b. Cape Town, South Africa, 9 October 1934. Grandmother played piano in church. Private piano lessons from age seven. He grew up with the hymns, gospel songs and spirituals of the American-influenced African Methodist Episcopal Church; also heard Louis Jordan and the Tympany Five popular hits blaring from the township ice-cream vans; and Duke Ellington's music was so familiar that he was 'not regarded as a foreign musician, but rather as something like a wise old man of our community *in absentia*'. His first professional job was with a vocal group, the Streamline Brothers, singing traditional songs, American popular songs, doo-wop, spirituals; then he played piano with the Tuxedo Slickers, followed by a period with the Willie Max dance band in 1959. 1960–1, he led his own band, the Jazz Epistles, which included Hugh Masekela (tpt) and Kippie Moeketsi (alto sax) and was the first black group in South Africa to record an LP.

He moved to Europe in 1962, playing for two years at the Café Africana in Zurich. February 1963, his wife-to-be Bea Benjamin persuaded Duke Ellington to hear him play, and Duke was so impressed that he fixed up a recording session for him. As a result of Ellington's sponsorship, Ibrahim played at the Antibes, Juan-les-Pins and Palermo festivals, 1963; 1964–5, he played at the Montmartre in Copenhagen. At Ellington's urging he went to the USA in 1965, played at the Newport festival and stayed on in New York for three years, getting deeply involved with the free (abstract) jazz scene and working with John Coltrane, Don Cherry, Ornette Coleman and Sunny Murray. He also played with the Elvin Jones quartet in 1966. From then until the mid-1970s he divided his time between Africa, Europe and the USA.

His early influences included Monk as well as Ellington, and also K. Moeketsi and his own African heritage, but all of these tended to become obscured during his involvement in free jazz. After his return to Africa in 1968 and his conversion to Islam, he rejected total abstraction and returned to his African roots, changing in the process from a very good musician into a great one. In his music of the 1970s and 1980s, composition and structure are as important as improvisation, a great variety of rhythms are explored, and there is a tremendous harmonic, melodic and emotional resonance. Having rediscovered his own identity, his art gains immensely in its power and projection, incorporating African chants, carnival music, rural laments, and the sonorities of church hymns – the inner-voicing of chords and the moving (and emotive) bass lines.

1970–6, he toured and played major festivals in Europe, the USA, Scandinavia, Japan, Australia and Canada. Most of his appearances were as a solo pianist, but in 1974 he toured with a 10-piece band in Germany, Italy and Switzerland. 1976, Ibrahim organized a South African jazz festival which flouted all the rules of apartheid, and a few days afterwards he left the country never to return. 1977, he moved to the USA, basing himself in New York, and since then has toured as solo performer, in duo, trio and quartet formations and with larger groups, his wife Sathima (Bea Benjamin) often appearing with him.

In 1982 he and Sathima spent two weeks on a cultural mission to Mozambique; the same year, Ibrahim's *Kalahari Liberation Opera*, a multimedia collage of drama, music and dance, was first performed throughout Europe; it has been called 'one of the most important artistic productions of the South African resistance'. In the mid-1980s he began leading a 7-piece ensemble called 'Ekaya' (= 'home' in several Southern African languages), and dedicating its work to the people of his home country still under the tyranny of apartheid. In Ekaya, Ibrahim leads and writes for his long-time associate Carlos Ward (alto sax and flute), Ricky Ford (tenor), Charles Davis (baritone), Dick Griffin (tmb), Ben Riley (dms) and Essiet Okon Essiet (bass), and Thomas Rome has commented, 'The creative challenges . . . are fuelling an intense but measured compositional outpouring on Ibrahim's part. As the members of the ensemble grow more and more intimate with Ibrahim's compositions, the harmonic brilliance of Ekaya's sound seems to be reaching audiences ever more profoundly.' [IC]

Solo piano, *African Sketchbook* (1973); big band, *African Space Programme* (1973); duo with Johnny Dyani, *Good News from Africa* (1973); trio, *Children of Africa* (1976); quartet, *Africa Tears and Laughter* (1979); duo with Dyani, *Echoes from Africa* (1979); quartet, *At Montreux* (1980); quartet, *Zimbabwe* (1983), all Enja; *Ekaya* (1983), Ekapa

Improvisation is the art of playing without premeditation, rather than necessarily 'making

Abdullah Ibrahim on soprano sax

it up as they go along'. It has been responsible for many of the innovations within jazz, whether early jazzmen departing from a given melody to decorate it or distort it, or the 1960s players who developed the art of 'free' improvisation. But neither the same embellishment repeated night after night, nor frequent free playing with the same group of musicians, will necessarily retain its freshness. With the best performers it does and, even if they are aware of quoting from their earlier efforts, they manage to convince the listener of their spontaneity: and, of course, quotation without being aware of it is often genuinely spontaneous. Nevertheless, most jazz performances are less than 100 per cent improvised, and some may be less than 5 per cent improvised and still be good jazz: it is the spirit (or illusion) of spontaneity which communicates.

Despite the mystique attached to improvisation, it is perfectly possible to learn playing without premeditation. Just like improvisation in comedy (or, indeed, in conversation) it requires a knowledge of the language; and it requires having something to say or, at least, a point of view (and, in performance involving two or more people, it requires a responsiveness to others' points of view). Above all, it is necessary to have a conviction that the act of improvisation is in some ways superior to making prepared statements, and that is something not easily acquired in Western societies – except by listening to jazz, which is also how the musical language is learned.

Whether it is possible to assimilate what is needed by following any particular teaching method is, however, highly debatable. Like other physical activities, it is only learned by example and by doing it. Given the magical aura of a satisfying group improvisation, it is somewhat ironic that in the US 'improv' is now an academic subject just like 'math'. [BP]

See Bailey, Derek, *Improvisation – its Nature and Practice in Music* (Moorland Publishing/ Incus Records, 1980)

Improvised Music, see FREE JAZZ.

Incus Records Founded in 1970 by Derek Bailey, Tony Oxley and Evan Parker with the financial and practical assistance of journalist Michael Walters. Now owned and run by Bailey and Parker. The label is devoted exclusively to abstract, freely improvised music created by Bailey and Parker and/or their associates. The greater part of its output has been produced without subsidy, but the Arts Council of Great

Britain gave financial assistance to make possible seven records involving larger ensembles, and the Commune di Pisa aided the production of another. [IC]

Ind, Peter, bass. b. Uxbridge, Middlesex, 20 July 1928. Studied piano and harmony at Trinity College, Cambridge, took up bass in 1947. Moved to USA in 1951, studied with Lennie Tristano, and played with Lee Konitz, Coleman Hawkins, Buddy Rich, Paul Bley, Roy Eldridge and others. 1963–6, he lived in Big Sur, California, and then returned to the UK, living in London freelancing and teaching. He started his own record company, Wave Records, and during the 1970s opened a recording studio and in the 1980s his own club, the Bass Clef, which presents jazz and related music. [IC]

With Tristano and Konitz; with Jimmy Raney, *Strings and Swings* (1957), Muse; with Rich, *Buddy Rich in Miami* (1958), Verve; *Great Jazz Solos Revisited* (1978); Ind/Martin Taylor, *Triple Libra* (1979); Ind/Buddy De Franco/Taylor/Tony Lee, *A Chip off the Old Bop* (1982), all Wave

Ingham, Keith, piano. b. London, 5 February 1942. He worked with most of the best British mainstream musicians from 1964 including Sandy Brown, Bruce Turner, Dick Sudhalter, Lennie Hastings, Ron Russell and others. He also formed a professional relationship with singer Susannah McCorkle from 1973 and built a reputation as a soloist with the help of producer-singer Chris Ellis for whom in the 1970s he recorded excellent solo albums for EMI. A natural choice for visiting Americans (including Red Allen, Pee Wee Russell, Charlie Shavers, Ben Webster and others) all of whom loved his sensitive accompanist's gifts, spectacular solo talent and knowledgeable repertoire, Ingham made an exploratory trip to New York accompanying McCorkle at the Riverboat Room in 1975 and three years later moved there permanently. He worked Eddie Condon's (with Ed Polcer and others), Benny Goodman and the World's Greatest Jazz Band, continued for a long period accompanying McCorkle, with whom he recorded several gold-standard albums, worked the rounds of hotels, piano bars and jazz festivals and by 1985 was touring Britain with the Eddie Condon Memorial band, led by Polcer, and collaborating with singer Maxine Sullivan (their album *Songs from the Cotton Club* (1984) was nominated for a Grammy). Ingham is a strong all-rounder equipped with an infallible classical-based technique whose tastes run from Bunk Johnson (in 1983 he was songwriting with Jabbo Smith) to John Coltrane and beyond. [DF]

Keith Ingham Plays the Music of Jerome Kern (1977), EMI

Irvis, Charlie, trombone. b. New York City, *c.* 1899; d. *c.* 1939. By the early 1920s he was regularly in clubs with, among others, Willie 'The Lion' Smith. He worked regularly with Bubber Miley, a boyhood friend, and by 1923, with Miley again, was introducing a revolutionary 'new sound' at the Bucket of Blood Club, a basement on 135th Street. Using a whole set of mutes, including (said Elmer Snowden) half a yo-yo, Irvis produced growling music that set a pattern for future specialists such as Tricky Sam Nanton and attracted the attention of famous leaders including Paul Whiteman. Young Duke Ellington hauled Irvis and Miley into Elmer Snowden's Washingtonians, soon to become Duke Ellington's, and began to write material for them. Ellington said later: 'He used an object that was very effective and he played in a different register of the horn. There was a kind of mute they built at the time to go into a trombone and make it sound like a saxophone but he dropped his one night and the darned thing broke – so he picked up the part that was left and started using it. That was his device and it was greater than the original thing. He got a great big fat sound at the bottom end of the trombone – melodic, masculine, full of tremendous authority.' Some of that sound can be heard on records Irvis made with Clarence Williams, Fats Waller ('Minor Drag'/'Harlem Fuss') and Jelly Roll Morton ('Tank Town Bump'/'Burning the Iceberg'): he went on working with Charlie Johnson and Miley into the 1930s but was inactive by 1939. [DF]

Isaacs, Ike, guitar. b. Rangoon, Burma, 1919. (Not to be confused with double-bassist Charles E. 'Ike' Isaacs. b. Ohio, 28 March 1923, who was married to Carmen McRae and worked with Erroll Garner and with Lambert, Hendricks and Ross, as well as leading his own trio.) He came to Britain in 1946 and worked over many years with Ted Heath and with the BBC Showband, as well as leading his quartet for the BBC's weekly Guitar Club in the 1950s: later he worked as a prolific studio man, and in the 1970s toured with Stephane Grappelli's quartet, the co-operative quartet Velvet (with Denny Wright, Len Skeat and Digby Fairweather) and played regularly in duo with Martin Taylor. From the early 1980s Isaacs – a master technician who for many years wrote about guitar technique in professional journals such as *Crescendo International* – moved to Australia to take up a professorship at Sydney Guitar School. [DF]

Isaacs/Taylor, *After Hours* (1979), JTC

Israels, Chuck (Charles H.), bass, composer. b. New York City, 10 October 1936. Studied music in USA and in Paris, becoming interested in jazz at age 18. Recorded with Cecil Taylor studio group (1958, reissued as by John Coltrane) and with Eric Dolphy (1961); regular working associations with George Russell sextet (1960) and Bill Evans (1961–6). Formed rehearsal band (1966) and had compositions played by European radio orchestras; founded the National Jazz Ensemble repertory group (1973–8) for which he conducted and (with others) arranged. Although no longer active full-time as a bassist, Israels's contribution to the Evans trio, far less flamboyant than other incumbents, amply demonstrated his fluency and responsiveness. [BP]

Bill Evans, *The Second Trio* (1962), Milestone

Izenzon, David, bass, composer. b. Pittsburgh, Pennsylvania, 17 May 1932; d. 8 October 1979. Took up bass in 1956, playing locally until 1961, when he moved to New York. He became deeply involved with the avant-garde, working with Paul Bley, Archie Shepp, Bill Dixon, Ornette Coleman, but also gigged with less abstract players such as Sonny Rollins and Mose Allison. He came to international prominence with the Ornette Coleman trio in the mid-1960s, touring and recording in Europe and Scandinavia. In the later 1960s, he led his own quintet in the New York area, and also worked with Perry Robinson, Jaki Byard and others. 1968–71, he taught music history at Bronx Community College. From 1972 he curtailed his playing in order to devote much time to his son Solomon who was born with severe brain damage. 1973, he received a Ph.D. in psychotherapy from Indiana Northwestern University, and started a private practice in New York. 1975, he composed and performed a jazz opera, *How Music Can Save the World,* dedicated to all those who helped care for his son. [IC]

With Bill Dixon, Archie Shepp, Sonny Rollins, Jaki Byard; with Ornette Coleman, *Chappaqua Suite* (1965), CBS; *The Great London Concert* (1965), Arista-Freedom; *At the Golden Circle, vols. 1/2* (1965), Blue Note

J

Jackson, Chubby (Greig Stewart), bass. b. New York City, 25 October 1918. Played clarinet at 16, then switched to bass, working professionally from 1937. With Charlie Barnet (1941–3) and Woody Herman (1943–6, 1948). Also with Charlie Ventura septet (1947), own small group (1947–8) and short-lived big band (1948–9). Then freelance and studio work in 1950s, also TV personality and songwriter. Worked briefly with Harold Baker (1963), own occasional groups in New York, Florida, Los Angeles and Las Vegas. Reappeared on jazz scene with Lionel Hampton all-star band (1978–9); his son Duffy Jackson played drums in both Hampton and Count Basie bands (early 1980s). Chubby's own sprightly bass work is still associated most strongly with the Herman band, to which he gave a tremendous rhythmic lift. He was also known, several years before Charles Mingus, for shouting out his encouragement of the band's soloists. [BP]

Woody Herman, *Carnegie Hall Concert* (1946), Verve

Jackson, Cliff (Clifton Luther), piano. b. Virginia, 19 July 1902; d. New York, 24 May 1970. 'He can beat sense into any box!' said Maxine Sullivan, talking about her husband and regular accompanist, one of the very greatest classic stride pianists. He came to New York from Washington in 1923 and after work with a variety of bands (including Elmer Snowden's) formed his own Krazy Kats in 1927. From then on – rather like Willie 'The Lion' Smith – Jackson made his name as a respected soloist (an early portrait of him by Snowden suggests that, on occasion, he would make short work of younger opposition like Duke Ellington), led his own bands, accompanied singers and made the rounds of clubs from the Radium to Café Society Downtown, where he was house pianist 1944–51. All the way through the 1950s Jackson survived New York unscathed, worked with such old friends as Garvin Bushell (1959), J. C. Higginbotham (1960) and Joe Thomas (1962) and by 1963 was resident at Jimmy Ryan's with clarinettist Tony Parenti. In 1965 he was prominent in Maxine Sullivan's return to live performance, worked Lou Terrazzi's club and he recorded solo in 1969, the year before he died of heart failure during a residency at the RX Room, Manhattan. [DF]

Cliff Jackson's Washboard Wanderers (1961), Swingville

Jackson, Milt(on) ('Bags'), vibes (and piano). b. Detroit, Michigan, 1 January 1923. Played in local groups alongside such players as Lucky Thompson, and studied music at Michigan State University. Moved to New York for work with Dizzy Gillespie sextet, in time for West Coast visit (1945–6). Then founder member of Gillespie big band (1946–7), followed by freelancing with Howard McGhee, Thelonious Monk, Tadd Dameron (also recording with first two). First sessions under own name (1948) during return visit to Detroit. Several months with Woody Herman (1949–50), later with new Gillespie sextet (1950–2). Recorded with own quartet (1951) for Gillespie's Dee Gee Records, then undertook live appearances including backing Charlie Parker and Ben Webster; further quartet records (and with guest soloists Lou Donaldson, Sonny Rollins and Horace Silver) led to abbreviation of Milt Jackson Modern Jazz Quartet to last three words, and establishment of regular group under musical direction of John Lewis (1954).

Throughout next 20 years, Jackson continued to work with MJQ and to make albums under his own name, collaborating with Frank Wess, Lucky Thompson, Coleman Hawkins, John Coltrane, Wes Montgomery etc. and guesting on records by Kenny Clarke, Miles Davis, Quincy Jones and others. Starting mid-1960s, also appeared in public with own quintets including James Moody, Jimmy Heath, Cedar Walton, Monty Alexander and former Gillespie colleague Ray Brown. Departed from MJQ bringing about its break up (1974, partly because he thought the members were being financially exploited), and from 1975 he appeared as guest artist or with own groups, e.g. in Montreux (1975, 1977), Japan (1976), London (1975, 1982). Then became regularly active with re-formed Modern Jazz Quartet, but toured Europe again with own group (1985).

Jackson's attempts to overcome the limitations of his chosen instrument have been remarkably successful: at the start of his career, the current model's mechanical problems were considerably greater than more recently manufactured models. Lionel Hampton and his followers had capitalized on its ringing tones and, at faster tempos, treated the vibes percussively like a recalcitrant piano, but Milt managed against the odds to make it sound more like a trumpet or saxophone. To that end he employs a great variety of attack in articulating his phrases, and allows the vibrato mechanism to emphasize the occasional longer note. This is especially true of the way in which he caresses a ballad or a slow blues, on which all of his melodic lyricism emerges in a seemingly unstoppable flow. Despite using a considerable quantity of notes, there is always an essential simplicity about Jackson's playing. It is no coincidence that his eponymous 12-bar blues 'Bags' Groove', and to a lesser extent 'Bluesology', are known the world over as easy but effective standards for jamming. [BP]

Milt Jackson Quartet (1954), Prestige/OJC; *Plenty, Plenty Soul* (1957), Atlantic; *Milt Jackson Big 4* (1975), Pablo

Jackson, Oliver, Jnr. ('Bops Junior'), drums. b. Detroit, Michigan, 1934. He played first in the Detroit area with r & b bands (one led by Gay Crosse featured a young John Coltrane) and signed his first union card in 1949. Thereafter he worked in trios – with Tommy Flanagan, Barry Harris and Dorothy Donegan – and in 1953, in a unique career-shift, formed a successful tap-dancing duo, 'Bop and Locke' with drummer Eddie Locke. They danced successfully at the Apollo and around the theatre circuit until Jackson signed with Tony Parenti's trio, working afternoons at the Metropole in 1954 and then evenings at the same venue with Henry 'Red' Allen, succeeding Cozy Cole. He stayed with Allen until 1961 when he joined Charlie Shavers, a constant working companion for the next ten years, in a Jonah Jones-patterned quartet which recorded widely and always beautifully. Jackson also worked with Earl Hines, Erroll Garner, Oscar Peterson (for a year) and in 1967 toured with a package show, *Jazz from a Swinging Era*, which teamed him with Roy Eldridge, Buck Clayton and Hines again. From 1969 he was a founder member of the JPJ Quartet, a group featuring Budd Johnson, Bill Pemberton and Dill Jones which played all over the USA in government-backed concerts for the John Manville Corporation; from 1975 he worked with Sy Oliver's fine new band at New York's Rainbow Room and led his own trio in New York and for European tours. In the 1980s Jackson played regularly with George Wein's Newport Jazz Festival All Stars, featuring Scott Hamilton and Warren Vaché, and in 1985 he toured the UK with Eddie Condon's Memorial group led by cornettist Ed Polcer. [DF]

With Charlie Shavers, *The Last Session* (1970), Black & Blue

Jackson, Preston (James Preston McDonald), trombone. b. New Orleans, 3 January 1902; d. Blytheville, Arkansas, 12 November 1983. He moved to Chicago at 15 after soaking up the music of his home town and was immediately enthralled with the challenging standards of ex-New Orleans men, who had moved on to greater things. 'I didn't play anything then,' he was to tell Shapiro and Hentoff, 'but I was thinking of taking the clarinet. We used to hang around Joe [King] Oliver's band [and] I used to sit behind Dutrey every night. He was wonderful about showing me fine points on the horn. I learned lots from him.' Jackson also took lessons from Roy Palmer and, after ten years working in territory bands (often around Milwaukee), came back to Chicago for ten more, playing and recording with Louis Armstrong (1931–2: he can be heard on 'You rascal you'), Carroll Dickerson, Jimmie Noone and Zilmer Randolph's big band. In the 1940s he took up a full-time union post but continued bandleading for fun, re-united with Lil Hardin Armstrong on record in 1959 and, at the end of his life, moved back to New Orleans. There he joined the Preservation Hall Band and, says John Chilton, died while touring with them.

Jackson was not only one of the most technically able and creative of the New Orleans trombonists but also an observant commentator on jazz history (Shapiro and Hentoff's *Hear me talkin' to ya* contains a number of his reminiscences and he wrote a regular column for *Jazz Hot* and *Hot News* magazines) as well as a capable administrator who from 1934 until 1957 served on the directors' board of Chicago's Associated Federation of Musicians. [DF]

Louis Armstrong, vols. 7 & 8 (1931), CBS

Jackson, Quentin Leonard ('Butter'), trombone, vocals, occasional string bass. b. Springfield, Ohio, 13 January 1909; d. New York, 2 October 1976. He first played violin and organ for hometown church services and in his school orchestra before taking up the trombone late, at 18 years old. But he progressed fast and was soon working with territory bands led by Gerald Hobson, Lloyd Byrd, Wesley Helvey (whose Troubadours sported an eminent succession of trombonists including J. C. Higginbotham and Vic Dickenson) and Zack Whyte. December 1930, he joined McKinney's Cotton Pickers, primarily to sing (Ed Cuffee was featured trombonist), replacing George 'Fathead' Thomas, who had been killed in a car crash. Don Redman was staff arranger for McKinney at the time and when he left to form his own band, Jackson (whom Redman named 'Butter' because he was 'kind of chubby') went with him, staying until the end of 1939 to play in a revolutionary three-trombone section that Duke Ellington liked and quickly copied. Then came eight years in Cab Calloway's band and 11 with Duke Ellington, replacing Claude Jones. From the late 1950s his career diversified with pit work under Quincy Jones's baton for *Free and Easy*, a tour with Jones's band through Europe, a year with Count Basie (replacing Al Grey), time with Charles Mingus (who had worked with Ellington for ten days while Jackson was there) which was to produce a classic Mingus album, *Black Saint and the Sinner Lady*, and later in the 1970s big-band work with Sammy Davis, Louie Bellson, Gerald Wilson and others. [DF]

Duke Ellington, *Such Sweet Thunder* (1957), CBS

See Dance, Stanley, *The World of Swing* (Scribner's, 1974, repr. Da Capo, 1979)

Jackson, Ronald Shannon, drums (and flute). b. Fort Worth, Texas, 12 January 1940. As teenager, played regular sessions in Dallas with Ray Charles sidemen James Clay and Leroy Cooper. Studied history and sociology in Texas, Missouri and Connecticut, then obtained music scholarship in New York (mid-1960s); recorded there with saxist Charles Tyler (1966) and worked with Albert Ayler, Betty Carter, Charles Mingus and Stanley Turrentine. Less involved in music in early 1970s, Jackson returned to the forefront with Ornette Coleman (1975–6) and Cecil Taylor (late 1970s). Then with James 'Blood' Ulmer group before forming his own Decoding Society, 1981. 1985–6, recorded and toured in Last Exit with Peter Brötzmann, Sonny Sharrock and bassist Bill Laswell. Jackson's style, initially focused by the influence of Milford Graves and Sunny Murray, proved adaptable to the further developments of Ornette's group approach. But, as with Coleman himself, Jackson seems to have simplified his music in the quest for greater popularity. [BP]

Man Dance (1982), Antilles

Jackson, Tony (Anthony), piano, vocals. b. Amelia Street, New Orleans, 5 June 1876; d. Chicago, 20 April 1921. He worked in bands well before the turn of the century (including Adam Olivier's) and spent some years in New Orleans entertaining at bagnios such as Gypsy Schaeffer's and Antonia Gonzales'. He was epileptic, homosexual and an alcoholic, with severe tooth decay, not one good feature to speak of and regular outbreaks of unsightly sores which he hid under his hat: he was also an enchanting singer-entertainer, who won the respect of even the most braggadocio denizen of New Orleans. 'He was the outstanding favourite of New Orleans,' admits Jelly Roll Morton.'We all copied Tony', said Clarence Williams. 'He was so original, and a great instrumentalist . . . certainly the greatest piano player and singer in New Orleans.' Jackson moved to Chicago in 1912, where he worked at cafés such as the DeLuxe and Pekin, his last engagement in 1921. As well as being an unbeatable one-man show he composed fine tunes, including 'Some Sweet Day', 'The Naked Dance' (recreated by Jelly Roll Morton) and his most famous, 'Pretty Baby', dedicated, said Alberta Hunter, 'to a tall, skinny fellow'. Jackson never recorded; he died, probably, of syphilis. [DF]

Illinois Jacquet

Jacquet, (Jean-Baptiste) Illinois, tenor sax (and bassoon). b. Broussard, Louisiana, 31 October 1922. Brought up in Houston, Texas, worked with Milt Larkin band (1939–40) including move to West Coast. Briefly with Floyd Ray (late 1940), became key member of new Lionel Hampton band (1941–2). Then with Cab Calloway (1943–4) and Count Basie (1945–6), also appearing in early Jazz at the Philharmonic concerts (1944) and subsequent national tours (1947, 1955). Had own 7-piece bands (1945, 1947 onwards). Later alternated between work as guest soloist and own groups, including trios with Milt Buckner (1966–74) and Wild Bill Davis (1972, 1977). Took part in all-star reunion bands with Hampton (1967, 1972, 1980) and made frequent solo tours of Europe. Also organized own Jazz Legends big band (1984 onwards).

Jacquet may be the essential encapsulation of the 'Texas tenor', for he managed to combine the mobility of the best blues players with the pungent yet fruity tone of more mainstream men such as Arnett Cobb and Buddy Tate. Despite a popular reputation for upper-register harmonics, Jacquet has had a considerable and usually unacknowledged influence on several generations of tenorists from Eddie Davis to King Curtis to Scott Hamilton. And, although not known for putting pen to paper as a composer, his 64-bar solo on the original Lionel Hampton record of 'Flying Home' (complete with quotation from Herschel Evans) is the longest example in existence of an improvisation which was then habitually incorporated wholesale into later written arrangements. [BP]

Swing's the Thing (1957), Verve; *Genius at Work!* (1971), Black Lion

Jam Although its origin is rather mysterious, 'jam' was probably a verb before it was a noun. In the 1930s and 1940s, 'jamming' often appeared to mean cramming as many musicians as possible into one room, but perhaps the concept of cramming the maximum number of ideas into each solo comes closer.

A 'jam' was the musicians' term for the occasion where such informal extended playing took place, away from the demands of the regular job; Duke Ellington's title 'Dinah's in a Jam' refers to a succession of solos on one of the favourite vehicles for jamming (as well as 'Dinah', other material regularly used included 'I Got Rhythm', 'Honeysuckle Rose', 'Lady Be Good' and the 12-bar blues). The phrase 'jam session', though doubtless uttered at some stage by a musician, was the description picked up by journalists and favoured by the fans.

The heyday of jamming came to an end in the US when the musicians' union (the AFM), worried about shrinking employment in the late 1940s, began to discourage members from doing informal unpaid sessions in front of even an invited audience. However, as recent attempts to revive this institution indicate, it served a valuable purpose in raising performance standards; young aspiring players were given the chance to match themselves against the best musicians of their area, and the best local players tried their luck against those with national reputations as they came through on tour.

Only rarely did these occasions turn into real 'cutting contests' and, even then, they were characterized by a marvellous combination of competition and camaraderie. [BP]

Jamal, Ahmad (Fritz Jones), piano. b. Pittsburgh, Pennsylvania, 2 July 1930. Like jazz-based vocalists, the jazz pianist who attains commercial success moves closer to the show-business world than most horn-players ever have the opportunity to do. Such is the case with Jamal, although his influence on jazz has been considerable. After touring with the St Louis-based George Hudson band, he formed his first group *c.* 1949, featuring Ray Crawford on guitar, and gained an early hit record with his arrangement of the folk song 'Billy Boy'. In the mid-1950s the guitar was replaced by drums and, with bassist Israel Crosby playing a prominent role, Jamal developed his distinctive sound on several best-selling albums. Never well-known in Europe, he continues to work sometimes with additional musicians, usually with just bass, drums and percussion.

Ahmad Jamal

Jamal's popularity was enhanced by the advocacy of Miles Davis and by the example of Miles's pianist of the mid-1950s, Red Garland. The bouncy left-hand voicings and tinkly, tantalizing right – contrasted from time to time with mobile block chords – were a streamlined version of fellow Pittsburgher Erroll Garner. But Miles went so far as to cover much of Jamal's repertoire (his composition 'New Rhumba' and numerous standards such as 'Autumn Leaves' and 'But Not For Me') and also to adopt the two-beat rhythm-section style and four-bar tags associated with the pianist. Given Davis's great influence on other musicians, the knock-on effect has been incalculable; not only later pianists with Miles (Wynton Kelly and Herbie Hancock particularly) but everyone who has imitated them as well reflect the work of Jamal to some degree. [BP]

At the Blackhawk (1961), Reactivation; *Awakening* (1970), Jasmine

James, Bob (Robert), piano, composer, organ, synthesizer. b. Marshall, Michigan, 25 December 1939. Received his master's degree in composition from University of Michigan, 1962. Worked for Maynard Ferguson for three months in 1963, then became pianist and arranger for Sarah Vaughan until 1968. James is a highly professional composer/arranger who has done much studio work, and arranged and performed with Quincy Jones, Dionne Warwicke, Roberta Flack. 1973, he was signed as exclusive arranger for CTI Records, and wrote albums for Eric Gale, Grover Washington, Hank Crawford,

Stanley Turrentine and others. Also made his own albums for that label. Later in the 1970s he was signed to CBS, making a series of highly produced albums with a disco flavour. [IC]

James/Earl Klugh, *One on One* (1979); Bob James, *"H"* (1980); *The Genie* (1983), all CBS

James, Harry Hagg, trumpet. b. Albany, Georgia, 15 March 1916; d. Las Vegas, Nevada, 5 July 1983. He began playing professionally at nine, in a circus orchestra led by his father, also a trumpet player: from Everett James, Harry learned technique (later the two men co-wrote a trumpet tutor), from the circus he learned how to make a show, and after an initial bout of lip trouble during a stint with Herman Waldman's band in Texas he was soon working all over Texas, with the enthusiastic backing of his proud father. By 1935, James – a skinny, voracious-looking teenager – had joined Ben Pollack, and even by then was a trumpet master, blessed with strength, steely control, concentration and a pugnacious creativity (his records of the period, for example 'Peckin'', suggest that he might be trying to blow the trumpet out straight). He was quickly accepted in New York's studio world, and almost as quickly by his jam session colleagues, black and white. 'James was pretty hostile at first as I remember him', says Billie Holiday. 'He came from Texas where negroes are looked on like they're dirt. It showed. We had to break him out of that – and also of the idea that he was the world's greatest trumpet player. [But] it only took a few earfuls of Buck Clayton's playing and Harry wasn't so uppity. He'd had his lesson and after that he came up to jam and loved it!' James's records then (with Teddy Wilson, Buster Bailey, Johnny Hodges and others, featuring on occasion marvellous boogie sides such as 'Boo Woo' and 'Woo Woo') make it clear that any prejudice was overcome early and his trumpet-playing confidence remained unshaken. In 1937 he left a chagrined Ben Pollack to join Pollack's younger rival Benny Goodman, and in two brief years his reputation was made. Not only was he Goodman's most brilliant-ever trumpet soloist ('he ripped hungrily at the solos', wrote the great Irving Townsend, 'as if he hadn't had one in weeks'), but he led the trumpet section with an unquenchable fire that would stay with him for life. He worked for Goodman for two years almost to the day, and a month later formed his own band which made its début at the Benjamin Franklin Hotel, Philadelphia: from then on James would be a leader for life.

In his time with Goodman he had already achieved idol status, and after a short consolidation period (during which Frank Sinatra joined him at Roseland Ballroom in July 1939) James began parading his limitless trumpet technique in a set of *tours de force* which are still unsurpassable: 'Concerto for Trumpet' (November 1939), 'Carnival of Venice' (March 1940), the revolutionary 'Flight of the Bumble-bee' (May 1940) and 'Trumpet Rhapsody' (March 1941). By this time he had lost Sinatra (amicably) to Tommy Dorsey and acquired the great Dick Haymes, but it was a trumpet feature from May 1941 which was to establish James as the most commercially successful jazzman of the 1940s. 'You made me love you', a James favourite which Judy Garland had sung in *The Broadway Melody of 1938*, introduced his new and revolutionary 'sweet style', a strong, sensuously vibratoed 'adoration of the melody' with generous embellishments and a sound like hot gold. Throughout the 1940s a string of successors turned him into a pop-music idol: at one stage Columbia, amid wartime shortages, was unable to press enough of his records to meet demand. James married and divorced a succession of wives (including Betty Grable), added strings to his orchestra, toured and broadcast constantly (by 1944 his band featured long-term members such as Willie Smith, 'Corky' Corcoran, Juan Tizol and singer Helen Forrest, with whom James shared a long love-affair) and made a number of films, including *Syncopation* (1942), *Bathing Beauty* (1944) and the marvellous *Springtime in the Rockies* (1942).

The swift changes in post-war jazz fashion briefly dented James's ongoing success story: he was neither modern enough for bebop nor rough-hewn enough for the revival, and his swing orchestra symbolized 'commerciality'. So he formed a small group, the Music Makers, featuring cornermen Smith, Tizol and Buddy Rich, and took time off to recoup energy and inspiration. But by 1957 he was touring Europe with a re-formed big band and from then on was seldom out of the spotlight. James's orchestra at the period was often unjustifiably regarded as a pale copy of Count Basie's for two reasons: Basie employed the young arrangers such as Neal Hefti and Ernie Wilkins that James had used *before* him but publicized them more, and sometimes James 'covered' Basie records ('M-Squad Theme' was one). In fact Harry James's show was quite different from Basie's: it featured a succession of familiar swing stars (such as Corcoran and Smith) rather than Basie's new-generation modern men, James's now-familiar 'sweet-style', a more catholic repertoire which returned happily to Armstrong as much as creating new material, and even a Dixieland front-line which gave his band the sound of a supercharged Bob Crosby. All this in 1958 terms was démodé: but James, as fierce as ever, was impatient with jazz fashion. 'What do you mean, "commercial"?' he demanded aggressively '. . . I don't believe we've ever played or recorded one tune that I didn't love to play – or I wouldn't have played it!' During the 1970s grandmaster James continued touring, his abilities an enviable legend to younger men, but he was ill in the 1980s and succumbed to cancer at 67. British trumpeter Kenny Baker, a comparable talent, was asked to take over his role but declined. [DF]

The Harry James Big Band (1943–6), Joker

Japan Jazz was banned in Japan during World War II, but after peace was declared the jazz scene there grew with astonishing vigour. Records of bebop and earlier jazz were available in the later 1940s, Norman Granz's Jazz at the Philharmonic toured Japan in the 1950s and from the 1960s US jazz musicians visited regularly; Art Blakey first toured there in 1961, Miles Davis in 1964 and John Coltrane in 1966.

Pianist Toshiko Akiyoshi went to the Berklee School in Boston, in the 1950s, and since then, many more Japanese musicians have studied there. Since the early 1970s many technically brilliant Japanese musicians have toured and recorded with leading Americans in the USA and Japan: trumpeters such as Terumasa Hino and Tiger Okoshi; a spate of gifted women pianists including Toshiko Akiyoshi, Aki Takase and Haruko Nara, as well as men such as Yosuke Yamashita and Masabumi Kikuchi; saxophonist Sadao Watanabe, and many excellent rhythm-section players.

Japanese jazz audiences also grew enormously, until, as concert-goers and record-buyers, they vied with the USA in the 1970s and by the mid-1980s probably led the world. Japan produces the largest monthly jazz magazine in the world: *Swing Journal* is as bulky as a longish novel. Since the early 1970s Japan has had reissues in their original covers of American LPs which were unavailable in the USA and Europe, with such success that in the mid-1980s the USA followed suit, reissuing, for example, the Blue Note catalogue in their original covers.

Japanese musicians, however brilliant, tend to be totally USA-oriented, and play American jazz. Their full creative maturity will come when they incorporate elements from their own musical culture and produce Japanese jazz. [IC]

Jarman, Joseph, sopranino, soprano, alto, tenor and bass sax, bassoon, oboe, flute, clarinets, piccolo, composer, voice, percussion. b. Pine Bluff, Arkansas, 14 September 1937. Family moved to Chicago when he was a child. Studied drums at high school, sax and clarinet in the army; further study at Chicago Conservatory of Music. 1965, began performing with AACM (see ABRAMS, MUHAL RICHARD). Had played bebop with saxist Roscoe Mitchell at college, and free improvisation with him in Abrams's Experimental Band. In the later 1960s he was leading a group which explored poetry and elaborate programme music with a strong theatrical slant. 1965, played his composition *Imperfections in a Given Space* with John Cage; 1966, recorded his first album, *Song For*, and premiered theatre pieces *Tribute to the Hard Core*. He gave the guest lecture for the Contemporary Music Society of the University of Chicago in 1967. Summer 1968, he was lecturer and director of music and theatre workshop at Circle Pine Centre, Delton, Michigan. 1969, he joined the *Art Ensemble of Chicago, and has played with it since then. [IC]

With AEC; *Song For* (1966), Delmark; *As if it were the Seasons* (1968), Delmark; *Sunbound* (1976), AECO; with Don Moye, *Egwu-Anwu* (1978), India-Navigation; *Black Paladins* (1979), Black Saint; *Earth Passage – Density* (1981), Black Saint

Jarrett, Keith, piano, composer, soprano sax. b. Allentown, Pennsylvania, 8 May 1945. Eldest of five brothers, all musically inclined. He was a child prodigy, studying piano from age three, and presenting a full-length solo recital when he was seven. He toured extensively as a child, performing solo recitals of classical music and his own compositions. He also took up drums, vibraphone and soprano sax. Although he had piano lessons throughout his childhood and adolescence, he received no training in orchestration or composition. At 17 he played a two-hour solo concert of his own compositions, and turned down the offer of a scholarship to study privately in Paris with Nadia Boulanger. After a year at the Berklee School on a scholarship, he left to lead his own trio in the Boston area. Then he moved to New York, playing with Tony Scott and others until he joined Art Blakey's Jazz Messengers, December 1965. Spring 1966, left Blakey to join the Charles Lloyd quartet, which included Jack DeJohnette and bassist Ron McClure. This was an important, trail-blazing group, and Jarrett stayed with it until 1969. With Lloyd, he toured Europe six times, the Far East once, and the Soviet Union – the first time that a group of modern jazz musicians had played there. They also played the International Jazz Festival in Prague, Czechoslovakia, where the Moscow Radio and TV Orchestra performed an arrangement of Jarrett's composition *Sorcery*.

The seeds of Jarrett's mature style can be seen in his work with the Lloyd quartet, which recorded several albums: his intensely rhythmic left hand, the brilliant right-hand linear runs, the emotional heat redolent of the blues and hot gospels; his exposure with the group also laid the basis for his national and international reputation. He left Lloyd in 1969 to lead his own trio with Charlie Haden and Paul Motian, starting with an extensive European tour. 1970–1, he played electric keyboards with Miles Davis, which further enhanced his reputation. He had recorded for various labels with his trio, but in 1972, after leaving Davis, he was signed up by CBS, only to be dropped unceremoniously two weeks later. However, that year he began his vital association with Manfred Eicher and the German ECM label, starting with the solo piano album *Facing You*, which made a big impact in Europe. As a result, Jarrett performed 18 solo concerts on a tour of Europe in 1973, and a triple album was released of his Bremen and Lausanne concerts. It caused a sensation and was voted 1974 Record of the Year in four influential organs of the US press: *Downbeat*, *Stereo Review*, *Time Magazine*, *New York Times*. It

Keith Jarrett

received three similar awards in Europe, and in Japan was awarded the *Swing Journal* Grand Prix (gold). His increasing recognition and burgeoning record sales resulted in a unique recording arrangement. He was signed by the American label Impulse to record with his US quartet (saxist Dewey Redman added to the trio), while he remained with ECM for solo LPs and special projects. But he also began recording for ECM with a European quartet (Jan Garbarek, Jon Christensen, Palle Danielsson) which many prefer to the US group.

As well as his solo and small group projects, he has written totally composed music. In the early 1970s he was awarded a Guggenheim Fellowship in composition, and the result was the double album *In the Light*, which has the string section of the Stuttgart Philharmonic, the American Brass Quintet, the Sonnleitner String Quartet and guitarist Ralph Towner, all performing with Jarrett. 1980, he recorded *The Celestial Hawk*, a 40-minute work featuring himself on piano with a symphony orchestra. During the rest of the 1970s and in the early 1980s there were more solo and quartet tours, and he then began to give performances of classical music.

Keith Jarrett is one of the very few people to begin as a child prodigy and slowly mature into a prodigious adult talent. His early influences were Art Tatum, Bud Powell, Bill Evans and McCoy Tyner, but he quickly absorbed them, becoming in the mid-1980s the most influential living jazz pianist. After his stint on electric keyboards with Miles Davis he turned his back on electronics and played acoustic piano; from this point, with the solo concerts, his fully mature work begins. The solo concerts were unique in that they were totally improvised: there were no preconceived themes or structures, and Jarrett attempted to begin them with a blank mind, so that audiences were witnessing the very act of creation. He seemed to be able to sustain his creative ecstasy throughout every concert, often egging himself on with little cries (a mannerism which irritated some critics). These marathons showed Jarrett to be one of the greatest improvisers in jazz, with an apparently inexhaustible flow of rhythmic and melodic ideas, one of the most brilliant pianistic techniques of all, and the ability to project complex and profound feeling. They also showed that though he is steeped in jazz lore and tradition, he is just as deeply versed in classical music, so his work combines exultant improvisation and powerful sustained rhythms with a tenderness and romantic melancholy that is European in origin. It was only after his relationship with ECM that his European strain was given free rein, and his persona became complete.

The new maturity also resulted in two masterpieces with his European quartet, the albums *Belonging* and *My Song*. The first leans more towards his wilder, intensely rhythmic side, but has two magnificent ballads; the second is more in his romantic vein. All the compositions on both are by Jarrett; they are superb, and the group performs them flawlessly. Jan Garbarek plays with an intensity which matches the leader's, and the rhythm-section (Danielsson and Christensen) is perfect. Keith Jarrett is one of a tiny handful of musicians who are admired by their peers and also have a huge popular following all over the world. [IC]

With Charles Lloyd, Miles Davis, Gary Burton and others; his recorded output is vast and much of his early work is good; his greatest mature works include: solo, *Facing You* (1971); *Solo Concerts Bremen and Lausanne* (1973) (3 LPs); *The Köln Concert* (1975) (double); *Sun Bear Concerts* (1976) (10 LPs, recorded in Japan); *Concerts (Bregenz/München)* (1981) (3 LPs); orchestral, *Arbour Zena* (1975); European quartet, *Belonging* (1975); *My Song* (1978); *Nude Ants* (live at the Village Vanguard, New York) (1979), all ECM; US quartet, *The Survivors' Suite* (1976), Impulse

Jarvis, Clifford Osbourne, drums, congas. b. Boston, 26 August 1941. His grandfather and his father both played trumpet, his father encouraging him to take up drums at the age of ten. Jarvis took a high school diploma and a diploma in electronics and then studied with Alan Dawson at the Berklee School of Music, Boston, 1958–9. He began playing professionally in Boston in the late 1950s with Jaki Byard and Sam Rivers, and went to New York at the end of the decade. There, during the 1960s, he played with Randy Weston, Coleman Hawkins, Eddie 'Lockjaw' Davis, Johnny Griffin, Sonny Stitt, Charles Mingus, John Coltrane. He joined Sun Ra in 1961, working with him throughout the 1960s. 1973, he left the USA, touring internationally with Sun Ra and with Pharoah Sanders. 1976–81, he was with Archie Shepp's group, after which he spent 14 weeks in Norway, appearing as a guest artist. 1983, he rejoined Sun Ra for an international tour with an all-star band which included Don Cherry, Lester Bowie and Shepp. Jarvis lists his main influences as Charli Persip, Sid Catlett, Art Blakey, Max Roach, Elvin Jones, Philly Joe Jones, Count Basie, Duke Ellington and Chick Corea. He has also worked in education, appearing as guest instructor at the University of Massachusetts and other New England colleges. [IC]

With Yusef Lateef, Sun Ra, Freddie Hubbard, Shepp, Randy Weston and Barry Harris; with Sanders, *Thembi* (1971), MCA

Jaspar, Bobby (Robert B.), tenor sax, flute. b. Liège, Belgium, 20 February 1926; d. 28 February 1963. After gigging at US army bases in Germany, moved to Paris (1950) and quickly established reputation. Worked and recorded with many US musicians such as Jimmy Raney and Chet Baker, then moved to New York with his wife, singer Blossom Dearie. Toured with J. J. Johnson quintet (1956–7), briefly with Miles Davis (1957). Member of Donald Byrd quintet on extended tour of Europe (1958), then in New York as guest soloist with Bill Evans (1959) and singer Chris Connor (1960). Further tour of Europe with Belgian guitarist René Thomas (1962); death following heart surgery was hastened by drug abuse.

A superior flute player who was highly valued during his American stay. His tenor work perhaps borrowed more than was the norm in the US from Lester Young, especially tonally, but his somewhat Rollins-tinged lines were notably individual. [BP]

Hank Jones, *Relaxin' at Camarillo* (1956), Savoy; Bobby Jaspar/René Thomas, *Live at Ronnie Scott's* (1962), Mole Jazz

Jaxon, Frankie Half-Pint, vocals, composer. b. Montgomery, Alabama, 3 February 1895. He worked around Chicago regularly from 1916 as a singer and show producer, as well as in Atlantic city at the Paradise Café until 1926. Then he based himself in Chicago and during the 1930s led his own Quarts of Joy, regularly appeared on radio and played the hotel circuit until 1941 when (according to John Chilton) he retired from the music business to work for the Pentagon in Washington. [DF]

Jazz at the Philharmonic Originally the billing for a 1944 concert organized by Norman Granz for victims of anti-Chicano rioting in Los Angeles; recordings of the concert were leased for an album of 78s, of which 'Blues Part 3' featuring Illinois Jacquet became a jukebox hit. Demand for more concerts and records was so great that, beginning in 1946, Granz was able to set up lengthy national (later international) package tours of star soloists such as Lester Young, Coleman Hawkins, Roy Eldridge, etc. Early editions traded for their success on r & b-inspired rabble-rousing, and were responsible for formularizing the idea of 'cutting contests' between two or more players of the same instrument; while much of this was released on record, much of a less obvious nature is apparently still in the can. Last of the annual US tours was in 1957 (with a follow-up in 1967) but the name continued to be used for Granz packages in Europe and Japan. [BP]

Bird and Pres/The '46 Concerts, Verve

Jazz Composers' Orchestra, see MANTLER, MICHAEL.

Jazz Crusaders, see SAMPLE, JOE.

Jazz-Rock-Fusion Towards the end of the 1960s the jazz scene in the USA and Europe found itself in a state of deep crisis. The more conventional forms – 'bebop', 'hard bop', 'modal jazz' etc. – seemed played out, and audiences were falling off. At the same time, the avant-garde music of the day – 'free jazz' and 'improvised music' – seemed unattractive to many musicians, and had not gained a new audience of any significant size. By 1967 rock had established itself as the current vernacular music, and was attracting huge audiences. Jazz seemed to have lost its social relevance, record sales slumped, clubs closed, people began muttering that jazz was dead and by 1968 even big names were drawing only handfuls of people.

The music itself was undergoing a severe identity crisis: was it related to the great ethnic musics of the world – African, Indian, oriental and European – in that it featured incisive rhythms, coherent structures, the disciplines of organized harmonies and/or scales and diatonic melodies which spoke of the human condition? Or was it now related more to the abstract music of the 20th-century classical avant-garde which was too 'serious' to accommodate the sensuous pleasure of ostinato rhythms or the comfort of tonality? The choice facing many musicians was an unappetizing one: they could either play in an established style, or throw out all the old rules, join the avant-garde and create abstract music. It became imperative to find a new identity and a fresh approach.

Jazz and rock both came from the same roots: the blues, hot gospels, worksongs and rhythm and blues. Nearly all American jazz musicians had started out with r & b bands, and in the 1960s many younger musicians had grown up with rock and roll, the Beatles and other rock groups. So it was perfectly natural that, throughout the decade, jazz musicians began to use and develop rock rhythms. Miles Davis's young rhythm-section with Tony Williams had played both spontaneous and premeditated rock rhythms in 1964 and 1965, and from the mid-1960s many people, including Gary Burton, Larry Coryell, Herbie Hancock, Keith Jarrett, Freddie Hubbard, Charles Lloyd, Don Ellis and

Bob Moses had made extensive and sometimes very subtle use of them.

The whole jazz-rock movement was crystallized and given its full momentum by three Miles Davis albums, *Filles de Kilimanjaro* (1968), *In a Silent Way* and *Bitches Brew* (both 1969), which produced an astonishingly fresh sound, combining rocky drum rhythms and bass riffs with sometimes three electric keyboards and guitar, creating and releasing tension in new ways and projecting the mysteriously sensuous and evocative atmosphere of the trumpeter's best music. The ensembles which recorded these albums included among others Herbie Hancock, Chick Corea, Joe Zawinul, Wayne Shorter, John McLaughlin, Tony Williams and Larry Young, all of whom afterwards led their own groups, producing their own particular brand of fusion and dominating the 1970s. Davis's three albums suggested lines of exploration and development which might be followed up in many different ways, and musicians all over the globe began to see a way out of the creative impasse. There was also a growing audience for the new music; with fusion, jazz had rediscovered its social relevance.

Nearly all the leading practitioners of jazz-rock were steeped in ethnic music of various kinds and were also schooled in European classical music, with the result that fusion not only combined jazz improvisation with rock rhythms – it also fused elements from ethnic and classical music in a tremendous explosion of creativity. John McLaughlin's Mahavishnu Orchestra often employed the scales and asymmetrical rhythms of Indian music, but also used amplified violin and rich chords which were redolent of the romantic melancholy of the European tradition. Zawinul's Austrian heritage could be heard in Weather Report – the wild spirit of gypsy music and the intense emotion of mid-European folk music. Chick Corea's Return to Forever had strong influences from Latin music, and African influences were apparent in the work of Miles Davis and others.

Jazz-rock-fusion had its most intense period of creativity 1969–75, although later in the decade one or two other peaks were reached by various groups. By about 1980, however, its heyday was over, it had become part of history and jazz was in its post-fusion period. The movement had many beneficial effects, and also vastly enriched the jazz language. It was, in part, a reaction against abstraction, which had tended to overemphasize the importance of improvisation at the expense of composition. Fusion restored the balance by reinstating composition as a vital factor, and this resulted in a wealth of inspired writing as well as brilliant playing. More was written for bass than ever before in jazz, and a rich new vocabulary of bass rhythms and phrases was created. In a sense, the bass was liberated from 'walking' – always playing four steady beats to the bar – without destroying the rhythmic coherence of the music, and even began in some cases (with Eberhard Weber and Jaco Pastorius, for example) to function as a melodic and featured solo instrument.

There were also radical structural and rhythmical innovations. The whole point of rock rhythm is that it works off a slow pulse, and the subdivisions of the pulse gave rise to an enormous number of asymmetrical rhythms – most of them new to jazz. The Mahavishnu Orchestra, and many other groups, began to function not only in common time (3/4 and 4/4), but in 5/4, 10/8, 7/8, 15/8, 19/8, and many other temporal subdivisions. In the best groups these times were handled not mathematically or mechanically, but with the fluidity of natural feeling. And this asymmetry also extended to whole structures which might include bars of unequal length, and/or irregular groupings of bars.

The use of *electronics also gave rise to a huge new vocabulary of sounds, textures and colours. [IC]

Jefferson, Eddie (Edgar), vocals. b. Pittsburgh, Pennsylvania, 3 August 1918; d. 9 May 1979, shot to death in front of a Detroit club after performing. Alternated between work as dancer and singer from an early age. Sang with Coleman Hawkins (*c.* 1940), but was discouraged from improvisation (scatting) by the excellent Leo Watson; instead, started creating lyrics to fit recorded instrumental solos by Hawkins, Lester Young, Charlie Parker, James Moody etc. First opportunity to record such material in Pittsburgh (1952) a few months after his then more popular imitator King Pleasure (aka Clarence Beeks, b. 24 March 1922). Replaced Babs Gonzales as vocalist and road manager of James Moody band (1953–7). Seemingly in obscurity during ascendancy of Lambert, Hendricks and Ross, he reappeared as a dancer in 1967, then rejoined Moody when the latter left Dizzy Gillespie (1968–73). Co-led Artistic Truth group with drummer Roy Brooks (1974–5), then worked regularly until his death with Richie Cole.

The quality of Jefferson's lyrics was always appropriate to the melodies he found in recorded improvisations, and these covered a wide stylistic range: from his famous versions of 'Parker's Mood' and 'Moody's Mood for Love' (he used different titles from those associated with King Pleasure, because of copyright conflicts) to solos by Miles Davis ('So What') and Horace Silver ('Psychedelic Sally'). The vocal group Manhattan Transfer recorded a posthumous tribute to Jefferson in their version of 'Body and Soul'. [BP]

There I Go Again (1953–69), Prestige

Jefferson, Hilton ('Jeff'), alto sax. b. Danbury, Connecticut, 30 July 1903; d. New York City, 14 November 1968. He began his career in 1926 with Claude Hopkins's soft and smooth ensemble and for the next 25 years was with most of the greatest big bands: Chick Webb, replacing Otto Hardwicke (1929–30), McKinney's Cotton Pickers (1931), Fletcher Henderson (1932–4), Hopkins, Henderson and Webb as well as freelance (1934–8) and just freelance (1938–40). His longest stay in one band (1940–9) was with Cab Calloway for whom he led the saxophone section and recorded one now-classic feature, 'Willow Weep For Me': a fine print of Jefferson at his poised, technically awesome best. 1949–51, he worked at Billy Rose's legendary Diamond Horseshoe in New York (a Fox musical was made about the club, starring Betty Grable and Dick Haymes; Gene Kelly was staff choreographer there and starlets such as June Allyson danced for Rose early in their careers). After this highly-paid period Jefferson joined Duke Ellington for 8 months in 1952–3, but soon after was working as a bank guard in New York to supplement irregular work with Rex Stewart's reassembled Fletcher Henderson orchestra and with his own small group. He continued to work spasmodically until the year he died.

Jefferson's translucent sound, harmonic ingenuity (he could run a chord progression into any other key at will) and graceful technique were objects of awe to musicians better known than he. For Ben Webster: 'I liked him for the playing of really beautiful things. When I first joined Fletcher in 1934 I've seen fellers at a party, away from home you know, made to cry by Jeff – people I didn't think had a tear in them.' [DF]

16 Cab Calloway Classics (1939–41), CBS

Jeffrey, Paul H., tenor sax, arranger. b. New York City, 8 April 1933. Worked in many different areas of USA (1956–60) with r & b singers Wynonie Harris, Big Maybelle and B. B. King. Also with Illinois Jacquet (1958) and, after return to New York, with Sadik Hakim, Howard McGhee, Dizzy Gillespie, Count Basie (1960s). Played with Thelonious Monk quartet (1970–2), conducted concert of Monk music at Newport festival (1974); arranged/conducted Mingus music on his last albums (1977–8) and at Newport (1978). Then head of Jazz Studies at Rutgers University (early 1980s). Jeffrey has also led his own octet and, though his ensemble writing is functional rather than inspiring, his infrequently heard tenor work was seemingly influenced by Sonny Rollins and promised greater individuality. [BP]

Electrifying Sounds (1968), Savoy

Jenkins, Leroy, violin, viola, composer, educator. b. Chicago, 11 March 1932. Began on violin at age eight, playing it regularly in church; basic musicianship with Walter Dyett at Du Sable High; took up alto sax at high school, playing bebop under the influence of Charlie Parker; graduated B.Mus. (violin) from Florida's A & M university, having now abandoned the alto; 1961–5, taught string instruments in Mobile, Alabama, schools; taught music in the Chicago school system, 1965–9, also working during that period with the AACM (see ABRAMS, MUHAL RICHARD). Jenkins developed into one of the most important musicians to emerge from the AACM. J. E. Berendt has written: 'His cluster-like, "pounded" violin sounds have a kind of manic drive. Jenkins uses the violin as percussion instrument or noise producer – without scrupling about the traditional rules of violin and harmony.' But Jenkins also fuses elements from the romanticism of the European classical tradition with his blues roots.

1969, there was an exodus of AACM musicians from Chicago, and Jenkins left for Europe with Anthony Braxton and trumpeter Leo Smith. In Paris, with drummer Steve McCall, they formed the Creative Construction Company. He also played with Ornette Coleman while there. He returned to Chicago, then, February 1970, moved to New York with Braxton, staying at Coleman's house and studying with him for three months. Played with Cecil Taylor, 1970; with Braxton, 1969–72. 1971–4, he also worked with Albert Ayler, Cal Massey, Alice Coltrane, Archie Shepp, Rahsaan Roland Kirk.

1971, he formed the Revolutionary Ensemble, with Sirone (Norris Jones) on bass and trombone and Jerome Cooper (drums and piano). The group stayed together until 1977, and Gary Giddins has written of it: 'It could be pastoral and urban, derivative and distinctive, bluesy and classical, baroque and austere.' After it broke up, Jenkins led a trio with Andrew Cyrille and Anthony Davis, which toured the USA and Europe in the late 1970s. [IC]

With Abrams, Braxton, Don Cherry, Carla Bley, A. Coltrane, Dewey Redman, Mtume, Kirk, Shepp, Rashied Ali; as leader, with JCOA Orchestra, *For Players Only* (1975), JCOA; *Solo Violin* (1977), India Navigation; *Revolutionary Ensemble* (1977), Enja; *The Legend of Ai Glatson* (1978), Black Saint

Jensen, Papa Bue (Arne), trombone, leader. b. Denmark. *c.* 1928. He formed his Danish jazz band in 1956 and achieved international recognition during the traditional jazz boom of the early 1960s. Featuring long-time sidemen such as Jorgen Svarre (clt) and Bjarne 'Liller' Petersen (banjo), as well as later additions like Keith Smith and Finn Otto Hansen (tpt), Papa Bue's jazz – New Orleans-based but with a likeable lilting swing and sophisticated soloists – won him a lasting reputation and during the 1960s and 1970s his band worked alongside a series of American visitors including Wingy Manone (1966–7), Wild Bill Davison (1975–7), Ed Hall, George Lewis, Albert Nicholas and Art Hodes. In the 1970s and 1980s he continued to record prolifically in and out of Denmark, played all the best Copenhagen venues and toured internationally for jazz festivals. [DF]

Jerome, Jerry, tenor sax, clarinet, flute, arranger, conductor. b. Brooklyn, New York, 19 June

1912. While still a medical student he was working with Harry Reser's Cliquot Club Eskimoes by 1935 and then abandoned thoughts of a medical career to concentrate on music. He joined an early Glenn Miller band in 1936 and stayed for a year until Miller broke up his organization, then joined Red Norvo (rather to Miller's chagrin). While Jerome was with Norvo, Miller offered him a sizeable one-third share in a new band, but Jerome refused. 'I was much too free-blowing a jazzman,' he told his friend George T. Simon later, 'and I needed more freedom.' He found it – at least to a degree – with Benny Goodman, 1938–40 (Goodman was later to write favourably about Jerome as 'our hot tenor man'), but still helped Miller by rehearsing his saxophone section and after a year with Artie Shaw (1940–1) he was to move further into the world of musical direction as a staff conductor for NBC, 1942–6. In later years he found fortune (if less fame) as MD/conductor at NBC, from 1950 for WPIX-TV New York and as a successful composer-producer of TV commercials and record company president. His free-blowing jazz creativity and fine, strong-toned solos were largely forgotten in the post-war jazz world. [DF]

Jerry Jerome Trio (1985)

Jeter–Pillars Orchestra After the breakup of Alphonso Trent's hugely successful territory band in Columbus, Ohio, in 1934, two of Trent's sidemen, James Jeter and Hayes Pillars – saxophonists of striking Mexican appearance, decided to form a band for themselves. 'They were very good musicians,' remembers Harry Edison, 'and they stressed quality in their band, which was more of a sweet band – there wasn't much room for playing solos!' The Jeter–Pillars Orchestra was nevertheless an important training ground for young musicians (including Edison, Walter Page, Jimmy Blanton, Sid Catlett, Charlie Christian and Jo Jones, who left to join Count Basie). To begin with they worked around Cleveland, Ohio, in the Magnolia Hotel Creole Bar. Later the co-leaders moved their operation further south to St Louis for three more years: during 1937 in Chicago, as the Jeter–Pillars Club Plantation Orchestra, they recorded four sides for Vocalion featuring (among others) Ike Covington (tmb), Floyd Smith (gtr) and Harry Ross (dms). Nearly 50 years on, in 1985, Hayes Pillars, fit and well, was interviewed by *Cadence* magazine. [DF]

Jive (1) A word which has carried many different shades of meaning, the common factor of which seems to be 'something not entirely serious'. Therefore, 'jive talk' originally covered both harmless tall-storytelling and deliberate attempts to mislead, while 'jiving' meant the use of jive talk. A 'jive' person, though, was at least untrustworthy (or unjustifiably egomaniac), while a 'jive-ass m—— f——' is still the ultimate to be avoided. The white journalists and fans who borrowed hip vocabulary and called it 'jive talk' fell into the latter category.

(2) It follows that no style of jazz was ever described by its players as 'jive music'. The term is used, however, by fans of a certain age to mean any music suitable for 'jive dancing' (also abbreviated to 'jiving'). This activity, still popular in some European circles, derives from the Lindy Hop and other dances associated with Harlem's Savoy Ballroom in the 1930s, and was presumably so named because the originators of these styles took such brazen (and humorous) liberties with the underlying rhythm. [BP]

Jobim, Antonio Carlos, composer, guitar, piano. b. Rio de Janeiro, 1927. He and his friend, guitarist João Gilberto, were the founders of the bossa nova movement which spread to the USA in 1962. Jobim is a composer of excellent songs, much favoured by jazz musicians as vehicles for improvisation. Some of his best-known pieces are: 'Chega de Saudade' (English title, 'No More Blues'); 'Desafinado'; 'One Note Samba'; 'The Girl from Ipanema'; 'Quiet Nights'; 'Wave'; 'Triste'; 'Jazz Samba'. His tunes have been played and recorded by Stan Getz, Dizzy Gillespie, Miles Davis, Gil Evans, and many others. [IC]

A Certain Mr Jobim (nda), Warner Bros; *Wave* (nda), A & M

Joel A, keyboards, vocal percussion, mridangam (two-sided drum), Carnatic (classical S. Indian) vocals. b. India, 29 January 1957. Grandfather professional musician, led western music bands in the courts of Indian princes. Father sings with Indian choral ensemble, Paranjoti Chorus. Studied Carnatic percussion with Sri T. R. Harihara Sarma, Carnatic vocals with Dr S. Ramanathan, western theory, composition and piano with A. C. Fernandes and other private teachers in Bombay. Played piano from age three. Started composing at six. First broadcast (solo piano) on All India Radio at seven. Local and national prizes for solo piano and composition. Graduated from Jaya Ganesh Academy of Rhythm, Madras. Formed the group J. G. Laya with Vikku Vinayakram in 1980, and has composed for it and performed with it since then, touring the Netherlands, 1983, and India, 1984. Joel A's ambition is to 'introduce Carnatic rhythms into the common vocabulary of improvised world music as has already happened with Afro-Latin rhythms'. Favourite pianists are Chick Corea, Bill Evans, Hilton Ruiz, Keith Jarrett and Art Tatum; on percussion he likes several Indian musicians including Subash Chandran and Vikku Vinayakram; and singers Balamurali Krishna, Bobby McFerrin, Stevie Wonder, among others. [IC]

Johnson, Bill (William Manuel), bass, guitar, banjo. b. New Orleans, 10 August 1872; d. 1972.

At 28 years old he switched from guitar to double bass and began working around the saloons of New Orleans and in parade bands (for which he doubled on tuba). In his late thirties he moved to California, and in 1914 teamed with Freddie Keppard to form the Original Creole Orchestra, a band which achieved headlining success on the Orpheum theatre circuit and, with Keppard's brilliant, versatile and high-powered trumpet, was an influence on young musicians everywhere. Johnson may have originated a now-standard convention of jazz bass. 'I think Bill, who travelled with Keppard, plucked the bass first,' says Ed Garland, himself often credited with the innovation, 'after a drunk broke his bow one night.' Later Johnson organized more bands, played with King Oliver, 1918–23 (the greatest period), and remained an influential senior figure on Chicago's music scene for another 30 years, a strong influence on young players such as Milt Hinton. His name is less familiar than that of Ed Garland or Pops Foster because, unlike them, he took a less active role in the post-war New Orleans revival. [DF]

Johnson, Budd (Albert J.), tenor, soprano and alto sax, clarinet, arranger. b. Dallas, Texas, 14 December 1910; d. 20 October 1984. Much of Budd's early career paralleled that of his elder brother, trombonist Keg Johnson (b. 19 November 1908; d. 8 November 1967), including work around Texas with Terrence Holder's 12 Clouds of Joy, whose personnel were taken over by Jesse Stone and then George E. Lee (1929–31). Both moved to Chicago (1932) and played with Louis Armstrong band (1933), then Budd began nine years' nearly continuous membership of the Earl Hines band (1935–42). Arranging for other bands began during this period and increasingly in the 1940s, but also playing for Dizzy Gillespie (1944, 1948), Billy Eckstine (1944–5), Sy Oliver (1947), Machito (1949) etc. In 1950s, arranged and produced many early rock and roll records, thanks to Jesse Stone, and partnered Al Sears in publishing such material and organizing house band for Alan Freed shows. Played with Benny Goodman (1956–7), Gil Evans (1959), Quincy Jones (1959–61) and Count Basie (1961–2). Further freelance playing and frequent quartet reunions with Hines (1964–9, including Russian tour with septet 1966), then took Hines rhythm-section and replaced Hines with Dill Jones to form own JPJ quartet (1969–75). Arranging and playing for Smithsonian Institution repertory project and New York Jazz Repertory Company (mid-1970s, including further Russian trip 1975), and Kool Festival tribute concerts from 1979. Also regular work as guest soloist, with many tours of Europe and visits to Nice festivals and Colorado Jazz Party, including 1984.

Johnson's arranging work was especially important during the 1940s, when he was musical director for Hines and then for the Billy Eckstine band. As in his freelance writing, for Gillespie and other bands, he was adept at combining a bebop influence with solid swing-era sounds. Budd's significance as a player only became evident to most listeners from 1959 onwards, when he was given more space by his bandleaders. The warmth of his mainstream approach was matched by a very contemporary-sounding fluency, and tonally he leaned towards the Lester Young side of the typical Southwestern sound, but with a restrained edge that was nevertheless very penetrating. [BP]

Let's Swing (1960), Prestige; *JPJ Quartet* (1972), RCA; *In Memory of a Very Dear Friend* (1978), Dragon

See Dance, Stanley, *The World of Earl Hines* (Scribner's, 1977)

Johnson, Bunk (Geary), trumpet. b. New Orleans, 27 December 1889; d. New Iberia, Louisiana, 7 July 1949. When young he played in and around New Orleans with early bands led by Adam Olivier, Bob Russell and Buddy Bolden (for whom he played second cornet). His talents as a second trumpet player at this time (in New Orleans, where jobs could last for six hours in a row, a second trumpeter was a vital backup) were well remembered: so were his melodic flair, feeling and gift for the blues. 'Bunk played funeral marches that made me cry!' said Louis Armstrong; Mutt Carey supplies more details: 'Bunk always stayed behind the beat – he wasn't quite the drive man that Joe Oliver and Freddie Keppard were.' Johnson also established (like Buddy Petit) a reputation for unreliability: Lawrence Marrero remembers him taking jobs for Red Duson's band agency, disappearing with the advance and forgetting to play the job. He left New Orleans *c.* 1915 and played all around the South in bands, theatres and clubs alongside entertainers as diverse as Louis Fritz (with whom he first met George Lewis), Ma Rainey and Julia Lee, until one night in 1931 when bandleader Evan Thomas was stabbed to death as he played alongside Johnson on the stand. The tragedy, however coincidentally, seems to have marked a slowing of Johnson's career: he was suffering from dental problems and soon after settled in New Iberia where (according to John Chilton) he worked at various trades including caretaking and truckdriving as well as, possibly, labouring in the ricefields.

In 1939 two young jazz researchers, Frederick Ramsey and William Russell, picked up references to Johnson (by Clarence Williams and Louis Armstrong) while researching their book *Jazzmen*, located him and began to correspond. By 1942 Russell had supplied his discovery with new teeth (Sidney Bechet's brother Leonard made up the plate) and a new trumpet, and recorded him with the aid of producer David Stuart in a room above Grunewald's Music Shop in New Orleans. Between 1942 and 1945, Johnson recorded nearly 100 sides: they created

Bunk Johnson with his wife

enormous interest and were hailed as a triumph for pure jazz over the commercial excesses of tired swing. Johnson became the apotheosis of the jazz revival, but was still playing only irregularly (a week at the Gary Theater, San Francisco, in May 1943, concert lectures with Rudi Blesh, recording and concerts with the Yerba Buena Jazz Band, nights with Sidney Bechet at the Savoy Café, Boston) and working daytime jobs in the meantime. By now his discoverers were aware that their protégé (like any man approaching 60) had his own decided – and sometimes anti-social – approaches to music and life. He drank as heavily as he once had in New Orleans: 'Bunk really got bad on my hands,' said Bechet of the Boston residency, 'full of liquor all the time! There was just no music to be gotten out of him.' (Johnny Windhurst finally completed the season.) More pointedly, Johnson had fixed ideas about the musical company he wanted to keep. When he re-opened at Stuyvesant Casino in April 1946 with a band including George Lewis, Jim Robinson and Baby Dodds, Johnson hated the sound of his sidemen and found it hard to make himself heard against Dodds's ferocious drums. He drank through his frustration, swore at his men onstage and, once at least, locked them out of their living quarters. (Contradictorily, Johnson was often the soul of charm: 'He was intelligent, gracious and sensitive', said Nesuhi Ertegun of the 'other' Johnson.) The group with Lewis disbanded and Johnson began working as a soloist in New York, Iberia and Chicago, until the following year he returned to New York to play and appear in a Hollywood fantasy, *New Orleans*, starring Louis Armstrong and Billie Holiday (all Johnson's scenes save one were later cut out of the film). Now a late aide, ex-GI Harold Drob, moved into the picture. He helped Johnson to assemble a band of latter-day swing-based players, including Ed Cuffee (tmb), Garvin Bushell (clt), Don Kirkpatrick (piano), who had arranged for Benny Goodman, Count Basie, Chick Webb and Cootie Williams, and Alphonse Steele, a more discreet drummer than Dodds. The new band played at Stuyvesant Casino again, recorded successfully in late 1947, and at last provided Johnson with the musical surroundings he had been hearing all along. Soon after, he went home to New Iberia where the following year he died after a succession of strokes. But history has made him – with George Lewis – the figurehead of revivalism and an inspiration to younger New Orleans jazz musicians ever since. [DF]

Bunk Johnson's Jazz Band (1942), Cadillac

See Sonnier, Austin, *Willie Geary 'Bunk' Johnson* (Crescendo, 1977); Williams, Martin, *Jazz Masters of New Orleans* (Macmillan, 1967, repr. Da Capo, 1979)

Johnson, Charlie 'Fess' (Charles Wright), piano, leader. b. Philadelphia, 21 November 1891; d. New York City, 13 December 1959. He is mainly remembered as the leader of a fine band that for over ten years was resident at Ed Smalls' Paradise in Harlem (the club was still operating in 1985). By the early 1930s Johnson's orchestra included Sidney de Paris, Leonard Davis, Benny Carter (who wrote arrangements), Billy Taylor (bass) and trombonist Dickie Wells, who draws a hilarious picture of the band in his autobiography *Night People*. 'Charlie's was one of the funniest bands I was ever in! Charlie loved to leave the piano and come out front to start his band so much that if only one cat had arrived he would still come out front and start him off, smiling as if the whole band were there! And he was a swell guy! Paynight there'd be a line around the booth and Charlie would sometimes be high and pay you twice!' Johnson's band recorded a few sides in the 1920s, but never achieved the reputation it deserved. 'With any sort of management it might really have been something,' said Eddie Condon later, 'a rival to Duke Ellington or anyone else.' After his orchestra broke up in 1938, Johnson continued playing around New York, but became ill in the 1950s and died in the Harlem Hospital after a long illness. [DF]

Johnson, Gus, drums. b. Tyler, Texas, 15 November 1913. He played the bass drum for hometown parades, then in cinema pit bands, before going to college in Kansas City, where he met and learned much from Jo Jones. After working in a variety of bands he joined Jay McShann, 1938, and stayed until army service intervened in 1943: after his release he played in New York with Jesse Miller's showband and with big bands led by Eddie Vinson, Earl Hines and Cootie Williams before joining Count Basie. The stay was short (Johnson was replaced by Butch Ballard) but later he rejoined Basie's small group at the Brass Rail in Chicago for $135 per week and later moved into the big band for another stay, after which Basie replaced him with Sonny Payne while Johnson was in hospital for an appendectomy. After his operation Johnson planned to concentrate on studio work, but soon after joined Ella Fitzgerald for a nine-year spell which he combined with more session work, Woody Herman's band in 1959 and club appearances accompanying everyone from Ralph Sutton to Stan Getz. From 1969, Johnson – a regular attender at Dick Gibson's Colorado Jazz Parties – was a member of the World's Greatest Jazz Band, continued his busy studio commitments and in the late 1970s was a star of Peanuts Hucko's Pied Piper Quintet. His presence in any jazz band is a hallmark of quality. [DF]

The World's Greatest Jazz Band at Massey Hall (1972), World Jazz

See Dance, Stanley, *The World of Count Basie* (Sidgwick & Jackson, 1980)

Johnson, Howard Lewis, baritone sax, tuba, composer, arranger, fluegelhorn, clarinets, bass sax etc. b. Montgomery, Alabama, 7 August 1941. Self-taught; started on baritone sax in 1954, tuba 1955. 1964–6, played with Mingus, Hank Crawford and Archie Shepp. From 1966, played on various instruments with Gil Evans orchestras. 1967, in Los Angeles working with Gerald Wilson, Big Black, Oliver Nelson. Has toured and played festivals in the US and internationally with Shepp, Evans and others. Influences, Clifford Brown, Mingus, Evans, Ellington, Herb Bushler. Johnson is at home with all styles and types of music, and is a strong soloist on several instruments. He has written arrangements for Taj Mahal, Gil Evans and B. B. King. [IC]

With Evans, *Svengali* (1973), Atlantic; *The Gil Evans Orchestra Plays the Music of Jimi Hendrix* (1974), RCA; *There Comes a Time* (1976), RCA; with Bob Moses, *Bittersweet in the Ozone* (1975), Mozown; *When Elephants Dream of Music* (1982), Gramavision

Johnson, James P(rice), piano, arranger, composer. b. New Brunswick, New Jersey, 1 February 1894; d. New York, 17 November 1955. By 1912 he was playing regularly in New York and the following year was established in the 'Jungle', a tough area between 60th and 63rd Streets, playing in clubs such as Jim Allan's, Barron's and Drake's Dance Hall. He was a big horse-faced man with a retiring manner, but despite his modesty his popularity and reputation grew quickly and in 1916 he began to cut piano rolls for the Aeolian Company, then for QRS which had a bigger circulation, and in the following year made his first record. All through the 1920s he recorded constantly with stars from Jabbo Smith to Bessie Smith (and directed music for her short film of 1929, *St Louis Blues*), appeared at clubs and rent parties, toured in England and elsewhere with *Plantation Revue* and worked as an MD. In 1923 he composed and orchestrated the score for a Broadway show, *Running Wild*, and by 1928 had written an extended work, *Yamecraw*, which although it was premiered at Carnegie Hall met the fate of most 'serious' music by black composers of the time. In the 1930s Johnson wrote stage works (including a collaboration with the famous black poet Langston Hughes) and composed a symphony, as well as occasionally assembling bands; from 1939 he was playing regularly in bands once more. In spite of progressive illness, he stayed reasonably active all through the 1940s, recording, playing at Jimmy Ryan's (in 1941 Ralph Gleason's *Jazz Information* devoted a double issue to him) and with bands such as Wild Bill Davison's and Eddie Condon's. By 1946 he was intermission pianist at clubs including Condon's and the Pied Piper, Greenwich Village, where he met the young Dick Hyman. In 1951 a severe stroke disabled him for the rest of his life.

James P. Johnson

'The father of stride piano', James P. Johnson is often cited as merely the teacher of Fats Waller, but there is evidence that he was in some respects a superior musician. 'His basslines', says Dick Wellstood, 'are better constructed, his right hand is freer and less repetitive, his rhythm is more accurate and his playing not so relentlessly two-beat.' Johnson was a highly trained pianist/musician (he studied the European school with Bruto Giannini) and based his music on a wide range of influences – church music, dances, ragtime, blues and reels (rags like 'Carolina Shout', featured by Fats Waller, are derived from square dances). Apart from the later extended works his famous compositions include 'If I could be with you one hour tonight', 'A porter's love-song to a chambermaid', 'Old-fashioned Love', 'Running Wild', and lesser-known beauties such as 'Caprice Rag' (a nocturne), 'Snowy Morning Blues' and 'Just Before Daybreak'. Twenty years after his death his pupil Dick Hyman retranscribed and re-recorded a celebration of Johnson's ageless music. [DF]

Piano Solos (1921–6), Joker; or any

Johnson, J. J. (James Louis), trombone, arranger, composer. b. Indianapolis, Indiana, 22 January 1924. After working with territory bands, joined Benny Carter band at age 18 (1942–5) and then Count Basie (1945–6). Small-group gigging in New York, and recording under own name and with Esquire All Stars (1946), followed by Illinois Jacquet group (1947–9) and brief stints with Dizzy Gillespie (1949, 1951) and Oscar Pettiford (1951). Out of music (1952), except for recordings with Miles Davis etc., then co-led quintet with fellow trombonist Kai Winding (1954–6, reuniting for European tour 1958 and for recording 1960, 1968). Worked with own quintet/sextet (1956–60), and toured with Miles Davis (1961–2) and with Sonny Stitt (in Japan and Europe 1964). Gaining reputation as a writer in late 1950s and 1960s, moved to Los Angeles (1970) to score film and TV background music, making only occasional records as player from then on.

Johnson adapted bebop to the trombone rather than the other way around, and achieved a quantum leap in what could be done with the unwieldy mechanism of the instrument. His immediate stylistic predecessors were people such as Trummy Young and Dickie Wells (whom he played alongside in the Basie band); their rhythmic concepts were firmly rooted in the swing era, but they easily overcame any limitations on their mobility or melodic thinking. The little-known and prematurely deceased Fred Beckett, trombonist with the Harlan Leonard and Lionel Hampton bands, was said by Johnson to have inspired his fast articulation, which for the 1940s was exceptionally clean and precise – while his contemporaries Kai Winding and Bill Harris both occasionally doubled on valve-trombone, J. J. never did but was often suspected of doing so.

Perhaps because of a certain blandness of tone, Johnson's early playing seems in retrospect a trifle academic, his choice of notes and especially of rhythms sounding somewhat stilted compared to leading modernists on other instruments. This approach also tends to carry over to his writing, which is at its best in relatively complex compositions such as 'Poem for Brass' and 'El Camino Real' (the latter in the album *J.J.!*); in more improvisatory contexts, even including the famous duo with Winding, his arrangements can be too fussy. However, Johnson's mature trombone work of the mid-1950s onwards, relieved of the need to prove itself alongside the beboppers, makes the instrument a more convincing vehicle for extended soloing than in the hands of almost anyone else. [BP]

The Eminent J. J. Johnson, vols. 1/2 (1953–5), Blue Note; Johnson/Winding, *The Great Kai and J.J.* (1960), Jasmine; *J.J.!* (1964), RCA

Johnson, Lonnie (Alonzo), guitar, vocals. b. New Orleans, 8 February 1899?; d. Toronto, 16 June 1970. He studied violin and guitar in New Orleans, and visited London for the first time in 1917 to work in revue. Returning home, he found that most of his family had died in a 'flu epidemic and left New Orleans for St Louis (where he worked with trumpeter Charlie Charlie Creath's band and in theatre orchestras) and Chicago. 1925, he won a talent contest for the Okeh record company, and became staff musician for the label, recording with emerging stars such as Duke Ellington, Louis Armstrong (classic sides include 'I'm not Rough' and 'Savoy Blues'), Eddie Lang, Victoria Spivey and Spencer Williams. 1932–7, he worked around Cleveland, playing for radio and working a day job; 1937–40, he teamed regularly with Johnny Dodds in Chicago and led for himself. For the next four years he was commuting between Chicago, Detroit and Kansas City, and by the mid-1940s was featuring amplified guitar and a contemporary ballad style which earned him a best-seller, 'Tomorrow Night', in 1948. When Johnson came to London in 1952, 'He seemed out of practice on his guitar,' *Jazz Journal* reported, 'and insisted on featuring too many of his own ballad compositions.' Johnson moved to Cincinnati at this time, then to Philadelphia (1958–62) where he worked as a chef, before touring in 1963 in a blues package with Otis Spann and others. From the mid-1960s he was living and performing in Toronto, a popular figure with local fans. [DF]

Lang/Johnson, *Blue Guitars, vols. 1/2* (1927–9), Parlophone

Johnson, Pete, piano. b. Kansas City, 24 March 1904; d. Buffalo, New York, 23 March 1967. A highly versatile pianist (Duke Ellington loved his work), he was mainly active as a soloist in 1930s clubs, accompanied Joe Turner and occasionally worked in bands. He was featured in the 1938 Carnegie Hall Spirituals to Swing concert featuring Albert Ammons and Meade 'Lux' Lewis and rode the boogie boom with Ammons at Café Society, New York (they also formed a highly successful trio with Lewis). He later worked again as a soloist and in the 1950s, despite a day job, he was still appearing occasionally at festivals and for Jazz at the Philharmonic, as well as accompanying Jimmy Rushing and getting together with Joe Turner for reunions until the early 1960s. [DF]

Johnson, Sy (Sivert Bertil), arranger, piano. b. New Haven, Connecticut, 15 April 1930. Studied music, played jazz in high school and in air force. Moved to Los Angeles, began freelance arranging but also involved with Ornette Coleman and Paul Bley; hoping to hear Bley in New York (1960), played in place of him for two weeks with Charles Mingus. Worked in New York with own trio, Rod Levitt octet, singer Yolande Bavan (1960s). Arranged for Mingus big band and small group (1971–8), also for Thad Jones–Mel Lewis and Quincy Jones. Wrote and occasionally played piano for Lee Konitz 9-piece band (1975–9). Involved in musical re-creations for film *The Cotton Club* (1984). Like most professional arrangers, Johnson does a considerable amount of non-jazz work, but the above associations demonstrate his versatility and wide knowledge of the jazz field. He is also an entertaining journalist and perceptive photographer of jazz subjects. [BP]

Charles Mingus, *Let My Children Hear Music* (1971), CBS

Jones, Carmell, trumpet. b. Kansas City, Kansas, 1936. After making his mark in student band contests in Kansas, moved to Los Angeles (1961), gigging and recording with Harold Land, Bud Shank and under his own name. Then to New York (1964) for more recording and touring with Horace Silver. Transplanted to Berlin (1965) for radio studio work, combined with solo appearances throughout Europe. In the 1980s returned to Kansas City. An interesting bop-oriented trumpeter who, through accidents of timing and geography, has been consistently underrated. [BP]

The Remarkable Carmell Jones (1961), Affinity

Jones, Claude B., trombone, vocals. b. Boley, Oklahoma, 11 February 1901; d. aboard SS *United States*, 17 January 1962. One of the trombone pioneers who helped free the trombone from its traditional role, he was a star of McKinney's Cotton Pickers (where his melodic improvisation and mobility reminded Quentin Jackson of Miff Mole), then worked with Fletcher Henderson from 1929 and Don Redman from 1931. His career went on to include years with Chick Webb, Cab Calloway and (from 1944) Duke Ellington among others: he left music in the early 1950s. [DF]

McKinney's Cotton Pickers (1928–9), RCA

Jones, Dave (David), clarinet, baritone sax. b. Ilminster, Somerset, 22 February 1932. He worked first around the East London area in the 1950s with bands such as Charlie Galbraith's before joining Kenny Ball's newly formed band in 1959. There his fruity, substantial tone, superior technique, powerful sound and driving approach became one of the strongest points of Ball's strong front-line and helped to establish a new high standard for British Dixieland of the period. Jones's clarinet was heard on all the Kenny Ball hits from 'I love you Samantha' onward (one of his greatest *tours-de-force* is the still unbeatable 'High Society' from *Invitation to the Ball*, 1961) and he became – like all the Ball band – a big star with an international reputation. After he left Ball in 1965 he became a freelance, worked with the Kinks in Britain and America (on baritone saxophone), and locally on the Dixieland scene with friends including Galbraith, Mike Cotton, Pat Mason and Bill Nile; he also subbed for Acker Bilk. In the 1970s he was often heard with bassist Ron Russell's small group (featuring Keith Ingham, Pete Strange and Digby Fairweather) and in the 1980s often played for drummer Laurie Chescoe's band. [DF]

Kenny Ball and his Jazzmen (1961), Pye

Jones, Davey (David), trumpet, mellophone, etc. b. Lutcher, Louisiana, *c.* 1888, d. Los Angeles, 1953. A multi-instrumentalist (he also played drums and saxophone), he worked in a Lutcher brass band from 1910 and in 1918 joined Fate Marable to work on the SS *Capitol*. During this time he played a part in young Louis Armstrong's musical education, helping him to learn to read music and possibly – in Danny Barker's estimation – more than that. 'Jones was a phenomenal musician', recalls Barker. 'He played trumpet, but his instrument really was the mellophone and French horn (!). Now I can appreciate what he was doing – I didn't then. He was running all kinds of strange changes and I think he was some help to Louis – cos Louis could see what could be done with that horn. Nobody had taken liberties, other than clarinet players – here was Davey Jones doing it on the mellophone.' Baker's remark about 'strange changes' suggests that Jones was a harmonically advanced player, and the degree of Armstrong's own harmonic sophistication by the time he joined King Oliver a year on in 1922 probably meant that Jones's early lessons at the very least did him no harm. Furthermore Oliver – 'a punch man' in George James's words – could hardly have been the inspiration for such flexible masterpieces as 'Cornet Chop Suey' or 'West End Blues' that Armstrong was effortlessly producing five years on. So Jones must be viewed as an appreciable influence in Louis's young life. He himself worked with Oliver in 1921 for a year, and by mid-decade was leading his own band at the Pelican Dance Hall, New Orleans: in 1929 (on saxophone this time) he cut four historic sides with the Jones–Collins

Elvin Jones

Astoria Hot Eight and later in the 1930s ran a student band (at one stage Joe Newman was a pupil member). As with Cuban Bennett, the full depth of his influence and originality is one of the casualties of jazz history. [DF]

New Orleans (1923–9; includes Jones–Collins Astoria Hot Eight sides), Collectors Classics

Jones, Dill(wyn Owen), piano. b. Newcastle Emlyn, Wales, 19 August 1923; d. New York, 22 June 1984. Played jazz while in navy (1942–6), then studied at music college in London (late 1940s). Was associated with wide variety of players including Joe Harriott, Don Rendell, Ronnie Scott, Jimmy Skidmore, Bruce Turner, Tommy Whittle during 1950s; also introduced BBC radio jazz series. Moved to New York (1961), working regularly with Yank Lawson, Max Kaminsky, Roy Eldridge, Bob Wilber, Jimmy McPartland and Gene Krupa quartet (1960s). Then with former members of Earl Hines quartet as the JPJ quartet led by Budd Johnson (1969–74). Resumed freelance activity, and made frequent solo appearances (including return trip to UK, 1983). The breadth of Jones's knowledge, from stride piano to 'modern jazz', was already evident during the 1950s when he was a 'mainstreamer' before the term was invented; by the time of his death from throat cancer, he had become a highly respected member of the New York jazz community. [BP]

Montreux '71 (1971), Master Jazz

Jones, Elvin Ray, drums, composer. b. Pontiac, Michigan, 9 September 1927. Younger brother of Hank and Thad Jones, but unrelated to other famous drummers Jo or Philly Joe Jones. After army service (1946–9), began playing locally in Detroit area in group led by Billy Mitchell, making record debut with them on two early 1950s sessions. Moved to New York (1955) and worked with Teddy Charles/Charles Mingus, Bud Powell trio and recorded with Miles Davis, Sonny Rollins. Joined new J. J. Johnson quintet (1956–7), Pepper Adams/Donald Byrd (1958), Tyree Glenn (1958–9), Harry Edison quintet (1959–60). Became member of the classic John Coltrane quartet, staying until early 1966, then started leading own trio/quartet/quintet. Among musicians working regularly for him have been saxists Joe Farrell, Frank Foster, George Coleman, Dave Liebman, Pat La Barbera; they have frequently chosen the group's repertoire, but some original material has been contributed by Elvin's Japanese wife Keiko Jones.

The dynamic drummer is an asset to any group and has done a certain amount of performing and recording in mainstream and all-star contexts, but he is particularly associated with Coltrane (and the post-Coltrane soloists of his own group). The driving, and psychologically driven, quality of his work was especially appropriate to the emotional climate of the new jazz in the 1960s, and it is difficult to imagine the eviscerating explorations of mature Coltrane without Elvin's percussive outpourings playing a simultaneous, indeed equal role. But, along with his all-enveloping energy and high volume level (that is, for someone playing unamplified pre-rock drums), there is an essential clarity to Jones's drumming, both tonally and rhythmically. The sounds he obtains from the standard kit are instantly recognizable and easy to follow, which is important since his rhythmic feel is very personal; the cross-rhythms, often complicated by omitting or underemphasizing the downbeat, may seem almost impossible to count aloud. Their ebb and flow, however, is so constant that they always come out sounding absolutely right in the end.

These stylistic innovations were a vital step beyond the polyrhythms of Max Roach and Art Blakey. Although he was not personally identified with either free jazz or jazz-rock-fusion, Elvin's contribution was crucial both for the multidirectional drumming of the former school and for the complex percussion of some fusion music. Throughout the varying fortunes of jazz itself in the last two decades he has maintained his own individuality, which is a considerable achievement in itself. And, in a more specific manner, his rhythmic independence (just like the sheer speed of Buddy Rich) is seen as an ultimate standard by which all other drummers are measured, and which affords them continual and limitless inspiration. [BP]

John Coltrane, *A Love Supreme* (1964), MCA; *Puttin' It Together* (1968), Blue Note; *Soul Trane* (1980), Denon; *Earth Jones* (1982), Palo Alto

Film: *Different Drummer* (dir. Ed Gray, 1979)

Jones, Hank (Henry), piano. b. Pontiac, Michigan, 31 July 1918. The elder brother of Thad and Elvin Jones, Hank was also the founder of the Detroit 'school' of pianists (Tommy Flanagan, Barry Harris etc.). Moved to New York in 1944 and worked with Hot Lips Page, Andy Kirk, Coleman Hawkins (1946–7) and Ella Fitzgerald (1947–53), which included touring with Jazz at the Philharmonic. Subsequently he took part in innumerable recording sessions with virtually every pre-'free jazz' soloist of any consequence (and in many non-jazz situations as well). A musician for all seasons with a distinctive but seemingly subdued style, which made him a superbly responsive accompanist. The strength and resilience of his contributions are often best savoured in recordings designed to feature others, but his solo playing, on which he concentrated from the mid-1970s, is worthy of close attention. [BP]

Ain't Misbehavin' (1978), Galaxy

Jones, Isham, saxes, bass. b. Coalton, Iowa, 31 January 1894; d. Florida, 19 October 1956. He led a famous band which worked Chicago's hotel circuit in the early 1920s, played at one stage for Streckfus Line steamers (along with Fate Marable and Ralph Williams) and recorded prolifically using fine players of the period such as Louis Panico (tpt), Leo Murphy (vln) and Roy Bargy (piano). By 1935 there were new stars in Jones's band including Pee Wee Erwin (tpt), Jack Jenney (tmb), singer Eddie Stone and staff arranger Gordon Jenkins, who called it later 'the greatest sweet ensemble of that time – or any other time!' Jones, a sad-faced leader, played his farewell engagement in 1936 opposite Benny Goodman and retired to concentrate on composition. His orchestra was taken over by sideman Woody Herman, who with the help of fluegelhornist-arranger Joe Bishop created his own first big band from it.

Isham Jones is remembered as the composer of fine songs including 'The one I love belongs to somebody else', 'Swingin' down the lane', 'On the Alamo', 'You've got me crying again', 'There is no greater love', 'Spain' and 'I'll never have to dream again'. His music has been recreated, among others, by Rusty Dedrick (see below). [DF]

Rusty Dedrick, *Twelve Isham Jones Evergreens* (undated), Monmouth Evergreen

Jones, Jo (Jonathan), drums. b. Illinois, 7 October 1911; d. 4 September 1985. 'Jo Jones reminds me of the wind', said Don Lamond in a familiar quotation. 'He has more class than any drummer I've ever heard: with Jo there's none of that dam' raucous tom-tom beating or riveting-machine stuff. Jo makes sense.' Jo Jones made sense in a lot of ways. Musically he was the finest, fastest drummer of the swing era: the pulse that powered Count Basie's unmatchable 'All-American Rhythm Section'. Personally he was the most pertinent (and sometimes painful) commentator on the jazz life for those prepared to lend an ear to an unquiet soul. 'As of today I don't know nobody I can talk to but Roy Eldridge, because there's nobody playing in the music business that's had the kind of experience he and I had!' said Jones not long before he died.

His earliest musical memories were often of

Hank Jones

fairgrounds – 'I remember my aunt taking me to a circus when I was a kid, and I can still feel that bass drum!' – and on the way up he worked successively in carnival bands (two important teachers of the period were bandleaders Henri Woode and Samuel Brothers, both from Omaha, Nebraska), territory bands and for such well-known leaders as Bennie Moten and Tommy Douglas. From 1934 he was, with one or two false starts, working for Count Basie ('I joined for two weeks and stayed for 14 years') and defining what modern jazz drummers were to do ten years later. 'He was playing that modern stuff and it sounded good', says Eddie Durham of that period. 'I don't know where he got it from!' Gus Johnson agrees: 'The way Jo played was something else, it was smooth as you'd want to hear anybody play and right easy! He was smiling doing little bitty things – and he wasn't working!' Like any great craftsman, the ever-smiling Jones made difficult things look easy, and the result was classic jazz's finest rhythm section ever. 'We worked at it to build a rhythm section every day and night', Jones recalled. 'If three were down, one would carry the three. Never four!' 'Basie's rhythm section had a kind of throb going – no one instrument louder than the other', explains Nat Pierce. Jones was with Basie until 1944, when he was called up, then again 1946–8, when he was replaced by Gus Johnson. By this time he was established as a star in his own right: a drummer of inimitable class and taste. He turned freelance, working with Illinois Jacquet and Lester Young, with Joe Bushkin's trio at the Embers, with such old friends as Teddy Wilson, Coleman Hawkins and Roy Eldridge, and with Jazz at the Philharmonic, as well as leading his own groups in clubs and for recording sessions arranged by John Hammond. 'I think Jo can do more things superlatively well than any drummer I ever heard,' said Hammond, 'he's always been my favourite. There was extraordinary wit in his playing.' The result of Hammond's enthusiasm was albums such as *Jo Jones Special* and *Jo Jones + 2* for Vanguard, which are still classics. By the mid-1960s, however, amid changing popular jazz fashions, the 'wide smile' that Jones had worn for so long was starting to be replaced by the quizzical look of a man marked for life: 'I'm a loner – a street boy – 50 years without a home!' was one regretful statement. 'Jo Jones has a quicksilver mind,' Stanley Dance observed while he was researching a book with Jones's help, 'and the interviewer soon discovers that he is not there to ask questions, but to be instructed!' In later years Jones brought a sensitive and keenly observant eye to the fallibilities of the jazz life, and tended to speak the truth with impatient non-compromise. He was a consummate professional, who dismissed the non-comprehension of followers: 'We haven't got time to explain our references.' In the 1980s Jones became ill: benefits were organized by drum-sons such as Jack DeJohnette, and the Master happily recovered but only for a while. [DF]

Jo Jones Special (1955), Vanguard

See Dance, Stanley, *The World of Count Basie* (Sidgwick & Jackson, 1980)

Jones, Jonah (Robert Elliot), trumpet, vocals. b. Louisville, Kentucky, 31 December 1908. He started his playing career with an alto horn in Louisville's Community Center Band and after an apprenticeship in local groups, worked with, among others, Horace Henderson and Jimmie Lunceford before beginning a partnership with Stuff Smith 1932–4, latterly at the Lafayette Theater. A year later Lil Hardin Armstrong took over the band and billed Jones remorselessly as 'King Louis II'. He rejoined Smith soon after, and when bandleader Dick Stabile offered the duo a residency at the Onyx on 52nd Street, their brand of knocked-out showmanship, combined with catchy hit songs such as 'I'se a muggin' ' and the reefer-happy 'If you'se a viper', made them a hot property, ensured a 16-month stay at the Onyx and four more successful years together. In 1941, Jones began an 11-year stay with Cab Calloway (who celebrated his arrival with a record, 'When Jonah joined the Cab', a cheeky reference to Raymond Scott's 'When Cootie left the Duke'). After 1952, Jones worked the Embers for a while with Joe Bushkin and his second stay there from 1955 (booked by Sam Berk, a veteran promoter) proved his biggest career step ever. A recording session for Dave Cavanaugh produced a throwaway end-of-session side: a shufflebeat paraphrase of 'On the street where you live' from *My Fair Lady*, which had opened that year on Broadway. The album featuring the track

(*Muted Jazz*, Capitol) sold more than a million copies, and was followed by a string of others including *I Dig Chicks*, *At the Embers*, *The Unsinkable Molly Brown* and *Jumpin' with Jonah* – all featuring Jones's singing and unmistakeable trumpet, full of veiled glissandi, attacking climbs and fuzzy vibrato. His group set a style for trumpet quartets for ten years after: with it he was the star of the Embers for seven years and an international star for six more after that, playing for President Johnson, Prince Rainier and network American TV with stars such as Fred Astaire. In the 1970s Jones played festivals and continued touring: in the 1980s his weathered trumpet was relaunched in a loosely swinging new format. [DF]

I Dig Chicks (1959), EMI

See Dance, Stanley, *The World of Swing* (Scribner's, 1974, repr. Da Capo, 1979)

Jones, Philly Joe (Joseph Rudolph), drums (and piano etc.). b. Philadelphia, 15 July 1923; d. 30 August 1985. Worked extensively in hometown (hence the nickname, bestowed to distinguish him from Jo Jones) before touring with Joe Morris, whose r & b group included Johnny Griffin and Elmo Hope. Played with Ben Webster (1949), then moved to New York, freelancing with Zoot Sims, Lee Konitz, Tony Scott (1953) and Tadd Dameron (1953). Partnership with Miles Davis (1952–5), who often used Philly Joe to bolster locally-based rhythm-sections when gigging outside New York; then with regular Davis quintet/sextet (1955–7, 1958, 1962). Many record dates during this period and early 1960s, also with Gil Evans band (1959) and own quintet (1959–62). Member of Bill Evans trio (1967, 1976). Moved to England (1967) and then France (1969–72), gigging and teaching all over Europe. Returned to Philadelphia for the rest of the 1970s, leading own groups. Formed 9-piece band Dameronia, dedicated to performing works of Tadd Dameron (1981–5). Also briefly replaced the deceased Kenny Clarke in Pieces of Time (1985, shortly before his own death).

Indelibly associated with the first classic Miles Davis quintet, Joe not only masterminded its rhythm-section but created one of its most distinctive (and most imitated) sounds, the once-per-bar rim-shot played with the heel of the drumstick, as in the title track of *Milestones*. Equally adept with the wire brushes, he was nevertheless at his best when using sticks to play an interactive commentary behind a suitably strong soloist such as John Coltrane. His style could be said to combine the intelligence of Max Roach with the power of Art Blakey, although in detail it was quite unique. Dismissing obliquely the criticisms of Joe's musical idiosyncrasy and drug-related unreliability, Miles once said, 'I wouldn't care if he came up on the bandstand in his BVDs and with one arm, just so long as he was there. He's got the fire I want.' [BP]

John Coltrane, *Blue Train* (1957), Blue Note; Miles Davis, *Milestones* (1958), CBS; *Look, Stop, Listen* (1983), Uptown

Jones, Quincy Delight, Jnr., composer, arranger, trumpet. b. Chicago, 14 March 1933. Moved to Seattle at age 10, played with locally-based teenager Ray Charles, who interested him in arranging. Early efforts recorded by Lionel Hampton, with whom he played two and a half years (1951–3, including European tour). Then freelance arranger, including many small-group record sessions. Musical director for Dizzy Gillespie big band (1956) before returning to freelance work. Spent eighteen months in France and Scandinavia (1957–8), studying composition and working for Barclay Records. Formed own all-star big band for European opening of show *Free and Easy* (1959) and, first in Europe and then in US, performed regularly for two years; also wrote albums for Count Basie and recorded backings for Sarah Vaughan, Dinah Washington, Billy Eckstine etc. Held executive post at Mercury Records, continuing with own albums but increasingly aimed at popular market. Since mid-1960s has written music for about 50 films, and since mid-1970s has run Qwest Productions, arranging and producing hugely successful albums by Brothers Johnston, Michael Jackson, Frank Sinatra.

Although now at a professional peak previously undreamed of for black musicians, Jones was also something of an innovator in the early and mid-1950s, using the concept of chords built in fourths long before McCoy Tyner (or even Richie Powell) discovered them as a piano device. In this way he obtained a sound as rich as that of Tadd Dameron or the arrangers for the Miles Davis band (and often with smaller forces at his disposal), and added a bluesy pungency that eluded other writers. To that extent, Quincy's work for such as Clifford Brown (during the Hampton European tour) predicted the strengths which pervaded collaborations with artists remote from jazz, and which made him capable of the farreaching fusions he has helped to create. [BP]

Clifford Brown Memorial Album (1953), Prestige/OJC; *This is How I Feel About Jazz* (1956), Jasmine; *Walking in Space* (1969), A & M

Jones, Richard M. ('Myknee'), piano, composer. b. Donaldsville, Louisiana, 13 June 1889; d. Chicago, 8 December 1945. He worked around New Orleans in clubs and cabarets in his teens and in 1919 joined Clarence Williams's publishing company. By 1925 he was A & R man for Okeh (producing the 'race' records which were popular with both black and white audiences in the 1920s) and later moved to Decca: he was a longtime friend of King Oliver, for whom he engineered recording contracts with Okeh, Columbia and other recording companies. Jones was also a fine pianist who recorded prolifically from 1923: and from 1925 with his own Jazz Wizards, which included such famous names as Albert Nicholas, Shirley Clay (cornet), Darnell Howard (clt), and Preston Jackson (tmb). He also composed famous tunes such as 'Trouble in Mind' and 'Riverside Blues'. From the 1940s he was most active as an arranger and talent scout for Mercury Records. [DF]

Jazz Sounds of the 20s, vol.4: The Blues Singers (1923–31), Parlophone

Jones, Rodney Bruce, guitar, bass, drums. b. New Haven, Connecticut, 30 August 1956. Family musical, an uncle was a pianist/conductor for church choirs. Went to City College of New York for two years, studying improvisation with John Lewis and playing in Lewis's ensemble. Private guitar lessons with various teachers including Bruce Johnson. 1966–73, Jones led his own small groups around the NY area. 1974–5, played with other groups in NY, doing many disco and Latin recordings. 1974, worked at the Five Spot with the Music Complex Orchestra led by Jaki Byard. 1975, recommended to Chico Hamilton by a friend of Arthur Blythe's and played with Hamilton for almost a year. 1976, joined Dizzy Gillespie's quartet, staying for almost three years. 1978–80, worked in USA with Chico Hamilton, Maxine Brown and numerous others, and formed his own group with Kenny Kirkland (piano), Ronnie Burrage (dms), Ben Brown (bass), which did a tour of Europe in 1979. 1980–3, worked with his group in NY area, did a world tour with the Subtle Sounds jazz group, and played with Darwin Gross in USA and Europe. 1983, guitarist for Lena Horne, writing and arranging her 'London Opener', and still with her in 1985. Jones has won two awards: Certificate of Merit from New Orleans, 1977, and a National Endowment for the Arts recording grant, 1983. His favourite guitarists are Wes Montgomery, Barney Kessel, Grant Green and Bruce Johnson, and other inspirations are Kenny Kirkland, Jaco Pastorius as a composer and Mahler. He has said, 'I try to bring out the subtle aspects of music when I play, and to make each note have a meaning.' [IC]

The Liberation of the Contemporary Jazz Guitar (1976), Strata East; *Articulation* (1978), Timeless; *When You Feel the Love* (1980), Timeless; *Friends* (1981), Joy of Sound; *My Funny Valentine* (1981), Timeless

Jones, Sam(uel), bass (and cello). b. Jacksonville, Florida, 12 November 1924; d. 15 December 1981. After moving to New York, worked with Tiny Bradshaw, Illinois Jacquet, Kenny Dorham (1955–6). Member of first Cannonball Adderley quintet (1956–7), then with Dizzy Gillespie (1958–9) and Thelonious Monk quartet (1959); as well as recording with the above, frequent album dates with such as Clark Terry, Bill Evans, Johnny Hodges–Duke Ellington etc. When Adderley re-formed, Jones was with him (1959–66) until replacing Ray Brown in the Oscar Peterson trio (1966–9). Thereafter freelancing in New York, and regular work with Cedar Walton trio plus various tenor players (from 1971). During last years of his life, led part-time 12-piece band. Despite occasional doubling on cello, in the manner of his forebears Brown and Pettiford, Jones made relatively little impression as a soloist. But in his partnerships with drummers Louis Hayes (in both the Adderley and Peterson groups) and Billy Higgins (via the Cedar Walton connection), he revealed himself as a rhythm-section player par excellence. Two of his tunes used by Adderley, 'Unit 7' and 'Del Sasser', have gradually become standard material. [BP]

Cannonball Adderley, *In San Francisco* (1959), Riverside/OJC; *Changes and Things* (1977), Xanadu

Thad Jones

Jones, Thad(deus Joseph), trumpet, cornet, valve trombone, arranger, composer. b. Pontiac, Michigan, 28 March 1923; d. Copenhagen, 21 August 1986. After working locally and in Oklahoma City, joined Count Basie (1954–63) and, though not generously featured as soloist, wrote many arrangements of original compositions. Left to become freelance arranger and studio player, and in the meantime started once-a-week rehearsal band of leading studio-band jazz musicians: the Thad Jones–Mel Lewis orchestra ran from 1965 to 1978 (continuing thereafter under Lewis alone), gained an international reputation and made several foreign tours. Jones then migrated to Denmark (1978–

84), writing for the radio orchestra and running his own jazz big band Eclipse. During this period, he also took up valve trombone and studied composition formally. In late 1984 he was contracted to work in USA with the Basie band following the death of its leader, but gave up touring and returned to Denmark a couple of months before his own death.

Jones's playing was unfortunately overshadowed by his arranging and bandleading ability, but the printed comment of Charles Mingus (1954) – 'The greatest trumpeter that I've heard in this life' – gives an idea of his stylistic freshness at the time. While with Basie, he appeared on several records (under his own name and with Mingus, Coleman Hawkins and Thelonious Monk) combining Gillespie's rhythmic alertness with an advanced approach to thematic improvisation. His big-band arrangements, especially post-Basie, employed similar rhythmic lines with astringent block-chord voicings demanding great virtuosity from the performers. They also incorporated some of the more recent freedoms of small-group work, especially when Jones directed his own music, and set new standards now aimed at by semi-professional and college bands. A few of his tunes have become extremely well-known (especially 'A Child is Born') but more attention should be devoted to absorbing the lessons of his recorded trumpet solos. [BP]

Thad Jones and Charles Mingus (1954–5), Prestige; Thad Jones/Mel Lewis: *At the Village Vanguard* (1967), Solid State

Joos, Herbert, fluegelhorn, trumpet, alphorn, composer/arranger. b. Karlsruhe, Germany, 21 March 1940. Studied music at Karlsruhe University. During 1960s, member of the Karlsruhe Modern Jazz Quintet which developed from hard bop to free jazz. 1974, took part in Baden-Baden Free Jazz Meeting; organized an NDR (Hamburg) Jazz Workshop; started fluegelhorn workshops for SDR (Stuttgart) with Kenny Wheeler, Ack Van Rooyen, Ian Carr, Harry Beckett; occasional leader of his own 10-piece band. 1975, member of the Mike Gibbs orchestra at the Berlin festival; with Hans Koller–Wolfgang Dauner Free Sound and Super Brass. January–February 1976, toured Africa with the New Jazz Ensemble for the Goethe Institute; December, recorded with Hans Koller and the classical Bläser Quintet for South West German TV. 1979, joined the Vienna Art Orchestra, touring India and the USA with them. 1984, he was awarded the South West German TV jazz prize. Joos also does drawings and paintings of jazz musicians. His main inspirations are Miles Davis, Gil Evans and Gustav Mahler. [IC]

Fluegelhorn/strings, *Daybreak* (1976), Japo/ECM; *Still Life* (nda), Extraplatte

Joplin, Scott, piano, composer. b. Texarkana, Texas, 24 November 1868; d. New York City, 1 April 1917. The popularly-accepted 'King of Ragtime', he taught himself the piano first, then at 11 years old acquired a German piano teacher. In his teens he left home and from 1885 to 1893 lived in St Louis, a centre for fine pianists, playing in local cabarets and saloons such as the Silver Dollar, and in 1894 for the World's Fair in Chicago (Joplin's band of strolling players performed on the outskirts of the fairground). From 1894 he settled in Sedalia, touring with a choir he had formed (the Texas Medley Quartet, which introduced many of his most famous compositions) and in 1896 enrolled at George Smith College, a black academy which enabled him to write down the ragtime music he heard: 'Joplin was the one and only ragtimer who had the nerve to put it down on paper', said Eubie Blake, years after. Joplin's rags became hits in the sporting houses of Sedalia's red light district, and in his local Maple Leaf club (a rendezvous for local piano professors); in 1899 'Maple Leaf Rag' was published by John Stark and sold 75,000 copies in the first year. It was soon followed by 'Swipsey Cake-walk', the success of which encouraged Stark to move to St Louis and expand his publishing activities; Joplin followed, but not before he had staged an extended ballet, *The Ragtime Dance*, at the Woods Opera House in Sedalia. The presentation was well received but the music, published soon after, made little impact: Joplin's ragtime opera of three years later, *The Guest of Honor*, although it may have been performed, was never published. By this time Joplin was producing a string of successful rags – 'Easy Winners', 'Élite Syncopations' and 'The Entertainer' – but the failure of his extended works was a preoccupying worry complicated by a marriage breakdown and the death of his baby daughter. By 1907, after a visit to Chicago and a second term in St Louis, he had arrived in New York, where he met and married a loving and supportive wife, Lottie Stokes, but there were still troubles to spare: he had contracted syphilis and was becoming ill. By 1910, talking with difficulty and almost unable to play, Joplin cut a sad figure amid the stylish society of young piano professors around New York. The year before he had split up with his old friend and publisher Stark over a royalty disagreement and he was to produce only three more rags before he died, along with the controlling obsession of his last years: a ragtime opera, *Treemonisha*. In 1915, Joplin financed a makeshift production of the work (without scenery, costumes or orchestra), but it met with indifference and the final blow to his classical aspirations was too much for him: syphilis took hold and in 1916 he was admitted to Ward's Island Hospital in Manhattan, where he died on April Fool's Day the following year. Recordings by Joplin, made in his declining years, sound sad and inept: scores of rare and unpublished works disappeared after the death of his wife.

The ragtime revival of the 1970s was boosted by a hugely popular film starring Robert Redford and Paul Newman, *The Sting* (1973), which used 'The Entertainer' as a theme tune and featured other Joplin rags. Soon after, in a ragtime boom, his works were recorded in scholarly sets by Joshua Rifkin and many others. [DF]

Ragtime King: Piano roll solos performed by Scott Joplin (1899–1914), Joker

See Janis, Harriet, and Blesh, Rudi, *They All Played Ragtime* (Music Sales, undated)

Jordan, Clifford Laconia, tenor sax. b. Chicago, 2 September 1931. Attended school with Johnny Griffin, Richard Davis etc., played in Chicago with r & b bands and gigged with Sonny Stitt. Briefly replaced Sonny Rollins with Max Roach (1957), then with Horace Silver (1957–8). Regular member of J. J. Johnson sextet (1959–60), Kenny Dorham quintet (1961–2), Max Roach quartet (1962–4 and 1965). Four months with Charles Mingus (1964, including European tour), further work in Europe as soloist and arranger (1966, 1969–70, 1974). Quartet with Cedar Walton (1974–5), also much educational work in public schools in New York.

Jordan's tenor style shows considerable individuality, particularly in terms of tone quality, although there are similarities to other Chicago tenors such as Griffin and Von Freeman. As the majority of his own records have been in a quartet format, his composing and arranging talents have been underplayed; the album below emphasizes these aspects as well as his excellent instrumental work. [BP]

These Are My Roots (1965), Atlantic

Jordan, Duke (Irving Sidney), piano, composer. b. Brooklyn, New York, 1 April 1922. Worked with Coleman Hawkins and the original Savoy Sultans during the early and mid-1940s, then one year with Charlie Parker (1947–8) and nine months with Stan Getz (1952). Periods of absence from the jazz scene have made for a rather erratic career, but Jordan was not only active but appeared on records regularly in the mid-1950s, early 1960s and the mid-1970s. The increased interest in jazz during the latter period led to well-received tours of Europe and Japan, and the recording of his complete output of compositions for the Danish label Steeplechase.

Several of Jordan's tunes have been taken up by other musicians; 'Jor-du' became a standard, while two of his originals (published by the copyright owners under the name of a fictitious composer) were popularized in the film *Les Liaisons Dangereuses* (1959). They reflect an inherently melodic style which, in improvisation, is enlivened by a delightfully crisp touch and unexpected turns of phrase. [BP]

Flight to Japan (1976), Steeplechase

Jordan, Louis, vocals, alto sax, leader. b. Brinkley, Arkansas, 8 July 1908; d. 4 February

Louis Jordan

1975. He came to prominence in New York, where he worked with Chick Webb on alto sax and as occasional vocalist, 1936–8. He formed his own group, the Tympany Five, an r & b outfit with a strong jazz slant, in 1938, working at Elks' Rendezvous in Harlem, and r & b venues. During the 1940s, he broke through to national and international stardom with a series of hit 78 rpm records, including 'Choo Choo Ch'Boogie' which sold a million, 'Saturday Night Fish Fry', 'I'm Gonna Move to the Outskirts of Town', and 'Ain't Nobody Here but us Chickens'. His version of 'Caldonia' was also a hit, and was later recorded by Woody Herman's mid-1940s band. Jordan recorded duets with Bing Crosby, Ella Fitzgerald and Louis Armstrong, and he and the Tympany Five were featured in one or two films. He was a great showman with an irrepressible personality and his singing was notable for its timing, its marvellous rhythms and its humour. His music always swung, was always well played and featured improvised solos, and it brought many people, including musicians, to jazz. His influence in this sense was considerable in the 1940s and 1950s. He was active in the 1960s, touring the UK in 1962 with Chris Barber, playing in the USA, and, after a long gap, resuming his recording career. In the 1970s he worked intermittently, leading a new version of his Tympany Five, and appearing at the Newport Jazz Festival, 1974. His is generally considered to have been a seminal influence on the rise of rock and roll. [IC]

Collections of hits from the 1940s and 1950s: *Louis Jordan and Friends*, MCA; with Tympany Five, *Jiving with Jordan*, Charly; *Jump and Jive*, JSP

Jordan, Sheila (Sheila Jeanette Dawson), vocals. b. Detroit, Michigan, 18 November 1928. Raised in Pennsylvania until age 14, singing in school and amateur shows on radio. Became interested in jazz in Detroit high school attended by Kenny Burrell, Tommy Flanagan, Barry Harris etc. Encouraged musically by Charlie Parker, she moved to New York (1950), studied with Lennie Tristano (1951–2), then married (1952), and later divorced, pianist Duke Jordan. Began singing regularly in small New York clubs (1959–65), and recorded with George Russell and her own first album (both 1962). Performed in churches and concerts with Don Heckman (late 1960s). Collaborations with Jazz Composers' Orchestra Association members such as Carla Bley (*Escalator over the Hill*) and Roswell Rudd (big-band and small-group records, 1973–4). Visits to Europe as soloist, including London (1966) and Norway (1970, 1977), led to increased reputation in US. Toured with Steve Kuhn trio from late 1970s, co-leading quartet on records; also performed album of music written by Steve Swallow (1981).

Entirely self-taught, Jordan resembles other prominent jazz singers only in the fact that she sounds like no one else. Her voice can sound alternately – or even simultaneously – bitter/sweet, soft/strained, pure/distorted (and all without any electronic treatment). Aptly described by trumpeter Richard Sudhalter as 'a difficult singer who demands much but is never less than absorbing', she relies on spontaneity to such an extent that a single performance can be full of ups and downs. Like her Detroit contemporary Betty Carter, she is equally capable of using scat, standard songs or little-known original material and making it all sound unique to her. [BP]

Portrait (1962), Blue Note; Kuhn/Jordan, *Last Year's Waltz* (1981), ECM

Jordan, Stanley, guitar. b. Chicago, 31 July 1959. Brought up in California, studying piano from age six, took up guitar at 11. Music degree from Princeton University (1977–81), followed by two years of practising and playing in small clubs or on the street. After living in Chicago area, moved to New York only months before invitation to play Kool Festival (1984). Also appeared in Europe at Montreux festival (1984) and on tour (1985). Jordan's is a highly promising but unrefined talent: his thoroughgoing use of the 'hammering-on' technique (instead of plucking his notes) may have opened up new avenues for the guitar, but so far his concept of what to play seems limited to the clichés of jazz piano. Guitar suffers in comparison to piano through its lack of variation in both volume and texture, even the occasional use of parallel octaves sounding less of a change than it would on a non-electric keyboard. A few things are easier to accomplish for Jordan than for pianists, such as playing a bass-line and chords with the left hand while improvising melodically with the right. Fortunately, there is ample time for both him and others to work out what to do with these possibilities. [BP]

Magic Touch (1984), Blue Note

Jordan, Steve (Stephen Philip), guitar. b. New York City, 15 January 1919. A pupil of Allan Reuss (the gifted swing guitarist who studied with George Van Eps and worked for Benny Goodman and others), he played with several big bands from the late 1930s, including Will Bradley's and Artie Shaw's, and after the war with Glen Gray, Stan Kenton and Boyd Raeburn. Jordan is best remembered as a rock-steady rhythm guitarist who seldom soloed but lent his sound to the 'All-American'-style rhythm sections that followed in Count Basie's footsteps during the 1950s, often on John Hammond's recording sessions. As well as studio work he completed three years with Benny Goodman (1954–7), but from then on was more regularly employed as a tailor until 1965, when he came back to regular work with Tommy Gwaltney's group at Chicago's Blues Alley. Jordan is one of a vanishing breed – the committed rhythm guitarist – and is often cited as a talent comparable to Freddie Green. [DF]

Vic Dickenson, *Showcase* (1953), Fontana

Jordan, Taft (James), trumpet, vocals. b. Florence, South Carolina, 15 February 1915; d. 1 December 1981. As a boy he was entranced by Louis Armstrong's revolutionary re-working of 'When You're Smiling' (inspired by high-note trumpeter B. A. Rolfe), took up the trumpet seriously and, after a time with a variety of Philadelphia-based bands, moved to New York. 1933, drummer Chick Webb heard him at a musicians' hangout, the Radium Club, and took him on to play with his band at the Savoy. Most bands of the day had their own Armstrong soundalike, and Jordan became Webb's, as well as playing lead, all the high notes, and most of the rest of the trumpet solos! (There are marvellous records of Jordan's work at this time, including small-group records featuring Webb alumni, recorded as 'Taft Jordan and his Mob'.) Jordan's centrestage role with Webb was later taken over by Ella Fitzgerald (from 'A-tisket a-tasket' onwards), but he stayed with the band until 1941, two years after Webb's death, and then, after a bandleading period at New York's Savoy, joined Duke Ellington in 1943 for four years. In the 1950s he was busy with studio work, and with bands led by Lucille Dixon (at the Savannah Club), Don Redman and Benny Goodman. By the 1960s he was playing on Broadway in the pit for such shows as *Hello, Dolly!*, led his own quartet and quintet, worked in studios again and, in the last 10 years before he died, played for the New York Jazz Repertory Company, as well as in a marvellous and fortunately recorded salute to Ella Fitzgerald at the Newport Jazz Festival, New York, 1973, and at the West End Café, New York, with Earl Warren in 1975. [DF]

Chick Webb, *King of Swing* (1937–9), Affinity

See Dance, Stanley, *The World of Swing* (Scribner's, 1974, repr. Da Capo, 1979)

Jump band A small group, especially of the late 1930s, which combined the verve of jazz with the compulsive repetition associated with blues. Bands such as the Harlem Hamfats, Stuff Smith's Onyx Club Boys and the somewhat slicker Louis Jordan Tympany Five shared a similar audience. They were the first small groups to imitate the power and directness of the newly popular big bands, and the first to start emphasizing the up-beat, both factors which were more pronounced in what became rhythm-and-blues. [BP]

K

Kahn, Roger Wolfe, leader, multi-instrumentalist. b. Morristown, New Jersey, 19 October 1907; d. New York, 12 July 1962. The millionaire son of a millionaire banker-cum-art dealer, he led a highly successful and influential dance band, 1924–33. Much of the music it played was for commercial consumption (Kahn worked a circuit of high-society hotels such as the Biltmore, New York, and the Southmour in Chicago before finishing up in his own, the Perroquet de Paris on West 57th Street, New York); but his orchestras, especially those assembled for recording sessions, often bristled with jazz talent: a shortlist from many names could include Leo McConville, Mannie Klein, Miff Mole, Joe Venuti, Arthur Schutt, Eddie Lang, Vic Berton and Jack Teagarden. Kahn featured his guest stars sparingly on record – one famous and delightful exception is Jack Teagarden's outing on 'She's a great great girl' from 1928 – but his orchestra was an object of interest and an influence on young men such as Benny Goodman. His string writing in particular intrigued Glenn Miller, who went to see Kahn every night for two weeks in 1927 to garner ideas which he later used in Ben Pollack's orchestra (and perhaps his own). Kahn's last stand was at the Hotel Pennsylvania in 1933; that year he left the music business to become a test pilot. [DF]

With Jack Teagarden, *Texas 'T' Party* (1928, one track), RCA

Kaminsky, Max, trumpet. b. Brockton, Massachusetts, 7 September 1908. He played his early gigs in the Boston area and studied (like Manny Klein) with a great local trumpet teacher, Max Schlossberg. Soon he was commuting between his home town, New York and Chicago, working with George Wettling, Red Nichols, Leo Reisman and others, and learning from friends such as Bud Freeman, Frank Teschemacher, and Wingy Manone. A quiet three years was followed by work with Joe Venuti and others, and in 1936 time with Tommy Dorsey. Kaminsky's reputation as a powerful, accurate lead-trumpeter, as well as a proficient small-band soloist, was spreading, and after turning down offers from Benny Goodman and Glenn Miller, he joined Artie Shaw in 1938, but a quarrel over leadership ended the partnership: Kaminsky joined Dorsey again, then Bud Freeman's Summa Cum Laude band, 1939–40, Tony Pastor, 1940–1, then Artie Shaw again in his 1942 navy band, which included Conrad Gozzo, Frank Beach, John Best, Dave Tough and Claude Thornhill. After discharge, he led his own band in Greenwich Village (including Frankie Newton), worked for Art Hodes at the Village Vanguard and, after a brief attempt at club owning in Boston, returned to New York to play Eddie Condon's for a year (his recordings with Condon from this period have become classics). It was an unhappy period: there was less work for a classic stylist in between two trends (bebop and New Orleans jazz) and clubs were closing all over. But he found work at the Village Vanguard, and even played with Charlie Parker for the opening night of Birdland. Throughout the 1950s Kaminsky carried on in big bands and small groups at Jimmy Ryan's and Eddie Condon's, travelled to Europe with Jack Teagarden and Earl Hines, 1957, and also worked with Teagarden the following year: after 1960 he was often to be found based in New York clubs, including a long residency at Jimmy Ryan's.

A forthright jazz trumpeter, a striking master of the plunger-mute and above all the grandmaster of an elusive Dixieland art, straight lead, Kaminsky wrote one of the most intelligent and informative of jazz autobiographies (see below). [DF]

Eddie Condon, *That Toddlin' Town* (1959), Warner Bros; Kaminsky, *Max Goes East* (1963), United Artists

See Kaminsky, Max, and Hughes, V. E., *Jazz Band: My Life in Jazz* (André Deutsch, 1964, repr. Da Capo, 1981)

Kamuca, Richie (Richard), tenor sax. b. Philadelphia, 23 July 1930; d. 23 July 1977. Big-band experience with Stan Kenton (1952–3) and Woody Herman (1954–6) was followed by small-group work on the West Coast with Chet Baker (1957), Maynard Ferguson (1957), Lighthouse All Stars (1957–8), Shorty Rogers (1959) and Shelly Manne (1959–61). Based in New York from 1962 with Gerry Mulligan band, Gary McFarland group and Roy Eldridge quintet (1966–71, including backing Jimmy Rushing); also occasional third tenor with Zoot Sims–Al Cohn. Did TV studio work in Los Angeles from 1972, remaining active in small-group jazz until shortly before his death from cancer. Kamuca was a firm adherent of the Lester Young approach, whose always sensitive playing was flexible enough to fit well in a number of different contexts. [BP]

Drop Me Off in Harlem (1977), Concord

Kansas City The commercial centre of the Southwestern USA was also an important musical centre in the 1920s and especially the 1930s. While the Great Depression decimated the entertainment industry except for radio, the corrupt municipal regime of Kansas City ensured a thriving nightlife and a constant demand for music. Therefore the city attracted all the best jazz players of the entire Southwest, and succeeded in incubating a new style of big-band music.

Early Eastern bands such as Fletcher Henderson, Duke Ellington and even McKinney's in Detroit attempted an extrovert but neatly organized version of jazz, justified in hindsight by the inclusion of hot solos, and so at first did Bennie Moten. But the 'territory bands' on which he drew for his sidemen had a rougher and more primitive blues-based style that gave the ensemble work more spontaneity, and eventually even introduced head arrangements. The fact that these were little more than riffs, and that opening themes were often interchangeable with backings for soloists, actually gave Kansas City bands (especially Count Basie's) greater stylistic unity and freedom. It is no coincidence that rhythmically repetitive riff-making was so central, for, in rhythm-section work too, the relaxed cohesion of the New Orleans groups found a new home in Kansas City.

It is no coincidence either that, by the late 1930s, exports from Kansas City had set the standard rhythmically for everyone else in the country to emulate and, in the innovations of Lester Young and Charlie Parker, they had an incalculable influence on developments in the 1940s and afterwards. [BP]

Katz, Dill (David Vandyl), bass guitar, double-bass, acoustic guitar. b. London, 12 January 1946. Mother and father both classical musicians. Studied double-bass and classical guitar at the Royal College of Music. 1962, became professional, playing with Irish showbands and doing general session work. With Dave MacRae's Pacific Eardrum in the mid-1970s. 1978–9, with Nucleus; 1979–82, Barbara Thompson's Paraphernalia. Left to form a trio with Nic France and pianist Colin Dudman, called 20th Century Blues. Has since worked with two African groups: Julian Bahula's Jazz Afrika and Brian Abrahams's District Six. Rejoined Nucleus, May 1984. Katz has worked a great deal in Europe with various people, also did a seven-week South American tour with Nucleus in 1984. He is very active in jazz education, and is Electric Bass Consultant at the Guildhall School of Music, London. Favourites are Jaco Pastorius and Scott La Faro. [IC]

With Barbara Thompson; with Nucleus, *Live at the Theaterhaus* (1985), Mood; with District Six, *Akuzwakale (Let it be heard)* (1984), D6 London

Kay, Connie (Conrad Henry Kirnon), drums. b. Tuckahoe, New York, 27 April 1927. Played with Sir Charles Thompson and Miles Davis (mid-1940s), with Cat Anderson Band (*c.* 1949). In early 1950s, gigging at Birdland with such as Stan Getz (1952), Davis (1952); also much r & b studio work (including hit records of 'Mama, He Treats Your Daughter Mean' by Ruth Brown and Joe Turner's 'Shake, Rattle and Roll'). Toured with Lester Young (1953–5), then spent 19 years with Modern Jazz Quartet (1955–74, plus reunions from 1981). During late 1970s, played in many semi-Dixieland contexts and with Benny Goodman (Carnegie Hall, 1978 and elsewhere). Kay is most strongly identified with the carefully detailed playing he contributed to the MJQ. He has not only managed to provide a light and bouncy swing suitable to the group's low volume level, but even – occasionally – to hint at his knowledge of r & b and Dixieland in this most demanding context. [BP]

MJQ, *Concorde* (1955), Prestige/OJC

Keane, Shake (Ellsworth McGranahan), trumpet, fluegelhorn. b. St Vincent, West Indies, 30 May 1927. Taught music by father from age of five. Also began writing verse at an early age, developing into an excellent poet: nickname is short for Shakespeare. While a schoolteacher in St Vincent, he had poems broadcast by BBC, and published two collections of verse. 1952, came to UK, playing with Mike McKenzie's Harlem Allstars which included Joe Harriott, and working with many other groups while spending two years studying English literature at London University. 1959–65, played with Joe Harriott, pioneering free (abstract) improvisation, and recording some classic and seminal albums with him. Toured Europe and played major festivals with the Harriott quintet. 1965, joined Kurt Edelhagen Orchestra in Cologne, West Germany, as featured soloist. 1970s, he went back to St Vincent where he was Minister of Culture for some years. Keane's main influences were Dizzy Gillespie and Miles Davis, but he had forged his own powerful and distinct identity by the beginning of the 1960s. His excellent technique and good range were at the service of a brilliant and unpredictable imagination, and he could handle anything from bebop to contemporary classical ensemble playing to austere and total abstraction. [IC]

With Harriott, *Free Form* (1960), Jazzland; *Abstract* (1962); *Movement* (1963); *High Spirits* (1964); *Indo-Jazz Fusions* (1966), all Columbia

Kellaway, Roger, piano, composer. b. Waban, Massachusetts, 1 November 1939. Began classical piano lessons at age seven; studied composition and piano at New England Conservatory, 1957–9. First professional jobs were on bass. He moved to New York, working as a pianist with Kai Winding, 1962, and Mark Murphy, 1963; also worked with Al Cohn–Zoot Sims. 1964–6, he led his own trio and also worked with Clark Terry and Bob Brookmeyer. He moved to Los Angeles, 1966, spending nine months with the Don Ellis band. He was music director for singer Bobby Darin, 1967–9. From 1967, regularly associated with Tom Scott for several years, first in a quartet with Chuck Domanico (bass) and John Guerin (dms), which was later augmented by Howard Roberts (gtr).

From the later 1960s he also began writing film music and composing for classical ensembles and for TV. 1973, he recorded with Gerry Mulligan, Tom Scott and others; his classical composition *Esque,* for trombone and double-bass, was recorded. 1974, he toured with Joni Mitchell and Tom Scott's LA Express in the USA, Canada and the UK. Since the mid-1970s he has been active as an arranger, and also as a producer and conductor. Kellaway is a technically brilliant pianist and an excellent composer. [IC]

With Tom Scott, Sonny Rollins and others; with Terry/Brookmeyer, *Tonight* (1965), Fontana; as leader, *Spirit Feel* (1967), Pacific Jazz

Kelley, Peck (John Dickson), piano. b. Houston, Texas, 1898; d. 26 December 1980. He led a famous band, Peck's Bad Boys, around Texas in the early 1920s, featuring soon-to-be stars such as Jack Teagarden, Pee Wee Russell and trumpeter Leon Prima. Kelley was a shy, kind man who took care of his musicians; he was also a virtuoso pianist, and his band played a famous residency at Sylva Beach on Galveston Bay in 1924: soon after he was persuaded to join Russell, Bix Beiderbecke and Frank Trumbauer at the Arcadia Ballroom, St Louis. But union problems prevented him getting a work permit and, says Russell, 'Peck went home more convinced than ever that it was a mistake to leave home!' From then on Kelley turned down offers from (among others) Paul Whiteman, the Dorseys, Rudy Vallee, Bob and Bing Crosby, and refused to record. He was seldom forgotten for long: a pop tune, 'Beat me daddy, eight to the bar' was said to have been written about him during the boogie boom, and in 1940 *Collier's Magazine* ran a feature. Kelley stubbornly stayed home, nonetheless, and worked locally: one of his last groups was a Shearing-style quintet, and after a final season at Houston's Dixie Bar in 1949 he retired. Much later *Downbeat* reporter Richard Hadlock interviewed him, tall, grey and nearly blind, in a dim, dusty house with only a practice keyboard and no piano in working order. 'I guess people think it's strange I didn't go with the big names in the 1930s', Kelley told Hadlock. 'Maybe the real reason was I never felt the need to entertain people – I like to play for myself!' Two sessions arranged by Kelley's latterday saxophonist Dick Shannon, recorded in 1957 and later reissued by Milt Gabler, reveal a fine but blunted talent. The old pianist at last went blind, contracted Parkinson's disease and died at 82. [DF]

Peck Kelley Jam, vols. 1/2 (1957), Commodore

Kelly, Chris, trumpet. b. Deer Range Plantation, Louisiana, *c.* 1890; d. 19 August 1929. One of the early trumpet kings of New Orleans, Chris Kelly never recorded and no photograph of him has ever been traced. He arrived in New Orleans somewhere between 1913 and 1915 and once other musicians had got over his eccentric dress – he was a raggedy man who came to work in whatever clothes he could find – they were struck by the power and originality of his playing. Soon Kelly was working every night, mostly in low-class joints where the poorest-paid strata of black New Orleans society gathered to dance and fight: at one such – Perseverance Hall – he worked regularly in the 1920s with clarinettist George Lewis. Kelly's famous feature was 'Careless Love' which (says researcher Len Page) he played into a plunger-mute at a time when the technique was new: the effect of the rendition (it was claimed) made men weep and women tear their clothes off. To at least one New Orleans citizen, Kelly's wife Edna, the song was really titled 'Kelly's Love', and so it became to his admirers, who knew his whispered, deep-muted variations note for note. Kelly became a musical hero, was constantly surrounded by fans and frequently took his band to venues in Biloxi and Mobile where – just possibly – Cootie Williams might have heard him. By the late 1920s Kelly was using relief trumpeters and in 1929 he died in the Algiers Naval Base Hospital: the consensus was that drink had ended his life by a heart attack. [DF]

Kelly, George, tenor sax, vocals, arranger. b. Miami, Florida, 31 July 1915. He was a successful bandleader in his teens around his home town Miami (his drummer was Panama Francis). At the period he was friends with young Fats Navarro, made a film with blues singer Mamie Smith and from 1941, in New York, worked with the band that Francis loved, the Savoy Sultans. From 1944 he was regularly leading his own groups again, arranged for Gene Krupa's orchestra, worked with the Ink Spots, joined Cozy Cole for touring in 1959 (after the success of Cole's hit record 'Topsy') and regularly subbed for Buddy Tate – whose style closely resembles Kelly's – in the Celebrity Club Orchestra. In the 1970s he rejoined Panama Francis in a newly re-formed Savoy Sultans, a move which for the first time drew international attention to his mature swing and was invaluable in helping him establish a soloist's reputation after 35 years of paying dues. In the 1980s Kelly was able to undertake tours of Europe (often organized, in Britain, by promoters Peter Carr and Dave Bennett) and produced solo albums which proved conclusively that great talents in American jazz can be easily overlooked: his plummy, hip singing (bringing Nat Cole to mind) was an unexpected bonus. [DF]

Stealin' Apples (*c.* 1982), Dharma

Kelly, Wynton, piano. b. Brooklyn, New York, 2 December 1931; d. 12 April 1971. An important stylist largely unrecognized except by fellow pianists, Kelly began working in the r & b field with Ray Abrams (1946) and recorded with Cleanhead Vinson, Hal Singer and Lockjaw Davis. Cut his own first album for Blue Note at age 19, and in 1951–2 worked with Dinah Washington, Dizzy Gillespie and Lester Young. After army service, rejoined Washington (1955) and Gillespie's big band (1957), also briefly with Charles Mingus (1956–7), then own trio. Four years with Miles Davis (January 1959–March 1963) led to the setting up of Miles's whole rhythm-section, completed by Paul Chambers and Jimmy Cobb, as the new Wynton Kelly trio. Frequently backing Wes Montgomery and other major soloists, the trio remained a regular unit for several years, although Kelly undertook other freelance accompaniment work until his death following an epileptic fit.

The pianist's mature style, hinted at in his earliest recordings and similar in origin to that of Horace Silver, combines boppish lines and bluesy interpolations, but with a taut sense of timing quite unlike anyone else except his many imitators. The same quality made his equally individual block chording into a particularly dynamic and driving accompanying style that was savoured by the many soloists he backed on record, such as Cannonball Adderley and Hank Mobley. [BP]

Kelly Blue (1959), Riverside/OJC

Kenton, Stan(ley Newcomb), piano, arranger, composer. b. Wichita, Kansas, 19 February, 1912; d. 25 August 1979. Raised in California from age five, played piano as teenager with high school group. Began touring at 18, worked in Las Vegas and Arizona, then in San Francisco and Los Angeles with locally-based bands including Gus Arnheim and Vido Musso (1938–9). Formed own first band in California, becoming extremely successful through broadcasts and then touring (1941–8); in this period, the band played for dancing as well as having a brash air of mild experimentation exemplified by such as 'Eager Beaver' and 'Intermission Riff' and, with the arrival of Shelly Manne (1946) and Art Pepper (1947), was described by Kenton himself as 'progressive jazz'. When he tried to earn his reputation as an experimentalist with the 40-piece Innovations in Modern Music Orchestra, including 16 strings (1950–2), he included some totally composed avant-garde works such as Bob Graettinger's 'City of Glass', and even the presence of improvisers such as Maynard Ferguson and Bud Shank hardly refuted accusations of Kenton's rampant pretentiousness.

Having alienated many of his fans, he thereafter decided that discretion was the better part of valour, reverting to updated swing and acquiring a particularly strong contingent of soloists in 1952–4 (Frank Rosolino, Lee Konitz, briefly Zoot Sims). He continued for the rest of his career in the same vein, except for such occasional ventures as the Neophonic Orchestra (1965–6) and a *Kenton Plays Wagner* album (1964), and retained the standard trumpets/trombones/saxes/rhythm configuration augmented only by a quartet of mellophoniums (1960–3) and a Latin percussionist (from 1968). Despite carefully contriving an impression of single-mindedness, Kenton was musically quite versatile in a rather heavy-handed way; he even recorded a couple of comedy numbers including 'Blues in Burlesque' and, though not noted for a sense of humour, was once heard to say in a live album, 'We've tried everything from playing music backwards; we've played three tunes at a time simultaneously, getting all kinds of polytonal effects; we've gotten so progressive that we went off the end and had to go back around and jump on again!' [BP]

Milestones (1943–7), Creative World; *New Concepts of Artistry in Rhythm* (1952), Capitol; *Cuban Fire* (1956), Creative World

See Easton, Carole, *Straight Ahead: The Story of Stan Kenton* (Morrow, 1973)

Keppard, Freddie, cornet. b. New Orleans, 27 February 1890; d. 15 July 1933. He was playing with John Brown's band from Spanish Fort by the time he was 12, and by 1906 led his own Olympia Orchestra (featuring Alphonse Picou). Soon after that he was New Orleans' newest trumpet king, who covered his hands with a handkerchief to keep his fingerings a secret, blew with huge power and could play for hours on end without faltering. Late in 1914 he left New Orleans and began working with Bill Johnson, George Baquet, Eddie Vinson and others in the Original Creole Orchestra, which toured the prestigious Orpheum circuit of theatres. Mezz Mezzrow heard them: 'That band really upset Chicago, and paved the way for the rest of the New Orleans jazzmen . . . Before harmon mutes were ever thought of he was getting his glissandos and tones with a water glass and a beer bottle too. Freddie's cornet was powerful and to the point: the way he led the ensemble breaking at the right breaks and carrying the lead there was never a letdown.' From 1918, Keppard settled in Chicago, first as a featured star with orchestras and bands led by Doc Cooke, Erskine Tate and Jimmie Noone, a regular drinking buddy: perhaps it was the sight and sound of younger men such as Louis Armstrong surpassing him that drove the older cornettist to drink more and more. By the mid-1920s, says Milt Hinton, 'he was blowing loud but not very good!' Keppard, his water-bottle full of whisky under his arm, became a notorious figure and later a mere sideman in lesser bands. He died of tuberculosis after a long illness in Cook County Hospital, Chicago.

Freddie Keppard is probably the closest recorded link with Buddy Bolden, but he was a more developed and sophisticated player than his forerunner: says Sidney Bechet, 'He played practically the same way as Buddy Bolden but he *really* played!' [DF]

Freddie Keppard (1923–8), Herwin

Kerr, Brooks (Chester Brooks, Jnr.), piano. b. New Haven, Connecticut, 26 December 1951. He graduated from the Manhattan and Juilliard Schools of Music and in the early 1970s became a close friend of Duke Ellington, subbing for him regularly and assisting him on teaching projects. Like Ellington he studied with Willie 'The Lion' Smith. Kerr is known as the leader of a small group featuring Russell Procope and Sonny Greer which after Ellington's death in 1974 worked all round New York in hotels and Greenwich Village clubs, playing a tribute programme and often starring Ellington alumni such as Ray Nance and Francis Williams. Kerr's eclectic piano talent (he could play 'Soda Fountain Rag' or 'Satin Doll' to order) made a strong and favourable impact. 'His style is steeped in Ellington,' wrote critic Lee Jeske in *Jazz Journal*, 'and he comes out with names, dates and places at a rate to make even Stanley Dance quiver! Duke couldn't ask for a finer quartet to keep his sound alive.' [DF]

Kerr/Greer, *Soda Fountain Rag* (undated), Chiaroscuro

Kessel, Barney, guitar. b. Muskogee, Oklahoma, 17 October 1923. First name job with big band fronted by Chico Marx. Settled in Los Angeles, worked with bands of Charlie Barnet (1944, 1945) and Artie Shaw (1945). Made first records under own name with Shaw sidemen Dodo Marmarosa and Herbie Steward (1945). Busy for the next 20 years with studio work, first in radio and then TV and films, but frequently appearing on jazz records, for example with Charlie Parker. Joined Oscar Peterson trio for one year (1952–3), including Jazz at the Philharmonic tours of US and Europe and many recordings arising therefrom. From 1953, regular albums under own name and playing jazz gigs as sideline to studio work; also from 1957, albums with the Pollwinners trio including Ray Brown and Shelly Manne. Toured Europe with Newport Festival package (1967), returning the following year to make records and perform in various European countries (1968–9). Back in US, resumed public appearances and became involved in teaching, with annual trips to Europe to give seminars. Also touring with occasional group including Herb Ellis and Charlie Byrd, under the name Great Guitars.

Frequently viewed as the most complete of the immediate inheritors of Charlie Christian (who was brought up in the same state of Oklahoma), Kessel's best work displays a lithe, boppish style with distinct blues overtones. These have sometimes been allowed to predominate, to the detriment of his overall playing, and the adaptability required in the studios has often caused him to sound too bland. But, given the right setting and stimulating colleagues, Kessel can be a brilliant jazz player. [BP]

Easy Like (1953–6); *Feeling Free* (1969), both Contemporary/OJC

Kikuchi, Masabumi, piano, composer. b. Tokyo, Japan, 19 October 1939. Piano lessons from age five; 1955–8, studied music at Tokyo University. Led his own trio in the early 1960s. 1962, toured with Lionel Hampton; 1968, toured Japan with Sonny Rollins. Went to the Berklee School, Boston, on a *Downbeat* scholarship, September 1968. Back in Japan, 1969, he led his own groups, and also (1969–71) worked with Woody Herman, Mal Waldron and Joe Henderson. Since 1970, has commuted between Japan and the USA, working with Elvin Jones until January 1974, and with others during the same period including McCoy Tyner. 1972, he played under Gil Evans's direction in a band of Japanese musicians plus Billy Harper and Hannibal Peterson, which gave concerts in Tokyo and recorded an album. From 1974, worked with Sonny Rollins; was also closely associated with Terumasa Hino in the mid-1970s. [IC]

With Elvin Jones, Masahiko Togashi; *Masabumi Kikuchi/Gil Evans* (1972), Japanese Philips; Kikuchi/Hino, *East Wind* (1974), East Wind; Kikuchi/Hino/D. Liebman/S. Grossman/R. Lucas/A. Jackson/Al Foster/Mtume, *Wishes/Kochi* (1976), East Wind

King, Peter John, alto, tenor and soprano sax, clarinet. b. Kingston upon Thames, Surrey, 11 August 1940. Entirely self-taught. Began playing clarinet at 15, soon changing to alto sax. 1959, his first important engagement when Ronnie Scott booked him to appear at the opening of the first Ronnie Scott Club in London; 1960, voted New Star in the *Melody Maker* Jazz Poll. 1960–1, worked with Johnny Dankworth orchestra. Since then he has worked with the big bands of Maynard Ferguson, Tubby Hayes, Harry South and Stan Tracey, and played in small groups with Philly Joe Jones, Zoot Sims, Al Cohn, Red Rodney, Hampton Hawes, Nat Adderley, Al Haig, Bill Watrous and others. He has also done a European tour with the Ray Charles band, and has worked with singers such as Jimmy Witherspoon, Joe Williams, Jon Hendricks, Anita O'Day. His favourite saxists include Charlie Parker, Stan Getz, John Coltrane, Lester Young. Among his influences he names Gillespie, Ellington, Bartók and Chick Corea. 1985, he recorded a broadcast as featured soloist and composer/arranger with the Brussels Radio big band. King is a brilliant soloist in the bebop tradition. [IC]

With Stan Tracey, Red Rodney, Jon Eardley, Maynard Ferguson, Philly Joe Jones, Jimmy Witherspoon, Al Haig and others; quartet, *New Beginning* (1982); quintet, *East 34th Street* (1983); *90% of 1%* (1985), all Spotlite

Kinsey, Tony (Cyril Anthony), percussion, piano, composer/arranger. b. Sutton Coldfield, Warwickshire, 11 October 1927. Parents both musical. He studied percussion with Tommy Webster (Birmingham) and Bill West (USA), composition and orchestration with Bill Russo (USA). Came to London in 1948 and worked with various small groups. He was a founder member of the Johnny Dankworth Seven, 1950–2. Then he led his own small groups featuring many of the finest British musicians. He has also accompanied Oscar Peterson, Ben Webster, Clark Terry, Billie Holiday, Ella Fitzgerald, Lena Horne and Sarah Vaughan. His favourite drummers include Kenny Clarke, Buddy Rich, Tony Williams, Phil Seamen, Max Roach, and he has gained inspiration from Duke Ellington, Miles Davis, Thelonious Monk and several European composers from Beethoven to Bartók. He writes music for TV shows, commercials, documentaries and films. Two of his best compositions are *Pictures*, an orchestral suite, and *The Colour Quadrant Suite*, pieces for string quartet and alto sax. [IC]

Quintet, *Jazz at the Flamingo* (1956); *Introducing the Tony Kinsey Quintet* (1957); *How to Succeed in Business* (1963), all Decca; big band, *Thames Suite* (1976), Spotlite

Kirby, John, bass, tuba, arranger. b. Baltimore, Maryland, 31 December 1908; d. Hollywood, 14 June 1952. He was originally the tubaist, and a good one, for Bill Brown's Brownies in New York, but changed over to bass after joining Fletcher Henderson's orchestra in 1930. From 1934 he was in and out of orchestras led by Chick Webb, Lucky Millinder and Charlie Barnet until in 1937 he moved into the Onyx Club on 52nd Street with a 6-piece band containing an old team, Frankie Newton and Pete Brown, soon to be replaced by Charlie Shavers and Russell Procope. Daily rehearsals, during which Kirby was officially appointed leader of the group, combined with Shavers's brilliant little arrangements (often of classical material such as Grieg's 'Anitra's Dance') quickly made John Kirby's sextet the talk of the Onyx, then of 52nd Street. Dressed in immaculate white suits, 'the biggest little swing band in the world' played all the best hotels (including New York's Waldorf Astoria), worked up and down Swing Street and landed a three-a-week radio series, Flow Gently, Sweet Rhythm for NBC, featuring Kirby's wife Maxine Sullivan. Their success lasted until the early 1940s, when Billy Kyle was drafted, drummer O'Neill Spencer was forced to leave for serious health reasons (Cliff Leeman replaced him), and Shavers finally left in 1944 to work in the studios. Charlie Holmes joined briefly three years later, by which time the band was in decline. Kirby – never much of a businessman or a disciplinarian – always paid his sidemen handsomely and seldom bothered to be ruthless: by 1950 his band had slipped out of fashion and a Carnegie Hall reunion concert attracted few customers. He went to California to plan a new band but died of diabetes with complications at 43. His band is remembered as the apotheosis of small band swing. [DF]

John Kirby and his Orchestra, 1941–2, RCA

See Stewart, Rex, *Jazz Masters of the 30s* (Macmillan, 1972, repr. Da Capo, 1982)

Kirk, Andy (Andrew Dewey), bass and baritone sax, tuba. b. Newport, Kentucky, 28 May 1898. He had been a postman/musician for more than ten years when in 1929 he took over leadership of Terrence Holder's Dark Clouds of Joy from Dallas. The band that year included young Buddy Tate and over the next ten years other keymen such as drummer Ben Thigpen, singer Pha (pronounced Fay) Terrell, electric guitarist Floyd Smith and saxophonists Dick Wilson and John Williams were to join; in 1931 Williams's wife, pianist Mary Lou Williams, became Kirk's staff arranger. 'I used to write with the flashlight on in the car when we did one-nighters,' she later told Stan Britt, 'and sometimes we didn't eat for four, five or maybe even six days, because we were afraid to stop at a particular city. After all they were lynching blacks! It was very difficult!' By 1936, when Kirk's band had a hit record, 'Until the real thing comes along' featuring Terrell, it was playing more in New York than down South, often at big venues such as the Savoy, and in 1939 took over the residency at the Cotton Club from Cab Calloway; but it was a brief stay: the club closed because of tax problems. All through the 1940s Kirk continued to lead successful bands: later keymen included Ken Kersey, Don Byas (who replaced Dick Wilson), Shorty Baker and Howard McGhee (who recorded 'McGhee Special' with Kirk in 1942). In 1948 the Clouds of Joy blew away forever and Kirk settled into a string of careers: hotel management, real estate and in the 1980s as a Musicians' Union official in New York. [DF]

Walking and Swinging (1936–42), Affinity

Kirk, Rahsaan Roland, tenor sax, flute, manzello, stritch, clarinet, composer, assorted whistles. b. Columbus, Ohio, 7 August 1936; d. 5 December 1977. Kirk was blinded soon after his birth, and was educated at Ohio State School for the Blind. He played saxophone and clarinet with a school band from age 12. By 1951 he was

Rahsaan Roland Kirk

leading his own group for dances, and playing with other bands around the Ohio area. At 16 he dreamed he was playing three instruments at once, and the next day went to a music shop and tried out all the reed instruments. He was taken to the basement to be shown 'the scraps', and found two archaic saxophones which had been used in turn-of-the-century Spanish military bands, the stritch and the manzello: the first a kind of straight alto sax, and the second looking a little like an alto, but sounding more like a soprano. Kirk took these and worked out a way of playing them simultaneously with the tenor sax, producing three-part harmony by trick fingering. As there were often slight tuning discrepancies between the three instruments, the resulting sound could be harsh, almost with the characteristic of certain ethnic instruments, and this gave Kirk's music an added robustness. He also used sirens, whistles and other sounds to heighten the drama of his performances.

He made his first album in 1956, but it went virtually unnoticed. Then in 1960, through the help of Ramsey Lewis, he recorded for the Cadet label, and immediately caused controversy. People accused him of gimmickry, and Kirk defended himself, saying that he did everything for a reason, and he heard sirens and things in his head when he played. He was, in fact, rooted very deeply in the whole jazz tradition; he knew all the early music, including the work of Jelly Roll Morton (and Fats Waller) in which sirens, whistles, car horns, human voices, had figured to brilliant effect. For Kirk, jazz was 'black classical music', and he was steeped in its wild, untamed spirit; in this he was 'pure' – there were virtually no detectable influences from European classical music in his work.

In 1961 he worked with Charles Mingus for four months, playing on the album *Oh Yeah* and touring with him in California. His international reputation was burgeoning, and after his stint with Mingus he made his first trip to Europe, performing as soloist at the Essen Jazz Festival, West Germany. From 1963 he began a series of regular tours abroad with his own quartet, and played the first of several residencies at the Ronnie Scott Club, London. For the rest of the 1960s and into the 1970s he led his group Vibration Society in clubs, concerts and major festivals throughout the USA, Canada, Europe, Australia and New Zealand.

In 1975, Kirk had a stroke which partially paralysed one side of his body. With tremendous courage he began performing again with one arm – an almost impossible handicap for a saxophonist – and he managed to tour internationally, play some festivals and appear on TV. In 1977 a second stroke caused his death.

Kirk was much loved, not only by his audiences, but also by other musicians. He was unclassifiable; a completely original performer, whose style carried in it the whole of jazz history from early New Orleans roots, through swing and bebop, to the abstraction of the 1960s and 1970s avant-garde. Throughout his career he recorded tributes to people he particularly loved, and they included Fats Waller, Billie Holiday, Duke Ellington, Lester Young, Thelonious Monk, Sidney Bechet, Don Byas, Roy Haynes, Charles Mingus, Clifford Brown, Barney Bigard and John Coltrane. Yet he could be classified neither as a traditionalist, nor as an avant-gardist; his music was always of the present, but contained the essence of past forms. Even in the 1980s his music does not sound dated – it sounds ever-present, beyond time. Playing one instrument – either tenor sax or the manzello – Kirk showed clearly that he was one of the great improvisers. He was an enthusiast who was always listening and learning, and he was generous in his encouragement of aspiring young musicians. He was a composer of memorable tunes: some of the better-known ones are 'From Bechet, Byas and Fats', 'No Tonic Pres', 'Bright Moments', 'Let Me Shake Your Tree', 'The Inflated Tear'.

J. E. Berendt said that Kirk had 'all the wild untutored quality of a street musician coupled with the subtlety of a modern jazz musician', and Michael Ullman wrote: 'Hearing him, one can almost feel that music, like the Lord in "Shine on Me", can "heal the sick and raise the dead".' [IC]

With Jaki Byard/Richard Davis and others, *Pre-Rahsaan* (1961–8), Prestige (double); *We Free Kings* (1961); *Domino* (1962); *Roland Kirk in Copenhagen* (1963), all Trip; *The Inflated Tear* (1968), Atlantic; with Mingus, *Mingus at Carnegie Hall* (1974), Atlantic

Kirkland, Kenny, piano, composer, b. Brooklyn, New York, 1957. Piano lessons at age six; attended Manhattan School of Music, studying classical piano performance for 18 months, then classical theory and composition, graduating as a teacher. He joined Michal Urbaniak's group on keyboards and synthesizer, touring Europe and Scandinavia in 1977. Back in the US, he played with Angela Bofill, Don Alias and others, 1979–81, then joined Terumasa Hino and toured in Japan where he met Wynton Marsalis. From 1982, worked with Marsalis, touring and recording several albums with him. November 1984, toured Japan with Jim Hall, Eddie Gomez and Grady Tate. 1985–6, with Branford Marsalis, Omar Hakim and Darryl Jones, Kirkland accompanied pop/rock musician Sting, recording *Dream of the Blue Turtles* (A & M) with him and doing a massive international tour. Main influences which brought him to jazz were Larry Willis – who played electric piano with Blood Sweat and Tears – Kenny Barron and Herbie Hancock. [IC]

With many people, including Urbaniak, Miroslav Vitous, Bofill, John Scofield, Chico Hamilton, Chico Freeman, David Liebman, Dewey Redman, Carla Bley; with Wynton Marsalis, *Think of One* (1983); *Hot House Flowers* (1984), both CBS

Kirkpatrick, Don (Donald E.), piano, arranger. b. Charlotte, North Carolina, 17 June 1905; d. New York City, 13 May 1956. A veteran of Chick Webb's and later Don Redman's bands in the first half of the 1930s, Don Kirkpatrick was as highly rated for his arranging talents as he was for his piano playing. He was one of the first to contribute scores to Count Basie's band at a time, in the 1930s, when it had relied largely on head arrangements: according to Dickie Wells, Kirkpatrick's work was complicated enough to defeat Herschel Evans (who would tear up the music accordingly). He also wrote regularly for top-class bandleaders such as Chick Webb, Alvino Rey and another great arranger, Don Redman. Surprisingly, Kirkpatrick's playing companions often included more hard-line traditionalists such as Mezz Mezzrow, and he had a solo spot at Nick's from 1944. Perhaps his most apparently dramatic change of stylistic course was a spell with Bunk Johnson in 1947 where he provided (for concerts and records) the kind of light, swing-based piano that Johnson by that time preferred. During the period 1952–5 he worked with Wilbur de Paris's 'New' New Orleans Jazz which – with its mix of old and new traditions – should have provided a perfect setting for Kirkpatrick's trained versatility. He died soon after of pneumonia. [DF]

Wilbur de Paris and his Rampart Street Paraders (1952), London

Klein, Manny (Emmanuel), trumpet. b. New York City, 4 February 1908. Like Max Kaminsky, he was a pupil of trumpet guru Max Schlossberg; later he was in boys' bands and New York's Junior Police Band. Klein was so good so young that, from 1928 onwards, he was in constant demand as a freelance, working on record and live with practically every important white band, from Roger Wolfe Kahn to Benny Goodman to Red Nichols. With very occasional breaks for isolated bandleading ventures (he co-led a technically staggering band with Frank Trumbauer in 1938), Klein remained a studio musician for the rest of his life, playing powerful lead, immaculate hot choruses or classical concertos to perfect order: it would be difficult to find a top-class studio trumpet-section of the 1940s and 1950s that did not include him and his long-time playing colleague Conrad Gozzo. Klein's trumpet featured on countless film soundtracks (including *From Here to Eternity*, 1953, for which he ghosted trumpet solos for Montgomery Clift, and *The Benny Goodman Story*, 1955, in which he doubled for a sick Ziggy Elman), on radio and TV and of course on records. In the 1970s he suffered a stroke which rendered him dyslexic and unable to read music, but he could still play as perfectly as ever. He is known affectionately as GOMOTS: 'Grand Old Man of the Trumpet Section'. [DF]

Manny Klein and his Sextet (1959), Imperial

Klink, Al (Albert), saxes. b. Danbury, Connecticut, 28 December 1915. One of the most stylish white swing saxophonists, he joined Glenn Miller, 1939–42 (he shares the tenor solo on 'In the Mood' with Tex Beneke but was under-featured in general), and then moved on to a succession of fine bands including Benny Goodman's and Tommy Dorsey's. Later in the 1940s he concentrated on studio work (for WNEW and later NBC) and appeared regularly on jazz albums too (including Ruby Braff's Billie Holiday tribute *Holiday in Braff*). As a freelance in the 1970s his work was heard more often, sometimes with the World's Greatest Jazz Band: an overdue return. [DF]

World's Greatest Jazz Band play Rodgers and Hart (1975), World Jazz

Knepper, Jimmy (James M.), trombone, arranger. b. Los Angeles, 22 November 1927. Early experience with band led by Chuck Cascales (brother of arranger Johnny Richards) and with saxist Dean Benedetti in mid-1940s. Toured with pianist Freddie Slack (1947), altoist Johnny Bothwell (1948) and other name bands, rehearsed and recorded in Roy Porter band (1948–9) alongside Eric Dolphy, fellow student at LA City College. Further big-band work including Claude Thornhill (1956) took him to

New York, where he immediately replaced trombonist Willie Dennis in Charles Mingus's Jazz Workshop (1957–8, rejoining him briefly in 1959, 1961 twice, 1976 and 1977). Spent a few months each with Stan Kenton (1958), Tony Scott (1958), Gil Evans (1960) and Benny Goodman (1962). Then following physical injury inflicted by Mingus in 1962, worked steadily in Broadway pit bands and session work, becoming member of Thad Jones–Mel Lewis band (1967–73) and of Lee Konitz nonet (1975–9). One of the regulars, and sometimes musical director, of Mingus Dynasty from 1979 onwards, also numerous tours abroad as soloist.

Knepper's solo work is most frequently associated with Mingus but is remarkably consistent, whatever the context. While taking account of the harmonic and melodic advances of bebop, he steered clear of the staccato attack of J. J. Johnson ('He plays the trombone fast like a fast trombonist rather than a machine-gunner; false slide positions are the secret', according to Mike Zwerin.) His extremely nimble technique enabled him to articulate more in the manner of a saxophonist, and at the same time to incorporate aspects of earlier trombonists, such as the slurs and tonal variations of Vic Dickenson. Since his re-emergence as a soloist in the mid-1970s, Knepper has become widely acknowledged as one of the leading performers on his instrument. [BP]

Idol of the Flies (1957), Affinity; *Cunningbird* (1976), Steeplechase; *Primrose Path* (1980), Hep

Koc, Dorota, see LAKA DAISICAL.

Koller, Hans, tenor and soprano sax, clarinet, sopranino, alto and baritone sax. b. Vienna, 12 February 1921. Studied clarinet at Vienna Music Academy, 1935–9. Entered German army, 1940, and was one of very few jazz musicians who played during Nazi dominance. He became one of the leaders of post-war jazz in Germany, forming the first important modern combo, which included Albert Mangelsdorff. Toured with Gillespie, Lee Konitz, Stan Kenton and others during the 1950s. He made a short film, *Jazz Yesterday and Today* for J. E. Berendt. Koller continued to lead his own groups during the 1960s and 1970s. His early influences were Lennie Tristano and Lee Konitz, and he later became inspired by John Coltrane. He appeared at many European festivals and won polls on tenor and soprano and for his group. Since 1957 he has been active as an abstract painter with national and international exhibitions. [IC]

Exclusiv (1963); *Vision* (nda); *Relax with my Horns* (1966); *Phoenix* (1972), all MPS/BASF

Konitz, Lee, alto sax (and soprano, tenor). b. Chicago, 13 October 1927. After meeting Lennie Tristano on commercial gigs in Chicago in the mid-1940s and studying under him, Konitz became deeply involved in jazz and toured with Claude Thornhill's band (1947–8). Settled in New York, working with Miles Davis (1948, and recordings during 1949–51). Recording for Tristano and under own name from 1949, was also member of Stan Kenton orchestra (1952–3). Since that time, apart from occasional reunions with Tristano and/or fellow student Warne Marsh, Konitz has been a freelance soloist and private teacher. Made regular trips to Europe from 1951, led own trio and nonet from mid-1970s.

Lee Konitz

The influence of Tristano was predominant in the early work of Konitz, so that in the late 1940s he was one of the few altoists of his generation not to be overwhelmed by the example of Charlie Parker. His playing instead was characterized by extremely long lines, with irregular but not strong accents and a thin, deliberately uninflected tone. Submitting to the demands of the Kenton band during his stay, he strengthened the tone and, in subsequent decades, allowed a much greater variety of emotion to be expressed by the sound quality alone. A similar development showed in the rhythmic accentuation and fragmentation of his lines, which gradually took on more vitality and complexity, demonstrating a thorough understanding of greats such as Armstrong, Young and of course Parker. A unique and immediately identifiable performer. [BP]

Timespan (1954–61), Wave; *Very Cool* (1957), Verve; *The Nonet* (1976), Roulette

Korner, Alexis, guitar, piano, vocals. b. Paris, 19 April 1928; d. London, 1 January 1984. Son of a Greek mother and an Austrian cavalry officer father. When Germany invaded France at the beginning of World War II, the Korner family fled from Paris, going via Switzerland and North Africa to the UK, where they settled. He had classical piano lessons from age five, but in 1940, age 12, he discovered a record by blues and boogie-woogie pianist Jimmy Yancey, and from then on was totally and passionately committed to playing blues and jazz. By the late 1940s Korner's blues quartet was part of trombonist Chris Barber's band, playing for 30 minutes in the middle of each of Barber's jazz concerts. However, Korner failed to fit into the fanatically purist traditional jazz scene; he also loved Charlie Parker and bebop because of the 'great blues feeling in it'. 1952, he again worked with Barber's band, playing in the skiffle group with the trombonist, Ken Colyer and Lonnie Donegan.

For the first time, American domination of the pop charts was broken. Skiffle was the new craze and the initial inspiration of most of the British rock groups of the 1960s, including the Beatles, and it was also the source of the whole British blues movement, spearheaded by Korner. In the mid-1950s Barber began to bring American blues artists such as Big Bill Broonzy and Muddy Waters to the UK, and for the third time he gave Korner a spot in his band, playing electric blues with Cyril Davis on harmonica. The heavily amplified music deeply offended traditional jazz purists, and Korner left to form his own band, Blues Incorporated, which rapidly became an inspiration and focal point of blues enthusiasts all over the UK. It provided a direct experience of the blues for young musicians who came to listen, to 'sit in' and sometimes to join the band: Mick Jagger, Charlie Watts, John Mayall, Eric Burdon, Long John Baldry, Paul Jones, Robert Plant and many others. And improvisation was so germane to Alexis's concept, that many of the most talented young jazz musicians of the 1960s worked with Blues Incorporated, including Jack Bruce, Ginger Baker, Graham Bond, John Marshall, Phil Seamen, John Surman, Ken Wheeler, Ray Warleigh, Dave Holland, Alan Skidmore, Art Themen and Dick Heckstall-Smith.

1968, Korner disbanded and went solo, touring with continental groups. 1969, he began a long and fruitful association with the Danish blues singer Peter Thorup, forming first a band called New Church, which included virtuoso bass guitarist (and singer) Colin Hodgkinson, and then the very successful bigger band CCS. Throughout the 1970s and into the 1980s Korner and Hodgkinson worked together as a duo a great deal. From the late 1970s until his death, he had his own Sunday night BBC Radio One show, on which he played and talked about records he liked. This programme reflected Korner's immensely broad tastes in vernacular music, covering everything from blues and rock to gospel music, folk and all eras and types of jazz, and its benign catholicity attracted a wide cross-section of listeners. He also wrote and recorded some excellent songs including 'Robert Johnson', 'Tap Turns on the Water', 'Lend Me Some Time'.

Alexis Korner's influence is incalculable. He was a passionate enthusiast who wanted to share his knowledge and experience with everyone. He was always generous with his help and advice, always quick to recognize quality in other artists and to preach their virtues. He brought direct experience of r & b to a whole generation of British rock and jazz musicians, and during the 1960s various of his disciples, such as the Rolling Stones, helped to make Americans aware of their own blues artists. [IC]

R & B From the Marquee (1962), Ace of Clubs; *Alexis Korner's Blues Incorporated* (1963), Ace of Clubs; *Red Hot from Alex* (1964), Transatlantic; *At the Cavern* (1964), Oriole; *Sky High* (1965), Spot; *I Wonder Who* (1966), Fontana

Kotick, Teddy (Theodore John), bass. b. Haverhill, Massachusetts, 4 June 1928; d. 17 April 1986. Moved to New York (1948), working among others with Buddy Rich, Buddy DeFranco, Artie Shaw band (1950). Played fairly regularly for Charlie Parker (1951–2) and with Stan Getz (1951–3). Recorded with Herbie Nichols (1956), Tony Scott (1956) and first album of Scott's pianist, Bill Evans (1956). Toured with Horace Silver quintet (1957–8), then freelancing in New York area. From early 1970s was again based in Massachusetts, one of his only recordings of recent years being with Allen Eager (1982). A light-fingered and light-toned bassist, Kotick in the early 1950s paralleled the development of Red Mitchell and predicted some of the innovations of Paul Chambers and even Scott La Faro. Both his walking and his occasional solos managed to avoid the obvious and nevertheless sound absolutely right. [BP]

Bill Evans, *New Jazz Conceptions* (1956), Riverside/OJC

Kress, Carl, guitar. b. Newark, New Jersey, 20 October 1907; d. Reno, Nevada, 10 June 1965. A brilliant and irresistible guitarist whose name is synonymous with the art of chorded guitar solos, he was discovered when he subbed at short notice for Eddie Lang, at the instigation of Bill Challis, on a Paul Whiteman recording date. From then on he was a New York studio habitué, recorded with Beiderbecke and Trumbauer on a Chicago Loopers session (with most of the best of the rest of the white studio fraternity, from Red Nichols to the Dorseys) and was rich enough by the 1930s to go into partnership with Joe Helbock as co-owner of the Onyx Club on 52nd Street at the height of its success (the partnership was later dissolved after a quarrel). Kress's guitar duets, recorded with such kindred spirits as Eddie Lang and Dick McDonough during the 1930s, are classics of their kind, and he remained a busy studio man until the 1960s working for radio and TV, including the Garry Moore programme, and duetting with a later partner, George Barnes, until his death.

Like many of his guitarist contemporaries (including his pupil George Van Eps), Kress played banjo first, and he continued to retain banjo tuning on the guitar's top four strings. He played banjo with Clarence Hutchenrider's trio in 1960, recording albums which were later to fetch collectors' prices. His wife was singer Helen Carroll, whom he backed regularly (with the Merry Macs). [DF]

Fun on the Frets (1934–41), Yazoo

Kriegel, Volker, guitar, composer, b. Darmstadt, Germany, 24 December 1943. Self-taught; began on guitar at 15; at 18 formed his own trio, which in 1963 was voted Best Band at the German Amateur Jazz Festival, Kriegel himself getting the Best Soloist award. Studied social science, psychology and some philosophy at Frankfurt University, and while there became involved with the scene centred on the Frankfurt Jazzkeller, which included Albert and Emil Mangelsdorff and bassist Peter Trunk.

In 1968 the US vibraphonist Dave Pike came to live in Europe, forming a quartet (the Dave Pike Set) which included Kriegel, Peter Baumeister (dms) and Austrian bassist Hans Rettenbacher. This group achieved immediate success, and Kriegel abandoned his university studies to become a professional musician. The DPS played concerts and festivals throughout Europe and twice toured extensively in South and Central America (1971, 1973) for the Goethe Institute. For their second tour the bassist was Eberhard Weber. Pike then returned to the USA, and in late 1973 Kriegel formed his own band, Spectrum, which included Weber on bass, Rainer Brüninghaus (keyboards), and Joe Nay (dms). 1976, Weber left to concentrate on his own band, Colours, taking Brüninghaus with him, so Kriegel formed an entirely fresh band called the Mild Maniac Orchestra, with very young and virtually unknown musicians including Hans Peter Ströer (bass gtr) and Thomas Bettermann (keyboards). MMO began as a quartet but eventually became a sextet with the addition of percussion and saxophone, and as such it continued into the mid-1980s.

Kriegel's early influences were Wes Montgomery, Jim Hall, Kenny Burrell, and later favourites include Pat Metheny, John McLaughlin, John Scofield. Other inspirations are Joe Zawinul, Gary Burton, Mike Gibbs, Albert Mangelsdorff; and Kriegel's work is also permeated with influences from rock, pop and ethnic music. His groups play jazz-rock-fusion, with a rare lightness of touch, and his music combines an often very subtle harmonic sense with great rhythmic deftness and invention. In his ballads there is a brooding romantic strain, while his up-tempo pieces can express unbridled joy. He is a prolific composer and has also written much music for TV programmes and animated films.

1975, Kriegel was a founder member of the United Jazz and Rock Ensemble; 1977, with Wolfgang Dauner, Albert Mangelsdorff, Ack Van Rooyen and Werner Schretzmeier, he co-founded Mood Records. With Spectrum he toured North Africa in 1974 and did his third tour of Brazil in 1975, spending one month teaching at the Goethe Institute in Salvador, Bahia. With MMO he has toured widely in Germany, played at Montreux, 1977, and in 1979, augmenting the group with Uli Beckerhoff (tpt) and Wolfgang Engstfeld (tenor sax), he did a two-month tour through 11 black African countries for the Goethe Institute. He has also worked as a sideman for other leaders including Klaus Doldinger and Peter Herbolzheimer. With UJRE he has played festivals all over Western Europe and at Sopot and Warsaw in Poland.

Kriegel is an established cartoonist with work published regularly in German papers and magazines; he is the author of two books (*Der Rock 'n' Roll König* and *Hallo*, both published in 1982); he is a regular radio broadcaster presenting analytical programmes on music. In 1980 he completed an animated cartoon film (*Der Falschspieler*) which was shown in many countries and won a prize at a Los Angeles film festival, and he has also directed two long TV documentary films about music. H. R. Gaines has written: 'Wit, consummate grace, humanity, these are the hallmarks of Kriegel's style in all his multifarious activities.' [IC]

Six with DPS and six with UJRE; *Spectrum* (1971); *Missing Link* (1972); *Topical Harvest* (1975); *Octember Variations* (1976); *Elastic Menu* (1977); *House Boat* (1978); *Long Distance* (1979), all MPS; *Journal* (1981); *Schöne Aussichten* (1983), both Mood

Kristian, Billy (Wiremu Aata Te Rangi-Amoa Karaitiana), bass guitar, percussion. b. Christchurch, New Zealand, 14 June 1943. Self-taught. Began in rock music, 1957–75, playing with various antipodean groups. Came to London, 1976. 1977–9, with Nucleus. Worked with Dave MacRae's Pacific Eardrum. 1979, toured USA with rock group Night. Then worked in London with various people. Returned to New Zealand in 1984. With Nucleus, Kristian toured in Europe and spent three weeks in India in 1978. Favourites are Eberhard Weber, Jaco Pastorius, Eddie Gomez, John Entwistle. [IC]

With Pacific Eardrum, *Pacific Eardrum* (1977), Charisma; *Beyond Panic* (1978), Charisma; with Nucleus, *In Flagrante Delicto* (1977), Contemporary; *Out of the Long Dark* (1978), Capitol; with Brian Smith, *Southern Excursion* (1984), Ode

Krog, Karin (Karin Krog Bergh), vocals. b. Oslo, Norway, 15 May 1937. From a musical family, she had private lessons with Anne Brown (Bess in the first *Porgy and Bess*). She began to appear in Oslo and Stockholm early

1960s with Jon Christensen, Jan Garbarek and Arild Andersen. 1964, performed at Antibes Jazz Festival. Played and recorded with Don Ellis orchestra and Clare Fischer trio in USA, 1967. She toured Japan in 1970 with a group of European poll-winners which included Albert Mangelsdorff, John Surman and Jean-Luc Ponty. Toured in the USA 1970, 1972, 1975, 1981. She did a world tour in 1975, and performed at the first Indian Jazz Yatra, 1978. She has also appeared throughout Europe at festivals and on radio and TV. 1974, she took a course in TV production and has since produced a number of jazz programmes for Norwegian TV. 1965–83, she won several prizes and awards in the USA and Norway. Her recordings with Dexter Gordon (*Some Other Spring*, 1971), and with Archie Shepp (*Hi-Fly*, 1977) were both voted jazz vocal record of their respective year in Japan. Influences range from Billie Holiday, Ella Fitzgerald and Sarah Vaughan to Oum Katoum and Cathy Berberian, and other inspirations are John Surman, Albert Mangelsdorff, Palle Mikkelborg and Dexter Gordon. Karin Krog has developed into one of Europe's most accomplished and original singers. Since 1978 she has concentrated on duo work with Bengt Hallberg, Red Mitchell and John Surman. 1985, she and Surman toured Australia. [IC]

With Garbarek/Andersen, *Joy* (1968), Sonet; with Gordon, *Some Other Spring* (1970), Sonet/Storyville; with Shepp, *Hi Fly* (1976), Compendium, Phonogram; with Surman, *Cloudline Blue* (1978), Polydor; with Red Mitchell, *Three's a Crowd* (1979), Bluebell; with Mitchell/Warne Marsh, *I Remember You* (1980), Spotlite; with Hallberg, *Two of a Kind* (1981), Four Leaf; with Surman, *Such Winters of Memories* (1983), ECM

Krupa, Gene, drums. b. Chicago, 15 January 1909; d. Yonkers, New York, 16 October 1973. Early on he worked in theatre bands, jazz groups and large dance orchestras: his first record in 1927 with the McKenzie–Condon Chicagoans was in itself a groundbreaker: 'I'm afraid Krupa's bass-drum and those tom-toms will knock the needle off the wax', said producer Tommy Rockwell. December 1934, Krupa joined Benny Goodman and became a riveting central figure whose innovatory drumnastics were dangerously likely to steal the limelight from his leader. 'Gene was as magnetic as a movie-star,' says Anita O'Day, 'filled with wild exuberance as his raven-coloured hair, flashing brown eyes and black suit contrasted with the snow-white marine pearl drums around him.' His image at the period was a cause for concern to middle-class America: 'He's much more normal at home!' promised a caption to his picture in Timme Rosenkrantz's 1939 *Swing Album.* In 1938 a distressing onstage fracas between Goodman and Krupa ended their partnership for the time being, and Krupa formed his own band for an April début at Atlantic City's Steel Pier. Soon after, following a drubbing from Jimmie Lunceford's orchestra, he augmented with Anita O'Day and trumpeter Roy Eldridge, who became two vital features of his show. Some of Krupa's creative spark focused itself on African percussion (he was fascinated by the Dennis Roosevelt expedition to the Belgian Congo) and one of his experiments featured every band member playing tom-toms in sectionally-arranged cross-rhythms: the memory of those experiments was to endear Krupa to modern drummers such as Max Roach. In 1943, an international star on record and in films, Krupa was arrested, ostensibly for employing an under-age bandboy, and briefly gaoled (society's correction, perhaps, for his larger-than-life image), but he was back with Goodman for an emotional reunion in September 1943 on which he played like a king, got a standing ovation, and cried. After Goodman he worked briefly with Tommy Dorsey's band, then re-formed his own for a second successful run from 1944 using new arrangers, including Eddie Finckel, Gerry Mulligan and George Williams, and young bop soloists such as Don Fagerquist, Lennie Hambro and Frank Rehak.

Gradually, however, the modern jazz revolution began to make Krupa's style sound inflexible and four-square, a problem that recurred when, after 1951, he formed a trio with pianist Dave McKenna and saxophonist Charlie Ventura: their attempts to re-create the excitement of Benny Goodman's quartet 15 years before sounded for once forced and contrived and ran at odds with the 'cool school'. From 1954 Krupa ran a drum school with Cozy Cole in New York and in 1959 the Hollywood film *Drum Crazy: the Gene Krupa Story* appeared. In 1960 he had his first heart attack, but he continued leading his own quartet and playing reunions with Benny Goodman until 1967 when he decided to take life more easily. Their last reunion was in 1973, the year of Krupa's death. Sadly, a fire destroyed his houseful of memorabilia shortly before he died.

In three ways at least Krupa was lucky in his career: he was born at the right time; he was a natural performer (unlike, say, Dave Tough, a contemporary of equal talents); and he was white – black showman-contemporaries such as Sid Catlett were never allowed the career opportunities that Krupa had. Musically his influence was colossal: 'I succeeded in doing two things,' he summed up later. 'I made the drummer a high-priced guy, and I was able to project enough so that people were drawn to jazz.' [DF]

Drummin' Man! (1938–49), Columbia (double, boxed set)

Kuhn, Joachim Kurt, piano, composer, alto sax. b. Leipzig, Germany, 15 March 1944. Brother clarinettist Rolf Kuhn. 1949–61, studied classical piano and composition privately, playing classical concerts throughout that period. Then became professional jazz pianist. 1962–6, led his own trio; 1966–9, co-led a quartet with his brother in Hamburg. 1969–71, with his own group in Paris. 1971–2, with Jean-Luc Ponty Experience; co-led group with Eje Thelin, 1972–3. With Association PC (1973–4) he toured Asia, North Africa, Portugal, Spain. Has toured and played festivals in Europe and the USA. In the 1980s he was also a member of the Tony Oxley quintet, with Enrico Rava, Gert Dudek and Ali Haurand. Influences Franz Schubert, Miles Davis, John Coltrane. [IC]

Boldmusic (1969); *Piano* (1971); *This Way Out* (1973); *Open Strings* (nda); with R. Kuhn, *Connection 74* (1973), all MPS

Kuhn, Steve (Stephen Lewis), keyboards, composer. b. Brooklyn, New York, 24 March 1938. Began piano lessons at age five. 1959–63, played with Kenny Dorham, John Coltrane, Stan Getz; 1964–6, with Art Farmer quartet and also led his own occasional trio. 1967–71, lived in Stockholm, working with his own trio throughout Europe. 1971, back in New York working with his own quartet. He played many festivals with Getz and Farmer, including Newport and Monterey; and with his own group, festivals in Finland and Europe. Kuhn is steeped in the whole jazz piano tradition and is a vastly accomplished player. His favourites range from Fats Waller and Art Tatum to Bud Powell and Bill Evans, and other inspirations are Charlie Parker, John Coltrane, Miles Davis. A fine example of his scope and style is his live quartet album *Last Year's Waltz* (1981, ECM), with Sheila Jordan (voice), Harvie Swartz (bass) and Bob Moses (dms). He is also a prolific composer. [IC]

With Dorham, Getz, Farmer, Gary Burton; solo, *Ecstasy* (1974); *Trance* (1974) (with Steve Swallow/Jack DeJohnette/Sue Evans); quartet *Motility* (1977); *Non-Fiction* (1978), all ECM

Kyle, Billy (William Osborne), piano, arranger. b. Philadelphia, 14 July 1914; d. 23 February 1966. He studied piano from the age of eight and was a professional at 18, playing with bands such as Tiny Bradshaw's as well as (briefly) his own and Lucky Millinder's. He joined John Kirby's band in 1938, and when he left in 1942 after call-up the loss was a severe blow to the band. After demobilization he rejoined briefly, then worked in pit bands for Broadway shows (including *Guys and Dolls*), led his own small group and worked for Sy Oliver. In autumn 1953, Kyle joined Louis Armstrong's All Stars (replacing Earl Hines) and for the rest of his life was to remain the perfect band pianist. 'In my opinion,' says Barney Bigard, 'Billy was the best piano player Louis ever had. He was strictly a band man – just straight comp. Of course he could solo too . . . One that he used to feature himself on a lot was "Pretty Little Missy" which he wrote.' With the All Stars, Kyle recorded classics such as *Plays W. C. Handy* and *Plays Fats*, appeared in the film *High Society* (1956) and weathered the touring until he died quite suddenly in Youngstown, Ohio, while on tour.

Although Billy Kyle never achieved the reputation of pianists such as Earl Hines and Teddy Wilson (whose approaches he somehow melded into one style), he was a brilliantly able pianist. His playing methodology resembled Wilson's, but Kyle produced a brighter sound and his style was more rhythmic and concise than the older man's legato approach. [DF]

Louis Armstrong, *Plays W. C. Handy* (1954), CBS

L

La Barbera, Pat (Pascel), tenor, soprano and alto sax, clarinet, flute. b. Mt Morris, New York, 7 April 1944. Parents musical; younger brothers are professional musicians: John plays trumpet and piano and is a composer/arranger; Joe plays drums. Pat La Barbera played with his father and brothers in the family band from age six. He studied with his father from 1952; attended Berklee, 1964–7; also studied with private teachers. Featured soloist with Buddy Rich band, 1967–73. Also led his own groups and worked with Louie Bellson and Woody Herman. He was with Elvin Jones from 1975. He did TV shows and played many international festivals with Rich. 1979, toured Europe with Jones, and appeared at the Messina (Sicily) festival. Influences include early Lee Konitz, John Coltrane, Sonny Rollins, Joe Henderson, Ira Sullivan, Joe Romano. [IC]

With Buddy Rich and others; with Jones, *Remembrance* (1979), PA/USA

Lacy, Steve (Steven Lackritz), soprano sax, composer. b. New York City, 23 July 1934. Started on piano with private lessons, took up clarinet, then changed to soprano. Studied with Cecil Scott; 1953, at the Schillinger School of Music (later Berklee); 1954, at the Manhattan School of Music, without finishing the course at either. He was inspired by traditional jazz – New Orleans, Chicago and Kansas City styles – and played that for a few years. But he spent several years rehearsing and playing with Cecil Taylor during the later 1950s. 1958–9, worked with Gil Evans, Mal Waldron and Jimmy Giuffre, and began studying Monk's music. 1960, he worked with Thelonious Monk's quintet for 16 weeks. Then led his own quartet with Roswell Rudd (tmb), Dennis Charles (dms) and various bassists, playing mostly Monk tunes. 1965, played at Café Montmartre in Copenhagen with Kenny Drew, and at the Bologna festival. In Italy he formed a quartet with Enrico Rava, and toured in South America for eight months, then went back to New York, working for a year with his quintet which included Rava, Karl Berger, Kent Carter and Paul Motian. 1967, he went back to Europe and settled there with his Swiss wife Irene Aebi.

He spent three years in Rome working in various contexts, including Musica Elettronica Viva, which combined improvised contemporary music with electronics, and experimented with sound and language. 1970, went to Paris; 1972, began playing solo soprano sax concerts. He has also led his own small groups and occasional bigger ensembles. As well as trips to Portugal, Holland, Italy, Japan and giving solo concerts in France, Germany and the UK, he has also worked in a whole variety of contexts including museums, schools, radio stations, clubs, theatres and cultural centres. In the later 1970s and the 1980s he worked intermittently with Derek Bailey and Evan Parker. At the beginning of the 1980s his quintet in Paris consisted of Kent Carter (bass), Oliver Jackson (dms), Steve Potts (saxes) and Lacy's wife Irene Aebi (voice, vln, cello): Lacy called his current music 'poly-free' because it was a mixed approach containing elements from the previous two decades – including abstract improvisation and more structured passages.

Lacy's whole career is a rare example of sustained artistic development which took him from total immersion in traditional jazz in the early 1950s, through bebop, Thelonious Monk's music and studies with Cecil Taylor, to the free improvisation of the 1960s and the pluralism of the 1970s and 1980s. In the late 1950s it was certainly his soprano playing which inspired Coltrane to take up the instrument, and his quiet but steely integrity has made him a contemporary force throughout his career. His soprano sound is more rounded than Sidney Bechet's, with less vibrato, and less reedy than Coltrane's, but Lacy has explored the tonal resources of the instrument far more than the other two. Lee Jeske has written: 'His work is interspersed with growls and short stop-time phrases which sound like dialogue in a Beckett play . . . Once in a while Lacy will hold a high, shrill squeak until it dissipates in the air . . . Sometimes his playing takes on a vaudevillian tone; elsewhere he uses slithery legato phrases. Then there are some two-tone train whistle effects, and occasionally he uses his corduroyed leg as a mute to produce a cow-like mooing.' He can also produce fresh and fleet lines of stark beauty.

In the late 1960s he began to go more deeply into composition, and has since written many pieces, including *Tao*, cycle for voice and quintet; *The Woe*, melodrama for quintet and tape; *The Sun*, litany for sextet and voice; *Shots*, eight pieces for sextet. He has also recorded prolifically, with over 50 albums as leader and over 45 as sideman. [IC]

With Gil Evans, Cecil Taylor, Monk, Jazz Composers' Orchestra, Globe Unity Orchestra, Gary Burton, Max Roach and many others; *Steve Lacy Plays Monk* (1969), Affinity; quintet, *Wordless* (1971), Musica; Lacy/Roswell Rudd, *Trickles* (1976), Black Saint; *Threads* (1977), Horo; solo soprano, *Clinkers* (1977), Hat Hut; quintet, *Stamps* (1978), Hat Hut; quintet, *Troubles* (1979), Black Saint

Ladnier, Tommy (Thomas J.), trumpet. b. Florenceville, Louisiana, 28 May 1900; d. New York City, 4 June 1939. A childhood pupil of Bunk Johnson, who played along with his teacher in several bands, he had come to Chicago by 1917, worked (with Gene Sedric, a frequent colleague) in St Louis trumpeter Charlie Creath's fine band, and soon after was back in Chicago again: Muggsy Spanier remembers duetting with him in a little hole-in-the-wall South Side club. For the next four years Ladnier worked with Chicago stars including Jimmie Noone and King Oliver (he was a later replacement, after Lee Collins, for Louis Armstrong) and in 1925 joined Sam Wooding's orchestra for the start of several years' spectacular globetrotting. In 1926 he joined Fletcher Henderson in New York for a year but in 1928 was back in Europe with Wooding again, rooming with Doc Cheatham. By this period Ladnier was already drinking heavily. Back in the USA in the post-depression years, times were hard: he opened a tailor's shop with Sidney Bechet and formed a great band with him, the New Orleans Feetwarmers which played in 1932 to a half-empty Savoy Ballroom but recorded classic sides for Victor. The low period combined with a broken marriage set him to heavier drinking, but in 1938, thanks to the determined promotion of Hugues Panassié, he recorded again after years in retirement, teaching and playing with a trio: classics such as 'Really the Blues', 'Jada' and 'Comin' on with the come on!'. The plain and simple trumpet of these sides is beyond price, but it was Ladnier at reduced power and while rooming with Mezz Mezzrow, he died from a heart attack. Mezzrow (who loved his guest and remembered 'the wonderful stories' he would tell) made a collection for the funeral and on 9 June Ladnier was buried in Frederick Douglas Memorial Cemetery, Staten Island. 'There's a guy who had a natural swing', says Buster Bailey. 'Listen to the way he plays – the way he takes a melody and swings it. That's what I mean by swing!' [DF]

The Panassié Sessions (1938–9), RCA

La Faro, Scott, bass. b. Newark, New Jersey, 3 April 1936; d. 6 July 1961. Only took up bass in 1953, began gigging in r & b groups. Toured with Buddy Morrow (1955), worked in California with Chet Baker (1956–7), Barney Kessel, vibist Cal Tjader etc. Moved to New York, playing with Benny Goodman (1959) and own group. Joined Bill Evans trio (1959–61), with which his name is still indelibly associated. Also recorded with Vic Feldman, Hampton Hawes, and two albums with Ornette Coleman (one replacing his close friend Charlie Haden). Played with Stan Getz at 1961 Newport festival immediately before meeting his death in a car accident.

La Faro has been, for both better and worse, one of the most influential bassists since Jimmy Blanton. During his brief period of prominence, he took for granted the new mobility which Mingus had demonstrated and, inspired in part by the style of Red Mitchell, constructed his solos entirely from the sort of boppish lines used by pianists and especially guitarists of the late 1950s. In his solo work with Evans he achieved a kind of parity with the pianist, audibly expanding the role of the bass in piano-led trios far beyond the then norm. To achieve this required a low action (i.e. strings lying close to the fingerboard, with correspondingly lower volume necessitating extra-close miking) which was contrary to standard practice at the time. But the facility gained in the upper range ensured that everyone would eventually follow the same path and that better amplification would become essential.

Less frequently noted is La Faro's rhythm playing in the same group which, in partnership with drummer Paul Motian, used a number of different gradations between straight-ahead and almost-out-of-tempo. This approach, quite distinct from either Ornette Coleman's rhythm-section with Charlie Haden or John Coltrane's, made a considerable impact on Miles Davis's 1963 group and, through them, on nearly everyone else. [BP]

Hampton Hawes, *Four!* (1958), Contemporary/OJC; Bill Evans, *Waltz for Debby* (1961), Riverside/OJC

Lafitte, Guy, tenor sax. b. St Gaudens, France, 12 January 1927. First became active in Toulouse area, then toured nationally with Big Bill Broonzy (1951), Mezz Mezzrow (1951–2), Bill Coleman–Dickie Wells (1952). Based in Paris from 1954, led own groups regularly and appeared with American musicians such as Emmett Berry (1956), Lionel Hampton (1959), Coleman (1973) and Wild Bill Davis (1985). Lafitte is a notably forthright soloist, whose early allegiance to Coleman Hawkins is particularly noticeable in terms of his tone quality. But his individuality has matured with the passing years and his playing, now sometimes spiced with the inflections of r & b, seems totally effortless. [BP]

Body and Soul (1978), Black & Blue

Lagrene, Bireli, guitar, electric bass. b. Alsace, France, 4 September 1966. A child prodigy on guitar (he was successfully recording by the age of 13), Lagrene has become known as an 'infant Django' to a generation of jazz fans who still regret Reinhardt's early death. Lagrene's background – he was born a Sinti gypsy and lives still in a caravan – uncannily resembles Reinhardt's, and so does his prodigious talent: he took up guitar at four and, encouraged by his father Fiso Lagrene, a well-known guitarist of the 1930s, was playing jazz by the time he was seven. In his teens he began touring Europe with musicians such as Diz Disley and Denny Wright and produced a string of beautifully produced solo albums, revealing his faultless technique, mature imagination and, above all, a rapidly-developing style which takes in contemporary musical trends as much as it harks back to the music of Reinhardt's era. [DF]

Routes to Django (1980), Island

Laine, Cleo (Clementina Dinah Campbell), voice. b. Southall, Middlesex, 27 October 1927. After singing semi-professionally, worked with Johnny Dankworth Seven and big band (1951–7). After marriage to Dankworth, continued to make guest appearances with band, but mainly involved in various stage shows including *The Seven Deadly Sins* by Kurt Weill, *Show Boat* and *Colette* (co-written by Dankworth) plus many acting-only roles. Since 1972, has undertaken many successful tours of US, including appearances at Carnegie Hall etc. Laine's performances since then have aimed for the middle-of-the-road audience, and her extraordinarily wide vocal range is easily admired. But, especially in her more intimate recordings, the sensitivity and phraseology still derive directly from her love of jazz [BP]

Laine/John Williams, *Best Friends* (1977), RCA

Laine, Papa Jack (George Vital), drums, alto horn, leader. b. New Orleans, 21 September 1873; d. 1 June 1966. Born at the dawn of jazz, Jack Laine – called 'Papa' because he was a father-figure to dozens of young white New Orleans jazzmen – formed his own ragtime band in 1888 and soon after was leading his own Reliance Brass Bands. Most of the later great names of early white jazz (Nick La Rocca and Tom Brown are two famous examples) worked with one of Laine's several bands, as did some of the best light-skinned 'Creoles of colour' such as clarinettist Achille Baquet. The demand for Laine's services around New Orleans was intense, and for a long time he exercised a monopoly in supplying live music for white upper-class New Orleans society and all over the neighbouring Gulf Coast States. Laine's bands played ragtime, by ear, and continued their successful spell until 1917 when he retired from music: his son Alfred was bandleading in New Orleans until the 1940s. During the revival of the 1940s and 1950s Laine – now tall, thinning and snowy-haired – was a familiar and revered figure. Records of Papa Laine's Children were reissued on various labels as well as a 'talking record', the forerunner of taped sessions, in the 1960s for Johnny Wiggs. [DF]

Any on Tempo/Southland labels (1951)

Laird, Rick (Richard Quentin), double-bass, bass-guitar. b. Dublin, 5 February 1941. Started playing piano at five. Family moved to Auckland, New Zealand, where he began playing bass in 1959. He moved to Sydney, Australia, and played with Mike Nock and others. Came to London in early 1960s, studying at the Guildhall School of Music and working with John Dankworth, Tubby Hayes, Ronnie Scott and others. 1966, emigrated to USA, studying at Berklee and working with Charlie Mariano, Phil Woods, Zoot Sims. Toured with Buddy Rich for 18 months. 1971–3, he was with John McLaughlin's first Mahavishnu Orchestra. In the later 1970s he freelanced in New York with John Abercrombie, Nock and many others. In the 1980s he worked with Chuck Wayne and a group called Timepiece, and did some teaching in New York. His main influences are Ray Brown, Paul Chambers and Scott La Faro, and the double-bass is his first love, but it was on bass-guitar that he made the first three trail-blazing albums with the Mahavishnu Orchestra. He has written one book: *Improvising Jazz Bass* (Amsco 1980). [IC]

With Mahavishnu Orchestra, *The Inner Mounting Flame* (1972); *Birds of Fire* (1973); *Between Nothingness and Eternity* (1973), all CBS; with Joe Henderson, *Soft Focus* (1979), Muse

Laka Daisical (Dorota Koc), piano, vocals. b. Oxford, 8 January 1953. Family musical. Piano from age three, cello for four years; played timpani in school orchestra. 1972–84, played with various pop groups, funk bands, small groups and big bands. 1983–5, with Annie Whitehead band. From 1982, with the Guest Stars, an all-women fusion group. Also 1982, organized the first British Women's Jazz Festival. 1984, the Guest Stars' first album was acclaimed in the UK, in September they toured the US East Coast, and December did a short UK tour. 1985, they were support group to Jan Garbarek for his London concert. Favourites, Don Pullen, McCoy Tyner, Betty Carter, Bobby McFerrin, Etta James, Patti Labelle, among others; also Mingus, John Taylor, Aretha Franklin, Annie Whitehead. [IC]

The Guest Stars (1984); *Out at Night* (1985), both Guest Stars; with Annie Whitehead, *Mix Up* (1985), Paladin/Virgin

Lake, Oliver, alto sax, composer, and flute, synthesizer. b. Marianna, Arkansas, 1944. Raised in St Louis. Started on percussion; began on alto in 1960. In the later 1960s he was involved with BAG (Black Artist Group), the St Louis equivalent of Chicago's AACM. Played in Paris in early 1970s. 1974, moved to New York.

1977, co-founder of the *World Saxophone Quartet. [IC]

With WSQ; as leader, *Heavy Spirits* (1975), Arista; *Holding Together* (1976), Black Saint

Lamare, Nappy (Hilton Napoleon), guitar, banjo, vocals. b. New Orleans, 14 June 1907. He began in New Orleans, where he played banjo in bands led by Sharkey Bonano, Monk Hazel and Johnny Wiggs, among others, and toured with Johnny Bayersdorffer and Billy Lustig, before joining Ben Pollack's band – a clearing-house for talent – in 1930. Five years later, Nappy (the nickname came from a childhood habit of over-sleeping) joined Bob Crosby's band of 'Pollack rebels' and for eight now classic years was an irreplaceable part of his rhythm-section. Then came a spell with Eddie Miller's reconstituted band along with working studios in the day, regular bands of his own, a year with Jimmy Dorsey (1948) and from 1947 part ownership of a Los Angeles club, the 47, which lasted until 1951. In 1950, Lamare, with his own band the Straw Hat Strutters, had begun a weekly TV show for KTLA: the successful touring that followed lasted for five years, then Lamare co-led a band with Ray Bauduc, the Riverboat Dandies, which ran a policy of high-entertainment Dixieland and recorded very successfully. From the early 1960s, following a severe car crash, he worked more sparingly but regularly, with Bauduc, clarinettist Joe Darensbourg and for Crosby reunions. In 1975 he toured with a package show, *A Night in New Orleans*, played again for Crosby, and ten years on was still reasonably active. A supremely talented guitarist, he belongs in the class of Carl Kress and Dick McDonough. [DF]

Mr Dixie: Nappy Lamare and his Band (1949), Vogue

See Chilton, John, *Stomp Off Let's Go!* (Jazz Book Services, 1983)

Land, Harold DeVance, tenor sax, flute. b. Houston, Texas, 18 February 1928. Brought up from age five in San Diego, California, worked there with trumpeter Froebel Bingham and used that group on his own first recording (1949). Moved to Los Angeles (1954) and toured nationally with Max Roach–Clifford Brown quintet (1954–5). Regular member of Curtis Counce quintet (1956–8), Gerald Wilson band (1955 onwards), Shorty Rogers Giants (1961), own quintet co-led with Red Mitchell (1961–2). Some studio work and live backing of vocalists (1960s), also composition and arranging. Co-led quintet with Bobby Hutcherson (1969–71, plus European tour 1983), which made several albums with changing rhythm-sections. One of the group's pianists, who has continued to work with his father more recently, is Harold Land Jnr. (b. 25 April 1950).

The tenor-playing Land first came to attention holding his own in the fast company of Roach and Brown, thanks to a thoughtful combination of interesting ideas and an insinuating tone. This somewhat undemonstrative approach was overtaken in the 1960s by a strong Coltrane influence, until he gradually began to achieve a satisfying balance between the two approaches. [BP]

Harold in the Land of Jazz (1958), Contemporary/Boplicity

Lane, Steve, cornet, bandleader. b. London, 7 November 1921. His revivalist band, the Southern Stompers, who have played around Britain's jazz clubs (and further afield) for more than 30 years, have always presented scholarly repertoire, immaculately rehearsed precision and a dedication to authenticity seldom to be found in contemporary bands: Lane himself plays hot cornet, combining discipline with conviction. His partnership in the VJM label, over the years with co-directors John Wadley and Trevor Benwell, has produced classic reissues of historic jazz music with enviable attention to detail as well as regular new albums documenting the progress of his own band, retitled, in 1985, the Red Hot Peppers. [DF]

Lang, Eddie (Salvatore Massaro), guitar. b. Philadelphia, 25 October 1902; d. New York, 26 March 1933. He began his career on violin at seven years old, later studied banjo and guitar, played his first duets with Joe Venuti in school and by 1923 had joined Venuti in pianist Bert Estlow's Atlantic City band. The following year he was with the Scranton Sirens (a hot band that featured the young Dorsey Brothers, and trombonist Russ Morgan), then joined the Mound City Blue Blowers, toured the USA and played a season at London's Piccadilly Hotel. By 1925, back in the USA, he was in constant demand for session work: the first of the twentieth century's new guitar heroes. 'He was the first fellow to do much single string guitar work', acknowledges Crosby (previously the guitar had been a rhythm instrument), and Lang's chiming rococo solo lines were superfast and machine-accurate. Never a great reader, when faced with a complicated big-band arrangement Lang would listen once, then add his own part – 'including the modulations' noted Frankie Trumbauer in wonder – the second time round: he was also a most skilful guitar duettist, recording classics with Carl Kress and (as 'Blind Willie Dunn') with Lonnie Johnson. By 1926, Lang was working with Joe Venuti's band, with Roger Wolfe Kahn's society orchestra (two regular connections all his life), toured with Jean Goldkette's band and when it broke up in New York joined Adrian Rollini's legendary (and short-lived) Club New Yorker band. From 1929, Lang and Venuti were teamed again in Paul Whiteman's orchestra, featured in the film *King of Jazz* in 1930, and from 1932, when Bing Crosby developed his solo career, Eddie Lang was his staff accompanist. In spare hours Lang visited the pool halls ('he made more at pool than he did accompanying me!' said Crosby) and in 1933 recorded classic sides with Venuti as the Blue Five, including 'Raggin' the Scale'. That year chronic throat trouble handicapped him: Crosby persuaded him to have his tonsils out, and Lang died of an embolism under the anaesthetic.

Eddie Lang was the greatest guitarist of his generation, invented a solo vocabulary for the guitar single-handed and was, says Bing Crosby, 'in the opinion of all the guitar players of his day, and many since, the greatest one of the craft that ever lived'. Lang's partnership with violinist Joe Venuti set gold-level standards for chamber jazz and for the format (Django Reinhardt and Stephane Grappelli who later adopted it were usually dismissed as a country-style parody of Venuti–Lang), and Lang's own plangent guitar was only temporarily superseded by the fashionable rise of electric guitar, and Charlie Christian, ten years on. [DF]

Lang/Johnson, *Blue Guitars, vols. 1/2* (1927–9), Parlophone

Lanphere, Don(ald Gale), tenor and soprano sax. b. Wenatchee, Washington, 26 June 1928. Studied music at Northwestern University, Illinois (1945–7), moved to New York at age 19 and made first of two recordings with Fats Navarro (1948). Worked with Woody Herman (1949), Artie Shaw (1949–50), also Claude Thornhill, Charlie Barnet, Billy May and Sonny Dunham. Arrested as a heroin user (1951), he returned home to run family music store and, apart from three years including playing with Herb Pomeroy and Herman again (1959–61) followed by further arrest, remained there until 1980s. His comeback albums beginning in 1982 resulted in playing visits to New York and Kansas City (both 1983) and Europe (1985).

Lanphere was impressed early on by Lester Young and Charlie Parker, his private recordings of whom have been issued on various labels. The great facility and interesting ideas of his own early work have grown considerably in recent performances, which display markedly unpredictable phrasing and a delightfully individual tone. [BP]

From Out of Nowhere (1982), Hep

Larkins, Ellis Lane, piano. b. Baltimore, Maryland, 15 May 1923. An elusive jazz aesthete of unimpeachable taste. His mother was a pianist, his father a violinist, and he was taught privately to a high standard. He made his début with the Baltimore City Colored Orchestra at 11 and was hailed as a prodigy. Graduation from the Peabody Conservatory and Juilliard School followed (a colossal achievement for a black musician at that time), and then Larkins began work as a jazz pianist with Billy Moore, Ed Hall and his own trio around New York, settling into a regular shuttle between the Village Vanguard and the Blue Angel which lasted 20 years (during the period he recorded two classic albums at least: duos with Ella Fitzgerald and Ruby Braff). From 1963, when the rock set in, Larkins worked in studios as a vocal coach and accompanist (including regular work with Joe Williams from 1968): other fine singers who benefited from his knowledge included Anita Ellis, Jane Harvey, Eartha Kitt, Georgia Gibbs and Harry Belafonte. In the 1970s his enormous talents were recorded at length by Ernie Anderson and by Hank O'Neil (with Braff again and alone) for Chiaroscuro, and he began regular club work at venues such as Gregory's and the Carnegie Hall Tavern which went on into the 1980s: commentators who have written sympathetically and knowledgeably about him in recent years include Lee Jeske and Whitney Balliett (see below). A 1980s TV documentary, *Anita Ellis: for the record*, was a rare showcase for Larkins's unobtrusive talents; the piano sound he achieves – pastel-brown, shaded, with interrogative lines and harmonies – is perfectly captured. He returned to his old haunt, the Carnegie Tavern, in autumn 1985. [DF]

Trio (1956), Brunswick/Ace of Hearts

See Balliett, Whitney, *Jelly Roll, Jabbo and Fats* (OUP, 1983)

La Roca, Pete (Peter Sims), drums. b. New York City, 7 April 1938. Born on same day as Freddie Hubbard and equally precocious, La Roca was recommended to Sonny Rollins at age 19 by Max Roach, working with Rollins until the latter retired (1957–9). Then with Jackie McLean (1959, 1961), Tony Scott quartet (1959), Slide Hampton octet (1959–60). Was first drummer of John Coltrane quartet (1960). Led own group (1961–2), also with Art Farmer quartet (1964–5), Freddie Hubbard quintet (1965), Mose Allison (1965), Charles Lloyd quartet (1966). Since that time, has been working under his Anglo name as a lawyer. As La Roca, however, he not only showed enormous promise but was the first person to record a totally free-tempo drum solo (May 1959, on the Jackie McLean album *New Soil*). His remarkably fluid backing of a very varied list of soloists was extremely impressive, and his departure from music a great loss. [BP]

Sonny Rollins, *St Thomas* (1959), Dragon; Art Farmer, *Sing Me Softly of the Blues* (1965), Atlantic

Lateef, Yusef (William Evans), tenor sax, flutes, oboe etc. b. Chattanooga, Tennessee, 1921. Went to school in Detroit, moved to New York (1946) and worked with Lucky Millinder, Hot Lips Page, Roy Eldridge etc. After nearly a year with Dizzy Gillespie band (1949), studied at Wayne University and led own Detroit-based group (1955–9) which made several albums for New York record labels. Again in New York,

Yusef Lateef

worked under own name and briefly with Charles Mingus (1960, 1961) and with percussionist Michael Olatunji (1961–2), then joined Cannonball Adderley sextet (1962–4). From 1964, alternated between leading own quartet/quintet and academic studies; holds MA and doctorate in education, and associate professorship. In the 1980s, has lived and taught in Nigeria.

Lateef's use in the 1950s of first the flute, then the oboe and various 'miscellaneous' instruments (including a 7-Up bottle) marks him as one of the earliest diversified talents. Though ultimately less dedicated to multi-instrumental excellence than Eric Dolphy or the generation who followed him, Yusef is certainly a brilliant flautist. The exotic aspects of his early work were a musical, and ideological, influence on many people such as John Coltrane, who said in 1960: 'Yusef Lateef has been using [Eastern music] in his playing for some time.' Interestingly, his tenor work has always retained the sound of straightahead blues-and-bebop, and indeed some of his late 1960s–1970s albums emphasized this to the point of banality. But when his compositional flair comes into play, and binds together the various strands of his music, the results are extremely impressive. [BP]

Jazz for Thinkers (1957), Savoy; *Live at Pep's* (1964), Impulse; *In Nigeria* (1984), Landmark

Latin Jazz, see AFRO-LATIN.

Laurence, Chris (Christopher Anthony), double bass. b. London, 6 January 1949. Grandmother and her sister harpists; father Tony Laurence a pianist; brother, Patrick Laurence, bassist with LSO. Studied at Royal Junior College of Music and the Guildhall School. Began in the later 1960s with many London-based musicians including Frank Ricotti; in the 1970s with Mike Westbrook orchestra, John Taylor sextet, Mike Pyne sextet; also with Kenny Wheeler's occasional big band and small groups. In the 1980s, also worked in trio format with Tony Oxley and Alan Skidmore, and with Oxley and Tony Coe. Laurence is equally at home with European classical music and with jazz and has always been active in both fields. During the 1980s he played second bass with the Academy of St Martin in the Fields chamber orchestra; from 1984, a member of the London Bach orchestra. His favourite bassist is Miroslav Vitous, and other inspirations are John Taylor, Keith Jarrett, Tony Coe and Chick Corea. A virtuoso player who is massively dependable. [IC]

With Ricotti, Norma Winstone, Taylor, Skidmore and others; with London Jazz Composers' orchestra, *Ode* (1972), Incus; with John Surman, *Morning Glory* (1972), Island; Coe/Oxley/Laurence & Co., *Nutty on Willisau* (1983), Hat Art

Laurie, Cy (Cyril), clarinet, vocals, leader. b. London, 20 April 1926. Originally a Johnny Dodds disciple, he worked around the London jazz clubs with his quartet, featuring Les Jowett (tpt) and Fred Hunt (pno), and by the early 1950s was producing influential albums such as *Cy Laurie Blows Blue-hot* (Esquire). His band, by a year or so later, achieved phenomenal success based at their Windmill Street premises – the 'Cy Laurie all-night raves' are still well-remembered by greying jazz *aficionados* – and with the added advantage of a first-class publicity agent Les Perrin (who later worked for the Beatles) produced a string of records which achieved best-selling status in jazz terms. 'Cy's band attracted and held all of Humph's disappointed revivalist fans,' points out George Melly, 'and won the adherence of the self-styled beatniks too.' Chris Barber's rise to fame was inexorable, however, and in 1960 Laurie left music to study meditation in India; little more was heard from him until the end of the 1960s. From then on he played regularly around the London jazz scene, briefly joined the Blackbottom Stompers, formed a regular band to work in the Essex area and for a time led a quintet with saxophonist Eggy Ley. By the 1980s he had based himself in the Southend area, working with musicians such as Terry Pitts (tmb), Hugh Rainey (banjo) and Dennis Field (cornet): *Shades of Cy* was his first album for 25 years. In 1985 he was touring Britain and Europe as a soloist and a show, *Mardi Gras*, in which he co-starred with Ken Colyer and Max Collie, sold out every venue it played. [DF]

Shades of Cy (1984), Sunstreamer

Laws, Hubert, flute, composer, and sax, guitar, piano. b. Houston, Texas, 10 November 1939.

Brother, Ronnie Laws (b. 3 October 1950), plays tenor and soprano sax. First professional job at 15 with Jazz Crusaders, staying with them until 1960. Also played symphonic music in his teens. During the 1960s he played with Mongo Santamaria, Gunther Schuller's Orchestra USA, Sergio Mendes, Lena Horne, Benny Golson, Jim Hall, James Moody, Clark Terry and many others. During the early 1970s he established an international reputation leading his own groups and touring world-wide. Laws was a member of the Metropolitan Opera orchestra, 1968–73, and also worked with the New York Philharmonic, 1971–4: he is a virtuoso player equally at home with jazz and classical music. Laws has attempted to create jazz adaptations of some classical music – compositions by Bach, Mozart, Debussy, Stravinsky, Ravel, Satie and others, and he has also made many jazz-rock and fusion records. He has won many jazz polls, and is in great demand as a studio musician. His early influences were Miles Davis, Gil Evans, Herbie Hancock, John Coltrane, Wes Montgomery, among others. [IC]

With Quincy Jones and others; *Wild Flower* (1972), Atlantic; *Afro-Classic* (1973), CTI; *At Carnegie Hall* (1974), CTI

Lawson, Yank (John Rhea), trumpet. b. Trenton, Missouri, 3 May 1911. He took up the trumpet in his teens, played with college bands and worked his way round the South with Wingy Manone before joining the Ben Pollack band, replacing Sterling Bose, in 1933. Two years later – following a famous disagreement over Pollack's determination to feature his girlfriend as band singer – Lawson freelanced in New York and then joined Bob Crosby's band, 1935–8. He left after a financial dispute with Gil Rodin, Crosby's business manager, and moved to Tommy Dorsey (who, as often, let his new sideman write his own cheque): the stay lasted a year, after which Lawson freelanced, worked briefly with Crosby again (1941), then with Benny Goodman, and from 1942 to 1968 continuously in New York studios and subsequently clubs. Like Manny Klein and Pee Wee Erwin, Lawson is a player of enormous strength, versatility and trained orthodox technique. From 1950 his trademarks – harmon-to-open muted technique, hectoring phrasing, a frank vibrato and (often muted) feeling for the blues recalling King Oliver – were paraded on marvellous records by the Lawson–Haggart Jazz Band, at Crosby reunions, in jazz clubs, on tour and from 1968 with the World's Greatest Jazz Band, where Lawson's acid, driving creations sat perfectly back-to-back with the shifting, more overt lyricism of Billy Butterfield. He was also regularly featured with Bob Crosby reunions and in the 1980s co-led the Lawson–Haggart band again, toured Europe as a soloist and played jazz festivals. Lawson's trumpet – more than any other instrument or player – *is* the sound of Bob Crosby's Bobcats. [DF]

See Chilton, John, *Stomp Off Let's Go!* (Jazz Book Services, 1983)

Laylan, Rollo, drums. b. Wisconsin, *c.* 1910. A capable big-band drummer (from 1938 he worked with Bunny Berigan, Paul Whiteman and, after the war, as relief drummer for Ray McKinley), Laylan led a highly successful Dixieland band in Florida under the title Preacher Rollo's Five Saints. They achieved a reasonable degree of fame on an international basis, recorded prolifically and, at various times, included such fine players as Tony Parenti (clt), Marie Marcus (piano) and a neglected cornettist, Tommy Justice. Laylan left professional music in the early 1970s. [DF]

Lee, Dave (David), piano, arranger, composer, vocals, leader. b. London, 12 August 1930. He won the *Melody Maker* poll for top jazz pianist when he was 16, and soon after joined John Dankworth's orchestra, with which he toured the USA and recorded prolifically. By the 1960s he was well established with his own trio, worked as musical director for Judy Garland for four years, issued a number of best-selling albums (including *New Big Band from Britain*, which was in the 'Cashbox' Top Ten for six weeks) and rapidly broadened his experience working as MD for TV shows such as That Was the Week That Was, BBC3, Not So Much a Programme etc. Lee's compositions also became famous: he wrote the scores for the musical *Our Man Crichton* (1965) and the film *The Solid Gold Cadillac* (1956) and a best-selling hit for Peter Sellers and Sophia Loren, 'Goodness Gracious Me' in *The Millionairess* (1960). In the 1980s he was still busily involved in writing for revue (a late hit was the theme tune for the long-running BBC TV programme That's Life) but re-emerged as a solo act at London venues such as Pizza on the Park and the Hampstead Theatre. Lee is a marvellous eclectic pianist whose work runs from Bud Powell to Earl Hines with equal ease. [DF]

Jazz Improvisations of 'Our Man Crichton' (1965), Colpix

Lee, Julia, piano, vocals, composer. b. Boonesville, Missouri, 31 October 1902; d. Kansas City, Missouri, 8 December 1958. She was the sister of George E. Lee, who led a novelty band which in the early 1930s worked in competition with McKinney's Cotton Pickers. Julia sang regularly with her brother's band until it broke up in 1934 (she also worked as a single on occasion) and then spent 14 years working clubs on Kansas City's 12th Street, sometimes with a drummer helping out. In 1944 she was 'discovered' by Capitol talent scout Dave Dexter, who recorded her regularly, first with Jay McShann's and Tommy Douglas's bands, later under the banner of Julia Lee's Boyfriends: the 'boyfriends' included such great men as Benny Carter, Ernie Royal, Vic Dickenson, Red Norvo, Red Nichols, Nappy Lamare and Douglas, and the salty songs they recorded (usually Lee's own compositions such as 'King Size Papa', 'Snatch it and grab it' and the immortal 'I didn't like it the first time!') often turned into hits. Julia Lee continued to work in Kansas City for most of the rest of her life, except for a year in Los Angeles, 1949–50. With artists such as Nellie Lutcher and Louis Jordan, her music represents one early transition for jazz towards rock and roll. [DF]

Party Time! (1947), Capitol

Lee, Phil (Philip Robert), guitar. b. London, 8 April 1943. Parents both musical, but he was self-taught. Played with various London-based groups in the 1960s including the Graham Collier sextet. Since the early 1970s has played with Henry Lowther's groups. In the mid-1970s was co-leader, with Tony Coe, of Axel. Also works with Michael Garrick and Jeff Clyne. 1979, toured with the Michel Legrand quartet; 1983, with Gordon Beck's nonet. Compositions: 'Third World Song', 'Your Dancing Toes', 'The Right Moment', 'Chapter One', 'Your Eyes are Love'. Lee's favourite guitarists range from Jim Hall and Wes Montgomery to John McLaughlin and Pat Metheny, and other influences are Bill Evans, Herbie Hancock and Charlie Parker. [IC]

With Tony Coe, *Zeitgeist* (1976), EMI; with Gilgamesh, *Another Fine Tune You've Got Me Into* (1978), Charly; with Andrew Boiarsky, *Play South of the Border* (1980), Spotlite

Leeman, Cliff (Clifford), drums. b. Portland, Maine, 10 September 1913; d. 29 April 1986. After work as a teenage percussionist with the Portland Symphony Orchestra he joined Artie Shaw at the State Ballroom, New York (he plays on all Shaw's hit records), then worked for Glenn Miller, Tommy Dorsey, Charlie Barnet and Woody Herman – a succession of great bandleaders at some of their peak years. 1944, at Charlie Shavers's instigation, he joined John Kirby's band (replacing O'Neill Spencer) and doubled with Raymond Scott's famous and short-lived 'integrated' studio band for CBS which included Johnny Guarnieri, Ben Webster, Trummy Young and Shavers. From 1945, Leeman worked with, among others, Jimmy Dorsey, Glen Gray's Casa Lomans, Jean Goldkette and Barnet again (this time uncomfortably, amid Barnet's reluctant bebop policy) and from 1950 was active in studios. From then his huge love and talent for Dixieland drums surfaced as he worked for Eddie Condon, Pee Wee Erwin, Billy Butterfield, Wild Bill Davison and the Dukes of Dixieland: his performance in this area was gold-standard and a lifelong influence on younger Europeans such as Lennie Hastings and Tony Allen. In the 1970s Leeman worked with Bobby Hackett, Joe Venuti, the World's Greatest Jazz Band, the European touring group the Kings of Jazz (featuring Pee Wee Erwin and Bernie Privin) and at Dick Gibson's Colorado parties: in the 1980s despite occasional hearing problems his gifts were undiminished, until kidney failure ended his life.

Cliff Leeman, whose formative years were spent in the shadow of Gene Krupa, had neither Krupa's flash nor the troubled intellectual image that somehow endeared Dave Tough to his followers. In every other way, though, he was their equal: he was one of the greatest classic drummers, and his records are preserved at Washington's Smithsonian Institution as the example of 20th-century jazz drums. [DF]

Bobby Hackett, *String of Pearls* (1970), Vogue (double)

Lemer, Pepi (Stephanie), voice. b. Ilfracombe, Devon, 25 May 1944. Her father sang in Russian choirs. She had singing lessons from the age of five with classical teachers, then went to stage school, studying singing and dancing, which led to theatrical work and cabaret in the UK and abroad. She has worked with John Stevens's SME, her then husband Pete Lemer's E, Keith Tippett's Centipede, Mike Gibbs, Barbara Thompson's Paraphernalia, and done session work with rock/pop stars including Alan Price and Mike Oldfield. During the 1970s she co-led Turning Point with Jeff Clyne; 1981, they did an Arts Council UK tour with featured guests, Allan Holdsworth and Neil Ardley. Her favourite singers are Urszula Dudziak, Ella Fitzgerald, Billie Holiday and Lambert, Hendricks and Ross, and Miles Davis is also an influence. Pepi Lemer has a very wide range, being able to handle anything from a popular song to the most difficult abstract lines and free improvisation. [IC]

The Shakespeare Birthday Celebration album recorded at Southwark Cathedral, London, *Will Power* (1974), Argo; with Turning Point, *Creatures of the Night* (1977); *Silent Promise* (1978), both Gull

Lemer, Pete (Peter Naphtali), piano, electric piano, synthesizers. b. London, 14 June 1942. He had private classical piano lessons when young, then went to the Royal Academy of Music, London. He later studied with Jack Goldzweig and took lessons from Paul Bley and Jaki Byard. During his first professional engagement in Haifa, Israel (1963), with Tony Crombie and Jeff Clyne, the latter introduced him to the music of Ornette Coleman and Scott La Faro. Back in London, began leading his own groups – trio, quartet, quintet, and E. Since the mid-1960s he has played with most leading UK musicians and groups including Barbara Thompson's Paraphernalia and Jubiaba, Harry Beckett, Don Rendell, SME, Amalgam, Baker Gurvitz Army, Mike Oldfield, Annette Peacock, Neil Ardley, Mike Westbrook. His favourite pianists range from Ellington, Zawinul and Twardzik to Sun Ra, Stevie Wonder and Meade Lux Lewis, and other influences are Coltrane and Ornette Coleman. Lemer's own concept covers a similarly broad spectrum and he is perfectly at home with free jazz, conventional jazz, or rock. He is also an excellent composer. [IC]

Quintet, *Local Color* (1965), ESP; with Annette Peacock, *X Dreams* (1978), Aura; with Pierre Moerlin's Gong, *Time is the Key* (1979), Arista; Peter Lemer avec la Troupe Populaire de G'Naoua de Asilah, *Asilah 80* (1980), limited edition by the Association Culturelle al Mouhit

Lemon, Brian, piano, arranger. b. Nottingham, 11 February 1937. He came south from Nottingham in the mid-1950s to join Freddy Randall's band, then moved to saxophonist Betty Smith's quintet. He quickly became the centre of attention among British mainstreamers – including the aristocratic echelons that included Kenny Baker, George Chisholm and their peers – and after a spell with the Fairweather–Brown All Stars began working all over; in Danny Moss's quartet, Dave Shepherd's quintet and small groups led by George Chisholm *et al.*, as well as subbing for Dudley Moore at the Establishment and accompanying an eclectic selection of visiting Americans (including Milt Jackson, Charlie Shavers, Ben Webster, Harry Edison, Lockjaw Davis, Buddy Tate and others), often at Ronnie Scott's Club. 'Professor' Lemon has long been a British figurehead for jazz piano playing that is correct in every vital musical aspect, taste, time and inspiration, and he works as easily with post-bebop players as he does with Dixieland music (for which he admits a special fondness). In latter years he has played for Benny Goodman, shared TV programmes with Ray Brown, organized his own small groups and large string ensembles for BBC sessions and worked with Alex Welsh and Peter Boizot's Pizza All Stars. [DF]

Our Kind of Music (1970), 77

Le Sage, Bill (William A.), piano, accordion, vibraphone, percussion. b. London, 20 January 1927. Self-taught, but had eight lessons with Lennie Tristano. 1945, his own sextet and with Johnny Dankworth quintet. 1945–8, played in army bands. 1950–3, with the Johnny Dankworth Seven, 1953–4, with Dankworth's big band. 1954–61, with Tony Kinsey trio; 1961–5, with Ronnie Ross. Since then he has led trios and quintets of his own, worked with many UK musicians, and also with leading US jazzmen such as Dizzy Gillespie, Benny Goodman, Red Rodney. Le Sage is also a composer/arranger and has written for various TV series. [IC]

With Dankworth Seven and Big Band, Tony Kinsey and Ronnie Ross; *Directions in Jazz* (1964), Philips; *Road to Ellingtonia* (1965), Philips; *Martin Drew Band* (1977), Lee-Lambert; with Dankworth quintet, *Gone Hitch-in* (1983), Sepia Repertoire

Lesberg, Jack, bass. b. Boston, 14 February 1920. From 1945 he doubled a bass chair in the New York Symphony Orchestra (under Leonard Bernstein) with a five-year residency at Eddie Condon's. From 1950, when he began freelancing, Lesberg's all-round talent took him at various times to Louis Armstrong's All Stars, on tour with Earl Hines and Jack Teagarden's band in 1957 to England, and regularly in and out of studios as a busy session man. His appearances on record are countless and in 1985 – a veteran of New York's club scene – he was still busy touring with the Eddie Condon Reunion Band, featuring Tom Artin, Ed Polcer, Kenny Davern, Keith Ingham and Oliver Jackson. [DF]

Any Lesberg record

Letman, Johnny (John Bernard), trumpet. b. McCormick, South Carolina, 6 September 1917. He first worked with Nat Cole in 1934 and through the 1940s with a succession of good big bands including those of Horace Henderson, Phil Moore, Lucky Millinder, Cab Calloway and Count Basie in 1951. In the 1950s he worked around with Eddie Condon, Wilbur de Paris, Claude Hopkins and others and led his own bands (an appearance on a highly-rated late 1950s collection, *Cascade of Quartets*, caused a stir at the time): by 1968 he was touring France with Tiny Grimes. In the 1970s he was still busy freelancing and sessions produced in New York at the period deserve to be issued. A fine strong-blowing trumpeter, Letman's recorded appearances are rare but his full sound, easy-flowing ideas and rhythmic drive make the search for his work worth while. [DF]

Any Letman record

Levallet, Didier, double-bass, composer, band leader. b. Arly sur Cure, France, 19 July 1944. Studied journalism at L'École Supérieure de Journalisme de Lille, 1963–6; studied bass briefly at Lille Conservatory, but otherwise self-taught. Professional début in Paris, 1969, working in clubs with Ted Curson, Chris Woods, George Arvanitas, Siegfried Kessler, Hank Mobley, Mal Waldron and others; toured France with Johnny Griffin, Kenny Clarke, Slide Hampton; 1970–7, worked with a free jazz quartet, Perception, touring in France, Belgium, Germany, Norway. 1976, founded and led ADMI (Association pour le Développement de la Musique Improvisée); also played in USA with saxist Byard Lancaster. Since the later 1970s, has formed and composed for several groups with unusual instrumentation, often using strings and including Didier Lockwood, Steve Lacy, Tony Coe, Marc Charig, Radu Malfatti, Tony Oxley. Levallet also played during the early 1980s with Archie Shepp, Frank Lowe and Chris MacGregor's Brotherhood of Breath. The Levallet–Marais–Pifarely string trio has joined 'A Little Westbrook Music' for concerts and festivals in France and the UK (1985–6), and with reed player Louis Sclavis is half of the Tony Oxley–Didier Levallet double quartet project (Bracknell, 1984, Paris, 1985, UK tour, March 1986). Levallet is also active in education, teaching at L'École Nationale de Musique in Angoulême. Since 1977, he has organized a week of workshops and concerts every summer in Cluny. 1975, he won the Académie du Jazz Boris Vian Prize for the Perception album *Mestari*; 1980, he won the same award for *Swing String System*. Favourites are Charlie Haden and Gary Peacock; other inspirations are Mingus, Ellington, Gil Evans. [IC]

Perception (1971), Futura; *Swing String System* (1978), Evidence; quintet, *Ostinato* (1981), In and Out; Levallet/Marais/Pifarely, *Instants Chavirés* (1982), Open; octet, *Scoop* (1983), In and Out; quintet, *Quiet Days* (1985), Evidence

Levine, Bobby 'Lips', clarinet, bass clarinet, saxes. b. Easton, Pennsylvania, 9 April 1923. He was a regular at Capitol Records for most of their greatest post-war years and made the rounds of a classy selection of contemporary big bands including Billy Butterfield's, Sam Donahue's recreated Tommy Dorsey Orchestra, Warren Covington (with whom he toured England), Vaughn Monroe, Sammy Kaye, Tex Beneke and Art Mooney, as well as playing for fine small groups led by Chris Griffin, trumpeter Ben Ventura, Parke Frankenfield (whom he first joined in 1954) and latterly Bob Crosby. 1974, he appeared with Sy Oliver in a Tommy Dorsey tribute at Carnegie Hall: 1985, he won the 'All Star Award' (for reeds) with Frankenfield's band at Sacramento's enormous jazz festival. An underrated talent. [DF]

Ben Ventura and the New York Jazz (1982), CP

Levine, Henry 'Hot Lips', trumpet. b. London, 26 November 1907. He lived in New York from the age of six months, learned the bugle in a Boy Scout troop, was taught by Max Schlossberg, graduated to trumpet soloist in Brooklyn Boys' High School, and thereafter worked with bands all over New York (a close friend then was trumpeter Phil Napoleon). From 1926 he replaced Nick La Rocca in the Original Dixieland Jazz Band, played with Vincent Lopez, and in 1927 joined Ambrose's band in London. Back in New York he worked for theatre orchestras and bandleaders, and from 1940, as a staffman for NBC, directed the Chamber Music Society of Lower Basin Street, an in-house Dixieland band which had its own programme, Strictly Dixie, and recorded with Dinah Shore, Jelly Roll Morton and others: the band included Levine, Gene Traxler (bass), Al Philburn (tmb) and Tony Colucci (gtr). In later years Levine became MD for Radio NBK and NBC TV in Cleveland and continued bandleading in Miami, Florida and Las Vegas. Now in retirement Levine deserves to be more widely known. [DF]

Chamber Music Society of Lower Basin Street (1940–1), RCA

Levitt, Rod(ney Charles), trombone, composer, arranger. b. Portland, Oregon, 16 September 1929. A member of Dizzy Gillespie big band (1956–7) and Gil Evans band (1959), Levitt made his living through studio work. Early 1960s, he formed his own octet with other studio-based players such as pianist Sy Johnson and trumpeters Rolf Ericson or Bill Berry, which made several concert appearances and four delightful albums. Now hard to find, the records feature a wide range of material, all written or arranged by Levitt himself and showing an intelligent blend of musicality and humour with influences as varied as Evans, Mingus and 1920s jazz. [BP]

Insight (1964), RCA

Lewis, George (George Louis Francis Zeno), clarinet, alto sax. b. New Orleans, 13 July 1900; d. 31 December 1968. He heard his first jazz early on as it blew across from neighbouring dance halls (Hope's was across the street) and bought his first clarinet around 1917 for $4. By 1919 he was working in brass bands, and small groups including trumpeter Buddy Petit, whom he idolized. Like Petit – and many other fine New Orleans players – Lewis never made the ambitious trip North and upriver to Chicago. All through the 1920s he led bands in New Orleans with Henry 'Red' Allen, Chris Kelly, Arnold Dupas and Sam Morgan, as well as Evan Thomas (another Lewis favourite, who was murdered onstage, alongside him, in 1932). In the 1930s came work with Kid Howard, Billie and Dee Dee Pierce and others and a period when Lewis – a convinced clarinettist – found himself out of instrumental fashion ('everyone was saxophone crazy then', he remembered later). By the end of the decade he was still playing regularly at night – with Jim Robinson, Lawrence Marrero, Howard and others – but working as a stevedore by day.

In 1941 researcher William Russell came to New Orleans, in search of the real jazz and Bunk Johnson, and at trombonist Robinson's suggestion, Lewis played clarinet on a 1942 recording session: a brief but memorable partnership with

Johnson was forged. For the next five years – with and without his new partner – Lewis played on and recorded for Russell (classics from the period include the 1944 'American Music' series with Johnson, Lewis-led masterpieces such as 'Burgundy Street Blues', recorded in his bedroom after an accident, and titles with Avery Kid Howard and others) and in 1945 took a band to New York to play a season at Stuyvesant Casino, a new venue opened for jazz by Russell and Gene Williams and starring Bunk Johnson. The band became a centrepoint for a new breed of post-war intellectual jazz followers who saw it as a vital restatement of the music's best and most honest qualities. The triumph lasted only a year: Johnson wanted to play with swing-style musicians, and Lewis wanted to go home. In 1946 he took his band back to New Orleans and the year after began a local residency at Manny's Tavern.

After Johnson's death in 1949 revivalist intellectualism needed a new saviour. In 1950 *Look* magazine ran a feature on Lewis ('The best New Orleans band in New Orleans'), his band moved up to Bourbon Street (New Orleans' commercial music centre) and from then on he was to remain the frail figurehead for hardline jazz revivalism. By 1952 he had left New Orleans again with his band, began an unrelenting round of major venues such as Beverly Cavern, Los Angeles, and San Francisco's Hangover Club (at $1000 a week), acquired a full-time manager, Dorothy Tait (she wrote his biography, *Call Him George*, under the pseudonym Jay Alison Stuart in 1961), and from the mid-1950s toured Europe and Japan as a soloist or in ensemble (in 1957 and 1959 he came to Britain, first with Ken Colyer then with his own venerable group). For much of his later life Lewis was musically a controversial figure. For lovers of New Orleans jazz everywhere he was often a Christ-figure: his music achieved a simple beauty which was otherworldly in its lack of artifice. Yet the natural occasional fallibilities which followed from the fact that Lewis was a natural talent, rather than a highly sophisticated one, often met with brickbats, even from his admirers. An occasional tendency to play out of tune was blamed on lack of judgement, rather than his obliging agreement to record with pianos that in the hot New Orleans climate were a semitone flat. And Lewis's musical philosophy was different from that of Dixieland, not simply a peasant simplification. 'It shouldn't be just one chorus ensemble then everybody takes down', he told Tom Bethell. 'It's a conversation: if you've got six men playing together then you've got a full band – enough to fit in everything. And it's rough music! You don't want nothin' smooth in it.' 'When I play music I like those people around me,' he said, 'especially people dancing. Then you don't think too much!' [DF]

George Lewis Plays Hymns (1964), Milneburg

See Bethell, Tom, *George Lewis: a Jazzman from New Orleans* (University of California Press, 1977)

Lewis, George, trombone, composer. b. Chicago, 1952. Took up trombone age nine, while at school, and three years later was copying tenor sax solos from a Lester Young–Oscar Peterson trio album. He took a BA in philosophy at Yale, playing with the Anthony Davis sextet while he was there. Entered the AACM School in 1971, and was taught theory by Muhal Richard Abrams. This experience led him, in 1973, to commit himself totally to music. He rapidly became a virtuoso on the trombone with terms of reference that covered everything from the tailgate style of classic jazz to the fleet lines of bebop to abstraction and the multiphonics (playing more than one note simultaneously) pioneered by Albert Mangelsdorff. Lewis has stated that the major influences on his playing are saxophonists Coltrane, Young and Parker, and in the 1970s he was also practising exercises out of Eddie Harris's saxophone books. Early 1976, he spent two months with the Count Basie band, which put the finishing touches to his basic education. Winter of 1976, he began his long and fruitful association with Anthony Braxton. He has also worked and recorded with Evan Parker, Derek Bailey, Dave Holland and others. He has toured Europe and Japan with Gil Evans, and also played with Randy Weston. [IC]

With Roscoe Mitchell, Anthony Davis, Anthony Braxton; as leader *Solo Trombone Record* (1976), Sackville; *Chicago Slow Dance* (1977), Lovely Music; *Homage to Charles Parker* (1979), Black Saint; with Evan Parker, *From Saxophone and Trombone* (1980); with Company (Bailey/Parker/Holland) *Fables* (1980); with Parker/Barry Guy/Paul Lytton, *Hook, Drift and Shuffle* (1983), all Incus

Lewis, John Aaron, composer, arranger, piano. b. La Grange, Illinois, 3 May 1920. After army service (1942–5), replaced Thelonious Monk in Dizzy Gillespie band at suggestion of Kenny Clarke (1946–8); following band's European tour, he and Clarke remained a few months in Paris. Also sat in and recorded with Charlie Parker (1947, 1948), arranged for and appeared (1948) with Miles Davis 9-piece band. Toured with Illinois Jacquet group (1948–9) and Lester Young quartet (1950–1). Much freelance recording with such as J. J. Johnson, Zoot Sims, Parker, Davis, singer King Pleasure etc. First recordings of Milt Jackson quartet (1951–2) with Lewis, Clarke and Ray Brown, the original rhythm-section of the Gillespie band, led to public appearances and then full-time Modern Jazz Quartet (1954, with Percy Heath instead of Brown and, from 1955, Connie Kay replacing Clarke); Lewis became musical director, composing or arranging all their material.

He also wrote soundtrack music for *No Sun in Venice* (1957) and *Odds Against Tomorrow* (1959), and for ballets, stage plays, TV documentaries. Was involved in forming Jazz and Classical Music Society (mid-1950s) and

Orchestra USA (1962–6), both ensembles comprising players fluent in jazz and European music, and both committed to using newly written 'third stream' compositions. Late 1950s, he organized jazz summer schools at Music Inn, and was musical adviser to Monterey Festival (1958–82). After Modern Jazz Quartet disbanded (1974), became professor of music at City College, New York (1977–) and, since 1980, has received honorary doctorates from University of New Mexico, Columbia College in Chicago and New England Conservatory. Reunion concert of MJQ (Japan, 1981) led to regular concert tours from summer 1982 onwards.

Lewis's reputation is identified almost totally with the Quartet, and his promising early compositions 'Two Bass Hit' for Gillespie and 'Rouge' for Davis were both re-written for the group, as 'La Ronde' and 'Delaunay's Dilemma' respectively. His choice of instrumentation, and the watercolour textures it produces, seem entirely appropriate to the dispassionate counterpoint of his pseudo-baroque writing. The key element in the Quartet is, in fact, not Milt Jackson but Lewis's own piano playing, delicate and even tentative as if picking at a dish he would rather not eat; even at his most convincing, he doesn't scintillate so much as insinuate. The fact that he has popularized a whole area of Bach-goes-to-town superficiality was acknowledged when the MJQ recorded an album with the Swingle Singers, and more recently Lewis (without the Quartet) has emulated his own imitator Jacques Loussier by tackling Bach's '48'. Among fellow musicians his very distinctive work seems to have aroused little enthusiasm, nor even very much hostility, although the tune 'Django' (in memory of Django Reinhardt) soon became a standard; jazz listeners, on the other hand, tend to be strongly divided about Lewis. [BP]

Modern Jazz Quartet, *Django* (1952–54), Prestige/OJC; *Afternoon in Paris* (1956), Atlantic; *The Golden Striker* (1960), Atlantic; *J. S. Bach Preludes and Fugues* (1984), Philips

Lewis, Meade 'Lux', piano, composer. b. Chicago, 4 September 1905; d. Minneapolis, 7 June 1964. The most famous of the boogie performers, he played around Chicago in the 1920s and worked with Albert Ammons in a taxi firm, where they sorted out their ideas on the owner's piano. In 1928, Lewis recorded 'Honky Tonk Train Blues', which was little noticed until recording executive John Hammond heard it and began advertising for Lewis's whereabouts. He was traced through Ammons (by that time Lewis was washing cars for a living) and after Lewis had begun playing regularly again Hammond teamed them both with Pete Johnson in the 1938 Spirituals to Swing Carnegie Hall concert that initiated an international boogie craze. From then on, with Ammons and Johnson and alone, Lewis remained a celebrity, living in California, working in Hollywood, up and down the West coast and for radio and TV. [DF]

Lewis, Mel (Melvin Sokoloff), drums. b. Buffalo, New York, 10 May 1929. Father was professional drummer, Mel began working full-time at 15. With several big bands including Boyd Raeburn (1948) and Stan Kenton (1954–6). Small-group work with Frank Rosolino (1955), Hampton Hawes (1955), own quintet with tenorist Bill Holman (1958). Involved in studio sessions in Los Angeles since leaving Kenton, also toured with Gerry Mulligan band (1960–3), Benny Goodman (1962), and deputized with Dizzy Gillespie quintet (European tour, 1961). Moved back to New York (1963), continuing studio work and forming band of top studio players co-led by Thad Jones (1965–78); originally a once-a-week venture, the band toured Europe in 1969, 1973, 1976, 1978 and, as it undertook more US work in the 1970s, employed younger, less well-known musicians. When Jones left (1978), Lewis continued to lead the Jazz Orchestra with further arrangements contributed by Bob Brookmeyer etc. Though often heard with small groups on record, less frequently in public, Lewis is thought of as pre-eminently a big-band drummer. His ability to underline and drive forward a complicated ensemble has been valued by many different leaders and is the equal of some more renowned players. [BP]

Mel Lewis and Friends (1976), Horizon; *Make Me Smile* (1982), Finesse

Lewis, Ramsey, piano, electric keyboards, synthesizers, composer. b. Chicago, 27 May 1935. Private piano lessons from age six; also studied at Chicago Music College and De Paul University. 1956, formed his own trio with bassist Eldee Young and drummer Red Holt, recording his first album for Argo Records (later renamed Chess Records). Lewis also recorded with Sonny Stitt, Clark Terry, Max Roach and others in the late 1950s. His trio album made a strong impact and in 1959 he played Randall's Island Jazz Festival, New York, followed by a residency at Birdland. 1965, he had a big hit with the title track of his LP *The In Crowd*, and both the single and the album gained gold discs for selling over a million copies. Lewis said; 'In June of 1965 we were earning something like $1,500 to $2,000 a week. By September we were earning something like $15,000 to $25,000 a week . . . After that we started finding problems with each other, dissension set in and then that trio broke up.' He formed a new trio, continued with Chess through the 1960s, then signed with CBS in 1971. Lewis's original influences were John Lewis, Oscar Peterson, Bud Powell and Art Tatum, but since the early 1970s he has produced MOR, easy-listening disco music. [IC]

Love Notes (1977); *Les Fleurs* (1983); *Ramsey Lewis/Nancy Wilson* (1984), all CBS

Lewis, Ted (Theodore Leopold Friedman), clarinet, vocals. b. Circleville, Ohio, 6 June 1892; d. New York, 25 August 1971. Known as the 'top-hatted tragedian of jazz', he was the clarinet playing leader of a vaudeville-based band show which was enormously successful over 30 years from 1917 and survived for 20 more after that. Lewis's playing exploited to the full the comedic possibilities of jazz clarinet (so did a lot of other 1920s reedmen, for example Barney Bigard early on, and Wilton Crawley), but it involved technique and kitsch-style: 'I'd never miss seeing Lewis when he came into town. He was fine!', said Coleman Hawkins. 'Lewis made the clarinet talk,' said Eddie Condon (who loathed show-offs), 'and it usually said, "Put me back in the case".' Like him or not, Lewis was hugely popular, and 'Shirt Tail Stomp', an irreverent imitation of his style by Benny Goodman's Boys was quite enough to achieve commercial success on its own: by the late 1920s Lewis – who 'talked' his songs and usually signed off all but his hottest records with a lugubrious 'Is everybody happy?' – was a radio and film star, and earning $10,000 a week. His bands, often staffed by such great jazzmen as Muggsy Spanier (who worked with Lewis for a dozen years off and on), George Brunis and Fats Waller, are fine jazz listening: his career was an important influence on later (sometimes inferior) comedy-based bands such as Harry Roy and Spike Jones. [DF]

Everybody's happy! (1927–31), Epic

Lewis, Willie (William T.), saxes, clarinet, vocals. b. Cleburne, Texas, 10 June 1905; d. New York, 13 January 1971. He was a graduate of European bands such as Will Marion Cook's and for seven years, 1924–31, Sam Wooding's, the best of its kind. After Wooding disbanded, Lewis formed his own orchestra, renamed it Willie Lewis and his Entertainers, and by 1934 had moved into a Paris nightclub, Chez Florence: a year later he was recording for Pathé, featuring such strong soloists as pianist Herman Chittison (a major talent), saxophonist/trumpeter/arranger Benny Carter and in 1936 trumpeter Bill Coleman. Along with other cornermen including Frank 'Big Boy' Goudie (tnr), June Cole (tuba) and George Johnson (alto) – as well as a legendary trumpeter, Arthur Briggs – Lewis's band continued touring and recording until 1941, when after wartime reversals he sailed for home. 'From then on he never made any serious effort to fit into the rapidly changing world of music again' (says Frank Driggs): despite an appearance in a Broadway play *Angel in the Pawnshop* (1951) he did little more in show business and ended up working as a waiter and bartender. [DF]

Willie Lewis and his Entertainers (1935–7), Swing

Ley, Eggy (Derek), soprano and alto sax, vocals, bandleader. b. London, 4 November 1928. He took up soprano saxophone in 1949, and led a top-rated Dixieland band in Germany in 1955–61. After returning to London he joined Radio Luxembourg and played resident at the Tatty Bogle Club (1961–9) before producing for BFBS (1969–83), freelancing and co-leading Jazz Legend (with Hugh Rainey 1973). From 1983 leading his own Hot Shots, Ley turned professional again, ran a 'small' jazz magazine *Jazzin' Around* and successfully recorded and toured abroad. He is one of the pioneers of classic soprano saxophone in Britain. [DF]

Come and Get It (1985), Veloce

Licks Jazz musicians usually begin by copying the phrases of players they like and admire. When a phrase is either copied and learned or habitually repeated, it is a lick. The finest musicians build up a vocabulary of their own rhythmic and melodic phrases – their own licks – and when inspired they can escape from the tyranny of their old licks and create new phrases – which of course may turn into licks. On uninspired occasions, they will of necessity fall back on their store of remembered licks, and this memory bank of phrases is part of every musician's identity, without which it would be impossible to function.

'Hot licks' was a racy term to describe some of the musical clichés of the 'hot' jazz of the 1920s and 1930s. [IC]

Liebman, Dave (David), tenor and soprano sax, flute, composer; also piano and drums. b. Brooklyn, New York, 4 September 1946. Mother musical; piano lessons as a child, then clarinet and later sax; began gigging at 14; inspired and helped by Bob Moses, with whom he was associated from 16. Liebman also studied privately with Joe Allard, Charles Lloyd, Lennie Tristano. He graduated from New York University in the later 1960s with a degree in American historyand a teaching diploma. First professional engagement in 1970 with the rock group Ten Wheel Drive; 1971–3, with Elvin Jones; 1973–4, with Miles Davis. April 1974, he formed his own group, Lookout Farm, with Richie Beirach (keyboards), Frank Tusa (bass), Jeff Williams (dms) and Badal Roy (percussion), which toured and played festivals in the USA and Europe. In the mid-1970s he was also playing in Open Sky, a group he and Bob Moses had first started at the end of the 1960s. Talking of Lookout Farm's music to Chuck Berg, Liebman said: 'I hear New York and I hear the Caribbean. Then, of course, I hear some Middle East stuff . . . And the East Indian with Badal. Then there's the African influence . . . There's the European thing with the acoustic piano, the chords and the way we associate with each other harmonically. In a way, it's a world music with all the elements that we have.'

In the later 1970s and early 1980s, Liebman led a very distinguished quintet with Terumasa Hino (tpt), John Scofield (gtr), Ron McClure (bass) and Adam Nussbaum (dms). The quintet did a two-month tour of Europe in 1979, taking in major festivals, and again toured Europe at the beginning of the 1980s, playing one concert in London. By the mid-1980s Liebman was touring as a soloist and appearing at European festivals with Albert Mangelsdorff, and others, and in 1985 played the Berlin festival with an all-star group led by Swiss trumpeter Franco Ambrosetti. He is also active in jazz education, giving personal tuition and conducting workshops – often internationally with the Jamey Aebersold organisation.

Dave Liebman is steeped in the work of John Coltrane, and other influences are Sonny Rollins, McCoy Tyner, Elvin Jones, Miles Davis and Wayne Shorter. He is one of the most gifted of the post-Coltrane saxophonists, and his work is always shot through with human feeling; his groups have created some of the most vital music of the 1970s and early 1980s. [IC]

With Elvin Jones, Steve Swallow and others; with John McLaughlin, *My Goal's Beyond* (1970), Elektra Musician; with Miles Davis, *Get Up With It* (1974), Columbia; as leader, *Open Sky* (1972), PMR; *Lookout Farm* (1974), ECM; *Spirit in the Sky* (1974), PMR; *Drum Ode* (1974), ECM; *Forgotten Fantasies* (1975), Horizon; quintet, *Doin' It Again* (1979), Timeless

Lightfoot, Terry (Terence), clarinet, alto sax, vocals, leader. b. Potters Bar, Middlesex, 21 May 1935. He formed his first band in 1955, turned professional in late 1956 and by 1959 had established a strong reputation: that year he toured with Kid Ory, played for the BBC's Festival of Jazz at the Royal Albert Hall and made a strong impression with his clean-cut, well-rehearsed act. A headliner through the 'Trad boom' years in Britain (he appeared in Dick Lester's 1962 fantasy *It's Trad Dad* and recorded prolifically for producer Denis Preston and others), Lightfoot set up strong competition to Bilk, Barber and Ball and always surrounded himself with an A-team of sidemen: at various times they included Colin Smith, Alan Elsdon and Dick Hawdon (tpts), John Bennett, Roy Williams, Phil Rhodes (tmb) and Colin Bates (piano). After the 'boom' finished he carried on very successfully through the 1960s, touring clubs and theatres (as well as playing private functions), appeared on radio and TV and for a year (1967–8) joined Kenny Ball. His band of the 1970s featured another strong brass team, Ian Hunter-Randall (tpt) and Mike Cooke (tmb), and stayed busy playing clubs and theatres: Lightfoot himself took on a pub, 1978–83, but never turned his back on performing. By 1983, fully professional again, he was touring with his own shows, recording again and teaming once more with Randall and Rhodes. [DF]

Personal Appearance (*c.* 1975), Windmill

Lincoln, Abe (Abraham), trombone. b. Lancaster, Pennsylvania, 29 March 1907. He began playing trombone at the age of five, played in the California Ramblers (replacing Tommy Dorsey) in 1926 and worked thereafter with a string of famous leaders including Paul Whiteman, Roger Wolfe Kahn and Ozzie Nelson before moving into studio work. In the 1940s and 1950s he was heard often in the company of Matty Matlock and arranger Paul Weston: his explosive contributions to Matlock recording dates for groups such as the Rampart Street Paraders – wide-intervalled, like a souped-up Miff Mole – are a reliable highspot. In the 1960s and 1970s he was still a busy freelance, working, among many others, with Pete Fountain and Wild Bill Davison.

Like Cutty Cutshall and Lou McGarity, Lincoln played for most of his life in the shadow of Jack Teagarden, but his roistering irreverent style and unique sense of humour showed no signs of inferiority, and on one famous date for Bobby Hackett (see below) there's recorded evidence of Lincoln playing Teagarden at his own game and making a home run. [DF]

Bobby Hackett, *Coast Concert* (1955), Capitol

Liston, Melba Doretta, trombone, arranger. b. Kansas City, Missouri, 13 January 1926. Family moved to Los Angeles (1937) where she studied trombone in high school. Played in theatre pit band led by Bardu Ali, former front-man for Chick Webb (1942–4); first arrangements written for this group. Member of Gerald Wilson big band (1944–7), later alongside Wilson in Count Basie band (1948–9). Joined Dizzy Gillespie in last year of one big band, then for whole lifespan of another (1950, 1956–7). Worked in New York and Bermuda with own all-women quintet (1958), and began freelance arranging. One of two women members of Quincy Jones touring band (1959–61, the other being pianist Patti Bown). Thereafter, occasionally active as player but busy as writer, including jazz albums for Randy Weston, Johnny Griffin, Milt Jackson etc, also arranging for singers and TV commercials. Teaching in Harlem and Brooklyn (late 1960s), Watts (early 1970s) and Jamaica, BWI (1974–9). Returned to full-time playing based in New York following second annual Kansas City Women's Jazz Festival (1979). Led 7-piece mixed group, Melba Liston and Company, in early 1980s.

Her 1947 recording with Dexter Gordon gives a favourable indication of Melba's potential as a jazz trombonist, but in her big-band playing she was rarely featured except on ballads. However her arranging, though not always credited, has created a considerable impression from the 1950 Gillespie band onwards. As Liston recalled, Gillespie asked her to bring an arrangement to her first rehearsal with the band, 'And of course they got about two measures and fell out and got all confused and stuff. And Dizzy said, "Now who's the bitch?" ' [BP]

Dexter Gordon, *The Chase* (1947), Spotlite; Randy Weston, *Uhuru Afrika* (1960), Roulette

Little, Booker, Jnr., trumpet. b. Memphis, Tennessee, 2 April 1938; d. 5 October 1961. Part of the 1950s Memphis jazz underground which included George Coleman, Charles Lloyd, pianists Harold Mabern and Phineas Newborn, Little moved to Chicago in 1957. Joined Max Roach (1958) and remained associated with him for most of his brief career, prematurely terminated by uremia. Also recorded and gigged with Mal Waldron, John Coltrane and Eric Dolphy (1960–1). Still highly regarded, despite having no chance to fulfil his great promise, Little had tremendous fluency and a bright, clear sound which, although descended from Clifford Brown, was more emotionally ambiguous. His harmonic approach was similarly adventurous, stretching the bonds of tonality without straining the logic of his lines. [BP]

Victory and Sorrow (1961), Affinity

Littlejohn, Alan, trumpet, fluegelhorn, bandleader. b. London, 4 January 1929. A veteran of the Eric Silk band, he has worked around the British jazz scene for over 30 years, leading a variety of bands including the Littlejohn–Milliner Sextet, featuring Lew Hooper (tenor) and an ambitious eclectic repertoire: in the 1960s they backed a series of visiting Americans, including Earl Hines, Ben Webster and Bill Coleman. Later in the 1970s Littlejohn's Jazzers, a 7-piece Dixieland group, was resident every Sunday at London's 100 Club. In between he worked often with co-trumpeter Al Fairweather, in the Sonny Dee (Stan Daly) Band, among others, and as a touring duo, and all around the club and pub circuit of London on his own as a soloist and sideman. A thorough student of classic jazz, with an infallible ear for what is or isn't good, Littlejohn reflects a natural identification with Billy Butterfield (his close friend) in performance: his fluegelhorn in particular carries the same overt flurries of lyricism that mark Butterfield's best latterday work. [DF]

Sonny Dee, *All Star Band* (c. 1965), SRT Productions

Litton, Martin Nicholas, piano. b. Grays, Essex, 14 May 1957. After a BA(Hons) in music at Colchester Institute, he worked with Steve Lane (1978–80), Harry Gold (1980–3) and, after a freelance period with George Melly, Ken Colyer, singer Johnny M and others, joined Kenny Ball, 1983–5. That year he left Ball and began freelancing, presenting a solo piano section in a 1985 Keith Nichols Jelly Roll Morton concert at Queen Elizabeth Hall, regularly accompanying Kenny Davern on British visits, recording with Kenny Baker and George Chisholm and subbing with Humphrey Lyttelton's band on records and live dates. A strong, sophisticated soloist with an eclectic repertoire and eye to presentation, he works naturally in the musical area of Jelly Roll Morton to Teddy Wilson. [DF]

Lloyd, Charles, saxes, flutes, composer, educator. b. Memphis, Tennessee, 15 March 1938. Began on saxophone at age ten; at first self-taught, later studying with private teachers. As a teenager played alto with r & b bands, including those of B. B. King and Bobby Bland. From 1956, studying composition at University of Southern California. After graduating he taught music until 1961, when he joined Chico Hamilton, switching to tenor sax and playing more flute. 1964–5, worked with the Cannonball Adderley sextet, touring and recording with the group, which brought him to international notice. 1966, he formed his own quartet with Keith Jarrett, Jack DeJohnette and Ron McClure (bass), which rapidly established itself as one of the most dynamic and successful groups of the later 1960s.

Lloyd's early influences were Coleman Hawkins, Ben Webster and Lester Young, and he also became steeped in the work of Sonny Stitt, Sonny Rollins and John Coltrane. By the mid-1960s he was a virtuoso performer whose passionate style incorporated elements from the whole tenor sax tradition, yet was unmistakably contemporary. His rhythm section of brilliant young virtuosi had a similarly broad concept, and the quartet's music covered everything from churchy gospel pieces, to blues, modal music, abstraction and rock. Lloyd and Jarrett did virtually all the composing, but the repertoire included the occasional Lennon and McCartney piece. Lloyd's quartet had a huge success at the Newport and Monterey Jazz Festivals, 1966, and in 1967 was the first jazz group to perform at one of the new cathedrals of rock music – the Fillmore Auditorium in San Francisco. Also 1967, Lloyd and his group were the first US jazz musicians to participate in an arts festival in the USSR. They also played at the International Jazz Festival in Prague, Czechoslovakia. 1966–9, the group toured Europe six times and the Far East once.

1969, Lloyd was the subject of a 60-minute documentary film, *Charles Lloyd – Journey Within*, which was shown at the New York film festival and on educational TV. During the early 1970s he toured and played festivals in the USA, and began undertaking more teaching and academic work. He also became a teacher of transcendental meditation. Since the later 1970s he has kept a low profile, but he did perform with Michel Petrucciani at the Montreux festival, 1982. Lloyd and his first quartet (1966–9), made an immense contribution to jazz at a very difficult time: when the entire scene was dominated by rock music he showed that it was possible to make music which could communicate to young audiences without having to cheapen itself in the process. [IC]

With Hamilton and Adderley; *Dream Weaver* (1965); *Forest Flower* (1966); *Love-In* (1967), all Atlantic

Lockwood, Didier, violin. b. Calais, France, 1956. Father a violin teacher. He began on violin at six, studying at the Conservatoire de Musique de Paris. While there he heard Jimi Hendrix, Johnny Winter and John Mayall, and began playing rock and blues. Jean-Luc Ponty's album with Zappa, *King Kong*, got Lockwood interested in jazz. 1972, at 16, he stopped his formal training, and soon after joined the famous French rock group Magma, recording a live double album with them. He began playing gigs in Paris with Daniel Humair, Aldo Romano and others. At the North Sea Festival he met Zbigniew Seifert and Stephane Grappelli, and was soon playing standards and doing tours with the latter. Lockwood was deeply immersed in the music of Coltrane, and at the same time formed a jazz-rock group called Surya. By 1979, he had diversified even more and was playing with five or six bands of jazz and rock persuasions, touring with Grappelli and recording with Tony Williams. Surya (= 'sun'), fused jazz and rock with classical overtones, following the work of Jerry Goodman, Michal Urbaniak and Jean-Luc Ponty, but unlike them, Lockwood does not play electric violin; he plays a 160-year-old instrument acoustically with a pickup. At the age of 24 he said, 'I'm more of a Coltrane fan than a bebop fan . . . bebop is past and we must see the future.' By the mid-1980s he had a solid international reputation and was touring regularly in the USA and Europe [IC]

With Magma; *New World* (1979) (with Tony Williams/Niels-Henning Ørsted Pedersen); *Live at Montreux* (1980), both MPS; *The Kid* (1982), JMS

Loose Tubes A 21-piece band of younger London-based musicians, one of the most joyously original large ensembles of the mid-1980s. Its orthodox big-band line-up is augmented by tuba, bass clarinet, flute and percussion, and is totally unlike the conventional jazz/dance orchestra. No bandleader fronts it and it functions democratically. It sets up in either a 'V' formation or in the round, thus affording the eye-contact which enables cues to be given by anyone in the band who is free to do so at that moment. The brilliantly assured writing is done largely by Django Bates (keyboards) and Steve Berry (bass), and occasionally by other members, and shows an understanding of the whole jazz tradition and of rock, African and other ethnic music. Rich melodies, sonorous harmonies, beautifully executed rhythms, are played with great fire, and several members are gifted soloists. First public performance was in London in June 1984, and since then it has played clubs, theatres and festivals in the London area. [IC]

Loose Tubes (1984), LTLP

Lovens, Paul, selected drums and cymbals, musical saw. b. Aachen, West Germany, 6 June 1949. He played drums as a child, and at the age of 14 worked with pop groups and jazz groups of different styles. Totally self-taught, from 1969 onwards he worked almost exclusively as a 'free' improviser and built his own individual drumset. Since then, he has played with almost all the leading musicians of the international 'free jazz' and 'free improvising' scene, and done concert tours in over 40 countries. He is a founder member of a musicians' co-operative, and in collaboration with Paul Lytton in 1976 he created his own record label, Po Torch Records. Since 1969 he has worked regularly with Alexander von Schlippenbach's trio, quartet, and Globe Unity Orchestra. Has also performed with Sven Ake Johansson, Günter Christmann, Evan Parker, and in duos with Paul Lytton and Martin Theurer. He lives in Genoa, Italy. [IC]

At least 40 LPs including *Alex Schlippenbach Trio* (1972), FMP; *Globe Unity Orchestra* (1976); *Lovens/Lytton* (1980); *Toshinori Kondo/Paul Lovens* (1980); *Schlippenbach Trio* (1981), all Po Torch; *Martin Theurer and Paul Lovens* (1981), FMP

Lowther, Thomas Henry, trumpet, fluegelhorn, cornet, violin, piano. b. Leicester, 11 July 1941. Brass band musicians on both his father's and mother's sides. He was taught cornet by his father and had private violin lessons; studied violin with Manoug Parikian at the Royal Academy of Music, London. As a jazz musician, self-taught. During the 1960s, he led various groups of his own, and also worked with Mike Westbrook, the New Jazz Orchestra, rock and blues bands such as John Mayall's and Keef Hartley's. During the 1970s, worked with many leading musicians in London including Mike Gibbs, Kenny Wheeler, Tony Coe, Norma Winstone, Michael Garrick, John Dankworth and others; in the 1980s with his own bands, John Surman, Gordon Beck, John Taylor, Gil Evans and London Brass Virtuosi. His inspiration comes from a broad spectrum including many classical composers, and jazz musicians such as Coltrane, Monk and Art Blakey. [IC]

With New Jazz Orchestra, John Mayall, Mike Gibbs, Neil Ardley and many others; with his own band, *Child Song* (1970), Deram; with Mike Westbrook, *Metropolis* (1971), RCA; with Tony Coe, *Zeitgeist* (1977), EMI

Lunceford, Jimmie (James Melvin), multi-instrumentalist, leader, arranger. b. Fulton, Mississippi, 6 June 1902; d. 12 July 1947. After school in Denver (where he studied music with Paul Whiteman's teacher-father Wilberforce) and a music degree at Fisk, Lunceford worked with New York bands led by Elmer Snowden, Wilbur Sweatman and others before taking up teaching (music and PE) at Manassa High School. At Manassa he formed a school dance band – Jimmy Crawford (dms), Moses Allen (bass) and Henry Clay (tpt) were founder members – and after augmenting with some old colleagues from Fisk, including Willie Smith (alto), Ed Wilcox (piano) and Henry Bowles (tmb), Lunceford took his well-drilled band of teenagers on the road. Four hard years of professional grind followed, living on morale and peanuts, until in 1933 the band was booked into New York's Lafayette Theater and four months later invited to play the Cotton Club. Touring from 1934 on quickly turned Lunceford's young band into the hottest property on the road. 'Willie Smith would put his bonnet on and sing a sort of nursery rhyme', remembers Eddie Durham. 'Eddie Tomkins hit the high notes and did a Louis Armstrong deal. Then they had a Guy Lombardo and a Paul Whiteman bit. Then the lights would go down and they'd all lay down their horns and come out and sing as a glee club!' The trumpeters threw their horns at the ceiling and caught them in regimented unison, or came down front for a dance routine, topping the show with a repertoire of rehearsed bows, Lunceford calling a number for each. Detractors, jealous of such panache, called Lunceford's band 'the trained seals'; discouragingly for the detractors, however, the band was musically perfect too. Individual section rehearsals were standard practice, and Willie Smith's saxophone team, inspired by its masterful boss, rehearsed the fine points of each bar. Powerful cornermen such as Smith, tenorist Joe Thomas and trombonist Trummy Young (who joined in 1937 and quickly established a star reputation) were soloists of premier quality, their talents powerfully featured by two arrangers: Sy Oliver (whose name is synonymous with Lunceford's) who did much to create his brilliant sound and Ed Wilcox, another fine arranger (his work for saxophones was especially outstanding) who after Oliver's arrival concentrated mainly on ballads and blues. The band was unbeatable, but it maintained a crippling succession of profitable one-nighters and by 1942 morale was starting to drop: Lunceford's men felt overworked and underpaid. 'We knew Jimmie was making a lot of money,' says Willie Smith, 'because he was forever buying planes, wrecking them and buying new ones.' An angry meeting at the YMCA, New York, at which Smith spoke up for the band, produced anger but no pay raise, and a succession of cornermen – including Young, Oliver and oldtimers such as Smith, Ed Wilcox and Moses Allen disappointedly moved on: the band never returned to full power. Lunceford treated his later sidemen more fairly and later claimed that his band manager had misled him over wages; it was a sad and misty issue. He collapsed and died a few years later, while signing autographs at a music shop in Seaside, Oregon. [DF]

The Complete Jimmie Lunceford 1939–40, CBS (4 records, boxed set)

Lusher, Don, trombone. b. UK, 6 November 1923. A virtuoso performer – his regular show-stoppers include Leroy Anderson's 'The Typewriter' played with machine-gun accuracy – he has been acknowledged as the master technician of British trombone since the 1950s. He worked with various bands, including Joe Daniels's and with orchestras led by Jack Parnell and Geraldo, then with the Squadronaires and with Ted Heath (where for nine years as lead trombonist he partnered Keith Christie to produce enduring and spectacular showcases such as 'Late Night Final'). From the 1960s, he worked in studios, toured world-wide with premier Americans including Henry Mancini, Nelson Riddle and Frank Sinatra, led his own big bands for radio, TV, records and live dates and made solo appearances. More lately he has toured with a jazz package show, 'The Best of British Jazz' featuring Kenny Baker and Betty Smith (in 1976 he was voted Musician of the Year by the BBC Jazz Society), subbed for Roy Williams in Peter Boizot's Pizza All Stars, played at Bill McGuffie's Niner Club, visited the USA and Australia to conduct master classes and continued his round of guest spots.

Lusher is a true gentleman-professional, respected by all who know him. He is a master-teacher, regular soloist with brass bands, old-hand studio man and expert classical performer, and has produced a striking autobiography/trombone textbook (see below). [DF]

Collection (1972–3), EMI

See Lusher, Don, *The Don Lusher Book* (Egon, 1985)

Lyons, Jimmy, alto and baritone sax, flute, composer. b. Jersey City, NJ, 1 December 1932; d. New York, 19 May 1986. 1941, he moved to New York, living with his grandfather in Harlem. He began on alto at 15, and was mainly self-taught. From 1960 onwards he was associated with Cecil Taylor, becoming identified with the free jazz movement. 1969, he played concerts with Taylor at the Maeght Foundation in France, and made his first record as leader for Byg records in Paris; 1970–1, he taught music for Narcotic Addiction Control; 1971–3, with Taylor, he was artist in residence at Antioch

Jimmie Lunceford

College, Ohio, and was orchestral director of the Black Music Ensemble. He said of this period: 'I continued writing and trying to develop a more compositional sense. At Antioch College I got a chance to hear the things that people like Fletcher Henderson, Coleman Hawkins, Ben Webster had done . . . I went back and listened to that music and really got turned on.' 1975, he was composer-instrumentalist and director of the Black Music Ensemble at Bennington College, Vermont. During the early 1970s he toured Japan twice with Taylor, and throughout the decade appeared with Taylor's groups at major festivals in Europe and the USA.

Lyons also worked with David Murray and with Mary Lou Williams, and in the 1980s collaborated in quartet formation with Andrew Cyrille, Joseph Jarman and Don Moye. After his untimely death from lung cancer, a concert tribute was organized in New York by his longtime associate Andrew Cyrille, and the performers included Archie Shepp, Sun Ra, Lester Bowie, Anthony Davis, Rashied Ali, among others. Lyons's early influences were Ernie Henry and Charlie Parker. [IC]

With Joel Futterman, Paul Murphy, Sunny Murray and John Lindberg, Andrew Cyrille and Jeanne Lee, Eddie Gale; with Cecil Taylor Unit, *Nefertiti, the Beautiful One has Come* (1962), Arista-Freedom; *Conquistador* (1966), Blue Note; *Great Concert of Cecil Taylor* (1969), Prestige; *Calling it the 8th* (1981), Hat Music; as leader, *Other Afternoons* (1969), Byg/Actuel; *Push Pull* (1978), Hat Hut; *Riffs* (1980), Hat Music; *Wee Sneezawee* (1983), Black Saint

Lyttelton, Humphrey, trumpet, clarinet, tenor horn, bandleader, author, broadcaster. b. Eton College, Berkshire, 23 May 1921. He emerged as a bright young trumpeter with George Webb's Dixielanders at Britain's revivalist shrine, the Red Barn, Barnehurst, after the war. By 1948 he had formed his own band from the remains of Webb's and recorded his first sides for London Jazz: over the next six years he was quickly established as Britain's premier revivalist, recording with Australian Graeme Bell and others in a variety of experimental contexts, and in 1954 producing the

Humphrey Lyttelton

first of several volumes of influential autobiography, *I Play As I Please*. 1954 was also the year that Lyttelton's musical policies broadened to encompass mainstream (a dramatic change at the time): by 1955 his band included saxophonist Bruce Turner, and four years after that a classic saxophone section including Tony Coe (alto), Jimmy Skidmore (tenor) and Joe Temperley (baritone). Lyttelton's records from this period are world-class: a great band with a great book of arrangements caught in the midst of constant performance. In the 1960s his career expanded: more writing, broadcasting, television presenting as well as trumpet playing, but his band continued to grow musically with a variety of new and familiar names – Dave Castle, Danny Moss, Tony Roberts and Eddie Harvey – all adding new chapters to his band's history. From 1970 a stabilized line-up and a long, productive contract with Black Lion Records refocused attention on Lyttelton's new band (now featuring Bruce Turner, Kathy Stobart and Mick Pyne) which he continued to run tirelessly while still producing books and articles, and appearing on TV and radio. In the late 1970s John Barnes and Roy Williams were new sidemen (they joined from Alex Welsh's ailing band) and in the mid-1980s, with Pete Strange replacing Williams and a new and effective drummer, Adrian Macintosh, Lyttelton's group (newly recorded on his own label, Calligraph) was flourishing again.

The career of 'Humph' is hard to summarize. Apart from his obvious talent as a trumpeter, which made him for Louis Armstrong 'the top trumpet man in England today', his contributions to jazz as an intelligent and acceptable communicator were vital to the music in its young roaring days. His successive volumes of autobiography were the first really intelligent writings from a jazz musician (apart from Eddie Condon's) and helped incalculably to establish jazz as a literate and intelligent art form in Britain: they also nipped in the bud a great deal of confused jazzthink that prevailed at the time. In his later years as Britain's senior jazz ambassador, there can be few people who have failed to be touched at some time by Lyttelton's wit, intelligence and humour, which he brings as easily to a BBC panel game as quizmaster, as he does to the concert platform. Above all, he is still an enthusiast. Any jazz venture involving him is guaranteed integrity, intelligence and an eye for the unusual: a late 1970s package show, 'Salute to Satchmo' featuring Alex Welsh and George Chisholm, was really his creation. [DF]

Any Lyttelton record

M

McBee, Cecil, bass. b. Tulsa, Oklahoma, 19 May 1935. After studying clarinet, began on bass at age 17; music degree from Ohio Central State University, and band director in army. Worked with Paul Winter sextet (1963–4), then with leading New York players such as Jackie McLean (1964) and Wayne Shorter (1965–6) on gigs and records. Main affiliations were with Charles Lloyd quartet (1966), Yusef Lateef (1967–9) and Alice Coltrane (1969–72). From 1975, led own group often featuring Chico Freeman, and worked also under Freeman's leadership; during same period, much in demand for work with musicians as varied as Abdullah Ibrahim, Joanne Brackeen and Harry Edison–Buddy Tate (Kool Festival, 1985). As well as having established a reputation for creative versatility in both 'free' and 'time' contexts, McBee has a rounded, expressive tone and an enviably strong pulse. [BP]

Live at Sweet Basil, vol.1 (1977), Enja

McCandless, Paul, oboe, English horn, bass clarinet, composer. b. Indiana, Pennsylvania, 24 March 1947. Parents public school music teachers; father taught him clarinet, mother taught him piano; at 13 he was playing and writing for a Dixieland band; educated at Duquesne University where he played both with the Pittsburgh Symphony and in jazz clubs; 1967, went to Manhattan School of Music to concentrate solely on oboe. 1968–73, with Paul Winter's Winter Consort which, from 1970, included Ralph Towner, Glen Moore and Collin Walcott; with these three, McCandless left the Winter Consort in the early 1970s and formed Oregon, one of the key groups of the 1970s (see TOWNER, RALPH). In 1980, McCandless also joined Gallery, with Michael Di Pasqua, David Samuels, David Darling. With Winter Consort, he toured and played festivals all over the USA, and with Oregon worked extensively on the international circuit. [IC]

With David Friesen, Billy Hart, John Scofield, Jerry Goodman, Zbigniew Seifert, Eddie Gomez, Bob Moses, Steve Gadd, Billy Cobham, Elvin Jones; *All the Mornings Bring* (1979), Elektra/Asylum; five albums with Winter Consort including *Road* (nda) A & M; with Gallery, *Gallery* (1981), ECM; with Eberhard Weber, *Later that Evening* (1982), ECM; 12 with Oregon including *Oregon* (1983), ECM

McCann, Les(lie Coleman), piano, vocals. b. Lexington, Kentucky, 23 September 1935. After studies and naval service, he accompanied singer Gene McDaniels in 1959, and formed his own trio just in time to profit from the popularity of soul-jazz. When in the 1960s he began featuring his own singing with the trio, he scored two sizeable hits ('Compared to What', written by McDaniels, and the standard 'With These Hands'). While eminently capable of setting up a compelling groove, his piano does little except pile cliché upon cliché and, like his dull singing voice, has few redeeming qualities other than confidence in its ability to entertain. [BP]

Swiss Movement (1969), Atlantic

McClure, Ron(ald Dix), bass, and piano. b. New Haven, Connecticut, 22 November 1941. Began on accordion at age five; piano in school band; studied bass, graduating from Julius Hartt Conservatory, Hartford, Conn., 1962. He worked with Buddy Rich, Maynard Ferguson, Herbie Mann, Don Friedman, Marian McPartland and others. Studied with Hall Overton in New York, 1965. Replaced Paul Chambers in the Wynton Kelly trio, 1965–6. Member of the Charles Lloyd quartet, 1967–9, which became one of the most successful jazz groups of the later 1960s and pioneered jazz-rock. 1969, he was a founder member of Fourth Way, which featured more sophisticated jazz-rock and toured in the USA and Europe. He left Fourth Way in 1970, working with Joe Henderson, Dionne Warwick, Gary Burton and Mose Allison, among others. 1971–2, he taught at the Berklee School of Music. 1971–4, he also freelanced with many people including Thelonious Monk, Keith Jarrett, the Pointer Sisters, Freddie Hubbard and Airto Moreira. 1974, he joined Blood Sweat and Tears. In the later 1970s and early 1980s he freelanced in New York. 1985, joined Al DiMeola's group (Al DiMeola Project), which included Danny Gottlieb and Airto, recording and touring in the USA and Europe. McClure's influences include Miles Davis, Bill Evans, Scott La Faro and Paul Chambers, and other inspirations are Charles Ives and Hall Overton. [IC]

With Maynard Ferguson, Pointer Sisters and others; with Lloyd, *Love In* (1967), Atlantic; *Charles Lloyd in the Soviet Union* (1967), Atlantic; with Fourth Way, *Sun and Moon* (1969),

Capitol; with Henderson, *In Pursuit of Blackness* (1971), Milestone

McCorkle, Susannah, vocals. She first heard Billie Holiday records in Paris around 1971, moved to England soon after and worked with, among others, Bruce Turner, Keith Nichols, Dick Sudhalter and pianist Keith Ingham, for several years her accompanist and musical director. Around then she played major concerts with visiting Americans such as Ben Webster, Dexter Gordon and Bobby Hackett (who called her 'the best singer since Billie Holiday') and in 1975 played a season at the Riverboat jazz room, Manhattan, to critical plaudits from Alec Wilder and his circle. After another year in England (during which she played Ronnie Scott's and recorded two solo albums of songs by Mercer and Warren, both with Ingham, both produced by Chris Ellis) it was back to America (with Keith Ingham) to live and perform. Later albums included a Yip Harburg tribute and a Grammy-nominated collection, *The people that you never get to love*. McCorkle's clear-sounding, natural voice combines Billie Holiday inflexions with a surprising occasional hint of Marilyn Monroe. An ambitious and intelligent performer, she also writes for the *New Yorker* and has published a number of short stories. [DF]

The Songs of Johnny Mercer (1977), Inner City

McCracken, Bob (Robert Edward), clarinet, saxes. b. Dallas, Texas, 23 November 1904; d. California, 4 July 1972. A highly musical player with an elegant 'timeless' style, in 1924 he worked in Jack Teagarden's company in Doc Ross's band and later based himself in Chicago where he worked from 1939 with musicians such as Jimmy McPartland and Wingy Manone. He is best remembered internationally for a brief spell with Louis Armstrong's All Stars in the early 1950s and time with Kid Ory later in the decade (it included touring in 1959). Later in his career he combined business interests with music, but kept up his playing with Teagarden (1962) and Wild Bill Davison (1967). [DF]

Henry 'Red' Allen and the Kid (1959), Metro (double)

McDonough, Dick (Richard), guitar, banjo. b. 1904; d. New York City, 25 May 1938. A pioneer of single-string solo guitar as well as the ringing 'chorded-solo' style that was a joyful aspect of 1930s jazz, he began as a banjoist (he played it regularly with Red Nichols), and from the late 1920s until his death was a constantly busy studio man, recording on guitar with musicians as varied as Nichols, Red McKenzie, the Boswell Sisters, the Dorseys, Benny Goodman, Joe Venuti, Mildred Bailey, Adrian Rollini and Glenn Miller (for Decca in 1937 he was guitarist for Miller's orchestral debut on record). McDonough, a sociable youngster who numbered Johnny Mercer among his many friends, was often to be found at the Onyx Club on 52nd Street in the early 1930s, discovering new music with his companions, playing – and drinking – the night away: one regular colleague was guitarist Carl Kress with whom McDonough recorded immortal duets and played a prestigious date, 'New York's First Swing Concert' at the Imperial Theater on 24 May 1936. Two years later McDonough collapsed at the NBC studios. 'Dick's dead for much the same reason as Bix and Bunny!' Artie Shaw was to say regretfully. [DF]

McDuff, Brother Jack (Eugene), organ (and piano, bass). b. Champaign, Illinois, 17 September 1926. Self-taught on piano, then moved to organ. Worked mid-1950s with Chicago-based groups, then on tour with Willis Jackson until 1959. Formed own trio; recorded under own name and (1961) with Roland Kirk. Employed as guitarist in his group Grant Green (1961) and George Benson (1962–5). Continued leading regular unit into 1980s, featuring himself on electric piano as well as organ and moving towards vocal-based soul music. Initially, like all the organists of his generation, McDuff was heavily indebted to Jimmy Smith. Unlike some of the more excitable players of this group, however, Jack had a less grating tone and a sober, coherent approach to improvisation. [BP]

The Honeydripper (1961), Prestige

McEachern, Murray, trombone, alto sax, trumpet etc. b. Toronto, Canada, 1915; d. Los Angeles, 28 April 1982. He was a child prodigy concert violinist and by his late teens had mastered clarinet, alto and tenor saxophones, trumpet, trombone, tuba and bass. He featured his array of instruments in Chicago floor shows by the mid-1930s and in 1936 joined Benny Goodman on trombone for just over a year. 1938–41, he was with the Casa Loma Orchestra and (after a year as assistant MD for Paul Whiteman) he moved to the West Coast where – understandably – he became an in-demand studio man, playing for films, TV, radio and records. A regular concert artist (with David Rose), McEachern often turned up as a soloist for TV specials as well as records and his work on any instrument suggested that he might have made a life-long study of that one alone (his trombone solos rival Tommy Dorsey for fluency, range, control and execution: his saxophone would grace such seasoned performers as Toots Mondello). In the 1970s he joined Duke Ellington for a short spell and led the re-formed Tommy Dorsey Orchestra: on its own an amazing feat for any musician. [DF]

Conrad Gozzo Sextet (1955), RCA

Macero, Teo (Attilio Joseph), composer, saxophones, producer. b. Glens Falls, New York,

30 October 1925. He attended the Navy School of Music in Washington, DC, 1943–4. He spent 1947 in Glens Falls, teaching and playing. Moved to New York in 1948, studying at Juilliard School and getting bachelor and master degrees in 1953. He began composing jazz-influenced atonal classical works, and over 100 performances of these were given 1955–60. He received two Guggenheim awards for composition, 1957, 1958. He also played and recorded with Mingus in the early and middle 1950s. From 1957 he joined the staff of Columbia Records, initially as a music editor and staying with the company until the end of the 1970s. At Columbia he began his long and fruitful association with Miles Davis in 1957, as producer of the trumpeter's albums. He continued in this role into the 1980s. Macero was the perfect producer for Davis, and his musical understanding, wisdom and vision helped the trumpeter in his quest for new forms and new standards of excellence. [IC]

With Mingus; as leader and composer, *Time Plus Seven* (1980), Finnadar

McFerrin, Bobby, voice. b. New York, 11 March 1950. Father an opera singer, mother a classical soprano. He began as a pianist, taking lessons from the age of six, attended Sacramento State and Cerritos College in California and afterwards began to get work as a pianist. He then worked as a singer/pianist, but soon abandoned the piano. He was discovered by Jon Hendricks with whom he sang some duets. Then he made a big impact at New York's Kool Jazz Festival and later toured the Kool circuit with George Benson and an all-star band. Since then he has toured internationally with Chico Freeman, Grover Washington Jnr. and Herbie Hancock's VSOP, among others. As a pianist, McFerrin was inspired by Keith Jarrett, and it was the latter's solo piano performances which made McFerrin think of singing unaccompanied, which he began doing in 1983. He also began studying the music of Bach and was soon invited to perform at festivals of classical music, both to sing pieces as they were written and to improvise variations on them.

McFerrin has an extraordinarily flexible voice with a good range, and he often uses it like a musical instrument. He has solved the problem of breathing by making musical notes when he breathes in, as well as when he expels air, and he can produce all kinds of rhythmic patterns by 'drumming' with his voice and keeping the pulse with his hand on his chest. [IC]

With Chico Freeman, Pharoah Sanders and Bob Dorough; *The Voice* (1981); *Bobby McFerrin* (1983); *The Young Lions* (1982), all Elektra Musician

McGarity, Lou (Robert Louis), trombone, violin, vocals. b. Athens, Georgia, 22 July 1917; d. 28 August 1971. He began on violin at seven (30 years on he was still playing it with the Lawson–Haggart Jazz Band), took up the trombone in his teens, moved to New York with Nye Mayhew's band, and then joined Ben Bernie's excellent and often jazz-influenced dance band towards the end of 'old maestro' Bernie's career (he died two years later, at only 46). McGarity's accurate lead and creative solos prompted an offer from Benny Goodman: he joined Goodman on 25 October 1940, to work with Cutty Cutshall in a champion-level trombone team. For McGarity it was a good period: he recorded influential and popular features with Goodman ('Yours' much influenced younger players such as George Masso), sang with Goodman's sextet ('Blues in the Night' was a feature), and appeared in a 1942 film, *The Powers Girl*. In 1942 he left Goodman to work with Raymond Scott at CBS, served in the US navy for four years and then joined Goodman again after discharge. By 1947 he was back in New York, working the studios and doubling Eddie Condon's: the 1950s were to produce a string of studio-based Dixieland recordings with the Lawson–Haggart Jazz Band which are amongst his finest. (Other McGarity classics from the period are found on big-band sessions such as 'The Big 18' and small-group sides with Muggsy Spanier, Cootie Williams, Neal Hefti and Wild Bill Davison.) Regularly with Condon until illness slowed him up in 1957, McGarity was visible in the 1960s in the studio orchestra for Arthur Godfrey's popular and longstanding TV show (backing, on occasion, latter-day talents such as J. J. Johnson), and working for Bob Crosby. A founder member of the World's Greatest Jazz Band (1968–70), he died of a heart attack in Washington, still at work. [DF]

Lawson–Haggart Jazz Band, *The Best of Dixieland* (1950s), MCA Coral

McGhee, Howard B., trumpet. b. Tulsa, Oklahoma, 6 February 1918. Main big-band affiliations with Charlie Barnet (1942–3) and Andy Kirk (1941–2, 1943–4); with the latter he wrote his own feature number 'McGhee Special'. Small-group playing with Coleman Hawkins (1944–5), then own groups in Los Angeles (1945–7) which sometimes included Charlie Parker. Back in New York, organized his sextet (1947), visiting the Paris Jazz Fair the following year, and briefly used Jimmy Heath's big band as his own (1948). Only sporadically active in 1950s owing to drug problems. Work after his comeback included short spell with Ellington (1965), own small groups and big band and recordings with both. A significant stylist of the 1940s, McGhee was a great admirer of Roy Eldridge but was also impressed by Fats Navarro and Dizzy Gillespie. More than capable of holding his own technically, he developed a compromise between the rhythmic approach of the swing-era players and the long lines of

Chris McGregor

bebop, which is not only musically successful but highly individual. [BP]

Maggie's Back! (1961), Contemporary

McGregor, Chris, piano, composer. b. South Africa, 24 December 1936. His father taught in Church of Scotland mission school in the Transkei province; among McGregor's earliest experiences were the hymns of the mission church and the music of the Xhosa people. He spent four years at Cape Town College of Music, studying Western European classical music by day, and at night playing jam sessions in local jazz clubs with white and African musicians.

1962, he formed the Blue Notes with Dudu Pukwana (alto sax), Mongezi Feza (trumpet), Nick Moyake (tenor sax), Johnny Dyani (bass) and Louis Moholo (drums). It became virtually impossible for racially mixed groups to function in South Africa, and when they were invited to play at the French Antibes festival in 1964, they left their country for good. Their compatriot Dollar Brand (now Abdullah Ibrahim) had preceded them to Europe and helped them find work there. They spent almost a year in Switzerland, playing at the Blue Note, Geneva, and the Afrikaner Café in Zurich, then came to the UK in 1965, playing at the Ronnie Scott Club and settling in London. 1966, McGregor and the band played a four-week engagement at the Montmartre Club in Copenhagen, which was then presenting most of the leading avant-garde players of the time including Albert Ayler, Archie Shepp and Cecil Taylor. From this point on, the music of McGregor and the Blue Notes was to fuse their African roots with elements from free jazz, creating a highly distinctive sound.

In 1970 McGregor augmented his band, calling the larger ensemble the Brotherhood of Breath. It toured the UK and Europe, playing many major festivals and gaining a solid international reputation. The Brotherhood also recorded the soundtrack for the film of Wole Soyinka's *Kongi's Harvest*. In the mid-1970s McGregor went to live in the south-west of France, commuting to engagements in Europe and the UK. In the early 1970s he toured Africa with the Blue Notes; the Brotherhood of Breath continued to function internationally; McGregor also plays solo piano concerts. 1983, he did an Arts Council Network tour of the UK with a very big band for which he had done all the composing and arranging. He is a consummate pianist with a style which often employs immense percussiveness. [IC]

With Blue Notes, *The African Sound* (1963), Gallo; *Blue Notes for Mongezi* (1975), Ogun; *Blue Notes in Concert, 1 and 2* (1978), Ogun; with Brotherhood of Breath, *Chris McGregor's Brotherhood of Breath* (1971), Neon/RCA; *Brotherhood* (1972), RCA; *Live at Willisau* (1974), Ogun; *Procession* (1977), Ogun; *Yes Please* (1982), In & Out; solo, *Piano Song, vols. 1/2* (1977), Musica

Machito (Raúl Grillo), voice, percussion, bandleader. b. Tampa, Florida, 16 February 1912; d. 15 April 1984. Brought up in Cuba, moved to New York (1930s) and sang with various Afro-Latin ensembles. Formed own band (1941), organized with his brother-in-law, trumpeter Mario Bauza (who had played with Chick Webb and Cab Calloway), and continued to lead this ensemble for 40 years. Although engaged full-time in Latin music, Machito was important in the Latin/jazz crossover of the mid- and late 1940s. The mambo style he helped to found (especially the brass-section work) represented the first major influence of jazz on Latin music and, in return, he inspired the Latin ventures of Stan Kenton and Dizzy Gillespie and backed Charlie Parker on records. As well as employing several jazz players on a long-term basis (such as Doc Cheatham), he remained open to later stylistic trends such as 'salsa' and, at the time of his death while working in London, had found a new younger audience. [BP]

Machito and his Salsa Big Band (1982), Timeless

Macintosh, Adrian Lynn, drums. b. Tadcaster, Yorkshire, 7 March 1942. He moved to London in 1966 and worked with pianist John Taylor's trio, 1966–8, before joining Alan Elsdon's band in late 1969. For the next 14 years he freelanced with a variety of leaders including Lennie Felix, Ted Beament and Brian Leake, as well as backing American visitors including Sonny Stitt, Red Holloway, Teddy Edwards, Cecil Payne, Jimmy Witherspoon, Doc Cheatham, Al Casey and Earle Warren. In May 1982 he joined Humphrey Lyttelton, becoming Lyttelton's most in-sympathy drummer for years. [DF]

Humphrey Lyttelton (with Wally Fawkes), *It Seems Like Yesterday!* (1983), Calligraph

McIntyre, Ken (Kenneth Arthur), alto sax, composer, educator, and flute, oboe, bass clarinet, bassoon, piano. b. Boston, 7 September 1931. Father a mandolin player. Classical piano lessons, 1940–5; studied sax with Gigi Gryce, Charlie Mariano and others. Bachelor's and master's degrees in composition from Boston Conservatory. He taught in New York schools in the later 1950s, leading his own group in clubs. 1960, he met and recorded with Eric Dolphy. He became an active member of the avant-garde, playing clubs and festivals. From 1961, became deeply involved in education, teaching in New York school systems until 1967; at Central State University in Wilberforce, Ohio, 1967–9; 1969–71, at Wesleyan. He received a doctorate in education from the University of Massachusetts and since 1971 he has been director of the African-American Music and Dance concentration at the State University of New York at Old Westbury, and also professor of humanities. 1970s, he recorded a series of albums on Steeplechase which show his originality as a composer and player. His compositions are full of surprises and odd twists; they often feature asymmetrical numbers of bars, and sometimes asymmetrical time signatures. It has been said that Ornette Coleman and Dolphy were influences on McIntyre, but he denies this – he is about the same age and was already mature when he met them. His main inspiration was initially Charlie Parker. [IC]

With Dolphy, *Fire Waltz* (1960), Prestige; as leader, *Hindsight* (1974); quartet (with Jaki Byard), *Home* (1975); *Open* (1975); *Introducing the Vibrations* (1976) (with Terumasa Hino); *Chasing the Sun* (1978), all Steeplechase

Mackel, Billy (John William), guitar. b. Baltimore, Maryland, 28 December 1912. He played guitar, banjo and ukulele around Baltimore at the start of his career and was leading a band in Club Orleans, Philadelphia, when in 1944 he was heard by Roy McCoy from Lionel Hampton's band. Hampton invited Mackel to play a concert with him, and from then on Mackel played guitar for Hampton, contributing to the nightly excitement of jazz's most exciting big band. He cites Charlie Christian and Wes Montgomery as his prime influences: in his funky, bluesy lines can be heard one dawn for rock and roll. [DF]

Lionel Hampton, *The Complete Paris Sessions* (1953), Vogue (double)

See Dance, Stanley, *The World of Swing* (Scribner's, 1974, repr. Da Capo, 1979)

McKenna, Dave (David J.), piano. b. Woonsocket, Rhode Island, 30 May 1930. He began with Charlie Ventura in 1949, worked with Woody Herman, 1950–1, and the year after found himself in Korea. After discharge in 1953 he spent the rest of the 1950s commuting between Gene Krupa, Stan Getz, Zoot Sims and Ventura, and most of the 1960s working with Bobby Hackett or Eddie Condon (fine records with Hackett's quartet include the classic *Blues With a Kick* on Capitol). In 1967, with his wife and sons, McKenna moved out to Cape Cod, near to Bobby Hackett (who called him 'the best piano player alive'), and began club work: seven years at the Columns, West Dennis, and later at the Lobster Boat towards Hyannisport. By the late 1970s he was back on the international circuit, touring and recording with Bob Wilber and Pug Horton, and by 1981 busily making the rounds of the festival circuit with Concord's Superband, including kindred spirits such as Warren Vaché and Scott Hamilton. Dave McKenna's solo recordings from this period and since are simply great two-handed jazz records: 'McKenna is his own rhythm section,' says Ira Gitler. [DF]

The Key Man! (1984), Concord

See Balliett, Whitney, *Jelly Roll, Jabbo and Fats* (OUP, 1983)

McKenzie, Red (William), vocals, kazoo. b. St Louis, Missouri, 14 October 1899; d. New York City, 7 February 1948. He was a jockey before he broke both arms in a fall, worked as a bellhop at the Claridge Hotel, St Louis, and there met guitarists Dick Slevin and Jack Bland. With them he formed a spasm-band, the Mound City Blue Blowers, which became a success working opposite Gene Rodemich's band in Chicago: Isham Jones engineered a recording date and their first single, 'Arkansas Blues', with McKenzie's red-hot comb and paper and plummy, punctilious singing, sold over a million copies. For the next eight years McKenzie – gingery, fast-talking, straight-speaking – led the Blowers playing for concerts, society parties and immortal recordings including 'Hello Lola' and 'One Hour' which, with guests including Coleman Hawkins and Glenn Miller, became classics. Two famous guitarists with the MCBB included Eddie Lang and Eddie Condon, who loved McKenzie's kindred cockfighting spirit and portrays it best in *We Called it Music*: McKenzie was a help to Condon, too, setting up his first record date (the McKenzie–Condon Chicagoans) and briefly in 1929 a band of rebel Chicago youth for Red Nichols. From 1932, McKenzie with Paul Whiteman for a year, worked 52nd Street and enjoyed success; but after his wife died he moved back to St Louis to look after his son and work as a beer salesman. He came back to record twice with Condon in 1944 (for World Broadcasting, reissued on Jazzology), and by 1947 was leading a band again at Jimmy Ryan's. Ed Hubble remembers: 'His death was the end of the band. It was a stomping band and Red was singing beautifully, but his personal life was very lonely – he was taking it out on the bandstand and drinking entirely too much.' He died of cirrhosis. [DF]

Bunny and Red (1935–6), Jazz Archives

McKibbon, Al(fred Benjamin), bass. b. Chicago, 1 January 1919. Raised in Detroit, played first in local bands. Then toured with Lucky Millinder band (1943-4), Tab Smith small group (1944-5). Further small-band work with J. C. Heard (1946), Coleman Hawkins (1946-7). Replaced Ray Brown with Dizzy Gillespie band in time for Carnegie Hall concert and European tour (1947-50). Briefly with Count Basie (1950), then George Shearing (1951–8) and vibist Cal Tjader (1958–9). Also recorded with Thelonious Monk (1951, claiming to have heard his music as early as 1939) and Herbie Nichols (1955); toured with Monk in the Giants of Jazz (1971–2). 1960s, settled in Los Angeles, busy with studio work and live appearances with singers, including Sammy Davis (1975). A veteran whose tone recalls the pre-amplification days of the 1940s, his lines similarly stick to the basics of the bop era without being too predictable. He proved extremely adaptable to the material of Monk and Nichols and, when playing Latin-jazz with Shearing and Tjader, submitted readily to the collective style of this type of rhythm-section. [BP]

Thelonious Monk, *Something in Blue* (1971), Black Lion

McKinley, Ray (Raymond Frederick), drums, vocals, leader. b. Fort Worth, Texas, 18 June 1910. 'Ray McKinley always was an amazing drummer,' says critic George T. Simon. 'He propelled a swinging beat, very often with a two-beat Dixieland basis, that inspired musicians to play better. [And] he spent more time on getting just the right sound out of his drums than any other drummer I can recall.' Simon's description clearly places McKinley in the class of contemporaries such as Cliff Leeman and Dave Tough, but more than either of them he was a vocational leader and all-round entertainer. Early in his career he had played in local 'territory-style' bands such as Duncan Marion's, Savage Cummings's and Milt Shaw's; later with Smith Ballew, the Dorsey Brothers and Jimmy Dorsey, with whom he stayed until 1939. That year he teamed with Will Bradley, a fine and very underrated trombonist, to form a famous big band which cornered the market for big band arrangements of boogie-woogie – the craze of the period. McKinley played drums, sang, co-led the band with Bradley and even composed special material: his biggest hit was 'Beat me Daddy, Eight to the Bar' and it was followed by others ('Scrub me mama with a boogie beat', 'Bounce me brother with a solid four!' and 'Fry me Cookie with a can of lard', as well as a trio hit 'Down the road apiece!'). After three years the co-leaders disagreed over material – Bradley, a smooth stylist, enjoyed playing ballads more than McKinley did – and the drummer formed his own band, then moved to Glenn Miller's AEF band, taking over leadership of the organization after Miller's death. It was a role he was to play again from 1956 for ten more years: in between, 1946–56, he led his own band again, featuring go-ahead arrangements by Eddie Sauter and cornermen such as Peanuts Hucko and guitarist Mundell Lowe, then worked as a solo singer/disc jockey. From 1965, McKinley semi-retired but worked regularly through the 1970s and in 1985 came to Britain for TV with old colleagues Hucko and Zeke Zarchy [DF]

Glenn Miller Time 1965 (with Bobby Hackett), EMI Epic

McKinney, Bill (William), drums, leader. b. Cynthiana, Kentucky, 17 September 1895; d. 14 October 1969. He took over the leadership of Milton Senior's Synco Septet (later the Synco Jazz Band) in Springfield, Ohio, where they were succeeding as a novelty band. ('We played typical dance music of the early 1920s,' remembered pianist Todd Rhodes, 'complete with paper hats and whistles!') In Detroit the band was heard by Jean Goldkette, who spotted their potential, booked them into his newly acquired Graystone Ballroom and changed their name to McKinney's Cotton Pickers. He also hired Don Redman away from Fletcher Henderson, at $300 a week, to build their repertoire, and a year later, in 1928 (after Goldkette threw a party for RCA Victor's boss at Edgewater Park Ballroom, Detroit), the band began recording for Victor: classic sides from that year, featuring John Nesbitt (tpt) and Prince Robinson (tnr/clt) include 'Cherry', 'Shimme sha wabble' and 'Four or five times'. The Pickers drew such crowds for their dances at Graystone Ballroom (they also appeared regularly on local Radio WJR) that when an offer came for the band to record in New York, Goldkette refused permission; after keymen including Claude Jones, Dave Wilborn, Joe Smith and Don Redman went anyway (they recorded marvellous sides featuring Coleman Hawkins and Fats Waller in November 1929) he relented and the band began touring and recording where they pleased. By 1931 the Cotton Pickers had left Detroit (and Goldkette) to work at Frank Sebastian's Cotton Club in Culver City, and Quentin Jackson had joined as singer replacing George Thomas. The same year several McKinney cornermen left with Don Redman to join his own new band: new members Rex Stewart and Benny Carter joined McKinney, and Carter took over musical direction. But he only stayed a year and after more touring the Cotton Pickers broke up in 1934. McKinney continued to lead bands and run an agency until the mid-1940s: the Cotton Pickers were enthusiastically re-created on record in the 1980s. [DF]

McKinney's Cotton Pickers (1928–9), RCA

McLaughlin, John, acoustic and electric guitars, piano, synthesizer, composer. b. Yorkshire, 4 January 1942. Mother a violinist; brothers and a sister all musical. Piano lessons at age nine, but mostly self-taught. Started on guitar at 11, playing blues and listening to Muddy Waters, Big Bill Broonzy and Leadbelly, and later Django Reinhardt with Stephane Grappelli, and Tal Farlow. Moved to London in early 1960s, playing in r & b groups with Alexis Korner, Graham Bond, Eric Clapton, Ginger Baker and others. Through Bond's influence, he joined the Theosophical Society, becoming interested in Eastern philosophy and religion and, after hearing Ravi Shankar, in Indian music. Later 1960s, worked with Gunter Hampel in Germany for six months, playing free jazz. 1969, his first album as leader, *Extrapolation*, with John Surman (reeds), Tony Oxley (dms) and Brian Odges (bass), was one of the classic albums of the decade. It was a virtual summary of current small-group playing techniques, it anticipated the jazz-rock movement of the 1970s and it showed that McLaughlin was already a very fine composer, as well as being a sublimely original guitar stylist. 1969, he went to New York to join Tony Williams's Lifetime, and recorded with Miles Davis, making a vital contribution to two of the latter's most influential albums, *In a Silent Way* and *Bitches Brew*. Lifetime included Jack Bruce (bass and vocals) and Larry Young (keyboards) and was one of the first jazz-rock bands, but it was dogged by bad luck and McLaughlin left in 1970. After some more recording sessions with Davis and some concerts with him, he started his own group, the Mahavishnu Orchestra, in 1971, with Jerry Goodman (vln), Billy Cobham (dms), Jan Hammer (keyboards) and Rick Laird (bass guitar). This was probably the very greatest jazz-rock band, and it was immensely successful, touring world-wide, playing major festivals everywhere and selling many albums. It was also revolutionary both as a phenomenon and musically.

In the spring of 1970, McLaughlin had become a disciple of the guru Sri Chinmoy, who suggested the name Mahavishnu ('divine compassion, power and justice'), so the band had a strong philosophical and spiritual basis. McLaughlin achieved inspiration by self-discipline and meditation, eschewing alcohol and drugs. This started a growing trend in the later 1970s and the 1980s towards self-discipline and clean living on the hitherto alcohol- and drug-ridden jazz scene. Musically the group deployed the resources of electronic sound superbly, and integrated drums with highly rhythmic melodies in a new way, used asymmetrical rhythms in a manner totally new to jazz, and juxtaposed immensely detailed and complex written passages with long sections of improvisation. It also combined extreme virtuosity with an Indo-European romantic lyricism and tenderness. Their first two albums, *The Inner Mounting Flame* and *Birds of Fire*, are masterpieces of the genre they virtually created.

Through the strains of massive success and internal conflicts, the band broke up at the end of 1973, and in 1974 McLaughlin started a new Mahavishnu Orchestra with Jean-Luc Ponty (vln) and Gayle Moran (vocals and keyboards). This toured internationally and made two albums before it disbanded in 1975. Since the early 1970s McLaughlin had been taking vocal lessons in Indian music, and lessons from Ravi

John McLaughlin

Shankar and other master instrumentalists. In 1973 he began playing with the violinist L. Shankar, Zakir Hussein (tabla) and Raghavan (mridangam). After the second Mahavishnu Orchestra disbanded, he concentrated on playing acoustic music with these Indian musicians, calling the group Shakti ('creative intelligence, beauty and power'). Again, new trails of energy, interplay and virtuosity were blazed, but this time the intensity was at low volume, though none the less dynamic. Shakti made a big impact internationally, recorded three albums, then disbanded in 1978. McLaughlin went back to electric guitar, making an album called *Johnny McLaughlin, Electric Guitarist*, which was a reunion with the Mahavishnu players. For a while he led another electric group, the One Truth Band, but then reverted to acoustic guitar, touring in the late 1970s and early 1980s in trio with either Paco De Lucia and Larry Coryell, or De Lucia and Al DiMeola, and in duo with French guitarist Christian Escoudé.

In 1975 he had moved back to Europe, living in France, because he felt that in Europe and Japan jazz is understood and respected as an art, whereas in America the music business regards it as a commodity. In 1984 he was playing electric guitar again in a new version of the Mahavishnu Orchestra which included ex-Miles Davis saxist Bill Evans. They toured in the USA and Europe, and recorded an album. McLaughlin also played on some tracks of Davis's heavily electric album *You're Under Arrest* in 1984. He was commissioned to compose a guitar concerto featuring himself with the Los Angeles Philharmonic, and Mike Gibbs orchestrated it in time for the première in November 1985. It is a densely composed, long (about 30 minutes) and complex piece, which includes passages of guitar improvisation.

McLaughlin is one of the most complete, gifted and influential guitarists in jazz, perfectly at home playing blues, bebop, free jazz, fusion, Indian music, or in a classical setting. He is equally dedicated to acoustic and electric guitar and is equally influential on both instruments. His 1970 album, *My Goal's Beyond*, featured him on one side playing standards on solo guitar, and it seems likely that this triggered off the spate of solo guitar records which followed. He is a visionary and a true artist, constantly searching and growing, who describes himself as 'a musician for people who are not musicians'. Like Miles Davis, Keith Jarrett and Weather Report, he has gained both a huge public following and the admiration of his peers. He is a prolific composer, and his music always communicates the warmest emotions, and very often beatific joy. [IC]

With Miles Davis, Carla Bley, Tony Williams, DiMeola/De Lucia, and others; *Extrapolation* (1969), Polydor; *My Goal's Beyond* (1970), Elektra Musician; *Johnny McLaughlin, Electric Guitarist* (1978); with Mahavishnu Orchestra, *The Inner Mounting Flame* (1971); *Birds of Fire* (1972); *Visions of the Emerald Beyond* (1974), all CBS; *Mahavishnu* (1984), Warner Bros; with Shakti, *Shakti* (1975); *A Handful of Beauty* (1976); *Natural Elements* (1977), all CBS

McLean, Jackie (John Lenwood), alto sax, composer. b. New York City, 17 May 1932. After studying with his neighbour Bud Powell and gigging with Thelonious Monk (late 1940s), was recommended by Powell for work with Miles Davis (1951–2). A year's formal music education at North Carolina A & T College (where Lou Donaldson and Dannie Richmond were also to become students) followed by gigs with Paul Bley (1954) and George Wallington quintet (1955). Further important affiliations with Charles Mingus (1956) and Art Blakey (1956–7). Became musician/actor in long-running stage play *The Connection* (1959–61, including performances in London and Paris). Toured Japan (1964) and Scandinavia (1966), then began part-time teaching and counselling users of narcotics, which had earlier interrupted his own career. From 1972, full-time head of department at University of Hartford, Connecticut, performing in public mainly during summer vacations, often with group led by his saxophonist son Rene McLean (b. 16 December 1946). Even before becoming an educator, Jackie made a practice of encouraging young musicians such as Tony Williams, Grachan Moncur III, Charles Tolliver, Woody Shaw and Cecil McBee.

Although they never recorded together, Jackie was a close friend of Charlie Parker and his style is an individual and oblique reflection of Parker, in which intensity replaces fluency and linear invention is more important than harmonic interest. McLean himself points to the example of Dexter Gordon and, in the 1960s, he was capable of absorbing creatively the influence of both Ornette Coleman (who recorded with him) and John Coltrane. Several of McLean's compositions have become standards, such as 'Dig' (aka 'Donna'), 'Dr Jackle' (or 'Dr Jekyll') and 'Little Melonae', all of which were recorded by Miles, and 'Hip Strut'. His uniquely tart sound and his forceful lines have also rubbed off on a whole generation of altoists such as Gary Bartz and Sonny Fortune. [BP]

4, 5 and 6 (1956), Prestige/OJC; *Jackie's Bag* (1959–60); *New and Old Gospel* (1966), both Blue Note

See Spellman, A. B., *Black Music: Four Lives* (Pantheon, New York, 1966; MacGibbon & Kee, London, 1967)

McLevy, John, trumpet, fluegelhorn. b. Dundee, Scotland, 2 January 1927. He became prominent on the British jazz scene in the 1960s after formative years in London hotel bands and at the BBC working for Cyril Stapleton. His humorous, hard-swinging style attracted huge attention when in 1970 he featured in Benny Goodman's British big band and toured Europe (on Bobby Hackett's recommendation) in Goodman's small group including Hank Jones, Slam Stewart, Bucky Pizzarelli and George Masso: a show-stopping rework of 'Baubles, Bangles and Beads' that he played on the concerts became a much-requested set piece for years after. In the 1970s McLevy worked on in studios (he played the Harry Edison role on 21 LPs with singer Max Bygraves), formed a highly successful quartet with accordionist Jack Emblow and worked the British circuit of jazz clubs (often with Kenny Baker and later Tommy McQuater). He visited the Nice Jazz Festival, 1981, with Kathy Stobart and Roy Williams, for *Jazz Journal International*. A middle-range trumpeter and fluegelhornist who never wastes a note, McLevy uses short, attacking phrases and a highly original approach; for example, he has adapted the in-and-out harmon-muted effect of Clark Terry to his own purposes with striking ingenuity. A trumpet-original in any language. [DF]

Roy Williams, *Royal Trombone* (1983), Phontastic

McPartland, Jimmy (James D.), trumpet. b. Chicago, 15 March 1907. He took up jazz seriously at Austin High School where, with fellow-students and outside friends known collectively as the 'Austin High School Gang', he learned New Orleans Rhythm Kings records note for note: later, with Al Haid's band in 1923, he heard Beiderbecke for the first time on Lake Michigan and in 1925 replaced him in the Wolverines in New York (Beiderbecke gave him a cornet and worked the first five nights with him). McPartland then worked with Ben Pollack and with Eddie Condon on seminal recording sessions with the McKenzie–Condon Chicagoans. In the 1930s he toured all over, settled in Chicago in 1937, working night clubs and hotels, and moved between there and New York until call-up in 1942: three years later he met his British wife Marian (below) in Belgium while playing *Bandwagon* (an ENSA service show), then worked back in Chicago and New York after demobilization. Clubwork at the Metropole and Nick's and a busy recording schedule continued (*The Music Man goes Dixieland* is a great McPartland record from the early 1960s), and at this time and on through the 1970s he played clubs, hotels and festivals, toured South Africa in 1971–2, toured again with Art Hodes in 1973, played the Newport Jazz Festival, 1974, and was regularly to be heard with Marian (although divorced they remained great friends) in the late 1970s. In 1981 the indefatigable McPartland toured Great Britain: in 1985, he starred at the Nice Jazz Festival.

With Wild Bill Davison, Jimmy McPartland is the last classic ambassador of jazz cornet. He was associated from very early on with Bix Beiderbecke, whom he revered; while McPartland never quite possessed the same elusive genius, he shared Beiderbecke's attractive tonal and melodic approaches, and could drive down a band with a force and excitement that sometimes recalled Muggsy Spanier as much as Bix. [DF]

Meet me in Chicago (1959), Mercury/World

McPartland, Marian (*née* Marian Margaret Turner), piano, songwriter. b. Windsor, Berkshire, 20 March 1920. She studied music at the Guildhall before working in music-hall with pianist Billy Mayerl's Claviers. In 1945, while in ENSA, she met and married Jimmy McPartland, returned to the USA with him and worked in the 1950s as a solo pianist at Condon's, the Embers, the London House, Chicago, and 1952–60 at the Hickory House, where she led a great trio for a while with Bill Crow and Joe Morello. The 1960s, an unsettling period for many jazz musicians, were unhappy for McPartland too; her marriage and a love affair both failed and a spell with Benny Goodman ended unhappily. By the end of the decade she was on an upswing: her new record label Halcyon (financed by Sherman Fairchild) made a conscious stand against the apathy of big record companies, and she was soon busily performing in clubs, concert halls and workshops; a sympathetic profile by Whitney Balliett (see below) portrays her aims and objectives at the period.

Besides being an important jazz pianist, Marian McPartland is a diversifier: her early educational work with black students in Washington predated most jazz educational work by five years, and continues today. She has served on a number of jazz boards, writes beautifully about her music and broadcasts: her Piano Jazz programme for NBC, New York, is regularly renewed. By 1985 she was busy playing and recording, including concerts with Robert Farnon's orchestra: an album from that year (see below), from music to cover design and striking notes by J. Tevere MacFadyen, is one fine testimony to her artistic overview of jazz. [DF]

Willow Creek and Other Ballads (1985), Concord

See Balliett, Whitney, *Alec Wilder and his Friends* (Houghton Mifflin, 1974)

McQuater, Tommy (Thomas Mossie), trumpet, fluegelhorn. b. Maybole, Ayrshire, Scotland, 4 September 1914. He was playing with Lew Stone by 1935, then with Ambrose (where he partnered George Chisholm as a jazz cornerman), and all through the period was creating a sensation as the brightest young trumpet soloist of his era, recording with Benny Carter while he was in England and with Chisholm, and playing in the short-lived but legendary Heralds of Swing in 1939. From the outbreak of war McQuater played lead trumpet with the Squadronaires and after 1945 worked as a freelance and with the BBC Showband, in studios and as a jazz soloist: although his post-war jazz reputation was occasionally eclipsed by the younger Kenny Baker, he remained a connoisseur's delight, played and recorded regularly with Chisholm (they also made a formidable comedy team) and by the late 1960s was still playing for Jack Parnell's band, lead at Elstree Film Studios, at the London Palladium, and making occasional jazz appearances. During the 1970s and 1980s McQuater's unfailing abilities turned him into a legend in his own time and he was still to be heard at Bill McGuffie's Niner Club, often with John McLevy, as well as in studios. McQuater is also a great teacher: his former pupils include

Ian Carr, Alan Elsdon and Digby Fairweather. [DF]

Swingin' Britain: the Thirties (1935–8), Decca (double)

McRae, Carmen, vocals (and piano). b. New York City, 8 April 1922. A keen student of piano and singers, she wrote the song 'Dream of Life', which was recorded by Billie Holiday when Carmen was 16. Worked with Benny Carter band (1944), and briefly with Count Basie. Married and divorced drummer Kenny Clarke in 1940s, sang under name of Carmen Clarke with Mercer Ellington band (1946–7). Later worked as intermission pianist/singer at various New York clubs. Began making records under own name, initially for small labels (1953) then successful albums for major companies. Since late 1950s has been accompanied by her own trio, featuring such pianists as Ray Bryant, Norman Simmons, Duke Pearson. International touring for nightclub and concert work, including appearances in England (1978, 1981) and frequent trips to Japan. Occasional acting work in films (*Hotel*, 1967) and television (*Roots*).

Although her admiration for Billie Holiday dates from the start of her career, there is never any hint of stylistic dependency and, in any case, Carmen's personal, rather acid tone-quality does much to disguise what little similarity there is. The chief legacy of Holiday, in fact, lies in her rhythmic expertise and in the depth of feeling which Carmen manages to extract from her interpretation of lyrics, an art which the majority of would-be jazz singers seem determined to ignore. [BP]

After Glow (1957), Brunswick: *At Ronnie Scott's* (1978), Pye

MacRae, Dave (David Scott), piano, electric piano, synthesizers. b. Auckland, New Zealand, 2 April 1940. Mother and father amateur musicians. Self-taught, with some study at Sydney Conservatory, Australia. 1960–8, worked in Australia. 1969, to USA, joined Buddy Rich band. 1971, came to UK working with many Americans at Ronnie Scott's, including Clark Terry, Chet Baker, Jon Hendricks, Gil Evans. 1971–3, with Nucleus. Later with Robert Wyatt's Matching Mole, Mike Gibbs, Mike Westbrook, Back Door and several other UK groups. 1978–82, with his wife, singer Joy Yates, co-led Pacific Eardrum. 1984, returned to Australia with Joy Yates. MacRae's influences range from Art Tatum, Wynton Kelly, Herbie Hancock and Bill Evans to Ellington, Monk and Zawinul, and his playing encompasses a similarly broad spectrum. [IC]

With Buddy Rich, Matching Mole; with Mike Gibbs, *Just Ahead* (1972), Polydor; with Nucleus, *Belladonna* (1972), Vertigo; *Roots* (1973), Vertigo; with Back Door, *Another Fine Mess* (1974), Warners; with *Pacific Eardrum* (1977) and *Beyond Panic* (1978), both Charisma

McShann, Jay 'Hootie' (James Columbus), piano, vocals. b. Muskogee, Oklahoma, 12 January 1909. Played piano from age 12, left home both for spells at college and for work with bands in Oklahoma, Arkansas, Arizona and New Mexico. Moved to Kansas City (mid-1930s), working with local groups and under own name, his 1938 group including Charlie Parker. When Kansas City nightlife slowed down, played briefly in Chicago (1939), then back to leading own KC group, enlarged to 12-piece band (1940–3). After army service, re-formed band (1945), later 8-piece group mainly active on West Coast (1946–50). Returned to Kansas City (1951), leading band (later trio) and singing numbers associated with his former band vocalists Walter Brown and Jimmy Witherspoon. Trips to France (1969) and Canada (1971) led to gradual increase in touring schedules, including several further European visits.

As well as his latter-day blues-singing, McShann is noted for his compelling solo playing with an indefinable blend of blues, boogie, Basie and a bit of Earl Hines. On occasion during the 1970s he was again able to call on the services of Gene Ramey and Gus Johnson who not only worked briefly together for Basie (1952–3) but were the foundation of McShann's 1938–43 band – and what a foundation! Their work then combined brilliantly with the leader's choice of blues-based section-players and forward-looking soloists such as Parker and trumpeter Buddy Anderson (who, though reported dead in 1944, was playing locally in the 1980s). It is this band which, despite its small recorded output, is likely to prove McShann's most enduring claim to fame. [BP]

Hootie's K. C. Boogie (1941–2), Affinity; *Vine Street Boogie* (1974), Black Lion

See Dance, Stanley, *The World of Count Basie* (Sidgwick & Jackson, 1980)

Film: *Hootie's Blues* (dir. Bart Becker, Michael Farrell, 1978)

Mainieri, Mike (Michael Jnr.), vibes, synthi-vibe, keyboards, percussion, composer. b. Bronx, New York, 24 July 1938. Began on vibes at age 12. Worked with Buddy Rich band until 1962, touring South America and Asia. Led his own groups from 1963; active as a studio musician from the later 1960s. During the 1970s he also wrote and arranged music for feature films and TV programmes. He invented an instrument called a 'synthi-vibe' which enables him to synthesize (treat electronically) the vibes sound. In the 1970s he set up his own recording studio in a converted barn at his home in Woodstock, New York. 1975, he formed a quartet. 1979, he became a founder member of the all-star group Steps, later Steps Ahead. It was formed to tour Japan and the original personnel included Steve Gadd, Eddie Gomez and Mike Brecker. When Gadd left, Peter

Jay McShann

Erskine came in on drums, and there have been various keyboard players. Steps Ahead became one of the most successful bands of the 1980s, touring and playing festivals all over the world. Mainieri's favourites are Milt Jackson, Dave Pike, Gary Burton, and other influences are Charlie Parker and Debussy. [IC]

With Wes Montgomery, Tim Hardin, Paul Simon and others; with Steps Ahead, *Steps Ahead* (1983); *Modern Times* (1984), both Elektra Musician

Mainstream (1) Term coined in the 1950s by Stanley Dance to describe the small-group swing still being produced by greats such as Coleman Hawkins and Ben Webster. These and other players were perceived as maintaining the same virtues they had displayed in the 1930s and early 1940s, before they were pushed aside in the enmity between the beboppers and the revivalists. Rhythmically and tonally, these 'mainstreamers' had changed little, although some had been at least touched by bebop and mainstream rhythm-sections, especially pianists and bassists, were often irretrievably bop-influenced. Similarly, swing revivalists of a younger generation such as Scott Hamilton have imported more 'modern' influences including that of rhythm-and-blues, but these tributaries inevitably become part of the mainstream as it flows ever on.

(2) Another mainstream has been identified within the last decade, sometimes called 'mainstream-modern' or 'modern-mainstream'. Broadly speaking, this consists of beboppers still active and bebop revivalists who, whether they realize it or not, play things that could not have been played 30 years ago, for the simple reason that they have absorbed influences from modal and free jazz. Nothing ever stays in the same place, but perhaps the lesson of the mainstream concept is that the more jazz changes, the more it's the same thing. [BP]

Makowicz, Adam, piano, keyboards, composer and bass guitar. b. Czechoslovakia, 18 August 1940. Mother, a piano teacher, gave him his first lessons. He attended the Chopin Secondary School of Music in Cracow, Poland. First jazz gig was in Cracow with Polish trumpeter Tomasz Stańko, 1962. He moved to Warsaw in 1965, leading his own trio; with Zbigniew Namyslowski and the Novi singers, he toured throughout Europe, Cuba, India, Australia and New Zealand. He began composing, arranging and writing music criticism in 1970. He joined Michal Urbaniak's group in 1971, playing many festivals and recording several albums; he also worked in duo with Urbaniak's wife, Urszula Dudziak, recording an album with her. 1974, he worked with the Tomasz Stańko trio touring extensively in Western Europe; 1975, formed the Tomasz Stańko and Adam Makowicz Unit, touring in West Germany. Makowicz has also worked with Ben Webster, Jan Garbarek and others. *Jazz Forum*'s International Readers' Poll voted him one of the five best European pianists in 1972. Favourites are Art Tatum, Oscar Peterson, Keith Jarrett, Herbie Hancock. [IC]

With Namyslowski, Novi singers; with Dudziak, *Newborn Light* (nda); with Urbaniak, *Michal Urbaniak Fusion* (1975), both Columbia

Malone, Linda (aka **Linda Da Mango**), congas, percussion, voice. b. Southampton, Hampshire, 19 April 1951. Family musical. Classical piano for a few years, and acoustic guitar. Influenced by African and West Indian music. 1978–84, played with UK small groups and big bands – funk, soul and Latin. Joined the Guest Stars in 1981. 1984–5, worked with a percussion group led by John Stevens. 1984, toured USA East Coast with Guest Stars, then did a UK tour. 1985, the Guest Stars were support group for Jan Garbarek at his London concert. Favourites, many Latin percussionists; also Abdullah Ibrahim and Chris McGregor. [IC]

The Guest Stars (1984); *Out at Night* (1985), both Guest Stars

Mance, Junior (Julian Clifford Jnr.), piano. b. Chicago, 10 October 1928. Active on the Chicago jazz scene with Gene Ammons (1947–8). After moving to New York, became pianist in Lester Young's bop-oriented group of 1949, then with Gene Ammons–Sonny Stitt touring band (1950–1) and, after army service, accompanied Dinah Washington (1954–5). Touring and regular recording with Cannonball Adderley's early quintet (1956–7), Dizzy Gillespie (1958–60) and the Lockjaw Davis–Johhny Griffin group (1960–1). Formed own trio, which also accompanied singer Joe Williams, and apart from a period of illness has worked steadily but recorded less prolifically in the past 20 years.

A strong accompanist, heard on record with performers as varied as Aretha Franklin and bluesman Buddy Guy, his trio and duo routines are sometimes predictable but very effective with a live audience. Known principally for a highly rhythmic, bluesy approach somewhat similar to that of Ray Bryant, Mance is capable in the right company of a much wider range of expression. [BP]

Glidin' and Stridin' (1981), Nilva

Mangelsdorff, Albert, trombone, composer. b. Frankfurt am Main, 5 September 1928. Father a classical music lover; grandfather and uncles were musicians; brother, Emil Mangelsdorff, a noted saxist in Germany. Jazz was banned by the Nazis, but with his brother he attended secret meetings at the Hot Club in Frankfurt, and in 1940, at 12, he decided that jazz was the kind of music he wanted to play. By then he had already started on violin, but switched to guitar, playing with local bands. Did not take up trombone until age 20, but played modern jazz (bebop) immediately, because after the war American Forces Radio in Europe broadcast Charlie Parker records. By the early 1950s he was listening to Lee Konitz and Lennie Tristano – in particular the latter's 1949 performance of 'Intuition', the first recording of free (abstract) jazz improvisation.

He played with Hans Koller and others, then began leading his own band, broadcasting regularly on Frankfurt radio. From 1954 he began to win polls in Germany. 1958, he played in the USA as a member of Newport International Band. 1960, he played with a specially organized group, the European All Stars. During the early 1960s, he played concerts with his own group all over Western Europe and also in Yugoslavia. In 1962, John Lewis called Mangelsdorff 'one of the three most important trombone players in jazz', and recorded an album with him (*Animal Dance*).

Albert Mangelsdorff

At the beginning of 1964, with his group, he did a three-month tour of Asia for the Goethe Institute, playing concerts in Turkey, Iraq, Iran, India, South Vietnam, Ceylon, Hong Kong and other places. 'Soon after that,' he said, 'my development towards free music began. We heard Indian music and played with Indian musicians . . . All of a sudden you could do without all this playing on chord structures and themes. So, my playing started to get freer all by itself.' He incorporated some of the Indian ragas into his own music and also recorded a work by Ravi Shankar. It was with these ethnic influences and the development of the freer, more abstract, side of improvisation that Mangelsdorff began to arrive at his full musical identity. He continued to tour with his own groups on a world-wide basis, playing festivals including Newport, 1965, 1967, 1969; New Orleans, 1968; Tokyo and Osaka, 1970; and in Western and Eastern Europe. From the late 1960s he was also a regular member of the Globe Unity Orchestra, a large ensemble devoted almost exclusively to free (abstract) music.

From the early 1970s he began to develop a radical new approach to trombone playing, a technique producing multiphonics (more than one note played simultaneously) on unaccompanied trombone. Mangelsdorff described the technique for J. E. Berendt: 'You play a note and you sing another, usually a higher note. In the interval between the played and the sung notes, overtones are created which become so audible that you end up with real chords – sometimes up to four notes. There are intervals that are easy to make and then there are others that are very difficult – all that has to do with how far you can control your voice.' After this discovery he began playing solo (unaccompanied) trombone concerts, appearing at several festivals including Monterey, 1975, Bombay Jazz Yatra, 1978, and Warsaw, 1982. He has also made several solo tours, often playing two-hour concerts of unaccompanied trombone, in South America (1976), Asia (1978), USA and Canada (1978), France (1979). Unaccompanied trombone playing led him to re-examine his jazz roots and to reject certain aspects of free jazz; he commented, 'To me jazz is rhythm; there were too many people who forgot that for a while.'

He worked with French saxist Michel Portal in a quartet and quintet, 1976–82. Since 1981, with French bassist J. F. Jenny Clark, he has co-led the French/German Jazz Ensemble, which is made up of young players from both countries. 1984, he toured Holland playing solo and with the Pierre Courbois quintet; 1985, he toured Sweden in a trio with Anders Jormin (bass) and Rune Carlsson (drums); and the same year he and Wolfgang Dauner were the soloists in a piece Dauner composed for trombone, piano and symphony orchestra. In the mid-1980s Mangelsdorff's group became a trio with Pierre Favre (drums) and Leon Francioli (bass); he also works regularly in duo with Dauner and since 1975 has been a regular member of the United Jazz and Rock Ensemble.

Albert Mangelsdorff has been voted Europe's 'Musician of the Year' more often than any other, and since 1962 has appeared in American polls more than any other musician not living in the USA. In 1985, at the North Sea Festival, he was given the 'Bird Award' for his contribution to the European jazz scene and to the trombone. As with Miles Davis, his career shows an extraordinary capacity for artistic growth allied to rigorous standards of self-discipline and self-criticism, and his progress is minutely documented in his huge body of recorded work. He is a major instrumentalist in jazz, an innovator and an influential stylist, with enormous physical and creative stamina. He is also a fine composer for small groups and larger ensembles. His compositions are full of drama and surprise; brilliant angular lines are juxtaposed with dense dissonant chords, displaced accents, sudden silences, percussive eruptions. His life and work have been a focal point and inspiration for other European musicians. [IC]

With Globe Unity, UJRE and others; quartet, *One Tension* (1963), L & R; Mangelsdorff/Attila Zoller/Lee Konitz, *ZO-KO-MA* (1967); quartet (with Heinz Sauer/Gunter Lenz/Ralf Hübner), *Never Let it End* (1970); solo trombone, *Trombirds* (1973); Mangelsdorff/Palle Danielsson/Elvin Jones, *The Wide Point* (1975); solo trombone, *Tromboneliness* (1976); trio (with Jaco Pastorius/Alphonse Mouzon), *Trilogue-Live* (1976); quartet (with Wolfgang Dauner/Jones/Eddie Gomez, *A Jazz Tune I Hope* (1978); trio (with Pierre Favre/Leon Francioli), *Triple Entente* (1983), all MPS; Mangelsdorff/Dauner, *Two is Company* (1983), Mood; quartet (with Dauner/Jones/Anders Jormin), *Hot Hut* (1985), EMI

Mangione, Chuck (Charles Frank), trumpet, fluegelhorn, keyboards, composer. b. Rochester, New York, 29 November 1940. Brother, Gap Mangione, is pianist and composer. Chuck studied at Eastman School of Music in his home town. 1960–4, with his brother Gap co-led Jazz Brothers. He moved to New York City, 1965, playing with Woody Herman, Kai Winding, Maynard Ferguson. 1965–7, worked with Art Blakey's Jazz Messengers. 1968–72, director of the jazz ensemble of the Eastman School of Music. He formed his own quartet in 1968, and in 1970, with the Rochester Philharmonic Orchestra, recorded a live album, *Friends and Love*, which blended jazz, rock, folk and classical elements; it received good critical notices and also sold well. The first track, a Mangione composition called 'Hill Where the Lord Hides', was released as a single and became a hit. 1972–3, he toured with his quartet, making appearances with various US and Canadian symphony orchestras, and recording *Land of Make Believe* with the Hamilton Philharmonic, Ontario. During the early 1970s he also toured extensively in the USA and Europe, playing at major festivals, and appearing at the Ronnie Scott Club in London.

1974, Mangione formed his own recording company in order to release records by his friends. He also published arrangements of his own compositions designed for high school choirs. His compositions have been recorded by jazz and pop artists including Cannonball Adderley, Herb Alpert, Ray Bryant, Mark Murphy, Percy Faith.

Mangione's favourites are Dizzy Gillespie, Miles Davis and Clifford Brown. He produces a lovely lyrical sound and, although he has a superb technique, he plays with great economy. As a composer and a player, he makes benign fusion music, often with a delicate Latin tinge. He also plays very 'tasty' piano. [IC]

With Blakey; *Friends and Love* (1970), Mercury (double); *Chuck Mangione Quartet* (1972), Mercury; *Land of Make Believe* (1973), Phonogram; *Chase the Clouds Away* (1975), A & M

Mann, Herbie (Herbert Jay Solomon), flute, sax, composer. b. Brooklyn, New York, 16 April 1930. Began on clarinet at age nine. He was in Europe with the US army and played with a band in Trieste for three years. 1954–7, he was active on the West Coast of the USA, playing and writing and directing music for TV dramas. 1959, he formed his Afro-Jazz Sextet; 1960, took it on a US State Department tour of 15 African countries. 1961, he played in Brazil, discovered the bossa nova style and began playing in this idiom. He had a best-selling album (*Herbie Mann at the Village Gate*) and a hit single ('Comin' Home Baby') in 1962. He played in Brazil again, 1962–3; 1964, toured Japan. He was by now established as the most popular flautist in jazz, and a winner of many polls.

As well as African, Latin, and Brazilian influences, he also incorporated elements from Arabian, Jewish and Turkish music into his performances. In the later 1960s, he brought in elements from rock, recording *Memphis Underground* with a group which included Larry Coryell, Miroslav Vitous and Sonny Sharrock. He continued exploring the jazz-rock-funk area in the 1970s, calling his band the Family of Mann. 1974, he recorded a reggae album with Tommy McCook; 1975, the Family of Mann had a disco hit. He also started his own record label, Embryo, in 1970, and produced albums by Ron Carter, Vitous, Attila Zoller and others.

Mann won the *Downbeat* Readers' Poll for 13 years running (1957–70) and his general popularity got him into bad odour with the critics. His music has always been closely related to the dance rhythms of the day, and his bands have usually included some of the most gifted up-and-coming young musicians. He has toured and played major festivals all over the USA and Europe. [IC]

Herbie Mann at the Village Gate (1962); *Herbie Mann Live at Newport* (1965); *Memphis Underground* (1968), all Atlantic; *Push Push* (1971), Embryo; with Bill Evans, *Nirvana* (1962), Atlantic

Manne, Shelly (Sheldon), drums, composer. b. New York City, 11 June 1920; d. 26 September 1984. Worked on boats to Europe (late 1930s), then with several leading big bands (1939–42); also with Joe Marsala group on 52nd Street (1940–41). While in navy (1942–5), played on and helped to organize sessions for Signature records with Coleman Hawkins, Barney Bigard etc. With Stan Kenton (1946–7, 1947–8, 1950–1) and Woody Herman (1949); also small-group work with Charlie Ventura (1947) and Bill Harris (1948). Leaving Kenton for the last time, settled in Los Angeles and became heavily involved in studio work, eventually not only as player but as composer of film and TV music. Simultaneously continued making small-group records and live appearances, billed as Shelly Manne and his Men. Ran successful nightclub, Shelly's Manne-Hole (1960–74), and was a founder member of the L.A.4 (1974–7).

An example of true versatility, Manne was widely respected in all the spheres he moved in: the West Coast experimentalists of the early 1950s, and the more vital jazz stylists he worked with before and after, all valued his musical contributions and his personal reliability – not to mention those who wielded power in the demanding world of the studios. His jazz drumming was marked by the kind of responsiveness which makes the life of other group members so much easier, and some of the unusual effects he came up with may have paved the way for the freer approach to drumming which surfaced in the mid-1960s. [BP]

The Three and the Two (1954), Contemporary/OJC; Sonny Rollins, *Way Out West* (1957), Contemporary/Boplicity; Bill Evans/Shelly Manne, *Empathy* (1962), Verve

Manone, Wingy (Joseph Matthews), trumpet, vocals. b. New Orleans, 13 February 1900; d. Las Vegas, 9 July 1982. He worked round the Southern states with leaders such as Peck Kelley and Doc Ross before going to New York in 1927 and then settling in Chicago. Fast-talking, amicable and ambitious, he toured in shows, recorded with Benny Goodman and Red Nichols and even appeared in a Red Indian revue (billed as 'the one-armed Indian': he had lost his right arm in a streetcar accident) during the late 1920s and early 1930s, but by 1934 was leading his own band in New York, and recording prolifically. One Manone title of the period, 'Isle of Capri', full of nonsense delivered in his appealing Italianate style, hit big and the formula made him a headliner on 52nd Street as well as in Chicago, New Orleans and Los Angeles – in fact country-wide. 'I'd like to be up at RKO myself', Manone sang in another anarchical re-write (of Dorothy Fields's 'A Fine Romance'):

Shelly Manne

by 1940 he was, for *Rhythm on the River* (starring Bing Crosby who befriended Manone and kept him as a court jester) and four other less successful low-budget movies including *Juke Box Jenny*, a more or less storyless excuse for a string of hit tunes. By now Manone, living in Hollywood, was the star he wanted to be and in 1948 he wrote a high-spirited jive-happy autobiography, *Trumpet on the Wing*. For most of the 1950s, living in Las Vegas, he was still warding off jazz fashion, bandleading and working with Crosby on radio shows. But by the 1960s, when he toured Britain, cracks were starting to show in his indomitable spirit. Nursing an ambition to write a suite based on his New Orleans memories, worried that his son might be drafted into Vietnam, he was near to disillusionment. 'You can't make it playing honest nowadays', he told a *Downbeat* reporter in 1970: a sad comment from the trumpeter who had billed his shows with the byline 'Come in and hear the truth!' Since then Manone's fine records of the 1930s have been issued as a chronology: a much happier epitaph. [DF]

A Chronological Study vols. 1–5, Rarities/Little Gem

See Manone, Wingy, and Vandervoort, Paul, II, *Trumpet on the Wing* (Doubleday, 1948, repr. 1964)

Mantler, Michael, composer, trumpet. b. Vienna, 10 August 1943. Studied trumpet and musicology at Academy of Music and Vienna University; 1962, moved to USA, studying at Berklee School of Music. 1964, moved to New York, playing trumpet with Cecil Taylor's group; involved in the formation of the Jazz Composers' Guild with Taylor, Bill Dixon, Roswell Rudd, Archie Shepp and others struggling for better working conditions and opportunities to present their new (abstract) music without compromise; together with Carla Bley, whom he later married, he formed a large orchestra to perform new compositions by members of the Guild. When the Guild broke up, he toured Europe twice, 1965–6, with Steve Lacy and Carla Bley in the Jazz Realities quintet. Back in the US, he formed the Jazz Composers' Orchestra Association (JCOA), a non-profit-making foundation to commission, perform and record new compositions for jazz orchestra.

1967, he played trumpet on the recording of Carla Bley's *A Genuine Tong Funeral* by Gary Burton and orchestra. 1968, he recorded a double album of his music for JCOA, featuring the JCO with soloists Cecil Taylor, Don Cherry, Rudd, Pharoah Sanders, Larry Coryell and Gato Barbieri. The album won several international awards including the Grand Prix, Académie Charles Cros, France; 1969, he conducted performances of several of his pieces by the orchestra and soloists at the Electric Circus, New York and also played on Charlie Haden's *Liberation Music Orchestra* album.

1970–1, Mantler also co-ordinated the recording of Carla Bley's long composition *Escalator Over the Hill* (see BLEY, CARLA), a triple album featuring the JCO with soloists Jack Bruce, John McLaughlin, Linda Ronstadt, Gato Barbieri, Don Cherry and others. 1972, he formed New Music Distribution Service (NMDS) as a part of JCOA, to provide adequate distribution for their own records as well as those of other independent producers. 1973, with Carla Bley, he formed Watt Works, a new record label and publishing company devoted to their own music, because JCOA was now releasing more records by other composers.

1975, he built a recording studio near Woodstock, New York, so that he and Carla Bley could function more autonomously. He received composition grants from the Creative Artists Program Service and the National Endowment for the Arts, and with the aid of a grant from the Ford Foundation's Recording-Publishing Program, he was able to record his *13* for two orchestras and piano. Since then he has recorded six more albums of his compositions featuring variously Robert Wyatt, Carla Bley, Terje Rypdal, Steve Swallow, Jack DeJohnette, Kevin Coyne, Chris Spedding, Ron McClure, Coryell and Tony Williams among others.

Since the mid-1970s, he has continued to manage, perform with and record with the Carla Bley Band, to compose new music, guide JCOA/NMDS as Executive Director, and run the affairs of Watt Works.

1982, he recorded and toured Europe with Charlie Haden's Liberation Music Orchestra. May 1984, his new orchestral suite *Twenty Five* was premiered in Cologne by the West German Radio Orchestra under the direction of Michael Gibbs and featuring Bill Frisell, Carla Bley, Steve Swallow, and Nick Mason. [IC]

Nine with Carla Bley; with Charlie Haden, *Ballad of the Fallen* (1982), ECM; as leader, *The Jazz Composers' Orchestra* (1968), JCOA; *No Answer* (1974); *The Hapless Child* (1976); *Silence* (1977); *Movies* (1978); *More Movies* (1980); *Something There* (1982); *Alien* (1985), all WATT

Marable, Fate, piano, calliope, leader. b. Paducah, Kentucky, 2 December 1890; d. St Louis, Missouri, 16 January 1947. One of the three bandleaders who led bands for the Streckfus riverboat line, Fate Marable – a light-coloured man with red hair who worked so long for Streckfus that he became known as 'Streckfus' son' – played on riverboats for most of his life. A bandleader by 1917, he was a highly talented piano and calliope player and a sternly disciplined leader, who reputedly kept his wild bunch of young musicians – many of them straight from rough-house New Orleans – in strict order. All of them had to be able to read music and tackle a varied repertoire (popular tunes, classical selections and singalongs to please the predominantly white clientele that rode the steamers) as well as play jazz, which more often came into its own on specially advertised 'coloured nights', when admirers stood six feet deep around the band. New music was rehearsed daily, band members were encouraged to listen to the orchestras on neighbouring boats and visits for the purpose were organized. The great musicians-in-the-making who worked for Marable included Louis Armstrong, Henry 'Red' Allen, Pops Foster, Jimmy Blanton, Gene Sedric, Zutty Singleton, the Dodds Brothers and mellophonist Dave Jones, who is said to have helped Louis Armstrong with technique and ideas: the music they produced had a colossal effect on still younger talents, two examples among hundreds being Bix Beiderbecke and pianist Jess Stacy who heard riverboat bands often at Cape Girardeau. Marable left only disappointing recordings made with a second-line band, Fate Marable's Society Syncopators, in 1924 in New Orleans, but his bands were a vital training ground. 'Fate knew that just by being around musicians who read music I would automatically learn myself', said Louis Armstrong: whether reading or improvising, Marable provided a free university to people who otherwise could never have seen one. [DF]

Marching Bands The history of marching bands predates jazz by many years, but they have remained up to the present day an integral part of jazz's culture. By the mid-1800s big brass ensembles were common all over America, and they were quick to embrace the ragtime repertoire that was popular by the century's end. Pianist Eubie Blake remembers such highly-trained bands 'raggin' the hell out of the music' in Baltimore by the 1890s, and New Orleans-based brass bands of the period often reached a standard which jazz listeners more accustomed to the sound of later ear-based groups, the Eureka and many others, might find surprising. An undated early recording by the New Orleans Military Band (on *Thesaurus of Classic Jazz*), probably staffed by Creole musicians, sets a standard that would be envied by any champion brass band in Britain's Midlands and North and reflects the fact that – back in jazz's early days – senior New Orleans players such as Lorenzo Tio and Manuel Perez had received thorough classical training. Such later brass bands as the Tuxedo, Eagle and Magnolia – all packed with young New Orleans stars from Henry 'Red' Allen to Louis Armstrong, King Oliver and hundreds of others – set up different traditions for themselves, playing marches, dirges and upbeat selections by ear for any variety of functions in the city but most usually for funerals: lodge members who had died would be buried with all the dignity of a full marching band playing a dirge en route to the burial and happy, faster selections on the way back. (New Orleans religious beliefs complied then – and still do, in theory at least – with the Old Testament philosophy 'Rejoice at the death and weep at the birth'.) For funerals as well as celebrations in general the New Orleans marching band achieved a legendary folk-status; similar bands have been organized in Europe by such New Orleans figureheads as Ken Colyer *et al.* and, broadly speaking, little has changed in the way they play over an 80-year span. But in the 1980s a new-generation marching band, the Dirty Dozens Brass Band, achieved widespread publicity (including a recording contract for George Wein, regular appearances at festivals in and out of New Orleans and so on) playing rock and roll and modern jazz repertoire, including Charlie Parker tunes. The Dirty Dozens, despite their huge success (and possibly because of it), have achieved only a mixed reception among diehard lovers of New Orleans jazz, but most other people will find their music a rewarding extension of an honourable jazz tradition. [DF]

Marcus, Steve (Stephen), tenor and soprano sax. b. New York City, 18 September 1939. After study at Berklee School, toured with Stan Kenton (1963) and briefly with Donald Byrd (1965). With Woody Herman (several times from early 1967), Jazz Composers' Orchestra (1968), Herbie Mann group (late 1960s) and Larry Coryell (1971–3): formed own Count's Rock Band (1973–5). Joined Buddy Rich (1975) and rejoined frequently, as featured soloist, in next decade. Marcus comes across as a contemporary version of the r & b 'tough tenor' and, although inevitably influenced by Coltrane, has much in common with his contemporary Sal Nistico; while he may prefer small-group work, he sounds highly appropriate in a big-band setting. [BP]

Lionel Hampton Presents Buddy Rich (1977), Kingdom Jazz

Mariano, Charlie (Carmine Ugo), alto and soprano sax, flutes, nadaswaram. b. Boston, 12 November 1923. Elder sister a pianist. He took piano lessons as a child, and started on sax at 17. Played in an army band, then attended Berklee School of Music, studied sax with Joe Viola. While at Berklee he played around Boston with Jaki Byard, Nat Pierce, Sam Rivers, Herb Pomeroy, Ray Santisi, Joe Gordon, Gigi Gryce, Quincy Jones, Jimmy Woode, among others. 1953–5, worked with Stan Kenton's band, then spent two and a half years in Los Angeles playing with Frank Rosolino, Shelly Manne and others. 1959, he married Japanese pianist Toshiko Akiyoshi and formed a quartet with her in 1960, playing in the US and Japan. 1962, he played and recorded with Charles Mingus. Then, with Toshiko, spent two years in Japan, returning to USA in 1965. Moved to Boston and taught at Berklee for six years, during which time he also played with Astrud Gilberto, going three times to Japan with her. He was also sent to Malaysia for five months on a US Government grant to coach the Radio Malaysia orchestra. While there, he began playing the nadaswaram, a South Indian wind instrument made of wood and with a double reed like an oboe. 1971–84, he lived in Europe working with groups such as Ambush (Stu Martin, Barre Phillips, Peter Warren), Eberhard Weber's Colours, Jasper van't Hof and Pork Pie, the United Jazz and Rock Ensemble (UJRE), a trio with van't Hof and Philip Catherine, and various other bands under his own name. 1973, he spent four months in India studying the nadaswaram, and subsequently made two more visits there to study and play.

He admires and has been inspired by very many musicians, but singles out for mention Johnny Hodges, Charlie Parker, John Coltrane, Miles Davis and the Indian musicians Bismillah Khan and Balachander. 1964, *Downbeat* voted him Talent Deserving Wider Recognition. Mariano's whole career is an object lesson in gradual artistic growth. Like Miles Davis, he has at every stage played *contemporary* music, always remained open to new ideas, never allowing his creative arteries to harden. He first made an international impression, in the early 1950s, as an impassioned alto soloist coming out of Parker, but already showing originality. By 1963, when he worked and recorded with Mingus on the two classic albums *Black Saint and the Sinner Lady* and *Mingus, Mingus, Mingus* (both Impulse), he was even more himself, and was described by critic John S. Wilson as 'a brilliant combination of authority, virtuosity and inspiration'. The years of teaching at Berklee made him examine the whole basis of his music, and this, with his profound interest in other (ethnic) musical cultures, broadened and deepened his vision, so that his very greatest work has been done since he reached 50. Living in Europe from the early 1970s, he found the environment conducive to his art: in Europe, competition – mere musical athleticism – plays very little part, but the creation of atmosphere and mood and the expression of emotion are of crucial importance. Mariano has made a major contribution to some of the key groups of the 1970s and 1980s, in particular Eberhard Weber's Colours, of which he was a regular member throughout its existence. In his compositions and solos, Mariano showed a much greater emotional range and a more finely poised artistry. His solos are often quite extraordinary – marmoreally sculpted, every note telling and every note meant, his soprano and alto sound projecting a powerful, almost anguished lyricism, as if the music were being wrung out of him. There are few parallels in jazz to the voluptuous austerity of Mariano's later work. [IC]

With Manne, Rosolino, Bill Holman, Toshiko, Elvin Jones; six with UJRE, which has some of Mariano's finest work; with Stan Kenton, *Contemporary Concepts* (1955), Capitol; with McCoy Tyner, *Live at Newport* (1963), Impulse; with Weber's Colours, *Yellow Fields* (1975); *Silent Feet* (1977); *Little Movements* (1980), all ECM; with Philip Catherine and van't Hof, *Sleep my Love* (1979), CMP; Mariano/Stu Goldberg/Don Alias/Gene Perla, *Crystal Bells* (1979), CMP; Mariano and the Karnataka College of Percussion, *Jyothi* (1983), ECM; *The Charlie Mariano Group* (1985), Mood

Marmarosa, Dodo (Michael), piano. b. Pittsburgh, Pennsylvania, 12 December 1925. Big-band work in late teens with Gene Krupa, Tommy Dorsey, Charlie Barnet (whose recorded 'The Moose' was his piano feature). After more than a year with Artie Shaw (1944–5) settled on the West Coast, as did fellow Shaw sideman Barney Kessel with whom Marmarosa had already recorded. Prolific freelance work including record dates with Lester Young and Charlie Parker. In 1950s inactive through illness and living in Pittsburgh, resurfacing in early 1960s to cut three albums (one with Gene Ammons) before returning to total obscurity. The brilliant sound and highly original bop-influenced lines of his 1940s playing made most of his contemporaries, and even his own later work, feel like an anticlimax. [BP]

The Dial Masters (1947), Spotlite

Marrero, Lawrence Henry, banjo, guitar. b. New Orleans, 24 October 1900; d. 5 June 1959. He was taught banjo by his brother John and from about 1919 played with leaders such as Wooden Joe Nicholas, Chris Kelly, Frank Dusen, John Robichaux; by the late 1930s he was working regularly with George Lewis, in clubs and cabarets in New Orleans. In 1942, alongside Lewis, he made the records for Gene Williams which were to help launch the revival and Bunk Johnson, and stayed on through the traumatic time in New York that followed until 1946, when Lewis went home and worked at Manny's Tavern, New Orleans 1947–8, with his own band. Marrero went with him and became inseparable from his leader (he called Lewis 'brother-in-law'). A simple, content-to-accompany banjoist with few tricks up his sleeve, Marrero was the ideal support for Lewis, and saw himself rise to unexpected stardom despite the onset of high blood pressure in the 1950s. Lewis replaced him in 1955 before a heavy spell of touring ('I knew Lawrence wouldn't last a month on the road') and for the rest of his life the old banjoist led his own bands in New Orleans. [DF]

Any with Lewis

Marsala, Joe (Joseph Francis), clarinet, saxes, composer. b. Chicago, 4 January 1907; d. Santa Barbara, California, 4 March 1978. When young he lived in a black neighbourhood of Chicago in a musical family and by 1937 had held down a wide selection of non-musical jobs as well as ten years in clubs and circus and touring bands in and out of New York and Chicago. That year he moved into 52nd Street's Hickory House, a steak joint owned by John Popkin: his band included Eddie Condon, Joe Bushkin, Ray Biondi (vln) and soon after – in a quietly revolutionary decision – Marsala brought in black trumpeter Henry 'Red' Allen to complete the group ('In the 1930s', says Leonard Feather, 'Joe was responsible in his quiet, unpublicized way for more attempts to break down segregation in jazz than Benny Goodman.' Allen was later replaced by another black player, Otis Johnson.) After illness in 1938, Marsala moved back into the Hickory House (this time featuring harpist Adele Girard, whom he later married) 'and from that time we were in and out of the Hickory House for the best part of ten years.' Apart from Girard, Marsala's group featured bright up-and-comers such as Carmen Mastren, Buddy Rich, Shelly Manne and Dave Tough, many of whom later joined Tommy Dorsey (Marsala once sent Dorsey a half-joking telegram: 'How about giving me a job in your band so

I can play with mine?') and singer Frankie Laine was another early protégé. In 1944, Marsala wrote the first of several hit tunes, 'Don't Cry Joe' (the hit was by Gordon Jenkins's orchestra); later ones included 'Little Sir Echo' and 'And so to sleep again'. But the winds of change were sweeping through jazz and Marsala (despite being open-eared enough to feature trumpeters Neal Hefti and Dizzy Gillespie in future projects) retired from full-time performing in 1948, went into music publishing and in 1962 was vice-president of Seeburg's juke-box-based recording company. Still bandleading occasionally in the 1960s, he made some intriguing late records featuring him with Bobby Hackett and singer Tony Bennett. [DF]

Joe Marsala and his Band (1944), Jazzology

Marsala, Marty (Mario Salvatore), trumpet. b. Chicago, 2 April 1909; d. 27 April 1975. He began in Chicago, where the New Orleans Rhythm Kings were an early inspiration, and worked locally before moving to New York in 1936 to join his brother Joe's band. On and off, with periods in between for leading his own band, touring with Chico Marx, 1942–3, and working with leaders such as Miff Mole and Tony Parenti, Marty was to be found with Joe up until 1946: by the late 1940s he was commuting more and more regularly between Chicago and San Francisco. With his powerhouse trumpeting, fine sense of humour and onstage presence, he became a much loved part of the jazz scene on the West Coast, appearing at Victor's and Roxie's, the Downbeat (where he backed Sidney Bechet) and at Doc Dougherty's Hangover Club with his own band and Earl Hines's. Marsala settled in San Francisco with occasional visits back to Chicago (for example to play Jazz Ltd in 1962), but became ill in the 1960s and gradually gave up music. While never a great individual in jazz terms, he offered a well-stirred mix of Muggsy Spanier, Wild Bill Davison and more technical players such as Don Goldie that is still appealing. [DF]

Earl Hines, *At Club Hangover, vol. 5* (1955), Storyville

Marsalis, Branford, soprano and tenor sax. b. New Orleans, 1960. Father Ellis Marsalis, pianist, composer and educator; brother Wynton Marsalis, trumpet player. He began on alto, replacing Bobby Watson in Art Blakey's band, 1981. He switched to tenor and soprano, joining his brother's band in 1982 and touring the USA, Europe and Japan with him. There were more international tours in 1984 and 1985. 1984, he played on some tracks of Miles Davis's album *Decoy*. 1985–6, with Kenny Kirkland, Darryl Jones and Omar Hakim, he accompanied Sting on the album *The Dream of the Blue Turtles* (A & M), and toured internationally with him. 1986, toured Europe with Herbie Hancock quartet. [IC]

With W. Marsalis; *Scenes in the City* (1983), CBS

Marsalis, Wynton, trumpet. b. New Orleans, 18 October 1961. Father Ellis Marsalis, a pianist, composer and educator. Brother Branford, a saxophonist. He was given his first trumpet when he was six, by Al Hirt; his classical studies began at age 12, at which point he also began to take a serious interest in jazz, practising and listening to albums. Studied trumpet with John Longo, who taught him to understand the concept behind the exercises. In his mid-teens he had extensive experience in marching bands, jazz bands, funk bands and orchestras with European repertoires. Throughout high school he played first trumpet in the New Orleans Civic Orchestra. At 17 he went to the Berkshire Music Center at Tanglewood for their summer school, where he received the Harvey Shapiro Award for Outstanding Brass Player, and impressed Gunther Schuller with his precocious knowledge of jazz. At 18 he went to the Juilliard School in New York, then a few months later joined Art Blakey's Jazz Messengers.

Summer 1981, he toured with the Herbie Hancock quartet in the USA, playing the Newport Jazz Festival/New York, then touring Japan, and this exposure established his international reputation. The quartet recorded a double album and Marsalis recorded his own first LP as a leader. By the spring of 1982 he was leading his own quintet and touring extensively in the US, playing concert halls, festivals and clubs. In the summer he was involved in a series of concerts with the Kool Jazz Festival All-Star lineups in the US, and in New York participated in the all-star tribute 'Musicians for Monk', and the 'Young Lions of Jazz' concert. Then, with his quintet, he did a long European tour playing major festivals in several countries, followed by a Japanese tour which was another triumph, and his summer itinerary ended with an extended stay in the UK, including dates at the Ronnie Scott Club. In December he was back in London to record his first classical album, of Haydn, Hummel and Leopold Mozart trumpet concertos with Raymond Leppard. While there he met the famous classical trumpeter Maurice André, who said that Marsalis was 'potentially the greatest [classical] trumpeter of all time'. 1983 and 1984 were also crammed with activity, tours in the US, Europe and the Far East, workshops, seminars, festivals and more jazz and classical recordings. Marsalis also did a classical tour in the summer of 1984, playing 24 concerts with symphony orchestras in the US, Canada, Hawaii and London. He also became the first instrumentalist to win two simultaneous Grammy awards in the categories of Jazz (Best Soloist) and Classical Music (Best Soloist with Orchestra). By now, awards and prizes were

Wynton Marsalis

coming thick and fast: he was winning jazz polls as Best Trumpeter and Jazz Musician of the Year (*Downbeat*), and he received the Netherlands Edison Award and France's Grand Prix du Disque. He was getting extensive media coverage in the US, and a documentary film was made about him for British TV. At the age of 22 he was already a superstar.

As a trumpet player, Marsalis is a technical genius: he has a beautiful sound, good range, superb articulation, brilliant control, a perfect ear, complete intellectual grasp of whatever music he is playing. As a player of composed music and as an improviser, he is a total virtuoso. As a jazz player, however, he has as yet done nothing new either stylistically or conceptually. His strongest discernible influences are first Miles Davis, then Freddie Hubbard, and he also likes Clifford Brown, Louis Armstrong, Don Cherry, Woody Shaw, Fats Navarro. It may be that, as with Joe Zawinul, Keith Jarrett and Eberhard Weber, his really great work will come later in his career, when he has fully absorbed his influences and found his own individual voice. He is the only trumpeter in history to have equally mastered the two disciplines of jazz improvisation and classical orchestral playing, and this in itself is an extraordinary achievement; but he has said, 'I'm a jazz musician who can play classical music', and the signs are that he is deeply committed to the jazz heritage of which, by now, he is an integral part. [IC]

With *Herbie Hancock Quartet* (1982); *Wynton Marsalis* (1982); *Think of One* (1983); *Hot House Flowers* (1984); *J Mood* (1986), all CBS; classical, *Wynton Marsalis, Raymond Leppard, National Philharmonic Orchestra* (1982), CBS Masterworks

Marsh, Warne Marion, tenor sax (and clarinet, flute). b. Los Angeles, 26 October 1927. Played with Hoagy Carmichael group (1944–5) before army service. Then toured with Buddy Rich (1948) and settled in New York, working with Lennie Tristano sextet (1949–52). Otherwise worked outside music except for recordings with Lee Konitz and under own name (mid-1950s). Reunions with Tristano (1959, 1964–5). Returned to California (1966), teaching music and swimming plus occasional playing. Early member of Supersax ensemble (1972). Two tours of Europe with Konitz, using local rhythm-sections (1975, 1976).

Marsh is an extremely fluent but not facile thinker, full of unusual turns of phrase despite a flow of notes that, in most other players, would hinder rather than encourage invention. He is, for instance, far more in command of high-speed technique than his frequent collaborator Konitz, but still manages to be nearly as interesting as him. Changing less over the years than Konitz, his later playing remains more obviously marked by his work with Tristano; in fact, the shifting accents and veiled tonality often make him sound like a saxophone transcription of Tristano's piano solos. The overall impression, though, is more vital, thanks to Marsh's unique tone – an acquired taste, which has tempted few other saxists apart from Teo Macero, but its glacial edge accords well with the otherworldliness of Marsh's lines. [BP]

All Music (1976), Nessa

Marshall, John Stanley, drums. b. London, 28 August 1941. Honours degree in psychology at Reading University. Began playing at school and became seriously involved with music at university. Private lessons with several teachers, including Allan Ganley and Philly Joe Jones. First regular engagement was with Alexis Korner's Blues Incorporated, 1964. With the Graham Collier sextet, 1965–70, during which time he played with John Surman, John McLaughlin, Dave Holland, Mike Westbrook, Graham Bond Organization, Joe Harriott, Indo-Jazz Fusions, Keith Tippett's sextet and Centipede, Alan Skidmore and others. 1969, he was a founder member of Nucleus, which won first prize at the Montreux festival the following year and played the Newport festival and the Village Gate in New York. At the beginning of the 1970s he also became a regular member of the Mike Gibbs orchestra. 1971, he left Nucleus to join the Jack Bruce Band; 1972, left Bruce and joined Soft Machine, becoming a permanent member and, in the later 1970s, co-leader with Karl Jenkins. During the 1970s he also played with many leading US and European musicians, including Larry Coryell, Gary Burton, Mary Lou Williams, Ronnie Scott, Ben Webster, Roy Eldridge, Milt Jackson, John Taylor, Norma Winstone, Volker Kriegel, Gordon Beck, George Gruntz's Piano Conclave. 1973, at the Baden-Baden Free Jazz Meeting, he met and began playing with Charlie Mariano, Jasper van't Hof and Philip Catherine. 1977, he joined Eberhard Weber's Colours, one of the most important and influential groups of its time, staying with it until it disbanded at the end of 1981. Since then he has rejoined Nucleus and worked with John Surman, Kenny Wheeler, the Gil Evans orchestra, van't Hof, Coryell, Anthony Braxton, Albert Mangelsdorff and many others.

Marshall is a drummer of consummate ability, able to handle difficult asymmetrical time signatures, as well as common time (4/4, 3/4) at any tempo, and he is at home with the whole gamut of contemporary styles: jazz, rock, ethnic, Indian, free improvisation, small group and big band. He is also a paradox: despite his intellect and wit, he is one of the most emotional drummers of all, and can erupt in an explosion of gargantuan energy. But he is capable of great subtlety, too, and it is this wide range of ability which has led to the extraordinary variety of his working contexts. He has performed with several classical groups playing composed works: 1973, he worked with Matrix; 1974, with Tim Souster and Roger Smalley, he played in a BBC Promenade Concert from the London Roundhouse; and he has performed for and with other contemporary composers. He frequently rehearses and performs new works with the Hamburg Radio Orchestra in Germany. He also does studio work, drum clinics and workshops, and has accompanied many singers including Sarah Vaughan, Leon Thomas, Elaine Delmar and Karin Krog. With Eberhard Weber's Colours he toured Europe, the USA (several times) and Australasia, and with Nucleus in 1984 he toured South America. He is one of the few European drummers with a solid international reputation.

Favourites include Elvin Jones, Tony Williams, Jack DeJohnette, Roy Haynes, Keith Moon and Phil Seamen. Other inspirations range from Charles Mingus and Miles Davis to Jack Bruce, Mike Gibbs and John Surman. [IC]

With Gibbs, Surman, Westbrook, Kriegel, Tippett; four with Nucleus, including *Elastic Rock* and *Solar Plexus* (both 1970), Vertigo; with Bruce, *Harmony Row* (1971), Polydor; with van't Hof's Pork Pie, *The Door is Open* (1975), MPS; nine with Soft Machine, including *Bundles* (1975) and *Softs* (1976), Harvest; with Weber's Colours, *Silent Feet* (1977); *Little Movements* (1980), both ECM

Marshall, Wendell, bass. b. St Louis, Missouri, 24 October 1920. While in college, played briefly with Lionel Hampton band (1942). Three years in army service, then with Stuff Smith trio (1946–7) and leading own group back in St Louis. Joined Mercer Ellington band (1948) followed by successful transfer to Duke Ellington (1948–55). Prolific recording session work from mid-1950s with such as Art Blakey, Donald Byrd–Gigi Gryce and Milt Jackson–Hank Jones–Kenny Clarke (together and separately). The bassist who replaced Oscar Pettiford in Duke's band took occasional solo features in a typical Blanton/Pettiford style, while his later jazz work concentrated almost exclusively on excellent rhythm playing. Interestingly, he was a first cousin of Blanton, inheriting one of Blanton's instruments, but sadly he was soon lost to the jazz scene as he specialized more and more in Broadway stage work. [BP]

Milt Jackson, *Jazz Skyline* (1956), Savoy

Masekela, Hugh, trumpet, fluegelhorn. b. Witbank, South Africa, 4 April 1939. Helped by the priest Father Trevor Huddleston, Masekela got his first trumpet from the Johannesburg Native Municipal Band, and his first lessons from its

John Marshall

leader Old Man Sowsa. Later he had lessons from saxophonist Kippie Moeketsi, and met trombonist Jonas Gwanga and Dollar Brand (Abdullah Ibrahim). Their musical experience consisted of their African roots – kwela and the music of the black townships – church music, and imported American records; they were listening to Ellington, Glenn Miller, Louis Jordan, Count Basie, Dizzy Gillespie and Charlie Parker. Together with Brand and Gwanga, Masekela formed the Jazz Epistles, the first black band to record a jazz LP in South Africa. The Jazz Epistles played 'township bebop', but had only a brief existence because of the worsening political situation. All gatherings of more than ten people were banned, which effectively prohibited public musical performances. John Dankworth and Harry Belafonte procured a passport for Masekela, and he left South Africa never to return. He studied for a few months at the Guildhall in London, then went to the Manhattan School of Music, New York. He began to record, and went to live in California, forming his own record label, Chisa Records. But living in US society and playing 'American' jazz made him lose his sense of identity to some extent and it became essential to re-establish contact with his African roots. He went to London with Makhaya Ntshoko (dms), Larry Willis (piano) and Eddie Gomez (bass), and with fellow SA emigré Dudu Pukwana on alto sax they recorded a dynamic album, *Home is Where the Music Is* (1972). Helped by Fela Ransome Kuti, he began to tour in Africa with an African group called Hedzoleh Soundz, then took it to California for some years, during which they recorded six albums. Again the US episode was not a success. 1980, he returned to Africa, living first in Zimbabwe, then in 1982 moving to Botswana. His 'Going Home' concert, with his wife, singer Miriam Makeba, was attended by 35,000 people. 1985–6, he played concerts and recorded in London. [IC]

Quartet, *Trumpet African* (1962), Mercury; *The Americanization of Ooga Booga* (1965), MGM; quintet with Dudu Pukwana, *Home is Where the Music Is* (1972), Chisa; with Hedzoleh Soundz, *I Am Not Afraid* (1974), Chisa; with the Kalahari Band, *Technobush* (1984), Jive Afrika

Mason, Harvey, Jnr, drums, percussion, piano, composer. b. Atlantic City, New Jersey, 22 February 1947. Father a musician. Began on drums at age four. Studied at Berklee; gained B.Ed. from New England Conservatory. Worked with Jan Hammer, George Mraz, Erroll Garner, George Shearing. Moved to Los Angeles in 1971, becoming very active as a studio musician and working with jazz and rock groups and symphony orchestras. Played with many leading musicians including Ellington, Quincy Jones, Freddie Hubbard and Gunther Schuller. Mason made an important contribution to Herbie Hancock's classic jazz-rock-funk album *Head Hunters* (1973); as well as playing drums, he was co-writer of the brilliant piece 'Chameleon', and he did a rearrangement of Hancock's old hit tune 'Watermelon Man' which was so imaginative that it amounted to virtual recomposition. [IC]

With Bobbi Humphrey, Shearing, Gerry Mulligan, Bobby Hutcherson, John Klemmer, Hubbard; with Donald Byrd, *Street Lady* (1973), Blue Note; with Hancock, *Head Hunters* (1973), CBS

Mason, Rod, trumpet, cornet, leader. b. Plymouth, Devon, 28 September 1940. He worked first with Cy Laurie in 1959 and by 1962 was working for Monty Sunshine, with whom he stayed four years. During the period he contracted Bell's palsy, a disease attacking the nerves of the lip (Sunshine kept him on full wages all through the illness), but an embouchure switch that became necessary coincidentally improved Mason's range and by 1970, when he joined Acker Bilk's band, he had turned into a world-class trumpeter with a phenomenal range, limitless endurance and a natural ability to sound like Louis Armstrong *c.* 1930. Later in the 1970s Mason led his own band and became well known in Europe, recording prolifically for the Dutch Riff label with musicians from Brian Lemon to Dick Wellstood and Bob Wilber. By the 1980s he had joined the prestigious Dutch Swing College Band, but left in 1985 to bandlead again in Europe. Mason's natural modesty and a light-hearted approach to jazz have tended to obscure his considerable talents for no good reason. [DF]

Great Having You Around (1978), Black Lion

Massey, Cal, composer, trumpet. b. Philadelphia, 11 January 1928; d. 25 October 1972. Brought up in Pittsburgh, toured briefly with Jay McShann (mid-1940s) before returning to Philadelphia (*c.* 1948). Some touring with Billie Holiday, Eddie Vinson, B. B. King and (in 1959) George Shearing big band. Contributed compositions to record dates by Charlie Parker ('Fiesta', 1951), John Coltrane ('Bakai', 1957; 'Nakatini Serenade', 1958; 'The Damned Don't Cry', 1961) and many others. Led own group in Philadelphia (from mid-1950s) including McCoy Tyner. Moved to New York, and co-led ROMAS big band (1970–2); worked with Archie Shepp in Europe (on trumpet, 1969) and collaborated with him on albums and on musical play *Lady Day* (1972). An under-recognized figure whose work was a considerable influence on certain free-jazz players. Cal's son Zane Massey has played saxophone (early 1980s) with Ronald Shannon Jackson's group. [BP]

Archie Shepp, *Attica Blues* (1972), Impulse

Masso, George, trombone, composer, leader, piano, vibes. b. Cranston, Rhode Island, 17 November 1926. The son of Tommy Masso, a well-known Rhode Island trumpet player, he was inspired to take up trombone in his teens by Lou McGarity's record of 'Yours' which he heard on the radio: Jack Teagarden and Trummy Young were also major influences and at 22 Masso found himself working with Jimmy Dorsey's band for two years, but gave up professional music for teaching to support his wife and family. In 1973, with his children grown up, he began to look at the possibility of professional music again, with the encouragement of friends including Bobby Hackett. He worked with Hackett, with Benny Goodman for a year and a half, with Bobby Rosengarden's band at the Rainbow Room and at Eddie Condon's. His numerous records in recent years – with his own quintet, Buck Clayton and the World's Greatest Jazz Band amongst others – reveal an elegant, highly gifted trombonist with a perfectly musical approach. [DF]

A Swinging Case of Massoism (1980), Famous Door

Mastren, Carmen (Carmine Niccolo Mastandrea), guitar, banjo, violin. b. Cohoes, New York, 6 October 1913; d. Valley Stream, Long Island, New York, 31 March 1981. He was a banjo player early on, as were George van Eps, Dick McDonough, Nappy Lamare and Carl Kress who, along with Mastren, perfected the art of chorded melodic solos which helped to liberate the acoustic guitar from its rhythmic function in the 1930s. Mastren's tight, fleet four-to-the-bar and agile ringing solos were first heard with Wingy Manone in New York in 1935 and the following year he replaced Mac Cheikes in Tommy Dorsey's orchestra for a five-year stay: by 1939 his work with Dorsey had put him at number one in *Downbeat's* guitar poll. Mastren – a capable reader and versatile creative soloist – was a natural for studio work, and from 1941 he worked regularly for NBC along with Raymond Scott and Bob Chester before joining Glenn Miller's AEF band to form part of the unbeatable rhythm-section that included Mel Powell, Trigger Alpert and Ray McKinley. After the war he returned to the studios and in 1953 rejoined NBC, where until 1970 he played for the Today and Tonight shows. Then, at 57 years old, he went freelance, writing jingles, playing with the New York Jazz Repertory Company and recording with them on guitar and banjo. (Mastren, like Herb Ellis, is now well known for his banjo playing, and his later LPs, such as *Banjo* for Mercury, now fetch collectors' prices.) By the late 1970s he was taking things easy and working round New York with (among others) singer Betty Comora. [DF]

Bechet/Spanier Big Four, 1940, Swaggie

Mathewson, Ron (Rognuald Andrew), double-bass, bass guitar. b. Lerwick, Shetland Isles, 19 February 1944. Father a pianist and arranger, mother a singer, brother Mat Mathewson a pianist. Began classical piano lessons at age eight, studying for eight years to advanced grade. Took up the bass at 15 and had six months' tuition to learn proper fingering and how to play arco (with bow). First professional job with a Scottish Dixieland band in Germany, 1962. Then played with various London-based traditional and r & b bands, 1963–6. Joined Tubby Hayes in October 1966, playing with him in all his active phases until his final illness and death in 1973. From the mid-1960s, Mathewson also played with groups led by Stan Getz, Charles Tolliver, Carmell Jones, Leo Wright, Budd Johnson, Joe Henderson, Ben Webster, Frank Rosolino, Roy Eldridge, Oscar Peterson, the Brecker Brothers, Philly Joe Jones, Bill Evans, among others; also with several UK bands, including the Kenny Wheeler big band, Stan Sulzmann quartet, Gordon Beck and John Taylor. He has also occasionally led his own groups, including the Ron Mathewson Six Piece, with Sulzmann and Alan Skidmore (saxes), Dick Pearce (tpt), Beck or Taylor (piano) and Spike Wells (drums). A regular member of Ronnie Scott's quartets and quintets from 1975. With Stan Getz he toured Scandinavia in 1970, and with Phil Woods toured the USA in 1971. With Scott he has toured and played festivals in the UK and internationally, including an Australian tour in 1979. Mathewson won several prizes for his classical piano playing, 1955–60. His favourite bassists are Scott La Faro and Ray Brown, and other inspirations are Bill Evans, John Taylor, Mike Pyne and his brother Mat. Mathewson's is a prodigious natural talent: he is blessed with good time, good ear, great speed of thought and execution. [IC]

With Tubby Hayes, *Mexican Green* (1967), Fontana; Beck/Mathewson/Daniel Humair, *All in the Morning* (1971), Dire-Italian; with *Francy Boland Orchestra* (1976), MPS; with Paz, *Kandeen Love Song* (1977), Spotlite; with Beck/Wheeler/Sulzmann/Oxley, *Seven Steps to Evans* (1979), MPS

Matlock, Matty (Julian Clifton), clarinet, saxes, arranger. b. Paducah, Kentucky, 27 April 1907; d. Los Angeles, 14 June 1978. He joined Ben Pollack, replacing Benny Goodman in 1929 as clarinettist and arranger, developed his arranging style from such gifted contemporaries as Fud Livingston, and stayed until 1934 when a band delegation for which he was spokesman complained to their leader over his musical favouring of singer-girlfriend Doris Robbins. After a 'freelance period' with the 'Pollack Orphans' in New York, Matlock joined Bob Crosby in 1935 as clarinettist: his enormous arranging gift was discovered by Gil Rodin and he was often seconded to stay in New York and write full-time for the orchestra and the Bobcats. In between (and making way for Irving Fazola, 1938–40), Matlock played with the band regularly until it broke up in 1942, then became a busy studio man, sideman and freelance arranger, writing for Eddie Miller's reconstituted Crosby band in 1943, for Bing Crosby's radio shows and all through the 1950s for skilled men such as Paul Weston (a constant associate), Billy May and Harry James: wherever perfect Dixieland scoring was required. In the 1950s this resulted in a string of now classic Matlock creations: the series *Pete Kelly's Blues* which started on radio, went to TV and in 1955 became a feature film (all the music arranged by Matlock featured trumpeter Dick Cathcart), albums by his Rampart Street Paraders (with Clyde Hurley this time), more by his Paducah Patrol (a Crosbyesque mid-size band and unbeatable), small-group sessions, and classic one-offs such as 'Coast Concert' for Bobby Hackett. In the 1960s Matlock took part in Crosby reunions, freelanced, played for Dick Gibson's jazz parties and sometimes led bands of his own.

Matty Matlock was, with Irving Fazola, the most inspired and spontaneous clarinettist in the Dixieland style, and as a truly original arranger he perfected the sound of 'arranged white Dixieland' as we know it today. [DF]

And his Dixie Men (1957), Storyville

See Chilton, John, *Stomp Off Let's Go!* (Jazz Book Services, 1983)

Maupin, Bennie, tenor sax, bass clarinet, flute, soprano sax, saxello. b. Detroit, Michigan, 29 August 1946. Extensive instrumental studies (1954–62) privately and at Detroit Institute of Musical Art. 1966–8, with Roy Haynes; 1968–70, with Horace Silver. 1971, joined Herbie Hancock, working with him for several years. Also worked with Lee Morgan, Miles Davis, McCoy Tyner, Freddie Hubbard. Influences are Yusef Lateef, Wayne Shorter, John Coltrane, Sonny Rollins, among others. His bass clarinet improvisations are an important ingredient on the Miles Davis album *Bitches Brew*, and Maupin also made a little jazz history when he played on Hancock's seminal album *Head Hunters*. One of the most accomplished players of the post-Coltrane period, he can handle any area from jazz to rock and abstraction. [IC]

The Jewel in the Lotus (1970), ECM; with Davis, *Bitches Brew* (1969), CBS; with Marion Brown, *Afternoon of a Georgia Faun* (1970), ECM; with Hancock, *Crossings* (1972), Warner Bros; *Head Hunters* (1973); *Thrust* (1974); *Man-Child* (1975); *Secrets* (1976), all CBS

Mauro, Turk (aka **Mauro Turso**), tenor and baritone sax. b. New York City, 11 June 1944. While in high school played clarinet and alto, gigged with Henry 'Red' Allen (1960). After involvement with organ trios and rock music, began working in late 1960s with Nat Pierce, Dave Frishberg, Roy Haynes and many others. Played with Dizzy Gillespie (1975–6), Buddy Rich band (1976–7, 1979–80). Small-group engagements alongside Al Cohn, Billy Mitchell (both from 1977) and vocalists Dakota Staton and Eddie Jefferson. Working mainly as soloist in 1980s including visits to Europe (1981, 1984, 1985). An admirer of Cohn and Zoot Sims, at whose funeral he played, Mauro is an exciting mainstreamer with a flair for showmanship. [BP]

The Underdog (1978), Jazzcraft

Maxwell, Jimmy (James Kendrick), trumpet. b. Stockton, California, 9 January 1917. From a long family line of brass players, he took up trumpet at age four and studied with a string of legendary American brass teachers, including Herbert Clarke over a ten-year period. Those studies – as well as the experience he gained afterwards – turned Maxwell into a trumpet teacher of guru-like knowledge whose advice has been sought by countless well-known players: from the 1970s he lectured regularly on brass technique for an august selection of colleges, conventions and clinics. Besides being a world authority on trumpet playing, Maxwell is a fine leadman, gifted soloist and informed music theorist who worked first with the young Gil Evans (1933–4), then with Jimmy Dorsey, Benny Goodman and others and, after the war, as a staffman for TV shows, including Perry Como's and the Tonight show as well as subbing, in spare moments, with famous big bands of the period.

Throughout the 1960s he stayed busy – with Gerry Mulligan, Quincy Jones, Goodman and many others – and in the 1970s was heard often on and off record with the New York Jazz Repertory Company (with whom he toured Europe), Dick Sudhalter's New California Ramblers, and in the 1980s with his own band. His trumpet manual *The First Trumpeter* was published in 1982. [DF]

Mayall, John, voice, harmonica, guitar, piano, composer. b. Macclesfield, Cheshire, 29 November 1933. Self-taught from age 13. Began as a commercial artist, playing blues in his spare time. Inspired and assisted by Alexis Korner, he came to London early 1960s and, after forming his Bluesbreakers, turned fully professional. He and his various groups sang and played the blues with conviction and authority, and helped to create the 1960s blues boom. By the end of the decade, Mayall had become immensely successful internationally. He went to live on the West Coast of the USA, doing one or two big tours a year. His UK bands included Eric Clapton, Jack Bruce, Jon Hiseman among others. His US groups often included leading jazz musicians such as Blue Mitchell, Victor Gaskin, Ernie Watts, Don Harris. 1965, he appeared in *Don't Look Back*, the film about Bob Dylan. 1969, he played at the Newport festival. His influences are Sonny Boy Williamson, Otis Rush, Django Reinhardt. [IC]

The Blues Alone (1967), Ace of Clubs; *Turning Point* (1969), Polydor

Mays, Lyle, keyboards. b. Wausaukee, Wisconsin, 27 November 1953. He grew up playing piano and improvising from an exclusively bebop point of view. 1975, he attended North Texas State University in Denton, Texas, joining the University Lab band for which he composed and orchestrated an album, the first by a college band to be nominated for a Grammy award. That same year he met Pat Metheny at the Wichita Jazz Festival and this was the beginning of their immensely fruitful association.

Mays made his first recording with Metheny's group in 1977 (*Watercolors*, ECM), and since then, with the guitarist, has co-written many of the compositions in their repertoire. They have also co-written film scores and background music for TV documentaries. Although Mays plays most of his solos on acoustic piano, he has developed a brilliant mastery of electronic sound which he deploys in Metheny's group to create different textures, moods, spatial densities. He was co-billed with Metheny on the Grammy-nominated album, *As Falls Wichita, So Falls Wichita Falls* (1981, ECM), and something of Mays's electronic artistry can be heard on the 20-minute title track. [IC]

With Metheny, *Pat Metheny Group* (1978); *Travels* (1983); *The Falcon and the Snowman* (1985); with Eberhard Weber, *Later That Evening* (1982), all ECM

Melly, George, singer, author. b. Liverpool, 17 August 1926. His first career, roistering around Britain in the 1950s with Mick Mulligan's band, is wickedly replayed in his first, still scandalous volume of autobiography, *Owning Up*, probably the funniest book ever written by a jazzman, and his epitaph to a singing career that he believed had been gazumped by rock and roll. In the early 1960s he was a freelance journalist, occasional TV and radio presenter and art critic. *Owning Up*, proud with permissiveness, brought Melly into line with the 'swinging sixties': contemporary critics (such as Chris Welch in *Melody Maker*) praised his occasional pub performances for their showmanship and likeable rudery (such songs as Eva Taylor's 'Hot Nuts' helped the publicity) and Melly's avowed bisexuality (now lapsed) corresponded to rock and roll's latest sexual preoccupation. By the time Melly had published another book of rock and roll criticism, *Revolt into Style* (he is the only traditional jazzman flexible enough to write well about rock music), his career had been relaunched in 1960s terms by Beatles publicist Derek Taylor with a handsome, if occasionally chaotic, 'live' album, *Nuts*. Melly's restoration to fame was helped by Jack Higgins, holding the managerial reins, and musical organization carefully handled by John Chilton, Melly's right-hand man and resident jazz authority. In the 1970s and 1980s Melly's neat and entertaining show, featuring Chilton, Steve Fagg (bass), Chuck Smith (drums) and talented pianists, including Collin Bates, became Britain's most successful jazz act of its kind, combining Melly's deeply loved classic repertoire (from Bessie Smith on) with new material by Chilton: regular tours of America, too, produced ecstatic press. Melly, with his mature art criticism, humour and ability to talk well about most things, became a TV personality: his later autobiographies, including *Mellymobile*, are the readable thoughts of a man of judgement who likes life. [DF]

See Melly, George, *Owning Up* (Weidenfeld & Nicolson, 1965, Penguin, 1970); *Revolt into Style* (Allen Lane, 1970, Penguin, 1972); *Mellymobile* (Robson, 1982, New English Library paperback, 1983)

Mercer, Johnny (John Herndon), singer, songwriter. b. Savannah, Georgia, 18 November 1909; d. Los Angeles, 25 June 1976. A dripping-with-charm white Southerner, he began singing with Paul Whiteman and writing special material for him in 1932: hits that emerged included 'Pardon my Southern accent' and 'Here come the British, bang bang!' (a jazzy epitaph for the Empire) as well as two immortal duets with Jack Teagarden, 'Fare thee well to Harlem' and its follow-up 'Christmas Night in Harlem'. (At this period a black social club from the South voted Mercer 'our favourite colored singer on radio'.) In the 1930s he made a film (*Old Man Rhythm*, a college farce with Betty Grable), recorded regularly with young stars such as Wingy Manone, Benny Goodman, Teagarden and Eddie Condon, and after leaving Whiteman became a radio personality, introducing Benny Goodman's band and Bob Crosby's orchestra on the 1939 Camel Caravan programmes and singing his special material with them. From 1943 he introduced his own series, Johnny Mercer's Music Shop, which lasted two years. In 1941 (the year he wrote 'Blues in the Night' with Harold Arlen, the greatest blues lyric after 'St Louis Blues') Mercer had founded Capitol Records, employing young talent such as Paul Weston, Matty Matlock and Eddie Miller as staffmen, signing young jazzmen such as Nat Cole, Stan Kenton and others to long contracts and recording duets with such as Wingy Manone, Bing Crosby ('Mr Meadowlark', like 'On behalf of the visiting firemen', is perfect), Cole and others. Later he gave up Capitol Records to concentrate on writing more great lyrics (and sometimes music), 'special material' for albums such as *Two of a Kind* (a collectable masterpiece with Bobby Darin) and *Bing and Louis*, for which he wrote all the lyrics and the sleeve note and sang one line on an out-take, 'Lazy River'. In 1961, with Henry Mancini, Mercer wrote probably his most famous song of all, 'Moon River', for *Breakfast at Tiffany's*. His 1960s solo albums (some recorded in London with Pete Moore) are reflective late Mercer with a strange yearning quality, implicit in his singing, more to the fore. [DF]

Sings Johnny Mercer (1942–50), EMI One Up

See Bach, Bob, and Mercer, Ginger, *Our Huckleberry Friend* (Lyle Stuart, 1982)

Merchan, Chucho (Alfredo), bass, electric bass, guitars. b. Bogotá, Colombia, 25 December 1953. From 1968, working in Colombia with salsa, Latin rock bands. 1970, he went to the USA to play and study. 1972–3, he was based in Colombia and toured in South America. 1974–9, he was in Britain studying music and taking a degree at Cambridge College of Arts and Technology. Then he came to London and, 1980–2, was with Nucleus. Formed his own band, Macondo, in 1980; 1983, it won the GLAA Young Jazz Artists of the Year and the European Young Jazz Artists of the Year; 1984, it played Detroit Kool Jazz Festival. Merchan has also played with the award-winning group Sunwind and has worked with various rock and pop stars as well as jazz musicians such as Mose Allison, Gordon Beck, John Taylor and Hank Crawford and with Working Week. [IC]

With Nucleus, *Awakening* (1980), Mood; with Sunwind, *The Sun Below* (1983), MMC; and *Working Week* (1985), Virgin

Metcalf, Louis, trumpet, vocals. b. St Louis, Missouri, 28 February 1905; d. Jamaica, Long Island, 27 October 1981. During the 1920s his impressive recorded work made him a well-remembered name who worked with most of the best of the period: they included Charlie Johnson, Sidney Bechet, Sam Wooding, Willie 'The Lion' Smith, Jelly Roll Morton, Duke Ellington, Luis Russell and King Oliver. Metcalf's approach was an original one, and his impressive range, tone and ideas won the respect of aspiring young bandleaders such as Charlie Barnet. By the early 1930s he was working regularly in Canada, then came back to New York to run his own Heatwave Club during the late 1930s and early 1940s as well as bandleading and playing riverboats; 1947–50 he was back in Canada again with his own club and band. During the 1950s he led at various New York clubs (including the Embers) and, says John Chilton, was resident at the Alibaba Club in the 1960s. Recorded examples of Metcalf in later years are regrettably scarce, although he made titles for Franwell Records in 1954–5 as well as a session for Stereocraft in 1958 and the album below. [DF]

At the Alibaba (1966), Spivey

Metheny, Pat, guitars, guitar synthesizer. b. Lee's Summit, Kansas City, Missouri, 12 August 1954. He played French horn throughout his time at high school and took up guitar when he was 13. At first he was totally under the influence of Wes Montgomery, but soon began to find his own personal style, inspired by the example of two local Kansas City musicians, a trumpet player called Gary Sivils and a drummer called Tommy Ruskin. He developed with amazing precocity and while still in his teens was teaching at both the University of Miami and Boston's Berklee School of Music. At 19 he joined Gary Burton's band, staying with it for three years (1974–7) and playing on three of Burton's ECM albums. After leaving he formed his own group with Lyle Mays on keyboards, and before the end of the decade had become a superstar, pulling in huge crowds wherever he played and his albums selling 100,000. Like Weather Report, he achieved this without in any way diluting his art or 'playing down' to the public.

Since the mid-1970s he has played and/or recorded with many of the most vital musicians in contemporary jazz including Paul Bley, Sonny Rollins, Steve Swallow, Dave Liebman, Eberhard Weber, Julius Hemphill, Jack DeJohnette, Mike Brecker, Charlie Haden and Billy Higgins. Metheny has also blossomed into a fine small-group composer as well as completing three film scores, including one for John Schlesinger's *The Falcon and the Snowman*

(1985). By 1985 he had recorded twelve LPs in nine years, three of them receiving Grammy awards. That year he also recorded with one of his idols, Ornette Coleman.

By the age of 30, Metheny had acquired a vast, world-wide audience for his music while at the same time enjoying the admiration of his jazz peers, and this puts him in a very select company of musicians with Keith Jarrett, Joe Zawinul, Wayne Shorter and the man Metheny seems most to admire – Miles Davis. The music of Pat Metheny's group has its roots in jazz, rock and country music and it is characterized by intensely melodic compositions (often co-written with Lyle Mays), clear rhythms perfectly executed, and an inexhaustible flow of melodic improvisation from the leader: Metheny has an extraordinary understanding of, and insight into, the making of improvised music. As with the handful of other really successful jazz groups, a great deal of thought goes into the presentation and the choice of programme. [IC]

Bright Size Life (1976); *Watercolors* (1977); *Pat Metheny Group* (1978); *New Chautauqua* (1979); *American Garage* (1980); *As Falls Wichita, So Falls Wichita Falls* (1981); *Offramp* (1982); *Travels* (1983); *Rejoicing* (1983); *First Circle* (1984), all ECM; with Ornette Coleman, *Song X* (1985), Geffen

Mezzrow, Mezz (Milton Mesirow), clarinet, saxes. b. Chicago, 9 November 1899; d. Paris, 5 August 1972. Eddie Condon, in his book *We Called It Music*, slandered Mezzrow so wickedly and funnily that he turned into a cartoon figure; *Really the Blues* by Mezzrow himself, full of Spillane-speak, Chicago wind and drumbeating, sealed the image. When Mezzrow was young he was often among the young white musicians of Condon's circle; his constant preoccupation with black players (Condon called him 'Southmouth') and determination to identify with them, however, was a source of embarrassment all round. 'When a man is trying so hard to be something he isn't,' said Sidney Bechet cruelly, 'then some of that will show in the music. The idea of it will be wrong.' As his career progressed, Mezzrow's projects more and more often included black players: during the 1930s he put together big bands containing Benny Carter, Pops Foster, Teddy Wilson *et al.*, but they seldom lasted long because of Mezzrow's waywardness, liking for drugs and legendary role as a marijuana supplier. 'Mezz got a big band together,' Condon recalled, 'to audition for some Bond Bread commercials. We all assembled and the bakers were sitting there waiting for him to give the downbeat. Just before he did Mezz turned round to the prospective sponsors and said, "Man, am I high!" We didn't get the job!' Many of Mezzrow's records, however, from his 1933 big band, to sessions with Frankie Newton, through the faultless sessions with Tommy Ladnier and Bechet for Hugues Panassié in 1938 to post-war Mezzrow–Bechet masterpieces on his King Jazz label, are marvellous, revealing his deep feeling for the blues, well-thought lines, frequent agility and appealing acid tone. Following his appearance at the Nice Jazz Festival, 1948, Mezzrow became a big star in Europe, touring regularly with bands including Buck Clayton, Gene Sedric and Jimmy Archey, recording in Paris with Lionel Hampton (sounding out of place at least proved that Mezzrow was no slave to fashion) and working part-time as tour gofer and marijuana supplier for Louis Armstrong. In 1986 his autobiography was scheduled for full-length filming, music by Bob Wilber. [DF]

The Panassié Sessions (1938–9), RCA

See Mezzrow, Milton 'Mezz', and Wolfe, Bernard, *Really the Blues* (Secker & Warburg, 1946)

Michelot, Pierre, bass, arranger. b. Saint Denis, France, 3 March 1928. Taking up bass at 16, soon began working with US musicians in Paris and making records with Coleman Hawkins (1949) etc. Regular gigging and recording with Kenny Clarke (from 1949), Miles Davis (1956, 1957), Bud Powell (1960–2) and many others. More involved in studio work and arranging for two decades, he took part in the filming of *Round Midnight* (1985). Michelot is a beautifully propulsive and melodic player, easily the best post-bop bassist that Europe has produced; while the opportunity to play with leading Americans clearly refined it further, his style was already perfectly balanced by the time he came to the fore. [BP]

Bud Powell, *A Portrait of Thelonious* (1961), CBS

Middleton, Velma, vocals. b. St Louis, Missouri, 1917; d. Sierra Leone, 10 February 1961. After working as a chorus girl she joined Louis Armstrong's big band in 1942 and remained with him all through the great days of the All Stars. A marvellous, good-humoured performer whom one critic described as looking like 'a sequinned football' on stage, she was always the female singer that Louis liked working with best and he featured her on such classic Armstrong records as *Plays W. C. Handy* and *Satch plays Fats*. 'She and I kinda lived life together,' he told *Cadence* magazine later. 'She was so *real*. She could smile.' Middleton's humour was perhaps her strongest point – 'Actually,' says Barney Bigard, 'she was a mediocre singer but one hell of an entertainer!' – but few Armstrong lovers could really dislike her amiable singing, which frequently turned up in hilarious duos with Armstrong like 'Baby it's cold outside' and 'That's my desire' and fitted admirably with the broad style of Armstrong's group. Her end was sudden and tragic: she had a stroke on tour with Louis in Africa, was too ill to be moved far and died in Sierra Leone three weeks later. [DF]

Any with Louis Armstrong's All Stars

Midnite Follies Orchestra Formed in 1978 by ragtime pianist Keith Nichols and arranger Alan Cohen to play big-band jazz of the 1920s and 1930s, Britain's best jazz repertory orchestra interpreted re-creations of important items by Ellington, Calloway, Wooding, Henderson and others, as well as imaginative originals composed by the leaders. Musicians featured within the MFO included, at various times, Alan Elsdon, Nick Stevenson, Dave Saville, Digby Fairweather (tpts), Gordon Blundy, Pete Strange (tmbs), John Barnes, Will Hastie, Olaf Vas, Mac White, Alan Cohen, Randolph Colville (reeds), as well as Keith Nichols (piano/soprano/trombone/vocals), Richard Warner, Keith Greville (gtrs), Bob Taylor (bass) Laurie Chescoe (dms). The 'Midnite men' were swiftly contracted to EMI after a historic first night at London's 100 Club, then appeared regularly on radio and TV, produced two well reviewed albums and played the jazz club circuit and festivals in Britain and Europe, as well as starring regularly in London concert halls, often in tribute concerts to Armstrong, Ellington and others. [DF]

Hotter than Hades (1978), EMI

Mikkelborg, Palle, trumpet, composer, conductor. b. Copenhagen, 6 March 1941. Self-taught as a trumpet player and composer, but studied conducting at Royal Music Conservatory, Copenhagen. Began to play trumpet in 1956 and from 1960 worked professionally. 1961–4, played at Club Vingaarden and Club Montmartre in Copenhagen; with Danish Radio Jazz Group, 1964–70, last four years as leader; and with Radio Big Band, 1965–71. During the 1970s he led the Radio Big Band for four periods, conducting his own compositions and interpreting the work of other composers. Began leading his own bands in 1965 and formed a quintet with drummer Alex Riel in 1966, which in 1968 won first prize at the Montreux Jazz Festival and played at the Newport festival. Since then he has continued to lead his own groups, V8 in the early 1970s, again with Alex Riel, and from the later 1970s to the mid-1980s his group Entrance. He was also a regular member of the Peter Herbolzheimer big band in the early 1970s. Mikkelborg has also worked for varying periods with George Russell, Dexter Gordon, Joachim Kuhn, Eje Thelin, Jan Garbarek, Terje Rypdal, Dollar Brand (Abdullah Ibrahim), Philip Catherine, Johnny Dyani, Charlie Mariano, Jasper van't Hof, Maynard Ferguson, Don Cherry, Yusef Lateef, Gil Evans, Bill Evans, Karin Krog, George Gruntz and others. He has won many other prizes and awards including Jazz Musician of the Year (Denmark), 1968, a Cultural Government Scholarship, 1969, the Lange Muller Prize, 1976, and the Danish Conductors' Society Prize of Honour, 1977. His main influence, both as a trumpet player and conceptually, is Miles Davis, but he also favours Clifford Brown, Chet Baker and Booker Little; as a composer other influences are Gil Evans, Bill Evans, Charles Ives and Olivier Messiaen. But he has absorbed his influences and created a way of making music that is all his own. He is a magnificent acoustic trumpet player with a lyrical sound and huge range, and he is also perhaps the very finest exponent of electric trumpet, deploying the new sounds and timbres with great artistry. A prolific composer, he has written long pieces for big ensembles. Some key works are: *Journey To . . .* (1978), for symphony orchestra and soloists; *Dis* (1981), for flute and percussion; *A Simple Prayer* (1981), for choir, gamelan ensemble and soloists; *Pictures* (1983), for bass, piano, soloists and symphony orchestra; *Aura* (1984), a tribute to Miles Davis, for big band and soloists, featuring Davis himself. [IC]

With Krog, Catherine, Gordon and others; *Ashoka Suite* (1970), Metronome MLP; with Terje Rypdal, *Descendre* (1979), ECM; with Gruntz, *Theatre* (1984), ECM; with Shankar/Garbarek, *Visions* (1984), ECM; with Entrance, *Entrance* (1977), MLP; *Live as Well* (1978), MLP; *Journey To . . .* (1985), Metronome

Miles, Lizzie (Elizabeth Mary Pajaud, *née* Landreaux), vocals. b. New Orleans, 31 March 1895; d. 17 March 1963. Her early work took her into medicine shows, tent shows and the vaudeville circuit and she became prominent in the 1920s, working first in Chicago, later in New York, and recording in New York from 1922 with stars such as Jelly Roll Morton and Clarence Williams, Louis Armstrong and Kid Ory. (Her first issues in the UK came out in 1923.) In 1924 she travelled to Europe with Alexander Shargenski's troupe, scoring a hit in Paris where she became known as 'La Rose Noire'. In 1925, back in the USA, she scored a big hit with a version of 'I'm Confessin''. Throughout the rest of the 1920s and 1930s she stayed busy (apart from a spell of illness in the early 1930s) and worked with Fats Waller briefly, but, as with many of her contemporaries, her blues singing slipped out of fashion in the early 1940s. A New Orleans DJ, Joe Mares (brother of the trumpeter Paul Mares) rediscovered her, recorded her with a trio and began regularly playing her records. Then she started singing again (at the Mardi Gras Lounge on Bourbon Street, with Paul Barbarin's band) and by 1955 was featured with Bob Scobey's hugely successful Dixieland band. She remained busy, working with bands such as Joe Darensbourg's at jazz festivals including Monterey, but retired in the late 1950s to study religion. [DF]

With Tony Almerico's Parisian Room All Stars (1954–6), Cook

Miley, Bubber (James Wesley), trumpet, composer. b. Aiken, South Carolina, 3 April 1903; d. Welfare Island, New York, 20 May 1932. He worked in clubs and cabarets around New York and toured with blues singer Mamie Smith. (In Chicago, while on tour with her, he heard King Oliver and went back every night for two weeks to listen and learn.) In 1923 Duke Ellington heard him in the basement of the Bucket of Blood club on 135th Street, New York, with trombonist Charlie Irvis. He joined Ellington in Elmer Snowden's Washingtonians at the Kentucky Club and caused a sensation: spies including Paul Whiteman and his featured trumpeter Henry Busse came to listen to his revolutionary, growling style, and to steal. As a cornerman of Ellington's new band, Miley, a handsome, good-time youngster who loved to make music and enjoyed battling with his competitors, was a strong team with 'Tricky Sam' Nanton: 'They were always blowing for each other and getting ideas for what they wanted to play', recalled Ellington. Miley helped Ellington to develop many of his compositions and occupied a central role in the band, but by 1929, he was drinking heavily, became unreliable and, when he did appear, was often unable to play. Cootie Williams took his place with Ellington and he left to freelance in Europe, working in France with Noble Sissle and at home with Zutty Singleton and Leo Reisman: Miley's records of the period show a disintegrating talent. By 1931 he was playing for revues, including Roger Dodge's *Sweet and Low* and Billy Rose's *Third Little Show*, and later that year had a show of his own, *Harlem Scandals*, built around his band by Ellington's manager Irving Mills. But tuberculosis set in while he was on the road with his show and he died at 29.

Bubber Miley was a central figure not only in Duke Ellington's first band, but to all Ellington's subsequent music. 'Our band changed character when Bubber came in', said Ellington. 'That's when we forgot all about the sweet music.' [DF]

Any with Ellington

Miller, Eddie (Edward Raymond Müller), tenor sax, clarinet, vocals. b. New Orleans, 23 June 1911. A second-generation New Orleans musician, he played the clarinet in home-town groups such as the New Orleans Owls before driving to New York in 1928 in a Model T Ford to work with bandleaders including Red McKenzie, the Dorseys and, from 1930, Ben Pollack. After Pollack's band broke up, Miller stayed with the re-formed unit under Bob Crosby until 1942, a strong cornerman with his blues singing, showmanship, gift for composition (a 1938 Miller tune, 'Slow Mood', with words added by Johnny Mercer, became a 1944 hit for them both), and urbane 'white tenor'. After Crosby's band split up, Miller led his own in 1943, then began a round of studio work, including nine years with Twentieth Century-Fox, staffwork for Capitol and other labels, and a lengthy association with clarinettist Matty Matlock for recordings, radio and the hugely successful *Pete Kelly's Blues* series on radio, TV and film. Bob Crosby reunions, a tour of the UK in 1967 with Alex Welsh and nine years with Pete Fountain's band back in New Orleans took Miller into the 1970s: in the 1980s he was with Crosby still, travelling Europe as a soloist, and as busy as ever. His frank, svelte saxophone is the smoothest graduate from Bud Freeman's school. [DF]

Bob Crosby, *South Rampart Street Parade* (1935–42), MCA

See Chilton, John, *Stomp Off Let's Go!* (Jazz Book Services, 1983)

Miller, Glenn (Alton Glenn), trombone, arranger, composer, leader. b. Clarinda, Iowa, 1 March 1904; reported missing after flight England–France, 15 December 1944. He flunked music at Colorado University, but achieved high grades in maths. His early trombone experience came with territory bands, and in 1926 he joined Ben Pollack as trombonist-arranger. Arranging mainly the sweet side of Pollack's book (he used Arthur Lange's method), the young trombonist's dual talent quickly became apparent (his writing for strings was influenced by Roger Wolfe Kahn's orchestra), but when Gil Rodin introduced Jack Teagarden's fluent gifts to the band, Miller – who hated being second best – tactfully moved on and by 1930 he was working for Red Nichols and others in pit orchestras, for shows including *Strike Up the Band* and *Girl Crazy*, arranging for radio and freelancing. In 1932, as MD for film star Smith Ballew's dance band, Miller polished his bandleading style ('He was a hard taskmaster,' said Ballew, 'often resented by musicians in the band'), and by 1934 was touring with the Dorsey brothers, singing 'Annie's Cousin Fanny', and studying in spare moments with Dr Joseph Schillinger. In 1935 he collaborated with Ray Noble to assemble an all-star band to play the Rainbow Room on top of the RCA Building in Radio City, New York, a job for which Noble paid him the high salary of $175 a week. In this band Miller found his elusive 'sound', when trumpeter Pee Wee Erwin, famed for his range and endurance, asked to play lead-alto parts transposed specially for his instrument; later players, less able than Erwin to play the parts, declined the pleasure and the music was handed to a clarinettist instead. By 1936, Noble and Miller – two strong characters – had parted company, and Miller began to make serious bandleading plans of his own. Early keymen such as Hal McIntyre and Rolly Bundock joined him; in 1937 the first, slow-moving records were made, and after a year of touring, playing hotels and running at a loss of $19 a week, Miller disbanded. In 1938 he re-formed with keymen including Willie Schwartz, Tex Beneke and singer Ray Eberle, made his first records for RCA Victor and took an arranger, Bill Finegan. Finegan, whose new boss stringently edited his work, liked Miller, but was bemused by his blunt reluctance to communicate: 'Glenn seemed to have the feeling that if he complimented a guy he would ask for a raise!' he remembered. By 1939 Miller's fame was growing: a spring season at Glen Island Casino (a teenage centre installed with broadcasting lines) broke records, and so did the one-nighters that followed. A string of singles for RCA helped, as did a radio series for Chesterfield Cigarettes, and by 1940 Miller had taken on more keymen: trumpeters Billy May and Ray Anthony, bassist Trigger Alpert, cornettist Bobby Hackett, the Modernaires vocal group and arranger Jerry Gray, whose creations such as 'Elmer's Tune', 'Chattanooga choo-choo' and 'I've got a gal in Kalamazoo' sealed Miller's success. By 1941 he was grossing more than any other bandleader (apart, strangely enough, from Kay Kyser) and that year the hugely successful film *Sun Valley Serenade* (starring John Payne and Sonja Henie) endeared him to audiences world-wide: it was followed by *Orchestra Wives* in 1942. By then Miller – a staunch patriot – had registered for the draft: later that year he was accepted as a captain in the US army. His band split up and Harry James took over the Chesterfield broadcasts, but Miller was soon appointed Director of Bands for the Army Air Force Technical Training Command (AAFTTC); keymen Alpert, Gray and Zeke Zarchy rejoined him, other new stars included Mel Powell, Bernie Privin and Carmen Mastren, and in 1944 the Glenn Miller AEF Orchestra sailed for England on the *Queen Elizabeth*. They arrived in London in the middle of the blitz and Miller insisted that his band be re-billeted out of London in Bedfordshire: their London quarters in Sloane Court were bombed to the ground the same night. Working for the BBC, Miller caused a stir (at one stage he insisted on tripling the number of microphones for a broadcast: the BBC responded with a battery of additional equipment, all unconnected), but he caused a musical sensation too. His Strings with Wings feature, broadcast every Saturday morning, was as much admired by his band as it was by Adrian Boult; his Uptown Hall Gang, featuring Privin, Hucko and Powell, was a small-group delight; and his full orchestra was simply better than anything heard in Britain before. In December 1944 Miller went ahead of his orchestra, which had been posted to Paris, to spy out the musical land. His plane disappeared, and a year later he was pronounced officially dead and received a posthumous Bronze Star. 'He left before we did – as he usually did!' says Peanuts Hucko. 'He didn't leave it to anybody; he didn't send out a scout. He *was* a scout.'

Glenn Miller himself was only an average trombonist ('pedestrian, and he knew it', said Benny Goodman) but he led the most commercially successful big band of the 20th century, and in jazz terms it would be absurd to dismiss all his output as merely disposable trivia. At its best, his orchestra, with Artie Shaw's, was the hardest-swinging white orchestra of its time; it introduced at least one totally original scoring device; and it featured stronger, more inventive material than any of Miller's rivals. His music has been kept alive in later years by American reassemblies (led by Hucko among others) and by British bandleader Syd Lawrence's orchestra, which re-interprets Miller with scholarly abandon. [DF]

The Glenn Miller Story RCA International Chronology (double albums: German issue)

See Simon, George T., *Glenn Miller and his Orchestra* (W. H. Allen, 1974); Butcher Geoffrey, *Next to a Letter from Home* (Mainstream, 1986)

Miller, Harry (Harold Simon), bass, cello. b. South Africa, 21 April 1941; d. 16 December 1983, following a car crash. Music lessons in South Africa, began playing with r & b groups there and with Manfred Mann. Came to the UK in 1961, played with various people, then joined Geraldo's Navy for 18 months on the New York run, which enabled him to experience jazz in New York. Back in London he worked with many leading musicians, including John Surman, Mike Osborne and with Mike Westbrook's small and big bands. He also joined Chris McGregor's Brotherhood of Breath. In the late 1960s and the 1970s he led his own group, Isipingo, and played with Stan Tracey, Keith Tippett, Elton Dean's Ninesense and Louis Moholo's Culture Shock. He helped to form Lambeth New Music Society which ran a regular jazz club (Grass Roots), and he was involved in the creation of the Ogun Record Company, for which he and many of his associates recorded. Miller was also a member of the Alan Skidmore quintet when it won the Press Prize at the Montreux festival in 1969. [IC]

With various associates, including Brotherhood of Breath *Live at Willisau* (1974) and *Live at Toulouse* (1977); *Children at Play* (1974); *Isipingo, Family Affair* (1977); *In Conference* (1978), all Ogun

Miller, Mulgrew, piano. b. Greenwood, Mississippi, 13 August 1955. Studied music at school and university, also playing in gospel and r & b groups. Toured with Mercer Ellington band (late 1970s including European visit 1977). Worked regularly with Betty Carter (1980), then member of Woody Shaw quintet (1981–3), plus prolific freelance work. Joined Art Blakey and the Jazz Messengers, 1983–6. Miller is a brilliant technician who has absorbed all the influences of 1960s–1970s jazz piano, and looks likely to add to the tradition. [BP]

Keys to the City (1985), Landmark

Miller, Punch (Ernest Burden), trumpet, vocals. b. Raceland, Louisiana, 14 June 1894; d. New Orleans, 2 December 1971. He was a Louisiana trumpeter who like many of his fellows (Guy Kelly, Joe Suttler) felt that they had unjustifiably been overshadowed by Louis Armstrong. While Miller's talent could never seriously be compared to Armstrong's, their early years at least show a striking similarity: a publicity shot of the time shows Miller handsome, young, in a brilliant white suit, looking uncannily like Louis. He was a powerful trumpeter who knew how to make show and was proud of his fly-fast fingering: 'Some of the men from that school had a few things that they did even better than Louis', says Milt Hinton. (In fact 'fast-fingering' is a spectacular but easy device which Armstrong consciously abandoned early on for something greater, on King Oliver's advice.) Miller's career, far from being territory-based, showed signs of following Louis, too: to Kid Ory's band in New Orleans, to Erskine Tate, Freddie Keppard and Earl Hines (for one night) in Chicago, and to New York by the mid-1930s with second-line bands such as Leonard Reed's. By the 1940s Miller was back in Chicago for clubwork, then tours with carnivals, circuses and rock and roll shows: apart from work with George Lewis, 1964–5, this was the pattern for the rest of his life, except for one fine final fling. *Till the Butcher Cuts him Down* (1971), perhaps the most moving jazz film of all, shows Miller, on leave from a terminal hospital stay, defiantly playing his show-stopping routine to an enthralled audience at Newport's Jazz Festival, with such great trumpeters as Dizzy Gillespie and Bobby Hackett in respectful attendance. [DF]

Tiny Parham, vol. 1 (1929–30), Collectors Classics

Millinder, Lucky (Lucius), leader. b. Anniston, Alabama, 8 August 1900; d. New York, 28 September 1966. He was a natural choice to take over Irving Mills's third band, the Mills Blue Rhythm Band, when it moved into the Cotton Club in 1934, replacing Cab Calloway. Like Calloway, Millinder was a high-powered frontman with a gift for showmanship and a canny eye for commercial appeal. He also had such a good retentive ear for music that reputedly he could conduct the hardest score after one hearing, including difficult and revolutionary arrangements for his band by Chappie Willett, which very early on featured such time signatures as 3/8, 5/8 and 12/8. (In reality Millinder worked hard on the scores, stayed up all night to study them and took advice from his deputy, 'straw boss' Bill Doggett.) Besides being 'the best conductor I've ever seen' (Dizzy Gillespie), Millinder was a popular and personable employer and ran a successful band: one great personnel from 1943 included Gillespie, Doggett, Freddie Webster and Tab Smith. In 1952 he retired to become first a liquor salesman and later a successful DJ. [DF]

Big Bands Uptown! (1931–43), MCA

Mills Blue Rhythm Band, see MILLINDER, LUCKY.

Mince, Johnny (John H. Muenzenberger), clarinet, saxes. b. Chicago, 8 July 1912. After an early spell with Joe Haymes's well-schooled band he worked for Ray Noble, Bob Crosby and, 1937–41, Tommy Dorsey. With all these bands he provided the technically able creative jazz clarinet that every swing band after Goodman and Shaw was expected to supply, with an attractive and recognizable grit-edged tone that he was to keep for life. During the war, Mince played for shows and after demobilization moved into studio work and television. His reappearances on the jazz scene were regular and welcome: he led his own bands, played at jazz festivals, toured with the Kings of Jazz (a 1974 package featuring Pee Wee Erwin, Bernie Privin and Dick Hyman) and others and collaborated regularly with Yank Lawson and Bob Haggart. His returns to recording were also frequent: with Bobby Hackett and Urbie Green among others in the 1970s. In the 1980s he was a featured star in Keith Smith's '100 Years of American Dixieland' package. [DF]

The Master Comes Home (1983), Jazzology

Mingus, Charles, Jnr., bass, composer (and piano). b. Nogales, Arizona, 22 April 1922; d. Cuernavaca, Mexico, 5 January 1979. Brought up in Watts, Los Angeles, and started on trombone and cello as a child, switching to bass at age 16. Played with high-school colleagues in Buddy Collette group, Al Adams band and rehearsal band of Lloyd Reese, with whom he studied piano and theory. Worked with Barney Bigard group in Los Angeles (1942) before touring briefly with Louis Armstrong band (1942–3); replaced his bass teacher Red Callender in Lee Young sextet (1943), then formed own Strings and Keys trio (1944–5). First records under own name (1945) and freelance playing, also stints with co-operative Stars of Swing (1946), Floyd Ray (1946) and Cee Pee Johnson (1947). Toured for a year with Lionel Hampton (1947–8), followed by Red Callender sextet (1948) and first period out of music. Joined Red Norvo trio (1950–1) and settled in New York, gigging with Miles Davis, Billy Taylor, Charlie Parker, Stan Getz, Lennie Tristano, Duke Ellington, Bud Powell, Art Tatum. Formed own company, Debut Records (1952–7),

Charles Mingus

later joined by Max Roach; co-founded Jazz Composers Workshop (1953–5) with Teo Macero, John LaPorta, Teddy Charles etc.

Began own quintet/sextet (1955), known for many years as the Charles Mingus Jazz Workshop, with frequently changing personnel despite virtual permanence of Dannie Richmond (from 1956) and front-line partnerships of Jimmy Knepper/Shafi Hadi (1957–8), Booker Ervin/John Handy (1958–9), Eric Dolphy/Ted Curson (1959–60). Summer 1960, musical director with Max Roach of 'alternative festival' at Newport; founder member of short-lived Jazz Artists Guild. After augmenting his group for record sessions, assembled big band for Town Hall concert (1962), 11-piece groups for club and record work (1962, 1963 and Monterey festival, 1964) and 8-piece group (1965–6). New attempt at own record label, then out of music for a year (1967–8). New quintet/sextet (from 1969) and publication of 'autobiography' *Beneath the Underdog* (1971) increased Mingus's popularity; big-band records (1971, 1977–8) and appearances (1972) aimed successfully at wider audience. Mingus's regular quintet activity halted (late 1977) by onset of sclerosis; within months of his death Mingus Dynasty group was formed, led first by Dannie Richmond, then by Jimmy Knepper.

Mingus was unlike any previous jazz composer, but his combination of egocentricity and generosity towards (some of) his sidemen resembled that of his idol Duke Ellington. Since he and his collaborators grew up during or after the bebop era, the structures Mingus evolved from the mid-1950s onwards had to be looser and lengthier than the majority of Ellington's work. As a result Mingus became one of the forces favouring the formation of 'free jazz', which he later deplored despite revelling in the concept of collective improvisation and encouraging the use of vocalized instrumental tone and similar colouristic devices. A couple of his recordings with enlarged small groups have become standard 12-bar blues, 'Goodbye Pork Pie Hat' and 'Wednesday Night Prayer Meeting' (or the related 'Better git it in your soul'); it should be emphasized, however, that no one else's versions, nor even his own remakes, sound anything like the 1959 originals.

Like Ellington too, Mingus was aware of the whole history of jazz. He was frequently not only adding to it but quoting from it, and his output contains somewhat sardonic tributes to such as Jelly Roll Morton, Fats Waller and of course Duke. Some listeners consider this a disadvantage, finding his major work, *Black Saint and the Sinner Lady*, too overtly Ellington-influenced, but it is in fact a marvellous conglomeration of everything from 19th-century piano to flamenco guitar. The only thing it lacks is Mingus's magnificent solo bass playing, which became influential in its own right because he was the first bassist of his generation to ignore the harmonic fundamentals when soloing and to imitate saxophone and piano lines. His larger-than-life personality, helped by his book, has made him both overrated and underrated, but his music was a unique contribution to jazz. [BP]

Pithecanthropus Erectus (1956), Atlantic; *Blues and Roots* (1959), Atlantic; *Mingus Ah Um* (1959), CBS; *Mingus Presents Mingus* (1960), Candid; *Black Saint and the Sinner Lady* (1963), Impulse; *Changes One* (1974), Atlantic

See Mingus, Charles, *Beneath the Underdog* (Knopf, New York, 1971, Penguin paperback, 1975); Priestley, Brian, *Mingus: A Critical Biography* (Quartet, London, 1982, Da Capo, 1983)

Film: *Mingus* (dir. Thomas Reichman, 1968)

Minton, Phil, trumpet, voice. b. Torquay, Devon, 2 November 1940. Father and mother both singers. Sang as choirboy and had trumpet lessons from local teacher. Worked with local bands around south Devon in late 1950s. 1962, moved to London and joined Mike Westbrook, leaving in 1964 to play with rock and blues bands in Europe. Rejoined Westbrook in 1972, and was involved in many of Westbrook's projects through the 1970s and 1980s, including the Blake songs, *Mama Chicago* and *The Cortege.* Also worked with Maggie Nicols and Julie Tippett in the vocal group Voice, performed in theatre and improvised duos with other singers. Also a member of Lindsay Cooper's Film Music and Trevor Watts's Moire Music. In the 1980s toured in Europe giving solo vocal concerts. With Westbrook and others, has toured in USA, Australia and extensively in Europe. [IC]

With Westbrook, *For the Record* (1976), Transatlantic; *Goose Sauce* (1978), Original; *Mama Chicago* (1979), RCA; *Bright as Fire* (1980), Original; *The Cortege* (1982), Original; *Voice* (1977), Ogun; solo, *A Doughnut in Both Hands* (1981), Rift; *AMMO* (with Roger Turner) (1984), Leo

Mintzer, Bob (Robert), saxes, clarinets, flutes. b. New Rochelle, New York, 27 January 1953. 1969–70, he attended Interlochen Arts Academy; 1970–4, Hartt College of Music and Manhattan School of Music. He began playing saxophone, flutes, clarinets and writing professionally in 1974, working with Deodato and Tito Puente. 1975, with Buddy Rich and Hubert Laws. 1977, with the Thad Jones–Mel Lewis Band, Sam Jones and Eddie Palmieri. 1978–80, worked with Ray Mantilla, Mel Lewis and his own (Bob Mintzer) band. 1980–2, played with Jaco Pastorius, Mike Mainieri, Louie Bellson and Joe Chambers. 1982–4, with Bob Moses, the New York Philharmonic, Brooklyn Philharmonic, American Ballet Theater, the Bob Mintzer big band and quintet, Liza Minnelli, the American Saxophone Quartet. 1982–4, he also appeared with the radio bands of Rome, Helsinki and Hamburg as a soloist and composer. He has written music for Buddy Rich, Mel Lewis, Art Blakey and Jaco Pastorius, as well as for more commercial ventures. He cites his main inspirations as Thad Jones, Herbie Hancock, Lester Young and Duke Ellington. [IC]

With Peter Erskine, Dave Sanborn, Moses, Lewis, Rich, Pastorius, Sam Jones, Philip Glass, Deodato, Blakey and John Tropea; *Horn Man* (1981); *The Source* (1982), both Canyon, Japan; big band, *Papa Lips* (1983), CBS Sony; *Incredible Journey* (1985), DMP

Mitchell, Billy, tenor (and alto, soprano, flute, clarinet). b. Kansas City, Missouri, 3 November 1926. Studied in Detroit, then toured briefly with Nat Towles, Lucky Millinder (1948), Woody Herman (1949, replacing Gene Ammons); record debut with Milt Buckner band (1949). Early 1950s, own group in Detroit backing visiting soloists. 1956–7, member of Dizzy

Gillespie big band, then replaced Lockjaw Davis with Count Basie (1957–61, 1966–7). Co-led six-piece group with Al Grey and sidemen such as Bobby Hutcherson (1961–4). Mid-1960s, musical director for Stevie Wonder. 1970s, busy with educational seminars and workshops. Also working as freelance soloist (including UK tour 1984), Mitchell has impressed consistently with his edgy but full-blooded tone and his fluent linear approach. [BP]

The Colossus of Detroit (1978), Xanadu

Mitchell, Blue (Richard Allen), trumpet. b. Miami, Florida, 13 March 1930; d. 21 May 1979. Work in r&b bands such as Paul Williams (1951), Earl Bostic (1952–5) and Red Prysock (1955). Later settled in New York and became firmly established during five years with the Horace Silver quintet (1958–64) which, when Silver re-formed, became the Blue Mitchell quintet with Chick Corea on piano (1964–9). Then toured with Ray Charles (1969–71) and John Mayall (1971–3) and did prolific freelance work in Los Angeles until his death from cancer. A forthright soloist, capable of making a personal contribution in a variety of situations. [BP]

The Thing To Do (1964), Blue Note

Mitchell, George, cornet. b. Louisville, Kentucky, 8 March 1899; d. Chicago, 27 May 1972. His dependable trumpet (he played trumpet-cornet after 1924) first showed up in Southern minstrel shows, where he was taught by Bobby Williams from Kansas City ('one of the outstanding brass bandleaders and very successful at that time', says Dickie Wells) and by 1920 he was working in Chicago with Tony Jackson. Mitchell is remembered mainly for his handful of classic recordings with Jelly Roll Morton, but they formed only a tiny fraction of his career as a busy Chicago session man. For the next 11 years he was an in-demand sideman touring out of town and working in Chicago with (among others) Carroll Dickerson, Doc Cooke, Lil Hardin Armstrong, Dave Peyton, Earl Hines (he was in Hines's first Grand Terrace band, sharing the trumpet book with Shirley Clay) and Jimmie Noone. 'Every so often George would come back home to Louisville from Chicago to help teach the kids in the Booker T. Washington youth band', remembers Jonah Jones, himself a former member. John Chilton points out that Mitchell retired from music in 1931 to become a bank messenger, not (as legend has it) a postman: later, says Chilton, he played with Elgar's Federal Concert Orchestra, but never (another legend) with the Chicago Symphony Orchestra. [DF]

The Complete Jelly Roll Morton, vols. 1/4, RCA

Mitchell, Red (Keith Moore), bass (and piano). b. New York City, 20 September 1927. Played piano while becoming established as bassist, and continued to use it occasionally. Piano in Chubby Jackson band (1949), then bass with Charlie Ventura (summer 1949) and Woody Herman (1949–51). Small-group exposure with Red Norvo trio (1952–3) and Gerry Mulligan quartet (1954–5). Settling in Los Angeles, worked regularly with Hampton Hawes trio (1955–7), his own quartet (1957) and Shelly Manne–André Previn (1957–61), while becoming involved in copious studio work. Co-led quintet with Harold Land (1961–2) and resumed partnership with Hawes (1965–6). Turning his back on commercial studio recording, moved to Scandinavia and gigged with similarly inclined Phil Woods (1968). Living in Stockholm ever since, freelanced successfully and led own groups, returning only occasionally to the USA.

Mitchell's early small-group work was strikingly unclichéd, both in accompanying and solo roles. His solos in particular sounded different from the then norm because of his varied articulation, often leaving notes to be heard simply through the change of left-hand fingering, without the right hand plucking the string at all. The result of this, and the choice of phraseology to go with it, was a distinctly horn-like approach which can be said to have foreshadowed the style of Scott La Faro. Perhaps in order to counteract his generally light sound, Mitchell in the 1960s re-tuned his strings exactly an octave lower than those of the cello, thus giving himself a bottom C as the lowest note on the bass, some years before Ron Carter and others acquired one.

Red's brother, Whitey (Gordon B.) Mitchell (b. 22 February 1932), also played bass, working in the rhythm-section of the band led by Oscar Pettiford (1956) among others, but moved out of the jazz field in the 1960s. [BP]

Presenting Red Mitchell (1957), Contemporary/OJC; *Jim Hall/Red Mitchell* (1978), Artists House

Mitchell, Roscoe, soprano, alto, tenor and bass sax, flute, piccolo, oboe, clarinet; also percussion, miscellaneous sounds, voice. b. Chicago, 3 August 1940. Played baritone sax in high school band and alto in his senior year. Played both instruments in army band during military service in Germany. After demobilization in 1961, played with Henry Threadgill in an Art Blakey-style group. Then joined Richard Abrams's Experimental Band and met Joseph Jarman, Anthony Braxton and others in an association which evolved into the AACM (see ABRAMS, MUHAL RICHARD). He led his own sextet in the middle and later 1960s: Graham Lock said of it, 'Just when you wondered how jazz could go any further, without smashing itself to pieces on these walls of febrile noise, Roscoe Mitchell – practically unknown outside his native Chicago – reasserted the elementary values of space and silence. His *Sound* and *Congliptious* LPs signalled a new attitude in the music: it stopped screaming and began to breathe. Sounds floated in and out of silence, cries and whispers would swell and fade in a complex ensemble dynamic.' 1969, with Jarman, Lester Bowie and Malachi Favors he formed the *Art Ensemble of Chicago, which became one of the most important groups of the 1970s and 1980s. Mitchell continued to perform and record solo projects. [IC]

With AEC; *Sound* (1966), Delmark; *Old-Quartet* (1967), Nessa; *Congliptious* (1968), Nessa; *Quartet* (1975), Sackville; *Nonaah* (1976/7); *LRG – The Maze S II Examples* (1978); *Snurdy McGurdy and her Dancin' Shoes* (1980), all Nessa; *More Cutouts* (1981), Cecma

MJQ, see LEWIS, JOHN.

Mobley, Hank (Henry), tenor sax. b. Eastman, Georgia, 7 July 1930; d. 30 May 1986. Raised in Newark, New Jersey, played there with Paul Gayten r & b band (1950–1) until discovered by Max Roach (1951–3). Also with Tadd Dameron, Dizzy Gillespie (1954) and Horace Silver quartet (1954), which merged into the Jazz Messengers (1954–6). Began prolific recording career under own name, while working with Silver (1956–7), Max Roach (1957–8) and Art Blakey (1959). Member of Miles Davis quintet (1961–2), between two absences through drug convictions. Continued from 1965 to work and record with Lee Morgan, Kenny Dorham, Elvin Jones etc. Toured in Europe as soloist (1967, 1968–70) and co-led quintet with Cedar Walton (1970–2). Moved from New York to Philadelphia (1975), where ill-health later forced him to abandon music. Made non-playing appearance at Blue Note re-launch concert (1985), and played briefly with Duke Jordan (1986) shortly before his death from double pneumonia.

Donald Byrd said in the mid-1960s, 'Hank is to me just as much a personality as Sonny Rollins. I mean, he has so definitely established his own sound and style.' Though far less flamboyant than Rollins, and therefore less widely appreciated, Mobley shared with him an extremely flexible rhythmic approach. This enlivened a choice of notes which would otherwise have come close to being banal but, with a suitably no-nonsense accompaniment, created an exciting air of brinkmanship. His somewhat introverted tone often made his lines seem a little too laid-back, but the logic of their construction amply repaid the dedicated listener. [BP]

Soul Station (1960); *No Room for Squares* (1963), both Blue Note

Modal Jazz implies improvisation on a series of scales instead of a sequence of chords. In practice there is an overlap between the two approaches, but the term describes specifically the style established in the late 1950s and early 1960s by Miles Davis's *Kind of Blue* and the John Coltrane quartet.

The themes used for modal jazz, although based on chords sounded by the keyboard accompaniment, deliberately avoided the amount of harmonic *movement* and harmonic *direction* of bebop sequences. Ample precedents existed for this, going back to the rather static harmonies of 'rhythm changes' and most 12-bar blues, while early Latin-jazz numbers such as 'Night in Tunisia' or Bud Powell's 'Un Poco Loco' also gave lower priority to chordal improvisation; certain pieces by Thelonious Monk ('Well You Needn't', 'Locomotive' etc.) and many by Charles Mingus had incorporated sections with no more than two chords continually alternating. The effect of this is to direct the soloist's attention towards melodic creativity and away from chord-derived 'filler' material, a trend that had been evident in Davis's own playing long before he gave birth to the modal 'school'. Interestingly, however, whereas the first modal recordings stimulated soloists by restricting them to the notes found in particular scales, Coltrane's quartet work found him reintroducing a kind of harmonic interest (by making passing reference to other scales, a technique known as side-slipping, for the sake of then resolving the tension with a return to the home scale).

The word 'modal' came into jazz terminology thanks to composer/theoretician George Russell, and derives from the seven 7-note scales (modes) used in Ancient Greece and which, together with certain 5- and 6-note scales, are the basis of all European music (the Ionian mode is identical to the so-called major scale, the Aeolian mode is one of the possible minor scales). It is a pity that widespread misapplication of Russell's theory by jazz educators has entrenched the belief that for every chord there is a scale and that knowledge of these is essential for improvising. The pathetic results of this kind of teaching tell their own story: as the old blues song put it, 'You've got the right key, but the wrong keyhole.' [BP]

Modern jazz A description whose built-in obsolescence did not prevent it gaining currency in the 1950s to describe bebop and post-bop. Chiefly used at the time by writers and fans who found the onomatopoeic word 'bebop' sounded childish and demeaning, 'modern jazz' is now mainly heard from diehard followers of swing and New Orleans; in their opinion, the term 'modernists' sounds equally demeaning, and covers indiscriminately anyone who arrived on the scene after 1940. [BP]

Modern Jazz Quartet, see LEWIS, JOHN.

Moffett, Charles Mack, drums (and trumpet). b. Fort Worth, Texas, 6 September 1929. Played as teenager with Ornette Coleman, Dewey Redman, Leo Wright etc., then after navy service (late 1940s), taught music in high school (1950s). Moved to New York (1961), joined Ornette Coleman trio (intermittently active 1962–7, including European tour). Also during this period with Archie Shepp and leading own group. In 1970s moved to San Francisco, teaching music again and gigging with the Moffett Family, including his several children (one of whom, bassist Charnet Moffett, later recorded with Wynton Marsalis and Stanley Jordan). In the 1980s he moved back to New York to teach mentally retarded children.

Moffett was very much a swing-oriented drummer but open to free styles of improvisation; as such, he certainly brought out the more traditional aspects of those 'avant-garde' soloists with whom he performed. [BP]

Ornette Coleman, *At the Golden Circle, vols. 1/2* (1965), Blue Note

Moholo, Louis T., drums, voice, cello, percussion. b. Cape Town, South Africa, 10 March 1940. Father a pianist, mother and sister both vocalists. Self-taught. 1956, co-founded a big band, the Cordettes. At the 1962 Johannesburg Jazz Festival, he received the Best Drummer award, and joined the Blue Notes, a band of local stars assembled by the white SA pianist Chris McGregor. Under apartheid, racially mixed bands were illegal, and as the reputation of the Blue Notes began to grow, it became almost impossible for the band to play together. They secured passports through an organization called Union Artists, and left in 1964 for Europe. They played at the Antibes Festival, appeared at some of the most important jazz centres in Europe and arrived in the UK in 1965, making their home in London. 1966, Moholo toured South America with Steve Lacy, recording with him and staying abroad for about a year, during which time he also played with Roswell Rudd, John Tchicai and Archie Shepp, among others. He returned to the UK in 1967, playing then and subsequently with McGregor's Brotherhood of Breath, Mike Osborne trio, Isipingo, Irene Schweizer trio, Peter Brötzmann trio and big band and with Keith Tippett, both as a duo and in the pianist's very large ensemble, the Ark. He has also led various groups of his own, including Moholo's Unit, Spirits Rejoice, Culture Shock, African Drum Ensemble and Viva La Black. Moholo, like his compatriot Dudu Pukwana, has made a very great contribution to the British jazz scene, bringing to it the whole ethos of African drumming and music-making: energy, passion, superb time, flexibility. He seems equally at home with jazz 4/4 time, free (abstract) improvisation and rock rhythms, which is why his presence has been felt in such a wide range of musical contexts. With the Brotherhood and other groups he toured and played festivals all over Europe. With Peter Brötzmann and Harry Miller he toured the USA in 1979, and with Chris McGregor and the Blue Notes toured Africa during the 1970s. His favourite percussionists are Tunji (Nigeria) and Bra Punk (Port Elizabeth, SA), and other inspirations are Eubie Blake, Harry Miller and three African composer/arranger/lyricists – Mnyataza, Tyhamzashe and Jolobe. [IC]

With Lacy, *Forest and the Zoo* (1966), ESP; with McGregor, *Very Urgent* (1967), Polydor; with Brotherhood of Breath, *Live at Willisau* (1974); *Procession* (1978); with Osborne trio, *Border Crossing* (1974); *All Night Long* (1975); with Blue Notes, *Blue Notes for Mongezi, vol. 1* (1975); Moholo octet, *Spirits Rejoice!* (1978), all Ogun

Mole, Miff (Irving Milfred), trombone. b. Roosevelt, Long Island, New York, 11 March 1898; d. 29 April 1961. He began his career in bands led by Gus Sharp and pianist Jimmy Durante but by 1923 was working with Phil Napoleon's Original Memphis Five: they produced dozens of highly-polished chamber jazz classics, and in turn influenced young Red Nichols, who heard Mole with Napoleon in Atlantic City that year. From 1925 for five years Nichols and Mole were virtually inseparable, producing irreplaceable on-record classics ('That's no bargain', 'Feeling no pain' and 'Boneyard Shuffle' are examples) under their own and a variety of other names: 'The Arkansas Travellers', 'The Redheads', 'Miff and Red's Stompers' and so on. Mole worked independently, too (with large society orchestras such as Roger Wolfe Kahn's), and by 1927, rather than join the roistering young band of Condon-led Chicago hopefuls making their first uncertain steps, had moved into studio work, first at WOR then at NBC (he played for Toscanini *and* Bessie Smith). In the 1940s illness complicated Mole's life: he worked with Benny Goodman and led a band at Nick's on and off for four years, but a period out of the limelight and the new omnipotence of Jack Teagarden (whose playing somehow seemed more charming than Mole's) presented major problems. Like Joe Sullivan (in some ways a kindred spirit), Mole worked less and less, and by the 1950s had become progressively more and more ill. By 1960, after six hip operations, he was working with Wingy Manone on Long Island and walking with a stick: that year a Newport concert featuring him and Henry 'Red' Allen was unceremoniously cancelled after riots, and Mole was sent home unrecognized. That winter he was seen selling pretzels in a New York subway: benefits organized by Jack Crystal at Central Plaza, New York, came too late and Mole died the following April.

'The J. J. Johnson of the 1920s,' in Dickie Wells's words, and 'one of the first fine technical trombones I heard', Mole was a revolutionary trombonist whose clean, quick technique may have been the first of its kind and, like Frankie

Thelonious Monk

Trumbauer's technically unsurpassable playing, made a deep impression on black and white players alike in the formative jazz years. [DF]

Thesaurus of Classic Jazz, vol 2 (1927–30), Philips; Columbia

Moncur, Grachan, III, trombone, composer. b. New York City, 1937. His father, Grachan Moncur II (b. 2 September 1915), was bassist with the original Savoy Sultans and on records with Billie Holiday, Mildred Bailey etc. The trombonist studied music, including at Manhattan School of Music and Juilliard School, and toured with Ray Charles band (1961–3) and with Art Farmer–Benny Golson (1962). Settled in New York, working and recording with Jackie McLean, Sonny Rollins and under own name. Played with Archie Shepp (1967–9, including European tour 1967 and Algiers 1969); also with drummer Beaver Harris in 360 Degree Music Experience. Wrote *Echoes of Prayer* for Jazz Composers' Orchestra Association (1974). Returned to Newark, where he was raised, to do educational work; also played there with organist John Patton, with whom he recorded again (1983). Toured Europe with the second edition of the Paris Reunion Band (1986). Unlike the expressionist exclamations of most trombonists involved in the 1960s avant-garde, Moncur's style was based on the approach of J. J. Johnson, which he successfully adapted to work in a free setting. [BP]

Evolution (1963), Blue Note

Monk, Thelonious Sphere, piano, composer. b. Rocky Mount, N. Carolina, 11 October 1917; d. 17 February 1982. Brought up in New York from age five, Monk took piano lessons at 11 or 12. Two years later, began playing at Harlem rent parties and accompanying his mother's singing in church. Led trio in neighbourhood bar (*c.* 1934) and then spent two years touring in quartet with an evangelist. Studied briefly at Juilliard School and freelanced with all kinds of groups. Played regularly with Keg Purnell quartet (1939), with Kenny Clarke at Minton's and at Kelly's Stables (1940–2). Also with Lucky Millinder band (1942), back at Minton's under Kermit Scott (1943), then regular pianist with Coleman Hawkins sextet (1943–early 1945), making record debut with him. Rehearsed with Dizzy Gillespie's first quintet (1943) and worked with Cootie Williams band (briefly, 1944), gigged with Skippy Williams band (1945) and then with Gillespie big band (1946). Began recording with own groups (1947) and appearing with them at Minton's, Royal Roost and Village Vanguard, sidemen in this period including Art Blakey, Milt Jackson, Sahib Shihab, Sonny Rollins. Imprisoned falsely for possession of drugs (1951), was deprived of New York employment for six years after release; continued recording with some regularity and occasionally gigging elsewhere, appearance at Paris Jazz Fair, 1954.

Summer 1957, assembled quartet with John Coltrane, Shadow Wilson (originally Philly Joe Jones) and Wilbur Ware for first of several long residencies at the 5 Spot. Collaborators included Johnny Griffin and Roy Haynes (1958), Charlie Rouse (1959–70); with the latter, Monk was presented in big-band concerts at Town Hall (1959), Lincoln Center (1963) and Monterey festival (1964). Reputation blossomed in US and then internationally, with first tours of Europe (1961) and Japan (1964). Toured Europe with octet (1967), but quartet continued to be usual format, featuring saxists Pat Patrick (1970) and Paul Jeffrey (1970–1) and, on drums, Thelonious Monk Jnr. Accepted fewer engagements in late 1960s and early 1970s, but toured widely with the Giants of Jazz (1971–2). Thereafter a combination of illness and voluntary inactivity kept Monk from public performance, one of his last appearances being at 1974 Newport Festival concert of orchestrated arrangements of his compositions.

No longer inevitably associated with his piano playing, Monk's tunes have enjoyed renewed interest since his death. But some of them were standard material as early as the mid-1940s: 'Round Midnight' was put on record by Dizzy Gillespie and Cootie Williams (who used Monk's 'Epistrophy' as his radio theme-song), '52nd St Theme' was recorded by Gillespie and Bud Powell, while Charlie Parker used both on broadcasts. In the 1950s Miles Davis's versions of 'Well You Needn't' and 'Straight, No Chaser' and Monk's own *Jazz on a Summer's Day* filmed performance of 'Blue Monk', succeeded in placing them in the same evergreen category. In fact these and the rest of his output always sound at their best when played by him and are best understood by reference to his piano style, and vice versa. Starting from an admiration for Teddy Wilson and the stride players, Monk achieved a much more economical and much more percussive manner; and the way in which he would analyse and develop the phrases of his own pieces in improvisation illustrated how they had been put together in the first place. Although he contributed harmonically to bebop, he criticized the boppers for being more interested in straight-ahead blowing than in exploring the ins and outs of his material.

Monk was equally frustrated by later generations of soloists, although Rollins, Coltrane and Griffin each approached his ideal from different directions. Steve Lacy, after working with him briefly in 1960, spent several years using only Monk tunes, and the motivic improvisation Monk favoured was quite prevalent in the 1960s avant-garde movement. In terms of influence, while the great majority of pianists always want to play the maximum number of notes, the select few who have followed Monk are more thoughtful and thought-provoking. [BP]

Genius of Modern Music, vols 1/2 (1947–52), Blue Note; *Thelonious Monk and Sonny Rollins* (1953–4), Prestige/OJC; *Thelonious Monk with John Coltrane* (1957), Jazzland/OJC; *At Town Hall* (1959), Riverside/OJC; *Something in Blue* (1971), Black Lion

Montgomery, Wes (John Leslie), guitar. b. Indianapolis, Indiana, 6 March 1925; d. 15 June 1968. Self-taught on guitar during teenage years, soon gigging on local scene. Toured with Lionel Hampton band (1948–50), appearing briefly in film short and taking first recorded solo on 'Moonglow' released in late 1970s. Returned to Indianapolis, working through most of 1950s at day job and playing every night at local bars such as the Flame and the Missile Room. Made record sessions in Chicago (1957) and Los Angeles (1958) with bassist Monk (William) Montgomery (b. 10 October 1921; d. 20 May 1982) and vibraharpist Buddy (Charles) Montgomery (b. 30 January 1930), who formed the Mastersounds group (1957–60, later known as the Montgomery Brothers, 1960–2).

Returned home again, working with own organ trio (1958–9) until cutting albums in New York under own name (1959 onwards). Lived in San Francisco with his brothers (1960–1), during this period briefly working also with John Coltrane sextet in SF and at Monterey festival,

Wes Montgomery

1960. Then toured with own trio/quartet, plus clubwork and TV with local rhythm-section during only British visit (1965); also recorded with Wynton Kelly trio (1962) and later played regularly in public with them (1965–6). Began series of albums with big-band backing, enjoying unprecedented success even for middle-of-the-road instrumentals (1964–8). 1967, made TV appearance with Herb Alpert, to whose record company he was contracted in the last year before his death from a heart attack.

Easily the most accomplished guitarist since the emergence of Charlie Christian, Montgomery had all the rhythmic verve associated with his original idol, and covered a wider range on the instrument. To this he added the four-note parallel chording that Barney Kessel had essayed and the unison octaves perfected by Django Reinhardt. Throughout his career he used his thumb to pick the strings (as opposed to the folky finger-style or the plectrum favoured by previous jazz stylists), which gave him a more mellow sound than anyone else except possibly Jim Hall. Although there was a predictable aspect to the way he constructed many of his solos, his work of the late 1950s–early 1960s still feels brilliantly alive. It is perhaps a pity that the mellow sound and the unison octaves were marketed so mercilessly during his last years, but the positive influence of his work on a whole generation of players is still strong. He was the subject of a Kool Festival all-star tribute concert at Carnegie Hall in 1985. [BP]

The Incredible Jazz Guitar (1960), Riverside/OJC; *Full House* (1962), Riverside/OJC; Wynton Kelly/Wes Montgomery, *Smokin' at the Half Note* (1965), Verve

See Ingram, Adrian, *Wes Montgomery* (Ashley Mark, 1985)

Montoliu, Tete (Vincente), piano. b. Barcelona, Spain, 28 March 1933. Born blind, Montoliu studied piano and became interested in jazz as a child. Played with Don Byas on his visits to Barcelona, began recording with US musicians such as Lionel Hampton (1956), Roland Kirk (1963) and Anthony Braxton (1974). From early 1960s worked regularly in Copenhagen and Germany, and visited the US (1967, 1979). Through his own albums, including duos with George Coleman and Chick Corea, Montoliu has gradually acquired an international reputation; possessing an excellent technique, his unaccompanied performances are less vacuous than other technical heavyweights, and he is also impressive in a group context. [BP]

Songs for Love (1974), Enja

Moody, James, tenor and alto sax, flute. b. Savannah, Georgia, 26 March 1925. Father was trumpeter with Tiny Bradshaw. Took up alto in 1941, tenor the following year, and played regularly in air force (1943–6). Joined Dizzy Gillespie band on tenor (1946–7 and 1948, including tour of Europe). Based in Paris (late 1948–1951), working with Miles Davis–Tadd Dameron and recording with Max Roach (1949) and touring throughout Western Europe. Returned to US, led own 7-piece group (1951–62), adding flute to his performances from mid-1950s. Briefly with three-tenor group including Gene Ammons and Sonny Stitt (1962), then featured in Gillespie quintet (1963–8, plus Gillespie big band in Europe 1968). Working as a single followed by Las Vegas backing bands (1974–80). Since re-emerging on jazz scene, has been in demand as soloist and has toured Europe (1982, 1983 and 1985).

Moody was one of the earliest tenor players to be at home playing bop in the mid-1940s, when he sounded a little like Dexter Gordon with a softer tone. He created a jukebox hit with his first-ever alto recording, the 1949 Swedish version of 'I'm in the Mood for Love', which demonstrated a fine command of ballads. He is also extremely fluent on flute, although the tenor still seems to be his most impressive instrument. A commitment to communicating with audiences comes across in his engaging stage presentation, even including the occasional vocal chorus. [BP]

Moody's Moods (1956), Prestige/OJC; *The Blues and Other Colors* (1967), Milestone

Moore, Brew (Milton Aubrey), tenor sax. b. Indianola, Mississippi, 26 March 1924; d. Copenhagen, 19 August 1973. Active in New York in the late 1940s with Claude Thornhill, Gerry Mulligan, Kai Winding etc, also recording under own name. Sessions with trumpeter Tony Fruscella (1953), then lived in San Francisco (1955–60). Based in Europe (1961–7), New York (1967–70), Canary Islands (1970), then back to Europe. Addiction to alcohol contributed to his fatal fall down a flight of stairs. Moore was the originator of the phrase, 'Anyone who doesn't play like Lester [Young] is wrong', and certainly his playing backed up the assertion. He never attained the fluency and unpredictability of the master, but he was definitely one of the most faithful followers. [BP]

Quintet (1955–6), Fantasy/OJC

Moore, Oscar Frederic, guitar. b. Austin, Texas, 25 December 1912; d. Las Vegas, 8 October 1981. He made a striking contribution to Nat 'King' Cole's hit-making trio in the 1940s: his use of electric guitar when that was still revolutionary and cool hip lines (recalling Charlie Christian) made him an innovator of the period, and hit recordings including 'Straighten up and fly right', 'Sweet Lorraine', 'Route 66' and 'It's only a paper moon' brought his work to international fame. Moore first met Cole after the pianist had been asked to assemble a quartet for a 1937 residency at the Swanee Inn, Santa Monica, and with bassist Wesley Prince (later replaced by Johnny Miller) began touring and clubwork: a 1942 contract for Capitol Records – and the hits that followed – did much to popularize electric guitar and Moore himself, who made a strong creative contribution to Cole's sound (including the use of unison piano/guitar passages). The partnership lasted until 1947, when he left Cole to pursue the possibilities of a band co-led with his guitarist brother John and was replaced in the trio by Irving Ashby. From then on very little was heard from Oscar Moore although (says John Chilton) he remained a busy freelance and returned to professional work in the 1960s after working as a bricklayer. 'He was a wonderful musician', says Maria Cole, Nat's widow. [DF]

Any with Nat Cole's trio

Moore, Russell ('Big Chief'), trombone, vocals. b. near Sacaton, Arizona, 13 August 1912; d.

Nyack, New York, 15 December 1983. He was taught the trombone by his uncle, lived in the Chicago area during the 1920s, played early jobs locally, was with Lionel Hampton's Los Angeles band in 1935, then with Eddie Barefield, and thereafter was active around New Orleans working with men such as Oscar Celestin and Paul Barbarin, as well as Noble Sissle and Harlan Leonard. 1944–7, he worked with Louis Armstrong's big band (which also featured young Dexter Gordon), played the Paris Jazz Festival, 1949, with his own band and by the 1950s was all over the jazz scene working with such names as Eddie Condon, Wild Bill Davison, Tony Parenti, Sammy Price, Buck Clayton, Don Byas, Hot Lips Page and Henry 'Red' Allen. Perhaps his most prestigious career step was to join Louis Armstrong for a year in 1964 (replacing Trummy Young); thereafter he led his own band again, gigged with Lester Lanin and was busy until 1981 when a tour of Europe with Keith Smith revealed, at last, an old tired Chief. [DF]

Louis Armstrong, *Hello Dolly* (1964), London

Morand, Herb, trumpet, vocals. b. New Orleans, 1905; d. 23 February 1952. Lizzie Miles's half-brother was broadcasting from New Orleans by the early 1920s and by 1925 had moved to New York to work with Cliff Jackson's band. For most of his career from the late 1920s he was Chicago-based, working with Joe Lindsey at Tony's Tavern, a regular stopping-off point for visiting celebrities (1934–5), recording with Frank Melrose and the Dodds Brothers (small classics like 'Piggly Wiggly' and 'Forty and Tight') and running the Harlem Hamfats, a mellow, entertaining group for which Morand was trumpeter-manager. (Hamfats, in Harlemese, were country boys who used ham fat to grease their valves: the Hamfats' great records, in fact, have just a trace of country style in them.) Morand was a latecomer to Chicago at a time when giants like Louis Armstrong were tearing up the town, and by the 1940s he was back in New Orleans leading resort bands and working with such as Joe Watkins and George Lewis. From 1950 he was plagued by illness complicated by obesity and he died during an engagement at the El Morocco Club, New Orleans, with Lewis. Frank Driggs reports that a disapproving older sister destroyed Morand's scrapbooks. [DF]

The Harlem Hamfats (1936–7), Queen-Disc

Morehouse, Chauncey, drums, percussion. b. Niagara Falls, New York State, 11 March 1902; d. Medford, New Jersey, 31 October 1980. He began work playing in silent-movie houses around Pennsylvania with his pianist father. Then came the Gettysburg College dance band and from 1922 the coveted drummer's chair with Paul Specht's Society Serenaders, who quickly came east from Detroit to New York. He recorded classic sides with Specht's band-within-a-band, the Georgians (led by Frank Guarente), but left three years on to work with Howard Lanin and Ted Weems, before joining Jean Goldkette at Detroit's Graystone Ballroom: Morehouse's records with Beiderbecke and Trumbauer from this period are classics. After Goldkette's band broke up in New York he joined Adrian Rollini briefly, then Don Voorhees for pitwork in a Broadway show, *Rain or Shine*. From then on (with a break for bandleading in 1938, for which he invented a set of chromatic tuneable drums), theatre and studio work was to be Morehouse's life pattern: he played for commercial radio and TV, wrote and recorded jingles, and later became house drummer for Decca Records. After retiring in the late 1960s he re-emerged in the 1970s to play for the New York Jazz Repertory Company Bix Beiderbecke tributes, for a Goldkette reunion at Carnegie Hall and elsewhere. [DF]

Bix Beiderbecke, *The Studio Groups – 1927*, EMI World

Moreira, Airto, percussion, drums, voice. b. Itaiopolis, Brazil, 5 August 1941. He studied acoustic guitar and piano, 1948–50, and at 12 was performing with groups. From 19 he spent three years playing in night clubs all over Brazil. He formed his own group, which included Hermeto Pascoal, and later the two of them formed the Quarteto Novo. During these early years, travelling through the various areas of Brazil, the Amazon jungle, the dry north-east and the Mato Grosso prairies, he collected and studied about 120 different instruments.

1968, he and his wife, singer Flora Purim, moved to the USA, and came to international notice with Miles Davis in 1970, playing on records and in live concerts. He worked with Lee Morgan early in 1971; and later that year played percussion in the first Weather Report with Joe Zawinul, Wayne Shorter, Miroslav Vitous and Alphonse Mouzon. 1972, with Flora Purim he was a member of Chick Corea's first Return to Forever. He became one of the most sought-after percussionists in the USA, working with many people in all sorts of contexts, including Stan Getz, Cannonball Adderley, Gato Barbieri, Don Friedman and Reggie Workman. He formed his own group in 1973, moving to Berkeley, California, with Flora Purim, playing on her albums and also recording under his own name. In the mid-1980s he was a member of the Al DiMeola Project, recording with it and touring in the USA and Europe. Moreira was the first of the contemporary Latin percussionists to work on the US scene and he has made the biggest reputation because he was in so many key groups at an extraordinarily dynamic time in jazz history. His influences include Gil Evans, Bill Evans, Miles Davis, Antonio Carlos Jobim, Pascoal, Wes Montgomery, Coltrane, Ravi Shankar. [IC]

With Getz, Adderley, DiMeola and many others; with Miles Davis, *At Fillmore*; *Black Beauty*; *Live-Evil* (all 1970); with *Weather Report* (1971), all CBS; with Corea, *Return to Forever* (1972), ECM; as leader, *Fingers* (1973), CTI

Morello, Joe (Joseph A.), drums. b. Springfield, Massachusetts, 17 July 1928. A near contemporary of Phil Woods, who was born in the same town, Morello was partly blind from childhood. After playing locally, toured with Glen Gray band (1950), then worked in New York with guitarist Johnny Smith (1952) and with Stan Kenton band. Regular member of Marian McPartland trio (1953–6) and of the best-known edition of the Dave Brubeck quartet (1956–67). Since then, his fairly infrequent appearances have been of an educational nature and/or promotional activities for drum manufacturers. His work with Brubeck might be seen in the same light, since he was the first drummer to make the group sound like a jazz band and, unlike its leader when he joined, Morello was an extremely precise player who nevertheless managed to be relaxed and swinging. As a result, he set standards of excellence for many young listeners who were just becoming interested in jazz, and prepared them to appreciate players such as Max Roach and Art Blakey. [BP]

Dave Brubeck, *Time Out* (1959), CBS

Morgan, Lee, trumpet, composer. b. Philadelphia, 10 July 1938; d. 19 February 1972, shot in a New York club where his quintet was performing, after a quarrel with a woman. His career had also begun with a bang, when at 18 he joined the Dizzy Gillespie big band, staying with it for two years (1956–8). He then joined Art Blakey's Jazz Messengers in one of the group's best phases (1958–61). Benny Golson was writing much of the material, and Morgan made a big impact internationally with brilliantly funky open horn solos on Golson's 'Blues March' and fine harmon mute work on 'Whisper Not'. He was a little overshadowed when Freddie Hubbard burst on the scene in the early 1960s, and he spent some years playing in the Philadelphia area with Jimmy Heath and others. 1964–6, he again toured internationally with Blakey, and was also recording regularly for Blue Note with his own groups. 1964, one of his compositions, a blues called 'The Sidewinder' was a hit, and the album of which it was the title track became a best-seller: this commercial success and popularity did not please the jazz critics. Morgan's instantly recognizable sound and style grew out of his main influences – Clifford Brown, Dizzy Gillespie and Fats Navarro. He had a fat, crisp tone, a good range, and he played with immense expressiveness and urgency – a style rooted in the inflexions of the blues, with slurred and bent notes, funky phrases, and great rhythmic momentum. [IC]

With John Coltrane's sextet, *Blue Train* (1957); several with Blakey; many under his own name, including, *At the Lighthouse* (1970); *Rumproller* (1965); *The Sidewinder* (1964), all Blue Note

Morgan, Sam, trumpet. b. Bertrandville, Louisiana, 1895; d. New Orleans, 25 February 1936. An important New Orleans trumpeter with a big local following, Morgan (the brother of bassist Al Morgan) played in and around the city for ten years at venues such as the Savoy on Rampart Street (George Lewis was an early sitter-in). In 1925 he suffered a severe stroke but by one year on had re-formed his band with keymen such as Jim Robinson (tmb), Rene Hall (banjo) and Isaiah Morgan (lead tpt). In 1927 the band made some now famous records for Columbia in New Orleans, at Werlein's Music Shop on Canal Street. 'Bogalusa Strut', 'Sing on' and every other title later became a respected classic of New Orleans jazz. The Morgan band played on until 1932 (they also ran a profitable sideline – a treasure hunting service complete with tents and divining rods) when Morgan had a second stroke. His band broke up a year later in 1933. [DF]

The Sound of New Orleans, vol. 3 (1925–45), CBS

Morrissey, Dick (Richard Edwin), tenor and soprano sax, flute. b. Horley, Surrey, 9 May 1940. Parents both musical, but he was self-taught. Began at school aged 16 on clarinet under the spell of Johnny Dodds, switched to sax when he played in a band with Peter King. Early 1960s, he was leading a quartet with Harry South, Phil Bates and Phil Seamen on drums. At the beginning of the 1970s he formed and co-led the jazz-rock band If with Terry Smith. He met Jim Mullen in 1976 and formed Morrissey–Mullen in order to record in New York City with the Average White Band. Then he continued in New York, playing with his own band and with Herbie Mann. Back in the UK his association with Mullen continued until 1985. His influences are Ben Webster, Lester Young, Zoot Sims, Hank Mobley, Sonny Rollins and Stanley Turrentine, and he derives inspiration from Louis Armstrong, Clifford Brown and Charlie Parker. In the USA he toured as a support group with Cannonball Adderley, and in the UK he has worked regularly at the Ronnie Scott Club. [IC]

Storm Warning (1967), Mercury; *Jimmy Witherspoon at the Bull's Head* (1966), Fontana; Morrissey–Mullen, *This Must Be the Place* (1985), Coda

Morton, Benny (Henry Sterling), trombone. b. New York City, 31 January 1907; d. 28 December 1985. A graduate of the Jenkins Orphanage Band (he was taught by Professor

Rohmie Jones), Morton's early influences included church music as well as Mamie Smith's star trombonist Dope Andrews. By 1923 he was working with Clarence Holiday's orchestra and gaining experience for Fletcher Henderson's which he joined in 1926. 'For a young person', Morton said (he was around 20 when he joined), 'it was like a school, because the youngest man close to my age was five years older and it went up to the first trumpet who was 20 years older.' Two stays with Henderson were followed by six years with Don Redman and three more with Count Basie: there are immortal records of Morton with Billie Holiday at this time, including 'My first impression of you'. After Basie, in the 1940s he worked with Teddy Wilson and with Ed Hall and led his own band, before playing in the pit for Broadway shows including *Guys and Dolls*, *Silk Stockings*, *St Louis Woman* and for Radio City Music Hall in 1959. Throughout the 1960s and 1970s he was back in high jazz society, including Wild Bill Davison, Bobby Hackett, the Saints and Sinners, replacing his friend Vic Dickenson, and the World's Greatest Jazz Band: in the 1980s, gentle, occasionally eccentric, self-effacing, Morton was busily working and touring still. Although he never boasted the spectacular technique of a Trummy Young or the humour of a Wells or Dickenson ('that's why Vic has been recorded two thousand times and I and others twenty times,' he once admitted), Benny Morton was one of the most sophisticated trombonists from the swing era. [DF]

Count Basie, *Swinging the Blues* (1937–9), Affinity

See Dance, Stanley, *The World of Swing* (Scribners, 1974, repr. Da Capo, 1979)

Morton, Jelly Roll (Ferdinand Lemott), piano, composer, arranger, vocals. b. New Orleans, 20 October 1890; d. Los Angeles, 10 July 1941. Around the career of Jelly Roll Morton there existed until recently a veil of mystique, grandiose claims and doubtful facts, many of them set up with delight by 'The Originator of Jazz Stomps and Blues' as Morton styled himself. Researchers such as Lawrence Gushee, John Chilton and Laurie Wright have now cleared the mists considerably, but Morton's career – full of pizazz, braggadocio and tireless self-promotion – remains one of the most colourful in jazz.

By 1906 he was playing piano in the Storyville brothels, hustling, playing pool and learning how to survive: these hard-won lessons were to involve him in vaudeville (he worked in a double act as 'Morton and Morton' with a partner, 'Rose'), music publishing with the Spikes brothers, running a tailor's shop, boxing promotion, pimping, black-face minstrel shows, work in cabarets, dance halls and gambling houses (as manager as well as pianist), and for a while running a club-hotel with his canny wife Anita, the sister of bassist Bill Johnson. (A splendid and detailed chronology of Morton's nomadic course at this time may be found in John Chilton's *Who's Who of Jazz*.) By 1923 he was in Chicago, and at the dawn of his greatest creative period: a good relationship with the Melrose brothers who published his tunes, and a string of successful piano solos recorded for Gennett (including 'King Porter Stomp', 'Kansas City Stomp' and 'The Pearls') drew early attention to his style. When not recording, Morton was touring with his own groups (and occasionally for other leaders such as Fate Marable and W. C. Handy, which he usually strenuously denied). In 1926, at the behest of Frank Melrose he recorded the classic 'Red Hot Peppers' sessions, acknowledged as his greatest. Baby Dodds supplies memories: 'There was a fine spirit in that group – at rehearsal Jelly used to work on each and every number until it satisfied him! You did what Jelly Roll wanted you to do, no more no less.' Morton would supply every last routine of the performance, always hired reliable men (preferably Creoles from New Orleans), paid generously for rehearsals ($5) and recording ($15) and maintained an easy but disciplined atmosphere: the results were such closely-worked masterpieces as 'The Pearls', 'Dead Man Blues' and 'Sidewalk Blues', which established the Peppers as Victor's number one hot band.

By 1928, Morton had followed his success to New York, but there – for the first time – he began to lose ground. The dawn of the big-band era could not accommodate his preference for small-band jazz and fondness for New Orleans, and his attempts over the next two years to hold together a big band were half-hearted and unhappy. By 1930 he was finding it hard to book the musicians and the kind of work he had been used to, his contract with Victor expired and was not renewed, and within two years he was working in theatre pits for musical revues and hanging out at the Rhythm Club over at Lafayette Theater, still talking and signifying. Four years on, in 1936, he was living in Washington and, in George Hoefer's memorable phrase, 'suing the world for recognition' as he played in a tiny second floor club to a clique of dedicated admirers, including Roy Carew. Later Alan Lomax, the curator of the Library of Congress folklore archives, joined them and in 1938 recorded Morton reminiscing at length in a small room in the library's music section: the records are a crazy quilt of memory, romance and invention. At the same period Morton (infuriated by a Robert Ripley radio programme which introduced W. C. Handy as 'the originator of jazz and the blues') fired off a letter to *Downbeat* magazine: 'I myself', he said, 'happened to be the creator of jazz in the year of 1902.' The controversy reminded people that Morton was still alive, although not well: in 1939, living in New York again – 'that cruel city' he called it – he recorded again, and once more in 1940. But that year, plagued with asthma and a heart condition, he drove to California in search of warm weather and perhaps success; the following year he died insensate in hospital. Ten years on the Jelly Roll Morton Society, at the instigation of Floyd Levin, finally marked his grave at Calvary Cemetery, Los Angeles.

Morton took classic small-band jazz to its artistic limits: 'Jelly Roll was to the small band what Ellington was to the large', says Art Hodes. His music assumed classic proportions and has been perpetuated in clubs, concert halls, theatres and on records by musicians and artists as varied as Dick Hyman, Pee Wee Erwin, Kenny Ball, Max Harris and choreographer Twyla Tharp. [DF]

The Complete Jelly Roll Morton, vols. 1/4, RCA

See Morton, Jelly Roll, with Lomax, Alan, *Mr Jelly Roll* (Evergreen, 1962); Shapiro, Nat, and Hentoff, Nat, *The Jazz Makers* (Rinehart, 1957, repr. Da Capo, 1979); Williams, Martin, *Jazz Masters of New Orleans* (Macmillan, 1967, repr. Da Capo, 1979); Balliett, Whitney, *Jelly Roll, Jabbo and Fats* (OUP, 1983)

Moses, Bob (Rahboat), drums, piano, vibes, bass clarinet, flutes, steel drums, log drums, kalimba, electric bass, synthesizer, voice, composer. b. New York City, 28 January 1948. Father, Richard Moses, was press agent for musicians including Charles Mingus, Max Roach and Rahsaan Roland Kirk, all of whom were close family friends and powerful influences on young Moses. Mostly self-taught. Began on drums (and piano and vibes) at age ten, and composing at 14. When he was about 12 he used to sit in with Mingus on Sunday afternoon sessions. His first professional gigs were as teenage vibraphonist on the NYC Latin music scene. 1964–5, he spent six months with Kirk, playing drums on two of the saxist's classic albums, *I Talk with the Spirits* and *Rip, Rig and Panic*. 1966, he helped to form Free Spirits with saxophonist Jim Pepper and Larry Coryell, which was perhaps the first electric jazz-rock group. 1968, he played briefly in Open Sky with Dave Liebman, then joined the Gary Burton quartet, which included Coryell and bassist Steve Swallow, leaving after 14 months in 1969. Moses then formed another jazz-rock band, Compost, 1970–3, with Jack DeJohnette and tenor saxist Harold Vick. He toured the UK with the Mike Gibbs Orchestra in 1974, then rejoined Gary Burton, staying until 1975. Then worked and recorded with Pat Metheny trio, with Jaco Pastorius, and Hal Galper's group with the Brecker brothers. 1978–9, he was again with Burton. 1980, formed an all-star quintet with Dave Liebman, Terumasa Hino, Steve Kuhn and Steve Swallow. 1981–3, with the Steve Kuhn–Sheila Jordan band; 1984, with the George Gruntz big band. 1984–5, formed his own quintet. In the mid-1970s he began composing for big ensembles, and created his own record label, Mozown Records, to release *Bittersweet in the Ozone*, for a line-up which included Randy Brecker, Eddie Gomez, Howard Johnson, Dave Liebman, Jeanne Lee, Billy Hart and Stanley Free. This was followed by two superb albums, *When Elephants Dream of Music* (1982) and *Visit with the Great Spirit* (1983), which showed Moses to be a highly accomplished and most original composer and orchestrator. He had always been an incipient visionary, and with these albums the seer came out in all his glory: he was now writing and reciting poetry and painting, and the album covers bore his texts and brightly coloured semi-abstract pictures. The music too had many resonances, from other periods of jazz, other cultures; it was dense and deft, but also full of wit and humour. The albums received universal critical acclaim, and Nat Hentoff wrote, 'No orchestral composer of this scope, mellow wit, and freshly distinctive range of colours has come along since Gil Evans.' As a drummer and as an orchestrator, Moses shows wide terms of reference, from Evans, Mike Gibbs, Mingus, Monk, Ellington and Miles Davis to African music, ethnic, Latin American, and the music he makes always swings. He has said, 'Several years ago, I got tired of playing subdued, non-physical, abstract music for a small audience of elite aficionados who sit there and politely applaud; I want to play some loud, powerful people's music . . . Everything I do I want to swing. I think music *needs* to swing, no matter how abstract it gets. In fact, the more abstract, the more intellectual it gets, the *more* it needs to swing, because that's the balancing factor.' [IC]

With Compost, *Life is Round* (1971), Columbia; with Mike Gibbs, *The Only Chrome Waterfall Orchestra* (1974), Bronze; with Steve Swallow, *Home* (1982), ECM; as leader, *Bittersweet in the Ozone* (1975), Mozown; *Family* (1979), Kama Sutra; *When Elephants Dream of Music* (1982), Gramavision; *Visit with the Great Spirit* (1983), Gramavision

Mosley, Snub (Lawrence Leo Mosely), trombone, slide sax, vocals. b. Little Rock, Arkansas, 29 December 1905; d. New York City, 21 July 1981. While he was never in the front rank of early trombone soloists such as Jimmy Harrison or even Claude Jones, Mosley was early on a talent to watch. 1926–33, he was featured soloist with Alphonso Trent's hugely successful territory band, where his stabbing, staccato attack and high register work attracted attention, and for the rest of the 1930s he worked in some of the best big bands, including Claude Hopkins's, Luis Russell's and (for a few months each) Fats Waller's and Fletcher Henderson's. From 1938 he led his own 6-piece band at hotels, clubs and on tour (for United Services Overseas among others) and produced at least one hit record, 'The Man with the Funny Little Horn!', featuring a remarkable 'slide saxophone': his own invention (it looked like a big metal Swanee whistle and produced a spectral sound). For 40 years, Mosley fronted his sometimes r & b-flavoured bands in and out of the New York area: he recorded in 1959 for Stanley Dance and 20 years on was touring Europe and the UK fronting Fred Hunt's trio, still making a brave and energetic show. [DF]

Live at Pizza Express (1978), Pizza

See Dance, Stanley, *The World of Count Basie* (Sidgwick & Jackson, 1980)

Moss, Danny, tenor sax, reeds. b. Sussex, 16 August 1927. He built his reputation in the best 1940s and 1950s British big bands, including Tommy Sampson's, Ted Heath's and John Dankworth's, in all of which he was a featured soloist. Although chronologically a member of the post-war bebop generation (and a master of it), Moss found himself by 1960 identifying more and more strongly with jazz's classic era and began returning deliberately to the vocabulary of Ben Webster and Coleman Hawkins, regularly sitting in with Dixielanders such as Alex Welsh and mainstreamer Sandy Brown. In the 1960s, with pianist Brian Lemon, he formed his quartet (now in existence for over 20 years), worked with Humphrey Lyttelton and by 1971 was regularly with Freddy Randall's Bobcats-style band (co-led by Dave Shepherd), was featured soloist again with Stan Reynolds's swing band, and worked only when necessary in studios. Moss – a jazzmaster of international standard – was by the 1980s working as easily for American singer Tony Bennett (as featured accompanist, a role previously filled by Bobby Hackett and Ruby Braff) and for drummer Bobby Rosengarden's New York band as he did for Peter Boizot's Pizza All Stars in Britain. Still occasionally underrated, Danny Moss did earlier in Britain what Scott Hamilton did later in America and to fewer fanfares, but he is an artist to treasure. [DF]

Any on Flyright label

Mossman, Michael Philip, trumpets, fluegelhorn, piccolo trumpet, piano. b. Philadelphia, 12 October 1959. BA in sociology/anthropology and B.Mus. in trumpet, both from Oberlin College, 1982; also post-graduate trumpet studies at Rutgers University. 1978, toured Europe with Anthony Braxton orchestra; toured Europe with Roscoe Mitchell, 1979, 1983; four months with Lionel Hampton orchestra, 1984, and one month with Art Blakey's Jazz Messengers; 1985, lead trumpet with Machito for Spanish tour, featured soloist with Gerry Mulligan orchestra and with two classical orchestras; co-leader of Blue Note Records Young Artist group Out of the Blue. Compositions, 'OTB', 'Piece for Double Bass and Trumpet', 'Isolation'. Favourites range from Miles Davis and Louis Armstrong to Maurice André, and influences are Mingus, Ellington, Coltrane, Donald Byrd, and particularly William Fielder, professor of trumpet at Rutgers University. [IC]

Roscoe Mitchell/Leo Smith Orchestra (1979), Moers Music; *Roscoe Mitchell Sound Ensemble* (1983), Black Saint; *Out of the Blue* (1985), Blue Note

Moten, Bennie, piano, leader, composer. b. Kansas City, Missouri, 13 November 1894; d. 2 April 1935. One of the three best-known Kansas big-band leaders of the 1920s – the other two were George E. Lee, his arch-rival, and Walter Page – Moten 'started out with just three pieces' (said Jimmy Rushing), playing ragtime and New Orleans-style jazz, and by 1923 had recorded for Okeh. His band policy, geared to public demand and specifically designed for dancing, made Moten very popular around Kansas (every year they played the local musicians' ball, and for a long time held down a residency at the El Torreon Ballroom) and by 1925 his band had augmented to six pieces. Three years on, when Moten came to New York for the first time, more big changes had occurred. 'When Walter Page had trouble with bookings,' remembers Rushing, 'Bennie began to take guys from his Blue Devils. Basie went first, then Lips Page and I. Later Walter Page broke up his group and joined Bennie too.' (So did guitarist Eddie Durham and accordionist Bus Moten, Bennie's young nephew.) The improvement was audible to all (apart from die-hard fans who resented his change in style) and gradually Moten's original men were replaced by new stars: Ben Webster and Eddie Barefield joined in 1932, Herschel Evans and Lester Young the year after. By 1935, Moten's 'first band' (he ran several others at the period) had reached a peak and travelled to Chicago for a booking at Rainbow Gardens and an audition for the Grand Terrace Ballroom. Moten stayed behind to have his tonsils out and died on the operating table: his band was taken over (after a struggle with Walter Page) by Count Basie – truly the start of something big. [DF]

Complete Bennie Moten, vols. 5/6 (1930–2), RCA

Motian, Paul (Stephen Paul), drums. b. Providence, Rhode Island, 25 March 1931. Gigging in New York (mid-1950s) with George Wallington, Russell Jacquet, then regular work with Tony Scott quartet (where he formed association with pianist Bill Evans, 1956–7). Also with Oscar Pettiford, Zoot Sims, Lennie Tristano, Al Cohn–Zoot Sims (late 1950s). Then with Bill Evans trio (1959–64), also Paul Bley trio (1963–4). Worked with Mose Allison (mid-1960s), other singers such as Morgana King, Arlo Guthrie, also with Charles Lloyd. Formed partnership with Charlie Haden in Keith Jarrett trio/quartet (1967–76), also recorded and toured with

Haden's Liberation Music Orchestra (1969, 1982, 1985). On record and in concert with Jazz Composers' Orchestra Association under different leaders such as Carla Bley, Don Cherry (1970s). Has led own trio/quartet/quintet since 1977, first appearing with it in UK in 1986.

Motian's ground-breaking work in the Bill Evans trio originally followed the example of Philly Joe Jones, but went much further in fragmenting the beat and interacting with the other members of the group. This ability lent itself extremely well to situations involving more 'avant-garde' soloists, and Motian developed to the point of playing authoritatively in all manner of contexts. He is still, however, very much underrated by most listeners. [BP]

Bill Evans, *Sunday at the Village Vanguard* (1961), Riverside/OJC; *It Should've Happened a Long Time Ago* (1983), ECM

Mouzon, Alphonze, drums, keyboards, composer, arranger, voice. b. Charleston, South Carolina, 21 November 1948. Involved with music from age four; drum lessons at high school where he also played in a band; went to New York at 17, working as an orderly in a hospital and going to night school studying to be a medical technician; also studied drama for two and a half years; at weekends, played with Ross Carnegie's Society Band; during his second year in NY, he played in the orchestra for *Promises Promises* on Broadway; the same year, 1969, he made his first record date – with the Gil Evans orchestra; 1968–9, freelanced in NY; 1970–1, with Roy Ayers; 1971–2, he was a member of the first Weather Report, with Joe Zawinul, Wayne Shorter, Miroslav Vitous and Airto Moreira; 1972–3, with McCoy Tyner; 1973–5, with Larry Coryell's Eleventh House. After leaving Eleventh House, Mouzon freelanced, playing festivals and touring with occasional groups. 1976, he played the Berlin festival with the Albert Mangelsdorff trio (Jaco Pastorius on bass); 1984, he was once more with Coryell, in a trio with French bass guitarist Bunny Brunel, which did a long European tour.

Mouzon is a flamboyant character and a drummer of great power who came to prominence during the jazz-rock-fusion movement. Although he can, and has, brought 'jazz polyrhythms to a rock pulse', to use his own words, his whole identity as a musician is more rooted in commercial rock than in jazz. [IC]

With McCoy Tyner, Roy Ayers and others; with *Gil Evans* (1969), Enja; with *Weather Report* (1971), Columbia; as leader, *Essence of Mystery* (1972); *Funky Snakefoot* (1973); *Mind Transplant* (1975), all Blue Note; with Coryell, *Introducing the Eleventh House* (1974), Vanguard; Mangelsdorff/Pastorius/Mouzon, *Trilogue – Live* (1976), MPS

Moye, Don, drums, congas, bongos, bass marimba, miscellaneous percussion, whistles, horns, voice. b. Rochester, New York, 23 May 1946. Percussion classes at Wayne State University, Detroit, 1965–6. Played with Detroit Free Jazz, going with it to Europe in 1968. Played with Steve Lacy in Rome, North Africa and Paris, where he also worked with the Gospel Messenger Singers, Sonny Sharrock, Dave Burrell, Gato Barbieri, Pharoah Sanders and Alan Shorter. 1969, joined the *Art Ensemble of Chicago in Paris and has been with it ever since. [IC]

With AEC; with Randy Weston, *Carnival* (1974), Arista; with Joseph Jarman, *Egwu-Anwu* (1978), India Navigation; *Black Paladins* (1979), Black Saint: *Earth Passage – Density* (1981), Black Saint

Mraz, George (Jiří Mraz), bass. b. Písek, Czechoslovakia, 9 September 1944. Leaving Prague around same time as Miroslav Vitous (both had played there with Jan Hammer), Mraz moved first to Munich (1966–7). After studies at Berklee School, worked with Dizzy Gillespie, Oscar Peterson trio (1972), Ella Fitzgerald (1972). Settled in New York, became replacement for Richard Davis with Thad Jones–Mel Lewis band (1972–6). Toured with Stan Getz (1974), then freelancing and studio work; also duo performances with pianists such as Jimmy Rowles, Tommy Flanagan and Barry Harris. Extremely reliable in the rhythm-section, Mraz's excellent harmonic sense also translates into marvellously melodic improvised solos. [BP]

Roland Hanna, *Sir Elf Plus One* (1977), Choice

Mullen, Jim, guitar. b. Glasgow, 1945. Started on guitar at age ten; switched to bass at 14, gigging locally. 1963, reverted to guitar, running his own bands in Glasgow. 1969, he moved to London, playing with Pete Brown until 1971. Played with Brian Auger's Oblivion Express, 1971–3; with Vinegar Joe and others, 1973–5. Worked in the USA, 1975–7, with Average White Band, Herbie Mann among others. He met Dick Morrissey in 1976 and formed Morrissey–Mullen in order to record in New York City with the Average White Band. 1977, back in the UK, his association with Morrissey continued until 1985. Favourites are Django Reinhardt, Charlie Christian, Barney Kessel, Kenny Burrell, John McLaughlin, among others. [IC]

Morrissey–Mullen, *This Must Be the Place* (1985), Coda

Mulligan, Gerry (Gerald Joseph), baritone (and soprano) sax, arranger, composer. b. New York City, 6 April 1927. Raised in Philadelphia and, after selling arrangements to a local radio band, specialized as a writer. First recorded works for Gene Krupa (1947) and Claude Thorn-

Gerry Mulligan

hill (1948); in both bands he also played alto briefly. Contact through Thornhill with Gil Evans led to writing and playing baritone for the Miles Davis band (1948); Mulligan later recorded with his own similar-sized groups in 1951, 1953 and 1972, and wrote for Stan Kenton (1953). Meanwhile he increased his performing reputation by organizing his popular quartet on the West Coast (1952–3 with Chet Baker, 1954–5 with Jon Eardley, 1956–7 with Bob Brookmeyer, 1958–9 with Art Farmer). Also led sextet (1955–6) with Eardley, Brookmeyer and Zoot Sims, and other small ensembles in mid-1960s and mid-1970s. Had own 12-piece big band (1960–3 and from 1978 intermittently to present), and appeared with Dave Brubeck group (1968–72) and as soloist in Italy (1974 onwards). Took part with Stan Getz in tribute to Zoot Sims at Chicago festival (1985).

Most of Mulligan's most popular tunes, such as 'Walkin' Shoes' or 'Line for Lyons', date from his 1950s quartets, which were the first regularly organized groups without a chord instrument (piano or guitar). His writing for larger bands, much of it original material but also including intelligent treatments of standards, is more absorbing. Whether using fully-voiced chords or unison lines, there is always a light-hearted and light-textured feel about Gerry's work. Typically, he operates at medium volume, always preferring two or three trumpets to everyone else's four, and the boring big-band blast-off is not his bag at all.

Sadly, this arranging style has not been as influential as his playing, which represents one of the few peaks of the baritone's history. By comparison with Serge Chaloff or later entrants, Mulligan has always sounded like a product of the swing era; indeed, in phraseology and timing, not much separates him from the bass-sax work of Adrian Rollini. Even the advanced harmonic knowledge in some of his arranging is usually banished from his own solos, whose rhythmic and melodic verve makes him 'the Zoot Sims of the baritone'. Given the ponderous nature of the instrument, there can be no higher praise. [BP]

Gerry Mulligan and Chet Baker (1951–65), Prestige; *Gerry Mulligan meets Johnny Hodges* (1960), Verve; *Walk on the Water* (1980), DRG

See Horricks, Raymond, *Gerry Mulligan* (Apollo, 1986)

Mulligan, Mick, trumpet, leader. b. Harrow, Middlesex, 24 January 1928. The Mulligan band was so wickedly – and funnily – documented in George Melly's book *Owning Up* that the music it produced is now lost under a tidal wave of (largely well-founded) legend. In fact Mulligan – a man of boundless charm and bawdy humour – was a sturdy Armstrong-style trumpeter whose music was later overshadowed by Alex Welsh's longer-lived organization. Occasionally chaotic in public performance (it seems), his band is marvellous on record: it featured two fine and latterly neglected players in Ian Christie (clt) and Frank Parr (tmb), as well as regular guests such as Betty Smith and Denny Wright, often dug into obscure and worth-while repertoire, played in an enjoyable 'timeless' style (in the best sense) and enjoyed a highly successful 15-year career. Their music deserves reassessment. Mulligan himself ran business concerns after 1962 and very occasionally played for fun. [DF]

Meet George Melly with Mick Mulligan (1959), Pye

Multiphonics The art of producing two or three notes simultaneously on an instrument not designed with this use in mind. Whereas it is child's play on all the keyboards and not much harder on stringed instruments, on horns it requires hard work and is at best a 'special effect'.

The construction of brass and reeds is intended for playing one note at a time (see HARMONICS). But the accidental sounds of inexpert players, and the deliberately 'dirty' tones of some jazz players, actually consist of two harmonics (or the fundamental note and a harmonic) sounding together. These instances, however, create one main note plus a subsidiary 'impure' note whereas, with sufficient practice, it is possible to produce two adjacent harmonics sounding equally strongly (though less strongly than a single 'pure' note), forming a two-note chord as in the later work of John Coltrane and his followers.

As a further refinement, Albert Mangelsdorff, Howard Johnson and others have shown that, by vocalizing their air-column (that is, humming a note into the instrument rather than just blowing), additional harmonics can be activated to form three- and four-note chords. [BP]

Muranyi, Joe (Joseph Paul), clarinet, soprano sax, vocals. b. Ohio, 14 January 1928. Of Hungarian descent, he did his first playing with a balalaika orchestra, and later attracted attention as one of the American post-war revivalists who flew in the face of jazz fashion by re-examining the music of Armstrong and Morton (two regular playing associates then, as now, were Marty Grosz and Dick Wellstood). In the 1950s he worked with bands led by Danny Barker as well as the Red Onion Jazz Band (while still only in his mid-twenties) and also successfully as a producer, sleevenote writer etc. for major record labels such as Atlantic, Bethlehem and RCA. Recording, club and festival work with senior partners such as Max Kaminsky and Jimmy McPartland helped to further Muranyi's reputation, and 1967–71 he hit a career peak as clarinettist with Louis Armstrong's All Stars, providing the observant, supportive role that Armstrong required and becoming a close friend in the process. The partnership was terminated only by the trumpeter's death, after which Muranyi moved into Jimmy Ryan's to work alongside another old master, Roy Eldridge, depped with the World's Greatest Jazz Band in 1975 and from 1983 became one-quarter of the Classic Jazz Quartet, a highly successful (and in its own way groundbreaking) quartet with cornettist Dick Sudhalter and old friends Grosz and Wellstood which plays determinedly at acoustic level, explores rare and original repertoire to great effect and, best of all, never takes itself too seriously. Muranyi – a witty intelligent commentator, beguiling composer and aspiring author – is a multi-faceted jazzman of great value: his swooping soprano and dry-toned clarinet call up the memory of Sidney Bechet and Jimmie Noone among more modern references. [DF]

Classic Jazz Quartet (1984), Jazzology

Murphy, Mark Howe, vocals. b. Syracuse, New York, 14 March 1932. Early experience with band led by elder brother. Began working at New York jazz clubs and appearing on TV, making albums under own name (from late 1950s) backed by arrangers such as Ernie Wilkins and Al Cohn. Toured UK and Europe as soloist (1964), then settled in Europe for next 10 years. Returned to US (1975), recording regularly and then working in Europe on tour (1984–5). Murphy's popular success with two different generations of young listeners, in the early 1960s and early 1980s, speaks well for his dedication. Stylistically very consistent, he frequently uses jazz-associated material for his own melodic improvisation and scat singing that sounds infallibly 'hip'. [BP]

Mark Murphy Sings (1975), Muse

Murphy, Turk (Melvin), trombone, composer. b. Palermo, California, 16 December 1915. After an apprenticeship with Mal Hallett, Will Osborne and cabaret bands he spent ten colossally successful years with Lu Watters's Yerba Buena Jazz Band, the figurehead of America's classic jazz revival in San Francisco. From 1940 to 1950 Murphy's racketing tailgate trombone was central to the rolling two-beat music of the Yerba Buenas: his natural gift for ensemble playing and forthright solos showcased in features such as his own 'Trombone Rag'. After the band broke up, Murphy formed his own, retaining ex-Yerbas such as Bob Helm and Wally Rose and digging – with a scholar's judgement – into the classic jazz repertoire. He also became a spokesman for revivalist jazz, well-known enough to be portrayed by Eddie Condon in his *Treasury of Jazz* ('a husky guy with a stir trim, somewhat like Fred MacMurray, who looks capable of staying a round or two!') and writing regularly and intelligently about his jazz in books and on record sleeve notes. Murphy's music – in contrast to his quick wit and verbal gifts – stayed close to the roots and was sometimes criticized: 'The music that I have been making for the past 15 years,' he wrote in 1956, 'has been the subject of a concerted critical animosity almost unanimous in the music trade press.' Murphy's music was actually great fun, and he weathered the criticism to play in New York at Child's Restaurant in the 1950s, as well as in New Orleans, and San Francisco where in 1960 his own famous club Earthquake McGoon's was to open: it became synonymous with his name. Murphy continued to play at his (later re-located) club when not appearing at Disneyland, at festivals (including the St Louis Ragtime Festival, 1977) or on the road. [DF]

And His Jazz Band at the Roundtable (1959), Roulette

See Goggin, Jim, *Turk Murphy: Just for the Record* (San Francisco Traditional Jazz Foundation, 1982)

Murray, David, tenor and soprano sax, flute, composer. b. Berkeley, California, 19 February 1955. Mother, a pianist in the Pentecostal Church, taught him elementary harmony. Played tenor from age nine. At 12 he became interested in r & b and led groups as a teenager. Studied at Pomona College, Los Angeles, with Stanley Crouch and Margaret Kohn (piano) for two years. 1975, went to New York and was soon leading his own groups, touring Europe regularly and making records. By the later 1970s he was working with James Blood Ulmer's harmolodic free-funk Music Revelation Ensemble, Jack DeJohnette's Special Edition and the World Saxophone Quartet. In the early 1980s he was leading his own octet and quartet and recording for the Italian Black Saint label. 1985, he performed at the Camden (London) festival with the World Saxophone Quartet. Murray began his professional career as a free player, sitting in with Cecil Taylor, Don Cherry and Anthony Braxton, and working with Sunny Murray. However, his music gradually moved back into the area of coherent swing and clear structures. Since 1984 has also led a big band which appeared at the Kool Festival. His main influence is perhaps Paul Gonsalves, whom he much admires and considers underrated. Other influences are Coleman Hawkins, Ben Webster, Albert Ayler, Ornette Coleman and Ellington. He is a player of outstanding plasticity and passion, and his music has all the fervour of hot gospel and the blues. He is also a gifted composer and arranger. [IC]

With World Saxophone Quartet, DeJohnette, Ulmer, James Newton, Amiri Baraka and Sunny Murray; as leader, over 20 albums including *Low Class Conspiracy* (1976), Adelphi; *Flowers For Albert* (1976), India Navigation; *Live at the Lower Manhattan Ocean Club* (1977), India Navigation; *Conceptual Saxophone* (1978), Cadillac; *3D Family* (1978), Hat Hut; *Ming* (1982); *Children* (1986), both Black Saint; *Home* (1983), Black Saint

Murray, Don, clarinet, saxes, violin. b. Joliet, Illinois, 7 June 1904; d. Los Angeles, 2 June 1929. A clarinettist who often played tenor saxophone, he is principally remembered as a colleague (and early champion) of Bix Beiderbecke who, after early work with a reconstituted New Orleans Rhythm Kings, played with Jean Goldkette's orchestra, with Adrian Rollini's short-lived New Yorker band and for bandleader Don Voorhees. His records with Beiderbecke under the banner of Bix and his Gang, as well as related small groups through 1927–8, are some of the greatest ever made, and his premature death, after hitting his head in a fall (while filming with Ted Lewis in 1928 in Hollywood) was a tragic loss to the 1920s jazz scene. [DF]

Bix Beiderbecke, *The Studio Groups – late 1927*, EMI World

Murray, Sunny (James Marcellus Arthur), drums. b. Idabel, Oklahoma, 21 September 1937. Moved to New York in 1956, worked with Henry 'Red' Allen, Willie 'The Lion' Smith, Jackie McLean, Ted Curson etc. Began playing with Cecil Taylor (1959–64, including European tour 1962). Meeting Albert Ayler in Scandinavia, formed trio with him and Gary Peacock (1964–5) which also toured Europe. Gigs with Don Cherry, John Coltrane, Ornette Coleman, Roswell Rudd, John Tchicai (mid-1960s). Based in France (1968–71), performing and recording with local musicians; also solo appearance in London (1968) and other countries, and work with visiting Americans such as Archie Shepp, Grachan Moncur including Pan-African Festival in Algiers (1969). Moved to Philadelphia (1970s), co-leader with vibist Khan Jamal of the Untouchable Factor, and working with Philly Joe Jones whom he had met in Paris.

Murray's pioneering work with Taylor found him building a bridge between a recognizable pulse and the totally abstract style typical of his period with Ayler. Though full of vitality, he was less domineering than many of the so-called 'energy' players and devoted considerable attention to the cymbals, from which he drew a great variety of tonal contrast. Although this was often submerged by the contexts in which he chose to perform, it is equally true that his example was not lost on European drummers of the 'free' persuasion. [BP]

Albert Ayler, *Spiritual Unity* (1964), ESP; *Applecores* (1978), Philly Jazz

Musso, Vido William, tenor sax, clarinet. b. Carrini, Sicily, 17 January 1913; d. Rancho Mirage, California, 9 January 1982. To the white tenor-saxophone vocabulary patented by Bud Freeman and carried on by such men as Tony Pastor and Eddie Miller, he brought a new Italianate fervour, a tone as big as a mountain and the rasping throat-growl that a generation later was to be adopted by rock and roll saxophonists everywhere. His career proper began with Benny Goodman in 1936 and he quickly became a crowd-pleasing favourite who moved on, over an 11-year period, to work with most of Swingdom's famous leaders: Gene Krupa (1938), Harry James (1940–1), Goodman again, Woody Herman (1942–3), Tommy Dorsey (1945) and Stan Kenton (1946–7). Musso's contribution to Kenton classics such as 'Painted Rhythm' and 'Artistry in Rhythm' are fondly remembered by jazz people, and had a powerful influence on younger modern jazzmen, including Ronnie Scott. But by the time he joined Kenton it was a sad fact that Musso sounded uncomfortable set against the harmonic advances of bop, the tight-lipped cool fashions of modern jazz and the austere empire of Kenton's innovations – in a word, he sounded dated and (perhaps because he was a 'natural' player who never learned to read music, nor studied a lot) found himself unable to do much about it. From 1947, Musso carried on bandleading on the West Coast but, despite fairly regular recording, somehow failed to maintain the reputation of his younger years. Perhaps he was simply born too early for rock and roll: jazz climates of the 1980s would have treated him better. [DF]

Featuring Vido Musso (1950s), Crown; any with Stan Kenton

Mutes are devices placed in the bell of a trumpet, trombone or other brass instrument to modify or alter the sound it makes. The commercial production of mutes was stimulated in the 1920s by jazz musicians who regularly used makeshift devices to produce revolutionary new effects: trumpeter Joe Smith used half a coconut, trombonist 'Tricky Sam' Nanton used half a yo-yo, and anything else that came to hand – from waterglasses to tin cans – was put to use. By the 1920s American manufacturers such as the Harmon Company had begun designing and marketing a big range of mutes to meet the demand: later European entrepreneurs such as British trombonist Lew Davis were to produce their own highly successful variants. In 1934 Nat Gonella was able to write: 'There was a time when a trumpet player was judged wholly by the variety and extensiveness of his mutes' but – as his statement implied – by then the demand had reached its height: in addition to the ubiquitous 'derby' mute (often originally made from a real hat, usually with a hole punched in the centre), the aspiring brassman could buy 'solotone' mutes, 'special effects' mutes and others, as well as the more standard 'cup', 'Harmon' and 'straight' designs. It was the last three that were to survive World War II most happily, in addition to the 'plunger' (really simply a rubber sink plunger and the marketed alternative to Joe Smith's coconut shell) and 'pixie' (a tiny straight mute used in conjunction with the plunger to produce a sour, choked sound). Post-war jazzmen such as Miles Davis and Harry Edison were to establish the Harmon mute (often with its central tube pulled out) as the most popular effect of its kind at the period. American companies including Humes and Berg continued to market full ranges of mutes into the 1980s, but in general the disappearance of new designs is regrettable, and isolated examples of attempts to find new sounds (by Peter Gane and bandleader George Evans, for two European examples) seem to have slowed down in the wake of developments in electronic music. [DF]

Muzak The name of a commercial company specializing in taped background music for restaurants, supermarkets, lifts, aircraft take-off etc. When this venture was still in its infancy (1935) they actually recorded Fats Waller but, since then, any jazz associations have been minimal.

With a small 'm', muzak is now the general term for sounds intended not to be listened to, even if jazz-influenced. Calling something muzak which was intended as jazz is, therefore, a deadly insult. [BP]

N

Namyslowski, Zbigniew, alto sax, composer, and flute, cello, trombone, piano. b. Warsaw, 9 September 1939. Began on piano at age four; music lessons at six; started on cello at 12; studied theory at High School of Music in Warsaw. He played trombone with a trad band and cello with a modern group, before taking up alto sax in 1960. With Andrzej Trzaskowski's Jazz Wreckers, he toured the USA and Europe, then left to form his own quartet in 1963. He toured in Europe, including the UK, India, Australia, New Zealand and the USSR. He has also played on film soundtracks and worked with C. Niemen, the Novi singers and Georges Arvanitas. Since 1971 he has led quintets and quartets. Namyslowski performed with his group at the first Indian jazz festival, Jazz Yatra in Bombay, 1978. He has composed and arranged for radio, TV and films; also a member of the Polish Radio Jazz Studio Band. Namyslowski's favourites include Charlie Parker, John Coltrane and Sonny Rollins, and J. E. Berendt calls him a 'timeless improviser in line with the great saxophone tradition in jazz'. But Namyslowski is more than that: he has created a music all his own, an impassioned Polish jazz compounded of his American influences and the rich heritage of Polish folk music. [IC]

With Novi singers and others; as leader, *Kujaviak Goes Funky* (1975), Muza; with Tony Williams and others, *Pop Workshop, vols. 1/2* (nda), EMI; *Namyslowski* (1977), Inner City; Air Condition, *Follow Your Kite* (1980), Muza

Nance, 'Ray' Willis, trumpet, violin, vocals, dancer. b. Chicago, 10 December 1913; d. New York, 28 January 1976. For most of the 1930s he worked in clubs around Chicago and for bandleaders such as Horace Henderson and Earl Hines. With them, and with his own little band around Chicago, he gained a reputation as a hard-swinging violinist, mellow cornettist and especially as an entertainer who could sing, dance, do comedy routines and front a show. After he joined Ellington (who nicknamed him 'Floorshow'), replacing Cootie Williams in 1940, Nance's talents were featured to the full: his cornet was teamed with 'Tricky Sam' Nanton for the growling role that Williams had in turn inherited from Bubber Miley, his violin featured on tone poems such as 'Moon Mist' and his jivey infectious vocals on appealing swing tunes such as 'A Slip of the Lip'. It was Nance, too, who on Ellington's 1940 record of 'Take the A Train' contributed passages of inspired solo work that soon became an integral part of the composition itself. In 1948 he came to Britain, as a natural choice for Duke Ellington's partner to tour variety theatres. Jack Fallon, who played bass, remembers: 'He was the king of stage presentation. When Duke would be playing he'd do a kind of jig, peckin' round the stage, and every time he'd shoot his cuffs he made his coat tail go up. Then he'd pull his coat down – and up went his cuffs! I used to go into hysterics every night. He used to carry a pile of 78s around of all his old friends, and I would say he was insecure, timid, though not aggressive. One time we got booked into a hotel and he looked around and just hated the decor – and changed hotels!' Nance stayed with Ellington until 1963, then led a solo career for a dozen years, toured Britain again in 1966 (a not so happy time) and carried on leading his own quartet, featuring his heavy-toned cornet and witty violin up to the time of his death. [DF]

Huffin' 'n' Puffin' (1971), MPS

See Dance, Stanley, *The World of Duke Ellington* (Scribner's, 1970, repr. Da Capo, 1980)

Nanton, Joe 'Tricky Sam' (Joseph N. Irish), trombone. b. New York City, 1 February 1904; d. San Francisco, 20 July 1946. Duke Ellington always loved his trombone section best of all, and of all his trombonists 'Tricky Sam' Nanton was the most inimitable, the least replaceable. Along with Bubber Miley, with whom he formed a keen team early on, Nanton, a plunger-mute master whose sounds were revolutionary then, never bettered after, played Ellington's growling jungle music best. 'Tricky had a perfect feeling for it and he could play the proper things to fit the plunger', says Mercer Ellington. 'That man could say as much as a human voice on his horn', agreed Dickie Wells; 'The wail of a newborn baby, the raucous hoot of an owl, the bloodcurdling scream of an enraged tiger, or the eerie cooing of a mournful dove!' remembered Rex Stewart.

Before he found Ellington in 1926, Nanton – a mild-mannered, cultured Anglophile who loved to read books and often set up a talking-table near the bar to discuss in his high-pitched voice anything from hand-made English clothes to Black American politics – had worked in cabaret bands such as Cliff Jackson's, Earl Frazier's and

Elmer Snowden's. Subsequently, he worked only for Ellington, refusing to appear or even record with lesser lights, and played on until he suffered a stroke in 1945. Within a few months he came back to tour California and was found dead one morning in his hotel bedroom: heavy drinking may have contributed to his early demise. Afterwards other fine players including Wilbur de Paris and Tyree Glenn tried to recreate Nanton's sound: for Ellington it was never quite the same again. [DF]

Any with Ellington

See Stewart, Rex, *Jazz Masters of the 1930s* (Macmillan, 1972, repr. Da Capo, 1982)

Napoleon, Marty, piano. b. Brooklyn, New York, 2 June 1921. A fine eclectic pianist, he received an all-round training in big bands before he joined Gene Krupa's in 1946. Then came time with his uncle Phil Napoleon's Original Memphis Five, and more with Charlie Ventura's big rebop band and quintet, beginning an association which lasted on and off for many years. Another long-term connection began in 1952 when Napoleon replaced Earl Hines in Louis Armstrong's All Stars, then came two years duetting with his brother Teddy (1955–6), followed by regular work at the Metropole in New York with Henry 'Red' Allen's band. 1966–71, Napoleon was with Armstrong again touring, recording and travelling; then he settled in New York for another brief period with Gene Krupa, as well as making solo appearances and playing festivals. He published a successful set of instructional tutors for piano in the mid-1970s. [DF]

Trio (1955), London

Napoleon, Phil (Filippo Napoli), trumpet. b. Boston, 2 September 1901. Like Red Nichols, he was a formally trained player who by the time he was 16 had recorded classical cornet set pieces, and early on was undecided whether to follow straight music or jazz as a full-time career. The jazz won. 'We'd listen to the best records we could get,' remembers Henry Levine, another underrated trumpeter of the period and Napoleon's friend, 'and whenever any good bands came to New York we'd hike across the river from Brooklyn to listen.' By 1922, Napoleon had formed the Original Memphis Five, one of the greatest white groups of that decade. Their first two sides ('My Honey's Lovin' Arms' and 'Gypsy Blues' from 1922) were to be followed by hundreds more: most of them were best-sellers, featuring the revolutionary trombone of Miff Mole as well as other young stars such as the Dorseys, Frank Signorelli and Jimmy Lytell. Napoleon's own clear-toned, clean jazz approach was to influence Red Nichols (who heard him in Kansas City) and Bix Beiderbecke who learned from him ('I'd take Bix outside and show him what I was doing', Napoleon told Dick Sudhalter): both men were, to some degree, to eclipse their inspiration. Napoleon broke up his band in 1928 and went to work in studios including NBC for leaders such as B. A. Rolfe, Sam Lanin and Leo Reisman. Apart from work with big bands (his own in 1938, Jimmy Dorsey's in 1943) he stayed there until 1949 when he re-formed the Original Memphis Five for a seven-year residency at Nick's Club. Soon after that he opened his own club, Napoleon's Retreat, in another hot spot, Miami, ran a band there (including trombonist Ed Hubble) and continued playing the strong, flexible and creative trumpet that jazz has so persistently tended to forget. [DF]

Masters of Dixieland, vol. 3 (1960), EMI Electrola

Napoleon, Teddy George, piano. b. Brooklyn, New York, 23 January 1914; d. 5 July 1964. Like his younger brother Marty, he was a fine and very versatile pianist who from the 1930s was active with society bands, and is remembered for a long association with Gene Krupa which lasted for 14 years from 1944. After a brief spell with bandleader Tex Beneke he moved closer to his uncle Phil Napoleon in Florida and worked with trios and visiting guests such as Bill Harris and Flip Phillips until his death in New York from cancer. [DF]

Gene Krupa and his Orchestra (various dates), Jazz Anthology

Naura, Michael, piano, Indian and Mexican flutes, composer. b. Memel, Lithuania, 19 August 1934. Studied philosophy, sociology and the graphic arts in Berlin; self-taught as a musician. He began leading his own groups in the early 1950s, always with Wolfgang Schlüter (vibes, percussion); at first they copied George Shearing, then Brubeck, the MJQ and Horace Silver, but evolved their own style in the 1960s which Naura describes as 'a collage of blues, bebop and European avant-garde'. By the beginning of the 1960s the two leading German groups were Albert Mangelsdorff's and the Naura quintet. Later in the decade he began working as an editor of music programmes for Norddeutscher Rundfunk (North German Radio), Hamburg. Since 1971 he has been head of the NDR Jazz Department (radio and TV), but continues to play, compose and record occasionally. With Schlüter he often accompanies one of Germany's leading lyric poets, Peter Rühmkorf, in poetry-and-jazz recitals.

Under Naura's influence the NDR developed the most dynamic jazz policy of all European radio stations, covering the whole spectrum from traditional jazz to swing, bebop and contemporary, and offering interviews, talks, record recitals and live concerts. Furthermore, it has afforded substantial patronage to leading

German and international musicians, with a programme of jazz workshops which Naura inaugurated: these concentrate on new contemporary music, and consist of four days of rehearsal in Hamburg and a recorded (sometimes filmed) concert on the fifth day. There have been on average just over ten of these workshops a year since the early 1970s, and the 200th took place in October 1985. Almost every contemporary US and European musician of note has taken part.

Naura is deeply interested in literature and painting, and he is president of PANDA – Performers and Artists for Nuclear Disarmament – in Germany. His favourites are Teddy Wilson, Art Tatum, Bill Evans, Keith Jarrett, and particular inspirations are John Lewis, Milt Jackson, Gil Evans, Ben Webster and Stravinsky. [IC]

Naura/Schlüter/Eberhard Weber (bass, cello), with Rühmkorf, *Kein Apolloprogramm für Lyrik* (1976); Naura/Schlüter, *Country Children* (1977), both ECM

Fats Navarro

Navarro, Fats (Theodore), trumpet. b. Key West, Florida, 24 September 1923; d. 7 July 1950. Played in territory bands as teenager, sometimes doubling on tenor saxophone, and toured with Andy Kirk (1943–4). Joined Billy Eckstine band, replacing Dizzy Gillespie (1945–6), then settled in New York. Recorded with Kenny Clarke, Coleman Hawkins, Eddie Davis and Illinois Jacquet (1946–7) and began association with Tadd Dameron. Toured with Jazz at the Philharmonic, Lionel Hampton band (1948); made one record (and rehearsed but never worked with touring band) led by Benny Goodman (1948). Worked regularly with Dameron sextet and 10-piece (1948–early 1949) and made records with Bud Powell (1949). Last public appearance (also recorded) was with Charlie Parker; like Parker a highly intelligent and articulate person who became a narcotics addict, Navarro contracted tuberculosis which proved fatal.

His premature death did not prevent Navarro from being seen as one of the leading soloists of the bebop era. The clarion quality of his tone is the most immediately recognizable factor distinguishing him from the Eldridge-inspired sounds adopted by Howard McGhee (whom he played alongside in the Kirk band) and by Gillespie; Navarro aimed for the fullness of tone associated with Charlie Shavers and Freddie Webster but with a brassy attack which claimed instant attention. His melodic lines gave the impression of being carefully sculpted, and avoided the apparent impetuosity of players such as Parker, Powell or even Gillespie, concentrating on classic and largely non-chromatic phraseology. For this reason, although Navarro's inventive ability was not outclassed even by Parker, he was most at home as soloist and lead trumpeter with Tadd Dameron, many of whose pieces were written with him in mind. Similarly the rhythmic content of his playing was conservative (though not stilted) and, had Navarro's lifestyle permitted more attention to furthering his music, he might have developed in the direction explored a few years later by his disciple Clifford Brown. [BP]

The Fabulous Fats Navarro, vol. 1/2 (1947–9), Blue Note; Charlie Parker, *One Night in Birdland* (1950), CBS

Neil, Steve, alto and tenor sax, guitar, Fender and Vox bass, string bass, drums. b. Dayton, Ohio, 16 November 1953. His mother played jazz, and as a child he went to see many jazz musicians, including Miles Davis, and was friendly with bassist Jimmy Garrison. At seven he studied sax and guitar, then at 13 he took up bass. First professional job was on bass guitar in Detroit with a band called Chairman of the Board in 1972. He toured the USA and UK with it in 1974, then was with Pharoah Sanders off and on for five years. 1977, joined Elvin Jones for a short time and then played with Yusef Lateef's band. He played on the West Coast with Harold Land, then on the East Coast with Mary Lou Williams. 1977, with Frank Foster big band; 1979, with Sun Ra. 1983, he did separate tours in Europe with Sam Rivers and Charles Tolliver. He has also toured Europe with Hannibal Marvin Peterson, 1976 and 1977, with Lateef, 1978, with Sanders, 1979, and with Beaver Harris, 1985. He has also worked and recorded with Gil Evans. In 1979, Neil received an award from CJOA (Consortium of Jazz Organizations and Artists, Inc.). Main influences are Sun Ra, Monk and Mingus. [IC]

With Hannibal Marvin Peterson, *Live in Berlin* (1976), MPS; *Live in Antibes* (1977), MPS; with Pharoah Sanders, *Pharoah* (1976), India Navigation; with Gil Evans, *Priestess* (1977), Antilles

Nelson, 'Big Eye' Louis, clarinet. b. New Orleans, 28 January 1885; d. 20 August 1949. One of the best Creole clarinettists in New Orleans (he was a Tio pupil), Nelson was a warm-toned, technically able performer. By 1900 he had played bass in Buddy Bolden's band, as well as violin and guitar for other leaders, but by 1904 was concentrating on clarinet (one report gave the reason that a clarinet was easier to run with in race-riot-torn New Orleans). For more than ten years after that Nelson was a familar sound of the city, working in the Ninth Ward band, Golden Rule Orchestra, Imperial Band, Superior Orchestra and others and specializing for a long period on C clarinet before moving over to the more familiar B-flat, on which George Lewis, at least, liked him less well. As a teacher – he taught Sidney Bechet for one – 'He'd show a youngster all he knew – but he knew how to be stern with those of us that were learning,' (Baby Dodds). In 1916, Nelson toured with Freddie Keppard's Original Creole Orchestra, but after a year he was home to stay and the rest of his life was spent in New Orleans cabarets, theatres and functions. The dawn of the revival brought renewed interest in Nelson's talent: in 1940 he recorded eight sides for Delta with Kid Rena's Jazz Band at the behest of Heywood Broun and two years after narrowly missed being selected by Bill Russell to record with Bunk Johnson (Russell heard him on a bad night at Luthjen's cabaret). In 1944, Nelson was the subject of a feature article by Robert Goffin in *Jazz Record*. He continued his residency at Luthjen's until 1948 and the following year – just in time – was recorded by Russell. [DF]

Nelson, Louis, trombone. b. New Orleans, 17 September 1902. After Jim Robinson, perhaps the best-loved New Orleans trombonist. A technically assured, velvet-toned player, he began his musical life playing alto horn, but had taken up trombone by the time he was 20 and worked regularly with Kid Rena, the Original Tuxedo Orchestra, then for 15 years with Sidney Desvigne's big band in New Orleans. It was probably his big-band training that led to his being equated by some local New Orleans musicians with such players as Tommy Dorsey. 'Louis Nelson plays a good trombone,' said George Lewis, 'but he plays nervous trombone, you know, on his out notes. That's because he never came up playing this music. He came up playing big-band music.' Nelson worked from 1944 with Kid Thomas's band and – despite the gentle criticism above – with George Lewis regularly in the 1950s in and out of New Orleans. He became, with Jim Robinson, a figurehead for New Orleans trombone, touring Europe with bands such as the Legends of Jazz and as a soloist, and appearing at home at Preservation Hall maintaining, at over 80, his reputation as New Orleans' most sophisticated slideman. [DF]

Any with George Lewis

Nelson, Oliver Edward, alto, tenor and soprano sax, arranger, composer. b. St Louis, Missouri, 4 June 1932; d. 27 October 1975. Worked in St Louis-based territory bands from 1947, and then played second alto in Louis Jordan big band (1951). Navy service followed by four years studying music at university. Moved to New York, working with Erskine Hawkins, Wild Bill Davis; briefly with Louie Bellson band on West Coast (1959), then on tenor with Quincy Jones band (1960–1, including European tour). 1959–61, recorded own compositions on six small-group albums, three including Eric Dolphy, and first big-band album. Then arranged first big-band recordings of Jimmy Smith (1962), also in similar capacity with Eddie Davis, Billy Taylor, Wes Montgomery and many others from early 1960s. Contributed arrangements to Buddy Rich band and other touring groups. Occasional live appearances with own all-star big bands (1966, Berlin festival 1970, Montreux 1971, New York and Los Angeles, 1975); led small group on tour of West Africa (1969). Moved to Los Angeles (1967), spending greater part of his time in writing for television and film soundtracks; died from a heart attack.

Although he did a certain amount of formal European-style composition, Nelson's jazz writing for both small group and big band was very close in spirit, and often in musical detail, to early Quincy Jones. He displayed many of the same virtues, sometimes spread too thinly for comfort, and it is a pity that his original themes were usually too formularized by comparison with the memorable 'Hoe Down' and 'Stolen Moments'. It is also to be regretted that after the early 1960s he had little time to further his forthright saxophone work. [BP]

Blues and the Abstract Truth (1961), Jasmine

Neo-bop is the musician's term for the kind of bebop played from the late 1970s onwards, following the revival of interest in the challenges bebop offers. Whether or not it reworks specific themes written in the 1940s, it differs considerably from early bop because later stylistic influences such as modal and free jazz (plus better amplification) affect the way the players relate to one another. [BP]

New Age is the generic term for the brand of easy-listening instrumental music identified with the American record company, Windham Hill. Associations with upwardly mobile lifestyles and slightly 'alternative' therapies cannot completely disguise its origins in the open-ended European-influenced improvisation popularized by Keith Jarrett *et al.* As with other jazz-derived muzak, it may assist in opening the ears of some listeners in the right musical direction. [BP]

Newborn, Phineas, Jnr., piano. b. Memphis, Tennessee, 14 December 1931. Along with his brother, guitarist Calvin Newborn (b. 27 April 1933), worked in r & b bands of Tuff Green and Phineas Snr. (late 1940s); touring with Jackie Brenston and B. B. King (early 1950s) and session work in Memphis, including piano feature on 'Rockin' the Boogie' with Lou Sargent (1951). Toured briefly with Lionel Hampton and Willis Jackson before army service (1952–4), then formed quartet and moved to New York (1956), making albums under own name. Also worked with Charles Mingus (1958) and Roy Haynes (1958–9), settled in Los Angeles and recorded with Howard McGhee and Teddy Edwards. Since then, Newborn's career has been extremely intermittent, partly as a result of a 1960s nervous breakdown. Like Chet Baker, he suffered from the extravagant praise of his early solo albums, which exhibited a dazzling technique and a rather superficial Petersonesque conception. Subsequent work, including late 1970s recording and a 1980 Montreux festival appearance, has been less overwhelming but, at its best, more considered and more affecting. [BP]

A World of Piano (1961), Contemporary/OJC

New Jazz Orchestra (1964–70) A British big band, led by composer/arranger Neil Ardley, which served as a crucible for the talents of many of the leading young musicians of the 1960s including Jon Hiseman, Jack Bruce, Mike Gibbs, Paul Rutherford, Trevor Watts, Barbara Thompson, Ian Carr, Kenny Wheeler, Henry Lowther, Harry Beckett and Michael Garrick. It featured original compositions and arrangements by Ardley, Gibbs, Rutherford, Garrick and other members, and also included in its repertoire occasional pieces by non-members such as Mike Taylor, one of the most gifted and original composers of the 1960s. The NJO played occasional gigs in London, and did a few broadcasts, UK tours and festivals. It made no impact abroad, but several of its members later became known internationally. [IC]

Western Reunion (1965), Decca; *Le Déjeuner sur l'herbe* (1969), MGM-Verve

Newman, Joe (Joseph Dwight), trumpet. b. New Orleans, 7 September 1922. He was born in a musical family in New Orleans and first took lessons from multi-instrumentalist David Jones, whose mellophone work with Fate Marable had influenced Louis Armstrong from 1919 on. While attending Alabama State College, Newman joined the college band, then took it out under his leadership and finally joined Lionel Hampton in 1941 for two years before Count Basie at the Lincoln Hotel signed him: with short breaks Newman stayed with Basie until 1947 when he teamed first with Illinois Jacquet in a touring unit, then with drummer J. C. Heard. From 1952 he was regularly with Basie for nine years: a period which focused international attention on Newman's crackling tone, 'neutralist-modern' approach (in Leonard Feather's words) and joyfully creative flair. It was then that he began a series of solo albums and recordings which were to establish him, just in time, as the last of Basie's classic trumpeters: an accessible player whose approach acknowledged such old masters as Louis Armstrong but was contemporary enough to match with fellow 'Basie-moderns' of the period such as Frank Foster and Frank Wess. 'Louis Armstrong was my first idol and the biggest influence of my whole career,' he told Stanley Dance, 'but if there's anybody to follow Louis it will be Dizzy Gillespie!' After he left Basie in 1961, Newman – a realistic businessman and self-promoter as well as a gifted player – became involved in Jazz Interactions, a non-profit-making trust devoted to jazz promotion and education which (under Newman's presidency from 1967) conducted master classes in schools and colleges, maintained a Jazz Information service and later formed its own Jazz Interaction Orchestra. For this orchestra and others Newman wrote extended jazz compositions (for example 'Suite for Pops', dedicated to Armstrong) and by the 1970s he was touring the international circuit as a soloist, guesting with the New York Jazz Repertory Company and recording solo for Pablo and other major labels. He was to continue this course in the 1980s, featuring a broad-based jazz presentation with homely vocals, eclectic repertoire and the same all-embracing style recalling all the best of the best. [DF]

Good 'N' Groovy (1961), IMS

See Dance, Stanley, *The World of Count Basie* (Sidgwick & Jackson, 1980)

New Orleans will be for ever associated with the crystallization of the first classic style of jazz in the early years of the 20th century. The favourable conditions for this development have often been linked to the French colonization of Louisiana, only formally ended in 1820; as in the Catholic Caribbean and South America, it condoned more racial intermixing with the slave population and more mutual musical tolerance (especially in the seaport of New Orleans) than in the predominantly Protestant USA.

The repertoire of the earliest New Orleans jazz bands is a matter for speculation: nothing

Joe Newman

was put on disc until the white 'Original Dixieland Jazz Band' in 1917. But, as with later bands that were recorded, it seems likely to have consisted of 'swinging' versions of European-style marches and dance tunes, the latter often requiring the use of a violin. Through lack of volume, the violin was soon dropped in favour of a front-line of one or more trumpets (or cornets), trombones and clarinets, with a rhythm-section including various combinations of guitar (or banjo), bass, drums and piano. But what was remarkable – and what took the white bands a long time to learn – was the improvised interweaving of simultaneous front-line melodies and the equally interlocking flow of rhythm-section instruments, as exemplified by the King Oliver Creole Jazz Band. This loose polyrhythmic flow tended to be minimized in later Chicago-style jazz and Dixieland, which is probably why they introduced more front-line solo work, whereas the classic New Orleans style is an ensemble style par excellence.

New Orleans is also the home of particular regional styles in both rhythm-and-blues and funk, the local recordings of which have often included jazzmen working as session musicians. In fact, even these days there is probably more interchange between players of different styles in New Orleans, and certainly less snobbishness between them, than in most other comparable centres of musical activity. [BP]

New Orleans Rhythm Kings Organized expressly for a Chicago residency at the Friars Inn by cornettist Paul Mares, the New Orleans Rhythm Kings – Georg Brunis (tmb), Jack Pettis (C-melody sax), Arnold Loyacano (bass), Louis Black (banjo), Elmer Schoebel (piano) and Frank Snyder (dms) – were a huge influence on young white Chicagoans: Jimmy McPartland, Frank Teschemacher, Bud Freeman *et al.* The Rhythm Kings, who filled the gap left in Chicago by the Original Dixieland Jazz Band after they moved on to New York, featured a high-powered programme (arranged by Schoebel, the only band member who could read music) laced with showmanship and clowning and built a huge reputation: New York promoters such as Sam Levin from Roseland made superior financial offers for the band, but no one wanted to leave Friars Inn, with its familiar clientele, swirling dancers and informal cabaret atmosphere. (As Friars Inn was gangster controlled, it is reasonable to assume that nobody could have left even if they had wanted to.) The New Orleans Rhythm Kings recorded for Gennett in 1922 (before King Oliver), but because they had no business manager, were all very young and often rushed into contractual and record deals their later career – by which time Mel Stitzel was playing piano, Ben Pollack drums – ended in a whimper in 1925. A recorded revival of the band in 1935 for Okeh records, featuring Jess Stacy on piano, is worth hearing: by the late 1930s Mares was a restaurateur. He died in 1949, planning a comeback. [DF]

Jazz Sounds of the 20s, vol. 2: Dixieland Bands (1922–5), Parlophone

See Williams, Martin, *Jazz Masters of New Orleans* (Macmillan, 1967, repr. Da Capo 1979)

Newton, Frankie (William Frank), trumpet. b. Emory, Virginia, 4 January 1906; d. New York City, 11 March 1954. By 1929 – neat, broad-shouldered and handsome – he was attracting attention with Cecil Scott's Bright Boys, quickly graduated to Charlie Johnson's band at Smalls' Paradise, then to Chick Webb and canny Elmer Snowden and by 1934 had recorded four classics (including 'Do Your Duty') at Bessie Smith's last recording session. From 1935 bouts of ill-health (some of it back trouble) were to ail him but in 1936 he was with Charlie Barnet's 'integrated' band (featuring John Kirby and a very young Modernaires) at Glen Island Casino, as well as with Teddy Hill's band at the Savoy, opposite Chick Webb. 1937, Newton recorded the hit 'Loch Lomond'/'Annie Laurie' with Kirby's wife Maxine Sullivan and worked for the last time with Kirby in his prototype of the soon-to-be-famous John Kirby Band: his rapid and unexplained departure from the Kirby project, with altoist Pete Brown, may have been his single most unlucky break. While Kirby's band spun to success, Newton played for Mezz Mezzrow and Lucky Millinder then led the band at Barney Josephson's new and integrated club Café Society (for Billie Holiday he was billed as 'trumpet-tootin' Frankie Newton' and he played on her best recording of 'Strange Fruit'). In 1940 he opened Kelly's Stables with Pete Brown again, but for this neglected trumpeter the 1940s were a slow and perhaps unplanned wind-down, with regular commuting from New York to Boston and elsewhere (with Sid Catlett, Ed Hall and James P. Johnson among others), and more time socializing with friends, fishing, playing tennis and taking care of himself. In 1948 a cruel fire destroyed his trumpet and belongings and, after a last summer season with his band at Boston's Savoy in 1950, he was more often to be found painting and reminiscing at his Greenwich Village home.

Frankie Newton's handicaps were bad luck, no hit records, occasional ill-health and mainly the kind of easy-going unambitious nature which, as Stanley Dance says, 'is seldom an asset in the world of jazz'. His gifts included a warm, plummy tone, the accuracy and control (though not quite the range) of a Charlie Shavers, and an imagination which, as Dickie Wells said, 'always believed in giving the people something different'. [DF]

Swingin' on 52nd Street, 1937–9, Jazz Archives

Newton, James, flute, alto and bass flutes. b. California, 1953. His grandmother and aunt sang Baptist hymns and taught him spirituals. In high school he started on electric bass, playing in rock and r & b bands. Then he became proficient on alto sax and bass clarinet, and took up the flute just before starting his last year at school. Inspired by Eric Dolphy's flute playing, he became interested in jazz, listening to Mingus, Ellington, Miles Davis and others. Studied music at California State College, playing in the classical ensembles as well as jazz groups. 1975, he received his degree in music, after which he went to New York, working with David Murray, Anthony Davis and many others. 1977, he gave up saxes and bass clarinet to concentrate entirely on flutes. By the early 1980s his reputation had burgeoned internationally, and he was generally recognized as a major exponent of the instrument. Newton is a virtuoso with a rich sound, and he has developed the simultaneous use of voice and flute to an unprecedented degree, by using special fingerings. He can sing in unison and harmony with it, which is not so unusual, but he can also improvise on a melody while he is singing it. He has said, 'I think very much in a contrapuntal sense, using both voice and flute. I have a piece called "Choir" that deals in four voices of holding a tone, singing a tone, and the different tones between the two. This is such a new field that classical flute players in Europe are always . . . asking how I get these sounds.' Newton remained active in classical music, both composing and playing it. [IC]

With Sam Rivers, David Murray, Anthony Davis, Arthur Blythe, Chico Freeman and others; as leader, *Axum* (1981), ECM; *Portraits* (1982), India Navigation; *The Mystery School* (1979), India Navigation; *Binu* (1977), Circle; *From Inside* (1978), BvHaast; *Flute Music* (1977), Flute Music Productions; *Echo Canyon* (1984), Celestial Harmonies

New York Despite claims to the contrary, New York still has some cause to consider itself the jazz capital of the world and, although reputations are no longer made and unmade there only, they are often reinforced by New York's acceptance.

'New York jazz' originally denoted 1920s bands which had not yet felt the impact of New Orleans music. And yet, what Charlie Parker once described as 'that fast New York style' undoubtedly existed in the late 1930s and early 1940s. It was typified by players, such as Roy Eldridge and Don Byas, whose technical and conceptual brilliance had outstripped their provincial upbringing so comprehensively that they had to 'make it' in the Big Apple.

This was the style that rapidly evolved into bebop and, since that time, most of the important schools of jazz have come to fruition there. Even styles pursued more persistently elsewhere (West Coast, European improvised music, ECM jazz) have taken their initial cue from New York trends. [BP]

Nicholas, Albert, clarinet, saxes. b. New Orleans, 27 May 1900; d. Basle, Switzerland, 3 September 1973. One of the mellowest New Orleans clarinettists (of course he was a pupil of Lorenzo Tio Jnr.), Nicholas played with all the early stars in his home town, served for three years in the US navy (his comrades-in-arms included Zutty Singleton and Charles Bolden) and by 1923 was back in New Orleans and leading his own band, which included Barney Bigard and Luis Russell, at Tom Anderson's cabaret on Basin Street. By early 1925 all three were working with King Oliver's Dixie Syncopators, but after two years Nicholas took work in the Far East (with Jack Carter), returned home the long way, spending another year in Cairo, and finally in 1928 rejoined his old friend Russell, whose New Orleans-based band was happily holding forth in New York including at Club Saratoga, millionaire Casper Holstein's personal indulgence. For the ten years after 1933 when he left Russell, Nicholas worked at the aristocratic end of New York jazz, including playing clarinet for John Kirby's quartet, reading Buster Bailey's difficult book with Kirby's sextet as first deputy, doubling on tenor in Louis Armstrong's sophisticated big band (led by Russell again) and in 1939 working for Jelly Roll Morton at Nick's. In 1941, a flat patch put him out of music and when he returned it was in the new musical context of the revival: by 1945 he was working for Art Hodes, Bunk Johnson (briefly), joined Kid Ory a year later and by 1948 – perhaps with relief – was at Jimmy Ryan's and with Ralph Sutton's Trio. In 1953 he settled in France and, like Sidney Bechet, the childhood friend with whom he had run the New Orleans streets, maintained a solo career thereafter. [DF]

Quartet (1959), Fona

Nichols, Herbie (Herbert Horatio), piano, composer, b. New York City, 3 January 1919; d. 12 April 1963. Played with Royal Baron Orchestra (1937) and other local bands before army service (1941–3). Gigging with a wide variety of leaders, including Herman Autrey (1945), Hal Singer (1946), Illinois Jacquet (*c.* 1946) and John Kirby (1948–9). Appeared on some obscure r & b record dates and, despite recording his own compositions in mid-1950s, worked always with other leaders such as Edgar Sampson, Arnett Cobb and Wilbur de Paris. Early 1960s, had club residency backing singers (Sheila Jordan and others less interesting), and had just been discovered by a new generation of musicians including Roswell Rudd and Archie Shepp (with whom he went to Scandinavia, 1962), when he died of leukaemia.

One of the many whose posthumous renown exceeds the reputation he achieved during his lifetime, Nichols's own compositions are completely at odds with the swing, r & b and Dixieland repertoire he played to earn a living. (He could apparently be surprisingly creative in that context too, but the records he made with Rex Stewart and trumpeter Joe Thomas do not provide enough evidence.) As a composer he was impressed by the early work of Thelonious Monk – indeed, he wrote the first article about him ever published – and may be said to have developed the linear, non-Ellingtonian side of Monk's playing. Not that he was uninterested in textures, for the ones he created were recognizably his, but his particular strengths lay in the use of melodic motifs and rhythmic ideas which were unique to him. This explains why, with the exception of 'Lady Sings the Blues', written for Billie Holiday, his tunes have seldom been adopted by others. But that hardly detracts from his importance, as the albums below (containing all the 28 originals he recorded) eloquently testify. [BP]

Third World (1955–6), Blue Note; *Love, Gloom, Cash, Love* (1957), Bethlehem

See Spellman, A. B., *Black Music: Four Lives* (Pantheon, New York, 1966; McGibbon & Kee, London 1967)

Nichols, Keith, piano, trombone, reeds, accordion, arranger, leader. b. Ilford, Essex, 13 February 1945. He was an All-Britain junior accordion champion and child actor and worked early on with Mike Daniels and a comedy-based group, the Levity Lancers. A ragtime authority with a particular *tendresse* for 1920s jazz, he rapidly gained a reputation in London jazz venues in the early 1970s, ran his own bands (such as the New Sedalia and a swing sextet) and by mid-decade was leading his own scholarly Ragtime Orchestra (featuring Paul Nossiter, Mo Morris and Richard Warner), playing in the New Paul Whiteman Orchestra and Dick Sudhalter's smaller bands, recording (with Bing Crosby, girl group Sweet Substitute and regularly as a soloist for EMI) and contributing scores to the New York Jazz Repertory Company, for Dick Hyman, and the Pasadena Roof Orchestra. From 1978 he co-led the Midnite Follies Orchestra (with Alan Cohen), toured shows of his own (including a Fats Waller tribute) and appeared on the South Bank presenting small-group concerts, including his Ragtime Trio, full-scale repertory presentations with the MFO (often featuring Ellington and Armstrong re-creations) and occasional one-offs including a Eubie Blake tribute. A tireless worker for the jazz he loves, Nichols is Britain's most methodical jazz preservationist: in 1985 he was fitting in work subbing with Harry Gold and leading his Paramount Theatre Orchestra between commitments. He plays most instruments well, but specializes on piano and trombone. [DF]

Ragtime Rules OK? (1976), One Up

Nichols, Red (Ernest Loring), cornet. b. Ogden, Utah, 8 May 1905; d. Las Vegas, Nevada, 28 June 1965. He was a child performer who played difficult set pieces for his father's brass band at 12: in his teens (to his father's annoyance) he idolized the Original Dixieland Jazz Band, Bix Beiderbecke and the Wolverines and Phil Napoleon – with whom he first met, in Atlantic City, his longtime partner and musical influence Miff Mole. In 1926, Nichols (already a busy session and studio man around New York) began a string of recordings with his Five Pennies: 'That was only a number we tied in with my name', he explained later. 'We'd generally have eight or nine, depending on who was around for the session and what I was trying to do.' The records were often made at the rate of ten to a dozen in a week under a variety of pseudonyms ('The California Redheads', 'The Charleston Chasers', 'The Arkansas Travellers' and 'Red and Miff's Stompers') and exerted a huge influence on black and white musicians alike, from Roy Eldridge, who thought Nichols had 'something different', to Gil Evans, whose first-ever transcription was of Nichols's 'Ida, sweet as apple cider': significantly, a close-voiced arrangement led by Adrian Rollini's dark-toned bass saxophone. By 1930, Nichols was a top bandleader who had worked for Whiteman ('My chair was taken by Bix,' he said later, 'and to me that's still the greatest honour I've ever received'), regularly directed Broadway shows such as *Girl Crazy* and *Strike Up the Band* and sometimes took bands on tour. On one such (at his friend Red McKenzie's instigation) he took a band of young Chicagoans who drank heavily, read badly, laughed at their leader's eye for commercial success and, through their spokesman Eddie Condon, questioned his decisions. Nichols – a strait-laced disciplinarian (a 1929 Vitaphone short shows his vocal group bowing to their leader before beginning their song) – sacked Condon for refusing to replay a request ('"Oh no, Red", I said. "Not 'Ida' again." "You're sacked!" he said. I was!': the seeds were sown for the unflattering portrait of Nichols in Condon's book). By the 1930s Nichols was on network radio, leading a fashionable big band and singing, and later (as Loring Nichols) conducting radio orchestras for Bob Hope and Ruth Etting. In 1942 he retired briefly and worked in a munitions factory: in contrast to Hollywood's version of his story, he was out of music for less than two years and by 1944 was star soloist again with Glen Gray's Casa Lomans (Nichols's record of 'Don't take your love from me' with Eugenie Baird and Gray's orchestra is an exquisite vignette). By 1945 – after Gray's promise of a 'band within a band' failed to materialize and Nichols had moved to the warmer climate of Los Angeles for his polio-stricken daughter's health – he re-signed with Capitol Records to lead a small group again (two years in advance of Louis Armstrong): until 1959 he led a comfortable career, bandleading in Los Angeles and around California, appearing on radio and TV (with Bing Crosby among others) and generally doing nicely. That year an often silly, sometimes marvellous Hollywood tribute, *The Five Pennies*, supercharged Nichols's career once again. Danny Kaye and Louis Armstrong starred in the film, Nichols, as silver-toned as ever, dubbed the music on his Selmer cornet and from then on a string of new records (featuring such old friends as Joe Rushton, Jack Coon, Manny Klein, Beau and Culver, all very underrated, all perfect) signalled a late blossoming. At 60 Nichols unexpectedly dropped dead in his Las Vegas hotel room. [DF]

And his Five Pennies, vols. 1/2 (1926–30), Coral

Nicols, Maggie, voice, piano. b. Edinburgh, 24 February 1948. Mother half French, half North

African (Berber), a singer. Self-taught. Began as a dancer at London's Windmill Theatre, 1964; first singing engagement in 1965. Worked with various musicians in London including John Stevens and Trevor Watts (SME), 1968–9, Keith Tippett's Centipede, 1971. Led her own group, Okuren, in early 1970s, and later co-founded the vocal quartet Voice with Phil Minton, Julie Tippett and Brian Eley. 1977, co-founded Feminist Improvising Group. Founded Contradictions, a workshop/performance group which has included many European musicians, for example Uli Lask, Conny Bauer, Irene Schweizer. Also composes, and has written the music for Common Stock Youth Theatre's production of Brecht's *The Caucasian Chalk Circle*, which gained the company's Best Music Award, 1982. Favourites range from Billie Holiday and Aretha Franklin to Julie Tippett and Phil Minton. Other inspirations, Bill Evans, Coltrane, Dolphy, Schweizer, Stevens and Watts. [IC]

With SME, *Oliv* (1969), Marmalade; Nicols/Tippett, *Sweet and Sours* (1982); FMP; with Ulrich P. Lask, *Lask I* (1982); ECM; *Live at the Bastille* (1982), Sync Pulse

Niehaus, Lennie (Leonard), alto sax, arranger. b. St Louis, Missouri, 11 June 1929. Played with Stan Kenton (1952, 1954–9), then concentrated on writing for television and educational activities. Also film music, mostly arranging for musical director Jerry Fielding but including, under own name, *City Heat* and *Pale Rider* (1985). Niehaus's alto work reflected that of Bud Shank and early Art Pepper, adhering to the West Coast orthodoxy of blending the styles of Charlie Parker and Benny Carter; an interesting comparison is afforded between Parker's 'Cherokee', recorded live with Kenton, and Niehaus playing the same Bill Holman arrangement. His own jazz writing revealed a talent for creating interesting original themes, and for finding fresh and sometimes contrapuntal approaches to arranging standard material. [BP]

The Sextet (1956), Contemporary

Nieman, Paul Terence, trombone. b. London, 19 June 1950. Father, Alfred Nieman, a composer, pianist, improviser. Studied music under Brian Richardson at Chiswick Polytechnic, then at Guildhall School of Music (1969–72) with Denis Wick. 1969–72, with National Youth Jazz Orchestra on lead trombone. Since then he has played with Mike Gibbs, George Harrison, London Jazz Composers' Orchestra, Soft Machine, John Surman, Keith Tippett, Stan Tracey, Mike Westbrook, Gil Evans, Diana Ross, among others. Also very active in education, teaching at jazz courses, and he is a professor at the Guildhall where he initiated the jazz course. He leads his own group, Elephant, for which he does much of the composing. Nieman is the complete trombonist, equally at home with early music and all contemporary styles, equally proficient as a lead player or a soloist whether working acoustically or with electronics. Influences range from Jimmy Knepper, Jack Teagarden and Bob Brookmeyer to Charles Mingus, the Brecker Brothers and Stockhausen. [IC]

With Westbrook, *Metropolis* (1971), RCA; with Don Rendell, *Earth Music* (1979), Spotlite; with Cayenne, *Roberto Who* (1981), Groove; with the Stranglers, *Aural Sculpture* (1984), CBS

Nistico, Sal (Salvatore), tenor sax. b. Syracuse, New York, 2 April 1940. Played with r & b bands in New York in the 1950s. Came to prominence with Chuck and Gap Mangione, 1960–1. Featured soloist with Woody Herman for several periods during the 1960s; also with Count Basie, 1965, 1967. With Don Ellis and others in Los Angeles in 1970. Briefly with Herman again, 1971, then freelanced with various small groups. Toured Europe with Slide Hampton. At the end of the 1970s, came to live in Europe, where he freelances, touring and playing festivals. Nistico's main influences are Charlie Parker, Gene Ammons and Sonny Rollins, and he has developed his own style in the post-bop idiom, a big-toned, fiery approach which swings intensely. [IC]

Several with Herman; *Neo/Nistico* (1978), Beehive

Noble, Ray, composer, leader. b. Brighton, Sussex, 1907; d. 1977. Probably England's most famous popular composer – he wrote 'The very thought of you', 'By the Fireside', 'The touch of your lips', 'Goodnight Sweetheart' (his signature tune), 'Love Locked Out', 'Love is the sweetest thing', 'Cherokee' (part of a *Red Indian Suite*) and many others – Noble was musical director of HMV, 1929–34, and in this capacity recorded hundreds of sides featuring an all-star house orchestra. The records, featuring British stars such as Nat Gonella, Freddy Gardner, E. O. Pogson and Tiny Winters, are much reissued classics full of brilliant writing (and playing) and set a standard bemusedly envied by American emulators. In 1934 Noble went to live in the USA (taking drummer-manager Bill Harty and singer Al Bowlly with him) and organized a band, for which Glenn Miller was musical director, to play at the Rainbow Room on top of Radio City in New York. His orchestra – featuring Johnny Mince, Pee Wee Erwin, Will Bradley, Claude Thornhill and George Van Eps among others – played from 9 pm to 3 am seven nights a week and lasted a year until Miller and Noble (a strong character of notable business acumen under a mild British

Sal Nistico

exterior) disagreed and the orchestra broke up after overtime and other political disputes: their records are seldom as good as those of their British predecessors. With his stars gone, Noble moved to Hollywood (with Harty) to work as musical director and straight man for the Burns and Allen Show (he appeared with them in RKO's *A Damsel in Distress*, 1937, starring Fred Astaire) and later worked in the same roles for comedian Edgar Bergen for 14 years. Noble remained a well-known radio personality and bandleader in America until the 1950s, when he retired with his wife to Jersey, in the Channel Islands; he went back to the USA to finish his life in Santa Barbara, California. Each month after he died his widow received a romantic legacy – a dozen red roses. [DF]

Nock, Mike (Michael Anthony), piano, electric keyboards, synthesizer. b. Christchurch, New Zealand, 27 September 1940. Lessons from his father for six months when he was 11, then mainly self-taught; but studied at Berklee, Boston, on a scholarship, 1961. 1962–3, he was house pianist in a Boston club, accompanying many jazz stars including Coleman Hawkins. 1964–7, toured with Yusef Lateef and worked with Booker Ervin, Stanley Turrentine, John Handy and others. 1968, formed Fourth Way, one of the first jazz-rock-fusion groups. Fourth Way toured internationally, appearing at many festivals including Montreux, 1970, before it disbanded in 1971, after which Nock became involved in electronic music and freelanced in San Francisco. [IC]

With Lateef, Handy, Steve Marcus; with Fourth Way, *The Sun and Moon Have Come Together* (1969); *Werewolf* (1970); *The Fourth Way* (1969), all Capitol; Nock trio with Eddie Gomez/Jon Christensen, *Ondas* (1982), ECM

Noone, Jimmie, clarinet, soprano and alto sax, leader. b. nr. New Orleans, 23 April 1895; d. Los Angeles, 19 April 1944. He had made the trip to nearby New Orleans by 1910 and took clarinet lessons from Sidney Bechet. A jolly, roly-poly man who loved to talk and socialize as well as to play, Noone was soon firm friends with his first bandleader Freddie Keppard and worked with him regularly as well as with other New Orleans stars such as Buddy Petit and Kid Ory, whose trumpet player at the time was Joe Oliver. When young Noone made his first trip to Chicago in late 1917 it was to join Keppard and a year later King Oliver, with whom he worked until 1920. Then came six years with Doc Cooke's Dreamland orchestra. 'That was a devil of a band,' recalls Barney Bigard, 'and Jimmie was the main one for me. While he was with Charlie Cooke he mostly played harmony parts, but after at the Nest he played mostly lead all night because the band was so small.' From 1926 the Nest – a famous Chicago nightspot – was renamed the Apex Club, and Noone who took up the residency that year with his little band, including Joe Poston (alto) and Earl Hines (piano), quickly became its star: records for Vocalion, especially 'Sweet Lorraine' and 'Four or Five Times', made him more famous still and soon he was recognized as the newest, most influential clarinet voice in all Chicago. Visitors from Benny Goodman to Joe Marsala came in to see Noone 'holding the horn over that great belly of his and playing like it was nothing' (in Marsala's words): so did Maurice Ravel. 'He showed up one night with the first clarinettist of the Chicago Symphony,' recalls Mezz Mezzrow, 'and they seesawed back and forth on their unbelief until the joint closed up!' Noone's pre-eminent position in clarinet history has occasionally been obscured because he never settled for long in New York, the jazz capital, but generally stayed around Chicago playing a kind of small-group jazz that by 1938 – with the dawn of swing – was temporarily out of fashion. But he stayed busy in Chicago, toured in 1938 and formed a big band for broadcasting in 1939. By 1944 he was living on the West Coast, and working with Kid Ory's band in the groundbreaking Standard Oil broadcasts. Then, quite suddenly, he dropped dead. 'He ate himself to death', says Jimmie Noone Jnr. (himself a successful clarinettist). 'He didn't drink or smoke but he couldn't leave food alone and he had very high blood pressure.' Noone was replaced by Barney Bigard, his great admirer: the band played 'Blues for Jimmie' in his memory on Ory's show a week after his death. [DF]

Jimmie Noone and Earl Hines at the Apex Club (1928), MCA

Norvo, Red (Kenneth Norville), vibraharp, xylophone. b. Beardstown, Illinois, 31 March 1908. Began his career as xylophone specialist (its 'novelty' characteristics are reflected in a couple of early recordings); spent time with Paul Whiteman in early 1930s. Formed own band (1935–44) with low-key approach modelled by arranger Eddie Sauter, tailored to the minimal decibel-count of Norvo's instrument and of the singing of his then wife, Mildred Bailey. Only in 1940s did Norvo follow the lead of Lionel Hampton and Adrian Rollini in concentrating on vibes, while retaining the rhythmically choppy style and terminal tremolos that made him the Jess Stacy of the mallets.

Keeping abreast of jazz developments without modifying his own playing, Norvo was responsible (during employment with Benny Goodman, 1944–5) for an all-star record session which introduced many listeners to the work of Dizzy Gillespie and Charlie Parker. After a year with Woody Herman (1946), settled on West Coast where the early 1950s found him leading a drummerless trio, initially with Tal Farlow and Charles Mingus; this group not only betrayed the influence of bebop but was the first of the 'chamber jazz' outfits which proliferated during that decade. Norvo remained active, frequently in Las Vegas, enjoying a brief semi-retirement in the mid-1970s. The 1980s saw him touring Europe several times with colleague Tal Farlow, his playing retaining its essential vitality and underlying humour. [BP]

Red Norvo and his All Stars (1933–8), Epic; *Red Norvo's Fabulous Jam Session* (1945), Spotlite; *Red Norvo Trio* (1950–1), Savoy

Nunez, Alcide 'Yellow', clarinet. b. New Orleans, 17 March 1884; d. 2 September 1934. One of the most highly trained New Orleans clarinettists – he was a Creole – Nunez worked all around New Orleans in cabarets, saloons and parade bands from 1902, including a stay with Jack Laine's Reliance Band, 1912–16. That year Nunez travelled to Chicago with drummer Johnny Stein and soon after joined the Original Dixieland Jazz Band under leader Nick La Rocca: after an argument with La Rocca, however, he traded places with Larry Shields in Tom Brown's group which had come back from New York after a none-too-successful comedy season. Nothing happened with Brown in Chicago, so Nunez went back to leading his own bands, toured with Bert Kelly and played for drummer Anton Lada at the Athenia Café, Chicago, before touring his quartet around the Midwest. By 1927 he was back in New Orleans and he later played with the New Orleans Police Band. [DF]

New York Jazz Scene, 1917–20, Riverside

Nussbaum, Adam, drums. b. New York City, 29 November 1955. Studied music at the Davis Center, City College of New York; started on piano, also bass and alto sax. 1978–83, with John Scofield; 1978–81, worked with Dave Liebman quintet; 1982–3, with Stan Getz; from 1983, with Gil Evans orchestra; from 1984, with Randy Brecker, Eliane Elias; 1984, also worked with George Gruntz Concert Jazz Band and Gary Burton. He has freelanced with Sonny Rollins, Joe Henderson, Art Pepper, Art Farmer, Lockjaw Davis, John Abercrombie, Bob Brookmeyer, Ted Curson, Al Cohn, Sheila Jordan, Hal Galper, among others.

Red Norvo

Nussbaum is one of the brightest drum stars in the American firmament. He has toured with Liebman, Scofield and Steve Swallow, playing major festivals in Europe and the USA. His favourites range from Baby Dodds to Sid Catlett, Shadow Wilson, Elvin Jones, Mel Lewis, Al Foster, among others, and particular inspirations include Armstrong, Coltrane, Miles Davis, Wayne Shorter, Gil Evans, Jimi Hendrix, Stevie Wonder, Jobim, João Gilberto. [IC]

With Dave Liebman, *If They Only Knew* (1980), Timeless; with John Scofield, *Shinola* (1981), Enja; *Out Like a Light* (1981), Enja; with Gil Evans, *Live at Sweet Basil* (1984), Electric Bird

O

O'Brien, Floyd, trombone. b. Chicago, 7 May 1904; d. 26 November 1968. In his early teens he was a ringsider at Lincoln Gardens for King Oliver's band, and was discovered by drummer Dave Tough at a University of Chicago fraternity dance in 1921. For the next ten years, although he became firm friends with the Austin High School Gang, he stayed around Chicago working for local leaders such as Charles Pierce and Thelma Terry, and for theatre orchestras. When he finally got to New York *c.* 1934, he made fine records with Eddie Condon, Fats Waller, Mezz Mezzrow and the Chocolate Dandies, but soon after joined comedian Phil Harris's big band and stayed until 1939 (that year he recorded George Wettling's classic *Chicago Jazz* set). Then came work with Gene Krupa, two years with Bob Crosby and time with Eddie Miller, before opening a shop on the West Coast, playing with Shorty Sherock's band, and finally moving back to Chicago in 1948. From then on O'Brien's career (apart from excellent records with Art Hodes in the late 1950s) was poorly documented, until a *Downbeat* obituary in 1968 told the full story.

O'Brien, one of the best Chicago-style trombonists, deserved to be better-known than he was, but, relative to his better-known peers, he made few records, based himself for much of his playing life outside New York, and for the ten years that he *was* around New York often played in big bands. [DF]

Condon/McPartland/Wettling, *Chicago Jazz* (1939–40), Coral

O'Day, Anita, vocals. b. Chicago, 18 December 1919. After singing with local Chicago groups in late 1930s, earned national reputation as member of Gene Krupa band (1941–3, 1945). Also worked with early Stan Kenton band (1944–5). Then established herself as a soloist, recording frequently; appeared with local rhythm-sections, her regular accompanist being from 1954 drummer John Poole. In a career marked by personal ups and downs (see her autobiography), her performance has been remarkably consistent and even well-known highlights such as the Newport festival, 1958, and Berlin festival, 1970 – captured on film and disc respectively – are only representative of her normal standards.

As well as making one of the first interracial vocal duets on record ('Let Me Off Uptown' with Roy Eldridge and the Krupa band), O'Day was the first (only?) feminist big-band singer, appearing in band-jacket and skirt rather than a dress. Musically, she more than earned the right to be treated as a band member rather than a visual exhibit, for her originality was a considerable asset and, after working solo, her style matured marvellously. On ballads there is a distant resemblance to Billie Holiday, while on up-tempo numbers, whether scatting or merely stretching the lyrics to breaking-point, she has a fine rhythmic sense and an ebullience which is hard to duplicate. Certainly, the many singers who emulated her ballad work especially (June Christy, Chris Connor, Helen Merrill etc.) came nowhere near to swinging as delightfully as O'Day. [BP]

Sings the Winners (1958), Verve; *At the Berlin Festival* (1970), MPS

See O'Day, Anita, and Eells, George, *High Times, Hard Times* (Corgi, 1983)

O'Farrill, Chico (Arturo), arranger (and trumpet). b. Havana, Cuba, 28 October 1921. Raised in Cuba and USA, studied music and played in Havana (1940–8), then settled in New York. As well as writing for Benny Goodman and Stan Kenton, did arrangements for Latin/jazz albums by Machito (with Charlie Parker and Flip Phillips, 1950), Dizzy Gillespie (1954, 1975), Art Farmer (1959) and Gato Barbieri (1974). Made a small number of albums under his own name, and (from 1965) other more conventional work for Count Basie, Clark Terry and many others. Although O'Farrill's big-band scoring is based on fairly banal US styles, he has an enviable knowledge of which Afro-Latin rhythms can blend with them. His son, Arturo O'Farrill Jnr., played keyboards with the Carla Bley band (early 1980s). [BP]

Dizzy Gillespie/Machito, *Oro, Incienso y Mirra* (1975), Pablo

Okoshi, Tiger (Toru), trumpet, synthesizer, composer, b. Ashita, Japan, 21 March 1950. Since 1972, has lived in the USA, playing with Gary Burton, Bob Moses and others, and also leading his own bands. His music is jazz-rock-fusion, and he calls it 'Baku' music after a mythical creature that eats bad dreams (= 'eating-nightmares' music). Okoshi is a highly accomplished player and composer. He has said of the trumpet, 'It is a limited, incomplete, very old-fashioned instrument – but I love it.' Miles Davis is a main influence, but more for his jazz-rock experiments on *Bitches Brew* (1969) than for his trumpet playing. [IC]

Tiger's Baku (1981), JVC; *Mudd Cake* (1982), JVC; with Gary Burton, *Times Square* (1977), ECM; with Bob Moses, *Visit with the Great Spirit* (1983), Gramavision

Oliver, Joe 'King', cornet, composer. b. Louisiana, 11 May 1885; d. Savannah, Georgia, 10 April 1938. Joe 'King' Oliver was a slow developer back in New Orleans. By 1905, although 'he had a book thicker than the Good Book with nothing but dates in it' (as Pops Foster remembers it), the future 'King' was still a thin-toned, restricted player with a lot of learning to do. Then, around 1914 (Preston Jackson recalls), he began to improve and to practise very hard; his own band began to cause a stir, and by 1917 Kid Ory was billing him as 'King'. By then – on parades, in cabarets and often fronting his own group – Oliver was cutting an impressive figure. 'I'll never forget how big and tough he looked,' says Ed Souchon, 'his brown derby tilted low over one eye, his shirt collar open at the neck and a bright red undershirt peeking out at the V.' Oliver was now a more than competent cornettist who played a strong, capable lead with plenty of volume and a battery of muted effects. 'Joe did most of his playing with cups, glasses, buckets and mutes', says Mutt Carey, who copied Oliver. 'He could make his horn sound like a holy roller meeting!' (He also used the tiny, now obsolete 'door-knob' mute beloved of Jabbo Smith.) Oliver was a canny and ambitious businessman who by 1919 knew that jazz was moving upstream to Chicago and that back home in New Orleans a new prodigy – Louis Armstrong – was ready to usurp every other king in the city. So that year he was pleased to join bassist-entrepreneur Bill Johnson (Buddy Petit had turned down the offer), as well as clarinettist Laurence Duhe, at the Dreamland Ballroom in Chicago. Soon after he took over Duhe's band and in 1921 took his new team (featuring Johnny Dodds, Honore Dutrey and Lil Hardin) to California. The trip was unsuccessful (Mutt Carey had got there first with Ory, and audiences saw Oliver as an imitator, rather than the originator, of Carey's muted tricks) and a year later Oliver, in fighting mood, returned to Chicago, where he opened at the Lincoln Gardens with his band and a new member up from New Orleans: Louis Armstrong. Armstrong – a young, generous New Orleans boy in search of a father – was far too good-natured to query his second-trumpet post, but it was one of Oliver's cannier moves. 'As long as I got him with me', he told pianist Lil Hardin, 'he won't be able to get ahead of me. I'll still be King!' The Creole Jazz Band was omnipotent. Nightly the Lincoln Gardens was packed with dancers and musicians listening to what George Wettling called 'the hottest band ever to sit on a bandstand', playing 45-minute versions of classics such as 'Riverside Blues', 'Working Man Blues' and 'Mabel's Dream', and featuring Armstrong and Oliver's staggeringly complex and apparently ad-lib 'hot breaks'. Oliver, at the centre of the band, was an imposing leader and a strict one: sidemen could drink only from a bucket of sugar water with a dipper in it, new boy Louis Armstrong was told to play 'more lead' and took the advice. At the Gennett Studios in Richmond, Indiana, in 1923 the first great sides by King Oliver's Creole Jazz Band were recorded. Everyone, apart from canny Lil Hardin, was nervous but the records (for, at various times, four different labels) are still some of the greatest ever made: Oliver's racketting, joyous lead is clearly audible in the pre-electric recording. (Although it may be that his best work never survived studio conditions: 'To tell the truth,' says Mutt Carey, 'I don't believe it is Joe playing on the records sometimes.')

In 1924, Oliver's greatest band broke up, after the Dodds brothers discovered that Oliver was 'creaming' money from his sidemen's salaries, and soon only Louis Armstrong was left, until Lil Hardin, now his wife, secured his departure. Oliver replaced him with Lee Collins, but by the end of 1924 was guesting with Dave Peyton's band. He took it over in February 1925 and formed his Dixie Syncopators, a band featuring the new and revolutionary saxophone team of Barney Bigard and Albert Nicholas. By 1927, Oliver had taken his new package to New York, but there – once again – time had beaten him to the punch. 'Everybody in New York then', said Louis Armstrong, 'was playing King Oliver – even me!' It was hard for the old King to accept. He continued quoting high fees and losing work (including a contract for the Cotton Club which Duke Ellington won), as well as overeating, which produced weight and dental problems. His last ten years (despite successful recordings) form a sad picture of a man reduced by jazz fashion, calling shots he could no longer afford to call, seeing such protégés as Armstrong relentlessly overtake him. And although Oliver's touring bands of the early 1930s were still successful, fashionable decline and recurrent pyorrhoea plagued the trumpeter and by 1936 he was janitor in a Savannah poolroom. 'He got stranded down there,' remembered Louis Armstrong, 'and ended up a very pathetic man.' Oliver's course was almost run: a letter to his sister in 1937 sounded like a goodbye: 'I know the Good Lord will take care of me. Goodnight dear!' He died in Savannah and was buried in the Bronx: a sad way to get back to New York. [DF]

Creole Jazz Band: The Okeh Sessions, 1923, World Records

See Allen, Walter C., and Rust, Brian, *King Joe Oliver* (Jazz Book Club, 1957)

Oliver, Sy (Melvin James), trumpet, arranger, vocals, composer. b. Battle Creek, Michigan, 17

December 1910. Oliver – his nickname was an abbreviation of 'Psychology' – originally wanted to be an attorney, but grew up in a houseful of music in which he learned to read notes as soon as he learned to read words. By his late teens he was working in territory bands led by Cliff Barnett, Zack Whyte and Alphonso Trent and perfecting his gift for orchestration; in 1933 he joined Jimmie Lunceford as trumpeter and co-staff arranger with pianist Ed Wilcox. With Lunceford, Oliver's writing – in arrangements such as 'T'ain't what you do!', 'Dinah' and 'Ain't she sweet' – was a dashing parade of innovation (it rivalled Ellington's for consistency and originality): when he joined Tommy Dorsey in 1939 (at $5000 a year more than Lunceford gave him) Oliver continued to write 'brilliant, full-blooded things', in Frank Sinatra's words, although as he said, 'I had to write down for the Dorsey guys because this was before the days when you couldn't tell the difference between a negro and a white musician.' ('Sunny side of the street' is one of Oliver's most famous for Dorsey.) From 1946, after a brief bandleading spell, he continued working as a freelance arranger (often for black artists) and – for Decca and other top record companies – produced a hugely successful *oeuvre* of recordings for (among many others) Ella Fitzgerald, Sammy Davis, Frank Sinatra and Louis Armstrong (two of Louis' finest albums, *Louis and the Good Book* and its lesser-known but superior companion *Louis and the Angels*, are Oliver's creations). From the late 1960s he returned to bandleading again: 1970, at the Downbeat Club in New York and, 1975–80, at the Rainbow Room with an all-star band for which he wrote a book of over 300 arrangements: 'At weekends when everybody gets high we play a lot of jazz', recalled Oliver Jackson. One of the most intense, intelligent and educated men of swing, Oliver remained as busy as ever in the 1980s. [DF]

The Complete Jimmie Lunceford (1939–40), CBS (4 records, boxed set)

See Dance, Stanley, *The World of Swing* (Scribner's, 1974, repr. Da Capo, 1979)

Original Original is what most jazz musicians would like to be, although it's easier said than done. 'An original' is a composition written by the same person who performs it, as opposed to 'a standard' which is something that anyone and everyone plays. Similarly, an 'original arrangement' is originated by a member of the group using it, as opposed to a 'stock arrangement' that could be bought off the shelf from a publisher. Neither an original nor an original arrangement has to be very original. [BP]

Original Dixieland Jazz Band Although their music now sometimes sounds quaintly dated, the ODJB (as they soon became known) played a vital part in a jazz revolution: their 1917 residency at Resenweber's restaurant in Columbus Circle, New York – which attracted all of New York's bright young society – really launched the jazz age of the 1920s. To musicians left behind in New Orleans the fast-working white publicity machine that advertised the (all-white) ODJB as 'the creators of jazz' must have seemed unfair and was. Its five members – Nick La Rocca (cornet), Larry Shields (clt), Eddie Edwards (tmb), Henry Ragas (piano), replaced after his death by J. Russell Robinson, and Tony Sbarbaro, or Spargo (dms) – were young New Orleans men who had played first with such senior New Orleans leaders as 'Papa' Jack Laine, then listened to and learned from older players like King Oliver ('the La Rocca boys used to hang around and got a lot of ideas from his gang', says Preston Jackson). In 1916, led by drummer Johnny Stein, La Rocca, Edwards, Ragas and clarinettist Alcide 'Yellow' Nunez (later replaced by Shields) worked for club-owner Harry James at Chicago's Booster Club then – with drummer Sbarbaro replacing Stein – at a rival café, the Del'Arbe, which put in a better offer. Soon after agent Max Hart gave La Rocca the chance to work at Resenweber's restaurant in New York's Columbus Circle and after a slow start the ODJB were soon packing in crowds with a high-powered jazz-based vaudeville act featuring Shields's fine playing interlaced with clarinet hokum (he was a prime influence on Ted Lewis), La Rocca and Edwards playing into each other's bell, a battery of tin can mutes, sock-cymbals and Swanee whistles, and Edwards playing the trombone with his foot. Their records from this time are a mixed bunch: hits such as 'Livery Stable Blues', full of trumpet-brays and clarinet cock-crows, and 'At the Jazz Band Ball', with its ritualized clarinet routines, remind us how young jazz was then, but other sides, including 'I've lost my heart in Dixieland' and 'Tell me' from two years after, are great by any standards. Every one of the records, in either case, was a seminal influence on a new generation of jazzmen from Bix Beiderbecke down. By 1919 the ODJB were the rude invaders of polite London society: they opened in Albert de Courville's *Joy Bells* revue at the Hippodrome, but were hastily removed from the bill at the instigation of George Robey and sent on a tour of variety theatres instead (including the Palladium). Then on 28 October 1919 they opened at the Hammersmith Palais. La Rocca's press announcements at the time must have sounded as controversial as punk rock players did in the 1970s: 'Jazz is the assassination of the melody – the slaying of syncopation. It's a revolution in this kind of music and I confess we're musical anarchists!' A nine-month stay at Hammersmith, however, proved that post-war Britain was ready for all the anarchy it could get, and when the group returned to the USA it was for a spell of busy touring and more recording. But jazz fashion was getting into gear and Paul Whiteman's

'Symphonic Jazz' concert at Carnegie Hall in 1924 in some ways sounded a trump for the ODJB. In 1925, La Rocca – a bundle of high energy, hard sell and ego – collapsed and retired to New Orleans exhausted (his place was briefly taken by Henry Levine) and for ten years the show was over. In 1936 the band re-formed for Ed Wynn's network radio programme, toured theatres, made a film and were written up in a perceptive article by J. S. Moynahan in the *Saturday Evening Post*: the ODJB, not Benny Goodman, said Moynahan, were 'the real jazz'. His article, and the reformed ODJB, came five years too early for the jazz revival: Shields developed heart trouble and La Rocca retired for ever to New Orleans and the building trade. Throughout the 1940s records by Edwards (featuring Bill Davison and Max Kaminsky on trumpets and Brad Gowans on clarinet) plus a tribute in Katherine Dunham's 1944 revue affectionately remembered the group: so – later and perhaps less likeably – did a book, *The Story of the ODJB* (see below), which set out to substantiate La Rocca's more grandiose claims and (of course) failed. But the band had left its mark on young players such as Phil Napoleon, Red Nichols and Beiderbecke and invented a style of presentation that was to live on in some Dixieland music to the present day. [DF]

ODJB (1917–36), RCA (double)

See Brunn, H. O., *The Story of the ODJB* (Sidgwick & Jackson, 1962); Williams, Martin, *Jazz Masters of New Orleans* (Macmillan, 1967, repr. Da Capo, 1979)

Original Memphis Five, see NAPOLEON, PHIL.

Ørsted Pedersen, Niels-Henning, bass. b. Örsted, Denmark, 27 May 1946. Mother a church organist. Studied piano, but was a prodigy on bass, playing with Danish groups at age 14; at 17 was asked to join Count Basie, but was unable to do so. Played with many Americans during the 1960s, including Sonny Rollins, Bill Evans and Roland Kirk. He was house bassist at Copenhagen's leading jazz venue, Club Montmartre; also member of Danish Radio Orchestra. He has won polls in Europe and the US. In the 1970s he formed a duo with pianist Kenny Drew. Since the mid-1970s he has been a regular and permanent member of the Oscar Peterson trio. Early 1980s, he hosted a jazz show on TV in the UK. He is a virtuoso double-bass player, equally capable as accompanist or soloist. [IC]

With Albert Ayler, Kirk, Dexter Gordon, Anthony Braxton and many others; several with Peterson; two duo albums with Drew; several albums recorded at Montreux festival, 1975, including *Dizzy Gillespie Big Seven* and *Oscar Peterson Big Six*, both Pablo

Niels-Henning Ørsted Pedersen

Ory, Kid (Edward), trombone, bass, cornet, alto sax, vocals, composer. b. La Place, Louisiana, 25 December 1886; d. Hawaii, 23 January 1973. While he was still playing the banjo in his home town La Place, 30 miles from New Orleans, he was already setting up musical picnics – and charging admission. When he arrived in New Orleans *c.* 1911 as a young trombonist, he quickly drummed up more business. 'I rented a furniture wagon, and told a fellow to make signs, "KID ORY", with address and telephone number. After that I began to get lots of calls!' Soon Ory – a very competitive leader who whipped opposition unmercifully and walked off the stage if the musical company failed to suit him – was spellbinding New Orleans with bands featuring strong trumpeters such as Mutt Carey (a lifelong colleague), Joe Oliver and young Louis Armstrong: in 1917 he received an offer to go to Chicago but was simply too busy. In 1919 his doctor advised a warmer climate: Ory moved to California, set up his band there, recorded the first-ever titles by an all-black jazzband ('Ory's Creole Trombone' for the Spikes Brothers' Sunshine label) and as early as 1921 was so busy again that he had to delegate a string of double bookings to Oliver's band. In 1925 he was back in Chicago with King Oliver and spent the next seven years playing for leaders such as Dave Peyton, Boyd Atkins and Clarence Black, and recording with (among others) Jelly Roll Morton, Ma Rainey, Tiny Parham, Luis Russell, and of course Louis Armstrong's Hot Five and Seven.

'When we made those records we didn't have any expectation that they would be so successful,' said Ory later. '. . . one thing that helped the sales was the fact for a while that the Okeh people gave away a picture of Louis to everyone that bought one.'

By 1933 music was slowing down and big bands taking over, and Ory retired from music to look after his brother's chicken farm; not much more was heard from him until 1942, when he came back to music with Barney Bigard's band (on trombone, not bass, as is often suggested) and a year later was playing concerts with his own group. In 1944 a series of weekly broadcasts hosted by Orson Welles for Standard Oil re-established him as the revival's most resilient star, and for the rest of his life Kid Ory was a prosperous and successful jazzman. In 1945 he began a long residency at the Jade Palace on Hollywood Boulevard, took a featured role in the Hollywood film *New Orleans* in 1947, toured nationally in 1948, and the following year moved to the Beverley Cavern back on the West Coast. After Carey left the band in 1948 (the year he died), Ory used a succession of brilliant trumpeters such as Teddy Buckner (who joined him from Lionel Hampton), Marty Marsala and Alvin Alcorn, and all through the 1950s continued to market his career with skill, vision and foresight (his Good Time Jazz albums of the period feature irresistible artwork and New Orleans recipes as well as notes about the band). A new hit version of his composition 'Muskrat Ramble' in 1954 made Ory richer still (in the early years of his career he had failed to collect royalties on the tune until Barney Bigard explained how), and that year he opened his club On the Levee in Los Angeles. 'Ory has the mentality of a French peasant, with all the charm, shrewdness and stinginess that that implies,' said Martin Williams at this time. (British trumpeter Colin Smith remembers Ory's reply to a fan who asked him for tips on trombone playing: 'Never do it for nothing!') Ory's primitive trombone – several observers, including Williams and British trombonist Alan Dean, believe that he was actually a far better player than he let on – was heard in Europe in 1956 and 1959: in the mid-1960s he moved to Hawaii, following the hot weather once more. A very old Ory appeared – but only to sing – at jazz festivals in the early 1970s. He died at 86 and was buried New Orleans-style: 'I know they played "Just a Closer Walk with Thee" over him,' remembers Barney Bigard, an old colleague, 'and cut down the hill with "Muskrat Ramble" and "Ory's Creole Trombone" and that was the end of an era.' [DF]

Any on Good Time Jazz

See Williams, Martin, *Jazz Masters of New Orleans* (Macmillan, 1967, repr. Da Capo, 1979)

Osborne, Mike (Michael Evans), alto sax, clarinet, piano. b. Hereford, 28 September 1941. Graduated at Guildhall School of Music, London. 1962–72, a member of Mike Westbrook's band. During 1960s and 1970s, a regular member of Chris McGregor's Brotherhood of Breath and the John Warren big band. Also worked with Mike Gibbs, Humphrey Lyttelton and Alan Skidmore. 1970, he began leading his own trio. Often associated with Stan Tracey, playing a series of duo concerts with him. He was, in 1973, a founder member of SOS (Surman, Osborne, Skidmore), an innovative 3-saxophone group which toured in Italy, Germany and France, and co-wrote and performed music for a ballet, *Sablier Prison*, at the Paris Opera House. With various bands, Osborne toured all over Europe and in Scandinavia. He was voted first on alto sax in the *Melody Maker* Jazz Poll each year 1969–73. His favourite altoists are Jackie McLean and Phil Woods, and Osborne's own playing has an intensity similar to theirs. He was ill and out of action from 1980. [IC]

With Westbrook, Gibbs, McGregor and others; *Outback* (1970), Turtle; *Marcel's Muse* (1977); *Border Crossing* (1974); *SOS* (1975), all Ogun

Osser, Glenn, arranger. b. Munising, Michigan, 28 August 1914. His career began in the 1930s, arranging ballad material for Bob Crosby's orchestra. Since then Osser has appeared in a huge variety of musical situations including jazz ones, notably for Bobby Hackett (he also played pipe organ in some post-Gleason recordings which are among Hackett's best), as well as special commissions for the World's Greatest Jazz Band, Teresa Brewer, and her husband, record producer Bob Thiele, and Joe Bushkin. [DF]

Bobby Hackett, *The Most Beautiful Horn in the World* (1961), CBS

Otis, Johnny (John Veliotis), drums, vibes, piano. b. Vallejo, California, 28 December 1921. Born of Greek parents, Otis lived his whole life in the black community of Watts. Starting as jazz drummer in 1939, worked with several name bands and recorded with both Illinois Jacquet (1945) and Lester Young (1946). Led own big band from 1945, gradually moving from jazz into r & b and featuring such singers as Little Esther Phillips, Willie Mae (Big Mama) Thornton; also recorded with Dinah Washington, using Ben Webster as guest with his band (1951). Became radio disc-jockey and hosted live r & b revue on weekly TV series (1956–61). Inactive in music in 1960s and late 1970s, including period as preacher in his own church. Successfully spearheaded r & b revivals in US (1969–75, 1984) and helped to relaunch careers of jazz-based singers Louis Jordan, Slim Gaillard, Eddie Vinson in early 1970s. [BP]

Johnny Otis Show Live at Monterey (1970), Epic

Overdubbing This technique was a by-product of the introduction of sound films, where music was only one of the elements along with the dialogue, sound effects, and the possibility of replacing an actor's speaking or singing voice with one more desirable (an example of the latter is Joe Turner's soundtrack appearance in the short film *Low Down Dog*).

Only gradually did the record industry take any interest, although Sidney Bechet's recording of five instruments in turn to make a 'one-man band' disc in 1941 was an early example. After Les Paul followed suit and then invented the multi-track tape machine, the industry never looked back. Even jazz musicians found uses for it, so that while in the early 1950s it was possible to add on an instrument that was originally missing or inaudible (e.g. Eddie Safranski in the Sonny Berman album *Beautiful Jewish Music*), by the early 1960s overdubbing could be a compositional tool (as in Charles Mingus's *Black Saint and the Sinner Lady*).

From there it was but a short step to the late 1960s habit (also known as 'tracking') of recording an ensemble arrangement first and then taping the improvised solos, several times if necessary; likewise, the early 1970s practice of 'layering', which built up a rhythm-section arrangement or a whole band by recording each instrument in turn, so that what was heard as simultaneous was perfected bit by bit. Though these technological facilities undoubtedly have their positive side, they are so far removed from live performance (even of synthesized sounds) that they encouraged the late 1970s swing of the pendulum back to acoustic post-bop played in real-time. [BP]

Owens, Jimmy (James Robert), trumpet, fluegelhorn, composer. b. New York City, 9 December 1943. Began on trumpet at age ten; attended High School of Music and Art, then studied composition with Henry Bryant and trumpet with Donald Byrd. During the 1960s he worked with many leading musicians, including Lionel Hampton, 1963–4; Hank Crawford, 1964–5; Charles Mingus, 1965–6; Herbie Mann, 1965–6; and spent briefer periods with Ellington, Gerry Mulligan, Max Roach and Count Basie. He was one of the original members of the Thad Jones–Mel Lewis orchestra. He toured Europe with the Dizzy Gillespie reunion band, 1968, and since then has done many other European tours with different groups and bands. 1974, he played with radio orchestras in Germany and Holland. Owens's initial influences were Miles Davis, Gillespie and Art Farmer, and he was already a highly polished performer by the mid-1960s, combining something of the sonority of Davis with a superb technique. At the 1970 Newport Jazz Festival celebration of Louis Armstrong's birthday, Owens was the youngest of a select group of trumpet players chosen to play in tribute to Satchmo; the others included Gillespie, Bobby Hackett and Joe Newman. But Owens was very much of the younger generation, and in 1973 was featured soloist on one of the classic jazz-rock albums – Billy Cobham's *Spectrum*. Later in the decade, Owens made his own fusion albums.

Owens is also active as a lecturer, lobbyist and educator. 1972–6, he served on the Jazz-Folk-Ethnic Music Panel of the National Endowment for the Arts; he is one of the founders of the Collective Black Artists, Inc., a non-profit-making, tax-exempt education and performance organization; he has been on the music panel of the New York State Council on the Arts; 1974, he was musical director of the New York Jazz Repertory Company. 1976, he received his Master's degree in education. [IC]

More than 80 with others, including Mann, James Moody, Gillespie, Archie Shepp, Booker Ervin; with Cobham, *Spectrum* (1973), Atlantic; with Billy Harper, *Capra Black* (1973), Strata-East; as leader, *Headin' Home* (1978), A & M/Horizon

Oxley, Tony, drums, percussion, electronics, composer. b. Sheffield, Yorkshire, 15 June 1938. Self-taught on piano from age eight, he did not get his first drum kit until he was 17. 1957–60, in Black Watch military band, he studied drums and theory. 1960–4, he led his own quintet in Sheffield; 1963–7, he collaborated with Derek Bailey in exploring freely improvised (abstract) music. 1966, he moved to London, becoming the house drummer at the Ronnie Scott Club, accompanying many visiting Americans including Sonny Rollins, Bill Evans, Stan Getz, Lee Konitz, Charlie Mariano, Joe Henderson, and continuing in this capacity until the early 1970s. 1968, with Ronnie Scott octet called the Band. Also played with Gordon Beck trio, Alan Skidmore and Mike Pyne trio. By the mid-1960s Oxley had mastered all the arts of conventional jazz drumming, and was already a virtuoso with superb time, and a brilliant technique, but he was losing interest in the accepted musical language of the period. He had resumed his association with Bailey, now also living in London, and was becoming deeply committed to abstract music as both a player and a composer. In 1969, he played on a classic album of the 1960s – John McLaughlin's *Extrapolation* – which was like a summary of small-group playing to date, with pointers to the future; some tracks anticipate the jazz-rock movement of the next decade. The same year, for CBS, he began recording his own severely abstract music with a quintet which included Bailey, Kenny Wheeler, Evan Parker and Jeff Clyne. Paul Rutherford (tmb) was added to make the group a sextet for a second album in 1970. With Bailey and Parker, he formed Incus Records, because it was already clear that major labels would not commit themselves to the austere new music. Oxley also became a member of the London Jazz Composers' Orchestra, formed by Barry Guy, and worked with Howard Riley in his trio and other groups. From 1973 he was organizing tutor at the Barry Summer School (Wales) of a course in Jazz and Improvised Music. 1974, he formed his own group, Angular Apron. He has also worked a great deal in Europe with leading European and American musicians. He has had several composing awards from the Arts Council of Great Britain. He worked with George Gruntz on music for the film *Steppenwolf* (1974). Although committed to abstraction, Oxley has in the 1970s and 1980s occasionally played in a more conventional way when accompanying others. However, his own quintet's concert at the Camden (London) Festival, 1985, was as abstract as ever. Further tours of the UK in 1986 with octet co-led by Didier Levallet, and a quartet with Tony Coe. Because there has been a larger audience for his music on the continent, Oxley has, since the mid-1970s, lived for much of the time in Western and Eastern Europe. He has been influenced by contemporary classical composers, and often uses graphic scores. Other influences are Eric Dolphy, Art Blakey, Elvin Jones, John Coltrane, Bill Evans. [IC]

With McLaughlin, *Extrapolation* (1969), Marmalade-Polydor; Oxley quintet, *The Baptised Traveller* (1969), CBS; *Tony Oxley 4 Compositions for Sextet* (1970), CBS; with LJCO, *Ode* (1972), Incus; *February Papers* (1977), Incus

Ozone, Makoto, piano, composer/arranger. b. Kobe, Japan, 1961. Father, Minoru Ozone, one of Japan's best pianists. Started on organ at age four; took up piano in his teens after hearing Oscar Peterson. 1980, went to Berklee, Boston, studying composing and arranging, and there Gary Burton immediately recognized Ozone's extraordinary qualities: great virtuosity, a born improviser, and his playing already a compendium of the entire jazz piano tradition. 1983, he opened the Kool Jazz Festival with a Carnegie Hall recital; 1984, recorded his first album as leader with Burton (vibes) and Eddie Gomez (bass). By 1985 he was a regular member of the Burton quartet, and also played a duo with the young French keyboard virtuoso Michel Petrucciani, at the Hollywood Bowl for the Playboy Festival. His main recent influences are Burton and classical pianist Vladimir Ashkenazy: Ozone is also studying classical piano playing. [IC]

Makoto Ozone (1984), CBS; with Burton quartet, *Real Life Hits* (1985), ECM

P

Page, Hot Lips (Oran Thaddeus), trumpet, mellophone, vocals. b. Dallas, Texas, 27 January 1908; d. New York City, 5 November 1954. 'You could take Louis Armstrong and put Lips in there and you couldn't tell 'em apart', said Budd Johnson. 'He learned to play every note Louis played on a record, note for note.' In fact, playing in his own style, Hot Lips Page was instantly distinguishable from his idol: his improvisation wilder and less monumental than Armstrong's, his singing more blues-filled and insidious. But the resemblance was close enough to strike Joe Glaser, who first heard Page while he was appearing with Count Basie at the Reno Club, Kansas City, in 1936, riding over the brass, as Louis did, in the final out-choruses. By that time 'The trumpet king of the West', as he was billed, had spent years backing blues singers such as Bessie Smith and Ma Rainey and starring in territory bands, including Walter Page's and Bennie Moten's, and had built a storehouse of confidence, showmanship and technique. Glaser, knowing that Louis Armstrong, his 'number one boy', was suffering with a disturbing patch of lip trouble and might be finished, signed Page to a long contract and when Basie left for Chicago with his new band the trumpeter stayed behind to front Bus Moten's group. For the last 18 years of his career, Lips – a handsome young hepcat, full of charm, talent and a Louis Jordan-esque fondness for rhythm-and-blues – led bands and appeared as a single up and down 52nd Street. But after Armstrong's lip recovered, Glaser rapidly lost sight of his second-string as a priority and Page had more reason to see himself determinedly as an Armstrong alternative. 'I went up to Lips at the Plantation,' recalls Ahmet Ertegun, 'and said "Would you please play 'Satchelmouth Swing'?" He looked at me and laughed and said "No, but I'll play 'Hot Lips' Page's special message to a young ofay!"' Page's career never achieved the status of Armstrong's: he remained a jam session habitué (something Armstrong never did) and often seemed haunted by bad luck (his hit record of 'St James Infirmary' with Artie Shaw came just as Shaw disbanded; a later best-seller with Pearl Bailey, 'Baby it's cold outside' backed with 'The Hucklebuck', launched Bailey but left Page unremembered). It would be rash to lay all the blame at Glaser's office door: Page was less talented than Louis Armstrong, and – relatively speaking – his career was a success, with a string of entertaining, often commercially slanted records to his name. But it is ironic that (as Greg Murphy points out) the first fullscale reissue of Hot Lips Page material on LP was 17 years after his death – the year that Armstrong died. [DF]

Oran 'Hot Lips' Page, vols. 1/2 (1942–53), Foxy

Page, Walter Sylvester, bass. b. Gallatin, Missouri, 9 February 1900; d. New York City, 20 December 1957. He worked with Bennie Moten, on and off from 1918, as well as leading his own Blue Devils (featuring Basie, Rushing and Hot Lips Page among others), 1925–31; that year Bennie Moten made room in his band for Page's young stars – and subsequently Page himself until 1934 – after they got stranded in Kansas City. After Moten died suddenly in 1935, Page came back to work for Basie, four years his junior, rather than vice versa, but he was to form a vital quarter of his new leader's 'All American Rhythm-Section'. 'Oh my goodness!' says Harry Edison. 'The whole band would be shouting and then all of a sudden everyone would drop out for the bridge, and there'd be just the rhythm with Page's bass going up and down.' 'Walter Page you could *hear*', agrees Eddie Durham. 'He didn't have the best ear in the world, but he worked hard. Walter Page invented that walkin', walkin'!' Page was a part of Basie's unbeatable section until 1942, when a dispute temporarily hardened him against Basie once more, but by 1946 he was back for three more years. Then he became a freelance with old friends Hot Lips Page (1949–51), Jimmy Rushing (1951–2) and regularly with Eddie Condon from 1952. He collapsed on the way to a TV Sound of Jazz recording, was rushed to hospital and died shortly after.

Jo Jones sets Walter Page in perspective. 'The greatest band I ever heard in my life was Walter Page's Blue Devils. Musically Page was the father of Basie, Rushing, Buster Smith – and me too, because without him I wouldn't have known how to play drums. For two years Page told me how to phrase. And aside from that he told me a few of the moral responsibilities that go into making up an artist's life.' Walter Page – or 'Big One' as he was known to the Kansas City jazz fraternity – was not only the last of the great pre-Blanton bassists, but a figure of authority. [DF]

Count Basie, *Swinging the Blues* (1937–9), Affinity

Palmer, Roy, trombone. b. New Orleans, 1892; d. Chicago, 22 December 1963. He worked all around his home town before making the pioneer jump to Chicago in 1917 to play with Sugar Johnny's headlining band in Chicago. All through the next decade he remained a busy freelance in the city, playing with Johnny Dodds, Hughie Swift, Jelly Roll Morton, Doc Watson and W. C. Handy, but left full-time music in the 1930s and by 1940 had opened a laundry. He is said to have influenced the young Georg Brunis: later (says John Chilton) he taught Albert Wynn and Preston Jackson, and he was still teaching trumpet, trombone and music theory in Chicago in the 1950s. [DF]

Parenti, Tony (Anthony), clarinet, saxes. b. New Orleans, 6 August 1900; d. New York, 17 April 1972. He was a child prodigy who by the age of 12 was playing in ragtime trios and soon after (Frank Driggs tells us) turned down offers from Paul Whiteman and the Original Dixieland Jazz Band because he was too young to go on the road. But he did work for 'Papa' Jack Laine's band, as well as on board riverboats (including the *Majestic* on Lake Pontchartrain and the *Capitol* for Streckfus, where young pianist Jess Stacy was an early partner). By the late 1920s Parenti was busy in New York, 'shackin' with my old friend Ray Bauduc' (another New Orleans man), and doing all the best work: playing for Ben Pollack in Benny Goodman's frequent absences, appearing on radio and records with leaders such as Fred Rich, and providing the jazz injection for society bands like Meyer Davis's. 'Those jobs accounted for us making a lot of money in those days', he recalled later. 'They wanted a man who could play a couple of choruses on the up-tempo things!' Throughout the 1930s Parenti, whose abilities in many respects rivalled Irving Fazola's, worked as staffman for CBS, and for the Radio City Symphony Orchestra, and from 1939 served alongside Muggsy Spanier in Ted Lewis's highly-paid show. After 1945 he became better known as a jazzman again, identifying strongly with the New Orleans revival and often recording with a mix of Chicago and New Orleans stars from Wild Bill Davison to Pops Foster. He was also regularly to be seen in New York at Dixieland strongholds such as Jimmy Ryan's, the Metropole and Central Plaza, spent four years in Florida with Preacher Rollo's Five Saints, and – perhaps surprisingly – subbed briefly for George Lewis in 1959. Parenti's heart was always in New Orleans jazz: 'Progressive jazz is really extemporaneous tricks: it lacks feeling and expression, and gives me a cold reaction.' In the 1960s, following Wilbur de Paris, Parenti led the house band at Ryan's for six years. [DF]

Tony Parenti's Talking Records (1958), Folkways

Parham, Tiny (Hartzell Strathdene), piano, organ, arranger, composer. b. Winnipeg, Manitoba, 25 February 1900; d. Wisconsin, 4 April 1943. One of the most quietly talented of the Chicago-based pianist-arrangers, Parham – called 'Tiny' because of his enormous girth – was touring the Pantages theatre circuit by 1925 and later directed music for a variety of clubs and theatres (including the Apollo Theater, Chicago, where he led a high-powered showband featuring high-note trumpeter Reuben Reeves). Parham's recording career was busy, too: he accompanied blues singers and led his own bands which – recording for RCA Victor, 1928–30 – maintained a constantly high standard (such titles as 'Dixieland Doings', 'Blue Island Blues' and 'Black Cat Moan' reveal an ingenuity comparable to early work from Ellington and Morton). A thoroughly schooled player – he arranged for King Oliver, Earl Hines and to order for club floorshows – Parham led bands all through the 1930s but never graduated to New York and by the end of the decade was playing the organ in theatres, cinemas and ice-rinks. [DF]

Tiny Parham, vols. 1/2 (1928–30), Collectors Classics

Parker, Charlie (Charles Christopher) ('Bird'), alto sax, composer (and tenor). b. Kansas City, 29 August 1920; d. 12 March 1955 in the home of jazz benefactor Baroness Pannonica de Koenigswater. One of the most striking performers in the entire history of jazz and one of the most influential, Parker became aware of the strong local music scene in Kansas City at an early age, even before he took up first the baritone horn and then the alto while in high school. Dropping out of school at 14, he concentrated all his efforts on mastering his instrument and watching locally-based innovators such as Lester Young and Count Basie. Learned much from employment by altoist/bandleader Tommy Douglas (1936–7) and Buster Smith (1937–8). In between, a few months out of town with the band of George E. Lee (1937) and subsequent trips to Chicago and New York contributed to his development, the seal of which was set by his tenure with Jay McShann (1938, 1940–2).

Played briefly in several more big bands including Earl Hines's (1942–3) and Billy Eckstine's (1944) before Dizzy Gillespie, his colleague under both Hines and Eckstine, helped to establish bebop on the small-group scene of New York's 52nd Street. Worked there with Gillespie (1944–5), Ben Webster (1944) and his own group (1945). While on the West Coast, Parker was featured with Jazz at the Philharmonic (1946) and Howard McGhee (1946–7), the latter period broken by six months recuperating from the previous ten years of heroin addiction. His return to New York in 1947 found him at the height of his powers, and leading a highly compatible quintet with Miles Davis, pianist Duke Jordan, bassist Tommy Potter and Max Roach. However, the popularity of his first

Charlie Parker with Tommy Potter (*left*)

recordings with strings, issued in 1950, led to public appearances with similar backing and a corresponding lack of challenge in even the rhythm-sections he employed. Parker spent the remaining years of his life gigging with local pick-up groups in different parts of the USA or touring as guest soloist in the unlikely company of the Woody Herman (1951) and Stan Kenton (1954) bands. His recording projects included a promising series with Latin-American accompaniment and an unpromising date with woodwinds and voices, both sabotaged by lack of adequate preparation. Approximately annual reunions with Gillespie and other key associates from the 1940s showed him still capable of superlative playing, but his re-addiction to narcotics, plus a huge intake of alcohol, eventually ended his growing musical frustration.

Although never excusing or recommending his own habits to others, Parker none the less set an example in this sphere as much as in his music, and the number of performers of his generation who lost several productive years, or in some cases their lives, is quite staggeringly high.

What made Parker truly charismatic, however, was his musical genius: the seemingly miraculous way in which he solved problems that were preoccupying his chief colleagues, and then proceeded to set up a whole new series of hurdles which he cleared with one hand tied behind his back, as it were. Parker's impact on saxophonists, from the time of his first records with McShann (1941) and his second arrival in New York (1942), may be likened to that of Art Tatum's on pianists. It is hardly coincidental that he was in fact influenced by Tatum, for he managed to give the same impression that executing any musical idea, however difficult, was childishly easy: and this facility bestowed the same, perhaps child-like, ability to conceive fantastic ideas which other, more rational beings would have dismissed as technically impossible. The net result of this was to take the fascinating rules of advanced European harmony (already being tapped by saxists Coleman Hawkins and Don Byas) and to deploy them at lightning speed, yet with all the linear grace associated with Lester Young. The effectiveness of the conception was made just that bit more authoritative by Parker's tone, which matched the daring of his structures and, once the listener has become accustomed to it, is as irresistible as a knife cutting through butter. His communicative powers surpassed the efforts of Hawkins, Byas and Young, who chiefly impressed other saxists – Parker impressed and influenced players of every instrument.

The new technical hurdles that he was largely responsible for introducing were above all rhythmic. As in the case of the harmonic extensions inherent in bebop, other leading thinkers such as Gillespie and Thelonious Monk were active in studying and perfecting the new rhythmic variations; but it was Bird who played them as to the manner born, and indeed he never had played any other way, to judge from his earliest recordings. For this reason, his most important collaborators were always drummers, whether the most flexible swing drummers such as Sid Catlett, or the best Latin percussionists of the day, or his ideal partner Max Roach. Miles Davis once illustrated Parker's freedom in this area by describing his (literally) off-beat entries: 'Every time that would happen, Max Roach used to scream at Duke Jordan not to follow Bird, but to stay where he was. Then, eventually it came round as Bird had planned and we were together again.' The full extent of his rhythmic virtuosity became the norm only in the 'free jazz' of the 1960s and the 'fusion music' of the 1970s (or at least in some instances of both): most of the 1970s revival of bebop fell far short in this respect.

One by-product of the bop revival, however, was the rediscovery of Parker's written lines and of their superiority to most other tunes of his era. The mere fact of executing themes such as 'Confirmation', 'Scrapple from the Apple', 'Cheryl' and 'Quasimodo' is a constant challenge to try and produce improvisation of equivalent quality to that of their composer. (One way of sidestepping the challenge was demonstrated in the early 1970s by the group Supersax, who transcribed and orchestrated Parker improvisations and played them as compositions, a treatment they are well able to withstand.) In many other ways, Bird is still very much a contemporary figure – either as the supreme example of the art of the soloist and therefore to be emulated, or as a superman whose contribution could only ever be equalled by drawing on the somewhat different strengths of the collective approach. No one individual apart from Louis Armstrong has cast such a long shadow over succeeding generations of jazz musicians. [BP]

The Savoy Years, vol. 2 (1945–7), Savoy; *Charlie Parker on Dial, vol. 1* (1946), Spotlite; *Charlie Parker on Dial, vols. 4/6* (1947), Spotlite; *Bird on Verve, vol. 1* (1948–9), Verve; *Bird at the Roost, vol. 1* (1948–9), Savoy; *One Night in Birdland* (1950), CBS; *Summit Meeting in Birdland* (1951–53), CBS; *Bird on Verve, vol. 7* (1952–3), Verve; *Jazz at Massey Hall* (1953), Debut/OJC

See Russell, Ross, *Bird Lives!* (Charter House, 1972; Quartet, 1973); Priestley, Brian, *Charlie Parker* (Spellmount, Hippocrene, 1984); Giddins, Gary, *Celebrating Bird* (Morrow, 1986)

Parker, Evan Shaw, soprano and tenor sax. b. Bristol, Somerset, 5 April 1944. Mother, an amateur pianist, introduced him to the delights of Fats Waller. Studied saxophone with James Knott, 1958–62. 1962–4, studied botany at Birmingham University, but dropped out to concentrate on music. Rapidly became interested in free (abstract) improvisation, playing occasional gigs with Howard Riley in the Birmingham area. 1966, came to London and worked with the Spontaneous Music Ensemble where he met Derek Bailey, his friend and long-time associate. 1968–72, Parker and Bailey co-led the Music Improvisation Company which also included electronics, percussion and voice; 1969, Parker joined Chris McGregor's sextet which later (augmented) became the Brotherhood of Breath; 1969–72, he was also with Tony Oxley sextet; from 1970, played with Alex von Schlippenbach's trio and quartet, from 1971 with Schlippenbach's Globe Unity Orchestra; 1979, with Derek Bailey's group Company; 1980, worked with Kenny Wheeler's quintet; from 1980, led his own trio and quartet with Barry Guy, Paul Lytton (and trombonist George Lewis). Since 1975, Parker has also played many solo (unaccompanied) concerts. He has a wide international reputation and has toured all over the world since the early 1970s, with Globe Unity and other groups, and also as a solo artist.

He is a master saxophonist and a radical experimentalist who has pioneered the use of harmonics, unusual note-groupings, and the production of new timbres by tonguing and by splitting up single notes into their component parts. By means of circular breathing he can produce an unbroken column of air for quite long periods of time and his solo concerts during the 1980s have often consisted of unbroken rhythmic and melodic patterns which undergo gradual and constant variations. The austerity of Parker's music makes it hard to realize that his original influence was Paul Desmond, while his current favourites are John Coltrane and Steve Lacy. In 1985 he wrote, 'I work in a form of free improvisation in which the theme and variations style has been replaced by spontaneous development.' Since 1970, Parker and Bailey have owned and run their own record label, Incus Records. [IC]

With Bailey/Han Bennink, *The Topography of the Lungs* (1970), Incus; with Schlippenbach/Paul Lovens, *Pakistani Pomade* (1972), FMP; with Paul Lytton, *Collective Calls (Urban) (Two Microphones)* (1972); with Bailey, *The London Concert* (1975); solo, *Six of One* (1982), all Incus

Parker, Johnny, piano, leader. b. Beckenham, Kent, 6 November 1929. He worked early on in bands led by Mick Mulligan and Humphrey Lyttelton (he played the boogie piano on Lyttelton's 'Bad Penny Blues') and very early on revealed a natural fine talent for ragtime and boogie-woogie. Later in the 1960s he worked for leaders as diverse as Alexis Korner and Monty Sunshine, as well as with Kenny Ball's band, and led his own small group – usually around the Islington area of north London – featuring Wally Fawkes (clt) and Chez Chesterman (tpt) among others. In the 1970s and 1980s he worked solo (delivering a highly entertaining one-man show) in clubs and piano bars, backed the vocal group Sweet Substitute for cabaret, organized his own bands and collaborated regularly with singer Beryl Bryden as well as recording regularly and broadcasting. [DF]

Johnny Parker's Boogie Woogie (1979), Dawn Club

Parlan, Horace Louis, piano. b. Pittsburgh, Pennsylvania, 19 January 1931. Worked in the r & b field and with Sonny Stitt, then moved to New York and almost immediately joined Charles Mingus (1957–9). Played in quartet with Booker Ervin (1960–1) and recorded frequently both as leader and sideman in the early 1960s. Was regular pianist with the Lockjaw Davis–Johnny Griffin quintet (1962) and with Roland Kirk (1963–6). Jazz work became scarce from the late 1960s and in 1973 Parlan took up residence in Copenhagen, where he has performed steadily and made a number of albums, including two duo sets with Archie Shepp.

Parlan's style derives musical strength from physical disability, arising from polio which partially crippled his right hand in childhood. By combining pungent left-hand chords with stark but highly rhythmic phrases in the right, he creates a very positive contribution to any situation in which he finds himself. Perhaps because of restricted mobility, he avoids blues clichés yet manages to sound more basically blues-influenced than many other pianists of his generation. [BP]

No Blues (1975), Steeplechase

Parnell, Jack, drums, leader. b. London, 6 August 1923. Nephew of the showbusiness tycoon Val Parnell. There were few points in his early career where his natural charm, charisma and talent failed to mark him out as a leader: very early on he co-led the Vic Lewis–Jack Parnell Jazzmen, featuring Billy Riddick and Ronnie Chamberlain, and as Ted Heath's drummer for seven years after the war he became a central feature of Heath's show, driving the orchestra from behind his kit and often singing, with fondly-remembered personality and natural style. Parnell is one of Britain's best but most often underrated mainstream drummers – primarily because he spent nearly 20 years as a highly successful bandleader, leading the staff orchestra for ATV and providing the music for countless peak-viewing television shows. In the late 1970s it was good to see him touring with a 'Best of British Jazz' package (featuring Kenny Baker and Betty Smith), drumming again in clubs and concerts and, in the mid-1980s, accompanying a close friend, Ruby Braff, at London's Pizza Express. [DF]

Big Band Show (1976), EMI

Pasadena Roof Orchestra Formed by bassist/bakery owner John Arthey in the mid-1960s, the PRO began as an authentic re-creation of a 1920s dance band but later – after enthusiastic publicity in the *Melody Maker* and elsewhere – widened their appeal, brought in cornermen such as singer John 'Pazz' Parry, clarinettist/saxophonist Mac White and trumpeters Clive Baker, Enrico Tomasso and Mike Henry and gradually built up a colossal European following which made them, with George Melly, the most commercially successful jazz-based act of the 1970s. Never really a jazz band in the full sense of the term, the PRO concentrated more on showbizzy re-creations of period material, but their staff arrangers included jazz pianist Keith Nichols, occasional solos added to the fun, and a great deal of their recorded work is still highly acceptable to ears attuned to 1920s hot dance music. [DF]

The Show Must Go On (1977), Metronome

Pascoal, Hermeto, piano, electric piano, flutes, guitar, saxes, composer. b. Lagôa da Canoa, Brazil, 22 June 1936. All his family were musical and he started in groups with his father and brother, but had no formal training. He worked with several small groups in Brazil, then, with Airto Moreira, formed the Quarteto Novo, which became very popular. He ventured out of Brazil in the early 1970s, going to New York City where he recorded with Miles Davis, and spending some time in California, but soon returned to his own country. Pascoal is the father-figure and inspiration of a whole generation of Brazilian musicians who, during the 1970s and 1980s, have worked in the USA and Europe making a considerable contribution to jazz – Moreira, Flora Purim, Milton Nascimento, Hugo Fatteruso, Dom Um Romao and others. Music flows out of Pascoal unquenchably and without apparent effort. He plays all his instruments with total virtuosity, he composes and arranges for all sizes of ensemble, from very big bands to small groups, and his orchestral writing is much admired by Gil Evans. Since the later 1970s he has led a sextet of young Brazilian musicians, and although his group rehearses almost every day, they still lack the time to perform many of the new pieces he is constantly producing. 1984–5, he toured Europe extensively with his group, making a big impact at festivals in Antibes (France), Pori (Finland), North Sea (Holland), and Camden (London). His musicians double on different instruments, so the sextet offers a very broad palette, and Pascoal makes full use of it. His concerts are notable both for very much writing and very much improvisation; and his music explores elements from jazz and rock, European art music, street music, ethnic and Brazilian folk music. The whole group exults in rhythm, performing with passionate energy, handling the most complex passages with consummate ease, and exuding the sheer joy of music-making. [IC]

With Miles Davis, Antonio Carlos Jobim, Duke Pearson, Airto Moreira and Flora Purim; *Hermeto* (1972), Muse; *Slaves Mass* (1977), Warner Bros; *Hermeto Pascoal Live at Montreux Jazz Festival* (1979), Atlantic; *Zabumbê – Bum – Á* (1979), Warner Bros; *Cérebro Magnético* (1980), Atlantic; *Hermeto Pascoal & Grupo* (1982), Som Dagente

Pass, Joe (Joseph Anthony Passalaqua), guitar. b. New Brunswick, New Jersey, 13 January 1929. After working with name bands including Tony Pastor before leaving high school, toured nationally with Charlie Barnet (*c.* 1947). Navy service was followed by a decade divided between serving time in Las Vegas backing groups and serving time for narcotics offences. Made first small-group recording with fellow patients at Synanon Foundation (1962). On discharge, began working regularly as soloist with West Coast-based groups and cutting albums under own name. Toured with George Shearing (1965–7) and Benny Goodman (1973), and did frequent studio work. Recommendation of Oscar Peterson led to international touring under Peterson's manager Norman Granz (from 1972), often with Peterson and/or Ella Fitzgerald; albums with both, also with Duke Ellington, Count Basie, Dizzy Gillespie, Milt Jackson etc.

A superbly competent guitarist, Pass has summarized all of the bop-based practitioners of the last 45 years (only the 'free' players and the prolific rock/fusion school have left him untouched). In addition to his abilities as a stylistic consolidator, he has quietly expanded the instrument's flexibility in a jazz context by his frequent work without bass and drums backing; as a result he has learned to simulate a bass-line counterpointing his simultaneous chords and melodic lines, and to swing as if he were an entire group. In this respect, and in most others, there are few living guitarists who can surpass Joe. [BP]

Intercontinental (1970), Memoir; *Genius* (1974), Pablo

Pastor, Tony (Antonio Pestritto), tenor sax, vocals. b. Middletown, Connecticut, 1907; d. New London, Connecticut, 31 October 1969. He was raised in New Haven, where a childhood friend was Artie Shaw, and played early on – often alongside Shaw – in John Cavallaro's band, Irving Aaronson's Commanders and with Austin Wylie. He led his own band for three years, 1931–4, but made his first real impact as the one-and-only tenor saxophonist with Shaw's band from 1936. 'Pastor's kidding around and screwy faces help to bring the crowds up to the bandstand!' reported George Simon. 'He's a vastly underrated hot tenor man with a splendid tone and a simple but pleasantly rhythmic style!' By 1940 Pastor was confident enough to start up his own band again and was soon resident at the Hotel Lincoln, where he paid to have radio lines installed: the reward was 18 broadcasts a week. By 1941, Max Kaminsky was leading Pastor's trumpet section (until he went back to Shaw), guitarist Al Avola was fashioning a stylish book of arrangements and a succession of singers including Eugenie Baird, Virginia Maxey (Mrs Matt Dennis), Rosemary Clooney with her singing sisters and Pastor himself were helping to produce a smooth and enjoyable show. By the mid-1940s Pastor was enlivening his library further with jazz arrangements by Budd Johnson and Walter Gil Fuller, and – with his natural gift for showmanship and near-comedy vocals – easily survived the demise of big bands until 1959, by which time a string of excellent big-band albums told his story. That year he formed a small group featuring his sons Guy, John and Tony Jnr. to play Las Vegas, and worked with them until 1968. [DF]

Pure Magic (undated, 1940s), Blue Heaven

Pastorius, Jaco (John Francis), bass guitar, composer, b. Norristown, Pennsylvania, 1 December 1951. Father a drummer and singer. 1958, family moved to Fort Lauderdale, Florida. His father was his model, but he had no lessons. First wanted to play drums, but at 13 he injured his right arm playing football, and it failed to heal properly. He also played piano, sax and guitar, and he learned by listening to local Florida musicians including legendary sax/trumpet player Ira Sullivan. He also accompanied visiting stars such as Wayne Cochran and the C. C. Riders, the Temptations, the Supremes and Nancy Wilson, on piano and bass. While still in his teens he began writing arrangements for a local big band and Ira Sullivan's Baker's Dozen. At 17 he had an operation to put his arm right; a year later it was strong enough to enable him to play the bass properly and from then on that became his main instrument. He got first-hand experience of Caribbean music by working as a show musician on tourist cruise ships off the southern tip of Florida and going for week-long trips to Mexico, Jamaica, Haiti and the Bahamas. In Florida he played country and western music, soul and reggae. There were no cliques of local young jazz musicians, so no peer group pressure to prejudice him against other types of music, and Pastorius attributes his later musical diversity to this freedom. He liked the Beatles, the Rolling Stones and other rock/pop groups as well as Max Roach. By the early 1970s he was playing with Ira Sullivan and also with the house band at Fort Lauderdale's Bachelors III Club. He also met and played with some visiting jazz musicians including Paul Bley and Pat Metheny.

In mid-1975, Blood Sweat and Tears were booked into the Bachelors III Club, and their drummer, Bobby Colomby, immediately arranged for Pastorius to record an album in New York. A few months later, with Colomby as producer and with the aid of Herbie Hancock, Mike Gibbs, Don Alias, Wayne Shorter and Hubert Laws, the album was made. By April 1976, Pastorius was a member of Weather Report, and by May he had also played on Pat Metheny's first album for ECM. Pastorius had arrived and he had done so fully formed, as a mature and original stylist and a composer/arranger with his own individual approach. He has always considered himself as much a composer as a bass player, and this is his great strength: he thinks, writes and plays orchestrally, which is why his music is so complete. As Eberhard Weber was already doing in Europe, Pastorius redefined the whole conception and role of the electric bass. He gave it the tonal characteristics and articulation of both an amplified acoustic guitar and an amplified double-bass producing an immensely resonant, lyrical sound. He has said, 'It sings . . . you have to know exactly where to touch the strings, exactly how much pressure to apply. You have to learn to *feel* it. And then it just sings.' He also uses the harmonics with brilliant imagination for both rhythmic and melodic colour. Like Weber, he gave the bass a new melodic role, often playing romantic themes or thematic fragments with delicate subtlety and expressiveness. But he also developed the rhythmic and linear aspects of the bass to new levels of complexity and ferocity, playing long rhythmic lines with perfect articulation at astonishing speeds.

He was with Weather Report through one of the group's most creative periods (1976–82) and his qualities contributed greatly to that success; his playing and persona were an inspiration to Joe Zawinul who wrote some of his finest pieces to feature Pastorius. After leaving Weather Report he pursued a solo career, recording and playing festivals with a big band. In this context, too, his writing shows marked individuality in the way it draws on elements of his musical heritage — jazz, blues, rhythm-and-blues, the classics, reggae riffs, and the Caribbean sound of the steel drum, which seems to be a staple ingredient of his music. [IC]

With Ira Sullivan and Paul Bley; *Jaco Pastorius* (1975), Epic; *Word of Mouth* (1981), Warner Bros; *Invitation* (1983), Warner Bros; with Weather Report, *Black Market* (1976); *Heavy Weather* (1977); *8:30* (1979); *Night Passage* (1980); *Weather Report* (1982), all CBS; with Pat Metheny, *Bright Size Life* (1976), ECM

Patton, 'Big' John, organ (and piano). b. Kansas City, Missouri, 12 July 1935. Played with Lloyd Price touring band (1954–9), then settled in New York. Switching to organ, worked with Grant Green *et al.* and made record debut with Lou Donaldson (1962). Records under own name and leading own trio from 1963, including at different times Clifford Jarvis and James 'Blood' Ulmer. Also capable of sitting in with Sun Ra's musicians in 1960s, Patton was initially inspired by Hampton Hawes, Horace Silver and Wynton Kelly, and managed to bring some of their linear invention to the frequently overblown art of jazz organ. Based since 1970s in East Orange, New Jersey, made new recording in 1983. [BP]

Blue John (1963), Blue Note

Paul, Emmanuel, tenor sax, banjo, vocals. b. New Orleans, 2 February 1904. He was trained in an orchestra organized by a New Orleans church foundation and played banjo regularly throughout the 1920s. During the depression –

when saxophones were starting to eclipse the clarinet as a fashionable instrument – he concentrated on tenor and began playing it regularly from 1940 on with the Eureka Brass Band. In 1942 he joined Kid Thomas Valentine's band and 40 years on was still partnering Valentine regularly at Preservation Hall, playing with huge vigour, unremitting swing and an approach falling somewhere between Benny Waters and Bud Freeman. [DF]

Paul, Les (Lester Polfus), guitar. b. Waukesha, Wisconsin, 9 June 1916. Did radio studio work in Chicago (1932–42) and toured with Fred Waring, recording under own name from 1940. Settled in California and formed own trio (1944), also making guest appearances on records by Red Callender, Jazz at the Philharmonic etc., often under pseudonym 'Paul Leslie'. Began (1948) recording best-selling discs as 'one-man band', thanks to primitive overdubbing techniques (with wife Mary Ford as vocalist); to further this success, created first multi-track tape machine. As a result of his pop hits Paul was lost to the jazz world, but he was a very capable Reinhardt-influenced improviser. In 1986 he was producing albums for Joe Bushkin. [BP]

Jazz at the Philharmonic, *Early Years, 1944–6*, Verve

Pavageau, Alcide 'Slow Drag', bass. b. New Orleans, 7 March 1888; d. 19 January 1969. Principally remembered as George Lewis's long-term double-bassist, Pavageau (he earned his nickname winning slow-drag competitions in dance halls in his youth) began as a street-corner guitarist and took up the bass when he was 40. 'I picked up a barrel on Orleans Street, between Robertson and Villere,' he told researcher Tom Bethell, 'and I made me a bass, a little bitty three-string bass, and that's how I learned myself to play.' He joined Lewis from Herb Morand's band (which played at the Silver Star Café, New Orleans) in 1944 and recorded with him that year, including a classic version of 'Burgundy Street Blues'. A beautifully-dressed French Creole, who smoked a big cigar and spoke in thick, almost incomprehensible patois, Pavageau was one of New Orleans' most relaxed and powerful slap-bassists and he worked hard for Lewis for 25 years (he was also officially known, on New Orleans street parades, as Grand Marshal of the Second Line). Afflicted with deafness by his mid-seventies, 'Slow Drag' was mugged on his way home from work and died soon after: his spectacular funeral was a tourist attraction. [DF]

Any with George Lewis

Payne, Cecil McKenzie, baritone sax (and alto). b. Brooklyn, New York, 14 December 1922. After army service, worked on alto with J. J. Johnson and baritone with Roy Eldridge band (both 1946). Then joined Dizzy Gillespie (1946–9), followed by Tadd Dameron tentet (1949). Worked with James Moody (1951), Illinois Jacquet (1952–4), then appeared on many jazz albums while also working at day job. Associated with Randy Weston (from 1956), appeared in play *The Connection* after original cast went to Europe (1961). Toured full-time with Machito (1963–6), Woody Herman (1966–8), Count Basie (1969–71). From mid-1970s performed regularly in duo with his vocalist sister Cavril Payne. Appeared at Berlin festival 'Battle of the Big Horns' (1985), taking place of honour among other baritonists; although less of an individualist than Serge Chaloff and largely unknown to the public, Payne was nevertheless one of the pioneers in adapting the instrument to bebop and post-bebop. [BP]

Bright Moments (1979), Spotlite

Payne, Sonny (Percival), drums. b. New York City, 4 May 1926; d. 29 January 1979. No relation to Sylvester 'Vess' Payne, drummer with the mid-1940s Cootie Williams band, Sonny was the son of Wild Bill Davis's drummer Chris Columbus (b. 17 June 1902). Worked with Hot Lips Page, Earl Bostic, Tiny Grimes (1947–9), also with Grimes bassist Lucille Dixon (1948). With Erskine Hawkins big band (1950–3), then long stay with Count Basie (late 1954–64). Rejoined Basie, 1965–6 and 1973–4, and toured with Illinois Jacquet (1976); in between and afterwards with Harry James band, with which he was working at time of death. A flashy and somewhat overexcitable performer: it was said that Basie's guitarist and timekeeper Freddie Green used to prod Payne with a drumstick when he rushed the tempo. Nevertheless, he possessed all the other qualities of a big-band drummer, and his showmanship was an asset to the Basie band during one of its vintage periods. [BP]

Count Basie, *The Atomic Mr Basie* (1957), Roulette/PRT

Peacock, Gary, bass, composer. b. Barley, Idaho, 12 May 1935. He studied piano while at school, and played piano in a US army band in Germany during the later 1950s. He stayed on in Germany after demobilization, now playing bass and working with Hans Koller, Attila Zoller and also Tony Scott and Bud Shank. 1958, he went to California working with leading musicians including Paul Horn, Terry Gibbs and Shorty Rogers. 1962, he moved to New York, becoming involved in more adventurous music and working with Paul Bley, Jimmy Giuffre, Roland Kirk, George Russell and Bill Evans. He also became associated with the avant-garde and worked in Europe with Albert Ayler and Don Cherry in 1964. He also worked with Roswell Rudd, Steve Lacy and Don Ellis. In the later 1960s he was briefly with Miles Davis, then with Bley again, after which he was inactive in music until the mid-1970s, when he once more resumed his association with Bley and also did some teaching. He began recording for ECM, leading his own trios and with trios led by Keith Jarrett.

Peacock is a technically brilliant bass player, and a master of both conventional structures and of semi- or total abstraction. His ECM recordings show this mastery and also reproduce his wonderfully resonant sound. [IC]

With Ellis, Clare Fischer, Bill Evans, Tony Williams and others; with Albert Ayler, *Spiritual Unity* (1964), ESP; *Paul Bley with Gary Peacock* (1970); Peacock/Jarrett/DeJohnette, *Tales of Another* (1977); Peacock/Art Lande (piano)/Eliot Zigmund (dms), *Shift in the Wind* (1980); with Keith Jarrett trio, *Standards, vol. 1* (1983); *Changes* (1984), all ECM

Pearce, Dick (Richard), trumpet, fluegelhorn. b. London, 19 April 1951. Father a singer, cousin a pianist and arranger. Private trumpet lessons at 13, but taught himself harmony. 1968–71, in a military band. 1971–2, with Graham Collier. 1973–80, played with the current younger generation of London musicians including Chris Biscoe, Dave Defries and Brian Abrahams. Later worked with Mike Westbrook, Keith Tippett, Dudu Pukwana, Gil Evans and others. 1981, joined Ronnie Scott's group. Leads his own occasional band. Favourites, Miles Davis, Art Farmer, Woody Shaw, Kenny Wheeler, Don Cherry. [IC]

With Graham Collier, *Portraits* (1972), Saydisc; Mike Westbrook, *The Cortege* (1982), Original

Pearson, Duke (Columbus Calvin Jnr.), piano, composer. b. Atlanta, Georgia, 17 August 1932; d. 4 August 1980. Gigging in home town before and after army service, Pearson had his tunes 'Tribute to Brownie' and 'Jeannine' recorded by Cannonball Adderley quintet. Moved to New York in 1959 and joined Donald Byrd, then Art Farmer – Benny Golson Jazztet (1960). 1963–70, assistant producer with Blue Note label, for which most of his own albums were made. Also in the late 1960s ran part-time big band in New York including musicians such as Randy Brecker and Chick Corea. Frequently employed as accompanist to singers (Nancy Wilson, Dakota Staton, Carmen McRae and Joe Williams), Pearson modelled himself on the work of Hank Jones and had an appropriately unflamboyant but lyrical solo style. [BP]

Introducing Duke Pearson's Big Band (1967), Blue Note

Pecora, Santo (Santo Joseph Pecoraro), trombone. b. New Orleans, 31 March 1902; d. 29 May 1984. Early in his 1920s career he worked with the New Orleans Rhythm Kings and by the 1930s was enough of an all-rounder to begin a period working in big bands including Will Osborne's, Ben Pollack's and Charlie Barnet's, as well as Dixieland groups such as Sharkey Bonano's (1936) and (after a move to the West Coast in 1938) in Hollywood film studios until 1942. For the last 40 years of his life he led bands of his own in New Orleans (and occasionally Chicago), often teaming with Bonano at Bourbon Street clubs including the Famous Door. [DF]

Recorded in New Orleans, vol. 2 (1956), Good Time Jazz

Pedersen, Niels-Henning Ørsted, see ØRSTED PEDERSEN, NIELS-HENNING.

Pepper, Art(hur Edward), alto and tenor sax, clarinet. b. Gardena, California, 1 September 1925; d. 15 June 1982. After working at age 17 on Central Avenue (the Los Angeles answer to 52nd Street) with otherwise all-black groups such as the Lee Young sextet (1943), joined Benny Carter and Stan Kenton bands briefly. During army service (1944–6), was heard jamming in London and then, after freelancing in Los Angeles, rejoined Kenton (1947–52). Recording under own name from 1952, his career interrupted by repeated imprisonment for drug offences (1953–4, 1954–6, 1961–4, 1965–6). Finally, after further work including a few months in 1968 with Buddy Rich band, was rehabilitated at Synanon Foundation (1969–71) and began slow comeback. Cut first new album (1975), played with Don Ellis band (1976), appeared at Newport festival (1977) and toured Japan for first time and Europe (1978), all to great acclaim. During remainder of his life, was much recorded and also found wider fame through his brutally honest book and film.

Pepper's playing, during his first popularity in the late 1940s, absorbed the influences of Benny Carter and Charlie Parker into a fluent and individual style. Especially in his own albums, the most affecting performances were often the slow ballads that showed an awareness of the melodic economy of Lester Young, which was also reflected in his 1950s work on tenor and clarinet. A period in the mid-1960s, not preserved on disc, was apparently dominated by Pepper's emulation of John Coltrane which, by the time Pepper was recording again, had been abandoned but had redoubled the intensity of his earlier work. [BP]

Meets the Rhythm Section (1957); *Smack Up!* (1960); *Living Legend* (1975), all Boplicity

See Pepper, Art and Laurie, *Straight Life* (Schirmer, 1979)

Film: *Notes from a Jazz Survivor* (dir. Don McGlynn, 1981)

Art Pepper

Perez, Manuel, cornet. b. New Orleans, 1879; d. *c.* 1946. The organizer of the Imperial Brass Band, Perez was a trained player – 'a military man who played on a Sousa kick', says Danny Barker – who read music fluently and expected his band to do the same: very few players in New Orleans of the period had his power, control and exceptional high register. 'He could hit those high notes', says Barker, in probably his only doubtful theory, '[because] he had eaten two pots of gumbo before he left! Most of them fellows who played the parades were full of whiskey!' Barney Bigard remembers Perez well, at a time when the trumpeter made one of his rare trips out of New Orleans to work with Charlie Elgar's orchestra in Milwaukee: 'He taught me a great deal. We would run down studies and reading and then Manuel was showing me how to transpose. He wasn't one of those fly trumpet players that you have nowadays. He was very tasty – a thorough musician.' Perez was New Orleans' trumpet equivalent to clarinettist Lorenzo Tio: one of the last of the town's old-style 'legitimate' teachers to work on into young jazz's rough and ready self-creation. In the 1930s he returned to his second profession of cigar-maker (a popular New Orleans trade): he was incapacitated in the early 1940s by a series of strokes. [DF]

Perkins, Carl, piano. b. Indianapolis, Indiana, 16 August 1928; d. 17 March 1958. Toured with Tiny Bradshaw and Big Jay McNeely, and settled on the West Coast in 1949. Member of the Oscar Moore trio (1953–4, 1955) and of the early Max Roach–Clifford Brown quintet (1954). Played with the hard-bop-inspired quintet led by bassist Curtis Counce from its formation in 1956 and, as well as these affiliations, was heard on records with Chet Baker, Jim Hall and Art Pepper. His career was not blessed with fame and was beset by drug addiction, but his 24-bar tune 'Grooveyard', cut at his last session in 1958 (led by Harold Land), has become a standard.

Like Horace Parlan, Perkins was a childhood victim of polio, which restricted his left-hand movement, but he made up for it with playing that resembled a heavier version of Hampton Hawes. Pianist Lionel Grigson wrote of Perkins: 'He rarely used double-tempo runs, preferring familiar phrases which he nevertheless inflected in an astonishingly horn- or guitar-like manner by the use of grace-notes, turns, doubling in octaves or fourths.' In this respect, he resembled the early blues pianists even more than Hawes or Horace Silver did, and was a considerable influence on Les McCann, Bobby Timmons etc. [BP]

Introducing Carl Perkins (1955), Boplicity

Persson, Aake, trombone. b. Hassleholm, Sweden, 25 February 1932; d. 4 February 1975. Acclaimed at age 18, began touring with bassist Simon Brehm (1951), then freelance gigging and recording, including with visiting US musicians such as Clifford Brown, Quincy Jones, Stan Getz. Then toured with Jones's European-based band (1959–60), followed by studio work first in Stockholm and Berlin, until his accidental death. Founder member of Clarke–Boland band (1961), featured on their records and subsequent live appearances. Persson was a brilliant improviser in a style which may be said to be inspired by J. J. Johnson but with a melodic grace and fire all his own. [BP]

Kenny Clarke/Francy Boland, *Jazz Is Universal* (1961), Atlantic

Persson, Bent, trumpet, cornet, leader. The star of fine Swedish bands such as Maggie's Blue Five, Kustbandet and Bent's Blue Rhythm Band, he came to prominence in Europe as the re-creator of *Louis Armstrong's Fifty Hot Choruses*, a written set of transcribed Armstrong solos published by Melrose Brothers in 1927, from long-lost cylinder recordings. Without reference to the recorded versions, the task of interpreting the old transcriptions as nearly as possible as Armstrong would have played them was far from easy, but Persson (over a four-volume set recorded from 1974 on) accomplished the job with what sounds like uncanny accuracy: the set forms a mine of previously unheard Armstrong diamonds. After this success Persson formed the Weatherbird Jazzband, collaborated with another fine re-creator, reedman Tomas Örnberg, for a variety of projects and in the 1980s was recording with Maxine Sullivan as easily as he continued his authentic re-creations of Armstrong, Beiderbecke and others. [DF]

Louis Armstrong's Fifty Hot Choruses for Cornet as re-created by Bent Persson, vol. 1 (1979), Kenneth

Peterson, Hannibal Marvin Charles, trumpet, composer. b. Smithville, Texas, 11 November 1948. Mother a pianist, sister Pat Peterson a singer. He studied harmony and theory 1962–5; played in local bands; 1967–9, studied at North Texas State. Moved to New York in 1970, working with Roy Haynes, Gil Evans, Elvin Jones, Pharoah Sanders, Archie Shepp, Rahsaan Roland Kirk and others. He formed his own Sunrise Orchestra in 1974. Peterson continued leading his own bands and working as a soloist throughout the 1970s and into the 1980s. He also continued his association with Gil Evans up to the mid-1980s, touring many times in Europe, Japan, and the USA and playing on some of Evans's most vital albums. 1976, Peterson played the Berlin festival with a group that included George Adams, and the concert was recorded by MPS. In the 1980s he toured in the UK with the Don Weller–Bryan Spring quartet. Peterson is a player of great dynamism with an excellent range, and his concept seems to embrace the entire jazz tradition from New Orleans to Coltrane. His influences include Gil Evans, Leadbelly, B. B. King, Coltrane, Ellington, Janáček, Sun Ra and Cecil Taylor. [IC]

With Richard Davis, Elvin Jones, Eric Kloss; with Gil Evans, *Svengali* (1973), Atlantic; *There Comes a Time* (1975), RCA; *Gil Evans Live at New York Public Theater* (1980), Japanese Trio (double); as leader, *Children of the Fire* (1975) (plus strings), Sunrise; *Hannibal in Berlin* (1976), MPS; *The Angels of Atlanta* (1980), Enja

Peterson, Oscar Emmanuel, piano, b. Montreal, 15 August 1925. Like many pianists, Peterson did not find fame first as a sideman and then branch out as a leader but, after a brief Canadian apprenticeship, was introduced to an unsuspecting US audience (1949) in his own right. It is therefore by his own groups that he is always judged and, despite differences of emphasis at various stages of his career, he has been remarkably consistent; the trios he led until 1959 invariably included a guitarist along with bassist Ray Brown, who remained for several more years when the third member was a drummer (first Ed Thigpen, then Louis Hayes). Since the 1970s Peterson does not maintain a regular group but appears variously in trio (often with Niels-Henning Ørsted Pedersen and Martin Drew), duo and unaccompanied formats, while continuing to record more prolifically than almost anyone else in jazz.

Inspired initially by the piano work of Nat 'King' Cole, he subsequently revealed the influence of Art Tatum (after the latter's death) and sometimes of Hampton Hawes or Bill Evans, while remaining instantly identifiable. The multiplicity of notes Peterson produces in even a relatively subdued context is undeniably exciting, as is the ease with which he works out harmonic variations. But one of the most impressive aspects of his work is an unfailing commitment to swinging which, although often achieved at the cost of repetition in the melodic line, is continually compelling. This is the quality that makes Peterson outstanding as an accompanist, at least to musicians stylistically rooted in the swing era, and the albums below should be compared with his backing work on Jazz at the Philharmonic concerts or on studio sessions with everyone from Louis Armstrong to Lester Young. [BP]

In Concert (1952–6), Verve; *Exclusively For My Friends* (1964–8), BASF; *The Trio* (1975), Pablo

See Palmer, Richard, *Oscar Peterson* (Spellmount/Hippocrene, 1984)

Petit, Buddy, cornet. b. White Castle, Louisiana, *c.* 1897; d. New Orleans, 4 July 1931. 'A dozen books should have been written about Buddy Petit', says Danny Barker. 'The way people rave over Dempsey, Joe Louis or Ben Hogan – *that's* how great Petit was when he played! The kids would come up and say "Can I shake your hand Mr Petit?" On parades they'd be ten deep around Buddy as he walked along blowing!' In New Orleans, Petit – small, with Indian features and a pronounced stammer – was Armstrong's nearest rival ('a hellion', said Louis), played funerals alongside him and set a fast pace with his superb control and warm, mid-register approach: 'Outside of Louis,' says George Lewis, 'Buddy was better liked and better known around New Orleans than any other trumpet player: the first one of all the men I've played with.' By 1916, Petit was co-leading a band with Jimmie Noone and worked constantly up and down the Gulf Coast playing one-nighters and daytime functions until he could no longer meet the demand: recalls Barney Bigard, 'Buddy was so popular that he'd take four or five jobs a night.' Petit always took a deposit, too, but spoiled his reputation by putting in other bands under his name: finally prospective bookers fought shy, as they could never be sure whether the band that turned up for the date would be his or someone else's. In 1917 Petit answered Jelly Roll Morton's call to work with him on the West Coast but the partnership foundered: Morton ridiculed his new employee's country-boy ways and eating habits (after he once tried to cook up red beans and rice at work) and the trumpeter returned threatening to kill Morton if their paths crossed again: the following year he refused an offer to go to Chicago to join Bill Johnson's band and King Oliver got the job instead. Petit continued working round the Coast all through the 1920s and later in the decade was regularly on the riverboats. He died at about 34 from the effects of over-eating and drinking at a New Orleans Independence Day picnic: Louis Armstrong was a pallbearer at the funeral. [DF]

Petrucciani, Michel, piano. b. Montpelier, France, 28 December 1962. Born with a rare bone disease which prevents growth to adult size, Petrucciani nevertheless began his professional career at age 15 by playing for Kenny Clarke and guesting with Clark Terry (1978). After visit to New York, toured France in duo with Lee Konitz (1980) then moved to US (1982). Visited Europe as member of Charles Lloyd quartet (1982), solo appearance at Kool Festival (1984) and frequent performances in duo and with own trio. A highly gifted performer still largely under the sway of Keith Jarrett, Petrucciani has a lyrical style and abundant technique which promise much for the future. [BP]

Live at the Village Vanguard (1984), Concord

Pettiford, Oscar, bass, cello. b. Okmulgee, Oklahoma, 30 September 1922; d. Copenhagen,

Oscar Peterson

8 September 1960. Began on piano and took up bass at 14, touring with family band led by father Harry 'Doc' Pettiford. (Of Oscar's many siblings, both trumpeter Ira and trombonist Alonzo worked in 1943 with Jay McShann.) Oscar joined Charlie Barnet for a few months (1942), then worked in New York with Roy Eldridge (1943), recording several key sessions with Coleman Hawkins (1943–4), Earl Hines (1944), Ben Webster (1944) etc. Co-led quintet with Dizzy Gillespie (early 1944) and led own small group, recording with Gillespie and own big band (both early 1945). Went to West Coast to work with Hawkins (1945), joined Duke Ellington (1945–8). After leading own trio in Los Angeles (1948), was with Woody Herman (1949). Then toured with Louie Bellson – Charlie Shavers (1950) followed by own groups, including residency at Café Bohemia (1955) and his occasional big band (1956–7); record dates under

own name and with Thelonious Monk (1955–6) and Art Blakey (1957). Went to Europe with 'Jazz from Carnegie Hall' package (1958), settled in Copenhagen and worked with Stan Getz (1959) and Bud Powell (1960) until his sudden death caused by 'polio-like virus'.

Pettiford became in 1950 the first musician successfully to adapt the pizzicato bass style to the cello, using it frequently on records and live. More strikingly, the exceptionally speedy acceptance from his elders during his first years in New York show that he was viewed, correctly, as a reincarnation of the recently deceased Jimmy Blanton. His characteristic melodic phrasing is preserved not only in countless recorded solos but in his written lines such as 'Bohemia After Dark', 'Trictatism' (*sic*) and 'Laverne Walk', the last two in particular being still viewed as test pieces by younger players. One such younger player, Buell Neidlinger, who compared Pettiford at first hand with all the top bassists of the 1950s, called him 'The greatest bass player who ever lived. The man was a monster – he had the most beautiful intonation and time.' [BP]

Bohemia After Dark (1955), Affinity; *Oscar Pettiford Orchestra in Hi Fi* (1956), Jasmine; *Blue Brothers* (1960), Black Lion

Phillips, Flip (Joseph Edward), tenor sax. b. Brooklyn, New York, 26 February 1915. Worked in Brooklyn on alto and clarinet (1934–9), then on clarinet with Frankie Newton (1940–1). On tenor from 1942, with Benny Goodman (1942), Wingy Manone (1943), Red Norvo (1943) and Woody Herman (1944–6). Toured with Jazz at the Philharmonic annually for next ten years, then moved to Florida and played with Herman and JATP colleague Bill Harris. European tour with Goodman (1959), followed by 15 years doing day job in Florida and leading own quartet. After occasional playing trips in early 1970s, moved to New York (1975) and worked more regularly, touring Europe in 1982.

Phillips came to the fore as a tenor star when all the other contenders idolized Lester Young, and he stood out from the crowd through his interest in Coleman Hawkins and especially Ben Webster. Always intensely rhythmic, he took the Southwestern-style shouting and honking common to both Webster and Young, and in the late 1940s threatened to outdo Illinois Jacquet as a JATP crowd-pleaser. The solid virtues of his playing were more evident, however, in less extrovert surroundings, and in particular his post-1975 comeback has been far more convincing than that of many others of his generation. [BP]

A Melody from the Sky (1944–5), Doctor Jazz; *Flipenstein* (1981), Progressive

Phillips, Sid, clarinet, piano, baritone sax, arranger, leader. b. London, June 1902; d. Chertsey, Surrey, 26 May 1973. He played early on in the Melodians, a band featuring his three brothers Harry (tpt), Ralph (bass) and Woolf (tmb), and later became baritone-saxophonist cornerman of Ambrose's orchestra (to which he contributed first-rate scores such as 'Cotton Pickers' Congregation', an intriguing mix of instrumental and choral passages, 'Escapada' and 'Bwangi': all as good in their way as the writing of Spike Hughes or Ray Noble). Phillips's first band of his own was organized for a Mayfair residency and included Max Goldberg (tpt), Max Abrams (dms), Bert Barnes, a longtime colleague (piano) and Ralph Phillips (bass); for the next 30 or more years he was to lead a succession of immaculately arranged, often hot Dixieland bands which at their best are as good as anything Bob Crosby ever did. Later sidemen who worked for Phillips included two fine trumpeters: the neglected Joe McIntyre (an Irishman whose best work is preserved on Phillips's records: he died early) and Kenny Ball. 'Sid's reputation as a hard-driving taskmaster, a perfectionist and to some almost a martinet was well-known,' says Ball, 'but this supposed hard man was so hard he not only employed and paid me, he sent me for reading lessons every week and paid for them as well.' Apart from being a fine arranger, Phillips composed *Symphonie Russe*, a full-length work which in 1946 was broadcast by the BBC Symphony Orchestra, conducted by Adrian Boult. His career continued unabated until the 1960s when his easy-to-like music was heard less often. Phillips's son Simon is a highly-rated session drummer: his nephew John Altman is Britain's most prolific writer of TV commercials, a popular-music authority and highly gifted reedman. [DF]

With orchestra and quintet, *Stardust* (undated, *c.* 1960s), Halcyon

Piano Rolls This early form of passive home-entertainment happens to offer the first mechanical reproduction of jazz musicians. Gramophone records only caught up with jazz from 1917 onwards (and not in any depth until the mid-1920s) but throughout the 1910s and 1920s performances were being cut by players such as James P. Johnson, Eubie Blake, Luckey Roberts, Fats Waller, Jelly Roll Morton and Earl Hines – in each case, piano rolls constituted their earliest solo recordings, while Scott Joplin's were the only records he made.

The barrel-organ-like process of cutting rolls provided a less faithful reproduction of the pianist's individual sound than disc recording (and sometimes they were overdubbed, as it were, with additional 'orchestration'), yet they not only entertained but educated other up-and-coming musicians like Duke Ellington. And, since the 1950s, they have been played back and re-recorded on albums, notably on the Biograph label, adding considerably to our overall picture of the period concerned. [BP]

Picard, John Francis, trombone, piano. b. Wood Green, London, 17 May 1934. He came to prominence with Humphrey Lyttelton's band of the mid-1950s where his pawky-toned, shouting declamations attracted huge attention and strongly recalled J. C. Higginbotham. But Picard was quick to broaden his approach and by the end of 1950s (after classic recordings with Lyttelton) was working not only with Bruce Turner's Jump Band but – just as notably – with Tony Coe's staggeringly brilliant contemporary-style quintet. Semi-professional in later years (he became a successful partner in an estate agency), Picard chose his musical surroundings with care and kept a watchful eye on the progress of modern jazz: later musical commitments he became involved in included a 1970s septet (featuring Colin Smith, Don Weller and Tony Coe) which played Mingus-style jazz as happily as Ellington; playing lead trombone with Stan Greig's London Jazz Band (for whom he produced stormy avant-garde-tinged scores such as 'Hooley dooley downhill lady', 'Meet Mr Rabbit' and 'Golden Apples of the Sun') and regular work in a hard-swinging rock and roll-based band, Rocket 88, featuring Alexis Korner, Don Weller, Colin Smith and sometimes Rolling Stones drummer Charlie Watts. From 1985 Picard – a thoughtful arresting musician – was a cornerman in Watts's big band. Meanwhile his son, tenor saxist Simon, had been in several groups including Stinky Winkles with Veryan Weston. [DF]

Humphrey Lyttelton, *Swing Out* (1956–7), Philips

Pick-up group (or **band**) means one not having a permanent existence, but put together for a specific appearance or recording. At worst it may sound like a bunch of strolling players (as Eddie Condon used to call them) picked up off the street, or at least out of the phone book. But if several of the members have worked together under other circumstances, it may have the benefits of a regular gigging group together with an added spontaneity. [BP]

Picou, Alphonse Floristan, clarinet, composer. b. New Orleans, 19 October 1878; d. 4 February 1961. The 'little big man' of New Orleans clarinet is most famous for his patenting of a piccolo descant written into a stock military band arrangement of 'High Society': Picou borrowed the theme, played it on his E-flat clarinet and the solo for ever after became a set piece for jazz clarinettists (and anyone else brave enough to try it). It was only one discovery in a 70-year career which by 1894 had begun in a bewildering variety of saloon and parade bands. He played for dance halls, functions, funerals, picnics, elections, birthdays, high days, holidays and Mardi Gras (where his speciality was a kazoo stuck down an E-flat clarinet which he fingered as he sang) in bands led by Buddy Bolden, Dave Peyton, Bunk Johnson, Manuel Perez and Wooden Joe Nicholas, as well as Oscar 'Papa' Celestin's Tuxedo Band, and the Olympia band led by Freddie Keppard . . . and often kept going for three days at a time. 'Sometimes my clarinet seemed to weigh a thousand pounds,' he remembered later, 'but those were happy days! Talk about wild and woolly! There were 2000 registered girls and must have been 10,000 unregistered. And all crazy about clarinet blowers!' Picou kept up the pace until 1932, then returned to his first trade of tinsmith at which he became prosperous: he acquired property, including several back-of-town bars. By 1940 he was playing again, and took part in Heywood Broun's first-ever recordings for the American jazz revival by Kid Rena's band on Delta Records. In 1944 he began a long residency at the Club Pig Pen, worked and recorded with Papa Celestin in the late 1940s (recreating his famous solo) and in the 1950s played again for Alexis' Tuxedo band, led his own group at the Paddock Club and – as the decade wore on – began to confine himself to guest appearances with the Eureka band. He died a prosperous property owner: nearly 2,500 people attended his funeral. [DF]

Pierce, Billie, piano, vocals. b. Marianna, Florida, 8 June 1907; d. New Orleans, 29 September 1974. She toured as a successful pianist/accompanist in the 1920s before she settled in New Orleans in 1930. In the 1960s she achieved international fame working in duo with her husband Dee Dee Pierce (Joseph de Lacrois, trumpet, vocals. b. New Orleans, 18 February 1904; d. 23 November 1973): Dee Dee was a prominent local trumpeter who worked with the Tuxedo band and others at venues such as Luthjen's and as a bricklayer in his spare time until he lost his sight. However, a string of albums for Atlantic, Riverside and others all through the 1960s assured the duo renewed success and a round of work at college and campus jazz festivals, regular appearances at Preservation Hall, New Orleans, and even tours of the Far East which they carried on until Dee Dee's death. [DF]

Jazz at Preservation Hall, vol. 2 (1962), Atlantic

Pierce, Dee Dee, see PIERCE, BILLIE.

Pierce, Nat(haniel), piano, arranger. b. Somerville, Massachusetts, 16 July 1925. After studying at New England Conservatory, worked with name bands in Boston and on the road. Then ran own part-time big band in Boston featuring Charlie Mariano (1949–51); also freelance writing for Woody Herman and Count Basie (1951–2). Toured as pianist/arranger with Herman band (1951–5). Based in New York thereafter, playing with such as Lester Young, Ruby Braff, Emmett

Berry, Pee Wee Russell. Also led occasional all-star band including Buck Clayton, Paul Quinichette, Gus Johnson (1957–9); arranging for the 'Sound of Jazz' TV special (1957), Ella Fitzgerald, Quincy Jones band (1959), Coleman Hawkins–Pee Wee Russell album (1961). Re-joined Herman (1961–6), followed by freelance work in Los Angeles for Carmen McRae, Louie Bellson, Bill Berry big band. Co-led Los Angeles-based big band Juggernaut, with drummer Frankie Capp, on and off during 1970s; also brief playing appearance in film *New York, New York* (1977). Made European tours as member of all-star packages the Countsmen (1980, 1983) and Louis Armstrong tribute (1984).

Pierce's writing has been predominantly associated with big bands, and has managed to retain the simplicity and drive of the best swing-era scores with a minimum of harmonic updating. In his long association with Herman, he was also the chief organizer of the band and even his piano playing had a functional, cheer-leading aspect. For this reason, he was adept at deputizing for pianist-bandleaders in times of illness such as Claude Thornhill and Stan Kenton (1972), and the originator of Nat's approach to ensemble playing, Count Basie, chose Nat as his deputy several times from the late 1950s and increasingly during his final years. [BP]

Big Band at the Savoy Ballroom (1957), RCA; Capp/Pierce Juggernaut, *Live at the Century Plaza* (1978), Concord

Pike, Dave (David Samuel), vibes, marimba, composer. b. Detroit, Michigan, 23 March 1938. Began on drums at age eight; self-taught on vibes. Moved to Los Angeles in 1954, playing with Elmo Hope, Carl Perkins, Curtis Counce, James Clay, Paul Bley, and leading his own quartets. Moved to New York, 1960; with Herbie Mann, 1961–4, touring Japan with him. Pike performed at the 1968 Berlin Jazz Festival, and stayed on in West Germany for five years, leading his quartet of German musicians, including guitarist Volker Kriegel and, for one tour, bassist Eberhard Weber. The Dave Pike Set toured throughout Europe and played major festivals. In the early 1970s, the group twice made extensive tours in South America for the Goethe Institute. After the second South American tour, at the end of 1973, Pike returned to the USA and settled in California. [IC]

With Mann, Bley and others; Dave Pike Set, *Noisy Silence, Gentle Noise* (1969); *The Four Reasons* (1969); *Infra Red* (1969); *Live at the Philharmonic* (1970); *Album* (1971); *Salamão* (1973), all MPS

Pine, Courtney, tenor and soprano sax, bass clarinet, composer. b. London, 1964. Began on clarinet; took up tenor sax, playing with reggae and funk bands while still at school. Inspired by Sonny Rollins and John Coltrane, he became interested in jazz. In the early 1980s he took part in some of John Stevens's weekly workshops, then graduated to occasional appearances with Stevens's Freebop band. By the mid-1980s Pine was teaching at his own workshops and had formed an organization called the Abibi Jazz Arts to help black musicians to take more interest in jazz. As an outcome of this project, he formed the Jazz Warriors, an all-black big band which includes the exceptionally gifted young flautist Philip Bent, and which has developed into a dynamic unit fusing elements from the jazz tradition with elements from West Indian music – calypso, reggae and ska. Pine also formed the World's First Saxophone Posse, a saxophone quartet, and from the mid-1980s has led his own quartet and quintet, both of which include the brilliantly promising young pianist Julian Joseph.

1986, Pine toured the UK with the George Russell orchestra, played with Art Blakey's Jazz Messengers at the Camden Jazz Festival and worked for several nights with Elvin Jones at the Ronnie Scott Club. He has established himself as a focal point and inspiration for young black musicians in London, and he is the first British-born black musician to set his imprint on the UK jazz scene. Other influences include Lester Young, Sidney Bechet and Albert Ayler. When he has fully absorbed all his influences and found his own identity, he may well become a major force in the UK and Europe; he is already a passionate and technically superb player. [IC]

Journey to the Urge Within (1986), Island

Pizzarelli, Bucky (John), guitar. b. Paterson, New Jersey, 9 January 1926. He was self-taught and very early on in his career tried out new ideas with Joe Mooney's small modern jazz group. He found no difficulty, however, in entering the demanding world of studio work in 1954, when he joined NBC, and over the next 12 years (during which he often toured with Vaughn Monroe) played regularly in studios moving to ABC around 1966 as a staffman for Bobby Rosengarden on the Dick Cavett Show. In the 1970s (rather as with Rosengarden himself) the guitarist's reputation as a jazzman started to blossom: he toured with Benny Goodman, formed a duo with George Barnes and all through the decade was regularly to be found at the centre of musical projects, recordings and concerts. Pizzarelli, who like George Van Eps plays a seven-string guitar, reveals the same all-music approach as his inspiration, and has worked with all the greatest latterday classicists from Bob Wilber (in the first days of the quintet Soprano Summit) to Bobby Hackett. In the 1980s Pizzarelli's son, John Jnr., has also become well known as a fine guitarist. [DF]

Love Songs (undated), Stash

Pletcher, Stew (Stewart F.), trumpet, mellophone. b. 1907; d. USA, 29 November 1978. A fine swing trumpeter prominent in the later 1930s, who worked with Red Norvo's band: his relaxed, Hackett-style playing is heard to advantage on Norvo sides such as 'Remember' (one of George T. Simon's nominations for the best record of 1937). After Norvo (with whom he also worked in an interesting drummerless, pianoless group at the Famous Door, featuring Dave Barbour on guitar), Pletcher worked with Tony Pastor, Billy Bissett and – between breaks from professional music making – with Jack Teagarden in 1945, Nappy Lamare (1949) and Teagarden again (1955).

Stew Pletcher's son, cornettist Tom, is one of the most interesting latterday revivalists with a strong affinity for Bix Beiderbecke. He works in the Beiderbecke-celebrating semi-professional Sons of Bix, which every year plays America's Beiderbecke convention and in 1978 toured the UK with Keith Nichols, John R. T. Davies, Nevil Skrimshire *et al.* Guitarist Skrimshire (a discerning Bixophile) praised Pletcher's 'beautifully controlled approach, mellifluous tone and intelligent repertoire'. Records by the Sons bear out this judgement, and since then he has toured internationally as a respected solo performer. [DF]

Stew Pletcher, *Red Norvo and his All Stars* (1933–8), Epic; Tom Pletcher, with the Sons of Bix, *Ostrich Walk* (1978), Jazzology

Pletcher, Tom, see PLETCHER, STEW.

Polcer, Ed (Edward Joseph), cornet, vibes. b. Paterson, New Jersey, 10 February 1937. A mellow mid-period cornettist who works the musical furrows of Hackett, Windhurst and Butterfield without copying any of them, he played early in his career with Stan Rubin's Tigertown Five at Princeton College while he was studying engineering. After graduation he was active on the jazz scene at Jimmy Ryan's and played at Carnegie Hall, but remained semi-pro, served his time in the US air force from 1960, then in 1963 toured Europe with Mezz Mezzrow. From then on he became a familiar sound to New York clubland, at Ryan's, subbing for Max Kaminsky, and worked for a time as house cornettist for Eddie Condon (although Condon was actually on stage for only about a score of the dates). In 1973, the year that Condon died, Polcer joined Benny Goodman, replacing Bobby Hackett (at Hackett's instigation), and when, two years later, Eddie Condon's club reopened at a new location, Polcer became house-cornettist, co-owner (with Red Balaban, in whose band he had worked from 1969), and, at last, a full-time musician. From then on his mellifluous, well-stirred trumpet style was heard more regularly in New York, and on fine, often out-of-the-way records by Jane Harvey, Peter Dean and the re-formed Eddie Condon house band. In the 1980s he visited Britain twice with his ensemble (featuring Keith Ingham and Kenny Davern), and in 1985 – the year of his second visit – was determinedly searching for new premises to accommodate Condon's historic 'Sign of the Porkchop'. [DF]

Red Balaban, *A Night at the New Eddie Condon's* (1975), Classic Jazz

Pollack, Ben, drums, leader. b. Chicago, 22 June 1903; d. Palm Springs, California, 7 June 1971. A fast-talking, kindly, but deeply ambitious man, he had already worked with such commercially successful bands as the New Orleans Rhythm Kings before forming his own in 1926. A musicianly Dixieland drummer ('one of the first to hit all four beats in a measure' said Benny Goodman), he possessed a fine ear for musical talent and saw much of it in the young white soon-to-be stars who lit up the music scene of the late 1920s. By 1928, at the Little Club, New York, Pollack's band was, as at most times in his career, a storehouse of young talent, featuring Benny Goodman, Jimmy McPartland, Glenn Miller and, soon after, Jack Teagarden. Although Pollack was never basically a tyrant, he soon found he had rebellious young tigers by the tail: his young protégés (often with Goodman, six years his junior, as their ringleader) laughed at Pollack's 'old-fashioned' commercial eye for presentation and plummy singing attempts, played practical jokes, took record dates without him and stood up to his views on and off the stand. Animosity built up and finally exploded over an apparently tiny but probably highly significant issue: 'Pollack said something to the effect that he didn't want anybody with dirty white shoes playing in his band', recalls Goodman. 'Jimmy turned in his notice and I followed.' Pollack survived the crisis (his records from the period, such as 'Bashful Baby', featuring white-hot Goodman, are wonderful) and by 1934 was leading another band of young stars, including Yank Lawson, Matty Matlock, Eddie Miller and an old ally, Gil Rodin: this time, however, Pollack made a more serious error of judgement. A new singer, Doris Robbins, who also happened to be Pollack's girlfriend, became his band's featured and favoured artist: 'She and Pollack used to sing moist-eyed duets that made the band cringe', Lawson told John Chilton. Pollack's reaction to the inevitable walk-out that followed was aggrieved and deeply angry, and he became angrier still at his protégés' rapid success without him under Bob Crosby's nominal leadership: fuel was added to the blaze as he saw another of his old employees, Benny Goodman, achieve commercial success that Pollack wanted but could only dream of. In 1936, Pollack's latest discovery, Harry James, left unceremoniously – to join Goodman. Over the next two years Pollack's fury boiled over. He sued Goodman, Bob Crosby, Paramount Pictures, Victor Records and Camel Cigarettes for $5,000,000 in estimated lost band earnings, a desperately angry move that died in the courts: another failure. For much of the 1940s, after a spell as MD for Chico Marx, Pollack ran a successful agency and record company (perhaps he saw it as a safer commercial option), but by the 1950s was bandleading again, on Sunset Strip in Los Angeles: he also made a (presumably) tight-lipped appearance as himself in the film *The Benny Goodman Story* (1956). By now most of the old rivalries had been filed away, and Pollack was once again successful in his own right: in 1964 his Pick-a-Rib Boys at the Disneyland Dixieland Festival attracted more than 20,000 people. But, in Richard M. Sudhalter's words, 'Pollack never overcame the feeling of bewilderment: never stopped asking what he should have done wrong that he shouldn't have received the rewards due to the Father of Swing.' Weighed down by a developing heart condition, Pollack eventually hanged himself in his Palm Springs bathroom. [DF]

And his Orchestra (1926–31), Sunbeam

Polo, Danny, clarinet, saxes. b. Toluca, Illinois, 22 December 1901; d. Chicago, 11 July 1949. Son of a clarinettist, he worked in a boys' duo with pianist Claude Thornhill, in Chicago with Elmer Schoebel and Merritt Brunies (at Friars Inn) and then all over with top American band leaders such as Ben Bernie, Joe Venuti and Jean Goldkette (he recorded with Bix Beiderbecke and Frankie Trumbauer under Goldkette's baton in 1927). That year Polo sailed to Europe with Dave Tough in George Carhart's New Yorkers (they made records for Tri-Ergon), toured Europe, formed a band in Paris for dancer Maurice Loupiau and ended up in London in 1929. The following year he joined Ambrose (who had just signed a new Decca contract with a strong jazz slant to it) and for most of the next nine years was a featured soloist with Britain's best orchestra of the period: records with Ambrose and with Polo's own groups including the Swing Stars (featuring Tommy McQuater, Eddie Macauley and Dick Ball) and the Embassy Rhythm Eight show him off to fine advantage. When at last he resettled in the USA, Polo was unforgotten. He recorded with Coleman Hawkins in 1940, doubled on tenor with Joe Sullivan's Café Society Orchestra ('a dry utilitarian style' says Charles Fox) and worked with Jack Teagarden's band, 1940–2: his marvellous playing can be heard on the soundtrack of Bing Crosby's film with Teagarden, *Birth of the Blues* (1941). For his last seven years Polo rejoined his old friend Claude Thornhill (replacing Irving Fazola) then led bands for himself, but was back with Thornhill by July 1949 when he collapsed and died within two days. [DF]

Ambrose, *Champagne Cocktail* (1935–9), Decca

Polyrhythm means the use of different rhythms simultaneously, and it is far more prevalent in jazz than the average listener (or even player) would readily admit. It covers not only the repetition of explicit patterns which interlock with one another (as in Afro-Latin and traditional African music) but the continual hinting at such patterns in jazz, even in unaccompanied jazz solos.

In most ensemble jazz the polyrhythmic element is fairly pronounced, although not explicit. For instance, the interplay between a single soloist and an apparently straightforward rhythm-section will be filled with all kinds of metrical juggling, including different accents from different members of the rhythm-section. But what transpires in an ensemble improvisation such as a traditional New Orleans band is considerably more complex, as a graph showing the accentuation patterns of all the instruments would demonstrate. Perhaps this is why many listeners choose to miss some of the details and concentrate on the underlying pulse as if they were dancing to it; but even dancers introduce cross-rhythms with different parts of the body.

The polyrhythmic sound within the jazz rhythm-section was already implicit in the New Orleans style, where the solid 4/4 beat of each of the rhythm instruments was sometimes supplemented by ragtime figures from the piano or similar double-tempo drum figures, usually on the wood-blocks. But its proliferation can be said to date from the late 1930s Basie band which, alongside the supple but single-minded bass and guitar, included the pianist's and the drummer's reactions to, and complications of, polyrhythms implied by the soloists. These developments were, of course, taken further in bebop and, yet again, in free jazz. If, in some respects, the average fusion or Latin-jazz rhythm-section seems more easily comprehended, it is still far looser and less regimented than the way 'authentic' Afro-Latin music is organized, and also far more interactive in a jazz sense than is granted by detractors of these developments. [BP]

Polytonality is the sound of different tonal areas (in other words, key-signatures) being used at once. This happens relatively rarely in arranged jazz and, apart from a few passages of Charles Mingus, examples worth remembering are even rarer. Bitonality, implying two simultaneous keys, has been more common in improvisation when the soloist departs temporarily from the tonal centre being used by the rest of the band; since this happens on a random basis, George Russell's term 'pantonality' is more accurate, but has not caught on. But whether arranged or improvised, polytonality is only ever used for brief moments and only makes an impact by contrast with the predominantly tonal nature of jazz. [BP]

Pomeroy, Herb, composer, trumpet, educator. b. Gloucester, Massachusetts, 15 April 1930. Studied theory, composition, piano and trumpet at Schillinger House (Boston) which later became the Berklee School of Music. He had extensive experience with jazz groups in the 1950s, working with Charlie Parker, Lionel Hampton, Stan Kenton and Charlie Mariano, among others. He joined the staff of the Berklee School in 1955, and continued as instructor there through succeeding decades into the mid-1980s. He also taught at the Lenox School of Jazz, 1959–60. He took time off from Berklee in 1962, in order to work for the US State Department in Malaysia, directing the Radio Malaya Orchestra. Pomeroy has also continued to lead his own bands, to host a jazz series on TV, and to teach at various summer schools. He has also composed for the Boston Ballet Company, the National Jazz Ensemble, and other organizations. [IC]

Ponty, Jean-Luc, acoustic and electric violins, violectra (baritone violin), composer, keyboards. b. Avranches, Normandy, 29 September 1942. Father a violin teacher, mother a piano teacher. Began studying violin at five, and at 13 left regular school to practise six hours a day to become a concert violinist. Studied at Conservatoire National Supérieur de Musique in Paris, and after two years gained the highest award for violin. Then spent two years with Lamoureux Symphony Orchestra. 1961–4, with Jef Gilson jazz group. After a big success at Antibes Jazz Festival, 1964, he committed himself totally to jazz, freelancing all over Europe. 1967, at John Lewis's invitation, he participated in the violin workshop at the Monterey Jazz Festival, USA, making another big impact. 1969, went to the USA, recording and working with Frank Zappa and the George Duke trio. 1970–2, back in France, he worked with his own group throughout Europe. 1973, he emigrated to the USA, working with Zappa and the Mothers of Invention. 1974, joined John McLaughlin's Mahavishnu Orchestra. From 1975, led his own groups. Early inspirations were first Stephane Grappelli, then Stuff Smith, but he also names Miles Davis, Clifford Brown, Parker, Rollins, Coltrane, Monk, Bill Evans and Ornette Coleman among his favourite musicians. In the early 1960s Stuff Smith said of Ponty, 'He is a killer! He plays on violin like Coltrane does on sax', and by establishing the instrument as a force in contemporary jazz, Ponty paved the way for others such as Jerry Goodman, Zbigniew Seifert and Didier Lockwood.

To be audible in a jazz context he had to be amplified from the very beginning, but from 1969 on, after working with Wolfgang Dauner and George Duke, he began to go deeply into the use of electronics. Ponty has said: 'The amplification and the weird sounds I got helped me . . . get away from the classical sound and classical aesthetics and forget what the teachers had been teaching me.' Yet his residual classicism is a stamp of his identity, because a strain of European romantic lyricism colours the sound of his groups. [IC]

With Mahavishnu Orchestra, *Visions of the Emerald Beyond* (1974), CBS; under his own name, *Upon the Wings of Music* (1974); *Aurora* (1975); *Imaginary Voyage* (1976); *Enigmatic Ocean* (1977), all Atlantic

Portal, Michel, clarinet, sax. b. Bayonne, France, 27 November 1935. Studied clarinet at the Paris Conservatoire. A powerful post-Coltrane player active in all areas of contemporary jazz. He played and recorded with John Surman's trio, 1970; 1976–82, he worked with Albert Mangelsdorff in quartet and quintet formations. He has also led his own groups. Influences include Mingus, Dolphy and Stockhausen. [IC]

On French labels under his own name; Portal/Surman, *Alors* (1970), Musica

Poston, Joe (Joseph), alto sax, clarinet, vocals. b. Alexandria, Louisiana, *c.* 1895; d. Illinois, May 1942. He was a graduate of Fate Marable's riverboat bands as well as Doc Cooke's Dreamland Orchestra and is well remembered as the alto-saxophonist with Jimmie Noone's Apex Club Orchestra which set a pace in Chicago, 1926–8, and featured the young Earl Hines. 'With Poston's lead carrying the melody,' says critic Martin Williams, 'Noone would improvise complex interweaving counter-themes [and] beneath this Hines provided not only harmony but sometimes a third counter-melody as well.' Classic recordings such as 'Apex Blues', 'Sweet Lorraine' and 'I know that you know' show Poston at his best. After leaving Noone he returned to Cooke briefly before illness ended his career in his late forties. [DF]

Jimmie Noone and Earl Hines at the Apex Club (1928), MCA

Potter, Tommy (Charles Thomas), bass. b. Philadelphia, 21 September 1918. Played piano and guitar before starting on bass in 1940. Worked in Washington, first meeting Charlie Parker there (1943), with pianist John Malachi; both joined Billy Eckstine band (1944–5). In between, with Trummy Young group (1944), later with John Hardee, Max Roach etc. Bassist with the classic Parker quintet (1947–50), also recording with Wardell Gray, Bud Powell (1949) and Stan Getz (1950). Performed regularly with Count Basie (1950, briefly), Earl Hines (1952–3), Artie Shaw (1953–4), Eddie Heywood (1955), Bud Powell (1956), Rolf Ericson (1956), Tyree Glenn (1958–60), Harry Edison (1960–1), Buck

Clayton (1963), Al Cohn–Zoot Sims (1965), Jimmy McPartland, Buddy Tate (late 1960s). Toured Europe and Japan with Parker 'tribute' package (1964). Left full-time music for work with hospital recreational facilities, but continued freelance gigging. Though he was rarely heard as a soloist, the melodic intelligence shown on those occasions was amply present in his backing work, and made a particularly fluid partnership with Parker's drummers Max Roach and Roy Haynes. [BP]

Charlie Parker, *On Dial, vol. 4* (1947), Spotlite

Powell, Bud (Earl) (Albert, according to one source), piano, composer. b. New York City, 27 September 1924; d. 31 July 1966. One of the most important figures in the history of jazz piano. Studied European music as a child, but was a keen observer of the beginnings of bebop in the early 1940s. Encouraged by Thelonious Monk, he joined the Cootie Williams band (1943–4) and made his record debut with them. After touring, became involved in the 52nd Street scene working (and, later, recording) with Charlie Parker. Hospitalized in 1945 as a result of alleged police brutality, Powell suffered recurrent mental instability and received electro-convulsive therapy in 1951–2. Active as trio leader from 1953 onwards, though often heavily tranquillized; took up residence in Paris with his wife and son (1959–64). Sanatorium treatment for tuberculosis and subsequent recuperation in 1962–3 led to invitation to work in New York for two months in 1964. Powell failed to return to Paris as planned and, after making concert appearances in early 1965, disappeared from view entirely, although for his funeral more than 5000 people lined the streets of Harlem.

Like his painful personal history, Powell's music parallels that of Charlie Parker. In Powell's case, his roots in pianists Teddy Wilson, Nat 'King' Cole and Billy Kyle (his particular favourite) are discernible in his earliest recordings and in the famous Massey Hall concert of 1953. His interpretation of ballads was often indebted to Art Tatum, but it was the intensity of his up-tempo right-hand lines which was unique; John Stevens once said metaphorically of Powell that 'He almost plays off the end of the piano', and there is a sense in which much of what he expressed, especially in the late 1940s, would have seemed more appropriate on a harsh-toned saxophone. Indeed, his glittering personal sound and brilliant percussive attack were the nearest thing to a piano equivalent of Parker's emotional message and instrumental authority. For this reason, his left hand was often most useful when at its most sparse, as was true of Kyle and Cole, although Powell's rhythmic interaction with bass and drums was seldom understood by antagonists of bebop. Nevertheless, he was the single most influential pianist of the period 1945–60 and has clearly marked the work of most players since then.

It must be said that Powell's command of the instrument was always more or less impaired during the last decade of his life, and only imperfectly reflected his earlier work. But there is often a subsidiary intensity caused by the diminished means of expression, which results in an even clearer distillation of his melodic gift. Equally, many of his compositions merely crystallize his improvisational style, such as 'Dance of the Infidels' (1949) or 'Hallucinations' (aka 'Budo') (performed by the Miles Davis band in 1948–9 but only recorded by Powell in 1951), and these have entered the general repertoire. A few are more ambitious, however: the driving mambo 'Un Poco Loco' (1951) and the macabre and haunting 'Glass Enclosure' (1953) are unlikely to be satisfactorily reproduced by other performers. The same may be said of his improvisation which, for all its wide influence, has an emotional atmosphere impossible to duplicate. [BP]

The Amazing Bud Powell, vol. 1/2 (1949–53), Blue Note; *Genius of Bud Powell* (1950–1), Verve; Charlie Parker, *One Night in Birdland* (1950), CBS; Quintet of the Year, *Jazz at Massey Hall* (1953), Debut/OJC

Powell, Mel (Melvin), piano, composer. b. New York City, 12 February 1923. His 'underground' reputation in mid-period jazz is gigantic: his short, phenomenal career is remembered with awe and the comparatively few records he made are constantly re-issued. A pianist of limitless technique who could play almost any style well, Powell played intermission piano at Nick's club while still in his teens, worked for Muggsy Spanier's big band soon after, and in summer 1941 (at George T. Simon's instigation) auditioned for Benny Goodman at MCA. 'I get more kicks out of Mel's playing than any other pianist in the business,' said Simon then, and Goodman was soon in agreement. By 1942, Powell was a staffman for Raymond Scott at CBS (along with a second pianist, Sanford Gold) and the year after joined Glenn Miller: in 1944 he came to Britain with Miller's AEF Band, where he featured with Miller's Uptown Hall Gang and broadcast for the BBC on Piano Party programmes. When he came back to the USA, however, Powell (in Nat Pierce's words) 'just disappeared'. After a brief spell in Hollywood studios he went to Yale to study composition with Paul Hindemith and piano with Nadia Reisenberg, graduated to teach theory at Queens College and composition at Yale, and by 1959 had been awarded a Guggenheim fellowship. More recently Powell's compositions (including a harpsichord concerto for Ferdinand Valenti) have been familiar items on American concert programmes, and in the 1970s he was Dean of Music at the California Institute of Arts. Powell's one recorded return to jazz, in 1954, produced classic albums such as *Thingamagig* (with Ruby Braff) and *Trio* (with Paul Quinichette): ten years on he could still be

Jean-Luc Ponty

spotted sitting in with Bobby Hackett in Connecticut and causing a sensation. (In 1986 Powell was heard again, playing for jazz cruises with cornettist Warren Vaché and others.) [DF]

Thingamagig (1954), Vanguard; *The Unavailable Mel Powell* (1947–8), Pausa

Powell, Richie (Richard), piano, arranger. b. New York City, 5 September 1931; d. 26 June 1956, in the same car accident as Clifford Brown. Younger brother of Bud Powell. After practising with near neighbour Jackie McLean, toured with r & b saxist Paul Williams (1952) and with the Johnny Hodges small band (1953–4). During the last two years of his life, began to reach musical maturity as a member of the Max Roach–Clifford Brown quintet. His only featured recordings were with this group, including a last session under Sonny Rollins's name, and demonstrate a certain lack of fluency amply compensated for by interesting ideas and a very individual sound. McCoy Tyner said, 'I was impressed by the harmonies Richard Powell used to play and by his use of the sustaining pedal on chords.' In fact, the chords built up of fourths which became a Tyner trademark ('quartal harmony' in the language of musical theorists) seem to have originated with Powell, who has thus exercised a considerable long-term influence on the following generation. [BP]

Sonny Rollins Plus Four (1956), Prestige

Powell, Rudy (Everard Stephen), alto sax, clarinet. b. New York City, 28 October 1907; d. 30 October 1976. 'He plays saxophone with a melodious singing tone and on clarinet he has a very pronounced growl' (Hugues Panassié). Powell was well known around New York by 1928 when he joined Cliff Jackson's Krazy Kats for three years, then worked with a variety of bands before starting a regular partnership with Fats Waller, live and on record, 1934–7. Much of the next 12 years he spent in big bands: Teddy Wilson (1939–40), Don Redman, Eddie South, Claude Hopkins, then Cab Calloway (1945–8) and Lucky Millinder (1948–50). During the 1950s he worked with Jimmy Rushing and for a long time with Benton Heath before spending years in the 1960s with Ray Charles and latterly the likeable Saints and Sinners which starred Herman Autrey and Vic Dickenson. In his last years he freelanced around New York. [DF]

Any with Waller

'Preacher Rollo', see LAYLAN, ROLLO.

Premru, Ray (Raymond), bass trombone, bass trumpet, composer. b. Elmira, New York, 6 June 1934. Parents both amateur musicians. B.Mus. at Eastman School of Music, 1956. Moved to London in late 1950s, playing with various British groups, and later with Friedrich Gulda's Euro-Jazz Orchestra. Since the 1960s, has been co-director of the Bobby Lamb–Ray Premru Big Band. He is active in symphonic music as well as jazz. Favourites are Jack Teagarden, Bill Harris, Bob Brookmeyer, J. J. Johnson, Charlie Parker, Bill Evans, Bill Holman and Gerry Mulligan. [IC]

Lamb/Premru Big Band, *Live at Ronnie Scott's* (1971), BBC

Previn, André, piano, conductor. b. Berlin, 6 April 1929. Family moved to USA when he was nine, father (Charles Previn) became musical director for *Flash Gordon* serial and other Hollywood films. André frequently active as jazz pianist, especially in mid-1940s (record debut at age 16) and mid-1950s. Wrote and conducted for films, then from the 1960s became internationally celebrated symphonic conductor and television personality. [BP]

Shelly Manne, *My Fair Lady* (1956), Contemporary

Prevost, Eddie (Edwin John), drums, percussion. b. Hitchin, Hertfordshire, 22 June 1942. He began as a teenager in traditional jazz bands, and later worked in 'imitation hard-bop groups'. 1965, co-founded AMM, a free improvising group, with Lou Gare and Keith Rowe, later to be joined by Cornelius Cardew. AMM has continued to perform over the years and has also included Christian Wolff, Christopher Hobbs, John Tilbury and Rohan de Saram. Since the early 1970s Prevost has also led a number of free-jazz groups latterly including Larry Stabbins, Veryan Weston and Marcio Mattos. He is also a member of Supersession with Evan Parker, Keith Rowe and Barry Guy. His main influences are Max Roach and Ed Blackwell, and other inspirations are the history of jazz, Sun Ra, Art Blakey, the Gagaku (ancient Japanese Court music) and David Tudor. He also writes and lectures on improvisation and related subjects. AMM toured the USA in 1968, 1972, 1983. [IC]

With AMM, *AMM Music* (1966), Elektra; *To Hear and Back Again* (1974), Matchless; *It had been an ordinary enough day in Pueblo, Colorado* (1979), ECM/JAPO

Price, Sammy (Samuel Blythe), piano, leader. b. Honey Grove, Texas, 6 October 1908. He studied the piano in Dallas, then joined local revues as a singer/dancer, was a Charleston dancer with Alphonso Trent's mighty band and toured on the TOBA circuit, 1927–30. That year he arrived in Kansas City and spent three years soaking up the music of Count Basie, Pete Johnson *et al.* before moving on to Chicago and Detroit. By 1938, in New York, he was hired as house pianist for American Decca, accompanying singers such as Trixie Smith and Sister Rosetta Tharpe, making boogie sides of his own (unlike many of his contemporaries, Price was versatile enough to survive the boogie phase) and leading his own band: a 1940 Decca date featuring his Texas Bluesicians (including Don Stovall and Emmett Berry) shows where Price was musically happiest to operate. After studio work slowed he began a busy career on 52nd Street, playing the Famous Door and Café Society, organized the first black-administered jazz festival, in Philadelphia, 1946, and visited the Nice festival in 1948 with Mezz Mezzrow (who called him 'the finest blues pianist I know'). After years in Texas again, Price came back to New York to work with Henry 'Red' Allen at the Metropole (he was also the Metropole's unofficial bouncer) and for the next ten years partnered Allen, in, for example, a classic album, *Feelin' Good* (1965, CBS), and a trip to England two months before Allen's death in 1967, as well as leading various teams of Bluesicians at home and in Europe in his own right. Price became a familiar soloist on the European circuit: in his spare time running a succession of companies (latterly, Down Home Meat Products) and taking part in local politics and community policing (as an honorary captain in the New York Police auxiliary): at various times he was also an undertaker, night club owner (twice), photographer and PR man, as well as a premier blues pianist. [DF]

And his Bluesicians (1955), Vogue

Priester, Julian Anthony, trombone. b. Chicago, 29 June 1935. Piano lessons at age ten for a year; baritone horn and trombone at Du Sable High School. 1953–8, he worked with Sun Ra, Lionel Hampton, Dinah Washington and others. Moved to New York, summer 1958, working with Max Roach and Slide Hampton. He continued with Max Roach in the early 1960s and the band included Eric Dolphy, Clifford Jordan and Booker Little. He freelanced in New York during the rest of the decade, including a six-month stint with Duke Ellington. 1970–3, he worked with the Herbie Hancock sextet, touring in the USA and Europe and playing major festivals. He moved to San Francisco in the mid-1970s, freelancing there and experimenting with electronic sounds and effects. 1980s, he was playing acoustically with the Dave Holland quintet which included Kenny Wheeler, and which toured extensively in the USA and Europe. Priester left the group in 1985. Early influences were J. J. Johnson, Charlie Parker, Sonny Rollins, Thelonious Monk, Dizzy Gillespie. [IC]

With Roach, Washington, Philly Joe Jones, Johnny Griffin; with Art Blakey, *Live* (1968), Trip; with Hancock, *Crossings* (1972), Warner Bros; with Billy Harper, *Capra Black* (1973), Strata East; Priester/Marine Intrusion, *Polarization* (1977), ECM; with Holland, *Jumpin' In* (1984), ECM

Priestley, Brian, piano, arranger, author, broadcaster. b. Manchester, 10 July 1946. Studied music from age eight and modern languages at university. Late 1960s, living in Oxford, accompanied visiting soloists and arranged for National Youth Jazz Orchestra. 1970, moved to London while working in bookshop management; gigged and broadcast with big bands led by Tony Faulkner and Alan Cohen, helping to transcribe 'Black, Brown and Beige' for Cohen (recorded with Priestley on piano, 1972) and Ellington's 'Creole Rhapsody' for New York Jazz Repertory Company (1977). Published solo transcriptions in *Downbeat* and book of Thelonious Monk (1977), four piano anthologies (1982–6). Assisted Cohen as musical director for TV specials of Ellington sacred music (1982) and Cotton Club celebration with Cab Calloway, Max Roach *et al.* (1985). Freelance since 1979, Priestley led quartet called Stylus, then own sextet/septet since 1980.

From 1977, ran jazz workshops (succeeding Stan Tracey) and piano classes (alongside Howard Riley) at Goldsmiths' College; from 1983, tutor in jazz history for Oxford University. A prolific contributor to periodicals since mid-1960s, Priestley in 1980s wrote three biographies – details under Mingus, Parker and Coltrane – and, continuously since 1971, has hosted an influential weekly programme on BBC Radio London. [JLS]

Alan Cohen, *Black, Brown and Beige* (1972), Argo

Prima, Louis, trumpet, vocals. b. New Orleans, 7 December 1911; d. 24 August 1978. His elder brother Leon Prima was one of the best New Orleans trumpeters and by 1923, Louis was the natural leader of a New Orleans 'kids' band' (it featured a ten-year-old Irving Prestopnik whom Prima later re-christened Fazola) and making connections all around the French quarter. By 1935 – an irresistible performer, and exuberant frontman – Prima had arrived in New York and was headlining at the Famous Door, where his husky vocals and musical partnership with Pee Wee Russell ('the most fabulous musical mind I have known') created a commercial sensation: society columnists such as Walter Winchell wrote him up, and the full club that resulted, plus a coast-to-coast radio show, *Swing It* (one of Prima's several catchphrases), turned him into the hub of 52nd Street. After the Mafia moved in on Prima he moved out and opened his own Famous Door in Hollywood with comedian Red Colonna: there his success was just as spectacular and by 1937 he was filming with Alice Faye (*You Can't Have Everything* for Twentieth Century-Fox), writing hits like 'Sing Sing Sing' and touring with his own big swing orchestra (featuring Russell and Sal Franzella). All the way through the 1940s Prima's big-band success continued: he recorded hits including 'There, I've said it again', 'One Mint Julep' and 'Angelina', and with the aid of a shrewd manager, Barbara Belle, weathered the big-band decline until 1954. That year he began his high-powered jazz-cum-rock-and-roll cabaret act with wife Keely Smith, Sam Butera and the Witnesses (featuring a secret weapon, James Blounty on trombone). It scored his biggest success yet on the New York, Chicago, Hollywood and Las Vegas circuits, but sometimes helped people to forget the fine jazz trumpeting (somewhere between Louis Armstrong and Jonah Jones) that adorns all but his very last records; Acker Bilk's 'Trad boom' best-sellers, as well as singing, were cast deep in the Prima mould. Prima remained highly successful into the 1960s (he divorced Keely Smith in 1961) and that 'hoarse, horny voice of his' (Sam Weiss's description) was teamed with an old 52nd Street crony, Phil Harris, in Walt Disney's cartoon film *Jungle Book* (1966): Prima's trumpet playing on the soundtrack, just as much as his singing, is worth the price of a seat. [DF]

And his New Orleans Gang (1934–5), Decca

Privin, Bernie (Bernard), trumpet. b. Brooklyn, New York, 12 February 1919. By 1938 he was attracting attention and good reviews in the Tommy Dorsey and Bunny Berigan big bands, and from 1938 for another year did the same with Artie Shaw, for whom Privin was a featured cornerman (his work can be heard on Shaw tracks such as 'One Night Stand' and 'My Heart Stood Still'). From 1940 he was with Charlie Barnet's informal and very successful big band and enjoying it (he worked for Barnet again in 1942) and thereafter spent time with Mal Hallett, Benny Goodman and Jerry Wald before joining Glenn Miller's AEF band in 1943. Miller had had his eye on Privin's biting, Armstrong-like solos for years and featured him both with the big band and as part of Mel Powell's Uptown Hall Gang, who had their own BBC radio show in Britain, but Privin found Miller's unblinking discipline hard to accept (especially when all band members wearing moustaches were ordered to shave them off) and was probably relieved to move into studio work, for NBC in 1946 and after 1950 for CBS, where he played for shows including Ed Sullivan's, Garry Moore's and Andy Williams's. From then on Privin's jazz gifts were heard more rarely (a delightful LP with Mundell Lowe's group was one 1950s exception): in the 1970s he was a welcome addition to a 'Kings of Jazz' tour around Europe (with Pee Wee Erwin, Johnny Mince

Russell Procope

and others). In the 1980s Privin was making the rounds of the jazz circuits again and playing jazz festivals. [DF]

Glenn Miller, *Uptown Hall Gang* (1944–5), Esquire

Procope, Russell, alto sax, clarinet. b. New York City, 11 August 1908; d. 21 January 1981. He grew up in a San Juan Hill household where records of Ted Lewis and Mamie Smith played, and went to school with Benny Carter. By 1929 he was playing in Carter's band, until his leader joined Fletcher Henderson, whereupon Procope joined Chick Webb: later, in a spectacular swap, their leaders exchanged sidemen and Procope worked for Henderson until 1934. He left (at the same period as Coleman Hawkins) at a time when Henderson's leadership was in question ('I got a bit disgusted'), then worked for Tiny Bradshaw, Teddy Hill and Willie Bryant before joining John Kirby's fleet sextet, replacing Pete Brown. With Kirby's band Procope's perfect playing found perfect expression and public recognition. In 1943 he followed Billy Kyle into the army and in 1946 joined Duke Ellington as one-fifth of Ellington's greatest-ever reed section. 'Otto Hardwicke had wandered off and got lost and Duke didn't know where he would find him!' remembered Procope: he subbed one night for Ellington in Worcester and stayed 28 years. In Ellington's orchestra he found two congenial qualities: a bandleader he respected musically and professionally, and a featured role he enjoyed. 'In Duke's band I could play more in the styles by which I had genuinely been influenced', he said: they included the deep, mellow aged-in-the-wood New Orleans-influenced clarinet sound that Ellington loved and featured on his 1950 'Mood Indigo' recording. 'Why did I stay 28 years? Because I loved the music! Besides which it was a chance to go round the world. Besides which it was security. To do what you like and get paid for it – isn't that what everybody wants? So I stayed with Duke until he died.' In the 1970s Procope toured with Ellington scholar Brooks Kerr's trio: a living memorial to his late great leader. [DF]

With Ellington; *John Kirby and his Orchestra, 1941–2*, RCA

See Dance, Stanley, *The World of Duke Ellington* (Scribner's, 1970, repr. Da Capo, 1980)

Profit, Clarence, piano. b. New York City, 26 June 1912; d. 22 October 1944. School friend of

Edgar Sampson, with whom he wrote the harmonically adventurous song 'Lullaby in Rhythm'. Led own big band during late teens, then with Teddy Bunn in the Washboard Serenaders (1930–1). His own trio, continuously employed from 1936 until his death, may have been the first to use the piano-guitar-bass format popularized by Nat 'King' Cole. Much admired by pianists of his generation but since forgotten, he employed the innovations of Art Tatum in a less overpowering and more straight-ahead style. He was the first to put on disc (five years before him) the Tatum-associated revised changes for 'I Got Rhythm', later used by Don Byas, Thelonious Monk and, occasionally, Charlie Parker. [BP]

Various (4 tracks by Profit), *Swing Street, vol. 2* (1939), Tax

Progressive Jazz A term first promulgated by Stan Kenton (to describe his own work, of course) and later applied by journalists and fans to such as Brubeck, the MJQ and 1950s 'cool jazz' in general. This usage is now outdated but, perhaps because progress is a phenomenon of fashion and because jazz was next fashionable when it became funky, 'progressive jazz' resurfaced in the 1970s as a term to describe jazz-funk-fusion. [BP]

Pseudonyms used to provide endless guessing games for dedicated record collectors, until the standard discographies (by Rust, Jepsen and Bruynincx) and reissued albums began giving away all the correct answers. The use of such disguises, incidentally, should be distinguished from the idea of whites of European extraction anglicizing their names (Terry Gibbs, Shorty Rogers) or black Americans adopting Islam: it is regrettably still possible to come across writers stating, for instance, that Yusef Lateef's 'real' name is William Evans. The only actual pseudonym apparently inspired by racial considerations was that of Eddie Lang (itself an adopted Anglo name), whose more funky records with Lonnie Johnson and King Oliver were credited to 'Blind Willie Dunn'.

Usually the fictitious names were concocted to cover a record session from which the participant should have been barred by an exclusive contract with another company. No sooner had Duke Ellington's manager/producer sold his services to one label (in 1929) than the band started appearing on other labels as 'The Jungle Band', 'The Harlem Footwarmers' and 'Mills' Ten Black Berries'. From the 1930s onwards, contracts tended to be a little more watertight, and the few pseudonyms that were required usually referred to a big-band leader doing a bit of small-group slumming, such as 'Shoeless John Jackson' (Benny Goodman) or 'Chicago Flash' (Gene Krupa). Often, however, the names reflected more mundane inspirations, as when Nat Cole (who also recorded as 'Shorty Nadine' and as 'A. Guy') appeared under the name 'Eddie Laguna', actually that of the session producer; Bobby Hackett once adopted the persona of 'Pete Pesci', owner of the club where he was working at the time. Some pseudonyms were in fact devastatingly prosaic, Cannonball Adderley becoming 'Ronnie Peters' and Eric Dolphy 'George Lane', each for one session only; but sometimes the musicians could not resist giving clues, such as the West-Coast-based altoist 'Art Salt' or the high-note trumpeter 'Buddy Maynard'.

The fun really started to go out of the name game in the 1960s, when it became more common to negotiate extra-contractual engagements 'by permission of So-and-So Records'. Ironically, now that it is the fashion to reissue albums in their original sleeves, it is once again important to know that, for instance, both of the two recordings of 'Charlie Chan' were actually done by Charlie Parker. [BP]

Pukwana, Dudu (Mtutuzel), alto and soprano sax, piano, composer. b. Port Elizabeth, South Africa, 18 July 1938. Father a pianist and vocalist, mother a singer. Self-taught with some lessons from his father. Began on piano at six. At 18, started on saxophone. 1962, played with his own group, Jazz Giants, at Johannesburg Jazz Festival and was awarded the prize for Best Saxophonist of the Year. The white pianist Chris McGregor formed his band the Blue Notes from the best musicians at that festival, with Pukwana on alto, Mongezi Feza (tpt), Nick Moyake (tnr), Johnny Dyani (bass) and Louis Moholo (dms). Under apartheid, racially mixed groups were illegal and it became impossible for the Blue Notes to work together, so in 1964 they left for Europe, where they played at the Antibes Jazz Festival, in Paris and in Switzerland, eventually arriving in London which they made their home after appearing at the Ronnie Scott Club. Pukwana began to work with a diversity of British groups including Keith Tippett's Centipede and the Incredible String Band, while continuing to write and play with the Blue Notes.

In 1970 McGregor enlarged his band, calling it the Brotherhood of Breath, and Pukwana also composed for this ensemble. The Brotherhood toured Britain and Europe, playing many major festivals. They also recorded the soundtrack for the film of Wole Soyinka's *Kongi's Harvest*. 1969, Dudu started his own kwela band, Spear, and toured in South Africa where he began a collaboration with trumpeter Hugh Masekela and trombonist Jonas Gwangwa. They played together in the USA and recorded as the African Explosion. Back in the UK, he formed a band called Assagai featuring black musicians from South Africa and elsewhere, and continued to work with reggae bands, as well as with the freer jazz improvisers such as drummer Han Bennink, Misha Mengelberg, John Surman and Mike

Dudu Pukwana

Osborne. 1977, he took Spear to Nigeria for Festac, the International Festival of Black Arts held in Lagos. 1978, he formed a new group, Zila, which has since toured and played major festivals all over the UK and Europe. Most of the Spear/Zila music is composed by Pukwana, and some of his best compositions are on the album *Blue Notes in Concert, vol. 1*.

Dudu Pukwana and his African associates have made an immense contribution to the British (and European) jazz scene, infusing it with a sense of urgency and purpose, re-invigorating the music with fiery improvisation and exultant rhythms beautifully executed, and inspiring successive generations of young British musicians. Pukwana's favourites are Ben Webster, Ornette Coleman, Archie Shepp, and he also gets inspiration from the current members of Zila, Chris McGregor, Dave Holland, Count Basie, Dollar Brand (Abdullah Ibrahim), Ahmad Jamal and others. [IC]

Four with Brotherhood of Breath; three with Johnny Dyani; with Bennink/Mengelberg; with Gwanga's African Explosion, *Who (Ngubani)* (1969), Ahmad Jamal Productions; with Masekela, *Home is Where the Music Is* (1972), Island; with Spear, *In the Townships* (1973); *Flute Music* (1974), both Caroline/Virgin; with McGregor, *Blue Notes in Concert, vols. 1/2* (1978), Ogun; with Zila, *Life in Bracknell and Willisau* (1983), Jika

Pullen, Don Gabriel, piano, composer (and organ). b. Roanoke, Virginia, 25 December 1944. Coming from a musical family, Pullen studied with Muhal Richard Abrams and reedman Giuseppe Logan, with whom he made record debut (1964). Worked with own groups and in duo with Milford Graves, producing self-distributed duo albums. Played in many r & b groups, mostly on organ; also with Nina Simone (1970–1) and briefly Art Blakey (1974). Member of Charles Mingus quintet (1973–5), then touring in own right including visits to Europe in 1976, '77, '78 and '79. Since 1979, has co-led quartet with George Adams, touring internationally and making several albums. As well as his great versatility, Pullen has a comprehensive technique that attracts attention in whatever setting he appears. Even when playing within relatively conventional structures, he is fond of rapid right-hand clusters which, though less percussive than Cecil Taylor, are more flowing and equally exciting. [BP]

Healing Force (1976), Black Saint; Adams/Pullen, *Breakthrough* (1986), Blue Note

Purim, Flora, voice, guitar, percussion. b. Rio de Janeiro, 6 March 1942. Father a violinist, mother a classical pianist. 1950–4, piano lessons; 1954–8, guitar lessons. She also studied percussion with Airto Moreira, whom she married. She worked with the Brazilian group Quarteto Novo, which was co-led by Moreira and Hermeto Pascoal. She went to live in the USA in 1967, toured Europe with Stan Getz in 1968; freelanced 1969–70; 1971, she worked regularly with the Gil Evans band, Chick Corea's group, and with Moreira. They were both, with Joe Farrell and Stanley Clarke, members of Corea's first Return to Forever band, touring the USA, Europe and Japan with it, and recording two classic albums, *Return to Forever* and *Light as a Feather*. 1973, Purim and Moreira left in order to start their own group which featured her as soloist under his leadership, and which combined elements from jazz, pop and Brazilian music in a rich mélange. 1974, she began making her own solo albums. 1974–5, she was imprisoned for over a year for a drug charge which was never proven. 1976, she was again working with Moreira. Her early inspirations were first Erroll Garner and then Miles Davis, Dinah Washington and Ella Fitzgerald. Her vocal range originally covered about three octaves but, under the guidance of Hermeto Pascoal, she gradually increased it to six octaves. Flora Purim sings her own and others' lyrics, but also wordlessly, blending her voice (often aided by electronics) with other instruments. [IC]

With Duke Pearson, George Duke, Carlos Santana, Pascoal and others; with Corea, *Return to Forever* (1972), ECM; *Light as a Feather* (1973), Polydor; with Moreira, *Fingers* (1973), CTI; as leader, *Butterfly Dreams* (1974); *Stories to Tell* (1974); *Open Your Eyes, You Can Fly* (1976), all Milestone

Purnell, Alton, piano, vocals. b. New Orleans, 16 April 1911; d. 1987. He was the pianist in Bunk Johnson's 1945 band and for the 12 years following was a mainstay of George Lewis's, providing the striding, raggy piano and vocals that Lewis loved to feature. In 1957, after a move to California, he worked with Kid Ory and a variety of other West Coast-based leaders including Joe Darensbourg, Teddy Buckner and (more surprisingly) Ben Pollack, before beginning in the early 1960s a life of solo performing which brought him to Europe many times (he also toured with packages such as the 1966 New Orleans All Stars). Purnell's industrious piano stride and jingling, jolly right-hand figures were set deep in the New Orleans traditions: his singing likewise. [DF]

Tribute to Louis (1971), CBS (double)

Purvis, Jack, trumpet, trombone, vocals, piano, multi-instrumentalist, composer. b. Kokomo, Indiana, 11 December 1906; d. San Francisco, 30 March 1962. The most generally remembered fact about Purvis is that in 1929 he had the *chutzpah* to record, for Tommy Rockwell and Okeh, a direct Louis Armstrong pastiche, 'Copyin' Louis'. Such a venture (at a period when Armstrong was at his technical best) suggests nerve as well as cocksure ability and Purvis – 'the swingin'est white trumpeter I ever heard', according to Rex Stewart – was loaded with both. In the disconnected periods of his life when he actually was involved with music full-time, Purvis repeatedly turns up playing brilliantly in unsurpassable company: sitting in with Fletcher Henderson's band to improvise fourth-trumpet parts (as difficult a task as it was a rare honour), recording a string of his own top-class compositions with an orchestra of his own (including such black heavyweights as Coleman Hawkins and J. C. Higginbotham, as well as Adrian Rollini), playing with Hal Kemp's orchestra (his replacement was Bunny Berigan) and – perhaps most incredibly of all – arranging for George Stoll and Warner Brothers (one of his compositions, 'Legends of Haiti', was composed for a 110-piece orchestra). For many musicians any one of these achievements would have been the joyful climax to a life in music: for Purvis, an uncommonly gifted 'natural' performer, they were intermittent activities in a life of adventure and crime which involved, at various times, climbing the Alps barefoot (said Eddie Condon), smuggling contraband country-to-country in a light plane, working as a hotel chef and fighting as a mercenary. By 1937 he was already a small legend: that year *Downbeat* published an article, 'What happened to Jack Purvis?', and the year after he was heard broadcasting from Texas State Penitentiary over Station WBAP, playing his own compositions with a prison band. Purvis's later years are misty. For a long time it was thought that he was incarcerated in Georgia for second-degree murder and died in gaol. Thanks to researcher Paul Larsen we now know that the corpse of an unemployed radio-repair man discovered in a gas-filled room in 1962 was Purvis's. His life is still insufficiently researched, but it makes a ripping jazz yarn. [DF]

Louis Armstrong/Purvis (8 tracks each), *Satchmo Style* (1929–30), Parlophone

See Barnet, Charlie, with Stanley Dance, *Those Swinging Years* (Louisiana State Press, 1984)

Pyne, Chris (Christopher Norman), trombone, valve trombone, piano. b. Bridlington, Yorkshire, 14 February 1939. Father a pianist, brother Mike plays piano and trumpet. Childhood piano lessons, but self-taught on trombone. 1960–1, RAF band with John Stevens, Paul Rutherford, Trevor Watts. 1963, came to London, playing with various bands including Alexis Korner, Humphrey Lyttelton, John Dankworth, Ronnie Scott, Maynard Ferguson, Tubby Hayes. Has done all Sinatra's UK and Europe tours, 1970–83; with John Taylor sextet, 1971–81; 1965–85, with many Kenny Wheeler groups; 1967–79, with all Mike Gibbs's UK bands. Toured with Gordon Beck, 1982, and John Surman, 1984. Also does much freelance work. Favourite trombonists are J. J. Johnson, Jimmy Knepper, Vic Dickenson, Frank Rosolino, Jack Teagarden. [IC]

With Dizzy Gillespie, Ella Fitzgerald, Sarah Vaughan, Mike Gibbs, Philly Joe Jones and others; with Dankworth, *Million Dollar Collection* (1967), Fontana; with Taylor, *Pause and Think Again* (1971), Turtle; with Pete Hurt, *Lost for Words* (1984), Spotlite

Pyne, Mick (Michael John), piano, keyboards, trumpet. b. Thornton-le-Dale, Yorkshire, 2 September 1940. Father a pianist, brother Chris plays trombone. Self-taught, with some help from his father. He came to London in 1961 and played with Tony Kinsey's quintet until 1962. 1965, with Alexis Korner's Blues Incorporated; 1966–73 with the Tubby Hayes quintet. Joined the Humphrey Lyttelton band in 1972, staying for 12 years. Pyne has always led his own groups – trios, quartets and bigger ensembles up to 12-piece. He has also worked with Hank Mobley, Joe Williams, Stan Getz, Philly Joe Jones, Roland Kirk, the Mike Gibbs Orchestra, Dexter Gordon, the Ronnie Scott quintet and Georgie Fame's 'Stardust Road' show (1983–5). His favourites are Art Tatum and Bill Evans and other influences are Louis Armstrong, Delius and John Coltrane. [IC]

With Mike Gibbs, Charles Tolliver, Philly Joe Jones, Alison Moyet; with Tubby Hayes quartet, *Mexican Green* (1967), Fontana; solo piano/cornet, *Alone Together* (1977), Spotlite; Jon Eardley/Pyne, *Two of a Kind* (1977), Spotlite; Lyttelton/Pyne, *Once in a While* (1976), Black Lion

Q

Quebec, Ike Abrams, tenor sax. b. Newark, New Jersey, 17 August 1918; d. 16 January 1963. Began on piano, changing to tenor only in 1940. Played with such bands as Benny Carter's, Coleman Hawkins's, Roy Eldridge's (1943), then with Cab Calloway band and small group (1944–51). From 'Cab Jiver' to cab-driver (literally), Ike was out of the music business for much of the 1950s. His comeback began in 1959, when he not only made records again but became assistant musical director for the Blue Note label, responsible for producing Dexter Gordon and new discoveries. This dual career was cut short by lung cancer.

Quebec will be chiefly remembered for his two periods of recording under his own name. In the mid-1940s his Websterish style fronted some beautifully cohesive sessions, including the jukebox hit 'Blue Harlem'. Fifteen years later, with only a slightly harder edge to his sound, he demonstrated the close connections between his earlier music (by now called 'mainstream') and the budding 'soul jazz' movement. At his best a moving performer, whose belated rediscovery has been amply justified. [BP]

Complete 40s Blue Note Recordings of Ike Quebec and John Hardee (1944–6), Mosaic; *Blue and Sentimental* (1961), Blue Note

Quinichette, Paul, tenor sax. b. Denver, Colorado, 17 May 1916; d. 25 May 1983. Played with many territory bands such as those of Nat Towles, Ernie Fields, and toured nationally with Jay McShann (1942–4), replacing Jimmy Forrest. Worked on West Coast with Johnny Otis (1945), then to New York with Louis Jordan group. Member of, among others, Lucky Millinder band (1948–9), Henry 'Red' Allen's group and Hot Lips Page septet (1951), before joining new Count Basie band (1952–3). Led own group for several years, also working briefly for Benny Goodman (1955), Nat Pierce (1957) and Billie Holiday. Left music in 1950s, returning in 1973 with Sammy Price, Buddy Tate etc. before being restricted by ill-health. Quinichette became known in the late 1940s–early 1950s as a Lester Young imitator (the 'Vice-Pres'), when all the other contenders for this honour were white. Although he had the makings of an individual soloist of the Southwestern school, the reputation of being a clone clung to him too closely. [BP]

On the Sunny Side (1957), Prestige/OJC

Quotation from another melody during an improvisation is an art whose value has frequently been disputed. It can arise for a variety of reasons, often indicating sheer high spirits (an early example: Louis Armstrong quoting 'Rhapsody in Blue' in his original record of 'Ain't Misbehavin''). Or the musical logic of a solo can suggest surprising similarities, as in some of Charlie Parker's more obscure quotations. Quite often there are traces of irony, even deliberate absurdity (such as Art Tatum employed) or the tone can be sardonic or sarcastic, sending up either the basic material or the passing reference or both (e.g. Dexter Gordon or Sonny Rollins). And there are different combinations of these aspects, depending on how the listener perceives the event in question.

Many soloists would say that the most pleasing quotations arise spontaneously and, even for the improviser, unexpectedly. Planned quotations have their place, but the players can easily sound bored and boring if they would prefer to be spontaneous. On the other hand, many of the early jazz soloists did not always improvise, and made self-quotation their stock-in-trade (see IMPROVISATION). Of course, written arrangements can also incorporate specific material from elsewhere, or can anthologize memorable phrases originally improvised on the same tune. But the transcription of whole solos (such as Leon Roppolo's in the McKinney's version of 'Milenberg Joys' or Thelonious Monk's 'Little Rootie Tootie' solo on his big-band Town Hall concert) has been done to death by groups such as Supersax.

It is not safe to assume that such possibilities are limited to harmonically-oriented jazz. Ray Smith has noted that one of Evan Parker's solo albums includes an accidental quotation from a recording of African tribal music. And the use of live African musicians in performances by Archie Shepp and Ornette Coleman also provides instances of quoting from an outside source (or were Shepp and Coleman being quoted by the Africans?) [BP]

R

Ragtime The origins of the wildly popular syncopated music that predated jazz but also ran alongside its early history lie, like those of jazz itself, in a complex set of roots that include (among other elements) black and white folk, dance, and brass band music. Its most notable characteristics were, first, deliberate use of syncopation in the right hand, often set against a simple, rhythmic bass in 2/4 or 4/4 (playing a tune this way was called 'ragging' it); and, second, a set of related themes in each piece, often linked by modulation (a direct link with band music). By the late 19th century ragtime was played by bands and solo pianists alike, but the greatest ragtime exponents were perhaps the high-toned 'piano professors' of the period. Eubie Blake recalled one such: 'One Leg' Willie Joseph, a virtuoso black pianist from Boston Conservatory who, because he was unable to succeed in the white man's musical world, devoted his colossal talents to playing ragtime in saloons. Willie's music was a spectacular rhythmic *tour de force*, probably nearly as complex as a Max Roach drum solo. 'Ragtime is syncopation – and improvising – and accents,' said Blake, 'and if you could have heard those old fellas play you would have *heard* ad lib – *and* those accents.' It seems possible that the creations of Joseph and his many contemporaries may have been simplified – even bowdlerized – in their later formalization by Scott Joplin and others. But such formalization was inevitable: by the turn of the century ragtime had created a huge demand for itself, and began to be published, sometimes in 'easy to read' versions for America's parlour fixture, the piano. The first rag to be published, Tom Turpin's 'Harlem Rag' in 1897, was quickly followed by a string of others from ragtime composers such as Joseph Lamb, James Scott and Scott Joplin. Joplin, possibly the most musically trained of the three (he studied with a German professor who may have been sent South under the USA's reconstruction policy), was one of the first who, in Eubie Blake's words, 'had the nerve to put ragtime down on paper' and his first composition, 'Maple Leaf Rag', published in 1899 by John Stark, sold 75,000 copies. It opened the floodgates for a deluge of ragtime piano publications (some good, some not) which in many cases usurped the place rightfully occupied by Joplin and his peers. By the dawn of the 20th century ragtime was being played by younger jazz musicians: New Orleans bands such as John Robichaux's and 'Papa' Jack Laine's took most of their repertoire from popular ragtime of the period published, in stock orchestrations, in the famous 'Red Back Book'. Within a few years, popular composers such as Irving Berlin were producing songs like 'Alexander's Ragtime Band' which owed little to true ragtime, and with the dawn of the jazz age a new, younger music was to catch the public fancy (Joseph Stark's house significantly discontinued publishing in 1922). For the next four decades ragtime was handled best of all by a small coterie of authorities such as pianist Wally Rose in post-World War II America and in the 1960s and after by Europeans such as Keith Nichols and Ron Weatherburn, as well as Americans such as Dick Hyman. Not every treatment of ragtime by jazz bands was a respectful one, but it can be said that scholarly recreations by such bands as Chris Barber's and Ken Colyer's helped to refocus attention on the music in the 1950s, and the revival of the late 1960s (consolidated by a Hollywood film, *The Sting*, which used Joplin's 'The Entertainer' as a theme tune) fully repositioned the music in public consciousness: the reworkings of Joshua Rifkin, Dick Hyman, Nichols and others thereafter at last restored ragtime to its rightful place in the music establishment. [DF]

See Janis, Harriet, and Blesh, Rudy, *They All Played Ragtime* (Music Sales, undated); Hasse, John Edward, ed. *Ragtime: Its History, Composers and Music* (Macmillan, 1986)

Rainey, Ma (*née* Gertrude Malissa Nix Pridgett), vocals. b. Columbus, Georgia, 26 April 1886; d. Georgia, 22 December 1939. 'Ma' Rainey is appropriately named, for in historical terms she really was 'Mother of the Blues': the recorded link between the street-corner style of early 'country' blues performers and such sophisticated later artists as her pupil Bessie Smith. Rainey began her career at 12 and in 1904 had married William 'Pa' Rainey with whom she toured for many years as a member of the Rabbit Foot Minstrels. (She was also known as 'Madam' Rainey.) In 1923 she began a string of more than 100 recordings with Lovie Austin's Blues Serenaders (her favourite accompanist was Tommy Ladnier) and their fabulous success helped her to set up her own tent shows which toured the South with great success throughout the 1920s; one show in 1927, *Louisiana Blackbirds*, a 1500-seater which spent a week in each town it visited, would have been like the one

Mary Lou Williams saw: 'Ma was loaded with diamonds, in her ears, round her neck, in a tiara on her head. Both hands were full of rocks, too: her hair was wild and she had gold teeth! What a sight!' Rainey may have sounded weird to Mary Lou's young ears, but she was the first great blues singer of all, whose poised cry sounded like plainsong. Although she was ugly, there was beauty in her smile and in the gentle personality which accepted taunts from her audience with great good humour, and she was a kindly and much loved employer: 'She treated her musicians so wonderfully,' says Lionel Hampton, 'and she always bought them an instrument.' Her vaudeville material included such showstoppers as 'Ma Rainey's Black Bottom': when she retired, after the death of her sister and her mother, in 1933, she could never have envisaged that 50 years on a Broadway show of the same name would be highly successful. Rainey spent her last years as an active member of the Friendship Baptist Church in Columbus, Georgia: her daughter, Ma Rainey II, also a blues singer, died in 1985. [DF]

Ma Rainey, vols. 1/2 (1923–5), VJM

See Stewart-Baxter, Derrick, *Ma Rainey and the Classic Blues Singers* (Studio Vista, 1970); Lieb, Sandra, *Mother of the Blues* (1981)

Ramey, Gene (Eugene Glasco), bass. b. Austin, Texas, 4 April 1913. He took lessons from Walter Page and, after several years of leading his own bands, joined Jay McShann, 1938–43. From 1944, in New York, he worked with a bewildering variety of leaders from Tiny Grimes to Miles Davis and in the 1950s was heard with Art Blakey as well as singer Eartha Kitt. In 1959 and 1961 he toured Europe with Buck Clayton's All Stars and in the ensuing two decades worked more regularly with mainstream-Dixieland stylists from Muggsy Spanier and Dick Wellstood to Jimmy Rushing and Peanuts Hucko. By 1979 he was once again a regular partner to Jay McShann: one of the most respected bassists in jazz. [DF]

See Dance, Stanley, *The World of Count Basie* (Sidgwick & Jackson, 1980)

Randall, Freddy, trumpet. b. Hackney, East London, 6 May 1921. He worked first with comedy bandleader Freddy Mirfield's Garbage Men, then quickly formed his own driving, Chicago-style band, through which passed most of the best British Dixielanders of the period: Lennie Hastings, Dave Shepherd, Bruce Turner, Roy Crimmins, Harry Smith, Betty Smith, Al Gay, Norman Cave, Eddie Thompson, Pete Hodge and others. A huge-toned trumpeter of exuberant technique, Randall – who in the early 1950s was resident at Cooks Ferry Inn in Edmonton, North London – became the figureheard for post-war Chicago jazz buffs, playing in a style which varied at will from the direct punch of Muggsy Spanier to the more florid creations of Harry James and Charlie Teagarden: late Teagarden and late Randall are nearly interchangeable. His records of the 1950s period – for Parlophone's Super Rhythm Style – are great jazz in any language. (BBC broadcasts from Cooks Ferry Inn are still well remembered, too.) Later, after a temporary lung disorder, Randall worked more sparingly. In the 1960s 'Trad boom' he briefly re-formed a band with Shepherd and trombonist Jackie Free: in 1971, with Shepherd again, he led the Randall–Shepherd All Stars (featuring Danny Moss and Brian Lemon) which broadcast in Britain on a near-daily basis, appeared on TV, played the Montreux Jazz Festival and recorded two excellent albums for Alan Bates and Black Lion. After the All Stars had dispersed, Randall – a sensitive man who disliked the traumas of bandleading and ran an old people's home later in his career – became more of a cult figure than ever, appearing when it suited him (but always brilliantly) in out-of-the-way pubs and clubs, often with less gifted bands, usually around his own East London territory. His admirers place him alongside Kenny Baker and Tommy McQuater as a British trumpet king. [DF]

His Great 16 (1951–6), Dormouse

R & B, see RHYTHM-AND-BLUES.

Randolph, Mouse (Irving), trumpet. b. St Louis, Missouri, 22 June 1909. He worked first with Fate Marable's riverboat bands and with a variety of territory bands (including Alphonso Trent's) before joining Andy Kirk in Kansas City, 1931–3. He moved to New York soon after and joined Fletcher Henderson (1934), Cab Calloway (1935–9) and then Ella Fitzgerald's band, which she had taken over from Chick Webb (1939–41). After a spell with Don Redman came a long stint with Ed Hall's sextet (1944–8) before time with Eddie Barefield (1950), Marcelino Guerra's Latin-American band and, from 1958, Henry 'Chick' Morrison's orchestra. A fine Armstrong-style player and versatile allrounder, Randolph has never received the credit due to him. 'He could always play', says Doc Cheatham. 'He had studied a lot and he played everything, especially good New Orleans music. He had a good conception and I could never understand how he could give up music, but I think it was just that he got tired and wanted to be more with his family.' [DF]

Raney, Jimmy (James Elbert), guitar. b. Louisville, Kentucky, 20 August 1927. Briefly in New York and then Chicago as teenager, working with local groups. Joined Woody Herman for nine months (1948), then in New York with Al

Haig, Buddy DeFranco, Artie Shaw, Terry Gibbs. Member of Stan Getz quintet (1951–2) and replaced Tal Farlow with Red Norvo trio (1953–4). Recorded regularly under own name in mid-1950s, but worked (1954–60) in supper club with pianist Jimmy Lyon (who earlier encouraged Farlow). Rejoined Getz (1962–3) but, after some studio work and backing singers etc., returned to Louisville to work outside music. Playing trips to New York (from 1972, including further recording) and gradual return to former reputation. Regular touring in Europe from mid-1970s, often in company with his guitarist son Doug Raney (b. 1957), a resident of Copenhagen for several years.

One of the few guitarists for whom the inspiration of bebop had a positive effect, Jimmy is not only extremely fluent but melodically lyrical as well. His best work usually requires the presence of inspiring collaborators, who can bring out all his latent rhythmic strength. A number of interesting original tunes, of which 'Signal' gained some currency with European groups, also mirror the qualities of which Raney is capable. [BP]

Jimmy Raney/Doug Raney, *Stolen Moments* (1979), Steeplechase

Rank, Bill (William C.), trombone. b. Lafayette, Indiana, 8 June 1904; d. Cincinnati, Ohio, 20 May 1979. From 1926 he was a regular musical companion to Bix Beiderbecke: in Jean Goldkette's orchestra, in Adrian Rollini's short-lived New Yorker band, in the famous 'Gang' records. Listening to Rank's brilliantly agile, full-toned trombone it seems hard to understand how his name has remained a collectable delight rather than achieving even the familiarity of Miff Mole's, but for more than a decade from 10 December 1927 he was with Paul Whiteman, leading his trombone section. Such a prestigious job was a plum for any young player, and Rank was good at his job. 'Jack Teagarden told me that Bill was a very fine lead player,' says Bob Havens, 'and he would sort of carry the lead as far as playing in the ensemble work. Bill would tell Jack and the rest of them: "You don't have to bother to count the bars – I'll let you know when it's time to come in!" ' After Teagarden joined Whiteman as featured soloist in 1933, however, Rank's solo talents were heard less often and, while (no doubt) working with Teagarden was a trombonist's education, Rank must sometimes have wondered what was happening to his own career. By the end of the war – with bebop in fashion – he was leading his own band in Cincinnati, and in the 1950s combined playing with work as an insurance man. (At this period it was sometimes fashionable to downgrade Rank after an off-centre comment by Eddie Condon that Beiderbecke recorded only with 'blood relations'.) In 1968 and 1969, Rank came to England to visit and play (and record) with his most famous Boswell, Dick Sudhalter, and in the 1970s, his talent intact, was a regular senior ambassador at jazz festivals. [DF]

Bix Beiderbecke and his Gang (1927–8), Parlophone

Rava, Enrico, trumpet, fluegelhorn. b. Trieste, Italy, 20 August 1943. His mother a classical pianist. Self-taught 'by listening to a lot of jazz records'. He started on trombone with traditional jazz groups and then took up trumpet. Later he studied with Carmine Caruso in New York. 1964, he played with the Gato Barbieri quintet. 1965–8, played with Steve Lacy groups, touring in Europe, South America and the USA. 1969–72, worked with Roswell Rudd's groups, with JCOA (Jazz Composers' Orchestra Association), Bill Dixon. 1975, he formed his own group with John Abercrombie, Palle Danielsson and Jon Christensen. 1976–7, his own quartet with altoist Massimo Urbani, J. F. Jenny Clark and Aldo Romano; 1978–9, his own quartet with Roswell Rudd, Giovanni Tommaso, Bruce Ditmas; 1980–3, his own quartet with Franco D'Andrea (piano), Furio di Castri (bass), Aldo Romano (dms). 1984–5, another quartet with Tony Oxley on drums. Rava has also worked with Gil Evans (1982) and toured with Cecil Taylor in Europe (1984). He has led big bands with special guests such as Rudd, Albert Mangelsdorff and Ray Anderson. In the early 1970s he divided his time between New York City, Italy and Buenos Aires, where his wife Graciela, a film-maker, lived.

Rava's quartet won a prize for the best group in Italy in 1982, and the Italian magazine *Musica Jazz* voted his ECM album *Opening Night* best record in Italy in 1983. In the same year his album *Ah* (ECM) was chosen in Brazil as one of the ten records of the year. Rava is influenced by Miles Davis, João Gilberto, Monk, Ellington, Charlie Parker, Chet Baker, Coltrane, Armstrong and 'all the greats'. He also loves cinema, literature and the visual arts, sometimes working with visual artists such as Michelangelo Pistoletto. In 1980 he collaborated on a project with Pistoletto and composer Morton Feldman in Atlanta, Georgia. Rava is also becoming more and more interested in composition and wrote the original score for the film *Oggetti Smarriti*, directed by Giuseppe Bertolucci. He has also written a big-band suite, 'F(rag)ments', for the Rome Opera. His own albums contain many of his original compositions. [IC]

With Dollar Brand (Abdullah Ibrahim), Rudd, Carla Bley, Lacy, Cecil Taylor, Jimmy Lyons, Barry Altschul, Lee Konitz; *Katchapari* (1973), MPS; *The Pilgrim and the Stars* (1975), ECM; *The Plot* (1976), ECM; *Quotation Marks* (1974), Japo; *String Band* (1984), Soul Note; *Enrico Rava Quartet* (1978), ECM; *Opening Night* (1982), ECM

Rayner, Alison, electric bass, b. Bromley, Kent, 7 September 1952. Family musical. 1957–

67, piano lessons; violin in school orchestra; singing lessons, also school choir; self-taught on bass guitar. 1976–84, played with various UK small groups and big bands. 1983, joined the Guest Stars, an all-women fusion band, which toured the US East Coast, September 1984, and the UK in December. 1985, the Guest Stars were support group to Jan Garbarek for his London concert. Favourites, Jaco Pastorius, Scott La Faro, Ron Carter, John Entwistle, Charles Mingus; also Aretha Franklin, Miles Davis, Joe Zawinul, Pat Metheny, Jimi Hendrix, and her associates in the Guest Stars. [IC]

The Guest Stars (1984); *Out At Night* (1985), both Guest Stars

Reardon, Casper, harp. b. Little Falls, New York, 15 April 1907; d. New York City, 9 March 1941. While the violin has – however tenuously – managed to survive the swiftly changing times of jazz history, very few harpists easily survived the 1930s. Perhaps because the instrument was impossible to amplify, and because of the practical difficulties of moving it around, only isolated players (American Corky Hale and Englishman David Snell, for example) still occasionally remind us of the irresistible sound of the harp in jazz. In the 1930s it was still possible to count jazz harpists on the fingers of at least half a hand. The most famous was Casper Reardon, who played first with the Philadelphia Symphony Orchestra and then became principal harpist with the Cincinnati Symphony, broadcasting regularly in his own time as a jazzman under the pseudonym 'Arpeggio Glissandi'. One of his earliest records with Jack Teagarden, 'Junk Man', demonstrates his admirable talent and by 1936 Reardon was featured with the Three Ts (Jack and Charlie Teagarden and Frank Trumbauer) and as a frequent guest with great orchestras from Paul Whiteman's on down. Reardon worked in Hollywood too, and led his own small groups in New York and Chicago until his premature death. [DF]

Rebop An early version of the word 'bebop', derived from imitating drum patterns as in the 1940 song 'Wham, Rebop, Boom, Bam'. Now a deliberately antiquated usage, it was already going out of favour by the time of Dizzy Gillespie's 1946 recording 'Ol' Man Rebop'. [BP]

Records It would be hard to exaggerate the importance of records in spreading and cultivating the appreciation of jazz. Even musicians, who always prefer to check out fellow performers by playing with them or at least hearing them live, cannot catch up with all those who specifically interest them; and for finding out about the greats now deceased, records are the only solution.

It should be remembered, however, that the process of making records is very different from playing live, whether for paying customers or for the performers' own pleasure. The clinical atmosphere of the studio is not inhibiting after a while, but the purpose (and the cost) of the venture is usually on somebody's mind and may inhibit everybody. Various strategies have been tried, from switching off all the lights to keeping the tape running continuously – even recording in front of an invited audience – but these do little to solve the basic dilemma of trying to document something that is usually at its most relaxed when not under such scrutiny. There is also the fact that artists invited to record often do not have control over the choice of material, and the company (in the shape of the producer) has the final say over what is released. Small wonder that a long list of musicians, from Fletcher Henderson onwards, have been described by their colleagues as being nowhere near their best on their records.

Some have, of course, learned to use the constraints of recording (for instance, careful sound balancing and, until the end of the 78 rpm era, enforced brevity) for artistic ends; some have even found good uses for facilities such as editing and overdubbing. Another technical consideration has provided, for those companies with large archives, a source of interesting historic material in the form of 'out-takes' (unused sequences) or 'alternate takes' (so-called from the pre-tape habit of keeping two master versions of each piece recorded, as a precaution against manufacturing problems). It has often been claimed that comparisons of these alternates shows how a given performer thought about the process of improvisation – which is true; but, even more so, they also show how the performer thought about trying to make a satisfactory record. [BP]

Redman, Dewey (Walter), tenor sax, clarinet, composer, educator, and alto sax, musette. b. Fort Worth, Texas, 17 May 1931. Began on clarinet at age 13; some lessons, but mostly self-taught; he played in his high school marching band, and fellow pupils were Ornette Coleman, Charles Moffett and Prince Lasha. In 1949 he attended Prairie View A & M studying industrial arts, with music as a subsidiary subject, and receiving his bachelor's degree in 1953. While there he switched from alto to tenor, playing in the marching band and the swing band. He received his master's degree in education from North Texas State in 1959. He taught in schools, 1956–9, then moved to Los Angeles. Shortly afterwards he settled in San Francisco, staying for seven years, leading his own groups and working with Pharoah Sanders, Wes Montgomery and others. Moved to New York in 1967, joining Ornette Coleman and staying with his group until late 1974. He also worked in the early 1970s with Charlie Haden's Liberation Music Orchestra, with Keith Jarrett and with his own groups. Redman recorded several albums with Jarrett, including a small masterpiece, *The Survivors' Suite* (1976). In 1976 he began working in a quartet with Coleman's old associates Don Cherry, Haden and Ed Blackwell. They toured in the USA and Europe, and took the name Old and New Dreams from an album they recorded in 1979. 1980, Old and New Dreams recorded a live album in Austria; the same year, Redman played on a studio album with Pat Metheny, in the company of Mike Brecker, Haden and Jack DeJohnette. Redman is a consummate player who can work with set structures and with semi- or total abstraction; he also incorporates elements from ethnic music into his work, and sometimes features the musette – a double-reed Arabian instrument. [IC]

With Haden, Cherry, Metheny, Carla Bley, Roswell Rudd; *Look for the Black Star* (1966), Arista Freedom; *Ear of the Behearer* (1973), Impulse; with Coleman, *Friends and Neighbours* (1970), Flying Dutchman; *Broken Shadows* (1971–2), Columbia; with Jarrett, *The Survivors' Suite* (1976); with *Old and New Dreams* (1979); *Playing* (1980), all ECM

Redman, Don (Donald Matthew), alto and soprano sax, multi-instrumentalist, vocals, arranger, composer. b. Piedmont, West Virginia, 29 July 1900; d. New York City, 30 November 1964. He was a conservatory-trained musician and multi-instrumentalist who came to New York with Billy Paige's Broadway Syncopators, a Pittsburgh-based band, in 1923: there he met Fletcher Henderson assembling his fledgeling band, and joined him at Harlem's Club Alabam as alto-saxophonist and staff arranger. Over the next four years Redman transformed the sound of Henderson's band, writing scores that were sometimes simple, always effective and ideal for the dancers at Roseland Ballroom: 'No matter how musical he arranges today,' said Coleman Hawkins, 'Don used to make some very good gutbucket arrangements! Rock 'n' roll with a little music behind it!' After Hawkins and Louis Armstrong had joined the band Redman's arranging took on a new enthusiasm, but in 1927 he was weaned away from Henderson by Jean Goldkette (at $300 a week) to arrange and direct for McKinney's Cotton Pickers. Redman rewrote the book, hired cornermen such as Prince Robinson (tnr) and Ralph Escudero (bass) and, in a long residency at the Graystone Ballroom, Detroit, transformed the Cotton Pickers into one of the best bands of the day: they also recorded in New York (initially without Goldkette's approval) augmenting with New York stars such as Benny Carter, Hawkins and Fats Waller. From 1931 for the next nine years Redman led his own band, recording such classics as 'Chant of the Weed' and 'Shakin' the African' and often writing with that same delicious economy. 'Some of Don's best arrangements were the simple ones', says Quentin Jackson. 'He used to say, "This is just a little something to get by!" And it would be beautiful!' From 1941, Redman gave up bandleading and opened an arranging office on Broadway, writing for bandleaders from Fred Waring and Paul Whiteman to Harry James and Jimmie Lunceford (he also arranged Jimmy Dorsey's hit 'Deep Purple'). In 1946, Redman organized the first band to visit Europe after the war (featuring such as Don Byas, Tyree Glenn and Peanuts Holland) and by 1951 was musical director for Pearl Bailey as well as arranging for orchestras all over New York. [DF]

Don Redman (1932–7), CBS Realm

Reece, Dizzy (Alphonso Son), trumpet, b. Kingston, Jamaica, 5 January 1931. Taking up trumpet at 14, moved to Europe and worked with Don Byas etc. (1949–54). Then based in UK (1954–9), recording regularly under own name including 1958 London session with sidemen Donald Byrd and Art Taylor. Settled in New York (1959), making occasional trips to Europe such as with Dizzy Gillespie big band (1968) and the Paris Reunion Band (1985). Reece is an extrovert but thoughtful post-bop stylist who, despite his nickname, does not sound like Gillespie or Navarro or Miles. Aspects of each are hinted at in his playing, but his tone and choice of phraseology are interestingly individual. [BP]

Duke Jordan, *Flight to Jordan* (1960), Blue Note

Reeds The reed instruments normally employed in jazz are the clarinet and the saxophones (alto, tenor and, to a lesser extent solowise, baritone and soprano, while occasional use has also been made of bass, contrabass, sopranino saxes and bass-clarinet). Some players of the aforementioned have often 'doubled' on other reeds such as oboe and bassoon, and (to a much greater extent, although it does not have a reed mouthpiece) on flute.

Because of the hybrid construction of the saxophone, it is also technically correct to call it a brass instrument. So, when one or more saxophones function in a section with trumpets and/or trombones, the 'horns' together are often referred to as a 'brass section'. [BP]

Reinhardt, Django (Jean Baptiste), guitar. b. Liverchies, nr. Charleroi, Belgium, 23 January 1910; d. Fontainebleau, France, 16 May 1953. He was born in a caravan in a shanty town, the son of a gypsy entertainer who worked as 'La Belle Laurence' in a travelling show based in France and Belgium. He learned first the violin, later the guitar, and when a serious caravan fire in 1928 deprived him of the use of two fingers of his left hand, he developed a revolutionary and spellbinding technique based on his limitations.

Dizzy Reece

Playing solo in cafés around Montmartre, he was discovered by a young French artist, Emile Savitry from Toulon, who found him work and introduced him to a young French star, Jean Sablon. For a while Reinhardt played Eddie Lang to Sablon's Crosby (Lang was Reinhardt's primary influence) until in 1934 he formed a quintet with violinist Stephane Grappelli, based on a band led by Louis Vola which appeared at Claridge Hotel, Paris, and the intimate little group attracted the attention of members of the Hot Club of France, a record society which occasionally put on concerts. Their next presentation – at the Salle Pleyel starring Coleman Hawkins – also featured the Quintette du Hot Club de France and successfully launched its career.

Within a year, Reinhardt, Grappelli and their group were becoming internationally famous and in the five years up to the war they recorded more than 200 sides. Most of the records, 40 years on, are acknowledged classics (even though at the time critics often downgraded the music as a country-style rehash of Joe Venuti and Eddie Lang's masterworks) and Reinhardt's work on them is as powerful as Louis Armstrong's best. An imposing man, colourfully dressed like a gypsy prince and with a powerful air of distinction, Reinhardt was an unpredictable handful. 'Ah, what trouble he gave me!' remembers Grappelli, then very much the hard-worked junior partner. 'I think now I would rather play with lesser musicians and have a peaceable time than with Django and his monkey-business.' But the music Reinhardt produced was worth all the trouble: the greatest European jazz so far, and a mystifying revelation to confident American originators: 'It was upsetting to hear a man who was a foreigner swing like that!' remembered Doc Cheatham ruefully.

The Hot Club quintet lasted until 1939, when Grappelli stayed in London for the duration of the war and Reinhardt once again went his own wandering way. On the road in his caravan, keeping clear of the Germans anywhere from Switzerland to North Africa, he stopped off to experiment with a big band, then dutifully formed a new quintet (with clarinettist Hubert Rostaing), but devoted a lot of his interest to a new challenge: 'He wanted to make it as a writer of serious music', says Gérard Levecque. Reinhardt's new compositions planned at this time (they were later transcribed by André Hodeir, among others) included a Mass for organ (never completed), a 'Boléro' and a symphony (which may well have been performed in the eastern bloc by a conductor with whom Reinhardt planned a performance and who was subsequently abducted by the Nazis): much of the best of this music was retained in a film for which Reinhardt supplied the soundtrack, *Le village de la colère* (1946). That year, back in his caravan, he received a cable from Duke Ellington inviting him to play concerts: despite the unreliability of Reinhardt's travelling habits he made it to the USA (his first question, stepping off the boat, was reportedly 'Where's Dizzy playing?') and played – on amplified guitar for the first time – a set of moderately successful concerts with Ellington, but it was a brief visit. Back home again, Reinhardt – by now playing amplified guitar and leaning towards bop idioms – spent his last years touring and recording with his quintet (sometimes including Grappelli again). But the critical feeling was that jazz fashion had taken the creative edge from him: that his determination to keep up with modern jazz developments had muted his passionate gypsy creativity. Certainly Reinhardt was disillusioned with his reception in the USA and found little to enjoy in the intellectualism of bebop; but his music stayed powerful to the end, which came with a stroke when he was only 43.

'The most creative jazz musician to originate anywhere outside the USA', says Mercer Ellington. More than 30 years on, and despite the huge upsurge in European creativity in jazz since 1960, there seems little reason to argue with him. Django Reinhardt's period of creative omnipotence was, in retrospect, brief: within a few years of his appearance the most cataclysmic development in 20th-century guitar – its electrification – was under way, and by 1942 a younger, more fashionable genius, Charlie Christian, had redefined the guitar's role for a generation. Yet Reinhardt's colossal impact – he was a genius – left an impression too deep to be forgotten, and his music has been perpetuated (appropriately in Europe) by a devoted salon of followers from Denny Wright and Diz Disley to Frenchman Bireli Lagrene in the 1980s. [DF]

50th Anniversary (1934–5), Vogue

See Delaunay, Charles, *Django Reinhardt* (Cassell, 1961, repr. Da Capo, 1982); Zwerin, Mike, *La Tristesse de Saint Louis* (Quartet, 1985)

Remler, Emily, guitar. b. New York City, 18 September 1957. Brought up in Englewood Cliffs, New Jersey, she studied at Berklee College (1974–6). Spent three years gigging and teaching in New Orleans (1976–9), working there and in New York with singers Nancy Wilson and Astrud Gilberto. Encouraged by Herb Ellis, made first album under own name (1980) and appeared at Kool and Berlin festivals (1981). Played in Los Angeles production of *Sophisticated Ladies* (1981–2), led own trio and quartet in New York. Formed duo with Larry Coryell (1985). While strongly marked by her appreciation of Wes Montgomery, Remler is also interested in the directions pursued by Pat Metheny and has impressed with her all-round competence. She is also well placed to make an important contribution to consolidating current trends into the mainstream. [BP]

Transitions (1983), Concord

Rena, Kid (Henry René), trumpet. b. New Orleans, 30 August 1898; d. 25 April 1949. He played alongside Louis Armstrong in the Colored Waifs' Home brass band and replaced him in Kid Ory's 1919 band. He was a flashy and spectacular trumpeter with high notes to spare and his band, featuring brother Joseph, a less than outstanding drummer, and young George Lewis on clarinet, was very popular in New Orleans by the mid-1920s: they played dances, functions and saloons, and featured a mixture of new jazz repertoire and loosely played ragtime from the stock 'Red Back Book'. While never the most highly-rated New Orleans trumpeter, Rena probably influenced young players such as Sharky Bonano and Louis Prima, and by the 1930s was leading a fashionable big band at the Gypsy Tea Rooms and by 1940 at the Budweiser Dance Hall. That year he was spotted by jazz researcher/journalist Heywood Broun, and at Broun's instigation recorded the first-ever sides (for Delta) to launch the American jazz revival: other players in Rena's band for this historic date included Big Eye Louis Nelson, Alphonse Picou and Ed Garland. Later in the 1940s Kid Rena played the Brown Derby Café with a hung-over jazz band: heavy drinking had dulled his spark and he was inactive for the last two years of his life. [DF]

Any with own band or George Lewis

Renaud, Henri, piano. b. Villedieu (Indre), France, 10 April 1925. Played (1949–50) with Don Byas, Buck Clayton, Roy Eldridge etc., then formed own small group. Performed on and helped to produce albums by visiting US musicians (early 1950s), and albums recorded in US for release in France (1954). Worked with Kenny Clarke quintet (1961) and, while still active as player, introduced regular radio series (from 1962) and later TV jazz spots. From 1964 became an executive of CBS Records (France), occasionally producing new sessions by such as Jean-Luc Ponty and organizing continuing series of jazz reissues. [BP]

Clifford Brown, *Paris Sessions, vol.1* (1953), Jazz Legacy

Rendell, Don(ald Percy), tenor and soprano sax, flute, clarinet. b. Plymouth, Devon, 4 March 1926. Parents both musicians, took up alto at 15. Worked alongside Americans in USO (1944), then with several big bands. Founder member of Johnny Dankworth Seven (1950–3), also with Tony Crombie (1955) and Ted Heath (1955–6). Toured Europe with Stan Kenton (1956, taking uncredited solos on *Live at Albert Hall* album) and with Woody Herman Anglo-American Herd (1959). First led own group 1953–5 and continuously from 1960, featuring such sidemen as Graham Bond (1961–2), Michael Garrick (1965–9), Barbara Thompson (1973–6) and Ian Carr who joined in 1962 and was

Django Reinhardt

co-leader of the Rendell-Carr quintet 1963–9. During this period, also worked and recorded with Neil Ardley, Garrick, Thompson etc. For last 20 years, prominent teacher of jazz (and Bible studies) including at Royal Academy of Music (1974–7) and Guildhall (from 1984).

Specializing on tenor from mid-1940s, Rendell was initially enamoured of Lester Young and later, though less audibly, John Coltrane. From these and other influences (Parker, Gillespie, Ellington, Monk, Holiday) he forged a style of great strength and resilience which has been an inspiration to many younger UK musicians. [BP]

Rendell/Carr, *Phase III* (1967), Columbia; *Earth Music* (1979), Spotlite

Revival (USA) A consciousness of the need to re-explore the musical fundamentals of classic jazz in the USA was detectable no more than six years after Louis Armstrong's Hot Five and Seven sessions had been recorded. The commercial aims of dance and swing band music in the mid-1930s were already leading young players such as Bob Haggart (bassist with Bob Crosby's orchestra) to aver: 'We play jazz, not swing. We always hated riff tunes and avoided them whenever possible.' Crosby's band revivals of Hot Five vehicles such as 'Savoy Blues' and 'Come back, sweet papa' were an early indication of one need to 'get back to the roots', but his orchestral formula – highly arranged, played with trained precision and a sophisticated tonal approach – was still closer to swing than to New Orleans jazz, and the same could be applied to his small group, the Bobcats, from two years later. Other revivalist whispers in the breeze came in 1936. That year an article by J. S. Moynahan in the *Saturday Evening Post* pointed out that the re-formed Original Dixieland Jazz Band (they came together for a radio show) played more 'authentic' jazz than Benny Goodman; again, in 1939, the Summa Cum Laude band (led by Bud Freeman), Muggsy Spanier's Ragtimers and others made conscious efforts on record to revive older repertoire and steer clear of the blander aspects of American swing. All these bands, however, re-interpreted old material in their own way, rather than studiously re-creating the original: that breakthrough belonged to the true figureheads of US revivalism, Lu Watters's Yerba Buena Jazz Band, in 1940. This band set out to re-create faithfully the two-trumpet format, rhythmic approach and repertoire of King Oliver's Creole Jazz Band, and set themselves consciously and intellectually aside from every commercial development of the previous 17 years. The emergence of the Yerba Buena band coincided with the researches of young missionary revivalists such as Heywood Broun, Frederick Ramsey and William Russell, who created an interest in the whereabouts of such forgotten New Orleans figures as Bunk Johnson, George Lewis and Kid Ory and then satisfied the interest by locating, interviewing, promoting and recording their subjects. The efforts of Broun, Williams, Russell, Eugene Williams and others created enormous controversy in a jazz world already split by fashion and factions; and their determined championing of primitive musicians such as Johnson caused bewilderment to ears more attuned to the sophisticated and rapid developments of Goodman, Hawkins and the swing era in general. But they initiated, and followed through, a highly necessary re-evaluation of jazz values at a time when the music had sometimes acquired an undesirably facile quality. The revival – in which 'authenticity' was the emotive keyword – set up rules which were to prove too restrictive for many of its early protagonists: leaders such as Bob Scobey (Watters's early crusading trumpet-partner) and Turk Murphy (his trombonist) subsequently found themselves working a jazz formula which, whether for business or musical reasons, dispensed with the most austere demands of revivalism. But because of the movement, a whole generation of New Orleans players were restored in the 1940s to glories greater than they ever achieved previously and an area of jazz which might otherwise have been forgotten forever was rightfully set back high in the music's hierarchy. Early recordings of revivalists such as Watters, and their originals such as Johnson and Lewis, possess a driving fervour which – set against most of Benny Goodman's 1944 records, for example – still clearly reveal how vital the need for a jazz revival was at that time. [DF]

Revival (Great Britain) The post-war British jazz revival (which, as with most British jazz history, echoed the American original) began for much the same reasons as it did in America. By 1944, British popular music, often commercially based to begin with, was ten years on from its most exciting innovations and conveyed by a BBC whose starched-collar presentation offered little to a young generation that was about to survive a world war. In terms of jazz activity, too, Britain had reached a level and none-too-exciting plane. Night clubs, rhythm clubs and record societies offered skilled dance-band musicians playing stylized choruses on chord sequences well established by ten years of jam sessions ('Sweet Sue', 'Honeysuckle Rose' and 'The Blues' were frequent choices). But there was a lack of fervour in the music, and the first re-explorations of New Orleans and its jazz by early revivalists promised gifts to spare: fresh repertoire, an intriguing sense of discovery, a tempting permissiveness, well away from the coy *double entendres* of Tin Pan Alley and, above all, a flushing away of music that belonged to an older, less bold generation for a neglected music of far superior quality and 'authenticity'. A great deal of debate has gone on as to who formed the first revivalist jazz band in Britain (Belfast's Ken Smiley band, which played Chicago-style jazz as early as 1938, is one contender), but the figurehead of the British jazz revival was and still is pianist George Webb, whose band – playing material by King Oliver and other New Orleans giants in the accepted two-trumpet format – was active in South London by 1944. The Webb band – which later included trumpeter Humphrey Lyttelton, as well as clarinettist Wally Fawkes and trombonist Eddie Harvey – established the principle of revivalism in Britain; but what exactly was being revived needed further definition. By 1950 – along with promising young revivalists such as Eric Silk and cornettist John Haim, who died early – three separate factions of British revivalism were clearly apparent: Freddy Randall (playing Chicago-style jazz at a North London venue, Cooks Ferry Inn), classic trumpeter Humphrey Lyttelton, who played the Armstrong/Bechet areas of jazz at the London Jazz Club, and – most intriguing of all – Ken

Colyer, who (slightly to the dismay of Armstrong-based revivalists) played strict New Orleans jazz. 'To ears attuned to Morton's Red Hot Peppers,' says George Melly, 'it was a horrible sound': his comment illustrates that for most early – and sometimes ill-informed – revivalists any pre-war jazz of black origins was an acceptable area for re-creation. It was Colyer, however, who was to make the most important long-term contribution to British New Orleans revivalism. Much as George Lewis and Bunk Johnson had done in the USA, Colyer created – and maintained for over 40 years – a climate in which New Orleans jazz could function in Britain as an independent entity. For most other revivalists, including Lyttelton, as well as hundreds of semi-professional bands around the country such as the excellent Merseysippi (Liverpool) and Avon Cities (Bristol) groups, the confines of revivalism pure and simple were too much of a creative strait-jacket. By 1960 most, apart from Colyer (and one or two kindred spirits like Eric Silk), had moved on to wider terms of reference (although many, notably Chris Barber, saw the re-creation of true New Orleans jazz as a continuing part of their brief). 'The battle had been won and therefore lost!' observed George Melly: New Orleans jazz had been thoroughly re-established in jazz's music spectrum and there was no longer any focus for a crusade. [DF]

Revivalism The conscious return, by a new generation of jazz musicians, to an earlier style or form of jazz. The term is most generally applied to the re-adoption of New Orleans jazz (either in its sophisticated Oliver/Armstrong incarnation or in the more basic styles of George Lewis and Bunk Johnson) by young musicians in the late 1930s in the USA and in the early 1940s in Great Britain and Europe, but has been used to refer to the bebop revival of the 1970s. [DF]

Rhythm (1) It seems an understatement to say that the use of rhythm in jazz is its most distinctive feature, and also its most subtle attribute by contrast with music in other ways comparable to jazz. For further discussion, see under AFRO-LATIN, BEAT, POLYRHYTHM, STOP-TIME, SWING, SYNCOPATION, TEMPO, TIME, TWO-BEAT.

(2) An abbreviation for the song title 'I Got Rhythm', since George Gershwin's chord-sequence was for many years the second most popular framework for improvisation (after the 12-bar blues). Therefore, the phrase 'Rhythm changes' does not mean changes in the rhythm of a performance, but rather the chord-changes of the Gershwin song as used in hundreds of jazz pieces such as 'Lester Leaps In', 'Anthropology', 'Rhythm-a-ning' etc.

(3) 'The rhythm' are also the rhythm-section players, as in the phrase 'brass, reeds and rhythm'. In the early New Orleans days, the rhythm often consisted of only guitar and bass, or only piano and drums; and, in much later periods, if the group's volume level was modest (e.g. the Benny Goodman trio or Bechet–Spanier Big Four), these duos were sufficient.

The first big bands of the 1920s, and indeed most small groups from the Armstrong Hot Seven onwards, had four rhythm (with banjo and brass bass for a while more popular than guitar or string bass, the situation being reversed from the early 1930s onwards). From the 1940s, the guitar became more marginal, as did the piano from the 1950s although, if they are in the group as soloists, they function as part of the rhythm when not soloing.

From the 1960s it became more common to add one or more Afro-Latin percussionists, and in the 1970s to include more than one keyboard player and/or more than one guitarist. The largest rhythm-section on disc, outside of Archie Shepp's and Ornette Coleman's recordings in North Africa, may well be that on Miles Davis's *On the Corner*, reportedly 11 strong. [BP]

Rhythm-and-blues A term for black popular music adopted by the US record industry in the late 1940s to replace demeaning descriptions such as 'race records' (1920s) and 'sepia series' (1930s). These names had, of course, covered nearly all of the early jazz issues which, it was naturally assumed, were only worth marketing for black listeners.

A lot of what is now thought of as rhythm-and-blues actually predated the term, and was a direct outgrowth of the blues groups and 'jump bands' of the late 1930s. But the rhythmic bounce and the saxophone-dominated instrumentation remained a constant thread at least up to the work of Earl Bostic, Fats Domino and Little Richard, although gradually more and more electric guitar sounds were absorbed (via West Coast blues) in the evolution of r & b into rock and roll. Much of the vocal work of the period was more influenced by gospel than blues, which is one reason why such a thorough-going mix made r & b the basis of all pop music since, in the same way that bebop simultaneously laid the foundation for all later jazz.

More than that, rhythm-and-blues has continued to interact with post-bebop jazz; where folk-blues had provided a touchstone for early jazz, now the relationship was closer. Not only had r & b been influenced by jazz, but most of the important jazz players of the hard-bop and free-jazz generation served their apprenticeship in r & b bands, even the great saxophone innovators John Coltrane and Ornette Coleman. [BP]

Rich, Buddy (Bernard), drums, vocals, leader. b. Brooklyn, New York, 30 September 1917. He was a performer at 18 months (he toured as 'Baby Traps' in his parents' vaudeville act, Wilson and Rich), danced and drummed on Broadway at

Buddy Rich

four, toured Australia as a single at six and by 11 was leading his own band. At 21 he replaced Danny Alvin in Joe Marsala's band and by then was already clearly a super-talent destined for the big bands which all his life were to remain his first love. 'Bunny Berigan's was my first,' he recalled later to Les Tomkins (in Britain's *Crescendo* magazine), 'and it was a whole different world opened up to me! "Oh so this is what music's all about!" ' A succession of great big bands followed for the young drummer – Harry James's, Artie Shaw's, and, from November 1939, Tommy Dorsey's – and Rich, with his abrasive tongue, fine ear for what was good and ruthlessly competitive edge – was a match not only for any other drummer within cutting distance but also for his usually indomitable leader. 'Dorsey's wasn't a hot band,' he coolly remembered later, 'it never professed to be. It was a dance band with good musicians. Then he hired Sy Oliver – started getting some jazz arrangements in, and then that band would kick as well as any for that time and period.' With Dorsey's orchestra Rich established a royal reputation and in 1945 he formed his own (at a time when big bands were in severe decline) and doggedly ran it for two years until the money finally ran out: 'We suffered! But even finally when there was no money that was a joy because we weren't bending to the big brains who said, "Big bands are out".' The attitude was typical of Rich, whose flint-hard convictions never allowed others to do his thinking for him. From 1947 he joined Jazz at the Philharmonic and for the next 13 years lent his talents to Charlie Ventura, Harry James, Dorsey again, cultivated a reputation as a stylish singer and led his own small groups and bands until by 1959 – slightly out of jazz fashion – he was contemplating a complete career switch to singing and acting. That year he suffered his first heart attack, but came back fighting, took up keep fit and some years later – well into his forties – achieved a black belt in karate! From 1961 for five years he worked for Harry James and in 1966, at the height of flower-power, Beatlemania and so on, re-formed his big band, at a time when the idea seemed ludicrous. 'Everybody said, "Who the hell wants a big band?" ' he remembers. 'But I said, "Well, who knows better than me? We don't know if the kids want it yet – they've never been exposed to it!" ' Rich's band – brilliant, featuring sensibly contemporary repertoire, a battalion of fine arrangers, including Bill Holman and Don Sebesky, and *tour de force* drum features such as a 10-minute 'West Side Story' broadside – became an international success, touring Japan, Britain, Australia and elsewhere, playing the best American venues, breaking into TV first in 1968 (replacing Jackie Gleason for a season) and recording best-sellers. Rich (like Tommy Dorsey 25 years before) was a ruthless (even cruel) taskmaster, but he got results, and his honest championship of fine music values, as he saw them, was a necessary re-affirmation of principles in an era of hype, overstatement, hard sell and pseudo-intellectualism. After heart bypass surgery in 1983 he cut his recuperation time from six months to two and was temporarily run down; but in 1985, back to full strength, he was once again touring nine months out of twelve, recording all-music spectaculars of his own for American public TV, and appearing with old friend-cum-sparring-partner Frank Sinatra for concerts. In 1986 he toured the UK to full houses, still with his big band. [DF]

The Man from Planet Jazz (1980), PRT

See Balliett, Whitney, *Improvising* (OUP, 1977)

Rich, Fred, piano, composer, leader. b. Warsaw, 3 January 1898; d. California, 8 September 1956. He was a capable studio pianist, arranger and bandleader who, in his capacity as musical director for studio orchestras on the Harmony, Okeh and Hit of the Week labels among others, recorded scores of sides from 1925 on. His regular sidemen included the cream of 1920s session and jazz players: a short list would include Leo McConville, Bunny Berigan, Tommy and Jimmy Dorsey, Carl Kress, Tony Parenti, Joe Venuti, Frank Signorelli, Dick McDonough, Joe Tarto, and Stan King; the records were issued under a bewildering variety of pseudonyms, including 'The Deauville Syncopators', 'Chester Leighton and his Sophomores' and 'The New York Syncopators'. By the late 1930s he was working mainly in radio: his last recording dates from 1940 included such as Roy Eldridge, Benny Carter, Clyde Hart and Hayes Alvis. From 1942, Rich worked on the musical staff for United Artists and from 1945 (says John Chilton) was partially paralysed as a result of a fall, but he continued his career up to the 1950s. [DF]

Fred Rich and his Orchestra, *Dance the Depression Away* (1929–31), World Records

Richards, Red (Charles), piano, vocals. b. Brooklyn, New York, 19 October 1912. He worked early on with players as varied as Tab Smith (for four years), Jimmy McPartland and Roy Eldridge and by the early 1950s had played for Sidney Bechet, his pupil Bob Wilber and Mezz Mezzrow, as well as a long stint with Muggsy Spanier (1953–7). Later in the decade he was regularly to be found among 'Chicago-style' jazzmen, including Wild Bill Davison, and as solo pianist at Eddie Condon's; from 1964 he co-led with Vic Dickenson the successful Saints and Sinners, featuring Herman Autrey. Later, after Dickenson left, Richards reduced to a quartet with clarinettist Herbie Hall, played club residencies, subbed with the World's Greatest Jazz Band and continued his solo piano work at Condon's, as well as touring Europe as a soloist. His fine rolling style, sympathetic backing talent and encyclopaedic knowledge of jazz piano history makes Richards one of the most satisfying classic pianists around: he deserves the kind of solo exposure which has been the good fortune of peers such as Ralph Sutton. [DF]

The Seventh Avenue Stompers, *Fidgety Feet* (1958), Savoy; or any solo album

Richardson, John, drums. b. London, 8 August 1932. He worked from the 1950s on with Alex Welsh, Acker Bilk, the Randall–Shepherd All Stars, Stan Greig's trio, John Picard's sextet and others for long periods, as well as freelancing and leading his own small groups. He plays in a high-powered, dynamic style which owes a lot to the most creative and colourful mid-period drummers such as Dave Tough, Cliff Leeman and Sidney Catlett: his exciting and driving talents are well-heard on the albums below. In recent years Richardson has freelanced, working in London pubs and clubs by night and as a postman by day. [DF]

Acker Bilk, *Expo '70*, Regal; *Randall–Shepherd All Stars* (1970), Black Lion

Richman, Boomie (Abraham Samuel), tenor sax, clarinet, flute. b. Brockton, Massachusetts, 2 April 1921. A very underrated tenor saxophonist in the style of Eddie Miller, he played his first dates around Boston and came to New York in 1942 to join long-time colleague Muggsy Spanier's big band. After work with Jerry Wald and George Paxton's orchestras he joined Tommy Dorsey for a six-year stay and became, along with Charlie Shavers, Pee Wee Erwin and Dave Tough, one of Dorsey's most outstanding cornermen, whose work is nicely captured on the Sentimental Gentleman's 1946 version of 'At Sundown'. After he left Dorsey in 1952, Richman worked in the studios and regularly for Benny Goodman (whom he met first on a 1946 Dorsey radio show for NBC), 1953–4, then again in 1955 and 1958 until Zoot Sims took over his chair. Recorded work from Richman is rarer than it should be: one fine date with Spanier (see below) shows off his tasteful swing skills to good advantage. [DF]

Muggsy Spanier (1954), Coral

Richmond, Dannie, drums (and tenor sax). b. New York City, 15 December 1935. Played tenor from age 13, toured with Paul Williams r & b band (*c.* 1955). Six months after taking up drums seriously, joined Charles Mingus with whom he was associated for 21 years, apart from a few interruptions (1956–67, 1969–70, late 1973–early 1978). Also worked in late 1950s with Chet Baker; in late 1960s with soul singer Johnny Taylor; and 1971–3 with Mark-Almond group, Joe Cocker, Elton John. Following his return to jazz, also did much freelance recording and gigging with Duke Jordan, Jimmy Knepper, Bennie Wallace etc. After Mingus's death, was original musical director of Mingus Dynasty (1979–80), worked with Chico Freeman quartet (1980) and George Adams–Don Pullen (1980–3, 1985). Own quintet has made several albums and European tours.

Richmond was typecast for many years as Mingus's drummer, and it is true that the qualities of all-round musicianship that he brought to the task made him ideally suited, as almost any record of them working together will demonstrate. Developing from a profound admiration for Max Roach and Philly Joe Jones, he perfected a style that was responsive both to the needs of a particular soloist at a particular moment and also to the overall structure of a composition. The combination of supportiveness and excitement he creates is equally adaptable to a piano trio or a big band, to a conservative mainstream context or a freely organized group improvisation, but this versatility is still under-recognized. [BP]

Mingus Ah Um (1959), CBS; *Dannie Richmond Quintet* (1980), Gatemouth

Ricotti, Frank, vibraphone. b. London, 31 January 1949. Father an ex-drummer. Studied at Trinity College of Music. Led his own quartet, 1967–71. Has worked with groups led by Mike Gibbs, Stan Tracey, John Taylor, Graham Collier. Favourites, Gary Burton, Claus Ogerman, Herbie Hancock, Tony Hymas, Kenny Wheeler, John Taylor. [IC]

Riel, Alex, drums. b. Copenhagen, 13 September 1940. Lessons in Copenhagen during the 1950s; one term at the Berklee School, Boston, 1966. During early 1960s he went deeply into free (abstract) jazz, working with John Tchicai, Archie Shepp, Gary Peacock among others. 1965, he was voted Danish Musician of the Year. With trumpeter Palle Mikkelborg, Riel formed a quintet in 1966, and in 1968 it won first prize at the Montreux festival and then played at the Newport festival. While in the USA (1966), Riel played with many musicians including Roland Kirk and Toshiko Akiyoshi. During the early 1970s he again co-led a group, V8, with Mikkelborg. Since then he has freelanced in Europe. [IC]

With Mikkelborg, Gary Bartz, Sahib Shihab, Stuff Smith, Herb Geller; with Jackie McLean, *Live at Montmartre* (1972); with Jackie McLean/Dexter Gordon, *The Meeting, vols.1/2* (1973); with Ben Webster, *My Man: Live at Montmartre* (1973); with Ken McIntyre, *Hindsight* (1974), all Steeplechase

Riff A repeated phrase of pronounced rhythmic character, often not strikingly melodic. Usually two bars in length, e.g. Basie's 'Swinging the Blues', or four bars as in 'One O'Clock Jump'.

Riffs can be found in solo work, especially from certain players who habitually think along such lines (such as Horace Silver or Illinois Jacquet), and even King Oliver's famous 'Dippermouth Blues' cornet solo begins with two riffs. But their use really found its logical home in the big bands of the late 1920s and 1930s, especially when one section of a band harmonized riffs as a cushion and a catalyst for someone else's solo. The Kansas City bands such as Bennie Moten's, Andy Kirk's and particularly Count Basie's were quite capable of creating new riffs on the spot, thus encouraging the soloist to continue for longer than was ever possible on records of the time, and this practice was readily incorporated into their off-duty 'jamming'. It even became so habitual that a jamming devotee such as Lester Young can be heard breaking out into one-man riffs behind others' solos even on quintet and sextet recordings.

The move to include riffs in bass lines dates back at least as far as 'Night in Tunisia' (and even Chu Berry's 'Christopher Columbus' from 1936 is just a bass riff used as the main melody). Thanks to the gradually increasing Afro-Latin influence on black popular music, and their combined influence on jazz, it was possible by 1970 for Miles Davis's *Jack Johnson* to contain three main themes, each of which consisted solely of a bass riff. And, especially since jazz bassists started to be properly amplified in the late 1960s, the relationship between the bass riff, the rest of the rhythm-section and the soloist is very similar to that created with section riffs in the big bands of 40 years earlier. [BP]

Riley, Howard (John Howard), piano. b. Huddersfield, Yorkshire, 16 February 1943. Father was a semi-pro dance-band pianist and encouraged Riley to play. BA and MA from University of Wales, 1961–6. M.Mus. from Indiana University, where he studied with Dave Baker, 1966–7. M.Phil. from York University, 1967–70. Yet Riley had no formal piano lessons, and was self-taught with some paternal help. He began at six and became interested in jazz in the mid-1950s. 1959 onwards, he played in jazz clubs around Yorkshire. While studying theory and composition formally during the 1960s, he also played jazz with his own trios and (1965) with the Evan Parker quartet, devoting himself almost exclusively to abstraction – free improvisation. Since 1967, he has played clubs and festivals in West and East Europe, USA and Canada. He led his own trio, 1967–76, and since then has done many solo performances.

He has also played with many groups including duos with John McLaughlin (1968), Keith Tippett (from 1981), Jaki Byard (from 1982), Eddie Prevost (from 1984), Elton Dean (from 1984); and quartets with Trevor Watts, Barry Guy, John Stevens (1978–81), Evan Parker, Guy, Stevens (from 1983); with Tony Oxley groups (from 1972); London Jazz Composers' Orchestra (from 1970); Barbara Thompson–Art Themen quintet (1969–70). Riley has also composed for the LJCO and New Jazz Orchestra and for his own groups. He has also composed formal (i.e. notated and non-improvised) pieces. His trio was the first jazz group to appear at an Albert Hall Promenade Concert (1969). He is interested and active in education and has taught jazz piano and taken workshops at the Guildhall School of Music (from 1969) and Goldsmiths College (from 1975) in London. 1976–7, he was Creative Associate at the Center of the Creative and Performing Arts, Buffalo, NY. 1970–4, he was a founder member of the Musicians' Co-operative in London. From 1969 on, he has had several Arts Council (UK) composition bursaries. His favourite pianists range from Bill Evans and Monk to Richard Twardzik and Art Tatum. [IC]

With New Jazz Orchestra (as composer), Tony Oxley, LJCO, Spontaneous Music Ensemble; *The Day Will Come* (1970), CBS; *Facets* (1979–81), Impetus (3 records, boxed set); *For Four on Two Two* (1982), Affinity

Rimington, Sammy (Samuel), clarinet, alto sax, leader. Of all the 'honorary' New Orleans citizens who happen to come from Britain, he is perhaps the most lyrically musical. A perfectly graceful and highly creative master of New Orleans jazz, he came to prominence with Ken Colyer's Jazzmen around 1960 and worked regularly with them thereafter as well as with like-minded musicians countrywide in Britain, Europe and America. In 1965 he moved to the USA, worked with Red Allen, Zutty Singleton, Herman Autrey and others, and soon after moved to New Orleans where he replaced Butch Thompson in the Hall Brothers' Band, recorded with Kid Thomas (George Lewis shared the sessions) and regularly collaborated with visitors like Don Ewell and Max Morath. 1971, he worked around Europe and in the next decade – with frequent returns to the USA – joined George Webb, Chris Barber and formed his own jazz-rock group, Armada. By 1985 he had played and recorded with every American and European New Orleans-style jazzman of note and – like a small number of other great British reedmen including Tubby Hayes or Pete King (albeit in a different style) – his name was a promise of quality, inspiration and flair. 'It's very difficult to express my feeling for this kind of music,' says Rimington, 'but I know after years of playing and experience that it's one of the most difficult forms of music to play well, due to its simplicity and relaxed rhythmic feel. I prefer the music to be quite free but controlled – also not to be restricted and tied down to sounding like a particular band on record.' [DF]

And Red Beans (1977), Dawn Club

Rivers, Sam (Samuel Carthorne), tenor sax, composer, soprano sax, piano, flute, and bass clarinet, viola. b. El Reno, Oklahoma, 25 September 1930. Grandfather, a minister and musician, published *A Collection of Revival Hymns and Plantation Melodies* (1882). Mother a pianist; father a Fisk University graduate, sang with Fisk Jubilee Singers and Silverstone quartet. Rivers heard spirituals and light classics at home; he began on piano at age five, then took up violin and also alto sax. At 12 he played soprano in a marching band. He took up tenor sax seriously at Jarvis Christian College, Texas. 1947, he went to the Boston Conservatory, studying composition and viola, and also playing the violin; at night he played sax in a bar. He also worked with Jaki Byard, Joe Gordon, Herb Pomeroy. His early influences were Lester Young, Coleman Hawkins and Eddie Davis, and later ones included John Coltrane, Charlie Parker and Sonny Rollins. 1955–7, he went to Florida, composing music for lyrics and working for singers and dancers; he also co-led a band with Don Wilkerson and accompanied Billie Holiday on tour. 1958, he was with the Herb Pomeroy big band in Boston, and also led his own quartet with 13-year-old Tony Williams on drums. At the beginning of the 1960s he was listening to Cecil Taylor and Ornette Coleman, and becoming interested in the abstract music of the avant-garde.

In the early 1960s he was also musical director of a band backing visiting artists such as Maxine Brown, Wilson Pickett, B. B. King, and toured with T-Bone Walker. 1964, he spent six months with Miles Davis, touring in the USA and playing in Japan where they recorded a live album. 1967, he moved to New York and began teaching at his own studio in Harlem. 1968–73, he played with Cecil Taylor. In 1971, with his wife Bea, he opened Studio Rivbea as a teaching and music performance centre, presenting his own group with guest artists such as Dewey Redman, Clifford Jordan and Sonny Fortune, and also presenting other groups.

Talking of music teaching, Rivers told Michael Ullman: 'I make sure that I'm not imitated. I make sure that my students come up with their own individual approaches to the music. My students write their own exercises.

They don't play anything but their own music – so how are they going to copy anybody?' As well as teaching at his own loft, Rivers was from 1968 composer in residence for the Harlem Opera Society, lecturer on Afro-American musical history at Connecticut College in 1972, and artist in residence at Wesleyan University, 1970–3.

January 1975, he was guest soloist with the San Francisco Symphony Orchestra; 1978, the Newport in New York Festival presented 'The World of Sam Rivers', in Carnegie Hall; 1979, he presented a piece for 32 musicians at New York's Public Theater. During the later 1970s Rivers was closely associated with Dave Holland in duo and trio formations. The trio toured the USA and Europe several times playing major festivals, and with it Rivers began to feature his piano playing and flute a great deal, and also sang the blues spiritedly.

Rivers is one of the 'universal' virtuosi in that his style is a compendium of the jazz tradition from the early blues to abstraction. In one sense, however, he is conservative – he has completely ignored the electronic revolution of the 1970s, and confines himself entirely to acoustic music. [IC]

With Cecil Taylor, Don Pullen and others; with Miles Davis, *Miles in Tokyo* (1964), CBS Japan; with Dave Holland, *Conference of the Birds* (1972), ECM; *Sam Rivers/Dave Holland, vols.1/2* (1976), Improvising Artists; Rivers/Holland/Barker/Daley, *Waves* (1978), Tomato; Rivers/Holland/Lewis/Barker, *Contrasts* (1980), ECM

Roach, Max(well), drums, composer. b. New Land, North Carolina, 10 January 1924. Brought up from age four in New York City, was given drumkit at 12. Played with teenage friends and studied theory and composition at Manhattan School of Music. Sitting in at Minton's and Monroe's, then replaced Kenny Clarke in Coleman Hawkins group, making record debut with Hawkins (1943). Worked with Dizzy Gillespie on 52nd Street (1944), deputized briefly with Duke Ellington and toured with Benny Carter band for a year (1944–5). Nightclub and recording work with Charlie Parker (1945, including Parker's first session under own name), Gillespie's big band (1945), Stan Getz, Allen Eager, Hawkins again (all 1946). Regular drummer in classic Parker quintet (1947–9), followed by freelance work (including Jazz at the Philharmonic) and own groups. Becoming a partner in Charles Mingus's Debut Records, appeared on several sessions including celebrated Massey Hall concert (1953). Worked in California (1953–4), then formed new quintet featuring Clifford Brown as co-leader (1954–6).

Surviving the tragic death of both Brown and Richie Powell, Roach maintained his group continuously to the present day, with, among many others, Donald Byrd, Kenny Dorham, Booker Little, Freddie Hubbard, Sonny Rollins, Hank Mobley, George Coleman, Stanley Turrentine, Billy Harper, Barry Harris, Ray Bryant, Mal Waldron, George Cables. He has also expanded his interests beyond the conventional horns-and-rhythm grouping, for specific projects incorporating choirs, solo singers such as Andy Bey and Abbey Lincoln (to whom he was married, 1962–70), and string quartets (including on occasion his daughter Maxine). He has performed duos with Archie Shepp, Anthony Braxton, Cecil Taylor and Dollar Brand (Abdullah Ibrahim) (late 1970s), and formed a regular group combining various drums and tuned percussion such as vibes and steel-pans, called M'Boom (from 1972). Although he has collaborated with various arrangers on some of these projects, he has been the composer of the greater part of material performed by his groups in the last 25 years.

It is no exaggeration, however, to say that Roach is composing each time he plays the drums. Not only are his solos models of structured development, but his manner of backing other soloists encourages or reinforces similar tendencies in them. This ability, which first surfaced alongside Parker (and during Rollins's 18 months with Roach), has become evident and perhaps more necessary in the marathon performances of the post-Coltrane era. And yet it is based on ideas arising from the work of Jo Jones and Kenny Clarke, who not only prompted the soloists but made them sound good within the ensemble. Even Max's own playing, while displaying extreme independence on each part of the kit (an influence in turn on Elvin Jones), always makes the whole greater than the parts.

Perhaps there is a parallel here with Roach's view of music's reflection of, and responsibility to, society as a whole. He marked the start of the 1960s with his *We Insist – Freedom Now!* suite and, while far from being the first musician to comment on the civil rights struggle, he has been the most consistent in his concern; more importantly, unlike much other politically inspired jazz, Max's work in this direction always stands up musically, even long after its initial impetus. And, from being a performer who organized protests and lectured audiences from the bandstand, he has been able since 1972 to combine his artistic and educational communication as professor of music at the University of Massachusetts. [BP]

Clifford Brown/Max Roach: *The Quintet, vols. 1/2* (1954–6), Mercury; *We Insist – Freedom Now!* (1960), CBS; *Lift Every Voice and Sing* (1971), Atlantic; *Survivors* (1984), Soul Note

See Haydon, Geoffrey, and Marks, Dennis (eds), *Repercussions: A Celebration of African-American Music* (Century, 1985)

Robert, Yves, trombone. b. Clermont-Ferrand, France, 17 January 1958. Studied at music school until age 18. 1977, played with hard bop groups in the Hot Club de Lyon; 1979, joined

Max Roach

the Nancy Jazz Action and the free jazz group Agapao; 1982, returned to Lyons to work with ARFI (Association à la Recherche d'un Folklore Imaginaire) and the big band La Marmite Infernale; 1984, moved to Marseilles and in the mid-1980s was working with GRIM (Groupe de Recherche et d'Improvisation Musicale), La Marmite Infernale, Didier Levallet quintet, and *Futurities*, a dance show led by Steve Lacy. Robert has also worked with the Brotherhood of Breath, touring the UK and Mozambique with them; with La Marmite Infernale he appeared at the New Jazz Festival in Moers. 1985, he joined the Orchestre National de Jazz led by François Jeanneau. [IC]

With André Jaume, *Musique pour 8: L'oc* (1982), Hat Hut; *Yves Robert Trombone Solo* (1983), Arfi Nove; with La Marmite Infernale, *Moralité Surprise* (1983), AM; with Denis Levaillant septet, *Barium Circus* (1984), Nato; with Didier Levallet quintet, *Quiet Days* (1985), Evidence

Roberts, Luckey (Charles Luckyeth), piano, composer. b. Philadelphia, 7 August 1887; d. New York City, 5 February 1968. After early days in vaudeville working as an acrobat and child juggler, he learned his profession in Baltimore playing in saloons and cabarets. A huge man – his fingers could stretch a record-breaking fourteenth on the piano keys – Roberts's formidable talent was well established in New York by 1913, the year that two of his most famous compositions, 'Pork and Beans' and 'Junk Man Rag', were published: like all of Roberts's output they became test pieces for such young hopefuls as Fats Waller, Duke Ellington and James P. Johnson (whom Roberts tutored) to live up to. Besides being one of the most technically dazzling piano soloists of the late ragtime era (his piano rolls, from 1916, are sensational), Roberts – a man of endless charm who, said Eubie Blake, possessed the remarkable gift of being able to cry at will to avert trouble – led his own band too: it worked on the vaudeville circuit as well as at hotels and high-society functions throughout the 1920s and 1930s, and Roberts quickly became a society favourite. Like Eubie Blake (who was a shade jealous of his young rival) Roberts was a prolific composer: he saw 14 of his own musical comedies successfully produced in the pre-war years and by 1939 was star of a concert at New York's

Carnegie Hall, then another at Town Hall, 1941. He was a featured artist on Rudi Blesh's This is Jazz series, recorded for Blesh in 1946, and by that time was writing extended works for his orchestra as well as semi-commercial hits such as 'Moonlight Cocktail' from 1941. In later years Roberts played often at his own Harlem bar, the Rendezvous: his music deserves re-examination (as does his small, fine recorded output) in the 1980s. [DF]

Roberts/Willie The Lion Smith, *Harlem Piano* (1958), Good Time Jazz

Robertson, Zue (C. Alvin), trombone. b. New Orleans, 7 March 1891; d. Watts, Los Angeles, 1943. (The nickname is thought to have come from 'Zoo', a reference to his regular work in carnivals and travelling circuses.) 'He was credited by many with setting the style for all who followed after on the slide trombone,' says Orrin Keepnews, 'but he was a rambler and irresponsible, which is probably why lasting fame eluded him.' Certainly Robertson's credentials (best researched, as always, by John Chilton) are impressive enough: he was working in Kit Carson's Wild West Show by around 1910, played with the great New Orleans trumpeter Manuel Perez and others and by 1917 was in Chicago where he teamed at various times with King Oliver, Jelly Roll Morton, W. C. Handy's highly-drilled band and Dave Peyton's theatre orchestra – all jobs requiring skill, musicianship and probably reading ability. From 1929, Robertson was settled in New York, where he played organ and piano at major theatres such as the Lincoln and the Lafayette; after a move to California in 1932 he concentrated on piano and bass. Chilton's researches indicate a musician to reckon with, but no records exist to prove the point. [DF]

Robichaux, John, violin, bass, drums, accordion, leader. b. Thibodaux, Louisiana, 16 January 1866; d. New Orleans, 1939. After early years as bass drummer with the Excelsior Brass Band he formed his first band in 1893 and, says the *New Orleans Family Album*, was 'the most continuously active dance-band leader in New Orleans history' until he died. Robichaux's group played for the élite of New Orleans society and used many of the city's greatest musicians, including Lorenzo Tio. He tends to be remembered in jazz history as the respectable dance-band leader regularly bested by Buddy Bolden's hotter jazz music, but according to Bud Scott (who joined Robichaux in 1904), the facts were different. 'Robichaux had the town sewn up. In about 1908 he had a contest with Bolden in Lincoln Park and Robichaux won. For the contest he added Manuel Perez [and] Bolden got hot-headed that night, as Robichaux really had his gang out.' Despite the obvious error in date (Bolden was taken out of circulation in 1907), Scott's story sounds plausible. 1918–27, Robichaux led the band at the Lyric Theater, New Orleans, and later at a popular restaurant, the Louisiane. [DF]

Robichaux, Joseph, piano. b. New Orleans, 8 March 1900; d. 17 January 1965. A nephew of bandleader John Robichaux, Joe took lessons from pianist Steve Lewis (a major influence) early on and played for parties before a brief exploratory visit to Chicago in 1918. He soon returned to New Orleans and worked with Lee Collins, the Black Eagle Band and travelling shows all through the 1920s as well as taking part in the classic Jones Collins Astoria Hot Eight sessions in New Orleans 1929. In the 1930s Robichaux formed a big band, recorded (for Vocalion) and all through the 1940s worked as a solo pianist in New Orleans clubs, before moving to the West Coast where, during the 1950s, he accompanied blues singer Lizzie Miles, then joined George Lewis, replacing Alton Purnell, for seven years from 1957. [DF]

Any with Lewis

Robinson, Jim (Nathan), trombone. b. Deer Range, Louisiana, 25 December 1890; d. New Orleans, 4 May 1976. He took up trombone late, at 25 while serving in France with the US army, after early years as a guitar player. When he came home in 1919 he studied with trombonist Sunny Henry, then worked part-time with bands such as the Golden Leaf Orchestra (featuring Lee Collins) and Tuxedo Band before joining Isaiah and Sam Morgan's band for over ten years. In the 1930s he worked a long residency at the La Vida Restaurant – really a dime-a-dance ballroom – where the hours were long and the tunes (necessarily) short: the routine bored Robinson and he took work as a shipyard labourer instead, playing part-time, with George Lewis, Kid Howard and others. When the great New Orleans revival began, however, he was quickly back in demand: first for Heywood Broun's records with Kid Rena, then for more records with Bunk Johnson, whose playing he liked and respected ('He had taste', explained Robinson, whose favourite sessions with Bunk were the famous 'American Music', below). From the late 1940s his brusque, direct trombone was more and more associated with George Lewis who, despite occasional criticisms, was partial to the Robinson style that Johnny Wiggs describes to Tom Bethell: 'Jim has a good sharp attack and a good crack to his notes, clarity, and he plays well-formed phrases. He's the top old-time trombone player. His solos [though] are nothing but background music – he comes from an era when solos weren't used.' In fact while Robinson was a fine ensemble player, his solos – full of saxophonic riffs and trumpet stabs as well as standard trombonistics

– are often startling. He came to Britain with Lewis in 1959 and continued to work with him and as a freelance throughout the 1960s, producing records of his own and guesting with Billie and Dee Dee Pierce, the Preservation Hall Jazz Band and touring groups. 'Big Jim' – a proud-faced, dignified man of strong African features – named his trombone 'Pearl', after his wife. [DF]

Bunk Johnson with George Lewis, 1944, Storyville

Robinson, Perry Morris, clarinet, b. New York, 17 August 1938. Son of composer Earl Robinson. Attended High School of Music and Art, New York, graduating in 1956; attended the Lenox School of Jazz, 1959, Manhattan School of Music, 1960–1. Associated with the avant-garde movement of the 1960s, he played with Sunny Murray, Paul Bley, Archie Shepp, Bill Dixon. He performed at the World Youth Festival, Helsinki, in 1967; also worked with the Jazz Composers' Orchestra in mid-1970s. 1968, worked with Roswell Rudd's Primordial Quintet, and in a trio with David Izenzon. At the end of the decade he played on Carla Bley's album *Escalator Over the Hill*. 1972–8, he worked with Gunter Hampel's Galaxie Dream Band. From 1973, with Dave and Darius Brubeck in their Two Generations band. Robinson's influences include Pee Wee Russell, Charlie Parker, Sonny Rollins and Tony Scott, and his approach is a composite of elements from abstraction, rock and all eras of jazz. [IC]

With C. Bley, Dave Brubeck and others; as leader, *The Traveller* (1977), Chiaroscuro; *Funk Dumpling* (1962), Savoy; with Hampel, *Cosmic Dancer* (1975), Birth

Robinson, Prince, clarinet, tenor sax. b. Portsmouth, nr. Norfolk, Virginia, 7 June 1902; d. New York City, 23 July 1960. 'We used to listen to Prince Robinson in those days. He was the tenor player with McKinney's Cotton Pickers – the one that really made it big on the tenor before anybody – but he was very underrated because he was like an old man when Hawk started playing!' Buddy Tate's description, and Coleman Hawkins's frequent citation of Robinson as a primary influence, have sealed an impression of Robinson as a dinosaur of the saxophone. In fact he was a year younger than Hawkins, led a very successful career until the late 1950s, and is probably badly underrated now because the impact of Hawkins was so cataclysmic from the 1920s onwards and because Robinson himself never recorded under his own name. After formative years with Elmer Snowden, Duke Ellington and others, however, he joined McKinney's Cotton Pickers and recorded with them: one famous session (which produced 'Four or Five Times', 'Milneburg Joys' and others) is recalled by Cuba Austin: 'In those days everybody took off their shoes – so the thud from beating the rhythm didn't ruin things. Now worst of all was Prince Robinson. Don [Redman] hit on the idea of lashing Prince's ankles and knees together with rope to hold him steady . . . Things went smoothly till Prince started a solo, then he began to bob up and down with his feet tied together and finally gave up . . . but finally we got by with a good one!' After he left McKinney in 1935, Robinson worked with Blanche Calloway, Willie Bryant and for two years with Roy Eldridge, then with Louis Armstrong's big band, then with bands led by Lucky Millinder, Benny Morton and Claude Hopkins as well as with Henry 'Red' Allen, his own quartet and the Fletcher Henderson reunion band assembled by Rex Stewart in the 1950s. Regrettably, it would be difficult to find many Prince Robinson solos recorded after 1935. [DF]

McKinney's Cotton Pickers vols. 1/2 (1928–9), RCA

Robinson, Scott, drums, piano, percussion, including mallets and tympani. b. Fort Thomas, Kentucky, 25 June 1966. Father, Glenn Robinson, principal percussionist in Cincinnati Symphony Orchestra, 1952–71. Studied drums with his father from an early age; at age ten he received a scholarship to the Charlie Parker Foundation, Kansas City, studying there for one year with Everett Brown. At 17 he received a full scholarship to Long Island University, NYC; January 1985, returned to Conservatory, University of Missouri, Kansas City, to study percussion; also studied piano. Robinson was a child prodigy, performing regularly in public from age nine. At ten he had already played with Clark Terry, Hank Jones, Zoot Sims, Milt Hinton, Charles Mingus and others, and performed a drum duet with Max Roach; from 13 he was leading his own quartet, which in 1981 was the subject of a 45-minute TV documentary; and also drumming with three big bands. 1983, spent three months with Carmell Jones quartet; 1984, spent eight months with Toshiko Akiyoshi's New York Orchestra. Favourites are Elvin Jones, Jack DeJohnette, Philly Joe Jones, Buddy Rich, Louie Bellson, Steve Gadd, Al Foster. [IC]

Toshiko Akiyoshi Jazz Orchestra, featuring Lew Tabackin, *Ten Gallon Shuffle* (1984), Ascent

Robison, Willard, composer. b. Shelbina, Missouri, 18 September 1894; d. 24 June 1968. Along with Alec Wilder, Robison is still the most undervalued of American popular songwriters – although seldom by jazz musicians who from Mildred Bailey to Dick Sudhalter have recorded definitive readings of important Robison tunes such as 'Old Pigeon-toed Joad', 'T'ain't so, Honey, t'ain't so!', 'Round my old deserted farm' and his biggest hit, 'A Cottage for Sale'. Many of Robison's songs are deeply localized in America's Midwest: while aspects of Johnny Mercer's work – and sometimes Hoagy Carmichael's – recall the scent of cornfields, waving trees and cotton-blossom clouds, Robison, more than either of them, wrote with a country pen and the effect is somehow audible in the music. 'Generally his songs were known only to a few singers and lovers of the off-beat non-urban song', says Alec Wilder. 'He, if ever there was one, was the maverick among songwriters.' Robison's 'Peaceful Valley' was an early theme song for Paul Whiteman in the 1920s (before 'Rhapsody in Blue' was written) and at the same time Robison himself recorded a handful of sides playing piano with his own groups: they included, at various times, Alcide 'Yellow' Nunez, Frank Trumbauer, Jack Teagarden and Bix Beiderbecke. [DF]

Jack Teagarden, *Think Well of Me* (1962), Verve

Rock For most non-rock musicians, the word 'rock' is now used indiscriminately as a shorthand term for all pop music since the arrival of rock and roll in the mid-1950s.

The latter was by and large a continuation of rhythm-and-blues with, in the work of leading performers such as Chuck Berry, a distinct flavour of country music (which itself had been influenced by swing and vocal blues since the 1930s). However, as soon as rock and roll was assimilated and anaesthetized by the music industry, the 1960s saw the twin phenomena of the first rhythm-and-blues revival and the emergence of so-called progressive rock; the situation paralleled that of jazz when, after the popularization of swing, there was a split between revivalists and beboppers. It was progressive rock with its incorporation of extended improvisation in the work of groups such as Cream or the Grateful Dead, which was first shortened to 'rock'; from there, it was only a short step to the various hyphenated forms including, of course, 'jazz-rock'.

There are a couple of generations of jazz fans for whom rock represents the absolute antithesis of what they thought jazz was all about, and yet all the forms of Afro-American music are closely related. Which is hardly surprising when you consider that the musicians who created the swing style all had a background of listening to traditional jazz; the beboppers had their background in swing and early rhythm-and-blues; and all the young jazz players of the last two decades (not merely the jazz-rock and fusion musicians) were brought up on the pop music of their youth, i.e. rock. [BP]

Rodin, Gil (Gilbert A.), saxes, clarinet, flute. b. Russia, 9 December 1906; d. Palm Springs, California, 17 June 1974. Although he was never even a competent jazz soloist (*Downbeat* magazine once wickedly published a spoof transcription of a Rodin solo: it consisted of one long note) his name, by association, is usually a guarantee of jazz quality. For eight years from 1926 Rodin was alto-saxophonist for Ben Pollack, and very much his right-hand man: he acted as talent scout for the band, shared an apartment with Pollack and advised him on key decisions. By 1934, however, after Pollack had determinedly ignored him over one or two important policies (including the vexed featuring of Doris Robbins, Pollack's new singer and girlfriend), Rodin found himself more in sympathy with sidemen than leader and, to Pollack's aggrieved surprise, followed them in the ensuing walk-out. To the younger men Rodin was already a father-figure and it was he who helped engineer the signing of Bob Crosby to their nominal leadership. For the next seven years Rodin was saxophonist and business adviser to the Bob Crosby orchestra, planned their campaigns and paid their money: despite one or two disagreements over wages (probably inevitable) he remained the well-liked power behind Bob Crosby's throne until the band broke up. In later years Rodin became a radio and TV producer and very successful, working for companies such as Universal, as well as occasionally helping Crosby to re-form bands for special occasions. [DF]

Bob Crosby, *South Rampart Street Parade* (1935–42), MCA Coral

See Chilton, John, *Stomp Off Let's Go!* (Jazz Book Services, 1983)

Rodney, Red (Robert Chudnick), trumpet. b. Philadelphia, 27 September 1927. Big-band experience as a teenager with many leaders such as Gene Krupa (1946), Claude Thornhill (1947) and Woody Herman (1948–9). First small-group recordings under his own name at age 19. Regular trumpeter of Charlie Parker quintet from late 1949 to 1951, with absence through illness. Later absences due to drugs involvement followed by brief returns and regular non-jazz backing work in Las Vegas throughout 1960s. Re-emerged on New York jazz scene in 1972, from then continued group playing including quintet co-led with Ira Sullivan from 1980. One of the first white trumpeters to show a grasp of bebop, Rodney was first noticed for brief solos on big-band records, but his exposure alongside Parker was not undeserved. A far more complete stylist in recent years, still with a bristling bebop edge to his playing. [BP]

Hi Jinx at the Vanguard (1980), Muse

Rogers, Shorty (Milton M. Rajonsky), trumpet, arranger. b. Great Barrington, Massachusetts, 14 April 1924. Following early work with Will Bradley and Red Norvo and subsequent army service, Rogers found his niche with Woody Herman (1945–6, 1947–9) and with Stan Kenton (1950–1). Having settled in Los Angeles, he became a figurehead of the West Coast period, writing and playing on his own records and many others'. Involvement in film and television in 1950s increased further in next decade, causing him to give up trumpet altogether. Resumed playing after tour with Britain's National Youth Jazz Orchestra (1982).

A distinctive if limited trumpeter, Rogers was always more influential through his writing. The rather fussy quality of his small-group charts, often a watered down version of the Miles Davis 1948 band, detracted from the lively performances he elicited from his colleagues. This aspect tends to triumph on big-band performances and, although none of his originals became standard material, some early items such as 'Keen and Peachy' (for Herman), 'Jolly Rogers' (Kenton) and his own big-band albums stand up extremely well. [BP]

Shorty Rogers plus Kenton and Christy (1950–1), Pausa; *Blues Express* (1953–6), RCA

Rollini, Adrian, bass sax, vibes, etc. b. New York City, 28 June 1904; d. Homestead, Florida, 15 May 1956. His prodigious talent (he played a Chopin concert at four years old at New York's Waldorf Astoria) may have been obscured by his fascination with such 'novelty' instruments as the goofus, hot fountain-pen, vibraphone – then a daring innovation – and bass saxophone, which he took up at manager Ed Kirkeby's suggestion soon after joining the California Ramblers in 1922 when he was 18. His newest instrument, which he learned in a week, became the envy of black stars such as Coleman Hawkins, who briefly struggled with one in Fletcher Henderson's orchestra; more successful learners who listened to Rollini in awe were Budd Johnson who bought one 'and used to play everything Rollini played', he said, and Harry Carney, who later remembered: 'I actually tried to get a sound as big as Adrian – so I suppose whatever sound I've got goes back to that!' After leaving the Ramblers, Rollini became a busy session man in New York – with Bix Beiderbecke, Red Nichols, Joe Venuti, Frank Trumbauer and others – then, after a brief bandleading disaster at the Hotel New Yorker, travelled to London to work with Fred Elizalde at the Savoy. Here British bandleader Harry Gold saw him: 'I used to slip behind the stage with a few pals at the Savoy and watch him. His sound and concept were my biggest influences.' Back in America by 1930, Rollini became a busy studio man, over the next decade recording with giants from Coleman Hawkins to Bunny Berigan and Bobby Hackett and in 1935 opened his own club in the basement of the Hotel President on West 48th Street, New York, Adrian's Tap Room; Wingy Manone with his quartet was a regular. From that time on Rollini concentrated on vibes (his four-mallet work uncannily resembles Gary Burton's two generations later) and worked hotels with his own smooth trio until 1955. Recent research suggests that his death the following year took place in mysterious circumstances. By that time he was running his own hotel, and his name was a stranger to top-flight jazz activity of the period, another crime to be laid at the door of jazz fashion. [DF]

Quintet/Trio, 1938–40, Tax

Rollins, Sonny (Theodore Walter), tenor sax (and soprano). b. New York City, 7 September 1929. Took up alto while in high school, then began gigging on tenor in 1947. First recordings with singer Babs Gonzales, J. J. Johnson and Bud Powell (all at age 19). Rehearsing and live appearances at this period with Thelonious Monk, Powell, Art Blakey (1949), Miles Davis and Tadd Dameron (1950). Records with Miles Davis from 1951, with Monk from 1953, under own name from 1951. After living in Chicago for a year (1954–5), joined Max Roach–Clifford Brown quintet (Nov. 1955–7). Leading own groups for two years, then two years' study with no public appearances. Formed quartet, Sonny Rollins & Co., featuring first Jim Hall (1961–2), then Don Cherry and Billy Higgins (1962–3, including European tour), and varying personnel thereafter; also work as soloist with local rhythm-sections, including in Europe (1965, 1966, 1967), and European tour as guest soloist with Max Roach (1966). Further period of public inactivity (1968–71) while studying in India and Japan, but from 1972 performed regularly with own quintet. Member of 1978 concert tour by Milestone All Stars (Rollins, McCoy Tyner, Ron Carter and drummer Al Foster). After being critical for some time of night-club conditions, virtually abandoned them in the 1980s in favour of concert-hall performances.

Inspired to take up the alto by Louis Jordan, Rollins soon came under the influence of Charlie Parker and, when he switched to tenor, Sonny Stitt and Dexter Gordon. These are all audible in his early work, but it is particularly the rhythmic freedom of Parker which marked Rollins's style, and the one occasion on which they recorded together (Miles Davis, *Collectors' Items*) showed Sonny on better form in this respect. By the mid-1950s, his partnership with Parker's former drummer Max Roach (producing numerous albums under both their names) revealed total command and total emancipation from the beat; each was able to stay in time while throwing outrageous rhythmic challenges to the other. Sonny's up-ending of other players' clichés and his general indirectness led to critical accusations of being sardonic or cynical, and his tonal distortions also increased the impression that he was impatient with the confines of post-bop.

Sonny never sought compositional solutions

Sonny Rollins

(despite having the composer copyright of the traditional calypsos 'St Thomas' and 'Don't Stop the Carnival', and writing several other minimalist tunes such as 'Doxy' and 'Oleo'). Instead he remained an improviser through and through, and the standard songs he favoured in the 1950s and 1960s were often reduced to melodic skeletons, the better to play with the bare bones. This motivic approach naturally led to a friendly interest in 'free jazz', but the most beneficial effect of this for Rollins was to vindicate his musical restlessness. Whereas some of his earlier extended solos seemed comparatively neatly structured, he now felt justified in changing direction several times in the course of one improvisation (see *Our Man in Jazz* and the originally unauthorized issue *There Will Never Be Another You*).

Since the 1970s Sonny has been engaged in what might be considered a sensible compromise. The short, recognizable melodies and the over-obvious rhythm-sections are now used more as a reference-point for audiences than for the soloist, who still feels free to get up to all his old tricks from time to time. This is frequently unsatisfying, like most compromises, but it allows him (like Miles Davis) to display his own playing more or less unchanged to a much younger audience. In doing so, he reminds us that his influence has been extremely widespread, and that he remains one of the most important musicians of the last 30 years. [BP]

Moving Out (1954), Prestige/OJC; *Freedom Suite* (1958), Riverside/OJC; *Our Man in Jazz* (1962), RCA; *There Will Never Be Another You* (1965), Impulse; *Don't Stop the Carnival* (1978), Milestone

Film: *Saxophone Colossus* (dir. Robert Mugge, 1986)

Romano, Aldo, drums. b. Sicily, 16 January 1941. Moved to France in 1947. Began on guitar while at school, then switched to drums. 1960, he began playing in clubs with Bud Powell, Jackie McLean, Stan Getz, J. J. Johnson and various French musicians. 1963, he began playing free jazz with Don Cherry and Gato Barbieri. At the end of 1966 he joined Carla Bley's group which broke up in 1967. He worked with Joachim Kühn for two years, playing most major festivals including Newport; joined Jean-Luc Ponty in 1970, touring throughout Europe. 1971–3, he formed his own rock group in which he played drums, guitar, sang and composed the music. 1973, he joined Pork Pie, which included Charlie Mariano, Jasper van't Hof, Philip Catherine and J. F. Jenny Clark. Romano left after two years, played some concerts with Catherine, and got back on the French scene, recording his first solo album and playing with the group Eyeball. [IC]

With Steve Lacy, Gordon Beck, Joachim Kühn and others; with Pork Pie, *Transitory* (1973), MPS; as leader, *Il Piacere* (1978), Owl

Romao, Dom Um, drums, percussion. b. Rio de Janeiro, 3 August 1925. Mother Portuguese, father African. Father a drummer. Dom Um Romao played drums with the Bossa Rio sextet, with Sergio Mendes on keyboards. Played drums with Cannonball Adderley in 1962 at Carnegie Hall, New York, then moved to the USA. 1965, he worked with Oscar Brown in Chicago. Worked for about a year (1966) in Los Angeles; 1967, he toured the world with Sergio Mendes and Brazil '66. He joined Weather Report when Airto Moreira left, playing percussion. He settled in New York in the early 1970s, opening his own rehearsal studio – Black Beans Studio. 1977, he worked extensively in Europe playing percussion with the Swiss group Om. [IC]

With Sergio Mendes/Brazil '66, Blood, Sweat and Tears, Om; *Dom Um Romao* (1972); *Spirit of the Times* (1973), both Muse, with Weather Report, *I Sing the Body Electric* (1972); *Sweetnighter* (1973), both CBS

Roppolo, Leon J., clarinet, composer. b. Lutcher, Louisiana, 16 March 1902; d. 14 October 1943. A handsome, high-powered young man who, in Eddie Miller's words had 'a tone all over the instrument', he was the son of a saloon-owner-cum-clarinettist who operated a music policy: young Leon – often a problem to his father – picked up the sound of jazz from visiting bands and took informal lessons from Eddie Shields (the piano-playing brother of clarinettist Larry) while working in his band at Toro's Club, New Orleans. More friends were the Brunies family and Roppolo worked with them, too, before travelling upriver to Chicago with George Brunies and cornettist Paul Mares in 1921 to form the great new band at Friars Inn – the soon-to-be-headlining New Orleans Rhythm Kings. Today's vision of Roppolo comes from then: playing the clarinet with a clear, singing sound all his own, experimentally bouncing that sound off the floors and pillars of Friars Inn (just as Sonny Rollins did 40 years later), often pausing to jot new phrases and themes on a shirt-cuff. (Sometimes, the story goes – like Rollins again – Roppolo would play out of doors, matching his sound to the wind in the wires.) By now he was drinking and smoking marijuana, but he kept working regularly until 1925 when – after bandwork which included a spell with pianist Peck Kelley – he came back to New Orleans to play with the NORK again and record (for Okeh) with Abbie Brunies's Halfway House Dance Orchestra. That year he broke down mentally and until he died was committed to an institution, for which in later years he led the jazz band. For his last 27 years Roppolo's music was seldom heard outside the walls of the home: in 1928 he played at the La Vida dance hall in New Orleans ('survivors still talk about his memorable saxophone chase choruses there with the younger "Scag" Scaglione', says Frank Driggs) and early in the 1940s (says John Chilton) he played a couple of nights with trombonist Santo Pecora and with old friend Abbie Brunies. [DF]

Jazz Sounds of the Twenties (1922–5), Parlophone

Rosengarden, Bobby (Robert M.), drums, percussion. b. Elgin, Illinois, 23 April 1924. 'We were playing the other night,' says British trombonist Roy Williams, ' "Bourbon Street Parade", and, you know, Bobby starts with *press-rolls*. You wouldn't catch a lot of drummers doing that! But Bobby loves everybody from Baby Dodds to Buddy Rich – and it shows! And of course it works!' Rosengarden, who attracted many jazz people's attention when he joined the World's Greatest Jazz Band, came from a highly professional background of studio work, and for a time was musical director for the Merv Griffin Show. 'He learned the hard way,' says Oliver Jackson, 'with the networks, the broadcasting people, CBS and others, in the studio bands. That's all finished now.' Since it finished, Rosengarden has become more and more associated with jazz activities: he took over the band at New York's Rainbow Room, plays with Kenny Davern and Dick Wellstood in a highly successful small group, the Blue Three, continues to work in studios on jazz and related projects and tours as a highly successful solo artist – an unusual feat for a drummer. Rosengarden's presentation goes from African talking drums (played on a bongo feature, 'Caravan'), via Baby Dodds and Sidney Catlett to the high-powered onslaught of a Buddy Rich in full flight. [DF]

Any with the World's Greatest Jazz Band

Røsengren, Bernt, tenor sax. b. Stockholm, 24 December 1937. Already active in Swedish jazz circles, Røsengren was member of Newport International Youth Band (1958). Played tenor solos on soundtrack of Polish film *Knife in the Water* (1962) composed by Krzysztof Komeda; appeared with him at Polish Jazz Jamboree (1961). Led own quartet and occasional big band. Worked and recorded (early 1970s) with Lars Gullin, including live album. Seemingly inspired at first by Chicago tenorists such as Gene Ammons, Røsengren then became adept at reproducing the sound of early John Coltrane; later, however, he absorbed a variety of influences into a convincing mature style. [BP]

Røsengren/Nisse Sandström, *Summit Meeting* (1984), Phontastic

Rosolino, Frank, trombone, vocals. b. Detroit, Michigan, 20 August 1926; d. 26 November 1978, committing suicide after first killing his children. His early big-band experience included Gene Krupa's bop-influenced 1948–9 line-up. With Georgie Auld quintet (1951), then joined one of Stan Kenton's more swinging outfits (1952–4). Living in Los Angeles, became prominent session musician but always ready for an opportunity to play jazz, making solo tours from 1973 onwards. Although aware of the style of J. J. Johnson, he seemed able to use the harmonic language of bebop with some of the bluster and gusto of Bill Harris. His free-ranging lines and musical humour often succeeded in disguising the immense adroitness of his playing. Though still associated in many people's minds with Kenton, Rosolino was in fact a soloist for all seasons. [BP]

Frankly Speaking (1955), Affinity

Ross, Annie (Annabelle Short Lynch), voice, songwriter, actress. b. Surrey, 25 July 1930. To Los Angeles, at age three, where she was brought up. She began acting as a child and studied drama in New York. 1947, she returned to the UK, working there and in France as a singer. Back in the USA, she came to prominence in 1952, when she wrote lyrics to a solo by saxophonist Wardell Gray on his tune 'Twisted' and recorded her vocalese version. In the mid-1950s she sang with the bands of Jack Parnell and Tony Crombie in the UK, then, with American singers Dave Lambert and Jon Hendricks, she formed Lambert, Hendricks and Ross, a vocal trio specializing in the technically brilliant vocalizing and verbalizing of jazz instrumental music. This brought her to international notice; the trio toured in the USA and Europe and played festivals, including the Playboy and Monterey jazz festivals in America. By the end of 1959 she was winning readers' polls in jazz magazines. Leonard Feather wrote of her: 'Technically she is the most remarkable female vocalist since Ella Fitzgerald.' Illness forced her to leave the trio in 1962.

She freelanced in the UK, 1962–6, singing on TV shows, with bands, in night clubs, and ran her own club, Annie's Room, for a while. She also appeared at the Ronnie Scott Club and played festivals throughout Europe. From the 1970s she began to take more acting roles, also performing in stage and TV plays and musicals. She starred in *The Threepenny Opera* with Vanessa Redgrave, appeared with André Previn at the Royal Festival Hall in a concert of Kurt Weill's music and played in Weill and Brecht's *The Seven Deadly Sins* for the Royal Ballet. 1985, she returned to the USA and was active in New York as a singer.

Annie Ross is a superb lyricist, combining dexterity, wit and black humour; and she is a consummate singer, able to handle anything from torch songs, and medium-paced swing, to breakneck tempos and intricate melodic lines. [IC]

With Lambert, Hendricks and Ross; solo albums of the 1950s on World Pacific and Prestige

Rouse, Charlie (Charles), tenor sax. b. Washington, DC, 6 April 1924. Briefly with Billy Eckstine band (1944) and first Dizzy Gillespie big band (1945), then with Tadd Dameron (1947) and several months each with Duke Ellington (1949–50) and Count Basie (1950). Freelancing in 1950s, also with Bennie Green (1955), Buddy Rich (1959) and co-leading own group Les Jazz Modes (1956–8). Permanent member of Thelonious Monk quartet (1959–70). Then further freelancing, including own groups, Mal Waldron quintet (early 1980s) and co-operative band Sphere (from 1979). Rouse has a very distinctive nasal tone, already discernible in his 1940s recordings with Dameron; so was his choppy rhythmic style which, though compared by some to that of Monk, sounded rather trite alongside him. In other contexts, however, Rouse stands out as a strong, individualistic player. [BP]

Sphere, *Flight Path* (1983), Elektra Musician

Rowles, Jimmy (James George), piano. b. Spokane, Washington, 19 August 1918. Moved to Los Angeles in 1940 and worked with Slim Gaillard, Lester Young, Benny Goodman and Woody Herman (all 1942) before army service. Late 1940s, with Goodman and Herman again, Les Brown and Tommy Dorsey, then busy freelance studio musician until he moved to New York in 1973. Known until then primarily as an accompanist with an encyclopaedic repertoire, Rowles made important contributions in this role, notably to records by Billie Holiday. The solo style revealed on his many later albums under his own name is quirky and totally unclassifiable, its relaxed wit matched by a sure sense of rhythmic brinkmanship. His daughter, Stacy Rowles (b. 11 September 1955), has appeared on record (with her father) as a promising trumpeter. [BP]

Plays Duke Ellington and Billy Strayhorn (1977), CBS

Rudd, Roswell Hopkins, Jnr., trombone, composer. b. Sharon, Connecticut, 17 November 1935. Studied French horn as a child. 1954–9, he played with traditional jazz groups in New York; early 1960s, began working with the avant-garde. 1960–2, with Herbie Nichols; Steve Lacy, 1961–3. From 1964, he worked with the New York Art Quartet, which included John Tchicai and Milford Graves and which visited Europe in 1965 for concerts, radio and TV. Rudd played the Newport festival the same year with the Jazz Composers' Orchestra. He also worked with Karl Berger, Perry Robinson, Charlie Haden and others. 1966–7, he worked with Archie Shepp, touring in the USA and Europe. He taught world music and jazz improvisation at Bard College, 1973–5. A graduate of Yale University, Rudd worked from 1964 as a musicologist in association with Alan Lomax, and ultimately became Professor of Music Ethnology at the University of Maine. His study of ancient music helped him in his activities as a composer and performer. He has said: 'Vocal techniques I had associated at one time only with the jazz singers of my own country were revealed to be common to the oldest known musical traditions the world over. What I had always considered the epitome of musical expression in America, the blues, could be felt everywhere in the so-called "folk world".' In the later 1970s Rudd had a fruitful association with trumpet player Enrico Rava, touring and recording with him in the USA and Europe.

Rudd's early favourites were Ellington, Monk, and the 'aboriginal music of the world', and he has consistently striven to make the connection between the jazz tradition, ethnic world music and the European classical heritage. He has composed jazz pieces, symphonic works and operas. [IC]

With NY Art Quartet, Archie Shepp and others; his symphonic work *Numatik Swing Band* (1973), JCOA; *Flexible Flyer* (1974); Rudd/Rava, *Inside Job* (1976), both Arista/Freedom; *Enrico Rava Quartet* (with Rudd/Aldo Romano/J. F. Jenny Clark) (1978), ECM

Rüegg, Mathias, composer, piano. b. Zurich, 8 December 1952. Studying composition and arranging in Graz and Vienna, while gigging on piano (1970s). Settled in Austria, founded Vienna Art Orchestra (1977) which recorded several albums, appeared at Berlin festival (1981); toured Asia (1984), USA and Canada (1984) and 15 European countries (autumn 1985). Has also formed Vienna Art Choir (1983) and written symphonic works. A competent pianist whose favourites include Bud Powell, Chick Corea and Uli Scherer, Rüegg's reputation rests on his writing. Despite admiration for Carla Bley, Gil Evans, J. S. Bach and Nali Gruber, he seems to belong rather to the theatrically inclined school of writers that also includes Mike Westbrook. Extremely eclectic, equally at home using themes by Mingus or Erik Satie, his arrangements have enough individuality to provide a framework yet allow considerable freedom to soloists such as Herbert Joos. [BP]

Vienna Art Orchestra, *Suite for the Green Eighties* (1981), Hat Art

Rushing, Jimmy (James Andrew), vocals, piano. b. Oklahoma City, 26 August 1902; d. New York City, 8 June 1972. His parents were both musical, his uncle played piano in a sporting-house, and in his early years 'little Jimmy' (known universally by his vital statistics as 'Mr Five-by-Five') was 'official pianist' at Wilberforce University hops. After school he was still making a living as a pianist although, as he remembered, 'I could only play in three keys. After a time everything began to sound alike to me and it was then they told me to sing.' From then on Rushing's voice – surprisingly high, intense and with a dramatic, near-operatic vibrato – became familiar all over the Southwest, in Walter Page's Blue Devils (he recorded 'Blue Devil Blues' with them for Vocalion in 1929), in Bennie Moten's band which took over most of Page's young stars including Count Basie and Eddie Durham, and finally, after Moten's death, in Count Basie's ad hoc group at the Reno Club in 1935. He stayed with Basie's band until 1948, by which time he had made films (from 'soundies' to the full-length *Funzapoppin* for Universal in 1943) with Basie, and recorded separately with Benny Goodman, Bob Crosby and others as well as his leader. When Basie reduced his band, Rushing took his own band on tour (it included

Buck Clayton and Dicky Wells), then in to the Savoy for two years where often he appeared opposite Basie and created a sensation. From then on, with frequent returns to his ex-leader for touring and special occasions, Rushing worked solo, producing a string of great recordings for John Hammond (*Little Jimmy Rushing and the Big Brass*, *Meets the Smith Girls*, *Jazz Odyssey of James Rushing Esq* and others) and singing his blues all around America and beyond. George Melly remembers him on a 1957 trip to England where he sang with Humphrey Lyttelton's band: 'Jimmy's bulk – and its attendant problems, getting in and out of cars for example – soon appeared irrelevant except to give his movements a deliberation, an almost balletic adjustment of weight in relation to gravity which suggested his inner calm.' Through the 1960s Rushing remained a busy solo performer working with Harry James, Benny Goodman and Eddie Condon as well as Basie, and later in the decade regularly at the Half Note with compatibles Al Cohn and Zoot Sims. Only occasionally did he find himself out of sympathy with a new generation of accompanists: 'I never thought the time would come', he said at this period, echoing Billie Holiday 15 years earlier, 'when I would go up on the bandstand, call this or that familiar number and have some of the cats on the stand say "I don't know it".' One or two of his later recordings reveal a little of that predicament including his last, *The you and me that used to be!* from 1971, on which Rushing's voice, tired though it is, still sounds too big for its buttoned surroundings. The record was nevertheless first choice for jazz critics in their *Downbeat* poll of 1972, the year that 'Little' Jimmy Rushing died of leukaemia. [DF]

Little Jimmy Rushing and the Big Brass (1958), CBS

See Dance, Stanley, *The World of Count Basie* (Sidgwick & Jackson, 1980)

Rushton, Joe (Joseph Augustine), bass sax, clarinet. b. Evanston, Illinois, 7 November 1907; d. California, 2 March 1964. The best-known American bass saxophonist, after Adrian Rollini, Rushton worked early on with the California Ramblers then all through the 1930s for a variety of American bandleaders, most of them based in the Chicago area. By then Rushton had already left music to work in the aircraft industry (he was also a motorcycle aficionado) and regularly returned to his second interest in between stints with Jimmy McPartland (1940), Benny Goodman (1942–3) and Horace Heidt (1944–5). From 1947 he formed his most famous association: with bandleader Red Nichols who featured him as a cornerman until the year Rushton died: his later contributions to Nichols's records – booming-toned, technically assured and smoothly rhythmic – are some of the most likeable sounds on the cornettist's fine late recordings. [DF]

Red Nichols, *Meet the Five Pennies* (1959), EMI Capitol

Russell, Curley (Dillon), bass. b. Trinidad, 19 March 1917; d. 3 July 1986. Played with big bands of Don Redman (1941), Benny Carter (1943). Became extremely busy in early bop period, working and recording with Dizzy Gillespie (1945) and Charlie Parker (1945, 1948, 1950). Regular member of Tadd Dameron group (1947–9), Buddy DeFranco quartet (1952–3). Also recorded with, among others, Bud Powell (1951), Horace Silver (1952), Thelonious Monk (1954) and Art Blakey quintet including Clifford Brown (1954). An extremely propulsive rhythm player, Russell was not featured as a soloist and, seemingly uninterested in the melodic mobility expected of bassists from the late 1950s onwards, dropped out of the jazz scene. [BP]

Art Blakey, *A Night at Birdland, vol. 1/2* (1954), Blue Note

Russell, George Allan, composer, piano, educator. b. Cincinnati, Ohio, 23 June 1923. Father professor of music at Oberlin University. Started on drums, playing in the Boy Scout Drum and Bugle Corps; he received a scholarship to Wilberforce University where he joined the Collegians, who included saxophonist/composer Ernie Wilkins. Russell was hospitalized at 19 by tuberculosis and learned arranging from a fellow patient. He joined the Benny Carter band on drums in Chicago, but was soon replaced by Max Roach, and began to concentrate more on arranging and composing than on playing the drums. After hearing Thelonious Monk's tune 'Round Midnight', he moved to New York where he became part of a coterie of young musicians, including Miles Davis and Gerry Mulligan, who gathered round Gil Evans to discuss their ideas. Russell was again hospitalized for 16 months, and while incapacitated he conceived the basic idea of his influential theoretical (and practical) work *The Lydian Concept of Tonal Organization*, which he finished writing in 1953, and of which J. E. Berendt has said: 'Russell's concept of improvisation, "Lydian" in terms of medieval church scales, yet chromatic in the modern sense, was the great pathbreaker for Miles Davis's and John Coltrane's modality.'

After leaving hospital he collaborated with Dizzy Gillespie in a composition which combined contemporary jazz with Afro-Cuban rhythms, 'Cubana-Be and Cubana-Bop', and which was first performed by Gillespie's band in September 1947. During the later 1940s he composed and arranged for various others, including Claude Thornhill and Artie Shaw, and in 1949 his

Pee Wee Russell

composition 'A Bird in Igor's Yard', which combined elements from Charlie Parker and Igor Stravinsky, was recorded by Buddy DeFranco's big band. Russell was also commissioned by Brandeis University to compose a 'serious' jazz work. 1958–9, he taught at the School of Jazz at Lenox, Massachusetts.

From 1960, Russell began leading his own sextets around the New York area and at festivals; he also toured throughout the Midwest and played at the Newport festival in 1964. During this time he recorded a series of albums of which *Ezz-thetics* has been perhaps the most influential; it featured Russell on piano, with Eric Dolphy, Don Ellis, Dave Baker, Steve Swallow and Joe Hunt, and it included one of the most evocative versions of 'Round Midnight' ever recorded – it begins and ends with abstract sounds, and the core is a solo feature for Dolphy on alto sax.

1964, Russell toured Europe with his sextet, appearing at the first Berlin Jazz Festival, and then lived in Sweden for five years. The Swedish Radio director of jazz, a trumpet player called Bosse Broberg, was an admirer of Russell, and during the latter's five-year stay, Broberg recorded everything Russell had ever written, and also gave him several new commissions including a Mass, music for a ballet based on *Othello*, and an orchestral suite combining tapes and improvisation with ensemble passages – *Electronic Sonata for Souls Loved by Nature.* Russell also taught his Lydian Concept in Stockholm, and toured in Europe with a sextet of Scandinavian musicians sometimes augmented with Americans such as Don Cherry. He also taught in Finland, Norway and Denmark, and performed his music with the radio orchestras of Oslo and Copenhagen.

1969, he returned to the USA to take up a permanent teaching post at the New England Conservatory in Boston. This post allowed him to continue touring and performing occasionally with his own groups, and in 1978 he led a 19-piece big band at the Village Vanguard in New York for six weeks; in the 1980s, he has regularly played the Bottom Line as part of the Newport Jazz Festival in New York; 1981, he toured Italy; 1983, he toured the West Coast of America. 1986, he made his first visit to the UK, touring for the ACGB Contemporary Music Network with an Anglo-American big band.

From the mid-1950s Russell has been an *éminence grise* of modernism and musical adventure. In the late 1950s and early 1960s his pupils included Art Farmer, Rahsaan Roland Kirk, Eric Dolphy and Carla Bley, and in the later 1960s his influence was pervasive in Scandinavia; Jan Garbarek, Terje Rypdal and Palle Mikkelborg among others worked with him and studied his Lydian Concept. Since 1967, *The Lydian Chromatic Concept* has been an official text at the University of Indiana Music School. The basic point about this concept is that it encourages improvisers to convert chord symbols into scales which best convey the sound of the chords. The next stage is the idea of the superimposition of one scale on another, which leads to pan-tonality, the presence of more than one key centre, but occurring within a dominant tonality. In other words, the music is not atonal (in no particular key), but it can accommodate some polytonality. Russell has said: 'Jazz is a music that is rooted in folk scales, which again are rooted strongly in tonality. Atonality is the complete negation of tonal centres . . . It would not support, therefore, the utterance of a blues scale because this implies a tonic.'

Russell's own music synthesizes elements from jazz, blues, gospel music with techniques from serialism, and abstraction. He says that he is not a revolutionary but an evolutionary: he did not negate the jazz tradition – he added dimensions to it. The blues and song structures, however they are seen through his creatively distorting mirrors, are, nevertheless, still structurally present in his work. In particular, his music is always immensely eloquent rhythmically, and his 1986 British tour showed that he had absorbed and transformed elements from African drumming and rock, integrating them with his own jazz heritage. [IC]

The Jazz Workshop (1956), RCA Victor; *George Russell Sextet at the Five Spot* (1960), Decca; *Outer Thoughts* (1960–2), Milestone (double); *George Russell Sextet at Beethoven Hall* (1965), MPS; *Othello Ballet Suite/Electronic Organ Sonato no. 1* (1968); *Electronic Sonata for Souls Loved by Nature* (1968); *Vertical Form* (nda); *Listen to the Silence* (1971); *The Essence of George Russell* (1968), all Soul Note; *The African Game* (1983), Blue Note

Russell, Luis Carl, piano, arranger. b. Careening Clay, nr. Bocas Del Toro, Panama, 6 August 1902; d. New York City, 11 December 1963. He used $3000 winnings from a lottery ticket to settle in New Orleans, by 1923 he was working for Albert Nicholas at Tom Anderson's Café and by 1927 – after an unsuccessful trip to New York with King Oliver – had taken over George Howe's band at the Nest Club and was forming his own from it, bringing in keymen such as Henry 'Red' Allen, Paul Barbarin and Albert Nicholas and founding, in the process, a happy New Orleans family. Soon after, amongst other work, he landed 'the best job in Harlem' (says Frank Driggs), playing at the Saratoga Club owned by millionaire Casper Holstein, a gambler who ran the premises for his own amusement and subsequently offered them to the band as a gift. 'I enjoyed playing in Luis' band more than any I performed in in those days', says Red Allen, and Charlie Holmes agrees: 'Luis was the nicest guy in the world. But you know they say nice people don't get nowhere!' In 1935 Louis Armstrong heard the band – now much improved after seven years of clubwork and touring – and took it over for two days at the Savoy: his young, ruthless manager Joe Glaser signed up the orchestra as Armstrong's backing group. The new discipline, the accompanying role and the mafioso shadow of Glaser took their toll: 'I didn't like working with the band then', says Holmes. 'It was OK when it was Russell's but afterwards it became very commercial and there was always this one and that one telling you what to do. But you have to be careful when it comes to naming people!' In 1940, on thin excuses, the band was dismissed by Glaser's office ('Jimmy Archey got told he was too short!' remembers Pops Foster, 'and I was too old!') but Russell was retained until 1943 as Armstrong's musical director. Then he formed his own band for touring and records, but by 1948 musical fashion was moving too fast. Russell opened a candy store in Brooklyn, then a gift shop, then worked as a booking agent for the Town Hall Club. He was a chauffeur-cum-piano teacher when he died of cancer. [DF]

And his Orchestra 1926–30/1930–4 (2 LPs) both VJM

Russell, Pee Wee (Charles Ellsworth), clarinet, saxes. b. Maple Wood, Missouri, 27 March 1906; d. Alexandria, Virginia, 15 February 1969. 'He is no virtuoso, and his tone is breathy and squeaky, but you forget those shortcomings when you hear the bliss and the sadness and the compassion and the humility that are there in the notes he plays': George Frazier, one of the great jazz writers, offering a key to the work of one of the greatest and most original jazz clarinettists who ever lived.

Russell spent 20 years working with the best company around St Louis, New York and the Midwest: stars such as Peck Kelley, Red Nichols, Bix Beiderbecke, Frank Trumbauer, Ben Pollack and literally dozens of others. 'I made God knows how many records in New York in the late 1920s and early 1930s,' he recalled later, 'and at night we lived uptown.' A 1929 Vitaphone short, 'Red Nichols and his Five Pennies', shows Russell's face fresh and unlined, but those nights uptown, as well as his huge capacity for liquor, were quickly to effect a change, in more ways than one. 'Pee Wee had to change his style, you know', opines Peanuts Hucko. 'I've heard some records and it's amazing, the technique he had as a young man. I think the booze just slowed him down completely!' By the time he worked for Louis Prima (who called him 'the most fabulous musical mind I've known') in 1935 Russell's aharmonic approach and fractured, cliffhanging style were, for whatever reason, fully formed: a brave and revolutionary artistic departure which not only upended the traditional musicology of clarinet tone but even cocked a snook at such fashionable and highly capable contemporaries as Goodman and Shaw. By 1937 he had begun his permanent residency in New York's clubland, working with all the best of the New-York-from-Chicago Dixielanders as well as their figurehead Eddie Condon. Condon loved Russell for his musical sincerity, serious approach and anti-commercial leanings, but was canny enough to see that Russell himself was potentially highly marketable. For the next 25 years he featured regularly on Condon's concerts, club dates, recordings and radio and TV appearances – as well as on club flyers and posters – and frequently in *Life* magazine and became a figurehead for Chicago jazz.

The accidental composite of Russell's clownish wrinkle-wracked features and eccentric clarinet style caused a number of people to like him for the wrong reasons. 'I'll bet you anything,' said critic George T. Simon in 1944, 'that Pee Wee's face is far more important to some young fans than what he plays – and commercially I daresay it's far more important to Pee Wee too.' Russell's account of this period contradicts him: 'I worked at Nick's and Condon's for ten years or more, and there's a sadness about that time. Those guys made a joke of me, a clown, and I let myself be treated that way because I was afraid. I didn't know where else to take refuge!' Russell was often irascible, often unhappy, often drunk, and by the late 1950s he was working in new surroundings such as George Wein's small group. In 1962 the progressive side of Pee Wee Russell came dramatically into view. That year, with trombonist Marshall Brown he formed a piano-less quartet reminiscent of Gerry Mulligan's which – with its determined use of contemporary tunes and album titles such as *New Groove* – announced plainly that Pee Wee Russell, progressive, was making his entry. Other then-revolutionary statements (including an album with Oliver Nelson) were to follow, but by the middle of the decade Russell had returned – willingly or not – to more familiar territory: touring as a soloist with Alex Welsh in England (where a gifted clone, Archie Semple, bemused him), playing again with Wein, Condon and an old friend, Bobby Hackett. His records, even late on, are all classics. He died of a liver complaint that had first laid him low in 1950. [DF]

Swinging with Pee Wee (1960), Fontana

See Shapiro, Nat, and Hentoff, Nat, *The Jazz Makers* (Rinehart, 1957, repr. Da Capo, 1979); Balliett, Whitney, *Improvising* (OUP, 1977)

Russian Jazz During the 1920s jazz was welcomed in the young Soviet Union. In 1926, Sam Wooding's band, with Tommy Ladnier on trumpet, and Benny Payton's Jazz Kings, featuring Sidney Bechet, both played in Moscow, and that same year pianist Leopold Teplitsky sailed to America with an instruction from the Commissariat of Public Enlightenment to: 'Master the techniques of American Jazz, buy up stock arrangements and all the necessary musical instruments and then put all to use in a new jazz orchestra for the city of Lenin's Revolution.' Teplitsky returned to Leningrad in 1927 with crates of recordings, over 20 Paul Whiteman arrangements and over 40 musical instruments. Russian jazz musicians soon began to appear, and though their names were not known in the West, some had considerable reputations in the USSR, and one in particular, trumpeter Eddie Rosner, was a legendary figure, and has been called 'possibly the greatest of Soviet jazzmen'.

The subsequent history of jazz in the Soviet Union is the story of successive periods of repression followed by grudging relaxations, according to the predominant ideology of the day. Was it a proletarian 'people's music' or a bourgeois and élitist phenomenon? Was it subversive or was it ideologically sound? There was no consistent party line on the matter. During one official campaign against jazz, Teplitsky was arrested and exiled. Eventually Rosner and his wife were arrested and tortured; he was exiled to Siberia, and made a non-person – his name never mentioned publicly.

In the 1950s Charlie Parker's influence percolated through, spawning a generation of Russian bebop musicians, and when, 1971–80, more than 60 well-established Soviet jazz musicians emigrated from the USSR, their technical competence astonished Western audiences. Trumpeter Valeri Ponomarev, for example, spent three years with Art Blakey's Jazz Messengers, and saxist Anatole Gerasimov recorded with Duke Ellington. But neither Ponomarev nor Gerasimov, nor any other expatriate Russian, made any significant mark on the international jazz scene.

At the beginning of the 1970s, however, free jazz, which had begun a decade earlier in the USA and Europe, began to find its disciples in the Soviet Union. The first wave of free improvisers were schooled classical players and included Vyacheslav Ganelin (piano), Vladimir Tarasov (dms) and Vladimir Chekasin (saxes) (see GANELIN TRIO), Anatoly Vapirov (saxes) and Sergey Kuryokhin (piano), among others. Their performances are often full of theatricality, irony, parody and burlesque.

Because of the general insulation of Soviet cultural life from that of the West, free improvisation is thriving there at a time when the international jazz scene is in both its post-abstract and its post-jazz-rock phase. Whereas in the rest of the world abstraction has become a dimension of jazz language in which rhythm, swing, tonality, harmony, etc., have been reinstated and transformed, the Russians regard these factors as 'characteristic features of light entertainment'. This high seriousness is mirrored in the grotesquely academic jargon of Soviet jazz criticism which is so abstruse that it seems a secret language. [IC]

Sergey Kuryokhin, *The Ways of Freedom* (1981); Anatoly Vapirov/Kuryokhin, *Sentenced to Silence* (1983); Vladimir Chekasin, *Exercises* (1983); Chekasin quartet, *Nostalgia* (1984); Vapirov, *Invocations* (1984); Siberian quartet, *Homo Liber* (1983), all Leo

See Feigin, Leo (ed.), *Russian Jazz: New Identity* (Quartet, 1985); Starr, S. Frederick, *Red and Hot: The Fate of Jazz in the Soviet Union 1917–80*, (OUP, 1983)

Russin, Babe (Irving), tenor sax, clarinet. b. Pittsburgh, Pennsylvania, 18 June 1911; d. California, 4 August 1964. A fine hot tenor soloist, he is best remembered for a long association with Benny Goodman which began in 1937 and was regularly renewed over a 20-year period. He worked first with the California Ramblers in 1926 and for the next ten years for a variety of prominent white bandleaders including Red Nichols, Roger Wolfe Kahn and Ben Pollack, as well as at CBS as a studio man. All the way through the big band years he worked for leaders such as Tommy Dorsey (1938–40) and Jimmy Dorsey (1942–4) and led his own orchestra in between, but after the war moved into studio work again in Hollywood, where he took part in jazz films including *The Glenn Miller Story* (1954) and *The Benny Goodman Story* (1955) as well as numerous sessions for soundtracks, radio and TV. [DF]

Session at Midnight (1955), Capitol

Rutherford, Paul William, trombone, euphonium. b. Greenwich, London, 29 February 1940. Parents very musical. He spent five years in an RAF regional band (1958–63) and four years at the Guildhall School of Music (1964–8). He started on alto sax in 1956, but switched to trombone and went to evening classes. When he joined the RAF he met John Stevens, Trevor Watts, Bob Downes, Chris Pyne and other kindred spirits. 1965, in London, with Stevens and Watts he founded the Spontaneous Music Ensemble (SME). 1964, he joined the New Jazz Orchestra (NJO), and from 1967 on, he was with Mike Westbrook's various bands. Rutherford has always been an indefatigable experimenter deeply immersed in the more abstract aspects of improvisation, and during the 1960s he was one of a tiny handful of people developing a new language for trombone; new sounds, new intervals, new textures. 1970, he formed his group Iskra 1903, and also became the principal trombone of the London Jazz Composers' Orchestra (LJCO). At that time he also became associated with Peter Brötzmann and Alex von Schlippenbach, playing with the Globe Unity Orchestra until he was sacked in 1981. Since 1973, he has been playing solo (i.e. unaccompanied) trombone. During the 1970s various magazines in the UK, USA and USSR voted him first in their jazz polls. For such an uncompromising avant-gardist, his taste in trombone players is surprisingly conventional: Jim Robinson, Jack Teagarden, J. J. Johnson, Bob Brookmeyer, Jimmy Knepper, Roy Williams. Rutherford also gets inspiration from musicians right across the contemporary spectrum, from John Coltrane and Eric Dolphy to Bartók and Varese. [IC]

With NJO and LJCO; *Iskra 1903* (1972), Incus; *Iskra 1903* (1974), Deutsche Grammophon; *Gentle Harm of the Bourgeoisie* (1976), Emanem; *Old Moers Almanac* (1978), Ring

Rypdal, Terje, guitar, flute, soprano sax, composer. b. Oslo, Norway, 23 August 1947. Father, Jakop Rypdal, a nationally renowned conductor of orchestras and marching bands. Studied piano from age five, guitar at 13. He began as a pop/rock guitarist, then, under the influence of Jimi Hendrix, moved towards improvisation and blues-based rock. In the late 1960s he played with Jan Garbarek's quartet, which included Jon Christensen and Arild Andersen. He also played with the George Russell sextet and big band, and studied Russell's *Lydian Chromatic Concept of Tonal Organization*, which helped him develop his improvisational abilities. At Baden-Baden Free Jazz Festival, 1969, he played in a big band led by Lester Bowie which featured most of the Art Ensemble of Chicago, and this enabled him to make his first real international impact. He played on Garbarek's first two ECM albums and then began recording for the label himself. 1972, performed with his own trio at Berlin Jazz Festival. In the mid-1970s, led his own group, Odyssey, which toured internationally. From the later 1970s into the 1980s he led a trio with Palle Mikkelborg and Jon Christensen. Rypdal is an important composer both for jazz small groups and for large orchestras, and has written symphonies, a piano concerto and also a composition featuring himself and Mikkelborg soloing (improvising) with a symphonic group. He has said, 'I find that a lot of rock guitarists have a more interesting tone than mellow type jazz guitarists', and though he cites Wes Montgomery as an influence, he has more affinity with rock guitarists in his brilliant use of electronic colours and textures. Rypdal is one of that new breed of European musicians who are deeply conversant with Western classical music without ever allowing it to undermine their natural sense of rhythm and their ability to improvise. [IC]

Whenever I seem to be Far Away (1974); *Odyssey* (1975); *Waves* (1977); *Terje Rypdal/Miroslav Vitous/Jack DeJohnette* (1978); *Descendre* (1979); Rypdal/Vitous/DeJohnette, *To be Continued* (1981); Rypdal/David Darling, *Eos* (1984), all ECM

S

St Cyr, Johnny (John Alexander), banjo, guitar. b. New Orleans, 17 April 1890; d. Los Angeles, 17 June 1966. He is remembered as the banjo player who played on Louis Armstrong's Hot Five and Seven recordings, with Jelly Roll Morton and others, while he was working for Doc Cooke's Dreamland Orchestra in Chicago. Around 1930 he returned to New Orleans, where he played regularly and worked as a plasterer and never moved from his home town again until 1955, when he went to the West Coast at age 65 to work with New Orleans-style bands for another ten years. His fascinating story was told in a lengthy *Jazz Journal* serial (with John W. Slingsby, Sep., Oct., Dec., 1966): a fine portrait of a great New Orleans musician. [DF]

Any with Louis Armstrong (1925–7)

Salsa A 1970s development of Afro-Latin music particularly associated with Hispanic New Yorkers (*nuevayoriqueño* is the adjective to describe the people and the music). Because of its geographical origin, this style initially had a tougher sound than some earlier Latin music and betrayed the influence of bebop and modal jazz. But, as used by non-specialists, the word has now become virtually a generic term for all Afro-Latin styles. [BP]

Sample, Joe (Joseph Leslie), piano, composer. b. Houston, Texas, 1 February 1939. Formed group with schoolfriends including Hubert Laws (1954), known after they moved to Los Angeles (1960) as the Jazz Crusaders; by this time they consisted of Wayne Henderson (tmb), Wilton Felder (tnr), Stix Hooper (dms) and a succession of bassists. Sample also worked with many other West Coast-based musicians such as Harold Land–Bobby Hutcherson (1967–8) and saxophonist Tom Scott (1973), and became heavily involved in studio work. From 1972 the Jazz Crusaders became the Crusaders, highly successful in the instrumental soul/funk field; Felder was now doubling on electric bass, and studio guitarists Arthur Adams, David T. Walker and later Larry Carlton were added for recording and touring. Sample also became involved in album production, and latterly songwriting for Minnie Riperton, Randy Crawford, B. B. King etc. Although his solo style with the Crusaders tends towards the superficial, his rhythm playing is always on target. His latent ability as a Tyneresque improviser was well demonstrated by some of the early Jazz Crusaders recordings and by the trio album below. [BP]

Try Us (1969), Sonet

Sampson, Edgar Melvin, alto and baritone sax, violin, arranger, composer. b. New York City, 31 August 1907; d. 16 January 1973. Played with many New York-based bands including Duke Ellington's (*c.* 1926), Fletcher Henderson's (1931–2) and Rex Stewart's short-lived big band (1933). Led sax section and arranged for Chick Webb band (1933–6, replaced by Louis Jordan on his departure). Then highly successful as freelance arranger for Benny Goodman, Artie Shaw, Red Norvo and many others. More regular playing in late 1940s, then writing and playing for top Latin bands such as Tito Puente (1950s). Led own occasional small group, but incapacitated by illness for some years before his death.

One of the most widely heard and least celebrated writers of the swing era, Sampson was no slouch as a player although featured infrequently in solo spots. But it was the arranging, and his dynamic but light-fingered way with the Webb band, which attracted the attention of others, especially Goodman who further spread the popularity of many Sampson charts previously done for Webb. These may seem too genteel for present-day tastes, but his original melodies are destined to remain immortal, and it would be difficult to think of anyone else who wrote five tunes as good as 'Stompin' at the Savoy', 'Don't Be That Way', 'If (When) Dreams Come True', 'Lullaby in Rhythm' (co-written with Clarence Profit) and 'Blue Lou'. [BP]

Swing Softly Sweet Sampson (1956), Jasmine

Samuels, David, vibraphone, marimba. b. Chicago, 1948. Began on drums at age six, graduated from Boston University, 1971, with a degree in psychology, and while there had also begun studying mallet instruments (vibes etc.); he taught at the Berklee School for two and a half years, where he worked with Pat Metheny and John Scofield. 1974, joined Gerry Mulligan's sextet, recording three albums with the group and touring Europe four times with it and the USA once. 1975, with Gerry Niewood, Rick Laird and Ron Davis, he co-founded the group

Timepiece, and also worked and recorded with Frank Zappa. In the later 1970s he was with Double Image until it split up in 1980, when, with Michael Di Pasqua, Paul McCandless and David Darling, he formed the group Gallery. Samuels has been a member of Spyro Gyra since the mid-1980s and is also active as a teacher in schools throughout the USA and Europe. [IC]

With Double Image, *Dawn* (1979); with Gallery, *Gallery* (1981), both ECM

Sanborn, Dave (David William), alto sax, flute. b. Tampa, Florida, 30 July 1945. Family moved to St Louis, where he was brought up. He contracted polio as a child, spending some time in an iron lung, and was advised to take up a wind instrument as physical therapy. He played alto sax in his school band. 1963–4, he studied music at Northwestern University; 1965–7, additional studies at University of Iowa. He moved to the West Coast, playing and recording with the Paul Butterfield band, 1967–71. He was with Stevie Wonder, 1972–3, touring with him in a Rolling Stones concert package. He began a long association with Gil Evans in January 1973, playing on several Evans albums including the classic *Svengali*. He worked with the Brecker Brothers in 1975 and also began leading his own groups that year.

Sanborn's influences include Hank Crawford, Jackie McLean and Charlie Parker, and he is steeped in the blues. He is a passionate, eloquent player with a tremendously expressive sound, and the ability to make melodies 'speak'. He has, apart from his work with Gil Evans, always been involved with electronic fusion music – often in the disco vein. During the 1970s and into the 1980s he was perhaps the most in-demand alto session player on the US scene, interpreting melodies and playing solos on dozens of albums. In the 1980s he continued leading his own groups and touring internationally; 1984, he performed with his quartet at the Montreux festival. [IC]

With Brecker Brothers, Hubert Laws, Wonder, David Bowie and many others; with Gil Evans, *Svengali* (1973), Atlantic; *Music of Jimi Hendrix* (1974), RCA; *There Comes a Time* (1975), RCA; as leader, *Taking Off* (1975); *Voyeur* (1981); *As We Speak* (1982), all Warner Bros

Sanders, Pharoah (Farrell), tenor and soprano sax, composer. b. Little Rock, Arkansas, 13 October 1940. Piano lessons from grandfather; studied drums, clarinet. Began on sax and flute at 16. He played with local r & b bands. 1959, he went to Oakland, California, on a music scholarship, playing with Dewey Redman, Philly Joe Jones and Vi Redd, among others. Moved to New York in 1962, working with Sun Ra, Rashied Ali, Don Cherry and others of the avant-garde. He came under the influence of Albert Ayler. 1966–7, worked with John Coltrane, and after Trane's death continued with Alice Coltrane until 1969. Sanders then began leading his own groups. He has toured and played many festivals in the USA and internationally. [IC]

With Coltrane, Alice Coltrane, Don Cherry; *Thembi* (1970–1), Jasmine; *Izipho Zam* (1972), Strata-East

Sangster, John Grant, composer, arranger. b. Melbourne, Australia, 17 November 1928. He began as a drummer/cornettist soon after the war and now specializes on vibraphone and marimbaphone, on which his improvised music is beyond reproach; but, as with Ellington, his best instrument is his arranger's pen. Major works from him in the 1970s and 1980s include *The Hobbit Suite*, a combination of irresistible tunes and near-avant-garde sound poems which features regular colleagues Bob Barnard (a brilliant all-round trumpeter), his brother Len Barnard (a drummer of similar ability) and clarinettist John McCarthy; a huge and appropriate 16-side follow-up, *The Lord of the Rings*, in which the writing moves from Ellington to Evan Parker and back with consummate ease; wholly original written tributes to Bix Beiderbecke and Ellington, which often mix washboards with electronic music to great effect; and numerous film soundtracks including *Fluteman* (1982), a charming fantasy. Sangster's writing may be the most eclectic in jazz today: he delights in two-beat as much as in the abstract use of atonal sound, and he also manages to work in existing disciplines with striking melodic and conceptual originality (his Beiderbecke tribute convincingly applies white 1920s voicing to original themes topped with electronic effects – a typical Sangster conceit). In the 1980s Sangster's position in the Australian jazz hierarchy is unassailable: it seems unfortunate that, because of international reluctance to accept that a non-American might make a contribution of real value, his position in world-class jazz circles is yet to be fully established. [DF]

The Hobbit Suite (1973), Swaggie

Sarmanto, Heikki, piano, composer. b. Helsinki, 22 June 1939. Three brothers are also musicians, including bassist Pekka Sarmanto (b. 1945). Studied languages and music at Helsinki University and Sibelius Academy (1962–4), music at Berklee College (1968–70, 1971) and with Serge Chaloff's mother. Named best pianist at Montreux festival (1971). Visited London (1975) with own 12-piece workshop ensemble, which then became independent big-band UMO from 1976. Sarmanto went on to write *New Hope Jazz Mass* (1978; also performed at Newport/New York, 1979), jazz ballet (1984), jazz opera etc. Played in South America (1985). Was

Pharoah Sanders

chosen by Sonny Rollins to arrange, orchestrate and conduct his saxophone concerto, premiered in Tokyo (1986). Influenced as a pianist by Bud Powell and Ran Blake, Sarmanto is a composer of immense competence in all fields, and his suite *Suomi* (featuring reedman Juhani Aaltonen and strings) is a contemporary equivalent of Sibelius's song of praise for his country. [BP]

Suomi (1983), Finlandia Records

Sathe, Keshav, tabla. b. Bombay, India, 31 January 1928. Brother played flute and religious music. Studied privately, 1947–52, with Pandit Joshi. 1951–5 accompanist to singer, Mr Kelkar Bombay. He came to the UK in 1956, playing tabla in Asian Music Circle (1957–9); also lecture recitals in schools and colleges with Bhaskar Chandavarkar (sitar). 1965–70, he worked with Joe *Harriott–John Mayer in their Indo-Jazz

Fusions. 1967, the Keshav Sathe trio worked with the Irene Schweizer trio, Barney Wilen and Manfred Schoof, in a 'Jazz Meets India' package which toured Germany and recorded an album. Through the 1970s and into the 1980s, he led his own trio and worked with Julie Felix, Danny Thompson, John Renbourn and others. Toured Europe and USA with John Renbourn and Friends, 1979, 1981. Favourites are Mahapurush Misra and Zakir Hussain. [IC]

With Indo-Jazz Fusions, *Indo-Jazz Suite* (1965), Columbia; Sathe/Jayashri Banerjee (sitar), *Kalawati* (1967), Polydor

Savoy Sultans The house band at the Savoy Ballroom, New York, for much of the swing-happy 1930s and 1940s, an efficient 8-piece unit who played simple and effective riff tunes for dancing. 'From the time they hit to the time they quit they were swinging!' says Panama Francis who, while he was with Lucky Millinder (1940–46), formed an attachment to the group which was to have a lasting effect. 'They had no big stars [but] put them all together, and look out!' The Sultans – who presented strong opposition for any 'star' band visiting the Savoy – included Pat Jenkins (tpt), Grachan Moncur II (bass) and Razz Mitchell (dms), one of the first drummers to introduce a riveted swizzle-cymbal to the jazz band: their two best soloists were Sam Massenberg (tpt) and Rudy Williams (alto), who was not only the youngest but (according to Francis) the 'most outstanding guy in the band'. The group broke up in the 1940s but were re-formed by Francis in the 1970s to play festivals, clubs and concerts, and make records: they scored an enormous success at the Nice Jazz Festival, 1979 and 1980, thereafter became headliners again and made a number of uniformly excellent albums. [DF]

Jump Steady (1938–41), Affinity; *Gettin' in the Groove* (1979), Black & Blue

Sbarbaro, Tony, see SPARGO, TONY

Scat The art of creating an instrumental-style improvisation vocally. This requires a vocabulary of vowels and consonants related less to identifiable words and more to the tone and articulation of jazz instrumentalists. Hence the trumpet-like 'Oop-Pop-a-Da' (by Babs Gonzales) or Sarah Vaughan's saxophonic 'Shulie-a-Bop'.

First done on records by Louis Armstrong (Fletcher Henderson's 'Everybody Loves My Baby' and then Louis's own 'Heebie Jeebies'), it is most closely associated by the general public with Ella Fitzgerald and her many imitators. Brought to an early peak of perfection by Leo Watson who, by introducing occasional real words inspired the development of 'vocalese', scat has scaled new heights of virtuosity with Bobby McFerrin. [BP]

Schifrin, Lalo (Boris), piano, composer. b. Buenos Aires, 21 June 1932. Piano lessons from age seven; harmony from age 16; he studied sociology and law at the University of Buenos Aires. In the early 1950s he studied music in Paris with a disciple of Ravel. 1956, back in Argentina, he met Dizzy Gillespie who heard Schifrin's work and admired it. 1957, Schifrin began writing for films. He moved to New York in 1958, leading a trio and writing arrangements for various bands including Xavier Cugat's. He spent three years, 1960–3, with Gillespie, touring the USA and Europe and coming to international notice. He wrote the suite 'Gillespiana' for Dizzy, and it was premiered at Carnegie Hall in November 1961, and 'New Continent' which was performed at the 1962 Monterey Jazz Festival. He also wrote and did most of the arranging on one of the most delightful Gillespie albums, *Dizzy on the French Riviera*.

After leaving Gillespie, he worked and recorded with Quincy Jones, and then began to concentrate on composing and arranging, writing innumerable film and TV scores. His *Jazz Suite on the Mass Text* was recorded by Paul Horn (RCA). 1969, he wrote *Dialogues for Jazz Quintet and Orchestra* for Cannonball Adderley. He taught composition at the University of California, Los Angeles, 1968–71, and scored many feature films including *The Cincinnati Kid* (1965), *The Good, the Bad, and the Ugly* (1966), *Bullitt* (1968) and *Dirty Harry* (1971).

Schifrin's piano influences include Thelonious Monk, Bill Evans, Oscar Peterson and Bud Powell, and among his composing influences are Gillespie and Stravinsky. [IC]

With Adderley and others; with Gillespie, *Dizzy on the French Riviera* (1962), Philips; *A Musical Safari* (1961), Booman; much recorded film music

Schneider, Moe (Elmer Reuben), trombone. b. Bessie, Oklahoma, 24 December 1919. He worked with a variety of pre-war bands including Alvino Rey's (he rejoined Rey in 1946 after army service), but most remarkably with a series of 'Dixieland academies', including Ben Pollack's band, before the war and after, and with Bob Crosby from 1949. Schneider's talent for classic jazz was enormous – he combined the tone of Jack Teagarden with the athletic rangy approach of Abe Lincoln – and some of his best work turns up on the recorded music from *Pete Kelly's Blues* in which he combined with Cathcart, Matlock *et al.* for radio, TV and a full-length feature film: the records are copybook 'white' Dixieland without ever sounding *too* precise. Later in his career Schneider combined work in studios (he also appeared in *The Five Pennies* and *The Gene Krupa Story* in 1959) with part-time accountancy; although his name is still really a collector's delight, his work is of top-grade standard. [DF]

Dick Cathcart, *The authentic music from 'Pete Kelly's Blues'* (1959), Warner Bros

Schoof, Manfred, trumpet, fluegelhorn, piano, composer. b. Magdeburg, Germany, 6 April 1936. Studied at Musikakademie, Kassel, 1955–8, and at Cologne Musikhochschule, 1958–63. Played in student groups with Alex von Schlippenbach, Gerd Dudek and others. 1963–5, with Gunter Hampel; led his own group from 1965. Free Jazz was burgeoning in Europe then and Schoof's quintet was one of the most important German groups in the abstract field, becoming, with the Peter Brötzmann trio, the nucleus for von Schlippenbach's Globe Unity Orchestra which was formed in 1966. 1968, he joined the Clarke–Boland international big band, staying until 1972. 1969–73, he led his New Jazz Trio, with Peter Trunk (bass) and Cees See (dms). 1975, Schoof's sextet and critic J. E. Berendt toured Asia under the auspices of the Goethe Institute, in a programme combining concerts and lectures. 1980, formed the Manfred Schoof Orchestra (big band). He has also worked with Albert Mangelsdorff, George Russell and others. Schoof is a very active composer and arranger, and has written for the Kurt Edelhagen Big Band at West German Radio, and also collaborated with various contemporary composers, working on a 1966 opera, *Die Soldaten*, and a 1969 trumpet concerto performed by the Berlin Philharmonic. He has also composed for small groups, and for film and TV. In 1977 his LP *Scales* received the German Record Critics' Prize, and in 1980 he was awarded first prize by the German Jazz Musicians' Union. He has performed at festivals all over Eastern and Western Europe; his composition 'Ode', for the Globe Unity Orchestra, was performed at Donaueschingen festival, 1970, and 'Kontraste und Synthesen', for Globe Unity and choir, was performed in 1974 at NDR (North German Radio). Influences are Miles Davis, Booker Little and Kenny Dorham, also Schoenberg, Anton Bruckner and Gil Evans. Schoof's playing and composing cover the whole spectrum of contemporary music: all forms of jazz from abstract to tightly structured, and areas of European 'art' music. He has also given performances of solo (unaccompanied) trumpet improvisation. [IC]

With Globe Unity, Stan Getz, Clarke–Boland, Mal Waldron; *Scales* (1977), ECM Japo; *Reflections* (1983), Mood; *Page One* (nda), MPS; *Page Two* (nda), MPS; *Horizons* (1978), Japo: *Light Lines* (1977), Japo; *Distant Thunder* (1975), Enja

Schroeder, Gene (Eugene Charles), piano. b. Madison, Wisconsin, 5 February 1915; d. 16 February 1975. He is well remembered for his 17-year partnership with Eddie Condon, which began at Nick's Club around 1944. Condon liked the sound of Schroeder right away: he played the right changes for Condon's style of music, knew how to integrate himself into a four-man rhythm-section featuring the straight four-to-the-bar of Condon's rhythm guitar, showed a gratifying lack of interest in the fashionable bebop trends that Condon hated and, unlike former colleagues Jess Stacy and Joe Sullivan, was neither committed to a big band nor intent on leading his own show. Schroeder played at the opening of Condon's own club in 1945, and for the next 17 years played pianistic Harry Carney to Condon's Ellington. 'There are few pianists in the business who can equal him,' said Condon, 'either as soloist or member of the rhythm-section', and this was, no doubt, because Schroeder enjoyed Condon's pool of musicians and their timeless jazz concepts. 'We had a sort of a huge roving clique of guys that played at a certain level,' he explained later, 'slightly modern but they knew all the old tunes. Most important, these were guys who knew how to swing' (the recorded evidence is there, on such Condon classics as *Bixieland* and *Jam Session, Coast to Coast*). After Schroeder left Condon he worked freelance and with a like-minded group, the Dukes of Dixieland, for whom he recorded fine albums such as *Now Hear This* and *Breaking it up on Broadway*, but by the late 1960s ill-health had immobilized him. [DF]

Eddie Condon, *Bixieland* (1955), Philips (reissued under various titles, e.g. *At the Jazz Band Ball*, 1985, CBS)

Schutt, Arthur, piano, arranger. b. Reading, Pennsylvania, 21 November 1902; d. San Francisco, 28 January 1965. One of the finest white pianists of the 1920s – he recorded with all the white stars of the period from Bix Beiderbecke to Benny Goodman – he was a trained musician and skilled reader who specialized in studio work and freelance arranging and became rich in the process. Always superbly dressed, with a carnation in his buttonhole, in photographs Schutt looks the very image of a successful 1920s society pianist; significantly perhaps, he was heard less of with the speedy passage of jazz fashion through the 1930s. But he continued to make a comfortable living in the studios, working for MGM, Columbia and others until the early 1960s, when ill-health took its toll. [DF].

Thesaurus of Classic Jazz, vol. 3 (1927–8), Philips

Scobey, Bob (Robert Alexander), trumpet. b. Tucumcari, New Mexico, 9 December 1916; d. Montreal, 12 June 1963. He worked his way up through dance orchestras, pit bands and night clubs in the 1930s and in 1938 met Lu Watters. From 1940 for nine years (apart from a 4-year spell in the army) he was second trumpeter to

Watters in the great Yerba Buena Jazz Band, but by 1949 was tired of the volume and two-beat concept that Watters loved and left to form his own band. For the next 15 years Scobey's career spiralled up. He was a natural leader, bubbling with ideas ('There was always something cooking,' remembered Art Hodes, 'new arrangements, rehearsals every week, fresh uniforms') and by the early 1950s his band was recording regularly for Good Time Jazz, headlining at the Dixieland festivals organized by Gene Norman and Frank Bull; they also played a three-year residency at Victor and Roxie's in Oakland. Scobey's ace in the hole all through the 1950s was banjoist Clancy Hayes, whose lazy Southern charm was central to the band's presentation: Hayes was co-billed with Scobey throughout their partnership. By the mid-1950s the band (augmented on record by stars such as Bing Crosby and superguests including Abe Lincoln, Manny Klein, Matty Matlock, Dick Cathcart and Frank Beach) had reached a recording and performance peak of top-drawer Dixieland.

In 1959, after a short experiment with a solo act, Scobey opened his own Club Bourbon Street in Chicago, making regular trips to Las Vegas, New York and San Francisco in spare weeks. At the club he played long sets (10 p.m. to 4 a.m.), pleasing the people and operating the show he believed in: 'I like the people who come and hear me to like what I play for them and to understand what I play and to go away happy. Like Louis!' he explained to Sinclair Traill that year. Scobey's band of the period featured ex-Ellington drummer Dave Black, whom he had hired after Black was incapacitated with polio: it was the generous move of a big man. Scobey finally succumbed to cancer. His supportive and hardworking wife Jan keeps his memory alive with a biography, an album on which she re-formed the band to sing some blues for her husband, and a regular reissue programme for Scobey albums. [DF]

Bob Scobey's Alexander's Jazz Band (1947–8), Dawn Club

See Scobey, Jan, *He Rambled Til' Cancer Cut Him Down* (Jansco, 1976)

Scofield, John, guitar, composer. b. Ohio, 26 December 1951, brought up in Wilton, Connecticut. Began on guitar at high school, playing in soul bands and r & b groups. At 15 studied with a local jazz player. He spent three years (1970–3) at the Berklee School, also playing around Boston, and recording two live albums with Gerry Mulligan and Chet Baker at Carnegie Hall, New York. 1974, he replaced John Abercrombie in Billy Cobham's band, staying with it for two years and recording four albums with it. 1976, he freelanced around New York and in 1977 recorded with Charles Mingus and then joined Gary Burton's quartet. The same year he formed his own quartet with Richie Beirach, George Mraz and Joe La Barbera, touring Europe and playing at the Berlin festival.

From the later 1970s to the early 1980s he was a regular member of the Dave Liebman quintet, touring world-wide with it and playing most major festivals. 1982, he joined Miles Davis, touring the USA, Europe and Japan in 1983, 1984, and 1985, and playing on three of Davis's albums. By 1984, Scofield was not only playing themes and solos with the band, but also collaborating with Davis in the composition of several of the pieces. Before he joined Davis, Scofield had also played or recorded with Zbigniew Seifert, Tony Williams, Ron Carter, Terumasa Hino and Lee Konitz. His main influences are Jim Hall, George Benson, Pat Martino, and to a lesser extent B. B. King and Otis Rush, but he has totally absorbed all these and arrived at a sound and approach all his own. He was always a player of consummate grace and inventiveness, conjuring melodic lines out of thin air, but during his stint with Miles Davis, his authority grew perceptibly, his rhythms becoming stronger, the lines more audacious and the emotional power of his work absolutely compelling. [IC]

John Scofield Live (1977), Enja; *Rough House* (1978), Enja: *Who's Who* (1979), Arista; with Davis, *Decoy* (1984), CBS

Scott, Cecil Xavier, clarinet, saxes. b. Springfield, Ohio, 22 November 1905; d. New York City, 5 January 1964. One of the most driving and creative first-generation saxophonists, Scott led a fine band which by the late 1920s was causing a stir at New York's Savoy Ballroom, where they often made short work of better-known opposition. 'They [Cecil and his brother Lloyd Scott] had brought their band to New York from Springfield, Ohio, in 1926', remembers Cab Calloway, whose first band, the Alabamians, could not equal Scott's. 'Cecil had developed his own style and was running the band himself. He was a bitch: those guys played gut-bucket, stomping, gutsy New York jazz. Cecil was one of the most exciting and fiery horn blowers in Harlem – and in addition to blowing up a storm they put on a hell of a show.' Scott later joined Calloway's new band, the Missourians, then worked with Fletcher Henderson, Vernon Andrade, with Teddy Hill (1936–7) and by 1942 had his own band again at the Ubangi Club. The swift passage of jazz fashion in the 1940s meant that Scott's initial impact was hard to maintain (he had also suffered a severe leg injury *c.* 1930 which at times put him out of action and subsequently necessitated an artificial limb) but his big sound and 'fiery dynamic style' (Panassié) guaranteed him a steady flow of work (including recording) all through the 1940s with leaders such as Art Hodes as well as with his own trio. In the 1950s he carried on his busy club activities around New York, working at Central Plaza, Ryan's, Stuyvesant Casino, and played at the Great South Bay Jazz Festival in 1957 and 1958: he continued to work regularly until his death. [DF]

Charlie Johnson, Lloyd Scott and Cecil Scott (1927–9), RCA (double)

Scott, Raymond (Harold Warnow), leader, pianist. b. Brooklyn, New York, 10 September 1910. He became well known on CBS radio, 1934–8, leading a quintet which played stylish novelties like 'Toy Trumpet', 'Dinner Music for a Pack of Hungry Cannibals', 'War Dance for Wooden Indians': the musicians who played this testing music included Dave Wade and Russ Case (tpts), Pete Pumiglio (clt), Dave Harris (tnr), Lou Shoobe (bass) and John Williams (dms). By 1938, Scott had established a strong reputation as an arranger, and a year later formed his own big band which toured and played residencies, 1939–42 (Shelly Manne was the drummer); that year he was asked to form the first desegregated staff orchestra in history, for CBS. On the face of it this was a good idea and Scott's orchestra corralled black musicians such as Cozy Cole, Charlie Shavers, Ben Webster and Benny Morton alongside white men such as Johnny Guarnieri and singer Frank Sinatra. But in 1945, after what Frank Driggs calls 'devious politicking' the whole ensemble, including Scott, was unceremoniously sacked. Thereafter Scott moved into a variety of commercial staff posts, ran his own record label (Audivox) and in the 1950s was musical director for Everest Records. By the 1970s he was running his own electronics research firm in Farmingdale, New Jersey, and later (John Chilton tells us) moved out to Van Nuys, California. [DF]

Scott, Ronnie (Ronald), tenor sax (and soprano). b. Aldgate, London, 28 January 1927. Gigging in small clubs at age 16, then touring with trumpeter Johnny Claes (1944–5) and Ted Heath (1946). Also with Ambrose band, Cab Kaye, Tito Burns and on transatlantic liners. Played at co-operative musicians' venue, Club 11 (1948–50), then with Jack Parnell band (1952). Formed own 9-piece group (1953–6), then co-led Jazz Couriers with Tubby Hayes (1957–9). Opened own jazz night club (1959), which rapidly became world-renowned. Continued to play regularly, leading quartet including Stan Tracey (1960–7), 8-piece band including John Surman, Kenny Wheeler etc. (1968–9), trio with Mike Carr (1971–5). Also member of Kenny Clarke–Francy Boland band (1962–73). From mid-1970s led quartets and quintets, usually with Ron Mathewson and Martin Drew.

Scott had already established himself as a forthright and committed jazz player long before the success of the pace-setting Jazz Couriers. Given the fact that most British musicians then tended to imitate the letter rather than the spirit of jazz, there was pointed praise in Charles Mingus's 1961 observation of the local scene: 'Of the white boys, Ronnie Scott gets closer to the negro blues feeling, the way Zoot Sims does.' The influence of Sims and countless others has moulded Ronnie's mainstream-modern style, both its phraseology and time-feeling being easily recognizable and effortlessly authoritative. Doubtless this is why he was awarded an OBE in 1981 by the sister of one of his club's celebrity customers. [BP]

Scott at Ronnie's (1973), RCA; *Serious Gold* (1978), Pye

See Fordham, John, *Let's Join Hands and Contact the Living* (Elm Tree, 1986)

Scott, Shirley, organ. b. Philadelphia, 14 March 1934. Studied piano as a child, also trumpet, then played piano in her brother's group. Changed to organ at same period as fellow Philadelphian Jimmy Smith (1955), became member of Eddie Davis trio (1956–60). Making records under own name from 1958, formed own trio and then toured with Stanley Turrentine, whom she married. Since ending that association, has led her own groups; recorded with Dexter Gordon (1982). While not perhaps as original as Smith, and not so blatantly battering the senses of the listener, Scott is a dynamic performer whose work is rhythmically compelling. [BP]

Hip Soul (1961), Prestige

Scott, Tom (Thomas Wright), alto, tenor and soprano sax, flutes, woodwinds, composer. b. Los Angeles, 19 May 1948. Mother a pianist, father a composer. Played clarinet at high school; self-taught as composer/arranger. His trio won a teenage jazz competition at the Hollywood Bowl. Scott was extraordinarily precocious, playing as a teenager with the Don Ellis and Oliver Nelson bands, and in orchestras on TV shows. When he was just 19 he recorded as featured soloist with Roger Kellaway's quartet on *The Spirit Feel* and also as leader (*The Honeysuckle Breeze*), and on both albums it is not his virtuosity which astonishes, but his artistic maturity at that early age – nothing is superfluous and every note tells. From his early twenties he wrote prolifically for TV shows and occasionally for feature films. He had a long and fruitful association with Kellaway, John Guerin, Chuck Domanico, Victor Feldman and others, playing clubs and concerts, and was part of the initial jazz-rock-fusion movement, forming his own band, Tom Scott and the L. A. Express, which became one of the most successful groups of the 1970s, touring in the USA and internationally, playing major festivals and winning various awards.

Scott's influences include John Coltrane, Charlie Parker, Gerry Mulligan, Phil Woods, Cannonball Adderley and King Curtis, and other inspirations include Indian music, the

Ronnie Scott

Beatles, Aretha Franklin, Ray Charles and early 20th-century classical music. [IC]

With Mulligan, Nelson, Carole King, Joni Mitchell and others; with Kellaway, *The Spirit Feel* (1967), Pacific Jazz; as leader, *Apple Juice* (1981), Columbia; *Tom Cat* (1974), Ode; *Tom Scott and the L.A. Express* (1973), Ode; *The Honeysuckle Breeze* (1967), Impulse

Scott, Tony (Anthony Sciacca), clarinet, saxes, composer/arranger (and piano). b. Morristown, New Jersey, 17 June 1921. Studied at Juilliard, 1940–2. During the next 13 years, Scott worked as a sideman with Buddy Rich, Ben Webster, Sid Catlett, Trummy Young, Earl Bostic, Charlie Ventura, Claude Thornhill, and (for a month) Duke Ellington; he also wrote arrangements for singers, including Billie Holiday and Sarah Vaughan, and did a nine-month stint as musical director for Harry Belafonte. From 1953 he led his own groups, winning polls as a clarinettist and establishing himself as an important new voice on the instrument. 1957, his group spent seven months touring in Eastern and Western Europe and in Africa. 1959, Scott left the USA and spent the next six years travelling and working in the Far East: explaining his departure from the scene, Scott said: 'The clarinet died, and I hate funerals.'

His main initial influences were Charlie Parker and Ben Webster, and although Scott was perfectly at home with mainstream and bebop musicians, his concept and style were, even at that time, beyond pigeonholes. He played the clarinet with immense power and expressiveness (Perry Robinson has called him 'the loudest of all clarinettists'), and the whole jazz tradition was evident in his work, but he was also one of the earliest experimenters in free improvisation and atonality. On his 1957 album *Scott's Fling*, two pieces, 'Abstraction No. 1' and 'Three Short Dances for Clarinet', are abstract improvisations, and he took part in a free collective improvisation on a 1958 programme, 'The Subject is Jazz'.

Scott was the first modern American jazz musician to make such a prolonged visit to the Far East. He visited Japan, Formosa, Okinawa, Hong Kong, Korea, the Philippines, Indonesia, Bali, Singapore, Malaya, Thailand and Saigon. Throughout the trip he was active as a player and teacher of jazz, but also immersed himself in the music and the culture of the countries in which he stayed. He recorded classical folk music of the Far East, and made concert appearances with indigenous musicians. He played at the first Hong Kong Jazz Festival, 1961, and the first Japanese festival, 1962; he played with a traditional Balinese orchestra in Bali, and with an Indian classical singer at Hindu and Sikh temples in Hong Kong. July 1965, Scott returned to the USA, leading a quartet in New York and incorporating elements from ethnic music into his jazz. 1967, with Collin Walcott on sitar and tabla, Scott gave a concert of Indo-jazz music for the Museum of Modern Art's 'Jazz in the Garden' series.

He moved to Italy in the 1970s, living in Rome and working with a group led by pianist Romano Mussolini. He has also led his own groups since then, and made many appearances as a soloist and with various groups at festivals all over Eastern and Western Europe.

Scott is a loner and a musical adventurer, and in a long and fascinating career he has anticipated several major new developments in jazz: the free jazz of the 1960s, Indo-jazz fusions, the gradual absorption by jazz of elements from ethnic musics and the progress towards the idea of 'world music'. [IC]

With Sarah Vaughan, Mel Powell, Milt Hinton, Billie Holiday and others; Tony Scott septet (with Gillespie/Webster/S. Vaughan and others), *52nd Street – vol. 1* (1945), Onyx; Scott/Walcott, *Music for Yoga Meditation and Other Joys* (1967), Verve

Sealey, Paul, guitar, banjo, bass guitar. b. Watford, Hertfordshire, 9 March 1943. His jazz career began in the 'Trad boom' of the early 1960s, when he worked with Bobby Mickleburgh's Confederates, Nat Gonella and others, but not until 20 years later, in the early 1980s, did his talents as a fleet acoustic guitarist, nimble banjoist (specializing in single-string solo work) and highly capable bass guitarist first become seriously noticed. At the period Sealey worked for an enormous number of local New Orleans-to-mainstream bands, and also – often at the behest of promoter Dave Bennett – for American visitors such as George Kelly, Benny Waters and Ruby Braff. Sealey's broad-based views and musical ear allow him to play with British talents as varied as traditional saxophonist Eggy Ley's Hotshots and Humphrey Lyttelton's eclectic band (as a regular deputy) and he often appears at British festivals such as Edinburgh and Brecon. [DF]

George Kelly/Sealey trio, *Fine and Dandy* (1982), Voca

Seamen, Phil (Phillip William), drums. b. Burton-on-Trent, Staffordshire, 28 August 1926; d. London, 13 October 1972. Legendary British drummer who came to prominence with big bands after World War II, playing and recording with the Ken Turner orchestra and Nat Gonella, 1946–7; Tommy Sampson, 1948; Joe Loss; Jack Parnell's band, early 1950s. 1955, he was with the Ronnie Scott orchestra, and in the later 1950s he played with the Jazz Couriers (co-led by Ronnie Scott and Tubby Hayes), the Tubby Hayes quartet and the Joe Harriott quintet. During the early 1960s he worked with Alexis Korner's Blues Incorporated and did gigs with Georgie Fame; he also did some teaching and one of his most illustrious students was Ginger Baker. 1964–8, he spent much time as resident drummer at Ronnie Scott's club, accompanying many US jazzmen including Johnny Griffin, Stan Getz, Roland Kirk, Freddie Hubbard. 1969–70, he worked with Ginger Baker's Air Force, recording LPs and touring with the group. The last two years of his life were spent playing in London pubs.

Phil Seamen arrived on the scene with the bebop movement, and he had from the beginning all the basic virtues: beautiful time, energy and an innate musicality; but it was the dynamism of his indelible spirit that made his work so exceptional. His abilities transcended bebop: he was with the glorious Joe Harriott quintet when it was creating the very first European free (abstract) jazz, 1959–60; and he was equally at

Phil Seamen

home with the rhythm-and-blues of Alexis Korner or the heavy rock of Air Force. He was also a man of great humour and trenchant wit. The drug addiction which caused his premature death also blighted his career, which had begun with magnificent promise. [IC]

With Dizzy Reece, Victor Feldman, Hayes, Scott, Jimmy Deuchar, Dick Morrissey, Harry South, Air Force and others; with Harriott, *Free Form* (1960), Jazzland; (talking and playing), *Phil Seamen Story* (1972), Decibel

Sears, Al(bert Omega), tenor sax. b. Macomb, Illinois, 22 February 1910. Worked in Buffalo, then replaced Johnny Hodges in Chick Webb band (1928). Played with Elmer Snowden (1931) and other leaders, led own band for most of 1933–43. Also with Andy Kirk (1941–2), Lionel Hampton (1943–4), then Duke Ellington (1944–9). Founder member of Johnny Hodges small group (1951–2), also recording with this group under own name. Recorded several rhythm-and-blues dates and founded music publishing company, also led house band for Alan Freed rock and roll shows during 1950s. Inactive as a player since then. Sears had a distinctive, rather querulous tone and an emphatic style of phrasing which became an important influence in rhythm-and-blues (his feature on Duke's gospellish 'A Gathering in a Clearing', 1946, cleverly used this style: 'Anybody can tell it was my riff, because there wasn't no preachers in the Ellington band till I joined,' said Sears). His own arrangement, 'Castle Rock' with the 1951 Hodges group, was a sizeable jukebox hit and pointed the direction of his future career. [BP]

Johnny Hodges, *Rabbit on Verve, vol. 1* (1951), Verve

Secrest, Andy, trumpet. b. Muncie, Indiana, 2 August 1907; d. California, 1977. Usually remembered as the trumpeter who replaced Bix Beiderbecke in Paul Whiteman's orchestra in 1928, he had been working in another chair vacated by Beiderbecke, with Jean Goldkette's organization, and it was a record of Secrest with Goldkette ('Here Comes the Showboat') which caught Whiteman's ear. While he was never the genius that Beiderbecke was, Secrest read quickly and sounded similar in tone and approach. 'You could say I was a pupil', Secrest told Richard Sudhalter later. 'I idolized the guy – thought his style and tone were way ahead of the times. I started playing that way because it was the style that I wanted to obtain.' When Secrest left Whiteman in 1932 he moved into studio work with orchestras such as Victor Young's and John Scott Trotter's (his cornet pops up on records by Bing Crosby from the period), and by the 1950s he was still active playing on many of the Hollywood-based Dixieland big-band broadcasts of the period. With the onset of rock and roll, however, Secrest left music and worked in real estate until he retired. [DF]

Section A group of instruments that functions together as a unit within a larger group. The 'rhythm-section', for example, can vary enormously in size and makeup – piano, banjo, tuba and drums; two guitars and bass; bass and drums, with or without piano; or several keyboard and guitar players, several percussionists and a couple of bassists – but they will always think of themselves, and be thought of, as a section.

Similarly, any organized (i.e. not 'jamming') group with four or five horns will have a sufficient ensemble power for them to be heard as the 'horn-section'. Anything larger, say with two trumpets, two trombones and two reeds, will tend to function at least part of the time as a separate 'brass-section' and 'reed-section'; whether the brass also sub-divide may depend on the nature of the music. In standard big-band formats, even if the arrangers persist in using them together all the time, the trumpets and trombones are located in separate rows called the 'trumpet-section' and the 'trombone-section'. [BP]

Sedric, Gene 'Honey Bear' (Eugene P.), tenor sax, clarinet. b. St Louis, Missouri, 17 June 1907; d. New York City, 3 April 1963. He worked in St Louis with trumpeter Charlie Creath's band in the early 1920s and 1925–32 was in Sam Wooding's globetrotting band. Sedric was one of Wooding's best soloists, and after leaving he worked for Luis Russell and Fletcher

Henderson before his big break came along: the years he spent with Fats Waller and his Rhythm, 1934–42. 'I was associated with Fats to the end,' he remembered, 'and from 1939 to 1942 we travelled all over the country, always on the move. Waller was one of the greatest box-office attractions of all time. The largest crowd we ever played to was at the musical fête held every year in Chicago at Soldier Field. It holds 120,000 people. And the largest dance crowd we ever played to was 20,000 in New Orleans at the Race Track.' With Waller, Sedric achieved the kind of career opportunities – radio and recording almost daily as well as films and plum concert bookings all round the USA – which would have been envied by many and after the pianist died Sedric continued his successful career, leading his own bands in New York clubs and on tour: in the 1950s he worked for leaders such as Jimmy McPartland, Bobby Hackett and Mezz Mezzrow as well as Conrad Janis (the trombonist who later became a Hollywood actor and starred in *Happy Days*), playing and recording. But the Sedric most jazz fans remember is the forthright tenor saxophonist and plummy chalumeau clarinettist on those irreplaceable Waller sides of the 1930s. [DF]

Any with Fats Waller

Segure, Roger, arranger, piano. b. Brooklyn, New York, 22 May 1905. Raised in Rhode Island and California, studied at universities of Nevada and California. Worked as pianist on boats to Orient, and played in China and Japan with singer Midge Williams (early 1930s). Moved to New York (1936) as freelance arranger for Louis Armstrong, John Kirby, Andy Kirk and Woody Herman before working full-time for Jimmie Lunceford (1940–2). After army service, during which he led his own group, further study, then teacher of arranging. Moved to California (1949), writing for Jerry Fielding and others (1950s) and then teaching. Still living in retirement in 1980s, Segure deserves more than the total lack of attention he has received. During his period of greatest jazz activity, he was a very influential arranger: his 1941 'Yard Dog Mazurka' for Lunceford was later borrowed for Stan Kenton's 'Intermission Riff'; even more remarkably, 'Little Miss', written in 1940 for Andy Kirk (and possibly inspired by the writing of Mary Lou Williams), uses the unison sound of the John Kirby group and turns it into almost fully-fledged chromatic bebop. Typically, neither of these tracks is available at the time of writing. [BP]

Jimmie Lunceford, *Rhythm Is Our Business* (1934–42), Affinity

Seifert, Zbigniew, violin. b. Cracow, Poland, 6 June 1946; d. 15 February 1979. He studied violin and alto saxophone at the Chopin School of Music in Cracow, and graduated from the Cracow Higher School of Music in 1970. His main inspiration was John Coltrane, and he began as a saxophonist, forming his own quartet in 1965. He gained rapid critical acclaim in Europe and won several prizes at jazz festivals – both for his group and for himself as soloist. He played with Swedish trombonist Eje Thelin, from whom he learned something of the art of 'free' improvisation. 1970, he joined Tomasz Stańko's group and played with it at the Berlin festival. It was with Stańko that Seifert began playing violin and gradually phasing out the saxophone. From 1973 on he appeared at many European festivals with Hans Koller and as a soloist. Then he played with Joachim Kuhn. Hamburg Radio commissioned him to write a 25-minute concerto for a violin, orchestra and jazz group. He played and recorded with Ralph Towner's group Oregon, and appeared live in duet with Philip Catherine. Seifert once said, 'I try to play as Coltrane would if he played the violin', and his playing has much of the passionate intensity and the fleetness of his idol. The last two years of Seifert's life were spent in a heroic battle against the cancer which ultimately killed him at the age of 32. He recorded his final album only three months before he died and yet it is ablaze with energy, passion and great playing from Seifert and the all-star group under his leadership, Jack DeJohnette, John Scofield, Eddie Gomez, Richie Beirach, Nana Vasconcelos. [IC]

With Volker Kriegel, *Lift* (1973), MPS; with Charlie Mariano, *Helen 12 Trees* (1977), MPS; with Oregon, *Violin* (nda), Vanguard: as leader, *Man of the Light* (1976), MPS; *Passion* (November 1978), Capitol; memorial album (eight performances by Seifert with various international groups, from radio broadcasts and festivals), *We'll Remember Zbiggy* (1974–8), Mood

Sellers, Roger John, drums, percussion. b. Melbourne, Victoria, 18 July 1939. Family musical. Studied percussion in Australia, New Zealand and later USA and UK. 1959, met and worked with Dave MacRae and Mike Nock. 1972, to USA for 18 months, then came to UK, 1974–80, with Nucleus. Also worked with many other UK musicians, including Ronnie Scott and Neil Ardley, and Americans such as Al Grey, Sonny Stitt, Art Farmer, Ernestine Anderson. 1981, went to New Zealand where he worked with local musicians and visiting Americans. With Nucleus he toured extensively in Europe and spent three weeks in India in 1978, playing at the first Jazz Yatra in Bombay and in Calcutta and Delhi. [IC]

With Nucleus, Neil Ardley and others; with Dave MacRae/Joy Yates, *Forecast* (1984); with Mike Nock, *Strata* (1984), both Kiwi Pacific

Semple, Archie (Archibald), clarinet. b. Edinburgh, 1 March 1928; d. January 1965. A spiritual son of first Ed Hall, later Pee Wee Russell,

Semple came south from Edinburgh in 1952 and, after year-long stays with Mick Mulligan and Freddie Randall, joined Alex Welsh. For the next decade his rambling, hushed creations provided the perfect foil for Welsh's forthright Chicago-style lead, and together with Roy Crimmins, Fred Hunt *et al.* they recorded British jazz classics such as *It's Right Here For You* (a Semple show-case) and small-group collectors' items such as *Night People*: on his own the clarinettist recorded quartet, trio and duo albums and (from 1962) a session with strings, directed by Johnny Scott, which might just be the best of its kind ever recorded anywhere. By the early 1960s Semple – a charming and immaculately-mannered man of deeply nervous disposition – was drinking heavily, though still playing brilliantly: a late tour with Pee Wee Russell in 1964 provided almost comedic proof of the similar talents – and dispositions – of the two. Soon after, one night at the Richmond Jazz Festival, Semple suffered a breakdown onstage, and never really played again. His death from alcoholism (four years before Russell's from the same cause) was a blow to Welsh's first great band. [DF]

Alex Welsh, *It's Right Here For You* (1960), Columbia

Serious music A term appropriated by admirers of European composition to distinguish it from all that lower-class popular music. If they choose to exclude jazz as being too popular, that is their problem. See also CLASSIC/CLASSICAL. [BP]

Session musicians are those who earn the greater part of their living working in record, radio, television and film studios. Each of the cities where these activities take place supports a pool of such players, who form a financial, and in some respects a musical, élite. For not all the music involved is necessarily 'commercial' in the derogatory sense: it can range from clever advertising jingles to complex pseudo-symphonic soundtracks. The great demands made on the players' skills, however, are often outweighed by the crucifying boredom of much of the work they have to carry out.

Since the 1920s, it has gradually become easier for musicians with a jazz background to gain entry into the exclusive ranks of the 'sessionmen' (the American terminology is now 'sessionists' as a result of the ranks slowly opening up to women musicians). Many of the players listed in this book have spent at least some of their career specializing in 'session work' but, for every Phil Woods or Bud Shank who returned to revitalized jazz playing, there are many who have been swallowed up and whose jazz reputation (and, indeed, jazz ability) has suffered as a result. [BP]

Shank, Bud (Clifford Everett, Jnr.), alto sax, flute (and baritone). b. Dayton, Ohio, 27 May 1926. Began on clarinet at age 10 and saxophone at 14, then after university moved to West Coast (1947). Joined Charlie Barnet (1947–8, on tenor) and Stan Kenton 40-piece band (1950–1). Regular member of Lighthouse All Stars group (1953–6), then own quartet. Making albums under own name from 1954, some (mid-1960s) of more middle-of-the-road music. Heavily involved in studio work, continued to appear regularly on jazz gigs. Founder member of L.A.4 group (1974), also toured Europe as soloist and with Shorty Rogers (1984, 1985).

Shank's early alto work reflected a polite blend of Charlie Parker and Benny Carter influences, with a touch of the early Art Pepper for flavouring; this was later roughened up considerably, in terms of tone quality and rhythmic emphasis. But it is perhaps his flute playing which is his most important achievement, for the instrument was hard to take seriously in a bebop context. Yet Bud's phrasing and articulation, and even more so his pliant tone, make the listener aware not of the flute's limitations in jazz but of its real communicative power. [BP]

Live at The Haig (1956), Concept; *Heritage* (1977), Concord

Shankar, Lakshminarayana, violin, composer. b. Madras, India, 26 April 1950. Father, V. Lakshminarayana, a noted violinist. At age two he was taught to sing ragas, and at five he began violin lessons with his father. His primary involvement was with Indian classical music, but he was always aware of Western influences and as a young boy heard many Western classical artists as well as groups such as the Beatles, and singers such as Elvis Presley and Frank Sinatra. 1969, he moved to the USA in order to play different kinds of music as well as to popularize Indian music in the West. He took a Ph.D. in ethnomusicology at Wesleyan University, and while working as a teaching assistant and concert master of the university chamber orchestra, he began meeting jazz musicians such as Ornette Coleman, Jimmy Garrison and John McLaughlin. From 1973, Shankar and McLaughlin studied together: 'John gave me a lot of jazz lessons and I gave him a lot of Indian lessons.' 1975, they co-founded and co-wrote the material for the group Shakti (see MCLAUGHLIN, JOHN), an acoustic group which created a unique synthesis of Indian classical music and Western jazz and brought Shankar to the notice of a world-wide audience. Shakti disbanded in 1978.

Shankar is a complete virtuoso with a vision of a pan-cultural musical synthesis – a slowly emerging world music – which he is helping to create. Chris Doering has written, 'Shankar executes the microtonal slurs of Indian music with liquid precision even in the highest octaves

Bud Shank

where fingering is difficult', and he is completely at home with Eastern secular and religious music and Western jazz and rock. He has also pioneered a new instrument: the ten-string, double-neck violin, a double-bodied instrument conceived and designed by Shankar and built by Stuyvesant Music in New York to his specifications. The necks can be played individually or collectively; when played individually, the strings of the other neck create sympathetic overtones. The double violin can cover the range of a whole string orchestra.

Shankar has also recorded with Frank Zappa, Phil Collins and Peter Gabriel among others. He performs for two months a year in India where he is a major recording artist, many of his albums of Indian classical music topping the charts there. [IC]

With Shakti, *Shakti* (1975); *A Handful of Beauty* (1976); *Natural Elements* (1977), all CBS; as leader, *Touch Me There* (1979), Zappa; *Who's To Know* (1980); *Vision* (1983); *Song for Everyone* (1984), all ECM

Shapiro, Art(hur), bass. b. Denver, Colorado, 1916. He took up bass in his teens and worked in 52nd Street's clubland as well as Washington throughout the 1930s. As a busy studio man he appears on a huge number of jazz records of the period (including classics such as Eddie Condon's Commodore Jam Sessions). 1938–41, with one break, he was with Paul Whiteman's pace-making orchestra, then he moved out to the West Coast and Hollywood and, after an army spell, joined Benny Goodman in 1947 for a brief stay. Afterwards, like many of his contemporaries, he moved full-time into studio work, safely away from the tides of jazz fashion. [DF]

Eddie Condon, *Jam Sessions at Commodore* (1938), Teldec/Commodore

Sharrock, Sonny, guitar, composer, and pedal steel guitar, banjo. b. Ossining, New York, 27 August 1940. Began on guitar at age 20; self-taught. Early experience singing with rock groups. Studied at the Berklee School of Music for four months when he was 21; studied composition for four months in 1963. From 1965 he worked with Olatunji, Pharoah Sanders, Sunny Murray, Don Cherry and others. He was with Herbie Mann, 1967–73, touring in the USA and internationally, and recording with him. He also played major festivals with Mann including Montreux and Newport, 1970. The same year, he played on side two of the Miles Davis album *Jack Johnson*, mostly just creating electronic textures. 1973, he formed a group with his wife Linda, and they also toured in the USA and Europe. 1985, he cut his first album in ten years and became a member of Last Exit, with Peter Brötzmann, Ronald Shannon Jackson and bassist Bill Laswell.

Sharrock came to prominence on the crest of abstraction and rock. With Mann's group he often played a non-tonal role, 'freaking-out' with feedback and other sounds, but this was all done in a rhythmically coherent context. Sharrock claimed to be the first guitarist to play free jazz, and so topsy-turvy had values become at the end of the 1960s that he actually boasted of his musical ignorance, saying he could write 'but not read music. Do not know any standard tunes or any other musicians' licks.' He won the *Downbeat* critics' poll in the category Talent Deserving Wider Recognition, 1970. [IC]

With Sanders and others; with Herbie Mann, several including *Memphis Underground* (1968), Atlantic; with Wayne Shorter, *Super Nova* (1969), Blue Note; with Linda Sharrock, *Paradise* (1974), Atco

Shavers, Charlie (Charles James), trumpet, arranger, vocals, composer. b. New York City, 3 August 1917; d. 8 July 1971. Before he was ten he was a natural dancer and played banjo and piano: the piano well enough to play in his teens at Tilly's Chicken Shack (a Harlem rib-joint), the banjo well enough to play duets with Bobby Hackett later for fun. By the age of 18, when he joined Tiny Bradshaw's band in New York, Shavers had mastered the trumpet so completely that he must have brought to near-despair a 1920s generation of trumpeters who had just got over worrying about Louis Armstrong and Roy Eldridge. By 1937, when he joined Lucky Millinder, his talent was fully grown and less than a year later – at the ripe age of 20 – he joined John

Kirby's new band at the Onyx, replacing Frankie Newton: it was Kirby's luckiest career move ever. For the next six years Shavers masterminded the Kirby operation, providing hit tunes ('Pastel Blue' and 'Undecided'), tiny, faultless arrangements and effortless, flighty trumpet. 'I really loved all the guys in that band,' he said later, in a monumental downgrading of his own contribution, 'and the reason it sounded so good was that we were all personal friends!' He left Kirby in 1944, by which time a year's work with Raymond Scott's integrated CBS staff orchestra had come and gone; the following year he joined Tommy Dorsey, who guarded his new cornerman jealously and (says Alun Morgan) on one occasion even sent a private detective to find Shavers after the trumpeter had tried to leave. He stayed 11 years, on and off, until Dorsey's death, but during the period Shavers's dynamic talent was heard all over: in the ranks of Jazz at the Philharmonic where he was (with Roy Eldridge) the most well-equipped trumpeter to deal with Granz's crucifying high-note finales, recording with all and sundry (as ever) from Charlie Parker to Billie Holiday (his bravura introduction to Holiday's 'My Man', full of *yiddische chutzpah*, makes everything after it sound flat), and producing classics of his own, like an immortal 'Stardust' from a 1947 Gene Norman concert featuring Lionel Hampton, which sums up jazz trumpet in one rib-tickling chorus. During all this time his trumpet playing contemporaries held him in awe ('after Charlie,' said Billy Butterfield once, 'there's nothing left to play!'), and it was left to critics joylessly frozen into the cool school or holed up in austere revivalism to brand his work as 'tasteless'. After Dorsey died in 1956, Shavers began leading groups of his own in New York and out (often he adopted the fashionable shufflebeat Jonah Jones format) and by 1963 was back with a re-formed Tommy Dorsey orchestra, led by saxophonist Sam Donahue and featuring Frank Sinatra Jnr: his act at this time – coming on late from the wrong side of the stage, gag endings, stopping half-way to blow his nose – was (as Owen Bryce points out) the epitome of trumpet cabaret. By the mid-1960s he was on tour with Sinatra again, regularly leading his own quintet (with Budd Johnson) and touring as a soloist, including a trip to England in 1969, during which he was gagging at full speed, playing brilliantly and vocally delighted to see electric sockets in hotel rooms marked 'For Shavers Only' ('Wait till Eldridge sees this!'). By 1970, however, the good humour and the trumpet perfection were beginning to slip as throat cancer took hold (an album, *The Last Session*, recorded in February 1970, shows unfamiliar strain creeping in) and he died the year after – two days after Louis Armstrong (his mouthpiece, at his request, was buried in Armstrong's coffin). Charlie Shavers might just be the best trumpeter the swing era ever produced. Others may have extended the trumpet's capabilities further in one direction (Cat Anderson played higher, Rex Stewart was perhaps more of a half-valve master) but Shavers had the perfect technique for whatever he wanted to do, and he did most things. [DF]

Live from Chicago (1962), Spotlite

Shaw, Artie (Arthur Jacob Arshawsky), clarinet, saxes, composer. b. New York City, 23 May 1910. He began his New York career as a lead-alto sessionman working for leaders such as Paul Specht, Vincent Lopez and Roger Wolfe Kahn, and on records with such as Fred Rich and Teddy Wilson (his clarinet sides with Billie Holiday, including 'Did I Remember' and 'A Fine Romance', are some of the best she made). After a concert in 1936 at New York's Imperial Theater, featuring a small string section, Shaw formed his first big band and over the next few years, in the wake of a re-formed high-powered orchestra and hit records such as 'Frenesi', 'Adios Mariquita Linda' and, of course, 'Begin the Beguine', he became a centre of swing-music attention, featuring saxophonist Tony Pastor (a boyhood friend), a string section again, and later on such black artists as Billie Holiday, Hot Lips Page and Lena Horne. Apart from his huge talent as a clarinettist, Shaw was sensitive, intelligent and (sometimes to his dismay) excellent copy. His career – especially in its early years – was littered with a string of famous wives (including Lana Turner), unexpected disbandments, disillusioned disappearances and frank public announcements proclaiming the inanity of the music industry and even of his young jitterbugging audiences. At the time the musical press in America and abroad found his outbursts mystifying and unsporting: in retrospect they were clearly the outpourings of a multi-faceted, sensitive nature all too aware that all was not what it could be down Tin Pan Alley. After one disbanding in 1939 Shaw re-formed a year later; his orchestra featured a much-loved and well-remembered small group, the Gramercy Five, including Johnny Guarnieri on harpsichord and Billy Butterfield on trumpet. By 1942 he was leading an all-star navy band which toured the Pacific. 'They went wild at the mere sight of us', recalls Max Kaminsky. 'It was like being back in the Paramount Theater again . . . those men went stark raving crazy. Even the fellows in the band were shaken!' From 1944, Shaw's bandleading career was more spasmodic. Jazz fashion was gravitating to bebop, big bands were on the decline and it was evident that Shaw would find it hard to fall in with jazz fashion just because it was there. But he carried on recording for another ten years, toured what remained of the big-band circuit, led a small string-based group at Bop City in 1949 and played Carnegie Hall in a classical programme the same year – accomplishing, in short, many of the same aims as Benny Goodman. But where Goodman was a stoic leader and an omni-directional musician who liked nothing

Artie Shaw

better than to play the clarinet all day, Shaw was a diversifier. By 1950 he had taken up Spanish guitar as a serious second instrument, gone into psychoanalysis and begun to realize that he was perhaps too bright to be just a jazzman. In 1952 he produced his long, romantic and thoughtful autobiography (see below) which (along with Sandy Brown's *McJazz Manuscripts*) is one of the most substantial self-portraits of a jazz musician. Shaw was to make his career as a writer from the mid-1950s, publishing an entertaining trio of short stories, *I Love You, I Hate You, Drop Dead*, in the 1960s and writing regularly for the theatre and for films. In the 1980s it was good to welcome him back to bandleading (as frontman for a re-formed orchestra led by Dick Johnson), and to see and hear him commenting on earlier triumphs for film documentaries including in 1985 a full-length documentary, *Time is all you've got*, a riveting study of a great musician with a fine mind.

Artie Shaw, along with Benny Goodman, was the leading clarinettist of the swing era. Because he achieved his first major success two years after Goodman, and his musical career was intermittent, his contribution is often considered secondary to Goodman's; but many jazz musicians find a warmth and creativity in Shaw's work that they miss in Goodman's, and many of his 1940s recordings ('Stardust' is one classic) stand alongside the best jazz music ever recorded. [DF]

Concerto for Clarinet (1938–45), RCA (double)

See Shaw, Artie, *The Trouble with Cinderella* (Farrar, 1952, repr. Da Capo, 1979)

Shaw, Arvell, bass. b. St Louis, Missouri, 15 September 1923. If only because of his skilful four bars in 'Now You Has Jazz' from the film *High Society* (1956), Arvell Shaw will always be associated with Louis Armstrong's All Stars, and might not wish for more. But Shaw (like Trummy Young and other All Stars who were selflessly happy to serve their leader) was himself an influential and highly progressive player who, when he was 'just a young kid' – three years after the death of Jimmy Blanton – was already impressing older hands such as Earl Hines with his power, creativity and speed at a time when most bass players offered much less. Shaw first worked with Armstrong in his big band in 1945, rejoined him when the All Stars were formed and (apart from a two-year break to study music at Geneva Conservatory) was with him up to 1956: his bass solos of the period – such as 'Blues for Bass' from the Crescendo sessions – are, right down to their audible in-time gasps for air, models of virtuoso performance. After *High Society* he worked with a variety of talents including Teddy Wilson's trio, Benny Goodman and Sidney Bechet, before rejoining Louis Armstrong with whom he then stayed and played (with short breaks) until the end. After 1971 he was active as a freelance and teacher, and by the 1980s was touring with Keith Smith's 'Wonderful World of Louis Armstrong', playing the bass as well as ever, singing in a pleasing, plummy baritone, and reminiscing in good-humoured tempo. [DF]

Louis Armstrong, *At the Crescendo* (1955), Coral

Shaw, Woody, trumpet, fluegelhorn, composer. b. Laurinburg, North Carolina, 24 December 1944. Family moved to Newark, New Jersey, where his father was a member of a gospel group, the Diamond Jubilee Singers. Started on bugle, then on trumpet at age 11. His teacher, Jerry Ziering, gave him classical lessons, but introduced him to the work of Dizzy Gillespie, Bix Beiderbecke and Bunny Berigan. He began to sit in locally with visiting guest stars, then at 18 he toured with Rufus Jones, after which he got his first big-time job with Willie Bobo in a Brooklyn club. The band included Chick Corea, Larry Gales, Joe Farrell and Garnett Brown. Then he joined Eric Dolphy's group until the saxophonist's sudden death in 1964. Shaw said of this period, 'Eric helped me to find my own individual approach to playing trumpet. He taught me to play inside and outside at the same time.' 1964, he went to Paris, working with Bud Powell, Kenny Clarke, Art Taylor, Johnny Griffin and Larry Young. He also played in Belgium and Germany before returning to the USA. 1965, he joined Horace Silver; 1968–9, he played on and off with Max Roach, touring the Middle East and performing at a festival in Iran. 1970–2 was a time of little work, during which he played with Joe Henderson and Gil Evans. 1973, he joined Art Blakey, then left, spending some time freelancing on the West Coast with Herbie Hancock and Bobby Hutcherson.

Back in New York in 1975, he recorded the third album under his own name, *Moontrane* (Muse), which got such favourable reviews and made such an impact that Shaw had enough viability to lead his own groups. Shortly afterwards, at Miles Davis's suggestion, Columbia signed him up, and a spate of fine albums ensued. He continued touring and playing festivals internationally with his own groups. 1985, he played the Camden festival, London, with a quintet that included Joe Farrell and the 'young lion' drummer Ronnie Burrage. Shaw's original influences were Gillespie, Miles Davis and Clifford Brown, and later Booker Little, Donald Byrd, Lee Morgan and perhaps most of all Freddie Hubbard. Other influences are McCoy Tyner, with whom he played and recorded in the late 1960s, and classical composers such as Debussy and Boulez. He is a superb player who had shrugged off most of the Hubbard influence by the mid-1970s, forging a highly individual style compounded of playing 'inside' (on the chords) and 'outside' (superimposing foreign notes on the chord). [IC]

With Dolphy, Tyner, Silver, Blakey and others; *Blackstone Legacy* (1970), Contemporary; *Song of Songs* (1972), Contemporary; *Little Red's Fantasy* (1978), Muse; *Stepping Stones* (1978); *Rosewood* (1978); *Woody III* (1979), all CBS

Shearing, George Albert, piano, b. Battersea, London, 13 August 1919. Blind from birth, Shearing began gigging in the late 1930s with the Ambrose dance band. Hotel, radio and record work with Harry Parry (1940–1) and Stephane Grappelli, then resident in London. Visited USA at end of 1946 and settled there permanently a year later. Formed extremely popular quintet (1949–67), and for the last two decades has led trio and then duo (currently with bassist Don Thompson). Shearing has made records under his own name since 1939, and in that time has successfully imitated boogie, Earl Hines, Bud Powell, Lennie Tristano, Latin-jazz,

Milt Buckner, Horace Silver, Bill Evans. In recent years, he has occasionally sung in public as well without denting his popularity. His 1952 tune, 'Lullaby of Birdland', is one of the most widely known jazz standards. [BP]

Live at the Café Carlyle (1983), Concord

Shepherd, Dave (David), clarinet, bandleader. b. East London, 7 February 1929. The most polished jazz clarinettist of post-war Britain is sometimes undervalued (in print, at least, if not by musicians), in part because his highly successful Benny Goodman-style quintet occasionally – and illogically – separates him from the general run of local jazz activity. In fact, Shepherd's musical terms of reference are much wider – they include Irving Fazola, Matty Matlock and Artie Shaw besides Goodman – and over 30 years he has played in a wide variety of British jazz settings: they include the 1950s 'Jazz Today' unit (with Bert Courtley, Johnny Rogers and others), Freddy Randall's and Joe Daniels's bands, Norman Granz's Jazz at the Philharmonic package for a British tour with Ella Fitzgerald, Oscar Peterson and others, and often with his own Dixieland-style groups. (He also backed Billie Holiday during her visit to England in 1954 and worked professionally in the USA around the same period on Long Island.) In the 1970s and 1980s he has toured internationally with Teddy Wilson, played numerous Edinburgh Festivals, Nice and Montreux and been heard with Lennie Hastings's band and Peter Boizot's Pizza All Stars, as well as with his own quintet, featuring Roger Nobes, Brian Lemon and Len Skeat, which regularly plays the club and festival circuit. Shepherd's immaculate style has earned him a music career including TV, radio and records, and in 1987 he was due to play solo concerts for the King of Thailand. By day he works in the film industry. His performances are always inspired, invariably tasteful and never lose their inbuilt sense of jazz decorum. [DF]

The Randall–Shepherd All Stars (1972), Black Lion; any with his quintet

Shepherd, Jim (James), trombone, bass saxophone. b. Dulwich, London, 29 March 1936. He worked with Steve Lane's Southern Stompers early in his career, then with bands led by Brian White, Dave Keir and Ian Bell. A close associate of clarinettist Alan Cooper, he subbed regularly with the Temperance Seven, played in the house band at Osterley Jazz Club, 1963–8, and from that year joined a great – and much underrated – British-based band, the Anglo-American Alliance (featuring Dick Sudhalter, pianist Henry Francis and singer Chris Ellis). In the 1970s he freelanced, playing with a resident group (including trumpeter Bob Kerr) at the Half Moon, Putney, and with violinist Dick Powell at the Redan, Queensway. After a brief spell of inactivity came work with the newly-formed Five-a-Slide trombone group, tours and recordings with a variety of visiting Americans such as Wild Bill Davison, Jimmy McPartland, Yank Lawson and Franc Williams, and in 1985 a short season with the American Harlem Blues and Jazz Band. One of the best British trombonists, with a strong eye to classic principles, he plays naturally in the style of white Americans such as Miff Mole and Bill Rank, as well as Jack Teagarden. [DF]

Anglo-American Alliance, *Sweet and Hot* (1969), EMI

Shepp, Archie, tenor and soprano sax, composer, educator. b. Ft Lauderdale, Florida, 24 May 1937. Brought up in Philadelphia. Started on piano, clarinet and alto; switched to tenor, playing with r & b bands. He met Lee Morgan, Cal Massey, Jimmy Heath and John Coltrane in Philadelphia. He studied drama at Goddard College, 1955–9, and after graduating he settled in New York. 1960, he worked with Cecil Taylor, playing concerts and also appearing in the play *The Connection*. He co-led a group with trumpeter Bill Dixon, then co-led the New York Contemporary Five with John Tchicai and Don Cherry, touring the USSR and Czechoslovakia with it in 1964, and appearing at the Helsinki World Youth Festival. From 1965 he began occasional associations with John Coltrane, working with him in various clubs, and recordings made by Shepp at the Newport Jazz Festival that year were coupled with a Coltrane performance in a release on the Impulse label called *New Thing at Newport*. This exposure, and the endorsement of his abilities by Coltrane, were enormously helpful in establishing Shepp in the USA and internationally. Also in 1965 he began establishing himself as a dramatist, and his play *The Communist* was performed in New York.

Shepp's main influences are Ben Webster, Coleman Hawkins, Charlie Parker, Coltrane, Sonny Rollins and Ornette Coleman. From the early 1960s he was closely associated with the avant-garde movement and with its manifestations as an expression of black solidarity. In December 1965, addressing himself to the white readership of *Downbeat* magazine, he wrote: 'I am an anti-fascist artist. My music is functional. I play about the death of me by you. I exult in the life of me in spite of you. I give some of that life to you whenever you listen to me, which right now is never. My music is for the people.'

Shepp's music has almost always been less abstract than that of the other avant-gardists, and his 1965 Newport concert revealed him to be a deft and highly original composer, as well as a distinctive new voice on tenor sax. His band which included Bobby Hutcherson (vibes), Barre Phillips (bass) and Joe Chambers (dms), featured rock rhythms, jazz swing, tonalities, harmonic structures, tightly composed

Archie Shepp

passages and occasional texts spoken by Shepp. His gruff tenor sound came out of Hawkins, but it included passionately vocalized tones, with falsetto passages sometimes tender, sometimes brutal, and he also showed an extraordinarily caressing way of handling a romantic melody – as if he were savouring and consuming it.

From the mid-1960s Shepp led his own groups, touring and playing festivals internationally. 1967, his octet album *Mama Too Tight* showed a rich eclecticism, overtones of Ellington and Ben Webster, r & b rhythms, street-band marches, lascivious parodies of popular ballads, non-tonal collective 'freak-outs'. All these elements were included in the music of his band which toured Europe that year and in London shared the bill with the Miles Davis quintet.

1969, he began collaborating with trumpeter and composer Cal Massey, playing his compositions and taking him on tour in Europe and North Africa, where Shepp appeared at the Pan-African Festival playing a concert with African musicians which was released on record. This attempt to get back to roots was, however, a disaster; Shepp's jazz sensibilities and the musical tradition of the African musicians found no common ground.

Shepp continued to be active in the theatre, collaborating with Cal Massey on *Lady Day: A Musical Tragedy*, which was performed at the Brooklyn Academy of Music in 1972. He also wrote other plays that were performed, including *Junebug Graduates Tonight*. 1972, he taught a course in playwriting at the University of Buffalo while holding the post of consultant in music, and from 1973 he lectured at the University of Massachusetts at Amherst.

He continued to tour and play major international festivals. In Europe, 1979, he toured with a group which included Mal Waldron, and at this point in his career, Shepp was featuring soprano as well as tenor, and he had reverted to playing bebop. 1985, he toured Europe with his group, and was once more playing post-bebop music – a kind of contemporary mainstream confection with strong roots in the blues; at one point he actually sang a blues. [IC]

With Coltrane, Cecil Taylor and others; Shepp/Roswell Rudd/Tchicai, *Four for Trane* (1964), Jasmine; *New Thing at Newport* (1965), Impulse; *Mama Too Tight* (1967), Impulse; quintet, *Montreux One/Two* (1975), Arista (double); *There's a Trumpet in My Soul* (1975), Arista; *A Sea of Faces* (1975), Black Saint; Shepp/Karin

Krog, *Hi Fly* (1976), Compendium/Phonogram; Shepp/Horace Parlan, *Goin' Home* (1977), Steeplechase; Shepp, *Trouble in Mind* (1980), Steeplechase

Sherock, Shorty (Clarence Francis Cherock), trumpet. b. Minneapolis, Minnesota, 17 November 1915; d. North Ridge, California, 19 February 1980. A child-student of cornet, Sherock – a fine and very neglected swing trumpeter – worked early in his career with Ben Pollack (1936) then with Jimmy Dorsey, Bob Crosby, Gene Krupa, Tommy Dorsey and others before forming his own band in 1945. He rejoined Jimmy Dorsey, replacing Charlie Teagarden in the Dorseylanders (1950), and then moved into studio work, playing for TV and radio: a valuable sample of his exciting solo approach turns up on the album below. [DF]

Session at Midnight (1955), Capitol

Shew, Bobby (Robert Joratz), trumpet, fluegelhorn, and slide, piccolo and pocket trumpets. b. Albuquerque, New Mexico, 4 March 1941. Largely self-taught. Spent one year at University of New Mexico, studying commercial art with some music classes. 1959–60, he attended Stan Kenton clinics. 1964–9, he worked with Tommy Dorsey orchestra, Woody Herman, Della Reese, Terry Gibbs, Robert Goulet, also in Las Vegas house bands and hotels. In the 1970s he toured as lead trumpet with Tom Jones and Paul Anka; also with Louie Bellson, Neal Hefti, Don Menza, Bud Shank and Art Pepper. Also active as a private teacher and a conductor of jazz clinics both in the USA and internationally. He is also a busy studio musician. His influences include Art Farmer, Dizzy Gillespie, Conte Candoli and Kenny Dorham. Shew is a fine section player and lead trumpet, and also a gifted soloist. [IC]

With Bellson, Herman, Toshiko Akiyoshi/Lew Tabackin and others; *Parallel 37* (1980), Ode

Shihab, Sahib (Edmund Gregory), baritone, alto and soprano sax, flute. b. Savannah, Georgia, 23 June 1925. Early experience with various territory bands, then studies in Boston (1941–2). Touring (on alto, as 'Eddie Gregory') with Fletcher Henderson (1944–5), Roy Eldridge band (1946). After working in Boston, gigging and recording in New York with Art Blakey (1947), Thelonious Monk (1947, 1951) and Tadd Dameron 10-piece band (1949). Out of music for few years, then on baritone with Dizzy Gillespie (1953), Illinois Jacquet (1954–5 including European tour), own group (1956), Oscar Pettiford big band (1957) and Dakota Staton (late 1950s). Went to Europe with Quincy Jones band (1959–60), settled there for next 12 years, as freelance soloist and with Kenny Clarke–Francy Boland (1961–72). Moved to Los Angeles (1973), working again in Europe and New York in 1980s. Shihab plays both flute and soprano with an individual approach, and not just for the sake of doubling. However, it is on baritone that he has made his most distinctive contribution. [BP]

Sentiments (1971), Storyville

Shorter, Wayne, tenor and soprano sax, composer. b. Newark, New Jersey, 25 August 1933. Studied music at New York University for four years, then in US army, 1956–8. Freelanced in New York until he joined Art Blakey's Jazz Messengers, 1959, staying with the group until he joined Miles Davis, summer 1964. During his four years with Blakey, he toured extensively in the USA, Japan and Europe and recorded several albums with the group, establishing himself as one of the most gifted of the younger saxists. His influences then were Sonny Rollins, John Coltrane and Coleman Hawkins, but he was already finding his own stylistic synthesis, and he was also composing pieces for the Messengers. He was with Davis through six crucial years (1964–70) of the trumpeter's career, and it was during this period that Shorter really found his own voice as both player and composer. Blakey's hard-driving, straight-ahead rhythms had brought out the muscularity in Shorter's tenor playing, but the greater freedom of the Davis rhythm-section allowed him to explore new emotional and technical dimensions. He said, 'With Miles I felt like a cello, I felt viola, I felt liquid, dot-dash . . . and colours really started coming.' The muscularity was still there when he wanted it, of course, as were the technique and speed of execution but, particularly on the studio albums with Davis, he began to practise a kind of understatement, often projecting an urbane melancholy and tenderness. Several of his compositions also bore these qualities, and his sound and style had a pervasive influence in the jazz world during the later 1960s and the early 1970s. His influence might have been even greater if the album he recorded with Davis in December 1965, *Live at the Plugged Nickel*, had been released at the time instead of more than ten years after the event. On this his playing is extraordinary; the influences of Coltrane, Rollins and Ornette Coleman have been totally absorbed, and Shorter shows a devastating originality which covers the entire technical and emotional spectrum. On solo after solo he seems to be reappraising the whole current saxophone vocabulary.

His compositions were an important part of the Davis repertoire until 1967, and subsequently several of them became part of the standard jazz repertoire – 'ESP', 'Footprints', 'Dolores', 'Nefertiti', 'Pinocchio' among others. Shorter left Davis in the spring of 1970, and later that year, together with Joe *Zawinul, formed Weather Report. Shorter is more a player who composes, and Zawinul more a composer who plays, and in its first stages Weather Report's approach was quite open and loose, featuring electronics and much rhythmic and tonal abstraction. But the whole tendency of jazz in the early 1970s was away from the overemphasis on improvisation which had unbalanced the music in the 1960s, and towards a greater emphasis on composition, clear tonalities and coherent rhythms. As Weather Report moved gradually in this direction, Shorter's role became reduced in it, with less solo space and fewer of his compositions in the band's repertoire. Explaining in 1982 why he was writing so little for the band, he said, 'Miles used to say that I was a great short story writer, but now we have epics and sagas.' During his time with Davis in the 1960s, and with Weather Report in the 1970s and 1980s, Shorter also recorded independently under his own name, writing most or all of the music for these albums, which is generally less radical and more conservative than the music of his two long-time associates, and often tinged with a Brazilian influence. However, Shorter is incapable of shallowness and, whether as leader or sideman, playing or composing or both, his music always has the larger view and is about the human condition. He is something of a visionary, with a knowledge of other cultures and other musics, ethnic and otherwise, and his striking use of imagery in conversation also points to his unusual sensibilities and viewpoint.

His playing and composing have inspired countless musicians on all instruments. With Davis, Shorter first played soprano sax on *In a Silent Way* and *Bitches Brew* (both 1969), producing such an ethereal, seductively forlorn sound, that he probably started the whole rise to prominence of the soprano with electronic fusion groups. He has appeared at all major festivals around the world with his various associates, and has won many polls in the US and internationally. [IC]

With Blakey; more than 12 with Weather Report (CBS); ten with Miles Davis (CBS); *Night Dreamer* (1964); *Speak No Evil* (1965); *Adam's Apple* (1966); *The All-Seeing Eye* (1965); *Juju* (1965); *Etcetera* (1965); *The Soothsayer* (1965); *Schizophrenia* (1967); *Super Nova* (1969), all Blue Note; *Native Dancer* (1975), CBS; *Wayne Shorter* (1959–62), GNP

Shotham, Ramesh, South Indian percussion: tavil, mridangam, ghatam, morsing and drum set. b. Madras, S. India, 7 May 1948. Mother an amateur Carnatic music violinist. Largely self-taught, but studied two years at Karnataka College of Percussion, Bangalore; also B.Sc. in zoology. With his brother, Suresh Shotham, in the late 1960s, formed a group called Human Bondage which lasted seven years and won several awards in India; he played at the 1978 and 1980 Jazz Yatras in Bombay with Louis Banks (keyboards) and Braz Gonsalves (reeds), forming the Jazz Yatra Septet (later called 'Sangam') with them. Sangam toured Europe (1980–1), playing festivals in Prague and Warsaw and recording in Germany, and in 1983 toured with Charlie Mariano. Shotham has lived in Europe since 1981, working with various people including Dutch flautist Chris Hinze, the group Embryo and Norwegian Jon Balke. He has conducted workshops all over Germany and was artist in residence at Bayreuth University. His favourites include Tony Williams, Elvin Jones, Billy Hart, Shannon Jackson, and several Indian and South American percussionists. [IC]

Sangam (1981), Eigelstein; *Jon Balke* (1982), ECM; with Chris Hinze, *Saliah* (1984), Keytone; *Jazz at the Opera House* (1985); *Flute Salad* (1985), both ABC, Australia

Sideman A sideman (not 'sidesman') is anyone who is not the group leader on a particular gig. In a big band, they may be section-men or soloists (who also play in a section, of course), but they are all sidemen.

There seems to be no non-sexist version of the term, largely because, in the present era of fewer and fewer full-time groups, the syndrome of 'always the sideman and never the leader' hardly exists any more; and, where everyone is a potential leader, no one is a sideman. Therefore, the term is now only heard on the lips of people who like jazz of a certain age. [BP]

Signorelli, Frank, piano, composer. b. New York City, 24 May 1901; d. Brooklyn, New York, 9 December 1975. A close friend and associate of Phil Napoleon for well over 30 years, he had a comfortably successful 40-year career which began when he assembled the Original Memphis Five in 1917 to play at the Balconnades Ballroom on 66th Street, New York. From then on he stayed busy, working with Napoleon, with Joe Venuti and with Adrian Rollini's New Yorker orchestra, as well as freelance and in studios, and during the 1930s he became a highly successful songwriter: 'I'll Never be the Same', 'Stairway to the Stars' and 'A Blues Serenade' are all Signorelli tunes. During the swing era and after he was a frequent soloist along 52nd Street, worked with a re-formed Original Dixieland Jazz Band and Paul Whiteman and by the late 1940s was working Nick's Club with Bobby Hackett and a similarly re-formed Original Memphis Five which continued to get together for records, radio and TV all through the 1950s. A fine pianist who worked naturally in a style reminiscent of Bob Zurke, Signorelli should be better known than he is. [DF]

Connee Boswell and the Original Memphis Five, *In Hi-Fi* (1956), RCA

Silk, Eric, banjo, leader. b. London, 19 May 1926; d. 17 April 1982. He worked first with John Haim's Jellyroll Kings, and after Haim's death assembled his own Southern Jazz Band in 1949 for a sensational appearance at Cooks Ferry Inn. Hand-picked to play New Orleans jazz (post-Armstrong), Silk's first band contained trumpeter Spencer Dunmore (soon to be replaced by a long-term partner, cornettist Dennis Field, and – for a while – trumpeter Alan Littlejohn) and clarinettist Teddy Layton. In 1951 his group began a long residency at the Red Lion, Leytonstone (the 'Southern Jazz Club'), played a succession of pioneering Riverboat Shuffles, and through the 1950s produced many records and broadcasts of their scholarly, well-rehearsed and nicely-played repertoire, with its early preoccupation with ragtime. The last of the determined amateurs ('I'm convinced that to turn professional you have to turn commercial,' he said), Silk gained a devoted following and produced at least one 'classic' British LP, *Off the Cuff*. By the end of the 1960s Field had left (replaced by Phil Mason), and in 1973 Silk (and his father, who managed the band throughout its life) disbanded; trombonist Alan Dean formed the Gene Allen Jazzmen from former band members including keymen Arthur Bird and Steve Nice. Silk became ill with pleurisy, and died of a heart attack at only 55. [DF]

Off the Cuff (1966), Polydor

Horace Silver

Silver, Horace Ward Martin Tavares, piano, composer. b. Norwalk, Connecticut, 2 September 1928. After gigging locally on tenor as well as piano, Horace's trio toured with Stan Getz, who became the first person to record Silver tunes (1950–1). Appearances in New York, often at Birdland, backing Terry Gibbs, Coleman Hawkins, Getz, Lester Young etc. (1952–3). Recording under own name with Art Blakey (1952–3), and albums with Blakey and Miles Davis (1954). Silver's own quintet recording (1954) led to formation of Jazz Messengers with same personnel (1955–6), then departure of Horace, Hank Mobley, Donald Byrd (initially for work with Max Roach) and Doug Watkins enabled Silver to form regular quintet, replacing Blakey with Louis Hayes. Apart from spending part of late 1970s–early 1980s in semi-retirement, has continued to lead a quintet ever since, including at various times Art Farmer (1957–8), Blue Mitchell (1958–64), Woody Shaw (1965–7), Randy and Mike Brecker (1973–4), Joe Henderson (1964–6) and, on record, Eddie Harris (1981–2). After recording albums on Blue Note for 28 years, some in mid-1970s with large ensemble backing and/or featured singers, Horace formed his own company, Silveto Records (1981).

His composing ability is pre-eminently as a stylistic consolidator, although one less academically inclined would be hard to find. In the mid-1950s he created the 'hard bop' writing style virtually single-handed, by taking for granted that even a fairly 'mainstream' rhythm-section would be heavily bop-influenced and contrasting this with simple swing-era phrasing for the front-line instruments. The rapid acceptance of his 'Opus De Funk' (the first use of the word in a tune-title) and 'Doodlin' ' by artists such as Woody Herman and Ray Charles illustrates the extent of this backward-looking fusion; the gospel influence of 'The Preacher' was achieved subtly (compared to others' later excesses) with a melody and associated riffs which had a natural, built-in back-beat. His equally fine 'Sister Sadie' (1959) bore a remarkable resemblance to the 1930s pop song 'Do You Wanna Jump, Children?' recorded by Count Basie and Cab Calloway, among others.

This joyously conservative approach stems directly from Horace's piano style (compare, for instance, the trio and quintet versions of 'Quicksilver') and, even when a tune is voiced in two-part harmony (eg 'Ecaroh' or 'Silver's Serenade'), it turns out to be just the top two notes of the full two-handed piano chords. Sometimes on record it seems that his improvisations flirt too much with the obvious, but to witness in the flesh their ease of construction – even down to the quotations – is completely captivating. Whether soloing or backing, Horace is first and foremost a rhythm player and has enjoyed excellent partnerships with Kenny Clarke (on records) and with Art Blakey; like Blakey, his accompaniment can be almost overwhelming, but its flowing compulsion cushions the soloists and forces them to say what they have to say. [BP]

Horace Silver Trios (1952–68), Blue Note; *Horace Silver and the Jazz Messengers* (1954–5), Blue Note; *Blowin' the Blues Away* (1959), Blue Note; *Live 1964*, Emerald

Simmons, Norman (Sarney), piano, arranger. b. Chicago, 6 October 1929. Regular work in the 1950s backing soloists visiting Chicago led to touring with singers Dakota Staton, Ernestine Anderson, Carmen McRae (1961) and, since 1979, Joe Williams. Arranged three albums for Johnny Griffin and worked with the Lockjaw Davis–Griffin group in 1960. Little known as piano soloist despite recordings under his own name, although a superior accompanist. His writing contribution to the album below, including superb arrangements such as 'Wade in the Water' (which preceded the Ramsey Lewis version), deserves wider recognition. [BP]

Johnny Griffin, *Big Soul Band* (1960), Milestone

Sims, Zoot (John Haley), tenor and soprano sax (and alto). b. Inglewood, California, 29 October 1925; d. 23 March 1985. Toured with several big bands during World War II, also small-group work with Sid Catlett (1944) and Bill Harris (including recording debut with Harris's pianist Joe Bushkin, 1944). After army service, member of Benny Goodman band (1946–7), together with trombonist brother Ray Sims (b. 18 January 1921). Then joined Woody Herman (1947–9), establishing reputation alongside fellow tenorists Stan Getz and Al Cohn, who also worked with him for Artie Shaw (1949–50). Several European tours with Goodman (1950, 1958, 1962, 1972, 1976), with Stan Kenton (1953), with Gerry Mulligan (sextet 1956, big band 1960), 'Jazz from Carnegie Hall' group (1958) and Jazz at the Philharmonic (1967, 1975). Took part in reunion concerts with Herman (1972, 1978). For the rest of the time, Sims was a freelance soloist, often (from 1957 onwards) in a two-tenor team with Al Cohn. He was the first US performer to play a season at Ronnie Scott's (1961) and returned several times between then and 1982. Made final tour of Scandinavia (late 1984) after hospitalization and diagnosis of his terminal cancer.

Zoot's tenor playing was one of the most delightful outgrowths of Lester Young's influence. While less emotionally ambiguous than Lester, Sims absorbed the rhythmic strengths of the parent style into his own self-propelled lines. Always intensely melodic, he developed over the decades a tone that was superbly sleek, though never flamboyant. This transferred well to the soprano, which he took up in the 1970s and which he turned into a much gentler instrument than in the hands of its previous practitioners. During his final years, his already economical approach became more spare and astringent than ever. [BP]

Zoot Sims

Cohn/Sims, *Al and Zoot* (1957), Jasmine; *Down Home* (1960), Affinity; Count Basie/Sims, *Basie and Zoot* (1975), Pablo

Singleton, Zutty (Arthur James), drums. b. Bunkie, Louisiana, 14 May 1898; d. New York City, 14 July 1975. Zutty Singleton was one of the most influential of all classic jazz drummers. He may have been the first to develop the idea of extended drum solos. He was a developer of percussive effects, for example the clicking temple-blocks and tiny choke cymbals that adorn records such as Louis Armstrong's 'My Monday Date' and 'West End Blues'. He was the first to introduce brushes to jazz drum vocabulary. And he was a huge influence on later drummers such as Cliff Leeman (who copied the 'tip' or 'ride' cymbal from Singleton) and Stan Greig, who still lists him as a primary influence. As if this were not enough, Singleton was always one of the personalities of the jazz era: 'the senior senator of the jazz community' in New Orleans (according to Milt Hinton) and a man who was held in respectful regard by all his fellows including Louis Armstrong. 'Even now,' said Hinton in the 1960s, 'Louis looks up to Zutty and Zutty looks down to Louis. Even though Zutty isn't doing very well.' Singleton never worked much for Louis Armstrong (once at least he was dropped from a band that Armstrong was leading at Connie's Inn) but this may be because he was – rather like Sid Catlett – too much of a leader for Armstrong, outgoing, extrovert, forceful in speech, too much of a personality in his own right. 'If you're not in a band with Zutty,' said Barney Bigard, significantly, 'he's the greatest guy in the world!' Singleton's approach to music strongly resembled Catlett's. He was as happy playing bebop as Dixieland (on Slim Gaillard's 'Slim's Jam' he can be heard tapping away alongside Dizzy Gillespie and Charlie Parker); he was a great show drummer and, like Catlett and Baby Dodds, heard drums as musical sounds. But perhaps more than either of them, Singleton was by vocation a leader.

One of his first bands in New Orleans, at the Orchard Club, featured Louis Armstrong and by the early 1930s he had worked with most of the biggest names in New York, too, but later in the decade, for whatever reason, he moved back to Chicago (careerwise he would have been better off in New York) working with Carroll Dickerson, whose name was ten years out of fashion, as well as with new, younger lions such as Roy Eldridge. In 1937 he came back to New York and was often bandleading there until 1943, when he moved out to Los Angeles to take a quartet into Billy Berg's: that year he made the first of three films, *Stormy Weather* with Bill Robinson, Fats Waller and Lena Horne (the others were *New Orleans* in 1946, with Louis Armstrong and Billie Holiday, and *Turned-up Toes* in 1949). Around LA, Singleton became a celebrity and until the 1950s he regularly led bands of his own (as well as working for other leaders such as Eddie Condon and Nappy Lamare), then he spent time in Europe with Bill Coleman, Mezz Mezzrow and others and finally came back to New York, where he took an apartment with his wife Marge and worked clubs including Jimmy Ryan's until the late 1960s. [DF]

Bill Coleman, *Rarities* (1952), Rarities

See Williams, Martin, *Jazz Masters of New Orleans* (Macmillan, 1967, repr. Da Capo, 1979)

Sissle, Noble Lee, leader, vocals, composer. b. Indianapolis, Indiana, 10 July 1889; d. Tampa, Florida, 17 December 1975. He is remembered primarily as a bandleader and solo performer of the 1920s (he recorded prolifically for Victor, Okeh and other companies during this period) and as the highly-gifted composer who collaborated with Eubie Blake, most notably in 1921, on the monumentally successful *Shuffle Along* (the first all-black Broadway revue), followed by *Chocolate Dandies* and others. His orchestras, usually formed as backing groups for his own routines, nevertheless often contained famous jazzmen: a short-list includes Buster Bailey, Tommy Ladnier, Frank Goudie, Sidney Bechet, Chauncey Haughton, Wilbert Kirk and co-singer Billie Banks. Sissle did little recording after the 1920s and consequently tends to remain a shadowy figure, mentioned only occasionally by the jazz community: Sidney Bechet says that later on his precoccupation seemed to be more with himself than with his sidemen and Earle Warren adds a possible confirmation ('I didn't care for the way he dominated his men'). Sissle remained highly successful, however, until the 1960s, by which time he was running not only a band but his own night club and publishing company. [DF]

Sissle and Blake's 'Shuffle Along' (1921), New World

Skeat, Len (Leonard), bass. b. East London, 9 February 1937. He worked up through Ted Heath's band, and later for singer Tom Jones, in Stephane Grappelli's trio, in studios and in London theatres, and values the traditional roles of jazz perpetuated by his close friend Ray Brown: acoustic-based sound, faultless time and chord changes and a primarily rhythm-based foundation. This has made him a natural choice for classic American entertainers visiting Britain – from Peggy Lee to Bob Wilber and Ruby Braff – and taken Skeat himself to America to work with, among others, Bobby Rosengarden's band. A British time-lord of bass, Skeat has long earned the respect he now enjoys.

His brother Bill, a gifted sessionman who plays woodwind and all the saxophones, while specializing on tenor, works regularly and to great effect around the British scene. [DF]

Skidmore, Alan Richard James, tenor and soprano sax, flute, alto flute, drums. b. London, 21 April 1942. Father, tenor saxophonist Jimmy Skidmore, gave him help and encouragement. Studied reading with Les Evans. 1958, began playing with dance orchestras and pop bands. 1961, first BBC Jazz Club broadcast. 1963, recorded with Eric Delaney and Louie Bellson (*Repercussion*, EMI). 1964, joined Alexis Korner's Blues Incorporated and recorded with John Mayall and Eric Clapton. 1965, with Ronnie Scott quintet. 1965–9, took part in several televised jazz workshops at NDR (North German Radio and TV), Hamburg, with Chick Corea, Dave Holland, Albert Mangelsdorff and John Surman among others; also guested with Maynard Ferguson orchestra and recorded film soundtrack music with Herbie Hancock. 1969, he formed his own quintet with Kenny Wheeler, Tony Oxley, Harry Miller and John Taylor, and at the Montreux festival won the International Press Award for best band and the Soloist Award. He also won a scholarship to Berklee School of Music, Boston, but did not take it up. 1970, joined Georgie Fame and the Blue Flames, worked with Weather Report on a NDR televised workshop, and played concerts in Hamburg and Berlin. 1971–2, worked with Mike Gibbs, Mike Westbrook, Chris McGregor's Brotherhood of Breath, and toured Italy with Nucleus. With John Surman and Mike Osborne he formed SOS, an innovative three-saxophone group, in 1973, and they toured in Italy, Germany and France. They also co-wrote and performed music for a ballet, *Sablier Prison*, at the Paris Opera House. 1974, formed his own trio with Chris Laurence and Tony Oxley. 1976–82, he was with the George Gruntz Concert Band which included Joe Henderson, Elvin Jones, Jimmy Knepper, Charlie Mariano, among others. 1978, formed SOH (Skidmore, Oxley, Ali Haurand), which toured Europe extensively for six years. 1981–4, he was guest soloist with WDR (West German Radio) Orchestra in Cologne, working with Gil Evans, Airto Moreira, Mel Lewis and others. With the WDR band, he toured India and South-East Asia for the Goethe Institute in 1984.

His favourite saxists are John Coltrane, Sonny Rollins, Dexter Gordon, Mike Brecker, Gerd Dudek and Ronnie Scott, and perhaps, like Brecker most of all, Skidmore is a 'man for all seasons', a player with immense physical and imaginative stamina, at home in any context, from tight structures to total abstraction, and with any tempo, from breakneck to slow. [IC]

With Stan Tracey, Graham Collier, Mike Westbrook, Mike Gibbs, Weather Report, Volker Kriegel, George Gruntz, Airto Moreira and many others; *Once Upon a Time* (1969), Deram; with John Surman, *Jazz in Britain* (1969), Decca; quintet, *TCB* (1970), Philips; *SOS* (1975), Ogun; *El Skid* (1977), Vinyl; *SOH* (1979), Ego; *SOH Live* (1981), View

Skidmore, Jimmy (James Richard), tenor sax. b. East Ham, London, 8 February 1916. After pre-war experience he worked with George Shearing early in both their careers, 1950–2, with Ralph Sharon's quintet (the misty tenor he contributed to their records of the period met with unanimous approval), with Vic Lewis and Jack Parnell, and regularly as a soloist on records and in clubs where his clean-toned, bop-influenced style created a sensation. By 1956 he was working for Humphrey Lyttelton, who in 1958 was still able to write: 'Jimmy is, for me, the finest player in the country.' Towards the end of his stay with Lyttelton, Skidmore was taken into hospital for a serious operation (his leader kept him on full pay throughout the period), but after leaving Lyttelton's band much less was heard from him than should have been. Various reasons could be guessed at: the relentless rise of young Tubby Hayes, who soon would meet Lyttelton's description of Skidmore, the emergence of avant-garde and rock and roll, perhaps above all Skidmore's easy-going nature and refusal to take anything, including jazz, too seriously. By the 1960s he was guesting around the country (including regularly at Southend Rhythm Club with old friend Bix Curtis) and working for a supermarket: a late album in the 1970s (disastrously titled *Skid Marks!* and ruined by atrocious engineering) did little to help. Skidmore's regular appearances at the Bell near Codicote, Hertfordshire, in the 1970s were late chances to enjoy his undiminished talent; in 1986 he was playing clubs more regularly. (Jimmy Skidmore's son is Alan, above.) [DF]

Humphrey Lyttelton, *Blues in the Night* (1960), Columbia

Skiffle A name apparently used only a couple of times in the whole history of American blues recording, 'skiffle group' was adopted by Ken Colyer as the description of his band-within-a-band. This specialized in the early 1950s in imitating early folk-blues drawn mainly from the recorded repertoire of Huddie Ledbetter and from the first European visit of Big Bill Broonzy.

The popularity of this music rapidly spread far wider than the world of traditional jazz and, by a freak of history, formed a bridge for British youth to cross over into rock and roll. Furthermore, the attempt of Alexis Korner to build a serious minority audience in the UK for the full range of blues and rhythm-and-blues actually succeeded; even more remarkably, it created a hybrid called 'British blues' which fed back into American rock music via the Rolling Stones, but also laid the groundwork for the late 1960s development in the US of jazz-rock-fusion. [BP]

Slim and Slam, see GAILLARD, SLIM; STEWART, SLAM.

Small group means anything that is not a big band or an unaccompanied solo. The smallest groups are usually not thought of as groups but are referred to as duos or trios. The borderline between a large small-group and a small big-band varies somewhat according to fashion and according to the attitude of the players involved. [BP]

Smalls, Cliff (Clifton Arnold), piano, trombone, arranger. b. Charleston, South Carolina, 3 March 1918. He was a graduate of Kansas Conservatory and afterwards worked, 1942–6, with Earl Hines's big band as relief pianist and trombonist before short stays with Lucky Millinder and Bennie Green. In 1948 he took the first of his jobs as MD/conductor for a singer – Billy Eckstine – and over the next 20 years was to perform the same service for Clyde McPhatter, Brook Benton and, in the 1960s, Smokey Robinson and the Miracles. Smalls's tastes ran naturally to rhythm-and-blues – he had worked with Earl Bostic during his controversial 'Flamingo' period which helped to usher in rock and roll – but by the 1970s had returned more regularly to his jazz side working with Sy Oliver and the New York Jazz Repertory Company. In the 1980s he toured Europe regularly with Oliver Jackson's trio. [DF]

Any with Oliver Jackson's trio

Smith, Bessie, vocals. b. Chattanooga, Tennessee, 15 April 1895; d. Clarksdale, Mississippi, 26 September 1937. 'She was a wild lady with her blues': Lester Young, gently bringing together the two facets of Bessie Smith, the 'Empress of the Blues'. First, she was the greatest American blues singer ever, whose rich, passionate contralto could fill a hall with the devastation of grief or the celebration of earthly joys, from gin, wine and pigs' feet to sexual ecstasy. Second, her hard-lived life was a prototype for wild women who sing the blues, right down to Janis Joplin who lived faithfully in her hard-drinking, hard-loving, bisexual image.

Bessie Smith was a protégée of Gertrude 'Ma' Rainey, sang in Rainey's minstrel show and by 1913 – when she was 18, strikingly beautiful and very black, with a belling blues cry stronger than her employer's – was stopping shows all around the South. By 1920 she had her own show in Atlantic City, and by 1923 had made the big career move to New York, where she lived in Harlem with her ne'er-do-well husband Jack Gee. At first her blues seemed too slow and measured for fast city audiences ('I'd go to the bathroom, come back and catch the rest of one verse', said bandleader Sam Wooding), but by the end of the year Bessie had signed for Columbia, produced her first issue ('Downhearted Blues' and 'Gulf Coast Blues' with pianist Fletcher Henderson) and begun a long year of clubwork and touring. More recordings – with Henderson's small group this time – soon established her further; so did a highly paid tour for TOBA, and by 1925 she was star of her own summer tent show, *Harlem Frolics*, which travelled the South in its own luxury railcar, thereby avoiding the dual problems of segregation ('We could just live on the train', said Maud Smith) and declining interest in the blues in symphonic-jazz-crazy New York. For the next three years *Harlem Frolics* grossed huge sums – in 1927, 1000 people were turned away from a performance in Kansas City – and Bessie Smith became the highest-salaried black star in the world: her new show a year later, *Mississippi Days*, had a cast of 45 and again grossed record amounts on TOBA. By then she had been recording for three years with such giants as James P. Johnson, Fred Longshaw, Fletcher Henderson, Louis Armstrong, Charlie Green and Joe Smith: the records that resulted – from 'St Louis Blues' (with Armstrong's speaking cornet and Longshaw's measured harmonium) to 'Backwater Blues' (which coincided with a huge flood disaster in the Mississippi delta) are required listening. From the late 1920s, however, popular fashion began to reject the matchless Empress of the Blues: talking pictures were drawing public attention from live shows, and the TOBA circuit was suffering like all the rest. Although Bessie appeared in a Broadway musical, *Pansy* by Maceo Pinkard in 1929 (it flopped), and made a film short (*St Louis Blues* for Phototone) the same year, her success was waning, and in 1931 she was dropped by Columbia: in 1932, after a spring tour of the South, she found herself back in New York with more clubs closing. But Spike Hughes, on a visit from England a year later, was still able to hear her: 'A mountainous woman who sang with pathos, humour and terrifying sincerity: there is little I've heard outside a Verdi opera that was so moving as her six-minute masterpiece called "Empty Bed Blues". She sang songs of everyday things in a black person's life – moving slowly across the stage towards the prompt corner to deliver her tag lines and disappear on a blackout.' In November 1933, Bessie made her last classic recordings for John Hammond (with Jack Teagarden, Coleman Hawkins, Benny Goodman *et al.*) and by 1934 was touring in *Hot from Harlem*, a show built around Ida Cox. In 1935 she played the Apollo, subbing first for Louis Armstrong, then in her own Christmas show; the year after she subbed again – for Billie Holiday this time – in *Stars over Broadway*: the reviews were ecstatic. By 1937 the Empress of the Blues was touring with the *Broadway Rastus* troupe, but on 25 September 1937 she was involved in a severe car crash and died the next day in Clarksdale Hospital after amputation of her right arm. 'If she had lived,' says Lionel Hampton, 'she would have been right up there with the rest of us – a national figure.' 7000 people attended her funeral, but her grave went unmarked until Janis Joplin and Juanita Green, once Smith's cleaner, financed a headstone in 1970: 'The greatest blues singer in the world', it read, 'will never stop singing.' [DF]

The Empress (1924–8), CBS.

See Albertson, Chris, *Bessie* (Abacus/Sphere, 1975); Feinstein, Elaine, *Bessie Smith* (Penguin, 1985)

Smith, Betty, saxophone, vocals, bandleader. b. Sileby, Leicestershire, 6 July 1929. She began her professional career with Freddy Randall's band in 1954, then formed her own quintet (with Brian Lemon) and quickly established a fine reputation as a swing saxophonist (her style in the early days came close to Eddie Miller and Bud Freeman; later it broadened and took on a harder swinging edge). In the 1960s and 1970s she worked regularly alongside Kenny Baker in a quintet, recorded as a soloist, singing as convincingly as she played, and from the mid-1970s was a central feature of the 'Best of British Jazz' package (also starring Baker and Don Lusher) which recorded, played concerts and clubs and appeared on TV. A club entertainer with a nice line in raunchy humour, Betty Smith remained as popular in the 1980s as she was 30 years before: she appears regularly with brass bands, as well as in jazz clubs, organizes groups for major shipping lines and collaborates musically with her husband, ex-Freddy Randall bassist Jack Peberdy. [DF]

Smith, Brian, tenor and soprano sax, flute, alto flute. b. Wellington, New Zealand, 3 January 1939. Family interested in music and drama; uncle ran a dance/jazz band in the 1920s. Four years' piano lessons; basically self-taught on clarinet and saxophone. Played in rock and roll, jazz and dance bands in NZ and Australia before coming to the UK in 1964, where his first job was with Alexis Korner's Blues Incorporated. 1966–7, worked at Ronnie Scott's Old Place with various blues and jazz musicians. 1969, began working with Tubby Hayes and Maynard Ferguson big bands. Autumn 1969, he was a founder member of Nucleus, staying with the group, except for two brief periods away, until 1982. 1970, with Nucleus, he played Montreux festival, where the group won first prize, and then the Newport festival and the Village Gate in New York. Also, extensive tours of Europe, particularly Germany and Italy with the group. 1972 and 1974, toured the USA with Maynard Ferguson and made a trip to Japan. Also tours with Nucleus in Scandinavia and Eastern Europe, then the first Jazz Yatra in Bombay, 1978, followed by concerts in Delhi and Calcutta. Smith has also worked with Gordon Beck, Annie Ross, Mike Gibbs, Graham Collier, Dave MacRae, Mike Westbrook, John Stevens, Keith Tippett and others. He moved back to NZ in 1982, where he plays with his own quartet and with drummer Frank Gibson's Space Case, and also does some teaching and studio work. 1984, he received the Australian Jazz Record of the Year award for his quartet album *Southern Excursion* (Ode). His favourite saxists are Sonny Rollins, John Coltrane, Charlie Parker, Wayne Shorter, Joe Henderson and Mike Brecker, among others. He names as other influences Herbie Hancock, Miles Davis, Wynton Kelly, Gil Evans, Louis Armstrong and Dizzy Gillespie. Smith is the complete musician – an all-rounder who is perfectly at home with anything from blues to rock, jazz and free improvisation. He also plays, and has recorded on, bamboo flute and percussion. [IC]

With Nucleus, *Elastic Rock* (1970), Phonogram Vertigo; *Belladonna* (1972), Vertigo; *Roots* (1973), Vertigo; *Awakening* (1980), Mood; with M. Ferguson, *World of Maynard Ferguson* (1974), Columbia; with Neil Ardley, *Kaleidoscope of Rainbows* (1976), Gull; with Pacific Eardrum, *Beyond Panic* (1978), Charisma; with Bobby Shew, *Parallel 37* (1980), Ode

Smith, Buster (Henry), alto sax, clarinet, arranger (and guitar). b. Ellis County, Texas, 26 August 1904. A key member of Walter Page's Blue Devils (1923–33) as lead saxophonist and arranger. Then worked for Bennie Moten (1933–5) before co-leading Count Basie–Buster Smith Barons of Rhythm at Kansas City's Reno Club (1935–6). Led own bands, including Charlie Parker among personnel, and moved to New York in 1938 as freelance arranger for Gene Krupa and Hot Lips Page and as altoist for Don Redman, Page, Eddie Durham and Snub Mosley, with each of whom he also recorded. Returned to bandleading in Kansas City (1942 onwards) and later in Texas, where his sidemen included future Ray Charles saxists Leroy Cooper and David (Fathead) Newman.

Smith's arranging contribution to the seminal Blue Devils must be taken on trust, since the band was virtually unrecorded, and likewise with the very early Basie band, although he was the uncredited co-composer of 'One O'Clock Jump' and others. On alto his influence may have been even more farreaching, for both he and Charlie Parker acknowledged the debt Parker owed to him; Jay McShann once said, 'When I heard Bird that night [on the radio] I thought I was listening to Buster Smith.' The disappointing contents of his one long-playing record (1959) make it all the more frustrating that Smith's early work is so sparsely represented on disc. [BP]

Various (3 tracks with Smith), *Original Boogie Woogie Piano Giants* (1938–41), Columbia; various (2 tracks with Smith), *Kansas City Jazz* (1940–1), Coral/MCA

Smith, Clara, vocals. b. Spartanburg, South Carolina, 1894; d. Detroit, Michigan, February 1935. No relation to Bessie Smith, but she ran a highly successful career in the shadow of the 'Empress of the Blues' all the way through the 1920s. 'Clara was the greatest for me', says Doc Cheatham. 'She wasn't an educated kind of person – very rough and mean, and the lower people who came to see her appreciated her because she spoke the language.' She had come up the hard way on Southern vaudeville circuits and by 1918 was playing big venues such as the Lyric Theater, New Orleans, and the Bijou in Nashville. When she arrived in New York in 1923 she was signed by Columbia (who wanted a second blues-singing Smith after Bessie on their books), began a recording career which totalled well over 100 sides and opened her own Theatrical Club which lasted for nine successful years. Perhaps because Clara's records only ever sold about half as well as Bessie's, Columbia sometimes teamed them on sides such as 'Faraway Blues' and 'I'm goin' back to my used-to-be': the relationship stayed friendly until 1925, when a fist-fight in New York put an end to the duo. Clara remained active in the 1930s in and around New York, Cleveland and Detroit where she died of a heart attack. [DF]

Louis Armstrong and the Blues Singers (1924–7), CBS

Smith, Colin Ranger, trumpet. b. London, 20 November 1934. An ex-clarinettist, he began his career in bands led by Cy Laurie and Terry Lightfoot and became well-known after joining

Acker Bilk, at the height of Britain's 'Trad boom' in 1960, replacing Ken Sims (the change-over produced storms of correspondence in the *Melody Maker* letter columns of the period). Two long stints with Bilk occupied Smith during the 1960s and 1970s (he also acted as Bilk's in-house musical director), but his musical approach quickly broadened, permitting long interim stints with – among others – John Picard's band (a mainstream-to-avant-garde 6-piece featuring Tony Coe), the London Jazz Big Band (for whom he initially played lead as well as solos) and in Peter Boizot's Pizza All Stars (from 1983). Smith works naturally in a Roy Eldridge-based swing style, but can move forward stylistically without noticeably donning a musical hat: his technique, harmonic flair and reliability are a musician's delight as well as becoming more generally known. [DF]

Dixieland All Stars, *Dixieland Now and Then* (1974), Line

Smith, Jabbo (Cladys), trumpet, trombone, vocals. b. Pembroke, Georgia, 24 December 1908. In the late 1920s, 'I remember several occasions when Jabbo came in to the Savoy when Louis was there,' says Milt Hinton, 'and he'd say something like "Let me play something with you! I'll blow you down!" ' Smith never managed to blow Louis down, mainly because his rival was a better and sounder trumpet player. But he was a considerable talent who, early on, played the kind of fast-moving, often stratospheric trumpet (he described it himself as 'running horn with lots of notes') which was later taken to its limits by Roy Eldridge. By 1929, Smith had worked for top bandleaders such as Charlie Johnson, Duke Ellington (on record) and James P. Johnson, and that year – at the Showboat in Chicago – he replaced Louis Armstrong as featured soloist with Carroll Dickerson's orchestra. What happened then, however, was prophetic, and must have secretly pleased Armstrong, who too often found Smith's trumpetistics buzzing round him like a persistent wasp. 'They got him the job and he blew it', recalls Hinton. 'He didn't show up.' Unreliability, complicated by girls a-million and hard drinking, were to be the downfall of handsome Jabbo Smith's early career: in 1928 he had been signed by Brunswick as an 'alternative' Louis Armstrong and the 19 resulting sides had been brilliant. But often he would turn up two hours late or not at all at the Chicago clubs that headlined him, and after the resulting fracas would use his home town Milwaukee as a bolthole: 'You get in a little trouble in Chicago, you run to Milwaukee. You get in a little trouble in Milwaukee, you run to Chicago!' By the late 1930s Smith's career, the victim of sexual fatigue and hard living in general, had slowed up; in 1941 he was heard at Newark Hot Club by Phil Stearn: 'He was kind of down and out. He was sickly and his lip was bad, and he had a miserable room in Milwaukee.' From the late 1940s very little more was heard from Jabbo Smith until the 1970s: he worked close to home, took day jobs and consciously recharged his batteries ('If I hadn't laid off 20 years I'd probably be burned out now,' he recalled later). In the 1970s he relaunched his career fulltime, played at Preservation Hall in New Orleans and then took a leading role in a New York musical, *One Mo' Time*. By the 1980s he was a celebrity again, songwriting alone and with British pianist Keith Ingham, appearing in film documentaries and telling his story to writer Whitney Balliett (see below). [DF]

Sweet and Lowdown (1927–9), Affinity

See Balliett, Whitney, *Jelly Roll, Jabbo and Fats* (OUP, 1983)

Smith, Jimmy (James Oscar), organ (and piano, vocals). b. Norristown, Pennsylvania, 8 December 1925. Won amateur contest at age nine, later appeared with entertainer father as duo. After navy service, studied bass and piano in Philadelphia. Worked with local Don Gardner group (1952–5), moving on to electric organ. Formed own trio, with John Coltrane joining for two weeks (1955). Following year, made New York debut and first trio albums; immediate success led to jam-session albums, with Smith joined by fellow Blue Note artists such as Art Blakey, Lou Donaldson, Lee Morgan, Jackie McLean (from 1957), and quartet dates with Stanley Turrentine and Kenny Burrell (1960). Changing to Verve label, redoubled his popularity with big-band backings arranged by Oliver Nelson and others (from 1962), even singing on a couple of albums. Toured Europe (1966, 1972, 1975) and, settling on West Coast, gave up touring and opened own night club. Renewed touring schedule in 1980s, including Atlanta festival (1983), Blue Note and Kool Festival concerts (1985) and European tours (1985, 1986).

It was Smith who defined the still standard approach to jazz organ by his work of the late 1950s and 1960s. Taking the organ/guitar/drums format (with optional saxophone) established by Wild Bill Davis and Milt Buckner, he replaced their big-band-inspired chording and substituted fast-moving bebop lines. With a shrill but punchy sound, he made sure his articulation was well defined at all tempos, so that the excitement of his concept was clearly communicated to audiences. Added to this was a distinct flavouring of blues phrases which was one of the factors feeding the fruition of 'soul jazz' in the late 1950s; by the mid-1960s it came to dominate Smith's work to the exclusion of all else, and from this time on he influenced not only former jazz pianists who took up organ but also all those keyboard players in blues and funk bands. There is only one Jimmy Smith, however. [BP]

Back at the Chicken Shack (1960), Blue Note; *Off the Top* (1982), Elektra Musician

Smith, Joe (Joseph C.), trumpet. b. Ripley, Ohio, 28 June 1902; d. New York City, 2 December 1937. 'I used to hate him when he came in, because otherwise I had the joint locked up!' remembered Roy Eldridge, his arch-competitor. 'Then he'd come in there and play so pretty!' Smith – a roamer, a wanderer, very much a wild man (unlike his brother Russell 'Pops' Smith) – was neither as quiet nor as reserved as his trumpet might have suggested. His speciality was a sweet and low-down plunger-mute style (Johnny Dunn was probably the very first to use a plunger rather than a water-glass for special effects) which – devoid of a growl-effect – produced the sound of a gently crooning human voice. By 1920, Smith was playing in New York, by 1922 he was accompanying Ethel Waters, then Mamie Smith and in 1924 he was musical director for Sissle and Blake's *In Bamville*, appearing on-stage at the end of the show to play the 'walking-out music'; his gentle preaching tone (played into a coconut-shell mute) effectively stopped the departing audience in their tracks, and people became jammed in the doorways. Smith's sensational new style was quickly noted by Fletcher Henderson, whom he joined from 1925 to 1928 (during the period he recorded classics with Bessie Smith and became her favourite accompanist): then, 1929–30, he worked with McKinney's Cotton Pickers. In the Pickers he became close friends (a rare event) with singer George 'Fathead' Thomas, but one autumn night in 1930, when they were both drunk, he drove his friend into a major car accident: Thomas was killed, and Smith never really recovered from the shock. Later details of his career are misty: he worked briefly with Henderson, Moten, McKinney and others, but in 1933 was picked up in Kansas City by Fletcher Henderson's band, who found him rambling and incoherent. They took him back to New York, where he died in a sanatorium after four years of progressive mental decline. [DF]

Fletcher Henderson, *A Study in Frustration* (1923–38), CBS (4 records, boxed set)

Smith, Keith John, trumpet, vocals, leader. b. London, 19 March 1940. From a back-to-the-roots trumpeter at the start of his career, Smith has developed steadily into one of Britain's most authoritative mainstream players. After a long formative spell with Papa Bue Jensen, he came back to Britain in the 1970s, formed his own band and revealed a new broad-ranged style with strong overtones of Henry 'Red' Allen, a primary influence, and Louis Armstrong. By the late 1970s Smith was leading his Hefty Jazz 6-piece, featuring his extra-talented front-liners Ron Drake (clt/saxes) and Mickey Cooke (tmb), which – under his canny leadership – quickly became the centre-point for a variety of well-packaged jazz shows including 'The Stardust Road' (a Carmichael tribute featuring singer Georgie Fame and female trio Sweet Substitute) and later '100 Years of Dixieland', featuring George Chisholm. Other of Smith's enterprises included 'The Wonderful World of Louis Armstrong' for which he re-assembled five of Armstrong's ex-All Stars to tour Britain and '100 Years of American Dixieland', another American package starring such fine players as Johnny Mince and Johnny Guarnieri. To back up his projects, Smith formed Hefty Jazz Agency, a small company, started his own record label, and by 1985 was heading a highly successful operation. That year he toured the USA with great success and received a well deserved award from the Overseas Press Club of America for 'creative and outstanding contributions to the international world of jazz'. [DF]

Ball of Fire (1978), Hefty Jazz

Smith, Lonnie Liston, piano, electronic keyboards, composer. b. Richmond, Virginia, 28 December 1940. Father and two brothers all singers. At high school he played trumpet in a marching band and sang bass and baritone in choirs. Graduated in music at Morgan State College, where he played tuba in a marching band and piano in the orchestra. Moved to New York and played with Betty Carter 1963–4; with Roland Kirk, 1964–5; Art Blakey, 1966–7; Joe Williams, 1967–8; Pharoah Sanders and Leon Thomas, 1969–71; Gato Barbieri, 1971–3; Miles Davis, 1973–4; then he formed his fusion group Cosmic Echoes, and his album *Expansions* became a hit, giving him star status overnight. Influences include Fats Waller, Art Tatum, Jelly Roll Morton, Duke Ellington, Miles Davis, Cecil Taylor, John Coltrane, Eubie Blake. With Barbieri and others he has played festivals on both coasts of the USA, and in Europe at Berlin, Nice, Milan, Hammerveld, Dusseldorf, Copenhagen. Smith is a prolific composer. [IC]

Two with Kirk, four with Sanders, five with Barbieri, two with Davis; *Visions of a New World* (nda); *Expansions* (nda); *Cosmic Funk* (nda); *Astral Travelling* (nda), all Flying Dutchman

Smith, Mamie (Mamie Robinson), vocals. b. possibly Cincinnati, Ohio, 1883; d. New York City, 30 October 1946. Mamie Smith occupies a key position in jazz history; it was her recording of 'Crazy Blues' for Okeh in 1920 which began the post-war craze for 'negro blues' and opened the floodgates for thousands of 'race records' aimed at the black audience in the 1920s. 'Crazy Blues' (composed by Perry Bradford, who arranged the session) was her second record: her first, 'That thing called love!' accompanied by white musicians, had sold only moderately well. But 'Crazy Blues' sold 7500 copies in the first week it was issued, and provided the ticket to success that Smith – a beautiful, very ambitious entertainer and (according to Willie 'The Lion' Smith, who played piano on the session) 'a pretty bossy gal' who had trouble keeping her musicians – had been waiting for. She formed her Jazz Hounds (they included, from time to time, stars such as Joe Smith and Coleman Hawkins) and, with regular appearances in New York and around the South for TOBA, became a hugely successful entertainer whose shows had 'crowds lined up for two blocks' (says Dave Dexter) waiting for tickets. By the mid-1920s Smith had more money than she knew what to do with. For her stage appearances she wore $3000 feathered gowns and she owned three palatial New York homes, each with luxury furnishings and a brand new electric player-piano in every room (the proceeds from these properties were later acquired by her manager Ocie Wilson). But although she appeared regularly in and out of New York through the 1930s and early 1940s, public interest in the blues was declining and she was suffering from a progressive arthritic condition: when her illness worsened, financial help from her manager Wilson never came. She died in poverty in a boarding-house room on New York's 8th Avenue after a long hospital stay and was buried on Staten Island. [DF]

Jazz Sounds of the Twenties, vol. 4: The Blues Singers (1923–31), Parlophone

Smith, Pine Top (Clarence), piano, vocals. b. Troy, Alabama, 11 June 1904; d. Chicago, 15 March 1929. A club and vaudeville entertainer, he worked on the TOBA circuit in the 1920s. 'Pinetop's Boogie-woogie', recorded in 1928, was a big hit after his death, and he is said to have invented the name for his eight-to-the-bar music. Shot in a Chicago dance-hall brawl over a woman, Smith missed the boogie boom by 10 years, as well as the success of his record. [DF]

(2 tracks by Smith), *Cutting the Boogie* (1926–41), New World

Smith, Russell T. 'Pops', trumpet. b. Ripley, Ohio, 1890; d. Los Angeles, 27 March 1966. Brother of Joe Smith (they came from a brass playing family), he played for Fletcher Henderson and others, 1925–42. Strictly a trained musician who left the playing of jazz to others, he was a steadying influence on many of the younger men around him (Benny Morton, for one, called him a 'father-figure'), seldom drank – it was said that he could make half a pint last a week – and kept regular hours. Consequently he led a long, successful playing life and after leaving Henderson worked for other respected leaders such as Cab Calloway and Noble Sissle until retiring to teach and play part-time in the 1950s. [DF]

Fletcher Henderson, *A Study in Frustration* (1923–38), CBS (4 records, boxed set)

Smith, Ruthie, tenor, alto and soprano sax, voice, cello. b. Manchester, 24 November 1950. Classical lessons as a child; degree in English and music at York University; self-taught on sax. 1972–84, played with various big and small bands including Brian Abrahams's District Six and Annie Whitehead's band. Founder member of the Guest Stars, an all-women fusion group. 1982, helped to organize the first British Women's Jazz Festival. The Guest Stars' first album received critical acclaim in the UK, and the group toured the US East Coast, September 1984, and the UK in December. 1985, they were support group to Jan Garbarek for his London concert. [IC]

With *The Guest Stars* (1984) and *Out at Night* (1985), Guest Stars; with District Six, *Akuzwakale* (1985), D6

Smith, Stuff (Hezekiah Leroy Gordon), violin, vocals. b. Portsmouth, Ohio, 14 August 1909; d. Munich, Germany, 25 September 1967. 'The cat that took the apron-strings off the fiddle.' Jo Jones's neat summing up says a lot about Smith's hard-bowing approach to the violin, which made him the most forceful swing fiddler in jazz history. 'It was just Louis who influenced me', Smith remembered later. 'I got some Venuti records and they were pretty,' (Venuti is still the nearest equivalent to Smith's unbuttoned approach) 'but they didn't push me enough. I use my bow the way a horn player uses breath control and I may hit a note like a drummer hits a cymbal!'

Smith came up in the 1920s with Alphonso Trent's orchestra, for whom he played a variety of sweet and hot features, including comedy 'point' numbers; later he married and settled in Buffalo. Here he met and teamed with trumpeter Jonah Jones, his life-long friend, and agent-bandleader Dick Stabile booked the two of them and their band into the Onyx Club on 52nd Street in 1936. The same year they recorded 'I'se a Muggin' ' (twice, followed by 'If You'se a Viper'), made a hit, and were soon the biggest attraction on Swing Street. But Smith – a temperamental talent who jealously guarded his own interests – could be hard to handle. After Joe Helbock, boss of the Onyx, had reluctantly released him to make a film, *Swing Street* (1938) in Hollywood, Smith was slow to come back, and by the time he did public attention had moved on. From then on his career levelled out: work with a trio was regular in New York and Chicago (where Smith opened a restaurant) but there was some evidence all through the 1940s of a mercurial temperament at work. 'Stuff's trio at the Onyx in 1944 was one of the greatest, most rhythmic trios I ever heard', says Billy Taylor. 'Their only records were made for Asch but they didn't show what the trio could do. They'd worked up some things for the session but then Stuff goofed and played some other things instead – as he was likely to do!' In the 1950s

Smith, working more often as a soloist, was California-based and often beset by health problems including pneumonia and ulcers ('The trouble with me and my liver was that I just couldn't stand food while I was drinking!') By the 1960s he was a familiar face in Europe, touring concert halls, clubs and festivals: his last recordings, as hard-swinging as ever, came from the year he died. [DF]

Stuff Smith (1957), Columbia

See Dance, Stanley, *The World of Swing* (Scribner's, 1974, repr. Da Capo, 1979)

Smith, Tab (Talmadge), saxes. b. Kinston, North Carolina, 11 January 1909; d. St Louis, Missouri, 17 August 1971. His lengthy jazz pedigree began in territory bands (starting with Henry Edwards's) and by 1936 he was experienced enough to come to New York and join Lucky Millinder, the new leader of Mills' Blue Rhythm Band, replacing Buster Bailey. He stayed with Millinder for two years, recording over two dozen fine sides, and also worked regularly with top-rankers such as Frankie Newton, Henry 'Red' Allen, Teddy Wilson and Eddie Durham before joining Count Basie in 1940 to work alongside Earle Warren. 'He was a formidable musician,' remembers Warren, 'and a nice guy to know, with an even personality, no animosity towards anyone. And he was happy with Basie.' After Smith left in 1942 he returned to Millinder for two more years and from then on led his own small groups, sometimes with singer Wynonie Harris, often recording for small r & b labels: several of his early 1950s sides were best-sellers. He continued to be successful until the early 1960s, when he retired to St Louis to develop the property his mother and sister owned: in later years he got involved in real estate, played the organ for fun and taught locally. Like Earl Bostic, guitarist Tiny Grimes and singer Dinah Washington, Smith was – just possibly – born too soon for rock and roll. [DF]

Coleman Hawkins, *Swing* (1944), Fontana

Smith, Tommy (Thomas), tenor and soprano sax, flute. b. Luton, Bedfordshire, 27 April 1967. Brought up in Edinburgh, took up saxophone at 12. Made national television debut at 15 backed by Gordon Beck and Niels-Henning Ørsted Pedersen and, within the next year, recorded two albums for different local labels. Gained scholarship to Berklee School and began studies there in 1984. Formed group Forward Motion with fellow students and graduates, bassist Terje Gewelt (from Norway), pianist Laszlo Gardonyi (Hungarian, replaced 1986 by Christian Jacob from France) and Canadian drummer Ian Froman; group made UK and European tours, 1985–6. Smith also became regular member of Gary Burton's quintet, 1986. Although his earliest recorded work was heavily marked by Coltrane (hence the album title *Giant Strides*), Smith's style has now largely transcended this direct influence, recalling players as different as Jan Garbarek and Bobby Wellins in his rapidly maturing work. [BP]

Forward Motion, *Progressions* (1985), Hep

Smith, Trixie, vocals. b. Atlanta, Georgia, 1895; d. New York City, 21 September 1943. In the 1920s there seemed to be just too many blues-singing Smiths. One of the most neglected – and also one of the most talented – was Trixie Smith, who brought a new polish to her often vaudeville-based material and recorded regularly – after she won Black Swan's 15th blues contest in 1921 – with a wide variety of jazz stars including Fletcher Henderson and his alumni, as well as Jimmy Blythe, James P. Johnson and Freddie Keppard. One of her most popular blues – 'The world's jazz crazy, Lawdy, so am I' – turned into a classic of its kind: another that should have done, in Sammy Price's opinion, was 'Freight Train Blues'. 'Her record of that is one of the greatest blues records ever made', says Price. 'Trixie had depth, real warmth and appeal. What was she like? She was just like another woman called Smith – but she could sing like hell!' [DF]

And Her Down Home Syncopaters (1925), London

Smith, Willie (William McLeish), alto and baritone sax, clarinet, vocals. b. Charleston, South Carolina, 25 November 1910; d. Los Angeles, 7 March 1967. A magnificent soloist and faultless section leader, he began on clarinet and later, after he had graduated in chemistry at Fisk University, joined Jimmie Lunceford's ambitious new band while they were working up country and down for cents, and suffering. Band morale was high, however, and Smith, who had known Lunceford while the older man was teaching at Fisk, took up his former teacher's cause with enthusiasm. Because he was popular – 'one of the warmest guys you could ever meet', says Harry Edison – Smith brought the best out of his saxophone section, which under his leadership became the most balanced, efficient and technically able of its time, playing the high-speed choruses written by pianist Ed Wilcox with spellbinding flair. Smith's own awesome solo ability, likeable personality and fine singing were soon spotted by Tommy Dorsey, and one night – on a job when the whole orchestra was playing for expenses – he offered the saxophonist whatever he wanted to move over. Smith refused. 'That was the spirit we all had in those days', he told Stanley Dance later. 'Nobody would quit, regardless of what happened.' But Lunceford's non-stop touring schedule (almost 365 days a year) laid the foundations of Smith's later drink problems, and suspicions were forming that Lunceford was creaming money from his sidemen's salaries. In 1942, shedding tears, Smith left, and after two years (one with Charlie Spivak, one in the navy) joined Harry James: for much of the rest of his life he was to play Johnny Hodges to James's Ellington (for one year in 1951 he did the same for Ellington himself). At that period Smith's driving, cutting-edged alto was also heard with Jazz at the Philharmonic, with Billy May's orchestra and in the studios, right up to the mid-1960s by which time his long battle with alcoholism was complicated by cancer. A less-than-perfect latterday Smith can be heard on Ella Fitzgerald's Johnny Mercer collection but almost all of his recorded work ranks with Benny Carter's or Johnny Hodges'. [DF]

The Complete Jimmie Lunceford (1939–40), CBS (4 records, boxed set)

Dance, Stanley, *The World of Swing* (Scribner's, 1974, repr. Da Capo, 1979)

Smith, Willie 'The Lion' (William Henry Joseph Bonaparte Bertholoff), piano, composer, vocals. b. Goshen, New York, 25 November 1897; d. 18 April 1973. With Jelly Roll Morton he was the most celebrated braggart of jazz piano, whose sometimes overwhelming gift for self-promotion was somehow at odds with the delicacy of his playing and compositions. But Willie 'The Lion' Smith – not to be confused with alto-saxophonist Willie Smith (above) – was a vital figure in piano jazz, and a great example of the school of pianists that seems to have originated on America's Eastern seaboard and became known – rightly or wrongly – as the Harlem stride school.

Smith grew up musically in the rough tough New York Jungles – an area between 60th and 63rd Streets full of clubs and dives – and for much of the rest of his life was to remain a native New Yorker. But he had the natural pizazz to survive in such surroundings: taking his style from the ragtime professors who preceded him, he dressed immaculately, carried a cane and always announced his arrival in a club with the warning growl, 'The Lion is here!' He quickly became a known influence on younger musicians such as Duke Ellington (who later dedicated a tune 'Portrait of the Lion' to him), ran regularly with fellow piano-masters James P. Johnson and young Fats Waller and saw active service in the war (according to his story he stayed at the front for 33 days, scored direct hits and acquired his nickname for valour). He then settled down to a jazzman's lifestyle including, variously, club-work, recording and (occasionally) touring with blues singer Mamie Smith (he played on the historic 'Crazy Blues' session), acting (he had one line in a Broadway play, *Four Walls*), working with Will Mastin's revue, hanging out at the Rhythm Club, playing rent parties and surviving. For much of his life after the 1920s the pattern was to repeat itself: in the 1930s Smith became well known on record (gentle, reflective solos like 'Morning Air' and 'Echoes of Spring' are classics) and from the 1940s on he was still bandleading, touring Canada and parts of Europe as a soloist, and starring at jazz festivals right up to the end of his days: in 1965 he published his likeably larger-than-life autobiography. 'The Lion has been the greatest influence on most of the great piano players who have been exposed to his fire, his harmonic lavishness, his stride – what a luxury', said Duke Ellington. 'Even the great Art Tatum – and I know he was the the greatest – showed strong patterns of Willie Smith-isms after being exposed to The Lion. I can't think of anything good enough to say about him.' [DF]

Music On My Mind (1966), BASF

See Smith, Willie, and Hoefer, George, *Music On My Mind* (MacGibbon & Kee, 1966)

Smythe, Pat, piano, composer/arranger. b. Edinburgh, 2 May 1923; d. London, 6 May 1983. He was a squadron leader in the RAF during World War II. After demobilization he practised as a lawyer in Edinburgh, but his heart was in jazz, and he gave up law at the end of the 1950s, moving to London. He played with trumpeter Dizzy Reece, then joined Joe Harriott's radically innovative quintet, which included Coleridge Goode (bass), Shake Keane (tpt) and either Phil Seamen or Bobby Orr (dms). Harriott pioneered the whole European free jazz movement, and Smythe made a great contribution in helping to formulate and organize the new ideas. He also went on to break other new ground with Harriott when they pioneered Indo-Jazz Fusions in the mid-1960s. The brilliantly creative work of Harriott's team of players is documented on a series of fine albums – some of which gained the maximum star-rating in the US magazine *Downbeat*. Smythe also had a long and fruitful association with Kenny Wheeler in big-band and small-group formations. He had a keen ear for outstanding young talent: his own small groups included bassist Dave Holland and guitarists John McLaughlin and Allan Holdsworth.

As well as being an excellent composer and arranger, Pat was a fine soloist and accompanist, conversant with the whole spectrum of contemporary jazz. He worked with Stan Getz and Paul Gonsalves (with whom he recorded), Ben Webster, Zoot Sims, Sonny Stitt and many others. He also accompanied Anita O'Day, Blossom Dearie, Tony Bennett, Annie Ross, Elaine Delmar and Mark Murphy.

After his death from cancer, a group of friends established the Pat Smythe Memorial Trust and Award in his memory, to provide an annual award for a young jazz musician. [IC]

With Harriott, *Free Form* (1960), Jazzland; *Abstract* (1961–2); *Movement* (1963); *High Spir-*

its (1964); *Indo-Jazz Suite* (1965); *Indo-Jazz Fusions* (1966); *Indo-Jazz Fusions II* (1967), all Columbia; *Sandra King Accompanied by Pat Smythe in a Concert of Vernon Duke* (1982), Audiophile

Snow, Valaida, trumpet, vocals. b. Chattanooga, Tennessee, or Washington, DC, 2 June *c.* 1900; d. New York City, 30 May 1956. From a Baltimore family of three girls (her sisters were named Lavaida and Alvaida, her mother was a – presumably eccentric – music teacher), she was headlining at Barron Wilkins's Harlem cabaret by the time she was 22 with an act in which she danced, sang, played the violin and topped off the show with revolutionary hot trumpet solos. For the rest of the 1920s she built her reputation around the USA; toured with Will Mastin (Sammy Davis Senior's partner) and his trio, made a trip to the Far East in 1926 to front Jack Carter's band, and in 1928 was top of the bill at Sunset Café, Chicago. There Louis Armstrong was impressed by her ('Boy, I never saw anything that great!' he said) and Earl Hines fell for her: 'I thought she was the greatest girl I'd ever seen.' Snow – a beautiful woman who loved life and liked the best of everything – kept on the move: she toured Europe, the Middle East and Russia from 1929, then took a starring role in Sissle and Blake's review *Rhapsody in Black*, and by 1933 was back in Chicago with Hines producing and starring in shows for Ed Fox at Grand Terrace Ballroom. (She featured a number of tap routines, including one in everything from tap shoes to Russian clogs, and often danced herself into near insensibility.) 'Valaida's shows were big productions like you see on TV, in Hollywood or at the Cotton Club,' says Quinn Wilson, 'with sixteen chorus girls, eight show girls, besides the acts!' For the rest of the 1930s Snow enjoyed her stardom, made three films, visited Britain (where in 1936 she recorded with George Scott-Wood, Reg Dare and others) and toured Europe: in 1941 she was interned in Nazi-occupied Copenhagen. 'I don't think she ever recovered, physically or mentally, although she kept working until she died', remembers Hines, who did not recognize his former lover when he met her again in 1943. Snow married her manager Earle Edwards, who had helped to nurse her, and carried on fronting bands and singing: she died of a cerebral haemorrhage soon after shows at the Palace Theater, New York, when she was 55. [DF]

Swing is the Thing (1936–7), EMI

Snowden, Elmer Chester, guitar, banjo, saxes, leader. b. Baltimore, Maryland, 9 October 1900; d. Philadelphia, 14 May 1973. A trained banjo player who could read in any key or clef – and a smart businessman – he worked with Eubie Blake in a dance school and first played with Duke Ellington in a Washington trio around 1919. He was, he made it clear later, none too impressed with the young piano player who only seemed to know one tune ('Soda Fountain Rag') and hung around asking to sit in. Ellington's opportunity came when Snowden was asked to take a band to New York, assembled Sonny Greer, Arthur Whetsol and Otto Hardwicke and when he got off the train in town found that his proposed pianist, Fats Waller, had disappeared. Snowden contacted Ellington, who joined his band at Barron's Club and rapidly impressed Greer, Whetsol and Hardwicke with his charisma and go-ahead ideas. These included bringing new talent – including Charlie Irvis and Bubber Miley – into the band: such apparent take-over tactics were probably prompted by a general suspicion that Snowden, in any case, was short-changing his employees. When the banjoist walked into the club and heard his band talking about getting rid of him, he complied with their wish (although just once, briefly, he came back at the request of Barron's club mafia). Snowden's future was secure enough without the Washingtonians: as a successful agent he was hiring out five bands a night, playing in productions such as the 1927 *Rang Tang Show* (featuring 48 banjo players), bandleading in other big clubs such as the Bamville and Smalls' Paradise, and earning money. In 1933, after a union dispute, he was barred from playing in New York (things were finally sorted out by John Hammond) and for the next 30 years led a highly successful career fronting his own groups: in 1963 he moved to California to teach at Berkeley for three years and by 1967 was touring Europe for George Wein. By that time the old rift with Ellington was healed and the greying Duke was even light-heartedly suggesting that Snowden might like to come back in the band. Once again the banjoist – one year younger than Ellington – declined, in tones that sounded more like an indulgent father figure. 'I was very close to Duke's father and he made me promise I would look out for his boy!' said Snowden. 'And Duke is still holding me to that promise!' [DF]

See Dance, Stanley, *The World of Swing* (Scribner's, 1974, repr. Da Capo, 1979)

Solal, Martial, piano, composer. b. Algiers, 23 August 1927. Born of French parents (not Algerian, as sometimes implied), he settled in Paris in late 1940s. Worked with expatriate US musicians such as Kenny Clarke, Don Byas, recorded with Sidney Bechet. Own trio from 1959 including drummer Daniel Humair. Since 1963 visit to New York and Newport festival, his reputation has been international, entailing solo and trio appearances all over Europe and occasionally USA. Has led an occasional big band in recent years, and written much film music (beginning with Jean-Luc Godard's *Breathless*, 1959).

Solal's piano style, although capable of sounding momentarily like anyone from Art Tatum to Bill Evans, is unique. Filled with glittering Gallic wit (or, according to his detractors, frigid French intellectualism), it is characterized by a restless abundance of ideas. Naturally enough, the technique required to execute these ideas is abundant too, as is Solal's harmonic knowledge, and both are perhaps best appreciated in his frequent demolition of popular song standards. But, not surprisingly, his original compositions are equally arresting and, as well as being immediately attractive, often have hidden depths. [BP]

Trio (1960), Pathé; *Big Band* (1981), Gaumont Musique

Solo (1) Any performance which is totally unaccompanied, the first non-keyboard example in jazz being Coleman Hawkins's 'Picasso'. There have been a multitude of other solo performances, especially in the last two decades, and in the piano jazz of all periods.

(2) A solo *in* a particular performance, or *on* a specific chord-sequence, is usually not unaccompanied. It merely refers to the passage where one person is engaged in prominent melodic improvisation, with some or all other members of the group providing a (usually partly improvised) accompaniment. Where (as is most often the case) the backing is by musicians who are equally capable of taking the lead, they may all take a solo in turn. Earlier generations of players used the phrases 'to take off' or 'to get off' before the European terminology was turned into a verb, 'to solo'. [BP]

Soloff, Lew (Lewis Michael), trumpet, fluegelhorn, piccolo trumpet. b. New York, 20 January 1944. Father a soft-shoe dancer, mother a vaudeville violinist. Piano lessons from age five until 13; took up the trumpet at school. 1955–61, attended Juilliard Preparatory Department; 1961–5, studied at Eastman School gaining B.Mus. in applied trumpet and music education; further studies at Juilliard, 1965–6. Until May 1968 he played with many Latin bands and also with Maynard Ferguson, Joe Henderson, Gil Evans, Thad Jones–Mel Lewis, Clark Terry, Chuck Mangione, Duke Pearson, among others. 1968–73, he worked with Blood, Sweat and Tears, touring world-wide. He has also been featured soloist on classical pieces, including Concerto for Trumpet and Orchestra by Alexandra Pakhmutova, with the New Orleans Symphony Orchestra.

From 1973, Soloff has been closely associated with Gil Evans, doing world-wide tours with him and playing on several albums. With Evans he has also played most major jazz festivals; and with Blood, Sweat and Tears he played most of the main rock festivals. 1975, he formed a quintet with fellow trumpeter Jon Faddis; 1977, Soloff was working regularly with a trio completed by Peter Levin (French horn) and Jeff Berlin (bass).

His influences include Gil Evans, Charlie Parker, Dizzy Gillespie, Miles Davis, Hannibal Peterson, Jon Faddis, Clifford Brown, Freddie Hubbard and Clark Terry. Soloff is a virtuoso who can handle any idiom or context; he has a brilliant technique and a magnificent range. [IC]

With BS & T, Gerry Niewood, Robin Kenyatta and others; several with Gil Evans, including *Parabola* (1978), Horo; *Live at New York Public Theater* (1980), Japanese Trio (double)

Soul (1) A quality first identified by jazz musicians, and which crept into writing about the music around the time (1956) that Milt Jackson appeared on a Quincy Jones album under the pseudonym 'Brother Soul'. It was important that he was a 'Brother', because being black was a necessary condition of having soul; whereas 'hard bop' was being adopted by whites as well as blacks in reaction to 'West Coast jazz', 'soul jazz' of the late 1950s and early 1960s was exclusively black. Musically, it implied a direct knowledge of gospel music and of its importance to the black community, and the ability to translate its phraseology into convincing instrumental jazz. In addition to Jackson, players as varied as Horace Silver and Jimmy Smith were thought of as part of this movement.

(2) Almost simultaneously, the word was applied to black popular music, as it began increasingly to reflect the influence of gospel. While this had already been a part of rhythm-and-blues vocals by such as Dinah Washington and Ray Charles, the blues element became in the 1960s the province of white 'folk' musicians sympathizing with the past travails of black people; but, as the civil rights movement gained strength, blacks rejected the connotations of blues and adopted the much more affirmative sound of gospel. Popular 'soul music' became so much like a straight transplant of secularized gospel that the music industry had to coin the expression 'blue-eyed soul' to cover would-be white exponents. The term 'soul' has now become a vast category encompassing virtually anything by black artists, whereas in jazz usage it is no longer a style but has reverted to being a quality, as in 'X has soul' or 'is soulful'. [BP]

South, Eddie, violin. b. Louisiana, Missouri, 27 November 1904; d. Chicago, 25 April 1962. A child prodigy, and later billed as 'the dark angel of the violin', he was a graduate of Chicago Music College in the early 1920s who received special jazz tuition (says Earl Hines) from Darnell Howard. South worked in bands around Chicago and New York before touring Europe with his own group, where he took time out to study in Paris and Budapest and when he got back to the USA, 1931, formed a big band, for which Milt Hinton – just out of high school – played bass. 'It was very good,' says Hinton, 'but it seemed as though the time wasn't right for a big band with a negro violinist standing in front playing ballads!' So South went back to a small group, played clubs such as the Rubaiyat and Congress Hotel in Chicago and then toured Southern towns on the Keith and RKO circuits, playing chamber jazz that was technically perfect, highly creative and ahead of its time. Says Hinton: 'This country wasn't prepared to accept his kind of continental saloon music. John Kirby's group had class and precision but Eddie's was before his and it was even more delicate!' As vaudeville and theatre circuits closed, South's career faltered and he went back to Europe (along the way he met Django Reinhardt and recorded classics with him), finally sailing back home for good with Benny Carter on the SS *Normandie* in 1938. All through the 1940s South's career moved comfortably along: he played clubs such as Kelly's Stables, toured with Billy Taylor ('a giant of a fiddler' said Taylor), worked for studio bands in New York at MGM and elsewhere and, as he gradually came into fashion, had his own radio series in the 1940s and regular TV in the 1950s with presenters such as Herb Lyons and Dave Garroway. But – perhaps because he was just too good – he never achieved the publicity of Stuff Smith (who was more of a clown) or Stephane Grappelli (who was white). In the mid-1950s South became ill: 'He took sick, started coughing, and died', said Billy Daniels. [DF]

And his Alabamians (1929–37), IMS

Spanier, Muggsy (Francis Joseph), cornet, b. Chicago, 9 November 1906; d. Sausalito, California, 12 February 1967. All through the 1920s he worked in Chicago in club bands, soaking up the lessons of Louis Armstrong, King Oliver and Tommy Ladnier, a player who – like Spanier – played economically and often in the middle register, with a big tone: 'When old Gabe blows that horn,' said Muggsy later, in a fit of Armstrong-esque good humour, 'he'll probably use the fingering that Tommy Ladnier taught him.' In 1929, Spanier joined Ted Lewis for seven years (the records are treasures), then Ben Pollack for two and, after a near-fatal illness (he collapsed on 29 January 1938 and was admitted to the Touro Infirmary in New Orleans for three months), formed in 1939 the great band for which he is best remembered, Muggsy Spanier's Ragtime Band. During a six-month stay at the Sherman Hotel, Chicago, that year, followed by a brief appearance at Nick's Club, New York, they recorded 16 sides for Bluebird – including a classic blues, 'Relaxin' at the Touro', commemorating Spanier's hospital stay – which are still known to jazz fans simply as 'The Great Sixteen': unparalleled and unequalled Chicago-

Muggsy Spanier

style Dixieland. But the Ragtimers disbanded soon after (it was the height of the big-band era) and Spanier rejoined Lewis, worked for Bob Crosby, briefly formed his own big band (which recorded just seven sides before the Musicians' Union recording ban bit) then went back to Lewis again in 1944. From then on – often at Nick's in New York – Spanier played for Miff Mole, led his own groups again for record dates and live appearances, and from 1950 was more and more on the West Coast, where he moved permanently in 1957 at the same time he joined Earl Hines at Club Hangover for a two-year residency. At the end of his life came five more years bandleading.

'The kind of guy Muggsy was? Direct, honest and vital!' says George T. Simon. The description fits Spanier personally and musically. His cornet encapsulates the art of direct musical lead (a quality which King Oliver, one of Spanier's idols, put first) and, while Muggsy was never the most technically startling player, no one knew better how to lead a Dixieland band with perfect economy, power, time and note-placement. Spanier – one of the kindliest and best-loved of Chicago jazzmen – also made big contributions to jazz trumpet vocabulary. 'I don't believe there was any other trumpeter to use a growl mute like he did', says Freddy Goodman. 'Muggsy influenced a lot of players. He had a beautiful tone and he played with a kind of natural feeling. Bunny Berigan was the only other white guy with that kind of feeling.' [DF]

The Great Sixteen (1939), RCA

Spargo, Tony (Antonio Sbarbaro), drums, kazoo. b. New Orleans, 27 June 1897; d. Forest Hills, New York, 30 October 1969. He was a regular colleague of Eddie Edwards and Nick La Rocca in Papa Jack Laine's bands back in New Orleans and went to Chicago with them in 1916 to form the Original Dixieland Jazz Band. For the next 40 years his name was to be much associated with the ODJB: he was in the 1936 re-creation with La Rocca, which he took over and led 1938–40, later in another (without La Rocca) for the Katherine Dunham Revue in 1943, and then another for Eddie Edwards in 1945–6. Before he retired in the 1960s Spargo worked regularly with Phil Napoleon, and showed that his drumming style had kept up well with the times: he also featured spirited kazoo playing, a central point of his jazz act. [DF]

Original Dixieland Jazz Band (1918–36), RCA (double)

Spikes Brothers A very influential family of jazz entrepreneurs, the Spikes brothers – Reb (Benjamin) and John – were active on and off for more than half a century. By the mid-1900s they ran a highly successful showband and travelling show (Jelly Roll Morton was in it for a while) and by 1919 had settled in Los Angeles. Here they opened a music store, a nightclub (the Dreamland Café), an agency and a publishing house (which handled their most successful composition 'Someday Sweetheart' and newly-written lyrics to 'Wolverine Blues'), and formed a band, the Majors and Minors, featuring singer Ivie Anderson, which played the Follies Theater on Main Street. In 1922 they were the first to record an all-black jazz band (Kid Ory's, on their home-recorded Sunshine label), in 1924 they wrote a show for Eddie 'Rochester' Anderson (*Stepping High*) and in 1927 they made a short sound film, *Reb Spikes and his Follies Entertainers* for Warner Bros, which predated *The Jazz Singer*. Gradually music fashions passed the Spikes Brothers by, John went blind, Reb became ill and by 1962 was an estate agent. But ten years on he was still working on a new revue, *The Heart and Soul of a Slave* (based on the story of Biddy Thomas, a slave who became a pioneer black capitalist): whether or not it was ever performed, the soon-to-be-popular TV series *Roots* had a similar theme and showed that Spikes's judgement was as sharp as ever. [DF]

See Feather, Leonard, *The Pleasures of Jazz* (Delta, 1976)

Spirits of Rhythm A five-man novelty group with a lot to offer the jazz listener, the Spirits of Rhythm – featuring Wilbur and Douglas Daniels (tipples/vocals), Teddy Bunn (gtr), Virgil Scroggins (dms/vocals) and Leo Watson (lead voice) – made their name in the 1930s working first at Chick Groman's Stables, New York, then at the Onyx Club. Charles Fox describes their act: 'Leo Watson moved his arm in and out just like a trombonist (Benny Morton was his idol) improvising one elaborate scat chorus after another, Teddy Bunn played guitar, there were three instruments called tipples, and Virgil Scroggins drummed on a paper-wrapped suitcase with a pair of whisk brooms.' The formula was just right for the Onyx Club and an America which had taken to novelty acts such as Red McKenzie's Mound City Blue Blowers (McKenzie was a regular colleague of the Spirits and recorded with them), but the Spirits produced a lot of enduring jazz and their records are frequently re-issued. 'They were full of joy and pep,' writes Max Jones, 'a fun group; and they were more than that – creative, and adventurous with it!' [DF]

The Spirits of Rhythm, 1933–4, JSP

Spivey, Victoria 'Queen', vocals, piano, organ, ukulele, composer. b. Houston, Texas, 1906; d. New York, 3 October 1976. She had an enormous hit in 1926 with 'Black Snake Blues', her first recording, which sold 150,000 copies in that year. From then on she was a big star, appearing at top New York theatres, and three years on in *Hallelujah*, a very successful all-black MGM musical (directed by King Vidor) which also featured Curtis Mosby's orchestra, Nina Mae McKinney and drummer Earl Roach. The success of the film, and Spivey's superior recordings of the period (including 'Funny Feathers', 'Make a country bird fly wild' and the immortal 'Organ Grinder', featuring such accompanists as Clarence Williams, Louis Armstrong and Henry 'Red' Allen), assured her a headlining career in vaudeville: during the 1930s she fronted Omaha trumpeter Lloyd Hunter's orchestra on tour and later married tapdancer Billy Adams, with whom she formed a team. By the late 1940s she was still well enough remembered to join Olsen and Johnson's *Hellzapoppin* show (which they toured in the wake of the successful 1941 film from Universal) and she returned to prominence again in the 1960s, after a temporary retirement, touring with packages, running her own recording company in New York and appearing with Turk Murphy's band. Spivey's work is first-rank, and her occasional neglect when great blues singers are discussed is hard to understand. [DF]

Jazz Sounds of the Twenties, vol. 4: The Blues Singers (1923–31), Parlophone

Spring, Bryan, drums. b. London, 24 August 1945. Several aunts played piano. Started on drums at six; self-taught, with some lessons from Philly Joe Jones. Began freelancing in London during early 1960s; from mid-1960s spent eight years with Stan Tracey's various groups; 1967–9, with Frank Ricotti quartet; 1972, with Klaus Doldinger's Passport; 1974, several months with Nucleus; from 1975, co-leader of the Don Weller–Bryan Spring quartet. Has also led bands of his own and continued to freelance in the London area. During the 1980s trumpeter Hannibal Marvin Peterson toured the UK as featured soloist with the Weller–Spring quartet. Spring has also worked with Jean-Luc Ponty, Tubby Hayes, Joe Williams, Charlie Shavers, George Coleman, Charlie Rouse among others. His favourites include Philly Joe Jones, Roy Haynes, Max Roach, Elvin Jones, Larry Bunker and Johnny Butts; other inspirations are Sonny Rollins, John Coltrane, Bill Evans, Miles Davis and Cannonball Adderley. A prodigious technician, he can handle any tempo and any area of the music. [IC]

With Doldinger, Nucleus and others; with Ricotti, *Our Point of View* (1969), CBS; with Tracey big band, *Seven Ages of Man* (1969), Columbia; with Tracey quartet, *Free an' One* (1970), EMI; with Tracey octet, *The Bracknell Connection* (1976), Steam; Weller/Spring, *Commit No Nuisance* (1979), Affinity

Spyro Gyra An American group begun in the mid-1970s by saxist Jay Beckenstein and pianist Jeremy Wall. Initially it was a studio phenomenon, making rock/pop instrumental records with a jazz tinge and featuring catchy melodies, neat rhythms, tight arrangements. 1979, the group's MCA album, *Morning Dance*, went gold and Spyro Gyra were launched internationally. They became a touring band and during the 1980s appeared at major international jazz festivals. Several subsequent albums also went gold. [IC]

Breakout (1986), MCA

Square One of the many jazz musicians' words to have gone into general usage. Before its application to virtually anyone lacking in awareness, 'a square' referred particularly to somebody unable to appreciate jazz. It has a specific rhythmic connotation, in that 'square music' lacks the complex polyrhythms of Afro-American styles and deals in what even European-trained musicians describe as four-square structures. Examples of square music are non-improvising marching bands and most pop of the pre-rock-and-roll era. [BP]

Stacy, Jess Alexandria, piano. b. Bird's Point, Missouri, 11 August 1904. One of the great swing pianists, whose sustaining right-hand tremolo is his unmistakable trademark, he began working on Missouri riverboats where he played piano (and sometimes the calliope) with bands such as Tony Catalano's Iowans, and by the mid-1920s had arrived in Chicago where he worked for numerous leaders in countless speakeasies, clubs and dance halls. Ten years later, at the instigation of John Hammond, he joined Benny Goodman and, apart from three years with Bob Crosby, 1939–42, stayed for nine years. With Goodman, Stacy became a star (a famous unscheduled solo at the close of Goodman's 'Sing, Sing, Sing' routine at Carnegie Hall, 1938, turned him into a legend in two minutes); but his unsuccessful marriage to singer Lee Wiley (which he later referred to, briefly and corrosively, as 'The Wiley Incident'), two short-lived big bands (one formed to back his wife), and irregular work after the 1950s made life less satisfactory. By that time he was recording less (*Tribute to Benny Goodman* by Jess Stacy and the Famous Sidemen from the 1950s is a late classic, nevertheless), playing piano bars and clubs and justifiably feeling neglected. In 1961 he retired to become a salesman for Max Factor and not until 1973, when he was persuaded to play soundtrack music for the film *The Great Gatsby*, was Stacy's individual piano heard again. The following year he played the Newport Jazz Festival to a standing ovation ('It took me all these years to find out who I am!' he told Bud Freeman afterwards), and subsequently appeared regularly at jazz festivals such as Sacramento, on TV and radio, and on records. [DF]

Tribute to Benny Goodman (1955), London

See Feather, Leonard, *The Pleasures of Jazz* (Delta, 1976); Balliett, Whitney, *Improvising* (OUP, 1977)

Standard Originally applied to popular songs of the 20th century whose popularity lasted beyond the period of their initial publication, despite the attentions of jazz players. Just sometimes, tunes have survived solely because of jazz treatments, e.g. 'What a Little Moonlight Can Do' or 'On Green Dolphin Street'.

Certain instrumental items written by jazz musicians have achieved a life far beyond the circumstances and personnel of their original performances, such as 'Perdido' or 'In a Mellotone', and have therefore become 'jazz standards'. [BP]

Stańko, Tomasz, trumpet, fluegelhorn, composer. b. Rzeszow, Poland, 11 July 1942. Father a musician. Studied violin and piano at school. From 1959, studied trumpet at the music high school in Cracow, graduating in 1969. He first heard jazz at a 1958 Dave Brubeck concert. He formed his first group in 1962 with pianist Adam Makowicz, calling it the Jazz Darings. He also worked with Krzysztof Komeda, and 1965–9 with Andrzej Trzaskowski. 1963–5, he did his first major tours in Czechoslovakia, Yugoslavia and Scandinavia. From 1965 he was voted best trumpeter every year in Poland. He took part in

Hamburg (NDR) jazz workshops, and also in Manfred Schoof's 'Trumpet Summit' in Nuremberg. 1970, he played with Alex von Schlippenbach's Globe Unity Orchestra at Donaueschingen Jazz Days, Warsaw Jazz Jamboree, the Berlin festival, Baden-Baden Free Jazz Meeting. Also 1970, he formed the Tomasz Stańko quintet, which included Zbigniew Seifert on alto (it was while he was with Stańko that Seifert switched to violin). 1971, Stańko played with Don Cherry, Albert Mangelsdorff, Gerd Dudek in the European Free Jazz Orchestra at Donaueschingen. The same year the *Jazz Forum* poll voted him Best European Jazz Musician.

The Tomasz Stańko quintet played all the major European festivals and also toured extensively in Europe, 1972–3. He and Makowicz played with Michal Urbaniak, 1974; 1975, he formed the Tomasz Stańko and Adam Makowicz Unit with Czeslaw Bartkowski on drums, touring Germany and receiving ecstatic press notices. J. E. Berendt has described Stańko as a 'white Ornette Coleman', but Stańko's music developed during the 1970s into a rich compound of all the jazz disciplines – rhythm, harmony, structure etc., plus the dimension of abstraction. He said in the mid-1970s: 'Our music may appear to be atonal and arhythmic, but it is not.' 1985, Stańko was featured in Graham Collier's 'Hoarded Dreams' at the Camden Festival, London. As a trumpet player, he is a virtuoso performer with an excellent range. [IC]

Quintet, *Music for K.*, (nda, Polish Jazz, vol. 22), Muza; *We'll Remember Komeda* (1973), MPS; Penderecki/Don Cherry/Stańko, *Actions* (1971), Philips

Stark, Bobby (Robert Victor), trumpet. b. New York City, 6 January 1906; d. 29 December 1945. Famous for his fine individual solo powers (and a distinctive trumpet embouchure set noticeably to one side), Stark was a noted freelance around New York from 1925: he worked in a number of bands (including Chick Webb's), then for Fletcher Henderson (1928–33) and Webb again (1934–9). 'No one sounded like Bobby Stark when he came back [to Webb] on trumpet', says Taft Jordan, who did an Armstrong act for the drummer-leader. 'His *wasn't* an Armstrong thing. That solo he used to play on "Squeeze me" was just Bobby, and no one else.' Stark was invalided out of the army in 1943 and (says John Chilton) worked with Garvin Bushell, Benny Morton and others in New York until his premature death. [DF]

Fletcher Henderson, *A Study in Frustration* (1923–38), CBS (double)

Stegmeyer, Bill (William John), clarinet, saxes, arranger. b. Detroit, Michigan, 8 October 1916; d. Long Island, New York, 19 August 1968. He was an early colleague of Billy Butterfield: they shared a room at Transylvania College and later worked together in Austin Wylie's band from 1937. From there Stegmeyer made rapid strides: he joined Glenn Miller in 1938 playing saxophone, and worked with Bob Crosby, 1939–40, by which time he was beginning to specialize as an arranger. From then on he continued to play regularly (for Butterfield and others) and led his own band at Kelly's Stables but broadened his activities, too, working for a Detroit radio station (WXYZ), 1948–50, and coming back to New York to work for TV and (from 1960) to conduct at CBS. His regular appearances on jazz records of the period were always so musically superior that his name is a guarantee of quality: one of the greatest Dixieland clarinettists, he rates with Matty Matlock, Irving Fazola and Heinie Beau. [DF]

The Best of Dixieland: The Legendary Lawson–Haggart Jazz Band 1952–3, MCA COPS (double)

Steig, Jeremy, flutes, composer. b. New York, 23 September 1942. Father is well-known artist William Steig. Began on recorder at age six; flute at 11 with lessons 1953–6; attended High School of Music and Art. 1961, worked with Paul Bley and Gary Peacock. 1966–7, with a jazz-rock group backing Tim Hardin. Began leading his own groups in 1967. Mike Mainieri and Eddie Gomez worked with him and, in 1970, Jan Hammer. In the 1960s his group was called Jeremy and the Satyrs and played jazz-rock; during the 1970s he made extensive use of electronics. He played the Berlin Jazz Festival several times during the 1970s, including Art Blakey's 'Orgy in Rhythm', 1972, and with Pierre Courbois' Association PC in 1974. Steig has also toured in Europe with his own quartets and quintets and as a soloist. He is a virtuoso, with a mastery of the whole flute family, from bass to piccolo, and a wide vocabulary of tonal devices. His work is also notable for his harmonic awareness and the intelligent integration of electronics with acoustic instruments. [IC]

With Bill Evans, Richie Havens and others; *Flute Fever* (1963), Columbia; *Jeremy and the Satyrs* (1967), Reprise; *Temple of Birth* (1974), Columbia; Steig/Gomez/Joe Chambers, *Lend Me Your Ears* (1978), CMP

Stevens, John William, drums, percussion, mini trumpet. b. Brentford, Middlesex, 10 June 1940. Father a tap/eccentric dancer. Studied at Ealing Junior Art School and Ealing College of Higher Education. 1958–64, in RAF bands, after studying at RAF School of Music. Early interest in skiffle, traditional and modern jazz. He sat in and played occasional gigs with various people including Francy Boland, Tubby Hayes, Derek Humble, Joe Harriott and Shake Keane. 1964–5, worked in London with Hayes, Ronnie Scott, Stan Tracey, and a quartet which included John McLaughlin, Jeff Clyne and Ian Carr. 1965, he began to lead his own groups, with a septet (which included Kenny Wheeler, Alan Skidmore and Ron Mathewson) and the Spontaneous Music Ensemble. With the septet, Stevens explored the jazz language of the day – harmonic structures, set bar-lengths, fixed tempos, composed tunes, and improvisation based on all these factors. With the SME he pursued his growing interest in the current avant-garde music – free or abstract improvisation with no fixed harmonies, bar-lengths or tempos. Stevens and the SME became the focal point for a new generation of British free improvisers which included Evan Parker, Derek Bailey, Trevor Watts, Paul Rutherford, Barry Guy, Howard Riley.

1970, he formed the Spontaneous Music Orchestra, a larger ensemble still dealing in abstraction. Then he began to move away from total abstraction and towards more clearly defined rhythms and structures, starting with the group Splinters, which he co-led in 1971 with Phil Seamen, and which included Hayes, Wheeler, Tracey and Clyne. 1974, he formed the John Stevens Dance Orchestra, 1975, his jazz-rock group Away, 1982, Freebop and Folkus. Stevens has also collaborated with Bobby Bradford, Steve Lacy, John Tchicai, Yoko Ono, Dudu Pukwana, Mongezi Feza and Johnny Dyani. 1968–85, he developed workshop techniques, and a manual of his workshop pieces was published in 1985. He has been musical director of the UK Jazz Centre Society's Outreach Community Music Project since 1983. (Stevens won the 1972 Thames Television Award for work within the community.) Favourites are Kenny Clarke, Phil Seamen and Elvin Jones, and trumpeters Chet Baker, Don Cherry, Louis Armstrong and Bobby Bradford. Other inspirations are Ornette Coleman, Gary Peacock, Bud Powell and Monk. [IC]

SME, *Challenge* (1966), Eyemark; *SME for CND for Peace for You to Share* (1970), A Records; Folkus, *The Life of Riley* (1983), Affinity; Evan Parker/Stevens, *The Longest Night, vols. 1/2* (1976), Ogun; SME, *Bio System* (1977), Incus

Stewart, Bob, tuba. b. Sioux Falls, South Dakota, 1945. Started on trumpet; scholarship to Philadelphia College of the Performing Arts and switched to tuba. Graduated with a teaching degree. 1968, moved to New York, teaching at junior high school as band director. Howard Johnson showed him the possibilities of the tuba as a solo instrument and he joined Johnson's Substructre, a tuba ensemble. 1971, with Collective Black Artists Ensemble. In the early 1970s he worked with Freddie Hubbard, Taj Mahal, Paul Jeffrey and others. Mid-1970s, he began working with three people who opened up even more opportunities for the tuba – Gil Evans, Carla Bley and Arthur Blythe. By the late 1970s he was gaining international recognition and winning polls on tuba. Stewart has also continued to teach, has played with the Globe Unity Orchestra and also co-led, with French horn player John Clark, the Clark–Stewart quartet. 1986, he toured with Lester Bowie's Brass Fantasy. [IC]

With Gil Evans, *There Comes a Time* (1975), RCA; with Carla Bley, *Dinner Music* (1976), Watt; *The Carla Bley Band European Tour, 1977*, Watt; with Arthur Blythe, *Illusions* (1980), CBS; *Elaborations* (1982), CBS

Stewart, Rex William, cornet. b. Philadelphia, 22 February 1907; d. Los Angeles, 7 September 1967. Stewart's major contribution to jazz in trumpet or cornet terms – he was also a successful part-time broadcaster/journalist in later life – was to develop the technique of 'half-valving' (pushing the trumpet valves half-way down to create quarter-tones and freak sounds) to its limit. Like most of his 1920s contemporaries, Stewart idolized Louis Armstrong – 'I tried to walk like him, talk like him, eat like him, sleep like him', he said later – but very early on he recognized the futility of trying to play as Armstrong did. The problem was presented in sharp relief when Stewart – at Armstrong's recommendation – replaced him in Fletcher Henderson's orchestra, and it became clear quite quickly to senior members such as Coleman Hawkins that Stewart was having to mug his way through musical passages that were beyond him. It may have been in sheer self-defence that Stewart – an unconventional and hard-blowing trumpeter who relied on energy as much as on legitimate training – developed his half-valving technique so definitively, and though other jazz trumpeters from Muggsy Spanier to Freddy Randall also used the device, Stewart's abilities were always way ahead. It was lucky for the cornettist that in Duke Ellington he found an orchestrator capable of framing his original talent to perfection: from 1934 to 1945, Stewart's weird half-vocal creations and walls-down blowing power were central to Ellington features such as 'Trumpet in Spades' and 'Boy Meets Horn', both written for him and both classics. After he left Ellington, Stewart's highly original 'alternative trumpet' talent earned him work as a soloist across America and Europe. In 1957 and 1958 he organized the Fletcher Henderson reunion band at South Bay's Jazz Festival, before working for Eddie Condon, 1958–9: his Condon recordings – often rough and fallible but filled with highly-charged energy – are a dramatic contrast to the more familiar sounds of Billy Butterfield, Bobby Hackett or Wild Bill Davison and clearly show Stewart's strong points as well as his weak ones. By the 1960s he was an established broadcaster, and writing marvellous articles for *Downbeat*, but a 1966 tour with Alex Welsh's band in Britain proved that he was finding it harder to deliver the goods. (Paradoxically a recording with Henri Chaix from the same year, including the eerie 'Headshrinker Blues' and 'Conversation Piece', is definitive late Stewart: unworried by the need to play difficult melodies or hold long notes, he disappears into a fantastical fantasy world of sound.) Stewart – a complex, competitive man of enormous charm and powerful personality – died of a brain haemorrhage at 60: his excellent book (really a collection of his *Downbeat* articles) contains a special word-portrait of him by Francis Thorne. [DF]

With Henri Chaix (1966), Polydor

See Stewart, Rex, *Jazz Masters of the 1930s* (Macmillan, 1972, repr. Da Capo, 1982)

Stewart, Slam (Leroy), bass, vocals. b. Englewood, New Jersey, 21 September 1914. In the 1930s he studied at Boston Conservatory, where (John Chilton tells us) he heard violinist Ray Perry – later a successful jazzman in his own right – singing in unison with his bowed lines. Stewart borrowed the idea (of course, he sang an octave up from the bass), worked on his bowing technique and by the time he joined Peanuts Holland's band in 1936 was in charge of a truly original idea. It appealed to Slim Gaillard (whom Stewart had met at a Harlem club, Jock's Place) and the two formed a duo, 'Slim and Slam', in 1937: by a year later a hit record, 'Flat Fleet Floogie' (later universally known as 'Flat Foot Floogie'), was one of the enduring hits of 52nd Street. Stewart stayed on the Street, working Kelly's Stables, the Three Deuces (in a trio with Art Tatum) and other clubs, and often ran his own trio which later – for three and a half years – featured the young Erroll Garner, who wrote bass features for his leader. The uncanny sound Stewart produced as he played them helped to mark him out as something special and provided a comedic effect which was to be emulated by fellow bassists Coleridge Goode, Major Holley and countless others. But although his invention had its funny side, Stewart was already a great musician, worked easily over 15 more years with Art Tatum (at regular intervals), Benny Goodman and other taskmasters and became a celebrity (he appeared in the film *Stormy Weather*, 1943, and won the *Metronome* poll in 1946). All through the 1950s and 1960s Slam Stewart continued his honourable career – with Tatum, Garner, pianist Beryl Booker, Roy Eldridge and later Rose Murphy – and by the 1970s was featuring as soloist with the Indianapolis Symphony Orchestra and giving master classes, some at Yale University, just as easily as he played and toured with fellow masters; he worked on the American Today show, wrote instructional tutors (*Styles in Jazz Bass*, Morris and Co, undated) and featured with the New York Jazz Repertory Company. In the 1980s Stewart was still just as busy as he wanted to be. [DF]

Slamboree (1975), Black and Blue

Stitt, Sonny (Edward), alto, tenor and baritone sax. b. Boston, 2 February 1924; d. 22 July 1982. Touring with Tiny Bradshaw band (on alto, 1943–4), during which he met (separately) the young Miles Davis and Charlie Parker, whose style Stitt had already partly assimilated. Settled in New York, working with Dizzy Gillespie (1945–6) and recording with the Bebop Boys and Kenny Clarke. Sonny then decided to specialize on tenor for the next few years, co-leading a band with Gene Ammons (1950–2) and then fronting own groups. Incorporating the alto into his performances again after the death of Parker, was regularly in demand as visiting soloist with local rhythm-sections. Also worked with Jazz at the Philharmonic (1957, 1959), Gillespie (1958), Miles Davis (1960–1), the Newport festival tributes to Parker (1964, 1974) and the Giants of Jazz (1971, 1972).

Stitt was a rewarding and extremely consistent performer, despite his debilitating struggles with narcotics and alcoholism. The question of his musical dependency on the contribution of Parker is a more thorny one; in tone and improvisatory approach he often matched the intensity, though not the intricacy, of his chief model. It was frequently observed that, on tenor, the sound and the lines were much closer to those of Lester Young, but there was much beneficial interaction between his later alto and tenor playing. Although more evenly-paced and less individual than either Young or Parker, Sonny was especially authoritative in a jamming context and always instantly recognizable. [BP]

Sonny Stitt/Bud Powell/J. J. Johnson (1949), Prestige/OJC; *Only the Blues* (1957), Verve

Stobart, Kathy (Florence Kathleen), tenor, soprano and baritone sax. b. South Shields, Co. Durham, 1 April 1925. Playing in touring band shows from age 14, then Newcastle ballroom residency. 1942, moved to London, working in nightclubs with such as Denis Rose, Jimmy Skidmore and visiting American servicemen Peanuts Hucko and Art Pepper; also many broadcasts with British AEF band. Between two stints with Vic Lewis big band (1948–9, 1951–2), led own regular group including Derek Humble, Dill Jones and trumpeter Bert Courtley (her second husband from 1951 until his death in 1969). Then casual gigging and guest spots (plus three months with Humphrey Lyttelton depping for Skidmore, 1957) while raising her family; later rejoined Humph on regular basis (1969–78). From 1974, own quintet with Harry Beckett, then (since 1979) with vibist Lennie Best. Guest appearances in New York (early 1980s) with Marian McPartland, Zoot Sims *et al.* Headlined first British women's jazz festival (1982); member of women's big band, Gail Force 17 (1986).

Always possessed of a robust tone and forthright style, Kathy has progressed from early 'modern jazz' to a timeless mainstream approach capable of taking on any musical situation. She has been very influential as a teacher of saxophone classes in London and Exeter and of London's City Lit band. Her position as a pioneer female jazzer was acknowledged by her inclusion in the US-compiled album *Jazz Women: A Feminist Retrospective*. [BP]

Lyttelton, *Kath Meets Humph* (1957), Parlophone; *Arbeia* (1978), Spotlite

Stop-time consists of a lengthy series of breaks, so that the rhythm-section marks only the start of every bar (or every other bar) for a chorus or more, remaining silent between each of the stop-chords; the soloist has to carry on regardless, however, and the effect is of an unaccompanied solo with marker-posts. The demands placed on the soloist's sense of time, not to mention invention, are of course considerable. Two of the most famous examples on records are Louis Armstrong's 'Potato Head Blues' and Sonny Rollins's contribution to the Dizzy Gillespie version of 'I Know That You Know'. [BP]

Straight music is still the preferred term among jazz and jazz-influenced performers to describe European-style composed music. Straight music is not the same as 'square music' but, like that term, 'straight' conveys a clear visual image of starched-shirt rectitude and no seductive polyrhythms.

On the other hand, 'straight ahead' can be a term of approval in a jazz context, implying the ability to incorporate the necessary polyrhythms and still convey a clear sense of direction in one's performance. [BP]

Strange, Pete (Peter Charles), trombone, arranger. b. East London, 19 December 1938. He joined Eric Silk's Southern Jazz Band in the late 1950s, then Ken Sims, then Teddy Layton, and finally (a coup) replaced John Picard in Bruce Turner's Jump Band. By then, Strange – an unassuming new star – was playing with confident technique in a style that took in all the best of Dickie Wells, Lawrence Brown and Tricky Sam Nanton: he made a good showing on Turner's 1963 album *Going Places* but, after Turner disbanded, took a Civil Service job and freelanced around London's club and pub scene working with such as Lennie Hastings, Stan Greig, Dave Jones and Colin Smith and regularly in the 1970s with Ron Russell's Dixieland band. In the late 1970s, long overdue, he turned professional again, and joined Keith Nichols's Midnite Follies Orchestra, Digby Fairweather's band (for whom he wrote the library), formed an ambitious 5-trombone ensemble Five-a-Slide (for which again he wrote the book) and joined Alan Elsdon's band. In 1983 he replaced Roy Williams with Humphrey Lyttelton, where his talent as trombonist and arranger found a perfect outlet and he achieved, at last, the recognition due to him. [DF]

Humphrey Lyttelton, *It Seems Like Yesterday* (1983), Calligraph

Strayhorn, Billy (William), composer, arranger, piano. b. Dayton, Ohio, 29 November 1915; d. 31 May 1967. A career summary is quickly accomplished for, after high school in Pittsburgh and private musical tuition, he started writing for Duke Ellington (1939). Playing piano briefly in Mercer Ellington's first band (1939), he then joined Duke's permanent staff and, until his death from cancer, wrote exclusively for his band and associated small groups. He played on occasional band recordings while Ellington himself directed, and more often on records by Duke's sidemen. Appeared as leader of Ellingtonian groups in Florida (1958) and at the Chicago Century of Negro Progress exhibition, backing the production *My People* (1963).

Before his Ducal association, Strayhorn had written music and lyrics of, among others, the remarkable song 'Lush Life' (*c.* 1938) and, in fact, joined Ellington initially as a lyric writer. Within a year he began arranging songs for the band, and then contributing instrumentals such as 'Day Dream', 'Chelsea Bridge' and 'Take the A-Train' (which, in early 1941, became the band's theme-tune). From 1945 onwards, some of Duke's extended works appeared with the credit 'Ellington–Strayhorn', which has made it easy for commentators and band-members to claim that the two writers' styles were indistinguishable. In fact the pieces credited to Strayhorn alone display clear differences from Duke's writing, whether in choice of rhythm or of texture, and they are somewhat more conventional in technique, though far from uninteresting. The two later became fairly adept at imitating one another, but some serious study needs to be spent on Strayhorn's individual contribution to Ellingtonia. [BP]

Cue for Saxophone (1958), Affinity; Ellington/Strayhorn, *Great Times* (1950), Riverside/OJC; Ellington, *And His Mother Called Him Bill* (1967), RCA

Strings The only stringed instruments regularly used in jazz are the guitar, bass-guitar and acoustic bass (sometimes known, almost correctly, as 'bass fiddle'). The first-named was replaced in New Orleans bands from around the 1910s by the somewhat louder banjo. In addition, a number of jazz soloists have specialized on violin, a few on cello and a couple on harp.

Occasional use of 'the strings' (in the European orchestral sense) dates back to the pretensions of Paul Whiteman; others such as Artie Shaw, Tommy Dorsey and Earl Hines later enlarged their big bands for brief periods with a 'string section', usually in a typically European configuration (i.e. two groups of violins, and far fewer violas or cellos) and usually with imitation European scoring. This is also the situation that has been foisted on those jazzmen (from Charlie Parker to Wynton Marsalis) who have appeared 'with strings' for specific recordings. The results, though undeniably attractive to fringe audiences, have done little for the soloists concerned, and the whole field of activity amounts to less than a footnote in the history of jazz. [BP]

Studer, Fredy, drums, percussion. b. Lucerne, Switzerland, 16 June 1948. Self-taught. Began on drums at age 16, playing all kinds of music – folk, rock, jazz-rock, r & b, hard bop, free jazz and experimental music. 1970, moved to Rome, playing with a rock trio. Consultant in the sound development of Paiste cymbals and gongs. 1972–82, with the electric jazz group Om. 1982–3, member of the rock group Hand in Hand. 1981–4, drummer in the trio Brüninghaus/Stockhausen/Studer. He has also played with Joe Henderson, Albert Mangelsdorff, Enrico Rava, Eberhard Weber, Kenny Wheeler, Joachim Kuhn, Tomasz Stańko and Miroslav Vitous. Currently with the Charlie Mariano–Jasper van't Hof band, and in the group Singing Drums, with Pierre Favre, Paul Motian and Nana Vasconcelos. He has played festivals all over Western and Eastern Europe, and at Monterey and he has performed concerts, held drum clinics and toured in North Africa, Central and South America, the Caribbean, Japan and the USA. He received the Lucerne Art Prize in 1977, and in 1983 the Jazz Prize of the German SWF radio station. His favourites are Elvin Jones, Tony Williams, Jack DeJohnette, Andrew Cyrille, among others. Jimi Hendrix, John Coltrane, Miles Davis and Wayne Shorter are also influences. [IC]

With Irene Schweizer, Barre Phillips, Wolfgang Dauner, John Tchicai, Didier Lockwood; *Om with Dom Um Romao* (1977), Japo; DeJohnette/Favre/Studer/Romao/Friedmann/Gruntz, *Percussion Profiles* (1977), ECM/Japo; Brüninghaus/Stockhausen/Studer, *Continuum* (1983), ECM; Favre/Motian/Studer/Vasconcelos, *Singing Drums* (1985), ECM

Studio group (or **band**) A studio group may be one of two rather different things. (1) A group which only worked as such for the purpose of recording, e.g. the Louis Armstrong Hot Five and Hot Seven, whose members were regularly employed with various other leaders, or the Ornette Coleman Double Quartet, which made the album *Free Jazz.* (2) A group assembled to record accompaniments for a star soloist, which may include his own group augmented (e.g. John Coltrane's *Africa/Brass*) or may consist entirely of *session musicians. As is the way with session musicians, some of them may have jazz credentials but, in the phrase 'Wes Montgomery playing with a studio group', they are merely there for backing purposes – or indeed, they may not be there, having recorded their parts previously, or they may be dubbed in next week. [BP]

Studio musicians, see SESSION MUSICIANS.

Subash, konnakol (vocal percussion), mridangam (two-sided South Indian drum), ghatam (clay pot), morsing (mouth harp), kanjira (like tambourine), dholak (two-sided drum). b. India, 1947. Father a legendary Carnatic (Southern Indian classical) percussion teacher. He was taught by a disciple of his father, Sri T. R. Harihara Sarma. Played Carnatic music concerts from age ten; worked with all the leading Carnatic soloists. In the West, he regularly accompanies Dr L. Subramaniam. Since 1980 he has been a member of J. G. Laya, performing regularly with them. In the late 1970s he toured the USA, Europe and Canada with L. Subramaniam, and taught percussion at California Institute of the Arts, Los Angeles; 1983, toured Netherlands with J. G. Laya; 1984, performed with the group throughout India and on national TV; represented India at Tal Vadya Utsav (International Percussion Festival) in India, 1985. In the early 1960s he won prizes as best mridangam and best ghatam player. Influences and inspirations are Vikku Vinayakram on ghatam and Brazilian percussionists in general. [IC]

Subramaniam, L., violin. b. Madras, India, 23 July 1947. Father a renowned Indian violinist and educator. Began on violin at age five, taught by his father; gave his first concert at age eight. At 16 he received the President's Award, one of the highest musical honours in India. At age 11, with his older brother and his younger brother, L. Shankar, he formed the Violin Trio and became famous in India. He also later graduated in medicine from Madras Medical College, then went to the USA and took his master's degree in music, studying how to play Western music and also how to compose. 1973–4, he recorded and toured with Ravi Shankar and George Harrison in the USA, Europe and Scandinavia to universal critical acclaim. 1980–1, with John Handy and Ali Akbar Khan in Rainbow. Like his brother Shankar, who played with John McLaughlin's Shakti, Subramaniam has thoroughly immersed himself in Western music. Talking to Lee Underwood, he has described the music on his own album *Fantasy Without Limit* as: 'The goal was to blend East and West in all forms. Some of the rhythms are 4/4, but others are very complex; some of the melodies are romantic and gypsy-like, but others are directly from Indian conceptions. Through it all, I use a wide variety of harmonies which should help the Western listener feel the music much better.' [IC]

Nearly 30 on EMI and Ganesh, mostly classical, some fusion; *Fantasy Without Limit* (nda), Discovery; with Stu Goldberg, *Solos-Duos-Trios* (nda), MPS; composed and played on one track, 'Spiritual Dance', on Larry Coryell's album *Standing Ovation* (1978), Mood

Sudhalter, Dick (Richard Merrill), cornet, alto horn, fluegelhorn, piano. b. Boston, 28 December 1938. A former UPI correspondent who spent his teenage years around Boston's jazz scene, he spent some of his formative years in England in the 1960s. There he worked regularly as a cornettist who identified strongly with Bix Beiderbecke but easily opened out into the musical territory of Bobby Hackett and Ruby Braff, organized Bix-related ventures such as the Anglo-American Alliance and the New Paul Whiteman Orchestra (a major triumph), led broad-based bands such as Commodore and Jazz Without Walls, toured with Hackett, worked in academic ensembles such as Keith Nichols's Ragtime Orchestra and formed a quintet with fellow-cornettist Gerry Salisbury. In addition, Sudhalter quickly revealed himself as a jazz writer whose natural passion, commitment and understanding set him in a class with rare literary talents such as George Frazier, Alec Wilder and Whitney Balliett: his regular contributions to the British jazz press of the period – equally informed in whichever jazz area and often hidden under the pseudonym 'Art Napoleon' – deserve reprinting. His writing talent and judgement, applied to the researches of Philip R. Evans and William Dean-Myatt, were to produce the first great jazz biography, *Bix: Man and Legend* (Quartet, 1974). Soon after he returned to the USA to play regularly with the New York Jazz Repertory Company, among others, and to exercise his jazz pen with the *New York Post*. Other regular New York activities include recording (often with kindred spirits such as Dave Frishberg): one such album – *Friends With Pleasure* by Dick Sudhalter's Primus Inter Pares Jazz Ensemble – right down to its tunes and title, is just one sample of Sudhalter's bright imagination and strong sense of history at work. Latterly he has worked regularly with the Classic Jazz Quartet (with clarinettist Joe Muryani, pianist Dick Wellstood and guitarist Marty Grosz, and also known as 'The Bourgeois Scum'), broadcasts and continues to write with the warm perception of a lover of the art. [DF]

Friends With Pleasure (1981), Audiophile

Sulieman, Idrees Dawud (Leonard Graham), trumpet, alto sax. b. St Petersburg, Florida, 7 August 1923. After touring with the Carolina Cotton Pickers and name bands such as Earl Hines's (1943–4), the trumpeter, already known by his Muslim name, became an early associate of Thelonious Monk, Mary Lou Williams and the beboppers. Recorded and gigged with Monk (1947–8), Coleman Hawkins (1957) and others during an intermittent career, until settling in Stockholm (1960s) and Copenhagen (1970s). Was regular member of the Clarke–Boland band, and in this period took up alto saxophone. Sulieman's main contributions have been made on trumpet and, despite being a variable performer, he sometimes produces inspired and highly individual work. [BP]

Now is the Time (1976), Steeplechase

Sullivan, Ira Brevard, trumpet, fluegelhorn, saxophones, flute, composer. b. Washington, DC, 1 May 1931. Father taught him trumpet; mother taught him sax. He moved to Chicago, working with Sonny Stitt, Howard McGhee, Wardell Gray, Lester Young, Roy Eldridge, Charlie Parker and many others. Later with Bill Russo, then briefly in 1956 with Art Blakey. He moved to Southern Florida in the early 1960s, working in Ft Lauderdale and Miami. With his own groups, he played concerts and clubs, and also in elementary schools, junior colleges and churches. Also a member of a large jazz ensemble, Baker's Dozen, in Miami, for which local boy Jaco Pastorius wrote some arrangements. Late 1970s, he moved to New York and began co-leading a quintet with Red Rodney. Sullivan is a legendary figure; one of the most gifted improvisers, he has chosen to maintain a low and local profile, rarely straying far from his base in Florida and hardly ever appearing internationally. His favourites on trumpet are Dizzy Gillespie, Miles Davis, Fats Navarro, Harry Edison and Clark Terry, and on saxophone Charlie Parker, Coleman Hawkins, Lester Young and Sonny Rollins. He began in bebop, but has expanded his concept over the years, incorporating elements from John Coltrane, abstraction and rock into his performances. [IC]

With Red Rodney, J. R. Monterose, Art Blakey, Roland Kirk, Eddie Harris and others; *Ira Sullivan* (1976), Horizon

Sullivan, Joe (Joseph Michael), piano. b. Chicago, 4 November 1906; d. San Francisco, 13 October 1971. A graduate of Chicago Conservatory, Sullivan was at the heart of the Chicago jazz scene all through the 1920s, recorded with the best (including Louis Armstrong and Eddie Condon: classics such as 'Knockin' a Jug') and while playing with the fly technique and topsy-turvy time-consciousness of the young Earl Hines, was far more than just an inspired copy ('I was playing my own way before I heard Earl', he later said flatly). By the 1930s he was in New

York with studio and jazz bands and playing solo (records for John Hammond at the period, including his own 'Little Rock Getaway', are outstanding), as well as accompanying Bing Crosby, and his finest hour should have come in 1936 when he joined Bob Crosby's band of kindred jazz spirits. Instead, Sullivan contracted tuberculosis and spent ten months in hospital: Bob Zurke replaced him and Sullivan in later years bitterly remembered his bad luck. By 1939 he was bandleading again at Café Society (with a strong multi-racial group featuring Ed Hall and Benny Morton) and all through the 1940s stayed busy enough with Eddie Condon (who said in 1940, 'There's no substitute for Joe Sullivan – he's unique'), Bobby Hackett and others and playing solo. By the 1950s solo piano had turned against his will into a permanent vocation, often at the noisy Club Hangover in San Francisco, a venue which – filled with noisy diners and expense-account clientele – often rubbed up badly against Sullivan's strong musical convictions. By 1963 people were starting to ask what had happened to him: in 1964 an article in *Downbeat* by Richard Hadlock, 'The Return of Joe Sullivan', celebrated his successful 1963 appearance at Monterey's Jazz Festival and helped to promote a new (listening) residency at the Trident Club, Sausalito, where people gave him the respect he deserved. Always a straight-talker, Sullivan's bitterness by now ran deep: 'It's not that I'm neglected,' he told Hadlock, 'it's more that I'm completely forgotten.' [DF]

New Solos by an Old Master (1953), Riverside

Sullivan, Maxine (*née* Marietta Williams), vocals, valve-trombone, fluegelhorn. b. Homestead, Pittsburgh, 13 May 1911. In 1937, early in her New York career, she was hired by guitarist Carl Kress to sing for intermissions at the Onyx Club. While she was working there arranger/bandleader Claude Thornhill (who had signed Sullivan and arranged a recording contract for her) put together arrangements of two Scottish songs, 'Annie Laurie' and 'Loch Lomond' – 'foreign-theme' popular tunes like Tommy Dorsey's 'Song of India' had set a trend – and after a feature in the *New Yorker* the young singer became a headliner. By then she had joined John Kirby's new band, the main attraction at the Onyx (she also married Kirby), and starred for two years on a CBS Radio programme, Flow Gently Sweet Rhythm. When it came to an end, along with her marriage, Sullivan pursued a highly successful solo career – with Benny Goodman, Glen Gray and others – and remained a popular solo act in night clubs until the 1950s when (by now married to pianist Cliff Jackson) she retired to a day job and family life. In 1958 she returned to performing and in 1965 Tommy Gwaltney invited her to work at his Washington club, Blues Alley: from then on – at Dick Gibson's Denver parties, with the World's Greatest Jazz Band and Bobby Hackett – Sullivan gradually rebuilt her career. Albums with Bob Wilber (such as *The Music of Hoagy Carmichael* and a later classic *Close as Pages in a Book*) received fine reviews, Sullivan featured valve-trombone and fluegelhorn in her armoury, and by the 1980s she was the best-loved singer of great jazz repertoire in her august circle, recording in Europe and back home in America with young kindred spirits such as Scott Hamilton and Keith Ingham. In 1985 her *Music from the Cotton Club* album was a best-seller: in 1986 she toured Europe again to full clubs. [DF]

Close as Pages in a Book (1969), EMI Parlophone

See Shaw, Arnold, *52nd Street* (Da Capo, 1971)

Sulzmann, Stan, soprano, alto and tenor sax; flute, alto flute, clarinet. b. London, 30 November 1948. He started playing with blues bands in clubs such as the Flamingo and the Marquee around 1963. 1964, he joined the first National Youth Jazz Orchestra. After trips to New York on the *Queen Mary*, he went to the Royal Academy of Music as a mature student. Subsequently he played in bands led by Graham Collier, Mike Gibbs and John Dankworth. He was an original member of the John Taylor sextet, and formed a quartet with Taylor in 1970. He did many broadcasts in the UK with Taylor, Kenny Wheeler, John Warren, and numerous small groups. In the mid-1970s he was with Gordon Beck's Gyroscope. With his own quartet, Sulzmann represented the BBC at the Molde (Norway) festival. Early 1970s, he was voted first in the *Melody Maker* New Star category. His favourite saxophonists are Sonny Rollins, Joe Henderson and John Coltrane, and on clarinet he admires Tony Coe; flautists he likes are James Moody, James Spaulding and Ray Warleigh. In the early 1980s he played and recorded with Gil Evans's London Band. [IC]

With John Taylor, Mike Gibbs, Gordon Beck, Clark Terry and the Kenny Clarke–Francy Boland band; *On Loan with Gratitude* (1977); *Krark* (1979), both Mosaic

Sun Ra (aka Herman 'Sonny' Blount; name at birth Herman Lee?), keyboards, composer. b. Birmingham, Alabama, *c.* May 1914. Studied music in college and with John 'Fess' Whatley, touring with his band (mid-1930s). Settled in Chicago (late 1930s) playing all kinds of piano jobs (as Sonny Blount), then involved in arranging for shows while pianist with Fletcher Henderson at Chicago's Club DeLisa (1946–7). Backed performers such as Coleman Hawkins, Stuff Smith, made record debut with bassist (and subsequent Brubeck sideman) Gene Wright (1948). Started own trio, gradually building rehearsal band with long-time associates John Gilmore, saxist Pat (Laurdine) Patrick etc. (early 1950s); a self-styled mystic, he renamed

Stan Sulzmann

himself Sun Ra and called his band the Arkestra. After making several albums (from 1956), moved briefly to Montreal and then New York (1961), financing organization through members' outside work (e.g. Patrick with Mongo Santamaria, Gilmore with Art Blakey); involved with Jazz Composers' Guild (1964–5). Gained international reputation based partly on exotic presentation, and made first of many tours of Europe (1970), eventually moving base of operations to Philadelphia (late 1970s). Formed prolific Saturn Records (late 1950s) to document his work since then and from earlier, some of it reissued by other labels.

Sun Ra's earliest body of recordings (mid-1950s) show him close to the flavour of Chicago hard bop, but writing attractive and individualistic themes on a similar Monk/Ellington tangent to that of Herbie Nichols, and capable at times of drawing a rich sound reminiscent of Tadd Dameron from his 10-piece ensemble. But by the end of the 1950s the band's music was more percussion-oriented, with results which were much more impressionistic and open-ended than in a conventional Afro-Latin band. Around this same period, the leader began to forgo his composed themes and, in one of the earliest responses to the idea of 'free jazz' (pre-dating Ornette Coleman and Cecil Taylor in this respect), he allowed the moods which he prescribed to be created entirely through solo and group improvisations. While this was the style for which he finally gained widespread recognition, and which enabled him in the late 1960s to increase the size of the Arkestra for a few years, in the mid-1970s Sun Ra decided to crown his own efforts by establishing conscious links with the tradition of composer/bandleaders, and henceforth expanded his repertoire with loose-limbed performances of classics by Jelly Roll Morton, Fletcher Henderson, Duke Ellington and Thelonious Monk.

As a keyboard player, Sun Ra tends to make a strong impression in live appearances, in a style which can veer from Earl Hines to Cecil Taylor, with rambling pseudo-European impressionism thrown in. In the 1950s he was a pioneer in the jazz use of electric keyboards such as the clavioline and what he called his 'rocksichord'; later, he gravitated naturally to the early versions of keyboard synthesizer. Again in the 1950s (ages before Ornette tried it) he was regularly using two bassists, one of whom played the then new electric bass. Similarly, his encouragement of the practice of hornmen playing additional percussion may have influenced its growing popularity in jazz, especially among the later Chicago avant-garde whose burgeoning in the mid-1960s was partly fuelled by Sun Ra's departure from the city.

The band's continuity has enabled his most faithful acolytes to remain longer than any sidemen except Ellington's, and there is a long list of musicians (such as Von Freeman and Julian Priester) who have worked with him briefly and then moved on. Perhaps this is because of Ra's notoriously stern discipline; he himself has said, 'I tell my Arkestra that all humanity is in some kind of restricted limitation, but they're in the Ra jail, and it's the best in the world.' His reputation in this area is matched by his reputation as an outlandish philosopher/showman, whose costumes and choreography reflect his early experience of Cotton Club-type extravaganzas. Nevertheless, the picturesque side of Sun Ra, like that of Monk, is dwarfed by the strength of his best music. [BP]

Sun Song (1956), Delmark; *The Nubians of Plutonia* (1959), Impulse; *The Heliocentric Worlds of Sun Ra, vols, 1/2* (1965), Happy Bird; *Pictures of Infinity* (1968), Black Lion; *Sunrise in Different Dimensions* (1980), Hat Hut

Film: *Sun Ra: A Joyful Noise* (dir. Robert Mugge, 1980)

Sunshine, Monty, clarinet, bandleader. b. London, 8 April 1928. A founder member of the Crane River Jazz Band in 1949 and later the clarinet star of Chris Barber's 1950s band, Sunshine contributed hugely to Barber's success (with his in-house recordings of clarinet features such as 'Hushabye' and 'Petite Fleur') then left in 1960 in a wave of publicity to form his own strictly New Orleans-style band. A string of solo albums followed – produced by Denis Preston and often featuring large studio groups and ambitious repertoire – and from the 1960s Sunshine maintained a highly successful career, playing the New Orleans jazz he loves best and touring all over Europe where his reputation achieved superstar proportions (a recent German album sleeve begins 'Although Humphrey Lyttelton has never reached the stardom achieved by Monty Sunshine . . .'). Regular sidemen who have worked with him include Rod Mason, Ian Hunter-Randall and latterly Alan Gresty (tpt), Charlie Galbraith, Eddie Blashfield and now John Beecham (tmb), Ken Barton, Barry Dew (banjo/gtr), Mick Ashman, Tony Baghot (bass), Geoff Downs (dms). In 1986, Sunshine was busy as ever, touring and recording at home and abroad. [DF]

Sunshine in London (1979), Black Lion

Surman, John Douglas, baritone and soprano sax, bass clarinet, synthesizers. b. Tavistock, Devon, 30 August 1944. Both parents musical, father a pianist. Studied at London College of Music, 1962–5, then London University Institute of Education, 1966. He began on baritone sax, joining Mike Westbrook in 1962, and also working with Alexis Korner in the early 1960s. His collaboration with Westbrook was particularly fruitful: as well as being the main featured soloist, Surman also composed and arranged pieces for both small groups and the larger orchestral works such as 'Marching Song'. He developed so fast as an instrumentalist, that by the later 1960s he had become a major innovative force on baritone, doing for that instrument what Eric Dolphy had done for the bass clarinet – dramatically increasing its mobility and flexibility, and actually creating, by mastery of the harmonics, an extreme upper register for the very first time. In 1968, when the Westbrook band took part in the competition at the Montreux festival, Surman won the Best Soloist award, and his international reputation grew rapidly after that. 1964–8, he also worked in the UK with Mike Gibbs, Graham Collier, Chris McGregor, Dave Holland, John McLaughlin and others. 1969, he played baritone and soprano on one of the classic albums of the decade, John McLaughlin's *Extrapolation*, with Brian Odges on bass and Tony Oxley on drums, and the same year Surman began leading his own groups, forming the Trio, with Barre Phillips (bass) and Stu Martin (dms). One of the most vital and acclaimed groups of its time, it toured and played festivals all over Western and Eastern Europe. 1970, he toured Japan with a group of European poll winners which included Karin Krog and Albert Mangelsdorff. 1973, he formed SOS with fellow saxophonists Alan Skidmore and Mike Osborne. With Surman's use of electronics and synthesizers, and Skidmore doubling on drums and Osborne on percussion, SOS managed to create a huge variety of sounds and textures. Surman also employed synthesizers with the Trio, and with Mumps, which was the Trio augmented by Albert Mangelsdorff. 1974–9, he collaborated regularly with the Carolyn Carlson Dance Theatre at the Paris Opera. He made duo recordings with pianist Stan Tracey (*Sonatinas*) and singer Karin Krog (*Cloudline Blue*) in 1978. 1979–82, he worked with bassist Miroslav Vitous's quartet. He toured Australia with Vitous, 1983, and with Krog, 1985. 1984, he collaborated with John Warren in composing and arranging *The Brass Project*, a series of pieces for brass ensemble and rhythm section, featuring Surman on reeds and piano. Since 1968, Surman has appeared at major festivals all over the world and has won jazz polls in many countries. Several of his LPs have received awards including *The Amazing Adventures of Simon Simon*, which was voted Record of the Year (Europe) in the *Jazz Forum* readers' poll, 1982, and received the maximum rating of five stars in the US magazine, *Downbeat*; *Upon Reflection* received the 1980 Italian Record Critics' award. His favourites are Sonny Rollins, Charlie Parker and Eric Dolphy, and other inspirations are Harry Carney, Ellington's music, John Coltrane, and his associates, Stu Martin, Barre Phillips, Skidmore and Osborne.

John Surman is that rare phenomenon in jazz, a musician who was brilliant and innovative at the beginning of his career and has gone on slowly evolving and maturing, so that in mid-career his music has great technical and emotional breadth and depth. Like Albert Mangelsdorff, he is a major figure who chose to remain in Europe. His compositions, and the evocative moods and atmospheres he creates with electronics, derive in part from his European heritage: his experience of church music as a choirboy, his awareness of folk and ethnic music such as Irish jigs, Scottish reels and laments, his knowledge of European classical music and brass bands. He has had many commissions for ballet scores and church music – all from outside the UK. His one British commission resulted in the album *Morning Glory*, for which he collaborated with John Taylor, and Terje Rypdal. [IC]

With Westbrook, Gibbs, Vitous; with McLaughlin, *Extrapolation* (1969), Polydor; under his own name, *The Trio* (1970), Pye; solo, *Westering Home* (1972), Island; *Morning Glory* (1973), Island; *SOS* (1975), Ogun; *Upon Reflection* (1979); *The Amazing Adventures of Simon Simon* (1981); *Such Winters of Memory* (1983), all ECM

Sutton, Ralph Earl, piano. b. Hamburg, Missouri, 4 November 1922. 'Ralph is without doubt the greatest, and he's just about alone with it now, because he's one of the few left from our finest and most creative piano eras.' Milt Hinton talking about Ralph Sutton, who in the 1980s is – with Dick Wellstood and Keith Ingham – the finest keeper of the great piano traditions set down by Fats Waller, Willie 'The Lion' Smith and Art Tatum. Sutton's career got under way post-war (he had played with Jack Teagarden while still at college in 1942) with appearances on Rudi Blesh's This is Jazz show, a trio with Albert Nicholas and eight years as intermission pianist (usually a thankless job anywhere) at

Eddie Condon's. Later he worked for Bob Scobey and, in 1963, was in the first Dick Gibson Jazz Party which was to pave the way for the formation in 1968 of the World's Greatest Jazz Band: Sutton was a founder member. In the 1970s the process of re-evaluating Sutton's career began in earnest: a lovingly-written biography by James D. Shacter began the operation, and soon after a multi-volume set of Sutton masterworks for Chaz Jazz (Charlie Baron's label), placing him in every context from solo to duo to band with such other masters as Ruby Braff and Kenny Davern, confirmed his jazz stature in the public consciousness. In the 1980s Sutton – a kindly, gentle bear of a man with a very occasional explosive temper – works regularly as a soloist and enjoys his hard-won reputation.

'Sutton is not an innovator', says William A. MacPherson, 'nor is he an imitator. He's simply a kindred spirit who lends himself as a meeting place for the happy ghosts of all the great Harlem pianists in whose style he has submerged his own.' [DF]

See Shacter, James, D., *Piano Man* (Hickox Productions, 1975)

Swallow, Steve (Stephen W.), bass guitar, composer. b. New York City, 4 October 1940. Began on piano and trumpet with private teachers; took up double-bass at 18. Joined the Paul Bley trio in 1960; also worked with George Russell, Jimmy Giuffre and Art Farmer in the early 1960s. 1965–7, with Stan Getz; 1967–70, with Gary Burton's quartet. Then he spent three years living in Bolinas, California, writing, and playing in San Francisco with pianists Art Lande and Mike Nock. 1973, he rejoined Burton and has worked with him intermittently ever since.

Swallow's original influences were Charles Mingus, Charlie Haden, Wilbur Ware and Red Mitchell, and he had most of their virtues and values. He was involved in the free (abstract) jazz scene during the early 1960s and in 1964 he won the *Downbeat* critics' poll as new star on bass. During the later 1960s, particularly with the Burton quartet, the music fused elements from jazz, rock and country music in a strongly electronic context, and it required bass guitar – not acoustic bass. Swallow began doubling on bass guitar and at the beginning of the 1970s he gave up acoustic bass altogether because he discovered that the two techniques were incompatible. Gary Burton told Charles Mitchell: 'He re-approached the [electric bass]; he plays it with a pick all the time, which few jazz players do; he changed the fingering system around to a more guitar-oriented style. He plays it on its own terms, so it doesn't sound like a plugged-in acoustic bass . . . he dropped all pre-conceived notions, finding his own voice on the instrument.'

Since the early 1970s, Swallow has also been intermittently associated with Mike Gibbs, recording and touring with him. Since the later 1970s, he has been a regular member of Carla Bley's various bands and has played on some of her finest albums. Swallow is a brilliant bass guitarist with his own sound and style; his concentration and dependability are legendary, and he is also a superb soloist. He always plays compositionally – with a comprehensive understanding of the music and his role in it – and this is probably because he is one of the finest and most fertile small-group composers. His pieces have been played and recorded by many musicians, including Gary Burton, Mike Gibbs, and Chick Corea. Some of his best-known compositions are: 'Arise Her Eyes'; 'Chelsea Bells'; 'Como En Vietnam'; 'Doin' the Pig'; 'Domino Biscuit'; 'Eiderdown'; 'Falling Grace'; 'General Mojo's Well Laid Plan'; 'Green Mountains'; 'Sweet Henry'; 'Hotel Hello'. [IC]

With George Russell, Steve Kuhn, Mike Gibbs, Paul Bley, Jimmy Giuffre; Swallow/Burton, *Hotel Hello* (1974); with Burton quartet, *Ring* (1974); *Picture This* (1982), all ECM; with Carla Bley, *Musique Mécanique* (1978); *Social Studies* (1981); *Live!* (1982); *Heavy Heart* (1984); *Night-Glow* (1985), all Watt; as leader, *Home* (music by Swallow to poems by Robert Creeley) (1980), ECM

Sweet Substitute A Bristol-based trio of singers, Sweet Substitute – Angie Masterson, Teri Leggett and Chris Staples, later replaced by Kate McNab – began their career in 1975 recreating the music of 'sister acts' such as the Boswells and the Andrews: later their approach broadened to include contemporary and rock-based material. A first album, *Something Special* (1978), teamed them with early associates Keith Nichols, MD Alan Cohen and a prototype of the Midnite Follies Orchestra (made up of studio musicians); thereafter the trio toured nationally (with organist Klaus Wunderlich among others), appeared on radio and TV specials, guested with Nichols's Midnite Follies Orchestra for live dates and played European jazz festivals: their MD during this whole period was guitarist/arranger Andy Leggett. When that association came to an end, Sweet Substitute worked regularly for Chris Barber's agency, toured and recorded with Barber's band, appeared in the USA and continued their successful career: a second album, *Sophisticated Ladies*, showed off their widely-based repertoire, as well as some witty Leggett originals. By mid-decade the group was touring for Keith Smith in shows such as 'The Stardust Road' (for which they teamed with Georgie Fame as well as Smith's band) as well as appearing in clubs, cabaret and on TV and radio. [DF]

Sophisticated Ladies (1980), Black Lion

Swing (1) Although the word was popularized as a noun (in Duke Ellington's 'It don't mean a thing if it ain't got that swing'), it was undoubtedly a verb first of all: a performance swings, a performer or a group or a tune swings, while even a less obvious tune can be swung. We all think we can recognize it when we hear it, but describing it is another matter entirely.

Most definitions of swing lay emphasis on the regularity of a pulse, despite the fact that a metronome or a ticking clock convey no sensation of swing. The latter in fact make compulsive listening only for people unable to hear them without superimposing melodies in their heads – which actually provides a clue to the nature of the sensation. Music only starts to swing when there is regularity *combined* with complex variation of the pulse, and when the listener participates mentally in maintaining the tension between the two. (This is indeed why the music of Bach is said to swing; Beethoven and Brahms do not swing, nor does Chopin, for they are too monorhythmic, but there are enough different things going on rhythmically in some of Bach for listeners to experience swing.)

Virtually all Afro-American music has the same quality to a greater or lesser extent, whether it be jazz, blues, gospel, soul etc. (the only exceptions are pieces, or parts of pieces, which are out-of-tempo or free-tempo). What is endlessly and delightfully variable is the amount of polyrhythmic interplay between members of a rhythm-section, and the amount that takes place between the front-line and the rhythm-section. This has not only varied in the different historical styles of jazz, but changes considerably in different performances within the same style, and indeed from bar to bar of a single performance. As a result of this, and of listeners' and performers' personal preferences, there is no objective standard as to what style of performance swings the most.

(2) Swing is also the name given to the style of big-band music formulated by Fletcher Henderson and Don Redman and popularized by the Casa Loma Orchestra, the Dorsey Brothers and Benny Goodman. Following Goodman's success in 1935 and until around 1945, more jazz-influenced music was more popular than at any time since. The 'swing era', however, did not have a monopoly on swinging; indeed, some of what was played then had as little to do with it as most music of the 1920s 'jazz age' had to do with jazz.

(3) What has proved more lasting, but was also referred to at the time as swing, was the small-group jazz typified by the clubs on New York's 52nd Street from the mid-1930s to the late 1940s. Hence the street was then known as (and has since been officially named) 'Swing Street'. Because of the way in which the big-band music soon became equated with pure nostalgia, however, the continuing vitality of the small-group style in the 1950s led to the adoption of the term 'mainstream' instead. [BP]

Syncopation A European term describing a European concept, namely a simple and steady pulse disrupted by an anticipated or delayed accent (the accent being called the syncope, which rhymes with 'hiccuppy'). This is rather misleading if applied to jazz playing, somewhat similar to describing New Orleans as polyphonic (i.e. employing simultaneous *sounds*) without even mentioning that it is also *polyrhythmic*.

So it is the least polyrhythmic Afro-American music, ragtime, which sounds the most syncopated; here the cross-accentuation, and the notes phrased in groups of 3 over a rhythm in 2, are most easily heard as deviations from a European-style march beat. The same principles are also at work in nearly all later jazz, but the cross-rhythms have become an integral part of the natural polyrhythmic flow of jazz. What a European-trained musician would see as syncopation if written down is usually not heard as such, except in the case of an extremely exaggerated example, for it is the flow rather than its constant disruption which is most valued by jazz lovers. [BP]

T

Tabackin, Lew (Lewis Barry), tenor sax, flute. b. Philadelphia, 26 May 1940. Philadelphia Conservatory of Music, 1958–62, B.Mus. majoring in flute. 1965, moved to New York, working with Maynard Ferguson, Clark Terry, Thad Jones–Mel Lewis, Joe Henderson and many others; also in small groups with Donald Byrd, Elvin Jones, Toshiko Akiyoshi and others. 1968–9, led his own trio, toured Switzerland, did a jazz workshop in Hamburg and was featured soloist with Danish Radio Orchestra. He married Toshiko Akiyoshi, touring Japan with her in 1970 and 1971. They moved to Los Angeles in 1972 and ran a workshop big band which evolved into the Toshiko Akiyoshi orchestra featuring Tabackin. It toured Japan several times, visited Europe, and played on the East Coast of the US, earning world-wide critical acclaim. 1982, Tabackin won the *Downbeat* poll on flute, and the same year he and Toshiko moved back to New York. Tabackin continues to work and tour with the band, but also leads his own trio and plays in other contexts. He and his wife also started their own US label, Ascent Records. He is one of the most gifted saxophonists on the current jazz scene and his influences include Sonny Rollins, John Coltrane, Lester Young and Ben Webster; he is also one of the finest flute players. [IC]

With Duke Pearson, Byrd, Attila Zoller and others; Lew Tabackin Trio, *Let the Tape Roll* (nda), RCA Japan; Akiyoshi Jazz Orchestra, featuring Tabackin, *Ten Gallon Shuffle* (1984), Ascent; with Freddie Hubbard, *Sweet Return* (1983), Atlantic

Tag A tag is a brief addition to the normal 8-bar sections of a 'chorus'. For example, the song 'I Got Rhythm' has a written 2-bar tag (listen to Benny Goodman's version), which is however usually dropped in most other jazz versions and certainly in jazz 'originals' based on 'Rhythm changes'. On the other hand, songs like 'My Funny Valentine' and 'All the Things You Are' have a 4-bar tag built into the melody and the chord-sequence, and which is therefore retained in each improvised chorus.

The earliest usage in jazz (and probably, in fact, the inspiration for the ending of 'I Got Rhythm') was the New Orleans practice of adding an improvised tag to the very last chorus of a long performance; this was expanded in the work of the first Chicago generation to a concluding series of 4-bar solos each followed by 4-bar ensemble tags. Such instances of tags at the very end of a piece correspond to the European term 'coda', but the 1950s–1960s Miles Davis quintet borrowed the idea when playing standards and added a series of tags at the end of each individual solo. [BP]

Takase, Aki, piano, Chinese koto, composer. b. Osaka, Japan, 26 January 1948. Mother, a piano teacher, gave her lessons from age three. She also played bass in her school orchestra; then studied piano at Toho Gakuen University in Tokyo. She heard records of Charles Mingus, Ornette Coleman and John Coltrane, then after hearing a friend improvising on 'Autumn Leaves' she began improvising herself. 1971, she got her first professional engagements; at 25 she began to lead her own groups. 1978, she made her first album as leader; 1981, she recorded with Dave Liebman; also made her first visit to Europe, performing with her trio at the Berlin festival.

May 1982, she worked in New York with Cecil McBee (bass), Bob Moses and singer Sheila Jordan; in June her solo piano concert was the high spot of the East-West Festival in Nuremburg. 1983, she formed her own quartet, touring Europe with it. Her influences include Bill Evans, Bud Powell, Herbie Hancock, Gary Peacock, Charlie Haden, and other inspirations include Ravel, Debussy, Satie and Bartók. Aki Takase is a brilliant performer who can handle all areas from conventional structures and harmony to semi- or total abstraction. She is steeped in jazz, but also uses elements from the Japanese musical tradition, and performs on Chinese koto, a 17-string zither. [IC]

Aki (1978), King; Takase/Liebman, *Minerva's Owl* (1981), Teichiku Continental; trio live at the Berlin festival, *Song for Hope* (1981), Enja; solo piano at East-West Festival, Nuremburg, *Perdido* (1982), Enja

Tate, Buddy (George Holmes), tenor sax. b. Sherman, Texas, 22 February 1913. He learned his craft playing with territory bands around the American Southwest in the early 1930s: they included McCloud's Night Owls (Booker Ervin Snr. played trombone), the St Louis Merrymakers (where he first met Herschel Evans), Terrence Holder (his first big band, later taken over

Buddy Tate

by Andy Kirk), Kirk's own group and Nat Towles's fine orchestra. In 1939 he was invited by Count Basie to replace Evans, who had died suddenly. 'I dreamed he had died,' Tate told Stanley Dance later, 'and that Basie was going to call me. It happened within a week or two: I still have the telegram!' He stayed with Basie for nine happy years, then worked with Lucky Millinder, Hot Lips Page, and Jimmy Rushing's Savoy band before entrepreneur Irving Cohen offered him the residency at the Celebrity Club on 125th Street in Harlem. Tate stayed at the club for 21 straight years 'until the clientele began to change: they wanted rock and didn't appreciate what we were doing so we quit.' But he had been canny enough to avoid being buried in his long residency: all through the 1950s he had recorded regularly, toured with Buck Clayton and kept himself in the public eye, so when he became a freelance again there were immediate keen offers for his services. On the European circuit he teamed with men such as Jim Galloway and Jay McShann and (after the death of Jimmy Forrest) formed a working duo with trombonist Al Grey: in America he worked the festivals including Dick Gibson's Jazz Parties and co-led a band with Bobby Rosengarden at the Rainbow Room. Seriously hurt when a hotel-room shower badly scalded him in 1981, Tate was soon back on the road, playing with the same broad-as-a-mile sound, thick vibrato and fine time. A direct successor, musical and spiritual, to Coleman Hawkins and Herschel Evans, Buddy Tate – an urbane and charming swing ambassador without an enemy in the world – is, in his own right, a giant of jazz tenor saxophone. [DF]

See Dance, Stanley, *The World of Count Basie* (Sidgwick and Jackson, 1980)

Tatum, Art(hur), piano. b. Toledo, Ohio, 13 October 1909; d. 5 November 1956. Virtually blind from birth, studied piano in early childhood and began gigging as a teenager in Toledo and Cleveland. Regular pianist for Adelaide Hall in New York and on tour (1932–3), making solo recording debut at this period. Career as soloist in clubs in Hollywood, Chicago, New York and briefly (1938) in Europe, until forming his own trio in 1943 with Tiny Grimes and Slam Stewart. From then until his death from uraemia, divided time between trio and solo work, and between night-club and concert appearances.

Like no other performer in the history of jazz piano, Tatum summarized everything that had preceded him stylistically, and did so in a supercharged manner which opened doors not only for succeeding generations of pianists but for practitioners of other instruments as well. Initially inspired by Fats Waller and by 'semi-classical' players, he was capable of making complex passages of 'stride piano' sound like simple exercises learned by heart and taken at suicidal speed, for the sheer joy of impressing and intimidating would-be competitors. Similarly, although not frequently associated with blues material, when boogie became popular he could produce a boogie speciality full of virtuoso pyrotechnics.

The chief source of Tatum's style, however, was the boundless invention which went into his reworkings of standard material. Like the best of the stride players, he was less of a pure improviser than the kind of flamboyant 'arranger' who preferred constantly to hint at the underlying theme while continuously decorating it (even overloading it, in the opinion of some lay listeners). His greatest strength in this area was his incessant rhythmic variation, which took discontinuity to even greater lengths than Earl Hines and, again for the layman, was sometimes just too much to follow. In this respect, he had a greater influence on the embryonic beboppers than on most of his fellow pianists, who attempted to emulate his surface characteristics and missed out on the rhythmic flexibility.

An even greater impact was made by Tatum's harmonic subtlety which, possibly influenced by Ellington's work of the early 1930s, incorporated the upper intervals such as 9ths, 11ths and 13ths, and an overwhelming variety of substitute and passing chords. It is no accident that this interested saxophonists especially, and all the harmonically forward-looking players such as Coleman Hawkins, Don Byas, Charlie Parker and, later, John Coltrane were deeply impressed by Tatum. And yet another facet of his general influence was pinpointed in this comment by Rex Stewart: 'One of the most significant aspects of Tatum's artistry stemmed from his constant self-challenge. At the piano, Art seemingly delighted in creating impossible problems from the standpoint of harmonies and chord progressions. Then he would gleefully improvise sequence upon sequence until the phrase emerged as a complete entity within the structure of whatever composition he happened to be playing.' [BP]

Pure Genius (1937–44), Affinity; *Solo Piano* (1949–52), Capitol; Tatum/Benny Carter, *Group Masterpieces, vol. 1* (1954), Pablo; Tatum/Ben Webster, *Group Masterpieces, vol. 6* (1956), Pablo

Taylor, Art(hur S.), drums. b. New York City, 6 April 1929. Gigged with Howard McGhee, Coleman Hawkins (1950–1, making record debut with Hawk). Toured with Buddy DeFranco quartet (1952), Bud Powell trio (1953, 1955–7), George Wallington trio/quintet (1954, 1955–6). Public appearances and records with Art Farmer (1955), Miles Davis (1955–7, including *Miles Ahead* album), Donald Byrd–Gigi Gryce (1957). Toured Europe with Byrd for several months (1958), then with Thelonious Monk (1959, including Town Hall concert). During late 1950s–early 1960s did copious freelance recording with such as John Coltrane, Jackie McLean, Hank Mobley, Lee Morgan etc. Moved to Europe (1963), working mostly with expatriate Americans such as Dexter Gordon and Johnny Griffin; also conducted interviews with American musicians (late 1960s–early 1970s), eventually published in book form. Living in New York again from 1980, more active as a performer. Organized concert tribute to Bud Powell, repeated and expanded at Kool Festival, 1985. Although his interviews are a significant contribution to the literature of jazz, his most important contribution is as a dynamic drummer displaying an admiration for both Art Blakey and Philly Joe Jones, interacting with soloists in the best sense of the word. [BP]

A.T.'s Delight (1960), Blue Note

See Taylor, Art, *Notes and Tones* (Perigree 1982, Quartet 1983)

Art Tatum

Taylor, Billy (William Jnr.), piano. b. Greenville, N. Carolina, 21 July 1921. Teenage trips to Harlem acquainted Taylor with pianists such as Art Tatum, Clarence Profit and the young Thelonious Monk. Moved to New York in early 1940s, worked with Ben Webster, Dizzy Gillespie, Stuff Smith and others. Led house rhythm-section at Birdland (1951), then own trio throughout 1950s. Taylor then became active (and better known) as writer, radio disc-jockey, television musical director, and educator; his book *Jazz Piano* (Wm. C. Brown, 1982) was based on one of his radio series. Co-founder of Jazzmobile organization, which provides free concerts in Harlem.

Taylor's piano style reflects informal tutoring

from Art Tatum plus the rhythmic approach of Nat 'King' Cole. While his right-hand lines sometimes seem overloaded, they are very impressive technically, and his close-voiced left-hand inversions may have influenced Ahmad Jamal and therefore countless others. [BP]

Billy Taylor Trio (1954), Prestige/OJC

Taylor, Cecil Percival, piano, composer, educator. b. New York, 15 March 1933. His mother was a dancer who also played piano and violin, and who died when he was quite young. He had piano lessons from age six. He attended the New York College of Music, then spent four years at New England Conservatory. While there he became influenced by Dave Brubeck's piano style – particularly his thick, multi-note chords. In later years, Taylor attempted to reverse the musical traffic, saying of Brubeck: 'I learned a lot from him. When he's most interesting, he sounds like me.' Other influences were Bud Powell, Horace Silver, Duke Ellington and Erroll Garner. In the early 1950s he worked with small groups led by Johnny Hodges, Hot Lips Page and Lawrence Brown, and then began to lead his own group, with Steve Lacy (soprano), Buell Neidlinger (bass) and Dennis Charles (dms). In 1956 this was the first jazz group to play regularly at the Five Spot Café, where they had a six-week residency. He was then still using chord changes and the usual jazz structures of 12 or 32 bars, but when his group appeared at the Newport Jazz Festival in 1957 the music had become much more abstract. (In fact he was booked there at one of the afternoon 'experimental' sessions, having already acquired the reputation of someone working on the frontiers of music.) By the early 1960s Taylor's music had become totally abstract – non-tonal and without any kind of conventional jazz rhythm.

The whole jazz scene in the late 1950s was ripe for a shake-up, which happened with the advent of free jazz, and Taylor should have played a very prominent role as one of the trail-blazers of abstraction; but the arrival in New York of Ornette Coleman, in the autumn of 1959, put Taylor completely in the shade, blighting his career for several years. As Thelonious Monk had done earlier, Taylor spent much of the 1960s at home practising. 1961, he had a booking at the Five Spot with his quartet, which included Archie Shepp, Neidlinger and Charles, and they also appeared in the play *The Connection*. 1962, he spent six months in Europe with Jimmy Lyons (alto) and Sunny Murray (dms), playing in Oslo and Stockholm and recording two albums at the Café Montmartre, Copenhagen. In Stockholm, Taylor met Albert Ayler, also beginning to find an audience for his music in Europe, and Ayler played with the group at the Montmartre, returning to the USA with them and continuing his association with Taylor until 1963. Back in New York, Taylor did not work again for almost a year. 1964–5, with Michael Mantler, Roswell Rudd, Bill Dixon, Archie Shepp and others he was one of the organizers of the Jazz Composers' Guild, which aimed to achieve better working conditions and opportunities to present the new music without compromise. By 1965, although still working very rarely, he was already an inspirational force in free jazz; pianists were becoming influenced by his style, and his example of integrity influenced musicians on all instruments.

Taylor has said that the more he plays, the more he becomes aware of the non-European aspects of the music, and he explained to John Litweiler: 'In white music the most admired touch among pianists is light. The same is true among white percussionists. We in black music think of the piano as a percussive instrument: we beat the keyboard, we get inside the instrument. Europeans admire Bill Evans for his touch. But the physical force going into the making of black music – if that is misunderstood, it leads to screaming . . .' As a pianist, Taylor has an exceptionally brilliant technique allied to phenomenal energy and stamina: people often talk about his playing more from a physical than from an aesthetic point of view. He can play the most intricate abstract lines and torrential atonal clusters with a blistering percussive attack, all at high volume, and he can sustain this kind of intensity for anything up to two or three hours. His groups too, reflect his energy, and are relentlessly abstract, and his music has virtually nothing in common with either the European classical tradition or the folk and ethnic musics of the world. It is not surprising that such a daunting and different music has taken a long time to find an audience.

In 1968, Taylor was a featured soloist on a Jazz Composers' Orchestra recording under the direction of Mantler. The same year, saxophonist Sam Rivers joined Taylor's group, staying with it until 1973, and in this period the pianist began to get more international bookings. The Cecil Taylor Unit toured Europe in 1969; Taylor himself played solo piano concerts at several festivals in the early 1970s, including the Newport Jazz Festival-New York and Montreux. 1975, his group with Jimmy Lyons and Andrew Cyrille played three weeks at the Five Spot. 1976, with his group he did a three-month European tour taking in almost all major festivals; 1977, he played a concert in duet with pianist Mary Lou Williams at Carnegie Hall.

He also became active in academic circles, first at the University of Wisconsin where, 1970–1, he taught a course in Black Music 1920–70 and directed the Black Music Ensemble, and then at Antioch College, Ohio, for two years, and Glassboro State College in New Jersey. He was awarded a Guggenheim Fellowship in 1973.

Taylor has always been interested in ballet and dance, and once said, 'I try to imitate on the piano the leaps in space a dancer makes.' He collaborated with dancer Dianne McIntyre in

1977 and 1979, and also in 1979 composed and played the music for a 12-minute ballet 'Tetra Stomp: Eatin' Rain in Space' featuring Mikhail Baryshnikov and Heather Watts. December 1979, the Cecil Taylor Unit with Lyons, Ramsey Ameen (vln), Alan Silva (bass) and Jerome Cooper (dms) did a ten-day workshop at the Creative Music Studio, West Hurley, New York, with 40 students; and the same month, Taylor played two duet concerts with Max Roach at Columbia University, and they were immediately inundated with offers to perform internationally. [IC]

Looking Ahead (1958), Boplicity; *The New Breed* (1961), Impulse; *Unit Structures* (1966), Blue Note; *Conquistador!* (1966), Blue Note; *The Great Concert of Cecil Taylor* (1969), Prestige; *Silent Tongues* (1974), Arista-Freedom; *Dark to Themselves* (1976), Enja; *Air Above Mountains (Buildings Within)* (1976), Enja; *Cecil Taylor Live in the Black Forest* (1978), MPS; *Cecil Taylor 3 Phasis* (1979), New World

Taylor, John, piano. b. Manchester, 25 September 1942. Self-taught. In the early 1960s he began working with dance bands. 1964, he went to London and was soon playing with the John Surman octet, the Alan Skidmore quintet, and Norma Winstone. He also worked with John Warren's band, John Dankworth and Cleo Laine, Marian Montgomery, and led his own trio and sextet in the later 1960s and the 1970s. For a while he was with the Ronnie Scott quintet, then in 1977, with Kenny Wheeler and Norma Winstone, he formed the trio Azimuth. In the later 1970s he worked with Jan Garbarek's quintet, Arild Andersen's quartet, and the Miroslav Vitous quartet, touring extensively internationally and appearing at many festivals. Taylor has absorbed all his influences and developed into one of the very finest pianists in jazz. The hallmarks of his style are long, flowing lyrical lines, and sonorous harmonies, and the same qualities are evident in his compositions. He is one of a handful of British musicians with a really solid international reputation. He is the driving force behind Azimuth, composing much of the music, and his piano usually performing the key role of setting up rhythmic or textural terms of reference. An influence on his whole approach, he once stated, was that of Mike Gibbs, whose scoring has affected Taylor's attitude to texture and dynamics. Other inspiration he derives from Bill Evans, and from his own associates, Wheeler, Winstone and Surman. [IC]

Sextet, *Pause and Think Again* (1971), Turtle; with Surman, *Morning Glory* (1973), Island; with Azimuth, *Azimuth* (1977); *Touchstone* (1979); *Départ* (1980); with Vitous, *Journey's End* (1982); with Kenny Wheeler, *Double Double You* (1983), all ECM

Taylor, Martin, guitar. b. Harlow, Essex, 1956. A guitarist of virtuoso technique, broad-based musical taste and mature approach, he was being widely noticed and praised by his early teens around the London jazz scene (one early Taylor coup was to sit in with Count Basie's orchestra during a jazz cruise) and soon after was working with discerning leaders including Lennie Hastings. In a regular partnership with Ike Isaacs in the late 1970s (they worked in duo at London's Pizza on the Park and recorded), Taylor's work showed a maturity beyond his years and regular work with Peter Ind at the same period indicated that he could move in the contemporary areas of jazz occupied by Pat Metheny and others with equal conviction. In the 1980s he regularly partnered Stephane Grappelli, recorded solo and continued to build his reputation from a home base in Scotland. Taylor possesses a rare double gift of brilliant musicianship and a business vision which enables him to keep a clear (though never pushy) eye on the business of making a living at jazz: even more admirably he has never in any way compromised his musical beliefs in order to go on doing so. [DF]

Taylor/Ind, *Triple Libra* (1981), Wave

Tchicai, John Martin, alto, tenor and soprano sax, bass clarinet. b. Copenhagen, 28 April 1936, of Danish mother and Congolese father. Studied music at conservatory while playing jazz; led own group at World Youth Festival, Helsinki, and with Jørgen Leth quintet at Warsaw Jazz Festival (both 1962). Moved to New York (1963), co-led New York Contemporary Five with Archie Shepp and Bill Dixon (later Don Cherry); toured Europe with this group (autumn 1963). Then formed New York Art Quartet with Roswell Rudd, Milford Graves (1964), with these and others in foundation of Jazz Composers' Guild; member of augmented John Coltrane group which recorded *Ascension* (1965). Returned to Europe (1966), working with Gunter Hampel, Don Cherry and own 17-piece Cadentia Nova Danica. Concentrating more recently on tenor, has also worked with guitarist Pierre Dørge and the New Jungle Orchestra (from 1982) and with the all-saxophonist sextet De Zes Winden. Tchicai was an interesting altoist whose tone, and even phraseology, were most often compared to Lee Konitz, which made a considerable contrast with other saxophonists of the 1960s avant-garde. As a result, he appeared to place less emphasis on the manner of his delivery and more on the content of his lines. [BP]

New York Art Quartet (1964), ESP-Disk; trio, *Real Tchicai* (1977), Steeplechase

Teagarden, Charlie (Charles), trumpet. b. Vernon, Texas, 19 July 1913; d. 10 December 1984. It was probably inevitable that Charlie

Teagarden would live his musical life in the shadow of his brother Jack. Although their talents were never dramatically different, Jack Teagarden, in the last analysis, was an innovator where Charlie was simply a very good and adaptable player; the trumpeter did sing for fun, but his voice never had the charm and hint of vulnerability that made his brother's great. It was a happy accident of jazz history – possibly less happy for Charlie's solo recognition – that wherever Jack was found (in Ben Pollack's band from 1928, with Whiteman in the 1930s, with the 'Three T's', featuring Frank Trumbauer, in 1936, and often later with his own bands) young Charles was often on hand too. Like Jack he had the perfect technique to deliver what he had: a hot-gold tone, the kind of fluid, carefree approach that would have graced a clarinet, let alone a trumpet, and a generous vibrato (like that of the young Harry James) which warmed up everything he played. Teagarden worked for James in 1946, later for Jimmy Dorsey (he shared the stage with a young tiger-ish Maynard Ferguson) and by 1948 had joined the Dorseyland Jazz Band: that year Dorsey gave him a picture inscribed to 'The most underrated trumpeter in the world'. 1950–8, Teagarden played for Ben Pollack and Bob Crosby in studios (there are records), led his own trio with Jess Stacy at Club Hangover, 1951–2, and played and recorded with his brother Jack to a new-found airy-creative level. By the 1960s he was living in Las Vegas, where he did the rounds of the hotel bands ('often six in a week'); then he took a group to the Silver Slipper where he stayed for three years. In the 1970s he was an officer in the Vegas local of AFM. 'My trumpet? Like me it's retired', he told Dave Dexter in 1984. 'But I have a jillion memories and I figure life's been good to me.' [DF]

Jimmy Dorsey, *Dorseyland Band* (1950), Hindsight

Teagarden, Cub (Clois Lee), drums. b. Vernon, Texas, 16 December 1915; d. 1969. The least-known of the Teagarden tribe, Cub played drums all round the Midwest in the 1930s and joined his elder brother Jack's big band, 1939–40. In the 1940s he worked with the Oklahoma Symphony Orchestra as well as his own band but left music in 1948 for a day job at the Long Beach branch of General Telephones and played for fun. [DF]

Teagarden, Jack (Weldon John), trombone, singer, leader. b. Vernon, Texas, 29 August 1905; d. New Orleans, 15 January 1964. He first came to local prominence with Peck Kelley's band in 1921 and his talent even then was enough to scare Pee Wee Russell: 'Look,' said Russell, 'I'm a nice guy 1000 miles from home and I'm outclassed! Just send me back to St Louis!' Over the next seven years – with Kelley, then with other leaders such as Willard Robison and 'Doc' Ross – Teagarden was developing ideas and a technique (including a set of close-to-the-chest slide positions, sadly never written down) which were to complete his armoury. By the time he joined Ben Pollack in 1928 his gifts had blossomed: a delicate, contoured tone in which every note sounded as if it were gift-boxed, effortless production (he was perhaps the first jazz trombonist to play softly, a method later adopted by the modern jazz generation of slidemen), a new, startling mobility of approach that used the slide as a means to an end rather than a comedic end in itself, seductive tricks with water-glass mutes and, above all, an innate perfection that made whatever he played sound naturally right. Other players, including Miff Mole, Bill Rank and Jimmy Harrison, had helped in the trombone revolution of the 1920s, but Teagarden's work capped theirs: Mole quickly moved into studio work, Bill Rank joined Paul Whiteman and Harrison, who died young, became the figurehead reserved for black followers.

Teagarden was with Pollack for five years (his arrival hastened Glenn Miller's voluntary departure) and then in 1933 signed a five-year contract as soloist for Paul Whiteman. Here he became something very close to a household name – with regular network radio from New York, prolific recording for Whiteman and of course copious 'special material' written for him by his friend Johnny Mercer and later by Bill Conway, whose Modernaires collaborated with Teagarden's friendly voice and deep-blue trombone on later radio shows for Chesterfield Cigarettes. But Teagarden found much of Whiteman's material tedious and shared the fashionable desire to lead his own orchestra. In 1939 he formed a big band, backed by MCA, which featured cornermen such as Charles Spivak (tpt), Allen Reuss (gtr) and Ernie Caceres (baritone); for the next seven years he led a succession of bands, often featuring such gifted soloists as clarinettist Sal Franzella and 'Pokey' Carriere (a very underrated soloist who dubbed the trumpet for Brian Donleavy in the 1940 Bing Crosby film *Birth of the Blues* in which Teagarden (on screen) and his band featured). But Teagarden's bands came late to the swing fray – his first was formed four years after Benny Goodman was already crowned 'King of Swing' – and, never a natural bandleader, he often found himself at the mercy of dishonest bookers, the US draft or simply an inability to think fast enough in business. In 1946 – after one or two bouts of heavy drinking – he disbanded and the following year joined Louis Armstrong's All Stars. Armstrong loved Teagarden to the end of his life – 'There'll never be another', Louis said – and the early years of their partnership produced fine music and records. But the regimented routines of Armstrong's All Stars, the cavalier management of Joe Glaser, which sometimes worked its members too hard, plus Teagarden's own memories of being (however tenuously) in charge of his

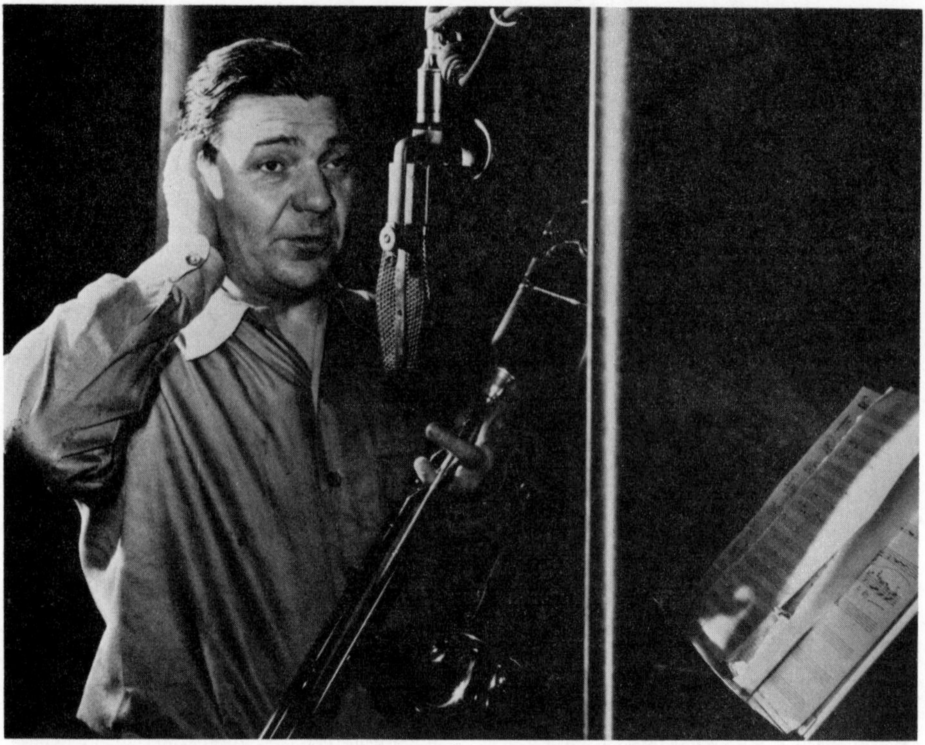

Jack Teagarden

musical fate over the previous decade, often led to the impression that he was fulfilling a role which he respected but, deep down, found hard going. (Later partners such as Trummy Young managed to play the support to Armstrong with more verve than Teagarden's talent would allow him.) In 1951 he left, and almost continuously for the last 13 years of his life led very successful bands of his own, featuring at first sidepersons such as his brother Charlie, his sister Norma, Ed Hall and Jimmy McPartland: from 1955 a contract with Capitol produced classic records with Bobby Hackett (*Coast Concert*) his own studio band (*This is Teagarden*) and others. In 1956, Teagarden formed his last great sextet which, with the addition of trumpeter Don Goldie ('The greatest I've heard', said the trombonist), toured, broadcast, played for the State Department in the Middle East, and recorded some autumn classics: their fine choice of material, perfect arrangements and vivacious solo work are gold-standard jazz. In 1957, with a determined co-leader, Earl Hines, Teagarden toured Europe: in 1960 a biography by Jay D. Smith and Len Guttridge was published (hugely sentimental, the book, like its subject, is hard to dislike). After three more years' touring, his heart stopped in a New Orleans motel: years of heavy drinking and stress had taken their last sad toll. 'I guess they didn't want anybody to see his face,' says Barney Bigard, 'it was so grotesque from all the drink. So the casket was closed.'

The name Jack Teagarden is a two-word definition of jazz trombone. 'It wasn't until a few years ago that I realized that Jack Teagarden *is* the best jazz trombonist', says Bill Russo. '. . . he has an unequalled mastery of his instrument which is evident in the simple perfection of his performance.' Teagarden set a new standard for his instrument in the 1920s and – like Louis Armstrong for the trumpet, and later Charlie Parker for alto saxophone – created a totally new approach. Before him the trombone had provided band harmonies or raised music-hall laughs: in jazz terms it most often sounded (in Vic Dickenson's words) like 'a dying cow in a thunderstorm'. After Teagarden, the trombone achieved a melodic status to match the heights being achieved by Armstrong, Bechet and the great masters of the early 20th century. Perhaps because of his colossal jazz achievement, Teagarden never quite achieved his second potential, as a pop star. Yet, more than any other great jazzman he possessed authentic star quality. His lazy Texan singing outcharmed contemporaries from Jimmy Rodgers to Bing

Crosby: hearing his early 1930s hits such as 'I ain't lazy, I'm just dreaming', 'Aintcha glad?' and 'I gotta right to sing the blues', right up to later pearls such as 'Say it simple' from 1947 and 'Meet me where they play the blues' from 1954, it is evident that Tin Pan Alley and the star-makers missed gold on the doorstep. [DF]

King of the Blues Trombone (1928–40), Columbia (3 records, boxed set)

See Waters, Howard J., *Jack Teagarden's Music* (Walter C. Allen, 1960); Smith, Jay D., and Gutteridge, Len, *Jack Teagarden* (Cassell, 1960); Lyttelton, Humphrey, *The Best of Jazz 2: Enter the Giants* (Robson, 1981)

Teagarden, Norma (Norma Louise Friedlander), piano. b. Vernon, Texas, 28 April 1911. Her reputation as a pianist unfortunately never emerged from the shadow of her older brother Jack Teagarden. From her earliest years in the late 1920s learning the ropes with territory bands, her piano talents were remarkable: a mature echo of solid Dixieland stylists such as Bob Zurke, coupled with a gift for delicate ragtime, learned from her mother early on. Norma worked all around Texas in the 1930s, led her own band in California from 1942 and, two years later, joined brother Jack's big band until 1946: from the late 1940s on she was commuting between all the best white Dixielanders from Matty Matlock and Pete Daily to Ben Pollack. 1952–5, she worked for Jack again (records such as the one below show her up as a sympathetic band pianist and occasional romping soloist) and from 1957, after moving back to San Francisco, played regularly with Turk Murphy, Pete Daily and others. In the 1970s and 1980s Norma Teagarden stayed busy: she was resident at the Washington Bar and Grill from 1975 to date, recorded, appeared as a guest on Marian McPartland's Piano Programme and in 1986 toured Britain with her own Marin County Band. [DF]

Jack Teagarden, *Big T's Jazz* (1947–55), Decca

Temperley, Joe (Joseph), baritone sax (and tenor, soprano etc.). b. Fife, Scotland, 20 September 1929. Worked with London-based dance bands, also (on tenor) Harry Parry (1949), Jack Parnell (1952–4) and (on baritone) Tommy Whittle (1955–6). Then played baritone exclusively while with Humphrey Lyttelton band (1958–65). Moved to New York (1965), where he has been a member of big bands led by Woody Herman, Buddy Rich, Thad Jones–Mel Lewis (recording with this band also directed by Charles Mingus), Clark Terry, Duke Pearson, Mercer Ellington etc. Has done considerable studio work, including soundtrack of film *The Cotton Club* (1984, performing solos associated with Harry Carney). Beginning with his work for Lyttelton and increasingly since moving to the USA, Temperley has forged an individual style and become one of the leading mainstreamers on his demanding instrument. [BP]

Temperley/Jimmy Knepper, *Just Friends* (1978), Hep

Tempo is literally the basic speed of a given piece, and can vary between different jazz performances more widely than is possible in most other music. The range is not merely from 'down tempo' (slow) to 'up tempo' (fast), but from 'way down' to 'way up' to 'ridiculous'. However, as much of the best jazz is polyrhythmic, there are often parallel tempos occurring simultaneously, so that an obviously slow tempo as defined by the rhythm-section may have the same tempo doubled or quadrupled by a soloist, or else different members of a rhythm-section may appear to be in different tempos.

'Out of tempo' covers everything from a slight relaxation of a previously fixed pulse, for instance just before the end of a ballad performance, to completely free rhapsodizing as in a long introduction (the European term 'rubato' is sometimes used) – either way, it only has meaning if preceded or followed by an in-tempo passage. On the other hand, 'free tempo' playing is very clearly in-tempo with a definite pulse, but 1-1-1-1 rather than 1-2-3, in other words without the need for regular spacing of bars or adhering to specific numbers of bars. [BP]

Terenzi, Danilo, trombone, composer. b. Rome, 2 March 1956. Grandfather a guitarist; began on guitar at age ten; studied trombone at the Conservatorio Musicale Di Santa Cecilia in Rome, 1969–75; 1977, began studying composition at the same conservatory. 1973, began professional career, forming quartet with Massimo Urbani and playing with Giorgio Gaslini and with Tommaso Vittorini's Living Concert Big Band. Has also worked with Enrico Rava, Steve Lacy, Paul Rutherford, Kenny Wheeler, Roswell Rudd, Albert Mangelsdorff, Lester Bowie, J. F. Jenny Clark, Archie Shepp, Mel Lewis and others. Many major festivals in Italy and internationally, and tours of France, Germany, Holland, UK, Switzerland and Yugoslavia. 1980, worked with Mike Westbrook's Brass Band; 1984, joined Westbrook's orchestra for performances of *On Duke's Birthday*; 1984 also took part in the Symposium on Jazz Pedagogy at Mulhouse. He teaches trombone in the Popular Music School of Testaccio in Rome, where he also conducts a big-band course. Compositions, 'Trees on the Sea', 'Nana', 'Amantide'. Favourites are Ray Anderson, Gary Valente and Albert Mangelsdorff. [IC]

With Gaetano Liguori, Rudd, Lacy, Riccardo Fassi; with Gaslini, *Message* (1973), BASF; with Westbrook, *On Duke's Birthday* (1985), Hat-Art

Territory Bands The bands that worked throughout the states of America without ever settling in a major city were the training ground in the 1930s for a whole generation of young musicians who later came to fame with the national-name bandleaders. One such – Alphonso Trent's band – was so popular around the Texas area that Trent was able to put out a second orchestra under his name (he called it TNT 2). They played in hotels, dance halls and sometimes just barns, decked up to look like a ballroom, in the middle of cornfields. Charlie Barnet remembers Trent's band well: 'He had a big reputation – but his band was nowhere near as disciplined as Fletcher's or McKinney's: it was exciting but there were weak links and it was terribly out of tune. The pianos you ran into in that section of the country were unbelievable – they hadn't been tuned since they were delivered.' Nevertheless, some of the early territory bands, from Jeter–Pillars (a sweet orchestra) to Nat Towles's band must have been exciting listening. In Towles's band, remembers Buddy Tate, 'we had Charlie Christian, Sir Charles Thompson, Henry Coker and Fred Beckett – he sounded just like Dorsey! We had about five arrangers – and two or three charts of each tune but unfortunately we never recorded and only worked in the Midwest'; even post-World War II, Towles trained young musicians, including successive saxists Jimmy Heath, Billy Mitchell and Oliver Nelson. In the early days, regular recording sessions were only offered to performers who commanded a widespread audience: the collection below (of early groups of the genre) gives only a small indication of how the music sounded. [DF]

The Territory Bands: 1926–9, EMI

Terry, Clark, trumpet, fluegelhorn, vocals. b. St Louis, Missouri, 14 December 1920. Early experience locally with various St Louis bands, and then in World War II with famous navy band which included players such as Willie Smith. Briefly with Lionel Hampton, then succession of name-band jobs with Charlie Barnet (1947–8), Count Basie (1948–51), Duke Ellington (1951–9) and Quincy Jones (1959–60). Became one of the first black musicians to be employed in a TV house band (led by former Barnet colleague Doc Severinsen) and during this period (1960–72) was occasionally featured in his own vocal speciality 'Mumbles'. At the same time was also extremely busy in recording session work, and co-led a part-time quintet with Bob Brookmeyer. Since late 1960s has led an occasional big band and, gradually undertaking less studio work, has participated in numerous jazz education clinics.

The creator of an irrepressibly bouncy style, Terry incorporates aspects of predecessors such as Charlie Shavers, Rex Stewart and Dizzy Gillespie, but his rhythmic verve is something entirely his own. His mellifluous tone is said to reflect an earlier school of St Louis players including trumpeter Joe Thomas, and is especially noticeable on fluegelhorn, an instrument which Terry virtually introduced as a jazz alternative to the trumpet. The very vocal nature of his sound (plus the use of the fluegel) were a direct influence on fellow St Louis native Miles Davis, and through him on a whole generation of trumpeters.

One of the special effects identified with Terry (heard for instance in 'Jim' from the Oscar Peterson album below), consists of holding fluegelhorn in one hand, muted trumpet in the other and alternating 'fours' with himself. His versatility with mutes and, when not muted, with articulation and inflection turns into affectionate satire when he sings the blues, often employing a personal brand of scat syllables. The good-humoured personality this demonstrates, which also comes across in his bandleading, makes Terry an important propagandist on behalf of jazz, as well as a significant player in his own right. [BP]

Serenade to a Bus Seat (1957), Riverside/OJC; *Oscar Peterson Trio with Clark Terry* (1964), Mercury; *Clark Terry/Bob Brookmeyer Quintet* (1965), Mainstream

Teschemacher, Frank, clarinet, alto, violin, arranger. b. Kansas City, Missouri, 13 March 1906; d. Chicago, 1 March 1932. Part of the original Austin High School Gang (in which he played alto, banjo and violin), he took up the clarinet in 1925, and by 1928 had come to New York with his Chicago friends. There he quickly made an impression. 'There used to be talk in those days,' recalls Max Kaminsky 'that Tesch could play Benny Goodman off the stand.' By 1928 the young clarinettist was certainly good enough to work with Ben Pollack and Sam Lanin in New York and – studious and solemn as he was – probably suited both leaders far better than some other of his rebellious Chicago colleagues. By the end of 1928, however, he was back in Chicago where he freelanced and played host to musicians such as Kaminsky who found themselves bedless: they usually found him practising hard, talking earnestly about music or dickering with violin and cornet as a rest from the clarinet. It seems strange that his few recordings – with Eddie Condon among others – are not more remarkable, but, says Kaminsky, 'Tesch had a phobia about making records: he'd freeze up in the studio and if he'd recorded more he would have overcome it!' 'He never made any records that did him justice', agrees Joe Marsala. Teschemacher died in a car crash when he was thrown out of Wild Bill Davison's Packard: 'Where', said Davison, dazed, 'will we ever get another clarinet player like Tesch?' [DF]

Chicago Jazz, vol. 1 (1928–30), Classic Jazz Masters

Tharpe, Sister Rosetta (*née* Rosetta Nubin),

Clark Terry

vocals, guitar. b. Cotton Plant, Arkansas, 20 March 1915; d. 9 October 1973. Began singing gospel music in church, and early on became a featured soloist. One of the star performers in Cotton Club revues (1938–9) backed by Cab Calloway band; toured with Calloway and then with Lucky Millinder, recording several singles of gospel and blues material with the latter (1941–2). After working in nightclubs (1942–4), decided to aim her records at growing gospel market, including duets with Marie Knight and with her mother, Katie Bell Nubin (who later made an album with Dizzy Gillespie's quintet). Rosetta continued to alternate between religious context and working for jazz audiences, especially on tours of Europe (from 1957).

Tharpe is the only fully-fledged gospel singer to cross over into the jazz field. At the time she was starting her rise to stardom, it would have been unacceptable to play a guitar in church;

and, even in the blues category, only one woman had attained any prominence as an instrumentalist (Memphis Minnie). Not only did Rosetta play gospel music with jazz groups and in a showbusiness context, but she effected a new stylistic fusion: although many folk-blues guitarists had also been evangelists, she was the first to incorporate the city-blues playing of the 1930s into gospel music. Like most important innovators, she was also a totally convincing and compelling performer. [BP]

Lucky Millinder (6 tracks with Tharpe), *Apollo Jump* (1941–2), Affinity

Thelin, Eje Ove, trombone. b. Jönköping, Sweden, 9 September 1938. Self-taught. Started in his teens as member of a popular Swedish Dixieland group, but soon graduated to more contemporary jazz. First important job with US drummer Joe Harris, 1958–9. Own group, 1961–5, made extensive tours all over Europe. Played at the Montmartre, Copenhagen, with George Russell, 1964. 1967–72, he taught at the Graz Jazz Institute. 1973–4, worked with John Surman in Europe. Based again in Sweden, he has been involved in teaching, playing with his own quartet and various other groups, and electronic experiments. He has performed at most European festivals including Antibes, 1963, and, with Barney Wilen, Roy Brooks and Palle Danielsson, at the Warsaw Jazz Jamboree, 1966. He has a pilot's licence and is a fanatical flyer. [IC]

Eje Thelin Group (nda), Riks; *Candles of Vision* (nda), Calig; *Live 76* (1976), CAP

Theme (1) The initial melody and chord-sequence of a jazz performance. This may be borrowed wholesale from a popular song, or it may be a new written melody based on someone else's chords. Or, in more recent jazz, it could be just a rhythmic figure of a few notes – a 'motif', according to European terminology. The theme will be what the soloists improvise 'on' or against, or else veer away from totally; either way, it will be a point of reference or, at the very least, something to start (and possibly end) the piece.

(2) The theme or theme-song of a particular group is the one used for identification at the start and/or end of each appearance. These were particularly prevalent when bands did a lot of broadcasting, and you can list your own favourites. One or two such pieces were identified with venues or eras rather than one group, such as 'Lullaby of Birdland' (written by George Shearing) or Thelonious Monk's '52nd Street Theme'. The piece called simply 'The Theme' has been used for 30 years by both the Art Blakey and Miles Davis bands, and is of indeterminate authorship. [BP]

Themen, Art (Arthur Edward George), tenor, soprano and sopranino sax. b. UK, 26 November 1939. Studied medicine at Cambridge, 1958–61, and St Mary's Hospital Medical School, London, 1961–4. Musically self-taught. Started with Cambridge University Jazz Group which won the UK inter-university jazz contests, 1959–62. He won the best soloist prize in 1959. On moving to London, he became involved with the early British blues movement, playing with Alexis Korner and Jack Bruce. Also a brief period with the pop session world, working with Rod Stewart, Joe Cocker, Charlie Watts, Long John Baldry. 1965, he was chosen to represent the UK in the international Peter Stuyvesant Jazz Orchestra at the Zurich festival. Late 1960s and early 1970s, played with Michael Garrick and Graham Collier bands. 1974, began a long association with Stan Tracey, playing in all his various groups. He has also toured with Al Haig, Red Rodney and Sal Nistico, and worked with Nat Adderley, George Coleman and Billy Mitchell. With Tracey and other groups he has toured India, the Middle East, Greece, South America, Switzerland, Indonesia and the Philippines, and played at most UK festivals. Themen, a consultant orthopaedic surgeon, is an immensely gifted saxophonist with a quirky, almost wilful originality. His favourites are Sonny Rollins, John Coltrane, Dexter Gordon and Don Weller, and his main inspirations are Thelonious Monk and Stan Tracey. [IC]

With Bruce, Collier, Garrick, Korner, Norma Winstone; with Stan Tracey quartet, *Captain Adventure* (1975), Steam; *Under Milk Wood* (1976), Transatlantic; with Tracey septet, *Spectrum* (tribute to Monk, 1982), Switch; with Al Haig, *Expressly Ellington* (1978), Spotlite

Thielemans, Toots (Jean Baptiste), harmonica, guitar, whistler, composer. b. Brussels, 29 April 1922. Started at age three on a home-made accordion, soon graduating to a proper one. Started on harmonica at 17 while studying maths at college. Hearing Django Reinhardt inspired him to take up guitar. After the war he gigged at American GI clubs and became interested in bebop. He was befriended by Charlie Parker, with whom he shared the bill at the Paris Festival International de Jazz, May 1949. He had visited the US in 1947, sitting in with groups on 52nd Street; 1950, he toured Europe with the Benny Goodman sextet. Emigrated to US in late 1951; worked with Dinah Washington, then joined the George Shearing quintet in early 1953, staying until the autumn of 1959. Formed his own group, but worked mostly as a freelance/studio musician.

In the early 1960s he began making regular trips to Europe. 1962, he recorded his composition 'Bluesette' which featured him on guitar and whistling, and this became a world-wide hit: there have been over 100 recorded versions of it. With this success, Thielemans was 'redisco-

Art Themen

vered' in the US, and was in constant demand for studio work on guitar, harmonica and whistling. From the mid-1960s he was closely associated with Quincy Jones, playing on the soundtracks of several films including *Midnight Cowboy* (1969), *The Getaway* (1972), *Sugarland Express* (1974) and *Cinderella Liberty* (1974), and on Jones's albums. 1972, he toured Russia with a quartet.

Since the 1970s he has divided his time between lucrative studio work and jazz gigs at clubs and festivals in the US and Europe. As a composer, he has written songs and background music for a Swedish cartoon film, *Dunderklumpen*, and composed and played harmonica on the theme music for the children's TV programme Sesame Street.

Thielemans is rooted in bebop, but his main

inspiration comes from Coltrane, and his work contains many resonances from the whole jazz tradition. He is a compelling performer who projects geniality and passion, and he has brilliantly developed the tonal qualities and expressiveness of the harmonica. Clifford Brown once told him: 'Toots, the way you play harmonica, they shouldn't call it a miscellaneous instrument!' [IC]

Several with Quincy Jones, including *Walkin' in Space* (1969), A & M; as leader, *Man Bites Harmonica* (1957), Riverside; *Toots Thielemans Captured Alive* (1974), Choice; with Oscar Peterson, *Big Six Live at '75 Montreux Festival*, Pablo

Thigpen, Ed(mund Leonard), drums. b. Chicago, 28 December 1930. Son of a noted drummer, Ben Thigpen (b. 16 November 1908; d. 5 October 1971), for 16 years a key member of the Andy Kirk band. Ed was brought up in Los Angeles, first toured with Cootie Williams group (1951–2) then, after army service, Dinah Washington (1954). Briefly with Lennie Tristano, Johnny Hodges band, Bud Powell trio (1955). Spent long periods with Billy Taylor trio (1956–9) and Oscar Peterson trio (1959–65). Freelanced in Los Angeles (late 1960s) and toured with Ella Fitzgerald (1966–7, 1968–72). Settled in Copenhagen (1972), performing with local musicians and visiting Americans and teaching drums. Although extremely versatile, Thigpen is particularly sensitive in a small-group setting, and his work with Taylor and Peterson showed him to be the epitome of a tidy, tasty trio drummer. [BP]

Out of the Storm (1966), Verve

Third stream describes the theoretical merging of two souls into one, those of jazz and European composed music. The unrequited love on both sides for the most incompatible characteristics of the other has resulted in many illicit encounters, and quite a few bastard offspring such as Paul Whiteman's 'Symphonic Jazz' and Stan Kenton's 'Innovations in Modern Music'. It is significant that this was no continuous lineage, growing in strength and numbers, for the 'third stream' was at the best of times never more than a trickle. As Billie Holiday said about love, 'Sometimes when you think it's on, baby, it has turned off and gone.'

Occasionally the liaison has been less fraught and one could point to a few near successes, in which either the European element predominates (e.g. Darius Milhaud's *La création du monde*) or the jazz justifies the exercise (as in Charles Mingus's 'Revelations'). Quantitatively, these are hardly enough to encourage further negotiations, let alone regular summit meetings.

The problem was that until recently the possible development was seen inevitably as a collaboration from two different sides of a very real fence. In fact, more often than not, the catalyst was not a jazz player but a European-trained writer such as composer/conductor/critic Gunther Schuller (who coined the phrase 'third stream'). Since the late 1960s, however, the consolidation of avant-garde jazz has helped to remove any lingering sense of inferiority about the structural aspects of jazz, as compared to European composed music. Moreover, with so much contemporary European-style writing being elaborately worked out, only to end up sounding like totally random improvisation, the jazz world has taken cognizance of its own comparative superiority and spontaneity. Perhaps as a result, a more regular flow of music has started to appear (from writer/performers such as Anthony Braxton, Anthony Davis and James Newton) which fulfils the conditions of the elusive third stream but, perhaps fortunately in view of the rather risible reputation of the terminology, is not usually called by that name.

Latterly also, an attempt has been made by Ran Blake to broaden the definition of the term by incorporating fusions with other music, often of an ethnic nature; this still arises from an academic impulse, however, as opposed to the more spontaneous development of 'world music'. [BP]

Thomas, Joe (Joseph Lewis), trumpet. b. Webster Grove, Missouri, 24 July 1909; d. New York City, 6 August 1984. He played in territory bands in the late 1920s and early 1930s before moving to New York to work at Smalls' with Ferman Tapp's band. For the rest of the 1930s he worked with Fletcher Henderson, Benny Carter and others and throughout the 1940s mainly with small bands, recording prolifically and establishing a fine reputation with Teddy Wilson (1942–3), Barney Bigard (1943–5, in a John Kirby-ish small group), Cozy Cole (1948) and Bud Freeman (1949). In the 1950s he often led his own small groups, as well as working with Eddie Condon in 1964 and Claude Hopkins two years after. 'One of the most underrated trumpeters of the swing era,' says Leonard Feather, '[with] a fine tone and relaxed style'. [DF]

Thomas, Joe (Joseph Vankert), tenor sax, clarinet, vocals. b. Uniontown, Pennsylvania, 19 June 1909. He began his professional career on alto saxophone with Horace Henderson after time working as a waiter, but changed to tenor after joining Stuff Smith in Buffalo and it was there that Jimmie Lunceford heard and hired him. Working for his new employer improved Thomas's sense of discipline and so did his section leader Willie Smith, who did a lot to improve the young recruit's musicianship. 'Joe had a lot of personality,' says pianist/arranger Ed Wilcox, 'and a lot of tricks on the horn. He had a way of slopping over notes, too, instead of making all the notes in a run. Willie wouldn't settle for that kind of stuff and sitting beside a man like that Joe naturally got better!' 'His solos are always built up in a way which permits the maximum swing,' said Hugues Panassié, 'but are none the less melodious for that. He really makes his instrument sing: his playing is full of feeling and his tone very moving.' Thomas stayed with Lunceford as featured tenor soloist long after many of his co-stars had left over money disagreements, and after Lunceford's death in 1947 he took over the band with Wilcox for a further year. By the 1950s he had left music and gone back to Kansas City to run a business concern, but returned to play the Newport Jazz Festival, New York, in 1968 with Count Basie, stole the show, and thereafter took up regular playing and recording again. [DF]

The Complete Jimmie Lunceford, 1939–40, CBS (4 records, boxed set)

Thomas, Leone (Amos Leon Thomas, Jnr.), voice, lyricist, and miscellaneous percussion and bottle. b. East St Louis, Illinois, 4 October 1937. Studied music at Lincoln High School. 1959, he moved to New York, working in a show at the Apollo Theater with Dakota Staton, Ahmad Jamal, Art Blakey's Jazz Messengers and others. He also worked with Randy Weston and Mary Lou Williams. 1961, he replaced Joe Williams in the Count Basie orchestra, staying, except for a break for army service, until 1965. With Basie, he sang at the inaugural balls of Presidents Kennedy and Johnson. 1969–72, he worked with Pharoah Sanders, writing lyrics to several of Sanders's tunes. May 1970, Thomas worked as a single at Ronnie Scott's club, London, backed by Nucleus. In June he appeared at the Montreux festival, again with Nucleus. During the 1970s he led his own groups, played occasional gigs with Sanders, worked with Santana and others. He added the ultimate 'e' to Leon in 1976. 1985, he was with the Joe Henderson quintet, touring internationally and playing major festivals.

Thomas sings in the blues/soul/gospel tradition, but has brought his own style and flavour to it; he has perfected a form of yodelling or voice 'shaking' which he uses to great effect, he creates infectious rhythms by blowing in bottles, and he is also an accomplished scat singer. [IC]

With Basie, Mary Lou Williams, Rahsaan Roland Kirk, Oliver Nelson; with Sanders, *Izipho Zam* (1972), Strata-East; as leader, *Blues and the Soulful Truth* (1972), Flying Dutchman; *The Leon Thomas Album* (1975), Flying Dutchman

Thomas, René, guitar. b. Liège, Belgium, 25 February 1927; d. 3 January 1975. Active in Paris from early 1950s, playing with visiting American musicians. Then followed example of compatriot Bobby Jaspar and emigrated to New York, working with Toshiko Akiyoshi and Sonny Rollins groups (1958). Settled in Montreal for two years, recording under own name in New York (1960). Busy in Europe again from 1961, appearing with Jaspar in London (1962) and performing with Kenny Clarke and others. Member of Stan Getz quartet including organist Eddie Louiss (1969–71); later recorded trio album with Louiss and Clarke. Thomas's career, which was terminated by a heart attack, was sadly under-documented on record; but he was highly praised by both Rollins and Getz, and his fresh, unhurried lines amply justify their enthusiasm. [BP]

Jaspar/Thomas, *Live at Ronnie Scott's* (1962), Mole; Stan Getz, *Dynasty* (1971), Verve

Thompson, Barbara (Barbara Gracey Hiseman), alto, tenor and soprano sax, flutes. b. Oxford, 27 July 1944. Grandfather a pianist and grandmother a cellist. 1965–8, studied clarinet, flute, piano and composition at Royal College of Music, saxophones privately. She joined the New Jazz Orchestra in 1965, where she met her future husband, drummer Jon Hiseman. From 1969 she led various groups of her own, but also worked for composers and bandleaders John Dankworth, Mike Gibbs, Wolfgang Dauner, Don Rendell, Neil Ardley and Manfred Mann among others. As a soloist, she has been featured frequently on TV and radio in Germany, Belgium, France, Italy, Yugoslavia, Spain and Norway, and she represented the jazz saxophone at the Adolphe Sax Centenary celebrations in Brussels. 1975, she joined the United Jazz and Rock Ensemble, started her own fusion group, Paraphernalia, and has worked with both ever since.

She is a prolific composer and has written three long works for a 20-piece jazz orchestra which have been recorded by the BBC. She also composes for radio, film and TV.

The main creative outlet for her composing and playing is Paraphernalia, which Jon Hiseman joined in 1979, and which has toured extensively in the UK, East and West Germany, Austria, Holland, Belgium, Switzerland and Scandinavia. The group has also appeared at festivals all over Europe. Barbara Thompson has been the featured flute and saxophone player on several of Andrew Lloyd Webber's stage, TV and LP projects, including *Variations*, *Cats*, and *Requiem*. Favourites include John Coltrane, Eric Dolphy, Oliver Nelson, Roland Kirk, Johnny Hodges, Mike Brecker, Dave Sanborn, and her tastes in music are very wide, ranging from funk and new wave to classical and ethnic music. 1979, BBC-TV made an hour-long documentary film about Barbara and Jon Hiseman and their two children, *Jazz, Rock and Marriage*. This examined the problems of parents who are also itinerant musicians.

Barbara Thompson

The Hisemans turn down work ruthlessly in order to have set periods with their family but their 24-track recording studio, which they opened in 1982, enables them to continue functioning while off the road. [IC]

With Howard Riley, NJO, UJRE, Colosseum, Neil Ardley, Manfred Mann, Don Rendell, Lloyd Webber; Paraphernalia, *Paraphernalia* (1978), *Wilde Tales* (1979); *Live in Concert* (1980), all MCA; *Mother Earth* (1983), TM; Thompson/Rod Argent, *Ghosts* (1983), MCA; *Pure Fantasy* (1984), TM; *Shadowshow* (1984), TM

Thompson, Eddie (Edgar Charles), piano. b. Shoreditch, London, 31 May 1925; d. 6 November 1986. A product of the same school for the blind as George Shearing, Thompson soon impressed the British scene in the late 1940s, recording with Victor Feldman and appearing at the Paris Jazz Fair, 1949, with Carlo Krahmer band. Work in the 1950s with Tony Crombie, Ronnie Scott, Vic Ash, Freddy Randall, Tommy Whittle and own trio, including as house pianist at Ronnie Scott's (1959–60). Emigrated to USA (1962), performing mostly solo and working steadily until permanent return to UK (1972). Solo and trio engagements, including with many American musicians at Pizza Express etc., and duo work with Roger Kellaway led to further appearances together in New York (1985). An extremely entertaining if eclectic improviser, Thompson at one time seemed too gifted for his own good; the earlier effects of undisciplined solo performances were hinted at by the outspoken Ruby Braff, who said in 1976, 'The first time I heard him in New York, I didn't think he could play . . . He's improved like a thousand per cent.' [BP]

Memories of You (1983), Hep

Thompson, Lucky (Eli), tenor and soprano sax. b. Detroit, Michigan, 16 June 1924. First toured with Trenier Twins (early 1940s). Worked briefly in New York with several bands including Lionel Hampton's, Don Redman's (both 1943), Billy Eckstine's, Lucky Millinder's (both 1944). Joined Count Basie (1944–5), then settled on West Coast, recording separately with Gillespie and Parker (1946); played with Boyd Raeburn, co-operative band Stars of Swing as well as many others. Returning to Detroit (1947) and then New York (1948), led band at Savoy Ballroom and became involved in rhythm-and-blues recording and songwriting, set up own publishing company. More active in jazz from mid-1950s, making albums with Oscar Pettiford, Quincy Jones, Milt Jackson (1956–7). After a visit to France (1956), cutting several albums and deputizing on tour with Stan Kenton, he settled there for two periods (1957–62, 1968–71). Though he taught at Dartmouth University (1973–4), has been inactive in music since then.

Thompson was one of the earliest and most dedicated of the relatively few Don Byas disciples. But his softer tone, in the mid-1940s especially, made his work quite distinctive and more mellifluous than Byas's. Later, by the period of his longest European stay, his sound had become more aggressive, but his individual time-feeling still made him quite different from anyone else, and his premature retirement represented a considerable loss to the scene. [BP]

Lucky Thompson featuring Oscar Pettiford (1956), Jasmine; *Lucky Strikes!* (1963), Prestige/OJC

Thompson, Sir Charles (Charles Phillip), piano, organ, arranger, b. Springfield, Ohio, 21 March 1918. He made his name as a soloist in the 1940s when he worked for Coleman Hawkins (1944–5), Lucky Millinder and Illinois Jacquet, and wrote a hit tune, 'Robbins' Nest'. In the 1950s he produced a set of albums with his trio and with bands and also worked in the very best mainstream company (Jimmy Rushing, Buck Clayton and others), often for the Vanguard label. During that period – when he acquired a reputation for sounding uncannily like Count Basie if required – Thompson played solo and led his own trios on the West Coast, toured Europe with Buck Clayton in 1961, and through the 1960s was regularly around New York playing piano rooms, jazz clubs and bars, as well as touring in Canada, Puerto Rico and elsewhere. After a period of illness in the 1970s he was active again, touring Europe and working in London for Peter Boizot's Pizza Express chain. He is also a talented arranger who in his formative years worked for Basie, Henderson, Jimmy Dorsey and others. [DF]

Quartet (1954), Vanguard

See Dance, Stanley, *The World of Count Basie* (Sidgwick & Jackson, 1980)

Thornhill, Claude, piano, arranger. b. Terre Haute, Indiana, 10 August 1909; d. 1 July 1965. Studied at music conservatory, then played in territory bands before moving to New York (early 1930s). Worked for various popular bands, including briefly for Paul Whiteman and Benny Goodman (1934), played and arranged for Ray Noble's American band (1935–6). Prolific session work including with Billie Holiday, some as musical director, e.g. his arrangement of 'Loch Lomond' for Maxine Sullivan; also recorded under own name and toured with Sullivan (1937–8). Helped singer Skinnay Ennis form West Coast band by taking over Gil Evans group (1938). Thornhill then led own touring big band (1940–2, Evans joining him 1941); after navy service, re-formed band (1946) briefly containing Lee Konitz and Red Rodney and more highly valued by musicians than by the public. Effects of nervous breakdown and alcohol consumption slowed his career in 1950s, but he continued to play for dancing, usually leading small or medium-sized groups.

Though his band was never a fully committed jazz organization, Thornhill's long-term influence was beneficial in a way that was not true of the more flamboyant and more financially successful Stan Kenton. Even viewed as a dance band, Claude's outfit was subtle and intelligent, making a mere slow foxtrot such as his original theme-song 'Snowfall' into a moody tone-poem (his more humorous 'Portrait of a Guinea Farm' was also widely admired); adding two French horns in 1941 and having all six reedmen play clarinet, Thornhill created some remarkably spacey effects. In 1947–8, when Evans and Gerry Mulligan wrote some of the arrangements, the jazz-oriented instrumentals swung without shouting and hinted at a bebop equivalent of early Basie and Lester Young (without being directly influenced, as Woody Herman was), and it was these arrangements that inspired Miles Davis to have Evans and Mulligan create a 9-piece version of the same sound, known retrospectively as the Birth of the Cool band. But Thornhill was not just historically significant – the original performances of his band stand up in their own right and are still as fresh as the day they were recorded. [BP]

The Real Birth of the Cool (1942–7), CBS-Sony; *Claude Thornhill, 1948*, Hep

Threadgill, Henry Luther, saxes, woodwind, composer. b. Chicago, 15 February 1944. Studied at American Conservatory of Music, Governor's State University. First professional job travelling with gospel music, church musicians and evangelists, then played with blues bands. Joined Richard Abrams's Experimental Band in 1962–3 and became closely associated with AACM (see ABRAMS, MUHAL RICHARD); active since then in education as music instructor and choir director. In the 1970s, with Fred Hopkins (bass) and Steve McCall (dms), he formed the group Air which developed into one of the most distinguished offshoots (after the Art Ensemble of Chicago) of the AACM. With Air he has toured and played festivals world-wide. Threadgill's influences include Sonny Rollins, Ornette Coleman, Gene Ammons and Howlin' Wolf. [IC]

With Air, *Air Time* (1977), Nessa; *Open Air Suit* (1978); *Montreux Suisse* (1978); *Air Lore* (1979), all Arista Novus; *80° Below '82* (1982), Antilles; as leader, *X75, vol. 1* (1979), Arista Novus

Tilbrook, Adrian, drums, b. Hartlepool, Durham, 20 July 1948. Father played tenor sax and clarinet. Studied drums for two years with Max Abrams. 1974, joined Back Door, with Ron Aspery (saxes) and Colin Hodgkinson (bass gtr). The group toured Germany and the UK and spent two seasons at Ronnie Scott's club. 1975, Back Door played the Berlin festival and toured Europe with Alexis Korner. The band split up in late 1975. Tilbrook has always been active as a percussion teacher, and has also worked with Allan Holdsworth, Don Weller, Lockjaw Davis, Al Grey, Jimmy Forrest, James Moody, Kai Winding, Al Casey, Jimmy Witherspoon and Stan Tracey. 1984, formed a quartet, Full Circle, with trombonist Rick Taylor. Influences, Elvin Jones, Tony Williams, Dannie Richmond, Tony Oxley, Billy Higgins. Other inspirations, John Coltrane, Miles Davis, Charles Mingus. [IC]

With Back Door, *Activate* (1975), Warner Bros; with Full Circle, *Beauty of the Unexpected* (1986), Full Circle Records

Time (1) The time-signature or metre of a piece, as in '5/4 time', '6/8 time' or 'common time' (i.e. 4/4).

(2) The ability to play 'in time' to the nearest microsecond, as used in the phrase 'X has good time' or 'Kenny Clarke had perfect time'. Nothing shows up an inexperienced or rusty musician so much as having lousy time; out-of-tune may be acceptable on occasion, but losing the time, never. Just to complicate matters, it is possible for two musicians to have good time but to have a different 'time feel' from each other. In a big band this is not a problem, because individual players should defer to section leaders and play according to the leaders' time feel, not their own; but in a pick-up group, or in an ill-chosen rhythm-section, there are often irreconcilable conflicts, and the more 'all-star' sessions you attend, the more often you can witness these conflicts between the time feel of different contributors. [BP]

Timmons, Bobby (Robert Henry), piano, composer (and vibes). b. Philadelphia, 19 December 1935; d. 1 March 1974. After work in Philadelphia, he was employed from 1956 successively by Kenny Dorham, Chet Baker, Sonny Stitt, Maynard Ferguson. Came to fame with Art Blakey (1958–9, 1960–1) and with Cannonball Adderley (1959–60). Own trio and regular recording from 1961 until shortly before his death from cirrhosis of the liver. Initially very much under the influence of Bud Powell, Timmons became popular by adopting the mannerisms of Red Garland and the phraseology of gospel and blues piano (though in more mechanical fashion than either Ray Bryant or Junior Mance). In this way he begat players such as Les McCann and Ramsey Lewis, but he is less likely to be remembered for his playing than for his originals such as 'Dat Dere' (lyrics added by Oscar Brown Jnr.) and 'Moanin' '. [BP]

This Here is Bobby Timmons (1960), Riverside/OJC

Tio, Lorenzo (Jnr.), clarinet, tenor sax, arranger, oboe. b. New Orleans, 1884; d. New York City, 24 December 1933. Tio's legendary reputation as New Orleans' best clarinet teacher is often mentioned before his own busy musical activities. He taught practically all of the great classic jazz clarinettists: a short list would include Barney Bigard, Albert Nicholas, Jimmie Noone and Johnny Dodds. Tio and his family were the most popular teachers, too: encouraging, honest and ready to give a young pupil his creative head. 'They all played clarinets,' Barney Bigard recalls, 'the great-grandfather, the grandfather, an uncle and a nephew.' (He forgot Tio's father, Lorenzo Snr., a fine trained player.) 'Lorenzo and his uncle taught me almost all the rudiments of clarinet – they were straightforward people and very nice. If a guy came to take lessons from them and they didn't see any possibilities in him they'd tell him right off.' Tio worked in orchestras, small chamber groups as well as brass bands and clubs and regularly in New Orleans (with Papa Celestin) and Chicago (with Manuel Perez); his most notable leader was Armand J. Piron, with whose orchestra he graduated to New York in the 1920s, recorded 20 fine titles for Victor in 1921 and worked the Cotton Club and Roseland (where they were later replaced by Fletcher Henderson) as well as back in New Orleans. Tio was a respected bandleader on 52nd Street by 1935 (Sidney Bechet worked alongside him); he died that year and was buried back home. [DF]

New Orleans (1923–9), Collectors' Classics

Tippett(s), Keith, piano, composer. b. Bristol, Somerset, 25 August 1947. Brass band players in the family. He was a chorister, and also studied piano and church organ privately, cornet and tenor horn with Bristol Youth Band. 1967, received a scholarship to the Barry (Wales) Summer School Jazz Course, where he met cornettist Marc Charig, Elton Dean, and trombonist Nick Evans. He formed a sextet which, helped by an Arts Council bursary, did many broadcasts and played concerts and festivals throughout Britain and Europe. 1970, he formed a 50-piece orchestra, Centipede, with an amplified string section to play his two-hour composition *Septober Energy*. This ensemble, comprising leading musicians from classical, jazz and rock backgrounds, performed in Britain and at festivals in Europe. 1972, he formed a small group, Ovary Lodge, with his wife Julie, Frank Perry and Harry Miller, which featured total improvisation as opposed to the use of pre-composed structures. 1973–8, he played with Elton Dean's groups and various other ensembles led by Charig, Harry Miller, Louis Moholo and Trevor Watts. He also performed a series of duets with Stan Tracey. 1978, he composed *Frames – Music for an Imaginary Film* for the Ark, a 22-piece ensemble of international musicians. 1984, he toured Britain with his septet. Among his influences are Jaki Byard, Cecil Taylor and Bill Evans, and other inspirations are Miles Davis, Mingus and Charlie Parker.

Tippett is a brilliant pianist and a fine composer, and he is at ease in all contexts: he does concert tours of solo piano improvisations, he works in duos, trios, quartets and with his big ensemble, the Ark. [IC]

Duo with Stan Tracey, *T'N'T* (1974), Steam; *Ovary Lodge* (1975); as leader, *Frames* (1977); Tippett/Charig, *Pipedream* (1978), all Ogun; Tippett/Moholo, *No Gossip* (1980); solo, *Mujician* (1981); *Tern* (1983), all FMP; duo with Howard Riley, *In Focus* (1984), Affinity

Tizol, Juan (Vincente Martinez), valve-trombone, arranger, composer, b. San Juan, Puerto Rico, 22 January 1900; d. Inglewood, California, 23 April 1984. He came to the USA in 1920 to work at the Howard Theater, Washington, with Marie Lucas's South American-staffed orchestra and stayed for nine years. Then he joined Duke Ellington who had become – and remained for life – his close friend, providing Ellington with another challenging new tone colour. 'One of the reasons Pop liked Tizol coming into the band was that he would write for him along with the saxophones', remembers Mercer Ellington. 'On valve-trombone he could move more quickly than Tricky Sam on slide.' Tizol was never a strong soloist, but musically he was one of the best-trained in the orchestra and a gifted composer who, over the years, provided Ellington with highly useable themes including 'Caravan', 'Perdido', 'Conga Brava', 'Bakiff', 'Pyramid', 'Sphinx', 'Keb-lah' and 'Moonlight Fiesta'. He was one of the band characters: punctilious over times – 'He gets everywhere an hour early, rarin' to go', said Willie Smith – drank little, smoked not at all, but took a lunatic delight in practical jokes, until someone set off a loud firecracker under his chair one night. (Another version of the story says that itching powder was the means of revenge.) In 1944, Tizol, who was getting tired of travelling, joined Harry James (at his friend Willie Smith's invitation) for seven years, and for the rest of his career commuted between the two leaders (Ellington 1951–3, James 1953–60, Ellington 1960) before retiring to Los Angeles in 1960, then to Las Vegas. He recorded again with Louie Bellson in 1964 and lived happily for 20 years more. A later (unusual) example of his recorded work is Nat 'King' Cole's 1956 Capitol session *After Midnight*, which teams Tizol with Smiths Willie and Stuff, and Harry Edison in a small group. [DF]

With Ellington; Nat 'King' Cole and his trio, *After Midnight* (1956), EMI

See Dance, Stanley, *The World of Duke Ellington* (Scribner's, 1970, repr. Da Capo, 1980)

Todd, Phil (Philip Donald), soprano, alto and tenor sax; piccolo, flute, alto flute; clarinet, bass clarinet. b. Borehamwood, Hertfordshire, 6 August 1956. Two-year music course at Hitchin College, then three years at Trinity College of Music, London. 1973–7, with National Youth Jazz Orchestra; 1978–82, with Jeff Clyne's Turning Point; from 1982, with Nucleus. Todd has also worked as a freelance musician in rock, pop and jazz contexts, and he is much in demand in the studios. Influences are David Sanborn, Phil Woods, Mike Brecker, Wayne Shorter and Evan Parker, but Todd has already developed into one of the most gifted and original of the remarkable new generation of British players. [IC]

With Nucleus, *Live at the Theaterhaus* (1985), Mood; with Mike Westbrook, *The Cortege* (1982), Original

Tomkins, Trevor Ramsey, drums, percussion. b. London, 12 May 1941. Cousin, Roy Budd, pianist and composer; other cousins and uncles musical. At first self-taught, then studied at Blackheath Conservatory of Music and Guildhall School of Music and Drama. Started on trombone in later 1950s, 1958–9, got first drumkit. First professional work with Rendell–Carr quintet in 1963, staying with it until its demise in 1969. In the later 1960s he also worked with the New Jazz Orchestra. Has worked with many UK musicians, including Keith Tippett, John Taylor, Michael Garrick, Kenny Wheeler, Tony Coe, Mike Westbrook and Barbara Thompson, touring and playing festivals in the UK and Western Europe. He has worked many times at Ronnie Scott's club, often with Americans such as Phil Woods, Sonny Stitt, Pepper Adams and Art Farmer. 1985, he toured the UK as a member of the Lee Konitz quartet. His favourites include Roy Haynes, Elvin Jones, Jack DeJohnette, Philly Joe Jones, Mel Lewis, Harvey Mason, and particular inspirations are Bill Evans, Miles Davis, Kenny Wheeler and Tony Coe among others. Tomkins is a brilliant teacher and regularly conducts clinics and workshops at the Guildhall School and elsewhere. [IC]

With Garrick, Nucleus, Westbrook, Thompson and others; with Rendell–Carr, *Shades of Blue* (1964), EMI; *Dusk Fire* (1965), EMI; with Neil Ardley, *Kaleidoscope of Rainbows* (1976), Gull; with Tony Coe, *Zeitgeist* (1977), EMI; *Coe-Existence* (1978), Lee/Lambert; with Gilgamesh, *Another Fine Tune* (1978), Charly Records; with Pat Crumly sextet, *Third World Sketches* (1984), Spotlite

Tommaso, Giovanni, bass. b. Lucca, Italy, 20 January 1941. He had private music lessons and began playing in Lucca with his brother, a pianist. They formed a group called Quartetto di Lucca which was initially influenced by the Modern Jazz Quartet. It became something of an institution in Italy, lasting from 1957 to 1966. Tommaso moved to Rome in 1967 and worked with many leading musicians including Johnny Griffin, Sonny Rollins, Chet Baker, Barney Kessel. 1971, he formed a jazz-rock group called Perigeo, which made six albums and toured all over the world including the USA and Britain (two weeks at Ronnie Scott's club). Perigeo broke up in 1977 and Tommaso joined Enrico Rava's quartet, staying with it until 1984, when he formed his own quintet with Massimo Urbani on alto sax. 1962, he received the Coppa Del Jazz prize for the best Italian jazz group, and in 1974 and 1975 he was voted number one as musician and leader of the group Perigeo. His influences are Paul Chambers, Scott La Faro, Charlie Parker, Sonny Rollins, Thelonious Monk, Bill Evans, Miles Davis. Tommaso has also composed over 100 hours of soundtrack music for silent films. [IC]

With John Lewis, Lee Konitz, Conte Candoli, Frank Rosolino; with Enrico Rava, *String Band* (1984), Soul Note; with Quartetto di Lucca, *Quartetto* (1962); with Perigeo, *Azimut* (1972); *Genealogia* (1974), all RCA

Tonality The fact of being in a particular key at a given time, which applies to much the greater part of Western music including jazz – and to much non-Western music, although the performers may not think of it in that way. Music of this kind is therefore described as 'tonal' music by contrast with 'atonal' music. (NB: 'tonal' is also the adjective deriving from 'tone', and it is important to distinguish between the two uses.)

Reference to 'a tonality' is to a specific key-signature, and easily identifiable tonal music may nevertheless proceed from one tonality to another, or may change quite frequently; for example, the standard song 'All the Things You Are' passes through five keys in 24 bars but is quite clearly an example of tonality, not atonality. There is a certain area of post-1960 jazz material inspired by Coltrane's 'Giant Steps', where no one key is retained long enough to be heard as the main key-centre of the piece, but the music is still tonal in nature. This is because of the predominant position given to harmony ('changes') in setting the direction of the performance, whereas in 'polytonality' the role of harmony is weakened and in atonality it is negligible. [BP]

Tone One of the key resources in all eras and styles of jazz has been the variety of instrumental tones employed. It has also been consistently underrated by commentators and educators, perhaps because there is no handy way of describing a performer's tone except with some rather emotive adjectives, and they, of course, are frustratingly vague.

At best, the situation has been oversimplified by statements such as, 'The tone used by jazz instrumentalists differs markedly from the sound required in European composed music, because it imitates the vocal tones of blues and gospel singers.' This is only true of some players: others imitate the tones and rhythms of Afro-American speech patterns. Equally, some other jazz players do produce a relatively Europeanized tone, especially on certain instruments (compare, say, Bill Evans and Thelonious Monk, and decide which one sounds closer to the European 'ideal' tone and which one more like West Indian steel drums). Even this is too much of a generalization, for (as in the vocal comparisons) a jazz instrumentalist will change or distort his tone on certain notes (syllables) for expressive effect, which though common in European folk-music is forbidden in academic music.

Listeners, fortunately, tend to respond

directly and without premeditation to the tone produced by an instrumentalist (or vocalist), whether it is somewhat Europeanized or not. The chief outcome of the variations of tone allowable in jazz, and the related variations of articulation and inflection, is the extremely personal nature of each performer's tonal repertoire. Not only do players from different eras, such as Johnny Hodges, Charlie Parker, Ornette Coleman and David Sanborn, sound quite different from one another on the same instrument, but so do performers who are stylistically much closer, for instance Hodges and Willie Smith, or Lee Konitz and Paul Desmond. Any listener familiar with one player from these pairs would not long mistake them for the other player concerned.

Sceptics may object that Hodges and Smith (or Konitz and Desmond) are, after all, trying to be different from each other and that their choice of notes is what is mainly responsible for their being easily distinguished. And yet a player may find it plain sailing to remember and reproduce whole series of phrases once chosen by Parker or Coltrane, but be immediately recognizable as an imitator because of the impossibility of recapturing the exact instrumental tone. A proviso, though, should be added about records: while the varying fashions in studio sound seldom betray a player's tone too seriously, it is certainly possible for an inferior bootleg album of Parker or Coltrane to sound like one of their imitators rather than the real thing. [BP]

Tonolo, Pietro, tenor sax. b. Mirano (Venice), Italy, 30 May 1959. Piano lessons at seven and at ten he switched to violin, studying it for eight years. At 16 he took up the saxophone and taught himself to play it. He came to jazz through jazz-rock and in 1978 first played with a group, in which his brother played piano. Since 1982 he has often been a member of Enrico Rava's groups. Summer 1982, he toured with the Gil Evans orchestra. He has played many European festivals including Nice and Berlin, and has worked with many other leading Italian and international musicians. His influences range from Ben Webster and John Coltrane to Thelonious Monk, Ornette Coleman and Miles Davis. [IC]

With Enrico Rava, *Andanada* (1983), Soul Note

Tormé, Mel(vin Howard), singer (and drums, piano). b. Chicago, 13 September 1925. Early involvement in showbusiness, singing on radio at age four and acting on radio from age nine. Began songwriting at 15 (enjoying considerable success over the years), and toured as vocalist with Chico Marx band (1942–3). Formed own vocal group, the Mel-Tones, recording under own name and with Artie Shaw (1945–6). After period of solo hit records, became in 1950s night-club attraction, singing and playing with a jazz slant. He has since shared billing with many famous big bands including Buddy Rich and, alone among jazz-inclined singers, has scored all his own arrangements for the last 15 years. In many ways the Mark Murphy of an earlier generation, Tormé has a light and airy tone and an almost instrumental precision which blended especially well with the West Coast-type backings of Marty Paich. [BP]

Lulu's Back in Town (1956), Affinity

Tough, Dave (David Jarvis), drums. b. Oak Park, Illinois, 26 April 1908; d. Newark, New Jersey, 6 December 1948. He was an associate of the Austin High School Gang in Chicago, and the son of a well-to-do Oak Park physician. An intellectual, who read widely and thought intensely about every aspect of life, Tough very early on showed signs of an uncomfortable brilliance in everything he set his hand to, including playing the drums. When not instilling his young friends with a good sense of time and dynamics ('We all got some of that bite from Dave', says Max Kaminsky), Tough was spearheading the Chicagoan campaign against bad commercial music: one night in Chicago he walked off the stand after eight bars with B. A. Rolfe's showband, shaking in anger. He was never slow to make his opinions public. All through the 1920s he was busy in Chicago, New York and Europe (with George Carhart's band) but in 1936, after at least one serious illness, he moved permanently to New York to work with a string of great bands such as Tommy Dorsey's, Benny Goodman's, Bunny Berigan's, the Summa Cum Laude, and from 1941 Artie Shaw's navy band. By that time Tough – a gaunt, hollow-cheeked man who in khaki fatigues (said Kaminsky) was 'a sight to make the blood run cold!' – was recognized as a drummer to set alongside Sid Catlett and ahead of Gene Krupa: a perfectly technical timekeeper and spectacular soloist capable of working in any musical surroundings. When he joined Woody Herman's shouting modern jazz big band in 1944, however, Tough the intellectual found himself pulled apart by jazz fashion, and instead of being able (like Sid Catlett) to weather the verbal rivalries between warring jazz schools by just going along with both, he nearly cracked up, suffered fits while with Herman and on one occasion went into print condemning George Brunis and Wild Bill Davison respectively as 'a clown and a musical gauleiter'. Unusually tense involvement with what now seems of little importance was Tough's great problem; the problems helped to make him ill again, and sometimes – for whatever reason – he would cry on the stand. In 1948, just after completing a residency with Muggsy Spanier, Tough (an outpatient at New Jersey Veterans Hospital) fell and fractured his skull after drinking. But he is still often cited as one of swing's greatest drummers. [DF]

Bud Freeman, *Chicagoans in New York* (1935–40), Dawn Club

Towner, Ralph N., 12-string and classical guitars, piano, synthesizer, French horn, composer. b. Chehalis, Washington, 1 March 1940. Mother a pianist and church organist; father played trumpet. From age three he improvised on the piano, and began on trumpet at five. 1958–63, studied theory and composition at University of Oregon; did post-graduate work, 1964–6. Studied classical guitar at Vienna Academy of Music, 1963–4, 1967–8. Played trumpet in a dance band at 13, later played piano in jazz clubs, while studying music; also lute and guitar with classical chamber groups, 1964–6. Replaced Larry Coryell in a Seattle band in 1966. Moved to New York in 1969, working with Jimmy Garrison, 1969–70, Jeremy Steig, 1969–71, Paul Winter's Winter Consort, 1970–1, Weather Report, 1971, Gary Burton, 1974–5. In 1971, Towner and three others (Collin Walcott, Glen Moore and Paul McCandless) broke away from Winter Consort to form Oregon, which was to become one of the key groups of the 1970s and 1980s. At first Towner composed much of the group's material, but once their identity and scope became clear, the others began to write more, and the band also featured some collective compositions. Oregon extended the whole idea of chamber-group jazz by assimilating elements and techniques from folk and ethnic music and classical music both ancient and modern. It toured extensively and played major festivals in Europe and the USA. After Walcott died in a road accident in 1984, the group re-formed in 1985 with Indian percussionist Trilok Gurtu.

In the later 1970s and the 1980s Towner also toured and recorded in duo with fellow-guitarist John Abercrombie, and this association has produced some exceptionally fine music. Towner is a composer with a recognizable style involving keyboard or guitar ostinati, resonant harmonies, lovely moving bass lines, and often an organ- or hymn-like sonority in his melodies. His work is always evocative and permeated with gentle human feeling; good examples are 'Icarus', 'The Rapids' and 'The Juggler's Etude'. His playing and his composing are all of a piece, homogeneous and complete. He told Joachim Berendt: 'I wasn't on the jazz scene until I got a classically oriented technique on guitar . . . I do find acoustic instruments more sympathetic than electric instruments . . . I treat the guitar quite often like a piano trio. If I'm playing alone, it's almost like a one-man-band approach.' [IC]

With Weather Report, *I Sing the Body Electric* (1972), CBS; as leader, *Trios/Solos* (1972); *Diary* (1973); *Solstice* (1974); *Old Friends, New Friends* (1979); Towner/Abercrombie, *Five Years Later* (1982); with Oregon, *Oregon* (1983), all ECM

Tracey, Clark, drums. b. London, 5 February 1961. Played informally with his father Stan Tracey (see below) and studied drums with Bryan Spring. Began working regularly with Stan's various groups as early as 1978, and gradually matured into a forthright and exciting rhythm-section player. Also undertook frequent work with saxist Mike Mower and pianist Tony Lee, and backed (among others) Buddy DeFranco, James Moody, Charlie Rouse, Sal Nistico, Art Farmer, Red Rodney and Benny Waters. Since 1984 has led his own quintet, including experienced young trumpeter Guy Barker, dynamic alto newcomer Jamie Talbot, pianist/composer Steve Melling, and bassist Alec Dankworth (another son of a famous father, but chosen for his musical compatibility). From starting out as a raw and relatively unskilled sideman, Clark has now moved front-and-centre, taking care of business both literally and musically. [BP]

Suddenly Last Tuesday (1986), Cadillac

Tracey, Stan(ley William), piano, composer, arranger (and vibes, accordion). b. Tooting, London, 30 December 1926. Professional musician at age 16. Jazz work in 1950s with Eddie Thompson (on accordion), Kenny Baker, Tony Crombie, Ronnie Scott, Basil Kirchin, also nearly two years with Ted Heath (1957–9). House pianist at Ronnie Scott's club, 1960–7, backing soloists such as Zoot Sims and Ben Webster (with both of whom he recorded), Sonny Rollins (cutting the *Alfie* film soundtrack with him, 1966) and many others. Formed own quartet *c.* 1964, first with saxist Bobby Wellins, then Peter King, Trevor Watts, and since 1974 Art Themen. Has also appeared and recorded in solo, duo (with Mike Osborne, John Surman or Tony Coe), trio, sextet, octet, tentet and big band. 1986, he was awarded the OBE in recognition of his services to British jazz.

Although international recognition was slow in coming, many US players such as Rollins spoke extremely highly of Tracey. In the last ten years, he has often visited continental Europe and is regarded as one of the most original of British musicians. Inspired by Ellington and Monk in that order, he soon created an idiosyncratic solo style which is instantly recognizable. This also translates into a very stimulating accompanimental approach (but only for those soloists who relish being stimulated). Equally interesting on standard material and original compositions, Tracey prefers the latter and, while his arranging for larger bands is less individual (occasionally recalling Gerald Wilson or Thad Jones), it mirrors his piano work in its pungent dynamism. [BP]

Under Milk Wood (1965); *Stan Tracey Now* (1983), both Steam; *Plays Duke Ellington* (1986), Mole Jazz

Trad An abbreviation of 'traditional jazz' and a curtailment of most of its essential virtues. This peculiarly European form of deviant Dixieland was mainly influenced by British bands, though it might be said to include the more commercial

Stan Tracey

side of the Dutch Swing College Band and several French and German groups.

The negative side of Trad was that, after the popular success of 'skiffle', there were a few hit-parade singles by such as Chris Barber, Kenny Ball and Acker Bilk (which made the charts in both the UK and the US). As a result the music industry took notice and signed up all the potentially money-making groups, and the gigs which they had been filling were immediately taken over by decidedly inferior musicians all hoping to reach the big time. Nothing like it had happened in the jazz world since the height of the swing era.

The positive side was that some of the leading musicians of the movement, by dint of constant work, eventually evolved from the tightlipped Europeanized sound of early Trad to something more like the relaxation of the real thing. And, perhaps inevitably because of its all-pervading presence, several young players came up through Trad who went on to quite other things, such as Ginger Baker, Jack Bruce, Klaus Doldinger, Ron Mathewson and Roy Williams. [BP]

Transcription (1) In the media, a transcription recording is one made specifically for a radio station and then copied for other member stations of the same network. The peak period of their use was the 1930s and 1940s (although such transcription services still exist today) and the material from that period has more recently provided many recordings that are now available publicly. It has to be said that, depending on the demands of the radio stations originally involved, the performances are often less jazz-oriented than the same band's commercial records of the same time, but they can offer insights into their repertoire that would otherwise be lost.

(2) The practice of arranging a composition for different instruments, e.g. a Joplin or Beiderbecke piano solo as played by a band, or an Ellington or other big-band work scaled down for a small group. Of limited application in a jazz context.

(3) The act of copying down a solo previously improvised either by the transcriber or (more likely) by someone better. These too may be used for group performance – again of limited application but for different reasons, since the original nuances of timing, tone and articulation are all ironed out in such a performance, while the linear and harmonic aspects assume an exaggerated importance. Many solo transcriptions, however, have been published with a view to private study, and may have greater value if used intelligently. Some of the greatest jazz soloists, at least from the second generation onwards, have made their own transcriptions from records as a learning process; but, since the main benefit lies in training the ears rather than the fingers, some have simply learned recorded solos directly on their instruments, thus eliminating the tedious task of writing them down. [BP]

Trent, Alphonso E., piano, leader. b. Fort Smith, Arkansas, 24 August 1905; d. 14 October 1959. Probably the most famous 'territory band' of all, Trent's orchestra featured stars such as Snub Mosley, Peanuts Holland, and drummer A. C. Godley – who may have been the first drum soloist/showman ever. Based in the deep South in the 1920s, Trent later played around Texas (his was the first black orchestra to play large hotels like the Adolphus in Dallas for long periods), broadcast over Radio WFAA, Dallas, and by that time was featuring such budding stars as Sy Oliver (tpt/arranging) and frontman Stuff Smith (vln/vocals). Occasionally Trent came in for patronizing publicity in those deep South states but he was successful enough to organize at least one other orchestra – TNT2 – which travelled the circuit simultaneously. A few records for Gennett, 1928–33, show something of Trent's orchestra's power. [DF]

Tristano, Lennie (Leonard Joseph), piano, composer. b. Chicago, 19 March 1919; d. 18 November 1978. Blind from childhood, learned piano at age four and later studied saxophone, clarinet and cello. B.Mus. from American Conservatory in Chicago. Worked in home town on various commercial gigs (sometimes on tenor) while perfecting own piano style. After moving to New York (1946), formed own trio with Billy Bauer and a succession of bassists; later expanded to sextet (1949–52) by addition of various drummers and saxists Lee Konitz and Warne Marsh. Both the last-named studied with Tristano when he began formal teaching (1951), and one or other was usually in attendance on his rare returns to night-club playing (1955, 1958–9, 1964, 1966). Appeared as soloist at Berlin festival (1965) and Harrogate festival (1968), but otherwise restricted activity to teaching.

His educational methods, which give primacy to developing the ear rather than sheer mechanical ability, have been influential through the teaching of his own students such as Konitz and Peter Ind (though, sadly, nowhere near as influential as the kind of big-band apprenticeship that passes for education in most institutions). He was also the first person on record who occasionally persuaded a group of players (the 1949 sextet) to improvise simultaneously without any pre-set limits as to key or duration, and to do so in public rather than merely in a studio. Not surprisingly, this was not the inspiration for the blues-derived 'free jazz' which Ornette Coleman and Cecil Taylor introduced in the late 1950s. Tristano may have indirectly encouraged the flirtation with modern European composers that led to 'third stream', thanks to the work of temporary Tristano followers Teo Macero, John LaPorta and Charles Mingus; his attempts to make improvisation less predictable and more open-ended certainly influenced European jazz players such as Albert Mangelsdorff and Martial Solal, as well as the 1960 'Blue Note school' including early Wayne Shorter and early Herbie Hancock.

Tristano's long-term influence on jazz piano has been considerable, not so much because of direct disciples like Sal Mosca and Connie Crothers, but through the clear effect he had on the much-imitated Bill Evans. But, unlike the romantic Evans, Tristano aspired to a pure, dispassionate piano sound (even recording one of his most down-to-earth improvisations, 'Requiem', at half-speed so that, when played back, it would have an other-worldly ring to it); he argued equally that his saxophonists should use a flat, uninflected tone so that their lines would stand or fall on the quality of their construction and not on emotional colouration. In doing so, his own playing moved away from the virtuosity of his earliest private recordings, which show fleetingly his roots in Earl Hines and Art Tatum (a progression that parallels Thelonious Monk's withdrawal from the Teddy Wilson style). Instead, he developed a unique approach which strikes many listeners as too cold for comfort, but has proved endlessly fascinating for others. [BP]

Earl Swope, *The Lost Session* (1945–6), Phontastic; *Crosscurrents* (1949), Capitol; *Lines* (1955), Atlantic; *The New Lennie Tristano* (1962), Atlantic

Trumbauer, Frankie, C-melody sax, multi-instrumentalist, vocals. b. Carbondale, Illinois, 30 May 1901; d. Kansas City, Missouri, 11 June 1956. The most brilliantly able white saxophonist of the 1920s, his influence (like Miff Mole's) was incalculable for black and white jazzmen alike. 'He was the baddest cat back in those days,' says Budd Johnson, summing up for his generation, 'and everybody was trying to play his stuff. He was boss of the alto like Hawk was boss of the tenor.' Trumbauer – 'Tram' for short – was spotted early on with the Benson Orchestra of Chicago (by Bix Beiderbecke among others) and soon the two of them were working for Jean Goldkette's orchestra, where Trumbauer confidently took on the job of musical director and produced super-technical light-toned solos to order ('To say the band was a killer would be putting it mildly', he recalled later). In these years Trumbauer and Bix recorded the greatest white jazz of its period in total harmony ('Singin' the Blues' is only one of many immortal titles) and by 1927 the friends were together again in Paul Whiteman's orchestra. 'Trumbauer was a sensation with Whiteman', recalls Earl Hines, and Buddy Tate also remembers him at the period: 'The first time I ever spoke to him he said, "Practise! You don't get this overnight!" ' Trumbauer flew his own plane to jobs, and Tate remembers, 'One night they were opening at some big hotel in St Louis. On the way his plane developed engine trouble and it ended up falling on the hotel they were to play!' Trumbauer worked for Whiteman 1927–32 and 1933–6, in 1936 he co-led the Three Ts (featuring the Teagarden brothers) and in 1938 co-led a band with Manny Klein. During and after the war, working for the Civil Aeronautics Authority, he still found time for music, working with Russ Case and in New York studios from 1945 and producing records of his own, but little more was heard from this giant in the modern-jazz crazy 1950s. Benny Carter, another master, reminds us how great Trumbauer was: 'My original influence was Frank Trumbauer. *I don't think I ever had his facility*. He was a great technician – but he wasn't an exhibitionist.' [DF]

Bix and Tram, 1927, EMI

Turner, 'Big' Joe (Joseph), vocals. b. Kansas City, Missouri, 18 May 1911; d. Inglewood, California, 23 November 1985. By the time he was 14 he was singing in the Kingfisher Club, Kansas City, while he worked behind the bar: there he met pianist Pete Johnson and the two of them worked together regularly through the 1940s, usually on the West Coast, where in 1945 they opened their own Blue Room club in Los Angeles. Turner's voice – rough, raw, often singing sexually direct lyrics – was one of the very first authentic rock and roll phenomena, and for a time in the 1950s he looked like becoming a rock star; but his approach was, simply, too black, too direct and too forceful for a white-dominated commercial music scene, and despite hit records on the Atlantic label, including 'Chains of Love' and 'Shake Rattle and Roll',

'Big' Joe Turner

he never made a permanent crossover. (He was also rather too old: 'Imagine Joe, six feet two and weighing 250lbs, belting out "Trendsetter" at 46', says Nick Kimberley.) Also in the 1950s Turner regularly re-identified himself with his jazz roots (not a wise move for a pop star then) and albums such as the classic *Boss of the Blues*, featuring Pete Brown, Lawrence Brown and Pete Johnson, clearly proved that he was a jazzman at heart. In the 1960s he moved back to New Orleans, but visited Britain in 1965 to tour with Humphrey Lyttelton: Lyttelton's account of the tour (including Turner's preference for the key of C and occasional liability to set fire to hotel rooms) in *Take It From the Top* is a revealing – and loving – portrait. Throughout the 1970s Big Joe sang for festivals, and signed a contract with Norman Granz's Pablo label which featured him in every context from jazz bands to down-home r & b bands. Just occasionally Turner sounded tired, and in 1981 he was hospitalized in Los Angeles with pneumonia and blood clots: by the year after, however, on crutches, he was back, playing Tramps' Room in New York City and singing (said Lee Jeske) in 'a voice so rich and clear and strong the walls shake, the plates rattle and the tables roll'. In 1985, Joe Turner sometimes appeared with kindred spirit Jimmy Witherspoon. [DF]

The Boss of the Blues (1956), Atlantic Jazzlore

Turner, Bruce, alto sax, clarinet, composer, leader. b. Saltburn, Yorkshire, 5 July 1922. He worked for Freddy Randall playing clarinet (he is, quietly, a world-class clarinettist), took advice from Lennie Tristano and lessons from Lee Konitz in New York and in 1953 joined Humphrey Lyttelton (the moment is encapsulated in a banner raised by defiant Birmingham traditionalists at the time reading 'Go home, dirty bopper!': 30 years on, a similar banner was ceremoniously re-waved by promoter Jim Simpson at a Birmingham jam session). Turner worked with Lyttelton until 1957 when he formed his first Jump Band, which broadcast, recorded, made a film, *Living Jazz*, for producer Alan Lovell in 1961, and toured the circuit, occasionally to hostile receptions from promoters who expected commercial traditional fare. But the band's music had a strong identity of its own, was often gorgeously arranged, and continually drew on the very best, most ambitious repertoire from the late 1930s swing era. Turner carried on with his band until 1966 – by which time they had toured with Americans such as Ben Webster, Bill Coleman, Don Byas and Ray Nance – when he decided to rest from bandleading and joined a kindred spirit, Acker Bilk: the records they made together (such as *Expo 70*, also featuring the dynamic Colin Smith) are a logical extension of Turner's own musical ideas, and immensely good. In 1970, Turner rejoined Humphrey Lyttelton, always his closest ally and best publicist, and 15 years on was still working regularly with Lyttelton's band. In 1984 he produced a gently-written, thoughtful autobiography which – much at odds with Turner's eccentric, cream-cake-loving *persona* – was a fascinating key to the real Bruce, stripped of his enjoyable eccentricities. Turner is one of British mainstream jazz's greatest and best-loved figures. A highly eclectic alto-saxophonist, he moves almost as easily into avant-garde situations (such as Dave Green's Fingers group from 1979) as he does into Dixieland. [DF]

The Dirty Bopper (1985), Calligraph

See Turner, Bruce, *Hot Air, Cool Music* (Quartet, 1984)

Turner, Joe (Joseph H.), piano, vocals. b. Baltimore, Maryland, 3 November 1907. A fine pianist-singer (not to be confused with blues singer Big Joe Turner, above) who worked steadily around New York in the 1920s, and in the 1930s was accompanist to Adelaide Hall. During the latter decade he spent much time in Europe and after the war (when he came back to the USA and served in the army) moved back to Hungary, then to Switzerland and at last to Paris. Most of his activities have been European-based since then: in the 1980s he has once again started recording for American labels and appearing in his home country. [DF]

Swing Sessions, vol. 1, 1937–9, Pathé

Turrentine, Stanley William, tenor sax. b. Pittsburgh, Pennsylvania, 5 April 1934. Father, Thomas Turrentine, played tenor with the Savoy Sultans in late 1930s. Stanley began on cello, took up tenor at age 11. Toured with Lowell Fulson (1950–1, including recording with band pianist Ray Charles), Tadd Dameron (1952), and, alongside trumpeter Tommy Turrentine Jnr. (b. 22 April 1928), with Earl Bostic (1953–4). After Stanley's three years in the army, both brothers in Max Roach quintet (1959–60). During this period, first albums under Stanley's own name; also recording partnership with Jimmy Smith, and touring with Shirley Scott, to whom he was married until 1971. Most albums since then in heavily arranged pop style, which met with great chart success, until reunion with Smith (1982) and own small-group recording with Smith, Les McCann, George Benson (1984). Turrentine's wide-open bluesy sound and terse phrasing made him a natural in the role of the 'Gene Ammons of the 1970s', but this has not detracted from his ability as a jazz player. [BP]

Straight Ahead (1984), Blue Note

Twardzik, Dick (Richard), piano, composer. b. Danvers, Massachusetts, 30 April 1931; d. 21 October 1955. Work in the Boston area including recordings with Charlie Mariano and Serge Chaloff, with whose mother he first studied piano. On tour with Lionel Hampton, then in the last months of his life with Chet Baker quartet; was in Paris with him when he died of a heroin overdose. As well as writing original material for Chaloff ('The Fable of Mabel') and Baker, Twardzik recorded one set of piano pieces of a notably individual character. Related to the Monk 'school' of pianist-writers but also reminiscent of Boston influence Jaki Byard, Twardzik's minimal output deserves rediscovery. [BP]

The Last Set (1954), Pacific Jazz

Two-beat A description of the rhythmic feel created by emphasizing the first and third beats of a 4/4 metre. Originally this was the usual feel prescribed for the European-style marches which went into the early New Orleans repertoire, and it was the feel borrowed for the strongly European-influenced compositions of early ragtime.

As the more even marking of all four beats became the norm, thanks to the example of the mature New Orleans style, the occasional continued use of a two-beat feel by some bassists in the late 1920s and early 1930s created pleasant polyrhythmic tensions, soon to be superseded by more complex factors in the work of the Count Basie band. Since the two-beat idea was then only associated with Dixieland bands seeking a deliberately antique style, the description 'two-beat' became a term of abuse used by those who found it quaint and stilted.

But a good idea is hard to keep down. Already it had found a musical welcome in the Jimmie Lunceford band, and it often proved a highly

McCoy Tyner

suitable accompaniment to the complex simplicity of Erroll Garner. Both of these had imitators who reduced it to a one-dimensional 'businessmen's bounce', but Garner's follower Ahmad Jamal inspired the 1950s Miles Davis quintet to rehabilitate the idea so successfully that it is still part of the standard rhythm-section arsenal to be able to play 'in two'. [BP]

Tyner, McCoy Alfred (Sulaimon Saud), piano, composer. b. Philadelphia, 11 December 1938. Mother, a pianist, encouraged him. His main early influences were the Powell brothers – Bud and Richie – who were neighbours. At 15, Tyner was leading his own teenage jazz group, and soon began gigging with local groups around Philadelphia. He first met John Coltrane there, working with him at the Red Rooster. 1959, Tyner spent six months with the Jazztet, which was co-led by Art Farmer and Benny Golson; 1960–5, he worked with the John Coltrane quartet, touring in the USA and world-wide and recording intensively. This was perhaps the most influential quartet in jazz history, and Tyner played a major role in its artistic success. After leaving Coltrane, he led his own trio in New York from 1966; also worked with Ike and Tina Turner, Jimmy Witherspoon, and others. He began recording for Blue Note, and his album *The Real McCoy*, with Joe Henderson, Ron Carter and Elvin Jones, is one of the loveliest LPs of the late 1960s.

From 1972, when he signed with Milestone Records and his album *Sahara* was voted record of the year by the *Downbeat* critics, Tyner began to tour regularly with his group in the USA, Europe and Japan. For the most part he led a quartet, with Sonny Fortune at first and then Azar Lawrence on reeds, but in the later 1970s he augmented the group with violinist John Blake. 1973, his double LP *Enlightenment*, recorded live at Montreux, with Lawrence, Alphonze Mouzon and Joony Booth (bass), won the Montreux Jury's Diamond Prize as record of the year. Tyner continued to tour and record throughout the 1970s and into the 1980s, his international reputation growing steadily until he became one of the most universally revered musicians in jazz. 1978, he took some time off from his own group to do an all-star tour with Sonny Rollins, Ron Carter and Al Foster. When Blue Note was relaunched in 1985, Tyner was filmed recording a solo piano album for a documentary about the label.

Tyner's main influences, apart from the Powell brothers (particularly Richie Powell) were Thelonious Monk and Art Tatum, but with the Coltrane quartet he rapidly established his own identity, developing one of the most original piano styles in jazz. Coltrane said of him: 'He gets a very personal *sound* from his instrument; and because of the clusters he uses and the way he voices them, that sound is brighter than what would normally be expected from most of the chord patterns he plays. In addition, McCoy has an exceptionally well developed sense of form, both as a soloist and an accompanist. Invariably in our group, he will take a tune and build his own structure for it.' In fact, Tyner has always played compositionally, with an overall view of the music and an unerring instinct for when to improvise uninhibitedly and when to play 'within the rhythm-section' in support of a soloist or to enhance a rhythmic pulse. Because of this, his music, no matter how wild, always 'breathes' properly, creating and releasing tension in a way which communicates to audiences. He is one of the most dynamic pianists of all, with awesome power and speed, yet he rarely 'goes free', preferring to play within tonalities and coherent rhythms which he pushes, with miraculous control, to their limits. His great love is acoustic piano (of which he has said, 'After a while it becomes an extension of yourself, and you and your instrument become one'); and he does not use electronics because his concept is more to do with the exploration of acoustic piano, lines and rhythms than with the exploration of texture for its own sake. Talking to J. E. Berendt, Tyner said that for him, all music is 'a journey of the soul into new, uncharted territory . . . I try to listen to music from many different countries: Africa, India, from the Arabic world, European classical music . . . all kinds of music are interconnected.' His music is an affirmation, an exultation in being alive. He is also a composer with tremendous melodic and rhythmic flair; some of his best-known pieces are 'Passion Dance', 'Contemplation', 'Blues on the Corner', 'Land of the Lonely', 'Celestial Chant', 'Enlightenment Suite', 'Desert Cry'. [IC]

With Coltrane and others; *Nights of Ballads and Blues* (1963), Jasmine; *The Real McCoy* (1967), Blue Note; *Sahara* (1972); *Enlightenment* (1973) (double); anthology, *Reflections* (1972–5), all Milestone

U

Ulmer, James 'Blood', guitar, flute, voice. b. St Matthews, South Carolina, 2 February 1942. He sang with a gospel group, the Southern Sons, from age seven until 13, and played guitar from an early age. 1959, moved to Pittsburgh freelancing professionally, and his outlook was broadened by local guitarist Chuck Edwards. 1964–6, he worked extensively with organ funk groups. 1967–71, in Detroit he studied, wrote music and practised regularly for four years with a group that included drums, bass, trombone and alto sax. 1971, he went to New York, playing six nights a week for nine months at Minton's Playhouse. He played briefly with Art Blakey, 1973, and also worked with Paul Bley, Larry Young and Joe Henderson. He met Ornette Coleman and studied with him for a year, and in 1974 they performed at the Ann Arbor Jazz and Blues Festival. 1977, he played with Coleman's group at the Newport Jazz Festival, and in 1978 recorded as a leader (*Tales of Captain Black*) with Coleman as sideman. During the late 1970s he continued to tour with Coleman, playing at major festivals and visiting the UK and Europe. In 1979 and 1980 he also played on two of Arthur Blythe's albums. 1980, he began working regularly with his own trio, making his first European tour in that year.

Ulmer is not really an innovator or a revolutionary player, but he has his own distinctive sound and approach. In fact he comes out of the long-established tradition of electric blues guitar playing with all its tonal distortions, its modally-based improvisations and its pitch-bending, which is often so extreme as to imply non-tonality. Ulmer's music is often dissonant and always strongly rhythmic – a kind of abstract funk – and his real identity lies in the emotional climate he projects; playing with an often dry, choked sound, he conveys a claustrophobic feeling of pent-up emotion fighting for expression. [IC]

With Larry Young, John Patton, Joe Henderson; *Tales of Captain Black* (1978), Artists House; *Are You Glad To Be In America?* (1980), Rough Trade; with Arthur Blythe, *Lenox Avenue Breakdown* (1979), CBS; *Illusions* (1980), CBS

United Jazz and Rock Ensemble Formed 1975 in Stuttgart, West Germany, by Wolfgang Dauner, to be the resident band of a young people's TV programme directed by Werner Schretzmeier, whose aim was to promote social and political awareness. In this programme he also presented little-known, talented singer/songwriters, as well as the band of leading jazz and rock musicians, hoping that such media exposure of two minority interests might bring them to a wider public. The programme became popular and the band rapidly gained a following. When it began touring and playing live concerts (January 1977), the personnel became fixed: Dauner (keyboards), Eberhard Weber (bass), Volker Kriegel (gtr), Jon Hiseman (dms), Albert Mangelsdorff (tmb), Charlie Mariano and Barbara Thompson (reeds and flutes), Ack Van Rooyen and Ian Carr (tpts); Kenny Wheeler (tpt) joined in 1979.

During the later 1970s and the 1980s, the UJRE toured widely in Germany and played major festivals all over Europe, including Sopot and Warsaw in Poland, the North Sea Festival and Antibes. 1984, it toured the UK and one reviewer wrote of '. . . that international 10-piece band which is so enjoyable to listen to that the serious [British] critics don't like it.'

1977, Dauner, Kriegel, Mangelsdorff, Van Rooyen and Schretzmeier formed Mood Records to release albums by the band, and by the mid-1980s more than 150,000 had been sold. In the autumn of 1985 a boxed set of the band's six LPs became a best-seller in West Germany. Writing in *Downbeat* in the later 1970s, J. E. Berendt called the UJRE 'the most successful European band since Django Reinhardt'. [IC]

Live im Schützenhaus (1977); *Teamwork* (1978); *The Break-Even Point* (1979); *Live in Berlin* (1981, double); *Opus Sechs* (1984), all Mood

Up (1) A fast tempo. Related to the same image as the use of the word 'uppers' in connection with amphetamines (another jazz expression that has gone into everyday language), though whether they help up-tempo playing is another matter entirely.

(2) The up-beat is the 2nd beat of a piece (and the 4th, 6th, 8th etc. if the time-signature is 2/2 or 4/4 – in 3/4 or 6/4, the up-beat is the 2nd, 5th, 8th, 11th etc.). Contrary to European musical practice, the up-beat in jazz is often felt to be stronger than the down-beat, hence the use of 'up-beat' as an adjective to mean affirmative or resilient. [BP]

Urbaniak, Michal, violin, lyricon, composer, and soprano and tenor sax. b. Warsaw, 22 January 1943. Studied at Academy of Music in Warsaw. He worked with various Polish groups in the early 1960s; 1965, formed his own group which included singer Urszula Dudziak, whom he later married. They toured throughout Europe and Scandinavia during the 1960s. 1969–72, they played festivals in Warsaw, Molde (Norway) and in France and Italy. He and Dudziak went to live in the USA in 1973. He formed a new jazz-rock group, Michal Urbaniak Fusion, which toured in the US and recorded for Columbia. He plays a custom-made five-string violin and violin synthesizer, and also the lyricon – a saxophone-like wind instrument, the sound of which is treated through a synthesizer. Urbaniak's favourites include John Coltrane, Miles Davis, Zbigniew Namyslowski and Lutoslawski, and he incorporates elements from Polish folk music into his music. In 1971 he was given the Best Soloist Award at the Montreux Jazz Festival and won a scholarship to the Berklee School of Music. Both he and his groups have won various European polls. [IC]

Fusion (1974), Columbia; *Atma* (1974), Columbia; *Urbaniak* (1977), Inner City; Urbaniak/ Dudziak, *Future Talk* (1979), Inner City

V

Vaché, Alan, see VACHÉ, WARREN, JNR.

Vaché, Warren, Jnr., cornet, fluegelhorn. b. New Jersey, 21 February 1951. A student of trumpeters Jim Fitzpatrick and Pee Wee Erwin (a much-loved friend and adviser), Vaché took a degree in music and soon after was working unflappably and brilliantly with Benny Goodman, playing lead trumpet and jazz solos, as well as at Eddie Condon's with Vic Dickenson, Red Balaban and Cats, with Bob Wilber, his father's group, and as a soloist all over. His first album, *First Time Out* for Monmouth Evergreen in 1976, revealed a cornettist of perfect control, with a singer's vibrato, a mobility around the instrument that recalled Ruby Braff (who loves his work) and, most noticeable, a revolutionary ability to play in high registers at the lowest volume level. Emerging on to the American mainstream scene at a time when it looked like gently winding down for ever, Vaché quickly became a star, and it says much for his strength of character and mental resilience that his performance – under the scrutiny of a hungry but picky mainstream generation of listeners – never faltered once. Regularly with Scott Hamilton he played festivals and toured Europe, and in the late 1970s signed a contract with promoter Carl Jefferson, producing a string of solo albums, band albums, and a regular job with Jefferson's Concord All Stars who toured world-wide to massive receptions. In the 1980s he consolidated his reputation with more recording, commuting world-wide for months at a time to play jazz venues and festivals and, when at home, worked clubs in New York and New Jersey (where he lives) in, among others, Bobby Rosengarden's band, and for a time at Condon's again. In 1984, Vaché was the victim of an accident in which tendons in his right hand were cut: undaunted, he played most of the jazz festivals (including Edinburgh in Britain) left-handed, and sounded as good as ever, in between commitments with George Wein's 'new' Newport All-Stars.

Warren is part of a talented jazz family. His father, Warren Vaché Snr., bassist, is a committed jazz historian, runs the active New Jersey Jazz Society, edits its newsletter, *Jersey Jazz*, runs a well-respected classic jazzband (which for a long time featured Pee Wee Erwin, replaced after his death by trumpeter Chris Griffin), masterminds the Annual Pee Wee Russell Jazz Stomp, and has produced a wealth of written jazz history including full-length biographies of Erwin and of Sylvester Ahola. His brother Alan, a highly gifted swing-style clarinettist, works with Jim Cullum's Jazz Band and has recorded at least one top-notch solo album (see below). [DF]

Warren Vaché, Jnr., *Midtown Jazz* (1983), Concord; Warren Vaché, Snr., *Jazz: it's a wonderful sound* (1977), Starfire; Alan Vaché, *Jazz Moods* (1982), Audiophile

Vaché, Warren, Snr., see VACHÉ, WARREN, JNR.

Valdambrini, Oscar, trumpet, composer, b. Turin, Italy, 11 May 1924. Father a violinist. Studied at Turin Conservatory. He came to prominence with a quintet he co-led with saxist Gianni Basso (the Basso–Valdambrini quintet) which played at the Taverna Mexico in Milan, 1955–60. The quintet, one of the best groups in Italy, remained active into the 1960s. Valdambrini also played with Lionel Hampton and Maynard Ferguson, and in 1967 and 1968 joined the Ellington orchestra for concerts in Milan. He and the quintet won Italian jazz polls in the 1960s and 1970s. [IC]

Buddy Collette in Italy with Basso–Valdambrini (1960s), Ricordi; *The Best Modern Jazz in Italy* (1960s), Italian RCA

Valentine, Kid Thomas, trumpet. b. Reserve, Louisiana, 3 February 1896. He worked in the Hall Brothers band in the early 1920s, then with Elton Theodore's band in Algiers, and from 1926 led his own band the Algiers Stompers. In later years he was a regular colleague of George Lewis (they worked in one another's bands and recorded together) and Lewis says: 'Thomas just plays the chords, but he's up there all the time, or he's doing something underneath, even just one or two notes you know what he's doing. He has the right idea of this type of music.' Valentine was still playing regularly at Preservation Hall, New Orleans, at well over eighty, his trumpet a mercurial mix of growls, note clusters and just plain sound. 'You know what I tell 'em?' says Valentine in a film documentary *Always For Pleasure*. 'I tell 'em I'm a hundred!

And I say, "If I knew I was gonna live that long I'd have taken better care of myself!" ' [DF]

The December Band, vol. 2 (1965), Jazz Crusade

Van Eps, George, guitar. b. Plainfield, New Jersey, 7 August 1913. Quite unobtrusively – he never achieved the mass reputation of an Eddie Lang or a Django Reinhardt – George Van Eps has become accepted (at least by guitar players the world over) as *the* master whose gently-chorded acoustic guitar is a guarantee of rare beauty. His father Fred Van Eps was a well-known banjo virtuoso who recorded often and, like other guitar players in his style, George studied banjo too before applying the techniques he had learned to guitar: his teacher later was Carl Kress. After early touring with another great banjo player, Harry Reser, then with the Dutch Master Minstrels, he worked with leaders including Smith Ballew, Freddy Martin, Benny Goodman and Ray Noble before taking up full-time studio work (he rejoined Noble 1940–1). On his solo work, later on, Van Eps – a highly creative mind – introduced one of his many inventions: a seventh bass string on which – by re-conceived fingering patterns – he could play his own bass line to accompany the elegantly chordal solos he played above them: the recordings he made using this invention are collectors' items. A regular associate of Paul Weston in the 1940s and 1950s, he and his super-artistry were featured on albums by Matty Matlock, Dick Cathcart and others, and he was staffman all through Cathcart's *Pete Kelly's Blues* successes. In the 1960s and 1970s the old master combined playing the guitar with time devoted to his second love – inventing – and despite occasional bouts of illness was still to be heard live. In 1986 he visited Britain to play the Soho Jazz Festival and tour nationally, sometimes appearing with clarinettist Peanuts Hucko. [DF]

Jess Stacy/Ralph Sutton (8 tracks with Van Eps), *Stacy 'n' Sutton* (1951–3), Affinity

Van Rooyen, Ack, trumpet, fluegelhorn. b. The Hague, Netherlands, 1 January 1930. Brother Jerry is a leading European composer/arranger. At 16 he did his first tour with a big band, entertaining troops in Indonesia (1946). Graduated 'cum laude' from The Hague Conservatory in 1949. 1950–2, joined Arnhem Symphony Orchestra and during military service played with air force band. 1953–6, toured with various orchestras in Germany, Denmark, Sweden and Belgium; recorded with Lars Gullin; studio work in Hilversum. 1957–9, moved to France, worked in Paris with Kenny Clarke, Lucky Thompson, Barney Wilen. 1960–6, moved to West Berlin, joining the SFB Big Band; sextet with Herb Geller, Jerry Van Rooyen, Cees See; jazz workshops with Friedrich Gulda, Hans Koller, Ake Persson. 1967–78, in Stuttgart, becoming a regular member of Erwin Lehn Orchestra, Peter Herbolzheimer's Rhythm Combination and Brass, and Wolfgang Dauner's Radio Jazz Group. South American tour with German All Stars, 1968; tour of Asia with German All Stars, 1972. 1975, he was a founder member of the United Jazz and Rock Ensemble. 1977, with Albert Mangelsdorff, Wolfgang Dauner, Volker Kriegel, he was the co-founder of Mood Records. 1979, he toured with Clark Terry, Gil Evans, Lee Konitz and others; taught at Musikhochschule in Stuttgart and Mannheim; took seminars at Remscheid Academy. 1980, moved back to Holland where he freelances, leads his own groups and teaches at The Hague Conservatory and at Hilversum Muzieklyceum. He tours and records every year with the UJRE, and has performed at the North Sea Jazz Festival with Shelly Manne, Dizzy Gillespie and his own groups, also did TV show with Gil Evans and Louie Bellson. His favourite trumpet players are Clifford Brown, Kenny Dorham, Don Cherry, Tom Harrell and Miles Davis, among others, and other inspirations are Gil Evans, John Coltrane and Bob Brookmeyer. Van Rooyen is one of the most lyrical soloists of all; he plays with extraordinary fluidity and flexibility, producing immensely long lines and bubbling streams of triplets. He is all quicksilver and wit, and his solos seem as natural as birdsong. [IC]

With Clarke–Boland band, Gulda, Peter Herbolzheimer, Slide Hampton, Jerry Van Rooyen's Festival Orchestra and others; with Eberhard Weber, *The Colours of Chloë* (1973), ECM; with UJRE, *Live im Schützenhaus* (1977); *Teamwork* (1978); *The Break Even Point* (1979); *Live in Berlin* (1981); *Opus Sechs* (1984); under his own name, *Homeward* (1982), all Mood

van't Hof, Jasper, piano, electric piano, organ, synthesizers, computer. b. Enschede, Netherlands, 30 June 1947. Father a jazz trumpeter, mother a classical singer. Private classical piano lessons for six years. One week studying piano with Wolfgang Dauner at the Jazzklinik, Remscheid, West Germany. 1969, he was a founder member of Association PC, with Pierre Courbois (dms), Toto Blanke (gtr), Siggi Busch (bass). 1973, he started his own band Pork Pie, with Philip Catherine, Charlie Mariano, Aldo Romano and J. F. Jenny Clark, which lasted some three years, worked extensively in Europe and made two albums. This was the beginning of his long association with Charlie Mariano which was still bearing fruit in the mid-1980s. Van't Hof has also worked with many other leading musicians such as Jean-Luc Ponty, Stu Martin, Archie Shepp, Alphonze Mouzon, Zbigniew Seifert, Manfred Schoof. Since 1977 he has continued leading various bands of his own: Eyeball, which included Didier Lockwood on violin; Pili-Pili, which comprised African percussion and computer; and several quartets with John Marshall, Bo Stief, or Aldo

Romano and J. F. Jenny Clark. Since 1978 he has been voted first in jazz polls in the USA and Europe. Influences are John Coltrane, Art Blakey, Elvin Jones and Charlie Mariano, and his favourite pianists are Chick Corea, McCoy Tyner, Michelangeli (classical) and Irene Schweizer. Van't Hof is an original stylist with an exhilarating speed of thought and execution and a complete mastery of both acoustic piano and electronics. He is also a prolific composer. [IC]

Selfkicker (1974); with Pork Pie, *The Door is Open* (1975); van't Hof, *However* (1976), all MPS; with Mariano/Catherine, *Sleep my Love* (1979), CMP; van't Hof/Archie Shepp duo, *Mama Rose* (1982), Steeplechase

Vasconcelos, Nana, Latin percussion (berimbaus, cuicas, gongs, corpos, bells, shakers, etc.). b. Recife, Brazil, 19–. Father a professional guitarist playing in a Latin band. Vasconcelos started in the band at age 12, playing bongos and maracas. He eventually graduated to drum set, playing bossa nova. In the mid-1960s he moved to Rio de Janeiro and worked with singer Milton Nascimento. He began to make a big reputation because he was at home with asymmetrical rhythms such as 7/4 and 5/4 which were common in north Brazil, whereas in Rio everything was in 6/8 and 4/4. He learned to play the berimbau, a Brazilian folk instrument which has been described as 'resembling an archer's bow stuck on to Edam cheese'. 1971, Gato Barbieri brought him to the USA and he played in New York, then toured Europe with Barbieri. At the end of the tour he stayed in Paris for two years, recording, playing and working intensively with handicapped children. During that period he occasionally played with Don Cherry in Sweden, and also recorded with Egberto Gismonti for ECM. 1976, he returned to New York. Since then he has toured Europe with Gismonti, played and recorded with Pat Metheny, and also with Codona, a co-operative trio consisting of himself with the late Collin Walcott and Don Cherry. [IC]

With Metheny, Garbarek, Gismonti; *Codona* (1978); *Codona 2* (1979); *Saudades* (1979); *Codona 3* (1981), all ECM

Vaughan, Sarah Lois, vocals (and piano). b. Newark, New Jersey, 27 March 1924. Singing in church and piano studies as a child. After winning amateur contest at Harlem's Apollo Theater, joined Earl Hines band as vocalist and second pianist (1943–4). When Hines colleague Billy Eckstine formed his big band, she became a founder member (1944–5), and began recording under her own name. Like Eckstine, she had many romantic hit records in late 1940s–1950s which gradually brought a large middle-of-the-road audience and accompaniments to match, at least on disc. Her usual public appearances, however, have been backed by piano, bass and drums (including players such as Roy Haynes and Jimmy Cobb) only occasionally augmented by larger bands including, since the 1970s, symphony orchestras.

In terms of vocal equipment and flexibility, Vaughan is one of the most gifted of all jazz-associated singers. As Betty Carter once observed, 'With training she could have gone as far as [operatic star] Leontyne Price . . . But I'm glad she didn't, because otherwise we would have lost what she is now.' Her comparatively rare scatting is rhythmically freer in conception than Ella Fitzgerald's and more effortless in execution, an excellent example being her improvisation 'Shulie a Bop' based on 'Summertime'. The rhythmic ease, in fact, underlies everything she does, just as the harmonic ear she acquired from playing the piano enables her to incorporate the added notes of bebop chords in her melodic lines. And she has a range of tone which changes (sometimes almost too abruptly) from a throaty 'hot' sound to a Europeanized head-tone, and the vowels that go with it. All this makes a fantastic medium for interpreting songs with an original style which has clearly extended the influence of jazz on popular music in general. [BP]

Summertime (1949–51), CBS; *Vol 2* (1962), Reactivation

Ventura, Charlie (Charles), tenor sax (and baritone etc.). b. Philadelphia, 2 December 1916. After gigging locally and jamming with visiting notables, joined Gene Krupa band (1942–3, 1944–6, 1952). Formed own big band (1946–7, 1949–51), in between led septet with Kai Winding, then Bennie Green and (1951) quartet with Buddy Rich. Managed night club in early 1950s, then continued playing either under own name or reuniting with Krupa. Still active in 1980s, Ventura attained popularity during first stay with Krupa, thanks to a touch of vulgarity that roughened up his initial Chu Berry-style approach. His late 1940s septet, partly inspired by the early rhythm-and-blues of Illinois Jacquet and others, was billed with some justification as 'Bop for the People' but stylistically he was the odd man out in his own group. [BP]

Bop for the People (1949–53), Affinity

Venuti, Joe (Giuseppe), violin. b. Philadelphia, 16 September 1903; d. Seattle, Washington, 14 August 1978. There are so many outrageous stories about Joe Venuti – pouring flour down the tuba during filming of Paul Whiteman's *King of Jazz*, eating Whiteman's violin, playing stark naked for a brothel full of madams in Philadelphia, pouring liquid Jello into a sleeping Bix Beiderbecke's bath, arrang-

Sarah Vaughan

ing a plate of salad round his penis to serve at Mildred Bailey's supper-party – that simply summarizing his life might seem an anti-climax. Encouragingly, even the story of Venuti's birth (whichever one he told) was usually larger than life: he was born, he said, on board ship as his parents emigrated from Italy to the USA. He grew up in Philadelphia, a boyhood friend of Eddie Lang, and by 1924 was directing Jean Goldkette's Book-Cadillac orchestra (with Lang): from September 1926 they made a string of recordings (together and apart) co-starring Arthur Schutt, Adrian Rollini, Lennie Hayton, Don Murray *et al.*, and (together and apart) worked for every important white leader of the period, from Red McKenzie to Roger Wolfe Kahn, as well as co-leading bands of their own. In 1929, Venuti joined Paul Whiteman (just in time for the *King of Jazz* film) and stayed a year: after that came four years of session work, including in 1933 the immortal 'Blue Four' sessions which produced such classics as 'Raggin' the Scale', 'Hey Young Fella' and 'Satan's Holiday'. In 1935, after a trip to Europe with guitarist Frank Victor, Venuti formed his own big band which featured at various times the young Barrett Deems (dms) and vocalist Kay Starr: only two sides were ever recorded, and the band was finally disbanded (after several trial runs) when Venuti was called up. When he had extricated himself from the US army the 'Mad Fiddler from Philly' (as he became known) returned to the studios, and by the 1950s was regularly on radio with Bing Crosby's General Electric-sponsored show. (His catchphrase was 'Is this the place?') By the early 1960s, however, he was an alcoholic, playing music lounges and recording not at all (his only records in the previous decade had been for a Whiteman reunion).

The 1967 Dick Gibson Jazz Party at which he guested restored public interest in what Venuti did; record producer Hank O'Neal followed up with albums and Venuti – by this time, 'a great, squat, square, bustling haystack of a man with a trombone of a voice and a huge Roman head' (Whitney Balliett's definitive description) – was a star for life. He played the Newport Jazz Festival, 1968, London's Jazz Expo, 1969, and for the next eight years – despite cancer, discovered in 1970 – led quartets at top New York venues such as the Roosevelt Grill and Michael's Pub, worked as guest of honour with the New York Jazz Repertory Company, and recorded with his own quartet and co-stars such as Zoot Sims. By 1977 he had been warned to take things easy but continued his punishing work round until August 1978. The day he was re-booked at Chicago's Holiday Inn the arch-joker of jazz violin died. [DF]

The Mad Fiddler from Phillie (1953), Shoestring

See Feather, Leonard, *The Pleasures of Jazz* (Dell, 1976)

Video, see FILM.

Vinayakram, Vikku, ghatam (clay pot), mridangam. b. India, 11 August 1942. He was taught by his father, Sri T. R. Harihara Sarma, a legendary teacher of Carnatic (South Indian classical) percussion. Vinayakram was a child prodigy, taking part in Carnatic music concerts from the age of 13 and playing with all the main Indian virtuosi of the 1950s and 1960s. In the mid-1970s he was invited by John McLaughlin to complete the quartet Shakti. In 1980, with Joel A., he formed the Indian jazz group J. G. Laya. In the mid-1980s Vinayakram was also principal of Jaya Ganesh Academy of Rhythm in Madras, the leading academy of Carnatic percussion. He has received several Indian classical music prizes and the formal titles of Nadasudarnava (1980) and Kalaimamani (1982) accorded to legendary musicians. He has done extensive international tours playing Indian music, and 1976–7 he toured the USA and Europe with Shakti. [IC]

With Shakti, *Handful of Beauty* (1976); *Natural Elements* (1977), both CBS

Vinnegar, Leroy, bass. b. Indianapolis, Indiana, 13 July 1928. School colleague of pianist Carl Perkins, joined him in Los Angeles (1954) after working in Chicago behind Charlie Parker, Sonny Stitt etc. (1952). Gigged and recorded with Stan Getz, Barney Kessel, Herb Geller (1955), Shelly Manne (1955–6). Regular work also with Teddy Edwards–Joe Castro (1959–61), Gerald Wilson band (1961–2), record dates with Sonny Rollins, Phineas Newborn, Jazz Crusaders, Kenny Dorham etc. Festival appearances including with Les McCann at Montreux (1969) and continued freelancing. Highly valued as a versatile rhythm player with a resilient, almost rubbery tone. Although not reluctant to solo when called upon, Leroy popularized the idea of playing his normal four-to-the-bar walking lines and making them as interesting as more complex solos. Occasional passing notes, unlike those of Mingus or Ray Brown which were played normally, resulted from Vinnegar plucking an open string with his left hand, which he described as: 'Like a little flip – actually feeding myself, like a drummer's accent.' [BP]

Leroy Walks! (1957), Contemporary/OJC

Vinson, Eddie 'Cleanhead', alto sax, vocals, composer. b. Houston, Texas, 19 December 1917. Played with Houston-based Chester Boone band from 1932 and Milt Larkin from 1936. Toured with Larkin musicians under Floyd Ray (1940–1), then star singer/saxist with Cootie Williams (1942–5). Formed own 16-piece band (1945–7) and later cut down to 7-piece, his 1947–8 group containing Johnny Coles, Red Garland and John Coltrane. Continued working under his own name through periods of obscurity and rediscovery. Made first European tour in 1969 and was featured with Johnny Otis rhythm-and-blues show at Monterey festival (1970). Recorded at Montreux festivals, 1971, 1974, and guested with Count Basie in Europe (1972). Still undertaking regular solo gigs in the mid-1980s.

A unique performer who convincingly straddles the jazz and r & b worlds, Vinson has a forthright alto style less indebted to Louis Jordan than to Charlie Parker, whom he met *c*. 1940. He was the composer of 'Tune Up' and 'Four', both originally attributed to and recorded by Miles Davis in the 1950s. While his vocal blues hits were usually authored by others, he created some memorable lyrics such as 'Alimony Blues' and 'Kidney Stew'. [BP]

Kidney Stew (1969), Black & Blue

Joe Venuti

Vitous, Miroslav Ladislav, bass, guitar, composer. b. Prague, 6 December 1947. Father a saxophonist. Studied violin from age six, piano 9–14, then started on bass. At Prague Conservatory he played with Jan Hammer (piano) and his brother Alan Vitous (dms) in a junior trio. He won first prize and a scholarship to the Berklee School of Music, Boston, at an international competition in Vienna organized by Friedrich Gulda. Vitous studied at Berklee August 1966–April 1967, then went to New York, working with Art Farmer, Freddie Hubbard and the Bob Brookmeyer–Clark Terry quintet. He worked very briefly with Miles Davis and then joined Herbie Mann, staying with him, apart from one tour with Stan Getz, until the end of 1970. 1971, he was a founder member of Weather Report, staying with it until late 1973. He moved to Los Angeles in 1974 and, apart from one appearance with Airto Moreira, did not play in public for over a year because he was practising a new instrument custom-made for him – a double-necked combination guitar and bass. 1976, he began leading his own groups, and continued doing so into the 1980s, touring world-wide, playing major festivals and recording for ECM. For the most part, Vitous's quartet was all-European with John Surman, Jon Christensen and John Taylor, but that particular group broke up in 1983. Since 1979, he has taught at New England Conservatory of Music, becoming head of the jazz department in 1983.

Vitous is a virtuoso player with a conception that embraces not only his jazz roots but also the folk music of his homeland. His initial influence was Scott La Faro, and then Ron Carter and Gary Peacock. [IC]

With Chick Corea, *Now He Sings, Now He Sobs* (1968), Solid State; with Weather Report, *Weather Report* (1971); *I Sing The Body Electric* (1972); *Sweetnighter* (1973), all Columbia; as leader, *Miroslav Vitous Group* (1980); *Journey's End* (1982); Terje Rypdal/Vitous/Jack DeJohnette, *To Be Continued* (1981), all ECM

Vocalese In jazz terminology, vocalese consists of singing lyrics to a previously existing instrumental tune or recorded solo. This extremely circumscribed exercise, which places great demands on the lyric-writer and even more so on the performer, is believed to have been developed as a serious diversion by Eddie Jefferson in the early 1940s (there was already a precedent, however, in a 1934 Marion Harris

Eddie Vinson

record of 'Singing the Blues' in which she sings words, writer unknown, to the Trumbauer and Beiderbecke improvisations). First popularized in the early 1950s by King Pleasure's recordings of 'Moody's Mood for Love' and 'Parker's Mood', other noted exponents include Annie Ross (with her version of Wardell Gray's 'Twisted') and Jon Hendricks, who seems to have versions of everything else ever recorded.

In writings about European music, the French term '*vocalise*' (pronounced the same as 'vocalese') denotes the exact opposite, i.e. wordless singing comparable to scat. [BP]

von Schlippenbach, Alex (Alexander), piano, composer. b. Berlin, 7 April 1938. Studied piano and composition at school, and jazz piano with Francis Coppieters. At 13 he was playing boogie-woogie and blues, then listened to Oscar Peterson, Thelonious Monk and Bud Powell. He became totally involved with free (abstract) improvisation in the 1960s. He was with the Gunter Hampel quintet in 1963; 1964–7, with Manfred Schoof quintet, during which time he started his *Globe Unity Orchestra. From 1970 he led his own quartet featuring Evan Parker, and during the 1970s and 1980s also led a trio, played in duo with Swedish drummer Sven-Ake Johansson, and performed solo piano concerts. With GUO and in his other capacities he has toured and played major festivals in Western and Eastern Europe and the Far East. 1978, he played solo piano at the first Jazz Yatra in Bombay, India, and in 1980 the GUO also performed there. Von Schlippenbach's influences range from Schoenberg to Charlie Parker, Monk and Cecil Taylor among others. [IC]

With Globe Unity Orchestra and others; solo, *Payan* (1972), Enja; trio (Parker/Lovens) *Pakistani Pomade* (1972); quartet (Parker/Kowald/Lovens), *Three Nails Left* (1974); duo (Johansson), *Alexander von Schlippenbach* (1976); *Piano Solo* (1977), all FMP

W

Wachsmann, Phil (Philipp John Paul), violin, electronics. b. Kampala, Uganda, 5 August 1944. Mother a singer, father an ethnomusicologist and amateur violinist. BA (1st class honours) in music at Durham University. 1965, scholarship to study violin and composition at Bloomington University, Indiana; 1968, scholarship to study in Paris with Nadia Boulanger for one year. 1969–70, lectured in contemporary music at Durham University, and set up improvisation workshop. Worked with Yggdrasil, a group playing Cage, Feldman, and doing mixed media projects. Started his own improvisation group, Chamberpot. From then on, he has worked almost exclusively in free (i.e. abstract) improvisation, with Fred van Hove, Tony Oxley, Paul Rutherford, Barry Guy and Derek Bailey. Also with London Jazz Composers' Orchestra, the Electric String Trio, and the Bugger All Stars. Continues to be interested in mixed media work. Started own label, Bead Records. Favourites, Joe Venuti and Itzhak Perlman. Influences, Berlioz, Berio, Webern, Cage. [IC]

Chamberpot (1976), Bead; *Sparks of the Desire Magneto* (1977), Bead; *Was macht ihr denn* (1982), SAJ; solo, *Writing in Water* (1985), Bead; Tony Oxley, *February Papers* (1977), Incus

Walcott, Collin, sitar, tabla, percussion, voice. b. New York City, 24 April 1945. d. 8 November 1984, in a road accident in East Germany. Mother a classical pianist. Studied violin for two years in grammar school; 1957–9, studied snare drum; also played timpani and sang madrigals at school. 1963, studied percussion at Indiana University. From 1967, studied sitar with Ravi Shankar and tabla with Alla Rakha. 1967–9, worked with Tony Scott. With Tim Hardin, 1968–9, then joined Paul Winter Consort, 1970. From 1971, he worked with Oregon, a splinter group from the Winter Consort which included Ralph Towner, Paul McCandless and Glen Moore. Walcott also worked with dancer/singer/composer Meredith Monk; and he toured and recorded from the late 1970s with Codona, a trio with Don Cherry and Nana Vasconcelos. Shortly before his death, he toured Europe with his own group which included Cherry and saxophonist Jim Pepper. His influences were Shankar, Rakha, Ali Akbar Khan, Mongo Santamaria, Herbie Hancock, and he admired John Coltrane's rhythm-section of Jimmy Garrison and Elvin Jones. His own groups and the other groups he worked with used elements from ethnic music, jazz and occasionally from European art music. Walcott's presence always gave groups a very special identity and atmosphere. He not only played sitar in the classical Indian manner, but could also produce walking bass lines on it, and improvise on jazz changes. He wrote some fine compositions including 'Song of the Morrow', 'The Swarm', 'Grazing Dreams', 'Walking on Eggs', 'Again and Again, Again'. He performed at festivals in Europe, Scandinavia and the USA. [IC]

Cloud Dance (1975); *Grazing Dreams* (1977); *Codona* (1978); *Codona 2* (1981); *Codona 3* (1983); *Oregon* (1983), all ECM

Waldron, Mal(colm Earl), piano, composer. b. New York City, 16 August 1926. After receiving BA in music and composing for ballet, worked with Big Nick Nicholas, Ike Quebec, Della Reese and r & b groups. Regular associate of Charles Mingus (1954–6 and occasionally later) and accompanist of Billie Holiday (1957–9), also frequent recording for which he did all the writing ('Soul Eyes' has become a standard). In the 1960s led own groups, backing John Coltrane in his first post-Davis gigs and later featuring Eric Dolphy, both live and on record. Wrote three US film scores and stage background music, then after film work in Europe (1965) settled there, with occasional trips to Japan and back to US.

Elements of Waldron's style can be traced to both Bud Powell and Thelonious Monk, although his sound is less bright and percussive than either. As with some practitioners of later styles, the impact of Mal's playing tends to be cumulative rather than constantly ebbing and flowing, and for this reason he has often worked successfully with soloists such as Steve Lacy, who also espoused 'free jazz' only gradually. For this reason too, his original compositions tend to be less memorable in themselves than as an effective stimulus to improvisation. [BP]

Waldron/Dolphy, *The Quest* (1961), Prestige/OJC; *Moods* (1978), Enja

Walking (1) An easy medium tempo, corresponding to walking pace.

(2) The various keyboard or bass styles most

suitable to this tempo. The term is now most usually associated with those bassists who, from Walter Page onwards, specialized in playing one note on each beat of the bar, sometimes using each different note for two adjacent beats (which sounds especially appropriate to the name) but also covering lines that were more wide-ranging provided the rhythmic pattern was unvaried. Many of the left-hand patterns of piano boogie were described as 'walking basses' (as opposed to 'stride') and in addition, since Lennie Tristano, pianists have also sometimes imitated bassists' lines with their left hand.

The Gene Ammons-derived tune entitled 'Walkin' ', especially as recorded by the Miles Davis All Star Sextet with Percy Heath, gives an excellent demonstration of the tempo and the bass style. [BP]

Wallace, Bennie, tenor sax. b. Chattanooga, Tennessee, 18 November 1946. As a teenager, played jazz and sat in with local country-music bands and black r & b combos, then studied clarinet at University of Tennessee. Moved to New York (early 1970s), worked with Monty Alexander and Sheila Jordan groups; record debut alongside Flip Phillips and Scott Hamilton (1977). Early gigs under own name featured bassist Glen Moore and drummer Eddie Moore (replaced by Eddie Gomez and Dannie Richmond, 1978). Appeared at Berlin festival as member of George Gruntz band (1979) and fronting NDR (North German Radio) big band (1981); many other appearances in Europe in early 1980s. Up to 1985 all his own recordings were cut in New York but released by German label.

Wallace has said, 'About 1973, I decided to spend one year totally away from modern music – I listened to all the guys with Duke's band, a lot of Johnny Hodges and Ben Webster, as well as to Don Byas and Coleman Hawkins.' This was done against a background of close acquaintance with John Coltrane, Sonny Rollins (especially) and, even more obviously, Eric Dolphy. The saxophone style that has emerged from this melting-pot is full of bizarre humour, but otherwise straight-ahead and rather intense. Recently Wallace has allowed his Southern roots in more popular forms to feed into his repertoire and into his improvisation, in an effort to become even more all-embracing. [BP]

Plays Monk (1981), Enja; *Twilight Time* (1985), Blue Note

Waller, Fats (Thomas Wright), piano, organ, singer, composer. b. New York City, 21 May 1904; d. 15 December 1943, in a train on his way back from Los Angeles to NYC. Father a clergyman who wanted Fats to follow a similar career; young Fats played organ in his father's church. After studying with private piano teachers he became a professional pianist at the age of 15. He worked in cabarets and theatres during the 1920s, accompanying Bessie Smith and other blues singers as well as playing organ and piano solos. 1925, he worked with Erskine Tate in Chicago. During the late 1920s, in collaboration with lyricist Andy Razaf, Waller made a reputation as a composer of popular songs for such shows as *Connie's Hot Chocolates*. He began broadcasting early, and made a brief trip to France in 1932. May 1934, he began a series of Victor record sessions with 6-piece groups known as Fats Waller and his Rhythm which featured his satirical treatments of current popular songs and which gained him a wide, non-jazz audience. The sextets usually featured either Herman Autrey or John 'Bugs' Hamilton on trumpets, Gene Sedric on clarinet and tenor, Al Casey on guitar, Cedric Wallace on bass and 'Slick' Jones on drums. All these performances are notable for a wonderful sense of time, rhythm and pacing, enormous fun and some glorious piano playing. Fats made jazz history by playing the organ in Notre Dame cathedral, Paris, and he recorded on the pipe organ and (1940–2) the Hammond organ, on which he recorded his composition 'Jitterbug Waltz'.

Waller came out of the James P. Johnson 'stride' piano style, but added to it a delicacy, a more powerful rhythmic intensity and a greater speed and deftness. He wore his genius lightly and his light-hearted music had a profound influence on subsequent generations of musicians. He could make an artistic and witty gem out of the tritest popular song; at the same time, his compositions and certain phrases he played vastly enriched the entire jazz repertoire, becoming part of the subconscious of all subsequent players. Waller compositions which have become standards are: 'Ain't Misbehavin' ', 'Honeysuckle Rose', 'Blue Turning Grey Over You', among others. Charlie Parker's bebop composition 'Scrapple from the Apple' and many other jazz originals are based on the harmonic structure of 'Honeysuckle Rose'. Fats appeared in several films, the most successful and influential of which was the all-black *Stormy Weather* (1943). Many of the more solemn jazz critics and fans, as they had done in the case of Louis Armstrong, lamented the fact of Fats's popularity and humour. They felt he was throwing his gifts away and that he should have devoted himself to more serious musical pursuits. But his occasional attempts at more sober composition (viz. his 'London Suite') were banal; his genius was for making immortal performances out of ephemeral popular songs. Over 40 years after his death, his biggest record hit, 'I'm going to sit right down and write myself a letter', is played frequently on the radio and sounds as delightfully fresh and humorous as ever. His influence on pianists has been huge and perhaps the most famous of his debtors are: Art Tatum, Teddy Wilson, Count Basie (who took lessons from Fats), Thelonious Monk, Erroll Garner, Bud Powell and Joe Zawinul. [IC]

The French RCA Black and White label has his piano solos (1929–41) and six volumes of his piano solos and sextets. The American label Giants of Jazz has *Fats Waller Live at the Yacht Club* (1938) and *Fats Waller Live, vol. 2* (1938)

See Waller, Maurice, and Calabrese, Anthony, *Fats Waller* (Cassell, 1978)

Wallington, George (Giacinto Figlia), piano, composer. b. Palermo, Sicily, 27 October 1924. Brought up in the US, gigged as a teenager and participated in Dizzy Gillespie's first 52nd Street group (1944). Freelancing with other leaders and own groups, recording under own name from 1949. 1955–6, led regular quintet of young stars-to-be, Donald Byrd, Jackie McLean (later Phil Woods), Paul Chambers and Art Taylor. Then left music business (1957), only re-emerging in the mid-1980s with new recordings and an appearance at Kool Festival (1985). His piano work is in the typical bebop manner and, though apparently developed independently from that of Bud Powell, differed little from his approach. Wallington wrote the bop standards 'Lemon Drop' and 'Godchild', as well as numerous other attractive but less well-known tunes. [BP]

Jazz for the Carriage Trade (1956), Prestige/OJC

Wallis, Bob (Robert), trumpet, vocals, leader. b. Bridlington, Yorkshire, 3 June 1934. He played trumpet for Acker Bilk briefly in the 1950s before forming his own Storyville Jazzmen in East London from members of Hugh Rainey's Storyville Band, including Pete Gresham (piano), Avo Avison (tmb) and Rainey (banjo). His high-pitched singing and hard-working, powerful trumpet (both influenced by Henry 'Red' Allen) achieved commercial success after a hit single, 'Come Along Please', and throughout the 'Trad boom' of the early 1960s his band worked successfully in Britain and Europe, including a successful year at the London Palladium. After the invasion of the Beatles in 1962, Wallis freelanced with various bands (including Monty Sunshine's), then built a new and successful career in Switzerland, working on into the 1980s with undimmed emergy. [DF]

Walters, John Leonard, composer, arranger, lyricon, computer synthesizers, soprano sax, flute, alto flute. b. Chesterfield, Derbyshire, 16 April 1953. Studied maths and physics at King's College, London University. Attended jazz summer schools with Graham Collier and Mike Gibbs, and studied privately with Neil Ardley, Don Rendell and others. Played in school folk/rock groups, and then university jazz group. 1974, formed his own band Landscape, which a year later became a co-operative 5-piece unit with Walters, Peter Thoms, Andy Pask, Chris Heaton, Richard Burgess. Landscape won the Greater London Arts Association Young Jazz Musicians' Award and the Vitavox Live Sound Award, both in 1976. The group's music combined the best elements of jazz and rock – a wide variety of perfectly executed rhythms, interesting structures, rich harmonies, strong melodies and much improvisation. Walters's composing and organizing abilities inevitably led him into record production and arranging work on the rock scene in collaboration with Burgess and others. [IC]

With Landscape, *Thursday the 12th* (1975), Jaguar cassette; *From the Tea-Rooms of Mars . . . To the Hell-Holes of Uranus* (1981), RCA; *Manhattan Boogie-Woogie* (1982), RCA

Walton, Cedar Anthony, Jnr., piano, composer. b. Dallas, Texas, 17 January 1934. Moved to New York in the late 1950s and worked successively with the sextet of J. J. Johnson (1958–60), the Benny Golson–Art Farmer Jazztet (1960–1) and Art Blakey (1961–4, 1973). Freelancing in New York with many different players and singers, Walton was also much in demand for recording, notably on Blue Note and Prestige. Frequent gigging and touring abroad since 1970, usually with own quartet including saxists Hank Mobley, George Coleman, Clifford Jordan, Bob Berg etc. and superior rhythm men such as Sam Jones and Billy Higgins. An excellent and stimulating accompanist, Walton is also an interesting writer whose tunes have begun to achieve standard status, e.g. 'Ugetsu' (aka 'Polar AC' or 'Fantasy in D'), 'Mosaic' and 'Bolivia'. A lively soloist whose long lines are the epitome of contemporary neo-bop piano. [BP]

First Set (1977), Steeplechase

Ware, Wilbur Leonard, bass. b. Chicago, 8 September 1923; d. 9 September 1979. Self-taught on banjo and a bass home-made by foster-father, Ware played in local string bands (claiming to have recorded with blues singer Big Bill Broonzy in 1936). Later worked professionally in groups led by Stuff Smith, Roy Eldridge, Sonny Stitt etc. (late 1940s). Led own groups intermittently from 1953, toured with Eddie Vinson (1954–5), Art Blakey (summer 1956), Buddy DeFranco (1957). Member of classic Thelonious Monk quartet (1957–early 1958), played with J. R. Monterose (1959). Returned to Chicago (1959), working locally then becoming inactive for a while. In New York again from late 1960s gigging with Monk (1970) and recording with Clifford Jordan (1969, 1976) and Paul Jeffrey (1972).

Ware had an instrumental sound redolent of the bop era, similar to certain players who flourished in the 1940s but were gradually left behind by later developments. However, Ware himself influenced those later developments through an idiosyncratic style which may have originated in getting around technical 'limitations' (the same allegation, of course, is made about Monk and Miles Davis). Either way, Wilbur's concentration on the lower range of the bass was considerably lightened by his rapid articulation which – especially though not exclusively while soloing – enabled him to break up the beat in a way that, while rather four-square rhythmically, was totally unexpected from a bassist. Equally, his devotion to the root-notes of chords was varied by his choice of unusual passing tones and substitutions. Taken together, these aspects of Ware's work set an example for Charlie Haden and other players of the 1960s who were diametrically opposed to the Scott La Faro school. [BP]

Thelonious Monk and John Coltrane (1957), Jazzland/OJC; Sonny Rollins, *A Night at the Village Vanguard* (1957), Blue Note

Warren, Earle Ronald, alto sax, clarinet, vocals. b. Springfield, Ohio, 1 July 1914. Count Basie's first great lead alto-saxophonist – he joined in 1937 in Pittsburgh, replacing Caughey Roberts – Warren was young, highly responsible and a first-class reader, who had led his own bands around Cleveland, Ohio. After he joined Basie he demonstrated (like Willie Smith, a kindred spirit) a natural gift for section-leading, a warm plummy voice, which Basie featured, and a devotion to Basie's early insecure course which often left him, as he said, 'without a nickel to ride the subway'. Warren's intense, orange-toned alto was a capable solo voice but later on – after Basie began to feature his saxophone tandem of Herschel Evans and Lester Young – he was heard more often as a brief shaft of light amid the battling tenors: 'I got all the bridges – eight bars in the middle of everything.' For the next 13 years – with occasional absences for bandleading and a bout of lung trouble in 1948 – Warren played and sang with Basie (his vocal features included 'I struck a match in the dark' during which once, in a Venuti-esque moment, Lester Young set fire to Warren's music, and 'Ride On'). In 1950 he struck out for a solo career; as a manager for top acts like Johnny Otis, as an MC, and regularly as bandleader and soloist, among others with Buck Clayton in 1959, 1961, and in 1969 in Europe with a package show, 'Jazz from a Swingin' Era', and vocal group, The Platters. In the 1970s and 1980s Warren was as busy as ever, often touring as a soloist and appearing with his own group the Countsmen, featuring swingmasters Dickie Wells and Claude Hopkins. [DF]

Count Basie, *Swinging the Blues* (1937–9), Affinity

See Dance, Stanley, *The World of Count Basie* (Sidgwick & Jackson, 1980)

Earle Warren

Washington, Dinah (*née* Ruth Jones), vocals. b. Tuscaloosa, Alabama, 29 August 1924; d. 14 December 1963. Sang gospel as member of Chicago-based Sara Martin Singers while a teenager. After winning an amateur contest, worked in Chicago night clubs (early 1940s) then joined Lionel Hampton band (1943–6) and began making records under her own name. Although her success in the burgeoning r & b field seldom diminished, she also made (from mid-1950s) albums with jazz groups and others benefiting from more middle-of-the-road packaging of her distinctive style. Turbulent private life involving several marriages and alcohol addiction led to her premature death.

The most influential female singer of the last 40 years, she achieved what Ray Charles did for the male vocalists: making the phrasing and tonal variations of gospel soloists an inescapable part of popular music. As early as the late 1940s her records were being 'covered' by white artists such as the derivative Kay Starr, so that her innovations were absorbed extremely rapidly; but it was she who paved the way for Aretha Franklin and Esther Phillips, not to mention gospel-influenced jazz singers who moved on to more popular work, for instance Ernestine Anderson and Nancy Wilson. Her most widely known records may have seemed rather mannered when the material was not very strong, but her interpretative qualities were at their best against a relaxed jazz backing. [BP]

The Jazz Sides (1954–5), Emarcy; *Sings Bessie Smith* (1957–8), Mercury

Washington, Grover, Jnr., tenor sax, composer (and alto, soprano and baritone sax, clarinet, electric bass, piano). b. Buffalo, New York, 12 December 1943. Father a saxophonist and family all musical; brother a drummer. Began on sax at age ten; claims to have been working in clubs by age 12. Studied at Wurlitzer School of Music, and played in high school bands on baritone. 1959–63, he toured with the Four Clefs; 1963–7, he spent two years in the US army, also working with organ trios and rock groups. During the 1970s he achieved enormous success with a series of fusion albums which topped the US charts in all categories – pop, r & b, and jazz. At least five of his albums 'went gold' with sales of 500,000 or more, and his double-Grammy-winning *Winelight* 'went platinum' with sales of over a million. Washington has achieved this success without ever having won a poll as an instrumentalist or a composer, and he has been savaged by critics and attacked by fellow musicians for 'corrupting' the young. His brand of fusion – a kind of disco with soul and blues – is really pop music with a jazz tinge, an innocuous type of MOR, and as such should not be judged by jazz criteria.

Washington is a technically excellent player with a sound that projects well, and his main influences are, ironically, from the heart of the jazz tradition: Coleman Hawkins, Don Byas, Wardell Gray, Dexter Gordon, Johnny Griffin, Sonny Rollins, Gerry Mulligan. He has done extensive international tours. [IC]

With Dexter Gordon, Dave Grusin, Bob James, Eric Gale, Lonnie Smith, Randy Weston and others; *The Best Is Yet To Come* (nda); *Come Morning* (nda); *Winelight* (nda), all Elektra/Asylum; *A Secret Place* (1976), Kudu

Waso A Belgium-based quartet of gypsy musicians, originally led by violinist Piotto Limburger, which works in the image of Django Reinhardt and the Hot Club of France. The group consists of Koen de Cauter (gtr/vln/reeds), Vivi Limburger, son of Piotto (piano/rhythm gtr), Michel Verstraeten (bass) and a brilliant and highly-rated acoustic guitarist, Fapy Lafertin, who in the 1980s has built himself a strong solo reputation. Leader Cauter took over from Piotto Limburger in the early 1970s, taking up the clarinet to lead the band because there was no one else to do it, and by the 1980s had built a strong European reputation: Waso is a guaranteed clubfiller and the group has recorded widely, usually on little jazz labels. [DF]

Watanabe, Sadao, alto sax, flute, sopranino, composer. b. Tochigi Prefecture, Japan, 1 February 1933. Father taught biwa (3–5-stringed pear-shaped lute), a traditional Japanese instrument. Began on clarinet at age 15 in the school band; then took up alto sax. 1953, he joined Toshiko Akiyoshi's quartet, taking over its leadership in 1956 when she left to study at Berklee. In 1962, Watanabe also went to the Berklee School, spending three years in the USA and playing and recording with leading US musicians including Gary McFarland and Chico Hamilton. Returning to Japan in 1965, he started a jazz school for young musicians the following year. He became one of the strongest musical influences in Japan, and his groups featured many fine musicians who came to prominence with Watanabe. 1968, he made his first appearance at the Newport Jazz Festival; 1970, he played at the Montreux and Newport festivals. He twice played in Africa, 1971, 1974; in 1975 he made his first visit to India. 1977, Watanabe became the first Japanese jazz musician to receive a National Award in Japan. 1978, he performed with his quintet at the first Jazz Yatra in Bombay, India, and also played there in Clark Terry's international big band.

Watanabe names Charlie Parker and Gary McFarland as his prime influences. He is a virtuoso performer on all his instruments, and a fertile composer, and he has won many prizes and awards as a bandleader, player, composer/arranger and for his records. [IC]

With Gabor Szabo, McFarland, Hamilton and others; *Pastoral* (1970), CBS/Sony; *Pamoja* (1975); *I'm Old Fashioned* (1976), both East Wind

Waters, Benny (Benjamin), saxes, clarinet, arranger. b. Brighton, Maryland, 23 January 1902. He had a sound musical grounding – he studied at Boston Conservatory for several years in the 1920s – and played with Charlie Johnson's band (1925–32) and recorded with Clarence Williams and King Oliver. He worked busily through the 1930s with well-rated bands such as Hot Lips Page's, and for several months in 1935 with Fletcher Henderson. During and after the war he spent a year with Claude Hopkins, months with Jimmie Lunceford, years as a bandleader, and by 1950 was with the band Jimmy Archey had inherited from Bob Wilber, but soon after left for Europe where in Paris in 1955 he joined Jacques Butler's band. For the next 15 years Waters's abilities were a European legend, and in the mid-1970s British promoter Dave Bennett set about re-marketing him in Britain. For Bennett, Waters toured annually, recorded, and made appearances at major jazz festivals such as Edinburgh, as well as keeping up an unrelenting round of European touring and making occasional visits back home to the USA. Short, squat and filled with a bustling energy, at well over eighty he still plays with the same creative fire and blistering intensity: his solo performances include high-speed re-runs of difficult test pieces like 'Cherokee' as well as standard swing tunes (on which he plays layered solos, full of complex runs, swiftly-delivered ideas and altissimo harmonics) and blues routines on which he sings and mugs like the professional jazz entertainer he is. [DF]

Any from 1980 on

Waters, Ethel, vocals. b. Chester, Pennsylvania, 31 October 1896; d. Los Angeles, 1 September 1977. 'She sang, man, she really sang', says Jimmy McPartland. 'We were enthralled with her. We liked Bessie Smith very much, too, but Waters had more polish, I guess you'd say. She phrased so wonderfully, the natural quality of her voice was so fine and she sang the way she felt – that knocked us out always with any artist.' During the 1920s Waters – a deeply religious woman who used God to keep her own violent demons at bay – toured with Fletcher Henderson's Black Swan Troubadors (her first record for Black Swan, 'Oh Daddy'/'Down Home Blues', she said, 'got Black Swan out of the red'), appeared at all the best theatres and nightspots, played revue, toured the TOBA circuit and was the first black singer to broadcast in the Deep South in the early 1920s. By the end of the decade she was a star as well as a jazz singer, recorded with Duke Ellington in 1932, Benny Goodman and others in 1933 ('It was a caper and a delight doing those records with those fellows who could ad lib my music round me') and toured with her husband, trumpeter Eddie Mallory, for the next six years. From then on – with films such as *Cabin in the Sky* (1943), revues such as *Laugh Time* and Broadway plays including *Mamba's Daughter* (1939), a triumph – Waters turned into a well-rated actress and was seldom out of the public eye for long, appearing on radio, TV and films, singing and working for religious charities and putting in live appearances, until she died at 80. Her autobiography, deeply disturbing, often violent, is the portrait of a cruelly persecuted black woman determined to succeed, with fists if necessary. It makes a vivid contrast to Billie Holiday's sad downward run and shows how two underprivileged and talented women of their time found different solutions to the same problem. [DF]

Greatest Years (1925–34), Columbia (double)

See Waters, Ethel, *His Eye is on the Sparrow* (W. H. Allen, 1951)

Watkins, Doug(las), bass. b. Detroit, Michigan, 2 March 1934; d. 5 February 1962. Left Detroit briefly touring with James Moody (1953), then in New York gigged separately with Kenny Dorham (1954) and others who became, along with him, the Jazz Messengers (1955–6). Joined Horace Silver quintet (1956–7), recording with them under Silver's name and those of Donald Byrd and Hank Mobley, and with many others such as Sonny Rollins, Lee Morgan, Jackie McLean during late 1950s. After a hiatus, reappeared in Charles Mingus group while Mingus played piano (1961). Was on the way to reside in San Francisco when a car accident ended his life.

Watkins was one of the important generation of musicians who came out of Detroit in the mid-1950s. He shared many of the characteristics of the great Paul Chambers, who was his cousin by marriage; although more reticent as regards solo work, his time playing showed the same combination of reliability and resilience. It is to be regretted that he was never in the limelight as much as Chambers and, since his death, his contribution has been largely overlooked. [BP]

Sonny Rollins, *Saxophone Colossus* (1956), Prestige

Watkins, Julius, French horn. b. Detroit, Michigan, 10 October 1921; d. 4 April 1977. Started playing at age nine, worked with Ernie Fields band (1943–6). Recorded for Kenny Clarke (with other Detroiters including Milt Jackson) and for Babs Gonzales (1949), member of Milt Buckner big band (1949). Much small-group work (recording with Thelonious Monk, 1953) and involved in many short-lived big bands led by Pete Rugolo, Oscar Pettiford, Johnny Richards and George Shearing. Co-led own occasional small group, Les Jazz Modes, with Charlie Rouse (1956–9). Also frequent studio work, including Miles Davis–Gil Evans albums, and recording and live appearances (1965, 1971) with Charles Mingus. Watkins was the first musician to show the possibilities of the French horn in bebop improvisation. Thanks to his punchy phrasing and pointed tone, he succeeded where (a few) others unwittingly underlined the difficulties of the instrument itself. [BP]

Thelonious Monk, *Quintet* (1953–4), Prestige

Watrous, Bill (William Russell, II), trombone, composer. b. Middletown, Connecticut, 8 June 1939. Father a musician. He played with Roy Eldridge, Kai Winding, Quincy Jones, Woody Herman, Johnny Richards, Count Basie and others. 1967–70, worked as a studio musician at CBS, and at ABC for the Dick Cavett show. 1971, he was a member of Ten Wheel Drive, then formed his own big band, Manhattan Wildlife Refuge. During the late 1970s and early 1980s he began touring internationally as a soloist with local/indigenous rhythm sections. Watrous is a technically brilliant performer. His influences include Clifford Brown, Charlie Parker, Carl Fontana, Vic Dickenson, Dizzy Gillespie and Brahms. [IC].

Bone Straight Ahead (1972); with Danny Stiles, *In Tandem* (1973), both Famous Door

Watson, Bobby (Robert Michael Jnr.), alto and soprano sax, clarinet, flute, piano, composer/arranger. b. Lawrence, Kansas, 23 August 1953. Father plays tenor sax, tunes pianos, repairs instruments. Graduated B.Mus. (theory and composition) from University of Miami (Florida), 1975. Began on piano at 10, clarinet at 11, and saxophone in the eighth grade, and playing rhythm-and-blues while at school. He began arranging and composing in high school for the concert band, and also organized the first school dance band, of which he was assistant director and for which he wrote all the music. 1970, started private lessons on clarinet with Carlo Minnetti. Mid-1970s, he went to New York City. 1977–81, played with and was musical director of Art Blakey's Jazz Messengers. After leaving Blakey he began a regular association with several groups: from 1981, the George Coleman octet, lead alto with Charli Persip and Superband; from 1982, Louis Hayes quartet; from 1983, 29th Street Saxophone Quartet. Also worked with Sam Riuck's Winds of Manhattan, Philly Joe Jones and Dameronia, Panama Francis and the Savoy Sultans. 1984, he helped Max Roach arrange music for a play, *Shepard Sets* by Sam Shepard, and the music won an award for the year's best music on off-Broadway. He also received a National Endowment for the Arts composer's grant in 1979. Has co-led groups with Curtis Lundy since 1973. His wife Pamela is a singer and composer and has sung and performed her songs with him. Watson likes any alto players with 'a great sound', but particularly Cannonball Adderley, Charlie Parker, Jackie McLean. Other inspirations are Art Blakey, Herbie Hancock, Stevie Wonder, George Coleman, Teddy Edwards and Eddie Harris. He has absorbed all these influences and arrived at a highly individual, extraordinarily fluid style imbued with powerful feeling. Compositions: 'Time Will Tell', 'In Case You Missed It', 'Wheel within a Wheel', 'Curious Child'. [IC]

With Art Blakey, *Gypsy Folk Tales* (1977), Roulette; *Estimated Time of Arrival* (1977), Roulette; *Live in Sweden* (1981), Amigo; *Straight Ahead* (1981), Concord; *Perpetual Groove* (1984), Red; *Beatitudes* (1984), Newnote/Hep; *Gumbo* (1985), Amigo

Watson, Leo, vocals, drums, trombone, tipple. b. Kansas City, Missouri, 27 February 1898; d. Los Angeles, 2 May 1950. He attracted attention after he joined Virgil Scroggins, Wilbur and Douglas Daniels and guitarist Buddy Burton in a novelty act in 1929: later, at the Onyx Club, New York, they were to find fame as the Spirits of Rhythm (by that time Teddy Bunn had replaced Burton). Watson's scat – he improvised melodies at the same time as lyrics with mind-boggling ease – caused a sensation and he was great to watch too: miming trombone as he created his whirlwind vocalese. Watson later worked briefly for big bands led by Artie Shaw, Gene Krupa (their record of 'Nagasaki' is, perhaps, the best ever version of the song) and Jimmy Mundy, as well as regularly in reincarnations of the highly successful Spirits, and in 1946 appeared with Slim (Gaillard) and Slam (Stewart) around Los Angeles. 'He was original', says Slim Gaillard. 'Everybody in Hollywood used to come and listen to him. And they'd follow everything he said, because he could sing about anything! He'd start singing about the walls, the rug, the table, ashtrays – he'd just sing!' His act made a deep impression on young singers including Mel Tormé, who saw Watson's 'total improvisation' as an unquestionable definition of 'jazz singing' – possibly the only one. For the last few years of his life (he died at 52 of pneumonia) Watson worked the cabaret circuit as a solo performer and sang and played drums for Charlie Raye's band. [DF]

The Spirits of Rhythm 1933–4, JSP

Watters, Lu (Lucious), trumpet. b. Santa Cruz, California, 19 December 1911. After being 'most promising bugler' at St Joseph's Military Academy, Sacramento, Watters formed his first jazz band in 1925, and all through the 1930s was working around San Francisco in small groups as well as with his own 11-piece, formed for a residency at Sweet's Ballroom, Oakland. By 1939 he was rehearsing nightly at the Big Bear in Berkeley Hills with Paul Lingle, Turk Murphy and other kindred spirits, then in December 1939 moved into the Dawn Club every Monday night with his new band playing back-to-the-roots King Oliver-style jazz. By 1940 his group was so successful that they officially re-titled themselves the Yerba Buena Jazz Band, and began a phenomenally successful career as America's first real revivalist band. 'It certainly is funny to hear those youngsters trying to play like old men!' said Bobby Hackett, but Watters was unstoppable: his band signed to the Jazz Man label, played and recorded with Bunk Johnson and packed the Dawn Club nightly with their stomping two-beat sound. 1942–5, Watters served in the navy (where he led a 20-piece band in Hawaii), then regrouped his Yerba Buenans and opened his own Dawn Club on Annie Street in March 1946 to continued success: in June 1947 the whole band moved to Hambone Kelly's Club in El Cerrito, where they remained until the very end of 1950. By that time the Yerba Buenans had gone about as far as they could go: the revival had been launched world-wide and they had broadcast and recorded regularly for ten years, but Watters had lost two keymen, Turk Murphy and Bob Scobey who had gone out on their own, and in 1950 contracted a painful hernia. He wound up his successful operation and later studied geology instead. [DF]

Yerba Buena Jazz Band, vol. 3: Stomps etc. and the Blues (1946), Good Time Jazz

Watts, Trevor Charles, alto and soprano sax, piano, bass clarinet. b. York, 26 February 1939.

His parents loved jazz and he heard it from an early age. Self-taught, except for one year at RAF School of Music. Began on cornet at 12 and took up sax at 18. 1958–63, played in RAF band. Demobilized in 1963, he went to London and joined the New Jazz Orchestra. 1965, founder member of Spontaneous Music Ensemble; 1967, formed his own group, Amalgam. 1972–3, with Pierre Jarre group; 1973, with Bobby Bradford; 1973–4, with Stan Tracey; 1972–85, London Jazz Composers' Orchestra; 1976, formed Trevor Watts String Ensemble; 1978, Universal Music Group. 1982, formed his Moiré Music and his Drum Orchestra. He has also played with many other UK musicians including Louis Moholo, Harry Miller, Keith Tippett. Watts has received several commissions and bursaries to compose for his various ensembles, and has played festivals and toured in the UK with Amalgam and Moiré Music. His taste in saxophonists ranges from Earl Bostic and Johnny Hodges to Ornette Coleman and Eric Dolphy, and other influences are Charles Mingus, John Coltrane and Thelonious Monk. He and his long-time associate John Stevens were given the Thames Television Award for schools teaching in 1972. [IC]

With NJO, LJCO, SME and others; String Ensemble, *Cynosure* (1976), Ogun; Amalgam, *Over the Rainbow* (1979), Arc; *Moiré Music* (1985), Arc

Weatherford, Teddy, piano. b. Bluefield, W. Virginia, 11 October 1903; d. Calcutta, 25 April 1945. 'A great pianist,' says Hugues Panassié, 'straightforward, with a powerful left hand. He played blues with a breadth and nostalgia proper to a musician from the South: he could also play good rags.' Weatherford, who arrived in Chicago in 1921 from New Orleans, could well have occupied the position in jazz history later taken by Earl Hines, who learnt an incalculable amount from the huge-handed pianist who starred with Erskine Tate's Vendome orchestra. But in 1926, after a trip back to California, Weatherford took up an advantageous offer from bandleader Jack Carter to visit Asia, and stayed to lead his bands all over the Near and Far East. By 1929 he was resident at the Candidrome Club, Shanghai, and in 1934 recruited Buck Clayton's band en bloc to play the season there: subsequently he worked in Singapore, Java and India, at the Taj Mahal Hotel and later the Grand Hotel, Calcutta. He died there of cholera, at only 41. [DF]

Louis Armstrong (two tracks with Weatherford), *Young Louis the Sideman* (1924–7), MCA; Various (5 tracks by Weatherford), *Piano and Swing* (1935–8), Pathé

Webb, Chick (William Henry), drums, leader. b. Baltimore, Maryland, 10 February 1909; d. 16 June 1939. One of the great drummer-bandleaders of the early swing era, hunchback Chick Webb presented a startling image. 'He was a tiny man,' describes Buddy Rich, 'and with this big face and big stiff shoulders. He sat way up on a kind of throne and used a 28″ bass drum which had special pedals for his feet, and he had those old gooseneck cymbal holders. Every beat was like a bell.' Webb had been bandleading around New York for half a dozen years, usually with a constant friend, his guitarist John Trueheart, before he moved into the Savoy in 1931 and quickly became a fixture. Constantly on the lookout for new talent (he was forever swapping good musicians for better with Fletcher Henderson), Webb was highly competitive: 'He'd tell you he was the best right quick', said Sandy Williams. He jealously defended his band's reputation at the Savoy – a beautiful ballroom with a sprung floor and a booth full of ten-cent partners – taking on all comers with an onslaught of speciality acts and tightly-rehearsed, newly-commissioned arrangements. 'Chick's was the greatest battling band,' says Harry Carney, 'and when Charlie Buchanan was at the Savoy he always saw to it that every new band hitting town battled with Chick.' In 1933, Webb hired arranger Edgar Sampson, a coup, and trumpeter Taft Jordan, whose Armstrong impressions were central to his show: by then he could hold off all opposition apart from Duke Ellington and the Casa Lomans. Finally, in 1935, Ella Fitzgerald – Webb's trump card – joined his band, a hit record, 'A-tisket, a-tasket', sealed both their futures, and from then on 'the little giant of the drums' (as Gene Krupa called him) was happy to build his show around his singer (he become her guardian, too, after Ella's mother died). Webb was a great drummer – 'the best up to that time' says Eddie Durham – but owing to the limitations of recording techniques at the period was highly restricted in what he could do in a studio. By the time engineers had learned how to cope with jazz drummers, Webb was ill: tuberculosis of the spine reduced his powers and by 1938 he was using Arnold Bolden to back support acts on theatre engagements. 'Just once towards the end,' says Sandy Williams, 'he was a little pitiful. "When I was young and playing for peanuts", he said, "I could eat anything you guys eat, but now I have all this money I can only eat certain things and can't even take a nip when I want to!" ' After a major operation in a Baltimore hospital Webb sat up in bed. 'I'm sorry,' he said, 'I've got to go,' fell back and died. Ella Fitzgerald, who took over leadership of his band for two years afterwards, sang 'My Buddy' at his funeral. [DF]

A Legend: 1929–36, MCA

See Dance, Stanley, *The World of Swing* (Scribner's, 1974, repr. Da Capo, 1979)

Webb, George, piano, leader. b. Camberwell, London, 8 October 1917. Father of the British post-war jazz revival. His band, featuring Wally Fawkes (clt), Ed Harvey (tmb), Reg Rigden and Owen Bryce (tpts), began playing at the Red Barn, Barnehurst (a South London suburb), in 1942 and quickly acquired a dedicated following. After the war Webb's band, playing a stomping two-beat recreation of Armstrong/Oliver/Henderson/Ellington music, acquired a regular sitter-in, Humphrey Lyttelton (who subsequently replaced Rigden and Bryce), a manager, Jim Godbolt, and began recording regularly, appearing on radio and playing London clubs (as well as regular concerts at King George's Hall, Tottenham Court Road) where their rough-and-ready approach symbolized jazz fans' post-war dissatisfaction with the glossier banalities of swing. Webb – a dedicated amateur – worked with Humphrey Lyttelton's band (which was formed from ex-Webb musicians) then led for himself again briefly, but during the 1950s and 1960s was equally active as an agent bringing American stars (like Jessie Fuller) to Britain and later representing singer Long John Baldry and a variety of others. After an unexpected failure (a projected Isle of Man Jazz Festival, in which he had invested, lost money after its venue burnt down), he returned in a wave of publicity in the early 1970s to lead a band including Dennis Field (cornet), Terry Pitts (tmb) and Sammy Rimington (clt), and led bands regularly thereafter. From 1976 he ran a pub in Stansted, Essex, and by then his 1940s recordings were the subject of scholarly re-issues: on 4 July 1985 a plaque was unveiled at the Red Barn commemorating Webb's musical achievements. [DF]

Dixielanders (1946), Jazzology

Webb, Speed (Lawrence Arthur), leader, drums, vocals. b. Peru, Indiana, 18 July 1906. He led a highly successful territory band for 17 years from 1925. By 1929 his new-formed group included Roy Eldridge, Joe Eldridge, Teddy Wilson, his trombonist brother Gus, and Vic Dickenson. No fewer than seven of the band members were excellent arrangers and Wilson often orchestrated Louis Armstrong, Bix Beiderbecke and Johnny Hodges in close harmony for the relevant section: a very early precedent for such later groups as Supersax and the New York Jazz Repertory Company. Understandably Webb's band often made short work of bigger visiting names and his own spectacular drumming, later in the 1930s, made him a natural frontman for a variety of groups which he assembled for special occasions under various names. In the 1940s Webb retired from music and became (John Chilton tells us) an embalmer. [DF]

Weber, Eberhard, bass, composer (and cello). b. Stuttgart, 22 January 1940. Father a cello and piano teacher. Began study of cello with him at age six, but in the mid-1950s switched to bass after becoming interested in jazz. Self-taught on bass and as a composer. As a young man, he sang with his sister in the Horst Jankowski Choir. In the 1960s he did a variety of jobs for a company which made TV commercials, and also freelanced as a director in theatre and TV, but played a lot of music in his spare time. He did not become a fully professional musician until 1972. 1962, he began playing with pianist Wolfgang Dauner, staying with him until the early 1970s. At first they had a trio influenced by Bill Evans and Scott La Faro, but soon began to explore the areas of free (abstract) improvisation. At the same time, Weber worked as a sideman in all styles of music. 1970, he spent some time with Dauner's Etcetera, a psychedelic rock-jazz outfit. 1972–3, he worked with the Dave Pike Set, which also included Volker Kriegel, and which toured and played festivals in Europe, and also did a long South American tour. 1973–4, he worked with Kriegel's Spectrum, a jazz-rock group. Weber had become one of the best and most experienced bass players in Europe, handling all styles – walking bass lines, free jazz, jazz-rock – with equal deftness, but from now on he was to evolve into an innovative stylist on his instrument and a major figure with his own musical identity and sound. He left Spectrum because, while Kriegel was deeply interested in rock rhythms, Weber was moving towards a concept which included spacey, electronic sounds with classical overtones, airy melodies with resonant harmonies and understated rhythms.

The key to his new identity is in the sound of the instrument he created which he calls an 'electrobass'. He redesigned an old Italian electric bass with a long neck and small rectangular soundbox, which looked like a bodyless acoustic bass. Then with the help of instrument makers and electronics experts, he further refined it, making a five-string version. This instrument had new qualities: it was more spacious and had more overtones, so that the sound was more brilliantly incisive and yet also more spread and more evocative, and it was capable of sustaining long notes. His new persona emerged on his first album as a leader, *The Colours of Chloë*, recorded 1973 and released the following year. It received instant critical recognition and popular success, and in 1975 was awarded first prize by the West German Phono-Akademie, which also voted Weber Artist of the Year. 1974, he also recorded with Gary Burton (*Ring*), and with Ralph Towner (*Solstice*), then did two US tours with Burton, 1975–6, as a front-line player, almost certainly the first time in jazz history that a bass player had toured as a featured soloist and melodist. The albums and tours immediately established Weber's reputation both in the US and Europe, and it was generally recognized that he had made a major contribution to the emancipation of the bass, opening up new dimensions for the instrument. One US critic called him a 'Mephisto of the bass, whose overwhelming technique and whose power of

Eberhard Weber

invention are awe-inspiring'. He was now able to form his group Colours (1975–82), one of the most important and influential groups of its time, with Charlie Mariano (soprano sax/nagaswaram/flutes), Rainer Brüninghaus (keyboards/synthesizers), and at first Jon Christensen, then from 1977, John Marshall, on drums. Since 1975, he has been a member of the United Jazz and Rock Ensemble and in 1982 he joined Jan Garbarek's regular group. In 1985, Weber began playing solo concerts. With Colours he toured all over Western and Eastern Europe, the British Isles, Scandinavia, Australia and New Zealand, and the USA (three times). His favourite bassist is Scott La Faro, and particular inspirations are Weather Report, Miles Davis and European classical music. As well as writing music for his own groups and albums, he has composed background music for films and TV. In his own music, composition is primary and improvised solos are simply a limited and controlled ingredient in his soundscape. The overriding atmosphere of his work is one of reflective melancholy and a warm romanticism, achieved by expansive chords, sustained notes, sonorous bass lines, hypnotically repeated figures, seductive melodies. [IC]

Over 60 as a sideman with other artists; *The Colours of Chloë* (1973); Colours, *Yellow Fields* (1975); Weber/Brüninghaus, *The Following Morning* (1976); Colours, *Silent Feet* (1977); Weber/Burton/singers, *Fluid Rustle* (1979); Colours, *Little Movements* (1980); Weber and group, *Later That Evening* (1982); Weber/Garbarek/Ralph Hübner, *Chorus* (1984), all ECM

Webster, Ben (Benjamin Francis), tenor sax, occasionally piano, arranger. b. Kansas City, Missouri, 27 March 1909; d. Amsterdam, 20 September 1973. After a grounding on violin he took to the piano naturally, Pete Johnson (a neighbour) taught him how to play blues and soon after Webster was playing for silent movies in Amarillo, Texas. Here, one night, he met Budd Johnson, who showed him the scale of C on saxophone – Webster had been intrigued with Frankie Trumbauer's 'Singin' the Blues' – and not long after he was playing saxophone in the Young Family Band (Lester Young and his father both supplied more tips), in Gene McCoy's band, then in Jap Allen's group (they specialized in McKinney's Cotton Picker re-creations) and for Blanche Calloway (where Johnny Hodges heard him first). By the winter of 1931, Webster had joined Bennie Moten as featured soloist and records such as 'Lafayette' and 'Moten Swing' first helped to get him recognized: for the rest of the 1930s the rough, gruff, sometimes unpredictable saxophonist was with a string of classy big bands (Andy Kirk, Fletcher Henderson, Benny Carter, Willie Bryant, Cab Calloway and Teddy Wilson) as well as doing the rounds of clubs to

Ben Webster

listen and cut, working on record dates and playing pool. Until then, Webster was often thought of as a Coleman Hawkins soundalike, but after he joined Duke Ellington in 1940 (the first major tenor saxophonist to do so), predictably enough, his true colours emerged: while Hawkins hustled through chords like a scientist with the wind behind him, Webster's approach moved between blustery fundamentalist *tours de force* and a sinuous, breathy sensuality topped with creamy vibrato. The approach recalled elegant alto-saxophonists like Benny Carter and Johnny Hodges (two of Webster's idols) but he replaced their cat-like sensuality with a brusque, tender sentiment like a sailor's kiss. His move to Ellington produced new enthusiasm among the saxophones. 'Ben brought new life to a section that had been together a long time', says Harry Carney. 'He was inspired and he inspired us so that we worked together.' Webster – sometimes charming, sometimes curtly rude to his employer – stayed with Ellington for three years, producing such masterpieces as 'All Too Soon' and 'Cottontail'; later tenor-saxophonists with Ellington, including Harold Ashby and Paul Gonsalves, knew his solos by heart when they arrived in the band. Webster left Ellington because one night he had been allowed to play piano with the band, stayed too long at the keyboard, and when Ellington took offence and refused to discuss the matter, Webster cut one of Ellington's best suits to bits. In 1944 he began working for other leaders such as Raymond Scott, John Kirby, Sid Catlett and Stuff Smith, led his own small groups up and down Swing Street, rejoined Ellington, 1948–9, and by the 1950s was working in studios as well as jazz clubs and JATP: for several years in the 1950s he lived permanently on the West Coast to be near his mother and sister (all through his career Webster, like Sid Catlett, was devoted to his mother and paid regular trips home). After their deaths he settled back in New York, playing clubs such as the Half Note, but by 1964, conscious of the tides of jazz fashion, moved to Copenhagen, and from there toured Europe regularly. It was now that Webster's unpredictability began to create a body of legend second only to Joe Venuti's. 'Ben had a habit of keeping two diaries in which he alternately wrote his bookings up', says journalist Henrik Iversen. 'Sometimes this resulted in double bookings – or close. A festival in Italy and a gig in Finland could be placed within a few hours' interval and since he would only travel by train' (in his cups Webster had been known to fall between the train and the platform) 'he could succeed in being several days late for gigs!' Webster also veered between two personae: easy-going, chatty and well-behaved when sober and terrifyingly unpredictable when drunk. 'I never forgot', says one British accompanist, 'watching Ben with his umbrella and topcoat on, at 3.30 a.m. in Trafalgar Square, racketing round and screaming up at the buildings for a whore: "I know you're there honey! Come on out!" ' Regular records from Sweden showed that Webster's late music had lost none of its passion and intensity: a marvellous album, *No Fool, No Fun* featuring Webster rehearsing the Danish Radio Big Band, is characteristic, funny and a master's dissertation on how to swing. Soon after his death, the Ben Webster Foundation, a philanthropic organization to support jazz music, was set up in Sweden by William Moore. [DF]

No Fool, No Fun (1970), Spotlite

See Dance, Stanley, *The World of Duke Ellington* (Scribner's, 1970, repr. Da Capo, 1980); Stewart, Rex, *Jazz Masters of the 1930s* (Macmillan, 1972, repr. Da Capo, 1982)

Webster, Freddie (Frederick), trumpet. b. Cleveland, Ohio, 1916; d. Chicago, 1 April 1947. An early associate of pianist-arranger Tadd Dameron, he worked with Earl Hines in Cleveland in 1938, then moved to New York around 1940; a year later he was once again with Hines's orchestra, having been noticed by the leader as one of the young bop innovators who 'played on a modern kick'. For six years more he worked in a string of fine big bands (including Lucky Millinder's, Jimmie Lunceford's, Benny Carter's and others), and as a regular player at jam sessions at Minton's and elsewhere was a big influence on younger players such as Kenny Dorham and Miles Davis, who remains his greatest champion in modern jazz history. 'I used to love what he did to a note', Davis recalled later. 'He didn't play a lot of notes; he didn't waste any. I used to try to get his sound. He had a great big tone like Billy Butterfield, but without vibrato.' Despite the warm recommendations of Webster's 'big pretty sound' (Kenny Dorham) he never achieved the international fame of Gillespie, or later Davis, never seems to have made much money (Davis taught him the lessons of Juilliard because 'Freddie didn't have any money to go') and later in his brief career was demonstrating alarming unreliability. 'You know when Freddie was supposed to join Count Basie?' says Leon Washington. 'When Count asked him what his price was he said, "After you've paid the rest of those m.f.s you and I split 50-50!" He was serious. He wasn't kidding. He was going down then, though, and he died shortly after that.' After brief spells with Dizzy Gillespie and Jazz at the Philharmonic, Webster collapsed and died of a heart attack at no more than 31. [DF]

Weller, Don, tenor, soprano and alto sax, clarinet. b. Croydon, Surrey, 19 December 1947. Started at 14 on clarinet, with private lessons; at 15, soloist in Mozart's clarinet concerto at Croydon Town Hall. Inspired by Kathy Stobart, he took up tenor sax and played in her rehearsal band. During the 1970s, he led his own jazz-rock group Major Surgery; also worked with Stan Tracey, Harry Beckett, and in quintet formation with Art Themen. In the 1980s he played with the Gil Evans orchestra in the UK, led a quintet with Bobby Wellins, and co-led a quintet with Bryan Spring. Weller also freelances as a soloist and on the London session scene. His favourites include Sonny Rollins and Charlie Parker, and other inspirations are Stan Tracey and Gil Evans. [IC]

With Tracey, *The Bracknell Connection* (1976), Steam; Weller/Spring, *Commit No Nuisance* (1979), Affinity

Wellins, Bobby (Robert Coull), tenor sax. b. Glasgow, 24 January 1936. Father played sax and clarinet, mother a singer. Started on alto sax with lessons from his father, who also taught him basic harmony on the piano. He later took a three-year course at Chichester College of

Bobby Wellins

Further Education, studying keyboard harmony. 1950–2, was taught clarinet at the RAF School of Music, Uxbridge. 1953 on, he worked with dance bands in the London area. In the late 1950s he began to specialize in improvisation and joined Tony Crombie's band Jazz Inc., in which he met Stan Tracey. He worked with Tracey's quartet during the early 1960s, playing on the classic album *Under Milk Wood*. Then Wellins's career was blighted by personal problems which kept him off the scene for almost ten years. He resurfaced in 1976, formed a quartet and, with Don Weller, a quintet, and began performing and recording again. He is also active as a teacher on various jazz courses. Wellins is, and has always been, an original. He has his own distinctive sound, a reedy, keening cry recalling the bagpipes of his native Scotland, and he phrases with immense elegance – every note is meant, none wasted. His taste in saxophonists runs from Charlie Parker, Lester Young and Zoot Sims to John Coltrane, Lee Konitz and Tony Coe, but, while embodying most of their virtues, he sounds like none of them. [IC]

With Stan Tracey, *Under Milk Wood* (1965), Steam; quartet, *Jubilation* (1978), Vortex; *Dreams Are Free* (1979), Vortex

Wells, Dicky (William), trombone, vocals, arranger, composer. b. Centerville, Tennessee, 10 June 1907; d. New York City, 12 November 1985. At a time in jazz history when the trombone was just starting *not* to be an object of comedy, it was brave of Dicky Wells to put the comedy right back. The trombone in his hands, and often played through a pepperpot mute of his own invention, usually sounded more like a voice than an instrument: full of blasé yawns, dismissive grunts and sudden yelps of surprise. It was a sophisticated set of tricks, a million miles from the music-hall humour of trombone features such as 'Lassus Trombone' which had only just started to disappear from trombone repertoire by the 1930s, and it took a man of wit to invent them. But Wells – for most of his life – kept a bubbling sense of humour intact: the cover picture of his autobiography (see below) shows Count Basie looking up from the piano stool with a delighted grin as Wells solos, and the book inside the covers is one of the funniest jazz autobiographies.

Wells worked his way up through fine New York bands led by Lloyd Scott, Benny Carter, Fletcher Henderson, Charlie Johnson and others: eight years with Count Basie from 1938 established Wells as a trombone stylist who had found an alternative to the approaches of Jimmy Harrison and Jack Teagarden. His account of the troubles encountered by black bands like Basie's in the Deep South (in *The Night People* below) is determinedly funny, but the problems he experienced were perhaps to help him along to alcoholism. After Basie he worked with Lucky Millinder, Sy Oliver, Willie Bryant and others and by 1959 was in Europe with Buck Clayton's All Stars where, just occasionally, he sounded tired. Drink affected his performance badly in the 1960s; a solo tour with Alex Welsh in 1965 in Britain was cut short, and soon after it he took a day job on Wall Street. But by 1973 his book had been published, he was working with Earle Warren's Countsmen (including Buddy Tate and Paul Quinichette), and in 1978 toured Europe with Warren and Claude Hopkins. Otherwise the decade was not noticeably kind to Wells – he was ill with pneumonia, mugged on two occasions and his wife died – but in the 1980s it was good to hear him on record again still managing to raise a smile. [DF]

Dicky Wells in Paris (1937), Prestige; Count Basie, *The Count and the President* (1936–9), CBS

See Wells, Dicky, as told to Stanley Dance, *The Night People* (Crescendo, 1971)

Wellstood, Dick (Richard MacQueen), piano. b. Greenwich, Connecticut, 25 November 1927. He came to New York in 1946 in a band led by Bob Wilber and a year later was working for Sidney Bechet in Chicago: in the two cities he heard most of the great pianists – from James P. Johnson to Bud Powell – on whom he was to model his own approach. Through the 1950s Wellstood worked with an impressive string of older, more established stars including Bechet, Rex Stewart, Charlie Shavers and, a primary influence, Roy Eldridge: in 1953 he was with a band led by actor Conrad Janis and by 1956 was

Dicky Wells

in the intermission band at Condon's. Later in the decade he was house pianist at the Metropole, New York (a university education for Wellstood who, at the club, was constantly surrounded by an eclectic parade of jazzmen), then moved to Nick's Club, then into Gene Krupa's quartet. By the late 1960s, Wellstood, now settled in New Jersey, was well established: besides working for classic men such as Roy Eldridge, Jimmy McPartland and the Dukes of Dixieland, he was going out solo at prestigious New York rooms including Michael's Pub and touring (subject to availability) with the World's Greatest Jazz Band. At this period he regularly recorded tasteful solo albums for Columbia, Chiaroscuro, Jazzology and others, played jazz parties and in odd moments wrote sleeve-notes which unobtrusively put him in the class of authors such as George Frazier, Whitney Balliett and Dick Sudhalter. A determined upholder of traditional standards Wellstood is pronouncedly against fashionable music trends ('All this electric junk's really beaten the s--t out of acoustic music', he told *Crescendo* magazine in a pithy interview during the 1970s): he was the subject of a sensitive pen-portrait by Whitney Balliett (in the book below) at the period. Into the 1980s Wellstood continued to play rooms, clubs, and festivals, and toured Europe with, among others, Bobby Rosengarden and Kenny Davern in a reconstituted Blue Three, worked with the Classic Jazz Quartet and – rather surprisingly – practised as a qualified attorney between times. [DF]

Wellstood/Marty Grosz, *Take Me to the Land of Jazz* (undated), Aviva

See Balliett, Whitney, *Jelly Roll, Jabbo and Fats* (OUP, 1983)

Welsh, Alex, cornet, vocals, leader. b. Edinburgh, 9 July 1929; d. London, 25 June 1982. The Alex Welsh Band – like many of the Chicagoans that Welsh adored – burned itself out too soon, but is remembered with more affection than almost any other British band, not only because it was arguably, in Bud Freeman's words 'the best small band of its kind in the world' but because its members formed a much-loved 'jazz family'. Welsh's first band settled down in the 1950s (after a few trial runs) with Archie Semple on clarinet, pianist Fred Hunt, trombonist Roy Crimmins and a top modern drummer of the period, Lennie Hastings, and began recording, broadcasting and playing clubs and concerts (their records such as 'Music of the Mauve Decade', 'Melrose Folio' and 'Echoes of Chicago' are now British jazz classics). In the early 1960s Welsh – one of the great lead Dixieland players who in 1957 turned down an offer to join Jack Teagarden – had to weather changes: Archie Semple collapsed and soon died, Roy Crimmins left to work abroad. Undeterred, Welsh re-formed – with John Barnes, Roy Williams, Jim Douglas, a fine bassist, Ron Mathewson (later replaced by the equally fine Harvey Weston), and shortly after Al Gay – and began his busiest period, touring with a stream of US visitors from Earl Hines to Ruby Braff, all of whom praised his new band as world-class. In 1967 they played the Antibes Jazz Festival to rapturous reviews, produced their first new album for three years, a classic, *Strike One*, and appeared at Newport the year after. For the next ten years, Welsh continued touring (later minus Gay again), playing clubs and concerts all over Britain and Europe, recording and perfecting his eclectic programme: mainstream arrangements (by Kenny Graham and others), banjo-based Dixieland, Mulligan–Brookmeyer interludes from Barnes and Williams, and warm solo features for Hunt and his leader. In 1977, Barnes left; the following year Williams followed; and for the last four years of his life Welsh (who had been ill in the 1970s from a recurrent hip injury, undiagnosed viral complaints and general wear and tear) played Dixieland pure and simple with a variety of sidemen including Campbell Burnap, Mick Cooke and finally Roy Crimmins (back again), Al Gay and pianist Barney Bates. He died after a long debilitating illness: at his funeral the church was packed. [DF]

In Concert (1971), Black Lion

Wertico, Paul, drums. b. Chicago, 5 January 1953. He took up drums at 12 and became a featured soloist with the Illinois High School Band. He was involved in the Chicago musical community for ten years and gained exceptionally wide experience, working with big bands, rock groups and two free-improvising groups, Earwax Control and the Spontaneous Composition Trio. He also accompanied Larry Coryell, Bunky Green, Jack Bruce, and Ellen McIlwaine. He joined Pat Metheny's group in 1983, and the guitarist has said of him: 'He can truly play in the variety of styles that we need, but he always sounds like himself, he always plays from the inside out.' Wertico cites Roy Haynes as his main influence, but also finds inspiration in ethnic music, particularly African field recordings. [IC]

With Metheny, *First Circle* (1984); *The Falcon and the Snowman* (1985), both ECM

Wess, Frank Wellington, tenor sax, flute, composer (and alto). b. Kansas City, Missouri, 4 January 1922. Played locally in Washington, DC, as teenager, and toured with Blanche Calloway. After army, worked in Billy Eckstine band (1946), then with Eddie Heywood, Lucky Millinder (1947–8) and former Millinder singer Bullmoose Jackson (1948–9). After studying flute, joined Count Basie band on tenor (and later alto) but making use of flute in solos (1953–64). Freelancing in New York since then, including theatre, television and recording work. Played and wrote for Clark Terry's occasional big band (from 1969) and founder member of New York Jazz Quartet (from 1974). Worked with Philly Joe Jones's Dameronia group (1981–5) and co-led quintet with Frank Foster (from 1984). Wess is a commanding though unflamboyant saxophonist, more renowned for his flute work. Using a basically pre-bop phraseology not very far removed from the pioneering efforts of Wayman Carver with the Chick Webb band, Wess helped the instrument to surpass the declining popularity of the clarinet by demonstrating that the flute too could be made to swing. [BP]

Wess/Foster, *Frankly Speaking* (1984), Concord

Westbrook, Kate (Katherine Jane Barnard), voice, tenor horn, piccolo, bamboo flute. b. Guildford, Surrey, 19–. Several members of her family gifted amateur musicians. She went to Dartington Hall School, then studied painting at Bath Academy of Art, Reading University and the University of London. Self-taught as a musician. Began as a painter, living and working in USA and having her first major one-person show at the Santa Barbara Museum of Art, California, 1963. She returned to the UK and taught at Leeds College of Art, 1964–73. 1974, she joined the Mike Westbrook Brass Band, giving up teaching to concentrate on the dual career of painter and musician. She and Westbrook married, and most of her musical work has been done with him. She joined his orchestra in 1981, and in 1982 formed the trio A Little Westbrook Music, with him and saxist Chris Biscoe. Kate Westbrook has also worked independently; during the 1970s she was guest soloist with the RAI Orchestra in Rome and with the Zurich Radio Orchestra, and in the 1980s she did several projects with Lindsay Cooper for TV films. With Westbrook she has four main roles: she works as a soloist and section player; since 1978 she has written the lyrics of many songs performed by the band; she has also worked (in collaboration with Westbrook and others) on scenarios for the Brass Band's jazz/cabaret productions for theatre and TV; and she performs songs in a number of European languages, adapting foreign texts for that purpose. For *The Cortege*, on which she worked with Westbrook, she adapted texts by Rimbaud, Lorca, Hermann Hesse, Belli, Blake and Saarikoski. The resulting triple album won the Montreux Grand Prix du

Disque, 1982. Since 1974 she has toured with various Westbrook groups, all over Western and Eastern Europe and Scandinavia, and performed at many major festivals including 'Britain Salutes New York' (New York), Jerusalem, Avignon, Pori (Finland). Inspirations are Billie Holiday, Karen Carpenter, Kathleen Ferrier, Phil Minton and, on valve trombone, Juan Tizol. She is also influenced by Brecht/Weill, Richard Strauss, Stravinsky and others, but writes: 'Perhaps the most important influences on my work have been poets, writers and painters: Goya, Monet, Lorca, Shakespeare, Blake.' [IC]

Eight with Mike Westbrook, including *The Cortege* (1982), Original; *A Little Westbrook Music* (1983), Westbrook; *Love for Sale* (1985), Hat Art

Westbrook, Mike (Michael John David), piano, tuba, bandleader, composer/arranger. b. High Wycombe, Buckinghamshire, 21 March 1936. Mother a qualified piano teacher, father an amateur orchestral tympanist and dance-band drummer. Studied painting at Plymouth Art School and Hornsey School of Art, London. Became seriously interested in music only after hearing jazz records at school. He had a little basic tuition on piano and trumpet, but was mainly self-taught; as a composer/arranger, entirely self-taught. 1960, he ran a jazz workshop at Plymouth Arts Centre with an 8-piece band that included John Surman. 1962, moved to London, eventually forming a regular 6-piece group that included Surman. The group played at the Montreux festival, 1968. He formed the Mike Westbrook Concert Band in 1967, which varied in size from 10 to 26 musicians, and which existed to perform the series of long compositions he was beginning to write. 1970–2, he co-led (with John Fox of Welfare State Theatre Group) the Cosmic Circus, a multi-media group. 1971–4, he led his Solid Gold Cadillac, a rock orientated group. 1973, he formed his Brass Band to perform jazz/cabaret productions for theatre and TV. 1979, he formed the Mike Westbrook Orchestra for his large-scale work *The Cortege*. With his wife Kate and saxist Chris Biscoe, he formed the trio A Little Westbrook Music in 1982. Again with his wife, in 1984 he formed Westbrook Music Theatre for more mixed-media productions.

Everything about Westbrook is on a massive scale: the number and variety of groups he has formed, the innumerable projects, his prolific output as a composer, the broad scope and long duration of the various works. Over the years he has developed a great mastery of orchestration and can handle everything from solo instrument to chamber group and very large ensemble. One of his greatest achievements is to have given jazz wider terms of cultural reference (relating it to poetry, theatre, the visual arts and the European classical music tradition) without in any way diminishing its own identity or vitality. Musically, too, he has enlarged the jazz concept by bringing to it a rich variety of influences – street music, ethnic music, rock, folk and European art music. His collaboration with his wife, since the mid-1970s, has been particularly fruitful, producing, among other things, his finest long work to date, *The Cortege*. The resulting triple LP, awarded the 1982 Montreux Grand Prix du Disque, is quintessential Westbrook, with tremendous plasticity and variety in the writing, an exceptionally broad emotional range and fine solos, particularly from Biscoe, Chris Hunter, Guy Barker, Dick Pearce and Phil Todd. Westbrook is not a virtuoso pianist; he says, 'I'm a composer really, and an adequate piano player.' His favourite pianists are Duke Ellington, Thelonious Monk and Jimmy Yancey, and as a composer his main influences are again Ellington and Monk, but also Charles Mingus, Jelly Roll Morton, Stravinsky, Brecht/Weill, and particularly all the people with whom he has worked. He has a wide international reputation, and has toured with his various groups all over Eastern and Western Europe and Scandinavia, performing at festivals there and also in Israel (Jerusalem), Australia (Adelaide), and the USA ('Britain Salutes New York'). He has also conducted performances of his work with radio orchestras in Rome, Venice, Stockholm and Copenhagen, and written and performed music for television plays and documentaries. All of his most important compositions are on record. [IC]

Celebration (1967); *Release* (1968); *Marching Song* (1969), all Deram; *Metropolis* (1971), RCA; *Citadel/Room 315* (1975), RCA; *Mama Chicago* (1979), Teldec/RCA; *The Westbrook Blake* (1980), Original/Europa; *The Cortege* (1982), Original; *On Duke's Birthday* (1985), Hat Art; solo, *Mike Westbrook Piano* (1978), Original

West Coast 'The Coast' (as it is called by all Americans, even those from there) was an established jazz centre by the 1920s, and the first black band to make records, Kid Ory's, did so in Los Angeles in 1922. But what is usually meant by 'West Coast jazz' is a particular type of mutant modernism which became popular in the early 1950s.

Its most typical sounds were associated with former sidemen of the Stan Kenton and Woody Herman bands (often of both, in fact) such as Shorty Rogers and Shelly Manne, who specialized in a brand of easily palatable, filleted bebop. The melodic, and especially rhythmic, predictability of much of their material was sometimes outweighed (as had been true of swing-era material) by superior soloists, in this case people like Bud Shank and Art Pepper, but the occasional use of European-style counterpoint and of instruments such as flute and oboe was greeted with more enthusiasm than seems in retrospect justified. Other, more distinctive, sounds from the groups of Gerry Mulligan and Dave Brubeck were classified for geographical reasons as West

Coast jazz, but the movement as a whole achieved the same watering-down of 1940s bebop as European Trad of the 1950s did for the 1940s New Orleans revival.

Probably more significant in terms of historical impact was the 'West Coast blues' movement of the late 1940s and early 1950s. Groups such as those of Roy Milton and Joe Liggins provided a considerable input into the newly-defined field of rhythm-and-blues, while leaders such as T-Bone Walker incorporated the style of amplified guitar work that was to become so crucial in the development of rock and roll. [BP]

Weston, Harvey, bass, b. London, 2 March 1940. He freelanced in London (at venues such as the Bull's Head at Barnes) before joining Alex Welsh's great band, 1967–74. From then on he pursued a busy freelance career, working with Kathy Stobart's quintet (featuring Harold Beckett), 1978–81, and with an enormous variety of visiting Americans: a short-list could include Eddie Vinson, Ruby Braff, Sonny Stitt and Red Holloway, Pepper Adams, Warren Vaché, Scott Hamilton and Roger Kellaway. A fast-thinking, creative soloist, sympathetic accompanist and excellent teacher, Weston turns up in a huge variety of jazz settings, always to their advantage. [DF]

Weston, Randy (Randolph E.), piano, composer. b. Brooklyn, New York, 6 April 1926. Began gigging in late 1940s with r & b bands including Eddie Vinson's (1953). Also with Kenny Dorham (1953) and Cecil Payne (1954), then formed own trio and quartet. Active as an educator and, after visiting Nigeria (1961, 1963) and West and North Africa (1967), settled in Morocco for next five years. Returned to USA, 1973, continuing to make solo, duo and band appearances there and in Europe and Japan.

Like many pianists initially inspired by Thelonious Monk, Weston often sounds at his best when playing his own compositions. Many of these became standards in the late 1950s, including 'Hi-Fly', 'Babe's Blues' and 'Little Niles', while there are many more worthy of investigation such as 'Niger Mambo'. 'Niles' was the nickname of his son Azzedin Weston (b. 12 August 1950), who has worked with Dizzy Gillespie, Ahmad Jamal and others. Randy Weston's piano work, perhaps through his interest in West Indian and African music, conveys a particularly dynamic and happy atmosphere, and deserves to be more widely recognized. [BP]

Blues to Africa (1974), Freedom

Wettling, George Godfrey, drums. b. Topeka, Kansas, 28 November 1907; d. New York City, 6 June 1968. After working around Chicago for ten years he went to New York (with British bandleader Jack Hylton's specially-formed orchestra), and thereafter worked with a string of fine bands including Artie Shaw's, Bunny Berigan's, Paul Whiteman's, Red Norvo's and Benny Goodman's – before moving into studio work for ABC. Wettling was an intellectual and a diversifier: he frequently led his own bands (a 1939 *Chicago Jazz* album is one of several top-notch recording sessions he organized), wrote stimulating and hard-hitting pieces for American magazines such as *Downbeat* and *Playboy* and – most unusual of all – was a gifted abstract painter (a close friend of Stuart Davis) who had several exhibitions, and was featured by *Collier's Magazine* in 1951 (they promoted a recording session, at which Wettling recorded 'Collier's Climb' and 'Collier's Clambake' among other numbers, as well as featuring pictures of the session and reproducing a Wettling abstract). For much of the 1950s Wettling was associated with Eddie Condon, as well as leaders such as Muggsy Spanier: in such surroundings his rattling, sometimes cavernous sound – much influenced by Baby Dodds and Zutty Singleton – produced the very best from his associates: 'There are many good kids playing drums today, but none of them has George's flexibility, imagination and virtuosity', said Condon at the period. For the last years of his life, Wettling led his own trio at New York's Gaslight Club and nursed a drink problem: 'One or two drinks was all it took to drive him out of his mind', says Bud Freeman. One of the great Chicagoans, he in a sense combined aspects of Cliff Leeman and Dave Tough in a single talent. [DF]

George Wettling's Jazz Band (1951), Columbia

Wheeler, Kenny (Kenneth V. J.), trumpet, cornet, fluegelhorn, pocket trumpet, composer. b. Toronto, Canada, 14 January 1930. Father, two brothers and a sister all musical. Began on cornet at age 12. Studied harmony and trumpet at Toronto Conservatory before he moved to the UK in 1952 where his first professional work was with big bands led by Roy Fox, Vic Lewis and others. With the John Dankworth Orchestra (1959–65) he did his first regular work as composer/arranger, studied composition with Richard Rodney Bennett for six months, and had some counterpoint lessons with Bill Russo. From the mid-1960s his reputation grew more rapidly and he played with Ronnie Scott, Joe Harriott, Tubby Hayes, Friedrich Gulda, and the Clarke–Boland big band. At the same time he became deeply immersed in free (abstract) improvisation, working first with John Stevens and the Spontaneous Music Ensemble, and later Tony Oxley's sextet. From 1969 he began to work with the Mike Gibbs Orchestra, which used electronic as well as acoustic instruments, often employed rock rhythms and was more formally organized. Subsequently he has work-

Kenny Wheeler

ed with groups that dealt in abstraction, such as (from 1972) the Globe Unity Orchestra and Anthony Braxton's quartet, and also with groups that favoured more formal structures, such as the trio Azimuth, of which he was a founder member with John Taylor and Norma Winstone in 1977, and the United Jazz and Rock Ensemble, which he joined in 1979. Since the 1960s, he has also intermittently led his own occasional big band and various small groups, and as he became more established internationally, particularly after he began to record for ECM in the mid-1970s, he had more opportunities to tour and perform as a leader. From 1983 he was a regular member of the Dave Holland quintet.

Although naturally reticent and self-effacing, Wheeler has always had the inner necessity and vision of the true artist, and this brought him early in his career to Europe, the perfect environment for him because it does not have the gladiatorial competitiveness of the American jazz scene. His instinct also led him to free jazz which gave his conception and his playing an added dimension. He became a complete brass virtuoso with a technical mastery of trumpets from the lowest to the highest registers, and tremendous stamina. He composes and arranges for very large ensembles and for small groups, and both his playing and his writing have a powerful individual atmosphere which has spawned many disciples – a kind of buoyant, romantic melancholy. Immensely self-critical, he finds it easier to like his writing than his playing, and has said, 'I don't have any solos of my own that I like completely, only those that are not as bad as others . . . perhaps the solos on *Deer Wan* I can live with.' Wheeler has toured and played festivals all over the world with his own and various other groups, and has performed his own compositions with the radio orchestras of Rome, Helsinki and Stockholm. He is also active in jazz education in Canada and Europe. He has won many jazz polls over the years in Europe and the USA, and his LP *Gnu High* won the German prize for the best jazz record of the year in 1976. He admires many musicians, but especially Miles Davis, Booker Little, Art Farmer, Benny Bailey and Freddie Hubbard, and particular inspirations are Gil Evans, Bill Evans, Duke Ellington. [IC]

With Pepper Adams, Mike Gibbs, George Adams, Rainer Brüninghaus, Anthony Braxton, Leo Smith, UJRE, Azimuth and many others; Wheeler Big Band, *The Windmill Tilter* (1968), Fontana; *Song For Someone* (1973), Incus; quartet with Jarrett/Holland/DeJohnette, *Gnu High* (1976); quintet with Garbarek, *Deer Wan* (1978); sextet, *Around Six* (1980); quintet with Mike Brecker/John Taylor, *Double, Double You* (1984), all ECM

Whetsol, Artie (Arthur Parker), trumpet. b. Punta Gorda, Florida, 1905; d. New York City, 5 January 1940. The original trumpeter with Duke Ellington's Washingtonians was a fine trained trumpeter and a consistently reliable performer, rather than a highly creative jazzman. 'The fact that he could sustain notes on the horn as long as he could with a pure sound that was almost violin-like in the range he was capable of,' says Mercer Ellington, 'that was very valuable.' It was particularly valuable to Ellington for the interpretation of early hits such as 'Mood Indigo' (one of the tunes that Whetsol always played better than most of his successors). Apart from a break to study medicine in the 1920s, Whetsol stayed with Ellington until 1937, when a developing brain disorder caused his premature retirement. Whetsol, tall, handsome, sophisticated, with a strong sense of correctness which once caused Barney Bigard to call him 'prissy', featured with Ellington in an award-winning film short, *Black and Tan Fantasy* (1929), although after Bubber Miley's arrival in the band in 1924 less attention was paid to him as a soloist. He remained, however, a vital 'lead voice' (especially in Ellington's sweeter repertoire): a pure tone colour which shone out often in Ellington's paintings. [DF]

Duke Ellington at the Cotton Club (1927–30), World

Whigham, Jiggs (Haydn), trombone. b. Cleveland, Ohio, 20 August 1943. 1961–4, with Glenn Miller orchestra under direction of Ray McKinley as lead trombonist and soloist; also with Stan Kenton. 1965, he freelanced in New York, then joined Kurt Edelhagen in Cologne, West Germany. He toured Africa with Edelhagen in 1966. During the 1970s he freelanced in Germany, then taught at the Music High School in Cologne. In the 1980s he became head of the jazz faculty there. [IC]

With Kenton, McKinley, Johnny Richards

White, Michael Walter, violin, electric violin. b. Houston, Texas, 24 May 1933. Brought up in Oakland, California. Began on violin at age nine. He came to prominence with the John Handy quintet at the 1965 Monterey Jazz Festival, and was one of the first violinists to adapt avant-garde techniques and ideas to that instrument. In the late 1960s he pioneered another direction with the group Fourth Way, one of the first jazz-rock outfits. From 1971 he began leading his own groups. He has also worked with Sun Ra, Prince Lasha, John Coltrane, Eric Dolphy, Wes Montgomery, Kenny Dorham, Richard Davis and others. His music combines oriental and classical elements with his jazz roots. His influences include Stuff Smith, Stephane Grappelli, Coltrane, Dolphy, Sun Ra, Duke Ellington, Charles Mingus, Thelonious Monk. [IC]

With Pharoah Sanders, Sonny Simmons, Jerry Hahn, McCoy Tyner and others; with Handy, *Live at Monterey* (1965), Columbia; with Fourth Way, *The Sun and Moon Have Come Together* (1969); *Werewolf* (1970); *The Fourth Way* (1970), all Capitol; as leader, *Spirit Dance* (1975), Impulse; *The X Factor* (1978), Elektra

Whitehead, Annie (Lena Anne), trombone, voice. b. Oldham, Lancashire, 16 July 1955. She had weekly music lessons at school and played in brass bands. 1969, she also played in local dance bands, and then at 16 joined Ivy Benson's band, staying with it for two years. During the 1970s she gave up music for six years, then in 1979 formed her own band to play ska, a precursor of reggae. 1981, she came to London and played numerous pop, reggae and soul sessions. 1982, she worked with various London-based bands and the following year toured Africa with Chris McGregor's Brotherhood of Breath and the USA with Fun Boy Three. 1984, she worked with John Stevens, with District Six, and formed her own group, the Annie Whitehead Band. Jimmy Knepper, Roswell Rudd and Lawrence Brown are among her favourite trombonists, and she has also been influenced by Charles Mingus, Chris McGregor and Hermeto Pascoal. [IC]

With John Stevens; *Mix-up* (1985), Paladin

Whitehead, Tim (Timothy George), tenor, alto and soprano sax, clarinet. b. Liverpool, 12

December 1950. He had music lessons on clarinet as a child but is otherwise self-taught, and began playing in a folk group while still at school. He took a bachelor's degree in law, but in 1976 gave up law and other pursuits in order to concentrate on music. His quartet South of the Border, which he co-led with guitarist Glenn Cartledge, won first prize in the Greater London Arts Association jazz competition in 1977; the same year, Whitehead toured Germany with Nucleus. 1978, he toured with Graham Collier's band. He then worked with various London-based bands and in 1980 formed his own quartet, Borderline. 1984, he joined Loose Tubes. His favourite saxophonists are John Coltrane, Wayne Shorter, Bob Berg, Mike Brecker, Dexter Gordon, and other inspirational figures for him are Keith Jarrett and Joe Zawinul. Whitehead's qualities as a composer and a player are well represented on the album below. [IC]

Borderline, *English People* (1982), Spotlite

Whiteman, Paul, leader, violin. b. Denver, Colorado, 28 March 1890; d. Doylestown, Pennsylvania, 29 December 1967. Paul Whiteman was once a figure of enormous controversy in jazz circles, more especially after a Universal film from 1930 sealed his previously-laid publicity campaign as *The King of Jazz*. By then he had been an internationally known showbusiness figure for ten years, who had promoted the first prestige jazz concert in history, 'An Experiment in Modern Music' at New York's Aeolian Hall in 1924 (featuring George Gershwin playing his own *Rhapsody in Blue*) and from then on was known for his fast-moving spectacular jazz presentations. Louis Armstrong gives a definitive word picture of what sort of thing went on at a Whiteman concert: 'Mr Whiteman went into the overture by the name of "1812" – and just before the end they started shooting cannons, sirens were howling like mad – and in fact everything was happening in that overture.' Not very much of what Whiteman presented ever had much to do with the unbowdlerized creations of jazzmen of the period, but he did contribute a great deal to the music. He publicized it, and did all he could to make it respectable and to popularize it. He created the idea of a band show: 'If you see that picture [*The King of Jazz*] he made in 1930,' says Lawrence Brown, 'you can see all the components [of a band show] that are still in use today.' Whiteman was a generous and discerning employer of the best. 'Don't ever make fun of Paul Whiteman', says Joe Venuti. 'He took pride in having the finest musicians in the world' (Venuti could more accurately have said 'the jazz world') 'and paid the highest salaries ever paid': Whiteman's star employees, from a long list, included, as well as Venuti, Bix Beiderbecke, Eddie Lang, Frank Trumbauer and Jack Teagarden. He was a kindly and much loved employer, who kept the sick Beiderbecke's chair open until the end, took a lot from 'difficult' bandsmen (like Venuti) with equanimity, and often released artists (for example the Modernaires) from their contracts if something good came up. Whiteman led a hugely successful band all through the 1930s but gave up regular bandleading in 1944 to become a director of ABC. Perhaps the most powerful argument for Whiteman, though, is how good a lot of his music (in retrospect) really was. The New Paul Whiteman Orchestra, organized by cornettist Dick Sudhalter in the 1970s specifically to play Whiteman's scores, proved the point: so of course do the King of Jazz's original recordings with Bix, Trumbauer, Bing Crosby *et al.*, which are charming at least, great at best. [DF]

The Bix Beiderbecke Legend (1924–30), RCA (double)

Whittle, Tommy (Thomas), tenor sax, reeds. b. Grangemouth, Scotland, 13 October 1926. He worked early in his career with Claude Giddings's band (including Ronnie Verrell, Pete Chilver, John Claes and Ralph Sharon) then with John Claes's Clay Pigeons, Lew Stone, Carl Barriteau and Harry Hayes. At 20 he joined the great Ted Heath orchestra, but left to develop his solo activities and skills with Tony Kinsey's trio, his own quintet (with Harry Klein) and soon after the BBC Show Band, with whom he was featured soloist: a film of the period, *Show Band Show*, spotlights his bright new talent. Some poll-topping followed, for *Melody Maker* and *New Musical Express*: Whittle formed his own 8-piece band which toured for 18 months and soon after he played solo and with his own small groups in France and the USA as the 'exchange' for Sidney Bechet and Gerry Mulligan's quartet. Then, after a spell of bandleading at the Dorchester Hotel, he joined Jack Parnell's famous ATV orchestra and remained working in studios regularly thereafter, coming out to play guest spots around the country (often with his wife, singer Barbara Jay), running – and sometimes playing at – a succession of jazz clubs in West London (including, for a long time, the Hopbine at Wembley), and appearing with the Jazz Journal All Stars (and Barbara Jay) at Nice, 1984. Whittle is a shining exception to the view that years of studio work dull the edges of jazz creativity. [DF]

Wilber, Bob (Robert Sage), clarinet, soprano sax. b. New York City, 15 March 1928. He began as a student clarinettist at Scarsdale High School, New York, where he soon formed a band (with Ed Hubble and Dick Wellstood among others), sat in at Jimmy Ryan's, and when still a teenager studied first under Sidney Bechet, then with Lennie Tristano. The extremes that his two teachers represented clearly indicated the eclecticism of Wilber's ideas (although he

Bob Wilber

recognized the stylistic limitations of bebop very early on) and in 1954, after periods leading bands of a Dixieland persuasion with such as Jimmy Archey, he formed The Six. 'We wanted to show', he explains, '. . . that we could use traditional material and modern material and new material: that there was no basic conflict between the old and the new.' Such a concept was perhaps over-intelligent for the jazz generation of the period, and when Wilber found his band sounding too much like the fashionable modern groups ('That was where the work was') he broke it up and joined Eddie Condon, with whom he toured England in 1957, then spent a year with Bobby Hackett's band playing clarinet (and a little vibraphone, behind Hackett's wandering ballads). From then into the 1960s Wilber was a freelance, working on classy recording projects with Ruby Braff, Bud Freeman and others and studying piano with Sanford

Gold; by now he was forming his own strong convictions about how jazz should be played. 'I have a feeling that jazz has got to be part of the pop music scene to survive,' he said in a *Downbeat* interview of the period, 'that there are some exciting things going on in the market place in music, more than in the rather introverted jazz scene.' The World's Greatest Jazz Band, filled with top-class musicians, prepared to play a wide repertoire, often drawn from contemporary sources, and offering an excitement in performance not always in evidence elsewhere, certainly took Wilber's fancy, and from 1968 (in the wake of Dick Gibson's jazz parties) he was a founder member of Gibson's cunningly-promoted brainchild. When he left in 1973 it was to form the first of his own well-thought-out projects, Soprano Summit, a quintet co-led with Kenny Davern which (like all his subsequent groups) presented unusual repertoire, well (but never over-) arranged, and performed with the kind of verve that was seldom still to be heard in an ageing jazz generation. Three years on, Wilber (who, with the aid of his canny, supportive and perceptive wife Joanne 'Pug' Horton, has always been good at knowing when to move on) broke up his group again: after nine albums, headlining success and poll-topping there seemed little left to do. For a while he formed a trio with Horton and pianist Dave McKenna (which toured widely), re-transcribed a set of Jelly Roll Morton titles for recording, worked with the New York Jazz Repertory Company and by 1981 had embarked on his latest project, the Bechet Legacy, a group which set out to re-create music that Bechet had played, in Wilber's own style. The 6-piece band – featuring a highly gifted New York trumpeter, Glenn Zottola (later replaced by Randy Sandke) – was, as usual, a glittering success for Wilber, whose projects were by now the focus of international jazz attention: he formed his own record company, Bodeswell, and used it as a means of regularly issuing more new projects, including a session with strings (*Reflections*, on which he played every part in a 5-man saxophone section as well as solos) and *The Music of King Oliver's Jazz Band*, a scholarly transcription of Oliver's 1923 sides. More transcriptions came when Wilber was asked to recreate Duke Ellington's 1927 Washingtonians for a Francis Ford Coppola movie *The Cotton Club* (1984): his work – sealing the success of the film – was uncannily close to the original. In 1985, Wilber visited England as musical director for the annual Duke Ellington Conference at Oldham, as ever planning new projects, including a re-formed Benny Goodman Orchestra of all-British players which toured widely in 1985–6. [DF]

Reflections (1983), Bodeswell

Wilder, Alec (Alexander Lafayette Chew), composer. b. Rochester, New York, 17 February 1907; d. December 1980. One of the songwriters whose talents have always inspired jazzmen. Wilder's often neglected compositions include 'It's so peaceful in the country', 'The Lady Sings the Blues', 'The April Age' and 'I'll Be Around'. He also wrote the definitive work *American Popular Song*, a highly readable, occasionally disputable, always loving analysis of great songs, written with never a boring sentence by an enthusiastic master of his craft. Wilder also wrote many compositions of a classical nature, while the jazz-tinged recordings of the Wilder octet from 1939 onwards are much-sought collectors' items. [DF]

Elaine Delmar Sings Wilder (1966), EMI Lansdowne

See Wilder, Alec, *American Popular Song: The Great Innovators 1900–1950* (OUP, 1972)

Wilen, Barney (Bernard Jean), tenor sax. b. Nice, France, 4 March 1937. Self-taught musician, made strong impression on Paris scene (mid-1950s); recorded there with John Lewis, and own first album at age 19. Worked with Miles Davis on *Lift to the Scaffold* soundtrack and in concert (1957), and with Art Blakey on *Les Liaisons Dangereuses* soundtrack and in concert (1959). Not continuously active as player, was later interested in free jazz (1966); appeared at Berlin festival, 1967, with Indian classical musicians, and acted as recording engineer for Archie Shepp's live performance in Algiers (1969). Wilen's early work absorbed the implications of Americans such as Sonny Rollins, but with a softer tone possibly influenced by Lucky Thompson's first visit to France. As well as demonstrating the maturity of the Paris scene, which was then a Mecca for visiting American players, Wilen himself sounds remarkably fresh and vital in retrospect. [BP]

Miles Davis, *Miles in Amsterdam* (1957), Jazz OP

Wiley, Lee, singer, composer. b. Fort Gibson, Oklahoma, 9 October 1915; d. New York City, 11 December 1975. 'Lee Wiley has class', says George Frazier. 'She makes you hurt more and more with the remembrance of other never-to-be-recaptured nights. Lee Wiley can do that to you – damn her! But damn her gently because she is, after all, the best we have – the very best.' Frazier was the singer's most passionate in-print advocate but most jazz people share a fondness, and often much more, for what she did.

In her teens she was temporarily blinded in a riding accident, recovered, came to New York around 1930 and by the time she was 17 was singing with Leo Reisman's orchestra. All the way through the 1930s she worked constantly on radio, recorded with Victor Young, John Green and the Casa Lomans, and from mid-decade began appearing in clubs with small jazz groups, including Eddie Condon's at the Famous Door (Condon's trumpeter was Bunny Berigan who became her lover). In 1939 and 1940 – an idea by songwriter John de Vries – she recorded albums of songs by Cole Porter and George Gershwin, accompanied by small jazz groups, in which her intimate, veiled voice, precise, almost tutored, diction and stroking approach to a note seemed guaranteed to turn strong men to jelly: 'I loved Lee Wiley,' said critic Stanley Green, 'even before I had any idea who she was, I loved her! She sang to me – just to me!' In June 1943, Wiley married Jess Stacy, and, for once, all was not as blissfully romantic as might have been expected: Stacy referred to his five-year marriage tersely as 'The Wiley Incident' and seldom said much more. By 1944, Wiley was still on radio but later left the business to marry a millionaire and – apart from a semi-documentary TV play starring Piper Laurie, *Something About Lee Wiley* (in the Bob Hope Presents series, 1963), very little more was heard from her until 1971. That year she recorded *Back Home Again* for Monmouth Evergreen, with Rusty Dedrick's band; the album was the last before her death, but her 1930s sides and broadcasts have never stopped being reissued. [DF]

Night in Manhattan (1950), Columbia

See Condon, Eddie, *Treasury of Jazz* (Davies, 1957)

Wilkins, Dave (David Livingstone), trumpet. b. Barbados, 25 September 1914. Anyone who likes the sides Fats Waller recorded in London (including 'Pent up in a penthouse', 'Flat Foot Floogie' *et al.* in 1938) is bound to like the sound of trumpeter Dave Wilkins too. He was born in Barbados, trained in the Salvation Army there, and then played in his family band before joining Richie Keith's Jazz Hounds in Trinidad, 1934. Soon after, he joined Ken 'Snakehips' Johnson's band in Port of Spain, and in 1938 arrived at the Glasgow Empire: a baptism of fire for the orchestra which they confidently survived. Johnson's band went on to make a big impact in London, Wilkins was spotted by Waller and asked to record, and by 1939 – via television, radio and coverage in the *Melody Maker* – he was well on his way. But although he survived the bomb that came down the steps of the Café de Paris in 1940, killing half of Johnson's band, very little more was heard of him, apart from recordings with Lord Kitchener and others during the 1950s calypso boom. In 1985 he was living in London, but inactive. [DF]

Fats Waller, *Memorial Album* (1938), EMI Encore

Wilkins, Ernie (Ernest Brooks), tenor, alto and soprano sax, arranger. b. St Louis, Missouri, 20 July 1922. After university study and navy service, worked with Earl Hines band (1947) and in St Louis area. Joined Count Basie (1952–5), playing alto and arranging. Left to become freelance writer for Basie, Dizzy Gillespie (in whose 1956 band he played briefly), Tommy Dorsey, Harry James; also arranger/musical director for countless albums with Sarah Vaughan, Buddy Rich, Oscar Peterson and many others. Career temporarily halted by drug problem (mid-1960s), after which played and wrote for Clark Terry big band and quintet (from 1969). Arranging and supervising sessions for Mainstream Records (1971–3). Worked in Europe from mid-1970s, recording with Art Farmer and Austrian Radio band, writing for other radio orchestras; from 1980, also leading own Almost Big Band, and touring as soloist.

Wilkins is an exciting and unfussy writer whose main historical importance lay in redefining the sound of the 1950s Basie band, which he was then expected to duplicate for freelance assignments (Basie is alleged to have said to Harry James at a joint appearance, 'Who's going to play my arrangements first, me or you?') This sound would have been widely imitated anyway, and it provided much encouragement for Wilkins's stylistic successor Quincy Jones; but it is a pity that Ernie himself, at least until recent times, has been so typecast. [BP]

Here Comes the Swinging Mr Wilkins (1959–60), Everest; *Almost Big Band* (1980), Storyville

Williams, Benny, see BLACK BENNY.

Williams, Clarence, piano, vocals, arranger, composer, leader. b. Plaquemine Delta, Louisiana, 8 October 1898; d. Queens, New York, 6 November 1965. As a child he was raised by a hotel-owning Plaquemine family, and quickly acquired a business eye: while playing the field in New Orleans and picking up tips from New Orleans pianists he ran a suit-cleaning service for the sharp-as-a-tack piano professors. Soon after that he was playing in Storyville as a solo entertainer, keeping a sharp ear out for new material and writing away to New York for the newest song-hits, as well as managing his own cabaret on the side. At the period he opened a small publishing company with Armand J. Piron (his regular partner) and in 1916, out of the blue, he received a $1600 cheque for a song he had almost forgotten about, 'Brownskin, who you for?', which had been recorded by a New York band for Columbia records. 'I believe it was the most money anybody ever made on a song in New Orleans', said Williams and from then on his course was clear. First he sold songsheets door-to-door around the District music shops (Lizzie Miles often sang the words), then he opened a music store in Chicago, and soon after established a highly successful New York publishing house for which, by 1919, Richard M. Jones was a regular employee. All the way through the next decade Williams was organizing record dates (including his classic 'Blue Five' sessions with Louis Armstrong, Sidney Bechet and others), playing, and accompanying a string of fine blues singers from Sippie Wallace to Rosetta Crawford and Bessie Smith (he also briefly managed Smith, an arrangement which collapsed suddenly after a royalty dispute), and composing a catalogueful of durable hits: 'Baby won't you please come home', 'Royal Garden Blues', 'Everybody loves my baby', 'West End Blues' and more. From 1923, Williams was also A & R man for the 'Race' division of Okeh records (a powerful position), regularly led bands of his own (often including Ed Allen, a fine and underrated trumpeter) and married blues singer Eva Taylor. As the decade progressed he went on recording (often with bigger bands) and stayed successful until – with the swift passage of jazz fashion – he found himself in less demand than before. In 1943, Williams sold his catalogue to Decca for $50,000 and opened a busy bargain shop in Harlem: by 1961, a devout Christian, he was living in Brooklyn still, but with failing sight. In 1965 he was knocked down by a taxi and killed on the New York streets. [DF]

With King Oliver and Bennie Moten (1927–8), Classic Jazz Masters

See Lord, Tom, *Clarence Williams* (Storyville, 1976)

Williams, Cootie (Charles Melvin), trumpet. b. Mobile, Alabama, 24 July 1910; d. New York City, 14 September 1985. He worked with Alonzo Ross, Chick Webb and Fletcher Henderson, before joining Duke Ellington in 1929, replacing Bubber Miley. To begin with Williams was never instructed to duplicate Miley's growling *tours de force*. 'But', he told Eric Townley later, 'I thought as I was taking Bubber's place I'd better learn how to growl . . . then one night when I had a solo to play on something I picked up the plunger and surprised the band with a growl solo. When we came off the stand Duke and the boys said, "That's it, that's it. Keep that in!" ' From then on Williams developed Miley's style into a vocabulary of his own (a side with Billie Holiday, 'Carelessly' from the 1930s, shows how) and featured his powerful horn on specially composed features such as 'Concerto for Cootie', which Ellington wrote for him in 1940. That year Williams – amid a blaze of publicity, media recrimination and even a Raymond Scott record commemorating the event – left the Duke to join Benny Goodman, a leader he much admired, and stayed a year. From then on he led his own big band (Ellington encouraged him to go out on his own when Williams asked to return to the fold), and over the years featured a string of bright young talents, including Charlie Parker, Bud Powell, Eddie 'Lockjaw' Davis, Ed Thigpen and Eddie

Cootie Williams

'Cleanhead' Vinson, before cutting down to a rhythm-and-blues-flavoured 6-piece at the instigation of Savoy manager Charlie Buchanan in 1948. By 1962, Williams – a trumpeter of unbending standards, strong opinions and inner tensions – was drinking more, developing high blood pressure and feeling the strain of leading his own band. So he rejoined Goodman briefly and, finally, Ellington for good in 1962. From then on his strong, immobile hatchet-features and masterful trumpet were centrepoints of Ellington's concerts until his leader's death; Williams carried on with Mercer Ellington's later re-creations, and a very late (unexpected) sample of Williams 1978 may be heard on the album *Teresa Brewer at Carnegie Hall*. [DF]

And his Rug Cutters, 1937–40, Tax

See Dance, Stanley, *The World of Duke Ellington* (Scribner's, 1970, repr. Da Capo, 1980)

Williams, Joe (Joseph Goreed), vocals. b. Cordele, Georgia, 12 December 1918, brought up in Chicago. Not to be confused with blues singer/guitarist Big Joe Williams (b. Clarksdale, Mississippi, 16 October 1903; d. 17 December 1982). Sang in Chicago night clubs with Jimmie Noone group and others (late 1930s), Coleman Hawkins and Lionel Hampton bands (early 1940s). Toured with Andy Kirk (1946–7), making first record with him in New York. Briefly with Albert Ammons–Pete Johnson, then with Chicago band of Red Saunders with whom he recorded under leadership of Hot Lips Page (1950). Worked in Chicago with Count Basie

Mary Lou Williams

septet (1950), then built reputation with first record of 'Every Day' (*c.* 1951) backed by King Kolax band. Became Basie's regular singer (1954–60), bringing himself and band to new popularity. Soloist from then, first with Harry Edison quintet (1961–2), then with own trios led by Chicago pianists Junior Mance, Norman Simmons etc. Regular appearances with all-star jazz groups (including African tour with Clark Terry quintet, 1979) and frequent reunions with Basie band (including in Europe, 1985). Williams's distinctive voice, deeper and darker than Billy Eckstine's, has been very effective on sophisticated blues performances, but he has also shown considerable versatility on jazz and ballad items. [BP]

Count Basie Swings, Joe Williams Sings (1955), Verve

See Gourse, Leslie, *Every Day: The Story of Joe Williams* (Quartet, 1985)

Williams, Mary Lou (*née* Mary Elfrieda Scruggs), piano, arranger, composer. b. Atlanta, Georgia, 8 May 1910; d. 28 May 1981. Playing by ear as a child, she first performed in public at age six. Brought up in Pittsburgh, she appeared in talent shows and from age 13 was working in carnivals and vaudeville. At 16 married carnival band member John Williams (who in 1940s was to play with the Cootie Williams and Earl Hines bands) and moved to Memphis, making her record debut with his Synco Jazzers; when Williams joined Terrence Holder's band (soon to become Andy Kirk's) she hired Jimmie Lunceford as his replacement and ran the group herself. When Kirk band settled in Kansas City (1929), Mary Lou first wrote arrangements for them, then deputized on piano for their initial recording (one of her compositions) and then (1931) became regular band pianist and chief arranger.

Though busy also as freelance arranger for Benny Goodman etc. (from mid-1930s) she remained with Kirk until 1942; having divorced and married Shorty Baker, left to co-lead sextet with him. When he joined Ellington, she led her own group (including Art Blakey, 1942) then also worked for Ellington as staff arranger. Settling in New York, began working regularly under own name; performed her 'Zodiac Suite' with New York Philharmonic at Town Hall (1946). Lived in England and France (1952–4) before retiring from music for three years. Guest appearance with Dizzy Gillespie at Newport festival (1957) followed by further regular playing and further composing. Toured Europe

(1968–9); concert appearances included duo with Cecil Taylor (1977), Goodman Carnegie Hall anniversary (1978) and Montreux festival, 1979. Was artist in residence at Duke University, North Carolina, from 1977 until shortly before her death from cancer.

In her last years, Mary Lou often gave a recital/demonstration of the history of jazz, most of which she had lived through and influenced. The early Andy Kirk band was a primitive blues-based organization just waiting to be overhauled and modernized by her writing and playing; at the keyboard, she was one of the first anywhere to pick up on the innovations of Earl Hines, whom she first heard before both left Pittsburgh. Always showing an affinity for boogie-woogie (the inspiration for her famous 'Roll 'Em', written for Goodman), she also adapted it to more modern patterns and voicings in her own performances of the late 1930s. Then, although she was partly behind the scenes, her friendship in the 1940s with Tadd Dameron, Bud Powell and Thelonious Monk (whom she had met when he visited Kansas City on tour) made her the virtual guru of the bebop movement.

Her interest in astrological titles had few follow-ups until the 'Age of Aquarius' suddenly made it an OK thing, but her subsequent Christian conversion and writing of religious works from the early 1960s set a precedent for those jazz musicians who then began performing in church, including Duke Ellington; although he only recorded the brilliant 'Trumpet No End' of the pieces she wrote for him, she was a close friend in later life and played at his funeral. But, more than with most musicians of historical importance and influence, the sheer enjoyment to be gained from her work is still vastly underrated. [BP]

Andy Kirk, *Walkin' and Swingin'* (1936–42), Affinity; *In London* (1953), Jazz Legacy; *Mama Pinned a Rose On Me* (1979), Pablo

See Dahl, Linda, *Stormy Weather* (Quartet, 1984)

Williams, Roy, trombone, b. Bolton, Lancashire, 7 March 1937. He began in Manchester playing tailgate trombone with a famous local band, Eric Batty's Jazz Aces. Soon after, he joined Mike Peters, then Terry Lightfoot for the duration of the 'Trad boom' in Britain, recording widely, appearing in films such as *It's Trad Dad* (1962) and impressing musicians in the know with his rapidly developing technique and fluent ideas. One such was drummer Lennie Hastings who, after Roy Crimmins's departure from Alex Welsh's first band, recommended young Roy Williams as the replacement, and he joined on 1 April 1965. An Alex Welsh album, *Strike One*, a fanfare for his new band, showed that almost overnight, it seemed, Williams had turned into a world-class talent, a perfect amalgam of Urbie Green and Jack Teagarden with a hint of Bob Brookmeyer here and there. For the next 13 years, Williams was a much-respected centrepiece of Welsh's great band, but left in 1978, joined Humphrey Lyttelton for four years, and then became a freelance. By now his reputation was unassailable: a regular winner of the *Jazz Journal International* readers' poll trombone section, he was visiting America to play for Dick Gibson's Colorado Jazz Parties and Don Miller's Phoenix festival, working with Bobby Rosengarden's band at New York's Rainbow Room, recording solo albums and appearing around the festival circuit as an in-demand soloist as well as playing club and concert dates with Peter Boizot's Pizza All Stars, the trombone group Five-a-Slide and the Alex Welsh Reunion Band. Williams is the natural heir to George Chisholm's crown: his talent – consistent, perfectly musical and, with its pianissimo close-to-the-microphone approach, recalling Jack Teagarden – is one of the joys of British jazz and has earned the respect and affection of the international jazz community. [DF]

Royal Trombone (1983), Phontastic

Williams, Rudy, alto, tenor and baritone sax, clarinet. b. Newark, New Jersey, 1909; d. September 1954. Was leading soloist with the original Savoy Sultans, on his main instrument the alto (1937–43), then briefly with Hot Lips Page, Luis Russell etc. Led own bands in New York and Boston (1944–51), also tours of Far East Service bases (1945–6, 1951–2). Periods of freelancing including with John Kirby (1945), Babs Gonzales (1947), Tadd Dameron (1948), Illinois Jacquet and Gene Ammons (both 1951), and at the time of his death in a swimming accident. Though not widely recognized, Williams was admired by fellow musicians for his 'advanced' work in the early 1940s. Broadly speaking, this can be described as applying the tenor style of Don Byas to the alto, and the link was especially noticeable when Williams played the tenor himself. [BP]

Al Cooper and the Savoy Sultans, *Jump Steady* (1938–41), Affinity

Williams, Sandy (Alexander Balos), trombone. b. Summerville, South Carolina, 24 October 1906. He learned to play in his Delaware school band and began his career working in theatre orchestras. It was then that he first became aware of Jimmy Harrison, the revolutionary trombonist with Fletcher Henderson ('I thought the sun rose and set on him – I had all his records') and began to be noticed himself as a stylish jazzman. In 1927 he joined Claude Hopkins for a season in Atlantic City and by 1929 was with Horace Henderson: three years on he was with Fletcher Henderson himself ('It was the height of my ambition to get in that band', he told Stanley Dance later). Williams – a natural practical joker – was sacked the following year for setting off a firecracker on stage, but then joined Chick Webb and stayed for seven years. He was then briefly with a string of other well-known bands including Duke Ellington's, but by 1943, 'the bottle was really starting to get to me', he recalled, and despite a drying-out period, he continued to drink heavily until in 1950 (after work with leaders including Roy Eldridge, Rex Stewart and Art Hodes) he suffered a complete health breakdown. When he got back into music later on in the late 1950s he found that embouchure problems caused by dental difficulties were making playing difficult and he was forced into inactivity. [DF]

Chick Webb, vol. 1: A Legend, 1929–36, MCA

See Dance, Stanley, *The World of Swing* (Scribner's, 1974, repr. Da Capo, 1979)

Williams, Spencer, composer, piano, vocals. b. New Orleans, 14 October *c.* 1889; d. Flushing, New York, 14 July 1965. He was a nephew of bordello owner Lulu White, in whose Mahogany Hall he lived after the death of his mother. In 1907 he worked in Chicago as a pianist, arriving in New York around 1916 where he quickly established himself with hits including 'Squeeze Me' (which he wrote with Fats Waller, a lifelong friend), 'I ain't got nobody' (one of a set of tunes for Bert Williams) 'Basin Street Blues', 'Royal Garden Blues', 'I found a new baby' and others. Spencer Williams was a frequent collaborator with Clarence Williams (they were unrelated) and by 1925 was successful enough to travel to Paris to compose 'special material' for Josephine Baker at the Folies-Bergère. In 1932 (after involvement in a murder trial; he was acquitted) Williams moved to the London area and then from 1951 to 1957 lived in Stockholm, comfortably, on his royalties. In 1957 he at last returned to New York, in poor health, and died eight years later. [DF]

Williams, Tony (Anthony), drums, composer. b. Chicago, 12 December 1945. Brought up in Boston; father played tenor sax. Started on drums at age ten, studying with Alan Dawson. Developed precociously, playing experimental concerts with Sam Rivers and the Boston Improvisational Ensemble in his early teens. December 1962, he moved to New York, playing with Jackie McLean. At the age of 17 he joined Miles Davis, staying with him for six years, 1963–9. With Davis, Williams made an immediate and sensational impact internationally, because he was already both a virtuoso and an original stylist. Technically he had everything: he could play superlative straight jazz 4/4 and 3/4 (and that rhythm-section with Ron Carter and Herbie Hancock is widely regarded as one of the greatest of all time-playing units), but he could also play with the utmost freedom, displacing accents, leaving spaces, producing counter-rhythms and polyrhythms, implying the beat and playing on the pulse of the music. After Philly Joe Jones and Elvin Jones, this was another crucial development of the role of the drums, and during his time with Davis, Williams perfected his approach, building up a whole new vocabulary of rhythmic devices and spawning imitators and disciples all over the globe.

While with Davis he also played with other groups and blossomed as a composer. 1965, he recorded his first album as leader, *Life Time* (Blue Note), which showed that his inclinations veered towards the avant-garde music of the day – abstraction. But he was becoming equally interested in the non-abstract rock rhythms of the time. His comment on Miles Davis in the late 1960s is true also of himself: 'He's trying to get further out (more abstract) and yet more basic (funkier) at the same time.' 1969, he left Davis and started his own jazz-rock group Lifetime with John McLaughlin, Jack Bruce and Larry Young. This was a wildly exciting and pioneering band playing loud, extremely complex music. Intricate written passages alternated with brilliant stretches of improvisation, and the drums not only played time (rock beat) but also were integrated in a new way with the rhythms of the melodies: this integration was to become a cliché of the jazz-rock movement in the later 1970s. Lifetime also offered a rich mixture of techniques and devices: chord-based playing, free improvisation with rock rhythms, modal improvisation and asymmetry in both metre and structure. Although it toured and played festivals in the US and Europe, Lifetime was dogged by bad luck and mismanagement. McLaughlin left to form his Mahavishnu Orchestra and, after his departure, Williams's personnel changed from year to year, and he seemed always to be denied the success and recognition which some of the later jazz-rock groups enjoyed.

In the later 1970s he toured internationally and recorded with VSOP, the reunited Miles Davis quintet (Hancock, Carter, Shorter) with Freddie Hubbard in place of Davis. In 1982, with the Herbie Hancock quartet (Carter and Wynton Marsalis), he toured in the US, Europe and Japan, and recorded a double album. In the mid-1970s Williams recorded with the Gil Evans orchestra, and one of his compositions, 'There Comes a Time', was the album's title-track.

Tony Williams's vital contribution to jazz has been as a player, not as a bandleader. He made an immense contribution to the music of Miles Davis in the 1960s, playing on about 17 of his albums, several of which are enduring classics. In terms of influence, he and Elvin Jones dominated that decade. His drumming with Lifetime fused the physicality and directness of rock with the complexity and flexibility of jazz, creating a precedent for subsequent groups. [IC]

With Lifetime, *Believe It* (nda) Columbia; *Emergency* (1969); *Turn It Over* (1970); *Ego* (nda); *Old Bum's Rush* (nda), all Polydor; with Davis, *My Funny Valentine* (1964); *Miles Smiles* (1966); *Nefertiti* (1967); *Miles in the Sky* (1968); *Filles de Kilimanjaro* (1968); *In a Silent Way* (1969), all CBS

Wilson, Dick (Richard), tenor sax. b. Mount Vernon, Illinois, 11 November 1911; d. New York, 24 November 1941. One of the briefest and brightest of jazz legends, Wilson was a pupil of reedman Joe Darensbourg and worked for territory bands in Portland, Oregon, and his home town before moving to the West Coast and Gene Coy's band, then to Denver, Colorado, where he worked with Zack Whyte and finally, in 1936, joined Andy Kirk's Twelve Clouds of Joy in Kansas City. For the last five years of his life he was the tenor star of Kirk's band, and before tuberculosis killed him at just 30 he had recorded enough evidence to prove that – with Jimmy Blanton's and Charlie Christian's – his death was the most bitter blow of the dawning modern jazz era. [DF]

Andy Kirk, *Walkin' and Swingin'* (1936–42), Affinity

Teddy Wilson

Wilson, Garland Lorenzo, piano. b. Martinsburg, West Virginia, 13 June 1909; d. Paris, 31 May 1954. He studied at Howard University, Washington, came to New York around 1930 and by 1931 was working at Covan's, a club close to the Lafayette Theater. At this time John Hammond agreed to finance a recording session for him via Frank Walker of Columbia: the results were issued on 12″ records, were reasonably successful and Hammond paid his protégé with an expensive watch. In 1932, Wilson, a heavy drinker, toured Europe as accompanist to Nina Mae McKinney, and all through the 1930s was a frequent familiar figure in England, playing solo and working with Jack Payne's orchestra (at the time, Derrick Stewart-Baxter remembers, Wilson would often find a piano in a pub between shows with Payne, and sit contentedly to drink and play). During his stays in England he recorded with Nat Gonella and as a soloist. In 1939 he returned to the USA for night-club work, returning to Europe in 1951, when he lived in Paris and commuted regularly to London, just as before. A modest man, he was inclined to underrate himself. 'Garland's best playing was away from the public in some darkened room', says Stewart-Baxter. After hearing the galloping, highly technical work that Wilson recorded, the remark turns into a high compliment. [DF]

The Way I Feel (1932–51), Collectors Items

Wilson, Gerald Stanley, trumpet, arranger. b. Shelby, Mississippi, 4 September 1918. Began on piano, learned trumpet while at college in Detroit. Worked there and on tour, then joined Jimmie Lunceford band (1939–42), playing and arranging. Settled in Los Angeles, working with Benny Carter and others before navy service. Formed own big band (1944) which has continued intermittently until present day, featuring many important West Coast-based musicians. Freelance arranging including for Dizzy Gillespie, Count Basie (both late 1940s) and Duke Ellington (from mid-1950s); occasional recording on trumpet with all three. Musical director on records and live appearances for numerous artists including Al Hirt and singer Nancy Wilson. Ran own jazz-based radio show in mid-1970s. Never prominent as a player although heard on albums by Leroy Vinnegar and others, Wilson has a distinctive style of writing, somewhat similar harmonically to Thad Jones. Even when played by Ellington, his arrangements are recognizably his and worthy of greater renown. [BP]

You Better Believe It (1961), Pacific Jazz

Wilson, Teddy (Theodore Shaw), piano, arranger. b. Austin, Texas, 24 November 1912; d. 31 July 1986. His perfectly honed playing – like the man himself – had an aura of graceful urbanity, a level dignity which somehow makes it less surprising that his father was head of English, his mother chief librarian, at Tuskegee University. By his teenage years Wilson had fallen in love with records such as Bix Beiderbecke's 'Singin' the Blues' and King Oliver's

'Snag It', and after a visit to Chicago in 1928 was so inspired by the jazz he heard that he determined to make it his living. The year after, he joined Speed Webb's band, for which he became one of seven staff arrangers, re-orchestrating, in close harmony, the solos by Beiderbecke and Hodges that had fascinated him on record (a very early example of the idea). In 1931 he teamed with Art Tatum in a regular duo: 'We would go out every night,' Wilson recalled later, 'and make the rounds of the places, playing on upright pianos until late morning and sometimes early afternoon.' Tatum's reputation was already legendary and the bright young pianist keeping up with him was quickly spotted; by, among others, Benny Carter and John Hammond, who heard Wilson one night in 1933 subbing for Earl Hines in a broadcast from Grand Terrace Ballroom. 'Hines's substitute, I suddenly realized,' said Hammond, 'was absolutely unique, with a cleaner and more elegant sound, never flashy but swinging, with an excellent left hand.' By then Wilson had been doing the rounds of bands (including Louis Armstrong's) and arranging for Hines, and it was Hammond – his greatest champion – who recommended him first to Benny Carter in New York, sent Carter the $150 needed to get Wilson there, and effectively launched the pianist's career with a recording date for the Chocolate Dandies led by Carter. From then on Wilson, often at Hammond's behest, was constantly recording with his own small groups, often featuring a singer about whom Wilson later had personally mixed feelings: Billie Holiday. But the Wilson–Holiday collaborations are a high-water mark, Wilson's steady direction, joyful piano and impeccable choice of sidemen setting off the young singer's ingénue genius to perfection. From Hammond came one more introduction: to Benny Goodman, whom Wilson met at a Victor recording date, and soon after – following a 1936 concert at Chicago's Hot Club, promoted by Squirrel Ashcraft – the pianist became the first black musician to join Goodman's band. At the time this caused immense publicity, but Wilson – cool, correct and impeccable – was a reassuring figure and for the next three years, seated amid the frantic activity of Goodman's frenetic quartet, he was a dignified ambassador for black music. Soon after, Goodman was to call him 'the greatest musician in dance music today, irrespective of instrument', and it was inevitable that Wilson, before long, should have thought about a big band of his own. The one he put together in 1939 caused (like Benny Carter's) a musical sensation – 'The most musical and cleanest big band outside of Ellington's', said Billy Strayhorn – but commercially it made little impact (due, said the leader, to a lack of showmanship) and from 1940 he was to confine himself to small groups. During World War II he led his own highly successful sextet at Café Society (featuring Benny Morton, Jimmy Hamilton and a variety of trumpeters including Bill Coleman), then rejoined Goodman and afterwards took a studio job at CBS and teaching posts at major colleges such as the Juilliard and Metropolitan Schools. By the 1950s he was still working the studios, leading his own trio, re-creating swing glories on classic sessions such as *Jazz Giants 1956* and *Prez and Teddy*, playing in Goodman reunions and building his solo reputation. In the 1960s he was more than ever a soloist, visiting Europe, Japan, South America and Australia, as well as holding down local residencies, and in the 1970s was regularly at Michael's Pub, New York, appearing annually at Newport Jazz Festival, New York, and still going abroad. The year before his death, despite recent severe illness, he was playing as impeccably as ever: enjoying a comfortable creative plateau from which he could proudly survey the achievements of five decades. [DF]

'The' Teddy Wilson (1935–41), CBS; any later solo or trio album

Windhurst, Johnny (John Henry), trumpet. b. Bronx, New York, 5 November 1926; d. November 1981. A hugely undervalued trumpeter, who mixed the delicacy of Bobby Hackett with the mobility of Ruby Braff and a feathery vibrato all his own, Windhurst was sitting in at Nick's in New York by the age of 15, and just four years on was playing alongside Sidney Bechet (as a late replacement for Bunk Johnson) at the Savoy Café, Boston. Such a talent should quickly have turned into a household name, but somehow Windhurst never did: in the omnipotent shadow of Armstrong, big talents were often underrated. Windhurst did well enough: he played regularly around his home area, Boston, often at the Storyville Club, worked at Gene Norman's Dixieland Jubilee with Louis Armstrong and spent time with Nappy Lamare's band. In the 1950s he led his own Riverboat Five around Columbus, Ohio, and Boston, worked and recorded with Eddie Condon (a 1950 Windhurst re-run of 'A Hundred Years from Today' is beautiful), played for George Wettling and Jack Teagarden in 1954 and by 1956 had taken an on-stage role with actor Conrad Janis in an off-Broadway musical, *Joy Ride*. After it closed Windhurst continued touring (often with trombonist Eddie Hubble) around his home patch: the odd records he made – with Barbara Lea, Walt Gifford's New Yorkers and his own quartet – indicate a young talent comparable at least to Ruby Braff. But whereas Braff stubbornly stuck to New York, Windhurst was seen there less often, apart from visits to Nick's Club, and by the late 1960s had moved out to Poughkeepsie with his mother. From 1970 he was resident at a local club, Frivolous Sal's Last Chance Saloon (a lovely old Victorian theatre) and lived contentedly. 'He won't do anything, won't travel, just wants to stay where he is', said Hubble. 'He should get out and let people know he's still alive.' In November 1981, Windhurst was invited to Manassas Jazz Festival, but died of a heart attack shortly before he was due to leave. [DF]

The Imaginative Johnny Windhurst (1956), Jazzology

Winding, Kai Chresten, trombone. b. Aarhus, Denmark, 18 May 1922; d. Spain, 7 May 1983. After emigrating to US with family at age 12, Winding began big-band work as a teenager and found fame with Stan Kenton (1946–7). Then active in small bands with Charlie Ventura (1947–8), Tadd Dameron (1948–9) and others. Co-led popular two-trombone quintet with J. J. Johnson (1954–6, plus occasional reunions), followed by own four-trombone septet (1956–60). Became musical director of Playboy Clubs in the 1960s. Two early 1970s tours with the Giants of Jazz (Gillespie, Monk *et al.*) were followed by semi-retirement in Spain. Also toured with Lionel Hampton (1979) and two-trombone group with Curtis Fuller (1980).

One of the earliest successful trombonists to be influenced by bebop, Winding also allowed some swing-era influences to be retained. Adopting a slightly coarser tone than his contemporaries, he achieved an individual style at a period when the trombone was generally an underrated instrument. [BP]

Winding/Fuller, *Bones 80*, Black & Blue

Winstone, Norma (Norma Ann Taylor), voice. b. London, 23 September 1941. 'Natural' singers on both mother's and father's sides, and much interest in music. She won a junior exhibition scholarship to Trinity College, London, studying piano and organ for three years. 1965, began singing with jazz groups and 1966 joined the New Jazz Orchestra, where she met Michael Garrick, whose group she also joined. She began working with John Taylor then, later marrying him. She has also worked with Neil Ardley, Mike Gibbs, Nucleus, John Surman, John Stevens, Kenny Wheeler, John Dankworth, and was in one of Mike Westbrook's groups for a number of years. She has worked quite extensively with various European radio big bands and orchestras. 1977, with John Taylor and Kenny Wheeler, she formed the group Azimuth, which records for ECM and has toured in Europe, appearing at many festivals. Norma Winstone is a singer of brilliant virtuosity and flexibility; she can handle very complex lines and wide intervals, improvise with the fluency of an instrumentalist and also breathe life into a simple song. Her favourite singers are Frank Sinatra, Joe Williams and Carmen McRae, and other inspirational figures for her are Bill Evans, John Coltrane, Kenny Wheeler and John Taylor. [IC]

With Michael Garrick, Mike Westbrook, Kenny Wheeler, Nucleus, Tony Coe and Eberhard Weber; *Edge of Time* (1971), Deram; with Azimuth, *Azimuth* (1977); *The Touchstone* (1978); *Départ* (1980), all ECM

Winter, Paul Theodore, Jnr., soprano and alto sax, composer. b. Altoona, Pennsylvania, 31 August 1939. Piano from age six. Attended Northwestern University in Chicago, organized his own band there which in 1961 won an intercollegiate competition. 1962, he took his sextet on a US State Department tour of Latin America, visiting 23 countries. His sextet was the first jazz group to perform at the White House – for the Kennedys in 1962. In the late 1960s Winter began leading his Winter Consort, which until 1971 included Ralph Towner, Collin Walcott and Glen Moore – all of whom left to form the group Oregon. During the 1970s Winter recorded some interesting albums, including *Common Ground*, which combined his plaintive soprano sound with animal noises and human voices, in a series of pieces which ranged from jazz and rock to country and folk. [IC]

Winter Consort (nda); *Something in the Wind* (nda); *Road* (nda); *Earth Dance* (nda); *Common Ground* (nda), all A & M

Winters, Tiny (Frederick), bass, vocals, leader. b. Hackney, East London, 24 January 1909. He taught himself bass to begin with (later he took lessons) and worked pre-war with Roy Fox, as a cornerman in Lew Stone's orchestra during all its greatest years, then with Ambrose and – on record – for Ray Noble, as well as with Nat Gonella's first Georgians (before they broke away from Stone's organization) and later with fine groups such as the short-lived Heralds of Swing. After wartime service in the RAF from 1940, his career continued unabated: as a sessionman for radio, TV and records as well as a succession of London stage productions including *Annie Get Your Gun* and *West Side Story* and regularly with the TV Black and White Minstrel Show, as resident bassist and featured comedian with George Chisholm's Jazzers. In the 1970s Winters continued to lead his own trio and orchestra, in 1982 began touring with a Nat Gonella tribute package, then formed and fronted his own Kettner's Five (featuring John Barnes, Keith Nichols, John Armatage, Digby Fairweather, Chris Ellis and Liza Lincoln) as well as continuing his South Bank appearances with an aristocratic Palm Court Trio and Café Society Orchestra. A regular broadcaster, sleeve-note contributor and one-man mine of information. [DF]

Lew Stone, *Coffee in the Morning* (1933–4), President

Witherspoon, Jimmy (James), vocals. b. Gurdon, Arkansas, 8 August 1923. Sang in church choir as a child, first blues singing during navy

Jimmy Witherspoon

service. On release, worked on West Coast with Jay McShann's band (1945–7), recording under McShann and own name; also recorded with backing by Buddy Tate group, Roy Milton band etc. (1947–50), extremely successful as solo attraction. A period of obscurity in mid- and late 1950s was ended by Monterey festival appearance (1959) with all-star jazz line-up, followed by frequent tours of Europe (beginning 1961, with Buck Clayton group). For a time in the early 1970s Witherspoon ran a disc-jockey programme, then enjoyed another performing comeback thanks to encouragement of British singer Eric Burdon. Further international touring in 1980s.

His singing, and one or two items of repertoire, are directly descended from Joe Turner, but Witherspoon's rich baritone foreshadowed the work of Joe Williams. His delivery is earthier, more in the Turner mould, but already by the time Spoon was making his mark, jazz-blues was becoming rhythm-and-blues. This has led to many attempts to cross over into the more general popular market, with a lot of ballads and a lot of unsuitable accompaniments, from which he has emerged unscathed. Witherspoon's importance derives from a great rapport with jazz players, and the flexibility of both his voice and his timing shows best in this context. [BP]

The Spoon Concerts (1959), Fantasy; *Jimmy Witherspoon and the New Savoy Sultans* (1980), Muse/Black & Blue

Wolverines Formed from the remains of a band resident at the Stockton Club, near Hamilton, Cincinnati, by clarinettist Jimmy Hartwell, the Wolverines (so named because of a fondness for Jelly Roll Morton's 'Wolverine Blues') are primarily famous as the first band in which cornettist Bix Beiderbecke attracted attention in 1923: a year later he was a regular associate of Jean Goldkette's orchestra which he joined under Frank Trumbauer in September 1925. The Wolverines, featuring George Johnson (tnr) and Dick Voynow (piano), as well as Beiderbecke, Hartwell and later drummer Vic Berton, had recorded a number of titles for Gennett which created a national sensation – including Hoagy Carmichael's first tune 'Free Wheeling', later retitled 'Riverboat Shuffle'. After provincial work in the Midwest they arrived in New York in September 1924 to play the Cinderella Ballroom on 48th and Broadway and attracted huge attention and rave reviews. But somehow they lost their impetus after Bix left (Jimmy McPartland replaced him) and broke up soon after. [DF]

The Complete Wolverines (1924), Fountain

See Sudhalter, Richard M. (with Evans and Dean-Myatt), *Bix: Man and Legend* (Quartet, 1974)

Wood, Mark Sinclair, guitar, guitar synthesizer. b. Newcastle upon Tyne, 29 August 1954. Great-uncle a composer and professor of music. Left school at 16 and was entirely self-taught as a musician. First professional job with Joe Harriott. Since then has toured extensively in Europe, USA, Scandinavia, Africa and the Far East, and played with Dudu Pukwana, Johnny Dyani, Charlie Mariano, Chris McGregor, Neil Ardley. Since 1981, has led his own band, Sunwind, which won the Greater London Arts Association's Young Musicians Award, 1982, and Capital Radio Musician of the Year, 1983. 1982, he joined Nucleus. Has performed at many festivals, including North Sea, Helsinki, Bologna, San Sebastian. 1984, toured South America and Mexico for seven weeks with Nucleus. Also does session work, and writes and produces music for film and TV. Favourite guitarists, Jimi Hendrix, Eddie Van Halen, Jeff Beck, and Zawinul on synthesizer. Other influences, Hermeto Pascoal, Frank Zappa, the Beatles. [IC]

With Sunwind, *The Sun Below* (1983), MMC; with Pukwana, *Zila Live* (1981), Jika; with Grand Theft, *One Step at a Time* (1979), EMI; with *Sound Barrier* (1984), Compact; with David Defries, *The Secret City* (1985), MMC; with Nucleus, *Live at the Theaterhaus* (1985), Mood

Woode, Jimmy (James Bryant), bass (and vocal, piano). b. Philadelphia, 23 September 1928. Nephew of arranger Henri Woode (b. 25 September 1909), co-writer of 'Rosetta'. Studied in Philadelphia and in Boston, where he returned after navy service. Gigging in Boston area with Nat Pierce etc. through late 1940s–early 1950s, except for touring with Flip Phillips, Sarah Vaughan and Ella Fitzgerald. Then five years with Duke Ellington (early 1955–early 1960), after which Woode relocated in Europe. Based for several years each in Stockholm, Cologne, Vienna, Munich, was very successful in studio work. Founder member of Clarke–Boland band (1961–73), also latterly involved in contracting for and producing studio sessions. In recent years, has done European tours with Arnett Cobb/Eddie Davis/Johnny Griffin (1984) and Paris Reunion Band (1985, 1986). An excellent rhythm-section player, less often heard in solo, Woode has been an important figurehead on the European scene. As standard-bearer for the 'friendly invasion' by US musicians, his influence has certainly been more helpful than harmful in terms of fostering the maturity of local players. [BP]

Paris Reunion Band, *French Cooking* (1985), Sonet

Wooding, Sam (Samuel David), piano, arranger. b. Philadelphia, 17 June 1895. One of the most important early black bandleaders, Sam Wooding led his Society Syncopators in a variety of New York clubs as well as for *Plantation Days* revue before travelling with his orchestra to Berlin in 1925 to accompany the show *Chocolate Kiddies*: for the next six years – with short trips back home – he was to build a huge reputation for his concert orchestra all over Europe. The orchestra – which at various times featured such stars as Tommy Ladnier, Doc Cheatham, Gene Sedric and Willie Lewis – was one of the best ever of its kind, recorded regularly for Pathé-Actuelle (in Paris), Deutsche Grammophon (in Berlin) and Parlophone (in Barcelona) and at the period was heard by the young Hugues Panassié: he was impressed. 'They played hot – terrifically hot,' he said, 'and I was amazed by their dynamism which was so much greater than white bands'!' Wooding played all the very best venues wherever he went and became a society favourite: great problems arose after 1931, however, when his band broke up in Belgium and he came back to the USA to find that, in New York, a host of big bands from Fletcher Henderson's on down were holding sway and, soon after, that younger white swing kings like Benny Goodman were following in hot pursuit. Wooding re-formed an orchestra, but found it hard to duplicate his European success: by 1935 he had disbanded and left full-time bandleading to study music at Pennsylvania University where he won his master's degree. From then on he pursued a busy career in teaching, but returned to performing regularly, ran his own record company in the 1950s and later in the 1960s formed a duo with singer Rae Harrison which toured the world. From 1968 Wooding, now semi-retired, made his home in Germany but came back regularly to perform in the 1970s. [DF]

Sam Wooding's Chocolate Kiddies, 1925–9, Biograph

Woodman, Britt, trombone. b. Los Angeles, 4 June 1920. His father, William O. Woodman, was trombonist who recorded with Sonny Clay (1925–6) and with Teddy Buckner (1955–6), and Britt's early experience was in the Woodman Brothers family band. Touring with West Coast outfits of Phil Moore (1938), Floyd Turnham (1938–9) and Les Hite (1939–42), followed by army service and work with Boyd Raeburn (1946) and Lionel Hampton (1946–7). Studies and some studio gigs led to joining Duke Ellington (1951–60), after which Woodman specialized in session work (New York in 1960s, Los Angeles in 1970s, New York again in 1980s). An admirer of Lawrence Brown, whom he replaced with Ellington, Britt has a more cutting tone which accords well with his occasionally boppish turn of phrase and excellent command of the extreme upper register. [BP]

The Ellingtonians (1950–1), Vogue

Woods, Phil(ip Wells), alto sax, clarinet. b. Springfield, Massachusetts, 2 November 1931. After studying at music school, touring jobs with big bands and then small-group work with Jimmy Raney (1955) and George Wallington (1956, 1957). Played with Dizzy Gillespie big band, including overseas tours (1956), and formed two-alto quintet with Gene Quill (1957). With Buddy Rich quintet (1958–9) and was founder member of Quincy Jones big band (1959–61). Also worked with Benny Goodman (1962) and did considerable amount of studio sessions in the 1960s. Moved to Paris with his then wife Chan Richardson (former consort of Charlie Parker) and formed his European Rhythm Machine quartet including Daniel Humair on drums and pianist George Gruntz, later Gordon Beck (1968–72). Back to US, doing some studio work in Los Angeles and then New York, but principally active with new quartet, which became a quintet in 1983 with the addition of Tom Harrell.

Woods's alto style helped to define one school of post-Parker players contemporary with that of Cannonball Adderley. The basic Parker vocabulary was lightened by somewhat broader phrasing, and the full tone occasionally decorated by growls and other bluesy inflections, where appropriate to the melody lines. A frequently exciting and always recognizable performer, Woods has managed to avoid the hysterical edge typical of many post-bop altoists. [BP]

Woodlore (1955), Prestige/OJC; *At the Vanguard* (1982), Antilles

Woodyard, Sam(uel), drums. b. Elizabeth, New Jersey, 7 January 1925. Playing locally with Paul Gayten band (1950–1) and Joe Holiday (1951–2), then worked with Roy Eldridge (1952) and Milt Buckner trio (1953–5). Joined Duke Ellington, remaining apart from short interruptions for 13 years (1955–68). After period of inactivity, played occasional gigs in early 1970s and was added (on congas) to Ellington band (1973) and Buddy Rich band (1974). Moved to France (1975), working with local musicians and touring Americans such as Buckner and Milt Hinton. Also made appearances in other European countries, including visit to England (1979). A somewhat uneven performer who nevertheless assisted the Ellington band through a peak period of its existence. His playing was often quite rudimentary, yet at its best swung effortlessly; on other occasions, it gave the impression of being laborious and insensitive. His work in Ellington's more subtle compositions drew less comment, simply because it was both effective and self-effacing. [BP]

Francis Biensan/Sam Woodyard, *Jumpin' With Sam* (1979), Black and Blue

World music The phrase describes the philosophy that all the 'folk' musics of the world are connected at a fundamental level; and the more or less conscious attempts from the 1960s onwards to prove that jazz, with its improvisatory directness, is best placed to bring out these fundamental connections.

After all, the earlier interest of both North and South American players in various kinds of African music was perhaps only to be expected, although the compatibility of these styles had not been a foregone conclusion. But for jazz musicians to assume that they had any reason or any right to start playing with musicians of other cultures implied a new self-confidence on the part of the jazz community, and could probably only have happened thanks to the 1960s climax of the civil rights movement.

John Coltrane may be said to have heralded this new pan-cultural approach, but it was Don Cherry who put the philosophy continually into practice. As well as being one of the first US musicians to collaborate with the South African pianist Dollar Brand (Abdullah Ibrahim), he was the first to play regularly with totally non-jazz musicians from several continents. But like many vital, or at least interesting, developments in jazz this was rapidly turned into something more soft-centred and commercial, by groups such as the Paul Winter Consort and Oregon. [BP]

World Saxophone Quartet Formed in 1977 by Hamiett Bluiett (baritone sax), Julius Hemphill (alto), Oliver Lake (alto), David Murray (tenor, replaced by John Stubblefield, 1986), who all double on other instruments. They perform mostly without a rhythm section, writing all the music they use, and working as a quartet, in trio, duo, and as unaccompanied soloists. They toured Europe in 1978, and since then have established a strong international reputation. By the mid-1980s they had appeared at most major festivals. [IC]

Point of No Return (1977), Moers Music; *Steppin' with the World Saxophone Quartet* (1978); *WSQ* (nda); *Revue* (nda), all Black Saint

World's Greatest Jazz Band Formed in 1968 by millionaire Dick Gibson after his sixth annual 'Jazz Party', the World's Greatest Jazz Band contained 'charter members' including Yank Lawson, Bob Haggart, Bob Wilber, Ralph Sutton and Billy Butterfield, who had previously played at Gibson's parties under the collective title the Nine Greats of Jazz and worked at the Elitch Gardens Trocadero in Denver for promoter Jack Gurtler. It was Gibson who launched the band under their new name (widely criticized, but excellent American-style hard sell, nevertheless) and after appearances at Manhattan venues such as the Riverboat, Trocadero and Roosevelt Grill, and successful radio and TV, the WGJB was on its way. For the next ten years it toured continuously, and on the whole happily, and early recordings of the band in full flight are hard to beat: live sessions including concerts at Massey and Carnegie Halls, and studio albums such as *Century Plaza* (all issued on the World Jazz label) are the WGJB in its prime. Later, after fluctuations in line-up and unexpected internal strife between co-leaders Lawson and Haggart (happily resolved) some of the initial enthusiasm inevitably left the project: the challenging contemporary repertoire which had graced early albums ('Up Up and Away' by the Fifth Dimension, 'Wichita Lineman' by Jim Webb, 'Alfie' by Burt Bacharach) was often replaced by ad-lib re-creations of standard repertoire, and just occasionally – even where arrangements were used in admirable 'concept' albums celebrating Cole Porter, George Gershwin and others – the band sounded what it emphatically never was: polite, with a tendency once or twice to write in Sammy Kaye-style codas. A very great deal of the WGJB's recorded music, however (including a magnificent 'Duke Ellington' tribute with Butterfield at his very greatest), is seminal music: the logical successor to Bob Crosby's band and the Lawson–Haggart band of the early 1950s. The band broke up in 1978 after Lawson and Haggart had finally decided to spend more time at home, but in the intervening ten years their band had done enormous amounts to re-popularize jazz and re-present some of its best artists as they deserved. [DF]

At Massey Hall (1972), World Jazz

Wright, Denny (Denys Justin Freeth), guitar, composer, arranger, conductor. b.

World Saxophone Quartet

Brockley, Kent, 6 May 1924. He turned professional in 1939 and in 1940 joined Cyril 'Happy' Blake at London's Jig's Club. In the 1940s his broad-based approach won him studio work (with Phil Green's house band for Decca), big-band work (with Carl Barriteau and others) and clubwork (he started London's first bop club, the Fullado, in 1945). By the 1950s Wright was playing for Kenny Graham's Afro-Cubists and the BBC Show Band (Latin section), founded the Hot Club of London and was musical director for a variety of night clubs before joining Lonnie Donegan and later Johnny Duncan for some hit-parading years (his was the solo guitar on their records). Later in the 1960s Wright worked in studios full-time (he produced dozens of albums for Music for Pleasure), but in 1973 rejoined Stephane Grappelli, with whom he had worked first in 1944, and stayed with him until 1978: that year he formed a quartet, Velvet (with Ike Isaacs, Len Skeat and Digby Fairweather), which toured for four years, recorded and won the *Jazz Journal* Small Group poll for 1981. In 1983, Denny Wright was awarded the BBC Jazz Society's Musician of the Year accolade and soon after re-formed his Hot Club of London group with John Van Derrick (vln) as well as Velvet with Fairweather in 1985. An irrepressibly creative soloist with a quicksilver mind, Wright's witty work reflects Django Reinhardt and George Barnes but his inspirations are all his own. [DF]

Velvet (1979), Black Lion

Y

Yamashita, Yosuke, piano, composer, author. b. Tokyo, 26 February 1942. He studied at Kunitachi Music University, 1962–7. At the beginning of the 1960s, with Terumasa Hino and Masabumi Kikuchi, he was part of a group which met at a jazz club called Gin-Paris, to play and discuss the finer points of jazz every night. Yamashita formed his own trio in 1969, with Akira Sakata on alto sax and Takeo Moriyama on drums, which played a violently abstract music. 1974, the trio made its first international tour – in Europe – during which it appeared at several festivals in East and West Germany and Yugoslavia. The manic energy of the group earned the label 'The Kamikaze Trio', a title which Yamashita relished. He said later: 'They caught on right. We were like kamikaze. We said: OK, let's show them our spirit. And we did just that.'

From 1974 the trio visited Europe every year throughout the 1970s. Then Yamashita disbanded it in 1983, because he felt he had done almost everything he could in trio form. He has since led a big band which combined swing music with free jazz, performed his own compositions with the Osaka Philharmonic Orchestra, played with Kodo, the Japanese drum group, performed solo piano concerts, and played his own iconoclastic versions of classical pieces such as Bach's Cello Suite no. 2 and the Italian Concerto (second movement). He has also written seven books and many essays for various magazines.

Although Cecil Taylor was an obvious early influence, Yamashita has arrived at his own concept and style. He has said: 'Let's use the words "in" and "out". I always stay "out" side. Playing solo piano or swing rhythm would be OK as long as I can stay on the "out" side. An "out" side approach is what jazz is all about. Jazz started out as "Africa approaching Europe". And be careful, it was not "Europe approaching Africa", but "Africa approaching Europe". That was the beginning of jazz – Europe had the system but Africa was alive with feeling. All the material I use belongs to the system, but as long as I can stand on the "out" side and approach things from the "out" side, I will never be suffocated.' [IC]

Trio, *Clay* (1974); Manfred Schoof with trio, *Distant Thunder* (1975); Yamashita/Adelhard Roidinger, *Inner Space* (1977); solo piano, *Banslikana* (1976); trio, *A Tribute to Mal Waldron* (1980), all Enja

Yancey, Jimmy (James Edwards), piano. b. Chicago, *c.* 1894; d. 17 September 1951. The father of boogie, he worked originally as a singing and dancing vaudevillian. A self-taught pianist, he played later at rent parties and clubs in Chicago from 1915 and is said to have passed on ideas to Albert Ammons and Meade 'Lux' Lewis. From 1925 he became a devoted baseball groundsman, but regained fame on an international scale after boogie came back into fashion in the late 1930s and played in Chicago and New York, often with his wife, blues singer Mama Yancey, as well as at Carnegie Hall in 1948. [DF]

Young, Lee (Leonidas Raymond), drums, vocals. b. New Orleans, 7 March 1917. He could scarcely have presented a more dramatic contrast to his famous brother Lester. 'They were like night and day', says bassist Red Callender. 'Probably the only thing they shared except their musical family background was their love of sport, particularly baseball. Lee was and is a leader, an extrovert, a consummate businessman, dependable, organized, health-conscious, a terrific golfer, a great drummer!' Apart from the last accolade, Young could scarcely have sported a worse set of qualifications for turning into a jazz legend, and he paid dearly for his thoroughgoing professionalism by being regularly ignored in the media. But in musical terms his career was as great as those of most other drummers of his generation, beginning in the 1930s with such bands as Mutt Carey's Jeffersonians and Buck Clayton's before moving into film work, first as an extra and later as the first black musician to be hired by Columbia for their staff orchestra. In 1941 Young co-led a band with his brother Lester at Billy Berg's Capri Club, worked in studios for ten years and later joined Nat 'King' Cole's trio, 1953–62. Then, says Callender, his close friend, 'At the height of his career Lee decided he didn't want anybody saying, "You should have heard Lee Young in 1954 or whatever year." So he went into the record business – it's the genius of Lee Young you hear in the Motown Sound and in many of the hit records of the late 1950s, early 1960s and 1970s.' [DF]

See Callender, Red, with Elaine Cohen, *Unfinished Dream* (Quartet, 1985)

Lester Young

Young, Lester Willis ('Pres' or 'Prez'), tenor sax, clarinet. b. Woodville, Mississippi, 27 August 1909; d. New York City, 15 March 1959. 'Prez was such a *nice* fellow, a beautiful, beautiful person.' Dicky Wells, talking about the greatest tenor-saxophonist (along with Coleman Hawkins) of the classic years. 'He was full of jokes, harmless, didn't bother nobody, loved everybody. He was the greatest.' 'The President' (he acquired the nickname in the 1930s from Billie Holiday) was the first to supply a viable alternative to the tenor saxophone vocabulary which cocksure young Coleman Hawkins had by 1930 finally defined: Young's answer, typically enough, was cool, light-toned, laid-back and avuncular, as far away from the charging, full-toned, macho Hawkins as it was possible to be.

The Lester Young formula represented a challenging alternative in the early days of his career with the Blue Devils (1932–3), Bennie Moten (1933–4) and with Count Basie's orchestra in 1934 (he had invited himself into the band with a telegram which Basie remembered as 'strange and urgent') and it met with wholesale approval at Kansas City jam sessions. Some months later, however, after he had joined Fletcher Henderson's orchestra, the reaction was very different. Henderson's wife played him records of Hawkins, praising the bigger sound, and even Billie Holiday, with whom Young was a welcome lodger and platonically close friend, tried to help him down an unlooked-for road ('We'll get us a tone!'). Young bore the idiocy with patience and fortitude – 'To each his own' was a favoured phrase – but after two more years of musical wandering, including a failed audition with Earl Hines, with relief he rejoined Basie at Kansas City's Reno Club. Once again he was accepted on his own terms – 'I just know we were all happy, always wanting to go to work and things like that' – and he was soon encouraged by Basie to set his talents against Herschel Evans, a highly gifted Hawkins follower who represented most of the saxophone options against which, by then, Young had quietly and determinedly set himself. Against Evans, a musical and personal opposite with whom he established a keen although amicable rivalry, Young could proudly display his own kind of music which, until lately, he had been instructed to suppress. In spare moments with Basie he enjoyed girlfriends ('I was tired of looking at chicks running in and out', says Buddy Tate), became the star pitcher in Basie's softball team, played practical jokes (including ringing a bell at any band member who made a mistake on-stage) and crawled back on the bus at the end of each night to what he called the 'sweet music' of rolling dice. 'Pres' invented, in return, a hip nickname for each band member (Harry Edison became 'Sweets', Buddy Tate 'Moon', the leader himself 'The Holy Main'), and recorded with Billie Holiday: 'She got me little record dates playing behind her, little solos and things like that', he minimized. Every side is a priceless gem.

In 1940, Young left Basie following a flat work patch for the leader, depression after the death of Herschel Evans and the wish to bandlead for himself. He freelanced and co-led a band with brother Lee before rejoining the Basie band for nine months from December 1943 until September 1944. He had just completed a short film, *Jammin' the Blues*, for Gjon Mili and Warner Bros (which was nominated for an Academy Award the following year) when, at the relaxed end of a night's work, he was spotted by a plain-clothes army official and summarily conscripted. From a star's position, in an albeit unacceptable line of showbusiness, he was flung into a world bewilderingly, horrifyingly strange. 'It was a nightmare – one mad nightmare', he said later. 'They sent me down to Georgia – that was enough to make me blow my top.' Young feared his racist captors, and he ended up in a disciplinary centre: when he emerged after an illness in 1945 he bore deep mental scars.

A new musical trend of bebop, fresh recording techniques and a flock of Young disciples who were achieving fame at his expense and with his ideas had to be faced: small wonder that at times his music seemed – like him – more heavy-lidded than before. Pres began to withdraw more, perfecting his own monosyllabic language and a set of speech formulae to cope with the threats of life ('eyes' for wanting, 'bells' for approval and so on). But in 1946 he was still a star, and just as creative with Jazz at the Philharmonic, happily playing against his old arch-rival Coleman Hawkins, and for the next 10 or more years he appeared regularly with Norman Granz's sometimes hysterical show as well as leading his own small groups. Poor health (including several hospital visits), heavy smoking and drinking often affected his performance from then on: more often, though, his approach – in contrast to the spunky young Turks of bebop – was simply and determinedly laid back. 'They say, "Oh Prez, he don't sound like he used to",' said Jo Jones, 'but then when they hear the album he made in 1956 with Roy Eldridge and Teddy Wilson and me they said, "Wow – that's different." It was a question of compatibility.' (Billie Holiday often sounds worse post-war for the same reason, in part at least, and complained about it in her book *Lady Sings the Blues*.) In his final years, Lester Young somehow got smaller: one year at Newport, very drunk, he told Buddy Tate: 'The other ladies, my imitators, are making the money!' In 1958 he was playing the Blue Note and planning an album with Gil Evans. 'He wanted to make the album, but he wanted to die more', Evans recalled. 'He came in from his home on Long Island and decided to stay at the Alvin Hotel, just across from Birdland. He never ate a thing. Then he got back from Paris, got in the hotel room again and had a heart attack.' Lester Young died; his old friend Billie Holiday followed him within a few months. [DF]

Lester Young Story (1936–9), CBS (all volumes)

See Shapiro, Nat, and Hentoff, Nat, *The Jazz Makers* (Rinehart, 1957, repr. Da Capo, 1979); Dance, Stanley, *The World of Count Basie* (Sidgwick & Jackson, 1980); Lyttelton, Humphrey, *The Best of Jazz 2: Enter the Giants* (Robson, 1981); Balliett, Whitney, *Jelly Roll, Jabbo and Fats* (OUP, 1983); Gelly, Dave, *Lester Young* (Spellmount, 1984)

Young, Snooky (Eugene Howard), trumpet. b. Dayton, Ohio, 3 February 1919. He took up the trumpet at five years old, and played in the Wilberforce College Band (without actually ever attending the college). Then, after time with Chic Carter's territory band in Michigan, he joined Jimmie Lunceford's orchestra at the behest of Gerald Wilson in 1939 and stayed for three years: his famous feature was 'Uptown Blues'. From 1942, when he briefly joined Count Basie, Young worked with Lee Young's band, Les Hite and Benny Carter, Basie again and Gerald Wilson, before rejoining Basie with whom he stayed 1945–7, replacing high-note man Al Killian. For the next ten years, in Dayton, Ohio, he led his own top-class band featuring players such as Slam Stewart and Booty Wood before rejoining Basie, 1957–62. From then on he was a busy studio player, and in 1979 for Concord produced a long overdue solo album. [DF]

Snooky Young – Marshall Royal Sextet (1982), Concord

See Dance, Stanley, *The World of Count Basie* (Sidgwick & Jackson, 1980)

Young, Trummy (James Osborne), trombone, vocals, composer. b. Savannah, Georgia, 12 January 1912; d. San Jose, California, 10 September 1984. He grew up in Washington – where he studied trumpet first – and made his professional debut in 1928 playing a revolutionary high-noted style of trombone. 'People used to say I was crazy,' he remembered later, 'and ask what I was trying to do.' One sympathetic bandleader, however, was Earl Hines, whom Young joined in 1933 and stayed with for four years, perfecting his trumpet style based on Louis Armstrong and the trombonist that Young adored, Jimmy Harrison. 'I worked very hard on . . . a sharper, brilliant sound.' But it was after he joined Jimmie Lunceford's orchestra – with its showmanship, strong discipline and regular chances for features – that Young became a figurehead for black (and white) trombonists everywhere. Says Dicky Wells, 'He really brought a modern turn to the trombone and it was unusual for a trombone player to be featured as much as he was.' With his jivey infectious voice and supercharged technique, Young was a natural cornerman for his leader and it was a pity that in 1943 Lunceford's low wages finally forced him to hand in his notice. But he worked on regularly for four years as bandleader in a variety of other bands (including Norman Granz's Jazz at the Philharmonic) before moving to Hawaii to live and play. Louis Armstrong heard him in Honolulu in 1952, Young joined Armstrong that year and for the next 13 years played the perfect supporting role to his leader, modifying his style accordingly. 'A lot of people don't understand what happened to Trummy's style when he joined Louis,' says Wells, 'but in Dixieland they don't want too many notes anyway. I don't think he ever got enough credit for it. But he had made such a big reputation in his career before that – it was a kind of sacrifice.' Young loved his role because he loved Louis. 'I try to keep him happy', he said. 'Louis' got more soul than anyone I ever met in my life!' He stayed until 1964 ('It was the road that caused me to quit') and then worked back in Hawaii, re-emerging for Dick Gibson's Colorado parties, special events and major jazz festivals such as Nice until he died – to everyone's dismay – of a heart attack. [DF]

The Complete Jimmie Lunceford, 1939–40, CBS (4 records, boxed set); any with Louis Armstrong's All Stars

Z

Zarchy, Zeke (Rubin), trumpet. b. New York City, 12 June 1915. Known to 1930s friends (and jazz critics) as 'Rubin from Brooklyn', Zarchy was a highly respected lead trumpeter of the swing era and after who, following an initial stint with Joe Haymes's tightly-disciplined orchestra in 1935, worked for Benny Goodman (1936), Artie Shaw (1936–7), Bob Crosby until he had a fighting disagreement with Irving Fazola (1937–9), Tommy Dorsey (1939–40), Glenn Miller (1940) and others. He has 'a whacky sense of humour', said George T. Simon in 1939, 'and he can play pretty fair jazz': unfortunately Zarchy's talents as a lead player often meant that the jazz was left to others, and after he moved into NBC as a staffman in 1940 there was even less chance to hear what he could do. In 1944–5 he was again playing for Glenn Miller's AEF band (Miller appointed him first sergeant and the two men were golfing buddies) but after the war Zarchy moved into TV, radio and recording in Hollywood. Far too little evidence of his jazz abilities was available until the 1980s, when he worked regularly with the Great Pacific Jazz Band and also, in 1985, visited Britain with Ray McKinley and Peanuts Hucko to play for VE Day anniversary celebrations with a re-formed Miller-style orchestra. [DF]

Zawinul, Joe (Josef), piano, keyboards, synthesizers, composer. b. Vienna, 7 July 1932. He was given an accordion at the age of six and played it for a year by ear – gypsy melodies and accompanying his family singing folk songs. From the age of seven he studied classical music at the Vienna Conservatory, but was unable to practise at home because his family had no piano. His first opportunity to practise regularly came in 1944, when he and other very gifted students were evacuated from Vienna to save them from the increasing Allied bomb attacks. They were sent to a private country estate in Czechoslovakia, where Zawinul had to practise the piano every day. Back in Vienna after the war, he had become interested in jazz, and when the film *Stormy Weather* (1943) arrived there, he saw it 24 times, and from then on wanted to play jazz with black musicians. 1952, he worked with the great Austrian saxophonist Hans Koller, which brought Zawinul to the notice of jazz audiences; 1953–8, he worked with various leading Austrian musicians, as well as playing at Special Service clubs in France and Germany with his own trio.

1959, he won a scholarship to the Berklee School of Music, Boston, and emigrated to the USA, where after only a week or so at Berklee, he joined Maynard Ferguson and toured with him for eight months. After working briefly with Slide Hampton, Zawinul was accompanist for singer Dinah Washington from October 1959 to March 1961. He played for a month with Harry Edison and Joe Williams, then joined Cannonball Adderley, becoming a key member of the group and staying with it until the autumn of 1970. During that period, he was also featured on recording sessions with many other leading US jazz musicians. 1966, he was a judge at the International Jazz Competition in Vienna; and with Friedrich Gulda, he recorded Gulda's Concerto for Two Pianos and Orchestra. Zawinul played a major part in the success of the Adderley group as composer of such hits as 'Mercy Mercy Mercy', which won a Grammy award for the best instrumental performance.

He also played an important part as both player and composer on four seminal Miles Davis albums (1969–70): *In a Silent Way* (the title-piece is Zawinul's tune), *Bitches Brew*, *Live-Evil* and *Big Fun*. This exposure with Davis brought Zawinul to the attention of a world-wide audience, and in 1971, with ex-Davis saxophonist Wayne *Shorter, he co-founded Weather Report. The other original members were Miroslav Vitous, Alphonze Mouzon and Airto Moreira, but throughout Weather Report's existence there have been several changes of personnel, Zawinul and Shorter being the only two constants. Weather Report (so named by Shorter after Zawinul's early description of the band's music as 'changing from day to day like the weather') rapidly established itself as one of the most vitally creative and influential units in jazz history. The group has been a perennial poll-winner, reaching enormous peaks of world-wide popularity without ever diluting its music or lowering its standards, and its fascinating artistic development (from the modish free improvisation plus electronics at the beginning of the 1970s to the more composed structures of its middle and later periods) is minutely documented on record. Its musical scope is huge, ranging from pure abstraction – non-temporal, non-tonal electronic and acoustic sounds – to brilliantly per-

Joe Zawinul

formed rhythms of tremendous variety, rich harmonies, indelible melodies, subtle variations of space and texture, and much improvisation. Its music is always of the heart, never merely of the glands.

Zawinul's career has reversed the usual jazz musician's pattern: instead of doing his most innovative work when he was young, the whole of his earlier life seems like a prolonged apprenticeship and preparation for the brilliant originality and sustained artistry of Weather Report, begun when he was nearly 40 and still peaking in his early fifties. Before Weather Report he was an excellent player and composer but perhaps a fairly peripheral figure on the jazz scene; his work with Miles Davis at the end of the 1960s made him a more central figure; then with Weather Report he became, with perhaps John McLaughlin, one of the first two Europeans since Django Reinhardt to have a major influence on the course of the music. He is generally recognized as being one of the finest composers in jazz, and his work has introduced a huge new vocabulary of compositional devices, new rhythms, new ways of making the music breathe. Zawinul claims Czech, Hungarian and gypsy blood in his ancestry, and his Austrian heritage has had a powerful effect on the nature and quality of his music; all the profound emotion of Central and Eastern European folk music is present in his work, and his compositions always have something to say about the human condition, conjuring up social scenes – marketplaces, families, gypsy celebrations, and also the inner landscapes of solitary individuals. Recalling the genesis of one of his most evocative pieces, he told C. Silvert: 'I wrote "Silent Way" in Vienna, in a hotel room overlooking the park. My kids were off with my parents, and my wife was asleep. The snow was falling down, and I looked out the window to the park, and took out the paper and wrote the whole thing in a few minutes.' He is one of the great masters of electronics, and his childhood memories of the accordion make him feel at home with synthesizers; he has likened his synthesized sounds to 'native instruments not yet discovered.' 1985, he toured in Europe and the USA playing solo acoustic and electric keyboards. Some of his other important compositions are: '74 Miles Away', 'Rumpelstiltskin', 'Dr Honoris Causa', 'Pharoah's Dance', 'Badia', 'Birdland', 'Man in the Green Shirt', 'A Remark You Made', 'Experience in E for Symphony Orchestra'. [IC]

Zawinul (1971), Atlantic; *Weather Report* (1971); *I Sing the Body Electric* (1972); *Tale Spinnin'* (1975); *Black Market* (1976); *Heavy Weather* (1977); *8.30* (1979); *Night Passage* (1980); *Weather Report* (1982); *Procession* (1983); *Domino Theory* (1984), all Columbia

Zeitlin, Denny (Dennis Jay), piano, synthesizer. b. Chicago, 10 April 1938. Piano lessons as a child, followed by studies with George Russell and others. Played jazz while in college and recorded first album (1964). Moved to San Francisco on graduating as psychiatrist, appeared at Monterey and Newport Festivals (1965) with trio including Charlie Haden. Retired from public appearances (late 1960s), resuming in mid-1970s. Has continued to perform regularly since then, sometimes reuniting with Haden. While his initial fame seemed inflated by his extramusical profession (there was also a jazz pianist/priest around the same time), he did produce several attractive pieces, among which 'Carole's Garden' was also recorded by other musicians. He can still sound glib and superficial as a soloist but these days he has a commanding presence at the keyboard. [BP]

Denny Zeitlin/Charlie Haden, *Time Remembers Time Once* (1982), ECM

Zoller, Attila Cornelius, guitar; and bass, trumpet. b. Visegrad, Hungary, 13 June 1927. Father, a conductor and music teacher, gave him violin lessons at age four; he took up trumpet at nine, playing in his school symphony orchestra. After World War II he began to play guitar with jazz groups in Budapest. 1948–54, he worked in Vienna; 1954–9, in Germany working with Jutta Hipp and Hans Koller, accompanying Bud Shank, Bob Cooper, Tony Scott, touring with Oscar Pettiford and Kenny Clarke. Summer 1959, he studied at the Lenox School of Jazz, Massachusetts. 1962–5, with Herbie Mann, then co-led a quartet with pianist Don Friedman. 1966, he worked with Red Norvo; 1967, with Benny Goodman, and leading his own group. From 1960 he toured Europe extensively every year into the 1980s. 1970, he toured Japan with Astrud Gilberto; 1971, again in Japan with Jim Hall and Kenny Burrell, as part of the guitar festival. He has also appeared at all major European festivals. Zoller has been active in jazz education. J. E. Berendt has written: 'Zoller is a master of sensitive, romantic restraint, and it is hard to understand why a man of such talent is still known only to insiders.' [IC]

With Koller, Albert Mangelsdorff, Martial Solal; *Gypsy Cry* (1971), Embryo

Zottola, Glenn, trumpet, alto sax. (nda) The son of a famous American brass mouthpiece manufacturer, jazz trumpeter Bob Zottola, he came to international attention in the 1980s with Bob Wilber's Bechet Legacy and has since established himself as a soloist, recording in America with small groups under his own leadership. Zottola plays trumpet in a warm and commanding Armstrong style which can, where necessary, take in more modern influences; his alto is a fluent amalgam of Benny Carter and Charlie Parker. [DF]

Live at Condon's (1980), Dreamstreet

Zurke, Bob (Robert Albert) (Boguslaw Albert Zukowski), piano, composer. b. Detroit, Michigan, 17 January 1912; d. Los Angeles, 16 February 1944. He achieved international fame after he joined Bob Crosby's orchestra, replacing Joe Sullivan in 1936. For three years he was central to Crosby's orchestra at the peak of its career, recording such classics as 'Old Spinning Wheel', 'Gin Mill Blues', 'At the Jazz Band Ball', 'Big Foot Jump' and 'Honky Tonk Train Blues' (his most famous feature). Zurke was a highly trained musician – he had played for Paderewski at the age of ten and, according to Bob Haggart, 'could read like a snake' – but a portrait in John Chilton's definitive history of Crosby's orchestra reveals him as a less than prepossessing man; overweight, a heavy drinker and a practised borrower of money. He was probably far from an ideal bandleader too, which explains why, from 1939, his own big band foundered in just 21 months. Zurke returned to solo piano work: his last date was at San Francisco's Hangover Club where he collapsed and died in hospital. [DF]

Bob Crosby, *Come On and Hear, vols. 1/2* (1936–40), Coral

See Chilton, John, *Stomp Off Let's Go!* (Jazz Book Services, 1983)

Zwerin, Mike (Michael), trombone, bass trumpet, author. b. New York, 18 May 1930. Studied violin in 1936; later attended High School of Music and Art. 1948, he played trombone with Miles Davis's 9-piece Birth of the Cool band during its residency at the Royal Roost. Zwerin spent several years in Paris, returning to the USA in 1958. He worked with Claude Thornhill, Maynard Ferguson, Bill Russo; 1962–5, he played with Orchestra USA and was musical director and arranger for a sextet drawn from the orchestra. He played with small groups around New York. 1966, he toured the USSR with Earl Hines. He was also very active as a journalist in the 1960s, writing for the *Village Voice*, *Rolling Stone* and *Downbeat* magazine. From 1960, Zwerin was also involved with the family steel business, Capitol Steel Corporation. 1969, he gave up regular playing and moved to the South of France to write novels and non-fiction works. In the later 1970s he moved to Paris, working as a journalist and author and occasionally playing trombone. He writes a regular jazz column for the *International Herald Tribune*. [IC]

With Miles Davis (1948 radio broadcast of the nonet), Orchestra USA, John Lewis/Gary McFarland, Maynard Ferguson

See his autobiography, *Close Enough for Jazz* (Quartet, 1983); Zwerin, Mike, *La Tristesse de Saint Louis: Swing Under the Nazis* (Quartet, 1985)

Acknowledgements

Ian Carr thanks all the musicians who returned their questionnaires; and Charles Alexander; Hugh Attwooll; Sandy Carr; John Cumming; James DeRigne of the Record Cabinet (USA); Dobell's Jazz Records Shop; John Elson; George Foster; Charles Fox; Mike Gibbs; Tony Middleton; Hazel Miller; Alun Morgan; Enrico Rava; Ray's Jazz Shop; Trevor Timmers and Circle in the Square; Valerie Wilmer; and for information and LPs, A & M; CBS; ECM; EMI/Blue Note; Enja; Downbeat Magazine; Island; IMS, London; Mood; Ogun; WEA.

Digby Fairweather thanks James Asman; John Barnes; Dave Bennett; Acker Bilk Agency; John Chilton; Dave Claridge; Bix Curtis; Chris Ellis; Jack Fallon; Jim Godbolt; Clarrie Henley; Fred and Brenda Hunt; Max Jones; Liza Lincoln; Adrian Macintosh; Keith Nichols; Paul Oliver; Len Page; Ed Polcer; Dave Shepherd; Jim Shepherd; Nevill Sherburn; Michael Sisley; Nevil Skrimshire; Warren Vaché Jnr; Warren Vaché Snr; Chris Wellard; Tiny Winters; Denny Wright; and all the British musicians who checked their own entries.

Brian Priestley thanks Roy Burchell (Melody Maker); John Chilton; Chris Clark (National Sound Archive); Roger Cotterrell; Michael Cuscuna; Vivienne Deighton; Pam Esterson; Pete Fincham (Mole Jazz); Graham Griffiths (Mole Jazz); Joan Gwinnell-Lee; Kevin Henriques; Adrian Lee; David Meeker (British Film Institute); Tony Middleton (Dobell's); Alun Morgan; Dan Morgenstern (Institute of Jazz Studies); Phil Schaap; Marion Scott; Ray Smith (Ray's Jazz Shop); Richard Sudhalter; Valerie Wilmer.

Photo Credits

The following photographs appear by permission of David Redfern:

Muhal Richard Abrams; Cannonball and Nat Adderley; Toshiko Akiyoshi; Louis Armstrong; Art Ensemble of Chicago; Derek Bailey (*Su Ingle*); Mildred Bailey (*William Gottlieb*); Count Basie; Sidney Bechet (*William Gottlieb*); Barney Bigard; Eubie Blake; Art Blakey; Carla Bley; Ruby Braff; Anthony Braxton; The Brecker Brothers; Gary Burton; Cab Calloway (*William Gottlieb*); Don Cherry; Kenny Clarke; Buck Clayton; Tony Coe; Ornette Coleman; John Coltrane; Ken Colyer; Eddie Condon; Chick Corea; Miles Davis; Paul Desmond; Vic Dickenson; Baby Dodds (*William Gottlieb*); Eric Dolphy (*Charles Stewart*); Tommy Dorsey (*William Gottlieb*); Roy Eldridge; Duke Ellington (*William Gottlieb*); Bill Evans; Gil Evans; Art Farmer; Pops Foster; Bud Freeman; Slim Gaillard; Erroll Garner; Stan Getz; Ghanaba; Mike Gibbs; Dizzy Gillespie; Al Grey; Bobby Hackett; Lionel Hampton; Herbie Hancock; Tubby Hayes; Woody Herman; Earl Hines; Johnny Hodges; Billie Holiday; Dave Holland; Daniel Humair with Bobby Jaspar and René Thomas; Abdullah Ibrahim; Ahmad Jamal; Bunk Johnson; James P. Johnson (*William Gottlieb*); Elvin Jones; Thad Jones; Louis Jordan (*William Gottlieb*); Rahsaan Roland Kirk; Yusef Lateef; Jimmie Lunceford (*William Gottlieb*); Humphrey Lyttelton; Chris McGregor; John McLaughlin (*Mike Cameron*); Shelly Manne; Wynton Marsalis; Charles Mingus; Thelonious Monk (*William Gottlieb*); Wes Montgomery; Gerry Mulligan; Fats Navarro; Sal Nistico; Red Norvo; Niels-Henning Ørsted Pedersen; Charlie Parker with Tommy Potter (*William Gottlieb*); Art Pepper; Oscar Peterson; Jean-Luc Ponty; Russell Procope; Dudu Pukwana; Dizzy Reece; Django Reinhardt (*William Gottlieb*); Buddy Rich; Max Roach; Sonny Rollins; Pee Wee Russell; Pharoah Sanders; Ronnie Scott; Phil Seamen; Bud Shank; Artie Shaw (*William Gottlieb*); Archie Shepp; Horace Silver; Zoot Sims; Muggsy Spanier; Buddy Tate; Art Tatum (*William Gottlieb*); Jack Teagarden; Clark Terry; Art Themen; Barbara Thompson; Stan Tracey; Big Joe Turner; McCoy Tyner; Sarah Vaughan; Joe Venuti; Eddie Vinson; Earle Warren; Ben Webster; Bobby Wellins; Dickie Wells; Kenny Wheeler; Bob Wilber; Cootie Williams; Mary Lou Williams; Teddy Wilson; Jimmy Witherspoon; World Saxophone Quartet; Lester Young (*William Gottlieb*).

The photograph of Eberhard Weber appears by permission of Marion Scott. Other photographs were provided by the subjects themselves or by Clarrie Henley who kindly made his collection available to the authors.